WORLD LITERATURE CRITICISM

1500 to the Present

WORLD LITERATURE CRITICISM
Advisory Board

———

WORLD LITERATURE CRITICISM

1500 to the Present

*A Selection of
Major Authors from
Gale's Literary
Criticism Series*

Cervantes-García Lorca

JAMES P. DRAPER, Editor

Gale Research Inc. · DETROIT · LONDON

STAFF

James P. Draper, *Editor*

Laurie DiMauro, Tina Grant, Paula Kepos, Jelena Krstović, Daniel G. Marowski, Roger Matuz, James E. Person, Jr., Joann Prosyniuk, David Segal, Joseph C. Tardiff, Bridget Travers, Lawrence Trudeau, Thomas Votteler, Sandra L. Williamson, Robyn V. Young, *Contributing Editors*

Catherine Falk, Grace Jeromski, Michael W. Jones, Andrew M. Kalasky, David Kmenta, Marie Lazzari, Zoran Minderović, Sean René Pollock, Mark Swartz, *Contributing Associate Editors*

Jennifer Brostrom, David J. Engelman, Andrea Gacki, Judith Galens, Christopher Giroux, Ian A. Goodhall, Alan Hedblad, Elizabeth P. Henry, Christopher K. King, Kyung-Sun Lim, Elisabeth Morrison, Kristin Palm, Susan M. Peters, James Poniewozik, Eric Priehs, Bruce Walker, Debra A. Wells, Janet Witalec, Allyson J. Wylie, *Contributing Assistant Editors*

Jeanne A. Gough, *Permissions & Production Manager*

Linda M. Pugliese, *Production Supervisor*
Paul Lewon, Lorna Mabunda, Maureen Puhl, Camille Robinson, Jennifer VanSickle, *Editorial Associates*
Donna Craft, Brandy C. Johnson, Sheila Walencewicz, *Editorial Assistants*

Victoria B. Cariappa, *Research Manager*

Maureen Richards, *Research Supervisor*
Mary Beth McElmeel, Tamara C. Nott, *Editorial Associates*
Andrea B. Ghorai, Daniel J. Jankowski, Julie K. Karmazin, Robert S. Lazich, *Editorial Assistants*

Sandra C. Davis, *Permissions Supervisor (Text)*
Maria L. Franklin, Josephine M. Keene, Michele M. Lonoconus, Denise M. Singleton, Kimberly F. Smilay, *Permissions Associates*
Rebecca A. Hartford, Shalice Shah, Nancy K. Sheridan, *Permissions Assistants*

Margaret A. Chamberlain, *Permissions Supervisor (Pictures)*
Pamela A. Hayes, *Permissions Associate*
Amy Lynn Emrich, Karla Kulkis, Nancy M. Rattenbury, Keith Reed, *Permissions Assistants*

Mary Beth Trimper, *Production Manager*
Mary Winterhalter, *Production Assistant*

Arthur Chartow, *Art Director*
C. J. Jonik, *Keyliner*
Kathleen A. Hourdakis, Mary Krzewinski, *Graphic Designers*

∞™ This book is printed on acid-free paper that meets the minimum requirements of American National Standard for Information Sciences— Permanence Paper for Printed Library Materials, ANSI Z39.48-1984.

ISBN 0-8103-8361-6 (6-volume set)
A CIP catalogue record for this book is available from the British Library
Printed in the United States of America
Published simultaneously in the United Kingdom
by Gale Research International Limited
(An affiliated company of Gale Research Inc.)

Table of Contents

Introduction

A Comprehensive Information Source
on World Literature

*W*orld Literature Criticism, 1500 to the Present (WLC) presents a broad selection of the best criticism of works by major writers of the past five hundred years. Among the authors included in *WLC* are sixteenth-century Spanish novelist Miguel de Cervantes and English dramatist William Shakespeare; seventeenth-century English poet John Milton and dramatist Aphra Behn; eighteenth-century Anglo-Irish novelist Jonathan Swift, English essayist Samuel Johnson, and French Enlightenment masters Jean-Jacques Rousseau and Voltaire; acclaimed nineteenth-century writers Jane Austen, William Blake, Emily Brontë, Lewis Carroll, Charles Dickens, Fyodor Dostoyevsky, Frederick Douglass, Gustave Flaubert, Edgar Allan Poe, Mary Shelley, Robert Louis Stevenson, William Wordsworth, and Emile Zola; and major twentieth-century authors W. H. Auden, James Baldwin, Albert Camus, Arthur Conan Doyle, Ralph Ellison, F. Scott Fitzgerald, Ernest Hemingway, James Joyce, Franz Kafka, Toni Morrison, Sylvia Plath, J. D. Salinger, Gertrude Stein, John Steinbeck, Virginia Woolf, and Richard Wright. The scope of *WLC* is wide: more than 225 writers representing dozens of nations, cultures, and time periods.

Coverage

This six-volume set is designed for high school, college, and university students, as well as for the general reader who wants to learn more about literature. *WLC* was developed in response to strong demand by students, librarians, and other readers for a one-stop, authoritative guide to the whole spectrum of world literature. No other compendium like it exists in the marketplace. About 95% of the entries in *WLC* were selected from Gale's acclaimed Literary Criticism Series and completely updated for publication here. Typically, the revisions are extensive, ranging from new author introductions to wide changes in the selection of criticism. A few entries—about 5%— were prepared especially for *WLC* in order to furnish the most comprehensive coverage possible.

Inclusion Criteria

Authors were selected for inclusion in *WLC* based on the advice of leading experts on world literature as well as on the recommendation of a specially formed advisory panel made up of high school teachers and high school and public librarians from throughout the United States. Additionally, the most recent major curriculum studies were closely examined, notably Arthur N. Applebee, *A Study of Book-Length Works Taught in High School English Courses* (1989); Arthur N. Applebee, *A Study of High School Literature Anthologies* (1991); and Doug Estel, Michele L. Satchwell, and Patricia S. Wright, *Reading Lists for College-Bound Students* (1990). All of these resources were collated and compared to produce a reference product that is strongly curriculum driven. To ensure that *WLC* will continue to meet the needs of students and general readers alike, an effort was made to identify a group of important new writers in addition to the most studied authors.

Scope

Each author entry in *WLC* presents a historical survey of critical response to the author's works. Typically, early criticism is offered to indicate initial responses, later selections document any rise or decline in literary reputations, and retrospective analyses provide modern views. Every endeavor has been made to include seminal essays on each author's work along with commentary providing current perspectives. Interviews and author statements are also included in many entries. Thus, *WLC* is both timely and comprehensive.

Organization of Author Entries

Information about authors and their works is presented through ten key access points:

- The **Descriptive Table of Contents** guides readers through the range of world literature, offering summary sketches of authors' careers and achievements.

- In each author entry, the **Author Heading** cites the name under which the author most commonly wrote, followed by birth and, where appropriate, death dates. Uncertain birth or death dates are indicated by question marks. Name variations, including full birth names when available, are given in parentheses in the caption below the **Author Portrait**.

- The **Biographical and Critical Introduction** contains background information about the life and works of the author. Emphasis is given to four main areas: 1) biographical details that help reveal the life, character, and personality of the author; 2) overviews of the major literary interests of the author—for example, novel writing, autobiography, poetry, social reform, documentary, etc.; 3) descriptions and summaries of the author's best-known works; and 4) critical commentary about the author's achievement, stature, and importance. The concluding paragraph of the **Biographical and Critical Introduction** directs readers to other Gale series containing information about the author.

- Every *WLC* entry includes an **Author Portrait**. Many entries also contain **Illustrations**—including holographs, title pages of works, letters, or pictures of important people, places, and events in the author's life—that document the author's career.

- The **List of Principal Works** is chronological by date of first book publication and identifies the genre of each work. For non-English-language authors whose works have been translated into English, the title and date of the first English-language edition are given in brackets beneath the foreign-language listing. Unless otherwise indicated, dramas are dated by first performance rather than first publication.

- **Criticism** is arranged chronologically in each author entry to provide a useful perspective on changes in critical evaluation over the years. Most entries contain a detailed, comprehensive study of the author's career as well as book reviews, studies of individual works, and comparative examinations. To ensure timeliness, current views are most often presented, but not to the exclusion of important early pieces. For the purpose of easy identification, the critic's name and the date of the critical work are given at the beginning of each piece of criticism. Unsigned criticism is preceded by the title of the source in which it appeared. Within the criticism, titles of works by the author are printed in boldface type. Publication information (such as publisher names and book prices) and certain numerical references (such as footnotes or page and line references to specific editions of works) have been deleted at the editor's discretion to provide smoother reading of the text.

■ Critical essays are prefaced by **Explanatory Notes** as an additional aid to readers of *WLC*. These notes may provide several types of valuable information, including: 1) the reputation of the critic; 2) the importance of the work of criticism; 3) the commentator's approach to the author's work; 4) the purpose of the criticism; and 5) changes in critical trends regarding the author. In some cases, **Explanatory Notes** cross-reference the work of critics within an entry who agree or disagree with each other.

■ A complete **Bibliographical Citation** of the original essay or book follows each piece of criticism.

■ An annotated list of **Sources for Further Study** appears at the end of each entry and suggests resources for additional study. These lists were specially compiled to meet the needs of high school and college students. Additionally, most of the sources cited are available in typical small and medium-size libraries.

■ Many entries contain a **Major Media Adaptations** section listing important non-print treatments and adaptations of the author's works, including feature films, TV mini-series, and radio broadcasts. This feature was specially conceived for *WLC* to meet strong demand from students for this type of information.

Other Features

WLC contains three distinct indexes to help readers find information quickly and easily:

■ The **Author Index** lists all the authors appearing in *WLC*. To ensure easy access, name variations and changes are fully cross-indexed.

■ The **Nationality Index** lists all authors featured in *WLC* by nationality. For expatriate authors and authors identified with more than one nation, multiple listings are offered.

■ The **Title Index** lists in alphabetical order all individual works by the authors appearing in *WLC*. English-language translations of original foreign-language titles are cross-referenced to the foreign titles so that all references to a work are combined in one listing.

Citing *World Literature Criticism*

When writing papers, students who quote directly from *WLC* may use the following general forms to footnote reprinted criticism. The first example is for material drawn from periodicals, the second for material reprinted from books:

Gary Smith, "Gwendolyn Brooks's 'A Street in Bronzeville,' the Harlem Renaissance and the Mythologies of Black Women," *MELUS*, Vol. 10, No. 3 (Fall 1983), 33-46; excerpted and reprinted in *World Literature Criticism, 1500 to the Present*, ed. James P. Draper (Detroit: Gale Research, 1992), pp. 459-61.

Frederick R. Karl, *American Fictions, 1940/1980: A Comprehensive History and Critical Evaluation* (Harper & Row, 1983); excerpted and reprinted in *World Literature Criticism, 1500 to the Present*, ed. James P. Draper (Detroit: Gale Research, 1992), pp. 541-46.

Acknowledgments

The editor wishes to acknowledge the valuable contributions of the many librarians, authors, and scholars who assisted in the compilation of *WLC* with their responses to telephone and mail inquiries. Special thanks are offered to the members of *WLC*'s advisory board, whose names are listed opposite the title page.

Comments Are Welcome

The editor hopes that readers will find *WLC* to be a useful reference tool and welcomes comments about the work. Send comments and suggestions to: Editor, *World Literature Criticism, 1500 to the Present*, Gale Research Inc., Penobscot Building, Detroit, MI 48226-4094.

WORLD LITERATURE CRITICISM

1500 to the Present

Miguel de Cervantes

1547-1616

(Full name Miguel de Cervantes Saavedra) Spanish novelist, short story writer, dramatist, and poet.

INTRODUCTION

*T*hrough his authorship of *Don Quixote* (1605-15) and other lesser known works, Cervantes has had an inestimable impact on the development of modern fiction. *Don Quixote* represents the first extended prose narrative in European literature in which characters and events are depicted in accord with modern realistic tradition, with the form of the work artfully constructed upon a complex of symbol and theme. Hence, *Don Quixote* maintains the distinction of being the original European novel, one from which all others, in some sense, are descended. Countless writers and scholars have viewed it as one of the most enduring masterpieces, as the deranged gentleman-turned-knight Quixote and his companion, Sancho Panza, assume archetypal importance for what they reveal of the human mind and emotions, Golden Age Spanish society, and the compass of earthly existence. Cervantes's short stories are also admired for their similar independence from stereotype and contrivance and are accorded high importance for their parallel development of the short fiction form.

Cervantes was born in Alcalá de Henares, near Madrid, into an itinerant apothecary-surgeon's family. Little is known of Cervantes's childhood, though it is assumed that his schooling was minimal and his comforts few, given the family's continual sojourn throughout the regions of Castile, Seville, and Andalusia as the father searched for work. The first documented evidence concerning Cervantes's life, other than his birth record, places him at the Estudio de la Villa de Madrid, a pregraduate liberal arts school, in 1568. While studying in Madrid, Cervantes probably wrote his first known works: elegiac verses on the death of Queen Isabel de Valois. Cervantes's schoolmaster, humanist Juan López de Hoyos, edited and published these and other poems, with approbatory reference to Cervantes, in

1569. By this time, however, Cervantes had removed to Rome to serve as steward to Cardinal Guilio Acquaviva. The following year, he enlisted with Spanish forces stationed in Italy that planned to help defend the countries of southern Europe against the burgeoning Ottoman-Turkish empire, which threatened invasion. In 1571, under the general command of Don John of Austria, Cervantes fought heroically in the naval battle of Lepanto off the coast of Greece. Although shot twice in the chest and once in his left hand—this last an injury which left him permanently crippled—Cervantes gloried in the victory for the duration of his life. His military career ended in 1574 and was followed by royal commendations. While returning from the Tunisian coast to Spain the following year, Cervantes and a group of fellow Spaniards were captured by Algerian pirates; for the next five years they remained imprisoned in North Africa, waiting for friends and family to meet the inordinately high ransom demanded by the leader of the Moorish captors. After four failed escape attempts organized by Cervantes and numerous setbacks to efforts on their behalf at home, the prisoners were finally ransomed, and the group returned to Spain as national heroes late in 1580.

Unfortunately, Cervantes soon found that his heroic efforts had been forgotten and that procuring official employment amidst a floundering national economy—due largely to ill-conceived war efforts in other regions of Europe—appeared impossible. In hopes of fame as well as fortune, he began writing plays for the Spanish stage in the classical tradition of Euripides and Aeschylus, though he focused on contemporary national concerns. It is believed that during the course of only a few years Cervantes wrote some thirty full-length plays, though only his first (*El trato de Argel; The Commerce of Algiers*) appears to have been produced, probably in 1580. The advent of the prolific young dramatist Lope de Vega and his lively comedies, replete with recognizable stock characters and sensational stories intended for a wide audience, eclipsed any possibility for success which Cervantes might have had in this field. An attempt at mastering the pastoral romance form with *La Galatea,* published in 1585 (the year of his marriage to Catalina de Salazar y Palacios), also met with little public notice. In 1587, in desperate need of a salaried job to support his wife, his two sisters, and an illegitimate daughter, Cervantes accepted a position as commissary agent for the Spanish Armada. Unfortunately, Cervantes was caught a short time later in the middle of a dispute concerning grain requisitions and was charged with malfeasance and jailed on at least two, and possibly three, occasions. During this troubled period Cervantes continued to write poems—some of which won great popularity, though small remuneration—and dramas, which he unsuccessfully attempted to have produced. Cervantes's position as commissary agent ended in 1597, though for several years afterward he was hounded by investigators charging him with further mismanagement while in his former job.

Remarkably, it was following this low point in his career that Cervantes—past fifty, impoverished, increasingly unhappy in marriage, and almost entirely unknown as a literary figure—undertook the composition of *El ingenioso hidalgo Don Quixote de la Mancha* (1605), the first part of the masterpiece from which virtually all fame during and following his life stemmed. Apparently, Cervantes's initial intention was to capitalize on the public's overwhelming interest in chivalric romances by writing a lively, salable parody of the genre. His own references to this work and its sequel clearly demonstrate that he viewed the prose narrative in general as a lower literary form, and that he believed his efforts in the forms he admired most—poetry, drama, and poetic romance—would one day earn critical acclaim. Nonetheless, both critical and popular welcome emerged rapidly after publication of the novel in 1605. Within a few months the hilarious exploits of the eccentric knight Don Quixote were being recited and discussed throughout Spain. However, Cervantes's and the publisher's reprint and royalty rights had been grievously unprotected so that, despite the appearance of more than a dozen editions throughout Europe during the next several years, Cervantes's monetary compensation was slight. As the creator of one of the most entertaining and vivid stories yet seen in European literature, though, Cervantes was now enabled to publish and command regard for several works heretofore neglected, including the burlesque poem "Viage del Parnaso" (1614; "Journey to Parnassus") and the dramatic collection *Ocho comedias y ocho entremeses* (1615); Cervantes also published *Novelas exemplares* (1613; *Exemplary Stories*), a collection of new and older material which, in many instances, anticipated in style and theme much of *Don Quixote.* In 1614, already far along in the composition of Part II to this work, Cervantes learned of a spurious imitation of his novel entitled *Segundo tomo del ingenioso hidalgo Don Quixote de la Mancha,* recently published under the pseudonym Alonso Fernandez de Avellaneda. Adapting the situation to his advantage through a clever discreditation of Avellaneda's work within a chapter he was currently drafting, Cervantes raced to complete the authentic version, publishing it the following year. Again, the reception was universally enthusiastic, and Cervantes's name now commanded great admiration throughout Europe, particularly in England, following the appearance of spirited translations by Thomas Shelton. This second part of the novel was as widely pirated as the first, however, and afforded Cervantes relatively little recompense. While *Don Quixote, Part II* (1615) signified a considerable advancement over *Part I* in terms of technique and narrative artistry, his final work, the posthumously published *Los trabaios de Persiles y Sigismunda* (1617; *The Travels of Persiles and Sigismunda*), reaffirmed the poetic romance form and an idealistic worldview, both of which *Don Quixote* deny. Shortly after completing *Persiles and Sigismunda*, Cervantes died of edema at the age of sixty-nine.

Few writers in world literature, aside from Shakespeare, are esteemed more than Cervantes. Yet, it is more truly said of Cervantes than of most major literary figures that his works vary widely in artistic value. The least of Cervantes's literary talents was that for writing poetry. In addition to his few individual poems, Cervantes generated through his verse dramas, two versified interludes, and the countless interpolated poems of his novels and short stories, a mass of poetic material which far exceeded the production of most noted Spanish poets of his era. His use of form and subject was wide, encompassing heroic and religious verse, elegies, and love poems. His most significant achievement in the genre is "Journey to Parnassus," the allegorical, self-deprecatory epic of Cervantes's trek to Parnassus's peak to seek recognition from Apollo and from Spanish colleagues for his poetic abilities. The poem is considered accomplished and occasionally lit by high humor and imagination. His verse in general, though, shows him a largely unimaginative poet unable to sustain extended, inventive lyric flights or sophisticated formulations of his thoughts and impressions.

As a dramatist, Cervantes was somewhat more successful according to modern evaluations. Only ten of his full-length plays survive: of these, only two—*The Commerce of Algiers,* which recreates his five years in captivity, and *Numancia* (1585?), a drama set in Classical Greece and reflecting Cervantes's desire for a renewed, heroic Spain—have been performed to moderate success since his death. Aside from a close adherence to the Aristotelian unities of action, time, and place—guidelines which Lope successfully chose to disregard—Cervantes's dramas may be distinguished by an overriding concern with characters in search of identities. Although Cervantes is credited for refusing to stereotype his characters, or to treat the drama form as a streamlined vehicle for light entertainment as did Lope, his dramas are considered drab theatrical exercises hobbled by discursive, moralistic dialogue, compared to most other Spanish Renaissance dramas. Unanimously acknowledged as Cervantes's highest achievement in drama are his eight *entremeses:* one-act comic interludes meant to be performed between the first and second acts of longer plays. Typically concerned with marital discord or the enactment of a clever swindle, Cervantes's interludes are praised for their swift pace and compelling entertainment and are still regarded as some of the best examples of this little-known form.

As with his other literary endeavors, Cervantes's early fiction stemmed from established generic models. *La Galatea,* considered an otherwise fairly good period romance, appears fraught with such pitfalls of the genre as contrived description and dialogue, melodramatic scenes, and a circuitous, confusing plot. Critics agree that Cervantes was considerably more successful in presenting artistically sound narrative in his later romance, *Persiles and Sigismunda.* This work, nearly as popular as *Don Quixote* throughout the seventeenth and early eighteenth centuries, gradually fell into disrepute until well through the first half of the twentieth century due to an increasing emphasis in fiction on realistic portraiture and thematically unified story, traits which the majority of scholars find absent from *Persiles.* However, a notable *Persiles* critic, Alban K. Forcione, has discovered significant meaning, unity, and masterful narration in the novel. He asserts that *Persiles*—a tale of the titular heroes' epic travels and records of self-discovery, culminating in their visit to the Holy See in Rome—is a "quest romance" mirroring humanity's difficult journey toward spiritual fulfillment. Aside from this central religious allegory, *Persiles* presents a multiplicity of secondary plots, which to most readers have seemed superfluous and disruptive. Nevertheless, Forcione has concluded that "the major effect of this structure is an accumulation of power in the statement of theme through ritualistic repetition. Moreover, through fragmentary narration Cervantes succeeds in superimposing the episodes on the main plot, creating a richly complex texture and heightening the effect of timelessness that springs from the recurrence of ritual." Although the literary merit of *Persiles* is still questioned, most scholars concede that it deserves serious study in order to understand Cervantes's circular development of the extended prose narrative: from the traditional pastoral romance of *La Galatea* to the modern satirical novel *Don Quixote,* to the epic, architectonic romance *Persiles and Sigismunda,* a work which has been said to represent Cervantes's final rejection of an increasingly science-oriented society in favor of the idealized beauty and grandeur of the Golden-Age Spain of his youth.

Perhaps most undeservedly overshadowed by Cervantes's masterpiece is his *Exemplary Stories.* Twentieth-century scholars recognize the stories as the first and, quite often, best examples of the traditional Spanish short story. Like few other works in his canon, the stories are considered virtually without flaw. Benefiting from the discernment of such Renaissance dramatists as Francis Beaumont and John Fletcher, who adapted Cervantes's skillfully managed plots to successfully entertain English audiences, many of the pieces have attained a wide and long-lived popularity. According to William Byron, Cervantes's foremost achievement with the stories was that "he placed his characters in society and gave them psychologies of their own with which to deal with their situations. The stories are open to the sights and sounds of everyday life, habits, clothes, attitudes, the random comings and goings of people and events in a lived-in world. His characters exist and act in the context of that world; their problems are created by it, its accidents change their lives and they in turn stir the general air." Despite such high evaluations, of greater importance to most Cervantists than the independent success of the stories is the fact that they strongly shaped the narrative style, characterization, and thematic scope of their longer counterpart, *The Ingenious Gentleman Don Quixote de la Mancha.*

It has often been claimed that, had he not written *Don Quixote,* Cervantes would undoubtedly be an obscure writer in world literature today. Judged by the overwhelming body of critical material devoted to this novel alone during the past three centuries, the assertion appears justified. Certainly the novel has, in addition to entertaining readers for centuries, wielded an incalculable literary influence and has been honored by a host of major literary figures: from Henry Fielding, who in his advertisement to *Joseph Andrews* (1742), one of the most influential early English novels, humbly acknowledged his work to be "in imitation of the manner of Cervantes," to Carlos Fuentes, who in 1986 labelled *Don Quixote* "the first modern novel, perhaps the most eternal novel ever written." The reasons for which *Don Quixote* has attracted such veneration are numerous and varied. Firstly, it is a novel of original, unforgettable characters, the first such of its kind. Don Quixote and Sancho Panza vie with the most memorable fictional personalities of all time in their larger-than-life existences—made so through their endlessly quotable speeches, distinctive mannerisms, and emblematic worldviews. Don Quixote is commonly understood, via his ludicrous exploits, perpetual endurance of personal suffering, missionary zeal, and blind refusal to reconcile reality with the ideals of a chivalric knight, as a composite of the tragic idealist, the unbridled imaginative genius, the suffering Savior, and the aging, psychosexually frustrated male. Sancho, conversely, is the ardent skeptic, the simple-minded expositor of rationality, and the would-be complacent individual (provided he is well-fed and reasonably comfortable). What largely elevates the novel to greatness, according to many scholars, is the close and complex bond that develops between these two characters. They share one another's perceptions of the world; they fuel each other's aspirations for fame; and they repeatedly share the pain and anguish that follow upon their brutal encounters with reality. Most importantly, each sustains the glorified existence—for they have crowned themselves roving apostles of truth and honor—of the other: without Sancho, Quixote is a knight lacking a squire;

similarly, Sancho, without Quixote, is a common farmer lacking any exalted sense of purpose in his life. Each supports the other and ultimately both sustain the entire imaginative framework of the novel.

Although the structural components in this long novel are numerous, perhaps most important is its novel-within-a-novel scheme. At the opening of Part II Cervantes firmly iterates such a structure, recalling that Cide Hamete Benengeli (Cervantes's created narrator, whom he brought forth periodically in Part I to undergird the authenticity of his narrative as well as to distance himself from his subject) has already brought fame to the wayward heroes Quixote and Sancho, for Part I has popularized the two throughout Spain. Although much may be said of the many divergent themes that have been uncovered in the novel, it is Cervantes's representation and examination of the fine line between real and imagined worlds, between sanity and insanity, between the world of the creative artist and the actual world, that becomes Cervantes's central theme.

This theme is continually brought to the fore by Cervantes through several techniques, among them his many interpolated, fantastic tales in the manner of Boccaccio, which serve to reinforce the reader's belief in the actuality of Quixote's more immediate exploits. Another technique Cervantes employed is the subtle discourse on the art of creative writing, that is, of how best to represent both reality and the imagination through the use of the narrator, or dual narrator, as well as through the dialogue of the characters. Cervantes's principal theme is, of course, fully embodied in the very character of Quixote, in his world-altering personality. Until recent times, Quixote was considered a laughable lunatic who unwittingly afforded readers a telling exploration of the human condition. Increasingly though, he has come to be regarded as a cunning, brilliant old man who, rather than acquiesce to lifeless existence in his retirement, decides to transform his own reality by fictionalizing his past, creating a maiden (Dulcinea del Toboso) whom he religiously serves and honors, and adopting a medieval worldview, a blindness to all but the sphere of his imagination. Joseph Wood Krutch has thus found that "the quixoticism of Don Quixote is more than mere chivalry and more than a generous folly in dealing with persons or events. It is the expression of a faith in the power of the human being to create values by virtue of his faith in them and to generate a world above the world of nature in which his human as opposed to his natural life may be led."

As ardent as the proponents of the work are, it has had prominent detractors. Among them is Lord Byron, who charged in *Don Juan* (1819-24) that Cervantes was responsible for extinguishing the chivalric spirit in Europe through his parodies of chivalric encounters, a charge repeated by Ford Madox Ford in 1938. More cutting than this and similar complaints, however, are those by Miguel de Unamuno and Giovanni Papini, who have regarded Cervantes's knight, respectively, as an eternal, miraculously conceived literary symbol, yet one virtually disassociated with its coincidental, marginally talented author; and as a cunning poseur, rather than a guiltless, lovable madman, who cruelly uses those about him for his own egocentric ends. The general trend in criticism has, however, been overwhelmingly favorable; from the seventeenth century onward, the work has progressively been regarded as more than a comic entertainment. Ultimately, it has been considered an epic masterpiece in which the aberrant psyche of the human mind, the friendship between individuals, the struggle to create lasting art out of drab existence, are dramatized in modern language and form.

As such, *Don Quixote* has had a vast influence on the development of the modern novel. It remains a watershed work of art which exerted undeniable impact on the fiction of Fielding, Alain René Le Sage, Tobias Smollett, and other early novelists; further, it anticipated, through its exemplary treatment of the comic outsider, satire of social convention, and exploration of the human psyche, countless later fictional masterpieces, including Gustave Flaubert's *Madame Bovary* (1857),

Fyodor Dostoevsky's *The Idiot* (1868), and Mark Twain's *Tom Sawyer* (1876) and *Huckleberry Finn* (1884). A harsh critic of Cervantes, Unamuno has nonetheless lauded his magnum opus (if not its creator) thus: "As much as we may meditate on *Don Quixote,* as the Greeks meditated on the Homeric poems or the English on the dramas of Shakespeare, we cannot consume all the marrow of wisdom that it contains." Vladimir Nabokov, a major twentieth-century proponent of Cervantes's enduring main character, has written: "He has ridden for three hundred and fifty years through the jungles and tundras of human thought—and he has gained in vitality and stature. We do not laugh at him any longer. His blazon is pity, his banner is beauty. He stands for everything that is gentle, forlorn, pure, unselfish, and gallant. The parody has become a paragon." Cervantes's authorship of *Don Quixote*, above all else, has established him as one of the greatest figures of world literature, one who pioneered the modern novel's construction and, in so doing, produced an indisputable literary classic.

(For further information about Cervantes's life and works, see *Literature Criticism from 1400 to 1800*, Vol. 6.)

CRITICAL COMMENTARY

THOMAS ROSCOE
(essay date 1839)

[Roscoe was a nineteenth-century English writer and translator who earned acclaim for his *Life and Times of Miguel de Cervantes*, the first comprehensive study of Cervantes to appear in English. In the following excerpt from this work, he enumerates the qualities of *Don Quixote* that afford its author an unequalled position among Spanish writers.]

To *Don Quixote* Cervantes owes his immortality. No work in any language ever exhibited a more delicate or a more lively satire, combined with a richer vein of invention, and wrought with happier success. Of this, every one who has really read this inimitable work, is pleasantly enough aware; and also that it is one which cannot be read in fragments, or analysed according to rule. To become acquainted with the knight of La Mancha we must have a full-length view of him; watch him poring over his books of chivalry, hear him holding parley with paladins and enchanters; and see him soaring beyond the little confines of reason in his fantastic and glorious moods. They who have read the histories

of Amadis and Orlando, in which he took so much delight, know best how to estimate his qualities when he mounts his lean and ancient steed, braces on his rusty armour, and traverses plains and mountains in quest of adventures worthy of his sword. They can see how every object is transformed by his vivid imagination, from windmills, country girls, and clowns, into giants, paladins, Dulcineas, and enchanters; and why all his vexations and reverses are insufficient to open his eyes. To them the exploits of the Don, with his faithful Rosinante, and his comic squire, Sancho, appear in their true colours, and with all the dignity which gives so rich a zest to their exploits. To value these and their genuine characters at their worth, we ought to enter into the circumstances of the previous histories supposed to have formed them, and into the views which actuated the author in commemorating their heroic deeds; into the essential and deep-seated satire of his entire work, and which, without the buoyant and merry spirit that animated him, would have been a serious labour, a disquisition upon the errors and follies of human nature and of his times. His pleasantry, on the other hand, induces us to think, and to make compan-

Principal Works

"Yo que siempre trabajo y me desuelo" (poetry) 1569; published in Historia y relación verdadera de la enfermedad, felicísimo tránsito, y suntuosas exequias fúnebres de la serenísima Reina de España Doña Isabel de Valois, nuestra señora, con los sermones, letras, y epitafios á su túmolo

La Galatea (romance) 1585

[Galatea: A Pastoral Romance, 1791]

*El ingenioso hidalgo Don Quixote de la Mancha (novel) 1605

[The History of the Valorous and Wittie Knight-Errant, Don Quixote of the Mancha, 1612]

Novelas exemplares (short stories) 1613

[Exemplarie Novells, 1640; also published as Exemplary Stories (partial translation), 1972]

Viage del Parnaso [adaptor; from the poem "Viaggio in Parnasso" by Cesare Caporali di Perugia] (poetry) 1614

[Voyage to Parnassus published in Voyage to Parnassus, Numancia, and The Commerce of Algiers, 1870; also published as Journey to Parnassus, 1883]

Ocho comedias y ocho entremeses (dramas) 1615

[Pedro, the Artful Dodger (partial translation), 1964; published in Eight Plays of the Golden Age]

*Segunda parte del ingenioso cavallero Don Quixote (novel) 1615

[The Second Part of the History of the Valorous and Witty Knight Errant, Don Quixote of the Mancha, 1620]

Los trabaios de Persiles y Sigismunda (romance) 1617

[The Travels of Persiles and Sigismunda. A Northern History. Wherein, amongst the Variable Fortunes of the Prince of Thule, and this Princesse of Frisland, are interlaced many Witty Discourses, Morall, Politicall, and Delightfull, 1619]

†El cerco de Numancia (drama) 1784

[Numancia, 1870; also published as The Siege of Numantia in The Classic Theatre, 1961]

‡El trato de Argel (drama) 1784

[The Commerce of Algiers published in Voyage to Parnassus, Numancia, and The Commerce of Algiers, 1883]

Obras completes de Cervantes. 12 vols. (novels, short stories, romances, dramas, and poetry) 1863-64

*These works have, since first publication and translation, appeared as the single work Don Quixote. Several English editions might be cited, in addition to those listed above. For general purposes, the three most often recommended for availability, textual integrity, and scholarly documentation are The Ingenious Gentleman Don Quixote de la Mancha, translated by Samuel Putnam (1949); The Adventures of Don Quixote, translated by J. M. Cohen (1968); and Don Quixote: The Ormsby Translation Revised, edited by Joseph R. Jones and Kenneth Douglas (1981).

†This work was written ca. 1585.

‡This work was performed sometime after 1580.

ions of wisdom and reflection by the way-side; and we laugh while we are taught. Even the most diverting adventures, told in the most humorous spirit, bear a moral with them at which the author never fails to point. If we wish to take as it was meant, the humour afforded by the singular heroism of the knight, contrasted with the terror of the squire, when, in the dead hour of night, they hear the sound of a fulling-mill, we enjoy the humour doubly from our knowledge of the peril of night adventures and attacks, and we unconsciously compare their situation with that of Homer's and Virgil's heroes, when plotting to surprise the enemy in their camps. To form a just opinion, the work must be understood and read as a whole. No extracts could convey an idea of the adventures at the inn which Don Quixote imagined was an enchanted castle, and where Sancho was thrown in a blanket. It is only in the work itself that we can enjoy the wit of the fine contrast between the gravity, the measured language, and the manner of Don Quixote, and the ignorance and vulgarity of Sancho. It must be left to the power of the narrative itself, to the interest and charm of the whole,

blending the liveliness of imagination which results from variety of adventures, with the liveliness of wit which displays itself in the delineation of character, to rivet the attention of the reader to such a book. This is shown by the indifference of those who have perused and relished it, to the best extracts which could be taken from it, and much is also lost without some acquaintance with the language, and with the customs and manners of the hero's country.

Another, and not the least striking feature in the composition of *Don Quixote,* is the continual contrast preserved between what has been called the poetical and the prosaic spirit. The imagination, the emotions, all the most generous qualities and impulses, tend to elevate Don Quixote in our eyes. Men of noble minds, we know, both before and since the age of the hero, made it the object of their lives to defend the weak, to aid the oppressed, to be the champions of justice and innocence. Like Don Quixote, too, they everywhere discovered the image of those virtues which they worshipped. They believed that disinterestedness, nobility, courage, and chivalry, were still in existence. Without calculating upon their own powers, they still exerted themselves for the welfare of the ungrateful, and sacrificed themselves to laws and principles, by many considered altogether illusory. The devotion of heroism, indeed, and the trials of virtue, are among the noblest and most exemplary themes in the history of man. They present the best subjects for the highest species of poetry, which is for the most part little more than the representation of grand and disinterested feelings. The same character, however, which excites our admiration when beheld from an elevated situation, becomes almost ridiculous when viewed from the level of the earth. We know that there is no more fertile source of entertainment than error, in other words, blunders and mistakes. These, which abound in the adventures of the hero, by producing the most comic juxta-positions, and what may be truly termed witty incidents, which speak for themselves, abound throughout the narration; for a man who sees nothing around him but what is heroic or chivalrous, must assuredly give frequent occasion for the play of strange combinations, odd situations, and novel events. Next to such pleasant mistakes are those contrasts still more productive, perhaps, of risible effects, for nothing can be more singularly contrasted than the poetry and the prose of life; the romance of the imagination, and the petty details of everyday occurrence; the valour and the great appetite of the hero; the palace of Armida and an inn; the enchanted princesses and Maritorna. (pp. 141-44)

The style of Cervantes, in his *Don Quixote,* possesses an inimitable beauty which no translation can approach. It exhibits the nobleness, the candour, and the simplicity of the ancient romances of chivalry, together with a liveliness of colouring, a precision of expression, and a harmony in its periods, which have never been equalled by any other Spanish writer. (p. 154)

Thomas Roscoe, in his *The Life and Times of Miguel de Cervantes,* Thos. Tegg, 1839, 412 p.

MIGUEL DE UNAMUNO

(essay date 1905)

[Unamuno was one of the most influential Spanish writers and thinkers of his era. In the following excerpt from an essay originally published in 1905, he argues that Cervantes "extracted Don Quixote from the soul of his people and from the soul of all humanity."]

[Today], there is scarcely a literature that yields less individual and more insipid works than that of Spain,

and there is scarcely a cultured nation—or one that passes for such—where there is such a manifest incapacity for philosophy. (pp. 446-47)

[This] philosophical incapacity which Spain has always shown, as well as a certain poetic incapacity—poetry is not the same as literature—has allowed a host of pedants and spiritual sluggards, who constitute what might be called the school of the Cervantist Masora, to fall upon *Don Quixote.*

The Masora was, as the reader will doubtless remember, a Jewish undertaking, consisting of critical annotations to the Hebrew text of Holy Scripture, the work of various rabbis of the school at Tiberias during the eighth and ninth centuries. The Masoretes, as these rabbis were called, counted all the letters which compose the Biblical text and determined the incidence of each letter and the number of times each one was preceded by one of the others, and other curious matters of this type.

The Cervantist Masoretes have not yet indulged in such excesses with *Don Quixote;* but they are not far off. As regards our book, all manner of unimportant minutiae and every kind of insignificant detail have been recorded. The book has been turned upside down and considered from every angle, but scarcely anyone has examined its entrails, nor entered into its inner meaning.

Even worse: whenever anyone has attempted to plumb its depths and give our book a symbolic or tropological sense, all the Masoretes and their allies, the pure litterateurs and the whole coterie of mean spirits, have fallen upon him and torn him to bits or have ridiculed him. From time to time, some holy man from the camp of the wise and shortsighted pedants comes along and informs us that Cervantes neither could nor would mean to say what this or that symbolist attributed to him, inasmuch as his sole object was to put an end to the reading of books of chivalry.

Assuming that such was his intent, what does Cervantes' intention in *Don Quixote,* if he had any intention, have to do with what the rest of us see in the book? Since when is the author of a book the person to understand it best?

Ever since *Don Quixote* appeared in print and was placed at the disposition of anyone who would take it in hand and read it, the book has no longer belonged to Cervantes, but to all who read it and feel it. Cervantes extracted Don Quixote from the soul of his people and from the soul of all humanity, and in his immortal book he returned him to his people and all humanity. Since then, Don Quixote and Sancho have continued to live in the souls of the readers of Cervantes' book and even in the souls of those who have never read it. There scarcely exists a person of even average education who does not have some idea of Don Quixote and Sancho. (pp. 448-50)

Cervantes wrote his book in the Spain of the beginnings of the seventeenth century and for the Spain of that time; but Don Quixote has traveled through all the countries of the world in the course of the three centuries that have passed since then. Inasmuch as Don Quixote could not be the same man, for example, in nineteenth-century England as in seventeenth-century Spain, he has been transformed and modified in England, giving proof thereby of his powerful vitality and of the intense realism of his ideal reality.

It is nothing more than pettiness of spirit (to avoid saying something worse) that moves certain Spanish critics to insist on reducing *Don Quixote* to a mere work of literature, great though its value may be, and to attempt to drown in disdain, mockery, or invective all who seek in the book for meanings more intimate than the merely liberal.

If the Bible came to have an inestimable value it is because of what generations of men put into it by their reading, as their spirits fed there; and it is well known that there is hardly a passage in it that has not been interpreted in hundreds of ways, depending on the interpreter. And this is all very much to the good. Of less importance is whether the authors of the different books of the Bible meant to say what the theologians, mystics, and commentators see there; the important fact is that, thanks to this immense labor of generations through the centuries, the Bible is a perennial fountain of consolation, hope, and heartfelt inspiration. Why should not the same process undergone by Holy Scripture take place with *Don Quixote*, which should be the national Bible of the patriotic religion of Spain?

Perhaps it would not be difficult to establish a relation between our weak, soft, and addled patriotism and the narrowness of vision, the wretchedness of spirit, and the crushing vulgarity of Cervantist Masoretism and of the critics and litterateurs of this country who have examined our book.

I have observed that whenever *Don Quixote* is cited with enthusiasm in Spain, it is most often the least intense and least profound passages that are quoted, the most literary and least poetic, those that least lend themselves to philosophic flights or exaltations of the heart. The passages of our book which figure in the anthologies, in the treatises of rhetoric—they should all be burned!—or in the selections for school reading, seem specially picked out by some scribe or Masorete in open warfare with the spirit of the immortal Don Quixote, who continues to live after having risen again from the sepulcher sealed by Don Miguel de Cervantes Saavedra, after the hidalgo had been entombed there and his death certified.

Instead of getting to the poetry in *Don Quixote*, the truly eternal and universal element in it, we tend to become enmeshed in its literature, in its temporal and particular elements. In this regard, nothing is more wretched than to consider *Don Quixote* a language text for Spanish. The truth is that our book is no such thing, for in point of language there are many books which can boast a purer and more correct Spanish. And as regards the style, *Don Quixote* is guilty of a certain artificiality and affectation. (pp. 451-53)

I have no doubt in my mind but that Cervantes is a typical example of a writer enormously inferior to his work, to his *Don Quixote.* If Cervantes had not written this book, whose resplendent light bathes his other works, he would scarcely figure in our literary history as anything more than a talent of the fifth, sixth, or thirteenth order. No one would read his insipid *Exemplary Novels,* just as no one now reads his unbearable **"Voyage to Parnassus,"** or his plays. Even the novellas and digressions which figure in *Don Quixote,* such as that most foolish novella, *Foolish Curiosity,* would not warrant the attention of any reader. Though Don Quixote sprang from the creative faculty of Cervantes, he is immensely superior to Cervantes. In strict truth, it cannot be said that Don Quixote is the child of Cervantes; for if Cervantes was his father, his mother was the country and people in which he lived and from which Cervantes derived his being; and Don Quixote has much more of his mother about him than of his father.

I suspect, in fact, that Cervantes died without having sounded the profundity of his *Don Quixote* and perhaps without even having rightly understood it. It seems to me that if Cervantes came back to life and read his *Don Quixote* once again, he would understand it as little as do the Cervantist Masoretes, and that he would side with them. Let there be no doubt that if Cervantes returned to the world he would be a Cervantist and not a Quixotist. It is enough to read our book with some attention to observe that whenever the good Cervantes introduces himself into the narrative and sets about making observations on his own, it is merely to give vent to some impertinence or to pass malevolent and malicious judgments on his hero. Thus, for example, when he recounts the beautiful exploit wherein Don Quixote addresses a discourse on the Golden Age to some goatherds who could not possibly understand it in the literal sense—and the harangue is of a heroic order precisely because of this incapacity—Cervantes labels it a "purposeless discourse." Immediately afterwards he shows us that it was not purposeless, for the goatherds heard him out with "openmouthed fascination," and by way of gratitude they repaid Don Quixote with pastoral songs. Poor Cervantes did not attain to the robust faith of the hidalgo from La Mancha, a faith which led him to address himself to the goatherds in elevated language, convinced that if they did not understand the words they were edified by the music. And this passage is one of many in which Cervantes shows his hand.

None of this should surprise us, for as I have pointed out, if Cervantes was Don Quixote's father, his mother was the country and people of which Cervantes was part. Cervantes was merely the instrument by which sixteenth-century Spain gave birth to Don Quixote. In this work Cervantes carried out the most impersonal task that can be imagined and, consequently, the most profoundly personal in another sense. As author of *Don Quixote,* Cervantes is no more than the minister and representative of humanity; that is why his work was great.

The genius is, in effect, an individual who through sheer personality achieves impersonality, one who becomes the voice of his country and people, one who succeeds in saying what everybody thinks though they have never been able to say it. (pp. 455-56)

There are lifelong geniuses, geniuses who last throughout their lives and who manage during all that period to be ministers and spiritual spokesmen for their country and people, and there are temporary geniuses, who are geniuses only once in their lives. Of course, that one occasion may be more or less long-lasting and boast greater or lesser import. And this fact should serve as consolation to us earthenware mortals when we consider those of finest porcelain. For who has not at some time been, even if only for a quarter hour, a genius of his people, and even though his people only number three hundred neighbors? Who has not been a hero for a day or for five minutes? And thanks to the fact that we can all be temporary geniuses, though it be only for a few moments, we can understand the lifelong, the lifetime geniuses, and be enamored of them.

Cervantes was, then, a temporary genius; and if he appears to us an absolute and lasting genius, as greater than most of the lifelong geniuses, it is because the work he wrote during his season of genius is a work not merely lifelong but eternal. (p. 457)

Consider what there is of genius in Cervantes, and consider what his inward relation is to his Don Quixote. Such considerations should indeed move us to leave Cervantism for Quixotism, and to pay more attention to Don Quixote than to Cervantes. God did not send Cervantes into the world for any other purpose than to write *Don Quixote;* and it seems to me that it would have been an advantage for us if we had never known the name of the author, and our book had been an anonymous work, like the old ballads of Spain and, as many of us believe, the *Iliad.*

I may indeed write an essay whose thesis will be that Cervantes never existed but Don Quixote did. In any case, inasmuch as Cervantes exists no longer, while Don Quixote continues alive, we should all abandon the dead and go off with the living, abandon Cervantes and follow Don Quixote. (p. 459)

Before finishing I must make a declaration to the effect that everything I have said here about Don Quixote is applicable to his faithful and most noble squire Sancho Panza, even worse known and more maligned than his lord and master. This disfavor blighting the memory of the good Sancho Panza descends to us directly from Cervantes, who, if he did not rightly understand his Don Quixote did not even begin to comprehend his Sancho, and if he was sometimes malicious as regards the master, he was almost always unjust to the servant.

One of the obvious truths which leaps to our attention while reading *Don Quixote* is the incomprehension shown by Cervantes of the soul and character of Sancho, whose sublime heroism was never understood by his literary father. Cervantes maligns and ill-treats Sancho without rhyme or reason; he persists in not seeing clearly the motivations behind his acts, and there are occasions when one feels tempted to believe that, impelled by incomprehension, he alters the facts and makes the good squire say and do things he never could have said or done, and which, therefore, he never did say or do.

So cunning was malicious Cervantes in twisting Sancho's intentions and shuffling his purposes that the noble squire has gotten an unmerited reputation, from which we Quixotists will redeem him, I trust, since a good Quixotist has to be a Sanchopanzist as well.

Fortunately, since Cervantes was, as I said, only in part—and in very small part—the author of *Don Quixote,* all the necessary elements to reinstate the true Sancho and give him the fame he deserves remain at hand in the immortal book. For if Don Quixote was enamored of Dulcinea, Sancho was no less so, with the difference that the master quit his house for love of glory and the servant did so for pay; but the servant began to get a taste for glory, and in the end he was, in the heart of him, and though he would have denied it, one of the most unmercenary men the world has ever known. And by the time Don Quixote died, grown sane again, cured of his madness for glory, Sancho had gone mad, raving mad, mad for glory; and while the hidalgo was cursing books of chivalry the good squire begged him, with tears in his eyes, not to die, but to go on living so they might sally forth along the roads in search of adventure.

Inasmuch as Cervantes did not dare kill Sancho, still less bury him, many people assume that Sancho never died, and even that he is immortal. When we least expect it, we will see him sally forth, mounted on Rocinante, who did not die either, and he will be wearing his master's armor, cut down to size by the blacksmith at El Toboso. Sancho will take to the road again to continue Don Quixote's glorious work, so that Quixotism may triumph for once and all time on this earth. For let there be no doubt that Sancho, Sancho the good, Sancho the discreet, Sancho the simple, Sancho who went mad beside the deathbed of his master dying sane, Sancho, I say, is the man charged by God definitively to establish Quixotism on earth. Thus do I hope and desire, and in this and in God do I trust.

And if some reader of this essay should say that it is made up of contrivances and paradoxes, I shall reply that he does not know one iota about matters of Quixotism, and repeat to him what Don Quixote said on a certain occasion to his squire: "Because I know you, Sancho, I pay no attention to what you say." (pp. 461-63)

Miguel de Unamuno, "Appendix: On the Reading and Interpretation of 'Don Quixote'," in his *Selected Works of Miguel de Unamuno: Our Lord Don Quixote, Vol. 3,* edited by Anthony Kerrigan and Martin Nozick, translated by Anthony Kerrigan, Bollingen Series LXXXV, Princeton University Press, 1967, pp. 445-66.

NORTHROP FRYE

(essay date 1949)

[A Canadian critic and editor, Frye wrote the highly influential and controversial *Anatomy of Criticism* (1957), in which he argued that literary criticism can be scientific in its methods and results and that judgments are not inherent in the critical process. In the following excerpt from a 1949 essay, he addresses several major themes of *Don Quixote.*]

Cervantes' intention in writing *Don Quixote* was, no doubt, to ridicule the stories of chivalry, with a result summarized in the Dewey Library Catalogue as: "immense vogue of books of chivalry despite legislation till publication of *Don Quixote;* thereafter only one written." But great art comes from harnessing a conscious intention to the creative powers beneath consciousness, and we do not get closer to the author's meaning by getting closer to the book's meaning. The greater the book, the more obvious it is that the author's consciousness merely held the nozzle of the hose, so to speak. For instance, we can see after the event what Cervantes can hardly have seen during it, that the tale of the crack-brained knight is one of the profoundest social parables in history. The feudal chivalric aristocracy has been caught at the precise moment of its departure from the European stage, caught with its armor rusty, its ideals faded to dreams, its sense of reality hopelessly lost. Elsewhere, in England, for instance, a new middle class not only seized its money and power but stole its ideals as well: the story of Quixote is the story of Spain, with its great culture destroyed by poverty and bigotry, with its weak middle class and its rabble of fanatically proud pauper-nobles. "And so, Sancho my friend," pleads Quixote, "do not be grieved at that which pleases me, nor seek to make the world over, nor to unhinge the institution of knight-errantry." But it's no use; the made-over world is already there.

However, the book has profounder levels than that of historical parable. Cervantes may be said to have defined a principle almost as important for fiction writing as charity is for religion: the principle that if people are ridiculous, they are pathetic; and if they have pathos, they have dignity. The Don is ridiculous chiefly when he is successful, or thinks he is: when he has routed a flock of sheep or set free a gang of criminals. But with every beating he gets, his dignity grows on us, and we realize how genuinely faithful he is to the code of chivalry. He is courteous, gentle, chaste, generous (except that he has no money), intelligent and cultured within the limits of his obsession, and, of course, courageous. Not only was the code of chivalry a real code that helped to hold a real civilization together, but these are real virtues, and would be if chivalry had never existed. It is this solid core of moral reality in the middle of Quixote's illusion that makes him so ambiguous a figure. As with Alice's Wonderland, where we feel that no world can be completely fantastic where such Victorian infantile primness can survive intact, we feel that the humanity of Quixote is much more solidly established than the minor scholastic quibble about whether the windmills are really windmills or not. So we understand the author's explanation of Sancho's fidelity very well: "Sancho Panaza alone thought that all his master said was the truth, for he was well acquainted with him, having known him since birth."

If we want satire on martial courage we should expect to find most of it in the army, and nobody could have written *Don Quixote* except an old soldier. But to satirize martial courage is not to ridicule it, but to show the contrast between the courage itself, which may be genuine and even splendid, and the reasons for its appearance—that is, the causes of war, which are usually squalid and foolish. And however silly the Don may look in his barber-basin helmet, the qualities that make him so haunting a figure are, in part, the qualities that make a lost cause glamorous. Yet a lost cause, even one so literally lost as Quixote's is pathetic as well as glamorous, and no one can miss the pathos in Quixote. Pathos arises when attention is focused on an individual excluded from a community. The child or animal whose affection is repulsed, the colored student whose offering of intelligence is rejected by a white society,

Gustave Doré's illustration of Don Quixote's ill-fated joust with the windmills.

the girl whose manners are laughed at by rich people   because she is poor—these are the figures we find pathetic—and with them is the mad knight whose enormous will to rescue the helpless and destroy the evil shows itself in such blundering nonsense.

As humanity is always trying to find human scapegoats, it dislikes having its attention called to their human qualities, and besides, the fear of being oneself isolated is perhaps the deepest fear we have—a much deeper one than the relatively cosy and sociable bogey of hell. Whatever the reason, long-sustained pathos is intolerable, and the story of Quixote would be intolerable without the fidelity of Sancho, who enables the knight to form a society of his own. Even so, it would be hard going without the good humor and charity of so many of the people they meet. There must have been times when Cervantes wished he had not made Quixote so pathetic. In the second part, the Don is in charge of a duke who has read part one, and who is responsible for most of the adventures, going even to the point of allowing the knight and squire to live for a time in an external replica of their fantasy. He does this purely to amuse himself, but still, a fundamental act of social acceptance underlies part two. One gentleman has recognized another, however much he has turned him into a licensed jester.

Don Quixote is the world's first and perhaps still its greatest novel, yet the path it indicated was not the one that the novel followed. Imitations of his pedantic crackpot and simple companion, such as we get in *Huckleberry Finn* or *Tristram Shandy,* do not constitute a tradition. The novel is an art of character study, and character study is mainly a matter of showing how social behavior is conditioned by hidden factors. Realistic novels select mainly the factors of class and social status; psychological ones select those of individual experience. Very few have followed Cervantes in tackling the far deeper problem of private mythology, of how one's behavior is affected by a structure of ideas in which one thinks one believes. Flaubert (in *Madame Bovary*) was one such follower, and Dostoyevsky another; but the full exploitation of this field has yet to come. One hopes it will come soon, as the shallower fields are nearly exhausted.

I have hinted that Quixote does not so much believe his fantasy as think he believes it: an occasional remark to Sancho like "upon my word, you are as mad as I am" gives him away. His fantasy is the facade of a still deeper destructive instinct, for at one level of his mind, Don Quixote is one of the long line of madmen, ending in Hitler, who have tried to destroy the present under the pretext of restoring the past. It is at this level that we find the puzzle of reality and appearance. The physical world rocks and sways as Quixote explains that his valiant deeds are real, but appear ridiculous through the artfulness of enchanters. It is difficult to know where a man will stop who regards the creator of "reality" as a magician to be outwitted. One feels at

times that Quixote rather enjoys the paradoxical clash of his inner and outer worlds, and that, like so many who have committed themselves to heroism, he finds that the damage he does is somthing of an end in itself.

But, the Don insists, he really has a positive mission: it is to restore the world to the Golden Age. In a passage of wonderful irony, he tells Sancho that the Golden Age would soon return if people would speak the simple truth, stop flattering their superiors, and show things exactly as they are. The childish element in Quixote, which breaks through in fantasy, believes that the Golden Age is a wonderful time of make-believe, where endless dreams of conquered giants and rescued maidens keep coming true. But then he comes across a group of peasants eating acorns and goat's cheese, who hospitably invite him to join them, and he suddenly breaks out into a long panegyric about the Golden Age, which, it appears, was not an age of chivalry at all, but an age of complete simplicity and equality. In such a kingdom, the social difference between himself and Sancho no longer exists, and he asks Sancho to sit beside him, quoting from the Bible that the humble shall be exalted. The bedrock of Quixote's mind has been reached, and it is not romantic at all, but apocalyptic. The childishness has disappeared and the genuinely childlike has taken its place, the simple acceptance of innocence.

This dream returns at the end, where Quixote and Sancho plan to retire to a quiet, pastoral life, and the author intends us to feel that by dying Quixote has picked a surer means of getting there. With this in our minds, we are not at all surprised that when Sancho, who has been promised the rule of an island, actually gets one to administer, he rules it so efficiently and wisely that he has to be yanked out of office in a hurry before he wrecks the Spanish aristocracy. We are even less surprised to find that Quixote's advice to him is full of sound and humane good sense. The world is still looking for that lost island, and it still asks for nothing better than to have Sancho for its ruler and Don Quixote for his honored counselor. (pp. 160-64)

Northrop Frye, "The Acceptance of Innocence," in his *Northrop Frye on Culture and Literature: A Collection of Review Essays,* edited by Robert D. Denham, The University of Chicago Press, 1978, pp. 159-64.

WILLIAM BYRON
(essay date 1978)

[In the following excerpt from his 1978 study *Cervantes: A Biography,* Byron comments on the innovation and appeal of Cervantes's *Exemplary Stories*.]

Like Shakespeare, Cervantes is a depressing figure for later writers to contemplate. This is partly because of his genius, of course. But partly, too, because so little had been done in literature before he came on the scene; the high likelihood is that no one ever again will have the chance to do so many new things that are important in writing as he did. Cervantes was not the first story writer, any more than Columbus was the first navigator or Copernicus the father of all astronomers. But we would not recognize our world as we do had his *Exemplary Stories* . . . not existed.

The stories, at any rate the seven best of them, confirmed how far ahead of his time he was. Again he is to be found going his own way, following the sources of a main stream of writing no one else in Spain then was able to find. Even today, a reader can still recapture the excited sense of formal adventure the stories exude. There is about them that experimental air, that tentative, step-by-step but confident probing of new regions of art that we perceive in a Leonardo painting or a Schoenberg opera. It was not simply that Cervantes' dialogue was solid, that his language was richer, his style purer, his ideas more complex than other prose writers'. What was important was that he brought a new dimension to prose fiction, the breakthrough structure which has carried it with relatively little fundamental change into the twentieth century. Like most such discoveries, it was deceptively simple: he placed his characters in society and gave them psychologies of their own with which to deal with their situations. The stories are open to the sights and sounds of everyday life, habits, clothes, attitudes, the random comings and goings of people and events in a lived-in world. His characters exist and act in the context of that world; their problems are created by it, its accidents change their lives and they in turn stir the general air.

This interaction between fictional characters and a real world seems so natural to us now that we do not easily see how it could not always have been so. But short stories before Cervantes occupied an almost airless middle distance; their personages lived closed in on themselves, concerned wholly with the dreamy universe in which their action evolved, vaguely conscious of the world as a hum of faraway bustle drifting through a farmhouse window. Boccaccio's people, trading their "in" gossip and their encapsulated anecdotes in their country hideaway, have nothing directly to do with life in plague-stricken Florence. Bandello's Romeo and Juliet dance their tragic ballet as though they were in the middle of an open, moonlit meadow, not in the thriving city of Verona. The Moor Abendarraez crisscrosses the Kingdom of Granada without ever encountering a peasant or a traveler. These were like the saints in Gothic paintings, dehumanized, oversized,

saved from caricature only by the gravity of the general values they represented.

In Cervantes' stories the world crowds in. Try as they may, his personages cannot prevent society from forcing its way into their lives. In the guise of Loaysa it thrusts its heedless snout into Leonora's cloistered existence. Andrés Caballero thinks he is sealed into the Gypsy hive, but the world is a constant, threatening presence which crashes into it with Clemente, with Juana Carducha. It is the random, spontaneous lust of Rodolfo that shatters Leocadia's world in **"The Call of Blood."** In **"The Glass Scholar,"** society is the tormentor, the street crowd that hectors Rodaja in his madness and persecutes him when he returns to sanity. **"The Illustrious Serving Wench"** is set in a roadside inn near Toledo and it is the shifting pageantry of normal inn life that provides the story's incidents. The moiling, shouting, struggling presence of society is the breath of these stories.

Yet, against all logic of the time, Cervantes did not disperse his narratives when he opened them to the unruly outside; despite their individual experiences, their personal problems, their almost journalistic reality, his characters' humanity enhances their universality instead of diminishing it. This was art working directly on personal experience, boldly exploring the unmarkable frontier between the "lie," or fiction, and "truth," or "history"—life itself. When Cervantes boasts in his prologue to the *Exemplary Stories* that "I was the first to write novelas in the Castilian tongue," he is exaggerating only in a semantic sense: he was redefining the "novela" to mean not a tale or an anecdote (Juan de Timoneda, for example, called his stories *patrañuelos*—tall stories), but longer, more complex pieces, closer in spirit to what we now call novelettes. He was very much the first to condense the broad vitality which he and Alemán and Quevedo were giving to the novel into the shorter, denser container of the story.

Scene after scene in these stories glitters with the lightning play of psychological insight: Loaysa's use of music to dominate the childishly amoral slave Luis, La Cariharta's row with her pimp Repolido, riotous as a modern musical comedy. Indeed, they are rightly thought of as scenes; an enemy of Cervantes shrewdly called the *Exemplary Stories* plays in prose and they do have a theatrical fascination which Cervantes was never able to convey intact to the stage; the silences, the descriptions, the subtleties so impressive in the stories become dead spots, loquaciousness, obscurities in his plays.

Not all of the *Exemplary Stories* are on this level, though there is not a dull story among them. Some (**"The Lady Cornelia," "The Liberal Lover," "The Two Maidens"**) are reworkings of early efforts which, despite revision, never achieved the level of sophistication the others reached. **"The Call of Blood"** may have been written around 1600, but its remodeling was more successful.

In at least one story, Cervantes' experimentation got out of hand. For all its potential power, **"The Glass Scholar"** is a failure because it lacks a framework of compelling action. It involves a Salamanca scholar driven mad by a courtesan's poisoned quince; he fancies he is made of glass. The idea was not original with Cervantes; there is a reference to such a case in Boccaccio's stories and in the writings of Frenchman Simon Goulart; there seems even to have been an actual case concerning an alchemist at the University of Valladolid, although there is no proof that Cervantes ever heard of any of these cases.

Since he is too fragile to work, Rodaja is reduced to roaming the streets hurling epigrams, to the delight of the crowds that flock behind him. Superficially, then, he is related to the court buffoons and the harlequins and *graciosos* ["wits"] of the theater whose supposed simplicity gives them license to tell home truths to the world.

But only superficially. We must not forget that Cervantes' seamless stories are not only experiments in prose alchemy, but they are designed to explore moral and philosophic problems. The prologue hints that the stories are to be taken both individually and as a group and that there is in them an esoteric meaning or system of meanings for elite readers to dig out:

I have given them the name *Exemplary,* and if you look closely, there is not one from which some fruitful example may not be drawn . . . if in any way I thought the reading of these stories were indeed to induce an evil desire or thought in whosoever reads them, I would rather cut off the hand that wrote them than expose them in public. At my age, one does not play tricks with the other life. . . .

The notes they strike reinforce—exemplify—the ideas in his other works: it is man's condition to live in society, but society is worldliness, corruption. This is how men are, and it is not their fault. They live locked into a world which is evil by definition. This theme of confinement, in its various aspects, runs through the great stories as, perhaps, it ran through Cervantes' mind on the roads and streets of Andalusia. Leocadia shuts herself up in her parents' house for fear "that her disgrace could be read in her brow." Leonora is cloistered by Carrizales, who himself is locked into his pinched and stunted values. Rinconete and Cortadillo confine themselves in Monipodio's warped brotherhood. Rodaja is twice confined, first in his madness, then in sanity. In all these cases, society is satanic in both its individual and collective incarnations, as Rodolfo the rapist, Loaysa the pícaro, the crowds around Rodaja. Life is hazard, mutely evil yet often joyous. The world has no patience with reason. Rodaja cured

of his madness pleads with the crowd to stop following him around. "Ask me now at home what you used to ask me in the squares and you will see that the man who gave you good improvised answers, so to speak, will give you better ones for having thought them out." It is no use. Reason is prudent; it is not amusing. He is forced to flee to Flanders, where he dies a soldier.

Notwithstanding the omnipresence in them of the world's unthinking evil, the *Exemplary Stories* are not pessimistic. . . . Cervantes prescribed a course of treatment of the disease: self-examination, cultivation of man's reason and his will, active pursuit of the ideal of love. None of this will change the world, but it will put man in readiness to receive the divine grace which will surely, sometime, be offered him. What was true for individuals, moreover, might also be true for societies, as Cervantes may have suggested in **"The Jealous Extremaduran."** In its story of a jealous authority (the aged husband Felipe de Carrizales) attempting to isolate a subject people (the child bride Leonora and her attendants) from the contamination of worldly evil (the pícaro Loaysa), we are surely meant to understand the uselessness—indeed, the offensiveness—of efforts to seal Spain off from foreign, i.e. heretical, thought. However carefully the doors are locked, Cervantes tells us, the outside will enter. Even the husband's name, *Philip,* is significant when we find that in his picaresque past he squandered his birthright in Spain, Flanders and Italy. Philip dies not of the truth, but of his false perception of the truth; it does not occur to him that Leonora, tempted by an alien seducer, might refuse to succumb to him. (pp. 485-88)

William Byron, in his *Cervantes: A Biography,* Doubleday & Company, Inc., 1978, 583 p.

EDWARD H. FRIEDMAN
(essay date 1981)

[In the following excerpt, Friedman discusses Cervantes's full-length comedies, focusing on their relationship to those of the author's rival, Lope de Vega.]

Cervantes is one of a group of Spanish writers, including Benito Pérez Galdós and Miguel de Unamuno, who yearned for success in the theater and failed to achieve it. Critics have blamed Cervantes, as later critics would blame Galdós, for a lack of technical skill in drama and an inability to transfer his novelistic genius to the stage. But, in essence, Cervantes has more in common with Unamuno, as the creator of a literary drama for a public less interested in thematic subtleties than in visual elements and movement. In the case of Cervantes, the divergence from popular tastes may be seen by comparing the success of Lope de Vega, whose *comedias* are based on rapid movement and the principle of unity of action, with Cervantes' general failure to please the managers of the *corrales* ["open-air theaters"] with plays less identifiable with a specific model and unified by a conceptual relationship between plot and episode.

Cervantes' plays fall into two periods. The first consists of twenty or thirty works, according to Cervantes himself, and coincides roughly with the date of publication of his pastoral novel, *La Galatea* (1585). The second group contains the eight full-length plays and the eight interludes, *Ocho comedias y ocho entremeses,* published in 1615, the same year as the publication of Part II of *Don Quijote.* Of the first group, the two extant plays are *La Numancia* and *Los tratos de Argel.* If one is to believe Cervantes, these plays and the others of that period were well-received by the public. . . . Cervantes left the theater for a time, and on his return, drama was a business and Lope's plays its most salable product. For the moment, at least, the public was the significant arbiter, and the public loved Lope. The *autores,* or theatrical managers, wanted plays by Lope or plays following the formula of Lope's *comedia.*

Although rejection left Cervantes embittered over the state of the theater, it seems evident from his references to drama that he believed in the intrinsic quality of his plays. When theatrical managers refused to buy the dramatic works of the second period, Cervantes awarded the final judgment to posterity by selling the *comedias* and *entremeses* to a bookseller willing to publish them. Unfortunately, posterity has not been as kind as Cervantes would have wished. Commentators on his plays from Leandro Fernández de Moratín early in the nineteenth century to contemporary critics stress the episodic nature of the *comedias.* Moratín's neoclassic orientation leads him to a condemnation of the structure of *Los tratos de Argel* because of a lack of correspondence between what the critic considers the single action of the play and the incidents isolated from this action. . . . Similarly, the numerous events of *La Numancia* produce a framework more proper to the epic than to drama, according to Moratín, who considers multiple action a defect in tragedy. . . . (pp. 1-2)

The first attempt at a comprehensive perspective of the *comedias* came in 1951 with the publication of Joaquín Casalduero's *Sentido y forma del teatro de Cervantes,* which E. C. Riley called on the occasion of its second printing in 1966 "still the most complete and important assessment of Cervantes's theatre since Cotarelo's ancient study." Casalduero establishes a progression from the Renaissance which he terms first and second Baroque periods. (p. 3)

In Lope's works, representative of the second pe-

riod, the scenes are related to a single action, united specifically by their respective roles in this action. . . . Cervantes, as a writer of the first Baroque period, structures his plays on the basis of what Casalduero refers to as "mental unity," a thematic connection between scenes.

Casalduero's conception of a thematic unity in the *comedias,* along with Alban K. Forcione's formulation of an analogic relationship between the episodes of Cervantes' prose epic, *Los trabajos de Persiles y Sigismunda* [see Sources for Further Study], leads to a primary contention of this study: that Cervantes achieves unity not by developing complications around a single action as do Lope and his followers, but through parallel episodes which form a conceptual unity. The point of contact between dramatic events may be shown to be a concept rather than a horizontal movement toward completion of an action. The *comedias* may be seen in terms of an archetypal pattern and structural modifications of this archetype; the archetype represents a radical innovation regarding the episodic plot, while the modifications reflect adherence to a successful formula. The powerful influence of Lope de Vega offers a perspective from which to analyze the full-length dramatic works of Cervantes. The early—prototypical—works establish the basis of Cervantes' conception of drama, and the later plays both develop this form and indicate his debt to Lope. In this way, the plays of Cervantes may be viewed individually and as part of a continually evolving dramatic tradition, having elements in common with preceding and newly introduced trends. The *comedias* are, as well, elements of the Cervantine literary universe, dramatic analogues of the multileveled vision of reality presented in the novels.

The Cervantine literary universe is nurtured by paradox. Rather than search for definitions in a system characterized by continual redefinition, one may rely on "approaches" to the works in order to elaborate syntheses, to indicate complementary and contradictory structures, and to delineate the paradox of multiperspectivism or, perhaps, the multiperspectivism of paradox. (pp. 4-5)

Cervantes wrote his ten full-length plays during a period marked by renewed interest in dramatic theory and often by divergence between theory and practice. The neo-Aristotelian theory which originated in Cinquecento Italy vied with the trend toward nationalization of the theater, culminating in Lope de Vega's formula for the *comedia.* Although Cervantes never fully elaborated a theory of drama, statements in his works indicate a knowledge of the major critical questions of his day, as well as an awareness of the supremacy of Lope. The interrelation of theory and practice in drama provides a point of departure for examination of the plays of Cervantes. Through analysis of two elements, unity and the episode, it is possible to define a structure of Cervantine drama and to note variations of conception within the plays.

Relying principally on Aristotle's *Poetics* and Horace's *Ars poetica,* the Italian theorists developed a compendium of literary principles. Theory merged with practical criticism in the debates centering on works representative of the major genres. The so-called ancients, who generally interpreted the classical sources in the most rigid way possible, were less flexible in their approach than the so-called moderns, who believed that time did and should bring change. Virtually all theorists conceded that a work must possess unity, but they disagreed as to criteria for unity. Consistent with an increasing emphasis on personal theoretical statements over strict textual exegesis, the commentators expanded the somewhat vague references to unity in the *Poetics* to include their own critical foundation for judgment of a work of literature. The resulting views range from Castelvetro's postulation of the three unities to Orazio Ariosto's contention that a poem need only have some type of unity. One aspect of unity, the relation of episodes to plot, led to opposing positions on the question of proportion and the incorporation of episodes into the main body of a work. Aristotle states that the epic allows for greater freedom with respect to episodes than the drama, that episodes should be written after the skeletal plot of drama and should be germane to it. While the ancients accepted these dicta, the moderns were inclined to be guided by Terence and other Roman writers, and even by their contemporaries.

Cinquecento theory and the literary quarrels influenced developments in drama outside of Italy. The Italian commentators could be disputed but not ignored. Spain's strong political and intellectual ties with Italy encouraged a tradition of drama modeled after classical tragedy and a preoccupation with dramatic theory, illustrated respectively in attempts to recreate tragic drama and in treatises such as Pinciano's *Philosophia antigua poética.* Through the three interlocutors of his work, Pinciano gives a rather literal reading of the *Poetics* with regard to episodes and unity. Like Aristotle, he concerns himself with the idea of unity of action, treating only randomly that of time and ignoring that of place. Lope revolutionizes the theater with his *comedia,* and in the *Arte nuevo de hacer comedias,* he professes to disregard classical principles while composing his plays. Nonetheless, he insists on a single action and the omission of all extraneous incidents.

Menéndez Pelayo, Riley, Forcione, and other critics recognize Cervantes' knowledge of Cinquecento theory and the literary polemics. The fundamentally ancient position taken by the canon in *Don Quijote* contrasts with the modernist position articulated by Comedia in *El rufián dichoso,* possibly demonstrating Cervantes' reconciliation to the success of Lope's comedia. Cervantes deals with the question of unity in Part II of *Don Quijote,* in the discussion of the interpolated novels of Part I and the subsequent modification of this format in the second part. By analyzing the diverse elements of the *Persiles,* Forcione finds structural unity based on analogy and recurrence and thematic unity based on the motif of the *trabajos.* Similarly, the relationship between plot and episode determines an approach to Cervantes' conception of unity in his plays.

A distinction must be made between the use of episodes in drama and Aristotle's classification of the episodic play. Aristotle criticizes the episodic play for weak or non-existent causal connection between episodes and for the use of episodes solely for quantitative purposes. Cervantes depends heavily on an episodic structure in the archetypal *comedias,* but the episodes fit into a preconceived conceptual framework which juxtaposes the main plot with events linked to it thematically rather than formally. The resulting unity, which may be termed conceptual unity, derives not from development of complications around a single action as in Lope's plays, but through parallel episodes which complement the central idea of the *comedia.* The episodes, as analogues of the sustained plot, represent the literary equivalent of variations on a theme. Cervantes, in essence, amplifies the analogic function of the episode by making it the structural nexus of his plays.

In the four plays which depict the struggles of Spanish Christians among their Moslem captors (*Los tratos de Argel, Los baños de Argel, El gallardo español, La gran sultana*), all episodes in the panoramic framework relate to the concept of captivity. An episode, often without direct formal relation to the linear base (in each case, a sustained love plot), may provide an additional dimension to the immediate action of the play, as through comic analogues or ironic parallels. Madrigal's love for a Moslem girl in *La gran sultana,* placed against the Gran Turco's love for Doña Catalina de Oviedo, is one such case. An episode may instead raise the incidents represented to a more transcendent level; in this instance, Cervantes establishes a microcosm-macrocosm correspondence between the dramatic events and the universal implications of these events. In the Argel plays, for example, the captivity motif is literal (in terms of the historical situation), figurative (in terms of the language of love), and spiritual (in terms of the conflict between the spirit and the flesh).

In *La Numancia,* Cervantes maintains a multiple frame of reference through a complex time scheme and emphasis on representation of the abstract by personified figures. Two historical periods, pre-Christian and Habsburg Spain, merge into the atemporal sphere of eternal glory, which serves as motivation for the play's action. Through a consciousness of history in the making on the part of the characters and a pattern of foreshadowing, as well as dependence on the familiarity of the audience with the historical material, Cervantes stresses the irony of the situation. Linguistically, he accentuates the play's major concept, that of victory in defeat, by extended use of antitheses.

Pedro de Urdemalas centers on the theme of identity, and Cervantes reinforces the repeated role-playing of the title figure with examples of the adaptability of other characters. Cervantes sets up a story-history dichotomy through the parallel actions of Pedro de Urdemalas and the gypsy-princess Belica. Pedro creates illusions and ultimately finds a definitive identity in the world of illusion, while Belica detaches herself from an identity unworthy of her noble birth to fulfil her historical destiny in the court.

The structure of three of the *comedias* shows the influence of Lope de Vega's model, with its emphasis on linear form and a single unified action. Each act of the saint's play, *El rufián dichoso,* signifies one stage in Cristóbal de Lugo's progression from sin to conversion to sainthood, and the work becomes an example of the type of drama criticized in *Don Quijote* (I, 48). Lope's *comedias de capa y espada* provide the formal pattern for *El laberinto de amor* and for its parodic and antithetical companion piece, *La entretenida.* The group betrothal in the first play is converted into collective failure in the second, as love truly conquers all.

The tenth *comedia La casa de los celos,* features an open-ended love plot, numerous and diverse characters, and episodes which fit into no apparent conceptual scheme. The elements which seem incompatible work together to make a statement about literature and the act of literary creation. Rather than a unifying concept, Cervantes presents the problem of the writer—his relationship with his work and with the world—as the basis of the play's structure. *La casa de los celos,* the least studied and least respected of Cervantes' *comedias,* closely approximates *Don Quijote* in its examination of literary reality. Some writers attempt to recreate reality, and others attempt to create their own reality. In Lope's *Lo fingido verdadero,* a man playing the role of saint becomes so engrossed in the role that he makes the part his genuine identity. The actor plays an actor who takes his role literally, while the spectator is asked to accept the validity of the theatrical illusion. The world is a stage, and the use of the theatrical metaphor within the *comedia* links life with literature. In Cervantes' plays on captivity, the world of historical reality makes its way into the work of art, and in *La Numancia,* the historical record merges with dramatic recourses to glorify an act and make it immortal. In its extreme form, the opposing tendency manifests itself in works which have literary points of reference. The external framework depends not on the historical and the realistic, but on literary multiperspectivism, on intertextuality. Literature is both microcosm and macrocosm, and the literary work becomes more complex by virtue of its autono-

my. Characters in *La casa de los celos* (and in Lope's *Las pobrezas de Reinaldos* and *El caballero de Olmedo*) find inward motivation from literature rather than outward motivation from the world of objective reality, and historical figures do not turn history into fiction but find history reduced to fiction.

The structure of Cervantes' *comedias* develops both during a period of interest in recreating classical tragedy and during the apogee of Lope de Vega's career. *La Numancia* and the archetypal plays in general seem to be influenced by the choral elements and subplots of the late sixteenth-century tragedies; Cervantes' method allows for integration of materials and increased emphasis on the episode, and may be seen as the culminating stage of a progression which begins with ornamental or extraneous episodes to accompany the main plot. Cervantes reverses priorities and establishes an episodic structure in which plot and episode work together to combine disparate elements into a unified whole. The ordering of episodes may be shown to relate to a given concept (which gives the play its specific direction), as opposed to a given action. The form of Cervantes' plays is concentric rather than linear, and the difference may be seen by comparing *Pedro de Urdemalas* with Lope's play of the same title. Cervantes' play offers a multifaceted vision of the theme of identity, and primary and secondary actions and episodes reflect the mutable nature of man, seen in the context of a society undergoing change. In Lope's play, a single action (the progression toward recovery of honor) defines the movement and use of conventions. Cervantes' *Pedro de Urdemalas* is a statement on identity, while Lope's *Pedro de Urdemalas* uses identity only as a means to complicate the plot, as a recourse by which the protagonists, by adopting numerous roles, may proceed to right a social wrong.

The emergence of Lope de Vega as the dominant force in the Spanish theater occurred during the period between the composition of *Los tratos de Argel* and *Los baños de Argel.* While the analogic structure of the two plays is primarily the same, certain changes suggest the influence of Lope's formula. The soliloquies and long argumentative speeches of *Los tratos de Argel* are generally eliminated in the later play, in which the literary and figurative evocation of captivity is replaced by greater emphasis on visual representation of the Algerian prison and faster pacing of events. The result is a more spectator-oriented form with equal stress on conceptual unity.

Two of the plays most directly influenced by Lope's model, *El laberinto de amor* and *La entretenida,* illustrate Cervantes' preoccupation with multiperspectivism and with what has been termed Baroque tension. Studied together, the *comedias* show the contradictory nature of social norms and ambiguities between the dictates of society and religious doctrine. A system of poetic justice which seems to apply to *La entretenida* does not apply to *El laberinto de amor,* and role-playing seems to adhere to two antithetical value systems. The lack of synthesis between the systems, rather than negate the presentation of man's role, serves to accentuate the problems inherent in the confrontation between inflexible codes and man's flexible nature.

The Golden Age *comedia,* initiated by Lope de Vega, is based on the principle of unity of action through development of events to form a single action. Each event has among its functions a part in the movement toward completion of the action. While Cervantes borrows elements from a number of dramatic traditions and while his work is affected by the success of Lope, the ten full-length plays neither belong to a particular tradition nor sustain a uniform pattern. In the majority of the plays, however, Cervantes offers a major structural innovation, a means of achieving unity through analogic episodes based on a single concept. This unifying concept allows for multiple visions of man and of the world around and beyond him. (pp. 133-39)

Edward H. Friedman, in his *The Unifying Concept: Approaches to the Structure of Cervantes' "Comedias",* Spanish Literature Publications Company, 1981, 185 p.

P. E. RUSSELL

(essay date 1985)

[In the following excerpt, Russell discusses the influence of *Don Quixote* on the modern novel.]

[Critics] from many lands have seen in *Don Quixote* the harbinger and sometimes the prototype of the modern novel. An impressive array of novelists themselves have expressed similar opinions. It is easy to see why eighteenth-century novelists like Fielding or Lesage did so, because they cultivated the burlesque epic style Cervantes had used. The connection between Cervantes's book and the forms taken by the novel in later times is, however, more elusive. A parodic or even a more generally comic stance is hardly the norm in the modern novel. Cervantes's attitude to contemporary reality in the book is certainly not that favoured by the great nineteenth-century realists. The daily scene appears in *Don Quixote* not because the author thinks it interesting or important in its own right; we have to turn to some of the *Exemplary Novels* for examples of that. In *Don Quixote* everyday reality is only brought to our notice in so far as the confrontational parody requires its presence. As the French novelist Gustave Flaubert, himself a great reader of Cervantes's book,

noted, the high roads of Spain on which so much of the action takes place are never described. The same can be said of the roadside inns which figure so largely in the book; we can infer a great deal about them from what happens there but they do not ever earn any description for description's sake. In Part II, though many chapters take place in the ducal palace, the reader would be hard put to it either to describe the palace, or what routine life there was like when neither Don Quixote nor Sancho was visiting. Nor does the book anticipate the assumption of later novelists that to understand a character's present we must know a good deal about his past. Cervantes resolutely refuses to tell us anything much about Don Quixote's life before middle age and madness came upon him and he treats the past of his other characters in the same way. This attitude must be deliberate. A long tradition of realistic fiction had existed in Spain since the end of the fifteenth century; Cervantes himself engaged in it in some of his other works. If he does not do so in *Don Quixote* it is presumably because, there, he is only concerned with catching his characters and their situations when they are highlighted by comedy. In those circumstances background description would have been not only an irrelevant but a positively counterproductive piece of authorial self-indulgence.

The ambiguity of the book is another feature that we scarcely associate with the modern novel. Novelists have usually sought to persuade their readers that the fictional tale they are looking at seems as if it were historically true even if they know it is not. Cervantes, anticipating experiments with the novel in our own time, deliberately sets out to warn his readers not to put too much trust in the authenticity of the text he offers them, or even in the authority of its various authors. Curiously enough the result of such frankness is to increase, not diminish, the conviction the book carries.

Ambiguity, which is built in to the book's formal structure as well as into its treatment of plot, characters, and theme, continues even after, at the end of Part II, Don Quixote recovers his sanity. We expect him then, in his recuperated personality as Alonso Quijano, to recognize that Don Quixote was a mere hallucinatory figment of his imagination. The dying man, however, merely says that he *was* Don Quixote and has become again Alonso Quijano. The final paradox is that Don Quixote cannot ever be displaced by his sane self. He is the chief figure of a book bearing his name and will continue to exist as long as men and women read novels. It is his 'real' self, Alonso Quijano, who is doomed to death followed by obscurity. It is hard not to believe that, when he wrote this scene, the ailing Cervantes was not aware of the affinity between the ex-knight's situation and his own but we, of course, get no overt suggestion of this.

Any discussion of the influence of *Don Quixote*

on the modern novel needs to start by accepting the premise enunciated by the critic Georg Lukaćs when he wrote of Cervantes's book that, like most great novels, it 'had to remain the only important objectivation of its type'. There have been a number of imitations of *Don Quixote*—the best of them being that of Avellaneda—but the imitations only serve to underline the uniqueness of Cervantes's genius. Yet, despite the differences just referred to, it is not difficult to see why novelists and critics alike have stressed the book's progenitive role in the history of the novel. There were other Spanish boks, all widely read and admired throughout sixteenth-century Europe, which seem, more than *Don Quixote* does, to anticipate the rise of the realistic novel of later times—works like the famous *Tragicomedy of Calisto and Melibea* (better known as *La Celestina*) or picaresque novels like *Lazarillo de Tormes* or *Guzmán de Alfarache*. But these do not have the mythical significance that gives to Cervantes's book its enigmatic and timeless appeal or the extra dimension it owes to the fact that, though parodying chivalric romance, like Ariosto before him, its author's mockery of the chivalry books is mingled with understanding of and respect for the ideas that they sought to express. There is a parallel here with the way in which the insane Don Quixote and the foolish Sancho, however laughable their ridiculous antics and utterances may be, are never quite stripped by Cervantes of his dignity in the case of the knight or his self-respect in the case of the squire. Thanks, too, to the fact that the book is written in the comic mode, which freed it from any obligation to bow to contemporary notions of literary (or social) decorum, Cervantes was able to show the potentially unrestricted scope of narrative registers at a novelist's disposal.

There are a number of other likenesses between *Don Quixote* and the modern novel. The book's underlying theme, the confrontation of illusion with reality, prefigures in its own special way a topic that has been a staple of later novelists. Cervantes's view in it that irony provides the most appropriate stance for a novelist to adopt in order to report on the human condition has also often proved a fruitful one in the subsequent history of the novel, as has his penchant, in this case not peculiar to *Don Quixote,* for showing the multiple perspectives which result when different characters view the same thing. Also important, specially for writers themselves, is the fact that, by his insistence on asking questions about the nature of fiction and about its difficult relationship to truth and to the reality it purports to portray and analyse, Cervantes made it obligatory for all subsequent novelists who take themselves seriously to think about the nature of the enterprise on which they are engaged. Nor should the liberating laughter that echoes through the greater part of *Don Quixote,* often at the expense of romance and other forms of literature, be allowed to obscure the fact that the book is an assertion of the power of literature as an art form. This is not only because, in the person of the knight, Cervantes shows us literature taking entire control of a life and through him greatly affecting the daily lives of many others; it is also because in it he demonstrated that, to be a writer of originality and genius, one did not have to hold new or interesting general beliefs or purvey some clear-cut intellectual message. What matters in *Don Quixote* is the artistic vision and its author's mastery of the techniques he needed to bring that vision to full fruition. In an age when, in Counter-Reformation Spain, dogma and certainty supposedly ruled, Cervantes demonstrated in his most famous book how ambiguity and uncertainity could lie at the centre of great art. He was only able to do so by showing that great art could be comic art. (pp. 105-09)

P. E. Russell, in his *Cervantes,* Oxford University Press, Oxford, 1985, 117 p.

SOURCES FOR FURTHER STUDY

Avalle-Arce, Juan Bautista. Introduction to *Three Exemplary Novels: "El Licenciado Vidriera," "El Casamiento engañoso," "El Coloqiuo de los perros,"* by Miguel de Cervantes, pp. 9-28. New York: Dell Publishing Co., 1964.

> Discusses prominent themes in three of Cervantes's *Exemplary Stories,* relating these concerns to parallel issues in *Don Quixote.*

Borges, Jorge Luis. "Partial Enchantments of the 'Quixote.'" In his *Other Inquisitions: 1937-1952,* translated by Ruth L. C. Simms, pp. 43-6. Austin: University of Texas Press, 1972, 167 p.

> Analyzes Cervantes's fusion of two realities in *Don Quixote:* the world of the reader and the world within the novel.

Forcione, Alban K. *Cervantes' Christian Romance: A Study of "Persiles y Sigismunda."* Princeton: Princeton University Press, 1972, 167 p.

> Evaluates the thematic unity of *Persiles y Sigismunda.*

de Madariaga, Salvador. *Don Quixote: An Introductory Essay in Psychology.* Translated by Salvador de Madariaga and Constance H. M. de Madariaga. 1934. Reprint. London: Oxford University Press, 1940, 159 p.

John Cheever

1912-1982

American short story writer and novelist.

INTRODUCTION

*C*heever is considered one of the most important twentieth-century American writers of short fiction. His well-crafted chronicles of upper-middle-class manners and mores, which describe the psychic unrest underlying suburban living, earned him the appellation "the Chekhov of the exurbs." Although such stories as "The Swimmer," "The Enormous Radio," and "The Housebreaker of Shady Hill" established Cheever as a skillful storyteller and a trenchant social commentator, the republication of sixty-one of his best stories in the 1978 collection *The Stories of John Cheever*—which received the Pulitzer Prize, the National Book Award, and the National Book Critics Circle Award—prompted serious scholarly appraisals of his works. Critics particularly noted Cheever's thematic interest in human morality and spirituality and praised his compassion and abiding belief in the redemptive power of love.

Cheever was born in Quincy, Massachusetts. His New England background is evident in the settings of his stories and in the traditions and values that inform them. He attended Thayer Academy, a preparatory school in Massachusetts, but his formal education ended when he was expelled at seventeen for smoking. The short story he wrote about the experience, "Expelled," published in 1930 in the *New Republic,* marked the beginning of Cheever's literary career. The theme of this piece, the conflict between the necessity for order and propriety and the desire for adventure and pleasure, recurs throughout Cheever's work. During the next several years, Cheever lived mainly in New York City, supporting himself with odd jobs, including a stint of writing book synopses for the Metro-Goldwyn-Mayer film studio, while remaining primarily interested in writing fiction. During the 1930s his short stories appeared in such magazines as the *Atlantic, Colliers,*

Story, the *Yale Review,* and, especially, the *New Yorker.* Cheever's connection with the *New Yorker* began in 1935 and lasted his entire life; well over one hundred of his stories were originally published in that magazine. Despite its advantages, this alliance also had a detrimental effect on Cheever's reputation, for critics associated his stories with the stereotypical *New Yorker* style: slick, facile, and self-conscious.

Cheever was serving in the United States Army during World War II when his first collection, *The Way Some People Live,* was published in 1943. Composed of thirty stories, many of them little more than sketches, the book garnered several positive reviews. After the war, Cheever wrote scripts for television series, including "Life with Father." In 1953 his second collection, *The Enormous Radio and Other Stories,* appeared. This volume illustrates Cheever's movement toward longer, more fully developed works. Mostly set in New York City, these pieces usually concern optimistic but naive individuals who experience culture shock after coming to the city. The much-anthologized title story exemplifies one of Cheever's predominant themes: that social proprieties and conventions cannot subdue emotional conflicts.

Cheever's fictional world commonly portrays individuals in conflict with their communities and often with themselves. His stories are remarkably homogenous, and most share similar settings and characters. The typical Cheever protagonist is an affluent, socially prominent, and emotionally troubled upper-middle-class WASP who commutes to his professional job in the city from his home in suburbia. Cheever's description of this milieu is realistic, but his stories extend beyond accurate depictions of a particular way of life. Into each picture of his idyllic suburbia, Cheever injected an element of emotional tension arising from the gap between the serene environment and individual passion and discontent. While this tension may take many forms, the most common problem in a Cheever story concerns marital conflict. Adultery, real or fantasized, is a motif, as Cheever's characters struggle with their simultaneous desires for emotional fulfillment and domestic and societal order. Cheever does not judge his characters; rather, he treats them with understanding and compassion. Although he obviously intended to satirize the stifling and hypocritical aspects of the lifestyle he depicts, Cheever clearly recognized that while the values of affluent suburbia may not address the individual's deepest concerns, they do reflect an admirable effort to impose stability on a chaotic world. Commentators observe that since Cheever's characters are ambivalent in their desires, so the stories themselves are ambiguous, presenting no clear resolution. The stories are generally realistic in setting and technique, but they are less complete tales than isolated slices of life briefly illuminated.

Recent critics have noted subtle but important phases in Cheever's career as a writer of short fiction. With *The Housebreaker of Shady Hill and Other Stories* (1958) Cheever moved his settings from New York City to the suburban world commonly associated with his work, and irony, wit, and narrative detachment become more evident. In *Some People, Places, and Things That Will Not Appear in My Next Novel* (1961), stories with European backdrops begin to appear. Critics noted a darker tone in *The Brigadier and the Golf Widow* (1964), in addition to a more experimental technique, particularly in "The Swimmer." Often regarded as Cheever's finest story, "The Swimmer" blends realism and myth as it follows Neddy Merrill's eight-mile journey, during which he attempts to swim in all the swimming pools of Westchester County. The image of the old athlete who tries to regain his lost youth through physical endeavor is common in Cheever's fiction. *The World of Apples* (1973) also has been termed somber, but some critics dispute this description, citing the title story as an unequivocal celebration of the triumph of human decency.

Cheever's novels share thematic concerns with his short fiction. *The Wapshot Chronicle* (1957), which won the National Book Award in 1958, episodically traces the disintegration of the eccentric Wapshot family in St. Botolphs, a small town in Massachusetts. The novel is divided into four parts: part one centers on Leander's feelings of uprootedness and subsequent loss of self-esteem induced by his sister and wife; parts two and three focus on his sons, Moses and Coverly, who leave their hometown for Washington, D.C., and New York only to find themselves comically ill-suited for big-city life; and part four ends optimistically, with both brothers producing their own sons, thus perpetuating the Wapshot lineage. In this work, as in its sequel, *The Wapshot Scandal* (1964), Cheever stressed the importance of family relationships and traditions. *The Wapshot Scandal,* often considered his darkest book, concerns the pervasive fear of death in contemporary life, which includes threats from nuclear weapons, auto accidents, cancer, as well as spiritual death from boredom and meaninglessness. Cheever's third novel, *Bullet Park* (1969), also presents a pessimistic view of contemporary America. The first section of the novel concerns Eliot Nailles, the archetypal suburban conformist, and his troubled relationship with his rebellious son, Tony. The experiences of Paul Hammer, the illegitimate son of a wealthy but unreliable businessman, are chronicled in the second section through his journal entries, which reveal his growing insanity. Hammer randomly chooses to crucify Tony Nailles as a sacrificial act he hopes will shake the suburban community of Bullet Park from its insular complacency. Mr. Nailles saves his son, however, and Hammer is institutionalized in a state hospital. The novel's conclusion suggests that Hammer's action has not affected Bullet Park. Several critics viewed in *Bullet Park* a shift in focus from Cheever's investigations of suburban manners to a greater interest in mythical and religious matters.

Cheever's next novel, *Falconer* (1977), introduces several changes into his fiction: a seamy environment, extensive Christian symbolism, and coarse language. In this work, a former college professor incarcerated in Falconer Prison for murdering his brother, experiences rebirth and redemption through overcoming his heroin addiction, engaging in a homosexual relationship, and miraculously escaping from prison. Janet Groth remarked: "[In] *Falconer*, John Cheever has written a stunning meditation on all the forms of confinement and liberation that can be visited upon the human spirit." Cheever's final work, the novella *Oh, What a Paradise It Seems* (1982), centers on business-

man Lemuel Sears's crusade to save a pond that represents the healthy innocence of his youth from industrial contamination. Sears's campaign is disrupted by heterosexual and homosexual affairs but he eventually resumes his interest in the cause and, with the help of a fanatical housewife, succeeds in thwarting the polluters and reviving the health of the lake.

(For further information about Cheever's life and works, see *Concise Dictionary of American Literary Biography, 1941-1968; Contemporary Authors*, Vols. 5-8, 106 [obituary]; *Contemporary Authors Bibliographical Series*, Vol. 1; *Contemporary Authors New Revision Series*, Vols. 5, 27; *Contemporary Literary Criticism*, Vols. 3, 7, 8, 11, 15, 25, 64; *Dictionary of Literary Biography*, Vol. 2; *Dictionary of Literary Biography Yearbook: 1980, 1982*; and *Short Story Criticism*, Vol. 1.)

CRITICAL COMMENTARY

STRUTHERS BURT

(essay date 1943)

[Burt was an American short story writer, novelist, and poet. In the following excerpt from a review of *The Way Some People Live*, he hails Cheever as an important and talented upcoming writer.]

Unless I am very much mistaken, [John Cheever] will become one of the most distinguished writers; not only as a short story writer but as a novelist. Indeed, if he wishes to perform that ancient triple-feat, not as popular now as it was twenty years ago in the time of Galsworthy and Bennett and their fellows, he can be a playwright too, for he has all the necessary signs and characteristics. The sense of drama in ordinary events and people; the underlying and universal importance of the outwardly unimportant; a deep feeling for the perversities and contradictions, the worth and unexpected dignity of life, its ironies, comedies, and tragedies. All of this explained in a style of his own, brief, apparently casual, but carefully selected; unaccented until the accent is needed. Meanwhile, he has published the best volume of short stories I have come across in a long while [*The Way Some People Live*], and that is a much more important event in American writing than most people realize.

The short story is a curious and especial thing; a delicate and restricted medium in which many have walked, but few succeeded. . . . Its strength, like the

sonnet's, comes from deep emotion and perception, and, when necessary, passion, beating against the inescapable form that encircles it. As in the sonnet, as indeed in all good poetry, not a word or line, or figure of speech, or simile, must be amiss or superfluous. The author has just so many minutes in which to be of value, and the contest—the selection—in his mind is between what he would like to say, and what he should say; the search is for the inevitable phrase and sentence and description that contain the final illumination but which, at the same time, seem inevitable and natural.

As a result, probably not more than a score of truly great short stories have ever been written. . . .

The present volume consists of thirty short stories and one can see the compression used, for the book is only two hundred and fifty-six pages long. Many of the stories are only a few pages in length, a thousand, twelve hundred words; and at least half of them are eminently successful; a quarter are far above the average; all are well done; and only a couple fail. **"Of Love: A Testimony,"** except for its title, is one of the best love stories I have ever read. There is a curious and interesting development in the book, and in the procession of the stories—the way they are placed—that ties the volume together and gives it almost the feeling of a novel despite the inevitable lack of connection between any short stories. The earlier stories have to do with the troubled, frustrated, apparently futile years of 1939 and 1941; and then there are some beautifully told

Principal Works

The Way Some People Live: A Book of Stories (short stories) 1943

The Enormous Radio, and Other Stories (short stories) 1953

The Wapshot Chronicle (novel) 1957

The Housebreaker of Shady Hill, and Other Stories (short stories) 1958

Some People, Places, and Things That Will Not Appear in My Next Novel (short stories) 1961

The Brigadier and the Golf Widow (short stories) 1964

The Wapshot Scandal (novel) 1964

Bullet Park (novel) 1969

The World of Apples (short stories) 1973

Falconer (novel) 1977

The Stories of John Cheever (short stories) 1978

Oh, What a Paradise it Seems (novella) 1982

The Journals of John Cheever (journals) 1991

stories of the average American—the average American with a college degree, the same suburbanite—actually at war, but still in this country. This gives the book the interest and importance of a progress toward Fate; and so there's a classic feeling to it. . . .

John Cheever has only two things to fear; a hardening into an especial style that might become an affectation, and a deliberate casualness and simplicity that might become the same. Otherwise, the world is his.

Struthers Burt, "John Cheever's Sense of Drama," in *The Saturday Review of Literature,* Vol. XXVI, No. 17, April 24, 1943, p. 9.

FREDERICK BRACHER

(essay date 1964)

[In the following excerpt, Bracher surveys Cheever's work from *The Way Some People Live* to *The Wapshot Chronicle,* focusing on the author's dominant themes and concerns.]

American fiction in the Forties and Fifties was dominated by the towering figures of Hemingway and Faulkner; the lesser writers—the foothill range from which the peaks emerged—were apt to be taken for granted, despite the very high level they achieved. Among these, John Cheever may well prove to have been the most sensitive to the temper of his times. Without attempting either a realistic picture or critical

analysis of American life, Cheever used his remarkable literary gift to catch the ephemeral quality and feel of life in a period of accelerating change. In his stories and novels he has demonstrated an acuteness of sensibility which establishes him among our most significant writers of comedy.

Cheever's early stories, collected in *The Way Some People Live,* are wry sketches of urban middle-class life, understated and occasionally sardonic. The stories in *The Enormous Radio* and *The Housebreaker of Shady Hill* show more warmth of feeling, a bittersweet sense of the absurdities of human life. In the novel *The Wapshot Chronicle* (1957) the humor is more apparent and more grotesque. The wry wit persists, but beyond the surface ironies that made Cheever's early stories "amusing," lies a view of life colored by the original, basic assumptions of comedy: a moral vision of continuity in which a tragic conclusion is not merely an unhappy ending but may be, also, a new beginning in the never-ending cycles of human existence.

Cheever's most recent work—*Some People, Places, and Things That Will Not Appear in My Next Novel* and *The Wapshot Scandal* (1964)—has become more somber in tone and more critical of our mechanized civilization. The atmosphere is reminiscent of Kafka—at once familiar, preposterous, and faintly sinister. Cheever has moved from the rich aura of the railroad station at St. Botolph's, where the dark smells of "coal gas, floor oil, and toilets" somehow magnify the lives of passengers, to the shiny emptiness of the glass-domed air terminal, efficient, unreal, and diminishing to the human spirit. To evoke such an atmosphere, Cheever pushes satire to the edge of burlesque, but he is clearly not content with a sardonic picture of a moral wasteland. Though the springs of human sensibility may be drying up in the desert of automated non-living, Cheever seems to be working toward the kind of implicit moral statement which distinguishes the serious writer of comedy from the mere entertainer.

Moral earnestness has been a pervasive element in all of Cheever's writing. Morris Freedman noted this in 1953: "Cheever, by reason of his New England background, has breathed into his system that Biblical concentration on the moral nature of reality . . . which we find in Hawthorne, Melville, and James." He might have added that Cheever's moral vision—as is appropriate for a writer of comedy, unwilling to rest in the depressingly familiar facts of human bondage—has been characteristically affirmative. In *The Wapshot Chronicle,* as in his earlier stories, Cheever is more concerned with man's possibilities than with his limitations; and throughout his fiction he depicts the sensuous surface of life "with candor and with relish" and celebrates love in all its forms. The novel also reminds us, despite its nostalgic evocation of the past way of life at St. Botolph's, that man has always had to face new and inhospitable environments and that change, with its concomitant reactions of surprise and shock, can be tonic as well as disturbing. Taken as a whole, Cheever's fiction constitutes, like the life of Leander Wapshot, "a gesture or sacrament toward the excellence and continuousness of things."

A basic metaphor for Cheever's vision of life is the voyage. . . . Cheever's characters move through experience, instead of resting in it. No matter how absorbing the present, it is flowing toward an unpredictable future and carrying the individual to a new stage of growth, to new possibilities of experience. Love and pain, passion and sorrow, are intense but transitory; nothing finally endures but the pattern of movement and change. (pp. 47-9)

In his most recent collection of stories, Cheever explicitly turns his back on some elements of his past writing. The superficial trappings of social comedy—glamor girls, scornful descriptions of the American scene, explicit accounts of sex, drunks, and homosexuals—are among the things that will not appear, if one takes the title at face value, in his next novel. They "throw so little true light on the way we live." Cheever singled them out to demonstrate "the unimportance that threatens fiction" if it continues to concern itself chiefly with the external events and outward surface of society. "We live at deeper levels than these and fiction should make this clear."

The deeper levels are personal and internal, and Cheever's new approach is defined in stories like **"The Bella Lingua," "Events of That Easter," "A Vision of the World,"** and **"The Embarkment for Cythera."** In these a realistic setting is only a framework, a point of departure for an expedition into the inner world of dream and fantasy. If successful, such explorations may arrive at truths that will redeem and give some reality to the preposterous surface of the mechanized suburbia in which most of us live. The writer's perpetual struggle "seems to be to tell the truth without surrendering the astringent atmosphere of truthfulness." As the actual world—supermarkets with piped-in music, highways lined with Smorgorama and Giganticburger stands, TV commercials advertising Elixircol for "wet-fur-coat-odor"—becomes increasingly unreal, the writer must turn inward to discover a vision of the world which has the atmosphere of truthfulness. (pp. 50-1)

In his most recent fiction, Cheever seems less concerned than in his earlier stories with the actual "taste of death"; his new material is more reminiscent of T. S. Eliot's unreal city: the sense of dissociation produced by living in the urban Wasteland. The setting has changed from the comfortable, if transitory, security of Shady Hill to the half-sinister irrationality of Proxmire Manor, a suburb so exclusive and conventional that within its boundaries it is illegal to die. Key images for the new stories are the supermarket and the superhigh-

way—two inhumanly efficient devices for satisfying basic human needs. Life in the supersuburb, where the Moonlight Drive-In has replaced old churches and homesteads, is disjointed and discontinuous; and the structure of the new stories makes a virtue of accidental or casual associations, the "broken lines of communication in which we express our most acute feelings." (pp. 51-2)

The difficulty of an adequate emotional response to our blaring mechanized environment is at least an implicit theme in all of Cheever's recent stories. (p. 52)

Before we can feel truly, we must be able to define the people, places, and things toward which our feeling is directed. In the past, language and literature have helped man to make some order out of the chaos of his external environment; but what language can do justice to the violence of recent change, the unreality of the supermarket? . . .

To sustain a vision of a world in which life flows freely, Cheever is relying more and more on the mythopoeic imagination. (p. 53)

For model and guide, Cheever reminds us, we have always had the dream—a nightly vision of the world which flouts the rational limitations of the waking mind and yet has its own authenticity. To grant our dreams their legitimacy means, ultimately, to accept the incomprehensible, as myth has always done, and to adapt ourselves, with the sanction of ritual if possible, to the next stage of the cycle. . . . Whether our desires are realizable or not, the important thing is to move ahead, to continue the cycle. On the moral level, Cheever would seem to agree with T. S. Eliot's imperative: "Not fare well, but fare forward, voyagers."

The last of the characters to be ousted in Cheever's **"A Miscellany of Characters That Will Not Appear"** is an aging writer in a shabby pensione in Venice. In an account of what this writer has lost, Cheever gives a strong hint of his own intentions for the future. He will try to preserve and exercise "the gift of evoking the perfumes of life: sea water, the smoke of burning hemlock, and the breasts of women." But this is no longer enough. "To celebrate a world that lies spread out around us like a bewildering and stupendous dream," one must manage to comprehend it through the imagination. The nearly impossible task of the writer is to make the world of the supermarket, in which we must live, congenial to the sensibility that makes life worth living. To reestablish the continuity of human experience, the writer must fare inward as well as forward, into the territory where the senses and the sensibility are reinforced by "the ear's innermost chamber, where we hear the heavy noise of the dragon's tail moving over the dead leaves." (pp. 56-7)

Frederick Bracher, "John Cheever: A Vision of the World," in *Claremont Quarterly,* Vol. 11, No. 2, Winter, 1964, pp. 47-57.

CLINTON S. BURHANS, JR.
(essay date 1969)

[Burhans is an American scholar and critic who specializes in nineteenth- and twentieth-century American literature. In the following excerpt, he analyzes the themes of continuity and human alienation in Cheever's short stories.]

Many qualities make John Cheever's writing appealing and interesting. Sinuous, mellow, evocative, capable of a surprising range of effects, his prose moves without apparent effort and convinces without fireworks. He has a keen eye for the bizarre and the eccentric; for the left-overs, the left-behinds, the left-outs; but more than this, a quiet acceptance of them all growing from an understanding that everyone is warped by life either more or less and in one way or another. He is a major chronicler of contemporary absurdity, especially in its upper middle-class urban and suburban manifestations; and he is a trenchant moralist who sees all too clearly into the gap between men's dreams and what they make of them. But in illuminating this absurdity and uncovering this gap, he neither derides the human beings trapped in both nor belittles their dreams. He has the long view of man: he sees that what we call progress has only drawn man deeper into the quicksand of his basic condition; that men are born more than ever into a world of chance, complexity, and ultimate loneliness; and that whatever the contemporary terminology, harpies still hover over man and devils ride his back. Cheever reflects this world in whimsy and fantasy, in irony and extravagance, but never at the cost of his deep compassion for those who must live in it with him; an unobtrusive decency shines everywhere in his writing.

Beyond these values and closely related to them, a provocative and significant theme seems to be emerging in Cheever's work, especially in the stories and novels of the past ten years or so. [In a 1959 essay included in *Fiction of the Fifties*] he pinpoints a shaping change in the attitudes underlying his thought and art:

The decade began for me with more promise than I can remember since my earliest youth. . . . However, halfway through the decade, something went terribly wrong. The most useful image I have today is of a man in a quagmire, looking into a tear in the sky. I am not speaking here of despair, but of confusion. I fully expected the trout streams of my youth to fill up with beer cans and the meadows to be covered with houses; I may even have expected to be separated from most of my moral and ethical heritage; but the forceful absurdities of life today find me unprepared. Something has gone very wrong, and I do not have the language, the imagery, or the concepts to describe my apprehensions. I come back again to the quagmire and the torn sky. . . .

The image is a powerful one; and Cheever's writing since the mid-fifties, especially in the Wapshot novels and in the stories collected in *The Brigadier and the Golf Widow*, seem at their deepest levels of meaning and value to be his groping both for a conceptual framework to explain his apprehensions and also for a language and forms to express them.

As Cheever's feeling that "something has gone very wrong" has deepened, so too has his sense of the past and of the indelible relationship between human beings and their socio-cultural matrix. His concern with contemporary absurdity is not that of an existentialist; his vision is not that of a Sartre or a Camus. He has the traditionalist's sense of a human nature and of its continuance in time and in experience; and he increasingly views man as a creature industriously but blindly cutting away the roots from which he grows and tearing up the soil which nurtures him. (pp. 187-88)

[For Cheever], man is a creature of the past both in his unchanging and unchangeable existential conditions and also in the tissue of historical, social, and familial forces and relationships which shape his responses to these conditions. (p. 189)

As the complex product of this tissue of interrelationships, of an immutable existential condition shaped by particular backgrounds in time and place, man pays a price and often a terrible one, Cheever feels, if he tries to deny his backgrounds and become something different or if he is cut off from these sources of his identity and values. Self-exiled from America because of a scandal, Anne Tonkin in **"A Woman Without a Country"** tries to make herself into an Italian, "but the image was never quite right. It seemed like a reproduction, with the slight imperfections that you find in an enlargement—the loss of quality. The sense was that she was not so much here in Italy as that she was no longer there in America." Refusing to be taken as a tourist, she claims to be Greek, and "the enormity, the tragedy of her lie staggered her. . . . Her passport was as green as grass, and she traveled under the protectorate of the Great Seal of the United States. Why had she lied about such an important part of her identity?" (p. 191)

This profound and complex sense of the past informs the deepest levels of Cheever's apprehensive concern with the present and the future and explains his perplexed feeling of standing "in a quagmire, looking into a tear in the sky." Given man's permanent existential condition and his inescapable relationship to his particular past, what, Cheever wonders, is man doing to himself in the present and what does it forebode for the future? Exploring these questions, Cheever centers on two predominant problems: *one,* the vast and unparalleled changes which characterize the contemporary world; and *two,* the rate of change which these reflect and its frightening significance.

In **"The Angel of the Bridge,"** the narrator recounts his mother's, his brother's, and his own bizarre responses to a contemporary world whose changes they find incomprehensible and subliminally unbearable. At seventy-eight, his mother skates at Rockefeller Center dressed like a young girl; she had "learned to skate in the little New England village of St. Botolphs . . . and her waltzing is an expression of her attachment to the past. The older she grows, the more she longs for the vanishing and provincial world of her youth. She is a hardy woman . . . but she does not relish change." She is afraid to fly, and "her capricious, or perhaps neurotic, fear of dying in a plane crash was the first insight I had into how, as she grew older, her way was strewn with invisible rocks and lions and how eccentric were the paths she took, as the world seemed to change its boundaries and become less and less comprehensible." Reflecting similar deep-seated anxieties, the narrator's brother is unable to use elevators because he is afraid the building will collapse while he is riding in one.

At first amused by these aberrations and feeling superior to them, the narrator suddenly finds himself terrified by large bridges. Convinced they will fall if he tries to drive across them, he goes out of his way to find "a small old-fashioned bridge that I could cross comfortably" and he feels "that my terror of bridges was an expression of my clumsily concealed horror of what is becoming of the world." (pp. 192-93)

Even more than by the nature of contemporary change, Cheever is disturbed by its velocity, by the rate of change and its chasmal incoherence. Shopping at a supermarket, the narrator of **"A Vision of the World"** thinks that "you may need a camera these days to record a supermarket on a Saturday afternoon. Our language is traditional, the accrual of centuries of intercourse. Except for the shapes of the pastry, there was nothing traditional to be seen at the bakery counter where I waited." Later, at the country club, he watches the daughter of a millionaire funeral director dancing with an indicted stock-market manipulator who had paid his fifty-thousand-dollar bail from the money he

Cheever (center) with fellow authors Yevgeny Yevtushenko and John Updike.

carried in his wallet. The band plays songs from the 1920's, and "we seemed," the narrator remarks, "to be dancing on the grave of social coherence." (p. 193)

The price contemporary man pays for too much and too rapid change appalls Cheever. The urban-suburban sprawl and the moral-esthetic collapse which the narrator of **"The Angel of the Bridge"** ultimately cannot stomach are more than simple ugliness evoking a good-old-days nostalgia: they reflect a way of life without roots or meaning or values, a quantitative life lacking any qualitative dimension. (p. 194)

For Cheever, then, the major casualties in the disruption of social coherence are traditional human values and relationships and the process by which they are sustained and extended. In **"A Vision of the World,"** the narrator is constantly struck and increasingly disturbed by the meaninglessness and incoherence of the contemporary world. Its chaotic discontinuities have the quality of a dream world; and, paradoxically, only in his dreams can he establish any relationship to the past and its traditional values. (pp. 194-95)

His dreams are largely of past events or people and traditional figures; and in each dream, someone speaks the words, " *'porpozec ciebie nie prosze dorzanin albo zyolpocz ciwego.'* " These apparent nonsense syllables are actually broken Polish and other Slavic derivatives from which relevant meaning can be extrapolated: "there are many good things in life; you should not search for the things that do not exist in life," or perhaps, "you have a good and pleasing life and should not cry for things you do not need." The relevance of these strange words becomes clear in the narrator's last dream:

> I dream that I see a pretty woman kneeling in a field of wheat. Her light-brown hair is full and so are the skirts of her dress. Her clothing seems old-fashioned—it seems before my time—and I wonder how I can know and feel so tenderly toward a stranger who is dressed in clothing that my grandmother might have worn. And yet she seems real—more real than the Tamiami Trail four miles to the east, with its Smorgorama and Gigantic-burger stands, more real than the back streets of Sarasota.

She begins to speak the mysterious eight words, and he suddenly awakes to the sound of rain. Sitting up, he too speaks eight words: " 'Valor! Love! Virtue! Compassion! Splendor! Kindness! Wisdom! Beauty!' The words seem to have the colors of the earth, and as I recite them I feel my hopefulness mount until I am contented and at peace with the night." The strange unfocussed words have become sharp and clear; they are "the virtues of conservatism," the "good things in life," the traditional values the narrator wants to make legitimate "in so incoherent a world." (p. 195)

In this complex feeling for the past, for man's re-

lationship to his backgrounds and his deep need for social coherence, Cheever is neither a nostalgic traditionalist nor a naturalistic determinist. He is thoroughly aware that man cannot return to or repeat the past, especially an imaginary past, however tempting an escape it may seem; and he views man in more than animal terms. To Cheever, man is the complicated product of his past, of heredity shaped by natural and cultural environment, and he is convinced that the identity and the values man lives by are rooted with him in that past. If man cannot return to or repeat the past, neither can he with impunity move very far beyond a coherent relationship to it. Deeply disturbed by his perceptions of vast change exploding in an apparently geometric progression, Cheever senses that man may be incurring a catastrophic penalty for progress, that the brilliance and power which have given man dominion over the earth may finally be operating to eliminate him from it.

Working at the heart of Cheever's complex concern with the past, then, is a profound insight into the contemporary human condition, a potentially tragic view of man which seems both electrifyingly relevant and poignantly accurate. As Cheever implicitly defines him, man is a biological creature who survives, like all organic life, by adapting to his environment. But man is also a cultural creature, a unique being who changes his environment; and in this uniqueness lies the potential for tragedy which Cheever has sensed. For if man changes his environment faster than he is capable of adapting to it, he is inevitably and self doomed.

Here is the "something" which for Cheever "has gone very wrong" in our time; man has released energies and developed technologies which together are changing his world far beyond his capacity to endure such change. . . . What can save a world, Cheever wonders, in which the needs and angers once vented in spears and arrows can now find outlet in nuclear missiles?

But life can end with a whimper as well as with a bang; and man can destroy himself just as surely, if more slowly, by violating the organic relationship to his natural and social environments through which he understands himself and his world and derives the values he lives by. . . . How, Cheever asks, can man adapt to a world he is changing faster than his capacity for comprehending and humanizing change?

In this provocative insight, which seems increasingly to be shaping his recent work, Cheever becomes more than the whimsical *New Yorker* satirist of urban and suburban absurdities, more than an austere but compassionate New-England moralist. . . . Fearing that contemporary man in his obsession with progress is destroying "the excellence and continuity of things," Cheever sees that he may ultimately pay the price of survival for the very brilliance of his own success. Emerging in Cheever's thought and art, this insight suggests a thoroughly contemporary and potentially major tragic vision of man and the human condition. If Cheever has not yet fully articulated it, if he has not yet found the most effective forms to express it, the promise is rich and worth exploring. (pp. 197-98)

Clinton S. Burhans, Jr., "John Cheever and the Grave of Social Coherence," in *Twentieth Century Literature,* Vol. 14, No. 4, January, 1969, pp. 187-98.

WILLIAM PEDEN

(essay date 1975)

[Peden is an American critic who has written on the American short story. In the following excerpt, he surveys Cheever's career as a short story writer from the publication of *The Way Some People Live* to that of *The World of Apples.*]

Much of the most important recent American short fiction has been in [the] province of the usual and the unexceptional. John Cheever, John O'Hara, Peter Taylor, and John Updike seem to me among the most representative of the many talented and perceptive writers who have for the most part concerned themselves with incidents in the lives of ordinary men and women in familiar or immediately recognizable situations, and have created a contemporary fiction of manners characterized by skill, urbanity, and insight.

Of these chroniclers of the unexceptional, perhaps the most distinguished is John Cheever. . . . [Many of the stories in his first collection, *The Way Some People Live,*] are brief fictional anecdotes or narrative sketches about a few moments or hours in the lives of a character or a group. Typical are **"Summer Theatre,"** in which a group of amateur prima donnas displays higher than average pre-opening-night jitters; **"Problem No. 4,"** in which a draftee training in South Carolina concentrates more on his wife back in New York than on his lieutenant's earnest adjurations concerning a security mission; **"The Law of the Jungle,"** with its effective contrast between older and younger generations in pre-World War II New York; and **"The Peril in the Streets,"** essentially a monologue delivered by an unhappy drunk in the presence of a bartender and a draftee. Longer, somewhat more ambitious stories include **"Of Love: A Testimony,"** a restrained and melancholy description of a love affair doomed to failure.

Though some of the stories in *The Way Some People Live* border on the trivial, the collection on the whole is an impressive one, and indicates the direction the author's subsequent stories were to take. Cheever

writes in a relaxed, seemingly casual but thoroughly disciplined manner; his general mood is a compound of skepticism, compassion, and wry humor; he is concerned with the complexities, tensions, and disappointments of life in a strictly contemporary world of little men and women, unheroic, unspectacular, unexceptional. Loneliness, perhaps the dominant mood of the short fiction of the forties, fifties, and early sixties, permeates the collection. (pp. 30-1)

[*The Enormous Radio and Other Stories*] was published ten years later, in 1953. It is unquestionably one of the major collections of the period. Gone are the occasional triviality and the sometimes studied informality of the earlier stories. With only isolated exceptions, Cheever has gained complete control of his medium; he is at all times and in all places on top of his materials. *The Enormous Radio* stories concern individuals similar to the people of his first collection, though they are often older and more mature—university graduates, World War II alumni, young businessmen on the way up or slightly older ones on the way down, and their anxious, frequently harried women. The scene is contemporary, usually in or around New York City. Cheever's subject matter continues to be the usual, but his treatment of it is far from commonplace. He is concerned with the loneliness that festers beneath the façade of apparently "happy" or "successful" individuals; he suggests the potential terror or violence inherent in the metropolitan apartment dweller's condition. Beneath the often placid, impeccably drawn surfaces of his stories there is a reservoir of excitement or unrest that is capable of erupting into violence; his well-mannered characters walk a tightrope that at any moment may break; the vast, shining city masks cruelty, injustice, and evil. (pp. 31-2)

Most of the people of *The Enormous Radio* stories are decent, respectable, fundamentally likable. Sometimes they win a temporary victory, like Ralph and Alice Whittemore of **"The Pot of Gold"**; only rarely do they become malignant, like Joan Harris of **"Torch Song,"** a "big, handsome girl" who leaves the Middle West to become a New York model. A modern vampire, Joan thrives on sickness and disaster, and well merits the cry of the man she helps destroy: "What kind of an obscenity are you that you can smell sickness and death the way you do?" For the most part the characters exist between these extremes, frightened and to all intents and purposes terribly alone, lost in a metropolitan no man's land from which most of the traditional guideposts have been removed; among the most memorable are the characters in **"The Season of Divorce," "The Summer Farmer," "The Superintendent,"** and, perhaps the best story Cheever has yet written, **"Goodbye, My Brother."**

Four of Cheever's pieces, written after the publication of *The Enormous Radio,* are included in *Stories:*

Jean Stafford, John Cheever, Daniel Fuchs, William Maxwell (1956). Except for **"The Bus to St. James's,"** with its account of the corrosive effect of big city mores and tensions, these stories display an extension of subject matter and theme and a considerably more leisurely technique than most of their predecessors. My own personal favorite, and I think the best of these stories, is **"The Day the Pig Fell into the Well,"** a warm-hearted and robust re-creation of the Nudd family at Whitebeach Camp in the Adirondacks. The story possesses a variety of character and incident more usually associated with the novella or the novel than with the short story; over this "chronicle of small disasters" hovers a kind of Indian summer warmth, as Cheever portrays the American equivalent of the English middle class with Galsworthian compassion and dislike, affection and irony. Almost as good are **"The National Pastime,"** part essay, part short story, a nostalgic re-creation of a New England boyhood, and the prizewinning **"The Country Husband,"** one of the best of Cheever's excursions into the suburbia, which was to furnish subject and theme for his next collection, *The Housebreaker of Shady Hill.* (pp. 33-4)

The title piece of the Shady Hill stories, with its mingling of humor, effective characterization, serious commentary, and suspense, is characteristic of the collection as a whole. (p. 34)

Except for the sadistic organization man of the merciless **"The Five-forty-eight,"** most of Cheever's nonheroes are essentially amiable men: one-time track star Cash Bentley, forty, who provides the climax for many a Saturday night Shady Hill party by hurdling sofas, tables, and firescreen; Francis Weed, who becomes infatuated with the Weed's babysitter but eventually, at the advice of a psychiatrist, finds solace through woodwork; Will Pym, whose only sin was marrying a flirtatious woman considerably younger than himself; and Charles Flint, "fugitive from the suburbs of all large cities" whose plea, written in his journal aboard ship, suggests the real villain of Cheever's world, Shady Hill itself, with its culture vultures, its inane activity, its joyless parties and meaningless love skirmishes, its pretentiousness and unending striving for status. (p. 35)

Like Johnny Hake or Charles Flint, some of these unheroic protagonists win a partial victory through love or by demonstrating a kind of courage or integrity; very rarely are they destroyed, like Cash Bentley. Most of the time they see things through; they muddle along, a little balder, a bit more short of breath, somewhat sadder today than they were yesterday. Sorrow and disappointment pervade the book: sadness for the loss of youth and love, for the gradual dimming of the dreams of the past, and for the nagging awareness of entrapment in an often comfortable present built upon an extremely flimsy moral foundation. Usually this is

implicit within the narrative framework of character and incident; only rarely does Cheever indulge in commentary like that of the misunderstood child of **"The Sorrows of Gin":** "the pitiful corruption of the adult world; how crude and frail it was, like a piece of worn burlap, patched with stupidities and mistakes, useless and ugly."

Cheever's fourth collection, *Some People, Places, and Things That Will Not Appear in My Next Novel,* contains **"The Death of Justina"** and **"Boy in Rome,"** which are among his best work; and even the slightest pieces in the book display Cheever's hallmarks, urbanity, wit, intelligence, and technical dexterity. As a whole, however, the book is a letdown, fatigued and written in an overcasual manner—at times almost a parody—of Cheever's earlier work. **"A Miscellany of Characters That Will Not Appear"** is a moving manifesto and declaration of intent, as much essay as short story. Among the clichés and bromides of character and incident that Cheever wishes to see eliminated from fiction—his own and that of his contemporaries—are "all scornful descriptions of American landscapes with ruined tenements, automobile dumps, polluted rivers . . . diseased elm trees . . . unclean motels, candle-lit tearooms, and streams paved with beer cans," all explicit descriptions of sexual commerce, all lushes, all parts for Marlon Brando, all homosexuals, all fake artistry. Cheever's exhortation, in spite of its levity of manner, is admirable; it would have more significance if it were not embedded in a collection that is the most uneven of Cheever's books, markedly inferior to *The Enormous Radio* and *The Housebreaker of Shady Hill,* and in some ways less impressive than *The Way Some People Live.*

On the other hand, his fifth collection of short stories, *The Brigadier and the Golf Widow* . . . , is perhaps Cheever's best. Over the years. Cheever's narrative method loosened up considerably, became more varied, more flexible: he is as adept in a brief anecdotal episode involving a son's last meeting with his divorced father (**"Reunion"**) as he is in relatively traditional narratives of people and incidents (the title story or **"A Woman without a Country"** and several others), or pieces like **"The Seaside Houses"** or **"Just One More Time,"** which are essentially fictional essays in which narrative hardly exists. In the setting, too—past or present, actual or filtered through the narrator's memories—we find considerable variety; it ranges from such familiar Cheever territory as Manhattan (**"Reunion"**) to suburbia (in **"Metamorphoses,"** Bullet Park, the scene of his novel of the same name) to the small New England village of St. Botolph's (**"The Angel of the Bridge"**).

Several of these stories are as good as any that Cheever has ever written: the title story with its expert delineation of a country-club militarist—"Bomb Cuba!

Bomb Berlin! Let's throw a little nuclear hardware at them"—and the "other woman," for whom, as for so many of the author's female characters, adultery is replacing bridge as the favorite national pastime; **"The Swimmer,"** one of the most conceptually interesting stories in the Cheever canon; though this story of Neddy Merrill's plan to "reach his home by water" hovers somewhat uneasily between realism and metaphor, it is nonetheless unforgettable; **"The Angel on the Bridge,"** memorable as much in the deft creation of the narrator's ice-skating-in-Rockefeller-Plaza mother, his brother, and the young hitchhiker he encounters as it is in the portrayal of the central character, who suddenly develops an obsessive fear of bridges; **"The Seaside Houses,"** a marvelous evocation of the influence of rented houses on those who own them and those who rent them, beautifully executed, with not a false word or jarring note until what seems to me an ending in which Cheever suddenly loses his touch; and **"The Music Lesson,"** too delicious to be summarized, perhaps the collection's most interesting variation of the tensions-of-marriage syndrome with which he has often concerned himself.

At the conclusion of **"Clementina"** the central character contemplates some of the recent events in her life: ". . . remembering the cold on her skin and the whiteness of the snow and the stealth of the wolves, she wondered why the good God had opened up so many choices and made life so strange and diverse." The last words can be applied to the author himself. With over a hundred successful stories behind him, Cheever has lost none of his zest, none of his wonderment in celebrating what he has termed "a world that lies spread out around us like a bewildering and stupendous dream."

The same can be said about Cheever's 1974 National Book Award fiction nominee, *The World of Apples.* **"The Jewels of the Cabots,"** a saga in miniature of life in St. Botolph's, is Cheever at his best, beautifully controlled, illuminated throughout by the effective juxtaposition of the trivial and the significant, the tragic and the comic. In the midst of the narrator's reminiscences of minor childhood experiences or recollections of love, adultery, and murder, we tend to remember most distinctly such asides and gratuitous comments as "when the ship sinks I will try to reach the life raft with an overhand and drown stylishly, whereas if I had used a Lower-Class sidestroke I would have lived forever."

Then there is the title story, a far remove from the world of St. Botolph's, a masterly portrait of an aging but very vigorous American poet in Italy. Or, in more familiar Cheever country, **"The Fourth Alarm,"** full of suburban *angst* and strain, growing out of a wife's sudden decision to perform in an off-Broadway skin show, or **"The Geometry of Love,"** in which the engineer protagonist is destroyed by the failure of his marriage.

The narrator of **"The Jewels of the Cabots"** comments that "Children die, beautiful women are mangled in automobile accidents, cruise ships founder, and men die lingering deaths in mines and submarines, but you will find none of this in my accounts." The statement is applicable to the body of Cheever's short stories. He is concerned with large contemporary and universal problems—hypocrisy, individual and societal idiocy, the absurdity of sham and pretentiousness, the need for love and understanding—but his approach to them is sophisticated, low-keyed, subtle. One of the most entertaining story-tellers and one of the most perceptive and urbane commentators on the contemporary scene, Cheever is a wry observer of manners and customs, more saddened than amused by the foibles he depicts with such understanding and grace. And in spite of the failures of so many of his characters and the disruptions in their personal and professional lives, the overall effect, particularly of his more recent work, is anything but somber. In its entirety it is animated by the sense of wonder implicit in Clementina's previously quoted comment and in the author's statement in an interview a few years ago:

> I know almost no pleasure greater than having a piece of fiction draw together disparate incidents so that they relate to one another and confirm that feeling that life itself is a creative process, that one thing is put purposefully upon another, that what is lost in one encounter is replenished in the next, and that we possess some power to make sense of what takes place.

(pp. 35-9)

William Peden, "Metropolis, Village, and Surburbia: The Short Fiction of Manners," in his *The American Short Story: Continuity and Change, 1940-1975,* revised edition, Houghton Mifflin Company, 1975, pp. 30-68.

ROBERT TOWERS

(essay date 1978)

[In the following excerpt, Towers examines several aspects of *The Stories of John Cheever*, including the author's moral purpose and narrative technique.]

For years many of us have gone around with bits and pieces of John Cheever stories lodged in our minds— oddities of character or situation, brief encounters, barely remembered passages of special poignancy or beauty. . . .

A reading of [*The Stories of John Cheever*] usefully corrected certain misconceptions of mine that had grown up over the years. Influenced no doubt by the popularity of **"The Swimmer"** and by the four novels, I had come to think of Cheever's work as far more sur-realistic and bizarrely plotted than it turns out to be. Of the sixteen or so stories that seem to me clearly first-rate (a high percentage, given the size of the *oeuvre*), twelve are distinctly within the bounds of realism, ob-serving the conventions of causality, chronology, and verisimilitude, with no untoward intrusions of the ar-bitrary or the fantastic.

Though Cheever disclaims a documentary pur-pose and (rightly) resents comparison to a social nit-picker like the later John O'Hara, his stories do have a powerful documentary interest—and why not? Docu-mentation of the way we—or some of us—live now has been historically one of those enriching impurities of fiction that only a mad theorist would wish to filter out. Less grand than Auchincloss, subtler and cleverer than Marquand, infinitely more generous than O'Hara, Cheever has written better than anyone else of that lit-tle world which upper-middle-class Protestants have contrived to maintain. . . .

Of course, Cheever, for all his fascination with manners, has never been primarily a documentary writer. His response to experience is essentially that of an old-fashioned lyric poet. In his preface to the new collection, he writes, "The constants that I look for in this sometimes dated paraphernalia are a love of light and a determination to trace some moral chain of being." While one might question Cheever's profundi-ty as a moralist, there can be no doubt about his preoc-cupation with—and celebration of—the shifting pow-ers of light. His stories are bathed in light, flooded with it; often his characters appear slightly drunk with it, their senses reeling.

Light, for Cheever, seems to have distinctly moral or religious properties. . . . Light seems to be associat-ed with a blessing, with a tender maternal smile fleet-ingly experienced, with all that is clean, tender, and guiltless, with the barely glimpsed immanence of God within His creation. At times Cheever appears to soar like Shelley's skylark toward the source of light, a be-lated romantic beating his luminous wings in the void.

But while the lyric impulse sometimes leads him into a slight (and often endearing) silliness—"The light was like a blow, and the air smelled as if many wonder-ful girls had just wandered across the lawn"—he is for the most part a precisionist of the senses. Though his imagery of light has the strongest retinal impact, Chee-ver's evocation of color and texture and smell is also vivid and persistent. He shares with two very different writers, Lawrence and Faulkner, an extraordinary abili-ty to fix the sensory quality of a particular moment, a particular place, and to make it function not as embel-lishment but as an essential element in the lives and moods of his characters. (p. 3)

The introduction of an element of the weird into a densely realistic setting is an old trick of Cheever's, going back to his beginnings as a storyteller. Nowhere does it work better than in **"The Enormous Radio."** . . . The social texture is every bit as thick and as accurately rendered as in any of the realistic stories; the husband's indictment of his wife, when at last the contagion spreads to the couple, is as grimly factual, as "class-specific," as if magic had nothing to do with the situation. The stories in which the two elements are successfully interwoven are among Cheever's most brilliant; they include not only the famous **"Torch Song"** and **"The Swimmer"** but also that superbly ma-cabre piece, **"The Music Teacher,"** in which a hus-band, driven to despair by a chaotic household and reg-ularly burned meals, resorts to an elderly piano teacher who has been recommended by a neighbor; she gives him a musical formula with which to tame his wife and then dies the ugly death of a witch. But on a re-reading they seem to me to veer toward slickness, to stand up less well than, say, a strongly felt and quietly impres-sive piece like **"The Summer's Farmer"** or **"The Bus to St. James's."**

Cheever is a writer whose faults have an unusual-ly close connection to his strengths. The imaginative identification with the upper-middle class which al-lows him to depict their mores and dilemmas with such vivacity entails a narrowness of social range and a sen-timental snobbery which can get the best of him when his guard is down. Unlike Faulkner, whose Snopeses and Bundrages are as lovingly rendered as his Comp-sons, Cheever is not at ease when he enters the thoughts and feelings of one of those retainers—usually an Irish-Catholic—who service the elevators and the doors of the East Side apartment houses. In **"Clancy in the Tower of Babel,"** **"Christmas Is a Sad Season for the Poor,"** and **"The Superintendent,"** he settles for faintly embarrassing stereotypes of those workers while displaying his usual keenness of obser-vation and sympathy for the apartment dwellers for whom they work. The absence of Jews in Cheever's New York world is striking; at times it seems a deliber-ate avoidance, as in **"O City of Broken Dreams,"** where a bus-driver-turned-playwright from Indiana is brought into a thicket of producers and theatrical agents of whom not even one has a Jewish name.

The most serious embarrassments occur when he attempts an identification with a really alien figure, as in **"Clementina,"** his story of a simple-hearted Italian girl who emigrates to America, or **"Artemis, the Hon-est Well-Digger,"** a late story in which he introduces a young digger of artesian wells to a sexually predatory matron of suburbia and then whisks him off on an im-plausible tour of Russia. His condescension to these characters is well meant, full of good will, and hard to swallow.

Cheever on novel writing:

I usually have a sense of clinical fatigue after finishing a book. When my first novel, *The Wapshot Chronicle*, was finished I was very happy about it. We left for Europe and remained there so I didn't see the reviews and wouldn't know of Maxwell Geismar's disapproval for nearly ten years. *The Wapshot Scandal* was very different. I never much liked the book and when it was done I was in a bad way. I wanted to burn the book. I'd wake up in the night and I would hear Hemingway's voice—I've never actually heard Hemingway's voice, but it was conspicuously his—saying, "This is the small agony. The great agony comes later." I'd get up and sit on the edge of the bathtub and chain-smoke until three or four in the morning. I once swore to the dark powers outside the window that I would never, *never* again try to be better than Irving Wallace. It wasn't so bad after *Bullet Park* where I'd done precisely what I wanted: a cast of three characters, a simple and resonant prose style and a scene where a man saves his beloved son from death by fire.

Cheever, in a 1969 interview with Annette Grant published in *The Paris Review* in 1976.

The snobbery is fairly innocent as snobberies go, attaching itself mostly to well-bred or even aristocratic ladies and causing little damage beyond a maudlin blurring of Cheever's usually sharp vision. (pp. 3-4)

Cheever's role as narrator is always obtrusive. He has, of course, never had any truck with the notion—once a dogma among certain academic critics—that an author should keep himself as invisible as possible, that he should show rather than tell. Cheever-as-narrator is regularly on stage, rejoicing in his own performance, commenting upon—often chatting about—his characters, dispatching them on missions, granting them reprieves or firmly settling their hash. At his most effective he can tell us things about a character with such authority that we never for a moment doubt that his comprehension is total, final. . . . He loves to generalize: "Walking in the city, we seldom turn and look back"—or: "It is true of even the best of us that if an observer can catch us boarding a train at a way station. . . ."

From these and a myriad other touches a composite image of Cheever-as-a-narrator emerges. . . . Cheever-as-a-narrator is a personable fellow—debonair, graceful, observant, and clever. His sympathies are volatile and warm. He is a good host—one who likes to entertain, to amuse, to turn a phrase. He is also a bit of a show-off, an exhibitionist. Beneath the gaiety and charm of his discourse, deep strains of melancholy and disappointment run. He is not, however, a cynic. Nor is he a profound moralist. He has no fun-

damental quarrel with the family or society as they now exist. For the ills of the flesh and spirit his sovereign remedy is the repeated application of love, love, love. . . .

Thanks to this volume, the best of Cheever's stories are now spread glitteringly before us. In our renewed pleasure in these, we can let the others—the trivial and the miscalculated—recede to their proper place. Cheever's accomplishment in his exacting art is proportionally large, as solid as it is brilliant, and likely to endure—a solemn thing to say (however true) of a writer who has so often flaunted the banner of devil-may-care. (p. 4)

Robert Towers, "Light Touch," in *The New York Review of Books,* Vol. XXV, No. 17, November 9, 1978, pp. 3-4.

SCOTT DONALDSON
(essay date 1986)

[In the following excerpt, Donaldson traces Cheever's increasingly pessimistic treatment of contemporary American society, identifying various symbols of despair in his novels.]

Asked why he wrote fiction, John Cheever used to answer that it was what he could do best, his craft, his usefulness. But he also wrote, he said, to "make sense of my life." The process was not so private as it sounds, for by attempting to make sense of his life Cheever provided his readers with insights into their own lives, their own times. What he wrote about, almost always, was the present, and it was a present he shared with his audience. No one else, as Joan Didion remarked in 1964, tells us so much about "the way we live now," and she did not mean as a social realist alone. What is remarkable about Cheever's attitude toward the world he confronted is how much it changed in the course of his career. There are many excellent writers, Saul Bellow has observed, who do not develop or expand. But, he added, "John Cheever was a writer of a different sort, altogether," one who went through a dramatic metamorphosis.

In *The Wapshot Chronicle* (1957), his first novel, Cheever contrasted a somewhat idealized and unrecapturable past with a less hospitable but not intolerable present. His tone ranged from genial to satirical without becoming bitter. Then, in his dark period of the 1960's, and particularly in *The Wapshot Scandal* (1964) and *Bullet Park* (1969), he adopted the narrative stance of a visiting anthropologist who, despite his apparent objectivity—"at the time of which I'm writing," the narrative voice would remark—regarded the ills of modernity with something verging on despair. Finally, in his last two novels—*Falconer* (1977) and *Oh What a Paradise It Seems* (1982)—this dismayed observer struggled toward acceptance of the deeply flawed universe, and even toward affirmation. Miracles could happen.

From these novels and from such well-known stories as **"The Death of Justina"** (1960) and **"The Angel of the Bridge"** and **"The Brigadier and the Golf Widow"** (both 1961), it would be easy to assemble a catalogue of the troubles besetting Americans in the third quarter of the 20th century. Technology can destroy the world. Our food, our entertainment, our homes, our very existences have become standardized and tasteless. We've lost our roots. Love gives way to lust, religion to psychiatry. Liquor and drugs anesthetize us against the fear of death. Cheever spells out no such bill of particulars, but it is implicit in the stories he tells and emerges through incident and conversation and symbol. Two dominant symbols in his work for this modern malaise are the superhighway and the supermarket.

Of the two, the superhighway is the most frequently and obviously invoked. Cheever's expressway that gouges through the landscape compares with the 19th-century railroad as the machine in the American garden. Emerson speculated that the railroad rides upon us and not the other way around, Thoreau feared that we had constructed a fateful engine beyond our capacity to control. A similar theme runs through much of Cheever's work, where the superhighway is the Atropos that levels the contours and obliterates the sights and smells of a fragrant past, and that in combination with trains and planes produces an incredible mobility at the expense of homelessness.

Uprootedness is at the heart of *The Wapshot Chronicle*, in which the two brothers Moses and Coverly Wapshot leave their native St. Botolphs to seek their fortunes in more thriving areas. All the young leave St. Botolphs, a dying seaport town. The movement is toward nomadism (a favorite Cheever term), toward a gypsy culture without roots, and the psychic costs—in loneliness and in yearning for roots—are heavy, especially for Coverly and his wife Betsey.

The young couple are assigned to Remsen Park, a government community where Coverly is employed in missile work, and Betsey—a small-town girl herself—is desperately lonely there. Bereft as she is, she is drawn to the supermarket, a modern artifact that has a more ambivalent symbolic import in Cheever's fiction than the superhighway.

> She walked out of Circle K and down 325th Street to the shopping center and went into the supermarket, not because she needed anything but because the atmosphere of the place pleased her.

There she strikes up a conversation with the pleasant young cashier who directs her to the electrical appliance store five doors down the street. There she strikes up a conversation with another man who promises to fix the cord on her iron and comes home, where she strikes up a conversation with a vacuum cleaner salesman who happens to ring her bell. Betsey can find friends only by way of these instrumental relations. Distraught, she decides to leave, and in her absence (for she will come back) Coverly "thought of her against scenes of travel—trains and platforms and hotels and asking strangers for help with her bags—and he felt great love and pity."

A relationship clearly exists between supertravel and supermarket. The fast cars and express trains and jet airplanes that make nomads of us all bear a certain affinity to the supermarket that is not really the friendly country store Betsey Wapshot wishes it were. (pp. 654-56)

The fear of death dominates *The Wapshot Scandal:* death by nuclear explosion, death by plane crash, death on the highway, death by cancer, above all the death-in-life of a meaningless and boring suburban existence that confronts Moses Wapshot's beautiful wife Melissa. Melissa, like the scientist Dr. Cameron who plays the violin while matter-of-factly contemplating the end of the world, seeks escape from mortality in lust. Dr. Cameron feels "the chill of death go off his bones" in the arms of his Roman mistress. Melissa purchases her own warmth in the form of the grocery boy Emile, and eventually they, too, go to Rome, on the wings of a supermarket promotion.

Fired from his job at an old-style grocery store because of his fornication with Melissa, Emile goes to work "at the new supermarket on the hill—the one with the steeple." To lure customers from the Grand Union and the A&P, the new store develops "an exploitation package." The store promises to distribute a thousand plastic eggs on Easter Eve, with certificates inside for a dozen real eggs, a bottle of French perfume, an outboard motor, and so on, with five golden eggs entitling the finders to "a three-week, all-expense vacation for two at a luxury hotel in Madrid, Paris, London, Venice or Rome." Emile is hired to hide the eggs between two and three on Easter morning, but word gets out and—in a scene Malcolm Cowley construed as "a Brueghel vision of hell"—he is pursued on his rounds by dozens of women in nightgowns and robes and curlers (they all appear "to be wearing crowns") who block the progress of his car and let the air out of his tires so that finally he is reduced to throwing eggs and dumping entire crates of them into a tract of empty land. But Emile keeps the golden egg for Rome in his pocket, on the way home leaves it on Melissa's lawn, and that—with bizarre complications—is why Melissa and Emile are living together in the Eternal City as the novel ends.

In effect they are exiles rather than expatriates in

Rome. Melissa's marriage has of course collapsed. The Italians whom she and Emile see socially treat them like the outcasts they are. She is last glimpsed in the Supra-Marketto Americano, pushing her way through the walls of food as solace for her bewilderment and grief. (pp. 658-59)

John Cheever was fully cognizant of the comic paradox of the supermarket in Rome, and liked to tell a story about meeting a rather assertive Bostonian at an embassy cocktail party there.

"What do you do, Mr. Shivers?" the Bostonian asked, having missed the name.

"Oh, I write. What do *you* do?"

"I'm a manager for Minimax in Boston."

"What brings you to Rome, then?"

"Well, Mr. Shivers," the Bostonian declared, "Rome needs Minimax and Minimax needs Rome. We're going to build a supermarket in Rome that will put the Pantheon to shame."

Though hardly a rival to the Pantheon, Cheever's modern supermarket is rich and strange indeed. "Except for the shapes of the pastry," the narrator of the 1962 story, **"A Vision of the World,"** remarks during his Saturday afternoon visit to the supermarket, "there was nothing traditional to be seen at the pastry counter." Then, having purchased his brioches, he is inspired by the cha-cha music to dance briefly with a homely stranger. But no such humor, no such momentary gaiety brightens the picture of Melissa at the Supra-Marketto, like Ophelia grieving unto madness.

Despite the darkness of *The Wapshot Scandal,* Cheever insisted in the *Time* cover story that appeared a few weeks after the novel was published that he felt "an impulse to bring glad tidings to someone. My sense of literature is a sense of giving, not a diminishment." And he emphasized that he did not intend to belittle anyone trapped in contemporary culture, like the woman obsessed with collecting plaid stamps, for example. "It is quite possible that a woman who goes to sleep and dreams of getting a new plaid-stamp book is not quite as undignified as she appears to be. People actually sidestep the pain of death and despair by the thought of purchasing things. . . . The time for levity or even making fun of people who go to bed and dream of having 17 plaid-stamp books full is over." Josephine Herbst, a writer Cheever had known and respected since the mid-1930's, could not agree. "You may be right about the plaid stampbooks and the utility of buying to stave off thoughts of death," she wrote him, but she could not "imagine life, anywhere, at any time, so pared down to that necessity." He was, she thought, celebrating the wrong values, and besides, *Time* had him all wrong as a facile celebrant. "You don't just celebrate life out of nothing, but out of a deep pessimism. Which makes it the more valid, for our time, for any time."

Herbst was absolutely right about that, for if in his later novels Cheever seems "suspended between a tragic pessimism and a raptured expectancy . . . [seems] to be listening for the tone of angels, as the earth smoulders beneath him," it was the tension between these polar outlooks, and the attempt to resolve them, that gave his writing power and dignity. The resolution did not come easily. His nearly impossible task was to make the world of the supermarket (and the superhighway) "in which we must live, congenial to the sensibility that makes life worth living."

More than anything else Cheever wrote, 1969's *Bullet Park* sings the sorrows of excessive mobility. The title refers, rather ominously, to a suburb not unlike Proxmire Manor in its pretended immunity from the rigors of life, but in fact Bullet Park is a dangerous place to live and represents a permanent home for almost no one. "The people of Bullet Park," the anthropologizing narrator observes, intended "not so much to have arrived there as to have been planted and grown there, but this of course was untrue." Everything is in flux in this apparently comfortable world. The novel opens on the scene of a small railroad station, but this is not like the wistful way stations of the past. The building, designed "with some sense of the erotic and romantic essence of travel," is now "a warlike ruin." On the station platform one morning, a waiting commuter is sucked under the Chicago express, leaving only "a highly polished brown loafer" to signify his passing. On that same platform, co-protagonist Eliot Nailles waits in terror for his daily ride to New York City. He has made the trip a thousand times, but now a phobia overtakes him and he cannot board the train unless he dopes himself with a massive tranquilizer that will float him "down the tracks into Grand Central."

The other protagonist, Paul Hammer, is a world traveler who settles in Bullet Park to awaken the world by murdering Nailles' son Tony (Cheever is little concerned with credibility in his late fiction). Obviously unbalanced, Hammer is subject to attacks of melancholy that overtake him on trains and planes and drive him to the brink of suicide. Then, however, he remembers that he has been inspired by his insane mother to commit a ritual murder and so shock America out of its drugged stupor. He does not succeed. In the end, Nailles rescues his son as Hammer prepares to immolate him on the cross of Christ's Church and, in a curiously ambivalent ending, brings matters back to normal. "Tony went back to school on Monday and Nailles—drugged—went off to work and everything was as wonderful, wonderful, wonderful, wonderful as it had been."

"Never, in the history of civilization," Hammer's mother proclaims, "has one seen a great nation single-mindedly bent on drugging itself " like the United

States. She chooses to live in Europe but on a trip to Los Angeles takes a ride on a freeway and there witnesses "another example of forgetfulness, suicide, municipal corruption and the debauchery of natural resources." Bullet Park itself averages 22 traffic casualties a year "because of a winding highway that seemed to have been drawn on the map by a child with a grease pencil." One Saturday morning, Nailles takes Hammer fishing, and they drive north on Route 61, one of the "most dangerous" and "most inhuman" of the new highways. (pp. 660-62)

Despite its emphasis on the stupefying effects of drugs and liquor and on the deadly pathways of rapid travel, *Bullet Park* offers a more hopeful picture than *The Wapshot Scandal.* Nailles is not terribly bright or capable, but he does manage to rescue his son. Moreover, as his reminiscence about the roads of yesterday suggests, he remains keenly attuned to nature. When he comes home to Bullet Park one night, the rain lets up, and he can distinguish the various sounds that the wind out of the northeast makes as it fills up different trees: "maple, birch, tulip and oak." What good is this knowledge? he reflects, and answers his own question. "Someone has to observe the world."

Exactly, and while he thinks this, the mysterious Swami Rutuola is upstairs with the teenager Tony who has troubles of his own, the murderous Hammer aside, and in a period of extended depression has refused to get out of bed. Neither conventional medicine nor psychiatry can rouse Tony, but Rutuola does. His method is to invoke an appealing image in Tony's mind and to reinforce that image with repetition. "I am in a house by the sea." the Swami has Tony repeat after him. "It is four o'clock and raining." "I am sitting in a ladder-back chair with a book in my lap." "I have a girl I love who has gone on an errand but she will return." "I am sitting under an apple tree in clean clothes and I am content." Next the Swami coaches Tony in the "love" cheer and the "hope" cheer—he says "love" over and over, as many as a hundred times, and the same with "hope"—and miraculously the treatment works and Tony is restored to health.

In effect the whole Cheever program for coping with the ills of modernity is summed up in these few pages. "Someone has to observe the world." Restoration comes with mountain air, the wind in the trees, the rain at the seashore, the scent of apples. It comes through love. And it will not come if we succumb to despair.

Ezekiel Farragut in *Falconer,* Cheever's widely publicized 1977 novel set in prison, conquers his drug addiction and escapes from confinement—again, miraculously—through giving himself in love and persistently yearning toward the light. Farragut's release from addiction and imprisonment paralleled Cheever's own 1975 victory over the confinements of alcoholism.

Thereafter the darkness that pervaded *The Wapshot Scandal* and, to a lesser degree, *Bullet Park,* gave way to radiance. Despite its forbidding subject matter, *Falconer* is full of blue sky, and there is nothing equivocal about its affirmative ending. Free at last, Farragut walks into the future in a coat a perfect stranger has just given him as protection against the rain and against detection. "Rejoice," he thinks to himself. "Rejoice." That there was more to celebrate than to bemoan became an article of belief for Cheever in his last years.

Yet as the title of *Oh What a Paradise It Seems* (1982) hints, the earth we inhabit is not really a paradise, or at least is not likely to remain one in an age of pollution. (pp. 663-64)

Cheever has been criticized for looking backward, for a nostalgia that by overvaluing a golden past ignores the question of how to confront the flawed present. But in his later work that is not at all true. He was every bit as aware in 1980 as in 1960 of the depradations that nomadism and commercialism (symbolized by superhighway and supermarket) had worked upon his culture. Yet in his last fiction he rejected negation as a contemptible attitude. In his most optimistic moods, he looked to the future rather than the idealized past for relief. Perhaps, he thought, the "automobile dumps, polluted rivers, jerry-built ranch houses" of the present were "not, as they might seem to be, the ruins of our civilization but . . . the temporary encampments and outposts of the civilization we—you and I—shall build."

In any event, so long as people could see the blue sky, feel the sea breeze, smell the sweet grass, and love one another, they should not succumb to despair. Life itself was the greatest of gifts. What he aimed to do, in *Falconer* and *Paradise,* was "to study triumphs, the rediscoveries of love, all that I know in the world to be decent, radiant, and clear." Was his writing getting better, a particularly dense television interviewer asked him in 1979? Well, not necessarily better, he answered, but he hoped there was a growth "as if one were discovering more light, if light is what one is after." This observation silenced his interviewer entirely, but those who read Cheever's fiction carefully and admire it, like John Updike, knew what he was talking about.

When Updike read *Paradise* in proof, certain images stuck in his mind: "The ecstatic ice skating, the wind chimes, the exultant evocation of the supermarket. This last place especially needed you to sing it," he wrote Cheever in December 1981. The previous month, the two writers made a joint appearance on the Dick Cavett show, but Updike felt he had not managed to articulate for television what he most valued in his colleague's work. "I kept saying radiant on Cavett but it's more like the little star inside a snowball on a sunny day." What Cheever had done during the 1960's was to tell us how we lived. In his last two novels he went beyond that. "You do that elemental thing only the rarely good writer can do"—Updike summed up the accomplishment—you "tell us how we are alive." (pp. 667-68)

Scott Donaldson, "Supermarket and Superhighway: John Cheever's America," in *The Virginia Quarterly Review,* Vol. 62, No. 4, Autumn, 1986, pp. 654-68.

SOURCES FOR FURTHER STUDY

Cheever, Susan. *Home Before Dark: A Biographical Memoir of John Cheever by His Daughter.* Boston: Houghton Mifflin Co., 1984, 243 p.

Reminiscences by Cheever's novelist-daughter, who writes in the preface: "I wanted to tell the story of a man who fought to adhere to some moral standard until the end of his life." Includes excerpts from John Cheever's journals as well as several pages of photographs.

Coale, Samuel. *John Cheever.* New York: Frederick Ungar Publishing Co., 1977, 130 p.

Biographical and critical study that discusses several of Cheever's short stories and all of his novels. Includes brief bibliography.

Collins, R. G. *Critical Essays on John Cheever.* Boston: G. K. Hall and Co., 1982, 292 p.

Collection of critical work on Cheever. The book includes interviews with Cheever, a representative selection of short reviews of his stories and novels, and a number of longer critical studies on various aspects of Cheever's fiction.

Donaldson, Scott. *John Cheever: A Biography.* New York: Random House, 1988, 416 p.

Thorough biography that is sometimes faulted for containing pedestrian literary criticism.

O'Hara, James E. *John Cheever: A Study of the Short Fiction.* Boston: Twayne Publishers, 1989, 161 p.

Chronicles the growth of Cheever's short fiction, "examining a representative selection of his stories to clarify significant developments in both the style and thematic content of his work from 1930 to 1981."

Waldeland, Lynne. *John Cheever.* Boston: Twayne Publishers, 1979, 160 p.

Full-length biographical and critical study of Cheever's career.

Anton Chekhov

1860-1904

(Full name Anton Pavlovich Chekhov; also transliterated as Chekov, Tchehov, Tchehoff, Tchekhof, Tchekhov, Čexov, Čekov, Čecov, Čechov, Chekhoff, and Chehov; also wrote under the pseudonym Antosha Chekhonte) Russian dramatist, short story writer, and novelist.

INTRODUCTION

*C*hekhov is the most significant Russian author of the literary generation that succeeded Leo Tolstoy and Fyodor Dostoevsky. Preeminent for his stylistic innovations in both fictional and dramatic forms, he is also known for his depth of insight into the human condition. While Chekhov's most characteristic writings begin with revelations of personal feelings and observations, they ultimately exhibit supreme emotional balance and stylistic control. It is precisely this detached, rational artfulness that distinguishes his work from the confessional abandons of Dostoevsky or the psychological fantasies of Nikolai Gogol. This artistic control made Chekhov one of the masters of the modern short story and the modern drama.

Chekhov's grandfather was a serf who bought his freedom, and his father was the owner of a small grocery business in Taganrog, the village where Chekhov was born. When the family business went bankrupt in 1876, the Chekhovs, without Anton, moved to Moscow to escape creditors; Anton remained in Taganrog until 1879 in order to complete his education and earn a scholarship to Moscow University. There he studied medicine and, after graduating in 1884, went into practice. By this time he was publishing sketches, mostly humorous, in popular magazines. Chekhov did this to support his family, and although he wrote literally hundreds of these pieces, he did not take them very seriously. In 1885, however, he moved to St. Petersburg and became friends with A. S. Suvorin, editor of the journal *Novoe vremja*, who encouraged the young writer to develop his obvious gifts. At this time, and for several years afterward, Chekhov's writings were profoundly influenced by Tolstoy's ideas on ascetic morality and nonresistance to evil. But after Chekhov visited the penal settlement on the island of Sakhalin, which he would make the subject of a humanitarian study, he rejected Tolstoy's moral code as an insufficient answer to human suffering. In the late 1880s Chekhov began to produce what are regarded as his mature works in the short story form. While he was also engaged in writing plays during this period, his first major work as a dramatist was not produced until 1896, when the Moscow Art Theater staged *Chayka* (*The Seagull*). The same company also presented the first performances of *Dyadya Vanya* (1899; *Uncle Vanya*), *Tri sestry* (1901; *The Three Sisters*), and *Vishnevy sad* (1904; *The Cherry Orchard*). In 1901 Chekhov married Olga Knipper, an actress with the Moscow Art Theater. Because of his worsening tuberculosis, from which he had suffered since 1884, Chekhov was forced to spend time in European health resorts and was often separated from his wife, who frequently performed in Moscow. He died in a Black Forest spa in 1904.

Chekhov's three periods in the short story genre—early sketches, stories influenced by Tolstoy, and later stories—comprise the major stages of his fiction. The early sketches display many of the traits of popular fiction: swift development of action, superficial yet vivid characterization, and surprise endings. But while many of these pieces were written as humor, they also contain qualities that led Maxim Gorky to call them "tragic humor." Gorky wrote of Chekhov: "One has only to read his 'humorous' stories with attention to see what a lot of cruel and disgusting things, behind the humorous words and situations, had been observed by the author with sorrow and were concealed by him." Chekhov's Tolstoyan period was influenced primarily by the older writer's ideas about sexual abstinence, devotion to the plight of others, strict antimaterialism, and nonresistance to the natural evil of the temporal world. During this period Chekhov believed that literature had the power to effect positive change in the world and that it was obliged to critique the lives of its readers. In consequence, stories like "Niscij" ("The Beggar") were written to convey a message, though this message is nonetheless delivered with the subtle artistry and restraint Chekhov cultivated throughout his career. This second period of Chekhov's fiction includes many features characteristic of all his works. "Step" ("The Steppe"), the author's first story to appear in a serious literary journal, substitutes for the mechanical tensions of plot a tightly-strung network of images, character portraits, and dense, actionless scenes of commonplace tedium. Rather than detracting from reader involvement, these qualities contribute to an overall effect of tense realism which serves its author's private vision of art and morality, a vision that led Chekhov to focus on the tragedies of everyday existence and portray them in a sympathetic yet unsentimental manner. In the final period of his fiction, Chekhov rejected and attacked his former master's ideas. "Duel" ("The Duel") critically examines the antisexuality message of

Tolstoy's *Kreutzer Sonata*, and "Moya zhizn" ("My Life") elaborates on the adverse effects of the Tolstoyan dogma. In "Palata nomer 6" ("Ward Number 6"), a story of madness and misery, Chekhov opposed the doctrine of nonresistance to evil by depicting the downfall of one of its proponents. This is considered the period of Chekhov's full genius in the short story form, the era in which his art and insight achieved the level that placed him among the greatest figures in modern literature.

Chekhov's interest and participation in the theater had its origins in his schooldays at Taganrog, when he acted and wrote for the local playhouse. His first serious effort in drama was written during his residence in Moscow. This work, *Pyesa bez nazvaniya* (1881; *That Worthless Fellow Platonov*), initiated the first of two major periods of the author's dramatic writings. The works of this first dramatic period are characterized by the theatrical conventions and subject matter of the times. *Platonov,* a long and somewhat declamatory social drama, features a leading character whose reformist ideals are negated by the indifference of others and by his own ineffectuality. Chekhov's next drama, *Ivanov* (1887), is less bulky and more realistic than its predecessor, though critics still view it as a theatrically exaggerated and traditional period piece. Written during the Tolstoyan phase of Chekhov's works, *Leshy* (1889; *The Wood Demon*) was his first attempt at the artistic realism fully achieved only in his later dramas. This didactic morality play on the theme of vice and virtue is criticized for the same dramatic faults as the other works of this period.

The dramas of Chekhov's second period constitute his major work in the theater. These plays are primarily noted for their technique of "indirect action," a method whereby violent or intensely dramatic events are not shown on stage but occur during the intervals of the action as seen by the audience. The main action, then, is made up of conversations alluding to the unseen moments in the characters' lives. In this way Chekhov was able to study and convey more precisely the effects of crucial events on a character's personality. The first drama done in this manner was *The Seagull*. Written seven years after *The Wood Demon*, *The Seagull* was a complete failure in its opening performance at St. Petersburg. Two years later, however, it was produced successfully in Moscow under the direction of Constantin Stanislavsky, who emphasized—some critics say overemphasized—the more dismal aspects of Chekhov's "art of melancholy." Critics attribute the artistic success of *The Seagull* to a subtle interweaving of theme and character. The resulting scenario is one in which viewed action is reduced to a minimum and in which nuances of pacing and mood become paramount to the full realization of dramatic tension.

In *The Seagull* and the dramas that followed—*Uncle Vanya, The Three Sisters*, and *The Cherry Orchard*—the mood and meaning hovers somewhere between the tragic and the comic. *Uncle Vanya*, a revised version of *The Wood Demon*, stresses the influence of economic and social conditions on everyday life and the inability of people to change. *The Three Sisters* is the closest to tragedy among Chekhov's dramas, the play that most heavily contributes to his reputation as a portrayer of futile existences and a forerunner of the modernist tradition of the absurd. Controversy has arisen over the interpretation of Chekhov's last play, *The Cherry Orchard*, which he subtitled "A Comedy," genuinely intending it to be viewed as such. Often perceived as a nostalgic parable on the passing of an older order in Russian history, this late work displays one of Chekhov's most important themes: the triumph of ignorance and vulgarity over the fragile traditions of elegance and nobility. Yet Chekhov was unhappy with the Moscow Art Theater's original production of *The Cherry Orchard*, which stressed, as many critics have, the pathos of the characters' situation. Dorothy Sayers, commenting on the inescapable humor of the play, wrote that "the whole tragedy of futility is that it never succeeds in achieving tragedy. In its blackest moments it is inevitably doomed to the comic gesture." Chekhov masterfully depicted the "ordinary drabness" of life, bringing to the stage a realism that eschewed the epic scale of traditional drama and a model of dramaturgy that demonstrated previously unrealized possibilities for the stage. Francis Fergusson wrote, "If Chekhov drastically reduced the dramatic art, he did so in full consciousness, and in obedience both to artistic scruples and to a strict sense of reality. He reduced the dramatic art to its ancient root, from which new growths are possible."

In comparison with the work of other great Russian authors, in particular the variety and vaulting ideological proportions of Tolstoy, Chekhov's stories and dramas are more uniform in mood and narrower in scope, frequently illustrating situations of hardship, boredom, and mundane suffering. The view of Chekhov as an utter pessimist, however, has always met with opposition, especially from those Soviet critics who see him as a chronicler of the degenerating landowner classes during an era of imminent revolution. The exact relationship between Chekhov and his work has long been a matter of interest for critics, and an attempt is often made to isolate the somber spirit of the stories and plays from the personal philosophy of their author. Critics such as Ronald Hingley have attempted to modify the view of a pessimistic Chekhov, while at the same time avoiding the equally erroneous image of an optimistic one. In either case, Chekhov's prominent stature in world literature is not a consequence of his philosophy or worldview as much as it is based on fiction and dramas executed with a phenomenal artistry that permanently altered the literary standards for these genres.

(For further information about Chekhov's life and works, see *Contemporary Authors*, Vols. 104, 124; *Short Story Criticism*, Vol. 2; and *Twentieth-Century Literary Criticism*, Vols. 3, 10, 31.)

CRITICAL COMMENTARY

MAXIM GORKY

(essay date 1906)

[Gorky, a Russian novelist and dramatist, is best known for his pivotal support of the Bolsheviks during the period leading up to the Russian Revolution. He knew Chekhov personally and greatly admired his literary works. In the following excerpt from his 1906 *Reminiscences of Anton Chekhov*, he evaluates Chekhov's motives and achievements as a writer.]

Anton Pavlovich in his early stories was already able to reveal in the dim sea of banality its tragic humour; one has only to read his "humorous" stories with attention to see what a lot of cruel and disgusting things, behind the humorous words and situations, had been observed by the author with sorrow and were concealed by him.

He was ingenuously shy; he would not say aloud and openly to people: "Now do be more decent"; he hoped in vain that they would themselves see how necessary it was that they should be more decent. He hated everything banal and foul, and he described the abominations of life in the noble language of a poet, with the humorist's gentle smile, and behind the beautiful form of his stories people scarcely noticed the inner meaning, full of bitter reproach.

The dear public, when it reads his *Daughter of Albion*, laughs and hardly realizes how abominable is the well-fed squire's mockery of a person who is lonely and strange to everyone and everything. In each of his

Principal Works

Pyostrye rasskazy (short stories) 1886

Ivanov (drama) 1887
[Ivanoff published in Plays, 1912]

Nevinnye rechi (short stories) 1887

V sumerkakh (short stories) 1887

Leshy (drama) 1889
[The Wood Demon, 1926]

Rasskazy (short stories) 1889

Chayka (drama) 1896
[The Seagull published in Plays, 1912]

*Dyadya Vanya (drama) 1899
[Uncle Vanya published in Plays, 1912]

Chekhov: Polnoe sobranie sochinenii (short stories and dramas) 1900-04

Tri sestry (drama) 1901
[The Three Sisters, 1922]

The Black Monk, and Other Stories (short stories) 1903

Vishnevy sad (drama) 1904
[The Cherry Garden, 1908; also published as The Cherry Orchard, 1912]

The Kiss, and Other Stories (short stories) 1908

Plays (dramas) 1912

The Darling, and Other Stories (short stories) 1916

The Duel, and Other Stories (short stories) 1916

The Lady with the Dog, and Other Stories (short stories) 1917

The Party, and Other Stories (short stories) 1917

The Wife, and Other Stories (short stories) 1918

The Witch, and Other Stories (short stories) 1918

The Bishop, and Other Stories (short stories) 1919

The Chorus Girl, and Other Stories (short stories) 1920

The Letters of Anton Chekhov (letters) 1920

The Horse-Stealers, and Other Stories (short stories) 1921

The Schoolmaster, and Other Stories (short stories) 1921

The Schoolmistress, and Other Stories (short stories) 1921

The Cook's Wedding, and Other Stories (short stories) 1922

Love, and Other Stories (short stories) 1922

†Pyesa bez nazvaniya (drama) [first publication] 1923
[That Worthless Fellow Platonov, 1930]

Polnoe sobranie sochinenii i pisem A. P. Chekhova (dramas, short stories, notebooks, diaries, and letters) 1944-51

The Oxford Chekhov. 9 vols. (short stories and dramas) 1964-80

*This work is a revision of the earlier Leshy.

†This work was written in 1881.

humorous stories I hear the quiet, deep sigh of a pure and human heart, the hopeless sigh of sympathy for men who do not know how to respect human dignity, who submit without any resistance to mere force, live like fish, believe in nothing but the necessity of swallowing every day as much thick soup as possible, and feel nothing but fear that someone, strong and insolent, will give them a hiding.

No one understood as clearly and finely as Anton Chekhov the tragedy of life's trivialities, no one before him showed men with such merciless truth the terrible and shameful picture of their life in the dim chaos of bourgeois everyday existence.

His enemy was banality; he fought it all his life long; he ridiculed it, drawing it with a pointed and unimpassioned pen, finding the mustiness of banality even where at the first glance everything seemed to be arranged very nicely, comfortably, and even brilliantly. . . . (pp. 107-09)

Reading Anton Chekhov's stories, one feels oneself in a melancholy day of late autumn, when the air is transparent and the outline of naked trees, narrow houses, greyish people, is sharp. Everything is strange, lonely, motionless, helpless. The horizon, blue and empty, melts into the pale sky, and its breath is terribly cold upon the earth, which is covered with frozen mud. The author's mind, like the autumn sun, shows up in hard outline the monotonous roads, the crooked streets, the little squalid houses in which tiny, miserable people are stifled by boredom and laziness and fill the houses with an unintelligible, drowsy bustle. (pp. 109-10)

There passes before one a long file of men and women, slaves of their love, of their stupidity and idleness, of their greed for the good things of life; there walk the slaves of the dark fear of life; they straggle anxiously along, filling life with incoherent words about the future, feeling that in the present there is no place for them.

At moments out of the grey mass of them one hears the sound of a shot: Ivanov or Treplev has guessed what he ought to do and has died.

Many of them have nice dreams of how pleasant life will be in three hundred years, but it occurs to none of them to ask themselves who will make life pleasant if we only dream.

In front of that dreary, grey crowd of helpless people there passed a great, wise, and observant man; he looked at all these dreary inhabitants of his country, and, with a sad smile, with a tone of gentle but deep reproach, with anguish in his face and in his heart, in a beautiful and sincere voice, he said to them:

"You live badly, my friends. It is shameful to live like that." (p. 111)

Maxim Gorky, "Anton Chekhov: Fragments of Recollections," in his *Reminiscences of Tolstoy, Chekhov, and Andreev,* translated by Katherine Mansfield, S. S. Koteliansky, and Leonard Woolf, The Hogarth Press, 1948, pp. 91-111.

PRINCE D. S. MIRSKY
(essay date 1926)

[Mirsky was a Russian prince who fled his country after the Bolshevik Revolution and settled in London. While in England, he wrote two important histories of Russian literature, *Contemporary Russian Literature* (1926) and *A History of Russian Literature from Its Beginnings to 1900* (1927). The following excerpt is from the latter work. Here, Mirsky examines Chekhov's development as a writer of short stories and outlines the characteristic features of his short fiction.]

Chékhov's literary career falls into two distinct periods: before and after 1886. The English reader and the more "literary" Russian public know him by his later work, but it may be safely asserted that a much greater number of Russians know him rather as the author of his early comic stories than as the author of **"My Life"** and *Three Sisters*. It is a characteristic fact that many of his most popular and typical comic stories, precisely those which are sure to be known to every middleclass or semi-educated Russian (for example, **"A Horse Name," "Vint," "The Complaint Ledger," "Surgery"**), were not translated into English. It is true that some of these stories are very difficult to translate, so topical and national are the jokes. But it is also evident that the English-speaking admirer of Chékhov has no taste for this buffoonery but looks to Chékhov for commodities of a very different description. The level of the comic papers in which Chékhov wrote was by no means a high one. They were a sanctuary of every kind of vulgarity and bad taste. Their buffoonery was vulgar and meaningless. They lacked the noble gift of nonsense, which of all things elevates man nearest the gods; they lacked wit, restraint, and grace. It was mere trivial buffoonery, and Chékhov's stories stand in no striking contrast to their general background. Except for a higher degree of craftsmanship, they are of a piece with the rest. Their dominant note is an uninspired sneer at the weaknesses and follies of mankind, and it would need a more than lynx-eyed critic to discern in them the note of human sympathy and of the higher humor that is so familiar to the reader of Chékhov's mature work. The great majority of these stories were never reprinted by Chékhov, but still the first and second volumes of his collected edition contain several dozen of the kind. Only a few—and all of them of a less crude variety—have had the honor of an English translation. But even in the crudest, Chékhov stands out as a superior craftsman, and in the economy of his means there is a promise of **"Sleepy"** and **"At Christmastime."** Before long, Chékhov began to deviate from the straight line imposed on him by the comic papers, and as early as 1884 he could write such a story as **"The Chorus Girl,"** which may yet be a little primitive and clumsy in its lyrical construction but on the whole stands almost on a level with the best of his mature work. *Parti-colored Stories*, which appeared in 1886 and laid the foundation of Chékhov's reputation in the literary circles, contained, besides many exercises in crude buffoonery, stories of a different kind that presented a gay appearance but were sad in substance—and that answered admirably to the hackneyed phrase of Russian critics, "tears through laughter." Such, for instance, is **"Misery"**: on a wet winter night a cabman who has just lost his son tries to tell his story to one after another of his fares and does not succeed in kindling their sympathy.

In 1886, as has been said, Chékhov was able to free himself from the comic papers and could now develop a new style that had begun to assert itself somewhat earlier. This style was (and remained) essentially poetical, but it was some time before he finally settled the main lines of what was to be the characteristic Chekhovian story. In his stories of 1886-8 there are many elements that have been yet imperfectly blended—a strain of descriptive journalism (in its most unadulterated form in **"Uprooted"**); pure anecdote, sometimes just ironical (**"The First-Class Passenger"**); sometimes poignantly tragi-comical (**"Vánka"**); the lyrical expression of atmosphere (**"The Steppe," "Happiness"**); psychological studies of morbid experience (**"Typhus"**); parables and moralities laid out in a conventional, un-Russian surrounding (**"The Bet," "A Story without a Title"**). But already one of the favorite and most characteristic themes asserts its domination—the mutual lack of understanding between human beings, the impossibility for one person to feel in tune with another. **"The Privy Councilor," "The Post," "The Party," "The Princess,"** are all based on this idea—which becomes something like the leitmotiv of all Chékhov's later work. The most typical stories of this period are all located in the country of his early life, the steppe between the Sea of Azóv and the Donéts. These are **"The Steppe," "Happiness," "The Horse-Stealers."** They are planned as lyrical symphonies (though the last one is also an anecdote). Their dominant note is superstition, the vague terror (Chékhov makes it poetical) before the presences that haunt the dark and empty steppe, the profound uninterestingness and poverty of the steppe peasant's life, a vague hope of a happiness that may be discovered, with the help of dark powers, in some ancient treasure mound. **"The Steppe,"** at which Chékhov worked much and to which he returned again after its publication, is the central thing in this period. It lacks the wonderful architecture of his short stories—it is a lyrical poem, but a poem made out of the substance of trivial, dull, and dusky life. The long, monotonous, uneventful journey of a little boy over the endless steppe from his native villiage to a distant town is drawn out in a hundred pages to form a languid, melodious, and tedious lullaby. A brighter aspect of Chékhov's lyrical art is in **"Easter Eve."** The monk on night duty on the ferryboat tells a passenger about his dead fellow monk, who had the rare gift of writing lauds to the saints. He describes with loving detail the technique of this art, and one discerns Chékhov's sincere sympathy for this unnoticed, unwanted, quiet, and unambitious fellow craftsman. To the same period belongs **"Kashtánka,"** the delightful history of a dog that was kidnaped by a circus clown to form part of a troupe of performing animals and escaped to her old master in the middle of a performance. The story is a wonderful blend of humor and poetry, and though it certainly sentimentalizes and humanizes its animals, one cannot help recognizing it as a masterpiece. Another little gem is **"Sleepy,"** a real masterpiece of concentration, economy, and powerful effectiveness.

In some stories of this period we find already the manner that is pre-eminently Chekhovian. The earliest story where it is quite distinctly discernible is **"The Party,"** on which Chékhov himself laid a great value, but which is not yet perfect; he confesses in a letter to Suvórin that he "would gladly have spent six months over **"The Party"**. . . . But what am I to do? I begin a story on September 10th with the thought that I must finish it by October 5th at the latest; if I don't, I shall fail the editor and be left without money. I let myself go at the beginning and write with an easy mind; but by the time I get to the middle, I begin to grow timid and fear that my story will be too long. . . . This is why the beginning of my stories is always very promising . . . the middle is huddled and timid, and the end is, as in a short sketch, like fireworks." But the essential of Chékhov's mature style is unmistakably present. It is the "biography" of a mood developing under the trivial pinpricks of life, but owing in sub-

stance to a deep-lying, physiological or psychological cause (in this case the woman's pregnancy). **"A Dreary Story,"** published in 1889, may be considered the starting point of the mature period. The leitmotiv of mutual isolation is brought out with great power. We may date the meaning that has come to be associated in Russia with the words "Chekhovian state of mind" . . . from **"A Dreary Story."** The atmosphere of the story is produced by the professor's deep and growing disillusionment as to himself and the life around him, the gradual loss of faith in his vocation, the gradual drifting apart of people linked together by life. The professor realizes the meaninglessness of his life—and the "giftlessness" . . . and dullness of all that surrounds him. His only remaining friend, his former ward Kátya, an unsuccessful disillusioned actress, breaks down under an intenser experience of the same feelings. And though his affection for her is sincere and genuine, and though he is suffering from the same causes as she is, he fails to find the necessary language to approach her. An unconquerable inhibition keeps him closed to her, and all he can say to her is:

> "Let us have lunch, Kátya."
> "No thank you," she answers coldly.
> Another minute passes in silence.
> "I don't like Khárkov," I say; "it is so grey here—such a grey town."
> "Yes, perhaps. . . . It's ugly. . . . I am here not for long, passing through. I am going on to-day."
> "Where?"
> "To the Crimea . . . that is, to the Caucasus."
> "Oh! For long?"
> "I don't know."
> "Kátya gets up and, with a cold smile, holds out her hand, looking at me. I want to ask her: 'Then you won't be at my funeral?' but she does not look at me; her hand is cold and, as it were, strange. I escort her to the door in silence. She goes out, walks down the long corridor, without looking back. She knows that I am looking after her, and she will look back at the turn. No, she did not look round. I've seen her black dress for the last time; her steps have died away! . . . Farewell, my treasure!"

This ending on a minor note is repeated in all Chékhov's subsequent stories and gives the keynote to his work.

"A Dreary Story" opens the succession of Chékhov's mature masterpieces. Besides the natural growth of his genius, he was now free to work longer over them than he could when he was writing **"The Party."** So his stories written in the nineties are almost without exception perfect works of art. It is mainly on the work of this period that Chékhov's reputation now rests. The principal stories written after 1889 are, in chronological order, **"The Duel," "Ward No. 6"** (1892), **"An Anonymous Story"** (1893), **"The Black Monk," "The Teacher of Literature"** (1894), **"Three Years,"**

"Ariadne," "Anna on the Neck," "An Artist's Story" (in Russian: "The House with the Maisonette"), "My Life" (1895), "Peasants" (1897), "The Darling," "Iónych," "The Lady with the Dog" (1898), "The New Villa" (1899), "At Christmas-time," "In the Ravine" (1900). After this date (it was the period of *Three Sisters* and *The Cherry Orchard*) he wrote only two stories, "The Bishop" (1902) and "Betrothed" (1903).

Chékhov's art has been called psychological, but it is psychological in a very different sense from Tolstóy's, Dostoyévsky's, or Marcel Proust's. No writer excels him in conveying the mutual unsurpassable isolation of human beings and the impossibility of understanding each other. This idea forms the core of almost every one of his stories, but, in spite of this, Chékhov's characters are singularly lacking in individual personality. Personality is absent from his stories. His characters all speak (within class limits and apart from the little tricks of catchwords he lends them from time to time) the same language, which is Chékhov's own. They cannot be recognized, as Tolstóy's and Dostoyévsky's can, by the mere *sound of their voices.* They are all alike, all made of the same material—"the common stuff of humanity"—and in this sense Chékhov is the most "democratic," the most "unanimist," of all writers. For of course the similarity of all his men and women is not a sign of weakness—it is the expression of his fundamental intuition of life as a homogeneous matter but cut out into watertight compartments by the phenomenon of individuality. Like Stendhal and the French classicists, and unlike Tolstóy, Dostoyévsky, and Proust, Chékhov is a student of "man in general." But unlike the classicists, and like Proust, he fixes his attention on the infinitesimals, the "pinpricks" and "straws" of the soul. Stendhal deals in psychological "whole numbers." He traces the major, conscious, creative lines of psychical life. Chékhov concentrates on the "differentials" of mind, its minor, unconscious, involuntary, destructive, and dissolvent forces. As art, Chékhov's method is active—more active than, for instance, Proust's, for it is based on a stricter and more conscious *choice* of material and a more complicated and elaborate disposition of it. But as "outlook," as "philosophy," it is profoundly passive and "nonresistant," for it is a surrender to the "micro-organisms," of the soul, to its destructive microbes. Hence the general impressions produced by the whole of Chékhov's work that he has a cult for inefficiency and weakness. For Chékhov has no other way of displaying his sympathy with his characters than to show in detail the process of their submission to their microbes. The strong man who does not succumb in this struggle, or who does not experience it, is always treated by Chékhov with less sympathy and comes out as the "villain of the play"— in so far as the word "villain" is at all applicable to the world Chékhov moves in. The strong man in this world

of his is merely the insensate brute, with a skin thick enough not to feel the "pinpricks," which are the only important thing in life. Chékhov's art is constructive. But the construction he uses is not a narrative construction—it might rather be called musical; not, however, in the sense that his prose is melodious, for it is not. But his method of constructing a story is akin to the method used in music. His stories are at once fluid and precise. The lines along which he builds them are very complicated curves, but they have been calculated with the utmost precision. A story by him is a series of points marking out with precision the lines discerned by him in the tangled web of consciousness. Chékhov excels in the art of tracing the first stages of an emotional process; in indicating those first symptoms of a deviation when to the general eye, and to the conscious eye of the subject in question, the nascent curve still seems to coincide with a straight line. An infinitesimal touch, which at first hardly arrests the reader's attention, gives a hint at the direction the story is going to take. It is then repeated as a leitmotiv, and at each repetition the true equation of the curve becomes more apparent, and it ends by shooting away in a direction very different from that of the original straight line. Such stories as "The Teacher of Literature," "Iónych," and "The Lady with the Dog" are perfect examples of such emotional curves. The straight line, for instance, in "Iónych," is the doctor's love for Mlle Túrkin; the curve, his subsidence into the egoistical complacency of a successful provincial career. In "The Teacher of Literature" the straight line is again the hero's love; the curve, his dormant dissatisfaction with selfish happiness and his intellectual ambition. In "The Lady with the Dog" the straight line is the hero's attitude towards his affair with the lady as a trivial and passing intrigue; the curve, his overwhelming and all-pervading love for her. In most of Chékhov's stories these constructive lines are complicated by a rich and mellow atmosphere, which he produces by the abundance of emotionally significant detail. The effect is poetical, even lyrical: as in a lyric, it is not interest in the development that the reader feels, but "infection" by the poet's mood. Chékhov's stories are lyrical monoliths; they cannot be dissected into episodes, for every episode is strictly conditioned by the whole and is without significance apart from it. In architectural unity Chékhov surpasses all Russian writers of the realistic age. Only in Púshkin and Lérmontov do we find an equal or superior gift of design. Chékhov thought Lérmontov's *Tamán* was the best short story every written, and this partiality was well founded. *Tamán* forestalled Chékhov's method of lyrical construction. Only its air is colder and clearer than the mild and mellow "autumnal" atmosphere of Chékhov's world.

Two of his best stories, "My Life" and "In the Ravine," stand somewhat apart from the rest of his mature work. **"My Life"** is the story of a Tolstoyan, and one cannot help thinking that in it Chékhov tried to approach the clearer and more intellectual style of Tolstóy. There are a directness of narrative and a thinness of atmosphere that are otherwise rare in Chékhov. In spite of this relative absence of atmosphere, it is perhaps his most poetically pregnant story. It is convincingly symbolical. The hero, his father, his sister, the Azhógins, and Anyúta Blagóvo stand out with the distinctness of morality characters. The very vagueness and generality of its title helps to make it something like an *Everyman.* For poetical grasp and significance **"My Life"** may be recognized as the masterpiece of Chékhov—unless it is surpassed by **"In the Ravine."** This, one of his last stories, is an amazing piece of work. The scene is the Moscow industrial area—it is the history of a shopkeeper's family. It is remarkably free from all excess of detail, and the atmosphere is produced, with the help of only a few descriptive touches, by the movement of the story. It is infinitely rich in emotional and symbolical significance. What is rare in Chékhov—in both these stories there is an earnestness, a keenness of moral judgment that raises them above the average of his work. All Chékhov's work is symbolical, but in most of his stories the symbolism is less concrete and more vaguely suggestive. It is akin to Maeterlinck's, in spite of the vast difference of style between the Russian realist and the Belgian mystic. **"Ward No. 6,"** the darkest and most terrible of all Chékhov's stories, is an especially notable example of this suggestive symbolism. It is all the more suggestive for being strictly realistic. (The only time Chékhov attempted to step out of the limits of strict realism was when he wrote the only story that is quite certainly a failure—**"The Black Monk."**) (pp. 372-79)

Prince D. S. Mirsky, "The Eighties and Early Nineties," in his *A History of Russian Literature from Its Beginnings to 1900,* edited by Francis J. Whitfield, Vintage Books, 1958, pp. 347-83.

VLADIMIR NABOKOV
(lecture date 1940-41)

[A Russian-born American man of letters, Nabokov was a prolific contributor to many literary fields. In the following excerpt from a lecture delivered in 1940 or 1941, he offers an evocative and reverent description of Chekhov's humor, style, and portrayal of the Russian national character.]

Chekhov's books are sad books for humorous people; that is, only a reader with a sense of humor can really appreciate their sadness. There exist writers that sound like something between a titter and a yawn—many of these are professional humorists, for instance. There are others that are something between a chuckle and a sob—Dickens was one of these. There is also that dreadful kind of humor that is consciously introduced by an author in order to give a purely technical relief after a good tragic scene—but this is a trick remote from true literature. Chekhov's humor belonged to none of these types; it was purely Chekhovian. Things for him were funny and sad at the same time, but you would not see their sadness if you did not see their fun, because both were linked up.

Russian critics have noted that Chekhov's style, his choice of words and so on, did not reveal any of those special artistic preoccupations that obsessed, for instance, Gogol or Flaubert or Henry James. His dictionary is poor, his combination of words almost trivial—the purple patch, the juicy verb, the hothouse adjective, the crème-de-menthe epithet, brought in on a silver tray, these were foreign to him. He was not a verbal inventor in the sense that Gogol was; his literary style goes to parties clad in its everyday suit. Thus Chekhov is a good example to give when one tries to explain that a writer may be a perfect artist without being exceptionally vivid in his verbal technique or exceptionally preoccupied with the way his sentences curve. When Turgenev sits down to discuss a landscape, you notice that he is concerned with the trouser-crease of his phrase; he crosses his legs with an eye upon the color of his socks. Chekhov does not mind, not because these matters are not important—for some writers they are naturally and very beautifully important when the right temperament is there—but Chekhov does not mind because his temperament is quite foreign to verbal inventiveness. Even a bit of bad grammar or a slack newspaperish sentence left him unconcerned. The magical part of it is that in spite of his tolerating flaws which a bright beginner would have avoided, in spite of his being quite satisfied with the man-in-the-street among words, the word-in-the-street, so to say, Chekhov managed to convey an impression of artistic beauty far surpassing that of many writers who thought they knew what rich beautiful prose was. He did it by keeping all his words in the same dim light and of the same exact tint of gray, a tint between the color of an old fence and that of a low cloud. The variety of his moods, the flicker of his charming wit, the deeply artistic economy of characterization, the vivid detail, and the fade-out of human life—all the peculiar Chekhovian features—are enhanced by being suffused and surrounded by a faintly iridescent verbal haziness.

His quiet and subtle humor pervades the grayness of the lives he creates. For the Russian philosophical or social-minded critic he was the unique exponent of a unique Russian type of character. It is rather difficult for me to explain what that type was or is, because it is all so linked up with the general psychological and social history of the Russian nineteenth century. It is not quite exact to say that Chekhov dealt in charming and ineffectual people. It is a little more true to say that his men and women are charming because they are ineffectual. But what really attracted the Russian reader was that in Chekhov's heroes he recognized the type of Russian intellectual, the Russian idealist, a queer and pathetic creature that is little known abroad and cannot exist in the Russia of the Soviets. Chekhov's intellectual was a man who combined the deepest human decency of which man is capable with an almost ridiculous inability to put his ideals and principles into action; a man devoted to moral beauty, the welfare of his people, the welfare of the universe, but unable in his private life to do anything useful; frittering away his provincial existence in a haze of utopian dreams; knowing exactly what is good, what is worth while living for, but at the same time sinking lower and lower in the mud of a humdrum existence, unhappy in love, hopelessly inefficient in everything—a good man who cannot make good. This is the character that passes—in the guise of a doctor, a student, a village teacher, many other professional people—all through Chekhov's stories.

What rather irritated his politically minded critics was that nowhere does the author assign this type to any definite political party or give him any definite political program. But that is the whole point. Chekhov's inefficient idealists were neither terrorists, nor Social Democrats, nor budding Bolsheviks, nor any of the numberless members of numberless revolutionary parties in Russia. What mattered was that this typical Chekhovian hero was the unfortunate bearer of a vague but beautiful human truth, a burden which he could neither get rid of nor carry. What we see is a continuous stumble through all Chekhov's stories, but it is the stumble of a man who stumbles because he is staring at the stars. He is unhappy, that man, and he makes others unhappy; he loves not his brethren, nor those nearest to him, but the remotest. The plight of a negro in a distant land, of a Chinese coolie, of a workman in the remotest Urals, affects him with a keener pang of moral pain than the misfortunes of his neighbor or the troubles of his wife. Chekhov took a special artistic pleasure in fixing all the delicate varieties of that pre-war, pre-revolution type of Russian intellectual. Those men could dream; they could not rule. They broke their own lives and the lives of others, they were silly, weak, futile, hysterical; but Chekhov suggests, blessed be the country that could produce that particular type of man. They missed opportunities, they shunned action, they spent sleepless nights in planning worlds they could not build; but the mere fact of such men, full of such fervor, fire of abnegation, pureness of spirit, moral elevation, this mere fact of such men having lived and probably still living somewhere somehow in the ruthless and sordid Russia of to-day is a promise of better things to come for the world at large—for perhaps the most admirable among the admirable laws of Nature is the survival of the weakest.

It is from this point of view that those who were equally interested in the misery of the Russian people and in the glory of Russian literature, it is from this point of view that they appreciated Chekhov. Though never concerned with providing a social or ethical message, Chekhov's genius almost involuntarily disclosed more of the blackest realities of hungry, puzzled, servile, angry peasant Russia than a multitude of other writers, such as Gorki for instance, who flaunted their social ideas in a procession of painted dummies. I shall go further and say that the person who prefers Dostoevski or Gorki to Chekhov will never be able to grasp the essentials of Russian literature and Russian life, and which is far more important, the essentials of universal literary art. It was quite a game among Russians to divide their acquaintances into those who liked Chekhov and those who did not. Those who did not were not the right sort.

I heartily recommend taking as often as possible Chekhov's books (even in the translations they have suffered) and dreaming through them as they are intended to be dreamed through. In an age of ruddy Goliaths it is very useful to read about delicate Davids. Those bleak landscapes, the withered sallows along dismally muddy roads, the gray crows flapping across gray skies, the sudden whiff of some amazing recollection at a most ordinary corner—all this pathetic dimness, all this lovely weakness, all this Chekhovian dove-gray world is worth treasuring in the glare of those strong, self-sufficient worlds that are promised us by the worshippers of totalitarian states. (pp. 252-55)

Vladimir Nabokov, "Anton Chekhov (1860-1904)," in his *Lectures on Russian Literature,* edited by Fredson Bowers, Harcourt Brace Jovanovich, 1981, pp. 245-95.

DAVID MAGARSHACK
(essay date 1960)

[In the following excerpt, Magarshack surveys Chekhov's development as a dramatist.]

[Chekhov's dramatic] work can be divided into two main periods. The plays belonging to one period differ from the plays belonging to the other, both in their structure and their final aim. There is an interval of about seven years between them during which Chekhov evolved the original type of drama which has made him famous. The first period includes four full-length plays, of which two have been preserved, and eleven one-act plays, eight of which are light comedies. All of them are characteristically direct-action plays, that is, plays in which the main dramatic action takes place on the stage in full view of the audience. The four plays of the second period, on the other hand, are indirect-action plays, that is, plays in which the main dramatic action takes place off stage and in which the action that does take place on the stage is mainly "inner action".

The Wood Demon does not strictly speaking belong to either of these categories and represents Chekhov's first attempt to write an indirect-action play or, as he first called it, a "lyrical" play. (p. 53)

The Wood Demon is essentially a morality play on Tolstoyan lines: it is not a play in which virtue triumphs over vice, but in which vice is converted to virtue. In this play Chekhov deals with the great theme of the reconciliation of good and evil by letting his vicious characters first defeat his virtuous ones and then realise the heinousness of their offence. At the same time, however, Chekhov wished to challenge the generally accepted view that stage characters ought to be "dramatically effective". He wished to show life on the stage as it really was and not as it was invariably contrived by the professional playwright. But, not surprisingly perhaps in view of the essentially "theatrical" nature of the main theme of *The Wood Demon,* what he finally produced was a revival of a romantic convention of a bygone age with all its incongruous crudities. And he did so chiefly because he failed to realise that the drama of indirect action he was attempting to write had its own laws which could be ignored only at the price of complete failure. When he discovered those laws, he transformed the crude melodrama he had written into a great stage masterpiece. (pp. 121-22)

[There are two] characteristic features of Chekhov's indirect-action plays that must be considered. The first concerns the difference between the dialogue of Chekhov's early plays and that of his late ones. The dialogue of the early plays is remarkable for the directness of its appeal to the audience, while in the late plays its appeal is indirect and, mainly, evocative. (pp. 159-60)

[Chekhov's dialogue is] a very subtle instrument for evoking the right mood in the audience and in this way preparing it for the development of the action of the play. It is no longer the colloquial prose Chekhov used in his early plays and in *The Wood Demon,* but a prose that is highly charged with emotional undertones, or, in other words, a poetic prose. . . . Tension in an indirect-action play is . . . one of the main motive forces of action. . . . [Chekhov conveyed tension] to his audience at the very beginning of the play. He did it by showing one of his main characters in a state of high nervous tension, like, for instance, Konstantin in

the opening scenes of *The Seagull* or Voynitsky in the opening scenes of *Uncle Vanya.* (pp. 162-63)

Another powerful impetus to action and movement is provided in an indirect-action play by the presence of "invisible" characters. . . . For instance, Nina's parents in *The Seagull,* Protopopov in *The Three Sisters,* and Mrs. Ranevsky's aunt and her Paris lover in *The Cherry Orchard.* In a play of direct action they would be allowed to take an active part on the stage, for they all occupy an important place in the plot and without them the final dénouement would be impossible. In an indirect action play, however, it is necessary that they, like the supernatural powers in a Greek play, should remain invisible, for their function is to supply a motive force for the action which is all the more powerful because the audience never sees them but is made to *imagine* them. (pp. 163-64)

The main elements through which action is expressed in an indirect-action play are: the "messenger" element, the function of which is to keep the audience informed about the chief dramatic incidents which takes place off stage (in a direct-action play this element is, as a rule, a structural flaw); the arrival and departure of the characters in the play round which the chief incidents that take place on the stage are grouped; the presence of a chorus which, as Aristotle points out, "forms an integral part of the whole play and shares in the action"; peripetia, that is, the reversal of the situation leading up to the dénouement, which Aristotle defines as "a change by which the action veers round to its opposite, subject always to the rule of probability and necessity", and which is the most powerful element of emotional interest in indirect-action plays and their main instrument for sustaining suspense and arousing surprise; and, lastly, background which lends depth to such plays. (p. 164)

[The most] remarkable thing about *The Seagull* is that in it Chekhov has achieved a complete synthesis of theme and character, and that the action of the play flows logically and naturally out of the interplay of the themes and characters upon each other. So complete is this synthesis that an illusion of real life is created, while in fact nothing could be further from reality than the events that happen in this play, or the situations out of which Chekhov so cunningly contrives its climaxes. Where in life would one come across such an absolute agglomeration of love triangles as in Chekhov's comedy? . . . And yet the love theme does not play any important, or any decisive part in the play: it is an ancillary theme introduced to give point to the comic elements in the play, though it is not the main comic element in it by any means. (p. 187)

Uncle Vanya is of course an adaptation of *The Wood Demon,* but Chekhov always maintained that it was an entirely new play, and it is in spite of the fact that the second and third acts of two plays are practically identical. For what did Chekhov do? He took one of the main themes of *The Wood Demon* and built an entirely different play round it. What must have struck him forcibly when he exhumed *The Wood Demon* six years after he had decided to bury it for good was that the dramatic relationships in that play were all wrong, mainly because they did not develop naturally, but were most commonly contrived by the playwright himself. Now that he had mastered the technique of the indirect-action play he could see clearly why it was so. The action, for one thing, did not unwind itself *inevitably* because it lacked the elements through which it is expressed in a play which depends for its final effect on the inner workings of the minds and hearts of its characters. The messenger element was most grossly mishandled; the chorus element was submerged in a flood of irrelevant detail because the playwright was too anxious to *copy* instead of *creating* it; the most vital peripetia element was not there at all, so that the dramatic movement of the play did not follow one single line of development, thus creating a most chaotic impression and resulting in a most unconvincing ending. Only the Serebryakov-Voynitsky incident seemed to hang together, and even that came to an abrupt end by Voynitsky's suicide. The play had therefore to be first of all disencumbered of all irrelevant matter and its action firmly based on the peripetia element. All unnecessary characters had to be dropped. . . . [A] vital change in the plot [changing a suicide to a bungled attempted murder] at once supplied Chekhov with the peripetia element of the new play: the whole action now centred round the reversal of the situation as it existed at the beginning of the play. (pp. 204-06)

The Cherry Orchard has been so consistently misunderstood and misrepresented by producer and critic alike that it is only by a complete dissociation from the current misconceptions about the play that it is possible to appreciate Chekhov's repeated assertions that he had written not a tragedy but "a comedy, and in places even a farce." Structurally, this last play of Chekhov's is the most perfect example of an indirect-action play, for in it all the elements are given equal scope for the development of the action. And in no other play is the peripetia element so important for a proper understanding of situation and character without which any appreciation of the comic nature of the play is impossible. (p. 264)

[In declaring] that there was not a single pistol shot in *The Cherry Orchard,* Chekhov overlooked another remarkable feature which distinguishes his last play from all his other plays, namely that there is not a single love triangle in it, either. Indeed, Chekhov seems to have been so anxious that nothing should obscure the essentially comic character of the play that he eliminated everything from it that might introduce any deeper emotional undercurrents. The play, it is true,

has plenty of emotional undercurrents, but they are all of a "comic" nature, that is to say, the ludicrous element is never missing from them. *The Cherry Orchard,* in fact, conforms entirely to Aristotle's definition of comedy as "an imitation of characters of a lower type who are not bad in themselves but whose faults possess something ludicrous in them". (p. 272)

The misinterpretation of *The Cherry Orchard* as a tragedy . . . is mainly due to a misunderstanding of the nature of a comic character. A "comic" character is generally supposed to keep an audience in fits of laughter, but that is not always so. No one would deny that Falstaff is essentially a comic character, but his fall from favor is one of the most moving incidents in *Henry IV.* Don Quixote, too, is essentially a comic character, but what has made him immortal is his creator's ability to arouse the compassion and the sympathy of the reader for him. The same is true of the chief characters of *The Cherry Orchard:* the sympathy and compassion they arouse in the spectator should not be allowed to blind him to the fact that they are essentially comic characters. (p. 273)

The main theme of the play is generally taken to be the passing of the old order, symbolised by the sale of the cherry orchard. But that theme was stale by the time Chekhov wrote his play. . . . What is new about this theme is the comic twist Chekhov gave it. (p. 274)

The symbolism of the cherry orchard, then, has nothing to do with its sale. All it expresses is one of the recurrent themes in Chekhov's plays: the destruction of beauty by those who are utterly blind to it. . . . The cherry orchard indeed is a purely aesthetic symbol which its owners with the traditions of an old culture behind them fully understand; to Firs it merely means the cartloads of dried cherries sent off to town in the good old days, and to Lopakhin it is only an excellent site for "development."

That the sale of the cherry orchard does not form the main theme of the play can also be deduced from the fact that the peripetia element has very little, if anything, to do with it. Indeed, the moment its owners appear on the stage, it ought to become clear to the discerning playgoer that they are certainly not going to save it. The whole dramatic interest of the play is therefore centred on Lopakhin, the future owner of the cherry orchard. (pp. 274-75)

Lopakhin can well afford to buy the estate on which his father has been a serf, but it never occurs to him to do so. At first he is absolutely genuine in trying to save the estate for its owners, but in the end it is he who becomes the owner of the estate—a complete reversal of the situation. It is the inner conflict between the son of the former serf and the rich business man round which the peripetia element in the play revolves. At the very beginning of the play Chekhov makes use of a device he used with equal effect in *The Three Sisters,* the device of the chorus element which gives the audience a vague hint of what the development of the plot is going to be while leaving the characters themselves completely in the dark. In *The Three Sisters* this device is associated with Protopopov and the two lines about the bear from Krylov's fable. In *The Cherry Orchard* it is more openly comic in character. (p. 276)

The contention, so frequently repeated and so firmly held, that Chekhov's favourite theme was disillusionment and that, moreover, he was, as [one critic] expressed it, "the poet and apologist of ineffectualness," appears in the light of the foregoing argument to be wholly untenable. Nothing, indeed, could be further from the truth than the opinion expressed by Bernard Shaw in his Preface to *Heartbreak House* in a reference to *The Cherry Orchard,* an opinion, incidentally, that has probably shaped the attitude to Chekhov in England more than any other critical appraisal of his plays. "Chekhov," Shaw wrote, "more of a fatalist than Tolstoy, had no faith in these charming people extricating themselves. They would, he thought, be sold up and sent adrift by the bailiffs; therefore, he had no scruple in exploiting and flattering their charm." Now, Chekhov was certainly not a fatalist, nor did he dream of exploiting and flattering the charm of his characters; that is done by the producers and actors who find themselves entirely at sea in face of a drama that seems to defy every canon of stagecraft and yet contains such wonderful stage material; therefore, they fall back on the more obvious and dramatically insignificant details, the mere bricks and mortar of a Chekhov play which, without its steel frame, is more of a picturesque ruin than an enduring monument to a great creative artist. (pp. 286-87)

David Magarshack, in his *Chekhov the Dramatist,* Hill and Wang, 1960, 301 p.

RANDALL JARRELL
(essay date 1965?)

[Jarrell was an American poet, critic, novelist, and translator. In the following excerpt from an essay written sometime before his death in 1965, he discusses the themes and structure of *The Three Sisters* and gives an act-by-act analysis of the play.]

In a sense *The Three Sisters* needs criticism less than almost any play I can think of. It is so marvelously organized, made, realized, that reading it or seeing it many times to be thoroughly acquainted with it is all one needs. In it Chekhov gives us a cluster of attitudes about values—happiness, marriage, work, duty, beauty, cultivation, the past, the present, the future—and shows us how these are meaningful or meaningless to people. Values are presented to us through opposed opinions, opposed lives; at different ages in life with different emotions; and finally, on different levels.

Take the ways, for instance, that marriage is presented: so obviously, so tenuously, so alternatively. All the marriages we see are disasters; but Vershinin's goes wrong for different reasons than Andrei's, and Andrei's goes wrong for different reasons than Masha's. Still, Chekhov can lump them into one generalization that we accept when Vershinin says, "Why is a Russian always sick and tired of his wife . . . and his wife and children always sick and tired of him?" Then he uses a generalization from particular experience when he has Andrei tell us, "People shouldn't get married. They shouldn't because it's boring." These are bold truths. And yet, surrounded by bad models (and in Kulygin's case, involved in one), Olga remains convincingly dedicated to marriage as an ideal—woman's role, woman's duty. And Kulygin never loses his faith in its value as a value, or as an "institution" to belong to for its own sake, and continues to encourage the single ones to marry.

"Love and Marriage" is a little ballet for Irina and Tuzenbach of coming together and parting, of going separate ways yet looking over shoulders. First they are on the same side about love. Both of them idealize it and want it, but while his dream of love is Irina, hers is Moscow where she'll meet "the real one." Later, when she gives up her dream, they come together on the marriage level (long enough to be engaged) but not at the love level. Theirs is a poignant pas de deux when, first, Irina truthfully declares it is not in her power to love this homely man and, after that, Tuzenbach's own sensitive drawing back from marriage on those terms. Both of them achieve their maximum substance as human beings at this moment. When he says to her, "There isn't anything in my life terrible enough to frighten me, only that lost key . . . " (the key to Irina's love), and when he puts love ahead of the imminent duel, Tuzenbach is ennobled. The ambiguities here make it possible for us to wonder whether the marriage would really have gone ahead the next day if he had not been killed, whether the "dead tree" allusion of Tuzenbach's meant he *knew* (by willing it) that he was going to die. (pp. 103-04)

There is a real geometry to *The Three Sisters.* It has an ideological, character, and chain-of-events organization that develops with an inevitableness akin to Greek tragedy. After making his logical skeleton Chekhov invents and *invents* plausible disguises that keep the play from having the Ibsen-well-made surface and the symbols from having the Ibsen starkness. Indeed, having so many symbols and leitmotivs prevents the most important of any of them from sticking out or being too differentiated from the rest of the surface. While the underlying organization is extremely plain, parallel, and symmetrical, it is masked by a "spot-surface" or expressed in terms of these "spots" themselves.

A visual counterpart of this very method uncannily exists in the work of the painter Vuillard. In certain of his indoor and outdoor scenes of French domestic life, the foundation areas on the canvas are made less emphatic by the swarms of particles that mottle the walls with rose-printed paper, the rugs with swirls, the lawns with pools of sun and shade. From such variation and variegation comes his cohesion. Vuillard commingles plaids and dappled things as non sequitur as the jottings in Chebutykin's notebook. He alludes to a mysterious darkness by leaving a door ajar. He baffles the viewer by a woman's ear glowing red. What does she hear? In the same way, Masha's eccentric line "By the curved seastrand a green oak stands / A chain of gold upon it . . . " baffles us. What *does* it mean?

These Vuillard "spots" are found in bizarre, grotesque, homey touches in a speech, a mannerism, a trait, an incident that add up to several dozen possibly. Solyony, Chebutykin, Kulygin, Natasha, and Ferapont are covered with them; Olga and Irina and Vershinin scarcely have any; with Masha and Tuzenbach they are used sparingly but memorably. Chekhov made such imaginative and original use of the indeterminacy principle on the microscopic level (the opposite of Ibsen) while maintaining on the macroscopic level firm causality. The more his themes and characters were contradictory, inconsistent, and ambiguous, the more the play got a feeling of the randomness and personalness of real life. (pp. 105-06)

In a certain sense *The Three Sisters* is as well-made as an Ibsen play in that everything is related to everything else, except that Chekhov relates things in a musical way, or in a realistic-causal, rather than geometrical-rhetorical-causal, way. The repeated use of Wagnerian leitmotivs occurs not only for characters but for themes, ideology, and morality. Diffusing the themes required more concentration, he wrote in letters when he was working on *The Three Sisters,* than for any other play. He perfected it to relax the essential structural framework the play is built on. In the exchange of themes, overly defined edges of characterization and situation are blurred and, to him, more realistic. In particular, Chebutykin's "What's the difference?" is his own special leitmotiv that, however, is borrowed by nearly everyone at sometime or other, just as themes of fatigue, happiness, boredom, etc., are shared.

Loneliness (hardly a value or a philosophy) becomes a sort of ghost that haunts Andrei all the time,

Irina until she gets older, and Solyony under cover of his Lermontov personality. (pp. 110-11)

[Chekhov] keeps us conscious of the loneliness underneath the general animation. At the birthday party in Act I, there is Vershinin's line about the gloomy-looking bridge in Moscow where the water under it could be heard: "It makes a lonely man feel sad." Later on we hear again when Chebutykin tells Andrei about being unmarried, even if marriage is boring: "But the loneliness! You can philosophize as much as you please, but loneliness is a terrible thing, Andrei. . . . " With the "good-bye trees" and "good-bye echo" and the embraces, tears, *au revoir's* and farewells, loneliness has built up like entropy as the good social group—that partly kept people from being lonely—has been broken into by the inferior outside world. The organized enclave of Act I, after being invaded by the relatively unorganized environment, loses its own organization like a physical system and runs down to almost nothing.

The musical side of Russian life, and Chekhov, comes into the play in every act: Masha whistles, the carnival people play off-stage, Chebutykin sings nervously after the duel. Specifically, Act I opens with Olga remembering the band's funeral march after the father's death and Act IV ends with the band playing a march as the brigade leaves and Olga has her last, summarizing speech. The "yoo-hoos" beforehand have imparted a faintly musical nostalgia to the scene, too. In Acts I and II there are guitar and piano and singing. "My New Porch" is a song everyone knows like "Old MacDonald Had a Farm," so that when Tuzenbach starts it off, even lonely Andrei and old Chebutykin can carry it along. Masha and Vershinin's duet becomes a witty—but entirely different—parallel of this formula. The camaraderie at the bottom of the first is countered with the romantic insinuation of the second. "Unto love all ages bow, its pangs are blest . . . " leaves nothing in doubt, and when Masha sings a refrain of this and Vershinin adds another, they make a musical declaration of love. This is an excellent preparation for Act III when, after Masha's love confession, it would have been awkward for Vershinin and her to appear together on stage. Their intimacy is even strengthened, in our minds, by his off-stage song to Masha which she hears, comprehends, and answers in song before leaving the stage to join him.

There was always a piano in Chekhov's house, and having someone play helped him to write when he got stuck. Rhythms came naturally to him, and just as he has varied them in the lines of *The Three Sisters*— from the shortest (sounds, single words) to the arias and big set speeches—similarly there is a rhythmic pattern like that on a railway platform where all the people know each other and little groups leave, say good-bye, meet.

To me, Davchenko's comment on the lack of spontaneity of this play is really a tribute to its extraordinary solidity of construction. How frail, spontaneously lyric, and farcical *The Cherry Orchard* is in comparison. Chekhov said of it, "I call it a comedy." It was the work of a dying man who had strength to write only a few lines a day, whereas *The Three Sisters: A Drama in Four Acts* is his crowning work. It is the culmination of his whole writing life. *Uncle Vanya* is the nearest thing, but nothing equally long (none of the short novels) is as good as *The Three Sisters*. (pp. 111-13)

Taking place at noon on a spring day before the first leaves come out, Act I is one of beginnings. Irina, the young girl whose birthday it is, is beginning her new year quite recovered from the death in the family and filled with happiness at the expectations of going back to Moscow soon. We see Baron Tuzenbach's beginning declarations of love for her. We see a friendship beginning in the meeting of Colonel Vershinin and the social group who, as Moscow speaking to Moscow, are immediately at ease with each other and like each other at once. With Masha's "I'm staying to lunch," we have the first intimation of her love affair with Vershinin. While there is mention made that their brother Andrei is beginning studies in Moscow to be a professor, he has actually begun—by his proposal of marriage that day to Natasha, "one of the local girls"—something quite different.

In this act occurs the establishment of a social situation that's mostly very pleasant; mostly there are happy expectations, mostly they are friendly and well-off. The Prozorovs and their extensions—Anfisa and Ferapont, the family servants; Chebutykin, the long-time family friend; Vershinin and the young officers who knew the family or of it—*all* make a little, foreign, cultivated, highly organized cell inside a provincial, crude city. The family is a father-organization that has lost its father. General Prozorov represented the days when they were governed, had their life and ideals prescribed for them, and revolt, or breaking free for a little space, was their only necessity. His censorship they obeyed, or fooled. With it gone they can say anything; but in this terrible freedom the vacancy of grown-ups who governed them has to be filled by themselves, the new grown-ups. They had a paradise in which they had only to follow the rules. Now they have to make the rules they follow—and they long to be in that earlier existence with Father. Moscow is their past, but just as definitely it is their future.

They are surviving partly happily, partly unhappily, in the midst of their uncultivated environment when the only son, who is the family's weakest element, introduces into it a powerful representative of the environment who manages to dominate him completely and, in the long run, to drive out the other members of the father-group. In the affectionate joking and teasing of part of the family by the rest are the first hints of anything troubling underneath the pleasant surface, and then we begin to see that Irina *is* partly troubled by life, that Masha is very much so, and that Olga is extreme and psychosomatic.

After Act I's spring, noon, Act II is between 8 and 9:30 at night in cold winter weather with the wind howling in the chimney. Act II begins with the continuation of the proposal: Here Natasha and Andrei are after a year or so of marriage, and the directness of their condition has a slap-in-the-face force. Here, also, is the continuation of Vershinin and Masha, of the "happiness" and "future" and meaning of life. The Andrei-Ferapont relationship is now fixed so that change can be indicated by change in it, i.e., Andrei's demanding to be called "your honor." There is a continuation of Tuzenbach's work-longing; with Irina there is the first dissatisfaction with her work. Act II is preparation for a party as is Act I, but a much more troubled preparation, which, when in full swing of beginning, is canceled out by Natasha (the provincial city element inside the little foreign cell, itself inside the provincial city), the element that's begun to destroy, grows and grows, and finally does destroy.

At the start of tea with singing, the little group is almost as pleasant as in the first act, but now needs the drunkenness, obliviousness, as in Act I it didn't. Being undermined by Natasha, the group continues more hectically with drinking and quarreling, and comes to nothing in a dreadfully anticlimactic, damped-out way. Solyony's declaration of love to Irina is unpleasant nothing to Irina, and results in unpleasant nothing to Solyony. The threat about successful rivals brings out in the open the unpleasantness toward Tuzenbach and Irina that finally kills Tuzenbach. Olga's exhaustion leads her straight to bed. The exhausted Kulygin doesn't get his evening in congenial company, and won't accompany Vershinin who (still tealess) has had nothing to eat all day, has to go out all alone. The act ends with most of them, and the carnival people, frustrated in some way; all, except Natasha, who gets her troika ride with Protopopov. Her temporary driving away of most of the family in Act II is foreshadowing what will happen permanently later. The stage is empty at the last with Irina alone, saying yearningly, "To Moscow! To Moscow! To Moscow!"

Just as the two preceding acts, [Act III] is a large *social* thing (Act I birthday dinner and Act II Mardi Gras preparations that are canceled). Act III is carried along by the arrangements necessitated by a social disaster, the fire in the town. The whole household is either taking part or avoiding taking part in it. We hardly notice what time of year it is. Under such unusual circumstances the unusual can be said or asked, and the extraordinary truth about most of the characters comes out at this extraordinary time.

With all the climaxes in Act III: Olga and Natasha's quarrel, Chebutykin's and Masha's confessions, Andrei's exposure, and Irina's breaking down, the first announcement is made of the brigade's leaving which will result in the departure of Vershinin and the military attachments of the Prozorovs.

The spring and birth beginnings of Act I have proceeded to the fall's prelude to winter, with the swans and geese flying south, departures, death, and conclusions.

The enclave's allies are leaving, the last remnants of the father-organization are gone. Natasha has complete victory in the house. Irina and Olga have been driven out, and Masha no longer enters the house. Natasha has all the rooms she wants, she can chop the trees down, and she has Protopopov there every day. Natasha, by being introduced into the family-society of *The Three Sisters,* destroys it, just as Yelena's introduction into the family-society in *Uncle Vanya* disrupts it. But Yelena leaves, and that society reforms and tries to go on as before. Natasha has broken to pieces the Prozorov society whose fragments go on as best they can.

What to make of a diminished thing, how to get partial satisfaction, get along, make life on a lower level of expectation? They now regard this existence as necessary, their fate, their lot (like growing old) rather than as something escapable (like leaving for Moscow). Not living in Moscow is accepted.

Olga does this with her impersonal schoolwork and being headmistress. No further mention of headaches and tiredness from her.

Irina plans to be satisfied without love, but with work away from home, and with marriage to a good man whom she doesn't love. This makes her feel happily anticipating again. When Tuzenbach is killed, the marriage part is removed, but she still sticks to the work ideal. Masha, after the partial satisfaction of the love affair with Vershinin, has to settle for continuing life without him but with Kulygin.

Chebutykin leaves for retirement, and Andrei surrenders in complete, abjectly nervous defeat.

In Act I Olga has the first lines and she recalled the band playing at the father's funeral. In Act IV Olga has the last lines to speak, and the band music accompanies her. As *The Three Sisters* ends, Olga puts her arms around the other two and makes a long speech that sums up her sisters' last words and one half of the play itself: the half that is about the meaning of life. She ends this speech by repeating the two Russian words that in an entirely literal translation would be *If knew, If knew!* and that in ordinary American English are *If only we knew, if only we knew!* Chebutykin once more

sings his nonsensical little song and then says twice over the two Russian words that have ended three out of four of his last speeches, words which sum up the meaningless, senseless, hopeless half of life. "What's the difference?" Olga repeats, "If only we knew, if only we knew," and the play is over. (pp. 156-60)

Randall Jarrell, "Chekhov and the Play" and "The Acts," in *The Three Sisters* by Anton Chekhov, edited and translated by Randall Jarrell, The Macmillan Company, 1969, pp. 103-13, 156-60.

J. L. STYAN
(essay date 1971)

[Styan is an English critic and educator who has written extensively on the theater. In the following excerpt, he comments on the major themes and techniques of *The Cherry Orchard*.]

Chekhov's advances in craftsmanship in *The Cherry Orchard* suggest a complete confidence in what he was doing at the last. One might point to the progress of the setting of the play from act to act, moving from the house out to the estate itself (almost, indeed, to the town beyond) and back to the house again; and, within the house, from the most intimately evocative room, the nursery, to more public rooms, and back again to the nursery. Parallel with these visual changes, Chekhov makes a more thematic use of the weather and the seasons, passing from the chill of spring with its promise of warmth to the chill of autumn with its threat of winter. In this, the lyricism of *The Seagull* returns to Chekhov's dramatic writing. The growth of the year from May to October is precisely indicated, and the cycle of the cherry trees, from their blossoming to their fruiting and their destruction, matches the cycle of joy and grief, hope and despair, within the family. As in *Three Sisters,* time and change, and their effects wrought on a representative group of people, are the subject of the play. But in feeling for this, Chekhov knows that the realism of the chosen convention can dangerously narrow his meaning until it seems too particular and finally irrelevant. He thus works hard to ensure that his play projects a universal image, giving his audience some sense that this microcosm of the cherry orchard family stands, by breadth of allusion and a seemingly inexhaustible patterning of characters, for a wider orchard beyond.

The cherry orchard is a particular place and yet it is more. It represents an inextricable tangle of sentiments, which together comprise a way of life and an attitude to life. By the persistent feelings shown towards it, at one extreme by old Firs, the house-serf for whom the family is his whole existence, and at another by Trofimov, the intellectual for whom it is the image of repression and slavery; by Lopahin, the businessman and spokesman for hard economic facts, the one who thinks of it primarily as a means to wiser investment, and by Mme Ranevsky, who sees in it her childhood happiness and her former innocence, who sees it as the embodiment of her best values—by these and many other contradictions, an audience finds that the orchard grows from a painted backcloth to an ambiguous, living, poetic symbol of human life, *any* human life, in a state of change.

Inseparable from these patterns are those into which the cherry orchard characters are woven by their brilliant selection. Chekhov claimed that his cast for the play was small, but in performance they seem curiously to proliferate. Offstage characters increase the complexity, like the lover in Paris, the Countess in Yaroslavl, Pishtchik's daughter Dashenka, Lyubov's drowned son Grisha. But the true reason for this sense of proliferation is because the same dozen players, each supplied with a character of three-dimensional individuality in Chekhov's impressive way, are encouraged to group and regroup themselves in our minds. He had always been meticulous in delineating the social background to his situation. Now he plans the play's context as a living environment. What is "a cross-section of society?" It may be a division by birth and class, by wealth, by age, by sex, by aspirations and moral values. Chekhov divides the people of the cherry orchard in a variety of ways, so that the orchard and its sale take on a different meaning for each group.

By birth and class, we see the members of the land-owning upper middle class, Mme Ranevsky, Gaev, Anya and, accordingly, the foster-daughter Varya, slipping from their security: we are made to feel what it is like to be uprooted. Lopahin, Epihodov, Yasha and Dunyasha, the servants and former peasants, are straining, comically it may be, to achieve a new social status. For some, Charlotta, Trofimov and Pishtchik for much of the play, their future security is in doubt. Forty years after the Emancipation, each character is still making a personal adjustment to the social upheaval according to age, sex or rank, and according to his lights. As a group, the cherry orchard people demonstrate the transition between the old and the new, bringing life to Chekhov's idea of an evolving social structure. The passing of time is thus represented *socially*. The three classes on the stage, owners, dependents and the new independents like Lopahin, are a social microcosm at a given point in time, so that any shift in the pattern of dependence forces an audience to acknowledge the reality of social time.

From economic considerations, the one-time wealthy landowners, Mme Ranevsky, Gaev and Pishtchik, are in great distress. The responsible ones, Lopahin, Charlotta and Varya, are intimately concerned: to those who must battle the real world, money matters. However, the new generation, Trofimov and Anya, are largely indifferent, and the servants are unaffected. But money is the least of it.

By age, those of middle years who live in and for the past, like Mme Ranevsky and Gaev, the sale of the orchard is a blow striking at their very souls. For Anya, Trofimov, Dunyasha and Yasha, the young who, naturally, live for the future, the event is an opportunity for enterprise of one kind or another, self-interested or altruistic as the case may be. For those who are neither young nor old, for Varya, Lopahin and Charlotta, those concerned with the pressing problems of the present, the auction is an urgent call for decisions and practical measures. Firs, aged eighty-seven, is beyond time. *The Cherry Orchard* is thus, in part, a "generations" play, marking the conflict between the old and the young, the substance of a thousand dramatic themes. To watch the interactions of the four age-groups is to watch the cycle of life itself. Time will be alive on the stage, and the characters will seem human milestones.

By sex, the departure from the orchard means an assessment of marital needs and opportunities, and the spinsters, Charlotta, Varya and Dunyasha, are troubled in varying degrees. But Pishtchik, Lopahin and Yasha, because of other pressures, fail to respond. While Anya and Trofimov claim idealistically to be "above love," at least for the time being, Mme Ranevsky is thrown back on her other resource, her Paris lover; as instinct or impulse brought her back to the orchard, so one or other drives her back to Paris. Only Firs has arrived at that time of life when nothing, neither status, money, past nor future, can affect him any more. With exquisite irony, it is he whose neglect by the family in the last act passes the final comment on them all.

This is not the best place to indicate the echoes and parallels and parodies built into this restless group of people: these are better observed as the action of the play proceeds. Mme Ranevsky finds her counterpart in the feckless optimist Pishtchik, the neighbouring landowner. Epihodov the clerk counters Pishtchik's trust in fate with an equally pessimistic fatalism. While Epihodov declares that he has resigned himself to his position, Yasha, who aspires to higher things than the life of a servant, is treading on necks as he climbs. When Gaev finds Yasha, a servant, playing his own aristocratic game of billiards, the valet's impertinence measures his master's own precarious status. Gaev, sucking his caramels, will, in spite of his disclaimers, never do a day's useful work, and Chekhov sets this weakness against the practical energies of Lopahin. And Lopahin against Trofimov. And Trofimov against Mme Ranevsky. *La ronde* continues ceaselessly.

Patterns of characters, then, make patterns of dramatic emphasis, and this "plotless" play is one with *too many* plots, however fragmentary, to permit analysis finally to untangle all its threads. In *Three Sisters,* Chekhov traced the passing of the months and years from scene to scene, and we watched the visible transformation of the people of the play. In *The Cherry Orchard,* time past, present and future are at the last all one, the play's last act an integrated moment of revelation. We know the orchard must go, just as surely as the curtain must fall, and in Act IV Chekhov counts out the minutes, as in the first three acts he counted out the days to the sale. As the minutes pass, we scrutinize the whole family. Every exchange, between Lopahin and Trofimov on their futures, between Mme Ranevsky and Pishtchik on the vagaries of fate, between Varya and Lopahin in their abortive proposal scene, refocuses the image of the play. When Varya seems to strike Lopahin with a stick, the notions both of differences in class and of sexual need are by one gesture violently yoked together, simultaneously reintroduced to contradict one another. When Trofimov refuses Lopahin's generous offer of a loan, the student's youth and idealism are in pathetic contrast with Lopahin's maturity and common sense. When Mme Ranevsky gives away her purse to the peasants at her door (her name "Lyuba" means "love"), we see in the gesture her failure to be realistic about her financial circumstances as well as her paternalistic affection for all the orchard stood for in the past. One incident comprehends and generates the next, endlessly, and the last act is a masterpiece of compact concentration.

"The entire play is so simple, so wholly real, but to such a point purified of everything superfluous and enveloped in such a lyrical quality, that it seems to me to be a symbolic poem." So wrote Nemirovich-Danchenko, early recognizing the gratifying contradiction that a play can be naturalistic and poetic at the same time. *The Cherry Orchard* has the poetic strength of simplicity. The interweaving in the play, the relationships between one generation and another, between master and servant, between the love-lorn and the less concerned, with the ebb and flow of such relationships, are the source of *poetic* energy in the play. But the subtle shifts across the social fabric are also the source of the play's *comic* energy, compelling its audience to remain both alert and amused as it watches. In *The Cherry Orchard,* Chekhov consummated his life's work with a *poetic comedy* of exquisite balance. (pp. 240-44)

J. L. Styan, in his *Chekhov in Performance: A Commentary on the Major Plays,* Cambridge at the University Press, 1971, 341 p.

SOURCES FOR FURTHER STUDY

Bruford, W. H. *Anton Chekhov.* New Haven: Yale University Press, 1957, 62 p.
> Examines Chekhov's literary works in relation to the social and political climate of nineteenth-century Russia.

Clyman, Toby, ed. *A Chekhov Companion.* Westport, Conn.: Greenwood Press, 1985, 347 p.
> Collection of seventeen essays on various aspects of Chekhov's works.

Emeljanow, Victor, ed. *Chekhov: The Critical Heritage.* London: Routledge & Kegan Paul, 1981, 471 p.
> Collection of short reviews of Chekhov's works from the time of their first appearance through 1945.

Hahn, Beverly. *Chekhov: A Study of the Major Stories and Plays.* Cambridge: Cambridge University Press, 1977, 350 p.
> Comprehensive overview of Chekhov's development as a writer.

Jackson, Robert Louis, ed. *Chekhov: A Collection of Critical Essays.* Englewood Cliffs, N. J.: Prentice-Hall, 1967, 213 p.
> Essay collection, with contributions by Russian scholars S. D. Balukhaty, G. Berdinov, Dmitri Chizhevsky, Boris Eichenbaum, Vsevolod Meyerhold, and V. Yermilov.

Rayfield, Donald. *Chekhov: The Evolution of His Art.* New York: Barnes & Noble, 1975, 266 p.
> Traces the development of Chekhov's literary career.

Jean Cocteau

1889-1963

(Born Jean Maurice Eugene Clement Cocteau) French dramatist, filmmaker, scriptwriter, poet, novelist, critic, essayist, librettist, and autobiographer.

INTRODUCTION

*A*mong the most versatile, innovative, and prolific literary figures of the twentieth century, Cocteau is best known for dramas and films in which he utilized myth and tragedy in modern contexts to shock and surprise his audiences. Identifying himself as a poet and referring to virtually all of his works as poetry, Cocteau rejected naturalism in favor of lyrical fantasy, through which he sought to create a "poetry of the theatre" consisting not of words but of such stage devices as ballet, music, and pantomime. The fantastic, or "le merveilleux," is made manifest in Cocteau's plays through inanimate objects and symbolic characters, which embellish our understanding of "reality" by making the impossible possible. Like Charles Baudelaire and Arthur Rimbaud, Cocteau made use of the romantic myth of the *poète maudit*—the poet blessed with artistic powers of creation yet cursed to remain a misunderstood social outcast. Alienation is an important theme in Cocteau's work; his related subjects include the origin of artistic creation and inspiration, the limitations of free will, and the relationships between such opposing forces as adolescence and adulthood, illusion and reality, and order and disorder.

Cocteau was born into a wealthy Parisian family from whom he gained an appreciation for the performing arts. Although he briefly attended the Lycée Condorcet in Paris, Cocteau detested school and left to pursue a writing career. His first volume of poetry, *Le lampe d'Aladin* (1909), consisted of traditional verse that Cocteau later suppressed and omitted from his collected works. His early circle of acquaintances included Marcel Proust and Léon Daudet. Through their influence, Cocteau became enthralled with the ballet, an interest which led to a friendship with Serge Diaghilev, Russian ballet impresario and director of the Ballet Russe de Monte Carlo. It was Diaghilev who inspired in Cocteau the philosophy he embraced throughout his artistic career: to shock and surprise his audience.

Towards the end of World War I, Cocteau entered the circle of the creative avant-garde, which included Pablo Picasso and composer Eric Satie, with whom Cocteau created the ballet *Parade* (1917). *Parade* depicts a festival and its promoters who attempt to entice an onstage audience to enter a mysterious tent; the ballet ends, however, without the spectators having entered the tent, implying that Cocteau's interest is not in the event itself but in the visual occurrences which surround it. Although a complete failure at its first production, *Parade* is generally regarded as one of the twentieth century's most innovative ballets.

Another valuable influence on Cocteau's career was the writer Raymond Radiguet, who became his teacher and lover. Radiguet steered Cocteau away from the avant-gardists and told him to "lean on nothing . . . and develop an attitude that consists of not appearing original." Radiguet's death in 1923 devastated Cocteau: grief-stricken, he turned to opium, an addiction that plagued him all of his life and was the subject of many of his writings, including a personal journal entitled *Opium: Journal d'une desintoxication* (1930; *Opium: The Diary of an Addict*, also translated as *Opium: The Diary of a Cure*). Hospitalized for opium poisoning in 1929, Cocteau met the anti-Bergsonian Catholic philosopher Jacques Maritain while at the clinic. Maritain's influence prompted Cocteau to turn briefly to religion. *Art and Faith: Letters between Jacques Maritain and Jean Cocteau* (1948) contains their correspondence on Catholicism.

Despite his involvement with central artistic figures of post-World War I France, Cocteau never allied himself with any school or movement. In his play *Antigone* (1922), Cocteau adapted Sophocles's tragedy to what he called "the rhythm of our times," thus initiating a lifelong preoccupation with contemporizing Greek mythologies. *Orphée* (1927; *Orpheus*) is among Cocteau's most innovative adaptations, focusing on the poet as interpreter of the supernatural and the poet's relationship to the source of inspiration. In this drama, objects, animals, and characters become symbols of ritual and acquire startling new associations. Cocteau also attempted several adaptations of the Oedipal myth during his career. The first, *Oedipus-rex* (1927), is an opera-oratorio on which he collaborated with composer Igor Stravinsky. *Oedipe Roi* (1928), a free adaptation that Cocteau revised in 1962 as an attempt at "total theatre," combines virtually all the performing arts to evoke lyric tragedy. Cocteau's best-regarded reworking of the Oedipal myth is *La machine infernale* (1934; *The Infernal Machine*), a drama exploring the relationship between free will and determinism that makes use of modern vernacular and musical forms. Unlike Sophocles, Cocteau opens his drama when Oedipus first enters Thebes—a free man about to realize his own mortality and unalterable fate. Henri Peyre called *The Infernal Machine* "the best modernization of the Oedipus story in our generation." Of his original dramas, *La voix humaine* (1929; *The Human Voice*) is probably Cocteau's most frequently performed work. Written as a "monodrama," a one-act play for a single character, the drama consists entirely of a woman's imaginary conversation with a boyfriend who has abandoned her.

Cocteau's films of the 1940s are regarded as his most accessible and engaging works. He found in the cinema a means superior to all other media in depicting his poetic view of death and the fantastic. Many of Cocteau's films, including *Les parents terribles* (1948) and *Les enfants terribles* (1948), are cinematic adaptations of his novels and plays. In such original works as *Orphée* (1950) and *Le testament d'Orphée* (1959), Cocteau employs classical legend and such visual effects as vanishing mirrors, vertical frames, and double images. Although some critics consider Cocteau's films difficult and obscure, he is generally regarded as a filmmaker of original talent and vision striving to realize his conception of film as "not a dream that is told but one we all dream together."

Throughout his career, Cocteau engaged in a variety of artistic ventures, ranging from decoration of public buildings to ceramics and the composition of music. His creative versatility prompted many of his contemporaries to contend that Cocteau had become too preoccupied with producing avant-garde works; as a result, Cocteau's critics often questioned his importance as an original and innovative artist. Henri Peyre commented: "It became customary to be entertained by Cocteau's chameleon-like metamorphoses and to treat him considerably as a 'juggler.'"

Although he rejected established schools of thought throughout his life, Cocteau maintained that the most radical act possible for a revolutionary was to ally oneself with the establishment. After Cocteau was elected to the prestigious Académie Française in 1956, he remarked: "They have imposed it on me. It would be discourteous not to accede."

(For further information about Cocteau's life and works, see *Contemporary Authors Permanent Series,* Vol. 2; *Contemporary Literary Criticism,* Vols. 1, 8, 15, 16, 43; and *Dictionary of Literary Biography,* Vol. 65: *French Novelists, 1900-1930.*)

CRITICAL COMMENTARY

NEAL OXENHANDLER
(essay date 1956)

[Oxenhandler is an American educator, novelist, poet, and critic who specializes in modern French literature. In the excerpt below, he discusses the films *Le sang d'un poète*, *La belle et la bête*, and *Orphée* as they relate to Cocteau's conception of "poetry."]

What Cocteau has attempted to do in his films is to convey, through the cinematic medium, the conception of poetry which exists in his purely literary works. Let me begin then by briefly characterizing this conception of poetry.

For Cocteau poetry is not primarily a dramatic representation of experience as in Racine, Baudelaire, Rimbaud. He is definitely in the tradition of "pure" poets for whom poetry is an end in itself and for whom morality is essentially an esthetic function. He insists in his poetry on purely verbal and syntactical manipulations. (p. 14)

Cocteau is not fundamentally interested in dramatic action; nor is he interested in ideas. His concern is less philosophical than that of other pure poets such as Mallarmé, Valéry or Giraudoux. He manipulates language like a kaleidoscope, creating new and surprising combinations, enjoying the illusion that poetry can change the face of reality.

Poetry has also a self-revelatory role for Cocteau, but it is a limited one. He reveals shifting states of consciousness rather than some fundamental human drama expressed in symbolic polarities. The drama is only revealed implicitly, by what the poetry leaves out, and by a study of the *dramatis personae* of his plays and novels. These characters are distinguished by their lack of involvement and for their ability to use language as a means of resisting any form of concrete solicitation to a course of action. The great human drama of Cocteau's plays and novels is never expressed. It is a drama of flight and negation, brilliantly disguised, yet masking a tragic human failure.

The movies offered Cocteau an ideal medium. To begin with, of course, he was not only a writer but also a pictorial artist. His sense of caricature and his feeling for the literary rather than the more painterly aspects of art were ideal equipment for a *cinéaste*. . . .

This is partly due to the fact that Cocteau thinks in images more directly than in words. . . .

Cocteau seems to feel freer in attributing sexuality to the actors in his films than to the characters of his books. It is his own emotions that he must inject into the characters of a book or play; working directly with the actor he seems to feel less fear that he will be held responsible for the emotions represented.

These observations are, I believe, sustained by the strong sexual overtones of all his films and primarily by *Le Sang d'un poète.*

There have been innumerable and contradictory exegeses of this film, including one which sees it as the history of Christianity. Cocteau himself has repeatedly refused to explain the film. (p. 15)

Le Sang d'un poète has no more unity than Cocteau's verse. Unity in the sense in which [C. G.] Wallis would find it in Cocteau is something that this poet is not especially concerned with. Instead of the traditional unity of an unfolding plot he achieves a kind of unity through the use of parallel themes. . . .

These themes run all the way through the film but the form of the film is such that a truly dramatic development is impossible. We pass from image to image in a kind of "qualitative progression" which does not attempt to produce anything like the classical dramatic structure of Purpose, Passion and Perception. What we are given is a series of astonishing and unforgettable images which to a large extent justify the conception of poetry here implied.

Cocteau has generously insisted on the role played by his technicians in the making of a film. They provide him with the mechanical resources that he modifies in his own ingenious way. . . . (p. 16)

The images of Cocteau's films defy the laws of nature. Props are always used suggestively with a hint that they themselves are part of the intimate life of the actors. The camera always finds the unexpected angle from which the event is illuminated in a new and true perspective. The image does not merely pass across the screen; it unfolds, using the full space of the screen, living organically with its background and every other object represented, painted in the infinite range of colors from white to black. . . .

Yet, in his later films, Cocteau has specifically chosen to dramatize a myth or to tell a story. In what sense then does this theory of "discontinuous poetry" still hold true for *La Belle et la Bête* and for *Orphée?*

La Belle et la Bête is a fairy-tale fantasy. What is

Principal Works

Parade (ballet) 1917

Le grand écart (novel) 1923

[The Grand Ecart, 1925; also published as The Miscreant, 1958]

Thomas l'imposteur (novel) 1923

[Thomas the Impostor, 1925; also published as The Impostor, 1957]

Opera: Oeuvres poetiques, 1925-1927 (poetry) 1927

Les enfants terribles (novel) 1929

[Enfants Terribles, 1930; also published as The Children of the Game, 1955, and The Holy Terrors, 1957]

*Les maries de la tour Eiffel (one-act play) 1924

[The Eiffel Tower Wedding Party (first publication), 1963; published in The Infernal Machine, and Other Plays]

Orphée (drama) 1927

[Orphée: A Tragedy in One Act (first publication), 1933; also published as Orphée, 1963]

Antigone (drama) 1928

[Antigone (first publication), 1961; published in collection Four Plays]

Opium: Journal d'une desintoxication (nonfiction) 1930

[Opium: The Diary of an Addict, 1932; also published as Opium: The Diary of a Cure, 1957]

Le sang d'un poete (film) 1930

[Blood of a Poet, 1949]

La voix humaine (play) 1930

[The Human Voice (first publication), 1951]

La machine infernale (play) 1934

[The Infernal Machine (first publication), 1936]

Les parents terribles (play) 1938

[Intimate Relations (first publication), 1962]

La machine à écrire (play) 1941

[The Typewriter (first publication), 1957]

La belle et la bête (film) 1945

[La belle et la bête, 1970]

L'aigle à deux têtes (play) 1946

[The Eagle Has Two Heads (first publication), 1948; also published as The Eagle with Two Heads, 1962]

La voix humaine (film) 1947

L'aigle à deux têtes (film) 1947

Les parents terribles (film) 1948

[Intimate Relations, 1952]

Les enfants terribles (film) 1948

Oedipus rex: Opera-oratorio en deux actes d'après Sophocles (opera) 1949

Orphée (film) 1949

Journals (nonfiction) 1956

Le testament d'Orphée (film) 1959

*This play has also been published as The Wedding on the Eiffel Tower in Modern French Plays, 1964.

more natural than that it should be told in a fantastic way? This is a point which has unfortunately not occurred to the producers of most of our films. How can the Bible stories or the wanderings of Ulysses or *Moby Dick* be filmed as if they had been written by Ibsen? Each image of *La Belle et la Bête* is framed for the viewer as the fable itself is framed in enchantment and wonder and lore. The camera-work in this beautiful film situates it in that area of imagination where we half believe the impossible, where metaphor is normal speech and miracle is a deeper truth than nature. (p. 17)

What exactly is the nature of the fantasy which is dramatized in *La Belle et la Bête?* A monster of abnormality wins a beautiful maiden. Cocteau's work is full of such monsters who eventually discover their own monstrosity. Self-knowledge he considers the height of moral beauty; hence it is not surprising that the monster, at the close of the film, becomes physically beautiful. Real beauty, in other words, is moral beauty and moral beauty is self-knowledge. This psychological process must of course be dramatized on the screen by a symbolic outward transformation.

This fable suggests to us, I think, the yearning of a man who has always secretly felt himself an exile from society and dramatizes his triumphant acceptance by society. At the same time it places this triumph in the impossible realm of fantasy. That is, Cocteau does not believe that the world will ever accept his personal morality; and perhaps he is right, for the world equates morality less with knowledge than with right action. (It might also be pointed out that the kind of self-knowledge that Cocteau proposes has a definitely Gidean ring—discovery and acceptance of one's total psychological diversity through the undifferentiated experience of life.)

The poetry of discontinuous images in this film is a product of a theory of lyric poetry which, as I have said, uses poetry as a means of evasion of responsibility. Poetry is a flight from and a substitute for action. But the theme of the film is itself an evasion of the real world and the facts of existence. It shows us the realization of a child's fantasy of reality. (p. 18)

Orphée, which is Cocteau's third poetic film, revives once more the theme of *Le Sang d'un poète.* Again we have a poet searching for the meaning of his vocation in the midst of love and death. The poet is more in love with Death . . . than with his wife, Eurydice; again it is implied that poetry brings us into contact with another world and that this other world is somehow more significant than the routine and responsibility of everyday life. (pp. 18-19)

Because *Orphée* is based explicitly on a myth it has more dramatic unity than *Le Sang d'un poète;* it is less of a poem and more of a plot. The question to be raised in regard to *Orphée* is this: does the story of Orpheus require such a special and distorted vision? Granted that we want to see this story as myth, are all the concomitants of motorcycles, mirrors, radios, etc., necessary to the mythic perspective?

Orphée is the poet and we have seen what Cocteau's special conception of the poet involves. The poet is a man who frees himself from the world by making images, by entering into an oneiric world where the freedom of language is equivalent to the freedom of action.

Most of the images of *Le Sang d'un poète* suggest confinement and enclosure—a room, a hotel corridor or the confinement of death. There is confinement in *Orphée* too, but there is also freedom. There are many more exterior shots, more movement. The poetry has become oriented, it has orchestrated itself upon a theme. That theme is, paradoxically, the absence of theme in life, the recognition of the dangers of involvement and the determination to flee them in the hall of mirrors which is pure poetry. The difference in the two films, the principle difference, is this recognition, this undoubtedly unconscious orientation by Cocteau towards his ultimate principle. We can call it "freedom" or "purity" as he does or by one of the less flattering terms used by his critics—"bad faith" or "sleight of hand" or "mystification." But here again, as in *La Belle et la Bête,* it must be conceded that the technique of the film is essential to its truth. Mirrors and motorcycles are its version of pure poetry. (p. 19)

The ultimate assessment of Cocteau's work is extremely difficult; perhaps it is enough that his films give a sharp and special pleasure, they can be and are seen over and over again. For they are poetry and that they be the ultimate in poetry is too much to ask. There have been few artists able to adapt the films to the expression of their own most intimate vision; and fewer still are able to narrow the gap between the profound intellectual concerns of literature and the filmy world of the screen. (pp. 19-20)

Neal Oxenhandler, "Poetry in Three Films of Jean Cocteau," in *Yale French Studies,* No. 17, 1956, pp. 14-20.

GERMAINE BRÉE AND MARGARET GUITON
(essay date 1957)

[In the following excerpt, Brée and Guiton discuss Cocteau's novels.]

The novel, as used by Cocteau, is somewhat experimental, halfway between the traditional nineteenth century novel and a totally new conception of the novel form. It is only with his last major novel, *Les Enfants terribles* (*The Children of the Game*), 1929, that Cocteau is altogether successful. And even here his theme is more restricted than in the case of his two best plays, *Orphée,* 1926, and *La Machine infernale* (*The Infernal Machine*), 1934. But from the point of view of the novel itself, the Cocteau novel is an interesting experiment.

The everyday world of recognizable people and places naturally plays a greater role in Cocteau's novels than in his poetry and theater. But Cocteau, by his choice of scene and atmosphere, sees to it that this world is fragmentized, disrupted, torn apart. (p. 141)

Disorder, for Cocteau, especially for Cocteau the novelist, is merely the "rejection of the conventional equilibrium" that precedes the poet's ascent to a higher and more intimate equilibrium of his own, an equilibrium found only in death, the symbolic death of the poet to the world. The theme of poetic "ascesis," which Cocteau apparently attempted to act out himself in his experiments with dadaism, opium and Catholicism, recurs in all his works. Even if the theme is not explicit, it is felt in the icy, mineral quality of Cocteau's imagery: his statues and snowballs, his demonic mechanical contrivances, his constant transposition of reality into artifice.

This latter device no doubt explains Cocteau's popular reputation as a literary charlatan. But for Cocteau, artifice is a serious matter. He sees in it that depersonalization, that dehumanization of reality, which to him is an essential attribute of poetry. (p. 142)

Jacques Forestier, the hero of *Le Grand Ecart* and the most directly autobiographical of Cocteau's fictional characters, represents the case of a potential drug addict who never finds his drug, a diver in his heavy diver's costume forgotten on the surface of the earth: "To rise again, to take off the helmet and the costume; that is the passage from life to death. But there comes to him through the tube an unreal breath that allows him to live and fills him with nostalgia."

This opening passage suggests interesting possibilities; but Cocteau never succeeds in deriving the substance of a novel out of Jacques's fatal unadaptability to life. What he has done is to graft this introductory theme onto the conventional story of an adolescent in the throes of disenchantment. And Cocteau, who specifically relates his hero to the typical Balzac adolescent arriving in Paris from the provinces, seems to have taken a good part of the story out of Balzac's *Le Père Goriot (Old Goriot).* Jacques Forestier, adrift in Paris, bears a fleeting resemblance to Eugène de Rastignac; the squalid pension where he lives, to the Pension Vauquer; his heartless mistress, Germaine, to the Baronne de Nucingen. Indeed, a principal cause of Jacques's final disillusionment is directly transcribed from Balzac's famous novel. Just as Balzac's baroness stubbornly refuses to believe that her father is dying, because she wishes to attend a fashionable ball, Germaine conceals a telegram informing her of her father's death, because she wants to go to the theater.

Cocteau's undisguised debt to Balzac is not in itself a weakness—Proust also has borrowed from Balzac—and Cocteau's treatment of the Balzacian theme of "lost illusions" is skillful. He knows how to turn the knife in the wound. Unfortunately, however, this theme is not really connected with Cocteau's original and more important subject: the poet's death to the world. The original subject recurs, somewhat abruptly, in the final pages of the novel when Jacques poisons himself and experiences a momentary illumination: "Jacques rises. He loses footing. He sees the other side of the cards. He is not aware of the system that he is disrupting, but he has the presentiment of a responsibility." But Jacques's attempted suicide is unsuccessful, and he returns to life, less as an exiled poet than as a disillusioned lover.

The unsuccessful suicide provides a more pathetic ending to this novel than death—the conclusion of Cocteau's two later novels—would have provided. Still, this element of human pathos, which no doubt stems from Cocteau's personal involvement in the story, is incompatible with his conception of the poet. Who *is* Jacques? the reader is left to wonder. A poet astray on the surface of the earth, or a nice, if somewhat spineless, young man who has fallen into bad company? And what *is* disorder? The eternal dissonance of poetry and life or the misplaced sentiments of an untidy heart? The universal and the particular in this novel are badly jointed. Instead of reinforcing one another, they rub and jar; and at these points of friction the fine edge of poetry is worn down to mere sentimentality, none the better for its superficial disguise of modernism, paradox and bravura. Cocteau's concluding sentence is worthy of de Musset at his very worst: "To live in this world one must follow its fashions, and the heart is no longer worn."

Thomas the Impostor, the hero of [*Thomas*

l'Imposteur], is another displaced adolescent, but one who has found an artificial equilibrium in a fictional existence. Guillaume Thomas, taking advantage of the confusion during the early months of the war, has lied about his age (sixteen), borrowed the uniform of a friend, and finally posed as the nephew of a famous general, Fontenoy. Cocteau hastens to inform us, however, that this is not an ordinary imposture, a vulgar means of "getting ahead." Guillaume, floating on the edges of a dream, is more at home, more himself, in a fictional than in a real existence. Aided by a Polish princess and her daughter, Henriette, Guillaume soon finds a place for himself in a hastily improvised ambulance service and is eventually expedited to his predestined environment, the fantastically camouflaged confusion of the northern front.

At the end of the novel the two conflicting personalities, Guillaume Thomas and Thomas de Fontenoy, are finally reconciled: Guillaume, who has volunteered to carry a message to another post under extremely dangerous conditions, is spotted by an enemy patrol and shot down.

" '—A bullet, he said to himself. I am lost if I don't pretend to be dead.' But fiction and reality, in him, were one. Guillaume Thomas was dead."

Thomas l'Imposteur, in contrast with *Le Grand Ecart,* is written with considerable detachment. Its hero is modeled not on Cocteau himself but on a young impostor that Cocteau encountered during the war. Self-pity thus gives way to sparkling irony. At first glance we seem to be confronted with a pure satirical fantasy in the early manner of Evelyn Waugh. We soon realize, however, that Thomas is actually another incarnation of the poet, a poet who succeeds in divesting himself of his human identity and whose "imposture" is ultimately authenticated by death.

The symbol is no doubt valid as a symbol, but is it anything more than an abstract symbol? We are quite willing to believe that artifice, under certain circumstances, can become real; lies, true; disorder, art. But has Cocteau really shown that this has happened? That Guillaume should die at the very moment he is pretending to be dead provides a neat conclusion to the novel. Does this, as Cocteau would apparently have us believe, really give retrospective reality to Guillaume's whole imposture? And the elegant detachment of Guillaume and his Polish patroness, their attempts to exploit the wartime situation in such a way as to enjoy the best possible view of the fireworks, the ambiguous emotional relationship that binds the two of them together—does this whole moral climate of exquisite snobbery really attain the "higher equilibrium" of poetry? It seems rather to be the Cocteau version of an atmosphere that Stendhal used for an entirely different purpose.

Here again Cocteau has taken an existing novel theme, that of Stendhal's *La Chartreuse de Parme (The Charterhouse of Parma)* as the vehicle for a totally unconventional novel subject. And here again the experiment, however interesting as such, is not entirely successful. Like one of those pioneering ventures in aviation, *Thomas l'Imposteur* never quite gets off the ground.

Cocteau's latest try, *Les Enfants terribles,* is, within its given limitations, a conspicuous success. His formula is simple: to push to their extreme consequences the fierce passions, strange tribal conventions and innocent perversions of a group of children living in a universe completely insulated from adult interference.

Childhood, Cocteau tells us, is a kingdom unto itself like the animal and vegetable kingdoms. In this novel the kingdom is constituted by the relationship of a young girl, Elizabeth, and her younger brother, Paul. Situated in their wildly disordered bedroom, "the room" as it is called, this private universe has its own language, fetishes and rituals . . . ; it offers a dangerous enchantment, of which Paul is the passive conductor and Elizabeth, the jealous guardian.

As Elizabeth is aware, this enchantment is constantly threatened by shifting relationships and loyalties—or the normal process of growing up. For this, however, she is prepared. Two possible threats, Paul's schoolmate, Gérard, and her own friend, Agathe, are neutralized by adoption and come to live in "the room." When Elizabeth realizes that Gérard has fallen in love with her and Agathe with Paul, she again neutralizes the two intruders by persuading them that each is morally bound to marry the other. (pp. 142-46)

The real danger to "the room" lies not in adult reality but in a counterenchantment; not in Agathe and Gérard but in Dargelos, a heartless, older schoolboy hopelessly adored by Paul. It is this external factor that originally sets the plot in motion and finally brings it to its catastrophic conclusion.

In a prologue to the novel, set in the enchanted light of a winter's afternoon, Paul wanders through an abandoned courtyard searching for his idol, Dargelos. Suddenly he is struck full in the chest and seriously hurt by a snowball that Dargelos has thrown. Unable to return to school, he lives from then on under Elizabeth's watch in "the room." At the close of the novel Dargelos happens to meet Gérard in the street, ironically asks after Paul, and, as a test of his own powers, sends Paul a package of poison—a "black pellet" counterbalancing the snowball of the prologue. Paul takes the poison, and a last-minute struggle sets in between Agathe, Elizabeth and the absent Dargelos for the final possession of Paul's soul.

At first it seems that Agathe will win out, for she arrives upon the scene before Paul dies, and Elizabeth stands by in impotent fury while the two lovers unravel the subterfuges that have hitherto kept them apart. In an excess of rage Elizabeth seizes a revolver, then suddenly controls herself, and with a feverish lucidity, a supreme effort of the will, rediscovers the magic words, associations and memories that will restore the charmed atmosphere of "the room." Paul's expression of hatred gives way to curiosity, curiosity to complicity, as Elizabeth, her finger on the trigger of the revolver, waits for her brother's death spasm. Paul's head falls back. Elizabeth presses the revolver against her forehead and pulls the trigger. But she has struck too soon. Paul is not yet dead, and Elizabeth, falling, brings down a screen hiding the window.

As the corrupt Danish court, in the last act of *Hamlet,* disintegrates at the sound of Fortinbras's martial trumpets, the perverse enchantment of "the room" is dissipated, for evermore, by the pale light of the frosty windowpane, by the ghostly spectators that lurk outside. Paul recognizes these spectators—the noses, the cheeks, the red hands, the capes, the scarves of the memorable snow fight of several years before—and resumes, in his last moments of consciousness, his original quest for Dargelos.

Les Enfants terribles, in striking contrast to Cocteau's earlier and more impressionistic novels, has the rigorous economy of means, the geometrical construction, the almost claustrophobic *unité de lieu* of a classical tragedy. As Cocteau himself reminds us in a number of incidental references, the theme is somewhat similar to that of Racine's *Athalie*—a pattern better adapted to Cocteau's purposes than that provided by a nineteenth-century novelist's treatment of the theme of adolescence. That necessity of a "rigorous equilibrium" for those who reject the conventional equilibrium, seems to apply not only to the poetic sensibility but also to the technique of novel-writing. This most ordered of Cocteau's novels also has the strongest poetic impact.

The basic ingredients are as down to earth, as credible, as one could wish. But they are also capable of unlimited expansion. . . . Elizabeth is entirely understandable as a passionate young girl who refuses to relinquish her childhood; but she is also the savage priestess-queen of *Athalie.* Dargelos is a thoroughly recognizable classroom criminal; but he is also the angel that preys on poets—the "Ange Heurtebise" of Cocteau's poem and of his *Orphée.* In contrast again with Cocteau's earlier novels, the universal and the particular, the poetic and the novelistic, are here indissolubly fused.

Les Enfants terribles was written in three weeks during a "cure." And the experiences that Cocteau describes, "the game," "the room" and the breath-taking poetic ascension that precedes the double suicide, are very similar to his descriptions of the effects produced by opium. It would thus seem possible that Cocteau, in his struggle to abandon opium, momentarily recovered the childhood reality for which opium had acted as an artificial substitute. "All children," Cocteau writes, "have a fairy-like power to change themselves into whatever they want. Poets, in whom childhood is prolonged, suffer greatly from losing this power. Indeed this is one of the emotions that drives them to use opium." This momentary return to childhood may provide the key to Cocteau's best novel; but it also shows the limitations of this novel, of the novel form itself as used by Cocteau: an incapacity to carry the poetic vision into the enlarged and more complex realm of adult consciousness. (pp. 146-48)

Germaine Brée and Margaret Guiton, "Escapes and Escapades," in their *The French Novel from Gide to Camus,* 1957. Reprint by Harcourt Brace Jovanovich, 1962, pp. 132-79.

JACQUES GUICHARNAUD AND JUNE BECKELMAN
(essay date 1961)

[In the following excerpt, Guicharnaud and Beckelman explore Cocteau's career as a dramatist. This essay first appeared in *Yale Romantic Studies* in 1961.]

Cocteau began to write for the theatre in 1916, when the battle for reform was at its most acute. He started as a revolutionary and continued as a revolutionary. And we know that in general, any immobility, any rigidity was distasteful to him. If his works often give more the impression of a great to-do and confusion than of revolution, it is because his desire for complete change was opposed to an unquestionable narcissism.

To the conflicts and struggles of Cocteau's subjects and themes are added the unexpected contrasts of the works as a whole. His theatre would seem to have covered all possible genres, from the avant-garde spectacle to commercial cinema, everything that could be represented or played by actors of every category. . . . Such diversity of means gives Cocteau's works a disparate appearance, a sort of Jack-of-all-trades or amateur aspect that makes him seem rather like [his character] Georges in *Les parents terribles.* Cocteau has tried to perfect already existing genres and make them more effective just as Georges, having tried other experiments, wants to perfect the spear gun and make it shoot bullets.

With each work, Cocteau plays the game he has chosen to play. In theatre he plays at being a play-

wright. . . . His prefaces often give the impression that . . . [each] work is an exercise in style, imposed by external circumstances. The "idea" of theatre comes first and varies according to the period, the year, the month. Every play is an example, a model, an illustration. Cocteau's works are presented as a group of occasional plays—to enhance actors or actresses, to satisfy a request from the Vicomte de Noailles, to scandalize a certain public.

Once he has decided to go along with such or such circumstance, Cocteau starts to work as if the genre of the play he is writing were the only one possible. In fact he is more actor than playwright. . . . He is an understudy of genius. When there is a comedy lacking on the French stage, Cocteau is ready to plug up the hole. He provides an avant-garde spectacle when needed. . . . [Cocteau] was the first of his generation, even before Giraudoux, to reinterpret Greek tragedy because the new era needed a Racine. *Bacchus* shows a certain fatigue in that respect, for there he was a follower. The general impression is that Cocteau has always something to do, if not always something to say. The problems he would seem to pose are of an aesthetic and even technical order, for he is more interested in the secrets of workmanship than in the actual material of the product.

If there is an evolution in Cocteau's works, it is based on a twofold movement: he wanted both to create fashions and revive them. In most of his prefaces he affirms the necessity of saying no to whatever is established, as soon as it is established. One must never become immobilized in a game. Once the rules are fixed, "the rules must be changed." His is indeed the psychology of a great dress designer. And in his perpetual invention of new rules, Cocteau constantly refers back to a certain past—now a lost naïveté, that of primitive theatre or childhood; now the bygone age of the theatre of actors, the sacred monsters. The ancient tunic is made old-fashioned by knight's armor; the suit, by Second Empire uniforms. Just as Antoine was right to have imposed "real quarters of meat and a fountain" on a public used to painted objects, Cocteau was to consider it his duty as an artist to impose painted canvas on a public accustomed to real quarters of meat, or to reinvent the Boulevard for a public that had come to demand modernist theatre. . . . The objective of such an operation is to keep the public's esthetic consciousness in a state of alert. However, a multiplicity of changes ends by resembling constancy. And in spite of the unexpected and the novelty, every one of Cocteau's plays can be recognized by a group of permanent features which might be called the writer's signature.

For Cocteau has more of a signature than a style. The handwriting is always the same, while the style changes. To whatever genre it may belong, a Cocteau play can be recognized by certain words, certain formulas, certain images. . . . (pp. 48-51)

On another level, we find that the milieu of nearly all Cocteau's plays is "the family." Doubtless it includes an idea of the couple in the manner of Giraudoux, but it also includes the idea of a household: the households of Orpheus, King Arthur, Jocasta, Yvonne, and Esther, all characterized by a feeling of bedroom slippers and slammed doors never found in those of Giraudoux's Alcmene, Clytemnestra, Lia, or Lucile. The novel *Les Enfants terribles* and the play *Les Parents terribles* have fixed the theme of family promiscuity at the center of Cocteau's works—a promiscuity of people (mother-son, sister-brother) and also of intimate objects. But even in the deliberately anti-naturalistic plays, Cocteau introduces a realism of intimacy through the mention of pieces of clothing, physical contact, and childish quarrels. (p. 52)

Intimacy and witchcraft often have a meeting point in the object—more or less ordinary—that lies about, goes astray, or behaves in unexpected ways. "Even the familiar objects have something suspicious about them," wrote Cocteau in his description of the stage set for *Orphée*. The objects that furnish his stage are therefore intimate or ordinary, but also magical. Whereas in *Les Mariés de la Tour Eiffel* the phonograph and camera are magical (the camera produces an ostrich and a lion that eats generals), the rest of his works are strewn with object-witnesses, chosen amongst the most ordinary and suddenly gifted with supernatural powers. . . . Sometimes the language and sometimes its physical aspect accentuate the object's mystery or secret in a kind of expressionism rare on the French stage until Adamov and Ionesco.

The objects often acquire their powers through disorder. Out of their usual places, they seem stripped of their usual functions, diverted from their roles in this world, and free therefore to assume new functions. The incongruity of the object not in its proper place creates an uneasiness in the spectator which comes from the consciousness of pure unjustified being. The transcendency of being that appears when being is stripped of the habitual relationships established with it becomes magic in the hands of a poet, the sign of, or a door opening onto, the supernatural. Through not belonging, the being of things becomes strange. The point at which consciousness bumps up against an impenetrable transcendency—a fact or an exceptional or monstrous relationship—is the point at which the poet, by an act of faith, affirms that *there* the world of poetry begins and that the imagination, the poet's "deep night," is called upon to give perceptible content to the ensuing uneasiness. (pp. 53-4)

An object which is not in its place can be poetic: a lion on the Eiffel Tower, theatrical costumes in a bourgeois house, even a stray shoe under an armchair.

The same holds true for the characters. Cocteau tries to poetize them by isolating them, displacing them, making them somewhat foreign. On the simplest level, he does it by a disparity of class: Stanislas in the Queen's room (*L'Aigle à deux têtes*); Hans, the poor mad peasant, chosen as king for a week (*Bacchus*). . . . In a more visual way, he disguises or masks the character in a decisive scene: Margo, in *La Machine à écrire,* is dressed up like Lucrezia Borgia during most of the first act; Esther, in *Les Monstres sacrés,* completely covers her face with cold cream when Liane confronts her with cruel facts. The displacement is complete in *La Machine infernale,* in which Jocasta speaks and gesticulates like a foreigner. . . . [Cocteau uses this device], as in the other cases, to isolate the character by an accidental peculiarity, or at least seemingly accidental.

In the same way, Cocteau hoped for revelations from certain coincidences, certain unexpected encounters. . . . [The] music of Bach as background to the film *Les Enfants terribles* was to furnish "accidental synchronisms" out of which the most original beauty would spring. At the beginning of every Cocteau play, a certain amount of chance, coincidence, and accident must be accepted in addition to the usual dramatic conventions: Orpheus' poetry dictated by a horse and his guardian angel in the form of a glazier . . . ; Stanislas as the image of the dead King. The process is similar to a combination of fairy-tale illusion and surrealist experiment. Cocteau's world is made up of disparate beings and elements, each one generally familiar but isolated from its context, whirling about in a vacuum, fastening on to one another as if by chance, and thus perhaps creating poetry. Cocteau has said that the great writer is he whose "aim is straight." He himself gives the impression of hoping to aim straight while closing his eyes, like the characters of certain comic films who haphazardly shoot in the air and out of the sky falls a duck or a balloon. In that way, Cocteau hopes to shoot down the blue bird.

More than a vision of the world, it is a device, and a device that can lead to every extravagance—legitimate to the extent that the incongruity of the combined elements is a protestation against the superficial coherence of psychological theatre or the theatre of ideas, and also against the traditions surrounding myth and certain great subjects. The poetry of *Les Mariés de la Tour Eiffel* consists in replacing traditional coherence by an inner chance that is quite contrary to the logic of everyday reality. "The scenes fit together like the words of a poem," says Cocteau in his preface. Here the poem would be a surrealist *divertissement* or, to be more explicit, a collage. Its interest lies both in its amusing absurdity and its challenge to accepted forms of poetry or painting. Cocteau counts on "the part that belongs to God" to make the symbol emerge, just as a chemist's apprentice might haphazardly choose two substances, mix them together in a test tube, and hope for an explosion. Of course there is the danger of obtaining no more than a bit of smoke and a change in color. (pp. 54-6)

Cocteau's experiment in *Les Mariés* in 1921 might seem old-fashioned today, for it is essentially a document, a polemic argument that took place during a quarrel, now established in history. It does not have the weight of either Jarry's *Ubu Roi* or Apollinaire's *Les Mamelles de Tirésias,* in which the revolution in form was accompanied by a true theme. Yet *Les Mariés,* in the intransigency of its conception, is still a call to order every time a resurgence of naturalism in the theatre begins to exercise its charms. It remains a warning against psychologism, earnestness, and want of imagination.

The plays that follow, from *Orphée* to *Bacchus,* and whatever the genre, reaffirm the poet's right to search for a synchronism of chance between elements drawn from the familiar world and the most exalted forms of myth or art. The Parisian vulgarity and banter of the demon Jinnifer in *Les Chevaliers,* the duality of Jocasta and the Sphinx in *La Machine infernale,* the great themes of incest and death embodied in Boulevard characters in *Les Parents terribles* are most striking examples of it. But do the shocks thus provoked have real dramatic value? There is no doubt that they create a tension between the play and the audience (surprise, indignation, irritation). However the determining factor is largely "the part that belongs to God," with the result that the juxtaposition of disparate elements may be rich in living tensions or turn out to be sterile, the spectator's interest being caught up in the play's ingeniousness or absurdity rather than in the drama itself.

A theatre of exorcism, Cocteau's works drive the demon out so effectively that there is hardly time to see him. The spectator is usually too busy watching the exorciser's pirouettes and incantations to think about the person possessed. Whence the clear division of public and critics into raving admirers and rabid disparagers, into those who see Cocteau's works as the reflection of a deep and intense drama and those who see Cocteau as the entertainer of a certain high society with a taste for anarchy.

Three managers organize the publicity. In their terrifying language, they tell each other that the crowd takes the parade for the inner spectacle, and they grossly try to make the crowd understand it.

No one enters. . . .

Such, in general, is the scenario of the ballet *Parade,* produced in collaboration with Picasso, Erik Satie, Diaghilev, and Leonide Massine. Besides its value as a manifesto, it has a theme that might serve as a symbol for the whole of Cocteau's works: Cocteau keeps his public outside. The true spectacle of the inner circus remains forbidden, despite the poet's innumerable invitations to enter. And perhaps that inner circus is no more than an absolute vacuum, as Eric Bentley has suggested.

Yet beyond the parade, beyond the enormous differences of style and tone that are so many theatrical variations of an outer ceremony, there is the suggestion of a real drama, if not its total realization. Almost all Cocteau's plays lead toward the same resolution. They are often directed toward a violent death and the hero generally appears more like a victim of the drama than the tragic master of his fate. Victims of either magic spells or very special circumstances, Cocteau's heroes submit to action more than they direct it. (pp. 56-8)

Cocteau is eminently representative of modern drama, which draws as near to tragedy as possible, yet most often remains on this side of it. Tragic heroism for the Greeks consisted in going all the way through an ordeal, to the point of giving any final acceptation the value of a challenge, and finding true grandeur in the catastrophe itself. Today this conception is replaced by a taste for victimization, still colored by Romanticism.

Cocteau uses the basic elements of tragedy in his dramas: the misunderstanding, a source of tragic irony, and the play of supernatural forces or obscure powers. Yvonne is mistaken about the meaning of her love for Mik just as Oedipus [in *La Machine infernale*] is mistaken about the oracle and the encounters in his life, and the interiorization of fate and its expression in psychological terms detract nothing from its transcendency. But either the characters, following in the path of fate, stop just on the edge of the revelation that might have elevated them (Yvonne dies without having really got to know herself, in *Les Parents terribles*); or the development of the action remains outside the character, who is victimized and then liberated without having had any determining effect on the drama (King Arthur, in *Les Chevaliers,* does no more than talk about the forces that "intoxicate" and then "disintoxicate" him); or, as is most frequently the case, the characters accelerate the final movement and precipitate their own deaths in gestures that are more evasive than fulfilling (Solange's suicide in *La Machine à écrire,* the anticipation of Hans who kills himself, in *Bacchus*).

Although the precipitated denouements are far removed from classical tragedy, they have two great merits. One, their theatricalism is effective. The foreshortening, the elements of spectacle, the effects of surprise and shock do create an unquestionable climate of finality. The spectacle is carried away by an increasingly rapid whirlpool of scenic movements and at the end death is imposed, so to speak, on the spectator's nerves. Two, they reveal a conception of freedom which is Cocteau's own. In the preface to *Les Mariés de la Tour Eiffel,* Cocteau wrote:

One of the photographer's lines could be used on the title page: *Since these mysteries are beyond us, let's pretend to be their organizer.* It is our line par excellence. The conceited man always finds refuge in responsibility. Thus, for example, he prolongs a war after the phenomenon that had been its deciding factor is over.

Freedom would then be shown in the acceleration or slowing down of the necessary developments, in their foreshortening or extension. Freedom is Cocteau's "pretense" and the others' "conceit." And Cocteau has no illusions about his own characters. When at the end of *Bacchus* Hans cries out "Free . . . ," his way of dying should be seen not as "tragic death par excellence, both fated and chosen" but as a pretense, a voluntary illusion. Hans' final freedom is in fact abstract. It consists only in anticipating an already determined event. (pp. 58-60)

Therefore what Cocteau's plays reveal is not a traditional tragic vision, but a particular conception of destiny very near to fatalism, wherein the best man can do is to live "as if " he were capable of controlling his fate. That "as if " can be found in all the eloquent affirmations, costumes, grand gestures, and at the extreme limit, in art itself. In *La Machine à écrire* many inhabitants of the city claim, at one point or another, to have written the anonymous letters. The play explains that in making the claim they hope to get out of the mediocrity in which they are imprisoned. They want to be recognized even in crime and their desire is so powerful that they end by believing their own lies. Actually their mythomania picks up the "pretense" and "conceit" of the preface of *Les Mariés.* Caught in a development of events that is beyond them and for which they are not responsible, they want to have themselves put in prison so that everything will happen *as if* the scandal was their own work. In short, the only escape from fate is in the lie. And the game of lying must be played to the very end, that is, all the way to total illusion, until the mask of freedom is seen as the very flesh of man. Man's only recourse is to deceive himself and others.

Death by suicide, in Cocteau's works, is the highest form of human pretense. By precipitating death, it often appears as an escape. The character disappears before the last illuminations of his ordeal. He wants to testify before it is too late and makes himself the martyr of certain values (poetry, love, grandeur, humanity) at the very moment that those values may be shown as impossible. As soon as the character realizes that the world has tricked him, he answers with the definitive trickery of suicide. He neither triumphs nor makes his peace. He retires. The deep and despairing cry of Cocteau's works is in the agitation of man who is caught and either ignores the fact or succeeds only in reconstructing a higher ignorance in the form of illusion. But although gilded by language and adorned with all the devices of mind and imagination, the trap remains merciless. By means of theatrical devices, Cocteau has invented a masked ball and he is the first to proclaim its vanity.

Cocteau's heroes—pure, still not disillusioned, preys to circumstance—are victims of chance, victims of a *fatalitas* often similar to that of melodrama. They believe that they benefit from it until, having gone too far in the game, they are seized with an unbearable mistrust which leads to a voluntary illusion. Cocteau's universe is not one of tragedy but of danger. The cosmos surrounding the characters is not that of a great moral order in the Greek manner, in conflict with man's affirmation of himself. It is a Coney Island contraption, a lay-out of pitfalls. . . . Those who fall into the traps—who are marked out for them—are the naïve and the pure in heart: poets, idealized adolescents, dewy-eyed revolutionaries. . . . Characterized by adolescence—a state of both grace and malediction, and a combination of impulsive acts, ignorance, purity, disorder, and youth—Cocteau's heroes are to a certain extent "going forces" in the Romantic manner, and "going" in a treacherous universe filled with every danger. Actually the adjective "Romantic" does somehow describe Cocteau's works. The variety of forms, the esthetic debates surrounding the plays, the justifying abstractions of the subject matter (poetry, youth, impure order, pure disorder) only partially disguise the underlying theme of isolation, an isolation of the individual destined for better and for worse. In *Scandal and Parade* Neal Oxenhandler emphasizes the theme of the *poète maudit*, the cursed poet, found throughout all of Cocteau's works. The ambiguity of benediction-malediction, generally identified with adolescence, is also, directly or indirectly, identified with the situation of the poet. (pp. 60-2)

The problem of the cursed protagonist is complicated by the fact that the young hero in each of his plays . . . cannot be considered individually. . . . The female role (mother, sister, queen) is just as important in Cocteau's plays as the leading male role, except perhaps for Eurydice in *Orphée,* who is a bit pale and simple-minded. Because of a kind of allegorical redistribution of qualities that somehow evoke Tennessee Williams and, in certain cases, Jean Genêt, Cocteau's hero can only be truly understood as part of the couple, young man-older woman. The poet-martyr's identification with his persecuted or rebel hero is obvious, but so is his identification with the feminine mask. "*I* am Yvonne," Cocteau might have said, paraphrasing Flaubert's "*I* am Madame Bovary." All more or less Jocastas, Cocteau's women are at once incarnations of the poet's feelings with regard to the young hero, and women-obstacles, now an outer obstacle (mother, wife, lover), now an inner one ("le fantôme de Marseille" in *Théâtre de Poche*).

The comparison with Tennessee Williams seems even more evident when we consider that Cocteau chose to adapt *A Streetcar Named Desire* for the French stage. . . . Obviously the heavy sexual atmosphere of Williams' works is foreign to Cocteau's, or at least considerably relieved in the major plays. Yet the general pattern—the duos, even the trios—are analogous. The unity of the couples reveals that they are but two faces of one basic individual—an eagle with two heads or with two sexes, as it were. In minor works such as *Le Fantôme de Marseille,* the hero remains undivided by also playing the part of a female impersonator. In fact the hero in Cocteau's dramas and certain of Tennessee Williams' plays is not one character but a couple, a divided hermaphrodite who tries to possess himself—an often impossible desire, and always tormenting.

The idea of the hermaphrodite can be seen in the complicity of intimacy so characteristic of Cocteau's atmosphere: the complicity of Yvonne and Mik, of Jocasta and Oedipus, of Maxime and Margot, of Maxime and Solange, of the Queen and Stanislas, of Hans and Christine, of Guinevere and Lancelot, parallel to that of King Arthur and the false Gawain. In Cocteau's theatre there are always at least two who are marked out—marked out for poetry, grandeur, disorder, or love. (pp. 63-4)

[Fate] serves as an archetype for the metaphors of danger and universal fatality which constitute the unchanging hidden drama in Cocteau's works. Each story consists in the search for union, realization, equilibrium, right up until the last scene, when an unexpected meaning breaks through in the form of catastrophe, a price to pay, a fatal incompatibility. The rest is surface effect. By means of a kind of baroque or rococo disproportion, the surface effects conceal the drama's underlying structure and are in fact taken for it—an obtrusive "parade," intentionally created by Cocteau who, through the diversity and exuberance of his talents, wanted both to disclose *and* to mask the danger in order to give the true equivalent of man's condition. (p. 65)

Mistrust is characteristic of Cocteau's sensibility and creates a primitive and somehow pre-tragic terror in his works. He never intellectualizes his fear but preserves it in its integrity, in its extreme discomfort. Theatre is one of man's maneuvers to appease a threatening Nature or super-Nature—an illusory maneuver, since despite all the embellishments and digressions, the universe can only be portrayed as implacable. Whereas Giraudoux resolved the problem of tragedy through intelligence, Cocteau, completely involved in a world for which the time of brilliant solutions is past or yet to come, does the dance of a man who is condemned to death, with no appeal possible. His masquerade is a staggering metaphor of the hesitation of a consciousness before its condemnation. Man can be seen innocently claiming freedom or the realization of values, desperately clinging to those desires, plunged in a defeat which is masked by a voluntary illusion. In a paral-

lel way, the playwright himself plays an analogous double game. He puts all his effort into raising the exalting or blinding illusion to the rank of reality while preserving enough illusionism to keep the reality from ever being reached.

Success—a synthesis of the hermaphrodite, the triumph of poets or lovers, the realization of a total and happy equilibrium, excluding all hazards or perils—is not of this world. It is in a beyond where Orpheus and Eurydice, Guinevere and Lancelot, Patrice and Nathalie (the Tristan and Isolde of the film *L'Eternel retour*) are reunited. The price for union is death. . . . In this world everything must be paid for and the deal is transacted above man and without his consent. (pp. 66-7)

A grim and anguished theatre, full of surface glitter that is no more than an illusion of esthetic satisfaction, Cocteau's plays are outwardly like entertainments of the twenties and thirties. He has used all the devices of the entertainment, from avant-garde forms to the Boulevard, in order to express the meeting between the illusionism of that time and the personal and sincere perception of a basic dimension of man's condition. Cocteau searched the present and a recent past for all the masks imaginable. Clowns, Music Hall stars, the favorite actors of the bourgeoisie and other classes are all buffoons in a masquerade addressed as much to the Prince de Beaumont as to the masses who attended vaudeville theatres during the time of the Popular Front. What gives Cocteau's theatre its value is its cry of warning addressed, whatever may be said, to all men.

Added to that is his fidelity to an uncompromising idea of theatre. He is a modernist not only when he concretizes psychological or metaphysical phenomena on stage, with the freedom of today's poets, but also in his "Boulevard" plays. Even *La Machine à écrire,* generally considered his worst play and one that he himself repudiated, is infinitely superior to plays of the same genre in that, while continuing to play the Boulevard game to the very end, Cocteau goes beyond the document on life in the provinces and succeeds, through dialogue and action, to actualize a theme of pure theatre: that of illusion, as both mask and instrument of the inexorable destructibility of man.

Cocteau has a love of the theatre which is evident from his general declarations, but which can also be found in the conception of his plays themselves. A metaphor of illusion, theatre should be presented with all the signs of illusion. At certain moments, the reality of what unfolds on stage must be forgotten so that the spectator may once again become conscious of the actor's number. . . . In *Les Parents terribles* the characters constantly remind us that they are acting out a play—vaudeville, drama, or tragedy, depending on the moment and situation. Allusions to dreams and magic, now represented by living beings or objects, now evoked by metaphors of language, should also be interpreted in the sense of a diversion from the real. What happens on stage is never absolutely true, despite appearances. Each play is presented as a trance or comedy, throwing man into a story that is fictional or dreamed up by some god.

A Protean theatre, it is the faithful image of a Protean universe. The number of forms that the traps of the universe can take is infinite; so are the forms taken by man's illusory defenses. The meaning of reality is finally lost in the game of lies and counter lies. Through an intransigence recalling the Baudelairian dandy, Cocteau, as the only possible affirmation of his identity, succeeded in immobilizing two elements of the confusion: theatre and the emotion of fear. His double game is tragic even though individually, his plays are not. It is a recognition, a voluntary act. For Cocteau, writing a play is taking man's part—but he takes it all in lucidity, for by resorting to devices and descriptive illusion, he affirms that he defends a lost cause. (pp. 67-8)

Jacques Guicharnaud with June Beckelman, "The Double Game: Jean Cocteau," in their *Modern French Theatre from Giraudoux to Beckett,* Yale University Press, 1961, pp. 48-68.

RENEE WINEGARTEN

(essay date 1989)

[In the excerpt below, Winegarten examines Cocteau's rejection of politics in his artistic works.]

What to do about Jean Cocteau? What to do about the critical dilemma of the respective claims of art and politics posed by his life and his work? These questions are renewed by the publication of his diaries for 1951-53 (a belated attempt to emulate Gide's), and of his letters to his friend and onetime companion, the actor Jean Marais (*Le Passé Défini,* vols. 1 and 2; *Lettres a Jean Marais*). It is surely time to reconsider Cocteau's position: last year marked the twenty-fifth anniversary of his death in October 1963; and the centenary of his birth, at Maisons-Laffitte in the environs of Paris, falls in July 1989.

Inextricably caught up in the jazzy twenties—a decade that he later came to regard as "the shirt of Nessus" from which he himself (and his reputation) could never win free—he was in many ways a product of aesthetic attitudes current during his boyhood and youth at the turn of the century, attitudes that endured at least up to 1939. All the same, he stood in the forefront of many of the innovatory tendencies that flourished in literature, music, and painting before and after the 1914-18 war. Either Cocteau was putting them into

practice in his own work, often before anyone else, or he was lauding and advocating those introduced by others. Poet, critic, novelist, librettist (for ballet, opera, and oratorio), dramatist, stage designer (of sets and costumes), actor on occasion, scriptwriter, filmmaker, caricaturist, illustrator, painter, designer of tapestries and pottery—Jean Cocteau is, for many, altogether too much.

Add to all this the fact that, when young, Cocteau was presented to the Empress Eugénie, widow of Napoleon III, and that he first came before the public at eighteen as a protégé of the homosexual actor, Édouard de Max, the friend of Oscar Wilde. Here is Cocteau dining with Proust, and there he is collaborating with Stravinsky and Picasso (both of whom he puffed). Nor should one forget the luminaries of fashion, stage, and screen with whom he associated throughout his life. The index of any biography of Cocteau reads like a twentieth-century *Who's Who.*

Yet it has to be admitted that after perusing biographical accounts of this famed magician, conjurer, acrobat, whether they be sympathetic to him or denigratory, the reader scarcely feels any nearer to the heart of the subject. Denigrators—and Cocteau has never lacked for them—would say that there is no heart or unifying core in the flutterings of this butterfly. He assisted opponents by declaring notoriously in a prose poem his sense of being a leper, a zero: "My blood has turned to ink. . . . I have stolen his papers from a certain J. C. born at M. L. (Maisons-Laffitte) on . . . , dead at eighteen after a brilliant poetic career. . . . Let them shut me up, lynch me. Understand who may: *I am a lie who always tells the truth*" (his italics). What precisely does that oft-quoted admission mean? Surely it does not signify that he is a liar (though he liked to embroider the truth), but a fictionist. And is it not the actor's role, as well as the poet's, to "lie" for what he likes to consider "a higher truth"? We readily acquiesce, for our delight or illumination.

The lack of a convincing sense of identity may characterize poet, dramatist, and actor. Keats felt this when speaking of himself, the great Shakespearian actor Edmund Kean, Shakespeare, and "negative capability." The ability to share—like Keats—in the existence of another creature, the bird that picks about the gravel, is one of the actor's talents also. With Cocteau, this is taken a step further in the idea that he has assumed the identity of another, that he is impersonating someone called Jean Cocteau (a notion encapsulated in his well-known words: "Victor Hugo was a madman who thought he was Victor Hugo"). Cocteau's story *Thomas l'Imposteur,* based on his own brief and idiosyncratic wartime career on the fringes of the conflict, traces the adventures of an obscure young man who, during the 1914-18 war, adopts the persona of General de Fontenoy's nephew. In keeping with the family military tradition, he volunteers to carry a message, and is gunned down by an enemy patrol: " 'A bullet,' he said to himself. *'I am lost if I do not pretend to be dead' "* (the novelist's italics). So in the performance of his role, the youth remains consistent to the last.

What certainly functions throughout Cocteau's work, alongside the numerous legends fostered by himself, and by others associated with the overexposed "frivolous prince," is a formidable industriousness together with a devout sense of discipline and order in art, if not in life. That high tone of devotion to art, reminiscent of Baudelaire or Flaubert, remains constant in his writings. Cocteau would later speak of his fidelity to his own path or personal line, along which he was directed by his unconscious. He began to write before the Marxian-style theory that everything is governed by politics and economics had taken hold. The artist's prime concern was beauty. As early as 1817 Keats had observed that "with a great poet the sense of Beauty overcomes every other consideration, or rather obliterates all consideration," though this was not his last word on the subject. The idea of "pure poetry" was in the air in France between the wars. Abbé Henri Bremond, profoundly influenced by A. C. Bradley's Oxford lectures *Poetry for Poetry's Sake,* upheld the notion of "la poésie pure" in the name of Baudelaire and Mallarmé. Cocteau could scarcely have been unaware of the controversy that ensued, in which ultimately the partisans of purity would be the losers.

Cocteau found a way of unifying all his diverse artistic activities by calling each one a form of poetry: somehow, this raised their tone. His numerous works are listed as "Poetry of the Novel," "Poetry of Criticism," "Poetry of the Theatre," "Poetry of the Cinema," "Poetry of the Graphic Arts." By this nomenclature, he doubtless wished to emphasize once and for all the preeminence of poetry, and the fact that he regarded himself primarily as "the Poet," indeed, as the heir of Baudelaire who sought to plunge into the Unknown in search of the *new.* Cocteau favors the image of the poet as a diver into the unknown. After rejecting his juvenilia from the canon, he composed some of the most exquisite poems in the language, poems whose rare quality inevitably eludes translation. Moreover, he went on writing poetry into old age. Yet the connecting link of poetry, chosen by himself, will not take one, perhaps, as far as the link of the theater. (pp. 436-37)

It is ultimately as "a performer," vulnerable, ever taking risks, acutely aware of a fickle public while professing indifference to it, yet anxious for its esteem and love, that Cocteau emerges from his multifaceted creations.

"Always hit the same spot in a different way," he advised the dancer Caryathis, otherwise Élise, wife and muse of his friend, the novelist Marcel Jouhandeau (an unprepossessing pair). What was the same spot in Cocteau's case? It was transience and death, a theme that obsessed him, not surprisingly, since his father—later suspected of being a secret homosexual—shot himself when the boy was barely ten years old, in 1898. Nobody knew why. Although Cocteau rarely spoke of his father and, indeed, the fact of the suicide did not become public knowledge until very late in the poet's life, it seems plain that this terrible and mysterious loss dominated his imagination.

For Cocteau, death is intimately connected with speed or the ultra-rapid passage of time. During the 1914-18 war he wrote a poem in prose entitled **"Visit."** It begins ominously like an opium dream: "I have some sad important news to tell you. I am dead. . . ." A description of the state of being dead follows: "With us, speed is much more vital than with you. I am not talking about the speed that moves from one point to another, but of the speed that does not stir, of speed itself. . . . Our speed is so powerful that it places us at a point of silence and monotony." Then the dead speaker continues:

> One of the earliest surprises of the adventure lies in feeling unfolded. Life only shows you a small surface of a sheet of paper folded many times over. The most superficial, freakish, crazy acts of the living are inscribed on this fragile surface. Within, mathematically, symmetry is taking shape. Death alone unfolds the sheet. . . .

The notion that there is a concealed mathematical order in life, rather as there is number in poetry (he uses the word *chiffre,* which can mean "code"), is essential to Cocteau. Access to this secret mathematical order is from time to time granted as a privilege to the poet. Images of death, of self-slaughter, the mystery of time, the secret folded beneath the visible page of life, will frequently be found throughout Cocteau's work, and conceivably they have their origin in his response to his father's mysterious suicide.

Associated with this tragic family secret, with his father's (putative) homosexuality and his own, is the theme of fate and free will. What in life is determined and what is choice? Already in his novel, *Le Grand Écart* (1923)—with its punning title meaning both the splits performed by the circus acrobat and, perhaps more significantly, a great distance, divergence, or deviation—Cocteau wrote: "We believe that we choose but we have no choice." (pp. 437-38)

At the age of fifteen, Cocteau had reputedly fled from his Parisian home and his cultivated bourgeois family. He claimed to have spent his time in Marseilles, among the sailors, the pimps and prostitutes, the bars, the opium dens, the male brothels with their transparent mirrors. Could his own bent be described as fate or choice? The most brilliant and sardonic denial of free will, adumbrated in *Le Grand Écart,* is exposed in his masterly play on the Oedipus legend, that tragic "farce atroce," *La Machine infernale* (1934), where the diabolic gods deceive mortals with false hopes, false clues, and supreme trickery. It is as if the malignant gods themselves have written a script to which the actors have to adhere, whatever contributions they mistakenly think they are making to the plot.

That Cocteau viewed his own course in such a determinist way seems plain. Naturally, by regarding himself as a person enacting a role in a play that had already been written, he reduced the element of human responsibility in affairs. How did he come to see life in such theatrical terms?

The theater is like a (harmless?) drug, and it can even become a kind of substitute religion. Those who have not acquired the addiction or the language of faith do not know the power of the experience. Here is not another form of business enterprise or an entertainment to pass the time, but a process that reminds us how the ancient Greek theater had its origin in religion and religious ritual, and how European drama, too, sprang from medieval mystery plays performed at church. Although the modern theater has traveled far from its spiritual source, at its best it can still come trailing clouds of glory from its distant home. Cocteau knew that well enough in his attempt to revive Greek drama for modern audiences. His play, *Antigone,* written in 1922, preceded dramas by Gide and Giraudoux on Greek themes, and inspired those of Anouilh and Sartre. Certainly, Anouilh acknowledged his debt to the creator of *Orphée.*

As Cocteau himself remarked (in *Opium,* 1930): "This truth of the theatre is the poetry of the theatre, something more true than the truth"—by which he presumably meant the actuality of everyday commonplace or ordinary vision. That paradox of Cocteau's, the projection of a theatrical truth "more true than the truth," which serves as a higher or more charged form of "reality," is essential to his view of the drama, indeed, of poetry and art in general. Evidently, it has nothing to do with the kind of drama that has largely predominated in the last thirty years or so: in the work of the admirers of the nihilistic minimalism of Samuel Beckett, for instance, or in the overly didactic plays of leftist political and social commitment written under the long shadow cast by Bertolt Brecht.

Cocteau acquired his love for the stage, and everything associated with it, in early childhood. It was from watching his mother and father leave to go to the theater that he was caught: "I contracted the red and gold sickness," he said later, an addiction to the gilt ornamentation and the crimson plush of the old Parisian theaters. (pp. 438-39)

It was not only circus artistes like the clowns Footit and Chocolat that Cocteau loved as a boy, but the larger-than-life actors and actresses, or *monstres sacrés,* who dominated the theater of his youth: Édouard de Max; Mounet-Sully, whom he saw in Victor Hugo's Romantic melodrama, *Ruy Blas* (which he would later adapt for the screen); and the immortal Sarah Bernhardt. Cocteau remembered the frenzy that greeted the great tragic actress when she took her curtain calls, with her right hand resting on the frame of the proscenium arch, in an attitude of exhaustion. The great performers have always known how to prolong a performance in their manner of receiving applause. Then there was Isadora Duncan, the celebrated American dancer, tragically strangled by her long scarf that caught in the wheels of her car, who inspired the strangulation-by-scarf that Cocteau would give to his Jocaste in *La Machine infernale.*

Of the famed Russian dancer Nijinsky, whose decline into madness was to be equally tragic, Cocteau wrote with amazement about his extraordinary transformation on stage. Nijinsky was short, and deformed by his profession, according to Cocteau: "In brief, one could never have believed that this little balding monkey . . . was the idol of the public. Yet he was, and rightly so. Everything about him was arranged to appear from a distance, under the lights. On stage, his excessively broad muscles turned slender. His height increased . . . , and as for his face, it became radiant. Such a metamorphosis is almost unimaginable for those who have not witnessed it." Actors, often barely recognizable in their everyday appearance, are like peacocks who only unfold their gaudy plumage on the boards, where they truly belong. Like the actor, the writer of poetry, fiction, or drama also assumes other identities and undergoes metamorphosis.

In his charming memoirs, *Portraits-Souvenir* (1935), which he brilliantly illustrated with his own caricatures, Cocteau tells how, in his youth, he was crazy about the theater, and that this passion was nourished at the school he attended. . . . Of the idols of his youth, like Sarah Bernhardt, Isadora Duncan, Édouard de Max, Cocteau would ask rhetorically: "What had these princes of impropriety to do with propriety, with tact, with restraint, these tigers who lick themselves and yawn in front of everyone, these forces of artifice at grips with that force of nature, the public?" It is no wonder that having been dazzled by these "tigers" he should write rich parts for the *monstres sacrés* of his maturity; for the enchanting Elvire Popesco (who took the role of Jocaste in the revival of *La Machine infernale* in the fifties); for the extraordinary Yvonne de Bray; for such talented creatures of physical beauty as Edwige Feuillère, Maria Casarès, and Jean Marais.

With *L'Aigle à deux têtes* (1946), that attempt to bring off a Romantic melodrama after Victor Hugo, Cocteau declared that common psychology was to be replaced there by "heroic or heraldic psychology." The two leading characters, the Queen and the Poet-assassin, or twin-headed eagle, were to bear the same relation to the everyday as heraldic unicorns and lions woven in tapestry bear to real animals. "Their behaviour . . . would belong to the theatre just as those fabulous beasts belong to escutcheons. . . . To make [such a work] visible, I needed décors, costumes, Edwige Feuillère and Jean Marais." In short, Cocteau was trying to reproduce in 1946, after the intense inbred "realism" of the family imbroglio in his play, *Les Parents terribles,* the kind of theatrical experience that had stunned him in his youth, and that happened to accord with a certain desire for poetic remoteness in an era of drab austerity and dread revelations.

When that great Russian impresario, Diaghilev, said to Cocteau: "Astonish me!" he was only encouraging the young man to pursue his own inclinations and gifts. He was treating the poet like a *premier danseur* of the Ballets Russes, a Nijinsky or a Massine, as a performer who takes risks and always surprises the audience. In a sense, the artist, whether on the stage or by means of the word, does take us by surprise; and we should not think much of the theatrical performer—or the literary creator—who did not do something other than what might be generally expected. Much of Cocteau's ability to surprise lies in his often marvelous and musical use of language, in that aspect of his art which can least be conveyed in translation, with his fondness for wordplay, for startling puns ("Mirrors would do well to reflect a little more before returning images"), coupled with a compelling simplicity. The amazingly rich vocabulary that he gave to the Sphinx in *La Machine infernale,* as she wraps Oedipe inextricably in the mysterious coils of the word, remains one of Cocteau's most astounding theatrical achievements.

Cocteau's passion for the theater pierces through the frequent theatrical metaphors in his novels, in *Thomas l'Imposteur,* in *Le Grand Écart,* and notably in *Les Enfants terribles,* that strange work written in a clinic where he was undergoing one of his periodic cures as an opium addict. Paul and Elisabeth, the doomed eccentric brother and sister, in revolt against the commonplace, who live together in bizarre disorder, served as models for the young of the 1930s (including—as Gustaf Gründgens would later assure Cocteau—Klaus Mann and his sister Erika). They also prefigure the anarchical youth and the dropouts of a later era. "The performance of the bedroom began at eleven o'clock at night. Except on Sundays, there were no matinees," we are told. None of the leading characters, not even the one who plays the spectator (Gérard) was aware of acting a part. The jinn of the room struck the three knocks that began the performance: ". . . the play (or bedroom if you wish) hovered on the brink of myth." Every night they enacted the same play. In the drama of their joint suicide, wearing "the buskins of

Greek actors, they depart from the hell of the Atrides," observes the narrator in his comment on the "death song" of brother and sister. At the end, the secret room itself becomes a theater open to an audience. All these theatrical allusions occur in a novel that ostensibly has little to do with the theater as such.

Several of Cocteau's films, like a number of his plays, are rooted in the same poetry of mystery and magic—*Orphée* (1949) being an adaptation of his play of 1926, which in turn had employed figures and imagery from his poems. French cinema, from the days of Georges Méliès, had been enchanted with magic. Cocteau, who loved this aspect of film, once declared that no filmic trick would ever take the place of the water-pantomime in the circus that he had first seen when he was seven years old; yet Cocteau spent his time trying to prove the opposite in his movies. What was *Le Sang d'un poète* but a series of mysterious visual devices, a performance designed to fascinate and astonish, based on his private poetic imagery? The cinematograph, as he liked to call it, reinforced his anxiety about time: it showed that a mere difference in tempo allowed people to believe nature was serene. Films now revealed that plants gesticulate; they uncovered the secret "of a bean in process of birth, of an exploding crocus." This concern with magic in film reached its apogee in the fairy tale *La Belle et La Bête*—the frightening yet serene human arms of the candelabra that project to light Beauty's path into the Beast's palace, the strange and touching sound made by the creature with his haunting eyes as he laps water. Cocteau's images remain indelibly in the memory, retaining their power to surprise and enchant at each viewing.

The difficulty of "placing" Cocteau does not become any easier with the passing of time. One obstacle is the legend he fostered while bemoaning it: the self-advertisement of his early years, neatly combined with his advertisement of the likes of Satie and Stravinsky, de Chirico and Picasso. Another is the notoriously long succession of handsome young men. Among these figured that precocious and ill-fated youth, Raymond Radiguet, author of *Le Diable au corps,* who (so Cocteau maintained) converted him to a neoclassical simplicity; the less talented but heroic Jean Desbordes (later tortured to death by the Gestapo); and not least, his adopted son and heir, the Yugoslav-born Edouard Dermit.

Some of Cocteau's young admirers and acolytes were said to climb the lamppost outside his residence in the rue d'Anjou, in quest of a glimpse of their idol. Others, like the outrageous Maurice Sachs, who purloined Cocteau's books and papers, followed him temporarily in his flirtation with the religious revival sponsored by the neo-Thomist philosopher Jacques Maritain—a movement qualified by a wit as "le pédérasthomisme." Goings-on at the Hôtel Welcome, on the waterfront of the picturesque Mediterranean fishing port of Villefranche-sur-mer, frequented by Cocteau and his friends, caused eyebrows to be raised. The poet said he took to opium in his total desolation at the sudden death of Raymond Radiguet—he could not bring himself to attend the funeral—but in all likelihood he had tried opium earlier, and he went on smoking what he called his "remedy" throughout his life, sometimes falling foul of the law.

Yet despite this bohemian air of disorder and scandal, nothing seems to have deterred Cocteau from seriously pursuing his varied literary and artistic tasks with constant professional ardor. He entitled a collection of reminiscences and reflections, *La Difficulté d'être,* after the dying words uttered by Fontenelle in 1757, commenting that where the centenarian writer's existential disquiet surfaced only in his last hours, "Mine has always been with me." That sense of not being at ease with himself or with life permeates Cocteau's work and, notwithstanding its surface dazzle, gives it an underlying gravity. The brevity of youth, so pertinent to his love of it, naturally exacerbates his obsession with the rapid passing of time, with mirrors that give back a declining image of the self and serve as a gateway to death.

If, for Cocteau, poetry is a kind of algebra, his idea of numerology is different from an accountant's. Do two and two make four—or twenty-two? he inquired, adding that "two chairs, two apples, do not make four." His awareness of a subtle incongruity, of all that remains unknown, would lead him in later years to believe in flying saucers and other dubious phenomena. Cocteau was not an intellectual. At every opportunity he tended, moreover, to denigrate the intellect. To Jean-Marie Magnan he wrote in 1958: "People have lost devout respect for the oracle—for the word obtained through a kind of alchemy suited to *reducing the role of the intellect* and to allowing the unknown to take root in this world (the Heurtebise attempt)." This—with his emphasis—was an allusion to the guardian angel, Heurtebise, whose wings are concealed under glass sheets as carried on a glazier's back, and who figures in Cocteau's poetry and dramatic work. A year later, writing to the same correspondent, Cocteau proclaimed: ". . . the intellect—our worst enemy." A purely intellectual approach to Cocteau is therefore likely to be self-defeating, and that is doubtless what some hold against him. Of course, this anti-rationalism of Cocteau's is convenient for him and can sometimes lead to nonsense (or worse) if taken to its logical conclusion. All the same, his constant reminder that there are more things in heaven and earth than are dreamt of in philosophy can be a timely corrective in a materialistic, technological age.

One reason why Cocteau does not fit easily into accounts of twentieth-century literature is because he was not associated with any prevailing group. He remained aloof from movements in a country where they play an important part in cultural life. At the same time, as panegyrist or contributor, he was on the fringe of such vital and influential forces as the Ballets Russes, the new jazzy modernism, the whole mode of experimentation as opposed to tradition. The Surrealists, who represented the most powerful element in French artistic life between the wars, gave him the cold shoulder. The great panjandrum of Surrealism, André Breton, loathed homosexuality and homosexuals and was at daggers drawn with Cocteau. As for André Gide, who ruled over the dominant journal *La Nouvelle Revue Française,* he found devious ways to wound the younger man, despite or maybe because of their homosexual tastes. The great debate and battle of the thirties that raged between anti-Fascists and adherents of Communism on one hand, and those tempted by Fascism and Nazism on the other, apparently did not touch Cocteau, the self-engaged poet and dramatist.

Opinions generally concur that the author of *Les Enfants terribles* was an egoist and narcissist, absorbed with himself, his art, his love affairs, and his friends. (pp. 439-42)

Simone de Beauvoir, much impressed when young by such Cocteau creations as the Eugènes of *Le Potomak,* met him for the first time not long before the liberation of Paris in 1944 and was fascinated by his dazzling virtuosity with the spoken word, by his astonishing monologue. She noted, "You realized at once that he was very concerned with himself, but this narcissism had nothing narrow about it and did not cut him off from others." It was to her, and to Sartre, both shortly to promulgate the influential doctrine of literary commitment to the Left, that Cocteau chose to hold forth about how the Poet must keep aloof from the age and remain indifferent to all the mad acts of war and politics. This was the attitude of fin de siècle aestheticism in which he had been bred. "The lot of them get on our nerves . . . the Germans . . . the Americans . . . ," he complained. That remark might be regarded as the understatement of the year concerning the brutally foul activities of the Nazis in 1944. Besides, he remained somewhat less aloof from the Germans than his words might suggest.

When France was defeated by Nazi Germany in 1940, Cocteau suddenly chose to remind himself of his esteem for Briand and Caillaux, politicians who had favored Franco-German entente. It would be absurd to suggest that the poet warmed to Hitler or to his French admirers and servants. Avowedly apolitical, he was essentially an anarchist-conservative or conservative-anarchist, here as in literature. During the Occupation, supporters of the breast-beating Vichy regime actually accused Cocteau of causing the *débâcle* by his moral turpitude (by which they meant his homosexuality). He was attacked in the notorious collaborationist paper, *Je Suis Partout,* by Lucien Rebatet (though he signed the appeal for that odious writer's pardon after the war). Once, Jean Marais, Cocteau's companion at the time, went so far as to strike the critic Alain Laubreaux for his scurrilous attack on the playwright (an episode later re-created in François Truffaut's film *The Last Métro*). Cocteau himself was beaten up when he declined to salute the flag at a parade of French volunteers who were departing to join the German forces on the Russian front.

Along with many others during the Occupation, however, Cocteau was involved in productions of his plays and films; and while these enterprises doubtless kept his head above water, they also required the imprimatur of the Germans. Nothing could be performed or published without it. Cocteau associated with the equivocal German writer and semi-official cultural ambassador, Ernst Jünger, whom he met at the home of his old friend, the novelist and Vichyite diplomat, Paul Morand. Cocteau penned a laudatory publicity article for an exhibition of the work of Arno Breker, Hitler's favorite sculptor. The author of *The Frivolous Prince* did not seem to realize how such associations would compromise him, or how little they accorded with his (unsuccessful) intervention on behalf of his friend, the poet Max Jacob, a Jewish convert to Catholicism, who died in Drancy prison. After the war, Cocteau paid a social visit to Arno Breker when in Germany in 1952 for the production of his play, *Bacchus,* in which Gustaf Gründgens played an important role. In his diary Cocteau remarked that the sculptor had saved both Picasso and himself from the worst during the Occupation. The poet was equally grateful to his Communist colleagues, Aragon and Éluard, for protecting him at the Liberation.

Like most of the littérateurs who had not hastily joined the bandwagon of Resistance literary groups, Cocteau had to face a *comité d'épuration,* or purge committee, though apparently without any ill effect. He began to moan a great deal, not just about the savage settling of old scores, but about the way things were going in post-war France. It seemed to him that he had been singled out for persecution. How was it, he wondered gloomily, that Paul Claudel, the Catholic poet and dramatist, had managed to get away with turning an ode to Marshal Pétain into one to General de Gaulle? Cocteau always felt that nobody took him seriously, at his proper valuation as an artist. "There is no writer as well-known, unknown, unappreciated as I am," he lamented. What he desired was *"respectful trust"* (his italics) owing to his years and his oeuvre. He wanted to know why he was left out when contemporaries like Malraux, Montherlant, Sartre, Camus, and Anouilh all received proper consideration. The repetition of this

dissatisfaction becomes embarrassing in the light of the honors that were to be showered upon him, including elevation to immortality in the Académie Française. No honors could ever be enough to prove to Cocteau that he was respected and loved as he wished.

There is something disproportionate in Cocteau's single-minded concern with finding a suitable vehicle for Jean Marais, with theater production, and filmmaking at a period of universal agony. Cocteau worried profoundly about those he loved and idealized, but his imaginative embrace was not large. He lacked a sense of evil where human conduct is concerned. The enmity of fate, the often touching folly and blindness of mortals—these result in human tragedy. What of responsibility for one's sins of commission and omission? The capacity of humankind for evil is eluded, and this ultimately serves as a limiting factor in his work.

For Cocteau, all the world is a stage, and all the men and women merely players. We may well be weary of a form of drama that ostentatiously thrusts the dramatist's tender social conscience, his "revolutionary" credentials, and his (predominantly leftist) sermonizing commonplaces upon us, but are we ready today to welcome a kind of drama like Cocteau's that often feeds upon itself? Would a return to his work, as distinct from his person, contribute to the long-awaited reaction against the current fashion of what he himself called "conformist anticonformism"? Must we be forever moving up and down on the seesaw of art for art's sake or an art that is politically and socially "committed"?

The dilemma is troubling. Cocteau himself complained to Jean Marais in 1954: "What a peculiar age when politics have a hand in anything and everything!" Two years earlier, he had remarked to Marais: "Like all ages, this age is subject to the false perspectives of actuality. One must understand it and swallow the pill. I often have it stuck in my throat, but I strive to stay within my line in spite of appearances against me." This was a respectable and once widely admired artistic standpoint, before Brecht and Sartre took command. It would be entirely admirable, if only actuality did not keep getting in the way of art and artists. As for ourselves, as readers or members of an audience, we naturally want to have it both ways. We esteem highly those fine artists who have devoted themselves single-mindedly to their art, and who have given us immense pleasure and enlightenment, but we are not at all happy if they choose a pernicious ideology or if—like Cocteau—they do not even seem to be aware that any moral choice is at stake. (pp. 442-43)

Renee Winegarten, "Reappraisal: In Pursuit of Cocteau," in *The American Scholar,* Vol. 58, No. 3, Summer, 1989, pp. 436-43.

SOURCES FOR FURTHER STUDY

Anderson, Alexandra, and Saltus, Carol, eds. *Jean Cocteau and the French Scene*. New York: Abbeville Press Publishers, 1984, 239 p.

> Contains essays on Cocteau's works in various genres and discusses his role in intellectual circles in twentieth-century France.

Crowson, Lydia Lallas. *The Esthetic of Jean Cocteau*. Hanover: University of New Hampshire/University Press of New England, 1978, 200 p.

> Close study of Cocteau's literary aesthetic. Includes bibliography.

Knapp, Bettina Liebowitz. *Jean Cocteau*. New York: Twayne Publishers, 1970, 179 p.

> Comprehensive study of Cocteau's life and works.

Oxenhandler, Neal. *Scandal and Parade: The Theater of Jean Cocteau*. New Brunswick, N.J.: Rutgers University Press, 1957, 284 p.

> Important early study of Cocteau's dramas.

Peters, Arthur King. *Jean Cocteau and André Gide: An Abrasive Friendship*. New Brunswick, N.J.: Rutgers University Press, 1973, 426 p.

> Comprehensive study of the written correspondence between Cocteau and André Gide.

———. *Jean Cocteau and His World*. New York: Vendome Press, 1986, 216 p.

> Detailed account of Cocteau's life supplemented by photographs and portraits of the writer.

Samuel Taylor Coleridge

1772-1834

English poet, critic, essayist, dramatist, and journalist.

INTRODUCTION

*C*oleridge is one of the most significant poets and critics in the English language. As a major figure in the English Romantic movement, he is best known for three poems, "The Rime of the Ancient Mariner," "Kubla Khan," and "Christabel," and one volume of criticism, *Biographia Literaria; or, Biographical Sketches of My Literary Life and Opinions* (1817). Although the three poems were poorly received during Coleridge's lifetime, they are now praised as classic examples of imaginative verse. His criticism, which examines the nature of poetic creation and stresses the relationship between emotion and intellect, helped free literary thought from the Neoclassical strictures of eighteenth-century scholars. Coleridge's analyses channeled the concepts of the German Romantic philosophers into England and helped establish the modern view of William Shakespeare as a master of depicting human character. Many of Coleridge's critical endeavors, like several of his poems, remain unfinished. Critics have often faulted his lack of sustained concentration, contending that he never attained his full literary potential. Although the recent publication of his voluminous correspondence and notebooks challenges the notion that Coleridge was unproductive, the extensive editing required to compile this work reinforces the argument that his disorganization contributed to years of critical disfavor.

Coleridge was born in Devon, where he lived until the age of ten, when his father died. The boy was then sent to school at Christ's Hospital in London. Later, he described his years there as desperately lonely; only the friendship of Charles Lamb, a fellow student, offered solace. From Christ's Hospital, Coleridge went to Jesus College, Cambridge, where he earned a reputation as a promising young writer and brilliant conversationalist. He accrued enormous gambling debts, however, and his financial difficulties, coupled with the pain of an unrequited romance, caused him to enlist in the army. Coleridge's brothers located him and paid his debts, and the next spring he returned to Cambridge. Further plagued by personal problems, he left in 1794 without completing his degree. Coleridge then traveled to Oxford University, where he befriended Robert Southey. The two developed a plan for a "pantisocracy," or egalitarian agricultural society, to be founded in Kentucky. For a time, both were absorbed by their revolutionary concepts and together composed a number of works including a drama, *The Fall of Robespierre,* based on their politically radical ideas. Since their plan also required that each member be married, Coleridge, at Southey's urging, wed Sara Fricker, the sister of Southey's fiancée. Unfortunately, the match proved disastrous, and Coleridge's unhappy marriage was a source of grief to him throughout his life. To compound Coleridge's difficulties, Southey lost interest in the scheme, abandoning it in 1795.

Coleridge's fortunes changed when in 1796 he met the poet William Wordsworth, with whom he had corresponded casually for several years. Their rapport was instantaneous, and the next year Coleridge moved to Nether Stowey in the Lake District, where he and Wordsworth began their literary collaboration. Influenced by Wordsworth, whom he considered the finest poet since John Milton, Coleridge composed the bulk of his most admired work. Because he had no regular income, he was reluctantly planning to become a Unitarian minister when, in 1798, the prosperous china manufacturers Josiah and Thomas Wedgwood offered him a lifetime pension so that he could devote himself to writing. Aided by this annuity, Coleridge entered a prolific period that lasted from 1798 to 1800, composing "The Rime of the Ancient Mariner," "Christabel," "Frost at Midnight," and "Kubla Khan." In 1798, Coleridge also collaborated with Wordsworth on *Lyrical Ballads,* a volume of poetry which they published anonymously. Coleridge's contributions included "The Rime of the Ancient Mariner," published in its original, rather archaic form. Most critics found the poem incomprehensible, including Southey, who termed it "a Dutch attempt at German sublimity." The poem's unpopularity impeded the volume's success, and not until the twentieth century was *Lyrical Ballads* recognized as the first literary document of English Romanticism.

Following the publication of *Lyrical Ballads,* Coleridge traveled to Germany, where he developed an interest in the philosophies of Immanuel Kant, Friedrich von Schelling, and August Wilhelm and Friedrich von Schlegel; he later introduced German aesthetic theory in England through his critical writings. Upon his return in 1799, Coleridge settled in Keswick, near the Lake District. The move to Keswick marked the beginning of an era of chronic illness and personal misery for Cole-

ridge. When his health suffered because of the damp climate, he took opium as a remedy and quickly became addicted. His marriage, too, was failing; Coleridge had fallen in love with Wordsworth's sister-in-law, Sara Hutchinson. He was separated from his wife, but since he did not condone divorce, he did not remarry. In an effort to improve his health and morale, Coleridge traveled to Italy but returned to London more depressed than before. He began a series of lectures on poetry and Shakespeare which helped establish his reputation as a critic, yet they were not entirely successful at the time because of his disorganized methods of presentation. Coleridge's next undertaking, a periodical entitled *The Friend,* which offered essays on morality, taste, and religion, failed due to financial difficulties. He continued to visit the Wordsworths yet was morose and anti-social. When a mutual friend confided to him Wordsworth's complaints about his behavior, an irate Coleridge, perhaps fueled in part by his jealousy of Wordsworth's productivity and prosperity, repudiated their friendship. Although the two men were finally reconciled in 1812, they never again achieved their former intimacy.

Coleridge's last years were spent under the care of Dr. James Gilman, who helped him control his opium habit. Despite Coleridge's continuing melancholy, he was able to dictate the *Biographia Literaria* to his friend John Morgan. The *Biographia Literaria* contains what many critics consider Coleridge's greatest critical writings. In this work, he developed aesthetic theories which he had intended to be the introduction to a great philosophical opus that was never completed. Coleridge published many other works during this period, including the fragments "Kubla Khan" and "Christabel," as well as a number of political and theological writings. This resurgence of productivity, coupled with his victory over his addiction, brought Coleridge renewed confidence. His newfound happiness was marred by failing health, however, and he died in 1834 of complications from his life-long dependence on opium. Upon learning that his old friend had passed away, Wordsworth remarked that Coleridge was the only "wonderful" man he had ever known.

Critical estimation of Coleridge's works increased dramatically after his death, but relatively little was written on them until the turn of the century. Opinions of his work vary widely, yet few today deny the talent evident in "The Ancient Mariner," "Kubla Khan," and "Christabel." "The Ancient Mariner" perhaps best incorporates both Coleridge's imaginative versification and the intertwining of reality and fantasy. The tale of a seaman who kills an albatross, the poem presents a variety of religious and supernatural images to depict a moving spiritual journey of doubt, renewal, and eventual redemption. The symbolism contained in this work has sparked diverse interpretations, and several commentators consider it an allegorical record of Coleridge's own spiritual pilgrimage. Critics also debate the nature of the Mariner's salvation and question whether the poem possesses a moral; Coleridge's own comment on this issue was that the poem's major fault consisted of "the obtrusion of the moral sentiment so openly on the reader. . . . It ought to have had no more moral than the *Arabian Nights'* tale of the merchant's sitting down to eat dates. . . . "

Coleridge's concern with religious themes is also evident in "Kubla Khan," which was published with a note explaining the strange circumstances of its composition. Coleridge wrote that he fell asleep while reading an account of how the Chinese emperor Kubla Khan had ordered the building of a palace within a walled garden. Three hours later, Coleridge awoke and began to write down the several hundred lines which he claimed to have composed during his sleep. However, he found that the rest of the poem had disappeared from his mind. In a later note appended to the text, he added that his dream was induced by opium and that it was "a sort of reverie." For many years, critics considered "Kubla Khan" merely a novelty of limited meaning, but John Livingston Lowes's 1927 study, *The Road to Xanadu: A Study in the Ways of the Imagination,* explored its imaginative complexity and the many literary sources which influenced it, including the works of Plato and Milton. Though Coleridge himself dismissed "Kubla Khan" as a "psychological experiment," the poem is now considered a forerunner of the work of the Symbolists and Surrealists in its presentation of the unconscious. In Coleridge's other poetic fragment, "Christabel," he combined exotic images with gothic romance to create an atmosphere of terror. Like "The Ancient Mariner," "Christabel" deals with the themes of evil and guilt in a setting pervaded by supernatural elements. Most critics now contend that Coleridge's inability to sustain the poem's eerie mood prevented him from completing it.

The *Biographia Literaria,* the most famous of Coleridge's critical writings, was inspired by his disdain for the eighteenth-century empiricists who relied on observation and experimentation to formulate their aesthetic theories. In this work, he turned to such German philosophers as Kant and Schelling for a more universal interpretation of art. From Schelling Coleridge drew his "exaltation of art to a metaphysical role," and his contention that art is analogous to nature is borrowed from Kant. While Coleridge acknowledged his debt to the Germans, he denied claims that he had plagiarized their theories. Of the different sections in the *Biographia Literaria,* perhaps the most often studied is Coleridge's definition of the imagination. He describes two kinds of imagination, the primary and the secondary: the primary is the agent of perception which relays the details of experience, while the secondary interprets these details and creates from them. The concept of a dual imagination forms a seminal part of Coleridge's theory of poetic unity, in which disparate elements are reconciled as a unified whole. According to Coleridge, the purpose of poetry was to provide pleasure "through the medium of beauty."

Coleridge's other great critical achievement is his work on Shakespeare. His Shakespearean criticism is among the most important in the English language, although it was never published in formal essays, instead, it has been recorded for posterity in the form of marginalia and transcribed reports from lectures. Informed by his admiration for and understanding of Shakespeare, Coleridge's critical theory allowed for more in-depth analysis of the plays than did the writings of his eighteenth-century predecessors. His emphasis on individual psychology and characterization marked the inception of a new critical approach to Shakespeare which had a profound influence on later studies.

In his roles as critic and poet, Coleridge displayed a concern for creativity as a guiding force both for the individual and for the universe. Literature, Coleridge concluded, required a combination of emotion and thought to be truly imaginative. His acknowledgement of the power of the imagination offered subsequent critics a new perspective for literary interpretation. Twentieth—century studies focus on various readings of Coleridge's poetry and criticism, and the controversies over the merit of his works have long since abated. Today, his problems of disorganization are largely ignored, and most critics agree that his writings constitute a seminal contribution to literature. While a few commentators, most notably J. Middleton Murry and F. R. Leavis, contend that both Coleridge's criticism and stature are overrated, most scholars acknowledge his poetic talent and insight and regard him as the intellectual center of the English Romantic movement.

(For further information about Coleridge's life and works, see *Nineteenth-Century Literature Criticism,* Vol. 9, and *Dictionary of Literary Biography,* Vol. 93: *British Romantic Poets, 1789-1832.*)

CRITICAL COMMENTARY

SAMUEL TAYLOR COLERIDGE
(essay date 1817)

[In the following excerpt from his 1817 *Biographia Literaria*, Coleridge offers his definition of imagination and fancy.]

The imagination . . . I consider either as primary, or secondary. The primary imagination I hold to be the living power and prime agent of all human perception, and as a repetition in the finite mind of the eternal act of creation in the infinite I AM. The secondary I consider as an echo of the former, co-existing with the conscious will, yet still as identical with the primary in the kind of its agency, and differing only in degree, and in the mode of its operation. It dissolves, diffuses, dissipates, in order to re-create; or where this process is rendered impossible, yet still, at all events, it struggles to idealize and to unify. It is essentially *vital*, even as all objects (as objects) are essentially fixed and dead.

Fancy, on the contrary, has no other counters to play with but fixities and definites. The fancy is indeed no other than a mode of memory emancipated from the order of time and space; and blended with, and modified by that empirical phaenomenon of the will which we express by the word *choice*. But equally with the ordinary memory it must receive all its materials ready made from the law of association. (p. 167)

Samuel Taylor Coleridge, "On the Imagination, or Esemplastic Power," in his *Biographia Literaria; or, Biographical Sketches of My Literary Life and Opinions*, edited by George Watson, 1817. Reprint by Dutton, 1960, pp. 161-67.

HENRY NELSON COLERIDGE
(essay date 1834)

[The following excerpt, by Coleridge's nephew Henry Nelson Coleridge, is from an essay that is widely recognized as the first serious study of Coleridge's poems, particularly "Kubla Khan" and "Christabel." Here, the critic praises Coleridge's technical skill and comments on the connection between the poet's metaphysical pursuits and his verse.]

[The best poems in *The Poetical Works of S. T. Coleridge*] are distinguished in a remarkable degree by the perfection of their rhythm and metrical arrangement. The labour bestowed upon this point must have been very great; the tone and quantity of words seem weighed in scales of gold. It will, no doubt, be considered ridiculous by the Fannii and Fanniae of our day to talk of varying the trochee with the iambus, or of resolving either into the tribrach. Yet it is evident to us that these, and even minuter points of accentual scansion, have been regarded by Mr. Coleridge as worthy of study and observation. We do not, of course, mean that rules of this kind were always in his mind while composing, any more than that an expert disputant is always thinking of the distinctions of mood and figure, whilst arguing; but we certainly believe that Mr. Coleridge has almost from the commencement of his poetic life looked upon versification as constituting in and by itself a much more important branch of the art poetic than most of his eminent contemporaries appear to have done. And this more careful study shows itself in him in no technical peculiarities or fantastic whims, against which the genius of our language revolts; but in a more exact adaptation of the movement to the feeling, and in a finer selection of particular words with reference to their local fitness for sense and sound. Some of his poems are complete models of versification, exquisitely easy to all appearance, and subservient to the meaning, and yet so subtle in the links and transitions of the parts as to make it impossible to produce the same effect merely by imitating the syllabic metre as it stands on the surface. The secret of the sweetness lies within, and is involved in the feeling. It is this remarkable power of making his verse musical that gives a peculiar character to Mr. Coleridge's lyric poems. In some of the smaller pieces, as the conclusion of the **'Kubla Khan,'** for example, not only the lines by themselves are musical, but the whole passage sounds all at once as an outburst or crash of harps in the still air of autumn. The verses seem as if *played* to the ear upon some unseen instrument. And the poet's manner of reciting verse is similar. It is not rhetorical, but musical: so very near recitative, that for any one else to attempt it would be ridiculous; and yet it is perfectly miraculous with what exquisite searching he elicits and makes sensible every particle of the meaning, not leaving a shadow of a shade of the feeling, the mood, the degree, untouched. . . . Mr. Coleridge has no *ear* for music, as it is technically called. Master as he is of the intellectual recitative, he could not *sing* an air to save his life. But

Principal Works

The Fall of Robespierre [with Robert Southey] (drama) 1794

Poems on Various Subjects (poetry) 1796; also published as Poems [revised edition], 1797

Ode on the Departing Year (poetry) 1797

Osorio [first publication] (drama) 1797; also published as Remorse [revised edition], 1813

Fears in Solitude (poetry) 1798

*Lyrical Ballads [with William Wordsworth] (poetry) 1798; also published as Lyrical Ballads [revised edition], 1800

Wallenstein [translator; from the dramas Die Piccolomini and Wallensteins Tod by Johann Christoph Friedrich von Schiller] (drama) 1800

Poems (poetry) 1803

Christabel. Kubla Khan: A Vision. The Pains of Sleep (poetry) 1816

The Statesman's Manual (essay) 1816

Biographia Literaria; or, Biographical Sketches of My Literary Life and Opinions (essays) 1817

Sibylline Leaves (poetry) 1817

Zapolya: A Christmas Tale (drama) 1817

The Poetical Works of Samuel Taylor Coleridge. 3 vols. (poetry, dramas, and translation) 1828

The Literary Remains of Samuel Taylor Coleridge. 4 vols. (poetry, essays, and drama) 1836-39

The Complete Works of Samuel Taylor Coleridge. 7 vols. (poetry, dramas, translation, and essays) 1853

Coleridge's Miscellaneous Criticism (criticism) 1936

Collected Letters. 6 vols. (letters) 1956-71

The Notebooks of Samuel Taylor Coleridge. 3 vols. (notebooks) 1957-73

*This work includes the poem "The Rime of the Ancient Mariner."

his delight in music is intense and unweariable, and he can detect good from bad with unerring discrimination. (pp. 7-8)

There are some lines entitled **'Hendecasyllables,'** . . . which struck us a good deal by the skill with which an equivalent for the well-known Catullian measure has been introduced into our language. We think the metrical construction of these few verses very ingenious, and do not remember at this moment anything in English exactly like it. . . .

The minute study of the laws and properties of metre is observable in almost every piece in these volumes. Every kind of lyric measure, rhymed and unrhymed, is attempted with success; and we doubt whether, upon the whole, there are many specimens of the heroic couplet or blank verse superior in construction to what Mr. Coleridge has given us. (p. 9)

[Whether] in verse, or prose, or conversation, Mr. Coleridge's mind may be fitly characterized as an energetic mind—a mind always at work, always in a course of reasoning. He cares little for anything, merely because it was or is; it must be referred, or be capable of being referred, to some law or principle, in order to attract his attention. This is not from ignorance of the facts of natural history or science. His written and published works alone sufficiently show how constantly and accurately he has been in the habit of noting all the phenomena of the material world around us; and the great philosophical system now at length in preparation for the press demonstrates, we are told, his masterly acquaintance with almost all the sciences, and with not a few of the higher and more genial of the arts. Yet

his vast acquirements of this sort are never put forward by or for themselves; it is in his apt and novel illustrations, his indications of analogies, his explanation of anomalies, that he enables the hearer or reader to get a glimpse of the extent of his practical knowledge. He is always reasoning out from an inner point, and it is the inner point, the principle, the law which he labours to bring forward into light. (pp. 12-13)

All this, whether for praise or for blame, is perceptible enough in Mr. Coleridge's verse, but perceptible, of course, in such degree and mode as the law of poetry in general, and the nature of the specific poem in particular, may require. But the main result from this frame and habit of his mind is very distinctly traceable in the uniform subjectivity of almost all his works. He does not belong to that grand division of poetry and poets which corresponds with paintings and painters; of which Pindar and Dante are the chief;—those masters of the picturesque, who, by a felicity inborn, view and present everything in the completeness of actual objectivity—and who have a class derived from and congenial with them, presenting few pictures indeed, but always full of picturesque matter; of which secondary class Spenser and Southey may be mentioned as eminent instances. To neither of these does Mr. Coleridge belong; in his **'Christabel,'** there certainly are several *distinct pictures* of great beauty; but he, as a poet, clearly comes within the other division which answers to music and the musician, in which you have a magnificent mirage of words with the subjective associations of the poet curling, and twisting, and creeping round, and through, and above every part of it. . . . [When] we point out the intense personal feeling, the self-projection, as it were, which characterizes Mr. Coleridge's poems, we mean that such feeling is the soul and spirit, not the whole body and form, of his poetry. For surely no one has ever more earnestly and constantly borne in mind the maxim of Milton, that poetry ought to be *simple, sensuous, and impassioned*. . . .The poetry before us is distinct and clear, and accurate in its imagery; but the imagery is rarely or never exhibited for description's sake alone; it is rarely or never exclusively objective; that is to say, put forward as a spectacle, a picture on which the mind's eye is to rest and terminate. You may if your sight is short, or your imagination cold, regard the imagery in itself and go no farther; but the poet's intention is that you should feel and imagine a great deal more than you see. His aim is to awaken in the reader the same mood of mind, the same cast of imagination and fancy whence issued the associations which animate and enlighten his pictures. You must think with him, must sympathize with him, must suffer yourself to be lifted out of your own school of opinion or faith, and fall back upon your own consciousness, an unsophisticated man. . . . From his earliest youth to this day, Mr. Coleridge's poetry has been a faithful mirror reflecting the images of his mind. (pp. 13-14)

No writer has ever expressed the great truth that man makes his world, or that it is the imagination which shapes and colours all things—more vividly than Coleridge. Indeed, he is the first who, in the age in which we live, brought forward that position into light and action. (p. 14)

The **'Remorse'** and **'Zapolya'** strikingly illustrate the predominance of the meditative, pausing habit of Mr. Coleridge's mind. (p. 23)

'Zapolya' is professedly an imitation of [William Shakespeare's] 'The Winter's Tale,' and was not composed with any view to scenic representation. Yet it has some situations of dramatic interest in no respect inferior to the most striking in the **'Remorse;'** the incidents are new and surprising, and the dialogue is throughout distinguished by liveliness and force. The predominant character of the whole is, like that of the **'Remorse,'** a mixture of the pastoral and the romantic, but much more apparent and exclusive than in the latter. . . . **'Zapolya'** has never been appreciated as it deserves. It is, in our opinion, the most *elegant* of Mr. Coleridge's poetical works; there is a softness of tone, and a delicacy of colouring about it, which have a peculiar charm of their own, and amply make amends for some deficiency of strength in the drawing. (pp. 26-7)

Mr. Coleridge's dramatic talent is of a very high and original kin. His chief excellence lies in the dialogue itself,—his main defect in the conception, or at least in the conduct, of the plot. We can hardly say too much for the one, or too little for the other. (p. 28)

[The] **'Ancient Mariner'** is, and will ever be, one of the most perfect pieces of imaginative poetry, not only in our language, but in the literature of all Europe. We have, certainly, sometimes doubted whether the miraculous destruction of the vessel in the presence of the pilot and hermit, was not an error, in respect of its bringing the purely preternatural into too close contact with the actual framework of the poem. The only link between those scenes of out-of-the-world wonders, and the wedding guest, should, we rather suspect, have been the blasted, unknown being himself who described them. There should have been no other witnesses of the truth of any part of the tale, but the 'Ancient Mariner' himself. This by the way: but take the work altogether, there is nothing else like it; it is a poem by itself; between it and other compositions, . . . there is a chasm which you cannot overpass; the sensitive reader feels himself insulated, and a sea of wonder and mystery flows round him as round the spell-stricken ship itself. . . . The **'Ancient Mariner'** displays Mr. Coleridge's peculiar mastery over the wild and preternatural in a brilliant manner; but in his next poem, **'Christabel,'** the exercise of his power in this line is still more skilful and singular. The thing attempted in **'Christabel'** is the most difficult of execution in the whole field of romance—witchery by daylight; and the success is complete. (pp. 28-9)

We are not amongst those who wish to have **'Christabel'** finished. It cannot be finished. The poet has spun all he could without snapping. The theme is too fine and subtle to bear much extension. It is better as it is, imperfect as a story, but complete as an exquisite production of the imagination, differing in form and colour from the **'Ancient Mariner,'** yet differing in effect from it only so as the same powerful faculty is directed to the feudal or the mundane phases of the preternatural.

From these remarkable works we turn to the love poems scattered through the volumes before us. There is something very peculiar in Mr. Coleridge's exhibition of the most lovely of the passions. His love is not gloomy as Byron's, nor gay as Moore's, nor intellectual as Wordsworth's. It is a clear unclouded passion, made up of an exquisite respect and gentleness, a knightly tenderness and courtesy,—pure yet ardent, impatient yet contemplative. (p. 30)

We know no writer of modern times whom it would not be easier to characterize in one page than Coleridge in two. The volumes before us contain so many integral efforts of imagination, that a distinct notice of each is indispensable, if we would form a just conclusion upon the total powers of the man. Wordsworth, Scott, Moore, Byron, Southey, are incomparably more uniform in the direction of their poetic mind. But if you look over these volumes for indications of their author's poetic powers, you find him appearing in at least half a dozen shapes, so different from each other, that it is in vain to attempt to mass them together. It cannot indeed be said, that he has ever composed what is popularly termed a *great* poem; but he is great in several lines, and the union of such powers is an essential term in a fair estimate of his genius. . . . It is the *predominance* of this power, which, in our judgment, constitutes the essential difference between Coleridge and any other of his great contemporaries. He is the most imaginative of the English poets since Milton. Whatever he writes, be it on the most trivial subject, be it in the most simple strain, his imagination, *in spite of himself,* affects it. (pp. 33-4)

We speak of Coleridge . . . as the poet of imagination; and we add, that he is likewise the poet of thought and verbal harmony. That his thoughts are sometimes hard and sometimes even obscure, we think must be admitted; it is an obscurity of which all very subtle thinkers are occasionally guilty, either by attempting to express evanescent feelings for which human language is an inadequate vehicle, or by expressing, however adequately, thoughts and distinctions to which the common reader is unused. (p. 34)

Henry Nelson Coleridge, "Coleridge's 'Poetical Works'," in *The Quarterly Review,* Vol. LII, No. CIII, August, 1834, pp. 1-38.

J. SHAWCROSS
(essay date 1907)

[In the excerpt below, Shawcross examines Coleridge's theory of fancy and imagination.]

The variety of motives which gave rise to the *Biographia Literaria* reveals itself in the miscellaneous character of the work. Intended in the first instance as a preface to the *Sibylline Leaves,* it grew into a literary autobiography which itself came to demand a preface. This preface itself outgrew its purposed limits, and was incorporated in the whole work, which was finally issued in two parts—the autobiography (two vols.) and the poems. Originally, no doubt, Coleridge's motive in writing the preface was to explain and justify his own style and practice in poetry. To this end it was necessary that he should state clearly the points on which he took exception to Wordsworth's [poetic] theory. All this, however, seemed to involve an examination of the nature of poetry and the poetic faculty: and this in its turn suggested, if it did not demand, a radical inquiry into the preconditions of knowledge in general. To Coleridge . . . the distinction of fancy and imagination was a distinction of equal import for philosophy and for poetry. But having thus been led to a consideration

of fundamental problems, there was danger that he would pursue them for their own sake; especially when the occasion was afforded him of attacking his old bugbear, the mechanical philosophy. (p. lv)

In the opening page of the work itself, Coleridge anticipates the charge of a personal motive in writing. 'The narration' (he writes) 'has been used chiefly for the purpose of giving continuity to the work, in part for the reflections suggested to me by the particular events: but still more as introductory to a statement of my principles in Politics, Religion, and Philosophy, and the application of the rules, deduced from philosophical principles, to poetry and criticism.' But it cannot be said that the narrative portion of the book, detached and fragmentary as it is, really fulfils this introductory purpose, or relieves the student from the task of reconstructing, from this and other sources, the gradual development of Coleridge's opinions to the point which they had now attained. Indeed, as Coleridge admits, the very narrative itself was made to serve three distinct ends, each of which was an obstacle to the fulfilment of the other two.

But enough has been said of the miscellaneous character of the *Biographia Literaria.* It remains to consider what definite contribution to Coleridge's theory of the imagination it actually contains. (p. lvi)

In tracing the origin of the theory in Coleridge's mind . . . , his early doubts as to the validity of the mechanical explanation of knowledge, if they did not originate in, were yet confirmed by, the testimony of the imagination in its poetic function. Its power to reveal a new aspect of things, and compel our faith in its revelation, naturally suggested a new attitude to the problem of knowledge. For although on the one hand the mind in its poetic interpretation of outward forms is limited and determined by the nature of those forms, yet it is equally free and creative in respect of them, in so far as it invests them with a being and a life which as mere objects of the senses they do not possess. Moreover, the basis of this activity being the desire for self-expression (not of the individual merely, but of the universal self), the fitness of the external world to be the vehicle of such expression pointed to its participation in a common reality with the self which it reflected. But the fact that the imagination is a restricted gift rendered it impossible to regard it as universally active in the process of knowledge.

At this point Coleridge became acquainted with Kant's works and found in his account of the mind a definite place assigned to the imagination as an indispensable factor in the attainment of knowledge. For since the understanding, as a purely intellectual faculty, was incapable of reaching the manifold of sense, it was necessary to call in the services of the imagination, which in virtue of its twofold nature presents that manifold in a form suitable for its subsumption under the categories. The imagination as thus operative is not a mere faculty of images: still less is it the faculty of poetic invention: its peculiar characteristic lies in the power of figurative synthesis, or of delineating the forms of things in general. Moreover, in performing this function it is subject to the laws of the understanding: its procedure, therefore, contributes nothing to our knowledge of the origin of phenomena. But for this very reason of its conformity to the understanding, its deliverances are objective, that is, valid for all thinking beings: and are in this respect to be distinguished from the creations of its reproductive activity, which as subject to empirical conditions (the laws of association) have merely individual and contingent validity. Finally, in the aesthetic judgement, the imagination, though still receiving its law from the understanding, is yet so far free, that its activity is determined not by the necessity of a particular cognition, but by its own character as an organ of knowledge in general.

Kant thus distinguishes three functions or activities of the imagination: as reproductive, in which it is subject to empirical conditions; as productive, in which it acts spontaneously and determines phenomena instead of being determined by them, but yet in accordance with a law of the understanding; and as aesthetic, when it attains its highest degree of freedom in respect of the object, which it regards as material for a possible, not an actual and impending, act of cognition.

For the first and last of these functions Coleridge had already found a name and a description. To Kant's reproductive imagination corresponds the fancy. To the imagination as poetic Coleridge assigns . . . a far greater dignity and significance than Kant could possibly allow it. For in Kant's view even the highest activity of the imagination (its symbolical interpretation of beauty) has no warranty in the supersensuous ground of things. Meanwhile the second of these three functions, to Kant by far the most important (as a universal factor in knowledge), presented Coleridge with fresh matter for reflection. Here, too, it was impossible for him to stop short with Kant. That insight into reality which characterized the imagination in its highest potency must also adhere to it in its universal use. The fact that the poet, in impressing his conscious self upon the world of objects, seemed to penetrate to the core of their being, might at least suggest the explanation of all knowledge as founded on a similar self-recognition of the subject in the object, and indicate the imagination as the organ of this recognition.

From Kant, however, Coleridge received no justification for such an hypothesis, though a suggestion might have been furnished in the unity of apperception as the basic principle of all acts of knowledge. On passing to the study of Fichte, he found a development of Kantean doctrine for which he had only a qualified approval. 'By commencing with an act, instead of a thing

or substance . . . , Fichte supplied the idea of a system truly metaphysical, and of a metaphysique truly systematic (i.e. having its spring and principle within itself). But this fundamental idea he overlaid with a heavy mass of mere notions. . . . Thus his theory degenerates into a crude egoismus, a boastful and hyperstoic hostility to Nature, as lifeless, godless, and altogether unholy.' It is not difficult to understand how little such a conception of nature would be welcome to Coleridge. Nor could the account of the imagination in Fichte's system commend itself to him. For having no external foundation for its activity, this faculty is consumed in the perpetual endeavour to outstrip the limits of self, in a restless self-torture which issues in unsubstantial mockeries of creation. Such a conclusion, however much it might appeal to certain moods in Coleridge as in us all, was certainly inimical to the faith which never wholly deserted him—the belief in a Spirit which spoke directly to the soul of man, but also revealed itself mediately through the forms of nature.

How far Coleridge's endeavours to find a philosophical expression for this faith had brought him when first his study of Schelling began, is a matter which cannot be accurately determined; nor what those 'genial coincidences' may have been, to which he alludes in the *Biographia Literaria*. The large verbal borrowings from Schelling in the course of the 'deduction of the imagination' suggest that when he began to write he had accepted Schelling's account of the faculty, or at least found his own conclusions happily expressed therein. (pp. lvii-lx)

Now to the imagination Schelling daringly assigns a function of high, indeed of the highest, dignity and importance. It is proclaimed as the organ of truth, and of truth not as the artist only, but as the philosopher apprehends it. And the quality, which makes it thus their common instrument, is the power of reconciling opposites in virtue of their inner unity; of discovering the ground of harmony between apparent contradictories. Such a reconciliation is demanded by transcendental philosophy. For the task of this philosophy is to discover *in consciousness itself* an explanation of the apparent contradiction involved in the fact, that the self or subject is conceived as both active and passive as regards the object, as both determining it and determined by it. Such a solution can take only one form: the recognition, namely, that these apparently opposed and unrelated activities are really but a twofold aspect of the same activity, that the power which determines is also the power which is determined. As the transcendental philosopher starts from the fact of consciousness, it is in consciousness itself that he must discover the original and prototype of this activity. And this he finds in the act of pure self-consciousness, in which the subject becomes its own object, and subject and object are therefore identical. Now from its very nature the apprehension of this pure self-consciousness, or pure activity returning upon itself, cannot be other than immediate and intuitive. Moreover, as reflecting the ultimate ground of all knowledge, it is productive and an act of the same power, whereby that ultimate principle is reflected objectively in the work of art. In either case the reflective or productive power is the imagination.

But the imagination, in this its highest potency, is itself identical in kind, though not in degree, with that very activity which it contemplates and reflects. For the original act whereby pure intelligence (the Absolute or Urselbst, as Schelling calls it) objectifies and limits itself in order to contemplate itself in its limitation, is an act of imagination, and indeed the primary act, an act which is subsequently repeated in the experience of every individual mind, in becoming conscious of an external world. This degree of imagination is common to all thinking beings. But as we rise in the scale of self-knowledge, the faculty reaches a higher intensity and is confined proportionately in extent, till in its highest power it pertains only to a chosen few. (pp. lx-lxi)

In attributing to the imagination the function in consciousness of reconciling opposites and so underlying all acts of knowledge, Schelling is but developing the conception of Kant, according to which the faculty mediates between the understanding and the senses. But to Kant this reconciling power implied no community of nature between the self and its object; the knowledge to which it contributed was valid only for the self from which it drew its unifying principle. When, however, the imagination is conceived as recognizing the inherent interdependence of subject and object (as complementary aspects of a single reality), its dignity is immeasurably raised. . . . Coleridge rightly apprehended the agreement of Schelling's conception, in its cardinal features, with his own; to unify and so to create is, in the view of both writers, the characteristic function of the imagination. And of this unification the principle is found in the self, conceived not abstractly but as the whole nature of man, or all that is essential to that nature. Thought and feeling, in their original identity, demand expression through an organ which itself partakes of both.

To Schelling's conception it has been objected, that in constituting the imagination the peculiar organ of philosophy, he countenances the claim of every visionary to a respectful hearing, be his system never so wild and fantastic. But this is to misinterpret his meaning, and to fall into the common error of confounding fancy with imagination. If the faculty of imagination be not equally active in all men, its activity is none the less independent of the idiosyncrasies of the individual, its witness is none the less a witness of universal validity. By calling it the organ of philosophy, Schelling means that philosophy must start from a fundamental experi-

ence, and that it is the imagination which renders this fundamental experience possible. And to Schelling this ultimate fact of experience appeared to be given, inwardly, in what he called the intellectual intuition, and outwardly, in the products of art. (pp. lxii-lxiii)

But at the same time Schelling acknowledged that of these facts one at least (the object of intellectual intuition) could not be made universally conscious. He therefore started from a datum which it was not in the power of all men to realize. No appeal to a universal spiritual faculty was here possible. All that lay open to him was to point to the creations of art, as the guarantee and evidence (evidence made visible to all) of that ultimate ground of all knowledge and being which the philosopher alone could directly contemplate.

Now, that poetry and philosophy, if their message be true, must be founded on the same spiritual experience, Coleridge would have readily acknowledged; indeed, it was the truth for which he had been contending throughout his life. To this truth, moreover, his own mental history bore witness; for he was conscious that the same impulse lay at the root of his poetic and speculative creation, the impulse to give again that which he had felt and known. By his own confession in later years, it was the same 'spirit of power' which had stirred him throughout—

> A matron now, of sober mien,
> Yet radiant still and with no earthly sheen,
> Whom as a faery child my childhood woo'd
> Even in my dawn of youth—Philosophy;
> Tho' then, unconscious of herself, pardie,
> She bore no other name than Poesy.

And his description of his poetic manner, given in that 'down of youth' which he here recalls, shows that he was conscious of his inclination to confuse these kindred modes of communicating truth. It was the conviction that in either case the whole self must be active in the apprehension of reality, which in the first instance opened his eyes to the error of the empiricists in their one-sided interpretation of a partial aspect of things. And it was to a poet (to *the* poet of the age) that he looked for a final confutation of this false philosophy. In Wordsworth's *Excursion* he had anticipated 'the first genuine philosophic poem', which in its conclusion was to have emphasized the message of which the age stood most in need. (pp. lxiv-lxv)

This task, however, Wordsworth had shown no inclination to undertake; and the sense that it was still waiting to be accomplished was present with Coleridge, when he was composing his literary life. And here the 'genial coincidence' of his opinions with those of Schelling stood him in good stead. For at this time at least he seems to have believed that in the transcendental philosophy was exemplified this process of 'true idealism perfecting itself in realism, and realism refining itself into idealism', and this through intuitions as 'alone adequate to the majesty of truth'. Hence it was that he incorporated into his book so much of Schelling's doctrines as suited his immediate purpose, without perhaps reflecting on their ultimate implications. (p. lxv)

After introducing, in chapter iv, the distinction of imagination and fancy, Coleridge proceeds to investigate it psychologically. He begins with an historical discussion of the theory of association, and compares Aristotle's theory with that of Hartley; the inadequacy of the 'mechanical theory' is then exposed, and the true nature of association explained. Having thus cleared the ground, Coleridge next purposed to show 'by what influences of the choice and judgement the associative power becomes either memory or fancy, and to appropriate the remaining offices of the mind to the reason and the imagination'. But this promise of a psychological treatment of the distinction is not fulfilled: indeed we hear little more of the fancy until, in the final summing up, it is defined side by side, or rather in contrast, with the imagination. After some intervening chapters of general or biographical interest, Coleridge advances to the statement of his system, from which he proposes 'to deduce the memory with all the other functions of intelligence', but which, as a matter of fact, he views in connexion with one faculty only—the imagination. In a series of theses he discovers the final principle of knowledge as 'the identity of subject and object' in 'the Sum, or I Am', which 'is a subject which becomes a subject by the act of constructing itself objectively to itself; but which never is an object except for itself, and only so far as by the same act it becomes a subject'. Originally, however, it is not an object, but 'an absolute subject for which all, itself included, may become an object'. It must, therefore, be an act. Thus it follows that consciousness in its various phases is but a self-development of absolute spirit or intelligence. This process of self-development Coleridge asks us to conceive 'under the idea of an indestructible power with two counteracting forces, which by a metaphor borrowed from astronomy, we may call the centrifugal and centripetal forces'. Such a power he 'assumes for his present purpose, in order to deduce from it a faculty the generation, agency, and application of which form the contents of the ensuing chapter'.

This faculty is the imagination or esemplastic power. (pp. lxvi-lxvii)

The distinction [drawn by Coleridge between the primary and secondary imagination] is evidently between the imagination as universally active in consciousness (creative in that it externalizes the world of objects by opposing it to the self) and the same faculty in a heightened power as creative in a poetic sense. In the first case our exercise of the power is unconscious: in the second the will directs, though it does not deter-

An illustration from "The Rime of the Ancient Mariner." The Mariner seeks absolution for killing the albatross.

mine, the activity of the imagination. The imagination of the ordinary man is capable only of detaching the world of experience from the self and contemplating it in its detachment; but the philosopher penetrates to the underlying harmony and gives it concrete expression. The ordinary consciousness, with no principle of unification, sees the universe as a mass of particulars: only the poet can depict this whole as reflected in the individual parts. It is in this sense (as Coleridge had written many years before) that to the poet 'each thing has a life of its own, and yet they have all our life'. And a similar contrast is present to Schelling when he writes that 'through the objective world as a whole, but never through a single object in it, an Infinite is represented: whereas every single work of art represents Infinity'.

With the definition of fancy which now follows we are already familiar. / 'Fancy has no other counters to play with but fixities and definites. The fancy is indeed no other than a mode of memory emanicipated from the order of time and space; and blended with and modified by that empirical phenomenon of the will which we express by the word choice. But equally with the ordinary memory it must receive its materials all ready-made from the laws of association.' . . . As connected by the fancy, objects are viewed in their limitations and particularity; they are 'fixed and dead' in the sense that their connexion is mechanical and not organic. The law, indeed, which governs it is derived from the mind itself, but the links are supplied by the individual properties of the objects. Fancy is, in fact, the faculty of mere images or impressions, as imagination is the faculty of intuitions. It is in this sense that Coleridge sees in their opposition an emblem of the wider contrast between the mechanical philosophy and the dynamic, the false and the true.

But with all this we have nothing of the promised 'deduction' of the imagination, still less that of the memory and other 'functions of intelligence'. The definition of fancy is founded, apparently, on the psychological discussion of the earlier chapters, not on the theory of knowledge propounded later on. As to the imagination, it seems at first sight, from the close coincidence of Coleridge's statement with that of Schelling, that he had accepted Schelling's system wholesale and with it his account of that faculty. But the sudden termination of the argument, and the unsatisfactory vagueness of the final summary, in which he does not really commit himself to Schelling's position, suggest that that position was not in fact his own. And this suggestion is confirmed by other evidence.

That Coleridge's attitude from the first to Schelling's philosophy was by no means one of unqualified approval, we have already seen. But in the *Transcendental Idealism* which he studied at a time when he was deeply engaged on aesthetic problems, he found a peculiar attraction. Here for the first time the significance of 'the vision and the faculty divine' seemed to be adequately realized. At first it appeared to Coleridge that he had met with a systematized statement of his own convictions, the metaphysic of poetry of which he was in search. But he was soon to find that the supposed concurrence did not exist—that the Transcendentalism of Schelling in fact elevated the imagination at the expense of other and more important factors in our spiritual consciousness.

No doubt the feature most unsatisfactory to Coleridge in the *Transcendental Idealism* and in Schelling's philosophy in general was its vague conception of the ultimate ground of reality. For Schelling's absolute, which is prior to and behind self-consciousness, from which self-consciousness originates, is conceived as mere self-less identity or total indifference, of which all that can be said is that it is neither subject nor object, but the mere negation of both. From such an abstract principle, it is evident, no living bond of union can be derived to hold together the complementary elements in self-consciousness when it is mysteriously generated: hence subject and object, intelligence and nature, appear as parallel lines of co-ordinate value, connected by a merely logical necessity. In such a system there was clearly no place for the God of Coleridge's faith, as a Spirit to whom self-consciousness is essential, a

Being 'in whom supreme reason and a most holy will are one with an infinite power'. Thus it is that in his own account in the *Biographia Literaria* Coleridge is all the time striving to identify Schelling's 'intellectual intuition' of subject and object in their absolute identity with the religious intuition, the direct consciousness of God.

But this, of course, involves him in contradictions. For the power of intellectual intuition, the philosophic imagination is, as Schelling conceived, a gift confined to a favoured few, not a state of being in which all can, by moral effort, raise themselves: his philosophy cannot therefore take the form of a moral appeal. And here Coleridge, so long as his thoughts are concerned primarily with the imagination and its deduction, is inclined to follow him. The solution of the problem is to discover 'for whom and to whom the philosophical intuition is possible'. For 'there is a philosophic no less than a poetic genius, which is differenced from the highest perfection of talent, not by degree, but by kind'. If, however, this intuition of the supersensuous is none other than the consciousness of God, it must evidently be regarded as a spiritual condition accessible to all: and in that case its organ must be in a faculty essential to the spiritual constitution of man. (pp. lxviii-lxxi)

J. Shawcross, in an introduction to *Biographia Literaria, Vol. I,* by S. T. Coleridge, edited by J. Shawcross, 1907. Reprint by Oxford University Press, London, 1958, pp. xi-lxxxix.

JOHN LIVINGSTON LOWES
(essay date 1927)

[In the following excerpt, Lowes confirms Coleridge's own assessment of "The Ancient Mariner" as "a work of pure imagination."]

'The Rime of the Ancient Mariner' is 'a work of pure imagination,' and Coleridge himself has so referred to it. And this study, far from undermining that declaration, is lending it confirmation at every turn. For a work of pure imagination is not something fabricated by a *tour de force* from nothing, and suspended, without anchorage in fact, in the impalpable either of a visionary world. No conception could run more sharply counter to the truth. And I question, in the light of all that is now before us, whether any other poem in English is so closely compacted out of fact, or so steeped in the thought and instinct with the action which characterized its time. Keats, in 'La belle Dame sans Merci,' distilled into a single poem the quintessence of mediaeval romance and balladry. And what 'La belle Dame sans

Merci' is to the gramarye of the Middle Ages, **'The Rime of the Ancient Mariner'** is to the voyaging, Neoplatonizing, naively scientific spirit of the closing eighteenth century. It has swept within its assimilating influence a bewildering diversity of facts in which contemporary interest was active. The facts are forgotten, and the poem stays. But the power that wrought the facts into the fabric of a vision outlasts both. And if we are rifling the urns where the dead bones of fact have long quietly rested, it is because the unquenchable spirit which gives beauty for ashes is there not wholly past finding out. (pp. 240-41)

When Coleridge set to work on **'The Rime of the Ancient Mariner,'** its plot, not unlike the budding morrow in midnight, lay . . . , beneath a queer jumble of fortuitous suggestions: an old seaman, a skeleton ship with figures in it, a shot bird, a 'spectral persecution,' a ship sailed by dead men, a crew of angelic spirits. The formative design of the voyage, surpassingly adapted as it was to the incorporation of masses of associated impressions, possessed in itself a large simplicity of outline. The supernatural machinery (at the outset a thing of shreds and patches) presented, on the other hand, a problem complex to the last degree. . . . [In] the moulding of the separate fragments that underlie the plot, subliminal associations and conscious imaginative control have again worked hand in hand. And when at last the poem was completed, the plot which Coleridge had wrought from his intractable and heterogeneous elements was a consistent and homogeneous whole.

For the action has a beginning, and a middle, and an end. In the first half of the poem the agency of an avenging daemon is in the ascendent; in the second, the prevailing power of an angel band. It is an overt act of the Mariner which precipitates the daemonic vengeance; it is an inner impulse counter to the act which brings to pass the angelic intervention; and in the end it is 'the penance of life' which falls upon the rescued wanderer, a fated wanderer still. Exciting force, rising action, climax, falling action, catastrophe—all are there. And through the transfer to the Mariner of the legendary associations of the Wandering Jew, undying among the dead, Cruikshank's dream—its figures metamorphosed into into Death and Life-in-Death—is built into the basic structure of the plot. And under the influence of another ship, sailed by an angelic crew, the suggestion of the navigation of the Mariner's vessel by the bodies of the dead is so transformed as to provide that cardinal antithesis of angelic and daemonic agencies on which the action of the poem turns. And finally, by a stroke of consummate art, ship and poem alike are brought back in the end to the secure, familiar, happy world from which they had set out. The supernatural machinery is a masterpiece of constructive skill. But only, I think, in the light of the genesis of its compo-

nent parts can the triumph of the faculty which shaped them into unity be fully understood. (pp. 293-94)

'During the first year that Mr. Wordsworth and I were neighbours,' the famous fourteenth chapter of the *Biographia Literaria* begins, 'our conversations turned frequently on the two cardinal points of poetry, the power of exciting the sympathy of the reader by a faithful adherence to the truth of nature, and the power of giving the interest of novelty by the modifying colors of imagination. *The sudden charm, which accidents of light and shade, which moon-light or sun-set diffused over a known and familiar landscape,* appeared to represent the practicability of combining both. . . . In this idea originated the plan of the **"Lyrical Ballads"**; in which it was agreed, that my endeavours should be directed to persons and characters supernatural, or at least romantic; *yet so as to transfer from our inward nature a human interest and a semblance of truth* sufficient to procure for these shadows of imagination that willing suspension of disbelief for the moment which constitutes poetic faith. . . . With this view I wrote the **"Ancient Mariner."** '

The far-reaching significance of the paragraphs from which I have just quoted has met with universal recognition. It is, however, their vital bearing on the interpretation of a single basic element of **'The Ancient Mariner'** which concerns us now. For if Coleridge's words mean anything, they mean that some interest deeply human, anchored in the familiar frame of things, was fundamental to his plan. What, in a word, *is* the 'known and familiar landscape' which, in the poem, persists unchangeable beneath the accidents of light and shade? Are there truths of 'our inward nature' which do, in fact, uphold and cherish, as we read, our sense of actuality in a phantom universe, peopled with the shadows of a dream?

Every mortal who finds himself enmeshed in the inexplicable or the fantastic reaches out instinctively to something rooted deep, in order to retain a steadying hold upon reality. That is the predicament of the reader of **'The Ancient Mariner.'** There before him, to be sure, are the tangible facts of a charted course beneath the enduring skies. But the broad bright sun peers through skeleton ribs, and the moon glitters in the stony eyes of the reanimated dead, and the dance of the wan stars is a strange sight in the element. The most ancient heavens themselves have suffered, with the sea, the touch of goblin hands. But Coleridge's sure instinct was not, for all that, at fault. For through the spectral *mise en scène* of **'The Ancient Mariner,'** side by side with the lengthening orbit of the voyage, there runs, like the everlasting hills beneath the shifting play of eerie light, another moving principle, this time profoundly human: one of the immemorial, traditional convictions of the race. And it constitutes the most conspicuous formal element of the poem.

The last stanza of each of the first six parts of **'The**

Ancient Mariner' marks a step in the evolution of the action. Let us isolate their salient phrases for a moment from their context.

> Part I: . . .with my cross-bow
> *I shot the* Albatross.

There is the initial act.

> Part II: Instead of the cross, *the Albatross*
> *About my neck was hung.*

And the consequences first attach themselves to the transgressor.

> Part III: Four times fifty living men . . .
> They dropped down one by one . . .
> *And every soul, it passed me by,*
> *Like the whizz of my cross-bow!*

The consequences pass beyond the doer of the deed, and fall upon his shipmates. And now 'Life-in-Death begins her work on the Ancient Mariner,' till at last the turning-point of the action comes:

> O happy living things! no tongue
> Their beauty might declare:
> A spring of love gushed from my heart,
> And I blessed them unaware:
> Sure my kind saint took pity on me,
> And I blessed them unaware.

And then:

> Part IV: The self-same moment I could pray;
> And from my neck so free
> *The Albatross fell off, and sank*
> *Like lead into the sea.*

And so the burden of the transgression falls. But its results march on relentlessly.

> Part V: The other was a softer voice,
> As soft as honey-dew:
> Quoth he, 'The man hath penance done,
> *And penance more will do.'*

But the voyage, at least, has a destined end, and with the Hermit's entrance, a new note is heard.

> Part VI: He'll shrieve my soul, *he'll wash away*
> *The Albatross's blood.*

But even absolution leaves the doer, now as before, 'the deed's creature.'

> Part VII: Since then, at an uncertain hour,
> That agony returns:
> And till my ghastly tale is told,
> This heart within me burns.
>
> *I pass, like night, from land to land;*
> I have strange power of speech;
> That moment that his face I see,

I know the man that must hear me:
To him my tale I teach.

The train of cause and consequence knows no end. The Mariner has reached his haven, and his soul is shrieved, and now (in the brief comment of the gloss) *'the penance of life* falls on him.' And with that the action of the poem, though not the poem, ends.

There, thrown into strong relief by the strategic disposition of the stanzas which disclose it, is the ground-plan of **'The Ancient Mariner,'** as a master-architect has drawn and executed it. Through it runs the grand structural line of the voyage; and with its movement keep even pace—like those Intellectual Spirits that walk with the comets in their orbits—the daemons, and spectral shapes, and angels which are also agents in the action. Each of the three shaping principles has its own independent evolution, and each is interlocked with the unfolding of the other two. The interpenetration and coherence of the fundamental unifying elements of the poem is an achievement of constructive imagination, seconded by finished crafts-manship, such as only the supreme artists have at-tained. 'I learnt from him,' said Coleridge of his old master, Boyer, 'that Poetry, even that of the loftiest and, seemingly, that of the wildest odes, had a logic of its own, as severe as that of science; and more difficult, because more subtle, more complex, and dependent on more, and more fugitive causes.' And that describes the logic of **'The Ancient Mariner.'** (pp. 295-98)

The sequence . . . which follows from the Mari-ner's initial act accomplishes two ends: it unifies and (again to borrow Coleridge's coinage) it 'credibilizes' the poem. Has it still another end, to wit, edification? I am well aware of Coleridge's homiletical propensity. Nevertheless, to interpret the drift of **'The Ancient Mariner'** as didactic in its intention is to stultify both Coleridge and one's self. . . . Coleridge is not intent on teaching (profoundly as he believed the truth) that what a man soweth, that shall he also reap; he is giving coherence and inner congruity to the dream-like fabric of an imagined world. *Given that world*—and were it not given, there would be no poem, and were it otherwise given, this poem would not be—given that world, its inviolate keeping with itself becomes the sole condition of our acceptance, 'for the moment,' of its validity. And that requirement Coleridge, with surpassing skill, has met.

But the fulfilment of the indispensable condition carries with it an equally inevitable corollary. For that inner consistency which creates the illusion of reality is attained at the expense of the integrity of the ele-ments which enter into it. They too, no less than the poet's own nature, are 'subdued to what they work in, like the dyer's hand.' And once wrought into keeping with each other and with the whole, by as far as they have taken on the colours of their visionary world, by so far have they ceased to be, thus coloured, independent entities, with a status of their own. Even poetry cannot transform reality and have it, untransmuted, too. And through the very completeness of their incorporation with the texture of **'The Ancient Mariner,'** the truths of experience which run in sequence through it have lost, so far as any inculcation of a moral through the poem is concerned, all didactic value.

For the 'moral' of the poem, *outside the poem,* will not hold water. It is valid only within that magic circle. The great loop of the voyage from Equator to Equator around the Cape runs true to the chart. But daemons, and spectres, and angels, and *revenants* haunt its course, and the Mariner's voyage, magnificent metamorphosis of fact though it be, can scarcely be regarded as a profitable guide to the fauna of equatorial and arctic seas. The relentless line of cause and consequence runs likewise, unswerving as the voyage, through the poem. But consequence and cause, *in terms of the world of reality,* are ridiculously incommensurable. The shooting of a seabird carries in its train the vengeance of an aquatic daemon, acting in cojunction with a spectre-bark; and an impulse of love for other living creatures of the deep summons a troop of angels to navigate an unmanned ship. Moreover, because the Mariner has shot a bird, four times fifty sailors drop down dead, and the slayer himself is doomed to an endless life. The punishment, measured by the standards of a world of balanced penalties, palpably does not fit the crime. But the sphere of balanced penalties is not the given world in which the poem moves. Within *that* world, where birds have tutelary daemons and ships are driven by spectral and angelic powers, consequence and antecedent are in keeping—if for the poet's moment we accept the poet's premises. And the function of the ethical background of **'The Ancient Mariner,'** as Coleridge employs it, is to give the illusion of inevitable sequence to that superb inconsequence. The imaginative use of familiar moral values, like the imaginative use of the familiar outline of a voyage, is leagues away from the promulgation of edifying doctrine through the vehicle of a fairy-tale.

It would be a work of supererogation thus to labour a point which Coleridge himself might be thought to have rendered fairly obvious, were it not that this rudimentary principle of the poem has been persistently misinterpreted. A distinguished modern critic, for example, after drawing from certain verses of Browning the inference that, in Browning's view, 'to go out and mix one's self up with the landscape is the same as doing one's duty,' proceeds as follows: 'As a method of salvation this is even easier and more aesthetic than that of the Ancient Mariner, who, it will be remembered, is relieved of the burden of his transgression by admiring the color of watersnakes!' Occurring as it does

in a justly severe arraignment of pantheistic revery as 'a painless substitute for genuine spiritual effort,' this statement, despite its touch of piquant raillery, must be taken seriously as an interpretation of what Coleridge is supposed to teach. It is immaterial that the Mariner's admiration of water-snakes is not the means of salvation . . . which the plain words of the poem state. The value of the criticism lies in its exposition of what happens when one disregards the fundamental premises of a work of art, and interprets it as if it were solely a document in ethics. Carried to its logical conclusion, such an interpretation makes Coleridge precisely to the same degree the serious exponent of the moral fitness of the 'ruthless slaying of the crew because the Mariner had killed a bird'—and that is the *reductio ad absurdum* of everything. Coleridge, in some of those all too frequent moments when he was not a poet, may well have betrayed an addiction to 'pantheistic revery.' But when he wrote **'The Ancient Mariner,'** he was constructing on definite principles, with the clearest possible consciousness of what he was about, a work of pure imagination. (pp. 299-301)

There is no mistaking the point of [Coleridge's commentary in an 1830 conversation concerning **'The Ancient Mariner'**]. Coleridge may (he felt) have carried his premises too far for safety in a world of Mrs. Barbaulds who yearn for a moral with their poetry, as they hanker after bread and butter with their tea. With the moral sentiment so patent in the poem they would be bound to put in their thumb and exultantly pull out their plum—as indeed they have. '*The obtrusion of the moral sentiment so openly on the reader* as a principle or cause of action in a poem of such pure imagination'—that was what gave Coleridge pause. 'The only, or chief fault' of the poem, as he saw it, was a fault of technique. Instead of procuring a momentary suspension of disbelief, he ran the risk of implanting firmly a belief ! Of the historic Mrs. Barbauld he need on that score have had no fear. For her, even in the Mariner's valedictory piety, which does, I fear, warrant Coleridge's (and our own) regret, the moral sentiment was not obtruded openly enough. Had the mariner shot a shipmate instead of an albatross, she would have understood—and there would have been no **'Ancient Mariner.'**

For the very triviality of the act which precipitates its astounding train of consequences is the *sine qua non* of the impression which the poem was intended to convey. The discrepancy is essential to the design. And I really know no better short-cut to the comprehension of the poem's unique art than to imagine (as I lightly suggested a moment ago) the substitution of a human being, as the victim, for a bird. A tale the inalienable charm of which (as Coleridge himself perceived) lies in its kinship with the immortal fictions of the *Arabian Nights,* becomes, so motivated, a grotesque and unintelligible caricature of tragedy. Springing from the fall of a feather, it becomes a dome in air, built with music, yet with the shadows of supporting arch and pillar floating midway in the wave. For its world is, in essence, the world of a dream. Its inconsequence is the dream's irrelevance, and by a miracle of art we are possessed, as we read, with that sense of an intimate logic, consecutive and irresistible and more real than reality, which is the dream's supreme illusion. . . . The events in a dream do not produce each other, but they *seem* to. And that is the sole requirement of the action of the poem. (pp. 302-03)

Is a poem like **'The Ancient Mariner'** merely the upshot of the subliminal stirrings and convergences of countless dormant images? Or is it solely the product of an unremittingly deliberate constructive energy, recollecting of its own volition whatever is necessary to its ends, consciously willing every subtle blending of its myriad remembered images? Or is the seeming discord susceptible of resolution?

Behind **'The Rime of the Ancient Mariner'** lie crowding masses of impressions, incredible in their richness and variety. That admits no doubt. But the poem is not the sum of the impressions, as a heap of diamond dust is the sum of its shining particles; nor is the poet merely a sensitized medium for their reception and transmission. Beneath the poem lie also innumerable blendings and fusings of impressions, brought about below the level of conscious mental processes. That too is no longer open to question. But the poem is not the confluence of unconsciously merging images, as a pool of water forms from the coalescence of scattered drops; nor is the poet a somnambulist in a subliminal world. Neither the conscious impressions nor their unconscious interpenetrations constitute the poem. They are inseparable from it, but it is an entity which they do not create. On the contrary, every impression, every new creature rising from the potent waters of the Well, is what it now is through its participation in a *whole,* foreseen as a whole in each integral part—a whole which is the working out of a controlling imaginative design. The incommunicable, unique essence of the poem is its *form.*

And that form is the handiwork of choice, and a directing intelligence, and the sweat of a forging brain. The design of **'The Ancient Mariner'** did not lie, like a landscape in a crystal, pellucid and complete in Coleridge's mind from the beginning. It was there potentially, together with a hundred hovering alternatives, in a *mélange* of disparate and fortuitous suggestions. To drive through that farrago, 'straightforward as a Roman road,' the structural lines of the charted voyage, and the balanced opposition of daemonic and angelic agencies, and the unfolding consequences of the initial act—that involves more than the spontaneous welling up of images from secret depths. Beyond a doubt, that ceaseless

play of swift associations which flashed, like flying shuttles, through Coleridge's shaping brain, was present and coöperating from the first. I am not suggesting that Coleridge, on or about the 13th of November, 1797, withdrew from the rest of himself into the dry light of a 'cool cranium' to excogitate his plan, and then and only then threw open the doors to his other faculties, and summoned the sleeping images from their slumber. All his powers, conscious and unconscious, at the inception of the poem no less than while it 'grew and grew,' moved together when they moved at all. And there are few pages of this study which have not disclosed, directly or indirectly, traces of creative forces operating without reference to the bidding of the will. The last thing I have in mind is to minimize that obscure but powerful influence. But the energy which made the poem a poem, rather than an assemblage of radiant images, was the capacity of the human brain to think through chaos, and by sheer force of the driving will behind it to impose upon confusion the clarity of an ordered whole. And over the throng of luminous impressions and their subliminal confluences 'broods like the Day, a Master o'er a Slave,' the compelling power of the design. Whatever their origin, the component images have been wrought into conformity with a setting determined by the conception which constructs the poem. Through that amazing confluence of associations out of which sprang the shining creatures of the calm, strikes the huge shadow of the ship, lending the picture the symmetry which is the secret of its balanced beauty, and at the same time locking it into the basic structure of the poem. The breathless moment when the sun's rim dips, and the stars rush out, and the dark comes at one stride—that magnificent cluster-point in the chaos of elements has its *raison d'être,* not in itself, but in the incredible swiftness which the downward leap of night imparts to the disappearance of the spectre-bark. The bloody sun stands right up above the mast in a hot and copper sky, not for its own sake as a lucidly exact delineation of a galaxy of images, but as a great sea-mark in the controlling outline of the voyage. The images which sow the poem as with stars owe their meaning and their beauty to a form which is theirs by virtue of the evolution of a plan. (pp. 304-06)

But Coleridge, it will be pointed out, has put himself on record against himself. For when the poem reappeared, revised, in 1800, he appended a sub-title: **'A Poet's Reverie.'** (p. 306)

[If] there is anything on earth which **'The Ancient Mariner'** is *not,* it is a reverie. (p. 307)

John Livingston Lowes, in his *The Road to Xanadu: A Study in the Ways of the Imagination,* Houghton Mifflin Company, 1927, 639 p.

L. S. SHARMA

(essay date 1982)

[In the excerpt below, Sharma assesses Coleridge's Shakespearean criticism, focusing on his treatment of *King Lear* and *Hamlet*.]

For Coleridge Shakespeare is the ideal poet, the greatest poet of all time. His treatment of Shakespeare is basically sympathetic, appreciative, rather 'bardolatrous' because he was fully convinced that Shakespeare was the greatest genius the world had ever witnessed. Shakespeare is the consummation of Coleridge's idea of an ideal poet.

Coleridge was jealously proud of his *Hamlet* criticism where he thought he had done really pioneering work. He did not only psychoanalyse Shakespeare's characters but also vigorously defended and praised Shakespeare for his skillful preparation of the audience for a successful dramatic illusion. The study of the audience-psychology was always a fascinating pursuit for Coleridge. Somehow only his superb character analyses have been so much praised and unfortunately his theatrical preoccupations have been ignored. He was not blind to the merits of the stage like many of his contemporaries, and he was quite fascinated by the adroit way Shakespeare managed the problems of presenting his plays to the audience. The study of manuscript marginalia proves that he is not a one-sided dramatic critic and had genuine sympathy for the technical and theatrical side of the play also. He has tried to prove Shakespeare's mastery of creating the illusion and maintaining it once it was achieved.

Nearly half of his entire attention to the play is concentrated on the first act of *Hamlet* perhaps because of his intense interest in the supernatural and the psychology of the people confronted with ghosts and witches but chiefly because of his interest in the "exposition". He is at his very best in the criticism of the first act of *Hamlet.* Apart from the subtle psychological analyses of the character, Coleridge here gives us a sensitive and imaginative insight into the dramatic descriptions and techniques which make the audience conscious of the dramatic illusion. His discussion of Shakespeare's presentation of the ghost in Scenes one and four proves his obsessing interest in the psychology of the audience. This is how he describes the scene one:

The language is familiar: no poetic descriptions of the night . . . yet nothing bordering on the comic on the one hand, and no striving of the intellect on the other. It is a language of sensation among men who feared no charge of effeminacy for feeling what they felt no want of resolution to bear. Yet the armour, the dead silence, the watchfulness that first interupts it, the welcome relief of guard, the cold, the broken expressions as of a man's compelled attention to bodily feelings allowed no man,—all excellently accord with and prepare for the after gradual rise into—but above all into a tragedy the interest of which is eminently ad et apud intra, as Macbeth . . . is ad extra.

He invites our attention to the accuracy of Shakespeare's pictures of watchmen's feelings and then he dwells upon the effect of the feelings of dramatis personae on the spectators. The problem most important to tackle is the belief in the ghost. (pp. 161-62)

Shakespeare attempting a ghost, in an age of disbelief in ghosts, was obliged to make it and the play credible, and therefore he elevates his style. The technique in *Hamlet* includes a gradual introduction in which Horatio, a sceptic who is soon going to be satisfied by the ghost, anticipates the doubts of the spectators. The atmosphere of the scene is established in such a way that even the arch sceptic Hume could not but have faith in the spectre dramatically. The emotion of the audience has been prepared. Bernardo's description of the previous appearance of the spectre also lends an appropriate solemnity and vividness to the scene and also serves to distract the attention of the audience at the last minute from the expected appearance of the ghost to make its return all the more surprising and sudden like its original appearance. There is a most appropriate interruption of the narration at the right moment. Coleridge praises Shakespeare's method in making the watcher's react. Shakespeare's judgement is superb in presenting two persons who have seen the spectre twice before while the sceptic is silent and after being twice addressed by them utters only two hasty syllables, "Most like" and appears horror-stricken. We all feel horror and wonder. Shakespeare, thus, succeeds in doubly bringing home to the audience the experience of seeing the spectre for the first time by their participation in the surprise of the watchmen and then by the contrast between Horatio's reaction and that of Bernardo and Marcellus.

The credibility of the ghost in the fourth scene becomes more difficult because the audience by now has become used to seeing the spectre. Yet Shakespeare once again applies the surprise technique and diverts the attention of the spectators just before the spectre's entry, but does so more elaborately. . . . Shakespeare hooks the attention of the audience in the nice distinctions and parenthetical sentences of *Hamlet,* and then completely taking them by surprise brings the spectre in with all the suddenness of its visionary nature. Coleridge has great admiration for the subtlety and economy of Shakespeare's art in the first and the fourth scene in preparing the audience for one thing while obviously preparing them for another. He was acutely conscious of the precarious nature of the willing suspension of disbelief by the spectators and therefore praises Shakespeare profusely in maintaining the illusion once he had achieved it. At many places in the Shakespearean plays the action becomes so improbable, distasteful or shocking as to threaten to destroy the illusion. Shakespeare takes great pains to prepare the audience for such trying moments, and maintains the illusion dexterously. As Coleridge observes, "Whatever disturbs this repose of the judgement by its harshness, abruptness, and improbability, offends against dramatic propriety." Sometimes Coleridge admits in spite of his "bardolatry", that Shakespeare's attempts at maintaining the illusion are not entirely successful.

The first scene of *King Lear* does not appear to Coleridge credible enough, yet it seems to him to be important to the play. This kind of improbability is unusual in Shakespeare. "It is", says Coleridge, "well worth notice, that *Lear* is the only serious performance of Shakespeare, the interest and situations of which are derived from the assumptions of a gross improbability." Though in the first scene the conduct of Lear may be incredible, yet the story of the division of the kingdom is a very well-known one rooted in the public mind and taken for granted and therefore without any effects of improbability. And at the beginning of a play the public is normally more tolerant and credulous, and the dramatist has exploited this psychological tendency of the audience to the full. "Many natural improbabilities are", says Coleridge of *The Tempest*, "innocent in the groundwork or outset of the play, which would break the illusion afterwards . . . a strong improbability in the story, founded on some known tradition, does not

offend in the outset of a play." The action of this scene does not seem to Coleridge essential to the plot. It serves merely as a canvas on which to paint the passions and characters, only an occasion not to be repeated as the cause of the incidents. Even if this scene is lost the interest of the tragedy would not be diminished and it will still be intelligible. The only condition for such scenes to succeed is that "the interest and plot must not depend upon that improbability." Why should then, the first scene have been used at all? Coleridge maintains that in the first six lines the division of the kingdom has been placed in the correct perspective: "It was not without forethought, and it is not without significance, that the triple division is stated here as already determined and in all its particulars previously to the trial of professions, as the relative rewards of which the daughters were made to consider their several portions." Shakespeare used the opening lines, Coleridge suggests, to discredit Lear's experiment and to tell us that the trial was but a trick and his anger was the direct result of the failure of this silly trick. With great economy of words this idea has been conveyed to the audience and to distract the audience from the improbability of the incident Shakespeare passes without delay to the main agent and prime mover. He introduces Edmund to us with great felicity of judgement and prepares the audience for his character in a casual, easy, and natural way. These are the arguments characteristic of Coleridge. Whenever he is faced with perplexing problems he resolves them by contending that Shakespeare is manipulating the audience for one purpose or another. (pp. 163-65)

L. S. Sharma, in his *Coleridge: His Contribution to English Criticism,* Humanities Press, 1982, 235 p.

SOURCES FOR FURTHER STUDY

Badawi, M. M. *Coleridge: Critic of Shakespeare.* Cambridge: Cambridge University Press, 1973, 222 p.

> Book-length study devoted solely to Coleridge's Shakespearean criticism. Badawi states that his intention is "to understand [Coleridge's] critical methods and assumptions on Shakespeare and . . . to define the nature of his contribution to the criticism of Shakespeare in England."

Knight, G. Wilson. "Coleridge's Divine Comedy." In his *The Starlit Dome: Studies in the Poetry of Vision*, pp. 83-178. 1941. Reprint. New York: Barnes & Noble, Inc., 1960.

> Discusses the central images in Coleridge's poetry, relating them to various religious symbols.

Richards, I. A. *Coleridge on Imagination.* 1934. Reprint. Bloomington: Indiana University Press, 1960, 236 p.

> Assesses Coleridge's definition of fancy and imagination which appears in the *Biographia Literaria.*

Schneider, Elisabeth. *Coleridge, Opium, and "Kubla Khan."* Chicago: The University of Chicago Press, 1953, 378 p.

> Investigates the background of "Kubla Khan" and questions Coleridge's contention that he composed it in a dream. After analyzing the effects of opium documented in medical literature, Schneider is skeptical of the poet's claims of semi-conscious composition inspired by opium.

Stephen, Leslie. "Coleridge." In his *Hours in a Library*, Vol. I, pp. 327-67. Rev. ed. New York: G. P. Putnam's Sons, 1904.

Maintains that Coleridge's poetry and criticism general-ly reject the artistic principles of seventeenth- and eigh-teenth-century poets, who infused their writings with moral and religious messages.

Warren, Robert Penn. "A Poem of Pure Imagination: An Ex-periment in Reading." In *The Rime of the Ancient Mariner,* by Samuel Taylor Coleridge, pp. 59-117. New York: Reynal & Hitchcock, 1946.

Repudiates John Livingston Lowes's reading of "The Ancient Mariner" as "a literal rather than symbolic in-terpretation" (see excerpt dated 1927). Unlike Lowes, Warren contends that the poem has a primary theme, which he terms "the theme of sacramental vision, or the them of the 'One Life,' " and a secondary theme, that of the imagination, which is "concerned with the context of values in which the fable is presented."

William Congreve

1670-1729

(Also wrote under pseudonym Cleophil) English dramatist, poet, librettist, novelist, and translator.

INTRODUCTION

Acknowledged as the greatest comic dramatist of the Restoration, Congreve is best known for the unflagging wit with which he infused a repertoire of plays still widely performed and read today. His skillful representations of human behavior in society—effected primarily through the brilliant banter of his characters in such celebrated plays as *Love for Love* (1695) and *The Way of the World* (1700)—have established his prominence within an age that considered intelligent and imaginative wit, particularly in comedy, of premier importance.

Born at Bardsey in Yorkshire, Congreve was the son of a country gentleman. His family was fairly well-off, so he enjoyed the benefits of a private education. After his father received a lieutenant's commission, the family moved to Ireland, where Congreve received his earliest schooling and, at age twelve, entered Kilkenny College. There he met Jonathan Swift, a fellow scholar. Congreve's curriculum—which included reading, writing, Greek, Latin, and theology—was rigid, but did not keep him from enjoying school holidays with Swift and other friends or regularly attending local dramatic performances by townsmen and by visiting Dublin players. In 1686 Congreve was admitted into Trinity College, Dublin, where he intensified his studies in theology and, particularly, the classics. Like many a restive student, Congreve, disposed to gregariousness and a love of amusement, availed himself of Dublin's many diversions, especially the theater. Congreve was there exposed to the most celebrated dramas of the time—among them Ben Jonson's *Volpone* and Thomas Durfey's *The Boarding House*—before such performances were suppressed during the reign of James II. He avidly read works on dramatic theory as well. Congreve was probably more familiar with the theater than most young gentlemen of his era by the time he came to

London in early manhood, a move precipitated, with James II's accession to the throne, by Irish Protestant fear of a resurgence of Roman Catholic repression.

In 1691 Congreve enrolled in the Middle Temple, London, to study law. He found this pursuit uninspiring, but London afforded him opportunities to meet other aspiring young writers. He soon established himself as a wit and promising writer with the novel *Incognita; or, Love and Duty Reconcil'd* (1692), and before long he joined the ranks of John Dryden's disciples at Will's Coffee House. Congreve eventually became Dryden's friend, legal adviser, and literary protégé; his legal acumen enabled him to negotiate arrangements between Dryden and publisher Jacob Tonson, while years of rigorous training allowed him to make numerous important contributions as translator to Dryden's editions of classical authors. Dryden, recognizing the younger man's sensitivity not only to good translation but to the nuances of his own language, predicted Congreve's literary success. This came in 1693 with the drama *The Old Batchelour,* which received enthusiastic acclaim. Although some complained that Congreve was merely a creation of his mentor, Dryden, most commentators, echoing the sentiments of English dramatist and translator, Peter Motteux, agreed that "the Wit which is diffus'd through [*The Old Batchelour*], makes it lose but few of those charms in the perusal, which yield such pleasure in the Representation."

Like the majority of plays produced during this period, *The Old Batchelour* was written with specific players in mind; it was performed with a cast of the most popular and accomplished thespians available. Many biographers surmise that Congreve created the role of the virtuous and witty ingenue, Araminta, specifically for actress Anne Bracegirdle, the object of his lifelong, though unrequited love. In later years, Congreve became romantically involved with Henrietta, Duchess of Marlborough, who bore him a daughter and, after Congreve's death, received his fortune.

Despite ringing endorsements from such notable figures as Dryden and Swift, *The Double-Dealer* (1693) inspired much less enthusiasm than its predecessor. Dryden's account of the drama's lukewarm reception includes a faithful summary of some typical audience reactions: "The Women think [Congreve] has exposed their Bitchery too much; and the Gentlemen, are offended with him; for the discovery of their Follyes: and the way of their Intrigues, under the notion of Friendship to their Ladyes Husbands." However, the overwhelming success of Congreve's next drama, *Love for Love* (1695) both redeemed Congreve's popularity and considerably increased his income, as he was given a full share in a new acting company under William III's protection. In 1696, traveling with dramatist Thomas Southerne, Congreve visited Ireland, where he received a master of arts degree from Trinity College and

was briefly reunited with his parents. It is believed that contact with Southerne, the author of several successful tragedies, may have prompted Congreve to test his ability in what most critics of the time considered a higher dramatic form. Ignoring gibes and unsolicited admonitions from fellow coffeehouse wits who were convinced his endeavor would fail, he wrote. *The Mourning Bride* (1697) which was praised liberally for its morality as well as its literary merit.

Given the prevailing encomiums attending his career thus far, Congreve was unprepared for Jeremy Collier's fervent attack on his work in *A Short View of the Immorality and Profaneness of the English Stage,* published in 1698. Collier, a clergyman, launched indictment after indictment against the profligacy he deemed clearly evident in Congreve's work. Congreve replied with *Amendments to Mr. Collier's False and Imperfect Citations* (1698) which professes the essential morality of all well-crafted art. This lucid rebuttal displays Congreve's characteristic wit but is colored by his own badly disguised contempt for Collier's fervent moralism and social standing—an emotionally charged tack that gave Collier the upper hand in the argument and spawned subsequent skirmishes as well. Weary of being drawn into further confrontations, Congreve concentrated on writing what was to be his last comedy, *The Way of the World.* Performed in 1700, it enjoyed moderate success but also revived certain criticisms that Congreve interpreted as indicating his work's opposition to the "general Taste."

Although Congreve's career had passed its apogee, it was by no means over. After several months on the Continent at health spas for treatment of gout and advancing blindness, he turned to the composition of a libretto, *The Judgment of Paris* (1701), which was well received despite the low esteem then accorded opera. Early in the eighteenth century, Congreve collaborated with fellow dramatist John Vanbrugh in the establishment of a new theater, the Haymarket. This project was financed by members of the Kit-Kat Club, a literary-political society that included among its members both Whig nobility and such renowned contemporaries of Congreve as Joseph Addison and Richard Steele. While the Haymarket soon failed, Congreve's association with influential members of the Kit-Kat Club proved profitable, enabling him to secure two government posts and a lifelong appointment as Secretary of Jamaica—sinecures that allowed him to remain an active man of letters. By 1706, however, ill health compelled Congreve to curtail much of his writing. No longer the prolific artist of his youth, he resided quietly in London until his death, visited to the last by friends and admirers.

Notwithstanding a modest reception by his contemporaries, *The Way of the World* has been long acknowledged as Congreve's masterpiece. Some critics have found the intricate plot difficult, though its derivations from comedic drama in general and comedy of the period in particular are unmistakable. *The Way of the World* relies on conventional devices of deception and misunderstanding to punctuate the author's wry evaluation of love, human relationships, and the institution of marriage—a favorite butt of Restoration humor. In the play, Millamant wishes to marry Mirabell, the only admirer who can capture her interest and match her wit. The two are initially denied permission by Millamant's aunt, Lady Wishfort, who finally consents after numerous events occur that expose human vanity, avarice, and lust yet proclaim the existence, amid corruption and marriages of convenience, of genuine values and real love. The play's paramount strength is its dialogue; Edmund Gosse remarked: "*The Way of the World* is the best-written, the most dazzling, the most intellectually accomplished of all English comedies, perhaps of all the comedies of the world." Conceding the almost nonexistent action of the plot, Gosse added judiciously: "The reader dies of a rose in aromatic pain, but the spectator fidgets in his stall, and wishes that the actors and actresses would be doing something. In no play of Congreve's is the literature so consummate, in none is the human interest in movement and surprise so utterly neglected, as in *The Way of the World.*"

The libertine sentiments expressed in *Love for Love,* another comedy replete with stock characters and predictable events, reflect the mores of Congreve's age and illuminate the author's underlying ideals. Gosse commented that this drama, while "not quite so uniformly brilliant in style as *The Way of the World* . . . has the advantage of possessing a much wholesomer relation to humanity than that play." And, as observed by Bonamy Dobrée, "amid all the flurry and pother and intrigue . . . [appears Congreve's] insistence that the precious thing in life—affection in human relations—must be preserved at all costs," a theme also stressed in *The Way of the World* and else-

where. *The Mourning Bride,* though a tragedy, utilizes some of the same elements found in Congreve's comedies. The popularity of this work has considerably abated since the day when audiences willingly unraveled such complexities of plot; barely fifty years after Congreve's death, Hugh Blair complained that *The Mourning Bride* was "too full of business." While most critics have considered the drama's plot laborious and its poetry faltering, many have, like Leigh Hunt, been pleased "to catch a man of the world at . . . evidences of sympathy with what is serious." If typified almost from its first appearance as poor declamatory tragedy, *The Mourning Bride* does contain several oft-quoted lines (among them, "Music hath charms to soothe the savage breast"), though, as Gosse has indicated, these are seldom attributed to their rightful source.

From the time of Collier's critical assault to the twentieth century, Congreve's critical reputation has been influenced by moral perception, even though the author's libertinism and antimatrimonial attitudes are considered intrinsic to his milieu. Yet despite his controversial libertine veneer and shortcomings as a dramatist, Congreve has managed to maintain his supremacy as the archetypal author of the English comedy of manners. To those for whom, in the words of Charles Cowden Clarke, "the comedy of furbelows and flounces" is impenetrable and the effervescence of Congreve's dialogue nothing more than froth, Dobrée has replied: "If you cannot translate the idiom of a past time—the idiom of behavior as well as of language—into that of your own, it may seem dull; if you can do so it appears highly relevant. Trivial? Only if you cannot see through to the universality that underlies every phase of the social mask."

(For further information about Congreve's life and works, see *Dictionary of Literary Biography,* Vols. 39, 84 and *Literature Criticism from 1400 to 1800,* Vol. 5.)

CRITICAL COMMENTARY

CHARLES LAMB
(essay date 1822)

[Lamb is best known for his many contributions to English Romantic literature and theory. In the following excerpt from his 1822 essay "On the Artificial Comedy of the Last Century," he counterposes the harmlessly amoral world of Congreve's dramatic

imagination with the mundane world of convention and moral necessity.]

The artificial Comedy, or Comedy of manners, is quite extinct on our stage. Congreve and Farquhar show their heads once in seven years only, to be exploded and put down instantly. The times cannot bear them. Is it for a few wild speeches, an occasional license of dialogue? I think not altogether. The business of their dramatic

Principal Works

Incognita; or, Love and Duty Reconcil'd [as Cleophil] (novel) 1692

The Double-Dealer (drama) 1693

The Old Batchelour (drama) 1693

Love for Love (drama) 1695

The Mourning Bride (drama) 1697

Amendments of Mr. Collier's False and Imperfect Citations from the "Old Batchelour," "Double-Dealer," "Love for Love," "Mourning Bride" (criticism) 1698

The Way of the World (drama) 1700

The Judgment of Paris (libretto) 1701

The Works of Mr. William Congreve. 3 vols. (dramas and poetry) 1710

A Letter to Viscount Cobham (poetry) 1729

The Complete Works of William Congreve. 4 vols. (dramas) 1923

William Congreve: Letters & Documents (letters and documents) 1964

characters will not stand the moral test. We screw every thing up to that. Idle gallantry in a fiction, a dream, the passing pageant of an evening, startles us in the same way as the alarming indications of profligacy in a son or ward in real life should startle a parent or guardian. We have no such middle emotions as dramatic interests left. (p. 178)

I confess for myself that (with no great delinquencies to answer for) I am glad for a season to take an airing beyond the diocese of the strict conscience,—not to live always in the precincts of the law-courts,—but now and then, for a dream-while or so, to imagine a world with no meddling restrictions—to get into recesses, whither the hunter cannot follow me—

—Secret shades
Of woody Ida's inmost grove,
While yet there was no fear of Jove—

I come back to my cage and my restraint the fresher and more healthy for it. I wear my shackles more contentedly for having respired the breath of an imaginary freedom. I do not know how it is with others, but I feel the better always for the perusal of one of Congreve's—nay, why should I not add even of Wycherley's—comedies. I am the gayer at least for it; and I could never connect those sports of a witty fancy in any shape with any result to be drawn from them to imitation in real life. They are a world of themselves almost as much as fairy-land. Take one of their characters, male or female (with few exceptions they are alike), and place it in a modern play, and my virtuous indignation shall rise against the profligate wretch as

warmly as the Catos of the pit could desire; because in a modern play I am to judge of the right and the wrong. The standard of *police* is the measure of *political justice.* The atmosphere will blight it, it cannot live here. It has got into a moral world, where it has no business, from which it must needs fall headlong; as dizzy, and incapable of making a stand, as a Swedenborgian bad spirit that has wandered unawares into the sphere of one of his Good Men, or Angels. But in its own world do we feel the creature is so very bad?—The Fainalls and the Mirabells, the Dorimants and the Lady Touchwoods, in their own sphere, do not offend my moral sense; in fact they do not appeal to it at all. They seem engaged in their proper element. They break through no laws, or conscientious restraints. They know of none. They have got out of Christendom into the land—what shall I call it?—of cuckoldry—the Utopia of gallantry, where pleasure is duty, and the manners perfect freedom. It is altogether a speculative scene of things, which has no reference whatever to the world that is. No good person can be justly offended as a spectator, because no good person suffers on the stage. Judged morally, every character in these plays—the few exceptions only are *mistakes*—is alike essentially vain and worthless. The great art of Congreve is especially shown in this, that he has entirely excluded from his scenes,—some little generosities in the part of Angelica perhaps excepted,—not only any thing like a faultless character, but any pretensions to goodness or good feelings whatsoever. Whether he did this designedly, or instinctively, the effect is as happy, as the design (if design) was bold. I used to wonder at the strange power which his *Way of the World* in particular possesses of interesting you all along in the pursuits of characters, for whom you absolutely care nothing—for you neither hate nor love his personages—and I think it is owing to this very indifference for any, that you endure the whole. He has spread a privation of moral light, I will call it, rather than by the ugly name of palpable darkness, over his creations; and his shadows flit before you without distinction or preference. Had he introduced a good character, a single gush of moral feeling, a revulsion of the judgment to actual life and actual duties, the impertinent Goshen would have only lighted to the discovery of deformities, which now are none, because we think them none.

Translated into real life, the characters of his, and his friend Wycherley's dramas, are profligates and strumpets,—the business of their brief existence, the undivided pursuit of lawless gallantry. No other spring of action, or possible motive of conduct, is recognised; principles which, universally acted upon, must reduce this frame of things to a chaos. But we do them wrong in so translating them. No such effects are produced in *their* world. When we are among them, we are amongst a chaotic people. We are not to judge them by our usages. No reverend institutions are insulted by their pro-ceedings,—for they have none among them. No peace of families is violated,—for no family ties exist among them. No purity of the marriage bed is stained,—for none is supposed to have a being. No deep affections are disquieted,—no holy wedlock bands are snapped asunder,—for affection's depth and wedded faith are not of the growth of that soil. There is neither right nor wrong,—gratitude or its opposite,—claim or duty,—paternity or sonship. Of what consequence is it to vir-tue, or how is she at all concerned about it, whether Sir Simon, or Dapperwit, steal away Miss Martha; or who is the father of Lord Froth's, or Sir Paul Pliant's chil-dren.

The whole is a passing pageant, where we should sit as unconcerned at the issues, for life or death, as at a battle of the frogs and mice. But, like Don Quixote, we take part against the puppets, and quite as imperti-nently. We dare not contemplate an Atlantis, a scheme, out of which our coxcombical moral sense is for a little transitory ease excluded. We have not the courage to imagine a state of things for which there is neither re-ward nor punishment. We cling to the painful necessi-ties of shame and blame. We would indict our very dreams. (pp. 179-82)

Charles Lamb, "On the Artificial Comedy of the Last Centu-ry," in his *The Essays of Elia,* edited by O. C. Williams, Oxford University Press, London, 1923, pp. 178-86.

LORD MACAULAY
(essay date 1841)

[Macaulay was a distinguished nineteenth-century English historian, essayist, and politician. In the fol-lowing excerpt from an essay originally published in 1841 in the *Edinburgh Review*, he takes issue with Charles Lamb's defense of Congreve's "pure com-edy into which no moral enters" (see excerpt dated 1822), then surveys the dramas of Congreve, favor-ably comparing his dramatic skill with that of William Wycherley.]

In the name of art, as well as in the name of virtue, we protest against the principle that the world of pure comedy is one into which no moral enters. If comedy be an imitation, under whatever conventions, of real life, how is it possible that it can have no reference to the great rule which directs life, and to feelings which are called forth by every incident of life? If what Mr. Charles Lamb says were correct [see excerpt dated 1822], the inference would be that these dramatists did not in the least understand the very first principles of their craft. Pure landscape-painting into which no light

or shade enters, pure portrait-painting into which no expression enters, are phrases less at variance with sound criticism than pure comedy into which no moral enters.

But it is not the fact that the world of these dram-atists is a world into which no moral enters. Morality constantly enters into that world, a sound morality, and an unsound morality; the sound morality to be insult-ed, derided, associated with every thing mean and hateful; the unsound morality to be set off to every ad-vantage, and inculcated by all methods, direct and indi-rect. It is not the fact that none of the inhabitants of this conventional world feel reverence for sacred institu-tions and family ties. Fondlewife, Pinchwife, every person in short of narrow understanding and disgust-ing manners, expresses that reverence strongly. The he-roes and heroines, too, have a moral code of their own, an exceedingly bad one, but not, as Mr. Charles Lamb seems to think, a code existing only in the imagination of dramatists. It is, on the contrary, a code actually re-ceived and obeyed by great numbers of people. We need not go to Utopia or Fairyland to find them. (pp. 360-61)

Congreve's writings are by no means pure; nor was he, as far as we are able to judge, a warm-hearted or high-minded man. Yet, in coming to him, we feel that the worst is over, that we are one remove further from the Restoration, that we are past the Nadir of na-tional taste and morality. (p. 387)

[Congreve's the *Old Bachelor* is] a play inferior indeed to his other comedies, but, in its own line, infe-rior to them alone. The plot is equally destitute of in-terest and of probability. The characters are either not distinguishable, or are distinguished only by peculiari-ties of the most glaring kind. But the dialogue is re-splendent with wit and eloquence, which indeed are so abundant that the fool comes in for an ample share, and yet preserves a certain colloquial air, a certain inde-scribable ease, of which Wycherley had given no exam-ple, and which Sheridan in vain attempted to imitate. The author, divided between pride and shame, pride at having written a good play, and shame at having done an ungentlemanlike thing, pretended that he had mere-ly scribbled a few scenes for his own amusement, and affected to yield unwillingly to the importunities of those who pressed him to try his fortune on the stage. (p. 389)

[Then] Congreve brought out the *Double Dealer,* a comedy in which all the powers which had produced the *Old Bachelor* showed themselves, matured by time and improved by exercise. But the audience was shocked by the characters of Maskwell and Lady Touchwood. And, indeed, there is something strangely revolting in the way in which a group that seems to be-long to the house of Laius or of Pelops is introduced into the midst of the Brisks, Froths, Carlesses, and Plyants. The play was unfavourably received. Yet, if the praise of distinguished men could compensate an author for the disapprobation of the multitude, Congreve had no reason to repine. Dryden, in one of the most ingenious, magnificent, and pathetic pieces that he ever wrote, extolled the author of the *Double Dealer* in terms which now appear extravagantly hyperbolical. Till Congreve came forth,—so ran this exquisite flattery,—the superiority of the poets who preceded the civil wars was acknowledged. (p. 390)

[*Love for Love* is] superior both in wit and in scenic effect to either of the preceding plays. It was performed at a new theatre which Betterton and some other actors, disgusted by the treatment which they had received in Drury-Lane, had just opened in a tennis-court near Lincoln's Inn. Scarcely any comedy within the memory of the oldest man had been equally successful. The actors were so elated that they gave Congreve a share in their theatre; and he promised in return to furnish them with a play every year, if his health would permit. Two years passed, however, before he produced the *Mourning Bride,* a play which, paltry as it is when compared, we do not say, with Lear or Macbeth, but with the best dramas of Massinger and Ford, stands very high among the tragedies of the age in which it was written. To find any thing so good we must go twelve years back to *Venice Preserved,* or six years forward to the *Fair Penitent.* The noble passage which Johnson, both in writing and in conversation, extolled above any other in the English drama, has suffered greatly in the public estimation from the extravagance of his praise. Had he contented himself with saying that it was finer than any thing in the tragedies of Dryden, Otway, Lee, Rowe, Southern, Hughes, and Addison, than any thing, in short, that had been written for the stage since the days of Charles the First, he would not have been in the wrong.

The success of the *Mourning Bride* was even greater than that of *Love for Love.* Congreve was now allowed to be the first tragic as well as the first comic dramatist of his time; and all this at twenty-seven. We believe that no English writer except Lord Byron has, at so early an age, stood so high in the estimation of his contemporaries. (pp. 391-92)

[*The Way of the World* is] the most deeply meditated and the most brilliantly written of all his works. It wants, perhaps, the constant movement, the effervescence of animal spirits, which we find in *Love for Love.* But the hysterical rants of Lady Wishfort, the meeting of Witwould, and his brother, the country knight's courtship and his subsequent revel, and, above all, the chase and surrender of Millamant, are superior to any thing that is to be found in the whole range of English comedy from the civil war downwards. It is quite inexplicable to us that this play should have failed on the stage. Yet so it was; and the author, al-

ready sore with the wounds which Collier had inflicted, was galled past endurance by this new stroke. He resolved never again to expose himself to the rudeness of a tasteless audience, and took leave of the theatre forever. (pp. 403-04)

Wycherley was a worse Congreve. There was, indeed, a remarkable analogy between the writings and lives of these two men. Both were gentlemen liberally educated. Both led town lives, and knew human nature only as it appears between Hyde Park and the Tower. Both were men of wit. Neither had much imagination. Both at an early age produced lively and profligate comedies. Both retired from the field while still in early manhood, and owned to their youthful achievements in literature whatever consideration they enjoyed in later life. Both, after they had ceased to write for the stage, published volumes of miscellanies which did little credit either to their talents or to their morals. Both, during their declining years, hung loose upon society; and both in their last moments, made eccentric and unjustifiable dispositions of their estates.

But in every point Congreve maintained his superiority to Wycherley. Wycherley had wit; but the wit of Congreve far outshines that of every comic writer, except Sheridan, who has arisen within the last two centuries. Congreve had not, in a large measure, the poetical faculty; but compared with Wycherley he might be called a great poet. Wycherley had some knowledge of books; but Congreve was a man of real learning. Congreve's offences against decorum, though highly culpable, were not so gross as those of Wycherley; nor did Congreve, like Wycherley, exhibit to the world the deplorable spectacle of a licentious dotage. Congreve died in the enjoyment of high consideration; Wycherley forgotten or despised. Congreve's will was absurd and capricious; but Wycherley's last actions appear to have been prompted by obdurate malignity. (p. 410)

Lord Macaulay, "Leigh Hunt," in his *Critical, Historical, and Miscellaneous Essays, Vol. IV,* Hurd & Houghton, 1880, pp. 350-411.

EDMUND GOSSE

(essay date 1924)

[In the following excerpt from his *Life of William Congreve,* Gosse provides a descriptive overview and favorable general assessment of Congreve's works.]

The Double Dealer contains some excellent characters. Sir Paul Plyant, with his night-cap made out of a piece of a scarlet petticoat, tied up in bed, out of harm's way, and looking, with his great beard, like a Russian bear upon a drift of snow, is wholly delightful; and Lady Froth, the charming young blue-stocking, with her wit and her pedantry, her affectation and her merry vitality, is one of the best and most complex characters that Congreve has created. Her doting affection for her child, "poor little Sappho," mingled with her interest in her own ridiculous verses, and set off by her genuine ability and power, combine to form a very life-like picture. Twenty years earlier she might have been supposed to be a study of Margaret, Duchess of Newcastle. Her astronomical experiments with Mr. Brisk are a concession on the poet's part to the worst instincts of his audience, and funny, as they undeniably are, they spoil the part.

A fault in the construction of *The Double Dealer* is that Lord and Lady Froth are not sharply enough distinguished from Lord and Lady Touchwood. In Cynthia, Congreve produced one of those gracious and honest maidens whom he liked to preserve in the wild satiric garden of his drama, that his beloved Mrs. Bracegirdle might have a pure and impassioned part to play. We owe to this penchant the fortunate circumstance that, while in Etheredge, Wycherley, and Vanbrugh there is often not a single character that we can esteem or personally tolerate from the beginning of the play to the end, in Congreve there is always sure to be one lady of reputation, even if she be not quite of the crystalline order of that more famous Lady, who walked among apes and tigers in the boskages of *Comus.* (pp. 43-4)

The comedy of *Love for Love* has been commonly accounted Congreve's masterpiece, and perhaps with justice. It is not quite so uniformly brilliant in style as *The Way of the World,* but it has the advantage of possessing a much wholesomer relation to humanity than that play, which is almost undiluted satire, and a more theatrical arrangement of scenes. In *Love for Love* the qualities which had shown themselves in *The Old Bachelor* and *The Double Dealer* recur, but in a much stronger degree. The sentiments are more unexpected, the language is more picturesque, the characters have more activity of mind and vitality of nature. All that was merely pink has deepened into scarlet; even what is disagreeable,—the crudity of allusion and the indecency of phrase,—have increased. The style in all its parts and qualities has become more vivid. We are looking through the same telescope as before, but the sight is better adjusted, the outlines are more definite, and the colours more intense. So wonderfully felicitous is the phraseology that we cannot doubt that if Congreve could only have kept himself unspotted from the sins of the age, dozens of tags would have passed, like bits of Shakespeare, Pope, and Gray, into habitual parlance. In spite of its errors against decency, *Love for Love* survived on the stage for more than a century,

long after the remainder of Restoration and Orange drama was well-nigh extinct. Hazlitt saw it played, and thus describes it:—

It still acts, and is still acted well. The effect of it is prodigious on the well-informed spectator. In particular, Munden's Foresight, if it is not just the thing, is a wonderfully rich and powerful piece of comic acting. His look is planet-struck; his dress and appearance like one of the signs of the zodiac taken down. Nothing can be more bewildered; and it only wants a little more helplessness, a little more of the doting, querulous, garrulity of age, to be all that one conceives of the superannuated, star-gazing original.

The plot of *Love for Love* forms a more interesting story than is usually the case with Congreve. His two first plays had possessed no plot at all, properly speaking, but only in the one case a set of amatory scenes, and in the other a series of satirical situations. (pp. 57-8)

It has been the habit to quote *The Mourning Bride* as the very type of bad declamatory tragedy. No doubt Dr. Johnson did it harm by that extravagant eulogy in which he selected one fragment as unsurpassed in the poetry of all time. But if we compare it, not with those tragedies of the age of Elizabeth, studded with occasional naïve felicities, which it is just now the fashion to admire with some extravagance, but with what England and even France produced from 1650 to the revival of romantic taste, *The Mourning Bride* will probably take a place close after what is best in Otway and Racine. It will bear comparison, as I would venture to assert, with Southerne's *Fatal Marriage* or with Crébillon's *Rhadamiste et Zénobie,* and will not be pronounced inferior to these excellent and famous tragedies in dramatic interest, or genuine grandeur of sentiment, or beauty of language. It has done what no other of these special rivals has done, outside the theatre of Racine, it has contributed to the everyday fashion of its country several well-worn lines. But it is not every one who says that "Music hath charms to soothe the savage breast" or that "Hell knows no fury like a woman scorn'd," who would be able to tell where the familiar sentiment first occurs. (pp. 75-6)

The blank verse of *The Mourning Bride* deserves some consideration, because it seems to be the model on which most eighteenth-century unrhymed iambics were formed. It is the parent of Thomson's, as that is of Cowper's and of Wordsworth's blank verse. When the heroic tragedies went out of fashion, and dramatic blank verse was reverted to by Dryden and Otway, those writers took the easy versification of Shakespeare's later time, with the incessant extra syllable, as their model. Lee, who was influenced by Milton, is much more sparing of this redundancy, and Congreve follows Lee rather than any other dramatist. His real model is, however, Milton, and it is curious to trace in his tragic blank verse a respectful study of that impeccable master. (p. 79)

The Way of the World is the best-written, the most dazzling, the most intellectually accomplished of all English comedies, perhaps of all the comedies of the world. But it has the defects of the very qualities which make it so brilliant. A perfect comedy does not sparkle so much, is not so exquisitely written, because it needs to advance, to develop. To *The Way of the World* may be applied that very dubious compliment paid by Mrs. Browning to Landor's *Pentameron* that, "were it not for the necessity of getting through a book, some of the pages are too delicious to turn over." The beginning of the third act, the description of Mirabell's feelings in the opening scene, and many other parts of *The Way of the World,* are not to be turned over, but to be reread until the psychological subtlety of the sentiment, the perfume of the delicately chosen phrases, the music of the sentences, have produced their full effect upon the nerves. But, meanwhile, what of the action? The reader dies of a rose in aromatic pain, but the spectator fidgets in his stall, and wishes that the actors and actresses would be doing something. In no play of Congreve's is the literature so consummate, in none is the human interest in movement and surprise so utterly neglected, as in *The Way of the World. The Old Bachelor,* itself, is theatrical in comparison. We have slow, elaborate dialogue, spread out like some beautiful endless tapestry, and no action whatever. Nothing happens, nothing moves, positively from one end of *The Way of the World* to the other, and the only reward of the mere spectator is the occasional scene of wittily contrasted dialogue, Millamant pitted against Sir Wilful, Witwoud against Petulant, Lady Wishfort against her maid. With an experienced audience, prepared for an intellectual pleasure, the wit of these polished fragments would no doubt encourage a cultivation of patience through less lively portions of the play, but to spectators coming perfectly fresh to the piece, and expecting rattle and movement, this series of still-life pictures may easily be conceived to be exasperating, especially as the satire contained in them was extremely sharp and direct. (pp. 122-23)

In *The Way of the World,* as in *The Old Bachelor,* Congreve essayed a stratagem which Molière tried but once, in *Le Misanthrope.* It is one which is likely to please very much or greatly to annoy. It is the stimulation of curiosity all through the first act, without the introduction of one of the female characters who are described and, as it were, promised to the audience. It is probable that in the case of *The Way of the World* it was hardly a success. The analysis of character and delicate intellectual writing in the first act, devoid as it is of all stage-movement, may possibly have proved very tedious to auditors not subtle enough to enjoy Mirabell's account of the effect which Millamant's faults have upon him, or Witwoud's balanced depreciation of his friend Petulant. Even the mere reader discovers that the whole play brightens up after the entrance of Millamant, and probably that apparition is delayed too long. From this point, to the end of the second act, all scintillates and sparkles; and these are perhaps the most finished pages, for mere wit, in all existing comedy. The dialogue is a little metallic, but it is burnished to the highest perfection; and while one repartee rings against the other, the arena echoes as with shock after shock in a tilting-bout. In comparison with what we had had before Congreve's time that was best—with *The Man of Mode,* for instance, and with *The Country Wife*—the literary work in *The Way of the World* is altogether more polished, the wit more direct and effectual, the art of the comic poet more highly developed. There are fewer square inches of the canvas which the painter has roughly filled in, and neglected to finish; there is more that consciously demands critical admiration, less that can be, in Landor's phrase, pared away.

Why, then, did this marvellous comedy fail to please? Partly, no doubt, on account of its scholarly delicacy, too fine to hold the attention of the pit, and partly also, as we have seen, because of its too elaborate dialogue and absence of action. But there was more than this. Congreve was not merely a comedian, he was a satirist also—*asper jocum tentavit* ("trying a harsh wit"). He did not spare the susceptibilities of his fine ladies. His Cabal-Night at Lady Wishfort's is the direct original of Sheridan's *School for Scandal;* but in some ways the earlier picture is the more biting, the more disdainful. Without posing as a Timon or a Diogenes, and so becoming himself an object of curious interest, Congreve adopted the cynical tone, and threads the brightly-coloured crowd of social figures with a contemptuous smile upon his lips. (pp. 124-25)

The reputation of Congreve has undergone many reverses, but will probably never again sink so far as it did half a century ago. In the early Victorian age, his plays almost ceased to be praised, and perhaps to be read, while every humanitarian passerby thought it easy to cast his stone of reproach at these "artificial," "heartless," and "immoral" comedies. Of late years the fame of our greatest comic playwright has been eloquently defended, and it is doubtful whether any critic of responsibility would, at the present day, be found to endorse the old strain of condemnation by the moral test. Charles Lamb, extreme and paradoxical as his famous essay on "Artificial Comedy" may have been, did infinite good in distinguishing the temper in which works of amusement and those of edification should be considered, and in defending the easy-going dramatists of the seventeenth century from the charge of being injurious to society [see excerpt dated 1822].

There is much to be said for Lamb's theory that

the stage of Congreve and Vanbrugh was never intended to represent real life, but merely created in order to form a "sanctuary and quiet Alsatia," where the mind could take refuge for a while when hunted by the casuistries of Puritanism. But the weak points of this argument are easily divined, and what is really valuable in Lamb's vindication is the appeal to another tribunal than the court where the Young Person sits enthroned, a Rhadamanthus of the minor morals. The result of Lamb's eloquent special pleading has been to make English critics feel that when it is said that Congreve is not "proper," the last word has not been spoken, and that though his standard of decency is not our own, nor ever likely to be resumed, his merits as an artist are not on that account to be overlooked or underrated. In this connection, and bearing in mind the fluctuations of sentiment upon this question of propriety, we may recollect that Voltaire . . . gives special praise to Congreve for the purity of his language. Decency of expression is mainly a conventional or comparative matter. In the seventeenth century divines said things to their congregations, and sons wrote anecdotes to their mothers, which to-day would sound crude in the smoking-room of a club, and it was rather Congreve's misfortune than his fault that he happened to flourish as a writer, at the very moment when, in all their history, Englishmen and Englishwomen were allowing themselves the broadest licence in expression, and the freest examination of scabrous situations. To dwell any further on this much-discussed difficulty in this place seems needless. It is enough to warn the lamb-like reader, if there be any longer such an one, that in the menagerie of the Restoration dramatists he must expect to find lions.

The position of Congreve in the brief and splendid series of our comic playwrights is easily defined. Etheredge led the van with his French inspiration, directly drawn from Molière, his delicate observation, his lightness of touch, his thin elegance. Wycherley followed with his superior strength, his massive dialogue, his pungent wit, his vigour, his invention. There could be no finer introduction to the art of comedy than was suggested by the experiments of these two playwrights. But they were merely transitional figures, they pointed the way to a greater master. Looked at as a final expression of a national art, the work of Etheredge would have seemed flimsy in its lightness, weak in its delicacy, while that of Wycherley was rough, hard, and unfinished. The natural complement of these two writers was a poet who should combine their excellences, be fine and yet strong, patient to finish as well as spirited to sketch. It was when the public had grown familiar with the types of writing exemplified at their best in *The Man of Mode* and *The Plain Dealer,* that Congreve came forward with his erudite and brilliant comedies, combining the quality of Etheredge with that of Wycherley, adding much from Molière, owing much to his own

trained and active fancy, and placing English comedy of manners for the first time on a really classic basis. By the side of the vivid characters in *Love for Love,* the group that dances round Sir Fopling Flutter seems a cloud of phantoms, and the Horners and Manleys no better than violent caricatures of humanity.

With all his genius, with all his opportunity of position, Congreve did not reach the highest level. The perfection of which we have been speaking is relative, and in comparison with Molière, the English comedian takes a second rank in all but wit. It is remarkable that while in most branches of literature the English have excelled in preserving the spirit of great writing while treating the forms and recognized types very cavalierly, in this one matter of the Comedy of Manners they failed to take the highest place precisely through their timid adherence to the rules of composition. If Congreve could have been forced out into a wider life, persuaded to disregard the restrictions of artificial comedy, obliged to draw men where and as he observed them, if, in other words, he could have written in a more English fashion, there is no apparent reason why he might not now stand close by the shoulder of Molière. The Englishmen who immediately followed him, Vanbrugh and Farquhar, with much less art than he, and genius decidedly inferior, have put themselves sometimes almost on a level with Congreve through their very audacity, their disregard of rules. Not one of their comedies, if carefully analyzed, reveals the science, the balance of parts, the delicate literary skill of Congreve, but their scenes are apt to be so much breezier than his, their characters have so much more blood and bustle, that we over-estimate their relative value in comparison with Congreve. Yet, with all his limitations, he remains the principal figure in English comedy of manners, one of the secondary glories of our language and literature, and in his own narrow kind unsurpassed even by such broader and more genial masters as Terence and Molière.

On one side the excellence of Congreve seems unique among the comic dramatists of the world. He is probably, of them all, the one whose plays are written with the most unflagging wit and literary charm. The style of Congreve lifts him high above all his English rivals, and there is no test so unfair to Wycherley or to Farquhar as that of comparing a fragment of their work with an analogous fragment of his. Hazlitt has excellently said that Congreve's comedies "are a singular treat to those who have cultivated a taste for the niceties of English style: there is a peculiar flavour in the very words, which is to be found in hardly any other writer." What we call his wit, that which makes his scenes so uniformly dazzling, consists, in a great measure, in this inexplicable felicity of phrase, this invariable selection of the unexpected and yet obviously the best word. In this art of diction he resembles none of his own sturdy contemporaries; the sentences are as limpid as Addison's, as melodious as Berkeley's, as highly coloured as Sterne's, and this quality of his style makes Congreve very interesting to the student. He stands on the threshold of the eighteenth century, and seems to have an intuition of all its peculiar graces.

Yet every admirer of Congreve has experienced the fatigue that this very brilliance, this unflagging glitter of style produces. It is altogether beyond not credibility only, but patience. The prodigality of wit becomes wearisome, and at last only emphasizes the absence of tenderness, simplicity, and genuine imagination. It is at such a moment that Thackeray steps in, and throwing the shutters suddenly open, floods the stage of Congreve with the real light of life, and in a few ironical pages disenchants us of his "tawdry playhouse taper." But we must not permit the intrusion. There is a sunshine that filters through the dewy hawthorn-branches, there is a wax-light that flashes back from the sconces of an alcove, but these are not compatible, and the latter is not justly to be extinguished by the former. In the comedies of Congreve we breathe an atmosphere of the most exquisite artificial refinement, an air of literary frangipan or millefleur-water. What we have to admire in them is the polish, the grace, the extreme technical finish, the spectacle of an intellect of rare cultivation and power concentrating itself on the creation of a microcosm swarming with human volvox and vibrion. If we are prepared to accept this, and to ask no more than this from Congreve, we shall not grudge him his permanent station among the great writers of this country. (pp. 169-74)

Edmund Gosse, in his *Life of William Congreve,* Charles Scribner's Sons, 1924, 181 p.

JOSEPH WOOD KRUTCH
(essay date 1927)

[Krutch is widely regarded as one of America's most accomplished literary critics. In the following excerpt from his introduction to *The Comedies of William Congreve,* he surveys Congreve's dramas.]

William Congreve, the last and perhaps the greatest of the Restoration comic writers, was one of those happy mortals whose annals are brief. Completely a man of the world, free from all the irritating vagaries generally associated with "artistic temperament," and finding the spirit of his age entirely in accord with his own, he fought no battles and suffered no disappointments more serious than those attendant upon finding some of his works less dazzlingly successful than others. At the beginning of his career he was eagerly hailed by the most admired writers of his time; at the end of it he received the homage of the most successful of the rising generation; and thus he was spared both the bitterness of the struggle for recognition and the greater bitterness of seeing that reputation fade away. Even those who, like Addison, were really on the other side of the moral fence seemed to wish to exclude him from the condemnation which they passed upon others who belonged in the same tradition with him and if we except the most fanatical of the reformers, whom he despised, he had no enemies. Desiring nothing which his world could not give him he received nearly everything that it could and he seems to have realized his singular good fortune. (p. vii)

Congreve's mind was of the sort which perfects rather than originates. This first comedy of his [*The Old Batchelour*] deviates in no essential respect from the type which the generation just before him had invented and it shows, in particular, the strong influence of Wycherley. Like all the best comedies of the time it is exclusively urban and exclusively gallant, assuming that the only world worthy of consideration is the world of fashionable society and that the chief interest of that world is the pursuit of love in the Ovidian sense. An amorous intrigue furnishes the basis of its plot, a satiric delineation of contemporary manners its substance, and from this formula his plays never deviated. And yet as he developed, Congreve managed to give the flavor of his own personality to work which continued to keep the essentials of a borrowed form. His second play, *The Double Dealer,* . . . was not at the beginning so well received as his first, partly because it is marked by that intricate confusion of plot into which Congreve had a tendency to fall; but in his third, *Love for Love,* . . . he reaches pretty nearly to his full maturity. Here the influence of Wycherley is no longer so obviously present and Congreve himself, at once the most intellectually brilliant and the most humanely tempered of the Restoration wits, is fully revealed.

Considered by themselves his comedies may seem both brutal and cynical but in comparison with the other most important plays of their time they are not so. Congreve was a member of a brutal and cynical society, he was familiar with the brutal and cynical literature which it produced, and his was not the type of mind which goes against the current of the age in which it lives; but on the whole he softened rather than intensified its tendency. Absolutely devoid of sentiment, he had no faith in man or woman and he sums up his attitude toward both in the concluding lines (borrowed from Ovid) of the song in *Love for Love:*

He alone won't betray in whom none will confide;
And the nymph may be chaste that has never been tried.

But he never descended, like Dryden or Mrs. Behn, to wallow in mere lubricity and he never pictured human depravity with Wycherley's ferocious relish. Amused and detached, he was content to let the world wag as it would and he was certainly untinged by any idealism, but his attitude was never any more harsh or corrupt than that appropriate to a man of the world.

This relative gentleness of tone is the first of the characteristics which distinguish Congreve from the other wits of his time and the second is the polish which he gives to his dialogue. For a whole generation before he began to write wit had been the supreme ideal of English society and of English literature. A score of writers had devoted themselves to the production of the witty phrase and Congreve, heir to this tradition, gave to it its final refinement. Here again he was not original, for his themes—the foppish vanity of men and the frailty of women—were the same as those upon which his predecessors had practiced their ingenuity, but his epigrams are always a little more felicitous than those of any of his rivals.

He was more completely literary than any of the others, and this fact offers a partial explanation of the impression which he gives of being less corrupt than his fellows. Charles Lamb's attempt to consider the comedy of the Restoration as something totally unrelated to real life cannot be accepted in so far as it applies to that comedy as a whole, for it was, in general, a genuine reflection of the manners and morals of the time, but Lamb's attitude is more nearly correct in regard to Congreve than in regard to any of the others [see excerpt dated 1822]. The world into which his plays conduct us is a Utopia of gallantry which has, to a considerable extent, detached itself from the real world and which is inhabited by exquisite creatures who play at love with the mind alone. If he judged from the world about him that virtue did not exist, he still believed in grace and he created an artificial world in which grace alone counted. He made no attempt to hide the fact that the persons of his comedy were utterly cold and utterly selfish; he even accepted the Restoration tradition that obscenity was acceptable material for wit; but he gave both his people and his epigrams a polish so exquisite that perversity of subject is lost in perfection of manner and exquisite gestures of mind and body alone remain. Restoration love was a game not infrequently played with heartless brutality, and Congreve purified it not by endowing it with either nobility or kindness, but by transferring it wholly to the mind and setting it to work upon fantastic creatures without bodies to be soiled or hearts to be wounded.

Love for Love, was tremendously successful and it kept a place upon the stage long after most of the plays written by his contemporaries and immediate predecessors had been forgotten, but his fourth and last comedy, *The Way of the World, . . .* had the ambigu-

Scene from a 1947 production of *Love for Love.*

ous fate of being a comparative failure upon the stage and yet to be regarded by many as his masterpiece. The reason for this comparative failure is not hard to understand for it was the most completely literary of its author's plays and represents the complete development of that tendency in Congreve, already referred to, to escape into a world of pure fancy. *Love for Love,* has a ludicrous and easily followed plot, there is in it a continual bustle of action and an abundance of broad comedy, while in *The Way of the World* the exceedingly complicated intrigue is too confused to be readily understood. There is almost no action whatever, and the characters are one and all completely intellectualized. Yet so exquisite is the polish of the dialogue and so delicate is the airy grace of the personages that admirers of Congreve consider this play his best because, in spite of its defects as a stage piece, it represents more completely than any other the qualities which are peculiarly his. *Love for Love* has still some faint connection with the real world; in it Miss Prue, at least, still has a body and the indecencies of the piece not only tickle the mind but warm the heart a little also. In *The Way of the World,* however, the slender thread which establishes a relationship between the characters and reality has snapped completely, leaving the personages to pursue their bloodless loves in a world of pure abstractions which lay not in the neighborhood of Covent Garden but somewhere east of the sun and west of the moon.

Fine as is the scene of *Love for Love,* in which Tattle teaches Miss Prue the art of saying "Yes" without unseemly promptitude, finer still is that in *The Way of the World* where Millamant and Mirabell, approaching crab-wise toward matrimony, lay down the conditions under which marriage would be tolerable. *Love for Love* is perhaps the best of Congreve's plays for the stage, but *The Way of the World* is supreme in the study. (pp. ix-xii)

Joseph Wood Krutch, in an introduction to *The Comedies of William Congreve,* edited by Joseph Wood Krutch, Macmillan Publishing Company, 1927, pp. vii-xv.

ELMER B. POTTER
(essay date 1943)

[In the following excerpt, Potter discusses factors affecting response to *The Mourning Bride* during the eighteenth century.]

Writers on the English theatre have noted an interesting paradox in the history of William Congreve's *The Mourning Bride.* Congreve is remembered today almost exclusively for his series of brilliant comedies, but it was in this, his only tragedy, that he achieved the greatest theatrical triumph of his career, and for the same play he has also been most severely criticized. (p. 977)

It is evident that *The Mourning Bride* never—either at the time of its first appearance or later—received the unqualified praise of the critics that many writers have suggested, but when we have established this fact we have solved only half of the paradox. However little the critics may have thought of Congreve's tragedy, the play *was* a popular and financial success. It brought its author more revenue than any of his other works, and the public came faithfully to see it performed for more than a century.

The audience which assembled at Lincoln's Inn Fields to witness the opening performance of Congreve's tragedy seems to have been friendly but skeptical. Memories of *Love for Love,* the author's most popular comedy, produced two years before, still lingered happily in the minds of London playgoers. They had not forgotten, however, the unfortunate results when Congreve had once before wandered from the light comic vein which in *The Old Bachelor* had established him in the theatre. The sombre comedy *The Double Dealer* had been coldly received by a baffled audience. Now the popular author of comedies had ventured into the unfamiliar field of tragedy, and his friends awaited the results with misgivings. The outcome, so far as the

general public was concerned, was as we have seen, a triumph for Congreve. The new tragedy, according to a London gentleman, "far exceeded what the world expected from him in that part of dramatic poetry." The same writer notes that the theatre "was full to the last."

The stage history of *The Mourning Bride* makes clear the reasons for its success. The play was skillfully adjusted to the playhouse and to the audience for which it was written. It brought together most of the elements which had proved popular in Restoration tragedies—heroic personages of high rank involved in a rivalry of love and hate, emotions of passionate intensity ranging from exaltation to despair, far away places and distant times, a background altering between palace and prison—all this clothed in the classical form which the average theatregoer of the times had been taught to expect. But taste for such matters eventually declined, and the *continued* success of the play was dependent rather upon the fact that it was eminently suited to the acting technique of an age of actors trained in the heroic drama of the period. *The Mourning Bride,* despite the opinion of at least one critic to the contrary, has proved itself outstandingly an acting play, and the eighteenth century was notable for its great actors.

Ingenious and original plotting, striking contrasts, vigorous movement, facile versification with occasional passages of grandeur—these are the timeless virtues of Congreve's tragedy, and these are the materials which the tragic actor requires to display his skill. Bombast and thinness of characterization—these are the principal faults of the play; yet these are the faults which the great actors of the period were best prepared to conceal. A well-trained voice could make the top-lofty sentiments sound like poetry, and a great imagination could clothe the characters in a semblance of reality. *The Mourning Bride* is indeed comparable to an opera libretto—dead stuff until supplemented by the musical delivery and creative powers of a skilled actor of the declamatory school. It is not surprising, therefore, that the play prospered in the theatre only so long as it served as vehicle for one or more of the great players of the century.

The Mourning Bride contains at least three characters, Osmyn, Almeria, and Zara, which provide the type of lines and situations in which the eighteenth-century actor appeared at his best. Each of the three served at various times as a stellar rôle to display the powers of some notable player, but the part of Zara especially attracted and challenged the greatest actresses of the time. In the years following the break-up of the extraordinary cast which first launched the play, the choice of a suitable Zara came to be of paramount importance in assuring its success. Indeed, the rise and fall of its popularity, except in one notable instance when Garrick was in the cast, seems to have been in direct relation to the skill of the actress playing the captive queen. In such a part great actresses like Barry, Porter, Pritchard, Younge, and Siddons could display the full range of their emotional powers, from the tenderness of love to despairing and frustrated rage; in such a part an actress of less ability would, as we shall see, inevitably move her audience to unseemly and unexpected mirth. (pp. 987-89)

The revolt against the neoclassic rules had been well under way before 1700. The schools of Addison and Johnson had established in their place the criterion of a "just imitation of nature"; i.e., the representation in essence of the general fundamental truths of experience. Such a criterion, in so far as it opposed bombast and exaggeration, accorded well with the practical-mindedness of the new society, a society in which the authority of a small aristocracy of taste had lost its force, and middle class traits had become dominant. By the end of the eighteenth century, critics, acting as spokesmen for the new tradition, (1) had become impatient with top-lofty sentiments of impossibly noble characters, and (2) demanded that every play expound a moral. At least a minor reason for the continued popularity of *The Mourning Bride* may be found in the manner in which the tragedy underwent small alterations to adapt it to this new society and to a changing theatre. The stage versions show progressive modifications involving (1) elimination of lines which critics found indecent, (2) elimination of passages of bombast and scenes of horror, (3) alteration of old stage directions which no longer applied to the changing styles of scenic design and theatre architecture, and (4) building up of the rôle of Zara. (p. 996)

It is evident that there is less paradox in the history of *The Mourning Bride* than many writers have implied. A mere reading of critical opinion, in its context and with background factors considered, disposes of the idea that there was at any time any sharp break from praise to censure. It is true that the public did not share the ill opinions of the critics, but that is no unparalleled situation in the theatre. Congreve's tragedy merely had the good fortune to suit the audience and the actors of the century in which it flourished. (p. 1001)

Elmer B. Potter, "The Paradox of Congreve's 'The Mourning Bride'," in *PMLA*, Vol. LVIII, No. 4, December, 1943, pp. 977-1001.

AUBREY L. WILLIAMS
(essay date 1979)

[In the following excerpt, Williams sketches the systems of justice and providence operating in Congreve's dramas.]

The plot, or "Fable," of *Incognita* is . . . "conventional." But far from being "no more than a useful compositional device," as Simon thinks, the plot of *Incognita* would have been recognized as an instructive emblem, as well as an "entertainment," a diverting parable, in romance terms, of the way man's wandering footsteps, amidst his living darkness, may be guided by Providence: a fanciful parable, indeed, in its most crucial episode and in almost fairy-tale terms, of the way man's very "stumblings" may be providentially directed for his salvation. And far from "building a world" in which his "art imposes its own pattern upon the flux of nature," as Novak argues, Congreve in his art rather accepts and reflects the Providentialist pattern thought to prevail not merely in nature itself but in all human affairs, even the most amorous and gallant, a pattern which affirmed, among other things, that when we are filled "with the apprehension of some great evil which is just ready to fall on us, either the evil does not come as we feared, or it proves no Evil, but a very great Good to us."

The existence of such an instructive pattern in so slight and charming a fiction as *Incognita* may come as a surprise to some today, especially to those who would separate the art of the age from the faith of the age. It nevertheless is present, the contextual frame as well as the informing design which will be seen as assuring that two sets of lovers, after a multitude of mistakes and rash designs of their own contriving, will in the end find their "Love and Duty Reconcil'd." (pp. 92-3)

An argument for a providentialist structure (and the vision it entails) is so "little" a "thing" as *Incognita* may seem odd or merely eccentric to some. But the real oddity is the argument that "*Incognita* relies heavily on chance," and that Congreve in it constructs "a world in which art imposes its own pattern upon the flux of nature." It is not chance which directs that Hippolito's thrusting sword, in the utmost darkness, shall go under Aurelian's arm instead of into his heart; it was, says Congreve as plainly as can be said, "the extraordinary Care of Providence in directing the Sword, that it only past under his Arm." It is not by chance that Aurelian stumbles and falls in the darkness at the moment when a pistol is fired at him: it is "by the greatest Providence in the World" that, "going backwards," he "fell down over some loose Stones that lay in his Way, just in that Instant of Time, when the Villain fired his Pistol." It is not chance that directs Aurelian to the "Ruins of an Old Monastery" or Hippolito to the Convent of St. Lawrence: in both instances they are said to have been directed, through the darkness in which they wander, by "Heaven."

The emblematic character of such episodes would have been unmistakable to readers reared in literature and fed by sermons which maintained that in "innumerable" instances of life "we drive on blindfold, and very often impetuously pursue that which would ruin us: and were God as shortsighted as we, into what precipices should we minutely hurry our selves." Such readers would have had minds well stocked with the idea and the image and the advice that "We ought always to appear before [God], like blind Men, who stretch out their Hands, to be conducted by Providence." Just as familiar and easily decipherable to them would have been the "sign" of God's providential interposition when an event "which in it self is not ordinary, nor could well be expected, doth fall out happily, in the nick of an exigency, for the relief of innocence." When the "relief of innocence" occurs in an old monastery, they would have seen it, moreover, as deliberately placed on God's own ground.

Such considerations as these are not put forward, of course, with the aim of overwhelming a sprightly story under a load of providentialist lumber. *Incognita* is a witty and charming and ingenious "Essay," as Congreve called his first work. But it is certainly worth remembering that it has its more somber content: two deaths by dueling, the near death of Claudio, two escapes from death by Aurelian, the near rape and death of Juliana. When we consider such elements, along with the multiple mistakes and mishaps and cross-purposes which characterize its "Fable," we may admire all the more the way Congreve gave to his novel the "Unity of Contrivance" he sought. We also may see, however, that his own admirable contrivances are closely reflective of a world where, it was assumed, there could be discovered another "admirable (though unsearchable) contrivance" in the "obscure administrations," by Providence, of even the most "casual, negligent, promiscuous Events."

Incognita is important in the history of the English novel, but not for the reasons usually given. It is also important as a prologue to the plays Congreve was so soon to write. There he would again illustrate, though in more subtle and complex terms, the ways in which men and women, even the most witty and urbane, may be thwarted by their own ingenuity, be delivered or defeated by seemingly casual or negligent events, find a guerdon, or meet disaster, through a "mistake." (pp. 105-06)

The Old Batchelour is a brilliant first play, one wherein a surpassing insight into human frailty is surpassingly displayed. If it seems a bit uncertain in its final ethical impress, this may be in part because, as Novak has said, Congreve "had not yet developed those ideal couples whose intelligence and sensibility seemed to promise an ideal match." Indeed, the couples of the play all seem curiously mismatched. Love is certainly inexplicable, but never again will Congreve stage a pairing so inexplicable as that of Araminta and Vainlove, where a woman so chaste, witty, honest, and above all, sensible, is presented as being in love with so self-regarding a man. It seems just as odd that Bellmour, the superior male of the play, should be yoked with a woman whose head, as Araminta drily understates the matter, is "a little out of Order." Marriages made on earth may not have been designed by heaven, but what seems unsatisfying about these pairings is their dramatic unaccountability: Araminta's love for Vainlove, and Bellmour's for Belinda, seem incongruous with their temperaments as established in the play.

Somewhat troubling also is the treatment accorded Heartwell. However much he is inclined to a surly pride, and however much his lust for Sylvia has turned him infatuate and hypocritical, his faults seem rather those of the rude plain-dealer and malcontent than anything else, more harmful to himself than to anyone else. Compared with Bellmour's deceitful debauching of Sylvia and his successful attempt on the honor of Fondlewife's house, the old bachelor's passion for Sylvia seems innocuous, no matter how absurd and unbecoming, and even more innocuous when set against Vainlove's narcissism and cold disdain for all women. Yet with his comparatively mild follies and failings, he is treated the most unmercifully of any character in the play. And while he is saved from his folly, it is not before he has undergone insufferable taunts from a circle of his "friends." As several critics have noted, the tormenting he receives "is in danger of becoming too serious for comedy," and though Congreve quickly restores a sense of mirth, one may still feel, when Heartwell is so provoked as almost to be ready to "draw upon a Woman," that the narrow verge between tragedy and comedy is nearly crossed—as it will continue to be; for Congreve's comedies, mirthful as they may be, are always turning up the darker undersides of life. (pp. 123-24)

It is my own view that *The Double-Dealer,* in spite of its Restoration esprit and gloss, is a genuine descendant of the English morality play tradition, and so I wish to give a rather heady measure of import to the way Maskwell's diabolism seems to recapitulate that of all the other incarnations of evil who appear, in one shape or another, at one or another time and place, in the English literary tradition, who there work their malevolent and destructive ends, and who are finally unmasked—only to reappear, we may be sure, in still another guise on still another stage. The satanism so insistently imputed to Maskwell by Congreve, along with a dazzling amount of demonological allusion hitherto unnoticed in critical discussions of the play, carries with it intimations of a world that simply cannot be reduced to the "naturalistic." On the contrary, the repeated association of Maskwell with "Hell" and "Damnation," along with all the occasions when Lady Touchwood not only is specifically categorized as a "Witch" but also is said to be "possess'd," would have been, to a contemporary audience, more than casual reminders of an ancient Adversary and of the human agents he might enter and subdue to his purposes—reminders, indeed, of an order of existence which for many still pressed closely upon the "natural" world. (p. 131)

[The] critics, by failing to see, or credit, the magnitude of the evil Maskwell was designed to represent, have continued to fault *The Double-Dealer* for what they consider to be Mellefont's inadequacies as a "hero." Holland thus states that "Ultimately, of course, the play fails because Mellefont is so woefully inadequate as a hero," and Birdsall finds that what "little pertinence" the play has for her study "lies, strangely enough, in its villain rather than in its hero, the latter being after all of very slight inherent interest." . . . Preoccupied, like so many others, with the wholly specious notion that the "hero" of a successful Restoration comedy is or must be a totally successful Machiavel, such critics simply overlook the basic fact that in no Congreve play after *The Old Batchelour* does the "hero" (whether Mellefont, Valentine, Alphonso, or Mirabell) succeed to a final reward as a result of his own cunning or maneuvering. (pp. 139-40)

We have seen, in *Incognita* and in *The Old Batchelour*, the ways in which "mistakes," fortunate as well as unfortunate, may serve providential ends. Here again, through an "Unfortunate Mistake" and "the unlucki'st Accident," a "Conspiracy," however low and tawdry, is "discover'd," and the reader has the choice of deciding here (as elsewhere in *The Double-Dealer*, and in plays to come) whether the discovery was due to Providence or to mere "chance." . . . But with *"the very matter of Fact"* set fully before Sir Paul's eyes, I do not see how it can be maintained, with Novak, that Providence would keep him "ignorant": Providence rather seems, in Sir Paul's words, as "constant" to him "in discovering this Conspiracy" as it had been in bestowing those blessings of life previously mentioned. Neither can it be, in my view, a reflection on Providence when, in the next few minutes, Sir Paul proves so much a cully as to be persuaded by his wife and Careless that the letter of assignation was intended only "to make trial" of a "suspected Vertue" which, on her ladyship's part, had proved "impregnable." Having done, one pre-

sumes, all that the most solicitous Providence could be expected to do, it surely is no impeachment of Heaven's care if Sir Paul should then ignore the "Ocular Proof" given him of his wife's infidelity and instead accept so spurious an explanation of the situation as is given him, exclaiming: "O Providence! Providence! What Discoveries are here made! Why, this is better and more Miraculous than the rest." (pp. 145-46)

The last "judgment" scene in *The Double-Dealer* establishes the pattern to be followed in the concluding scenes of Congreve's two remaining comedies; after *The Old Batchelour* he apparently acquired a deeper sense of the judgmental endings which occur in so many plays of his English dramatic forefathers, and was able to give what I consider the greatest possible imaginative turn to his own: in the last scenes of both *Love for Love* and *The Way of the World* the presiding judges or vicarious ministers of providential justice will be seen in the shape of women, one young and witty and beauteous, the other old and decayed and absurd of person—a surprising fact at first, perhaps, but not too much so if such precedents as Rosalind and Portia are brought to mind. In either case, whatever their fleshly form, they come forth in the end, as does Lord Touchwood, as reminders of a kind of justice still at work in the world. (pp. 153-54)

The world of *Love for Love* is, for the most part, so enigmatic as to defy comprehension by most of the characters, a world of secrets and ambiguities, where people, in Ben's words, "look one way" and yet "row another," and where a woman "is harder to be understood than a Piece of *AEgyptian* Antiquity, or an *Irish* Manuscript." It is a world in which people, like "a Witches Pray'r, and Dreams and *Dutch* Almanacks," are "to be understood by contraries." It is a world where things may seem, in Sir Sampson's foolish opinion, "as plain as the Nose in one's Face," and it is also a world where a Foresight, for all his pride in reading the stars and others' physiognomies, may be cuckolded while poring over his own face in a mirror. As these illustrations should suggest, it is a fictive world that once again evinces Congreve's close familiarity with the vocabularies of various occult arts and practices: judicial astrology, witchcraft, divination by dreams as well as by "sieve and shears," physiognomy, chiromancy, omens and prognostications.

In this world the character of Foresight is unusually instructive; the highly exaggerated example of a man who, in spite of his boasted ability both to "tell and foretell," is yet totally bewildered by goings-on that seem not only to defy all augury but also all his "Consideration, and Discretion, and Caution." His very name, of course, is a literal translation of "providence," a matter Congreve has amusingly underscored in the name of his "chitty fac'd" and hoydenish daughter Prue (the diminutive of Prudence, from Latin *pru-*

dens, contraction of *providens*). The family nomenclature is important, but not as a mere punning witticism or as a derogation of Providence itself. Just the reverse, for by using it Congreve promptly points to the real folly and impiety of Foresight's faith in astrology. . . . (pp. 159-60)

Foresight's role or function thus seems somewhat analogous to that of Sir Paul in *The Double-Dealer,* for he serves not at all to discredit Providence itself but rather to discredit wrong notions of it. In the jargon of his tribe, as well as in his perplexity of spirit despite all his "Science," he moreover contributes to Congreve's construction of a baffling and largely undecipherable world wherein both persons and events may be "kept secret" even "from the piercing Eye of Perspicuity," even indeed "from all Astrologers, and the Stars themselves," where anyone may "have a wrong Notion of Faces," where "Grey Hairs" may "cover a Green Head," where, in sum, and in his own words, *"Humanum est errare."* (p. 163)

The traditional Christian paradox of wordly wisdom as folly is sustained and enriched throughout *Love for Love* by an extraordinary Congrevean display of those oxymoronic expressions and contrary (not to say dizzying) pronouncements to which the human mind resorts when it tries to affirm or resolve the conflicting claims of spirit and flesh, mind and matter, love and self-love—utterances, for example, so cross and contrary, and yet so relevant to the whole play, as this from Proverbs 13:7: "There is that maketh himself rich, yet hath nothing; there is that maketh himself poor, yet hath great riches." (pp. 169-70)

In terms of the play's central paradox, Valentine essentially is "confined" by his acceptance of the precepts and practices of the "wisdom of this world," two of the outward signs of which, as South had noted in a sermon on 1 Corinthians 3:19, are "a constant, continual Course of Dissimulation," and a making of a man's self "the chief, if not the sole End of all his Actions." But it is not, as we have seen, by this kind of "wisdom" that Valentine can hope to win Angelica, or the "Blessing" she comes to represent, and so it is necessary for him to accept another kind of "wisdom"—the Epictetan kind, for example, that he had been able to mouth at the start of the play but was unwilling to incorporate in his own behavior. The way "out" of his "Confinement" is before him, indeed, throughout the play, implicit in all the paradoxes—Epictetan, Pauline, and otherwise—that are tossed about so frequently, so wittily, so lightly. But he cannot take the way "out" of his self-imposed "confinement" until he accepts the actual import of all such paradoxes, and so lays aside all his stratagems, all his dissimulation, all his self-interest, and thereby becomes the living proof of one who, in the earlier and scoffing but nevertheless presaging

words of Scandal, would "die a Martyr to Sense in a Country where the Religion is Folly."

With his decision, out of love for Angelica, to sign away any remaining right of inheritance, Valentine may be seen as having played a last card of "most price" in the game of "hearts" so important to us all. In doing so he takes leave of the conventional "wisdom of the world": as Angelica says, "How few, like *Valentine,* would persevere even unto Martyrdom, and sacrifice their Interest to their Constancy!" In a play where the very qualities of wisdom and folly are strained to the utmost, Valentine becomes the dramatic embodiment of that paradoxical man who becomes "a fool, that he may be wise," and also that paradoxical man "that maketh himself poor, yet hath great riches." (p. 172)

The world of *The Mourning Bride,* in the words of Gonsalez, has "somewhat yet of Mystery" in it. Faced with its mystery, man may be "amused," or blinded, by his own sight, just as he may "exceed in thinking" and be "blinded by [his] Thoughts." It is also a world, on the other hand, where a grief-stricken and dying father may, "in some Hour of Inspiration," read in Heaven's "Book of Prescience," and there find a way to leave the "Example of his Resignation" by which his son, with all the "afflictions" heaped upon him by an inscrutable Providence, will be strengthened and confirmed in his faith—and thereby deserve not only his release from a dark and underground dungeon cell (as close an analogy to a tomb as one could find), but also deserve to be given "again from Death" to his mourning bride. (p. 186)

The "legibility" of Providential sovereignty in the play is made the more certain by the way the wicked, with all their power and craft, are unable to enforce their own sovereignty over human nature and event. If Almeria and Osmyn are represented as baffled and amazed by the way their misfortunes are inexplicably, or "miraculously," turned into blessings, their oppressors are represented as equally perplexed by the way things turn out. They are represented, indeed, as frustrated by their own designs and actions, as being, in Zara's castigation of Selim,

> officious in contriving,
> In executing, puzzled, lame, and lost.
>
> (pp. 188-89)

All of the plotters—Manuel, Zara, Gonsalez, and Selim—have been drawn, by their own purposes, from their usual setting, the well-lighted "Room of State," into the cell which Gonsalez describes as being all "dark within, save what / A Lamp that feebly lifts a sickly Flame, / By fits reveals." In this so emblematic darkness, the feeble light of human reason is proven insufficient for its own purposes—but instrumental nevertheless in the accomplishment of the "just Decrees of

Heav'n." The "legibility" of such events seems to me indisputable: in them "the finger of God doth point out and indicate itself." (p. 191)

Over the past decade or so it has become the fashion among critics to perceive the principal character of *The Way of the World* as "Machiavellian Mirabell," the "Machiavellian poet as maker of society," as the "omniscient hero" who manipulates "the elements of polite society as cleverly as a Horner," as the man who has gained the greatest "mastery of conventions," as the character "who is held up for our admiration as the most accomplished manipulator," the one who "is victorious at the end of the play not because of any particular moral qualities he may have, but rather because he is a better lawyer than Fainall, and has made sure that his threats and his bargains are legally enforceable."

Such perceptions of Mirabell seem badly skewed to me, and for several reasons. They ignore, in the first place, the very basic fact that all of the schemes set forward by this so-called Machiavellian master of convention and society are shown, in the play itself, as countermined and frustrated. They further ignore the equally basic fact that Mirabell gains Millamant's hand and fortune only after his very ungentlemanly schemes against Lady Wishfort have proved unsuccessful, and also only after he has agreed to appear before her ladyship and profess his "sincere remorse" for the "many Injuries" he has "offer'd to so good a Lady." They furthermore, out of some strange and aberrant esteem for an amoral Machiavellian craftiness and exploitation of others, would move *The Way of the World* off any moral center at all, as may be seen most clearly perhaps in Birdsall's view of Mirabell as the "kind of hero from whom unprincipled behavior is to be expected in such a life-and-death matter as [he] has in hand"—a view which would certainly have confirmed Collier in his conviction that Congreve and other Restoration playwrights, in spite of their protests, were offering up for audience admiration a set of rake-heroes whose pursuit of a fortune justified any means, however mendacious, they might employ.

Such critical perceptions of Mirabell seem to me to originate, finally, from the widespread current assumptions that the world of Congreve's art is governed by some dubious amalgamation of Hobbesian, nihilistic, "Epicurean" premises, and that in consequence any supremacy in such a putative moral jungle could only be won, or even merited, by a "hero" in the Machiavellian mode—despite the fact that the Machiavellian Maskwell in *The Double-Dealer,* so much the honest Mellefont's superior in guile and stratagem, is exposed and expelled from the Touchwood estate at the end of the play; or that Valentine, in *Love for Love,* wins Angelica only when he renounces his impostures and his self-interest; or that Manuel and Gonsalez and Zara, in *The Mourning Bride,* are shown as finally destroyed not only by the "just Decrees of Heav'n" but also by their own inordinate cunning.

So intent, indeed, have been the critics on demonstrating that the "resolution of the play depends entirely on Mirabell's wit, charm, and knowledge of the ways of the world," or on proving that the "secular strength of his solution must not be diminished by mere luck," that they have ignored or depreciated the very large number of seemingly quite fortuitous, yet also extremely "opportune," discoveries in the play—"discoveries" which, in the end, may be seen not only as having frustrated Mirabell's own more unpalatable schemes during the course of the play but also as providing Mrs. Fainall, in the end, with the moral courage to face, and face down, a vile and mercenary husband. The chance discoveries by which Mirabell's impostures are thwarted, as well as those by which his final success is forwarded, are inconsistent with the idea of his being the consummate Machiavellian master of his milieu; they are consistent, on the other hand, with the pattern evinced in Congreve's other plays, where we find that protagonists never succeed by their own unaided devices and strength, but are rather moved, if morally disposed, through a course of defeats, mistakes, seeming coincidence, and apparently chance discovery, to ultimate reward. (pp. 193-94)

Strange as it may seem on first thought, the final scene of *The Way of the World,* like the final scenes of *The Double-Dealer* and *Love for Love,* must be regarded as another scene of "judgment," and in the tradition of such scenes in English dramatic history as we have noted before. Only Holland seems to have observed the "judgmental" nature of the scene, when he remarks that in the finale Lady Wishfort "becomes a kind of tribunal before whom the opposed forces in the play plead their causes." And while my emphasis is quite different from Holland's, his comment is right in the main, for however improbable and ridiculous a tribunal she may seem, Lady Wishfort is nevertheless the head, however disordered her own head may be, of the large family whose members make up most of the characters in the play: all relationships in the play center on her, and so there is an appropriateness, however comic, in the fact that the main transgressors against her honor and her person, whatever its dilapidations, are brought to judgment before her. (p. 197)

I would stress, in conclusion, the way the failings and transgressions of most characters in *The Way of the World* are placed within a framing diction which accentuates the very human fact, even the human weakness, of "forgetfulness"—and also accentuates the value and even the necessity of such "forgetting." One may, as Witwoud does, forget what one "was going to say," or even, as he also does, forget the half-brother he has not seen "since the Revolution." One may forget one's gloves or the "Motto" on one's "Crest," as Sir

Wilfull does, or forget, as does Lady Wishfort, that her nephew will be coming for dinner. One may even forget one's own self, as Waitwell fears he may do in his transformation into Sir Rowland, as Foible is said to do in her new "Preferment" as Waitwell's wife, or as Lady Wishfort apologizes for doing: "As I'm a Person I am in a very Chaos to think I shou'd so forget my self."

So human a failing, however, may also be put to the most virtuous and saving of purposes, and most especially when one endeavors "to forget" past injuries, or to "stifle" a "just resentment," as Lady Wishfort does after Mirabell has begged that the past "be forgotten" and that he "be pitied first; and afterwards forgotten." And indeed, as Sir Wilfull maintains, you must "Forgive and Forget," most especially "you must, an you are a Christian." By the end of *The Way of the World* a goodly number of characters have shown that our acts of "forgetfulness" may be something more than mere foibles or signs of infirmity—they may be the best evidence we can give of a most estimable human trait. (p. 214)

Aubrey L. Williams, in his *An Approach to Congreve,* Yale University Press, 1979, 234 p.

LOUIS AUCHINCLOSS
(essay date 1986)

[In the following excerpt, Auchincloss examines the nature of courtship in Congreve's dramas.]

Congreve through the generations has found himself constantly spanked for his morals, or lack thereof, from contemporary parsons who denounced him from the pulpit, to Thackeray, that king of Victorians masquerading as an eighteenth-century wit, who could not help wondering if the great dramatist, whose art seemed to justify a seat on the very peak of Parnassus, would not bring disapproving sniffs to the noses of the properer gods already there.

We can laugh at this in our own liberated day, but have you read him recently? He does go rather far. Making full allowance for the latitude of comedy, or even of farce, his heroes and villains still strut with astounding arrogance around a sleazy barnyard. Consider two of the former: Bellimour in *The Old Bachelor* and Mirabell in *The Way of the World.* Both are viewed as sympathetically by their creator as he seems capable of viewing men. They have charm and wit, and they are very much in love with equally charming and witty girls. Yet Bellimour, while wooing his Belinda, is quite as intently plotting the seduction of Mrs. Fondlewife, the spouse of an old fool whose name is proof, in a

Congreve world, that the gods themselves will smile on his cuckolding. Mirabell is more constant to his enchanting Millament, yet he is represented, before the action of the play, as having deliberately hoodwinked the villain Fainall into marrying his discarded mistress, whom he believes—erroneously, as it turns out—to be pregnant by himself. Here is how he justifies this conduct to his old love who, understandably enough, finds herself wretched in her new union:

> If the familiarities of our loves had produced that consequence of which you were apprehensive, where could you have fixed a father's name with credit, but on a husband? I knew Fainall to be a man lavish of his morals, an interested and professing friend, a false and designing lover; yet one whose wit and outward fair behaviour have gained a reputation with the town enough to make that woman stand excused who has suffered herself to be won by his addresses. A better man ought not to have been sacrificed to the occasion; a worse had not answered to the purpose.

What the standards of the barnyard seem to boil down to is that Fainall is fair game to be cheated because he is a creep, and that Mirabell is justified in cheating him because he has charm. And as for Bellimour, is a healthy young man to give up sex while he is obliged to go through the lengthy ritual of courtship? Of course not. Such virtue is expected only of the impotent.

I suggest that Congreve is not entirely joking when he tells us through the mouths of his female characters that men are inconstant creatures who will marry their inamoratas only if the latter stick it out. The game of courtship has perfectly definite rules. For the man it is to huff and to puff, to breathe deathless passion which neither he nor the woman addressed believes, and to do everything in his power to seduce her—as he is simultaneously seducing others. The woman's game is to hold him off with enticing mockery and yield not so much as a kiss until she has led him firmly to the altar. The penalties in the game are all for the woman; she who yields prematurely is labeled a "whore" by all, including her conqueror, nor can she ever thereafter hope to marry a gentleman unless she resorts to the subterfuge suggested by Mirabell. Yet the word "whore," at least as used in *The Old Bachelor* to describe the unfortunate Silvia, is without any sharp pejorative sense. She has been caught offside and been penalized, so to speak, a fatal number of yards. She has lost the game, to be sure; she is now a whore. But there are plenty of nice whores. One doesn't whip them at the cart tail. Silvia in the end is even allowed to marry a minor and ridiculous character.

What has probably most shocked people through the ages about Congreve is that he seems really to have accepted this concept as a valid social system. We have recently learned in a biography of Velásquez that even the greatest artist may care more for fashion than anything else in life. To Congreve it was bad to be a cuckold, no matter how little one cared for one's wife. Why? Society decreed it. And it was bad to lose one's maidenhead before marriage, although perfectly acceptable to commit adultery afterward. Why? Society ordained it. Today he would violate *our* fashion, because it is still fashionable to believe in enduring love after marriage, however rare it may be becoming.

Or *did* he believe in it? Is that the one note of sen-

timent that leaks through? He never, like Oscar Wilde, tries to reconcile his cynical characters in the last act to the wedded bliss of the late Victorian illusion. But he seems to allow us to speculate that Mirabell and Millament may have a happy life together. Or is his ghost laughing up his sleeve at me? Who knows? All that I can be sure of is that he had a passionate faith in the power of language. Only Shakespeare himself had a cadence in his prose like Congreve's. (pp. 83-4)

Louis Auchincloss, "Courtship in Congreve," in *The New Criterion,* Vol. V, No. 2, October, 1986, pp. 83-4.

SOURCES FOR FURTHER STUDY

Corman, Brian. " 'The Mixed Way of Comedy': Congreve's *The Double-Dealer.*" *Modern Philology* 71, No. 4 (May 1974): 356-65.

    Traces patterns of comedy in *The Double-Dealer.*

Erickson, Robert A. "Lady Wishfort and the Will of the World." *Modern Language Quarterly* 45, No. 4 (December 1984): 388-49.

    Analyzes Lady Wishfort as a victim of will in *The Way of the World.*

Kaufman, Anthony. "Language and Character in Congreve's *The Way of the World.*" *Texas Studies in Literature and Language* XV, No. 3 (Fall 1973): 411-27.

    Suggests that dialogue mirrors characterization in *The Way of the World.*

Mueschke, Miriam, and Mueschke, Paul. *A New View of Congreve's "Way of the World".* Ann Arbor: University of Michigan Press, 1958, 85 p.

    Detailed study of Congreve's artistry in *The Way of the World.*

Muir, Kenneth. "The Comedies of William Congreve." In *Restoration Theatre,* edited by John Russell Brown and Bernard Harris, pp. 221-37. Stratford-upon-Avon Studies, No. 6. London: Edward Arnold, 1965.

    Chronicles the development of Congreve's skill as a dramatist.

Woolf, Virginia. "Congreve's Comedies." In her *Collected Essays, Vol. I,* edited by Leonard Woolf, pp. 76-84. New York: Harcourt Brace Jovanovich, 1967.

    Attests to Congreve's wealth of memorable characters and his "genuis for phrase-making" in his dramatic works.

Joseph Conrad

1857-1924

(Born Tedor Josef Konrad Nalecz Korzeniowski) Polish-born English novelist, short story writer, essayist, dramatist, and autobiographer.

INTRODUCTION

Conrad was an innovative novelist as well as one of the finest stylists of modern English literature. His novels are complex moral and psychological examinations of the ambiguous nature of good and evil. His characters are repeatedly forced to acknowledge their own failings and the weakness of their ideals against all forms of corruption; the most honorable characters are those who realize their fallibility but still struggle to uphold the dictates of conscience. To examine these dilemmas, Conrad devised narrative techniques that more completely involve the reader in the conflicts of his characters than did traditional novels.

Conrad was born in 1857 in a Russian-ruled province of Poland. He was exiled with his parents to northern Russia in 1863 following his parents' participation in the Polish independence movement. His parents' health rapidly deteriorated in Russia, and, after their deaths in 1868, Conrad lived in the homes of relatives, where he was often ill and received sporadic schooling. At sixteen, Conrad pursued a career as a seaman, sailing to Martinique and the West Indies. Although he knew very little English at the time, he joined the British merchant marines in 1878; during his ten years of service, he became a naturalized British citizen, traveled to Africa, Australia, India, and the Orient, rose to the rank of Captain in the service, and mastered the English language.

Poor health forced Conrad to retire from the merchant marines. In 1894, he began a career as a writer, basing much of his work on his experience as a seaman. Conrad wrote much of his first novel, *Almayer's Folly* (1895), while he was still in the service. Regarding its publication in 1895, Conrad later remarked: "the only doubt I suffered, after the publication of *Almayer's Folly*, was whether I should write another line for print. . . ." Conrad struggled for the rest of his life to earn a living as a writer. In addition to his financial diffi-culties, he found writing in English to be a slow and ag-onizing ordeal, and many critics have noted the effects upon his work of such lifelong conditions as neurasthe-nia and fear of inadequacy. While the 1913 novel *Chance* was Conrad's first financial and critical suc-cess, his novels and short stories published during the first decade of the twentieth century are currently re-garded as his most important and enduring works. Conrad suffered a heart attack and died in his home in Kent, England, in 1924.

Throughout his career, Conrad examined the im-possibility of living by a traditional code of conduct: his novels postulate that the complexity of the human spirit allows neither absolute fidelity to any ideal nor even to one's conscience. In Conrad's work, failure is a fact of human existence, and every ideal contains the possi-bilities for its own corruption. This is portrayed most ef-fectively in *Nostromo* (1904), which deals with revolu-tion, politics, and financial manipulation in a South American republic. All of the characters in this novel are corrupted by their ambitions, which range from greed to idealistic desires for reform, and all their ambi-tions lead to disaster—the nobler the ideal, the greater their self-disgust.

Most of Conrad's greatest works take place on a ship or in the backwaters of civilization. A ship or a small outpost offered an isolated environment where Conrad could develop his already complex moral prob-lems without unnecessary entanglements that might obscure the concentration of tragedy. The two greatest examples of moral tragedy in his work are *Lord Jim* (1900), which examines the failures of a man before society and his own conscience, and *Heart of Dark-ness* (1899), a dreamlike tale of mystery and adventure set in central Africa that is also the story of a man's symbolic journey into his own inner being. In both of these novels an understanding of the role of the narra-tor, Marlow, is crucial to a more complete comprehen-sion of Conrad's intentions. Marlow offers a tentative view of a complex and ambiguous world. He is the most refined example of Conrad's use of an unreliable narra-tor, but in all of his works he relies upon time shifts, flashbacks, and multiple perspectives to portray the unreliability of human perception. The reader is con-stantly forced to interpret and reinterpret the informa-tion that Conrad's characters present. In his preface to *The Nigger of the "Narcissus"* (1897), an essay that has been called his artistic credo, Conrad expressed his intention of forcing the reader's involvement in his work: "My task which I am trying to achieve is, by the power of the written word, to make you feel—it is, be-fore all, to make you *see*. That—and no more, and it is everything."

Nostromo is widely recognized as Conrad's most ambitious novel. An account of a revolution in the ficti-tious South American country of Costaguana, *Nostro-mo* examines the ideals, motivations, and failures of several participants in that conflict. Critics agree that *Nostromo* represents an important development in Conrad's career. His earlier works, including *Lord Jim* and *Heart of Darkness*, provide an intense analysis of a few characters, while in the political novels, begin-ning with *Nostromo* and including *The Secret Agent* and *Under Western Eyes*, Conrad widened his scope to examine an entire society. Conrad himself referred to *Nostromo* as his "largest canvas," and many critics consider the novel one of the greatest of the twentieth century.

Conrad's current reputation rests with such rela-tively early works as *Lord Jim, Heart of Darkness,* and *Nostromo,* in which imagery, symbolism, and shifts in time and perspective combine to create an intriguing, mystical series of fictional settings. In his later works, Conrad's examination of the ambiguity of good and evil is generally considered too stylized and heavy-handed. His most highly regarded works, however, are acknowl-edged as masterpieces of English literature and contin-ue to generate significant critical commentary.

(For further information about Conrad's life and works, see *Contemporary Authors,* Vol. 104; *Dictionary of Literary Biography,* Vols. 10, 34, 98; and *Something about the Author,* Vol. 27.)

CRITICAL COMMENTARY

JOSEPH CONRAD
(essay date 1897)

[In the following excerpt from his preface to *The Nig-ger of the "Narcissus"* (republished in 1914 as *Jo-seph Conrad on the Art of Writing*), Conrad discuss-es his theories concerning the artistic effects of fic-tion.]

A work that aspires, however humbly, to the condition of art should carry its justification in every line. And art itself may be defined as a single-minded attempt to

Principal Works

Almayer's Folly (novel) 1895

An Outcast of the Islands (novel) 1896

The Nigger of the "Narcissus" (novel) 1897

Tales of Unrest (short stories) 1898

Lord Jim (novel) 1900

The Inheritors: An Extravagant Story [with Ford Madox Ford] (novel) 1901

"Typhoon" (short story) 1902

*Youth: A Narrative, and Two Other Stories (short stories) 1902

Romance [with Ford Madox Ford] (novel) 1903

Nostromo: A Tale of the Seaboard (novel) 1904

The Mirror of the Sea: Memories and Impressions (autobiography) 1906

The Secret Agent (novel) 1907

A Set of Six (short stories) 1908

Some Reminiscences (autobiography) 1908; also published as A Personal Record, 1912

Under Western Eyes (novel) 1911

'Twixt Land and Sea (short stories) 1912

Chance (novel) 1913

Victory: An Island Tale (novel) 1915

Within the Tides (short stories) 1915

The Shadow Line (novel) 1917

The Arrow of Gold (novel) 1919

The Rescue (novel) 1920

Notes on Life and Letters (essays) 1921

Notes on My Books (essays) 1921

The Rover (novel) 1923

The Nature of a Crime [with Ford Madox Ford] (novel) 1924

Collected Works of Joseph Conrad. 21 vols. (short stories, novels, essays) 1925

Suspense: A Napoleonic Novel (novel) 1925

Tales of Hearsay (short stories) 1925

The Sisters (short stories) 1928

*This collection includes the novella Heart of Darkness.

render the highest kind of justice to the visible universe, by bringing to light the truth, manifold and one, underlying its every aspect. It is an attempt to find in its forms, in its colours, in its light, in its shadows, in the aspects of matter, and in the facts of life what of each is fundamental, what is enduring and essential—their one illuminating and convincing quality—the very truth of their existence. The artist, then, like the thinker or the scientist, seeks the truth and makes his appeal. Impressed by the aspect of the world the thinker plunges into ideas, the scientist into facts. . . . (p. 49)

It is otherwise with the artist.

Confronted by the same enigmatical spectacle the artist descends within himself, and in that lonely region of stress and strife, if he be deserving and fortunate, he finds the terms of his appeal. His appeal is made to our less obvious capacities: to that part of our nature which, because of the warlike conditions of existence, is necessarily kept out of sight within the more resisting and hard qualities—like the vulnerable body within a steel armour. His appeal is less loud, more profound, less distinct, more stirring—and sooner forgotten. Yet its effect endures for ever. The changing wisdom of successive generations discards ideas, questions facts, demolishes theories. But the artist appeals to that part of our being which is not dependent on wisdom; to that in us which is a gift and not an acquisition—and, therefore, more permanently enduring. He speaks to our capacity for delight and wonder, to the sense of mystery surrounding our lives; to our sense of pity, and beauty, and pain; to the latent feeling of fellowship with all creation—and to the subtle but invincible conviction of solidarity that knits together the loneliness of innumerable hearts, to the solidarity in dreams, in joy, in sorrow, in aspirations, in illusions, in hope, in fear, which binds men to each other, which binds together all humanity—the dead to the living and the living to the unborn.

It is only some such train of thought, or rather of feeling, that can in a measure explain the aim of the attempt, made in [*The Nigger of the "Narcissus"*], to present an unrestful episode in the obscure lives of a few individuals out of all the disregarded multitude of the bewildered, the simple, and the voiceless. For, if any part of truth dwells in the belief confessed above, it becomes evident that there is not a place of splendour or a dark corner of the earth that does not deserve, if only a passing glance of wonder and pity. The motive, then, may be held to justify the matter of the work. . . . (pp. 49-51)

Fiction—if it at all aspires to be art—appeals to temperament. And in truth it must be, like painting, like music, like all art, the appeal of one temperament to all the other innumerable temperaments whose subtle and resistless power endows passing events with their true meaning, and creates the moral, the emotional atmosphere of the place and time. Such an appeal to be effective must be an impression conveyed through the senses; and, in fact, it cannot be made in any other way, because temperament, whether individual or collective, is not amenable to persuasion. All art, therefore, appeals primarily to the senses, and the artistic aim when expressing itself in written words must also make its appeal through the senses, if its high desire is to reach the secret spring of responsive emotions. . . . And it is only through complete, unswerving devotion to the perfect blending of form and substance; it is only through an unremitting never-discouraged care for the shape and ring of sentences that an approach can be made to plasticity, to colour, and that the light of magic suggestiveness may be brought to play for an evanescent instant over the commonplace surface of words: of the old, old words, worn thin, defaced by ages of careless usage. (p. 51)

To snatch in a moment of courage, from the remorseless rush of time, a passing phase of life, is only the beginning of the task. The task approached in tenderness and faith is to hold up unquestioningly, without choice and without fear, the rescued fragment before all eyes in the light of a sincere mood. It is to show its vibration, its colour, its form; and through its movement, its form, and its colour, reveal the substance of its truth—disclose its inspiring secret: the stress and passion within the core of each convincing moment. In a single-minded attempt of that kind, if one be deserving and fortunate, one may perchance attain to such clearness of sincerity that at last the presented vision of regret or pity, of terror or mirth, shall awaken in the hearts of the beholders that feeling of unavoidable solidarity; of the solidarity in mysterious origin, in toil, in joy, in hope, in uncertain fate, which binds men to each other and all mankind to the visible world. (p. 52)

Joseph Conrad, "The Nigger of the 'Narcissus'," in his *Conrad's Prefaces to His Works,* edited by Edward Garnett, J. M. Dent & Sons Ltd., 1937, pp. 49-54.

H. L. MENCKEN

(essay date 1917)

[Mencken was an American social and literary critic whose irreverent outlook on life and vigorous, invective-charged writing style helped establish the iconoclastic spirit of the Jazz Age. In the following excerpt, he praises Conrad's works for their realism.]

Conrad's predilection for barbarous scenes and the more bald and shocking sort of drama has an obviously autobiographical basis. His own road ran into strange places in the days of his youth. He moved among men who were menaced by all the terrestrial cruelties, and by the almost unchecked rivalry and rapacity of their fellow men, without any appreciable barriers, whether of law, of convention or of sentimentality, to shield them. The struggle for existence, as he saw it, was well nigh as purely physical among human beings as among the carnivora of the jungle. Some of his stories, and among them his very best, are plainly little more than transcripts of his own experience. He himself is the enchanted boy of **"Youth"**; he is the ship-master of *Heart of Darkness;* he hovers in the background of all the island books and is visibly present in most of the tales of the sea.

And what he got out of that early experience was more than a mere body of reminiscence; it was a scheme of valuations. He came to his writing years with a sailor's disdain for the trifling hazards and emprises of market places and drawing rooms, and it shows itself whenever he sets pen to paper. A conflict, it would seem, can make no impression upon him save it be colossal. When his men combat, not nature, but other men, they carry over into the business the gigantic method of sailors battling with a tempest. *The Secret Agent* and *Under Western Eyes* fill the dull back streets of London and Geneva with pursuits, homicides and dynamitings. *Nostromo* is a long record of treacheries, butcheries and carnalities. **"A Point of Honor"** is coloured by the senseless, insatiable ferocity of Gobineau's "Renaissance." *Victory* ends with a massacre of all the chief personages, a veritable catastrophe of blood. Whenever he turns from the starker lusts to the pale passions of man under civilization, Conrad fails. **"The Return"** is a thoroughly infirm piece of writing—a second rate magazine story. One concludes at once that the author himself does not believe in it. *The Inheritors* is worse; it becomes, after the first few pages, a flaccid artificiality, a bore. It is impossible to imagine the chief characters of the Conrad gallery in such scenes. Think of Captain MacWhirr reacting to social tradition, Lord Jim immersed in the class war, Lena Hermann seduced by the fashions, Almayer a candidate for office! As well think of Huckleberry Finn at Harvard, or Tom Jones practising law.

These things do not interest Conrad, chiefly, I suppose, because he does not understand them. His concern, one may say, is with the gross anatomy of passion, not with its histology. He seeks to depict emotion, not in its ultimate attenuation, but in its fundamental innocence and fury. Inevitably, his materials are those of what we call melodrama; he is at one, in the bare substance of his tales, with the manufacturers of the baldest shockers. But with a difference!—a difference, to wit, of approach and comprehension, a difference abysmal and revolutionary. He lifts melodrama to the dignity of an important business, and makes it a means to an end that the mere shock-monger never dreams of. In itself, remember, all this up-roar and blood-letting is not incredible, nor even improbable. The world, for all the pressure of order, is still full of savage and stupendous conflicts, of murders and debaucheries, of crimes indescribable and adventures almost unimaginable. One cannot reasonably ask a novelist to deny them or to gloss over them; all one may demand of him is that, if he make artistic use of them, he render them understandable—that he logically account for them, that he give them plausibility by showing their genesis in intelligible motives and colourable events.

The objection to the conventional melodramatist is that he fails to do this. It is not that his efforts are too florid, but that his causes are too puny. For all his exuberance of fancy, he seldom shows us a downright impossible event; what he does constantly show us is an inadequate and hence unconvincing motive. In a cheap theatre we see a bad actor, imperfectly disguised as a viscount, bind a shrieking young woman to the railroad tracks, with an express train approaching. Why does he do it? The melodramatist offers a double-headed reason, the first part being that the viscount is an amalgam of Satan and Don Juan and the second being that the young woman prefers death to dishonour. Both parts are absurd. Our eyes show us at once that the fellow is far more the floorwalker, the head barber, the Knight of Pythias than either the Satan or the Don Juan, and our experience of life tells us that young women in yellow wigs do not actually rate their virginity so dearly. But women are undoubtedly done to death in this way—not every day, perhaps, but now and then. Men bind them, trains run over them, the newspapers discuss the crime, the pursuit of the felon, the ensuing jousting of the jurisconsults. Why, then? The true answer, when it is forthcoming at all, is always much more complex than the melodramatist's answer. It may be so enormously complex, indeed, as to transcend all the normal laws of cause and effect. It may be an answer made up largely, or even wholly, of the fantastic, the astounding, the unearthly reasons of lunacy. That is the chief, if not the only difference between melodrama and reality. The events of the two may be, and often are identical. It is only in their underlying network of causes that they are dissimilar and incommensurate.

Here, in brief, you have the point of essential distinction between the stories of Conrad, a supreme artist in fiction, and the trashy confections of the literary artisans—*e.g.*, Sienkiewicz, Dumas, Lew Wallace, and their kind. Conrad's materials, at bottom, are almost identical with those of the artisans. He, too, has his chariot races, his castaways, his carnivals of blood in the arena. He, too, takes us through shipwrecks, revolutions, assassinations, gaudy heroisms, abominable treacheries. But always he illuminates the nude and amazing event with shafts of light which reveal not only the last detail of its workings, but also the complex of origins and inducements behind it. Always, he throws about it a probability which, in the end, becomes almost inevitability. His *Nostromo,* for example, in its externals, is a

mere tale of South American turmoil; its materials are those of "Soldiers of Fortune." But what a difference in method, in point of approach, in inner content! Davis was content to show the overt act, scarcely accounting for it at all, and then only in terms of conventional romance. Conrad penetrates to the motive concealed in it, the psychological spring and basis of it, the whole fabric of weakness, habit and aberration underlying it. The one achieved an agreeable romance, and an agreeable romance only. The other achieves an extraordinarily brilliant and incisive study of the Latin-American temperament—a full length exposure of the perverse passions and incomprehensible ideals which provoke presumably sane men to pursue one another like wolves, and of the reactions of that incessant pursuit upon the men themselves, and upon their primary ideas, and upon the institutions under which they live. I do not say that Conrad is always exhaustive in his explanations, or that he is accurate. In the first case I know that he often is not, in the second case I do not know whether he is or he isn't. But I do say that, within the scope of his vision, he is wholly convincing; that the men and women he sets into his scene show ineluctably vivid and persuasive personality; that the theories he brings forward to account for their acts are intelligible; that the effects of those acts, upon actors and immediate spectators alike, are such as might be reasonably expected to issue; that the final impression is one of searching and indubitable veracity. One leaves *Nostromo* with a memory as intense and lucid as that of a real experience. The thing is not mere photography. It is interpretative painting at its highest.

In all his stories you will find this same concern with the inextricable movement of phenomena and noumena between event and event, this same curiosity as to first causes and ultimate effects. Sometimes, as in **"The Point of Honor"** and **"The End of the Tether,"** he attempts to work out the obscure genesis, in some chance emotion or experience, of an extraordinary series of transactions. At other times, as in **"Typhoon,"** **"Youth,"** **"Falk"** and *The Shadow Line,* his endeavour is to determine the effect of some gigantic and fortuitous event upon the mind and soul of a given man. At yet other times, as in *Almayer's Folly, Lord Jim* and *Under Western Eyes,* it is his aim to show how cause and effect are intricately commingled, so that it is difficult to separate motive from consequence, and consequence from motive. But always it is the process of mind rather than the actual act that interests him. Always he is trying to penetrate the actor's mask and interpret the actor's frenzy. It is this concern with the profounder aspects of human nature, this bold grappling with the deeper and more recondite problems of his art, that gives him consideration as a first-rate artist. He differs from the common novelists of his time as a Beethoven differs from a Mendelssohn. Some of them are quite his equals in technical skill, and a few of them, notably Bennett and Wells, often show an actual superiority, but when it comes to that graver business which underlies all mere virtuosity, he is unmistakably the superior of the whole corps of them.

This superiority is only the more vividly revealed by the shop-worn shoddiness of most of his materials. He takes whatever is nearest to hand, out of his own rich experience or out of the common store of romance. He seems to disdain the petty advantages which go with the invention of novel plots, extravagant characters and unprecedented snarls of circumstance. All the classical doings of anarchists are to be found in *The Secret Agent;* one has heard them copiously credited, of late, to so-called Reds. **"Youth,"** as a story, is no more than an orthodox sea story, and W. Clark Russell contrived better ones. In *Chance* we have a stern father at his immemorial tricks. In *Victory* there are villains worthy of Jack B. Yeats' melodramas of the Spanish Main. In *Nostromo* we encounter the whole stock company of Richard Harding Davis and O. Henry. And in *Under Western Eyes* the protagonist is one who finds his love among the women of his enemies—a situation at the heart of all the military melodramas ever written.

But what Conrad makes of that ancient and fly-blown stuff, that rubbish from the lumber room of the imagination! Consider, for example, *Under Western Eyes,* by no means the best of his stories. The plot is that of "Shenandoah" and "Held by the Enemy"—but how brilliantly it is endowed with a new significance, how penetratingly its remotest currents are followed out, how magnificently it is made to fit into that colossal panorama of Holy Russia! It is always this background, this complex of obscure and baffling influences, this drama under the drama, that Conrad spends his skill upon, and not the obvious commerce of the actual stage. It is not the special effect that he seeks, but the general effect. It is not so much man the individual that interests him, as the shadowy accumulation of traditions, instincts and blind chances which shapes the individual's destiny. Here, true enough, we have a full-length portrait of Razumov, glowing with life. But here, far more importantly, we also have an amazingly meticulous and illuminating study of the Russian character, with all its confused mingling of Western realism and Oriental fogginess, its crazy tendency to go shooting off into the spaces of an incomprehensible metaphysic, its general transcendence of all that we Celts and Saxons and Latins hold to be true of human motive and human act. Russia is a world apart: that is the sum and substance of the tale. In the island stories we have the same elaborate projection of the East, of its fantastic barbarism, of brooding Asia. And in the sea stories we have, perhaps for the first time in English fiction, a vast and adequate picture of the sea, the symbol at once of man's eternal striving and of his eternal impotence.

Here, at last, the colossus has found its interpreter. There is in **"Typhoon"** and *The Nigger of the "Narcissus,"* and, above all, in *The Mirror of the Sea,* a poetic evocation of the sea's stupendous majesty that is unparalleled outside the ancient sagas. Conrad describes it with a degree of graphic skill that is superb and incomparable. He challenges at once the pictorial vigour of Hugo and the aesthetic sensitiveness of Lafcadio Hearn, and surpasses them both. And beyond this mere dazzling visualization, he gets into his pictures an overwhelming sense of that vast drama of which they are no more than the flat, lifeless representation—of that inexorable and uncompassionate struggle which is life itself. The sea to him is a living thing, an omnipotent and unfathomable thing, almost a god. He sees it as the Eternal Enemy, deceitful in its caresses, sudden in its rages, relentless in its enmities, and forever a mystery. (pp. 40-51)

H. L. Mencken, "Joseph Conrad," in his *A Book of Prefaces,* Alfred A. Knopf, 1917, pp. 11-66.

MARVIN MUDRICK
(essay date 1958-59)

[In the following excerpt, Mudrick discusses Conrad's verbal and structural techniques.]

Everything Conrad wrote recalls everything else he wrote, in a pervasive melancholy of outlook, a persistency of theme ("the plight of the man on whom life closes down inexorably, divesting him of the supports and illusory protection of friendship, social privilege, or love"), and a conscientious manipulation of innovational method; yet what marks Conrad as not a mere experimentalist or entertainer but a genuine innovator occurs only sporadically in his full-length novels, with discretion and sustained impulse only in several long stories or short novels: in *The Nigger of the Narcissus,* in *Typhoon,* in Part I of *Under Western Eyes,* and—with most impressive rich immediacy—in *Heart of Darkness.*

Conrad's innovation—or, in any case, the fictional technique that he exploited with unprecedented thoroughness—is the double-plot: neither allegory (where surface is something teasing, to be got through), nor catch-all symbolism (where every knowing particular signifies some universal or other), but a developing order of actions so lucidly symbolic of a developing state of spirit—from moment to moment, so morally identifiable—as to suggest the conditions of allegory without forfeiting or even subordinating the realistic "superficial" claim of the actions and their actors.

Heart of Darkness—at least until we reach Kurtz and the end of the journey—is a remarkable instance of such order: details intensely present, evocatively characteristic of the situations in which they happen, and prefiguring from moment to moment an unevadable moral reality. The equatorial incubus of inefficiency, for example, is created and consolidated by a set of details memorable in their direct sensuous impact, almost farcical in the situations whose absurd disproportions they discover, and wholly dreadful as a cumulative cosmic denial of mind: the warship (" 'It appears the French had one of their wars going on thereabouts' "), its men dying of fever at the rate of three a day, " 'firing into a continent' "; the forsaken railway truck, looking " 'as dead as the carcass of some animal,' " rusting in the grass " 'on its back with its wheels in the air' "; the fat man with the moustaches trying to put out a blaze in a grass shed with a quart of water in a leaking pail; the brickmaker idling for a year with no bricks and no hope of materials for making them; the " 'wanton smashup' " of drainage pipes abandoned in a ravine; burst, piled-up cases of rivets at the Outer Station, and no way of getting them to the damaged steamboat at the Central Station; the " 'vast artificial hole somebody had been digging on the slope, the purpose of which I found it impossible to divine. It wasn't a quarry or a sandpit, anyhow. It was just a hole.' " . . . (pp. 545-47)

In this world of the fortuitous, acutely realized details of nightmare, such efficiency as can survive will be of a very special kind; like the accountant's—

Hair parted, brushed, oiled, under a green-lined parasol held in a big white hand. He was amazing, and had a penholder behind his ear. . . . His appearance was certainly that of a hairdresser's dummy; but in the great demoralization of the land he kept up his appearance. That's backbone. . . .

In this climate, where life for a clot of exasperated foreigners contracts itself to the exploitation of the hopelessly alien, it is also difficult to guard against certain explicit moral errors; among them, a cruelty as ordained and unimpassioned as in " 'the gloomy circle of some inferno.' " . . . (p. 547)

[Work] defines and embodies itself in its reluctant functionaries, starched accountant as well as dying natives; it has its particular countersign and gleaming talisman (" 'The word "ivory" rang in the air, was whispered, was sighed. You would think they were praying to it. A taint of imbecile rapacity blew through it all, like a whiff from some corpse' "); in its tangible promise of easy gratifications, it indifferently victimizes both the unwilling natives and their incompetent overseers, it prescribes the tableau of cruelty in the grove of death, it provides its own corresponding niche for every stage of opportunism from the novice exploiter (weight 224 pounds) who keeps fainting, to the manager of the Central Station. . . . (pp. 547-48)

The general blight and demoralization are inextricable, they do not detach themselves for scrutiny, from the developing order of actions that intensely brings them to mind; they have no independent symbolic existence, nor do any other of the spreading abstractions and big ideas in the narrative. Even the journey into the heart of darkness—the more obvious broad symbolic provocations of which have given joy to so many literary amateurs—insofar as it has artistic (rather than merely psychoanalytic) force, is finely coincident with its network of details; its moral nature steadily reveals itself not in the rather predictable grand gestures of Conradian rhetoric (" 'Going upriver was like going back to beginnings, when vegetation rioted and the big trees were kings' "), but in the unavoidable facts of suspense, strangeness, vigilance, danger, and fear: the difficulties of piloting the patched fragile steamer past hidden banks, snags, sunken stones upriver; the sudden " 'glimpse of rush walls, of peaked grass roofs, a burst of yells, a whirl of black limbs, a mass of hands clapping, of feet stamping, of bodies swaying, of eyes rolling, under the droop of heavy and motionless foliage' "; the honest, " 'unmistakably real' " book mysteriously discovered in the abandoned hut; the terrified savage tending the boiler, who " 'squinted at the steam gauge with an evident effort of intrepidity' "; the arrows from nowhere; the death of the black helmsman . . . ; and, most shocking of all in its evocation of mind at an intolerable extremity, the climactic farcical detail of Marlow's panic to get rid of his shoes and socks overflowing with a dead man's blood. . . . (pp. 548-49)

When Conrad is called, with a clear confidence that the judgment is general and will not be challenged, "perhaps the finest prose stylist" among the English novelists, it is doubtless such passages as these that the critic has in mind. . . . Qualifying his account of Conrad as one of the four masters of English fiction, Dr. Leavis makes the definitive comment on this sort of thing: "Conrad must here stand convicted of borrowing the arts of the magazine-writer (who has borrowed his, shall we say, from Kipling and Poe) in order to impose on his readers and on himself, for thrilled response, a 'significance' that is merely an emotional insistence on the presence of what he can't produce. The insistence betrays the absence, the willed 'intensity' the nullity. He is intent on making a virtue out of not knowing what he means."

Qualification, however, is not enough. Conrad's lapses of this sort are not rare or incidental, they do not merely weaken his master style but schismatically parallel it in a style of their own. The "finest prose stylist" in English fiction has in fact two styles: the narrative-descriptive, in which explicit details triumphantly cohere with implicit moral moments in an accumulating point-to-point correspondence (a style whose purest, if not most imposingly complex, manifestation may be examined in **"Typhoon"**); and the oracular-ruminative, which dotes on abstractions, exclamations, unexpressive indirections, pat ironies ("the arts of the magazine-writer"), a style which takes over, especially in the large-scale works, whenever Conrad loses faith in the power of his details to enforce both their own reality and the symbolic substructure whose contours they are intended to suggest—so Marlow cries out as he and his author signalize, in a joint loss of faith, their drift from master to meretricious style, " 'I've been telling you what we said—repeating the phrases we pronounced—but what's the good?' "

Conrad's symbolism, and his moral imagination, are, after all, as unallegorical as possible. When they function and have effect they are severely realistic: they nourish themselves on voices heard and solid objects seen and touched in the natural world, they contract into rhetoric as soon as the voices and objects begin to appear less than independently present; when Conrad is not describing, with direct sensuous impact, a developing sequence of distinct actions, he is liable to drift into the mooning or glooming that for some critics passes as Conrad's "philosophy" and for others as his style in its full tropical luxuriance.

Moreover, to assume, as Dr. Leavis seems to assume, that all symbolism works *only* as it is anchored to a record of immediate sensations, that it must totally coincide with "the concrete presentment of incident, setting and image," is to transform Conrad's limitation (and gift) into a condition of fiction. To compare Conrad's symbolic method, his two-ply plot, with the methods of, say, Dostoievsky and Kafka is to become aware of radically different possibilities: on the one hand, Conrad's realistic mode; on the other, moral imaginations not necessarily anchored to objects and places, symbolic means capable of producing, for example, those vibrations of clairvoyant hallucination in Dostoievsky, and of meaningful enigma in Kafka, which move through and beyond immediate sensations into a world of moral meanings almost as independent as, and far more densely populated than, the other side of the mirror of traditional allegory. Of such effects, beyond the capacities of even the most evocative realism, Conrad is innocent; yet when, in *Heart of Darkness,* he approaches the center of a difficult moral situation (desperately more troublesome than the simple choices permitted the characters in **"Typhoon"**), when facts and details begin to appear inadequate as figurations of the moral problem, it is just such effects that he is at length driven to attempt.

The problem is, of course, Kurtz. It is when we are on the verge of meeting Kurtz that Marlow's "inconceivables" and "impenetrables" begin to multiply at an alarming rate; it is when we have already met him that we are urged to observe "smiles of indefinable meaning" and to hear about "unspeakable rites" and "gratified and monstrous passions" and "subtle horrors"—words to hound the reader into a sense of enigmatic awfulness that he would somehow be the better for not trying to find a way through. . . . (pp. 549-51)

The problem, as Conrad sets it up, is to persuade the reader—by epithets, exclamations, ironies, by every technical obliquity—into an hallucinated awareness of the unplumbable depravity, the primal unanalyzable evil, implicit in Kurtz's reversion to the jungle from the high moral sentiments of his report. . . . Unhappily, though, the effect of even this minor irony is to bring to mind and penetrate Conrad's magazinewriter style as well as the hollowness of Kurtz's sentiments. Besides, Kurtz's sentiments must, to help justify the fuss Conrad makes about their author, radiate at least a rhetorical energy; yet all Conrad gives us of the report is a phrase or two of mealy-mouthed reformist exhortation that would not do credit to a Maugham missionary let alone the "extraordinary man" Kurtz is supposed by all accounts to be, so that the "irony" of the scrawled outcry at the end of the report—'Exterminate the brutes!'—is about as subtle and unexpected as the missionary's falling for the local call-girl.

In the effort to establish for Kurtz an opaque and terrifying magnitude, Conrad tends to rely more and more oppressively on these pat ironies. The very existence of the incredibly naïve young Russian is another such irony: the disciple who responds to Kurtz's abundant proofs of cruelty and mean obsession with the steadfast conviction—and no evidence for the reader—that Kurtz is a great man (" ' "he's enlarged my mind" ' "—another irony that cuts more ways than Conrad must have intended). And if the culminating irony of the narrative, Marlow's interview with Kurtz's Intended, is expertly anticipated long before . . .—it is all the more disheartening, after such anticipation, to encounter in that interview sighs, heart stoppings, chill grips in the chest, exultations, the cheaply ironic doubletalk (" 'She said suddenly very low, "He died as he lived." "His end," said I, with dull anger stirring in me, "was in every way worthy of his life." ' ") as well as the sentimental lie that provokes not only her " 'cry of inconceivable triumph and of unspeakable pain' " but the final cheap irony (" ' "I knew it—I was sure!" She knew. She was sure.' ")—a jumble of melodramatic tricks so unabashed and so strategic that in any less reputable writer they might well be critically regarded as earning for the work an instant oblivion.

Still, in *Heart of Darkness* at least, Conrad is neither cynical nor laxly sentimental in his failure of imagination and corresponding failure of technique. The theme itself is too much for him, too much for perhaps any but the very greatest dramatists and novelists. The sense of evil he must somehow project exceeds his capacity for imagining it; he strains into badness while reaching for verifications of a great and somber theme that is beyond his own very considerable powers. (pp. 551-52)

[*Heart of Darkness*] is in fact one of those mixed structures whose partial success (not so neatly separable as, for example, Part I of *Under Western Eyes*) is so profound, so unprecedented, and so strikingly irreplaceable as to survive a proportion and gravity of failure that would sink forever any other work.

It is one of the great originals of literature. After *Heart of Darkness* the craftsman in fiction could never again be unaware of the moral resources inherent in every recorded sensation, or insensitive to the need of making the most precise record possible of every sensation: what now appears an immemorial cliché of the craft of fiction has a date as recent as the turn of the century. If Conrad was never quite equal to his own originality, he was at least the first to designate it as a new province of possibilities for the novelist; and, in *Heart of Darkness,* the first to suggest, by large and compelling partial proof, the intensity of moral illumination that a devoted attention to its demands might generate. The suggestion was an historical event: for good and bad novelists alike, irreversible. After *Heart of Darkness,* the recorded moment—the word—was irrecoverably symbol. (p. 553)

Marvin Mudrick, "The Originality of Conrad," in *The Hudson Review,* Vol. XI, No. 4, Winter, 1958-59, pp. 545-53.

FREDERICK R. KARL

(essay date 1969)

[Karl is one of the foremost authorities on Conrad. In the following excerpt, he discusses *Heart of Darkness* as a quintessentially modern depiction of the absurdity of experience and equates Conrad's exploration of the mind with the work of Sigmund Freud.]

Conrad himself recognized that [*Heart of Darkness*] penetrated to those areas of darkness, dream, indeed nightmare with which he tried to define the substance of his world. Written when he was still a fledgling novelist, *Heart of Darkness* helped solidify a vision that rarely wavered in Conrad's later work, and one we now accept as uniquely modern. Here he limned the images one usually encounters in dreams or in war, and here he found that discontinuous, inexplicable, existentially absurd experience which was to haunt his letters and his work.

Based on personal impressions, his own Congo journey, *Heart of Darkness* welled out. As he wrote apologetically and hesitatingly to Elsa Martindale (Mrs. Ford Madox Ford):

> What I distinctly admit is the fault of having made Kurtz too symbolic or rather symbolic at all. But the story being mainly a vehicle for conveying a batch of personal impressions I gave the rein to my mental laziness and took the line of least resistance. This is then the whole Apologia pro Vita Kurtzii—or rather for the tardiness of his vitality. (unpublished letter, December 3, 1902)

The novella, then, contains a vision so powerful that Conrad excuses himself for being unable (he thought) to control it. It was also, as Freud wrote of his own *Interpretation of Dreams,* an insight that falls to one but once in a lifetime. The reference to Freud and to *Dreams* is not fortuitous. It was of course chance that Freud and Conrad were contemporaries; but chance ends when we note the extraordinary parallelism of their achievements. (pp. 136-37)

Chance is further reduced when we recognize that literature and a new style of psychological exploration have been first cousins for the last hundred years, that both Conrad and Freud were pioneers in stressing the irrational elements in man's behavior which resisted orthodox interpretation. Conrad's great contribution to political thought is his insight into the irrationality of politics, its nightmarish qualities which depend on the neurosis of a leader, in turn upon the collective neuroses of a people. Such an insight is timeless, but particularly appropriate for developments since 1900. For when has man tried so carefully to preserve life while also squandering it so carelessly? Conrad caught not only hypocrisy (an old-fashioned value), but the illogic of human behavior which tries to justify itself with precision, only to surrender to explosive inner needs. "Exterminate all the brutes," Kurtz scrawled at the bottom of his report. This is the politics of personal disintegration, uncontrollable personal needs, ultimately paranoia.

Confronting similar material, the scientist Freud was concerned with a logical analysis of seeming illogic—the apparent irrationality of dreams, on occasion of nightmares. Both he and Conrad penetrated into the darkness—when men sleep, or when their consciences sleep, when such men are free to pursue secret wishes, whether in dreams, like Freud's analysands, or in actuality, like Kurtz and his followers. The key word is darkness; the black of the jungle for Conrad is the dark of the sleeping consciousness for Freud.

In still another sense, Marlow, in his trip up the Congo, has suffered through a nightmare, an experience that sends him back a different man, now aware of depths in himself that he cannot hide. The tale he narrates on the *Nellie* is one he is unable to suppress; a modern Ancient Mariner, he has discovered a new world and must relate his story to regain stability. The account is a form of analysis—for him and for Conrad. In a way, it provides a defense against Kurtz's vision. (pp. 137-38)

[Freud's] great discovery, like Conrad's, was surely that dreams, despite the various barriers the conscious mind erects, are wish-fulfillments of the hidden self. This sense of wish-fulfillment is evidently never far from Marlow—for the very qualities in Kurtz that horrify him are those he finds masked in himself. Kurtz's great will to power, Nietzschean and ruthless in its thrust, is also Marlow's. The latter, however, can hold back, his restraint, for Conrad, a mark of his Englishness. Marlow, however, only barely restrains himself, for, irresistibly, he is drawn toward Kurtz, readily accepting the latter's ruthlessness as preferable to the bland hypocrisy of the station manager. Even Marlow is seduced—he, too, hides secret wishes and desires, his dreams curiously close to Kurtz's; and so are the dreams of us all, Conrad suggests. Kurtz's savage career is every man's wish-fulfillment, although by dying he conveniently disappears before we all become his disciples.

The secret longing, the hidden desire, the hypocritical defense, the hate covered superficially by love, the artfully contrived lie—all of these are intertwined in dreams. In this sense, Marlow's experience is a nightmare for creator, narrator, and reader. The jungle, that thick verdant cover, disguises all, but most of all hides a man's real existence from himself.

As a connoisseur of dreams, Conrad is a "dark" writer in the sense Rembrandt was a dark painter, Milton a dark poet. They begrudged the light, husbanded it, squeezed it out in minute quantities, as if it were filtered from between densely packed trees in a jungle setting. So the light in Kurtz's heart barely appears, overwhelmed as it is by the darkness of his needs, the exigencies of his situation. Light and dark, in this vision, are polarized; their antagonism runs parallel to the struggle for life in nature itself, a Darwinian battle for growth, power, supremacy.

The yellowish, wispy light, indeed the white of the ivory, later of Kurtz's very bald skull, exists against the fragmented darkness of the jungle—the contrast of colors giving Conrad a vast symbol for moral, political, and social values. And yet such is the knottiness and ambiguity of his symbol that the result is blurred, filled artfully with the illusions and deceptions that Conrad makes us accept as the pathos of existence. (pp. 138-39)

To create order from such shards of nihilism, negativism, distortion, deception, savagery, and, ultimately, fear, Conrad offered a dubious restraint. Somehow, one must find it within. It is an individual matter, and evidently either one has it or one doesn't. It is not solely a European quality by any means, since Kurtz, that pan-European, lacks it, and the Congolese tribal natives have it. Restraint—a kind of muscular courage not to do—marks the difference between civilization and capitulation to savagery. Yet where does it come from? How does one obtain it? Does the lack of it always brutalize? Such mysterious reckonings make it impossible for us to see Conrad as a meliorist. Society as constituted means little—only the responsible individual counts. Possibly one acquires restraint as the sum total of what he is. Yet decency, indeed the future of civilized society, hangs in the balance. (pp. 139-40)

[The] gnarled seaman [Marlow] is surely one of the keys to the story, and much has been written about him, including much nonsense. He is, at least here, Conrad's Everyman, Bunyan's Christian updated. What he suffers and experiences is analogous to what we as judicious democrats would feel. Conrad made Marlow sentient, somewhat intelligent, but, most of all, courageous—about himself, about life, about man's social responsibilities—yet at the same time sufficiently cynical; in brief, very much like Conrad himself. But the two are not congruent; among other things, Conrad possessed a literary intelligence that his narrator did not. He surrounds Marlow as well as enters him. But even if he is foremost a man of action, Marlow should not be taken too lightly. His intelligence is displayed in his moral sensibility. With a certain dogged charm, reminiscent of many American presidents and statesmen, he wishes to see the world based on English (or American) democracy. He accepts private enterprise—with personal restraints. He believes that imperialism must justify itself with good deeds. He expects all men to be fair and decent. Such are Marlow's preoccupations, and here Conrad demonstrated to good purpose the contradictions and rifts between modern belief and modern practice. And here also is the source of Conrad's irony—a quality that gives him considerable advantage over Marlow. (pp. 140-41)

Like Conrad, he accepts the status quo, but one maintained, he trusts, by just men. For both, this is the sole basis of the human contract—one does things in an enlightened manner and develops his moral sensibilities. This is a solid nineteenth-century philosophy, although for us somewhat naive. Marlow rarely questions whether particular work is necessary; for example, he never asks whether white men should be in the Congo—for whatever reason. Rather, he assumes they should be—since they are—but they must come as friends, as helpers, and bring enlightenment. Even while they rape, they must be benevolent. He sees them as solid, progressive Englishmen, who helped to develop countries the better to plunder them, nineteenth-century "ugly Americans." (pp. 141-42)

The long river that informs this world is described, like the Styx, in treacherous, serpentine terms—"deadly—like a snake," "resembling an immense snake uncoiled." The river is essentially a woman: dangerous, dark, mysterious, concealed, with the jungle also feminine, personified by Kurtz's savage mistress. Marlow is overwhelmed; his ideal of womanhood is clearly the girl back in Brussels, or his aunt—the brainwashed public—that naive woman who believes "the labourer is worthy of his hire." Such womanly illusions Marlow wishes to preserve. But his experience includes a treacherous, feminine river, an equally perfidious jungle that conceals its terrors, and, finally, a savage mistress—in all, an unspeakable sexual experience. Though the reticent, chivalrous Marlow never speaks directly of sex, it lies heavily on the story, in every aspect of nature—in *his* fears, in *its* demands. As much as Marlow fears the attraction of power, he shies away from the temptation of orgiastic, uncontrollable sex. He retreats into neutral shock. (pp. 142-43)

Heart of Darkness . . . is concerned with moral issues in their most troubling sense: not only as philosophical imperatives, but practically as they work out in human behavior. In a m ˙hanical universe—"evolved out of a chaos of scr ˛ of iron"—what is flesh? The profusion of metallic ˛nd mechanical images indicates that resistant objects have superseded softness, flexibility, humanity itself; that, clearly, one must become an object, tough and durable, in order to survive. (p. 144)

The sense of human waste that pervades the story is best unfolded in the ivory itself. It is an object for the rich—in decorations, for piano keys, for bibelots—hardly necessary for physical or mental survival. In a way, it is like art, a social luxury, and it is for art that the Congo is plundered and untold numbers slaughtered brutally, or casually. This view of ivory as art was surely part of Conrad's conception; a utilitarian object would have had its own *raison d'être*. A relatively useless item or one selective in its market only points up the horror; surely this, too, is part of Kurtz's vision. Possibly Kurtz's artistic propensities (he paints, he collects human heads, he seeks ivory) make him so contemptuous of individual lives; for art and life have always warred. In the name of art (pyramids, churches, tombs, monuments, palaces), how many have died, gone without, worked as slaves? Traditionally, beauty for the few is gained with blood of the many.

Where art rules, artifacts are a form of power. The art object takes on magical significance, becoming a kind of totem, the fairytale golden egg. Knowing this, Kurtz gains his power, indeed his identity and being, from the ivory he covets. In a world of art, the most greedy collector is often supreme; matter, not manner, counts. One source of Kurtz's fascination for Marlow is the former's will to power, Nietzschean, superhuman, and brutal. Kurtz has risen above the masses—of natives, station managers, even of directors back in Brussels. He must continue to assert himself, a megalo-

maniac in search of further power. Marlow has never met anyone like him, this Kurtz who represents all of Europe. The insulated Englishman now faces east, toward the continent. . . . "All Europe contributed to the making of Kurtz," we read.

He is indeed Europe, searching for power, maneuvering for advantage; and he finds the lever in the colonial adventure of ivory. No wonder, then, that his hunger for acquisition is so overwhelming. Having gratified forbidden desires, he is free of civilized taboos. In the Congo, where the white man—the civilized Belgian—ruled, he could do anything. His only prescription: produce results, send back ivory. Indeed, his very will to power, his confident brutality made him appear a kind of god—to the natives and other agents who feared him, to the Russian sailor who believed in him.

The ultimate corruption is that Kurtz can go his way without restraint. All human barriers are down. Only power counts—no matter whether political or economic. In the jungle, as in enterprise, only the strong survive, and Kurtz obviously is one of the strong. He brings European power—all of Europe—into the jungle; his weapons encompass 2000 years of western civilization. And the consequence: corruption of self and death to "inferiors" on a monumental scale.

When a journalist informs Marlow that Kurtz would have been a "splendid leader of an extreme party," Marlow understandably asks, "What party?" "Any party," his visitor answers, "he was an—an extremist." With that Conrad presents his grandest insight into the politics of our time—superficially totalitarian, but extending also to democratic powers. (pp. 144-144b)

In this conception of Kurtz, Conrad's powers as an artistic thinker were at their strongest. . . . As an artistic thinker . . . he was at once caustic, subtle, broad. His conception of Kurtz, slim on the surface, broadening beneath, is a Cassandra's view of European progress, a view both realistic and ironic. (pp. 144b-144c)

The Congo had been, since 1875, the private preserve of Leopold II of Belgium. . . . Kurtz, or his type of exploiter, was the rule, not the exception. . . . Conrad's journey, as he relates in his Congo diary, was real, Kurtz and his type prevailed, the land and the natives existed, the facts are undisputed. Even if Conrad used symbols to excess, as he feared, each symbol is solidly grounded in fact. Here is white against black, entrenched against primitive, have against have-not, machine against spear, civilization against tribe.

If Conrad's novella is to have artistic as well as political significance, it must make broad reference to human motivation and behavior. One evident part of the application comes with Kurtz's double shriek of "The horror! The horror!" The cry is far richer and more ambiguous than most readers make it. We must remember that Marlow is reporting, and Marlow has a particular view and need of Kurtz. As Marlow understands the scream, it represents a moral victory; that is, on the threshold of death, Kurtz has reviewed his life with all its horror and in some dying part of him has repented. Marlow hears the words as a victory of moral sensibility over a life of brutality and prostituted ideals. This "Christian" reading of the words is, of course, what Marlow himself wishes to hear; he is a moral man, and he believes, with this kind of bourgeois religiosity, that all men ultimately repent when confronted by the great unknown. Kurtz's cry, in this interpretation, fits in with what Marlow wants to know of human nature.

We are not all Marlows, however, and we should not be seduced into agreeing with him, even if he is partially right. More ambiguously and ironically, Kurtz's cry might be a shriek of despair that after having accomplished so little he must now perish. His horror is the anguish of one who dies with his work incomplete. In this view, Kurtz does not repent; rather, he bewails a fate which frustrates his plans. Indeed, at the very moment of death, he challenges life and death and tries to make his baffled will prevail. (pp. 144c-144d)

The irony of the story comes full turn. Returning from the world of the dead, Marlow—our twentieth-century Everyman—cannot admit the full impact of the indecency he has witnessed, of the feelings he has experienced. Even this most honest of men must disguise what he has seen and felt. Like a politician he must bed down with lies. Only Conrad, who is outside both Marlow and Kurtz, can admit the truth, can limn the lie and see it as a lie. (pp. 144d-144e)

In this and other respects, *Heart of Darkness* is a masterpiece of concealment. Just as Marlow has concealed from himself the true nature of his own needs, so too we can find concealment—in art, in nature, in people—in virtually every other aspect of the novella. The jungle itself, that vast protective camouflage barring the light of sun and sky, masks and hides, becoming part of the psychological as well as physical landscape. Like the dream content, it forms itself around distortion, condensation, and displacement.

Post-Darwinian and overpowering, the jungle is not Wordsworth's gentle landscape, by no means the type of nature which gives strength and support in our darkest hours. Rather, it runs parallel to our anxieties, becomes the repository of our fears. The darkness of the jungle approximates darkness everywhere, adumbrating the blackness of Conrad's humor, the despair of his irony.

The persistence of the color sets the tone and elicits our response. (p. 144e)

Kurtz's final words, his death, the report by the manager's boy, the darkness surrounding all, the frantic run out of the Congo, the meeting with Kurtz's Brussel's fiancée—connected to all such events is the shimmer and nightmare of dream, Conrad's definition of modern life. No less than Kafka, he saw existence as forms of unreality stubbled with real events. And no little part of the dream-like substance of the tale is the Russian follower of Kurtz, like Marlow a mariner. Dressed in motley, he seems a figure from another world, and yet with his ludicrous appearance he is a perfect symbol for Marlow's Congo experience. Befitting someone who worships Kurtz like a god, the Russian forgives his worst behavior and argues that a common man like himself needs someone to follow. He is persuaded that Kurtz's will to power draws in all those less capable, conveys hope and substance to them.

There is, in his view, a void in every man that only someone like Kurtz can fill. Without Kurtz, the sailor says, he is nothing. "He made me see things—things." His ordinariness is balanced by Kurtz's superiority—every disciple needs a god. Like the natives, like the superb native mistress who forgives Kurtz everything, the sailor follows power. Conrad's prescience was never more trenchant.

To Marlow's accusation that Kurtz is insane, simply mad, the Russian offers Kurtz's great intelligence, his ability to talk brilliantly, his charismatic qualities. To our objection that the sailor himself is mad, Conrad offers his influence upon Marlow—he strikes in Marlow precisely the note of love-hate that Conrad's narrator has come to feel for Kurtz. Although Marlow would like to anchor himself solidly in the Russian's sea manual and reject the vapidity of the Russian, he too is drawn into Kurtz's orbit. He senses what the sailor voices.

In this strangely insane world, all alignments defy logic. Loyalties, beliefs, love, women themselves take on new shapes and attractions. Marlow, that neuter bachelor, is fascinated by the jungle woman, by her wanton, demanding display of sex, by the "fecund and mysterious life" she embodies, by the deliberate provocation of her measured walk. He is further drawn to her sense of reality; without illusion, without question, she accepts Kurtz for what he is, as integrated with the very savagery which enfolds her.

For Marlow the pull of the primitive comes full circle. Again and again, he breaks off his narrative to assure his listeners that all this really happened. Even while he talks, this modern mariner, he must convey the depth of his experience, try to convince that it was as profound as he claims. Marlow knows what happened—yet to find the precise words is almost impossible. (pp. 144f-144h)

Possibly in some areas the language is too heavy, but to labor this point is to lose sight of the story as a whole. One might, in fact, argue the very opposite: that the words—adjectives and all—beat upon us, creating drum-like rhythms entirely appropriate to the thick texture of the jungle, a more sophisticated version of Vachel Lindsay's "Congo." When one confronts the artistry of the complete piece, Conrad's reliance on verbal embellishment appears a minor consideration.

The story in fact has form: from the opening frame, with Marlow's somewhat ingenuous listeners, to the closing sequence, with Kurtz's innocent fiancée confirming her illusions. The use of a first person narrative, through the agency of Marlow, was necessary so that Conrad could gain aesthetic distance and the reader could identify with an average man thrown into an abnormal situation. We must, Conrad realized, go through it with him and Marlow. Lacking the narrator, the story would appear too distant from the immediate experience—as though it had happened and was now over, like ancient history. (pp. 144h-144i)

So, too, in other respects did Conrad work out the shape of the story, in large and in details: through doubling of scenes and characters, through repetition, analogy, duplicating images, through difference of tone. From the beginning, when the ancient Romans on the Thames are contrasted with the modern Europeans on the Congo, Conrad used heightening and foreshortening, contrast and comparison to give the novella form. Most obviously, Marlow's peaceful setting on the *Nellie* is set off against his nightmarish Congo riverboat setting; in a different way, Kurtz's two fiancées are contrasted, each one standing for certain values, indeed for entire cultures, in conflict; further, the jungle is set off against the river, with jungle as death, river as possible relief; in another way, Kurtz is compared with other forms of evil, with the deceptive smoothness of the station manager, with the hypocrisy of the pilgrims; the pilgrims in turn are ironically compared with the savages they condemn, with the pilgrims less Christian than the pagan natives; within the natives, the tribal savages are contrasted with those exposed to civilization, detribalized as it were, the latter already full of wiles and deceit; light and dark, the painter's chiaroscuro, hover over the entire story, no less important here than in Milton's Christian epic; day dream and night dream form contrasts, worked out in the play between expectation and consequence, between professed ideals and realistic behavior, between Kurtz's humanitarianism and his barbarism, between Marlow's middle class sense of English justice and the Congo reality, between the fluctuating love-and-hate which fill both Kurtz and Marlow.

Out of the infinite possibilities facing Conrad, he chose these to give unity to his language and ideas. Such devices shape our thoughts and give form to our responses; they, too, become the substance of our awareness. (pp. 144i-144j)

What makes this story so impressive is Conrad's

ability to focus on the Kurtz-Marlow polarity as a definition of our times. European history as well as the history of individual men can be read more clearly in the light of Conrad's art; for he tells us that the most dutiful of men, a Marlow, can be led to the brink of savagery and brutality if the will to power touches him; that the most idealistic of men, Kurtz, can become a sadistic murderer; that the dirty work of this world is carried out by men whose reputations are preserved by lies. Conrad's moral tale becomes, in several respects, our story, the only way we can read history and each other. (pp. 144j-144k)

Frederick R. Karl, in his *A Reader's Guide to Joseph Conrad,* revised edition, Farrar, Straus and Giroux, 1969, pp. 91-144ee.

DOUGLAS HEWITT
(essay date 1975)

[In the following excerpt, Hewitt examines the political aspects of Conrad's major works.]

We cannot fail to observe, if we approach Conrad's work without preconceptions, that in almost all his earlier books a penetrating scrutiny is directed against the simple virtues of honesty, courage, pity and fidelity to an unquestioned ideal of conduct. (p. 16)

In particular we notice the recurrence of one situation which, though it occupies a subordinate place in two or three of the works, dominates many—the situation in which a man who relies on these simple virtues is confronted by a partially apprehended sense of evil against which they seem powerless. The mere realization of the existence of this evil overwhelms him with a sense of insecurity and casts doubt on the supposedly secure foundations of the ideals themselves; the virtues at last become suspect. Moreover, because of the peculiar structure of Conrad's works, the sharp immediacy of the problems which the confrontation raises and the clear knowledge of the significance to others of the main character's actions combine to prevent these realizations from being disregarded as vague self-questionings or moods which can be ignored. This awareness is often brought about through the recognition by the central character of an obscure link between himself and a manifestation of the evil which he cannot fail to know for what it is. (p. 17)

The choice of the word 'evil' to describe this seems inevitable. I have used the word . . . without apology and without explanation. This is not merely because it is the word which Conrad himself so often uses, but because it corresponds to his entire outlook on moral issues. We can discuss many novelists without using this term, speaking of aberrations of conduct, regrettable failings, weaknesses of character and the like, but the most cursory glance at Conrad's work is enough to convince us that he has a conception of a transcendental evil, embodying itself in individuals—a sense of evil just as great as that of any avowedly Catholic or Calvinist writer. (pp. 22-3)

In a chronological study of a writer who, like Conrad, did his best work comparatively early, we may be left with a sense of disappointment. Such a feeling should be dissipated when we reflect that, though his reputation rests upon part only of his output, it is not a particularly small part—certainly not less than four novels and rather more tales of varying length. Not many English novelists can claim more. The only point of noting a decline is to emphasise what he declined from.

His work is remarkably varied; the books between 'Youth' and *The Secret Agent* manifest a restless exploratory energy. But they share . . . an individual vision, a cast of mind, which confronts us, upsettingly, with certain repeated situations. Conrad's concern is with a powerful sense of potential weakness and betrayal lurking under an apparent confidence in an established code of behaviour and waiting for the right circumstances of stress to emerge, often with devastating power. His technical method of isolating his characters enables him to project these states of mind very forcefully through objects and circumstances which are both physical, natural, inevitably imposed by the real world, and at the same time symbolic of the plight of the characters.

To put matters thus may suggest that Conrad is essentially a systematic metaphysical thinker. This seems to me to be inaccurate. Certainly he employed large quasi-metaphysical terms, especially in his least successfully rhetorical moments, and he speaks of human behaviour roundly in terms of good and evil. Certainly, too, he encountered at second and third and fourth (and occasionally perhaps even at first) hand metaphysical doctrines which were being discussed at the time, and we can sometimes trace echoes of them in his work. But this is a very different matter from being a systematic metaphysical thinker. . . . There are, of course, occasions when, rather unconvincingly, he offers general statements as if he believes that they encapsulate meanings. The Marlow of *Chance* is given to this indulgence, but so, more damagingly because the novel has more in it to be damaged, does the Marlow of *Lord Jim.* But when he is writing at the height of his powers Conrad's individual vision is presented in a remarkably complex and often indirect manner, involving not only such basic fictional methods as engaging our sympathies, often surprisingly, with his characters and generating suspense and resolving it, but also shifts of tone and disconcerting juxtapositions of hap-

penings. When we harden this dense and complex effect into doctrines it is often because of a tendency to support our view by what seem appropriate quotations. (pp. 129-30)

What lies at the heart of Conrad's work is surely not metaphysics but politics—politics understood in the widest sense. Much of private life—sexual relationships, family, neighbourly friendships, domestic rhythms—is of little interest to him, and when he writes about such matters, as in *Chance* and *Victory,* he displays his weaknesses rather than his strengths. His interest lies in the interplay of groups, the conflict between personal feelings and professional duties; he sees men as fulfilling public roles as well as leading private lives and he focuses attention upon their shared efforts and their conflicts of interest. Few novelists have written so much about work as Conrad, though the fact that the work is so often that of ship-handling—an exotic task for most readers—has tended to make us overlook the fact. But his tales of the sea are essentially about what we might call the politics of shipboard life. Even so apparently private a study of self-doubt as **'The Secret Sharer'** gains its force from the narrator's awareness of professional responsibilities and his rela-

Inscription in a copy of the first edition of *The Secret Agent.*

tionship with the crew over whom he has power but whose judgements he cannot ignore. (pp. 130-31)

There is, however, one characteristic of [Conrad's sea] stories which distinguishes them from the strictly political novels, *Nostromo, The Secret Agent* and *Under Western Eyes;* in them at least one limited aim is clear and unquestionable—to navigate the ship and to preserve life at sea. The isolation of the situation concentrates the problems and convincingly limits them; Conrad does not have to consider such matters as the economic issues of the trade in which they are engaged nor the morality of sending men to sea in leaky ships. . . . Nothing is allowed to question the simplicity of the immediate task—as, indeed, nothing would in real life. It is interesting to observe in **'Heart of Darkness'**, where the morality of the trading is an issue and therefore the purpose of the voyage, that even though Marlow speaks of the therapeutic value of getting his ungainly steamboat to work he comes back down the river ill, a passenger and not a commander.

The pessimism of the sea stories is thus modified because Conrad's positive values, a belief in doing one's job properly, in fairness, in courage, in the stoic acceptance of blows, have a real, if limited, value. His protagonists may find themselves thrust into situations where the code by which they regulate their conduct seems precarious, unlikely to defend them against all the forces which may be arrayed against them, but at least in the situations which immediately confront them their duty is clear and they can win a limited victory.

In the overtly political novels there is no such unquestioned aim. There may be actions in which the practical virtues remain unquestionable but they are subsumed under larger themes where the end cannot claim legitimacy. Conrad's political view is one of gloomy scepticism, spiced with the sardonic humour of one who watches the futility of all political effort. (pp. 131-32)

But in truth his scepticism is more corrosive than we may think; attempts to change society may be futile but authority has no moral force. Nowhere is this more clearly shown than in Winnie Verloc's attempt to explain to Stevie the function of the police. He, in his pity for the cabman and his horse, has formulated his judgment as 'Bad world for poor people' and invokes the police as agents for righting wrongs—'He had formed for himself an ideal conception of the metropolitan police as a sort of benevolent institution for the suppression of evil'. Winnie feels the need to put him right and she also knows that the word 'steal' upsets him; she chooses, therefore, a formula upon which the Professor could hardly improve: 'They are there so that them as have nothing shouldn't take anything away from them who have.'

This view of politics—one which has no faith in the legitimacy of established order but also no faith in progress through political development and which sees men as almost inevitably corrupted by the public roles which they have to play—finds expression most fully in Conrad's masterpiece, *Nostromo.* (pp. 133-34)

But if *Nostromo* is, as many believe, the best political novel in the language this is not just because of the shrewdness of its analysis of the exploitation of an underdeveloped country by the invested capital of the 'Anglo-Saxon' powers, but rather because the complex form of the book does justice to the double vision of men and women as both individuals and as socially determined beings. The very frustrations which this arouses in the reader serve the meaning of the book.

In all substantial novels there is an inherent tension between our perception of form, of controlling structure, and our interest in the characters as individuals. In *Nostromo* this tension is very powerful; there are many elements in the book which are potentially or actually frustrating or irksome but to which, in the long run, we give our assent. The tension thus set up is in effect a political statement. (p. 134)

It is, of course, by the omnipresent symbolism of the silver of the mine, with which is linked the legend of the treasure seekers of Azuera, that the political judgement of the book is most enforced. There are times when this, too, may seem overdone, when its predetermining power constrains the characters' freedom so that they are perilously close to seeming puppets. As one gets to know the book better one realises that they are, indeed, puppets, but not those of a puppet-master novelist so much as of a political situation whose central controlling symbol seems not imposed by the writer but elucidated by him from the facts of the situation.

The structure, with its great use of time-shifts and changes of viewpoint, also functions to show the futility of the struggles of individuals within a political and economic situation which dwarfs them. The book's method is to plunge us into situations where we feel for characters faced by danger or the need to make decisions and then, without comment, to see these personal predicaments as part of a process which diminishes them. (pp. 135-36)

Nostromo does not merely express a political attitude; it embodies it, in the sense that the process by which the reader comes to understand it, changing his viewpoint and coming to terms with certain muddles and disappointments, is the political statement itself. It is this, above all, which gives the novel its extraordinary impression of density, solidity, which can only come from a large theme which finds its appropriate form. Maturity of outlook and originality of technique are perfectly matched. Had Conrad written nothing else his place would be assured. When we add to it **'Heart of Darkness'**, *The Secret Agent*, *Lord Jim* and half a dozen other works we recognize a body of work which makes all but a handful of other English novelists look superficial. (p. 136)

Douglas Hewitt, in his *Conrad: A Reassessment*, third edition, Rowman and Littlefield, 1975, 142 p.

SOURCES FOR FURTHER STUDY

Crankshaw, Edward. *Joseph Conrad: Some Aspects of the Art of the Novel.* London: John Lane, 1936, 248 p.

> Important early study of Conrad's literary artistry that treats his novels as wholly unified artistic achievements.

Gillon, Adam. *Joseph Conrad.* Boston: Twayne, 1982, 210 p.

> Biographical and critical study.

Karl, Frederick R. *Joseph Conrad: The Three Lives.* New York: Farrar, Straus and Giroux, 1979, 1008 p.

> Comprehensive biography of Conrad.

Jacobs, Diane. "Coppola Films Conrad in Vietnam." In *The English Novel and the Movies,* edited by Michael Klein and Gillian Parker, pp. 211-17. New York: Frederick Ungar, 1981.

> Discusses Francis Ford Coppola's 1979 film *Apocalypse Now* as an interpretation of Conrad's novella *Heart of Darkness.*

Teets, Bruce. *Joseph Conrad: An Annotated Bibliography.* New York: Garland, 1990, 786 p.

> Comprehensive bibliography of critical writings about Conrad and his works.

Watt, Ian. *Conrad in the Nineteenth Century.* Berkeley: University of California Press, 1979, 375 p.

> Important study of the first half of Conrad's career. Watt provides in-depth readings of the early novels and relates Conrad's artistic accomplishments to contemporary developments in literature and the arts.

Hart Crane

1899-1932

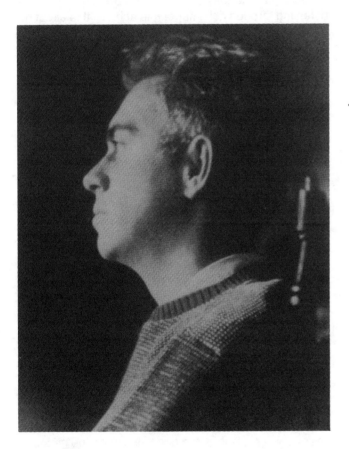

(Full name Harold Crane) American poet and essayist.

INTRODUCTION

Although he left only a small body of work, Crane is important as a lyric poet in the tradition of the romantic visionary. As such, his work is often compared to that of William Blake, Samuel Taylor Coleridge, and Charles Baudelaire. A man acutely conscious of the transitory nature of life, Crane sought salvation from the spiritual pains of existence through art. His poetry chronicles a quest for love and beauty that would lift him above life's miseries. Thus, his work is at once an expression of despair over the disintegrative processes of life and a cry of exultation for his occasional transcendence of despair through art. Though he was never able to sustain his brilliance throughout a single work, Crane is considered one of the greatest lyric poets of his generation.

Crane was born and grew up in Garrettsville, Ohio, where his father was a businessman who produced chocolates. As the only child of estranged parents, Crane was often the victim of their mutual antagonism. Biographers generally consider the violent incompatibility of Crane's parents and his support of his gentle, artistic mother over his pragmatic father to be an important influence in his life, contributing to his highly strung nature. When Crane's mother suffered a nervous collapse in 1908, he moved to his grandmother's house in Cleveland. There he spent most of his formative years and showed his first enthusiasm for poetry. His grandmother's library was extensive, featuring editions of complete works by poets such as Robert Browning, Ralph Waldo Emerson, and Walt Whitman, who became major influences in Crane's poetry. During his mid-teens Crane continued to read extensively, broadening his interests to include such writers as Plato, Honoré de Balzac, and Percy Bysshe Shelley. Crane's formal education, however, was continually undermined by family problems that led to prolonged absences from school. Finally, in 1916, he left high school without graduating and moved to New York City to attend Columbia University, which he hoped to enter upon passing an entrance examination.

Once in New York City, however, Crane abandoned any pretense of acquiring a college education and began vigorously pursuing a literary career. Through a painter he knew in Cleveland, Crane met other writers and gained exposure to various art movements and ideas. Reading the works of the French Symbolists, English Elizabethan poets, Whitman, William Butler Yeats, and especially T. S. Eliot and Ezra Pound, writing, and socializing with other artists left Crane little time or energy for work.

Struggling financially, Crane sold magazine advertising to supplement the financial support he received from his parents. Although he consistently abused alcohol and engaged in promiscuous homosexual activity during this period, Crane still managed to diligently work on his poetry and publish some of his early pieces in the local journal *Pagan.*

Crane returned to Cleveland in 1917, working first in a munitions plant and later as a reporter for the *Cleveland Plain Dealer.* After working in his father's company for a short time, he worked in various advertising firms in Cleveland; finding similar work in New York, he moved again to the city. By 1922, Crane had already written most of the poems that would comprise his first collection, *White Buildings* (1926). Inspired by his relationship with Emil Opffer, Crane next composed his "Voyages" sequence, a group of poems in praise of love. By the time he finished "Voyages" in 1924, he had already commenced his epic poem *The Bridge* (1930).

Crane reconciled with his father in 1928, but his parent's death soon afterward plunged the poet into depression. With the money he inherited, Crane traveled to Paris, where he associated with prominent figures in the city's American expatriate community. Crane wrote little in Europe, indulging instead in alcohol and carousing. When he returned to the United States he wallowed further in heavy drinking and unrestrained sexual relations. Furthermore, his self-confidence was shaken by the disappointing reception accorded *The Bridge* by critics, many of whom expressed respect for his effort but dissatisfaction with his achievement. Crane had entered a creative slump from which he would not recover. Perhaps sensing a decline in his literary skills, he applied for a Guggenheim fellowship with intentions of studying European culture and the American poetic sensibility. After obtaining the fellowship, though, Crane traveled to Mexico and continued his self-destructive behavior. During this time he wrote only infrequently, producing largely inferior work that only confirmed his own fear that his talent had declined significantly. Finally, in 1932, his

despair turned all-consuming, and on April 27, while traveling by ship, Crane killed himself by leaping into the Gulf of Mexico.

Crane's poetry is often difficult to comprehend, primarily because of the author's poetic theory. According to Crane, logic should not be allowed to divest experience of its complexity, for "the entire construction of the poem is raised on the organic principle of a 'logic of metaphor,' which antedates our so-called pure logic." Thus his poems are often laden with private symbolism and emotions inspired by the sounds of words. He was more concerned with the illogical connotations and associations inspired by words than he was with their definitions, which he felt would limit the perceptions of his poems. Throughout his career Crane aimed at spontaneity of expression and crystallization of feeling through rich imagery; to achieve this effect he often wrote while drinking and listening to jazz. This type of composition best served his lyric poetry, which was unencumbered by any philosophical abstractions requiring careful logical development. Of the poems in *White Buildings,* "Voyages," an evocation of lost love, stands out as his lyrical masterpiece.

Crane's major work, *The Bridge,* planned as a reply to T. S. Eliot's *The Waste Land,* is essentially a series of lyrics on a single theme. *The Bridge* was meant to counteract the pessimism of Eliot's poem with an exuberant affirmation of experience. Crane intended to provide a myth for American life, but his lack of formal education resulted in social analysis and criticism that displayed a deficient knowledge and understanding of the American past. Early critics, while recognizing the greatness of individual passages, considered the poem as a whole to be a failure. Most found *The Bridge* to have no formal unity or logical exposition of ideas; its symbolic structure was considered incoherent and poorly conceived. Later critics, however, have reassessed the poem. They agree that as an epic expression of American history and an affirmative myth of American experience, the poem fails. But they contend that *The Bridge* succeeds admirably as the portrayal of a spiritual quest for a new mythic vision. The poem's subject is thus the quest itself and the necessity for such an intense examination of experience by every individual. Whether or not the quest succeeds in providing a new vision is of secondary importance. Though uncertain about its ultimate merit, most critics agree that *The Bridge* is a major achievement in many of its parts and that Crane is one of the most important American poets since Whitman.

(For further information about Crane's life and works, see *Concise Dictionary of Literary Biography, 1917-1929; Contemporary Authors,* Vols. 104, 127; *Dictionary of Literary Biography,* Vols. 4, 48; and *Twentieth-Century Literature Criticism,* Vols. 2, 5.)

CRITICAL COMMENTARY

HART CRANE AND HARRIET MONROE

(correspondence date 1926)

[Monroe, an American editor, poet, and critic, is best known as the founder of *Poetry* magazine, the first periodical devoted primarily to this genre. The following excerpt is taken from correspondence between Monroe and Crane regarding Crane's poem "At Melville's Tomb."]

From the editor to Mr. Crane:

Take me for a hard-boiled unimaginative unpoetic reader, and tell me how *dice* can *bequeath an embassy* (or anything else); and how a calyx (*of death's bounty* or anything else) can give back a *scattered chapter, livid hieroglyph;* and how, if it does, such a *portent* can be *wound in corridors* (of shells or anything else). . . .

All this may seem impertinent, but is not so intended. Your ideas and rhythms interest me, and I am wondering by what process of reasoning you would justify this poem's succession of champion mixed metaphors, of which you must be conscious. The packed line should pack its phrases in orderly relation, it seems to me, in a manner tending to clear confusion instead of making it worse confounded. . . .

From Mr. Crane to the editor:

Your good nature and manifest interest in writing me about the obscurities apparent in my Melville poem certainly prompt a wish to clarify my intentions in that poem as much as possible. (p. 35)

[Though] I imagine us to have considerable differences of opinion regarding the relationship of poetic metaphor to ordinary logic (I judge this from the angle of approach you use toward portions of the poem), I hope my answers will not be taken as a defense of merely certain faulty lines. I am really much more interested in certain theories of metaphor and technique involved generally in poetics, than I am concerned in vindicating any particular perpetrations of my own.

My poem may well be elliptical and actually obscure in the ordering of its content, but in your criticism of this very possible deficiency you have stated your objections in terms that allow me, at least for the moment, the privilege of claiming your ideas and ideals as theoretically, at least, quite outside the issues of my own aspirations. To put it more plainly, as a poet I may very possibly be more interested in the so-called illogi-

cal impingements of the connotations of words on the consciousness (and their combinations and interplay in metaphor on this basis) than I am interested in the preservation of their logically rigid significations at the cost of limiting my subject matter and perceptions involved in the poem.

This may sound as though I merely fancied juggling words and images until I found something novel, or esoteric; but the process is much more predetermined and objectified than that. (p. 36)

Its paradox, of course, is that its apparent illogic operates so logically in conjunction with its context in the poem as to establish its claim to another logic, quite independent of the original definition of the word or phrase or image thus employed. It implies (this *inflection* of language) a previous or prepared receptivity to its stimulus on the part of the reader. The reader's sensibility simply responds by identifying this inflection of experience with some event in his own history or perceptions—or rejects it altogether. . . . Much fine poetry may be completely rationalistic in its use of symbols, but there is much great poetry of another order which will yield the reader very little when inspected under the limitation of such arbitrary concerns as are manifested in your judgment of the Melville poem, especially when you constitute such requirements of ordinary logical relationship between word and word as irreducible. (pp. 36-7)

You ask me how a *portent* can possibly be wound in a *shell*. Without attempting to answer this for the moment, I ask you how Blake could possibly say that "a *sigh* is a *sword* of an Angel King." . . . I ask you how Eliot can possibly believe that "Every street *lamp* that I pass *beats* like a fatalistic *drum!*" . . . [My] metaphors may fall down completely. I'm not defending their actual value in themselves; but your criticism of them . . . was leveled at an illogicality of relationship between symbols, which similar fault you must have either overlooked in case you have ever admired the Blake and Eliot lines, or have there condoned them on account of some more ultimate convictions pressed on you by the impact of the poems in their entirety.

It all comes to the recognition that emotional dynamics are not to be confused with any absolute order of rationalized definitions; ergo, in poetry the *rationale* of metaphor belongs to another order of experience than science, and is not to be limited by a scientific and

Principal Works

White Buildings (poetry) 1926

The Bridge (poetry) 1930

The Collected Poems of Hart Crane (poetry) 1933

Complete Poems and Selected Letters and Prose (poetry, letters, and essays) 1966

arbitrary code of relationships either in verbal inflections or concepts.

There are plenty of people who have never accumulated a sufficient series of reflections (and these of a rather special nature) to perceive the relation between a *drum* and a *street lamp*—*via* the *unmentioned* throbbing of the heart and nerves in a distraught man which *tacitly* creates the reason and "logic" of the Eliot metaphor. They will always have a perfect justification for ignoring those lines and to claim them obscure, excessive, etc., until by some experience of their own the words accumulate the necessary connotations to complete their connection. (pp. 37-8)

If one can't count on some such bases in the reader now and then, I don't see how the poet has any chance to ever get beyond the simplest conceptions of emotion and thought, of sensation and lyrical sequence. (p. 38)

Not to rant on forever, I'll beg your indulgence and come at once to the explanations you requested on the Melville poem:

> The dice of drowned men's bones he saw bequeath An embassy.

Dice bequeath an embassy, in the first place, by being ground (in this connection only, of course) in little cubes from the bones of drowned men by the action of the sea, and are finally thrown up on the sand, having "numbers" but no identification. These being the bones of dead men who never completed their voyage, it seems legitimate to refer to them as the only surviving evidence of certain messages undelivered, mute evidence of certain things, experiences that the dead mariners might have had to deliver. Dice as a symbol of chance and circumstance is also implied.

> The calyx of death's bounty giving back, etc.

This calyx refers in a double ironic sense both to a cornucopia and the vortex made by a sinking vessel. As soon as the water has closed over a ship this whirlpool sends up broken spars, wreckage, etc., which can be alluded to as *livid hieroglyphs*, making a *scattered chapter* so far as any complete record of the recent ship and her crew is concerned. In fact, about as much definite

knowledge might come from all this as anyone might gain from the roar of his own veins, which is easily heard (haven't you ever done it?) by holding a shell close to one's ear. (pp. 38-9)

From the editor to Mr. Crane:

No doubt our theories and ideals in the art differ more or less fundamentally, yet I would not deny to the poet the right to take certain of the liberties you claim. I think he can take as many as he succeeds with without mystifying his particular audience; for mystery is good, but not mystification.

I think that in your poem certain phrases carry to an excessive degree the "dynamics of metaphor"—they telescope three or four images together by mental leaps (I fear my own metaphors are getting mixed!) which the poet, knowing his ground, can take safely, but which the most sympathetic reader cannot take unless the poet leads him by the hand with some such explanation as I find in your letter. . . .

I don't get this effect from Blake or Eliot in the lines you quote or others that I have read. . . .

My argument comes down, I suppose, rather to your practice than your theory. Or, more specifically, your practice strains your theory by carrying it, with relentless logic, to a remote and exaggerated extreme. You find me testing metaphors, and poetic concept in general, too much by logic, whereas I find you pushing logic to the limit in a painfully intellectual search for emotion, for poetic motive. Your poem reeks with brains—it is thought out, worked out, sweated out. And the beauty which it seems entitled to is tortured and lost. (p. 40)

Hart Crane and Harriet Monroe, "A Discussion with Hart Crane," in *Poetry,* Vol. XXIX, No. 1, October, 1926, pp. 34-41.

ALLEN TATE

(essay date 1932-37)

[Tate is best known for critical essays on modern poetry, Southern traditions, and the legacy of the American Civil War. In the following excerpt from a two-part essay begun in 1932 and completed in 1937, he examines the themes and style of *The Bridge* and asserts that Crane's sensibility was essentially Romantic.]

Rimbaud achieved "disorder" out of implicit order, after a deliberate cultivation of "derangement," but in our age the disintegration of our intellectual systems is accomplished. With Crane the disorder is original and fundamental. That is the special quality of his mind that belongs peculiarly to our own time. His aesthetic problem, however, was more general; it was the historic problem of romanticism. (p. 310)

It is probable that he was incapable of the formal discipline of a classical education, and probable, too, that the eclectic education of his time would have scattered and killed his talent. His poetry not only has defects of the surface, it has a defect of vision; but its great and peculiar value cannot be separated from its limitations. Its qualities are bound up with a special focus of the intellect and sensibility, and it would be folly to wish that his mind had been better trained or differently organized. (p. 311)

Every poem is a thrust of [his locked-in] sensibility into the world: his defect lay in his inability to face out the moral criticism implied in the failure to impose his will upon experience. (p. 313)

[Crane's] vagueness of purpose, in spite of the apparently concrete character of the Brooklyn Bridge, which became the symbol of his epic, he never succeeded in correcting. The "bridge" stands for no well-defined experience; it differs from the Helen and Faust symbols only in its unliterary origin. I think Crane was deceived by this difference, and by the fact that Brooklyn Bridge is "modern" and a fine piece of "mechanics." (pp. 314-15)

The fifteen parts of *The Bridge* taken as one poem suffer from the lack of coherent structure, whether symbolic or narrative: the coherence of the work consists in the personal quality of the writing—in mood, feeling, and tone. (p. 315)

It was a sound impulse on Crane's part to look for an American myth, some simple version of our past that lies near the center of the American consciousness; an heroic tale with just enough symbolism to give his mind both direction and play. The soundness of his purpose is witnessed also by the kind of history in the poem: it is inaccurate, and it will not at all satisfy the sticklers for historical fact. (p. 316)

The impulse in *The Bridge* is religious, but the soundness of an impulse is no warrant that it will create a sound art form. The form depends on too many factors beyond the control of the poet. The age is scientific and pseudo-scientific, and our philosophy is Dewey's instrumentalism. And it is possibly this circumstance that has driven the religious attitude into a corner where it lacks the right instruments for its defense and growth, and where it is in a vast muddle about just what these instruments are. Perhaps this disunity of the intellect is responsible for Crane's unphilosophical belief that the poet, unaided and isolated from the people, can create a myth. (p. 317)

Crane was a myth-maker, and in an age favorable to myths he would have written a mythical poem in the act of writing an historical one. (p. 318)

His pantheism is necessarily a philosophy of sen-sation without point of view. An epic is a judgment of human action, an implied evaluation of a civilization, a way of life. . . . At one moment Crane faces his predicament of blindness to any rational order of value, and knows that he is damned; but he cannot face it long, and he tries to rest secure upon the intensity of sensation.

To the vision of the abyss in **"The Tunnel,"** a vision that Dante passed through midway of this mortal life, Crane had no alternative: when it became too harrowing he cried to his Pocahontas, a typically romantic and sentimental symbol:

Lie to us—dance us back our tribal morn!

It is probably the perfect word of romanticism in this century. When Crane saw that his leading symbol, the bridge, would not hold all the material of his poem, he could not sustain it ironically, in the classical manner, by probing its defects; nor in the personal sections, like **"Quaker Hill,"** does he include himself in his Leopardian denunciation of life. He is the blameless victim of a world whose impurity violates the moment of intensity, which would otherwise be enduring and perfect. He is betrayed, not by a defect of his own nature, but by the external world; he asks of nature, perfection—requiring only of himself, intensity. The persistent, and persistently defeated, pursuit of a natural absolute places Crane at the center of his age.

Alternately he asserts the symbol of the bridge and abandons it, because fundamentally he does not understand it. The idea of bridgeship is an elaborate blur leaving the inner structure of the poem confused.

Yet some of the best poetry of our generation is in *The Bridge*. Its inner confusion is a phase of the inner cross-purposes of the time. Crane was one of those men whom every age seems to select as the spokesmen of its spiritual life; they give the age away. (pp. 319-20)

The Bridge attempts to include all American life, but it covers the ground with seven-league boots and, like a sightseer, sees nothing. With reference to its leading symbol, it has no subject matter. The poem is the effort of a solipsistic sensibility to locate itself in the external world, to establish points of reference. (p. 320)

Crane had, in his later work, no individual consciousness: the hard firm style of **"Praise for an Urn,"** which is based upon a clear-cut perception of moral relations, and upon their ultimate inviolability, begins to disappear when the poet goes out into the world and finds that the simplicity of a child's world has no universal sanction. From then on, instead of the effort to define himself in the midst of almost overwhelming complications—a situation that might have produced a tragic poet—he falls back upon the intensity of consciousness, rather than the clarity, for his center of vision. And that is romanticism.

His world had no center, and the thrust into sensation is responsible for the fragmentary quality of his most ambitious work. This thrust took two directions—the blind assertion of the will, and the blind desire for self-destruction. The poet did not face his first problem, which is to define the limits of his personality and to objectify its moral implications in an appropriate symbolism. Crane could only assert a quality of will against the world, and at each successive failure of the will he turned upon himself. . . .

Crane instinctively continued the conception of the will that was the deliberate discovery of Rimbaud. A poetry of the will is a poetry of sensation, for the poet surrenders to his sensations of the object in his effort to identify himself with it, and to own it. (p. 321)

The Bridge is an irrational symbol of the will, of conquest, of blind achievement in space; its obverse is **"Passage,"** whose lack of external symbolism exhibits the poetry of the will on the plane of sensation; and this is the self-destructive return of the will upon itself. (p. 322)

The Bridge is a failure in the sense that "Hyperion" is a failure, and with comparable magnificence. Crane's problem, being farther removed from the epic tradition, was actually more difficult than Keats's, and his treatment of it was doubtless the most satisfactory possible in our time. Beyond the quest of pure sensation and its ordering symbolism lies the total destruction of art. By attempting an extreme solution of the romantic problem Crane proved that it cannot be solved. (p. 323)

Allen Tate, "Hart Crane," in his *Essays of Four Decades,* Swallow, 1968, pp. 310-23.

R. P. BLACKMUR

(essay date 1935)

[Blackmur was a leading twentieth-century American literary critic. Linked to the New Critics, he believed that a literary work consititutes an independent object to be analyzed closely for its strictly formal devices and internal meanings. In the following excerpt, he comments on Crane's style in the light of various influences on his poetry.]

These notes intend to examine certain characteristic passages of Hart Crane's poems as modes of language and to determine how and to what degree the effects intended were attained. The rationale is that of poetic language; the weapons are analysis and comparison. (p. 122)

[Crane] wrote in a language of which it was the virtue to accrete, modify, and interrelate moments of emotional vision—moments at which the sense of being gains its greatest access,—moments at which, by the felt nature of knowledge, the revealed thing is its own meaning; and he attempted to apply his language, in his major effort, to a theme that required a sweeping, discrete, indicative, anecdotal language, a language in which, by force of movement, mere cataloguing can replace and often surpass representation. He used the private lyric to write the cultural epic; used the mode of intensive contemplation, which secures ends, to present the mind's actions, which have no ends. The confusion of tool and purpose not only led him astray in conceiving his themes; it obscured at crucial moments the exact character of the work he was actually doing. At any rate we find most impenetrable and ineluctable, in certain places, the very matters he had the genius to see and the technique to clarify: the matters which are the substance of rare and valid emotion. The confusion, that is, led him to content himself at times with the mere cataloguing statement, enough for him because he knew the rest, of what required completely objective embodiment. (pp. 126-27)

[The] nature of the influences to which he submitted himself remained similar from the beginning to the end and were the dominant ones of his generation. It was the influence of what we may call, with little exaggeration, the school of tortured sensibility—a school of which we perhaps first became aware in Baudelaire's misapprehension of Poe, and later, in the hardly less misapprehending resurrection of Donne. Crane benefited, and was deformed by, this influence both directly and by an assortment of indirection; but he never surmounted it. He read the modern French poets who are the result of Baudelaire, but he did not read Racine of whom Baudelaire was himself a product. (p. 127)

Crane fitted himself for the exploitation of the peculiar, the unique, the agonised and the tortured perception, and he developed language-patterns for the essentially incoherent aspects of experience: the aspects in which experience assaults rather than informs the sensibility. Yet, granting his sensibility, with his avowed epic purpose he had done better had he gone to school to Milton and Racine, and, in modern times, to Hardy and Bridges—or even Masefield—for narrative sweep.

Crane had, in short, the wrong masters for his chosen fulfillment, or he used some of the right masters in the wrong way: leeching upon them, as a poet must, but taking the wrong nourishment, taking from them not what was hardest and most substantial—what made them great poets—but taking rather what was easiest, taking what was peculiar and idiosyncratic. That is what kills so many of Crane's poems, what must have made them impervious, once they were discharged, even to himself. It is perhaps, too, what killed

Crane the man,—because in a profound sense, to those who use it, poetry is the only means of putting a tolerable order upon the emotions. (p. 128)

[Despite] the confusion and positive irrationality of Crane's language the general tendency is sound, the aspiration sane. He wanted to write good poetry and his archetype was Dante; that is enough. But in his prose thinking he had the wrong words for his thoughts, as in his poetry he had often the wrong themes for his words. (p. 129)

[In] reading Hart Crane we must make allowances for him . . . whereby we agree to supply or overlook what does not appear in the poems, and whereby we agree to forgive or guess blindly at those parts of the poems which are unintelligible. (p. 130)

Merely because Crane is imperfect in his kind is no reason to give him up; there is no plethora of perfection, and the imperfect beauty, like life, retains its fascination. And there is about him, too—such were his gifts for the hearts of words, such the vitality of his intelligence—the distraught but exciting splendour of a great failure. (p. 140)

R. P. Blackmur, "New Thresholds, New Anatomies: Notes on the Text of Hart Crane," in his *The Double Agent: Essays in Craft and Elucidation,* 1935. Reprint by Peter Smith, 1962, pp. 121-40.

MALCOLM COWLEY

(essay date 1951)

[Cowley is best known for his studies of twentieth-century American literature. In the following excerpt, he offers a brief assessment of Crane's poetry, commenting on his occasional vagueness and praising his emotional power.]

There were many poets of the 1920s who worked hard to be obscure, veiling a simple idea in phrases that grew more labored and opaque with each revision of a poem. With Crane it was the original meaning that was complicated and difficult; his revisions brought it out more clearly. He said, making fun of himself, "I practice invention to the brink of intelligibility." The truth was that he had something to say and wanted to be understood, but not at the cost of weakening or simplifying his original vision.

Just what were these "meanings" and these "visions"? They were different, of course, in each new poem, but it seems to me that most of them expressed a purpose that was also revealed in his method of composition. Essentially Crane was a poet of ecstasy or frenzy or intoxication; you can choose your word depending on how much you like his work. Essentially he

was using rhyme and meter and fantastic images to convey the emotional states that were induced in him by alcohol, jazz, machinery, laughter, intellectual stimulation, the shape and sound of words and the madness of New York in the late Coolidge era. At their worst his poems are ineffective unless read in something approximating the same atmosphere, with a drink at your elbow, the phonograph blaring and somebody shouting into your ear, "Isn't that grreat!" At their best, however, the poems do their work unaided except by their proper glitter and violence. At their very best, as in **"The River,"** they have an emotional force that has not been equaled by any other American poet of our century. (pp. 230-31)

Malcolm Cowley, "The Roaring Boy," in his *Exile's Return: A Literary Odyssey of the 1920's,* The Viking Press, 1951, pp. 221-34.

SAMUEL HAZO

(essay date 1963)

[Here, Hazo discusses the poems in *White Buildings* and *The Bridge* in terms of the maturation of Crane's lyrical style.]

Most of the critics who admire Crane's poetry are unanimously high in their praise of his lyrical talent. And even those critics who have reservations about Crane's achievement as an American poet are usually willing to concede that he has written a durable number of short poems or that certain parts and lines of *The Bridge* are notable lyrical moments.

Crane's versatility as a lyric poet in his first published book, *White Buildings,* is best examined and most readily seen in stages. The first stage would include those relatively simple poems which reveal a strong influence of the Imagists. Crane's purpose in these poems is the evocation of a single, dominant mood through the use of sensation-creating tropes, as in **"Legend," "My Grandmother's Love Letters," "Garden Abstract," "In Shadow," "The Fernery," "North Labrador," "Pastorale,"** and **"Sunday Morning Apples."** Included in the second stage are those poems in which Crane is indebted to the Elizabethans and the French Symbolists, as well as the Imagists. These are poems like **"Black Tambourine"** and **"Stark Major"** where Crane's imagistic ability fuses with the careful conceits of the Elizabethans and the rapid, symbolic transitions characteristic of Laforgue, Mallarmé and Rimbaud. The third stage represents the fullest realization of Crane's lyrical talent. The influences of the Imagists, the Elizabethans and the French Symbolists are still apparent, but they are integrated into and transcended by an idiom that is unmistakably Crane's own. (p. 17)

Among the poems related to the imagistic stage of Crane's lyrical development is the first poem in *White Buildings.* "Legend" is not only a poem of affirmation but a synthesis of some of Crane's Platonic beliefs and poetic imperatives. Its theme evolves from the tension between death and renewal, giving and receiving, immolation and transfiguration. (p. 18)

The technique of "Legend" is predominantly impressionistic. Crane came to rely on this technique more and more in his later poems but with added dimensions. At first, however, he was content to let the impressionism of his work reveal itself through a blending of imagery. But even in a poem like "Legend" one is able to see that Crane is already at work developing the technique of relating multiple images in a thematic progression, as in the development of the image of the moth into that of the lover and, finally, the poet. (p. 19)

Stylistically, "My Grandmother's Love Letters," like "Legend," shows Crane at an early stage of his development. The reliance upon imagery tends to dominate all other aspects of his talent. (p. 21)

The two most representative poems of Crane's second lyrical stage are "Black Tambourine" and "Stark Major." . . . [He] relies more and more upon the symbol and the symbolic metaphor. It is left to the imagination of the reader to supply the many transitions that Crane has deliberately omitted. (pp. 24-5)

Clues of Crane's maturation as a lyric poet are evident in "Black Tambourine" in the flexibility of diction and image, the functional reversals and substitutions within the traditionally regular verses of the poem, and the abrupt shifts of focus from stanza to stanza without transitional aids. Crane is literally daring the imagination of the reader to make the transitions that he has not written into the poem in order to heighten the impact of each of the three stanzas as they are read.

The style of "Black Tambourine" suggests that Crane had reached a truce with impressionism when he wrote the poem. He was willing to use impressionistic devices but only within the bounds established by his own propensities for metrical regularity and for the riches of metaphors and symbols. "Black Tambourine" is a step beyond impressionism. It is Crane's commitment to avoid Dadaism, which he regarded as the "dying agonies" of the impressionistic movement. (p. 26)

The poems in the third stage of Crane's lyrical development reveal the true Hart Crane. In these poems he has integrated his talents and influences so that the voice we hear is definitely his own. The rhetoric is

there, but it is no longer Marlovian; it is Crane's. The symbolic metaphors are there, but they are no longer the metaphors of Verlaine or Laforgue; they are Crane's. The blank verse is no longer a mimicry of the blank verse of the great Elizabethans; it is Crane's.

In poems like "Praise for an Urn" and "At Melville's Tomb" Crane is a poet in complete possession of his powers. (p. 28)

From a technical point of view "Praise for an Urn" is enriched by a number of significant contrasts. First, there is the contrast of the bittersweet and Pagliacci-like humanity of Pierrot with the raucous laughter of Gargantua. This is followed by the image of the final "thoughts" of a dying man which are capable of becoming "riders of the storm." There is the implied but omnipresent urn of human ashes contrasted with the remembered "gold" of Nelson's hair. Finally, there is the central paradox of the poem itself as an attempt to remember a dead man "living still" against the implied futility of the poet's trying to commemorate anything at all. . . . These involved contrasts are not unique to "Praise for an Urn." They are more or less typical of all of the poems in this third stage of Crane's lyricism. (p. 31)

"Lachrymae Christi" typifies the extremes to which Crane could go at this third stage of his development. The range of association is so daring here that it becomes at times simply puzzling. The transitions are so abrupt that they tend to mystify. (p. 38)

Whether or not Crane thought "Lachrymae Christi" a poem that could justifiably be called difficult is unknown. It is significant to note, however, that he never wrote another poem exactly like it. Perhaps he felt that he had taken too inordinate a gamble with the sensitivity and imagination of even his most sympathetic readers. The remaining poems in *White Buildings* that are at this third level of Crane's lyrical development—"Repose of Rivers," "Passage," "Paraphrase," "Possessions," "Recitative," "The Wine Menagerie," "For the Marriage of Faustus and Helen," and "Voyages"—are, though difficult, not quite as puzzling in their idiom or their development as "Lachrymae Christi." (p. 39)

One of the finest testaments of Crane's ability to metamorphose images and themes through the symbolical and chromatic scales of sound and color is "The Wine Menagerie." . . . "The Wine Menagerie," apart from the three-part "For the Marriage of Faustus and Helen" and the six-part "Voyages," is one of the most perfect single poems in *White Buildings* and one of the best examples of Crane's mature style. (p. 43)

Except for the two longer poems in *White Buildings*—"For the Marriage of Faustus and Helen" and "Voyages"—all of these shorter poems from "Legend" to **"The Wine Menagerie"** constitute Crane's initial lyrical moment. (p. 46)

There are many who believe that the enduring value of Hart Crane as a poet will be based upon his achievement in the best of these early lyrics. . . . Important to a consideration of these claims, however, is the realization that Crane did not simply leap from the composition of shorter works to the composition of longer ones. **"For the Marriage of Faustus and Helen"** and **"Voyages"** . . . are particular cases in point. He proceeded mosaically in all of his poems, regardless of length, beginning with the splicing of image and image in the unifying and transfigurative moment of inspiration and working until he thought he had achieved an organic whole. (pp. 46-7)

In reading *The Bridge,* as in reading most of the poems of Crane's third and most mature period, it is necessary to "read" with more senses than the eye. This becomes an almost indispensable prerequisite when one realizes that Crane was a poet whose concern for language was multidimensional. Words created for him a beauty that transcended both their denotative and connotative meaning; this beauty arose from the sounds of words both singly and together, from the feelings created by sound as well as sense and, finally, from the often unnoticed texture of the alphabetical pigment itself. Crane exploited each of these capacities of language. (p. 118)

If, as some of Crane's critics have suggested, *The Bridge* is weakened by passages where the meters seem forced and the images willed into position, it was not because of the faltering of Crane's lyric talent in the face of an epic challenge. If an epic is regarded in part as the testament of a people or a culture, *The Bridge* is simply not an epic, despite the persistence of some critics to treat it and subsequently condemn it as such and despite Crane's early Pindaric ambitions for it. Instead, *The Bridge* is the personal testament of one twentieth-century poet within the framework of his own and his country's past, present, and future as they appeared to him. The symbols that Hart Crane chose from various periods of American history and literature to incarnate his vision have their true meaning in their relationship to him. They are, we must assume, those things that appeared significant to Crane's sensibility. Their hierarchic importance in the historical sense is not in question here. The primitivistic themes of **"The Dance"** or Crane's Nietzschean faith in the poet as a type of redemptive hero in **"Cape Hatteras"** and **"Atlantis"** may or may not be regarded as crucial aspects of American culture, but they were to Crane. As such, they are reflective of his own vision. Thus the success or failure of some parts of *The Bridge* cannot be made answerable to any other criterion but their success or failure as poetry. If we discuss the work in terms of history, we are measuring the poem by a nonpoetic standard. If we dis-

cuss the poem in terms of its inadequacy as an American epic, we are ignoring its true nature and attempting to judge it as something which it most certainly is not. In the same sense, if passages in *The Bridge* fail at times because the lines seem "manufactured" and the poetic moments adulterated by rhetoric, it is simply because manufactured lines and adulterated poetic moments are never consistent with good poetry. Crane was as vulnerable to such lapses as any poet, and we must criticize him in that context. Occasional lapses should not blind us to the true significance of *The Bridge* as a revelation of Crane's sensibility coming to terms with itself and the world confronting it. (pp. 122-23)

Crane's best poem in *Key West: An Island Sheaf* is **"The Broken Tower."** It is not only a memorable poetic achievement; it is Crane's last will and testament, containing that moment of sudden brightness that came to him before his suicide. In it there is the poetic power and versatility that reveal Crane at his very best. (p. 129)

"The Broken Tower" is simultaneously a dirge and an epiphany. What is revealed is not only the naked spirit of Crane in near despair but also his commitment of poetry as his final hope of salvation. In its agony the poem recalls the beauty of Hopkins' "terrible sonnets" and the last poems of Keats; in its hope of redemption there is an echo of Shelley's "The Cloud." Crane's poem reveals the poet polarized, that is, crucified on the cross of his suffering as well as on the cross of his hope.

The dominant symbol of the poem is the tower, but it is important to remember at the outset that this is a broken tower. If this tower symbolizes the poet, it suggests not only the creative but the destructive aspect of his talent. It perpetuates, too, the Dionysiac, Orphean, and Christ-like symbols that are common to poems like **"Lachrymae Christi"** and **"The Dance"**— the concept of the poet as one who sacrifices himself in the very act of creation as his entire being yields to the higher necessity of poetic expression. (p. 130)

If the tower is seen as a counterpart of the poet, the bells can be regarded as the inspired songs that must rely both on the "bell-rope" and the "tower" to be sounded forth and heard. The songs will find their release even if it means that they will "break down their tower" in so doing. In this image Crane alludes to the dynamism of poetic knowledge; poems will *out* even at the poet's expense. (p. 131)

In **"The Broken Tower"** Crane has succeeded in dramatizing not only the mystery of poetic creation in the style and idiom of his best poetry, but he has also succeeded in dramatizing himself and what he considered to be his mission. If the tower symbolizes the poet, it cannot help but symbolize Crane. . . .

If Crane in his less impressive poems seems like

a man intent on satirizing himself, he is in his best poems a poet intent on transcending himself. (p. 132)

Samuel Hazo, in his *Hart Crane: An Introduction and Interpretation,* Holt, 1963, 146 p.

R. W. B. LEWIS
(essay date 1967)

[In the following excerpt, Lewis traces Crane's search for a new poetic vision in the "Voyages" poems, commenting that his treatment of homosexual love in that sequence is "representative of every kind of human passion."]

Taken as a whole, **"Voyages"** is undoubtedly Crane's lyrical masterpiece. . . . (p. 148)

"Voyages" from its beginning to its end unfolds a story—a love story, needless to say—that in its rhythm and content is altogether familiar and expertly conventional.

"Voyages," that is, presents a clear enough and a continuing action, and one that belongs recognizably to an age-old tradition of romance. In it, by convention, the experience of earthly love reaches its peak of excitement only to be broken off by the departure or death of the beloved, whereupon the poet-lover finds consolation and a more permanent kind of gratification in a vision of transcendent beauty or of God or paradise; and in his own poetic narrative of the entire affair. Petrarch and Sidney come to mind as notable early practitioners of this genre; Keats's "Ode on a Grecian Urn" and Whitman's "Out of the Cradle Endlessly Rocking" are perhaps the later poems in English with which **"Voyages"** has most in common. . . . Crane's sequence . . . was rooted in the joy and pain of a homosexual love affair and its culmination; and it similarly described, in a series of highly metaphoric projections, the experience of psychic death leading to the discovery of the language of vision—that is, to poetry. At times, **"Voyages"** almost dissolves this "story" in the sheer flow of its sensuous imagery; at other times, its suggestive allusions, taken out of context, seem to carry us into the realm of myth, or into some boundless domain of splendid un-reason where opposites consort and nameless forces or disembodied pulsations dance out their uninterpretable allegory. But we should hang on to the traditional, even the archetypal, story in it; to do so may, at any given moment, seem to reduce the poem's range, but it is in fact and over all to perceive more fully the beauty, the poignance, and the power with which the entire work is endowed.

"Voyages I" introduces the theme of experi-

ence—represented, for Crane as for Herman Melville, by the dangerous but inviting sea and taking the specific form of a sea-journey which at the same time is and stands for a journey into love. The heart of the poem is in its final stanza, in the poet's would-be address to the "bright, striped urchins" he sees—evidently in a picture or poster of some sort—playing on the beach. . . . The urchins, as we see, are swiftly transformed by metaphor into ships alerted for departure: their bodies are "spry cordages" or lively ship's rigging. But Crane urges them *not* to put out to sea—not to voyage into a crueler and more encompassing love, but to stay safely on shore or in harbor; to be satisfied with "fondl[ing]" their playthings in innocent affection, and not to submit to caresses from a sea which, in its largeness and power, may dash them against the lichen-covered rocks. (pp. 150-52)

But this was only a warning to the uninitiated (Crane called it a " 'stop, look and listen' sign"). It was no more Crane's final exhortation about experience than it had been Melville's. We recall, in **"Faustus and Helen II"** the invitation to make the daring plunge into life: "to fall downstairs with me / With perfect grace and equanimity"; or, closer to the symbolism of **"Voyages,"** to "scud past" those "shores" where the trimmers sit in pious safety. Just such bold "shoreless" venturing was commended by Melville. . . . (pp. 153-54)

Melville, of course, was speaking about a voyage of thought, of "deep, earnest thinking"; the daring effort of the mind to retain its freedom and to journey through the tempestuous appearance of things to the nature of ultimate reality. Crane was speaking about a (for him) no less daring voyage of love, the effort of flesh, feeling, and imagination to travel to the last reality and meaning of the erotic life. And for Crane, the sea plays a more ambiguous and shifting role. In **"Voyages II,"** it is a still mightier being than in **"I,"** but it is no longer the cruel and destructive lover of the human who submits to it. Instead, as the actual love affair—*"our* love"—gets under way, the sea becomes an imperious rival in love, an absolute and godlike monarch (evidently a queen) whose boundless love and huge embrace of the moon at first make mockery of the limitations of the merely human lovers. The new identification of the sea emerges . . . from the "combination and interplay" of the connotations of words as they impinge on our consciousness; and from a rhythmical energy that, as against **"Voyages I,"** seems suddenly supercharged. In **"I,"** however effective its content, the tone was flat and prosaic, and kept at a low key by a number of monosyllabic grammatical binders . . . that in his later and more highly pressured verse, such as **"Voyages II,"** Crane would do without. The rhythm in **"II"** is a remarkable mixture of the sense of flowing and that of marching: or better, it suggests a flowing movement that has been stiffened and accentuated into a march—just as the coined word "processioned" visually transforms the rising and breaking waves into disciplined figures marching by in some pageant or parade.

"Processioned," meanwhile, is also one of the important words whose impinging connotation interacts with others to beget the new image of the sea. . . . What is being stressed about this royal lover in the opening stanza is the absolute nature of her love and the derision she visits, in consequence, upon the finite love-possibilities of man. (pp. 155-56)

But the authority and the arrogance of the sea do not, after all, overpower or disempower (through laughter) the human love. The action in **"Voyages"** is, as I have suggested, an interlocking double action: the progress of the human affair as it is dialectically involved with the shifting relation between the poet and the sea. This is Crane's dazzlingly original treatment of an old, essentially a Romantic, convention of love poetry: whereby "nature" (here, chiefly, the sea and the sky) reflects or frustrates, sympathizes with or opposes the movements of human emotion. In **"Voyages III,"** the sea as lover will become the reverent mimic of human sexual behavior; here, in the second stanza of **"Voyages II,"** the two elements—the infinite lover and the finite—grow matched and even. (pp. 156-57)

Human love is mortal: it exists in time, and time is passing; the relentless passage of time is just what the sea-tides, timeless as they are, continuously measure— "her turning shoulders wind the hours," like a clock. And so. . . .

Hasten, while they are true,—sleep, death, desire,
Close round one instant in one floating flower.

Those lines have the kind of utter finality—as of some deep and serious emotion perfectly realized in language and cadence—that a lyric poet would be lucky to achieve half a dozen times in his life. The rhythm that hurries briefly and then slows to the solemn tread of "sleep, death, desire," continuing in the soft funereal count of the second line; the countering of imperative and statement; the play, almost the wash, of words against each other; the alliterations and repetitions; even the dimness of syntax and allusion—all gives us poetry in intimate touch with a feeling (about love and death) that is on the far side of logical formulation but that communicates immediately. The entire experience and all its many elements are quietly concentrated in a single entity or image: "one floating flower."

And yet the very beauty of the lines has, I believe, caused a certain misapprehension about **"Voyages II"** and, by their influence, about a larger range of Crane's poetry. It is true that in the sequence "sleep, death, desire," sleep and death determine the reference of desire—which becomes, exactly, a desire *for* sleep and death; a yearning for oblivion. Crane is indeed saying in some untranslatable way that he and his lover must

hasten to enjoy their love while the sea's bounty is still available ("while they"—the bent foam and wave— "are true")—as the setting which gives their love its ultimate and awesome nature. For he knows that, like Keats, he is half in love with easeful death, and perhaps all men are; before death closes sweetly upon them, they must seize the day of love. But, to put it as unequivocally as possible, **"Voyages II"** is not a *Liebestod;* it is not an expression of the so-called death-wish; it is no evidence of a suicidal impulse. It gives rise, quite on the contrary, to a remarkably firm prayer for life. . . . (pp. 158-60)

This prayer would be very definitely answered in the conclusion of the **"Voyages"** sequence—when, in **"Voyages VI,"** the poet passes through a kind of death (symbolized as death at sea), through the grave of his love, to rest his own visionary gaze upon a paradise of timeless beauty, an unearthly shore called Belle Isle. . . . [Then] the floating flower of death would become the "petalled word" of creation.

It occurs to me that the presumptive manner of Crane's actual death in 1932 has been a blinder on the understanding of his poetry. Because he died by his own hand as it seems, and at so relatively young an age, there has been a temptation to find in his writing the constant expression of a suicidal urge, or at least a yearning for nothingness; a profound and dominant desire to be released from this mortal world. But the proudest imperatives of his characteristic poems are directed against the escape from the temporal world and toward the praise of it. . . . That Crane had a fervent consciousness of death is undeniable; he would scarcely have been a very interesting poet without it. But the force and beauty of [his poetry] come directly from his committed *resistance* to that consciousness. (p. 161)

The life he spoke for, and we cannot insist upon it too often, was life enlarged and illuminated by a divine energy: or by a human energy raised to a higher power. This is the life realized as the intoxicated fulfillment of love in **"Voyages III,"** where death is mentioned only to be utterly denied. **"Voyages III"** is the most riotous poem, emotionally, in the whole sequence. . . . The poet's sea-journey is now a journey *to* his beloved (the title of the sequence, we remember is **"Voyages"** in the plural); a movement—toward perfect union—that becomes enormously accelerated. The poetry swirls with gerunds of breath-taking activity, and at a speed too great for normal punctuation. And where, at the start of **"Voyages II,"** the human love saw itself derided by the boundless erotic swellings of the sea, now on the contrary it is magnified beyond measure—since the erotic act of the lovers has become the model imitated by the universe at large. (pp. 161-62)

The poet's love for his friend is blood-brother to the love discernible between the elements of nature throughout infinity; at once a model for and portion of that love. The sea mounts the sky's proffered breast in a sexual union identical with that of the lovers. . . . The image is huge and startling; but the convention, sometimes and disapprovingly called the pathetic fallacy—natural elements behaving in sympathetic imitation of human beings—is probably as old as love poetry. . . . But perhaps never have the elements engaged in so fierce a mimicry of human sexual combat as in "Voyages III." . . . (pp. 162-63)

All the forms of love—as it were, the various and strenuous embraces of the universe—reach their culmination in the sexual embrace of the beloved. This is the end of the journey: which, through the preceding lines, had been steadily gathering momentum. (p. 163)

"Voyages III" represents the peak of the love experience, and the moment when the sense and the sound of song are most powerful. With "IV," a change sets in; and soon the poetic attention will shift from love to loss, and from song to vision. (p. 165)

The general sense of "Voyages IV" we make out without undue exertion; but there is in it a notable slackening of poetic muscle. The compact vigor of "III" is dissipated; and the first and third stanzas in particular seem for all their brevity to thicken interminably, piling phrase upon phrase with a loss rather than an accumulation of meaning and intensity. Crane seems here to be poetically grinding his gears, as though he were trying to move the action forward but had not found the way to do so. (p. 166)

Homosexual symbolism also hovers inescapably in the imagery of "Voyage III" and infuses "Voyages V"; it is present wherever hands or oars are referred to, and in one perspective it can be seen pervading the whole sequence. This is perhaps the moment to remark that "Voyages," despite its flaws, is not only that rarity in American literature—genuine and personal love poetry; it is also the only truly moving and beautiful poetry of male homosexual love in English with which I am acquainted. It is so because Crane has succeeded in making the passionate love of male for male representative of every kind of human passion: "the secret oar and petals of *all* love." (p. 168)

"Voyages VI" is in its own right one of the truly splendid poems in English; and it concludes the "Voyages" sequence with a poetic splendor so appropriate as in effect to provide the subject matter of this final moment. It is a poem of intense visionary straining, sight and blindness are of its essence, and eyes constitute its key reference; and it is a work of the utmost rhetorical magnificence. Vision and poetry: these are what "Voyages VI" is about; vision and poetry as the answer to the death of love and the shattering bewilderment it produced. Out of the vortex of love's grave, the shipwreck of his love, the poet sees and hears the

long-awaited answer to "the seal's wide spindrift gaze toward paradise." And the answer ("Voyages VI" consists, structurally, of a prayer and an answer, an "unbetrayable reply") is a glimpse of the paradise of the poet's own aspirations—his creative aspirations; for as he comes to perceive Belle Isle, he also hears issuing from it the "petalled word" of "creation." In Crane's compelling treatment of this greatly traditional movement, the sea is again a decisive agent. The sea that had threatened and laughed at him, that had rivaled, imitated, and turned against him, that had wrecked or drowned him, now exerts its power to rescue and restore the poet. (p. 172)

We have moved, geographically and spiritually, from the warm Caribbean to icy northern waters; as it turns out, from the heat of emotional and physical experience to the cool zone where emotion may be recollected in tranquillity. . . . As "Voyages VI" opens, the poet finds himself in a region and within a complete poetic figure where swimmers struggle through chill ocean rivers toward morning, under skies that are strange to them, and with "eyes" that are "lost." The poet is one of those swimmers, or like them. He too is lost; he does not recognize the new surroundings, the shifting borders; and he has lost his ability to see—that is (again, as it turns out), his capacity to understand the actual world, its excitement and its pain, in the light of an envisioned ideal world. "Voyages VI" begins on the note of desolating incomprehension with which "Voyages V" ended.

It also begins with a tight paradox and an eloquent prayer. The poet is like a drowned and eyeless swimmer; two stanzas later, he is also like a blind sailor on an abandoned ship—he is even that ship itself. . . . He had, against all the warnings of "Voyages I" embarked on the dangerous love-journey; he had trusted his "spry cordage," the vessel of his body, to the cruel sea—had, in "Voyages III," descended to the depths of the sea to experience the whole fierce grandeur of human love; but after that grandeur had come the separation and with it the sense of psychic incarceration and of death. And yet it is exactly that imprisoning and destructive sea whose *guest* the poet is, and whose "dungeons" (according to the poem's surprising syntax) can "lift" the "lost morning eyes" of swimmers like the poet. The sea possesses the power to restore life and light and vision, which is why its icy dungeons are also "bright"; for it is through just such a descent, just such a sea-death, that the adventurous and questing spirit may reach an ultimate perception forever denied to the emotionally landlocked. One must lose one's vision in order to find it. In the poem, the poet knows this; even as Crane knew it to be the inevitable outcome in the poetic tradition he was following; and the voice in "Voyages VI" prays to the ocean rivers that he too may be resurrected and re-enlightened. . . . (pp. 172-74)

It is a prayer for an end to the exhaustion of voyaging, a prayer for peaceful rest (later: "unsearchable repose"); for a spiritual haven and a phoenix-like rebirth. It is above all, a prayer for spiritual vision that can once more give rise to poetic utterance. In lines that surge and fall, that pound almost audibly to a turbulent oceanic pulse, the poet urges the sea-waves to "rear" for him an immense poetic theme. . . . [The] new subject is the death or fragmentation of poetic vision itself: it is "a splintered garland for the seer" which at the same time, by transposition, is a garland for the splintered seer.

This endlessly reverberating passage contains, among other things, as direct and dramatic a statement as one can find about the nature of the Romantic tradition—one is inclined to say, about the nature of modern poetry, and of a large range of modern literature generally. It bespeaks what is probably the key historic event in that tradition: the emergence of the poet—replacing the king or prince—as the hero of poetry; and of the exacting processes of the creative imagination as the drama that most absorbs the poet's attention. No less in the Romantic tradition . . . , the prayer is in great part answered in the very eloquence by which it gets uttered. The sweeping intensity of the poet's address to the waves indicates how far he has recovered his lost powers. (pp. 174-75)

R. W. B. Lewis, in his *The Poetry of Hart Crane: A Critical Study,* Princeton University Press, 1967, 426 p.

MARGARET DICKIE UROFF
(essay date 1974)

[In the following excerpt, Uroff isolates and discusses five major image patterns in Crane's poetry.]

Abandoning the division by genre [his lyric poems and epic poem], one can see in Crane's poetry as a whole a recurrence of patterns and can explore more fully the ways in which Crane's imagination worked. Crane has been regarded as a poet of broken efforts, of varied creative aims, but a study of his poetry reveals that his is rather a work of unusual continuity, of patterns recurring with obsessive frequency. Although Crane made great claims for the originality and ambition of *The Bridge,* it is the product of the same imagination that produced the lyrics, and its connections with them are multiple. Some poetic concerns dominate his work from beginning to end and seek expression in varied patterns throughout his career. (pp. 5-6)

The poet whose consciousness is the center of Crane's imaginative world defines himself again and again by two separate and in some ways opposing patterns of impulses: the impulse to violence and the impulse to possession. These are the two extreme responses of the creative self aware of its isolation yet agonizingly moved to enter into communion with the larger life around it. As soon as Crane discovered his poetic vocation, which was almost coincident with his discovery of self, he saw also the connection between art and violence. To create is to violate the certainties of the world, to free oneself and to move beyond all accepted limits; but it is also to suffer the violence of self-expenditure as well as the torment of the world's scorn. In his apprentice poems Crane imagines the artist as the supreme sufferer. (p. 6)

But as Crane's poetic powers developed, so did his confidence in the victory to be won from the violence of art. Although he imagined himself throughout his career as violated, burning, breaking, and in agony, he came to regard his suffering as purgative, redemptive, worthy. The attitudinizing and maudlin self-pity of his apprentice works give way to a deeper awareness of the artist's strength to endure. The suffering and self-expenditure of the poet lead, Crane came to see, not to exhaustion and defeat but to a new vision. The poet who unleashes his imaginative force spends it, but he also breaks through the deadened and restrictive forms of the world, releases the life hidden within them, and achieves thereby a new freedom and an apprehension of the world that is an expansion of ordinary consciousness. The poetic act is thus liberating. The "white buildings" of poetry, unlike the stultifying enclosures of the city's skyscrapers, are open to the light. To dwell in them is to be free. The bells of the imagination "break down their tower; / And swing I know not where," Crane said in a late poem, **"The Broken Tower,"** where he celebrates the liberating and barrier-breaking power of the imagination. (p. 7)

The pattern of violence in Crane's poetry is intricately interwoven with a second pattern: the urge for possession. Violence is a means to possession. To violate the world and thus possess it is one way of imaginative access to an otherwise resistant reality. The fire that burns in Crane's poems, the wind that razes "All but bright stones wherein our smiling plays," the bells that break down the tower, all are analogues of the imagination's violent power to wrest from experience a new and purified meaning. But the poet who perpetrates violence is also consumed by an unassuagable lust and agonized by his loneliness. In his isolation and suffering he is tormented by a desire to possess the miraculous spirit that has the power to transform the ugliness and torpor of the quotidian world and the unbearable solitude of his own experience into something whole, perfect, pure. This spirit is imagined in Crane's poetry as an elusive female figure. To possess her is to claim her gift of beauty, grace, vision, poetry.

The pursuit of this seductive but tantalizingly remote figure is traced in three of Crane's best series of poems: **"For the Marriage of Faustus and Helen,"** **"Voyages,"** and the section of *The Bridge* entitled **"Powhatan's Daughter."** The pattern repeated in variations in these long poems starts with a dreamlike vision of a beatific presence who inspires the poet with feelings of love and insight and harmony but who fades or disappears almost as soon as the poet senses her illuminating powers. She is awesome, and the poet is overpowered by his initial glimpse of her. Although he desires an intimate contact with her, he realizes that this exalted figure cannot be possessed, that, in fact, she possesses him. Still he longs for her. Energized by her presence, yet frightfully lonely and uncertain of his own powers, the poet sets out on a quest for her. She eludes him, and in the course of his pursuit he vents his frustration and rage, purifies himself of his purely sexual desires, and survives to claim, if not the object of his desires, the reward of new life and vision that she bestows. (p. 8)

The third pattern evident in Crane's poetry is that of flight, a pattern involved in much of his poetic action. In his poems of violence the poet races from all restrictions, moves through purgatorial fires, breaks barriers. His desire for possession propels him toward pursuit, hurries him along in his quest, and leads him to moments of ecstatic transport. The poet himself seems driven to flee, compelled by forces at the depth of his psyche. But he also experiences flight as a new and liberating sensation. His moments of most intense consciousness are caught in images of ascension, of spanning, of weightlessness. If patterns of flight serve to express certain psychic situations in Crane's poetry, they are also used in what seems a totally different way to detail the sensations of the twentieth century. Flight was, Crane felt, the revolutionizing experience of the modern world. The speed attainable in the conveyances of the machine age excited Crane's imagination with a new sense of illimitable power while it terrified him with its destructive potential. (pp. 9-10)

Flight is not the only experience of the modern world in Crane's poetry. The dynamism of speed was exhilarating, but Crane also sensed moments of stasis, times when he felt rooted in space, enclosed in a world of hardened forms, oppressed by the resistant bulk of the material world. . . . Images of stasis occur throughout Crane's poetry to describe moments when he feels balked, dejected, trapped, uncreative, but these moments are usually transitory in the process of the poems and give way quickly to movement. However, Crane did write a series of poems devoted to the poet's sense of stasis. (p. 11)

Violence and possession, flight and stasis, these

Crane in 1916.

are the alternating and inextricably intertwined patterns in Crane's poetry. The tension between them is extreme, yet it is tautly held by the work's intensity of feeling and the powerful control of Crane's artistry. There was in Crane's imagination a fervent longing to see these patterns as part of a larger pattern, to see his intensely private sensations as cosmically meaningful. As he develops each pattern, he attempts to expand its significance beyond the immediate experience and to give it a larger value. In his violence and suffering the poet spends himself, Crane imagines, to win for the world the "bright logic" of the imagination. His desire for possession moves beyond the beautiful object of his dreams and expresses his longing to call into the world the spirit of beauty and harmony. The pattern of flight traces not only the speed and destruction of the machine age but the vast potential for a new perspective of time and space, "New verities, new inklings." Even Crane's poems of stasis trace a pattern, however terrifying, which he senses operating in the world.

Throughout Crane's poetry from beginning to end is the persistent effort to give direct expressive form to those moments of intense consciousness in which he felt he had attained the "pattern's mastery."

The last pattern of his poetry to be explored details the poet's sense of mastery. To describe it, he uses terms of religious, liturgical, and ritualistic significance, but he detaches them from their orthodox and dogmatic meaning, uses them freshly to detail the sense of awe that attended the greatest flights of his imagination. In this process Crane's intention is not so much to revitalize the outworn language of religious belief as it is to affirm and celebrate his own conception of the creative power, of Creation's power. . . . Unlike traditional religious poets, Crane did not have the assuring belief in God's presence, the sense of reciprocity between the human and the divine. Although feelings of awe and mastery are direct and overpowering in his poems, the meaning of those feelings is questioned even while it is being affirmed. While this is Crane's most overarching and celebratory pattern, it is also his most tentative. In it he poses directly the central question of the modern poet: can it be true?

These five patterns may be understood as Crane's persistent efforts to give form to the deepest and most complex urgings of his imagination. (pp. 12-13)

Margaret Dickie Uroff, in her introduction to her *Hart Crane: The Patterns of His Poetry,* University of Illinois Press, 1974, pp. 1-17.

HAROLD BLOOM
(essay date 1982)

[In the following excerpt, Bloom analyzes Crane's "Repose of Rivers" and "Passages" in light of the poet's developing sensibility.]

O Thou steeled Cognizance whose leap commits
The agile precincts of the lark's return . . .

I remember reading these lines when I was eleven years old, crouched over Crane's book in a Bronx library. They, and much else in the book, cathected me onto poetry, a conversion or investment fairly typical of many in my generation. I still have the volume of Crane that I persuaded my older sister to give me on my twelfth birthday, the first book I ever owned. Among my friends there are a few others who owned Crane before any other book. Growing up in the thirties, we were found by Crane's poetry, and though other poets followed (I went from Crane to Blake) the strength of first love still hovers whenever they, or I, read Crane.

The Marlovian rhetoric swept us in, but as with Marlowe himself the rhetoric was also a psychology and a knowing, rather than a knowledge, a knowing that precisely can be called a gnosis, transcending the epistemology of tropes. What the Australian poet Alec

Hope, echoing Tamburlaine, perceptively called: "The Argument of Arms," is as much Crane's knowing and language as it was Marlowe's. "Know ye not the argument of arms?" Tamburlaine calls out to his protesting generals before he stabs his own son to death for cowardice. As Hope expounds it, "the argument of arms" is poetic warfare, the agonistic interplay of the Sublime mode:

There is no middle way and no compromise in such a world. Beauty is the rival of beauty as force of force, and only the supreme and perfect survives. Defeat, like victory, is total, absolute, final.

This is indeed Marlowe's knowing, and it would be pointless for a humanist critic to complain that such a vision is human-all-too-human. *Power* is the central poetic concept in Marlowe as it will be in Milton, and as it came to be in the American Milton, Emerson (a prose Milton, granted) and in Crane as a kind of American Marlowe. Hope rightly points to Hazlitt on *Coriolanus* as the proper theorist of the union of the Argument of Arms and the Argument of Poetry. Hazlitt also would not gain the approval of the natural supernaturalist kind of critical humanist:

The principle of poetry is a very anti-leveling principle. It aims at effect, it exists by contrast. It admits of no medium. It is everything by excess. It raises above the ordinary standard of sufferings and crimes.

But Crane is a prophet of American Orphism, of the Emersonian and Whitmanian Native Strain in our national literature. His poetic of power is therefore best caught by the American theorist proper:

. . . though Fate is immense, so is Power, which is the other fact in the dual world, immense. If Fate follows and limits Power, Power attends and antagonizes Fate. We must respect Fate as natural history. For who and what is this criticism that pries into the matter? Man is not order of nature, sack and sack, belly and members, link in a chain, nor any ignominious baggage; but a stupendous antagonism, a dragging together of the poles of the Universe . . .

This might be Melville, meditating upon his own Ahab, but of course it is the uncanny Sage of Concord, satirized by Melville as Plotinus Plinlimmon and as Confidence Man, yet the satire was uneasy. Crane is not very easy to satirize either, and like Shelley, with whom his affinities were deep, Crane goes on burying his critical undertakers. Whitman and Dickinson, Frost and Stevens all had time enough, but Crane, perhaps more gifted than any of them, was finished at an age when they had begun weakly or not at all. A gnosis of Man as a stupendous antagonism, Orphic and Promethean, needs time to work itself through, but time, reviled by all gnostics with a particular vehemence, had its literal triumph over Crane. As with Shelley and Keats, we have a truncated canon, and yet, as with them, what we have is overwhelming.

I am concerned here with Crane's "religion" *as a poet* (not as a man, since that seems an inchoate mixture of a Christian Science background, an immersion in Ouspensky, and an all but Catholic yearning). But by poetic "religion" I mean American Orphism, the Emersonian or national religion of our poetry, which Crane inherited, quite directly, from his prime precursor Whitman. True precursors are always composite and imaginary, the son's changeling-fantasy of the father that his own poetry reinvents, and there is usually a near-contemporary agon as well as a struggle with the fathering force of the past. The older contemporary antagonist and shaper for Crane was certainly Eliot, whose anti-Romantic polemic provoked in Crane an answering fury of High Romanticism, absurdly undervalued by Crane's critical contemporaries, but returning to its mainstream status in the generation that receives the recent abundance of poetic maturation in Ashbery, Merrill, Ammons and others.

The governing deities of American Orphism, as of the ancient sort, are Eros and Phanes, Dionysus or Bacchus, and Ananke, the Necessity who appears as the maternal ocean in Whitman and Crane most overtly, but clearly and obsessively enough in Stevens also. Not so clear, though just as obsessive, must be our judgement upon Melville's representations of an Orphic Ananke in the great shroud of the sea. Melville's "that man should be a thing for immortal souls to sieve through!" is the apt epigraph of a crucial chapter on Greek Shamanism in E. R. Dodds' great book, *The Greeks and the Irrational.* Dodds traced to Scythia the new Orphic religious pattern that credited man with an occult self of divine origin. This self was not the psyche, but the daemon; as Dodds says, "the function of the daemon is to be the carrier of man's potential divinity and actual guilt." Crane's daemon or occult self, like Whitman's, is the actual hero and victim of his own poetry. Crane as American Orpheus is an inevitable image, exploited already by writers as diverse as Winters in his elegy for Crane and Tennessee Williams in *Suddenly Last Summer.* The best of the Orphic hymns to Crane is the astonishing "Fish Food" of John Brooks Wheelwright, except that Crane wrote his own best Orphic elegy in **"Atlantis,"** his close equivalent of Shelley's *Adonais.* But I narrow my subject here, of Crane's "Orphism," down to its visionary epistemology or Gnosis. Crane's Eros, his Dionysus, above all his Whitmanian Ananke, remain to be explored, but in these pages I concern myself only with Crane as "daemon," a potential divinity knowing simultaneously its achievement and its guilt.

The assumption of that daemon, or what the poets of Sensibility called "the incarnation of the Poetic Character," is the inner plot of many of the lyrics in

White Buildings. The *kenosis* or ebbing-away of the daemon is the plot of the **"Voyages"** sequence, where the other Orphic deities reduce Crane to a "derelict and blinded guest" of his own vision, and where the "ocean rivers" churn up the Orphic heritage as a "splintered garland for the seer." Certainly the most ambitious of the daemonic incarnations is the sequence **"For the Marriage of Faustus and Helen,"** which is Crane at his most triumphantly Marlovian, but so much else is at play there that I turn to two lesser but perfect hymns of Orphic incarnation, **"Repose of Rivers"** and **"Passage."**

Crane is a great master of transumptive allusion, of achieving poetic closure by a final trope that reverses or sometimes even transcends both his own lyric's dominant figurations and the poetic tradition's previous exploitations of these images. So, **"Repose of Rivers"** concludes:

> . . . There, beyond the dykes
> I heard wind flaking sapphire, like this summer,
> And willows could not hold more steady sound.

The poem's opening stanza gives a more complex version of that "steady sound" because the synaesthetic seeing / hearing of "that seething, steady leveling of the marshes" is both an irony and an oxymoron:

> The willows carried a slow sound,
> A sarabande the wind moved on the mead.
> I could never remember
> That seething, steady leveling of the marshes
> Till age had brought me to the sea.

Crane is recalling his version of a Primal Scene of Instruction, a moment renewing itself discontinuously at scattered intervals, yet always for him a moment relating the inevitability of sexual orientation to the assumption of his poethood. The slow-and-steady dance of the wind on the marshes became a repressed memory until "age" as maturation brought the poet to the sea, central image of necessity in his poetry, and a wounding synecdoche here for an acceptance of one's particular fate as a poet. The repressed reveals itself as a grotesque sublimity, with the second stanza alluding to Melville's imagery in his story, "The Encantadas";

> Flags, weeds. And remembrance of steep alcoves
> Where cypresses shared the noon's
> Tyranny. They drew me into hades almost.
> And mammoth turtles climbing sulphur dreams
> Yielded, while sun-silt rippled them
> Asunder . . .

The seething, steady leveling of the mammoth turtles, their infernal love-death, is a kind of sarabande also. In climbing one another they climb dreams of self-immolation, where "yielded" means at once surrender to death and to one another. The terrible slowness of their love-making yields the frightening trope: "sun-silt rippled them / Asunder," where "asunder" is both the post-coition parting and the individual turtle death. Crane and D. H. Lawrence had in common as poets only their mutual devotion to Whitman, and it is instructive to contrast this stanza of **"Repose of Rivers"** with the Tortoise-series of Lawrence in *Birds, Beasts and Flowers.* Lawrence's tortoises are crucified *into* sex, like Lawrence himself. Crane's Melvillean turtles are crucified *by* sex. But Crane tells a different story about himself: crucified *into* poetry and *by* poetry. The turtles *are* drawn into a sexual hades; Crane is *almost* drawn, with the phrase "hades almost" playing against "steep alcoves." Embowered by steep alcoves of cypresses, intensifying the dominant noon sun, Crane nearly yields to the sexual phantasmagoria of "flags, weeds," and the sound play alcoves / almost intensifies the narrowness of the escape from a primary sexuality, presumably an incestuous heterosexuality. This is the highly oblique burden of the extraordinary third stanza:

How much I would have bartered! the black gorge
And all the singular nestings in the hills
Where beavers learn stitch and tooth.
The pond I entered once and quickly fled—
I remember now its singing willow rim.

What he would have bartered, indeed did barter, was nature for poetry. Where the second stanza was a *kenosis,* an emptying-out, of the Orphic self, this stanza is fresh influx, and what returns from repression is poetic apperception: "I remember now its singing willow rim," a line that reverberates greatly against the first and last lines of the entire poem. The surrendered Sublime here is a progressive triad of entities: the Wordsworthian abyss of birth of "the black gorge"; "the singular nestings" instructive of work and aggression; most memorably the pond, rimmed by singing willows, whose entrance actually marks the momentary daring of the representation of Oedipal trespass, or perhaps for Crane one should say "Orphic trespass."

If everything heretofore in **"Repose of Rivers"** has been bartered for the antithetical gift of Orpheus, what remains is to represent the actual passage into sexuality, and after that the poetic maturation that follows homosexual self-acceptance. Whether the vision here is of an actual city, or of a New Orleans of the mind, as at the end of **"The River"** section of *The Bridge,* the balance of pleasure and of pain is left ambiguous:

And finally, in that memory all things nurse;
After the city that I finally passed
With scalding unguents spread and smoking darts
The monsoon cut across the delta
At gulf gates . . . There, beyond the dykes
I heard wind flaking sapphire, like this summer,
And willows could not hold more steady sound.

The third line of the stanza refers both to the pa-

thos of the city and to Crane's own sexual initiation. But since "all things nurse" this memory, the emphasis must be upon breakthrough, upon the contrast between monsoon and the long-obliterated memory of sarabande-wind: "like this summer," the fictive moment of the lyric's composition, the monsoon of final sexual alignment gave the gift of an achieved poethood, to hear wind synaesthetically, flaking sapphire, breaking up yet also distributing the Shelleyan azure of vision. In such a context, the final line massively gathers an Orphic confidence.

Yet every close reader of Crane learns to listen to the wind for evidences of *sparagmos,* of the Orphic breakup, as omnipresent in Crane's winds as in Shelley's, or in Whitman's. I turn to **"Passage,"** *White Buildings'* particular poem of Orphic disincarnation, where the rite of passage, the movement back to unfindable and fictive origins, is celebrated more memorably in the opening quatrain than anywhere else even in Crane, who is clearly the great modern poet of *thresholds,* in the sense definitively expounded in Angus Fletcher's forthcoming book of that title:

Where the cedar leaf divides the sky
I heard the sea.
In sapphire arenas of the hills
I was promised an improved infancy.

The Fletcherian *threshold* is a daemonic crossing or textual "image of voice," to use Wordsworth's crucial term. Such a chiasmus tends to hover where tropes collide in an epistemological wilderness. Is there a more outrageously American, Emersonian concept and phrase than "an improved infancy"? Crane presumably was not aware that **"Passage"** centered itself so directly at the Wordsworthian heart of the crisis poem, in direct competition with "Tintern Abbey" and the "Intimations of Immortality" ode. But the American version as established in the *Seadrift* poems of Whitman was model enough. Crane, inland far though he finds himself, hears the sea. The soft inland murmur promised Wordsworth so improved an infancy that it became an actual intimation of a more-than-poetic immortality. But for Whitman the secret of the murmuring he envied had to be listened for at the water-line. Crane quests for the same emblem that rewarded **"Repose of Rivers,"** but here the wind does not flake sapphire in the arenas of these inland hills, where the agon with the daemon, Whitman's dusky demon and brother, is to take place.

In Whitman's great elegy of Orphic disincarnation, "As I Ebb'd with the Ocean of Life," the daemon comes to the poet in the shape of a sardonic phantom, "the real Me," and confronts Whitman, who may hold his book, *Leaves of Grass,* in hand, since the phantom is able to point to it:

But that before all my arrogant poems the real Me
stands yet untouch'd, untold, altogether unreach'd
Withdrawn far, mocking me with mock-
congratulatory signs and bows,
With peals of distant ironical laughter at every word
I have written,
Pointing in silence to these songs, and then to the
sand beneath.
I perceive I have never really understood any thing,
not a single object, and that no man ever can.
Nature here in sight of the sea taking advantage of
me to dart upon me and sting me,
Because I have dared to open my mouth to sing at
all.

In Crane's **"Passage"** the sulking poet, denied his
promise, abandons memory in a ravine, and tries to
identify himself with the wind, but it dies, and he is
turned back and around to confront his mocking daemon:

Touching an opening laurel, I found
A thief beneath, my stolen book in hand.

It is deliberately ambiguous whether the real Me
has stolen the book, or whether the book of Hart Crane
itself is stolen property. Unlike the abashed Whitman,
Crane is aggressive and his phantom is lost in wonderment:

"Why are you back here—smiling an iron coffin?"
"To argue with the laurel," I replied:
"Am justified in transience, fleeing

Under the constant wonder of your eyes—."

But nature here, suddenly in sight of the sea, does
take advantage of Crane to dart upon him and sting
him, because he has dared to open his mouth to sing at
all:

He closed the book. And from the Ptolemies
Sand troughed us in a glittering abyss.
A serpent swam a vertex to the sun
—On unpaced beaches leaned its tongue and
drummed.
What fountains did I hear? What icy speeches?
Memory, committed to the page, had broke.

The Ptolemies, alluded to here as though they
were a galaxy rather than a dynasty, help establish the
pyramid image for the serpent who touches its apex in
the sun. The glittering abyss belongs both to time and
the sun, and the serpent, drumming its tongue upon the
beach where no Whitmanian bard paces, is weirdly
prophetic of the imagery of Stevens' "The Auroras of
Autumn." The penultimate line glances obliquely at
Coleridge's "Kubla Khan," and the poem ends appropriately with the broken enchantment of memory, broken in the act of writing the poem. It is as though, point
for point, **"Passage"** had undone **"Repose of Rivers."**
(pp. 198-206)

Harold Bloom, "Hart Crane's Gnosis," in *Hart Crane: A Collection of Critical Essays,* edited by Alan Trachtenberg, Prentice-
Hall, Inc., 1982, pp. 198-213.

SOURCES FOR FURTHER STUDY

Hazo, Samuel. *Hart Crane: An Introduction.* New York:
Barnes & Noble, 1963, 146 p.

General introduction to Crane's poetry.

Lewis, R. W. B. *The Poetry of Hart Crane: A Critical Study.*
Princeton: Princeton University Press, 1967, 426 p.

A seminal interpretation of Crane's work.

Schwartz, Joseph. *Hart Crane: An Annotated Bibliography.*
New York: David Lewis, 1970, 276 p.

Comprehensive bibliography.

Sugg, Richard P. *Hart Crane's "The Bridge": A Description
of Its Life.* University: University of Alabama Press, 1976,
127 p.
An important reading of *The Bridge.*

Trachtenberg, Alan, ed. *Hart Crane: A Collection of Critical
Essays.* Englewood Cliffs, N.J.: Prentice-Hall, 1982, 224 p.
Includes famous essays by such critics as Yvor Winters, William Carlos Williams, Marius Bewley, and others.

Unterecker, John. *Voyager: A Life of Hart Crane.* New York:
Farrar, Straus and Giroux, 1969, 787 p.
A respected biography of Crane.

Stephen Crane

1871-1900

(Also wrote under pseudonym Johnston Smith) American novelist, short story and novella writer, poet, and journalist.

INTRODUCTION

*C*rane was one of America's foremost realistic writers, and his works have been credited with marking the beginning of modern American Naturalism. His Civil War novel *The Red Badge of Courage* (1895) is a classic of American literature that realistically depicts the psychological complexities of fear and courage on the battlefield. Influenced by William Dean Howells's theory of Realism, Crane utilized his keen observations, as well as personal experiences, to achieve a narrative vividness and sense of immediacy matched by few American writers before him. While *The Red Badge of Courage* is acknowledged as his masterpiece, Crane's novella *Maggie: A Girl of the Streets* (1893) is also acclaimed as an important work in the development of literary Naturalism, and his often-anthologized short stories "The Open Boat," "The Blue Hotel," and "The Bride Comes to Yellow Sky" are among the most skillfully crafted stories in American literature.

Born in Newark, New Jersey, Crane was the youngest in a family of fourteen children. His desire to write was inspired by his family: his father, a Methodist minister, and his mother, a devout woman dedicated to social concerns, were writers of religious articles, and two of his brothers were journalists. Crane began his higher education in 1888 at Hudson River Institute and Claverack College, a military school where he nurtured his interest in Civil War studies and military training. Throughout his college years, Crane wrote; he worked as a freelance writer for his brother's news service, and it is thought that he wrote the preliminary sketch of *Maggie* while still at Syracuse University. In 1891, deciding that "humanity was a more interesting study" than the college curriculum, Crane quit school to work full time as a reporter with his brother and part time for the New York *Tribune*. In New York he lived a bohemian existence among the local artists and became well acquainted with life in the Bowery; from his first-hand knowledge of poverty during this period he was able to realistically depict tenement life in his writings. In 1893 Crane privately published his first novella, *Maggie,* under a pseudonym after several publishers rejected the work on the grounds that his description of slum realities would shock readers. According to Crane, *Maggie* "tries to show that environment is a tremendous thing in the world and frequently shapes lives regardless." Critics suggest that the novel was a major development in American literary Naturalism and that it introduced Crane's vision of life as warfare: influenced by the Darwinism of the times, Crane viewed individuals as victims of purposeless forces and believed that they encountered only hostility in their relationships with other individuals, with society, with nature, and with God. Also prominent in his first novel is an ironic technique that exposes the hypocrisy of moral tenets when they are set against the sordid reality of slum life. Although *Maggie* received the support of such literary figures as Hamlin Garland and Howells, it was not a success. It was not until 1896, after Crane tempered the brutalities in a second edition, that the work received wide recognition.

Crane's second novel, *The Red Badge of Courage,* won him international fame. His vision of life as warfare is uniquely rendered in this short, essentially plotless novel. Often compared to Impressionist painting, *The Red Badge of Courage* is a series of vivid episodes in which a young soldier, Henry Fleming, confronts a gamut of emotions—fear, courage, pride, and humility—in his attempt to understand his battlefield experiences; in this respect, Fleming represents the "Everyman" of war. Crane's work employs a narrative point of view that distinctively offers both an objective panorama of the war as well as the more subjective impressions of the young soldier. Since he had never been to war when he wrote *The Red Badge of Courage,* Crane claimed that his source for the accurate descriptions of combat was the football field; when he finally experienced battle as a war correspondent, he said of the novel, "It was all right." Critics have long debated whether *The Red Badge of Courage* should be considered a product of any specific literary movement or method. The work has been claimed by several schools and referred to as Realistic, Naturalistic, Symbolistic, and Impressionistic. Proponents of Realism view *The Red Badge of Courage* as the first unromanticized account of the Civil War and find Fleming's maturation from an inexperienced youth to an enlightened battle-worn soldier to be truthfully depicted. Defenders of a Naturalistic reading contend that the youth's actions and experiences are shaped by social, biological, and psychological forces and that his "development" as a character is incidental to Crane's expert depiction

of how these forces determine human existence. Stylistically, Crane's novel contains elements of both Impressionism and Symbolism. For example, some critics note that *The Red Badge of Courage* is laden with symbols and images, while others explain that Crane's episodic narrative structure and his consistent use of color imagery are indicative of an Impressionistic method. A succinct estimate of this debate is offered by Edwin H. Cady: "The very secret of the novel's power inheres in the inviolably organic uniqueness with which Crane adapted all four methods to his need. *The Red Badge*'s method is all and none. There is no previous fiction like it."

Shortly after the publication of *The Red Badge of Courage,* Crane published the poetry collection *The Black Riders, and Other Lines* (1895). Although not widely known, this volume of free verse foreshadowed the work of the Imagist poets with its concise, vivid images. During this time Crane continued to work as a journalist, traveling throughout the American West and Mexico for a news syndicate, and later using his experiences as the basis for fictional works. Returning to New York, Crane wrote *The Third Violet,* a story of bohemian life among the poor artists of New York. This novel is considered one of his least accomplished works and some early critics believed that it was an indication of Crane's failing talent.

In 1897 Crane met Cora Taylor, the proprietor of the dubiously named Hotel de Dream, a combination hotel, nightclub, and brothel. Together as common-law husband and wife they moved to England, where Crane formed literary friendships with Joseph Conrad, H. G. Wells, and Henry James. Shortly after this move, Crane left to report on the Spanish-American War for the New York *World,* an assignment he accepted, in part, to escape financial debts he and Cora had accrued. Although Crane was ill when he returned to England, he continued writing fiction in order to satisfy his artistic needs and to earn money. With *Active Service* (1899) he produced another flawed work. This war novel, based on his experiences as a war correspondent in the Greco-Turkish War, is often described as uneven and sprawling. By 1900, Crane's health had rapidly deteriorated due to general disregard for his physical well-being. After several respiratory attacks, Crane died of tuberculosis at the age of twenty-eight.

Although Crane achieved the pinnacle of his success with *The Red Badge of Courage,* many critics believe that he demonstrated his greatest strength as a short story writer. His major achievements in this genre are "The Open Boat," "The Blue Hotel," and "The Bride Comes to Yellow Sky." "The Open Boat" is based on Crane's experience as a correspondent shipwrecked while on a filibustering expedition to the Cuban revolutionaries in 1897. The Naturalistic story pits a handful of men against the power of the indifferent but destructive sea. Crane's characteristic use of vivid imagery is demonstrated throughout this story to underscore both the beauty and terror of natural forces. According to critics, Crane is at his best in "The Open Boat," maintaining an even tone and fluent style while conveying a metaphysical identification between God and nature. Crane's facility with imagery is again displayed with telling effect in the tragic story "The Blue Hotel." In this deceptively simple Western tale, "the Swede," one of Crane's most interesting characters, becomes the inevitable victim of his own preconceptions about the "Wild West"—fearing a lawless, uncivilized world, his violent reactions to Western life result in his own death. Thomas Gullason described Crane's depiction of "the Swede" as "almost Dostoevskyean in its psychological penetration." In another Western story, the comic "The Bride Comes to Yellow Sky," Crane parodies the "shoot 'em-up" Western myth as the characters Jack Potter and Scratchy Wilson fail to fulfill romantic illusions through a gunfight. In these short stories, as in most of his work, Crane is a con-summate ironist, employing a technique that most critics find consistently suggests the disparity between an individual's perception of reality and reality as it actually exists.

Commentators generally agree that for the most part Crane disregarded plot and character delineation in his work and that he was unable to sustain longer works of fiction. However, with the proliferation of Crane scholarship during the last twenty years, Crane's literary reputation has grown. Critics contend that despite his minor flaws, Crane's artistry lies in his ability to convey a personal vision based on his own "quality of personal honesty." In so doing, he pioneered a modern form of fiction which superseded the genteel Realism of late nineteenth-century American literature.

(For further information about Crane's life and works, see *Contemporary Authors*, Vol. 109; *Dictionary of Literary Biography*, Vols. 12, 54, 78; *Twentieth-Century Literary Criticism*, Vols. 11, 17, 32; and *Yesterday's Authors of Books for Children*, Vol. 2.)

CRITICAL COMMENTARY

H. G. WELLS

(essay date 1900)

[Wells, a close friend of Crane, is best known today, along with Jules Verne, as the father of modern science fiction and as a utopian idealist who correctly foretold an era of chemical warfare, atomic weaponry, and world wars. Throughout much of his career he wrote and lectured on the betterment of society through education and the advance of scientific innovation. The following essay, originally published in 1900 in *The North American Review*, is considered one of the most important early critical assessments of Crane's works.]

[Stephen Crane's] success in England began with the *Red Badge of Courage,* which did, indeed, more completely than any other book has done for many years, take the reading public by storm. Its freshness of method, its vigor of imagination, its force of color and its essential freedom from many traditions that dominate this side of the Atlantic, came—in spite of the previous shock of Mr. Kipling—with a positive effect of impact. It was a new thing, in a new school. When one looked for sources, one thought at once of Tolstoy; but, though it was clear that Tolstoy had exerted a powerful influence upon the conception, if not the actual writing, of the book, there still remained something entirely original and novel. To a certain extent, of course, that was the new man as an individual; but, to at least an equal extent, it was the new man as a typical young American, free at last, as no generation of Americans have been free before, of any regard for English criticism, comment, or tradition, and applying to literary work the conception and theories of the cosmopolitan studio with a quite American directness and vigor. For the great influence of the studio on Crane cannot be ignored; in the persistent selection of the essential elements of an impression, in the ruthless exclusion of mere information, in the direct vigor with which the selected points are made, there is Whistler even more than there is Tolstoy in the *Red Badge of Courage.* (pp. 662-63)

I do not propose to add anything here to the mass of criticism upon this remarkable book. Like everything else which has been abundantly praised, it has occasionally been praised "all wrong"; and I suppose that it must have been said hundreds of times that this book is a subjective study of the typical soldier in war. But Mr. George Wyndham, himself a soldier of experience, has pointed out in an admirable preface to a reissue of this and other of Crane's war studies that the

Principal Works

Maggie: A Girl of the Streets (A Story of New York) [as Johnston Smith] (novella) 1893; also published as Maggie: A Girl of the Streets [revised edition], 1896

The Black Riders, and Other Lines (poetry) 1895

The Red Badge of Courage: An Episode of the American Civil War (novella) 1895

George's Mother (novel) 1896

The Little Regiment, and Other Episodes of the American Civil War (short stories) 1896

The Third Violet (novel) 1897

The Open Boat, and Other Tales of Adventure (short stories) 1898

Active Service (novel) 1899

the Monster, and Other Stories (short stories) 1899

War Is Kind (poetry) 1899

Whilomville Stories (short stories) 1900

Wounds in the Rain: A Collection of Stories Relating to the Spanish-American War of 1898 (short stories) 1900

*The O'Ruddy (novel) 1903

The Collected Poems of Stephen Crane (poetry) 1930

†The Sullivan County Sketches of Stephen Crane (sketches) 1949

Stephen Crane: Letters (letters) 1960

The Works of Stephen Crane. 10 vols. (poetry, short stories, novels, and journalism) 1969-72

Stephen Crane: Prose and Poetry (novels, novellas, short stories, sketches, journalism, and poetry) 1984

*This work was completed by Robert Barr.

†This work was originally published serially in the newspaper New York Tribune and the journal The Cosmopolitan in 1892.

hero of the *Red Badge* is, and is intended to be, altogether a more sensitive and imaginative person than the ordinary man. He is the idealist, the dreamer of boastful things brought suddenly to the test of danger and swift occasions and the presence of death. To this theme Crane returned several times, and particularly in a story called *Death and the Child* that was written after the Greek war. That story is considered by very many of Crane's admirers as absolutely his best. I have carefully reread it in deference to opinions I am bound to respect, but I still find it inferior to the earlier work. The generalized application is, to my taste, a little too evidently underlined; there is just that touch of insistence that prevails so painfully at times in Victor Hugo's work, as of a writer not sure of his reader, not happy in his reader, and seeking to drive his implication (of which also he is not quite sure) home. The child

is not a natural child; there is no happy touch to make it personally alive; it is THE CHILD, something unfalteringly big: a large, pink, generalized thing, I cannot help but see it, after the fashion of a Vatican cherub. The fugitive runs panting to where, all innocent of the battle about it, it plays; and he falls down breathless to be asked, "Are you a man?" One sees the intention clearly enough; but in the later story it seems to me there is a new ingredient that is absent from the earlier stories, an ingredient imposed on Crane's natural genius from without—a concession to the demands of a criticism it had been wiser, if less modest, in him to disregard—criticism that missed this quality of generalization and demanded it, even though it had to be artificially and deliberately introduced.

Following hard upon the appearance of the *Red Badge of Courage* in England came reprints of two books, *Maggie* and *George's Mother*. . . . Their reception gave Crane his first taste of the peculiarities of the new public he had come upon. These stories seem to me in no way inferior to the *Red Badge;* and at times there are passages, the lament of Maggie's mother at the end of *Maggie,* for example, that it would be hard to beat by any passage from the later book. But on all hands came discouragement or tepid praise. The fact of it is, there had been almost an orgy of praise—for England, that is; and ideas and adjectives and phrases were exhausted. To write further long reviews on works displaying the same qualities as had been already amply discussed in the notices of the *Red Badge* would be difficult and laborious; while to admit an equal excellence and deny an equal prominence would be absurd. But to treat these stories as early work, to find them immature, dismiss them and proceed to fresher topics, was obvious and convenient. So it was, I uncharitably imagine, that these two tales have been overshadowed and are still comparatively unknown. Yet they are absolutely essential to a just understanding of Crane. In these stories, and in these alone, he achieved tenderness and a compulsion of sympathy for other than vehement emotions, qualities that the readers of *The Third Violet* and *On Active Service,* his later love stories, might well imagine beyond his reach. (pp. 663-65)

The Open Boat is to my mind, beyond all question, the crown of all his work. It has all the stark power of the earlier stories, with a new element of restraint; the color is as full and strong as ever, fuller and stronger, indeed; but those chromatic splashes that at times deafen and confuse in the *Red Badge,* those images that astonish rather than enlighten, are disciplined and controlled. "That and *Flanagan,*" he told me, with a philosophical laugh, "was all I got out of Cuba." I cannot say whether they were worth the price, but I am convinced that these two things are as immortal as any work of any living man. (p. 666)

The Open Boat gives its title to a volume containing, in addition to that and *Flanagan,* certain short pieces. One of these others, at least, is also to my mind a perfect thing, *The Wise Men.* It tells of the race between two bartenders in the city of Mexico, and I cannot imagine how it could possibly have been better told. And in this volume, too, is that other masterpiece—the one I deny—*Death and the Child.*

Now I do not know how Crane took the reception of this book, for he was not the man to babble of his wrongs; but I cannot conceive how it could have been anything but a grave disappointment to him. To use the silly phrase of the literary shopman, "the vogue of the short story" was already over; rubbish, pure rubbish, provided only it was lengthy, had resumed its former precedence again in the reviews, in the publishers' advertisements, and on the library and booksellers' counters. The book was taken as a trivial by-product, its author was exhorted to abandon this production of "brilliant fragments"—anything less than fifty thousand words is a fragment to the writer of literary columns—and to make that "sustained effort," that architectural undertaking, that alone impresses the commercial mind. (pp. 668-69)

It was probably such influence that led him to write *The Third Violet.* I do not know certainly, but I imagine, that the book was to be a demonstration, and it is not a successful demonstration, that Crane could write a charming love story. It is the very simple affair of an art student and a summer boarder, with the more superficial incidents of their petty encounters set forth in a forcible, objective manner that is curiously hard and unsympathetic. The characters act, and on reflection one admits they act, *true,* but the play of their emotions goes on behind the curtain of the style, and all the enrichments of imaginative appeal that make love beautiful are omitted. Yet, though the story as a whole fails to satisfy, there are many isolated portions of altogether happy effectiveness, a certain ride behind an ox cart, for example. Much more surely is *On Active Service* an effort, and in places a painful effort, to fit his peculiar gift to the uncongenial conditions of popular acceptance. It is the least capable and least satisfactory of all Crane's work.

While these later books were appearing, and right up to his last fatal illness, Crane continued to produce fresh war pictures that show little or no falling off in vigor of imagination and handling; and, in addition, he was experimenting with verse. In that little stone-blue volume, *War Is Kind,* and in the earlier *Black Riders,* the reader will find a series of acute and vivid impressions and many of the finer qualities of Crane's descriptive prose, but he will not find any novel delights of melody or cadence of any fresh aspects of Crane's personality. (pp. 669-70)

In style, in method, and in all that is distinctively *not* found in his books, he is sharply defined, the ex-

pression in literary art of certain enormous repudiations. Was ever a man before who wrote of battles so abundantly as he has done, and never had a word, never a word from first to last, of the purpose and justification of the war? And of the God of Battles, no more than the battered name; "Hully Gee!"—the lingering trace of the Deity! And of the sensuousness and tenderness of love, so much as one can find in *The Third Violet!* Any richness of allusion, any melody or balance of phrase, the half quotation that refracts and softens and enriches the statement, the momentary digression that opens like a window upon beautiful or distant things, are not merely absent, but obviously and sedulously avoided. It is as if the racial thought and tradition had been razed from his mind and its site plowed and salted. He is more than himself in this; he is the first expression of the opening mind of a new period, or, at least, the early emphatic phase of a new initiative—beginning, as a growing mind must needs begin, with the record of impressions, a record of a vigor and intensity beyond all precedent. (p. 671)

H. G. Wells "Stephen Crane from an English Standpoint," in *The Shock of Recognition: The Development of Literature in the United States Recorded by the Men Who Made It,* edited by Edmund Wilson, Farrar, Straus and Cudahy, 1955, pp. 661-71.

AMY LOWELL
(essay date 1924)

[Lowell was a leading proponent of Imagism in American poetry. In the following excerpt from a 1924 essay, she assesses Crane's *The Black Riders* and *War Is Kind,* finding that Crane's poetic talents waned as he matured.]

Crane spoke of his poems as waiting to be "drawn off." And this is an excellent expression. Once freed from the unconscious, capable of taking on words and becoming disengaged from their author, all the pent-up energies of creative thought, or rather all such pent-up energies as were ripe enough to become creative thought, came in a rush [in *The Black Riders*], and he could hardly draw them off quickly enough. Hitherto, Crane's writing had been objective. His forte was description; but along with this description went a keen, impressionistic perception of people and things. There had been no place for personal comment, no time for introspective ejaculations. Probably he was scarcely aware of the need for them. But Crane felt too vividly, he touched life too curiously and tenderly, his reactions were too bitter, his sensibility too avid, for him to remain for ever the onlooker, the recorder of other men's lives. At some time in his career, a personal speech must have forced itself upon him. The only question was when and for how long.

Crane's life was too short for the critic to hazard a positive statement, and yet I think there is strong reason to believe that, in spite of much poetry in his prose books, he was not primarily a poet. His genius lay in prose sketches, even when these expanded themselves into novels. His was not a largely imaginative talent. Even his prose tales, to be done at his best, must be solidly founded upon experience. *The Red Badge of Courage* is the one exception, and in this case he merely augmented the football games he had seen by digesting innumerable accounts of battles told by eye-witnesses. His art was tied to himself, and he was extremely dependent upon a period of gestation. Granted this period, he could produce marvellous work; without it, he was almost helpless. He was the last man in the world who should ever have attempted newspaper writing. To enable him to continue at his best, he should have been able to proceed slowly, and at every stage reached been permitted to discharge the accumulations of thought and sensation proper to that stage. Then, and then only, would he have maintained his level and advanced.

When he suddenly started writing poetry, he had in himself a full reservoir of intimate, personal experiences to tap. And he tapped them until he found that his spring had run dry. Thereafter it was necessary to wait until the energy of living had filled him up again, and this precisely because his was not a nature of inexhaustible subjective reactions. Youth is prone to express itself in verse, and, Crane being a youth of genius, and of a highly original genius, his verses were sure to be eminently worth while. But, after all, I think it cannot be gainsaid that his poetry is far more adolescent than his prose, and this leads to the obvious corollary that, as adolescence waned, so would the poetry wane. Indeed, it seems to have done so. His poetry was static. It came amply clothed, and it never improved. On the contrary, it retrograded. His second book, *War is Kind,* in spite of the fact that it contains a few pieces which surpass anything in *The Black Riders,* is as a whole less vital, less spontaneous, and less original than the earlier book.

How did Stephen Crane stumble on his form? That is really a very interesting question. It is a form with which we are all too familiar to-day. The *Vers Libre,* or Free Verse, war has rammed it down our throats in season and out of season. . . . [Crane's] contemporaries thought the form "odd," but were willing to let it be. What baffled them was his use of suggestion. And here possibly lies his chief technical debt to Emily Dickinson, for she was past mistress of suggestion. This and, to a lesser degree, irony were what Crane derived from her, but his was no such light gossamer touch. Crane's irony clanks by heavily clad in steel and bran-

dishing a molesting spear, Crane is conscious of an enemy with whom he is out to do battle—most adolescent of attitudes! Emily Dickinson's irony brushes as inconsequentially as a butterfly's wing; she is unconscious of any audience. The world exists for her solely as she sees it, and her carelessness in the matter of whether she exists for her readers or not is wholly admirable. This is maturity. This is the poet who is chiefly such and no other thing. In one poem only does Crane really remind us in the slightest of Emily Dickinson. This is it:

> A man said to the universe:
> "Sir, I exist!"
> "However," replied the universe,
> "The fact has not created in me
> A sense of obligation."

If Emily Dickinson cannot be made to stand for Crane's form, where did he find it? I think in the Bible. The son of a mother who was also a Methodist preacher must have been extremely familiar with the Bible. Its cadences, its images, its parable structure cannot have failed of being ground into his consciousness. When he came to expressing himself as shortly and as poignantly as his thoughts demanded to be presented, he fell back on the rhythms which were stored in his head, and these rhythms were the completely natural ones of Biblical cadence. The Old Testament is full of the most beautiful cadenced verse, if once we learn to read aside from the hampering typography of arbitrary divisions.

Crane was so steeped in the religion in which he was brought up that he could not get it out of his head. He disbelieved it and he hated it, but he could not free himself from it. A loathed and vengeful God broods over *The Black Riders.* Crane's soul was heaped with bitterness, and this bitterness he flung back at the theory of life which had betrayed him. His misery and his earnestness made the book, and the supreme irony of all is that it should have been issued as an aesthetic knick-knack and its author hailed as an "affected ass." . . . Crane handed the world the acrid fumes of his heart, and they howled at him for an obscene blasphemer, or patted him on the back as a "cracker-jack" on whom they "doted," a cranky and unexpected star beaming above the amateur magazines and proud to shed its light upon East Aurora.

Reading the book now, thirty years afterwards, one is tempted to neither reaction. What chiefly impresses is the volume's sincerity. Strangely enough, it is almost devoid of those pictorial touches which make Crane's prose so striking. Such passages, for instance, as this, of horses at a fire, kicking "grey ice of the gutter into silvery angles that hurtled and clicked on frozen stone." Crane seems to have had no time for such things as these when he was writing verse. He seems concerned so greatly with *what* he has to say that embroidery of any sort is a hindrance. He speaks in symbols, far out-distancing his time, and his method is starkly epigrammatic. . . . (pp. xv-xx)

Crane's theme in *The Black Riders* is two-fold. It is at once the cruelty of universal law, and the futility of hope. It is a creed of gall and aloes, and Crane believed it. It is the key to his life. Gentle and kind, yet he was weak, a man who needed something beyond himself to bolster him up.

War is Kind adds little to our interest in Crane's poetry. The Roycroft poems [from *The Roycroft Quarterly*] were included in it, and they were the best things in the book. The first poem, **"War is Kind,"** is a satiric comment on war, in which Crane voices what so many poets of a later generation have felt and said. The poem has pathos, but the tone is subdued. The man who wrote it was profoundly weary. Occasionally Crane rises to something of his old fire in such poems as **"Have you ever made a just man?"** or **"Forth went the candid man,"** but on the whole the volume is disappointing. This man is evidently destined to abandon poetry in no long while. The last part of the book is taken up with a long love poem, **"Intrigue."** There is no question of its sincerity, and how much Crane had "felt" it, but it is not memorable as poetry, however important it may be as biography. And, oddly enough, it shows Crane, as a pioneer, breaking down. His bright modernity is fading. **"Intrigue"** is full of "thee's" and "thou's," the refrain is "Woe is me," and the poet is constantly declaring "Thou art my love." This will do for some men, but not for Stephen Crane. We see that he is losing his grasp, that poetry is sliding from him, that it had been no more with him than a breath of adolescence. (pp. xxvii-xxviii)

What then is Stephen Crane, in so far as his poetry is concerned? A man without a period, that is at once his plume and his forfeit. He sprang from practically nowhere, and he has left only the most isolated of descendants. There were forerunners of his type of verse, but he had never heard of them. He is that rarest of artistic phenomena, a man who creates from inner consciousness alone. The men from whom he might have learned, who spoke his speech and might have led him on, were the French *Symbolistes,* but he did not know of them; and the Chinese and Japanese poets, but he knew nothing of them either, and there were only the scattered translations of Lafcadio Hearn even if he had sought to know. The usual translations of the period would have done him no good.

Crane saw life through individual eyes, and he dared write as he pleased; therein rests his abiding merit. So short a time as twelve years after his death, a type of poetry extremely like his came suddenly into being. By all rights he should have been its direct parent, but he was not, simply because most of the practitioners of it had based themselves upon French precedent and William Blake before they knew anything of

Crane. In the decade which began with 1912, Crane would have been in his element, perfectly understood, wisely praised, forced to take the position of leader. He died too soon. He did much, but the temperature of the world he lived in was unsuitable. He ranks in America somewhat as Chatterton ranks in England. A boy, spiritually killed by neglect. A marvellous boy, potentially a genius, historically an important link in the chain of American poetry. (pp. xxviii-xxix)

Amy Lowell, in an introduction to *The Work of Stephen Crane: 'The Black Riders and Other Lines', Vol. VI* by Stephen Crane, edited by Wilson Follett, 1926. Reprint by Russell & Russell, 1963, pp. ix-xxix.

━━━━━━

JOHN BERRYMAN
(essay date 1950)

[Berryman is an American poet, essayist, and biographer. In the following excerpt from his biography of Crane, he assesses Crane's literary style and comments on his place in American literature.]

Crane I daresay is one of the great stylists of the language. These words "master" and "great" will trouble some readers, as they trouble me. But they seem unavoidable. The trouble we feel arises from several causes, which are worth examination. Crane's works that matter are all short. We don't see how works so little can be with any decency called great. Greatness of prose-style, however, does not require length for display. . . . Another trouble is that Crane was writing greatly, if he ever did, in his early twenties. We are told that prosewriters mature slowly; scarcely anyone writes prose worth reading under thirty. . . . A third trouble is just that he is comparatively recent; this matters less. Then there are the words themselves, grandiose. We have no objection to calling the boy Keats a master, Rimbaud a master, but the word "great" sticks a little. It looks like a catchword. Our major troubles, though, I think are two, both of them proceeding from the nature of his work and of its historical situation. There is first the relation of his style to prose style in English and American before him, and second the relation of his general art-form, the story, to Western fiction before him. (The term Western is unsatisfactory because it must include Russian fiction, but no other seems better.) Though these troubles are closely related, we must take them separately.

Nothing very like Crane's prose style is to be found earlier; so much will probably be granted at once by an experienced reader. Here I must observe that Crane wrote several styles. He had even an epistolary style—extended, slow, uninflected, during most of his life, curter and jotty towards the end—but we are interested in his narrative styles. He began with the somber-jocular, sable, fantastic prose of the **"Sullivan County Sketches"** and the jagged, colored, awkward, brilliant *Maggie*. *Maggie* he probably revised much barbarousness out of before anyone except brothers and friends saw it, and he abandoned deliberately the method of the sketches—though fantasy, and fantasy in the quality of the prose, remained intermittently an element in his work to the end. A movement towards fluidity increases in *The Red Badge* and the **"Baby Sketches"** he was writing at the same time and produces a Crane norm: flexible, swift, abrupt, and nervous—swift, but with an unexampled capacity for stasis also. Color is high, but we observe the blank absence of the orotund, the moulded, which is Crane's most powerful response to the prose tradition he declined to inherit. In the fusion of the impassive and the intense peculiar to this author, he kept on drawing the rein. **"Horses—One Dash"** and **"The Five White Mice"** lead to the supple majesty of **"The Open Boat,"** a second norm. *The Monster*, much more closed, circumstantial, "normal" in feeling and syntax, is a third. Then he opened his style again back towards the second norm in the great Western stories, **"The Bride Comes to Yellow Sky"** and **"The Blue Hotel,"** and thereafter (for his two years) he used the second and the third styles at will, sometimes in combination, and the third usually relaxed as his health failed but peculiarly tense and astonishing in **"The Kicking Twelfth."** In certain late work also, notably in **"The Clan of No Name,"** a development toward complexity of structure is evident, which death broke off. Nevertheless we may speak of "Crane's style" so long as we have these variations in mind, and my point is that it differs *radically* both from the tradition of English prose and from its modifications in American prose. Shakespeare, Dryden, Defoe, Johnson, Dickens, Arnold, Kipling, as these develop into Edwards, Jefferson, Hawthorne, Melville, James—Crane writes on the whole, a definite and absolute *stylist*, as if none of these people had ever existed. His animation is not Kipling's, his deadpan flatness is not Mark Twain's. He is more like Tacitus, or Stendhal in his autobiography, say, than like any of the few writers of narrative English who actually affected his development. He was a rhetorician who refused to be one. In Crane for the first time the resources of American spareness, exaggeration, volcanic impatience, American humor, came into the hands of a narrative author serious and thoughtful as an artist as Hawthorne or James, and *more* serious than any others of the New England-New York hegemony. Thus he made possible—whether by way of particular influence or as a symbolic feat in the development of the language—one whole side of Twentieth Century prose. It is hard to decide that a boy, that anyone, did this, and so we feel uncom-

fortable about the word that characterizes the achievement with great justice.

The second difficulty with "great" is the newness of his form. I am not referring to the immense burst of talented story-writing in England and America during the 'nineties, though this is relevant; the short story had scarcely any status in English earlier, and we are less eager, naturally, to concede greatness to its artist than to crown a novelist. (pp. 283-85)

Crane's stories are as unlike earlier stories as his poems are unlike poems. He threw away, thoughtfully, plot; outlawed juggling and arrangement of material (Poe, Bierce, O. Henry); excluded the whole usual mechanism of society; banished equally sex (Maupassant) and romantic love (Chekhov—unknown to him); decided not to develop his characters; decided not to have any conflicts between them as characters; resolved not to have any characters at all in the usual sense; simplified everything that remained, and, watching intently, tenderly, and hopelessly, blew Fate through it—saying with inconceivable rapidity and an air of immense deliberation what he saw. What he saw, "apparently." The result is a series of extremely formidable, *new,* compact, finished, and distressing works of art. Mencken dated modern American literature from *The Red Badge of Courage.* The new *Literary History of the United States,* coming to hand as I write, dates it from the reissue of *Maggie* in 1896. It must come from about there, apparently.

Of course Crane did nothing such as I have just described. He was interested, only, in certain things, and kept the rest out. It is the ability to keep the rest out that is astounding. But the character of the deliberate in his prose too is conspicuous. . . . [This] was absent from his poetry, and it is time to come to the difference. The difference is that between presentation (in the poetry) and apparent presentation (in the prose); in the figure of the savage's dream that we were employing, between *rehearsal* and *investigation.* The poem can simply say what the dream (nightmare) was; at once it gets rid of the dream, and is solaced in hearing it said. An effect of style is undesirable. To *study* the dream, to embody it, as in a story—this is another matter. One needs a suit, a style, of chain armor to protect the subject from everything that would like to get into the story with it: the other impressions of life, one's private prejudices, a florid and hypocritical society, existing literature. The style of the prose aims at the same thing as the unstyle of the poetry, namely, naked presentment, but its method is ironic. Other authors are saying what things "are," with supreme falsity. Crane therefore will only say what they *seem* to be.

The youth turned, with sudden, livid rage, toward the battlefield. He shook his fist. He seemed about to deliver a philippic.

Title page of the first edition of *The Red Badge of Courage.*

"Hell—"

"The red sun was pasted in the sky like a wafer."

Half of Crane's celebrated "coldness" is an effect of this *refusal to guarantee.* "He seemed about to deliver a philippic." It sounds as if he weren't going to; but he is; but he isn't; but—one does not know exactly where one is. The style is merely honest, but it disturbs one, it is even menacing. If this extremely intelligent writer will not go further than that insistent "seemed," says the reader nervously to himself, should *I*? The style has the effect of obliterating with silent contempt half of what one thinks one knows. And then: a policeman begins "frenziedly to seize bridles and beat the soft noses of the responsible horses." In the next sentence the noses are forgotten. But to tell us about the horses if the author is not going to commiserate with them seems brutal. It makes the reader do the feeling if he wants to; Crane, who cared more for horses than any reader, is on his way. Again the reader is as it were rebuked, for of course he *doesn't* feel very strongly about horses—he

would never have put in that "soft" himself, much less clubbed it in with "responsible." (pp. 286-88)

This is supposed, by the way, to be Realism or Naturalism. Frank Norris, who was a romantic moralist, with a style like a great wet dog, and Stephen Crane, an impressionist and a superlative style, are Naturalists. These terms are very boring, but let us agree at least to mean by them *method* (as Howells did) rather than *material* (as Norris, who called his serious works "Romance," did). "Tell your yarn and let your style go to the devil," Norris wrote to somebody. The Naturalists, if there are any, all *accumulate,* laborious, insistent, endless; Dreiser might be one. Crane selected and was gone. "He knew when to shut up," as Norris put it. "He is *the only* impressionist," said Conrad in italics to Garnett, "and *only* an impressionist." This is not quite right either: Crane's method shows realistic and also fantastic elements. But it would be better, as a label for what has after all got to be understood anyway in itself, than the categorical whim established now in the literary histories. Crane was an impressionist.

His color tells us so at once. This famous color of his plays a part in his work that has been exaggerated, but it is important. Gifted plainly with a powerful and probably very odd sense of color, fortified then by Goethe, he did not refuse to use it; sometimes he abused it, and he increasingly abandoned it. Most authors use color. "The sun emerges from behind the gray clouds that covered the sky and suddenly lights up with its bright red glow the purple clouds, the greenish sea . . . the white buildings." So Tolstoy at the end of *Sevastopol,* and it bears no relation whatever to Crane's use of color. "At this time Hollanden wore an unmistakable air of having a desire to turn up his coat collar." This is more like one of Crane's colors than Tolstoy's actual colors are. Color is imposed, from an angle, like this apparently physical and actually psychological detail. Crane was interested in what Goethe called the "moral-sensual effect of color." He owes nothing whatever, apparently, to painting. The blue hotel "screaming and howling"—"some red years"—"fell with a yellow crash." The color is primitive. So with adverbs, metaphors. A man leans on a bar listening to others "terribly discuss a question that was not plain." "There was a general movement in the compact column. The long animal-like thing moved slightly. Its four hundred eyes were turned upon the figure of Collins." Here there is none of Crane's frequent, vivid condensation; and yet the eyes are not human eyes. It is primitive, an impression. A psychologist lately called red the most panicky and explosive of colors, the most primitive, as well as the most ambivalent, related equally to rage and love, battle and fire, joy and destruction. Everywhere then, in style, a mind at stretch.

We may reach toward the subject of all this remorseless animation through his characters. They are very odd. To call them types is a major critical error, long exposed, ever-recurrent. The new *Literary History* describes the hero of *The Red Badge* as "impersonal and typical," for which read: intensely personal and individual. George Wyndham (and Wells after him) fifty years ago showed the boy an idealist and dreamer brought to the test. Pete in *Maggie* is not a bartender, but Pete. Billy Higgins in **"The Open Boat"** is not an oiler, but the oiler. Crane scarcely made a type in all his work. At the same time, he scarcely made any characters. His people, *in* their stories, stay in your mind; but they have no existence outside. No life is strongly imaginable for them save what he lets you see. This seems to me to be singular, to want explanation. I think he is interested in them individually, but only as a crisis reaches them. The "shaky and quickeyed" Swede of **"The Blue Hotel"** is certainly an *individual* mad with fear, one of Crane's most memorable people, but it is as an individual *mad with fear* that he grimly matters. "Stanley pawed gently at the moss, and then thrust his head forward to see what the ants did under the circumstance." When this delightful thing happens, a lovescene is taking place two feet away, one of the most inhibited and perfunctory ever written. It is only or chiefly in animals that Crane can be interested when a *fate* is not in question. Once it is, he is acutely and utterly present with the sufferer, attending however to the fate.

"Apparently" the state of the soul in crisis: this is his subject. The society against the person will do; he uses the term "environment" in regard to *Maggie,* and this is more generally dramatized in *The Monster,* more particularly dramatized in **"The Bride Comes to Yellow Sky."** But one has less feeling in these works, and in a number of others like them, that the men are themselves against each other, than that they have been set simply facing each other—not by Crane—by a fate. War is the social situation that does this most naturally and continually, so he possesses himself of it; in imagination first, again and again, and then in fact. **"The Open Boat"** is his most perfect story partly because here for once the fate is in the open: one is *fully justified* in being afraid, one can feel with confidence that one is absolutely tested. The antagonist will not fail one, as another man might, as even society might. The extraordinary mind that *had* to feel this we shall look at in the next chapter; here we are concerned with the art. Now these states of crisis, by their nature, cannot persist; so Crane succeeded only in short work. *The Red Badge of Courage,* as most critics have noticed, is not really a novel at all, but a story, and it is a little too long, as Crane thought it was. His imagination was resolute in presenting him with conditions for fear; so that he works with equal brilliance from invention and from fact. To take **"The Open Boat,"** however, as a *report* is to misunderstand the nature of his work: it is an action

of his art upon the remembered possibility of death. The death is so close that the story is warm. A coldness of which I was speaking earlier in Crane is absent here. Half of this I attributed to the stylistic refusal to guarantee. The other half is an effect from far in the mind that made the art, where there was a passion for life half-strangled by a need for death and made cold. Life thaws under the need when the death nears. In the eggshell boat, the correspondent knew even at the time, under dreadful hardship, that this was "the best experience of his life"—the comradeship, he says this is, but it was really something else: "There was a terrible grace in the move of the waves, and they came in silence, save for the snarling of the crests. . . ."

The immense power of the tacit, felt in Crane's accounts of Maggie's brother's nihilism, her mother's self-pity, Henry Fleming's self-pride, George's dreams, gives his work kinship rather with Chekhov and Maupassant than Poe. "I like my art"—said Crane— "straight"; and he misquoted Emerson, "There should be a long logic beneath the story, but it should be carefully kept out of sight." How far Crane's effect of inevitability depends upon this *silence* it would be hard to say. Nowhere in **"The Open Boat"** is it mentioned that the situation of the men is symbolic, clear and awful though it is that this story opens into the universe. Poe in several great stories opens man's soul downwards, but his work has no relation with the natural and American world at all. If Crane's has, and is irreplaceable on this score, it is for an ironic inward and tragic vision outward that we value it most, when we can bear it. At the end of the story a word occurs that will do for Crane. "When it came night, the white waves paced to and fro in the moonlight, and the wind brought the sound of the great sea's voice to the men on the shore, and they felt that they could then be interpreters." Crane does really stand between us and something that we could not otherwise understand. It is not human; it is not either the waves and mountains who are among his major characters, but it acts in them, it acts in children and sometimes even in men, upon animals, upon boys above all, and men. Crane does not understand it fully. But he has been driven and has dragged himself nearer by much to it than we have, and he interprets for us.

For this reason, as well as for his technical revolution, he is indispensable. By a margin he is probably the greatest American story-writer, he stands as an artist not far below Hawthorne and James, he is one of our few poets, and one of the few manifest geniuses the country has produced. (pp. 288-92)

John Berryman, in his *Stephen Crane: A Critical Biography,* 1950. Reprint by Octagon Books, 1975, 347 p.

CHARLES CHILD WALCUTT
(essay date 1956)

[In the following excerpt, Walcutt discusses *The Red Badge of Courage,* finding evidence of Crane's Naturalism in his depiction of moral delusions, his impressionistic style, and in his "deterministic accounting for events."]

The Red Badge of Courage . . . , Crane's Civil War story, is the most controversial piece in his canon. It has been much discussed and most variously interpreted, and the interpretations range about as widely as they could. Is it a Christian story of redemption? Is it a demonstration that man is a beast with illusions? Or is it, between these extremes, the story of a man who goes through the fire, discovers himself, and with the self-knowledge that he is able to attain comes to terms with the problem of life insofar as an imperfect man can come to terms with an imperfect world? It is tempting to take the middle road between the intemperate extremes; but let us see what happens before we come to the paragraphs at the end that are invoked to prove each of the explanations. . . . (p. 75)

The book opens with a scene at a Union encampment in which the uninformed arguments of the soldiers are described in a manner that recalls the mockery of "infantile orations" in *Maggie.* The phrase pictures a squalling child colorfully, while it conveys the author's private amusement at the image of a shouting politician. In *The Red Badge* there is continually a tone of mockery and sardonic imitation of men who are boisterous, crafty, arrogant, resentful, or suspicious always in an excess that makes them comical, and the author seems to delight in rendering the flavor of their extravagances. An element of the fantastic is always present, the quality apparently representing the author's feeling for the war, the situations in it, the continual and enormous incongruities between intention and execution, between a man's estimate of himself and the way he appears to others, between the motivations acknowledged to the world and those which prevail in the heart. It is with these last that the book is centrally concerned—with the problem of courage—and it is here that the meaning is most confusingly entangled with the tone. (pp. 75-6)

[Henry Fleming] has "dreamed of battles all his life—of vague and bloody conflicts that had thrilled him with their sweep and fire. . . . He had imagined peoples secure in the shadow of his eagle-eyed prowess." He had burned to enlist, but had been deterred by his mother's arguments that he was more important on

the farm until—the point is sardonically emphasized—the newspapers carried accounts of great battles in which the North was victor. "Almost every day the newspapers printed accounts of a decisive victory." When he enlists, his mother makes a long speech to him—which is presented by Crane with no trace of mockery—but he is impatient and irritated. (pp. 76-7)

Vanity amid dreams of Homeric glory occupy him thenceforth—until battle is imminent. Then he wonders whether he will run or stand; and he does not dare confide his fears to the other men because they all seem so sure of themselves and because both they and he are constantly diverted from the question by inferior concerns. (p. 77)

Approaching the first engagement, the youth perceives with terror that he is "in a moving box" of soldiers from which it would be impossible to escape, and "it occurred to him that he had never wished to come to the war . . . He had been dragged by the merciless government." He is further startled when the loud soldier, a braggart, announces with a sob that he is going to be killed, and gives the youth a packet of letters for his family. The engagement is described with terms of confusion: the youth feels "a red rage," and then "acute exasperation"; he "fought frantically" for air; the other men are cursing, babbling, and querulous; their equipment bobs "idiotically" on their backs, and they move like puppets. The assault is turned back, and the men leer at each other with dirty smiles; but just as the youth is responding in "an ecstasy of self-satisfaction" at having passed "the supreme trial," there comes a second charge from which he flees in blind panic: "He ran like a blind man. Two or three times he fell down. Once he knocked his shoulder so heavily against a tree that he went headlong." As he runs, his fear increases, and he rages at the suicidal folly of those who have stayed behind to be killed.

Just as he reaches the zone of safety, he learns that the line has held and the enemy's charge been repulsed. Instantly he "felt that he had been wronged," and begins to find reasons for the wisdom of his flight. "It was all plain that he had proceeded according to very correct and commendable rules. His actions had been sagacious things. They had been full of strategy. . . . He, the enlightened man who looks afar in the dark, had fled because of his superior perceptions and knowledge. He felt a great anger against his comrades. He knew it could be proved that they had been fools." He pities himself; he feels rebellious, agonized, and despairing. It is here that he sees a squirrel and throws a pine cone at it; when it runs he finds a triumphant exhibition in nature of the law of self-preservation. "Nature had given him a sign." The irony of this sequence is abundantly apparent. It increases when, a moment later, the youth enters a place where the "arching boughs made a chapel" and finds a horrible corpse, upright against a tree, crawling with ants and staring straight at him. (pp. 77-8)

The climax of irony comes . . . , when, after a stasis of remorse in which he does indeed despise himself (albeit for the wrong reason of fearing the reproaches of those who did not flee), he sees the whole army come running past him in an utter panic of terror. He tries to stop one of them for information, and is bashed over the head by the frantic and bewildered man. And now, wounded thus, almost delirious with pain and exhaustion, he staggers back to his company—and is greeted as a hero! . . . He is now vainglorious; he thinks himself "a man of experience . . . chosen of the gods and doomed to greatness." Remembering the terror-stricken faces of the men he saw fleeing from the great battle, he now feels a scorn for them! He thinks of the tales of prowess he will tell back home to circles of adoring women.

The youth's reaction to his spurious "red badge of courage" is thus set down with close and ironical detail. Crane does not comment, but the picture of self-delusion and vainglory is meticulously drawn. In the following chapter Henry does fight furiously, but here he is in a blind rage that turns him into an animal, so that he goes on firing long after the enemy have retreated. The other soldiers regard his ferocity with wonder, and Henry has become a marvel, basking in the wondering stares of his comrades.

The order comes for a desperate charge, and the regiment responds magnificently, hurling itself into the enemy's fire regardless of the odds against it. . . . (pp. 79-80)

Heroism is "temporary but sublime," succeeded by dejection, anger, panic, indignation, despair, and renewed rage. This can hardly be called, for Henry, gaining spiritual salvation by losing his soul in the flux of things, for he is acting in harried exasperation, exhaustion, and rage. What has seemed to him an incredible charge turns out, presently, to have been a very short one—in time and distance covered—for which the regiment is bitterly criticized by the General. The facts are supplemented by the tone, which conveys through its outrageous and whimsical language that the whole business is made of pretense and delusion. . . . (p. 80)

What it all seems to come to is that the heroism is in action undeniable, but it is preceded and followed by the ignoble sentiments we have traced—and the constant tone of humor and hysteria seems to be Crane's comment on these juxtapositions of courage, ignorance, vainglory, pettiness, pompous triumph, and craven fear. The moment the men can stop and comment upon what they have been through they are presented as more or less absurd.

With all these facts in mind we can examine the Henry Fleming who emerges from the battle and sets about marshaling all his acts.

He is gleeful over his courage. Remembering his desertion of the wounded Jim Conklin, he is ashamed because of the possible disgrace, but, as Crane tells with supreme irony, "gradually he mustered force to put the sin at a distance," and to dwell upon his "quiet manhood." Coming after all these events and rationalizations, the paragraphs quoted at the beginning of this discussion are a climax of self-delusion. If there is any one point that has been made it is that Henry has never been able to evaluate his conduct. He may have been fearless for moments, but his motives were vain, selfish, ignorant, and childish. Mercifully, Crane does not follow him down through the more despicable levels of self-delusion that are sure to follow as he rewrites (as we have seen him planning to do) the story of his conduct to fit his childish specifications. He has been through some moments of hell, during which he has for moments risen above his limitations, but Crane seems plainly to be showing that he has not achieved a lasting wisdom or self-knowledge.

If *The Red Badge of Courage* were only an exposure of an ignorant farm boy's delusions, it would be a contemptible book. Crane shows that Henry's delusions image only dimly the insanely grotesque and incongruous world of battle into which he is plunged. There the movement is blind or frantic, the leaders are selfish, the goals are inhuman. One farm boy is made into a mad animal to kill another farm boy, while the great guns carry on a "grim pow-wow" or a "stupendous wrangle" described in terms that suggest a solemn farce or a cosmic and irresponsible game.

If we were to seek a geometrical shape to picture the significant form of *The Red Badge,* it would not be the circle, the L, or the straight line of oscillation between selfishness and salvation, but the equilateral triangle. Its three points are instinct, ideals, and circumstance. Henry Fleming runs along the sides like a squirrel in a track. Ideals take him along one side until circumstance confronts him with danger. Then instinct takes over and he dashes down the third side in a panic. The panic abates somewhat as he approaches the angle of ideals, and as he turns the corner (continuing his flight) he busily rationalizes to accommodate those ideals of duty and trust that recur, again and again, to harass him. Then he runs on to the line of circumstance, and he moves again toward instinct. He is always controlled on one line, along which he is both drawn and impelled by the other two forces. If this triangle is thought of as a piece of bright glass whirling in a cosmic kaleidoscope, we have an image of Crane's naturalistic and vividly impressioned Reality. (pp. 81-2)

Charles Child Walcutt, "Stephen Crane: Naturalist and Impressionist," in his *American Literary Naturalism, a Divided Stream,* University of Minnesota Press, 1956, pp. 66-86.

JAMES DICKEY
(essay date 1984)

[Dickey is considered one of America's foremost contemporary poets. He is also the author of the bestselling novel *Deliverance* (1970). In the following excerpt, he argues that Crane's literary style is the natural, unaffected product of a many-sided personality and talent.]

[It] is difficult to pin down exactly wherein Crane's uniqueness lies. It is not, despite **"The Open Boat,"** his overall comprehensive or dramatic power as a writer of fiction that gives him value, but his peculiar laconic turn of personality in the single insight or phrase, which can and does occur in anything he put down, from business letters to novels; that is to say, as a fragmentary but authentic poet. The spontaneity is quite real, not a device but a part of Crane's way of going, and gets into his words in a manner that is uncannily involving, though at first it seems to stem from the most extreme detachment. To Crane's unorthodox animism, battleships are thus:

> These great steel animals sat in a little bay, menacing with their terrible glances a village of three rows of houses and a dock and vast stretches of hillsides, whereon there was not even a tree to shoot at for fun. A group of vicious little torpedo boats also waited impatiently. To one who did not care to feel that there was something in this affair as much as a planet it would be a joke of a kind. But it was the concert of Europe. Colossi never smile.

Crane's offhandedness would be irritating if it were studied, for affectation dates rapidly, but once the reader surrenders to the odd-angled brilliance he is likely to want more, a lot more. Crane shoots from the hip, but he is deadly accurate. His short, bitterly humorous phrases, tossed off as though in passing, are the kind of thing that somebody ought to be able to do; the effect is that an inspired remark made out of the side of the mouth or to one's self has come to rest on paper as a kind of mistake; that is to say, as a perception threatened by darkness and only by miracle preserved. (pp. 1, 9)

He must surely have understood that a shrugging negligent irony, natural to him, was his strong suit, his full-house, and as an inveterate gambler he knew it to be best that he depend on the luck of that particular draw, which makes the writing of masterpieces, in the accepted sense, unlikely if not impossible; *The Red Badge of Courage* is uneven indeed, and verges on the

scrappy, but it is full of fiery revelations. The good side of things is that this gambler's daring also makes everything Crane wrote, even the veriest hack-work, of great interest; there is no telling when he will blindside you with stunning and illuminating force, as though there were nothing to it.

Despite Crane's insistence on the "truth," that he only wrote what he "saw," *The Red Badge of Courage* remains, along with Coleridge's "Rime of the Ancient Mariner," among the most striking examples of works of pure imagination. Its "seeing" is not literalism or naturalism, and it is amusing to note Howells' dismissal of *The Red Badge* as a book based on material which the author did not know at first-hand. The qualities we now esteem are those supplied not by Crane's eyes but by his invention, and it is pertinent here to remember Coleridge's belief that the symptoms of poetic power are most evidenced in depictions of events and actions which the author has not witnessed but summoned up from the depths of himself.

The poetry is not, in the main, as memorable as the prose, though since it is Crane it is still valuable. No one deals with its qualities better than John Berryman . . . : "His poetry has the inimitable sincerity of a frightened savage anxious to learn what his dreams mean." And, "Crane's poetry is like a series of primitive anti-spells." This is maybe going it some, but Berryman is right in citing the enigmatic, heavily ironic, allegorical nature of those verses as essentially, "primitive" or not, a casting-out. The source from which they come is not defiance or supplication, but fear, and there is the suspicion that, though compulsively said, they don't work; they are incantatory spin-offs; the genius is incidental. (p. 9)

James Dickey, "The Casual Brilliance of Stephen Crane," in *Book World—The Washington Post,* August 19, 1984, pp. 1, 9.

BETTINA L. KNAPP
(essay date 1987)

[Knapp is an American educator and critic who has written numerous critical studies, chiefly of French literature. In the following excerpt from her *Stephen Crane*, she provides an overview of stories in Crane's *The Open Boat, and Other Tales of Adventure.*]

In his short stories, Crane adheres to Poe's dictum: the tale should form a "totality . . . there should be no word written, of which the tendency, direct or indirect, is not to the one pre-established design." Like a poem, each tale forms a complete unit, every portion contributing to its final impact and effect upon the reader. Each tale is a self-contained drama. Some have a sting to them; others have an epigrammatic quality that intensifies their momentum and shattering climax. Excitement is generated by controlled, barely sensed actions, which may be nothing more than a minor occurrence, such as a blizzard. Crane's tales aim at realism. They deal with the conflict between illusion and reality or the inner and outer worlds. Neither romantic nor charming, as are Washington Irving's *The Sketch Books,* Crane's stories show detachment, coldness, and a remote quality, lending a mythical touch to such tales as **"The Bride Comes to Yellow Sky"** or **"The Open Boat."** A feeling for nature and for natural man is molded directly into his colorful landscapes and precise descriptions of people and things. The earthiness of his terse, colloquial dialogue is alternately humorous, sardonic, and searing. The stories' musicality also lends them a poetic and incantatory quality.

Crane did not probe his characters' souls as Hawthorne did. Instead he silhouetted them in the light of specific situations or through character traits, giving brief insights here and there. Like Twain, he injected humor into his stories—not *Huckleberry Finn*'s light-hearted banter, but rather satire wedded to bold similes. Unlike Twain, he never romanticized his protagonists nor alluded to nostalgic moments. Crane banished sentimentality and gushy romance, opting for realistic optical images, which under scrutiny reveal the truth of a situation. In this art form, Crane is on a part with masters such as Maupassant, Flaubert, Chekhov, Tolstoy, Gogol, Melville, Hawthorne, James, and Conrad. He knew how to use form, color, and drama to heighten the desired effects. Crane was a superb verbal photographer. His close-up and distant shots, possessed of some indefinable magical powers, remain indelibly fixed in the mind's eye.

"The Pace of Youth" (1895) is situated in the seaside resort of Asbury Park, New Jersey, where the twelve-year old Crane lived with his widowed mother. It focuses on a single image of intense appeal to a child: a glittering and exciting merry-go-round, which dominates not only the events but the characters as well. Stimson is the owner of the "Mammoth Merry-Go Round," with its "whirling circle of ornamental lions, giraffes, camels, ponies, goats, resplendent with varnish and metal that caught swift reflections from windows high above them." The fabulous carousel elicits excitement and ebullience from the children, who cling to the animals on which they ride. Amid all of this joy stalks Stimson, who has learned of his daughter Lizzie's elopement with Frank, his impresario. Despite his wife's pleading, he takes his revolver and runs "hatless" to hail a hack. Once inside, he orders the driver to gallop through the streets and catch up with the buggy that Lizzie and her lover had taken moments earlier. Excitement is intensified as the two vehicles race each other. But when Stimson realizes his hack is falling behind, his hopes of stopping his daughter are dashed. "His whole expedition was the tottering of an old man upon the trail of birds," Crane explains. Age has intervened; the generation gap has made inroads in his relationship with his daughter. He represents a dying past; she, the joyous future. Stimson gives up the race. It is no use. As he makes "a gesture of acquiescence, rage, despair" he suddenly becomes aware of the fact that he forgot his hat. This detail is of monumental importance since it makes him realize that he is no longer in the running.

"One Dash—Horses" (1896) was the first of a group of tales Crane wrote about his trip to the West and Mexico. For some years he had dreamt of seeing those open spaces and endless skies. He was fascinated by the myth of this land of promise and excitement with its very different codes, customs, and characters.

"One Dash—Horses" is based on a real incident in which Crane and his guide, riding into Mexican back country, spent the evening in a local adobe tavern. When Crane saw a drunken bandit, Ramon Colorado, eyeing him, obviously thinking Crane was a "rich" American, he reached for his revolver and stared unflinchingly at the bandit. Ramon Colorado, stunned by the courage of this foreigner, seems then to have changed his mind. The arrival on the scene of girls and musicians draws the bandit's attention away from Crane and his guide, permitting them to slip out of the tavern, mount their horses, and ride away. Soon, however, they notice they are being pursued by the bandit and his cohorts. The terror in their hearts encourages them to gallop on until they meet a troop of rural militia.

Crane does not emphasize the men in his tale; instead he focuses on and humanizes the horses. For example, when the narrator, fearing for his life, drives his steed to incredible speed he looks at the animal with deep confidence, as if it also knew the danger at stake: "The little animal, unurged and quite tranquil, moving his ears this way and that way with an air of interest in the scenery, was nevertheless bounding into the eye of the breaking day with the speed of a frightened antelope." Having reached safety, the narrator again stares at his little horse and becomes aware of his deep love for the animal.

The protagonist's terror is depicted as a race against time. The speed of hoofbeats as bits and pieces of landscape flash by, the rhythmic noise of the dashing horses, the sweat and breathlessness generated by the tremendous effort being expended symbolize the chaos of the unresolved situation. In the tavern scene, for example, fear is built up by foreboding reds and lambent hues: "the deep silence of the pale rays of the moon" as opposed to "the red spears of the fire," shedding their tones in a room "slowly flooded to its middle with a rectangle of silver light." Through economy of words Crane achieves a work of powerful impact. (pp. 145-48)

"The Five White Mice" (1896) is a wry story that . . . features two gun-slinging, venturesome, jocular youths, the San Francisco and New York Kids. . . . After rolling up more and more aces, the New York Kid finds himself and his two drunken companions, the San Francisco Kid and Benson, facing some Mexican desperados on a street, "as dark as a whale's throat at deep sea." The sober Kid is terrified; he remembers what easterners had said about western lawlessness, about the cruelty of cowboys and desperadoes. He sees himself dead and his family grieving for him. He waits, motionless, as he observes his enemies. He is terrified at the thought that he might not be able to draw his gun quickly enough. What if he drops it at the crucial moment or it gets entangled in his coat tails? "The sober Kid saw this [Mexican] face as if it were alone in space—a yellow mask smiling in eager cruelty, in satisfaction, and above all it was lit with sinister decision." The Kid suddenly decides to step forward. He grips his revolver. Crane increases the suspense by taking a moment out to caricature the entire incident, inviting the reader into the Kid's imaginary world. "He recalled that upon its black handle was stamped a hunting scene in which a sportsman in fine leggings and a peaked cap was taking aim at a stag less than one eighth of an inch away." The contrast between the gravity of the Kid's present situation and the romantic visions carved on the holster of his revolver encourages wry laughter along with feelings of fright at the thought of the dangers at stake. "At the supreme moment the revolver came forth as if it were greased and it arose like a feather. This somnolent machine, after months of repose, was finally looking at the breasts of men." The reader learns, in a form of interior monologue, why the Kid was filled with rage as he took aim. The Mexicans "slunk back, their eyes burning wistfully," never giving him a chance to prove his courage. "The whole thing had been an absurd imposition." They all leave. "Nothing had happened". Nothing, yet everything is compressed into that one traumatic incident: fear, self-pity, courage, and will power.

"A Man and Some Others" (1897) also deals with the trauma of sustained terror and the serenity that follows the acceptance of one's mortality. A sheepherder, Bill, decides to fight the murderers stalking him. Feelings of anxiety and alienation build as Crane focuses his camera's eye on stark background images: "Dark mesquit spread from horizon to horizon. There was no house or horseman from which a mind could evolve a city or a crowd. The world was declared to be a desert and unpeopled." Crane now fills the reader in on Bill's past, giving the present situation a sense of perspective. Bill was once the owner of a rich mine

in Wyoming, but lost the mine playing poker. He then became a cowboy, gambled again, and once again found himself destitute. He then worked as a bouncer, a killer, and, finally, a sheepherder in Texas. The story now pursues its course in the present. A Stranger approaches Bill, who warns him to leave because killing is in the offing. Minutes later, some Mexicans charge Bill. The Stranger screams. "As the guns roared, Bill uttered a loud grunt, and for a moment leaned panting on his elbow, while his arm shook like a twig. Then he upreared like a great and bloody spirit of vengeance, his face lighted with the blaze of his last passion." Bill is dead.

A sense of compassion, greater, perhaps, than in Crane's previous stories, prevails in **"A Man and Some Others."** Bill's past and his laconic statements to the Stranger let the reader understand the dignity of a man who once was a killer and the ease with which life may be ended. At the end of the tale, the Stranger looks at the "body contorted, with one arm stiff in the air" that lies in his path. "Slowly and warily he moved around it, and in a moment the bushes, nodding and whispering, their leaf-faces turned toward the scene behind him, swung and swung again into stillness and the peace of the wilderness."

"The Open Boat" (1898), one of America's finest short stories, describes the adventure that satisfied Crane perhaps most fully. He said once that he wanted to go "to some quarter of the world where mail is uncertain." He did just that when he accepted Bacheller's assignment in November, 1896 to cover the Cuban Revolution. Thick fog enshrouded the St. Johns River as the Commodore set sail from Jacksonville with Crane aboard. Although Captain Edward Murphy had taken the precaution of hiring a local pilot to help the vessel out of the harbor, it struck a sand bar. The following morning, the Commodore was towed free, but Murphy neglected to review the damage done the ship, which continued on into deeper waters. By the time the leak was discovered, there was no hope of saving the ship. Although the Captain tried to steer it back to the harbor, the pumps and engines gave out and it foundered. Passengers and crew were ordered into the lifeboats. Crane's conduct during this harrowing ordeal was superb: he soothed frightened men, helped bail out water, and acted like a born sailor. After the crew was in the lifeboats, Crane, the Captain, the cook and the oiler climbed into a ten-foot-long dinghy.

Although the boat managed to stay afloat on the high seas, Crane's harrowing experience was far from over. The mate's lifeboat capsized and the men on it drowned. Crane was deeply moved by the courage of the sailors who drowned: no shrieks, no groans, only silence.

The remaining lifeboats reached land the following day. The dinghy, however, could not get ashore because of the rough surf and so remained out at sea. No one on shore could see or hear the men in the dinghy. The captain fired his pistol but to no avail, and the men were forced to spend another night in the dinghy, rowing frantically to prevent being swallowed up by the rough seas. They then decided to row to Daytona Beach and try to make it through the breakers there. But the boat overturned, and they had to swim. A man on the beach saw what happened and ran for help. All but the oiler were saved. (pp. 149-52)

Its poetry and rhythmic schemes make **"The Open Boat"** the match of Melville's "White Jacket" and the best of Jack London and Joseph Conrad. This tale's unusually punctuated sentences of contrasting length simulate the heart beat of man under extreme stress, producing an incantatory quality. Crane's sensual images of man struggling against the sea remain vivid long after the reading of **"The Open Boat."** The salt spray and deafening roar of the waves pounding against the dinghy can almost be tasted and heard.

"Flanagan and His Short Filibustering Adventure" (1898) also focuses on the sea. Written under intense pressure, the story is entertaining, but not comparable to **"The Open Boat"** in either technique or subject matter.

"The Bride Comes to Yellow Sky" (1898), however, is another masterpiece of restraint, concision, and heart-stirring drama. The action takes place mostly in the mind of Sheriff Jack Potter, who goes off to San Antonio to bring back his bride to Yellow Sky. Disquietude and guilt seem to mark his every thought and gesture during the long train trip home with his new wife. The "heinous crime" that torments Sheriff Potter is that he has not informed his friends—the citizens of Yellow Sky—about his forthcoming marriage. The personality of the groom—in contrast with the usual image of the Western sheriff who with gun and badge imposes order on a lawless society—is revealed as he looks at his bride tenderly and shyly shows her "the dazzling fittings of the coach." Although trying to impress her, the sheriff remains modest and humble. He then slips into town via the back entrance in order to keep out of sight. The couple has almost reached their home when a drunken outlaw, Scratchy Wilson, approaches them and pulls out his gun. He intends to settle his affairs by fighting Potter. "I ain't got a gun on me, Scratchy," answers the Sheriff. Scratchy doesn't believe him. How could a sheriff be unarmed? "If you ain't got a gun, why ain't you got a gun? Been to Sunday-school?" When Potter tells him he has just been married, Scratchy Wilson is stunned—he "was like a creature allowed a glimpse of another world. He moved a pace backward, and his arm with the revolver dropped to his side."

Sheriff Potter broke the frontier code in two respects: by his marriage, and being gunless. His image tarnished, he is no longer a role model. Scratchy Wilson can not conceive of living in a town with a married sheriff. As for Potter's not carrying a gun: "There ain't a man in Texas ever seen you without no gun." Like the Sheriff, whose train trip was so filled with anxiety, Scratchy is also caught in a maze. This new situation spells trepidation. A single incident serves to point up the meaning of dread, not the dread encountered in **"The Open Boat,"** but the fear of change and apprehension that comes with the shattering of illusions and preconceived notions. With humor and irony, Crane demolishes the images of the brash, aggressive, loud-mouth sheriff and the blood-thirsty outlaw and creates instead the two unforgettable characters of **"The Bride Comes to Yellow Sky."** (pp. 155-56)

"The Blue Hotel" (1898), which takes place at Fort Romper, Nebraska, is another of Crane's finest tales. It has many facets. Each character plays a role in keeping with his personality. Although the narrator apprehends only some of the truths implicit in the tale, the reader, through the metaphor of the blue hotel, is able to grasp the entire picture.

The Palace Hotel in Nebraska is painted blue, a fact of utmost importance: "a light blue, a shade that is on the legs of a kind of heron, causing the bird to declare its position against any background." This premonitory image, offered the reader at the very outset of the tale, implies metaphorically the fixity and intractability of the protagonist's view of people.

A Swede enters the Blue Hotel. Like the heron in the opening image, he is anchored to his unalterable preconceptions. He is certain that the people frequenting the Blue Hotel are lawless and cruel and that he may even be killed here. He masks his terror by adopting a swaggering gait and behaving in an arrogant manner. Like several other of Crane's characters, the Swede is an easterner prejudiced against the Wild West by dime novels and not by real life. Scully, the proprietor of the hotel, reveals himself to be just the opposite of the Swede's notion of the gun-happy Westerner; in fact, he looks "curiously like an old priest." He offers the Swede warmth, hospitality, and a drink in a show of friendliness, but to no avail. The Swede continues to act aggressively and defiantly. He even insults the proprietor and the habitués. "A guest under my roof has sacred privileges," Scully says. But the friendliness Scully offers the Swede is rejected. The Swede is convinced that the Blue Hotel, which looks more like a church with its icons and stained glass windows, spells violence and death.

Scully persists; he offers the Swede a fine meal and encourages him to join a group of friendly card players. The Swede then accuses the host's son, Johnny, of cheating, and a fight breaks out. Of course, Johnny is no match for the Swede. He is knocked to the ground almost immediately and the Swede would have continued hitting him had the others not intervened.

The Swede, convinced that he is in *real* danger, leaves the Blue Hotel in a blizzard to search for a safe place. "In front of it [another bar] an indomitable red light was burning, and the snow-flakes were made blood-color as they flew through the circumscribed territory of the lamp's shining." Another premonitory image: the red light presages blood and death. The Swede enters the "sanded expanse before him" and pours himself a whiskey. He then begins boasting of having "thumped the soul out of a man down here at Scully's hotel." Those present "encased themselves in reserve" and when the Swede invites the guests—a gambler, businessmen, a district attorney, and others—to drink with him, they refuse with "quiet dignity." Enraged by their rejection, the Swede virtually explodes. Putting his hand on the shoulder of the gambler, he invites him once again to drink with him and is once again refused. "What? You won't drink with me, you little dude! I'll make you!" the Swede roars, holding the gambler by the throat and dragging him from his chair.

There was a great tumult, and then was seen a long blade in the hand of the gambler. It shot forward, and a human body, this citadel of virtue, wisdom, power, was pierced as easily as if it had been a melon. The Swede fell with a cry of supreme astonishment.

The story does not end with this. Crane must add his dash of irony. The gambler is given three years in prison for murder. As for Johnny of the Blue Hotel, he *had* cheated, the reader learns, but because "the game was only for fun." The guest who actually saw the sleight of hand had said nothing. Everyone, then, is guilty of the Swede's murder, Crane suggests—the criminal who did the stabbing as well as the collective who did nothing to prevent it.

Fear, masked by arrogance, and the impossibility of modifying role models are the themes of **"The Blue Hotel."** The fierce, graphic descriptions of the howling blizzard reproduce the nerve-shattering momentum

built up within the hotel. The tale revolves around the Swede, who harangues and assaults the other guests, projecting his own inadequacies upon them. Because he wants to give the impression of being strong and virile, he has built up a paranoic system of defenses against presumed enemies. Scully, the spiritual leader of the hotel group, prevents an outbreak of violence as long as it is humanly possible. The Swede's heavy drinking, begun in the Blue Hotel, continues in the saloon. He feels manic elation over his victory in his fight with Johnny. The blinding snowstorm symbolizes the Swede's lack of vision, his inability to see into himself and, therefore, into others. He is unable to assimilate the kindness he was shown at the Blue Hotel; nor can he interpret the harsh atmosphere of the saloon. Like the heron of the opening image, he stands fixed in his ideas, oblivious to his surroundings, and it is his rigidity and blindness that cause his death.

Like **"The Open Boat," "The Blue Hotel"** deals with the theme of brotherhood as well as that of hostility. The Swede is given shelter from the storm, and is invited into a community of friendly people. But because they failed to understand the meaning behind the Swede's hostile behavior, the other characters are as blind and set in their ways as the Swede. As Crane suggested, **"The Blue Hotel"** is "a whirling, fire-smitten, ice-locked, disease-stricken space-lost bulb"—a microcosm of society and the world.

Fascinated by the dichotomies of eastern and western landscapes, of wild and churning seas, Crane, like Melville, Poe, and Conrad, uses his painter's eye to reveal strikingly vast spaces and war-torn areas. His verbal canvases, marked in blues, whites, reds, ochres, browns and blacks, portray scrubby ranges, low hills, blinding snows, and ferocious seas. He uses the detail to reveal the whole; he scrutinizes the isolated incident to explain the larger drama. He reveals a personality type in a swift and often elliptical manner, a situation in stonelike, language divested of all extraneous elements. (pp. 158-62)

Bettina L. Knapp, in her *Stephen Crane,* Ungar, 1987, 198 p.

SOURCES FOR FURTHER STUDY

Bloom, Harold, ed. *Modern Critical Views: Stephen Crane,* New York: Chelsea House Publishers, 1987, 167 p.

    Contains essays on Crane's life and works by noted scholars in American literature.

Ellison, Ralph. "Stephen Crane and the Mainstream of American Fiction." In his *Shadow and Act,* pp. 60-76. New York: Random House, 1964.

    Examines *The Red Badge of Courage* and several Crane short stories as expressions of Crane's moral struggle and his depiction of social reality.

E. E. Cummings

1894-1962

(Full name Edward Estlin Cummings; also wrote as e. e. cummings) American poet, novelist, essayist, and dramatist.

INTRODUCTION

Cummings's innovative and controversial verse places him among the most popular and widely anthologized poets of the twentieth century. While linked early in his career with the Modernist movement, he wrote poems with themes that more closely resemble the works of the New England Transcendentalists and English Romantics. Rejecting what he perceived as the small-mindedness of "mostpeople," Cummings's work celebrates the individual, as well as erotic and familial love. Conformity, mass psychology, and snobbery were frequent targets of his humorous and sometimes scathing satires. Cummings was also a painter and a student of such modernist art forms as cubism and futurism. His knowledge of the visual arts led him to experiment with punctuation, idiomatic speech, compressed words, dislocated syntax, and unusual typography, line division, and capitalization in order to capture the particulars of a single movement or moment in time. Discussing Cummings's technique, Randall Jarrell explained: "Cummings is a very great expert in all these, so to speak, illegal syntactical devices: his misuse of parts of speech, his use of negative prefixes, his word-coining, his systematic relation of words that grammar and syntax don't permit us to relate—all this makes him a magical bootlegger or moonshiner of language, one who intoxicates us on a clear liquor no government has legalized with its stamp."

Cummings grew up in Cambridge, Massachusetts, where his father was a sociology professor at Harvard and a noted Unitarian clergyman. Demonstrating a strong interest in poetry and art from an early age, Cummings enjoyed the full support and encouragement of his parents. He attended Harvard from 1911 to 1915, studying literature and writing daily. He eventually joined the editorial board of the *Harvard Monthly*, a college literary magazine, where he worked with his close friends S. Foster Damon and John Dos Passos. In his senior year he became fascinated by avant-garde art, modernism, and cubism, an interest reflected in his graduation dissertation, "The New Art." In this paper, Cummings extolled modernism as practiced by Gertrude Stein, Ezra Pound, Amy Lowell, and Pablo Picasso. He also began incorporating elements of these styles into his own poetry and paintings. His first published poems appeared in the anthology *Eight Harvard Poets* in 1917. These pieces feature experimental verse forms and the lower-case personal pronoun "i"—symbolizing both the humbleness and the uniqueness of the individual—that became his trademark. The copyeditor of the book, however, mistook Cummings's intentions as typographical errors and made "corrections."

In 1917 Cummings moved to New York, was employed very briefly at a mail-order book company, and soon began working full-time on his poetry and art. With World War I raging in Europe, he volunteered for the French-based Norton-Harjes Ambulance Service. He spent time in Paris upon his arrival and was completely charmed by the city's bohemian atmosphere and abundance of art and artists. He was particularly impressed by the sketches of Pablo Picasso, whose cubist techniques later helped shape much of his work. Because of a misunderstanding, Cummings spent four months in an internment camp in Normandy on suspicion of treason, an experience documented in his prose work *The Enormous Room* (1922). Making use of his contacts in government, Cummings's father was able to secure his son's release. Cummings was drafted shortly after he returned to New York in 1918 and spent about a year at Camp Danvers, Massachusetts. During the 1920s and 1930s he traveled widely in Europe, alternately living in Paris and New York, and developed parallel careers as a poet and painter. Politically liberal and with leftist leanings, Cummings visited the Soviet Union in 1931 in order to find out how the system of government subsidy for art functioned there. *Eimi* (1933), an expanded version of his travel diary, expresses his profound disappointment in its indictment of the regimentation and lack of personal and artistic freedom he encountered. From that time, Cummings abandoned his liberal political views and social circle and became an embittered, reactionary conservative on social and political issues. He continued to write prolifically and received the Shelley Memorial Award for poetry in 1944, the Charles Eliot Norton Professorship at Harvard for the academic year 1952-53, and the Bollingen Prize for Poetry in 1958. He composed miscellaneous prose pieces, drama, and a ballet. Cummings reached the height of his popularity during the 1940s and 1950s, giving poetry readings to college au-diences across the United States until his death in 1962.

Cummings's first book, *The Enormous Room,* is a novel/memoir based on his experiences in the French internment camp; it concerns the preservation of dignity in a degrading and dehumanizing situation. This work, widely considered a classic of World War I literature, introduced themes that Cummings would pursue throughout his career: the individual against society, against government, and against all forms of authority. Cummings used words in both French and English to create a witty, satirical voice that lampoons the war itself as well as military bureaucracy. Cummings's father's efforts to obtain his son's release is documented in the book's preface, which reprints correspondence with U.S. and French authorities.

All of Cummings's poetry attests to the author's neverending search for fresh metaphors and new means of expression through creative placement of words on the page, new word constructions, and unusual punctuation and capitalization. He originally intended to publish his first collection as *Tulips & Chimneys,* but was forced to publish the poems from the original manuscript as three separate volumes: *Tulips and Chimneys* (1923), *XLI Poems* (1925), and *&* (1925). The "tulips" of the first volume are free-verse lyric poems that present a nostalgic glance at his childhood. The poem "in Just-" celebrates youth in playful, imaginative and creative contractions—"mud-/luscious" and "puddle-wonderful," for example—while the poem "O sweet spontaneous" revels in nature that can only be appreciated fully through the senses rather than through science, philosophy, or religion. The "chimneys" are a sustained sonnet sequence that identifies the hypocrisy, narrow-mindedness, and stagnation Cummings saw in the society around him. The sequence includes the well-known poem "the Cambridge ladies who live in furnished souls"—women who, according to Cummings, "are unbeautiful and have comfortable minds." The poems excised from the original manuscript that were later collected in *XLI Poems* and *&* are generally more erotic in content.

The thematic concerns of Cummings's first three volumes of verse are repeated in *is 5* (1926), in which the author also included satiric and anti-war pieces, notably "my sweet old etcetera" and "i sing of Olaf glad and big," a poem about the death of a conscientious objector. *ViVa* (1931) contains sonnets and other poems attacking conservative and uncreative thinking. Along with his barbs at society, Cummings also composed such lyrical poems as "somewhere I have never travelled, gladly beyond," in which he extolled love, nature, the mystery of faith, individualism, and imaginative freedom. The collection *No Thanks* (1935), written in response to his trip to the Soviet Union, treats the theme of artistic freedom in an especially powerful manner. *50 Poems* (1940) contains such popular pieces as "anyone lived in a pretty how town" and an elegy to his father, "my father moved through dooms of love." *1 x 1* (1944) solidified Cummings's reputation as one of America's premier poets. It presents a more optimistic, life-affirming viewpoint than do the poems written during Cummings's period of personal and political disaffection in the 1930s. Structured in a pattern of darkness moving toward light, *1 x 1* begins with poems that denigrate businessmen and politicians and ends with poems praising nature and love. In his late verse— *XAIPE* (1950), *95 Poems* (1958), and the posthumously published *73 Poems* (1963)—Cummings effects a softer, more elegiac note, recalling his early affinity for New England Transcendentalism and English Romanticism.

Critical opinion of Cummings's poems is markedly divided. Beginning with *Tulips and Chimneys,* reviewers described Cummings's style as eccentric and self-indulgent, designed to call attention to itself rather than to elucidate themes. Some critics also objected to Cummings's explicit treatment of sexuality, while others labeled his depictions of society's hypocrisy and banality elitist. When his *Collected Poems* were published in 1938, Cummings's sharp satires caused some reviewers to call him a misanthrope. His later, more conservative poetry came under attack for anti-semitism, a charge that is still debated. Critics have noted, too, that Cummings's style did not change or develop much throughout his career. Some commentators speculate that Cummings early found a style that suited him and simply continued on with it; others, however, have faulted the author for insufficient artistic growth. For example, many critics censured *50 Poems,* accusing Cummings of relying too much on formulaic writing and habitual stylistic mannerisms. A group of scholars posited that Cummings's verbal pyrotechnics and idiosyncratic arrangement of text actually draw readers' attention from the poetry itself. Despite these negative assessments, Cummings remains an extremely popular poet, and his poems are widely anthologized.

Cummings remains one of the best-known and best-loved poets of the twentieth century. He is remembered for his innovative, playful spirit, his celebration of love and nature, his focus on the primacy of the individual and freedom of expression, and for his treatment of the themes, in his own words, of "ecstasy and anguish, being and becoming; the immortality of the creative imagination and the indomitability of the human spirit."

(For further information about Cummings's life and works, see *Contemporary Authors,* Vol. 73-76; *Contemporary Literary Criticism,* Vols. 1, 3, 8, 12, 15; and *Dictionary of Literary Biography,* Vols. 4, 48.)

CRITICAL COMMENTARY

RICHARD P. BLACKMUR

(essay date 1931)

[Blackmur was a leading American literary critic of the twentieth century. His early essays on the poetry of such contemporaries as T. S. Eliot, W. B. Yeats, Wallace Stevens, and Ezra Pound were immediately recognized for their acute and exacting attention to diction, metaphor, and symbol. In the following excerpt from an essay first published in 1931, he places Cummings with "the anti-culture group" of artists, criticizing his sentimentality and superficial, imprecise diction.]

Mr. Cummings is a school of writing in himself; so that it is necessary to state the underlying assumptions of his mind, and of the school which he teaches, before dealing with the specific results in poetry of those assumptions.

It is possible to say that Mr. Cummings belongs to the anticulture group; what has been called at various times vorticism, futurism, dadaism, surrealism, and so on. Part of the general dogma of this group is a sentimental denial of the intelligence and the deliberate assertion that the unintelligible is the only object of significant experience. . . . It is argued that only by denying to the intelligence its function of discerning quality and order, can the failures of the intelligence be overcome; that if we take things as they come without remembering what has gone before or guessing what may come next, and if we accept these things at their face value, we shall know life, at least in the arts, as it really is. Nothing could be more arrogant, and more deceptively persuasive to the childish spirit, than such an attitude when held as fundamental. It appeals to the intellect which wishes to work swiftly and is in love with immediate certainty. (pp. 1-2)

The central attitude of this group has developed, in its sectaries, a logical and thoroughgoing set of principles and habits. . . . Jazz effects, tough dialects, tough guys, slim hot queens, barkers, fairies, and so on,

Principal Works

The Enormous Room (novel) 1922

Tulips and Chimneys (poetry) 1923

& (poetry) 1925

XLI Poems (poetry) 1925

is 5 (poetry) 1926

ViVa (poetry) 1931

Eimi (travel diary) 1933

No Thanks (poetry) 1935

Collected Poems (poetry) 1938

50 Poems (poetry) 1940

1 X 1 (poetry) 1944

XAIPE: Seventy-One Poems (poetry) 1950

i: six nonlectures (lectures) 1953

95 Poems (poetry) 1958

100 Selected Poems (poetry) 1959

73 Poems (poetry) 1963

Selected Letters of E. E. Cummings (correspondence) 1969

are made into the media and symbols of poetry. Which is proper enough in Shakespeare where such effects are used ornamentally or for pure play. But in Cummings such effects are employed as substance, as the very mainstay of the poetry. There is a continuous effort to escape the realism of the intelligence in favour of the realism of the obvious. What might be stodgy or dull because not properly worked up into poetry is replaced by the tawdry and by the fiction of the immediate. (pp. 2-3)

By denying the dead intelligence and putting on the heresy of unintelligence, the poet only succeeds in substituting one set of unnourished conventions for another. What survives, with a deceptive air of reality, is a surface. That the deception is often intentional hardly excuses it. The surface is meant to clothe and illuminate a real substance, but in fact is is impenetrable. We are left, after experiencing this sort of art, with the certainty that there was nothing to penetrate. The surface was perfect; the deceit was childish; and the conception was incorrigibly sentimental: all because of the dogma which made them possible.

If Mr. Cummings' tough-guy poems are excellent examples of this sentimentality, it is only natural that his other poems—those clothed in the more familiar language of the lyric—should betray even more obviously, even more perfectly, the same fault. There, in the lyric, there is no pretence at hardness of surface. We are admitted at once to the bare emotion. What is most striking, in every instance, about this emotion is the fact that, in so far as it exists at all, it is Mr. Cummings'

emotion, so that our best knowledge of it must be, finally, our best guess. It is not an emotion resulting from the poem; it existed before the poem began and is a result of the poet's private life. . . . This is the extreme form, in poetry, of romantic egoism: whatever I experience is real and final, and whatever I say represents what I experience. Such a dogma is the natural counterpart of the denial of the intelligence. (pp. 3-4)

Assuming that a poem should in some sense be understood, should have a meaning apart from the poet's private life, either one of two things will be true about any poem written from such an attitude as we have ascribed to Mr. Cummings. Either the poem will appear in terms so conventional that everybody will understand it—when it will be flat and no poem at all; or it will appear in language so far distorted from convention as to be inapprehensible except by lucky guess. In neither instance will the poem be genuinely complete. It will be the notes for a poem, from which might flow an infinite number of possible poems, but from which no particular poem can be certainly deduced. (p. 4)

The question central to [this] discussion will be what kind of meaning does Mr. Cummings' poetry have; what is the kind of equivalence between the language and its object. The pursuit of such a question involves us immediately in the relations between words and feelings, and the relations between the intelligence and its field in experience—all relations which are precise only in terms themselves essentially poetic—in the feeling for an image, the sense of an idiom. . . . In the examination of Mr. Cummings' writings the grounds will be the facts about the words he uses, and the end will be apprehended in the quality of the meaning his use of these words permits. (pp. 4-5)

If a reader, sufficiently familiar with these poems not to be caught on the snag of novelty, inspects carefully any score of them, no matter how widely scattered, he will especially be struck by a sameness among them. This sameness will be in two sorts—a vagueness of image and a constant recurrence of words. . . . In *Tulips and Chimneys* words such as these occur frequently—thrilling, flowers, serious, absolute, sweet, unspeaking, utter, gradual, ultimate, final, serene, frail, grave, tremendous. . . . [None] of them, taken alone, are very *concrete* words; and . . . many of them are the rather *abstract,* which is to say typical, *names* for precise qualities, but are not, and cannot be, as *originally important* words in a poem, very precise or very concrete or very abstract: they are middling words, not in themselves very much one thing or the other, and should be useful only with respect to something concrete in itself. (pp. 6-7)

[One example, the word "flower," is used repeatedly and in a variety of usages, such as flower-terrible, flowers of kiss, and world flower.] The question is, whether or not the reader can possibly have shared the experience which Mr. Cummings has had of the word; whether or not it is possible to discern, after any amount of effort, the precise impact which Mr. Cummings undoubtedly feels upon his whole experience when he uses the word. (p. 8)

[In] his use of the word "flower" as a maid of all work [Mr. Cummings has let his ideas run away with him]. The word has become an idea, and in the process has been deprived of its history, its qualities, and its meaning. . . . In Mr. Cummings' poetry we find [that] the word "flower," because of the originality with which he conceives it, becomes an idea and is used to represent the most interesting and most important aspect of his poem. Hence the centre of the poem is permanently abstract and unknowable for the reader, and remains altogether without qualifications and concreteness. It is not the mere frequency of use that deadens the word flower into an idea; it is the kind of thought which each use illustrates in common. By seldom saying *what* flower, by seldom relating immitigably the abstract word to a specific experience, the content of the word vanishes: it has no inner mystery, only an impenetrable surface.

This is the defect, the essential deceit, we were trying to define. Without questioning Mr. Cummings, or any poet, as to sincerity . . . it is possible to say that when in any poem the important words are forced by their use to remain impenetrable, when they can be made to surrender nothing actually to the senses—then the poem is defective and the poet's words have so far deceived him as to become ideas merely. (pp. 9-10)

Mr. Cummings has a fine talent for using familiar, even almost dead words, in such a context as to make them suddenly impervious to every ordinary sense; they become unable to speak, but with a great air of being bursting with something very important and precise to say. "The bigness of cannon is *skilful* . . . enormous rhythm of *absurdity* . . . *slimness* of *evenslicing* eyes are chisels . . . electric Distinct face haughtily vital *clinched* in a swoon of *synopsis* . . . my friend's being continually whittles *keen* careful futile *flowers,*" etc. With the possible exception of the compound *evenslicing* the italicized words are all ordinary words; all in normal contexts have a variety of meanings both connotative and denotative; the particular context of being such as to indicate a particular meaning, to establish precisely a feeling, a sensation or a relation.

Mr. Cummings' contexts are employed to an opposite purpose in so far as they wipe out altogether the history of the word, its past associations and general character. To seize Mr. Cummings' meaning there is only the free and *uninstructed* intuition. (p. 16)

The general movement of Mr. Cummings' language is away from communicable precision. If it be argued that the particular use of one of the italicized words above merely makes that word unique, the retort is that such uniqueness is too perfect, is sterile. If by removing the general sense of a word the special sense is apotheosized, it is only so at the expense of the general sense itself. The destruction of the general sense of a word results in the loss of that word's individuality. . . . (pp. 16-17)

When Mr. Cummings resorts to language for the *thrill* that words may be made to give, when he allows his thrill to appear as an equivalent for concrete meaning, he is often more successful than when he is engaged more ambitiously. . . . Thrill, by itself, or in its proper place, is an exceedingly important element in any poem: it is the circulation of its blood, the *quickness* of life, by which we know it, when there is anything in it to know, most intimately. To use a word for its thrill, is to resurrect it from the dead; it is the incarnation of life in consciousness; it is movement.

But what Mr. Cummings does, when he is using language as thrill, is not to resurrect a word from the dead: he more often produces an apparition, in itself startling and even ominous, but still only a ghost: it is all a thrill, and what it is that thrilled us cannot be determined. (pp. 22-3)

[There] is an exquisite example of the proper use of this strangeness, this thrill, in [a] poem of Mr. Cummings: where he speaks of a cathedral before whose face "the streets turn *young* with rain." While there might be some question as to whether the use of *young* presents the only adequate image, there is certainly no question at all that the phrase is entirely successful: that is, the suggestive feeling in *young* makes the juncture, the emotional conjugation, of streets and rain transparent and perfect. . . . Just because reference is not commonly made either to young streets or young rain, the combination here effected is the more appropriate. The surprise, the contrast, which lend force to the phrase, do not exist in the poem; but exist, if at all, rather in the mind of the reader who did not forsee the slight stretch of his sensibility that the phrase requires—which the phrase not only requires, but necessitates. This, then, is a *strangeness* understood by its own viableness. No preliminary agreement of taste, or contract of symbols, was necessary.

The point is that Mr. Cummings did not here attempt the impossible, he merely stretched the probable. The business of the poet who deals largely with tactual and visual images, as Mr. Cummings does, for the meat of his work, is to escape the prison of his private mind; to use in his poem as little as possible of the experience that happened to him personally, and on the other hand to employ as much as possible of that experience as it is data. (pp. 25-6)

The proper process of poetry designs exactly

what the reader will perceive; that is what is meant when a word is said to be inevitable or *juste*. But this exactness of perception can only come about when there is an extreme fidelity on the part of the poet to his words as living things; which he can discover and control—which he must learn, and nourish, and stretch; but which he cannot invent. This unanimity in our possible experience of words implies that the only unanimity which the reader can feel in what the poet represents must be likewise exterior to the poet; must be somehow both anterior and posterior to the poet's own experience. The poet's mind, perhaps, is what he is outside himself with; is what he has learned; is what he knows: it is also what the reader knows. So long as he is content to remain in his private mind, he in unknowable, impenetrable, and sentimental. All his words perhaps must thrill us, because we cannot know them in the very degree that we sympathise with them. But the best thrills are those we have without knowing it. (p. 27)

Richard P. Blackmur, "Notes on E. E. Cummings' Language," in his *The Double Agent: Essays in Craft and Elucidation,* 1935. Reprint by Peter Smith, 1962, pp. 1-29.

JOHN ARTHOS

(essay date 1943)

[In the following excerpt, Arthos discusses the peculiarities of Cummings's style, pointing out that the poet used language both as a means of rebelling against convention and to expand the range of his poetry.]

E. E. Cummings is one of the few modern poets who write about beautiful things simply. Much contemporary poetry is concerned with the analysis of states of mind for the sake of philosophic or social comment. . . . There are exceptions, of course, but most modern poets are not concerned very much with declaring that the beauty of their experience is proof of the power of beauty. . . . Cummings is surely the modern poet who has most consistently aimed at lyric expression in the direct manner. . . . He has remained a lyric poet because he has not been interested in questioning and doubting; he has been constantly searching but he has always known what he is searching for. (p. 372)

Cummings's career in print began with a novel, *The Enormous Room.* . . . After graduating from Harvard he had served with an ambulance corps in France before the United States entered the war, and there through one of the blunders of the French he and a friend were confined to a concentration camp near the

Pyrenees for some months, confined with people who by the record might appear to have been the scum of the earth. But Cummings found some of them to be characters of overpowering excellence. . . . Here Cummings discovered and re-created such virtue and beauty as are hardly to be found in any other contemporary writer. And here he seems to have taken a direction he was never to give up, a strict and rich attention to the particular beauty that belongs to the humble.

But in the strange world of New York and Paris after the war such simple service was very often undertaken as part of the revolt against a society that for many people no longer seemed to deserve much loyalty. As after any great collective effort when individuals are closely confined in their personal aims, there was the reaction to extreme individualism and much disillusionment. Cummings was one of those swept by this anarchic surge. . . . Still believing in virtue, he seemed to assert it was to be found only among the downtrodden, which is a rather comfortable way of escaping from Brattle Street. Insofar as he was rebelling against complacency and dullness and arrogance he was being true to himself, but in exaggerating the virtues of the underworld he submitted himself to an unnecessary strain and artificiality. (pp. 373-74)

He has spent his feeling, then, with some confusion, and it is useful for any consideration of his poetry to examine how he has done this. It is significant that many of the chapter headings of *The Enormous Room* are taken from *The Pilgrim's Progress.* Several of the late poems are explicitly religious, but without these we may see many indications that he has consistently striven to be pious. In spite of himself he has remained a Puritan, though for him despair, his Valley of Despond, has been the hatred of the senses Puritanism approved and fostered. . . . As fortune would have it, some of his intensity of feeling is guarded by the singleness of mind that provides one of the great strengths of Puritanism, so much so that he is led by the same virtue to become a missionary, to make beauty a cause. He is sometimes obliged, praising whatever is Spring-like, to worship defiantly. . . . To do justice to the claims of the senses he turned to the world Brattle Street considered most debased, and he did this in a conscientious and Puritan way. (p. 374)

His love poems, which show both his loyal intentness and his unhappy confusion, describe countless affairs, crude as well as fine. Sometimes they are very beautiful, and at other times they are detached and hard. Sometimes they are merely obscene jokes. He told Puritanism off even while shocking himself, and this became a habit. It was right and necessary to tell his Puritan ancestors that the life of the senses is good, but it does the senses no favor to consider their restlessness their essential virtue. Their value consists really in their aptitude for constancy, in service that is rewarding to the whole individual, whereby the attachment of the senses is deeply and lastingly fixed.

His paganism, then, is corrupted with an idea, that the casual experience of the senses provides a sufficient truth for living. Falling in love, he is really serving this idea, and his experience of what is more deeply human is restricted. (p. 375)

In the very earliest poems, **"Puella Mea"** and **"Epithalamion,"** Cummings began with the praise of love, with sensuous and fragrant language and a kind of delicacy that is like Catullus. Later he was to make epigrams in the manner of the Latin poet, but here the stronger reminiscences are of Spenser and Keats, with here and there, curiously enough, a tone that seems to come from Milton. . . . [There] is much that is clumsy, and sometimes the language is pitifully insecure. But they are left as a remainder of a genuine striving. The surer grace came in certain sonnets, where there is a kind of fragile charm. . . . (pp. 376-77)

What is immediately striking here is the language of the images, more perhaps than the images themselves: the *threaded moment,* the *shadowy sheep,* eyes *frailer than dreams.* Something of this same love of language is in Spenser and Milton, where abstract words are treated like material ones, *the very skillful strangeness of your smile.* The method seems to be to use the abstraction to express the essential quality of a thing, and a sensuous or material epithet is attached in order to clinch the image referred to in such a way that all the associations implied in the abstraction are drawn on. When unsuccessful, such phrasing points to a kind of vagueness of language and perhaps feeling. But the failures only indicate the nature of the successes, which seem to prove that any beautiful particular depends upon something ineffable, something not exclusively comprehended in the image alone—*eyes frailer than most dreams are frail.* (p. 378)

I think one of Cummings's first inclinations must have been to write in a convention, even while he was intent on forming an individual style. He must have taken forms from the past that were roughly adapted to the things he had to write about. He found these forms of course in the poets he admired, Spenser and Keats, the Spenserian stanza, the sonnet, the iambic rhythm. And in the beginning he found a language there he wanted, and a way of phrasing. However fresh the feelings he had to express seemed to him, he knew that it was impossible merely to take over the language of daily speech with no wider knowledge of its capacity than is to be gained in conversation. He has had an extraordinary gift of his own with which to extend our language, and it is understandable that at times he should have distorted language beyond recognition. (pp. 378-79)

A Protestant rebelling against Protestantism, he

has a particular stake in asserting the value of his feeling, and he has the conjunct necessity to establish a language worthy of his rebellion. (p. 379)

His failures come most often when he relies on a strident exaggeration of language to express feelings that are unripe for expression, when he is confusedly intent. I think it can be said that his obscure poems are bad, and they are bad because he is in them affirming the values of his sensibility at the expense of his conviction. This is like the hope of most adolescent writers that personal feelings may be communicated with images whose connotations are not supported by the logic of the syntax. . . . There is still something else to be said, I think, about the insecurity of Cummings's language, and about his persistent crudeness next door to excellence. (pp. 380-82)

The punctuation Cummings employs often distracts and antagonizes readers, but at times it can be shown to serve a useful purpose. (p. 383)

At times his scheme certainly causes the reader to pay special attention to the sound of the words. But at other times it seems to provide a puzzle of such complexity that interest in the poem is lost for the sake of the puzzle. At times Cummings is merely thumbing his nose at convention and at the reader. Occasionally I think Cummings is making jokes, and I for one am amused, but then, some of these are threadbare jokes.

When this unorthodox punctuation is good, it is excellent. When it is less than that it is of doubtful value, for I think that ambiguity in these matters indicates a lack of interest in the poem by the poet himself. The punctuation is worked out in terms of a word or phrase, or two or three phrases, and almost never is there a logic to it which supports the meaning of the whole poem. (The Buffalo Bill poem, as an exception, is a very short poem.) Very often those poems in which the punctuation is most complicated are poems which fall apart, which are without unity of meaning. And conversely, those poems which are sustained and unified are most simply punctuated. In general, I think, his unorthodox punctuation is most successful when it leaves out signs. It is most often unsuccessful when it elaborates on the conventional scheme by amplification.

However obscure Cummings's language may become at times and however absurd his typography, it is clear that he is an intelligent poet. He is not interested in intellectual subtleties as Eliot and MacLeish are, and on the other hand he does not belong to the cult of unintelligibility. Actually his intellectual position is respectable and rather coherently maintained. He is a Platonist, absorbed in the discipline of contemplation and devoted to the perception of being. Existence means more to him than action. The highest praise he can give to people is to say they are; the Zulu Is. That which is alive in the truth, and is capable of growth and fulfillment, Is. (pp. 387-88)

In [his latest] poems I find a firmness and strength which is new to Cummings. All along he has maintained his knowledge of the invaluable worth of the individual . . . , and some of his limitations of belief have hindered him from social comment. But now I think he more clearly understands the nature of the rebellion he has been waging; it is clearer to him, and his experience can be put to wiser use. . . . His imagery and his thought are more frequently informed with Christian doctrine. I do not believe Cummings yet has a fully reasoned philosophy, but it is evident that he is now able to express more serious convictions by virtue of greater sympathy with Christianity. The judgments in the recent poems are not perhaps profound, but they are never foolish. They are responsible judgments. He is now more sure that he belongs to the world of all of us. This, I think, is growth, and provides a means whereby Cummings may now avoid errors he once made, and develop more fully what was originally sound in his perceptions. As from the beginning he has given us things of immeasurable worth, so I think he will continue to increasingly.

He should not be allowed to fall from sight, or to be remembered only as one of the wild experimenters who came along after the last war. For he represents even now, in a more terrible war, something that is valid and sweet in the human spirit, and something profound and strong—in short, beauty. (pp. 389-90)

John Arthos, "The Poetry of E. E. Cummings," in *American Literature,* Vol. 14, January, 1943, pp. 372-90.

JAMES DICKEY

(essay date 1959)

[Dickey is a prominent American poet and critic. In the following excerpt from an essay originally published in 1959, he emphasizes the individuality of Cummings's style.]

[I] think that Cummings is a daringly original poet, with more virility and more sheer, uncompromising talent than any other living American writer. I cannot and would not want to deny, either, that he dilutes even the finest of his work with writing that is hardly more than the defiant playing of a child, though the fact that he does this with the superb arrogance of genius has always seemed to me among the most attractive of his qualities. I love Cummings's verse, even a great deal of it that is not lovable or even respectable, but it is also true that I am frequently and thoroughly

bored by its continuous attitudinizing and its dogmatic preaching. I have often felt that there must be something hiddenly wrong with his cult of spontaneity and individuality, that these attributes have to be insisted upon to the extent to which Cummings insists on them. I feel, also, that "love" and the other well-known emotions that Cummings tirelessly espouses are being imposed on me categorically, and that I stand in some danger of being shot if I do not, just at that moment, wish to love someone or pick a rose or lean against a tree watching the snowflakes come down. . . .

Cummings has felt the need, and followed it, of developing absolutely in his own way, of keeping himself and his writing whole, preferring to harbor his most grievous and obvious faults quite as if they were part and parcel of his most original and valuable impulses which perhaps they are. . . . His excesses are, most certainly, enormous, as one feels they should be in a genuine poet. Cummings is without question one of the most insistent and occasionally one of the most successful users of pathetic fallacy in the history of the written word. He is one of the most blatant sentimentalists, one of the most absurdly and grandly overemotional of poets, one of the flimsiest thinkers, and one of the truly irreplaceable sensibilities that we have known, with the blind, irresistible devotion to his exact perceptions, to *his* way of knowing and doing, and to his personal and incorruptible relation to the English language that an authentic poet must have. Immediacy and intensity are Cummings's twin gods. . . . Whether or not successful in every instance, all of Cummings's skill, so special to himself that we cannot imagine anyone else making use of it, has gone to establish and consecrate the *moments*. . . .

He is so strongly of a piece that the commentator feels ashamed and even a little guilty in picking out flaws, as though he were asked to call attention to the aesthetic defects in a rose. It is better to say what must finally be said about Cummings: that he has helped to give life to the language. . . . Cummings belongs in the class of poets who have done this, not by virtue of his tinkering with typography, but because of his superior insight into the fleeting and external moments of existence: not because of words broken up into syllables and strewn carefully about the page, but because of right words with other right words. . . .

James Dickey, "E. E. Cummings (1959)," in his *Babel to Byzantium,* Farrar, Straus and Giroux, 1968, pp. 100-06.

RUSHWORTH M. KIDDER
(essay date 1979)

[In the following excerpt, Kidder surveys Cummings's poetic career, focusing on the development of his themes and style.]

It is important to recognize . . . that the spatial arrangements of [Cummings'] poems are the work neither of a whimsical fancy nor a lust for novelty. Poetry and visual art grew, in Cummings' mind, from one root; and while their outermost branches are distinct enough, there are many places closer to the trunk where it is hard to know which impulse accounts for a piece of work. Throughout his life he labored to articulate, in his essays and especially in his unpublished notes and journals, the relationship between literature and the visual arts. A number of his poems, too, deal verbally with visual ideas—not only with transcriptions of visual patterns (a common enough phenomenon in poetry) but with attempts to articulate visual thinking and bring into poetry the aesthetic principles of the painters.

The portrait that gives us the man in the round, then, must include proper emphasis on Cummings as a man of feeling and as a man of visual responsiveness. But it must do more. Primarily and essentially it must also portray him as a man of thought. For underneath the antirational guise, which delights or disgusts readers according as they see in it the purely childlike or the merely immature, lies a core of knowledge and a capacity for abstract and analytic thought strongly buttressed by something that can only be called scholarship. (pp. 3-4)

[Cummings gives a strong place] to feeling: to intuition, to the sensibilities, to the human capacity for responding to metaphysical reality in ways that are beyond the rational. . . . [But Cummings also possessed a] lively sense of the dangers inherent in the antirational. These are the sort of dangers that surface when what Eliot called "the general mess of imprecision of feeling" and the "Undisciplined squads of emotion" find expression in forms that are commonplace and sentimentalizing. The fact is that Cummings uses logic, thought, and a great deal of calculated skill in writing poems which assert that feeling is first. Surely there is a paradox worth investigating here. And surely the investigation must consist of a close and thorough reading of individual poems—word by word, syllable by syllable, and in many cases letter by letter. Such a reading recognizes that there is much that cannot be grasped by limiting our study to syntax and semantics alone. But it also recognizes that we can only touch the substance of the poet's feeling by beginning with the structure of his thought as it appears in the arrangement of his words. That arrangement is all a poem gives us to look at; we cannot reach through to feeling by ignoring structure. (pp. 7-8)

To make such a choice is not to affirm, however, that Cummings is to be seen only as an intellectual. His importance lies in the skillful combination of feeling and intelligence in his work. Always laboring to be as articulate as possible, he nevertheless refused to allow the thrust toward articulation to sweep aside the delicate moments of feeling. (p. 9)

One other detail needs to be added to the portrait here. Cummings wrote—it will not do to mince words—some bad poetry. Moreover, he occasionally published it. The same is true in his painting. He seemed unwilling to consider the wastebasket his ally. Perhaps he was not a sound critic of his own work—which may mean no more than that he could not take the proper distance on it. . . . The task for the reader, then, is one of sorting. If he is willing to trust his own discriminations, and if he is willing to read carefully, he need not be put off by the occasional inferior piece as he locates and appreciates the many excellent ones, nor need he labor to defend the indefensible. (pp. 9-10)

Tulips and Chimneys (1923), Cummings' first collection, gathered together only some of his many early poems. (p. 16)

[His choice of title] suggests a number of oppositions: the country to the city, the organic to the lifeless, the natural to the manmade, and the beautiful to the ugly, as well as (in shape) the female to the male and (in the pun on *tulips* and the waste-disposing function of chimneys) the oral to the anal. It may well suggest, too, the essential division in the book: the section headed "Chimneys" comprises only sonnets, while "Tulips" includes a good deal of free verse.

Beyond this major division, *Tulips and Chimneys* is further segmented into fourteen sequences, each containing from one to ten poems. Cummings' interest in conjoining short individual poems into larger sequences persists throughout his career; his practice of identifying these sequences by separate titles, however, continues only through *is 5* (1926). . . . His interest in these patterns is nevertheless instructive. Always fascinated by the happy accidents of individual words—the puns, the multiple meanings, the words-within-words—he was also fascinated by the ways in which whole poems, since they always appeared to a reader within a context, inevitably and somewhat accidentally interacted with that context. In his collections of poems, sequence determined context and provided a means for making larger statements. A thoughtful examination of his sequences reveals that Cummings had much more to say than could be said in individual short poems.

It is equally clear, too, that Cummings' talent did not run to long poems. *Tulips and Chimneys* begins with **"Epithalamion,"** an extended poem as traditional in its structure as it is classical in its reference. Here Cummings . . . proves his mastery of the poet's traditional domain of rhyme, rhythm, metaphor, assonance, consonance, and a host of other literary devices listed in most handbooks of prosody. Here, too, he tactfully opens his assault on the conventions of poetry with an uncontroversial overture, saving the shock and dazzle for later. (pp. 17-18)

For all its propriety, the poem is nevertheless a kind of cold frame for Cummings' later style. The overt subject (praise of sensual delight) and the metaphor (spring) will grow up to become Cummings' favorites; even the suggestion in the final lines that this is a poem about poetry has parallels in numerous later pieces. (p. 19)

"Tulips" gathered together a rather broad cross-section of Cummings' early work. . . . "Chimneys," however, is a tightly composed work. The seventeen sonnets, most having something to do with love, are divided into three groups: "Sonnets—Realities," "Sonnets—Unrealities," and "Sonnets—Actualities." (pp. 31-2)

The best of ["Sonnets—Realities"] . . . is the first, **"the Cambridge ladies who live in furnished souls."** "Cambridge," here, is a word charged with significance. Having grown up under the shadow of Harvard, Cummings knew well the kind of old New England intellectual strain represented by these arbiters of social life. Apparently espousing the liberal humanitarian causes, they remain rigidly conservative. . . . [The] poem is essentially about the failure to make distinctions between the significant and the trivial. (p. 32)

The next sequence, "Sonnets—Unrealities," comments on the idealized and sentimentalized aspects of love. It moves toward the metaphysics of its concluding poem (**("a connotation of infinity"** . . .), which anticipates Cummings' later transcendent bent so well that it seems oddly out of place in this early work. . . .

"Sonnets—Actualities" is a sequence which, ostensibly praising love and the lover, is really rather acidulous. To speak of a kiss in so anatomical a phrase as "the little pushings of the flesh" . . . , and to speak of love as "building a building" . . . where, in a kind of dungeon, the lover's "surrounded smile / hangs / breathless," is surely to treat the lover with more mockery than affection. (p. 34)

Early in 1925 the remainder of the poems from the original *Tulips and Chimneys* manuscript were published in two volumes, *&* and *XLI Poems*. . . .

XLI Poems is [as described by Cummings] "harmless"—a charming, if slightly effete, collection. While it indulges in some experimental word disruptions and typographical oddities, it presents none of the extraordinary curiosities of **&**. . . . (p. 36)

The other 1925 volume, *&*, spells its title in the names of its three sections: "A," "N," and "D." . . .

[While] it is not entirely accurate to classify the poems in **&** as either new, prurient, or poor, it is apparent that the sensual poems are among the liveliest here. If the overall tone of *XLI Poems* tended to pale into polite comment, the tone of **&** errs on the side of ribaldry: neither had the other for balance.

Essential to the interpretation of many of these poems, especially those in "Sonnets—Actualities," is a recognition of the importance of Cummings' dedication of the volume [to Elaine Orr]. (p. 44)

The first fourteen poems [in **&**], comprising the "Post-Impressions" sequence, have no convenient common denominator. Some are clearly impressions of scenes; some seem more like portraits; and some are love poems or meditations. They are difficult poems from the outset. . . . (p. 46)

The twelve poems in "Portraits" suggest what later volumes will make clearer: Cummings rarely wrote about sexual relationships in a wholly approving manner. While most of these poems are explicitly sensual, none is in any way a love poem or a poem of praise. He seems to have glimpsed rather vividly the death's-head at the feast of the flesh: even those poems ostensibly celebrating sensual endeavors frequently employ an imagery and diction that undercuts the praise. (p. 48)

In respite from the prevailing sensuality, two of the best poems in the sequence take up quite different topics. The portrait of the barroom pianist (**"ta"** . . .) is in subject simply a quick imagist impression. Once the fractured words are reassembled, it reads: "tapping toe—hippopotamus Back—genteelly lugubrious eyes LOOP-THE-LOOP as fat hands bang rag." But the poem no more appears through such paraphrase than a Cubist portrait can be approximated by a photograph of the sitter: the effect is less in subject than in execution. A poem about rag, it captures the dislocations of jazz in its first stanza:

ta
ppin
g
toe.

(pp. 50-1)

The individual sonnets in the "D" section of *&* generally require little explication. The larger statements they make, however, deserve analysis. The two sequences in the section, "Sonnets—Realities" and "Sonnets—Actualities," are, superficially, of opposing

Hyatt H. Waggoner on Cummings's critical reception:

Cummings' poetry is romantic, intuitive in precept and in method, and rhetorical as opposed to Imagist-Modernist. It is essentially a "poetry of statement," as Wordsworth's was and as Emerson's was—but very complex, personal, ambiguous, and dense statement, at its best, statement which challenges the reader to complete it by first participating in the making of it and then carrying it on in himself, as his own, the gift to his self of another self. New Critical techniques of analysis do not work with such verse. There is nothing that literary positivism can get hold of—just Emersonian "Primary intuitions" and despised rhetoric to help their transfer. No wonder all the New Critics ignored Cummings for thirty years, except Blackmur, who damned him for not writing the way Ransom and Eliot had taught poets to write, for using general instead of specific words, for being, in short, a "Romantic" poet instead of a Modernist.

Hyatt H. Waggoner, in his 1968 study *American Poets from the Puritans to the Present.*

tones and attitudes. . . . "Sonnets—Realities" are, for the most part, poems of plain venery, withholding no detail of the sexual act; and they are so intentionally gross as to repulse the reader by their very surfeit of sensuality. (p. 55)

"Sonnets—Actualities" is no less explicit about sexual relations. But the blatant repugnance toward the act is lessened. These are more meditative sonnets, poems about "i" and about "my love" which are less patently ironic in their praise. The imagery, nevertheless, casts a peculiar pall over the subject of love. Buried in the most apparently complimentary catalogues of the lover's attributes are images surprising for their animality or . . . notable for their unfeeling hardness. (p. 56)

The fact that the vast bulk of his sensual poetry in these years blended the sexual with the repulsive suggests that his attitudes were far more complex than they are usually taken to be. A careful assessment of the imagery in these early poems reinforces the conviction that, while they are obscene, ironic, and often very witty, they are hardly to be written off as the graffiti of a goatish mind. To misread them and view Cummings as a youth unashamedly mesmerized by eroticism is to convict him of a tastelessness and an immaturity which neither his age—he was thirty when **&** was published—nor the genuinely affectionate tone of his letters at this time can support. It is also to erect formidable barriers to an understanding of his later development toward a transcendence that moved him leagues beyond the worship of unrelieved physicali-

ty—because such a misreading posits a personality that changed rather suddenly from prurience to refinement. In an odd and inverted way, these poems are pleas for purity and balance, stifled cries for a higher vision of human love coming out of a wilderness of sensual indulgence. Much as his diatribes against conformity reinforce his celebrations of individuality, these assertions that flesh is at worst gross and at best slightly unsatisfactory prepare the way of his later metaphysic: to show the repulsiveness of carnality is to prove the need for its opposite. For even in his most sensual early work, the seeds of his mature ethic were planted—sometimes too deep, and sometimes upside down, but planted nonetheless. (pp. 58-9)

[Cummings' forward to *is 5*] addresses itself to "my theory of technique." Comparing his art to that of burlesque, he observes that he is "abnormally fond of that precision which creates movement," and notes that the poet is "somebody to whom things made matter very little—somebody who is obsessed by Making." Here, too, he confesses his "Ineluctable preoccupation with The Verb." Behind these statements lies his concern for the active and living over the fixed and inert. . . . (p. 60)

The ramifications of his "theory of technique" show up in *is 5* somewhat more clearly than in his earlier volumes. Here, as Norman Friedman says [in his *E. E. Cummings: The Growth of a Writer*], "there is an organic relation between the poet's technique and his purposes." Noting that the satirical vein is mined to a new depth in *is 5*, Friedman also observes that "in general Cummings uses metrical stanzas for his more 'serious' poems, and reserves his experiments by and large for his free verse embodiments of satire, comedy, and description. Parody, pun, slang, and typographical distortion are called into being by the urgencies of the satirical mode, which requires the dramatic rendition of scorn, wit, and ridicule. Violence in the meaning: violence in the style." The poetry may, as Friedman points out, have taken some flavor from Cummings' concurrent prose writings: he had published a number of satires in *Vanity Fair* during the eighteen months preceding the publication of this volume. The requirements of writing for that monthly, noted for its debunking manner, had quite naturally sharpened the satirical edge of Cummings' style. (pp. 60-1)

[Cummings] discovered in *is 5* a voice distinctly his own. The freshness of that discovery informs these poems. . . .

Satire enters forcefully in "One," the first of the five sequences in the volume. Earlier poems, taking their tone from Eliot and the Ash Can painters, had been content to present physical degradation with neither praise nor blame; these poems do not hesitate to condemn, in unmistakable terms, physical and moral corruption. They are generally more complex and thoughtful poems than the earlier ones: the same verve and élan characterize the language, but the thought behind them now extends into various dimensions. Here, more regularly than before, we are reminded that the poet is at work trying to sort out and articulate the tremendous diversity of responses facing him. (p. 62)

War and its effects are the subjects of the ten poems in the next sequence, "Two." The first (**"the season 'tis, my lovely lambs"**) begins with a fine sarcasm on topical allusions. . . . Cummings' objection here is not so much to the specifics of [social control of vice] . . . (although he inalterably opposed literary censorship and prohibition) as to the progressive interference by government in the lives of individuals. (p. 71)

The poems in the next sequence, "Three," are interrelated by their interest in distinctly European scenes and by their references to sunsets or sunlight. Each is in some way a meditation on the significance of a natural scene. (p. 73)

The last three poems in "Three," in which the narrator questions the nature of existence and moves toward a tentative resolution, also form something of a set. Poem V asks searching questions about why the poet is where he is. In poem VI (**"but observe; although"**) he considers the difference between an inner and an outer life. . . . The final poem (**"sunlight was over"** . . .) sees in sexual consummation a kind of resolution: bright sunlight turning to sunset, two lovers becoming one, and "what had been something / else carefully slowly fatally turning into ourselves." These two last poems strike a significantly new note: without being sonnets, they praise sexual love with little of the undercutting so noticeable in **&.** In this way, they provide a fitting introduction to the fourth sequence.

The eighteen poems in "Four," a well-knit cycle of love poems, come into clearest focus when seen through the lens of Cummings' relationship with Elaine Orr, his former wife. They form a loose progression in subject (innocence through sexual experience and on to separation) and in imagery (night through daylight and on into evening). . . . (pp. 74-5)

In **"since feeling is first"** ("Four" . . .), Cummings brings to ripeness the ironic *carpe diem* mode in one of his surest pieces. Taking grammar as his metaphor, the poet notes that those who pay attention only to "the syntax of things"—the logic, the intellectual aspects of experience—can never involve themselves so thoroughly in love as to "wholly kiss you." (p. 76)

The last poems in the sequence [are] perhaps too full of sentiment to convey real feeling. . . . Taking themselves a little too seriously, they have neither the distancing self-awareness nor the grandeur of vision that inform his better poems. They are interesting confessional statements for the biographer; but even their

convolutions of syntax and surprises of diction cannot overcome their somewhat softboiled moistness.

By contrast, the five sonnets composing the last sequence, "Five," are less mawkish and more resolved. (pp. 78-9)

The final poem in the volume, **"if i have made, my lady, intricate,"** shows Cummings at his finest. Although written before his divorce from Elaine, it takes on an added poignancy by its placement at the end of a book dealing so centrally with that separation. Tinged with regret, it becomes a gallant valediction to a lady no longer his. Yet as an ending to the volume it provides resolution: it is, after all, a poem about poetry, a poem which redeems his experience by transforming it into art. (pp. 80-1)

Even in such a poem, however, the underlying irony is apparent. I cannot write poems of praise, says the poet, who, saying so, manages to write one of the finest poems of praise in the century. And if the poem seems less than that, it is perhaps because of the success enjoyed by certain of its devices in more recent verse. The technique behind such phrases as "the ragged meadow of my soul"—the coupling of a concrete substantive with a modifying phrase containing an abstraction—has become the staple of current songwriters, and our sense of the purity of this poem may be a little jaded by jukebox verse built on such lines as "the bright illusive butterfly of love" and a hundred similar phrases. (p. 82)

[The topics of the poems in *ViVa*] are characteristic: there are love poems, portraits, impressions, low-life sketches, and a generous helping of satires. The collection was similar enough to his earlier volumes that William Carlos Williams dismissed it as "definitely an aftermath" and objected that Cummings sounded too much like Cummings, that he "reminds one very much of him." (p. 84)

ViVa reveals, in fact, a great deal more patterning than at first appears. . . . The design he builds into the second half reflects his tribute to the individual, and the lack of cohesion (indeed, even of coherence at times) in the first half manifests his low estimate of man as a social animal. (pp. 84-5)

The literary community in which Cummings lived in the early thirties had, almost to a man, sworn allegiance to socialism. . . . [It] had expended too much of its own rancor in denouncing capitalism to listen openmindedly to alternatives. Into this context came *Eimi,* Cummings' account of his thirty-six-day trip to the Soviet Union. There, for those willing to unravel its remarkable prose, was a report of the grim inhumanities of the Soviet system, of repression, apathy, priggishness, kitsch, and ennervating suspicion.

Shortly after its appearance there came, to various publishing houses, a manuscript of poems by its author. The rejections that followed could hardly have been based on quality alone. *No Thanks* is no less competent a collection than *ViVa*. It makes more progress toward experimental forms; but it provides nothing so radically different nor indefensibly bad as to justify rejection on merit. It is, in many ways, standard Cummings: the age, not the man, had changed.

Like *ViVa*, *No Thanks* [printed privately in 1935] is designed on a numerological pattern, with sonnets occurring at regular intervals. . . . There is . . . a general thematic development throughout the volume, which progresses in the first half downward toward the poems of defeat at its center, and thereafter moves upward into more transcendent ideas. (pp. 105-06)

Collected Poems [1938] begins with an introduction, a prose statement akin to but much more extensive than the one introducing *is 5*. Here he identifies his villains, the "most-people" who prefer inertia to activity. Describing them, he happens upon a word for their essential attribute—"passivity." The metaphor characterizing their behavior is of the womb. What "most-people" want is "a guaranteed birth-proof safetysuit"; what they fear most is being born. For "ourselves," on the other hand, "birth is a supremely welcome mystery," and "We can never be born enough." The entire introduction is built on this opposition—as, indeed, are many of his poems. Apart from the diction (which is his own particular invention) and the sometimes pretentious or condescending tone (which is his own occasional failing), the piece has an odd flavor of the pulpit. . . . The introduction builds to its culmination in reaffirming the poet's commitment "never to rest and never to have: only to grow." And it ends with an ambiguity worthy of his poems—"Always the beautiful answer who asks a more beautiful question"—a sentence which means both "[there is] always the beautiful answer [for him] who asks a more beautiful question" and "the beautiful [people, ideas] always answer [the person] who asks a more beautiful question." (pp. 125-26)

Unlike the bulk of his contemporaries in the arts, [Cummings] never saw in government subsidies an answer to his [financial] problems, but felt instead that the preservation of individuality and the acceptance of New Deal handouts were irreconcilably opposed. This opposition is the burden of *50 Poems* (1940), which contains some of his best-known poems praising individuality and condemning the state: **"as freedom is a breakfast-food," "the way to hump a cow is not," "anyone lived in a pretty how town,"** and **"my father moved through dooms of love."** (p. 134)

[The justly famous poem] **"my father moved through dooms of love"**—presents a figure expressly heroic. Like **"anyone lived,"** it too is introduced by a poem (**"one slip-slouch twi"** . . .) which anticipates some of its themes and prepares the way. (p. 146)

The world, in **"my father moved through dooms of love"** . . . , needs redemption: it is a place of "scheming" and "passion," of stealing, cruelty, fear, and doubt, and of "maggoty minus and dumb death." Unlike some of Cummings' poems, however, this one emphasizes not primarily this corruption but the nature of the individual who redeems it. And unlike other poems, this one presents an individual who finds answers not in transcendent escape but in direct engagement and correction of the world's wrong. It is a poem about love. But like the Gospels—in which the word "love" appears with surprising infrequency—the poem does not so much explain as demonstrate. Defining the attributes of love not in exposition but through narrative, it echoes the technique of the Gospel writers by showing how love is exemplified in the works of a single man. Fittingly, the word "love" occurs only twice in the poem—in the first and last lines.

Commentators have generally assumed that the poem is biographical. . . . Certainly the poem describes in some ways the Reverend Edward Cummings. Essentially, however, it describes qualities of feeling and habits of mind which have fathered Cummings' own mental set. Not simply recording the ideals of a real man, the poet chooses to embody his own highest ideals in a fictionalized character, describe him in action, and claim a sonship with him which makes clear his own intellectual and spiritual heritage. (pp. 147-48)

Where some of Cummings' poems are aggressively complex and others patently simple, this one erects a smooth facade which, significant in itself, reverberates inside with more profound meaning. Apparently simple, it nevertheless rewards close reading. (p. 149)

Most of the remaining poems develop themes raised in **"my father moved through dooms of love"**: individuality, love, and redemption from the world's assertive evils. (pp. 150-51)

With the publication of *1 x 1* in 1944, Cummings' format returns to the explicit divisions that marked his first four books of poetry. The fifty-four poems in this volume are grouped into three sections, titled "1," "X," and "1," and arranged in progressive seasonal imagery. (p. 154)

While using this seasonal framework as a strategy for organization, Cummings was not enslaved by it: several poems in the second section (**"dead every enormous piece"** and **"when god decided to invent"** come to mind) seem equally at home among the satires in the first section. Generally, however, the sense of direction here is more evident than in earlier volumes, which either had no obvious structural scheme (as in *50 Poems*) or a pattern of recurrent sonnets (as in *ViVa* and *No Thanks*) sometimes more ingenious than helpful. The volume demonstrates that Cummings, having outgrown the simpler divisions ("Post Impressions," "Portraits," "Sonnets—Realities," and so forth) in the original manuscript of *Tulips and Chimneys,* now focuses his discernment more finely. (p. 155)

Behind these poems lies Cummings' evident interest in arithmetic significance. Throughout his work he pays great attention to numbers, letting them determine the formats of some of his volumes and founding some of the poems on a strict counting of lines and even, at times, of syllables. This volume, in fact—the work of a poet generally thought of as rebelling against the restraint of reason—includes no completely free verse. Even poems whose lines appear most casual—**"a-,"** for example, or **"ygUDuh"**—are arranged in stanzas. It is perhaps this achievement of design in matters large and small which leads Friedman to assess *1 x 1* as "a distinctively crystallized book, both in art and in vision—a highly-wrought and mature achievement." Where the earlier Cummings was satisfied by gathering poems into selfcontained sections, the poet here interweaves the sections themselves, anticipates and recalls their images, and appears to conceive of the volume less as a bricked accretion than as a fluid whole. (p. 156)

The final poem [of *1 x 1*] (**"if everything happens that can't be done"** . . .) restores the lyric to its predominant position. Natural process, whereby things simply "happen," asserts itself over the human "doing" of things. If miracles arise, that only proves that the lovers are "one times one." Each of the five stanzas puts down "books" as it sets up experience: not unlike the Wordsworth of "Up, up, my friend, and quit your books," the poet here notes that "anything's righter / than books / could plan." The irony, of course, is that he says so in a book; but a deeper irony may be directed at the reader who fails to notice that this is the last poem before the book quits. Having come through poems of autumn, winter, and spring, through satires, meditations, and lyrics, the poet closes the book and sings the praises of the world beyond books, the summer itself where life is not for reading but for living. The deepest irony of all, however, is that even this exhortation to plunge into experience is made through words. Our very capacity to experience life, after all, is conditioned by the language through which we come to terms with life. And if we have in any way absorbed Cummings' poems, we are to that extent incapable of putting aside the book: some part of us will see experience through his insights. The "we" in this poem, then, refers not only to the lovers. It may also stand for the reader and the poet, "one times one" in their common outlook. (pp. 173-74)

[*Xaipe,* a Greek word meaning "rejoice" or "greetings," is the title of Cummings' next volume of verse, published in 1950. It is an appropriate title], for the book registers a decrease in poems that scorn and satirize and a corresponding increase in poems of praise. Here, for the first time, is the Cummings who writes of the religious and transcendent not as an antidote to the evil of the world but because it alone is coming to seem the most real. The change in emphasis affects his choice of subjects. Of the seventy-one poems, only one addresses itself directly to the "infinite jukethrob" of seamy city life. The values and images of country life are increasingly attractive to the poet. . . . (p. 175)

One of Cummings' best-known sonnets, **"i thank You God for most this amazing"** . . . , is good enough that one wishes it were better. Revealing itself cleanly on a single reading, it has been dismissed, in Robert Graves' words, as "intrinsically corny." A religious poem, it has neither the vibrant intellectuality of Hopkins, the cool ambiguity of Eliot, nor the resonance of Thomas. It depends, especially in the third stanza, on assertion rather than demonstration, and is finally a bit too facile. Nevertheless, it has some very good moments. The first line, for example, makes excellent use of the transposed adverb. We expect "most" to modify either "thank you" ("i thank you most, God") or "amazing" ("for this most amazing day"). Splitting the difference, Cummings places the word in a position where it does double duty. And the progression in the fourth line—"everything / which is natural which is infinite which is yes"—crescendoes toward abstraction, affirmation, and simplicity all at once. Perhaps for Cummings it is what "And death shall have no dominion" was for Thomas: a statement of faith that is too clear, too simplified, and hence too dishonest. In any case, it stands as a significant marker in the path of Cummings' development of transcendental and religious themes. (pp. 193-94)

95 Poems (1958), Cummings' longest volume, brings together eight years' work. Earlier volumes had come more frequently, never more than six years apart. Here, as he exercises more patience, he expresses a quieter and more meditative outlook. Turning his attention largely to things held in high regard (Joy Farm, Washington Square Park in the rain, the less physical aspects of love), he does not shrink from those things—the cosmeticized mother, the apathetic reader, the bickering housewife—which deserve ridicule. But it is to Horace rather than Juvenal that the few satires here owe their allegiance: only **"THANKSGIVING (1956)"** recalls the rancor of earlier years. . . . It is a volume full of praise for human goodness and wonder at nature's marvels.

As such, it is Cummings' most risky volume. Praise, as a glance at the best of modern literature attests, does not come easily to our age. (p. 197)

Yet Cummings, after years of practice at distinguishing the merely sentimental from the genuinely affirmative, the "pansy heaven" from the "heaven of blackred roses" . . . , had learned his balance well. Refusing to give over his skills at organization, his ear for nuance, and his fertile metaphoric imagination, he welded this book into a collection which helps demonstrate Robert Creeley's proposition that "FORM IS NEVER MORE THAN AN EXPRESSION OF CONTENT." Here, it seems, is proof that a poet can refuse conformity to the "poetical" subject matter favored by his age and still attain a high standard of craftsmanship. (p. 198)

Cummings' last volume was published the year after his death in New Hampshire on September 2, 1962. Like earlier volumes, *73 Poems* intermixes new work with poems previously published in periodicals. Unlike earlier volumes, the contents were not arranged by Cummings but by his bibliographer, George Firmage. (p. 219)

While nothing of Cummings' intentions can be deduced from the sequence, the volume does mark a certain progress beyond *95 Poems.* Although it levels its share of satiric darts—at "mrs somethingwitz / nay somethingelsestein" . . . , at the "fearlessandbosomy . . . / gal" of eighty . . . , and even at Aphrodite, Hephaestus, and Ares . . .—these pieces tend to be soft at the tip, written less in biting anger than bemused aversion. The world, with its "Mostpeople" who scream for "international / measures that render hell rational" . . . , is still a "sub / human superstate" . . . descending on "the path to nothingness." . . . But that world, for Cummings, is no longer too much with us: he looks with increasing serenity at a better one. (pp. 219-20)

As conviction increased, so did limpidity. Syntax here is less demanding, vocabulary less challenging, and words are less often fragmented than in earlier volumes. There is a growing proportion of extremely short poems, poems with no more than thirty words and sometimes no more than ten. It is a simplicity born not of senility but of wisdom, a capacity for concise statement coupled with lyric evocation. Fittingly, a number of these poems recall earlier ones: Cummings in these years was of a mind, it seems, to reexamine his earlier successes. In many ways it is a poetry of triumph, marking the victory of the feeling he always preached over the thinking he struggled to refine. (p. 220)

The two last poems in the volume are, in very different ways, among the finest in the canon. The three pentameter lines of **"wild (at our first) beasts uttered human words"** . . . compress into twenty-four words a compendious history of the world. Ascending from "beasts" to "birds" and on into "stars," the images move progressively upward and away from earth. In the beginning, says the poet, we were children uttering strangely wordlike sounds. In maturity our presence made "stones sing like birds"—made the inanimate universe take on the qualities of animation, joyousness, and freedom. Cummings, again, implies that the things

of the world—stones, in this case—have no expressive qualities of their own. Hence they have no meanings until given them by the user of language who, like the banished duke in *As You Like It*, finds "sermons in stones." The first two lines, then, account for human life; but the poem has a third line, moving on to considerations of immortality. Where life for the early Cummings was a matter of birth, maturity, and decay, for the late Cummings it consists in birth, maturity, and transcendence. The "star-hushed silence" is our third state, an ascendent condition in which, words and songs quieted, the silence of a deeper communion prevails. This is the silence that appears at the end of "all which isn't singing is mere talking" . . . : there, "the very song . . . / of singing is silence," for as singing is superior to talking, so silence is the very essence of the power of song. (pp. 232-33)

As silence is the keenest quality of sound, so a vision of love is the sharpest focus of sight. And just as no human ear will be adequate to the first, so mere worldly seeing will not encompass the second. That is the message of the last poem, **all worlds have halfsight, seeing either with."** . . . For Cummings, "worlds" are limited and loveless places inhabited by mostpeople and utterly without grace. Worlds are places made not by fact but by consent, not by matter, society, or time but simply by belief. Seen for what it is, the world can be rendered harmless. . . . (p. 234)

This sort of poem demands a reading in context. Isolated from the slowly developing themes that progress through Cummings' earlier poetry, it appears somewhat plain. But in that context there are very few words used here that do not come to this poem charged with significance. The idea of halves versus wholes, the distinction between the seeming and the real, the words "steep," "beauty," "truth," "timelessly," and "merciful," derive their impact from use in numerous prior poems; each draws sustenance and originality from the accretion of definition built up throughout Cummings' entire career. Most notable is the word "love." If Cummings has one subject, that is it. It begins in *Tulips and Chimneys* as an echo of popularly romantic notions, and it grows in early volumes to a sometimes amorphous phenomenon seasoned by a not entirely unselfish lust. By these last poems, however, it has come to be a purified and radiant idea, unentangled with flesh and worlds, the agent of the highest transcendence. It is not far, as poem after poem has hinted, from the Christian conception of love as God. It is this sense of God that Cummings' poems of praise have celebrated, this sense that his satires have sought to protect. It is this sense that Cummings, whose entire body of work is finally an image of himself, would have us see as the source of his own being. (pp. 235-36)

Rushworth M. Kidder, in his *E. E. Cummings: An Introduction to the Poetry,* Columbia University Press, 1979, 275 p.

MILTON A. COHEN
(essay date 1983)

[In the following excerpt, Cohen examines the effect of Cummings's use of deliberately ambiguous language on the meaning and themes of his poetry.]

Of the many novel and disconcerting techniques that E. E. Cummings devised in his early poems, one of the most curious is his structuring of a phrase so that it can be read in two ways simultaneously. Consider this passage from the poem, **"the skinny voice."** A Salvation Army captain asks onlookers (including the speaker) to contribute another quarter to reach an even dollar,

> whereupon
>
> The Divine Average who was
>
> attracted by the inspired
> sister's howling moves
> off

Is the speaker, a Whitmanesque "Divine Average," attracted to the sister's "howling moves" or "howling"? Cummings intentionally suggests the first reading ("moves" as noun) by constructing "howling moves" as a phrase that closes the line. Then the adverbial "off" appears, claims "moves" as a verb, and leaves "howling" as the sole noun. This ambiguous shift in grammar temporarily upsets the reader's perceptions, as first one meaning, and then another, emerges. (p. 33)

[In] **"a blue woman . . ."** the ambiguity of the first two lines governs the entire poem:

> a blue woman with sticking out breasts hanging
> clothes. On the line, not so old
> for the mother of twelve undershirts (we are told
> by is it Bishop Taylor who needs hanging
>
> that marriage is a sure cure for masturbation).
>
> A dirty wind, twitches the, clothes which are
> clean
> —this is twilight,
> a little puppy hopping be-
> tween
> skipping
> children
> (It is the consummation
> of day, the hour) she says to me you big fool
> she says i says to her i says Sally
> i says
> the

mmmoon, begins to, drool

softly, in the hot alley,

a nigger's voice feels curiously cool
(suddenly-Lights go! on, by schedule

Until "clothes" appears, the woman has hanged *herself,* her face already blue from strangulation. This reading lingers as the poem reveals the hopelessness of her life: a young mother of twelve trapped by a church (in the metonomy of Bishop Taylor) with feudal ideas about sex, marriage, and birth control; stifled by deadening routines conveyed in the repetitive actions of hanging clothes, skipping rope, droning empty voices ("she says i says") and lights going on "by schedule." In this context of futility, "blue" acquires its colloquial meaning of "depressed."

The poem's thematic climax, "(It is the consummation / of day, the hour)" is therefore triply ironic, as it alludes to the fruits of the mother's sexual consummation, twelve children, to the *un*fulfillment of a life that consumes her and makes her "blue," and to the possibility of her ending it—consuming it—by suicide. The initial ambiguity controls the entire poem, concealing the woman's grim future, hanging, within her hopeless present, hanging clothes.

Technically, the ambiguity of "blue woman" results from the intermingling of two meanings on two consecutive lines without intervening punctuation. The same arrangement appears in **"i am a beggar always,"** only here the ambiguity is more evenly divided between the two readings and twists the poem's thematic direction from the middle of the narrative. In this bitter apostrophe, the speaker portrays himself as a blind beggar panhandling from his love "just enough dreams to live on" and "a little love preferably":

> then he will maybe (hearing something
> fall into his hat) go wandering
> after it with fingers; till having
>
> found
> what was thrown away
>   himself
> taptaptaps out of your brain, hopes, life
>
> to (carefully turning a
> corner) never bother you any more.

Perceptually and thematically, "himself" is the crux of the poem. Seen as a subject ("himself / taptaptaps out of your brain"), it continues the established theme. But seen as the referent of "what" ("what was thrown away / himself"), it provides the missing fact that explains the poem: the speaker has been jilted by his lover, metaphorically blinded, reduced to begging from her some scrap of their former love. What he finds in his hat is "himself," a self-discovery born of pain but strong enough to let him "turn. . . . a corner" and put the blighted affair behind him. Lacking punctuation to clarify its grammatical function, "himself " pivots both ways and imparts two meanings simultaneously.

These ambiguous constructions can generate new ideas, impossible if the motifs were completed by syntax and separated by punctuation:

A cat waiting for god knows makes me

wonder if i'm alive

Either "waiting for [something], god knows," or "waiting for God knows *what* " would fill out the phrase and separate the ideas. As is, "makes" attaches itself to "knows"—both are present-tense, singular, active verbs—and forms two new motifs: "god makes me" and "god makes me wonder if i'm alive."

Finally, Cummings may close a poem with an ambiguity, wrenching the thematic progression from its expected course and achieving an effect akin to a surprise ending in fiction. The conclusion of **"lis/-ten"** offers the homonym "no" in place of the expected "know":

lis

-ten

you know what i mean when
the first guy drops you know
everybody feels sick or
when they throw in a few gas
and the oh baby shrapnel
or my feet getting dim freezing or
up to your you know what in water or
with the bugs crawling right all up
all everywhere over you all me everyone
that's been there knows what
i mean a god damned lot of

people don't and never
never
will know,
they don't want

to

no

The ambiguous "no" suggests two related but distinct meanings at once. First, those who were not in the trenches cannot, and do not want to, "know" how terrible it was. And consequently, they refuse to say "no" to the political machinery that makes wars: the draft, the patriotic appeals, the national chauvinism and xenophobia. Concluding the poem, "no" gives a shock of the unexpected that forces the reader's attention to this thematic ambiguity.

While all of these ambiguities can be described as structural, it is important to recognize that they are primarily perceptual: they control the speed and manner in which a line is perceived. Typically, the reader perceives a thematic motif and expects its progression, only to have an ambiguous swing word lead to quite a different meaning. Momentarily thrown off by the unexpected turn, the reader must accommodate the new idea, either by reconciling it with the original, or by maintaining both in suspension, as it were. The result is often a balanced tension, as the competing themes struggle for dominance in the reader's eye and mind, with first one reading, and then the other, ascendent. Such a tension precludes a comfortable, monothematic reading and requires, instead, an unstable and shifting perception of a thematic complex. (pp. 33-5, 38)

Milton A. Cohen, "E. E. Cummings' Sleight-of-Hand: Perceptual Ambiguity in His Early Poetry, Painting, and Career," in *University of Hartford Studies in Literature*, Vol. 15, No. 1, 1983, pp. 33-5, 38-46.

SOURCES FOR FURTHER STUDY

Friedman, Norman. *E. E. Cummings: The Art of His Poetry.* Baltimore: Johns Hopkins University Press, 1960, 209 p.

Respected study of Cummings's oeuvre.

———, ed. *E. E. Cummings: A Collection of Critical Essays.* Englewood Cliffs, N. J.: Prentice-Hall, 1972, 185 p.

Collection of seminal critical essays on Cummings and his poetry.

Kennedy, Richard S. *Dreams in the Mirror: A Biography of E. E. Cummings.* New York: Liveright, 1980, 529 p.

Recent biography of Cummings.

Marks, Barry. *E. E. Cummings.* Minneapolis: University of Minnesota Press, 1969, 156 p.

Introductory overview of Cummings's works.

Rotella, Guy L. *E. E. Cummings: A Reference Guide.* Boston: G. K. Hall, 1979, 212 p.

Annotated bibliography of critical writings on Cummings from 1922 to 1977.

Wegner, Robert E. *The Poetry and Prose of E. E. Cummings.* New York: Harcourt, Brace, 1965, 177 p.

Detailed critical study of Cummings's work.

Robertson Davies

1913-

(Full name William Robertson Davies; has also written under pseudonym Samuel Marchbanks) Canadian novelist, essayist, dramatist, short story writer, editor, journalist, and critic.

INTRODUCTION

Davies's reputation as a leading figure in Canadian literature was firmly established by his novels *Fifth Business* (1970), *The Manticore* (1972), and *World of Wonders* (1975), collectively published as *The Deptford Trilogy* (1983). Like all of his fiction, these novels are densely plotted and display Davies's knowledge in a wide range of subjects. Davies often directs satirical humor towards Canadian provincialism, which he perceives as a hindrance to Canada's cultural development. While his novels are firmly rooted in realism and are presented in traditional forms, Davies introduces such elements as magic, supernatural events, and religious symbolism to underscore the mystery and wonder of life. His novels are infused with a Jungian sensibility that informs his characters' search for identity. Central to Davies's novels is his belief that a particular action may produce consequences of infinite possibility and irreversible effect. *The Deptford Trilogy*, for instance, is structured around the single act of a charactor throwing a snowball, an event that shapes the destiny of the trilogy's three protagonists.

Born in Thamesville, Ontario, Davies later moved to Renfrew, a small town in the Ottawa Valley, and then to Kingston, Ontario. These settings provide the backdrop for all of Davies's fiction. Influenced by his father, a newspaper publisher, and his mother, Davies cultivated an early interest in writing and dramatic pursuits. He attended Queen's University in Kingston from 1932 to 1935 and then enrolled in Balliol College, Oxford, England, where he became active in student theatre productions and contributed to university magazines. After graduating from Balliol in 1938 with a degree in literature, Davies remained in England and joined the Old Vic theatre troupe. Following his marriage in 1940, Davies returned to Canada and contributed to the liberal journal *Saturday Night* before assuming editorship of the *Peterborough Examiner* newspaper in 1942. Davies assumed the positions of vice-president and publisher of the *Examiner* in 1946 and served with the newspaper until 1962. During this time, he also helped found the Canadian Stratford Shakespearean Festival and was elected governor on its board of directors in 1953. In 1960 Davies began teaching English literature at Trinity College in Toronto, and in 1961 he was appointed first master at Massey College, a graduate school at the University of Toronto, where he taught until his retirement in 1981.

During his years with the *Peterborough Examiner,* Davies wrote many journalistic essays under the pen name Samuel Marchbanks. A curmudgeon who has been likened to Samuel Johnson and Canadian satirist Stephen Leacock, Marchbanks is often humorously excessive in his bitter attacks on such topics as Canadian politicians and social movements. These essays have been collected in *The Diary of Samuel Marchbanks* (1947), *The Table Talk of Samuel Marchbanks* (1949), and *Samuel Marchbanks' Almanack* (1967); portions of these collections were edited and republished in *The Papers of Samuel Marchbanks* (1985). During this period, Davies also wrote and directed numerous plays, among them *Overlaid* (1947) and *Fortune, My Foe* (1948). Involving such themes as the relationship between art and life and the consequences of repressed hopes, these works reflect Davies's interest in psychology and signal important ideas that are central to his fiction.

In the 1950s, Davies began writing novels, a genre for which he has received his greatest recognition. His first three novels, *Tempest-Tost* (1951), *Leaven of Malice* (1954), and *A Mixture of Frailties* (1958), comprise *The Salterton Trilogy* (1986), which examines life in a small Canadian university town. *Tempest-Tost* recounts the attempts of Salterton's amateur theater group to stage Shakespeare's *Tempest.* The company's ineptitude and churlish behavior are the source of much of the novel's humor and represent factors limiting Canada's cultural growth. The plot of *Leaven of Malice* revolves around the placement in Salterton's local newspaper of a false engagement announcement linking a young man and woman from rival families. The pretentiousness of the two families is satirically exposed as they go to great extremes to humiliate each other. Love triumphs, however, and the couple eventually marry. *A Mixture of Frailties* concerns a young Salterton woman who travels to Europe to train as a singer. Her development from a rustic small-town girl to a sophisticated woman reflects Davies's belief that education and experience are important elements for a complete life.

The *Salterton Trilogy* was followed by Davies's acclaimed *Deptford Trilogy* (1983). The novels in this trilogy focus on the individual's need to accept the irrational, unconscious side of the self in order to achieve completeness. The trilogy centers on the seemingly inconsequential incident of a thrown snowball that ultimately alters the lives of three men. In *Fifth Business* (1970)—the first of the three novels—Dunstan Ramsey, who dodged the snowball, suffers remorse and guilt because the snowball that missed him struck a pregnant woman. He attempts to rationalize the experience through an interest in saints, magic, and psychology. *The Manticore* (1972) recounts the psychoanalysis of David Staunton, the son of the boy who threw the snowball. In this novel, Davies employs Jungian archetypes and ancient myths to unravel the mysteries of the subconscious which contribute to Staunton's self-awareness. *World of Wonders* (1975) is the story of Paul Dempster, whose mother was hit by the snowball, causing his premature birth and her mental breakdown. Dempster's life is shaped by magic and illusion after he is kidnapped as a child by a carnival magician and eventually becomes the world-famous prestidigitator, Magnus Eisengrim. The dominant themes displayed in these novels reflect Davies's concern with the individual's quest for identity and the moral necessity to examine all facets of life. Of *The Deptford Trilogy,* Claude Bissell declared: "These novels comprise the major piece of prose fiction in Canadian literature—in scope, in the constant interplay of wit and intelligence, in the persistent attempt to find a pattern in this 'life of marvels, cruel circumstances, obscenities, and commonplaces.' "

Davies's reputation was further enhanced by the novels that comprise *The Cornish Trilogy: The Rebel Angels* (1981), *What's Bred in the Bone* (1985), and *The Lyre of Orpheus* (1988). *The Rebel Angels* centers on a group of professors at a Toronto university who serve as executors of the estate of Francis Cornish, a collector and patron of the arts. Among the eclectic subjects touched upon by Davies in this novel are the works of French satirist François Rabelais and Swiss alchemist Philippus Paracelsus, gypsy customs, and "filth therapy." *What's Bred in the Bone* explores the influence of external forces upon one man's life. Ostensibly a biography of Francis Cornish as narrated by two angels, *What's Bred in the Bone* also contains a frame story involving characters from *The Rebel Angels.* Like Davies's other novels, this work concerns the protagonist's pursuit of self-discovery and is infused with supernatural, psychological, and religious elements while being firmly rooted in realism. *The Lyre of Orpheus* again centers upon the story of Francis Cornish. In this novel, Cornish's biographer, Simon Darcourt, discovers that a painting that had been attributed to a sixteenth-century artist in *What's Bred in the Bone* is actually the work of Cornish. Concurrent with this plot are events that revolve around characters who are attempting to reconstruct an opera begun by E. T. A. Hoffmann as commissioned by the Cornish Foundation. While the opera production is accepted as an obvious attempt to complete Hoffmann's work and imitate his style, Cornish's painting, originally construed as the genuine work of a medieval artist, is later regarded as a fake with no artistic merit. Several critics consider *The Lyre of Orpheus* a culmination of Davies's own artistic philosophy that is rooted in nineteenth-century Romanticism rather than in aesthetics of contemporary fiction. David Lodge noted that *The Lyre of Orpheus*

"has all Davies' wit, learning, and inventiveness in abundance, and brings to a satisfying conclusion a trilogy that stands as a major fictional achievement independent of literary fashion."

(For further information about Davies's life and works, see *Contemporary Authors*, Vols. 33-36; *Contemporary Authors New Revision Series*, Vol. 17; *Contemporary Literary Criticism*, Vols. 2, 7, 13, 25, 42; and *Dictionary of Literary Biography*, Vol. 68: *Canadian Writers, 1920-1959.*)

CRITICAL COMMENTARY

JUDITH SKELTON GRANT

(essay date 1978)

[In the following excerpt, Grant explores the use of myth, psychology, and moral philosophies in Davies's works, especially in the novels of *The Deptford Trilogy.*]

That there is a market in these days of tight publishing budgets for a bibliography of works by and on Robertson Davies, a study of his plays, and a collection of his "Pronouncements" is an index of Davies' current popularity. This popularity is based on his second trilogy—*Fifth Business, The Manticore,* and *World of Wonders*—for in these books Davies has created vivid and distinctive central characters whose eccentric interests have both popular appeal and a philosophic undercurrent. (p. 56)

[Davies'] childhood love of theater bore fruit in his excellent Oxford thesis, published under the title *Shakespeare's Boy Actors* (1939) and in a stream of plays from the mid-forties on. Fourteen of these have been published and some ten others produced. His early plays earned him a permanent place in the history of Canadian drama. (pp. 56, 58)

Some of [Davies'] witty and irascible comment on the passing scene published in the *Peterborough Examiner* under the pseudonym Samuel Marchbanks was collected in *The Diary of Samuel Marchbanks* (1947), *The Table Talk of Samuel Marchbanks* (1949), and *Marchbank's Almanack* (1967). Some of the *Saturday Night* book review articles constitute the core of *A Voice from the Attic* (1960). Here Davies first reveals the idiosyncrasy and breadth of his reading. His knowledgeable discussion of aspects of popular culture from Shakespeare's day to our own, ranging over subjects like joke books, sex manuals, popular science, health tracts, and melodrama is not only diverting reading but the first

real hint of the resources Davies brings to his recent novels. The Marchbanks books and *A Voice* are the mere iceberg tip of Davies' writing for periodicals. (p. 58)

[His first trilogy: *Tempest-Tost* (1951), *Leaven of Malice* (1954), and *A Mixture of Frailties* (1958) is] in the mode of the satiric romance. Davies' long experience as critic, dramatist, and journalist gave them an astonishingly impressive finish. His dialogue rooted in comedy of manners is lively; his plots are tight and workmanlike. But these surface strengths cause problems. The plot of *Tempest-Tost* permits significant development for only one of the half dozen characters Davies brings convincingly to life. The frame devices of the first two novels, though interesting and lively, jar, because they differ in subject or tone from the rest of the books. And there are technical problems with the omniscient narrator. But Davies learns and develops as he moves from book to book. The third in the series, *A Mixture of Frailties,* is a very fine novel indeed. Here Davies holds satire to a minimum, keeps his narrative stance consistent, focuses attention on one developing central character, and tackles his theme, the value of culture, seriously and openly. (p. 59)

The three volumes of the Deptford trilogy—*Fifth Business, The Manticore,* and *World of Wonders* . . . were well worth waiting for. Davies had avoided first-person narration in his early novels because he felt uncomfortable with the self-revelation and direct communication he associated with the technique. Now he used it masterfully. The intertwined stories of Dunstan Ramsay, Boy Staunton, and Magnus Eisengrim are told by three distinctive and convincing first-person narrators who compel the reader's interest in the story that begins when the stone-laden snowball thrown at Dun-

Principal Works

Shakespeare's Boy Actors (nonfiction) 1939

Shakespeare for Young Players: A Junior Course (nonfiction) 1942

The Diary of Samuel Marchbanks [as Samuel Marchbanks] (journalism) 1947

Overlaid (drama) 1947

Fortune, My Foe (drama) 1948

Eros at Breakfast, and Other Plays [first publication] (drama) 1949

The Table Talk of Samuel Marchbanks [as Samuel Marchbanks] (journalism) 1949

At My Heart's Core (drama) 1950

*Tempest-Tost (novel) 1951

A Masque of Aesop (drama) 1952

Renown at Stratford: A Record of the Stratford Shakespeare Festival in Canada, 1953 [with Tyrone Guthrie and Grant Macdonald] (nonfiction) 1953

A Jig for the Gypsy (drama) 1954

*Leaven of Malice (novel) 1954

Twice Have the Trumpets Sounded: A Record of the Stratford Shakespearean Festival in Canada, 1954 [with Guthrie and Macdonald] (nonfiction) 1954

Thrice the Brinded Cat Hath Mew'd: A Record of the Stratford Shakespearean Festival in Canada, 1955 [with Guthrie, Boyd Neel, and Tanya Moiseiwitsch] (nonfiction) 1955

*A Mixture of Frailties (novel) 1958

†Love and Libel (drama) 1960

A Voice from the Attic (nonfiction) 1960; also published as The Personal Art: Reading to Good Purpose, 1961

A Masque for Mr. Punch (drama) 1962

Samuel Marchbanks' Almanack [as Samuel Marchbanks] (journalism) 1967

‡Fifth Business (novel) 1970

Stephen Leacock (nonfiction) 1970

Hunting Stuart, and Other Plays [first publication] (drama) 1972

‡The Manticore (novel) 1972

Question Time (drama) 1975

‡World of Wonders (novel) 1975

One Half of Robertson Davies: Provocative Pronouncements on a Wide Range of Topics (addresses, lectures, and short stories) 1977; also published as One Half of Robertson Davies, 1978

The Enthusiasms of Robertson Davies (journalism and essays) 1979

§The Rebel Angels (novel) 1981

The Well-Tempered Critic: One Man's View of Theatre and Letters in Canada (addresses, essays, and lectures) 1981

High Spirits (short stories) 1982

The Mirror of Nature (lectures) 1983

The Papers of Samuel Marchbanks (journalism) 1985

§What's Bred in the Bone (novel) 1985

§The Lyre of Orpheus (novel) 1988

Murther and Walking Spirits (novel) 1991

*These works were published as The Salterton Trilogy in 1986.

†This drama is an adaptation of the novel Leaven of Malice.

‡These works were published as The Deptford Trilogy in 1983.

§These works are collectively referred to as The Cornish Trilogy.

stan by Boy hits Mrs. Dempster and causes the premature birth of Magnus.

Davies centers each story in a different kind of knowledge. In *Fifth Business* the consequences of the snowball lead Dunstan to saints and myth; in *The Manticore* they lead David Staunton (Boy's son) into Jungian analysis; in *World of Wonders* they lead Magnus to magic and stagecraft. These provide the thematic core of each book; but only in *Fifth Business,* the master work of the trilogy, does Davies create an organic whole from his disparate materials. All the lore on saints and myth is firmly connected to the central character, reflecting his interests, showing how he thinks, influencing his life, and playing a part in his interpretation of events. That this is not the case in *The Manticore* is partly intentional. David Staunton has held his life together by banishing some things from conscious-

ness, acting in stereotyped patterns, and blunting his feelings with alcohol. When his father's suicide shatters his customary defenses, he needs outside help if he is to find a meaningful pattern in his life, and he finds this help at the Jung Institute in Zurich. There is thus an initial inevitable division between the narrated life and the Jungian theory supplied by his analyst. . . . *World of Wonders* likewise falls short of the standard set by *Fifth Business* and again the problem centers in Davies' handling of data which occupies long stretches of the book. (pp. 59-60)

Though flawed when compared with *Fifth Business, The Manticore* and *World of Wonders* are intriguing and challenging works. With *Fifth Business* they contain the self-revelation compelled by first-person narration that Davies had earlier avoided. What constitutes self-revelation is not autobiography but philosophy. The ideas that overarch the Deptford trilogy are of two kinds: the speculations about myth and psychology pertain to natural philosophy; those on saints and magic, good and evil, God and the Devil to moral philosophy. With the first Davies feels sure of his ground as he follows in the footsteps of such trail blazers as Frazer, Freud, and Jung; with the second he is tentative and suggestive.

Let us begin with his natural philosophy. In the first and third volumes, perceptive characters find in myth a tool for understanding character and for anticipating patterns of human behavior. In the middle volume, David's Jungian analyst explains why myth lays bare the core patterns of character and action as she tells David how he could dream of a manticore, a mythic creature unknown to him:

> People very often dream of things they don't know. They dream of minotaurs without ever having heard of a minotaur. Thoroughly respectable women who have never heard of Pasiphae dream that they are a queen who is enjoying sexual congress with a bull. It is because great myths are not invented stories but objectivizations of images and situations that lie very deep in the human spirit; a poet may make a great embodiment of a myth, but it is the mass of humanity that knows the myth to be a spiritual truth, and that is why they cherish his poem.

In other words, myth gives insight into human behavior because its ultimate source is the psyche. (p. 60)

Davies' use of this material goes far beyond the mythic interpretation of character and events and the revelation of the source of myth's interpretive power. It also influences the nature of the reality in each book. In *Fifth Business,* the world is that of every day reality; myth interprets but does not transform Dunstan's world. In *The Manticore,* David deserts the ordinary world. As he learns new ways of thinking about his life, he finds his dreams presenting glimpses of a myth-like psychic life, hitherto unimagined. In *World of Wonders,* Magnus' daily life in Wanless's World of Wonders, in the old-fashioned traveling troupe, and in the gothic house and household he joins at the end of his story, is mythic. The heroic world David is challenged to find in the depths of his own psyche at the end of *The Manticore* is the world in which Magnus lives, for he has the "Magian World View" where the archetype of the Magus and the myth of Merlin are one and the same, and exist in broad daylight.

About the relation of God and the Devil to the natural world, Davies is exploratory and tentative. . . .

[In] Davies' world, individuals continue to make meaningful choices, though always in the presence of absolute Good and Evil. (p. 61)

Where Dunstan moves toward God and Boy toward the Devil, Magnus experiences both. He seems to represent psychic wholeness, and the possibility of a rich middle ground where man, conscious of the vigor and omnipresence of the forces of good and evil, lives an heroic life.

And is this "wholeness" which seems to be Davies' ideal, a balancing of opposites? I think not. Rather it seems to be what a character in *Fifth Business* has in mind in saying that meeting the Devil is educational and what David's analyst in *The Manticore* means when she urges the value of reclaiming, examining and getting to know one's Shadow (the dark side of the self). For not everything that has been labeled Evil proves to be so, nor all that has been repressed ought to remain so. And the genuinely evil and justifiably banished are weaker if faced and understood. Together with the vigorous, lively and eccentric narrators of the last trilogy, these moral and the earlier mythic and psychological ideas have given these books a place among the dozen significant works of fiction published in Canada during the seventies.

One Half of Robertson Davies (1977) is a selection of pieces read aloud on occasions ranging from convocation to All Hallow's Eve celebrations. It is not as fruitful a totality as *A Voice from the Attic* because it lacks the sustained argument of the earlier collection and because some of the selections are slight. Nonetheless, five lectures constituting the heart of the volume are compelling, meaty reading. "Jung and the Theatre" approaches the Jungian material in *The Manticore* from a different angle; the four lectures called "Masks of Satan" tackle evil and good. Idiosyncratically, Davies approaches the latter subject through the medium of melodramas and novels of the nineteenth century, ghost stories and novels of the twentieth. The main lines of his argument will surprise no thoughtful reader of his late fiction, but such a reader will find his grasp of Davies' religious beliefs enriched and broadened and will find himself ruminating about some of Davies' pronouncements. He talks illuminatingly about poetic justice (Magnus' Great Justice?). He declares that the greatest art is created by those who believe in the existence of absolute Good and Evil, in God and the Devil. He talks of the necessity of opposites. He talks with a vigor that persuades one to expect more books plumbing the riches of Jungian psychology and speculating about the impact of God and the Devil on man's life. (pp. 62-3)

Judith Skelton Grant, "Robertson Davies, God and the Devil," in *Book Forum,* Vol. IV, No. 1, 1978, pp. 56-63.

DAVID STOUCK
(essay date 1984)

[Stouck is a Canadian critic and educator. In the following excerpt, he analyzes what he considers Davies's "search for wisdom" in his works.]

Davies has attracted public attention throughout his career by his witty, often satiric observations on Canadian life and by his cultivation of a theatrical personality. The high esteem in which this author is held, however, has a more solid foundation in certain philosophical concerns which have informed Davies's writings for many years and which give his work as a whole a coherency of purpose and statement.

A list of Davies's subjects would be almost endless, for he has an insatiable interest in all manner of knowledge and information. In his plays we learn about such curious matters as Bohemian puppetry, jest books, Victorian photography, while in the novels we are made to consider such diverse subjects as hagiography, Jungian psychoanalysis, heraldry, and the stagecraft of the illusionist. What is impressive is the way Davies's out-of-the-way lore is made to yield real knowledge about human life.

Although there is great range and diversity to his interests, certain themes recur consistently in all of Davies's writings. As a Canadian Davies frequently attempts to define the essential character of life in Canada, pointing to those special traits of a people with a northern geography and limited political power. More generally, as a critic of contemporary manners, Davies is concerned with attacking the narrow-mindedness and philistinism of any society hostile to individuality and the imaginative life. In this regard Davies frequently aims his barbs at women, who, in his opinion, often embody the stultifying influences of conformism and self-righteousness. But the serious core of Davies's writing is a concern with the values of the carefully examined life. He has long been fascinated with Jung's theories of wholeness in human personality and with the importance of myth in explaining the patterns of individual lives. Davies has also been much attracted to the Swiss psychologist's idea that evil is an embodiment of the unlived life, those things that an individual has repressed in himself. In Davies's public voice there is an aristocratic disdain for the majority of people, but there is also admiration expressed for the individual who tries to understand his thoughts and feelings fully, who places feeling on the same plane of importance as reason, and whose life's goal is not the pursuit of hap-

piness, but of self-knowledge. Indeed, we might say that the program of all of Davies's writing is the search for wisdom.

Davies's development as a writer began with the creation of Samuel Marchbanks, an irascible Johnsonian eccentric, whose scathing opinions on humankind were first voiced in the columns of the *Peterborough Examiner*. In 1947 Davies assembled the sketches in book form as *The Diary of Samuel Marchbanks.* The book's success resulted in a sequel, *The Table Talk of Samuel Marchbanks* (1949), and twenty years later *Samuel Marchbanks' Almanack* (1967). Marchbanks is a crusty old bachelor who lives alone in Skunk's Misery, Ontario, from which vantage point he passes judgment on society in general and on Canadians in particular. With typical comic acerbity he observes: "Most Canadians dislike and mistrust any great show of cheerfulness. If a man were to sing in the street he would probably end up in jail." Marchbanks believes Canadians are essentially puritans who frown on pleasure in any form. A Canadian woman, he says, "is a dowdy and unappetizing mammal, who is much given to Culture and Good Works, but derives no sinful satisfaction from either," while "the Canadian male is so hounded by taxes and the rigors of our climate that he is lucky to be alive," much less have sex appeal. It is the uncertainty of the weather, says Marchbanks, which "makes Canadians the morose, haunted, apprehensive people they are." Ibsen's plays, he adds, reflect the Canadian spirit admirably, a favorite observation by Davies over the years. Marchbanks's own life as a Canadian is dramatized in his winter-long battle with his furnace and his struggle in summer with the weeds in his garden. Marchbanks is an admirer of eccentric individuality; he rails against the present, with its ideals of conformity and machine-age efficiency. He claims to be a democrat, but admits: "The idea that a gang of anybodies may override the opinion of one expert is preposterous nonsense. Only individuals think, gangs merely throb." It has been suggested that Marchbanks's exaggerated and often outrageous observations represent a parody of Davies himself—his own iconoclastic spirit, arrogant misanthropy, and antifeminist feelings. The suggestion is fitting, for Davies comes to assert in his later critical writings that fictional characters often represent something the author has been forced to suppress in himself. The Marchbanks books are often reminiscent of Davies's favorite Canadian author, Stephen Leacock. They are sometimes ponderous and sometimes trivial, but for Davies they represent an important apprenticeship with the techniques of humor.

The second phase in Davies's development saw him turn to the theatre as a vehicle for comedy and for presenting his ideas and social comments. In the years 1947-54 he wrote and produced more than a dozen plays, several of them for the Peterborough Little Theatre. The published plays include *Overlaid* (1948), *Eros at Breakfast and Other Plays* (1949), *Fortune, My Foe* (1949), *At My Heart's Core* (1950), and *A Jig for the Gypsy* (1954). The subjects and settings of these plays vary greatly—*Fortune, My Foe* is about an immigrant from Prague who wants to start a puppet theatre in Canada, while *A Jig for the Gypsy* deals with politics and magic in nineteenth-century Wales—but a constant theme in the plays, indeed in all of Davies's writings, is the importance of art to civilization. Perhaps the liveliest and most amusing treatment of this theme is in the brief, one-act play *Overlaid.* Here Pop, an old Canadian farmer, and his middle-aged daughter, Ethel, argue as to how Pop should spend a $1,200 windfall from a paid-up insurance policy. Pop, who describes himself as "the Bohemian set of Smith township, all in one man," dreams of going on a spree in New York City, where he would enjoy a gourmet dinner, sit in the front row at the Metropolitan Opera, and wind up at a night club show, perhaps giving fifty dollars for the stripper's brassiere. When his daughter, however, is persuaded to confide her inner dream of spending the money on a huge granite tombstone that would give solidity and dignity to the family name, Pop yields to what he calls her "power of goodness" and gives her the money. Pop's love of theatre and opera and his dream of a good time is "overlaid" by the tombstone; Davies wants the audience to view this very Canadian symbol of "goodness" in a negative light.

The conflict between the world of imagination and a sober, utilitarian environment is strongly emphasized in *At My Heart's Core,* which is set in the backwoods society of Upper Canada in 1837. The central characters include the Strickland sisters—Catherine Parr Traill and Susanna Moodie—who were willing to sacrifice personal needs and comforts in order to achieve certain cultural goals. The play, however, develops another theme, one that becomes of central importance in Davies's later works. As in *Overlaid,* the central characters (the Strickland sisters and a third pioneer woman, Frances Stewart) are each brought to confess their innermost dreams. Mrs. Stewart admits a romantic regret for an aristocratic social life that she lost when she rejected a suitor in Ireland, Mrs. Traill admits an ambition to become an acknowledged botanist, and Mrs. Moodie confesses her desire to be a famous writer. Cantwell, the man who elicits these confidences, does so in order to betray the women publicly and revenge himself on their "tight, snug, unapproachable little society," from which he and his wife are excluded. One of the minor characters in the play calls Cantwell the devil, pointing to an important idea in Davies's writing—namely, that we identify as evil any embodiment or open expression of our secret longings. To the three women in the play Cantwell is the devil incarnate because he has successfully tempted them to

give voice to their repressed thoughts and wishes. In addition he has stolen their peace of mind by making them feel that their dreams can perhaps be realized. Davies's early plays are fascinating to read in the light of his later fictions, for one can trace in embryos the development of certain ideas that were to gain importance as he continued to write. But the plays are not wholly satisfying in themselves because characters are always secondary to ideas and remain very much one-dimensional types.

The third phase in Davies's work was the writing of three related novels about the social, moral, and artistic life of a small Ontario city called Salterton. These novels, published in the 1950s, are essentially comic and contain many lively and entertaining scenes, but like the early plays suffer from flatness of characterization. The plot of *Tempest-Tost* (1951) turns on an outdoor production of Shakespeare's *Tempest* by Salterton's little theatre group, a plot rich in comic ironies because Shakespeare's play is served up in a bumbling amateur production. Davies's chief purpose in the novel is to satirize the cultural immaturity of Canada, where aesthetic standards must take second place to the ambitions and narrow-minded prejudices of the people. (pp. 197-201)

In *Leaven of Malice* (1954) Davies continues to make fun of Canadian provincialism, but in this deftly plotted comedy he probes that more serious theme—the nature and operation of evil. The plot turns on the repercussions which ensue when a false engagement announcement is placed in the Salterton newspaper. This bit of malice works in the community to bring all the major characters into a series of conflicts with each other. In accord with Davies's idea that evil is actually an expression of one's suppressed fears and wishes, the characters in the novel are shown to be freed by the false announcement and its implications. (pp. 201-02)

A Mixture of Frailties (1958), the third and most ambitious novel in the *Salterton Trilogy,* is a study of the development of an artist, a *Künstlerroman.* Although the novel begins and ends in Salterton and continually refers to its values, its focus is on Monica Gall, a young Salterton woman sent to England to train as an opera singer. Monica seems an unlikely heroine because of her family's working-class background and fundamentalist religion. The special interest of the novel, however, is the relationship between the artist and her life, how she gradually substitutes the universal values of art for the specific and limited values of her Salterton background. . . . In spite of its important themes, the novel is not wholly successful. The farcical tone of the Salterton scenes does not mesh with the serious portrait of the artist. The Canadian setting is the world of childhood and comedy, while England and Europe are the place of art, education, and wisdom. Unfortunately,

Monica's consciousness does not comprehend and integrate both worlds fully.

In *A Mixture of Frailties* Monica's mentor, Sir Benedict, describes the theme of a certain opera as "the metamorphosis of physical man into spiritual man." This summary describes exactly the intent and achievement of *Fifth Business* (1970), an expansive and complex book which has been a bestseller and may be Davies's masterwork. The first of a trilogy of novels whose principal characters originate in the small Ontario town of Deptford, *Fifth Business* takes the form of a long letter written by a retired schoolteacher, Dunstan Ramsay, who is intent on revealing to the headmaster of the school that he is not the colorless person his colleagues always assumed him to be, that his life on the contrary has been wide-ranging and eventful. (pp. 202-03)

[The] unifying thread has been a lifetime involvement with two characters from his childhood, Boy Staunton and Mary Dempster. In the novel's opening scene, Ramsay, a boy of ten, ducks to avoid a snowball (containing a stone) thrown at him by his friend and rival, Boy Staunton. The snowball instead strikes pregnant Mary Dempster, the Baptist preacher's wife, who falls, gives birth to a son, Paul, prematurely, and is said to have been made "simple" by the accident. (p. 203)

The problems of tone and point of view that seriously mar *A Mixture of Frailties* are solved in *Fifth Business* by Davies's choice of Dunstan Ramsay as first-person narrator. In the earlier novel the characterization of Monica Gall is not large enough to unite the serious episodes concerning her development as an artist and the farcical treatment of Salterton. But Dunstan Ramsay is a narrator whose sensibility, similar to the author's, includes both satirical delight in the foibles of human nature and religious awe at the unfathomable mysteries of human experience. *Fifth Business* accordingly is a hybrid of unlikely literary modes—satire and romance. Such writing is not easily done, because the author is working with forms of experience that are poles apart. A romance portrays a hero's quest for some kind of ideal, while satire focuses on the incongruities that exist between a professed ideal and what actually happens. But satirical romance describes exactly the double nature of this book and its hero, and one of the most impressive feats in *Fifth Business* is the way Davies indulges the satirist's delight in human folly without ever destroying the solemn, religious mood of the hero's romantic quest. (p. 204)

The popular and critical success of *Fifth Business* encouraged Davies to explore the Deptford material in two more novels. *The Manticore* (1972) is narrated by Boy Staunton's son, David, who has had a nervous breakdown after his father's death and is undergoing therapy at the Jungian Institute in Zurich. David examines his life chronologically so that a completely differ-

ent perspective is taken on many of the events narrated by Ramsay in *Fifth Business*. The novel, however, focuses on David's breakdown and the process of establishing a meaningful pattern for his life again. . . . *World of Wonders* (1975) is the story of Paul Dempster, known professionally as Magnus Eisengrim, and the consequences of the snowball thrown at the beginning of *Fifth Business* are viewed from yet another perspective. Magnus, now in his sixties, is a world-celebrated magician, and Ramsay, as a historian, is making a record of his life which includes not only Paul Dempster's own account of his transformation into Eisengrim but the thoughts and reactions of important admirers such as the Swedish film director Jurgen Lind and the members of his film crew. Fascinating though they are, neither *The Manticore* nor *World of Wonders* is as successful as the first volume in the trilogy. The problem is that the wealth of information about Jungian analysis and the stagecraft of magic is not wholly integrated with the central character studies in these novels; it is interesting material, but not given the fully developed dramatic purpose that the study of the saints' lives is given in *Fifth Business*.

Davies's principal weakness in his plays and his novels is that Shavian propensity to explain his ideas at length rather than dramatize them fully through character and action. In *Fifth Business* both Padre Blazon and Liesl are splendid characterizations, but their conversations with Ramsay have a homiletic cast. The nature of Jungian analysis and the importance of magic are subjects presented even more clinically in the subsequent novels. However, to cite this flaw in Davies's writing is also to draw attention to his strength, which is that he is a writer with important ideas for us to consider. Davies's ideas have international origins and universal application, but as a comic writer Davies approaches humor in a peculiarly Canadian way. He sees satire, not as an agent to destroy the formal structures of society, but as a means of changing society for the better—as a leavening agent (to use one of his favorite metaphors) in creating a better and wiser world. The realm of wisdom is always Davies's vision and goal. (pp. 209-10)

David Stouck, "Robertson Davies," in his *Major Canadian Authors: A Critical Introduction,* University of Nebraska Press, 1984, pp. 197-211.

DAVID LODGE

(essay date 1989)

[Lodge is an English novelist, critic, short story writer, and dramatist known for critical works dealing with literary theory and for novels that satirize religious and academic practices. In the following review of *The Lyre of Orpheus*, he surveys Davies's literary development and position in contemporary fiction.]

Robertson Davies started writing novels fairly late in life, and has come into his prime as a novelist at an age when most men are glad if they can summon up enough energy and concentration to read a book, let alone write one. Born in Thamesville, Ontario, in 1913, he was an actor (with the London Old Vic company), then a playwright, theater director, essayist, and newspaper editor for many years before (and after) he published his first novel, *Tempest-Tost* (1951). This and its sequels, *Leaven of Malice* (1954) and *A Mixture of Frailties* (1958), which make up the so-called Salterton trilogy, aroused little interest outside Canada. *Fifth Business,* which appeared more than a decade later (1970), and the Deptford trilogy, which it inaugurated, continued in *The Manticore* (1972) and completed by *World of Wonders* (1975), enjoyed some success in America, but made little impact in England. I have to confess that the first time Robertson Davies impinged on my own consciousness was when I was asked (by an American journal) to review *The Rebel Angels* in 1982.

What's Bred in the Bone, a related, though freestanding novel, was widely praised, and was short-listed for the Booker Prize in 1984. It put Robertson Davies in that small group of novelists whom anyone professing a serious interest in contemporary fiction has to read. His impressively bearded countenance, staring challengingly from the review pages of newspapers and magazines like a reincarnation of Tolstoy (whose birthday he shares, to his obvious pleasure, along with Goethe and Saint Augustine), has become a familiar literary icon. The publication of *The Lyre of Orpheus,* which completes another, as yet unnamed, trilogy, is an important literary event.

There are several possible reasons why Robertson Davies's novelistic reputation has ripened so slowly. One is that he is Canadian, and the Anglo-American world has only recently begun to take seriously the idea of a Canadian literature. He was once told by the secretary of a famous London theatrical management to whom he had submitted one of his plays, "Mr. Davies, you must realize that nobody—literally nobody—is interested in Canada." Such an attitude is not unknown in the United States—some years ago an American magazine competition to invent the most boring book title imaginable was won by *Canada—Our Neighbor to the North.*

This dismissive attitude toward Canadian culture becomes increasingly difficult to sustain in the presence, literal or metaphorical, of writers like Margaret Atwood, Alice Munro, and Robertson Davies himself,

but it is not without some historical foundation, as Davies would readily acknowledge. When he returned to his native country in 1940, after completing his education and theatrical apprenticeship in England, Canada seemed to him "like a dull, ill-rehearsed show that someone should put on the road," and his novels are peppered with satirical observations on the Canadian ethos that have not endeared him to his fellow countrymen.

The narrator of *The Lyre of Orpheus* says of his characters, "They were not wholly of the grey majority of their people. . . . They did not murmur the national prayer: 'Oh God, grant me mediocrity and comfort; protect me from the radiance of Thy light.' " This is something of an understatement: any foreigner who took Robertson Davies's novels as his only guide to Canadian society would acquire a somewhat distorted image of it. Davies deals for the most part with rich, eccentric, artistic, and scholarly personages, who enjoy good food and good wine, old books and old masters, and engage each other in witty and learned conversation—characters who seem to have strayed out of the pages of Thomas Love Peacock or George Meredith rather than the kind you might meet at, say, a neighborly barbecue in a Toronto suburb.

The affinity with bookish nineteenth-century writers suggests another reason why Davies's novels have taken a long time to find a large appreciative audience. When he hit his stride as a novelist, in the 1970s, new fiction claimed attention by being formally "experimental" in the postmodernist style (lots of discontinuity, fragmentation, contradiction, randomness, and "metafictional" openness of form) and/or by a boldly explicit exploration of sexuality and sexual politics. Though Robertson Davies's novels are not without their erotic, sometimes kinkily erotic, passages, he has made clear, both in these texts and outside them, that he regards the contemporary Western obsession with the physical mechanics of sexual intercourse, and especially with what an uncouth character in *The Lyre of Orpheus* calls "the organism," as encouraging a fatally limited view of human relationships. As for literary experimentalism, he has characteristically observed:

We all know what the avant-garde was. It was the group that was sent forward to encounter the worst of the fire, and to fall bravely in the service of their country, and then the real army came up and took over and won the battle. And I think that's what happens in literature. Those who want to be in it, are just inviting their destruction, because the avant-garde has changed its clothes and its uniform and its underwear three or four times in my lifetime. Who wants to get into that?

Certainly there is at present a lull, indicating either exhaustion or disillusionment, in the polemical and creative struggles of postmodernism, and a literary

climate, therefore, receptive to the old-fashioned pleasures of texts like *What's Bred in the Bone* and *The Lyre
of Orpheus.* Robertson Davies has observed that "great
literature always has plots," and although he likes to
group his novels in sequences of three, each has a beginning, a middle, and an end in true Aristotelian fashion. He has called them "romances," perhaps acknowledging that he takes some liberties with probability in
the interest of narrative complication or symbolic design, and uses supernatural machinery (for example the
interventions of the Recording Angels in *What's Bred
in the Bone,* and of the limbo-confined composer Hoffmann in *The Lyre of Orpheus*), but it is all done in a
style hallowed by traditional literary convention, and
does not in any way subvert or challenge ways of reading derived from the classic realist text. The word that
constantly comes to mind in reading Davies is "gusto":
he seems to have taken huge pleasure in the creation of
his imagined world, and this pleasure conveys itself in-
fectiously to the reader. His prose is brisk, supple, and
well-balanced. The enigmas of the narrative, and the
amusing, cultivated chatter of the characters, draw us
effortlessly through the text, intrigued and stimulated,
if seldom deeply moved. His novels are (I do not regard
this as faint praise) the thinking man's good read.

The sequence completed by *The Lyre of Orpheus*
may become known as the Cornish trilogy, since its
stories revolve around the enigmatic figure of Francis
Cornish, a well-to-do Canadian art connoisseur who
has left his mysteriously acquired fortune to found a
charitable trust for patronage of the arts, administered
by his businessman nephew, Arthur Cornish, and a
number of other trustees drawn from the University of
Toronto—in particular from the College of St. John and
the Holy Ghost, which seems to bear some humorous
resemblance to Massey College, of which Robertson
Davies was master from 1962 to 1981. *The Rebel Angels*
concerns the intrigues and struggles between several of
these academics for possession of a rare collection of
holograph letters from Rabelais to the Renaissance
magus Paracelsus.

What's Bred in the Bone backtracks in time to relate the life of Francis Cornish and explain some of the
mysteries of his life. This is a more serious and ambitious novel than its predecessor, moving confidently in
time and space, vividly evoking the hero's childhood in
provincial Ontario, his aesthetic and sentimental education in England, and his experiences during World
War II, when he served on an Allied commission for
tracing and identifying old paintings. One of the works
he discovered was a depiction of *The Marriage Feast of
Cana* by an unidentified genius of the sixteenth century
known as the Alchemical Master, following an explication of the painting's esoteric symbolism by an art critic
associated with Cornish.

One of the main plot strands of *The Lyre of Or-*

pheus concerns the discovery by Simon Darcourt, a
theology professor and Anglican clergyman who is
writing a biography of Francis Cornish, that this interpretation of the painting is quite mistaken. The other
strand concerns the production of an opera subsidized
by the Cornish Foundation—not so much a production,
in fact, as the reconstruction and completion of a complicated original work by the German Romantic composer E. T. A. Hoffmann. The subject of the opera is the
story of King Arthur, and Hoffmann's working title
was *Arthur of Britain, or the Magnanimous Cuckold.* Its theme
was to be "King Arthur's recognition of the love of
Lancelot for Guinevere, and the great pain with which
he accepts that love." The project foundered because
Hoffmann was unable to reach agreement with his
London-based librettist, Planché. All that survives (in
Francis Cornish's valuable manuscript collection) are
Hoffmann's notes and rough drafts of the score, and the
correspondence with Planché.

On the basis of these documents, Hulda Schnakenburg, a brilliant if unprepossessing graduate student of music at Toronto, undertakes to reconstruct the
opera as a Ph.D. project, supervised by the Swedish
composer and musicologist Dr. Gunilla Dahl-Soot (Davies's gusto is very evident in his invention of names).
Darcourt supplies the libretto (deftly plagiarized from
Sir Walter Scott) and the performance is directed by the
ambitious and eloquent Welsh director Geraint Powell.
The ghost of the composer himself watches over the
whole enterprise with some excitement, from his vantage point in the limbo of forgotten artists from which
the production promises to release him.

Robertson Davies makes full use of his theatrical
experience in relating the story of this production, and
the account of its first night is genuinely thrilling even
to a reader (like myself) who has little enthusiasm for
opera. One acquires from this book a great deal of fascinating information about the history of operatic
form, early-nineteenth-century stage design, and the
mechanics of libretto writing ("Do you know a two-
syllable word meaning 'regret' that isn't 'regret'? Because 'regret' isn't a word that sings well if it has to be
matched up with a quarter-note followed by an eighth-
note"), not to mention Arthurian legend, the Tarot
pack, art history, pony breeding, old Ontario figures of
speech, and Romany proverbs. The apparently effortless deployment of specialized and arcane knowledge
about many different subjects is one of Davies's great
strengths as a novelist.

The production of the opera is enmeshed in various amorous intrigues. The lesbian Dr. Gunilla Dahl-
Soot seduces Hulda Schnakenburg, who falls in love
with Geraint Powell, who, by a device reminiscent of
the bed tricks in Shakespeare's problem plays, impregnates Arthur Cornish's barren wife, Maria (née Theotoky, a former graduate student of the College of St.

John and the Holy Ghost, and a major character in *The Rebel Angels*). By magnanimously accepting the child, Arthur Cornish reenacts the theme of Hoffmann's opera—Maria corresponding to Guinevere and Powell to Lancelot.

"Let us, I entreat you, explore the miraculous that dwells in the depths of the mind," Hoffmann writes to Planché. "Let the lyre of Orpheus open the door of the underworld of feeling." The lyre of Orpheus stands metonymically for music and mythopoeia, which break through the crust of rationality and materialism concealing our real desires and fears from ourselves. Davies, a self-confessed Jungian, invokes archetypes in his novels for the same purpose. The fact that the characters are all well aware of these archetypes makes the mythic level of the novel seem somewhat artificial and contrived, but Davies tries to mitigate this effect by a kind of mythic overdetermination. Thus it is not only the Grail legend but also the Tarot pack that offers clues—confusing clues—to the fortunes of the characters. Darcourt, for instance, who supposes himself to be the Hermit in the pack, turns out to be the Fool.

But a wise fool, whose disinterested pursuit of the truth about Cornish, to the point of endangering his own reputation (it entails his stealing some drawings from the National Gallery in Ottawa), enables him to unravel the mystery of *The Marriage Feast of Cana*. It proves to be the work of Francis Cornish himself, executed in a flawless imitation of sixteenth-century painting, every figure of which is a portrait of some member or associate of the artist's family.

Darcourt feels that his discovery "establishes Francis as a very great painter. Working in the mode of a bygone day, but a great painter nonetheless." Arthur Cornish is not so sure: "He may be a great painter, but that makes him unmistakably a faker." This exchange seems to bear obliquely on the art of Robertson Davies himself, which some critics have seen as skillful pastiche of an obsolete fictional style rather than an authentic contribution to modern literature.

The Lyre of Orpheus ends with a discussion of Keats's remark "A Man's life of any wroth is a continual allegory"; and in the invented life of Francis Cornish Davies seems to be writing an allegory of his own artistic career. Like Cornish, Davies has "dared to be of a time not his own"; like Cornish he has been fascinated by the figural tradition in late medieval and early Renaissance art and literature, "all that allegorical-metaphysical stuff, all that symbolic communication" that, according to Darcourt, post-Renaissance Europe rejected. Through the theme of the fake or imitation painting which is indistinguishable from its revered models, Robertson Davies seeks to undermine the arrogant historicism of modern aesthetics that would condemn his highly crafted and highly enjoyable novels as "irrelevant."

The Lyre of Orpheus is not perhaps as powerful and *surprising* a novel as *What's Bred in the Bone*, but it has all Davies's wit, learning, and inventiveness in abundance, and brings to a satisfying conclusion a trilogy that stands as a major fictional achievement independent of literary fashion. Davis's own spiritual home, however, is not so much the sixteenth century as the early nineteenth. He is essentially a latter-day Romantic who believes in man's unconquerable mind, and the expressive function of art. *The Marriage Feast of Cana*, when decoded by Darcourt, turns out to be a work not of alchemical symbolism but of Romantic biography and autobiography, rather like Benjamin Haydon's huge canvas *Christ Entering into Jerusalem*, in which Haydon himself and most of his acquaintances, including Keats, were portrayed. Does this imply that underneath the highly contrived plotting and archetypal patterning of the Cornish trilogy there is a kind of confessional, autobiographical novel waiting to be discovered? Davies has hinted as much, and in the process given another explanation for the late maturing of his formidable talent. In a very recent interview he told Herbert Denton of *The Washington Post* that "he was able to write more frankly as he grew older because 'people died.'" We must be grateful for his own vigorous longevity. (pp. 35-6)

David Lodge, "Hermits and Fools," in *The New York Review of Books*, Vol. XXXVI, No. 6, April 13, 1989, pp. 35-6.

GEORGE WOODCOCK
(essay date 1990)

[A Canadian educator, editor, and critic, Woodcock is best known for his biographies of George Orwell and Thomas Merton. He also founded the influential literary journal *Canadian Literature*. In the following excerpt, he examines the novels in Davies's *The Cornish Trilogy*, maintaining that the works embody the author's conservative artistic philosophy.]

With the publication in the autumn of 1988 of *The Lyre of Orpheus*, Robertson Davies has completed the third of his fictional trilogies, each centred on a different Ontario town, and each dominated by a central group of characters through whose varying perceptions and memories the current of events that characterizes the trilogy is perceived.

The completion of the triple triad is, as Davies has undoubtedly recognized, an event that stirs a multitude of numerological, folkloric, and mythological echoes. Nine was one of the three mystical numbers of the Pythagoreans, and though three was a perfect number which Pythagoras made the sign of the deity, nine had its specific significance as a trinity of trinities, the perfect plural. For Pythagoras, and later for the great classical astronomer Ptolemy, the universe moved in nine spheres. In various contexts we find the number particularly associated with inspiration and imagination. There were nine Muses, nine Gallicenae or virgin priestesses of the Druid oracles, and nine Sibylline books transmitted from Cumae to Rome. Echoed constantly in Davies' novels is the ancient concept of a nine day's wonder: as the old proverb has it, "A wonder lasts nine days, and then the puppy's eyes are open." But most relevant of all in considering *The Lyre of Orpheus* as the last Davies novel to date—and perhaps the last of the kind to which we have become accustomed since *Fifth Business* appeared in 1970—is the role which nine plays in music, for nine was the Pythagorean *diapason,* man being the full chord, or eight notes, and nine representing the deity, ultimate harmony.

The Lyre of Orpheus is not merely a novel about music; it is a novel about the nature of art in general and its relation to reality and time and the human spirit. But the main plot carrying this theme concerns a musical event, and in doing so it takes us back with striking deliberation to the first group of Davies novels, the Salterton series. For, like the last of that series, *A Mixture of Frailties* (1958), *The Lyre of Orpheus* is built around a family trust which offers a phenomenally generous grant to a young woman musician from a Philistine background, and finds itself sponsoring a controversial opera, so that a contribution is made to the art of music in a general way at the same time as the young musician, aided by wise teachers, undergoes an inner transformation that opens to her what in Davies terminology one might call "a world of wonders"; in Jungian terms she is taken out of the anonymity and personal incompleteness of common life and achieves individuation.

There are indeed important ways in which *The Lyre of Orpheus,* written thirty years later, goes beyond *A Mixture of Frailties.* While Monica Gall in the earlier novel is a singer whose talents are trained by inspired teachers, and the opera in which she becomes involved is the original work of another—a wayward modern genius—in *The Lyre of Orpheus* we edge nearer to the creative role, for the musician, Hulda Scknackenburg (generally called Schnak), is a composer engaged not in an original composition but in a task of inspired reconstruction. She is making an opera, *Arthur of Britain,* out of scattered fragments left by E. T. A. Hoffman (better known as a Gothicist tale-teller than as a musician) of an opera he was unable to complete before his early death from the nineteenth-century endemic, syphilis. At the same time the priestly scholar Simon Darcourt (one of the narrators of an earlier Davies novel, *The Rebel Angels*) constructs the libretto around which the score that Schnak develops from Hoffman's fragments

is built up. Schnak and Darcourt, with their various collaborators, manage to recreate an authentic sounding early nineteenth-century opera which pleases the spirit of E. T. A. Hoffman who makes a ghostly appearance in the comments from the underworld that appear as interludes between the narrative chapters.

Related to this major plot is a strikingly similar sub-plot devoted to the visual as distinct from the audial arts. As well as acting as pasticheur-librettist, Simon Darcourt is engaged on a biography of Francis Cornish, the celebrated connoisseur and art collector whose bequest has funded the preparation and production of *Arthur of Britain.* Darcourt stumbles on the clues which reveal to him what readers of **What's Bred in the Bone** already know, that Cornish was actually the painter of a famous triptych, *The Marriage of Cana,* done so authentically in the fifteenth-century German manner that it has been plausibly attributed to an unknown painter working five centuries ago who was given the name of the Alchemical Master.

Simon Darcourt manages to convince everyone involved, including the owners of the painting and the reluctant mandarins of the National Gallery to which it is eventually given, that a work done sincerely and without intent of fraud in the style of a past age is not a fake and can be as authentic as the best work in a contemporary manner. The argument put forward by Darcourt's colleague Clement Hollier, an expert on myths, is not only interesting in itself but important for what it tells us about Davies' own attitudes towards the arts and about his own literary achievement. Here is Darcourt's paraphrase of Hollier's statement:

> If a man wants to paint a picture that is intended primarily as an exercise in a special area of expertise, he will do so in a style with which he is most familiar. If he wants to paint a picture which has a particular relevance to his own life-experience, which explores the myth of his life as he understands it, and which, in the old phrase, "makes up his soul", he is compelled to do it in a mode that permits such allegorical revelation. Painters after the Renaissance, and certainly after the Protestant Reformation, have not painted such pictures with the frankness that was natural to pre-Renaissance artists. The vocabulary of faith, and of myth, has been taken from them by the passing of time. But Francis Cornish, when he wanted to make up his soul, turned to the style of painting and the concept of visual art which came most naturally to him. Indeed, he had many times laughed at the notion of contemporaneity in conversation . . . , mocking it as a foolish chain on a painter's inspiration and intention.

> It must be remembered . . . that Francis has been brought up a Catholic—or almost a Catholic—and he had taken his catholicity seriously enough to make it a foundation of his art. If God is one and eternal, and if Christ is not dead, but living, are not

fashions in art mere follies for those who are the slaves of Time?

In musical terms the chapter in which these matters are resolved can be regarded as a coda, a concluding passage after the main pattern of the work has been developed and completed; it states the theme of the novel more definitely and succinctly than in early renderings. *Arthur of Britain* has been completed and successfully launched as a new work in the operatic repertoire, Schnak had found herself and her career, and now, three years later in a chapter free of the ghostly voice of E. T. A. Hoffman (a ghost now actually laid), we can consider what is the meaning of it all, assisted by our reflections on Francis Cornish's strange master work. And so, just as *The Lyre of Orpheus* as a whole, with its deliberate reordering and retelling of the plot of *A Mixture of Frailties,* completes the circle of Davies' mature fiction, so this final chapter of the latest of his novels acts, I suggest, as a veiled *apologia pro vita sua,* a justification for the uncontemporary aesthetic underlying Davies' life work.

George Orwell once remarked on the striking fact that the best writers of his time—and among them he included the great apostles of literary modernism—have in fact been conservative and even reactionary in their social and political attitudes. This is certainly true of most of the great moderns in the Anglo-American tradition; Eliot, Pound, and Wyndham Lewis were all to be found politically somewhat to the right of old-style Toryism, and James Joyce failed to join them only because of a massive indifference to anything outside his own linguistic experiments.

Robertson Davies has not spoken of his political views in any detail or with much directness. I have no idea how he votes, though it is clear that he has the kind of Tory mind which judges politics ethically; his treatment of Boy Staunton's political career in *Fifth Business* suggests that he probably has little patience with what passes for a Conservative cause in late twentieth-century Canada.

What distinguishes Davies from the reactionary modernists is that his Toryism runs into his art as well as his political ethics. He is an unrepentent cultural élitist. "There is no democracy in the world of intellect, and no democracy of taste," he said in *A Voice from the Attic* (1960) and he has not since shown a change of attitude. He has never posed as an avant garde writer of any kind. In spite of occasionally expressed admiration for *Ulysses* as a great comic work, he has never followed Joyce's experiments in language, and despite a loosely stated interest in Proust, he has never tried to emulate Proust's experiments in the literary manipulation of time and memory. Indeed, in this respect he has been far less experimental than other writers we do not regard as particularly avant gardist, like Margaret Lau-

rence and Marian Engel. Though in his two later trilogies he may view the same sequences of events in different novels through different eyes, he still tends within each novel to follow a strictly chronological pattern, with effect following cause, whether the causes are the inner ones to be dragged out by Jungian analysis or the outer ones which we see a character's social ambiance and physical environment imposing on him.

Not that, even taking into account the clear, serviceable and declarative prose that Davies writes, we should regard him as a plain realist. If he is a realist, it is not in the documentary sense, but in the theatrical sense of wishing to give plausibility to the implausible, in his early novels to farce and in his later ones to melodrama. There is always in his writing a heightening of the use of language that goes beyond the demands of ordinary realism, and, given his special interests, Davies might justly be called a magic realist rather than a surrealist. It is true that he shares with the surrealists a preoccupation with depth psychology and its resources of imagery, but while most of the surrealists tended to put their faith in Freud, Davies has found Jung a richer source.

Just as his magicians are technicians of illusion rather than true thaumaturges, so Davies himself takes a pride in artifice, yet he is too conservative a writer to fit in with the postmodernists, metafictionists and destructionists of our own day. Far from being destructionist, indeed, his novels are as Edwardianly well-made as Galsworth's Forsyte novels or Arnold Bennett's fictional chronicles of the Five Towns, while among his contemporaries the one novelist he has regarded as undeniably great, and whom he has admitted to be an influence, is Joyce Cary, whose virtues lay not in his experimental daring, but rather in a zest for the language, "a reaffirmation of the splendour and sacredness of life," and the same kind of restless and active erudition as Davies displays in his own fiction.

While recognizing that a novel is a work of artifice in which verisimilitude is part of the illusion, and often using contrived fictional devices, Davies manifests little of that preoccupation with the relationship between writers, readers, and the work which has led metafictionists ever since Cervantes and Sterne in their smoke-and-mirror games with reality. He is too didactic, too much concerned with developing lessons about life, and with displaying knowledge and expertise, to subordinate the central narrative, the line of purpose in his works, to any speculative process that might seem to weaken its validity. He is, essentially, a novelist in the central English tradition of Fielding and Dickens and Cary, intent on using artifice to entertain and to instruct. He is brilliantly inventive and has an extraordinary power of assimilating information and presenting it acceptably. But he has little formal originality, little of the power of imaginative transfiguration, so that his novels are still influenced by the conventions of the theatre where he began his writing career, and large sections of them are dominated by the kind of didactic dialogue we used to associate with Bernard Shaw and his disciples. Art comes, when it does, at the end of the process, in the accidental way which also accords with the main English fictional tradition. The kind of deliberate artistry that distinguished the main French tradition from Flaubert onwards, and the tradition of deep social criticism that distinguished the central lineage of Russian fiction from Turgenev onwards, find no place in Davies' books.

Nor, for that matter, does one find much in common between Davies' novels and those of the writers, like Hugh MacLennan and Sinclair Ross and Margaret Laurence, whom we regard as most faithful in their projection of the climate and character of Canadian life and its relation to the land. Davies' novels are restricted geographically to a tiny fragment of Canada—Toronto and the small towns of western Ontario—and to a restricted social milieu of Old and New Money, of the false and true intellectual and artistic aspirations of the middle class, and working-class people are introduced only for comic relief, as in the case of the Morphews in *Leaven of Malice* or the elder Galls in *A Mixture of Frailties,* or on condition that they become transformed and find their way into the cultured bourgeoisie, as Monica Gall does in *A Mixture of Frailties* and Hulda Sckneckenburg seems about to do at the end of *The Lyre of Orpheus.*

Davies did indeed define his attitude to Canada in an interview in *Maclean's* in 1972, two years after *Fifth Business* was published, when he replied to the complaints he had heard that "my novels aren't about Canada."

> I think they are, because I see Canada as a country torn between a very northern, rather extraordinary mystical spirit which it fears and its desire to present itself to the world as a Scotch banker.
>
> (pp. 33-8)

[*The Rebel Angels, What's Bred in the Bone,* and *The Lyre of Orpheus* . . .] are partly at least *romans à clef,* based on Davies' experiences of educational and cultural institutions, so that readers in the know have had no difficulty recognizing some of the people whom Davies has embellished into often bizarre characters: John Pearson transmogrified into John Parlabane in *The Rebel Angels,* for instance, and Alan Jarvis made over into Aylwin Ross in *What's Bred in the Bone.* Such mergings of fact into fiction always arouse doubts in one's mind about the writer's motives and ultimately about the nature of his achievement. Is he playing metafictional games with the reader? Or is he lazily offering us memory half raw? As distinct from the youthful autobiographical novel, which is a *rite de passage* many readers undergo in the development of their fic-

tional imagination, the *roman à clef,* in the hands of an experienced novelist, is always an equivocal achievement in which the power of imagination remains in doubt.

Still, the three novels are more than *romans à clef;* if the Deptford series is concerned with the relationship between illusion and reality as mediated by artifice, this later group tends to be dominated by the relationship between true art and artifice, played out, as in the earlier novels, against the shifting scenes of a stage where history and myth are seen as merging.

In a literal way the central figure is Francis Cornish, whose life is told in the middle novel, *What's Bred in the Bone.* Cornish is known to the world as a discriminating connoisseur and a voracious collector of art. In the first volume, *The Rebel Angels,* he has just died and left to three professors the task of sorting the great accumulation of objects he has acquired and of distributing them in accordance with his will. The narrative is a curiously divided one, part of it being written by one of the three professors, Simon Darcourt, as a gossiping journal of academic life he called "The New Aubrey," and alternating chapters forming a kind of interior diary of Maria Theotoky, a half-Polish, half-Gypsy graduate student; she thinks herself in love with Clement Hollier, the second of the professors, a great mythographer who has seduced her in a fit of absent-mindedness. The third professor, the leading villain, is an unprincipled academic poseur, Urquhart McVarish, who steals from the Cornish collection a remarkable unknown Rabelais manuscript after which Hollier lusts academically.

These high eccentrics, consumed by scholarly passions and academic greeds, and reinforced by such colleagues as the sinister ex-monk John Parlabane, present academe as the terrain of such strange conflicts that one feels often Davies is trying to compensate for his frustration with the dullness of real Canadian academic life. The action mounts to a suicide (Parlabane's) and a bizarre murder (of McVarish by Parlabane) among sexual orgies as strange in their own way as anything in Petronius. The novel slides—as so many of Davies' do—into the serene harbour of a happy ending, out of tone with the rest of the book, in which Maria, having recovered from her infatuation with her professor, marries Arthur Cornish, the rich nephew of Francis and the real administrator of the Cornish estate.

Once again we are treated to displays of knowledge. There is a fascinating oddity about the arcane lore of gypsies rejuvenating and faking old violins which provides some of the most entertaining pages of the book. There is also an unfortunate bit of stale derivativeness when the Sheldonian theory of the effect of physique on temperament is warmed up in a weakly humorous scene when Ozias Froats expounds his theories on the qualities and virtues of human excrement.

It is a more disunited novel than any of Davies' previous works; the central intrigue over the Rabelais papers is too weak to carry the burden of so many extraneous interests, and no character—not even wicked Parlabane or the brooding offscene presence of Francis Cornish is sufficiently realized to sustain one's interest.

Francis Cornish comes fully onstage in *What's Bred in the Bone,* which is really a classic *bildungsroman,* in form, language, and in the handling of the trilogy's central theme, the relationship between artifice and art. A whimsical structure, in which the chapters are interspersed with angelic conversations, does not disguise the fact that the novel is told in a very conservative third-person narrative. Cornish's life begins in Blairlogie on the Ottawa River, which is clearly a fictional presentation of Renfrew, where Davies spent much of his childhood, and the money that will eventually finance Francis as a collector comes originally from the destruction of the northern Ontario forests. Like Ramsay's [in *Fifth Business*], his childhood is dominated by an obsession, in this case with "the Looner," his idiot brother, the first Francis, whose survival has been concealed and who becomes one of the earliest subjects of the second Francis's pencil when he begins his lonely apprenticeship as an artist.

Following a picaresque line, the novel takes Francis to Oxford, where he falls in with the famous restorer of classical paintings, Tancred Saraceni; he eventually joins Saraceni at a castle in Bavaria where their task is to restore—and improve in the restoring—a cache of German late medieval paintings which are passed on to the credulous Nazis in exchange for authentic Italian masterpieces from German collections. Here—and the opportunity is not lost for a display of the knowledge Davies has acquired of the methods of the old masters and how their effects can be reproduced in materials now available—Francis perfects his grasp of the technique of painting. When he has reached this point Saraceni proposes to test his aesthetic imagination by leaving him to paint—on an old ruined altarpiece—the work that will show he is a true artist as well as a fine artisan. The result is *The Marriage of Cana* which, when it surfaces before a commission established to send European paintings back to their proper homes, Saraceni proclaims to be an original by an unknown early painter, whom he calls The Alchemical Master; later Aylwin Ross publishes an analytical essay that seems to set the picture firmly in the political and social context of the times. What we—as readers—know to be the work of a modern man has been accepted by the artistic establishment as the work of a man five centuries before, and we enjoy the ironies that our knowledge allows us.

But Davies is after more than irony. There is serious business on foot here, as *The Lyre of Orpheus* reveals. I have already shown, in opening this essay, how in plot *The Lyre of Orpheus* circles back to the early Davies novels, as if to signify that a cycle is being closed, and how, thematically, it brings to a conclusion questions regarding the nature of literary art that are implicit in Davies' fiction from the beginning.

Here, in this most recent novel, the artistic conservatism of Robertson Davies is clearly displayed, in argument and in practice. Once again the narrative is a traditional third-person one, given a touch of metafictional contrivance by the introduction of the beyond-the-grave commentaries of Hoffman, which in fact deepen the conservatism of the narrative by presenting the views on art of a nineteenth-century musician, which the twentieth-century musicians in the novel are seeking to bring to fruition. The enthusiastic account of Schnak's dedicated toil in completing another musician's work abandoned so long ago is a clear denial of the cult of originality that has dominated western art and literature since the days of the romantics. Allied to the cult of originality is that of contemporaneity, the idea that the true artist must speak of his time in its own verbal or visual language; Darcourt's triumphal assertion of Francis Cornish's genius, which finds in *The Marriage of Cana* an expression that is neither original nor contemporary but is true to his talents and his life, is a negation of that doctrine too.

Thematically, *The Lyre of Orpheus* projects a viewpoint that is reactionary rather than classicist in formal terms, for, though Davies has adhered increasingly in his most recent English novels to the traditional methods of mainstream English fiction, his interests have placed him on the verge of Gothic romanticism in selecting his content, while his approach to characterization has brought him close to a comic tradition in fiction that, as we have seen, runs from Fielding through Peacock and Dickens to Joyce Cary. In denying the importance of originality and contemporaneity he is in fact guarding his own territory, for he is neither a strikingly original novelist, nor, in the sense of representing any avant garde, a notably contemporary writer.

Here lie the main reasons for the popularity of Robertson Davies, which some critics have found offensive to their ideas of what Canadians should be expecting of their writers. It resembles the current popularity of realist painters like Alex Colville, Christopher Pratt, Ivan Eyre, and Jack Chambers. Most people, in Canada and elsewhere, are artistically conservative; only the avant gardes of the past are—though not invariably—acceptable to them. It is true that the permissiveness of the 1960s made the broader public open to certain kinds of content that were once unacceptable. But, as the totalitarians have always known, it is in the formal aspects of a work that the deepest rebellion declares itself, and it is at this point that general readers, feeling the boundaries of normal speech and perception slipping away, become disturbed; the nihilism of much of modern art and literature bewilders and repels them. They need reassurance, and the novels of Robertson Davies, which present no real formal challenges, and whose essential optimism is shown in upbeat endings, with quests completed, wishes fulfilled, evil routed, and villains destroyed, are admirably suited for the calming and comforting of uneasy Canadians. They exist on the edge of popular fiction, where Pangloss reigns in the best of possible worlds. (pp. 45-8)

George Woodcock, "A Cycle Completed: The Nine Novels of Robertson Davies," in *Canadian Literature,* No. 126, Autumn, 1990, pp. 33-48.

SOURCES FOR FURTHER STUDY

Davis, J. Madison, ed. *Conversations with Robertson Davies.* Jackson: University Press of Mississippi, 1989, 285 p.

> Collection of interviews arranged chronologically from 1963 to 1988.

Lawrence, Robert G., and Macey, Samuel L., eds. *Studies in Robertson Davies' Deptford Trilogy.* Victoria, B. C.: University of Victoria, 1980, 123 p.

> Includes nine essays on various topics concerning content, theme, and motifs in *The Deptford Trilogy,* as well as an introduction by Davies.

Monk, Patricia. *The Smaller Infinity: The Jungian Self in the Novels of Robertson Davies.* Toronto: University of Toronto Press, 1982, 214 p.

> Examines Davies's affinities with Jungian psychology as expressed in his fiction and nonfiction.

Oates, Joyce Carol. "Books Considered." *The New Republic* 178, No. 15 (15 April 1978): 22-5.

> Unfavorable review of *One Half of Robertson Davies,* in which Oates challenges Davies's reputation as "Canada's leading man of letters."

Peterman, Michael. *Robertson Davies.* Boston: Twayne Publishers, 1986, 178 p.

> Biography focusing on critical discussion of Davies's journalistic works, dramas, and novels up to the publication of *The Rebel Angels.*

Stone-Blackburn, Susan. *Robertson Davies, Playwright: A Search for the Self on the Canadian Stage.* Vancouver: University of British Columbia Press, 1985, 249 p.

> Study of Davies's dramas examining aspects of melodrama as well as his analysis of the human consciousness.

Daniel Defoe

1660?-1731

(Also DeFoe and De Foe; born Daniel Foe) English novelist, essayist, poet, journalist, historian, and satirist.

INTRODUCTION

Defoe has been called the "father of the English novel." He is also one of the most prolific authors in world literature. Although scholars disagree as to the exact number, as many as 545 works have been attributed to his pen. Among these are a select group of novels and histories considered classics, including *The Life and Strange Surprising Adventures of Robinson Crusoe, of York, Mariner* (1719); *The Fortunes and Misfortunes of the Famous Moll Flanders* (1721); and *A Journal of the Plague Year* (1722). However, more significant than the quantity of Defoe's works is his impact on the development of fiction as we know it today. Combining elements from the spiritual autobiography, the Christian allegory, and the rogue biography, Defoe fashioned realistic narratives that utilized techniques—such as dialogue, setting, characterization, symbolism, and irony—common to the modern novel form. Many critics consider Defoe the first "realist" in literature, and contend that his sensitivity to detail gave his art a quality of believability unknown before his time. Coupled with this realism, Defoe's use of common language and his simple, direct style helped to popularize the novel form among the growing middle class in England and Europe. In addition to his influence on fiction, Defoe also played a major role in the development of modern journalism. *The Review*—a journal he single-handedly wrote and edited during the reign of Queen Anne—is considered the forerunner of the *Tatler* and *Spectator* and the most advanced newspaper of its time. But Defoe achieved literary immortality primarily as a novelist, particularly with his masterpiece *Robinson Crusoe*, which Edmund Gosse has called "one of the most beautiful of the world's romances."

Defoe was born in London, the son of Nonconformist, middle-class parents. The Nonconformists, or Dissenters, were protestant sects that opposed the official state religion of Anglicanism and consequently suffered persecution. Despite the oppression of Nonconformists during his youth, however, Defoe enjoyed a relatively secure and religious upbringing. At the age of fourteen his parents sent him to the famous academy at Stoke Newington kept by Charles Morton, where most of the students were Dissenters. At this time he was intended for the ministry, but after three years he forfeited this ambition and turned to business. Around 1683, he established himself as a hosiery merchant and traveled throughout England and the continent. During this period he acquired an expert knowledge of trade and economics and began speculating in a number of financial ventures. One such speculation backfired and in 1692 Defoe filed for bankruptcy, his debts mounting to over 17,000 pounds. Though he paid off all but 5,000 pounds to his creditors, Defoe was haunted throughout his life by unsatisfied debt collectors. While spending time in the debtor's refuge of Whitefriars—where arrest warrants could not be served—Defoe first came into contact with the thieves and prostitutes who would become the subjects of much of his later fiction. After declaring bankruptcy, Defoe took a position as secretary at a brick factory near Tilbury, England. He gradually improved his position until he became chief owner of the brickworks. During this time Defoe published his first essays, the most prominent of which was *An Essay upon Projects* (1697). In this work he used all his experience as a businessman and traveler to suggest radical reforms for the British nation, including an advanced road system, mental hospitals for the insane, the recognition of women's equality with men, military colleges, and a national bank. These suggestions—many of which were eventually enacted over the next two centuries—show that Defoe was an acute social observer and prescient thinker.

The first decade of the 1700s marked a period of increased political involvement for Defoe. Heretofore, he had been active in political questions and social struggles, such as the Monmouth uprising of 1685 and the succession of King William of Orange in 1689. But the new century brought increasing political hardships for Dissenters and fresh attacks on King William, whom Defoe staunchly supported. After the poet-journalist John Tutchin ridiculed the king in his poem "The Foreigners," Defoe published perhaps his best-known verse, *The True-Born Englishman* (1701). In this work he satirized the prejudice of his fellow citizens and declared that the English were a race of mongrels, bred from the castaways of Europe. Rather than inciting his opponents, the poem was warmly received and sold more copies in a single day than any other previously published poem in English. However, Defoe's next major work, *The Shortest Way with the Dissenters* (1702), was not greeted with the same success. In this anonymously written satire, Defoe set out to discredit,

through ironic impersonation, the Tory leaders and high churchmen who continued to press for stricter measures against Dissenters. Defoe had hoped that by exaggerating their point of view he could reduce their arguments to absurdity. Instead, both Dissenters and high churchmen alike mistook the satire for an honest proposal, and both groups became equally enraged when they discovered that the work was a hoax. Defoe was eventually arrested and charged with seditious libel. He was found guilty and sentenced to a term in prison, to be served at the queen's pleasure and only after he spent three consecutive days in the pillory, a punishment which occasionally ended in death. Although Defoe managed to turn this event to his favor—by publishing his *A Hymn to the Pillory* (1703) and thereby convincing the crowds of the injustice done to him—critics generally believe that the pillory had a lasting effect on Defoe, making him a bitter man and an outcast in his own society.

After a brief prison term, cut short with the assistance of Secretary of State Robert Harley, Defoe became an instrument of the government, serving as a secret agent and political propagandist for the Tories. With funds from Harley, he began *The Review* in 1704 and continued as its sole writer for ten years. Although *The Review* served as a vehicle for Harley's Tory beliefs, which promoted Anglicanism and resisted religious toleration and foreign entanglements, Defoe's essentially Whiggish beliefs were developed in private, particularly his identity with and support of the rising English middle class. In 1706 Defoe worked behind the scenes during the secret negotiations for the union of Scotland and England. He acquired a vast amount of knowledge on the subject, which he later published as *The History of the Union of Great Britain* (1709), a work still valued by historians for its accuracy and scope, though often attacked by literary critics for its lack of color. With Queen Anne's death in 1714 and the fall of the Tory government, Defoe disappeared from public view. He reappeared in 1716 as editor of *Mist's Weekly-Journal,* a Tory-Jacobite periodical which, as a secret Whig agent, Defoe was hired to sabotage.

Throughout these years of political activity, Defoe continued his imaginative writing. He began to experiment with realistic dialogue, setting, and characterization in *The Family Instructor* (1715), one of his many books on religious and moral conduct; but it was not until the publication of *Robinson Crusoe*—followed by its sequels *The Farther Adventures of Robinson Crusoe* (1719) and *Serious Reflections during the Life and Surprising Adventures of Robinson Crusoe* (1720)—that Defoe discovered a successful formula. Partly inspired by the true adventures of an ill-disciplined sailor named Alexander Selkirk, *Robinson Crusoe* was extremely popular, particularly with the middle and lower classes for whom Crusoe was an appealing model.

Robinson Crusoe stands apart and above Defoe's other novels, mainly because its subject and setting lent themselves so well to the author's descriptive talents. The novel has been interpreted as an allegorical presentation of the growth of the British empire, as an attack on economic individualism, as an adaptation of the traditional spiritual autobiography, as an allegory of the author's own life, and—to Defoe's contemporaries—as simply the true story of one man's unusual life. No matter how critics have interpreted the novel, most agree that *Robinson Crusoe* is one of the world's most engaging stories.

For Defoe, the years 1719 to 1724 marked the most productive period of his career. In addition to journalistic and political writings, he wrote a series of novels in the same mold as *Robinson Crusoe,* including *The Life, Adventures, and Pyracies of the Famous Captain Singleton* (1720); *Memoirs of a Cavalier* (1720); *Moll Flanders; The History of the Most Remarkable Life and Extraordinary Adventures of the Truly Honourable Colonel Jacque, Vulgarly Called Colonel Jack* (1722); *A Journal of the Plague Year;* and *The Fortunate Mistress* (1724) (commonly known as *Roxana*). Among these works the most frequently discussed are *Moll Flanders, A Journal of the Plague Year,* and *Roxana.* The first is a study of poverty and crime similar to the rogue biographies of the seventeenth century, but much more complex in theme and characterization. As with *Robinson Crusoe,* Defoe published *Moll Flanders, Colonel Jack,* and *Roxana* as actual biographies with certain well-defined moral messages attached. However, his use of the first-person narrator and the development of his protagonists often undercut his moral themes, resulting in a group of stories whose plots flatly contradict their endings. Such is the case with *Moll Flanders,* which has raised a critical debate over whether Defoe meant to be sincere in stressing the immorality of a life of crime or simply ironic, suggesting that economic circumstance is responsible for the protagonist's decline. Despite the uncertainty of Defoe's intentions, most contemporary critics agree that in *Moll Flanders,* as well as *Colonel Jack* and *Roxana,* the author was writing an unfavorable critique of capitalistic society, and not simply stressing the virtues of a moral life. *A Journal of the Plague Year* is considered Defoe's most successful novel after *Robinson Crusoe.* In the later work he imagined numerous recorded incidents to present a strikingly realistic picture of life in London during the Great Plague. *A Journal of the Plague Year* avoids the moral trappings and character reversals of Defoe's other stories. It is told in an objective, matter-of-fact manner through the narrator, "H. F.," often assumed to be based upon Defoe's uncle, Henry Foe. Though the book is often factually incorrect, *A Journal of the Plague Year* demonstrates Defoe's understanding of the powerful role nature plays in shaping human destinies.

Roxana was Defoe's last major work of fiction. After this he concentrated solely on travel essays and history, such as *A Tour through the Whole Island of Great Britain* (1724-27) and *The Political History of the Devil* (1726). During the mid-1720s his journalistic employment came to an end, perhaps because James Mist, the owner of *Mist's Weekly-Journal,* discovered Defoe was a government agent and notified other editors. Scholars are uncertain about Defoe's final years. It is known that he left his home at Stoke Newington and disappeared from public view once again, but the reason has never been determined. Some critics suggest that he was hiding from Mist, who sought revenge for Defoe's tampering with his newspaper; others believe that, having lost governmental protection, Defoe was forced to escape from his creditors. Whatever the reason, Defoe spent his final years alone and died in London near the place of his birth.

Defoe has always enjoyed a wide popularity among the reading public. From critics and scholars, however, he has received ambivalent reactions. It was nearly a hundred years after his death before Walter Scott presented the first favorable account of Defoe's merits as a novelist. During his lifetime, Defoe was looked upon as an imaginative writer at best and was usually considered a swindler and moral invalid. Because of his dealings with both the Whigs and the Tories, he earned the trust of neither, and he quickly acquired the reputation of a literary hack willing to do anything for a fee. His novels did nothing to enhance his reputation. *Robinson Crusoe* was considered un-Christian and attacked for its improbabilities and misconceptions concerning life at sea. His so-called secondary novels, despite the author's moral pretext, were viewed as unworthy of literary consideration. Much of the early criticism of Defoe's fiction failed to realize the innovative nature of the novel form, though Defoe compounded the problem by insisting that his novels were real biographies. Even such later critics as Theophilus Cibber and George Chalmers, while praising Defoe for his vivid imagination and literary talents, held firmly to the eighteenth-century theory that literature should delight and instruct when appraising his works. Thus, criticism of Defoe's work during the eighteenth century focused strictly on its authenticity and moral implications—two standards poorly suited for an appreciation of Defoe.

Scott's essay signaled a major shift in Defoe criticism. Although Scott felt uneasy about the subject matter of such novels as *Moll Flanders, Colonel Jack,* and *Roxana,* he believed that Defoe was successful due to his ability to present an "appearance of reality" in his works, particularly *Robinson Crusoe.* Other critics began to praise Defoe for his simple style, his common language, his lack of affectation, even his unstructured method of writing, for all these contributed to the sense of reality conveyed by his narratives. After Scott, Charles Lamb resurrected *Moll Flanders, Colonel Jack, Captain Singleton,* and *Roxana,* which he considered just as important as *Robinson Crusoe.* Throughout the first half of the nineteenth century Defoe's works were the subject of a heavy amount of critical attention, especially when compared to the previous century. His stature rose from an obscure literary mountebank to one of England's greatest authors, superior even to Jonathan Swift according to Samuel Taylor Coleridge. But by the 1850s Defoe's reputation once again began to wane. Critics of this period, including W. C. Roscoe, argued that Defoe was a skillful writer, but hardly an imaginative or creative genius. Many concluded that *Robinson Crusoe* was the only novel in which he demonstrated any degree of artistry whatsoever. Others assailed his characters for their psychological shallowness and argued that Defoe lacked the imaginative scope necessary to produce truly memorable portraits of life.

Twentieth-century critics of Defoe's works have tended to be more concerned with structure and meaning than with the author's character. Most often discussed is Defoe's use of irony, his dependence on conventional morality, his economic theories, and his debt to the traditional autobiography. Perhaps the biggest debate concerns the sincerity of Defoe's moral themes—whether he considered them integral to his novels or whether he artificially imposed them on his work as a convenient device for making his stories palatable to the public of his day. Some critics, such as Mark Schorer, contend that while the moral of Defoe's novels was always based on the rewards of virtue and the punishment of sin, his narratives suggested exactly the opposite: his heroes and heroines would become rich and independent through crime or immorality, then repent and accept their guilt without ever sacrificing their security for this redemption. These critics suggest that this discrepancy is due to Defoe's irony, that in reality he was questioning the moral values of his day when middle-class security, acquisitive behavior, and the Puritan conscience were so easily reconciled. On the other hand, Ian Watt argues that although Defoe's moral themes often contradict his narratives, his novels, in particular *Moll Flanders,* are not ironic because the author never sees the action differently from his protagonists. For Watt, if it is irony, it is irony of an unintentional kind, merely suggesting an unresolved conflict within the author's thought.

Modern critics agree that Defoe has been undervalued as an artist by those who take the works and ideas of Swift, Alexander Pope, and Joseph Addison as the standard of eighteenth-century literature. His economic and social interests, his powerful imagination and inquisitive mind, combined with his experience as a journalist and international merchant, enabled him to give in fiction an unparalleled account of life in the eighteenth century, while his masterpiece, *Robinson Crusoe,* continues to fascinate people of all ages and nationalities.

(For further information about Defoe's life and works, see *Dictionary of Literary Biography,* Vol. 39: *British Novelists, 1660-1800; Literature Criticism from 1400 to 1800,* Vol. 1; and *Something about the Author,* Vol. 22.)

CRITICAL COMMENTARY

JEAN-JACQUES ROUSSEAU
(essay date 1762)

[A French philosopher and essayist, Rousseau has been called "the father of Romanticism." In the following excerpt, originally published in 1762 as part of his *Émile; ou, De l'éducation,* he discusses the instructive value of *Robinson Crusoe.*]

Since books are absolutely necessary, there is one which to my taste supplies the happiest introduction to natural education. This will be the first book my Émile will read. For a long time it will constitute his entire library by itself, and it will always retain a distinguished place there. It will be the text on which all our discussions of the natural sciences will be merely a gloss. It will serve as a check on the state of our judgment as we proceed, and in so far as our taste remains unspoilt, we shall always take pleasure in reading it. What is this wonderful book then? Is it Aristotle, or Pliny, or Buffon? No—it is *Robinson Crusoe.*

Robinson Crusoe on his island, alone, deprived of the help of his fellows and of all artificial aids, yet providing for his own support, for his own safety and even achieving a sort of well-being—this is a matter of interest for any age, which can be made enjoyable to children in a thousand ways. . . . This state, I admit, is not that of man in society, and most probably it will not be

Principal Works

An Essay upon Projects (essay) 1697

The True-Born Englishman (poetry) 1701

The Shortest Way with the Dissenters; or, Proposals for the Establishment of the Church (satire) 1702

A Hymn to the Pillory (poetry) 1703

The History of the Union of Great Britain (history) 1709

The Family Instructor (handbook) 1715

*The Life and Strange Surprising Adventures of Robinson Crusoe, of York, Mariner: Who Lived Eight and Twenty Years All Alone, in an Uninhabited Island on the Coast of America, Near the Mouth of the Great River Oroonoque (novel) 1719

*The Farther Adventures of Robinson Crusoe: Being the Second and Last Part of His Life; and the Strange Surprising Accounts of His Travels Round Three Parts of the Globe (novel) 1719

The Life, Adventures, and Pyracies of the Famous Captain Singleton (novel) 1720

*Serious Reflections during the Life and Surprising Adventures of Robinson Crusoe, with His Vision of the Angelick World (novel) 1720

The Fortunes and Misfortunes of the Famous Moll Flanders (novel) 1721

The History of the Most Remarkable Life and Extraordi-

nary Adventures of the Truly Honourable Colonel Jacque, Vulgarly Called Colonel Jack (novel) 1722

A Journal of the Plague Year: Being Observations or Memorials of the Most Remarkable Occurences, as Well as Publick as Private, which Happened in London during the Last Great Visitation in 1665 (fictional history) 1722

† The Fortunate Mistress; or, A History of the Life and Vast Variety of Fortunes of Mademoiselle de Belau, Afterwards Called the Countess de Wintselsheim, in Germany: Being the Person Known by the Name of the Lady Roxana, in the Time of King Charles II (novel) 1724

The Political History of the Devil, as Well Antient as Modern (fictional history) 1726

The Works of Daniel Defoe. 16 vols. (novels, history, essays, fictional history, fictional journal, fictional memoirs, and poetry) 1903-04

Defoe's Review: 1704-13. 22 vols. (essays and journalism) 1938

The Letters of Daniel Defoe (letters) 1955

*These works are collectively referred to as Robinson Crusoe.

†This work is commonly referred to as Roxana.

Émile's: but it is through this state that he will come to value all others. The surest way of rising above prejudice and ordering one's opinions according to the real relations of things is to put oneself in the place of a solitary man, and to judge everything as he would, having regard to its particular utility.

Stripped of all its nonsense, beginning with Robinson's wreck off his island and ending with the arrival of the ship which is to take him away, this novel will be both instruction and delight to Émile during this period. I would like him to be quite infatuated with it; to busy himself constantly with his stockade, his goats and his crops. I want him to learn in detail everything one would have to know in such a case, not through books but through things. I want him to identify himself with Robinson, to see himself dressed in skins, with a big hat and a broadsword—the whole grotesque paraphernalia of his appearance, except the parasol which he will not need. (pp. 52-3)

The child, when urged to equip himself for the island, will be keener to learn than the master to teach him. He will want to know everything useful, and nothing else; you will no longer have to guide him, only to restrain him. Moreover, we must hurry to set him up on the island, whilst it is enough in itself to satisfy him. For the day is coming when, if he wishes to live there

still, it will not be alone; and when Friday, who scarcely concerns him now, will no longer suffice for any time. (p. 53)

Jean-Jacques Rousseau, "Rousseau on 'Robinson Crusoe'," translated by Pat Rogers, in *Defoe: The Critical Heritage,* edited by Pat Rogers, Routledge & Kegan Paul, 1972, pp. 52-4.

SIR WALTER SCOTT

(essay date 1827?)

[Scott was a nineteenth-century Scottish novelist, poet, and essayist. In the following excerpt, he outlines reasons for Defoe's enduring popularity.]

[Before] proceeding to attempt a few observations on *Robinson Crusoe* in particular, it may be necessary to consider what is the particular charm which carries the reader through, not that *chef-d'oeuvre* alone, but others of De Foe's compositions, and inspires a reluctance to lay down the volume till the tale is finished; and the desire, not generally felt in the perusal of works of fiction, to read every sentence and word upon every leaf, instead of catching up as much of the story as may enable us to understand the conclusion.

It cannot be the beauty of the style which thus commands the reader's attention; for that of De Foe, though often forcible, is rather rendered so by the interest of a particular situation than by the art of the writer. In general the language is loose and inaccurate, often tame and creeping, and almost always that of the lower classes in society. Neither does the charm depend upon the character of the incidents; for although in *Robinson Crusoe,* the incidents are very fine, yet in the *History of the Plague* the events are disgusting, and scarce less in those works where the scene lies in low life. Yet, like Pistol eating his leek, we go on growling and reading to the end of the volume, while we nod over many a more elegant subject, treated by authors who exhibit a far greater command of language. Neither can it be the artful conducting of the story, by which we are so much interested. De Foe seems to have written too rapidly to pay the least attention to this circumstance; the incidents are huddled together like paving-stones discharged from a cart, and have as little connexion between the one and the other. The scenes merely follow, without at all depending on each other. They are not like those of the regular drama, connected together by a regular commencement, continuation, and conclusion, but rather resemble the pictures in a showman's box, which have no relation further than as being enclosed within the same box, and subjected to the action of the same string.

To what, then, are we to ascribe this general charm attached to the romances of De Foe? We presume to answer, that it is chiefly to be ascribed to the unequalled dexterity with which our author has given an appearance of REALITY to the incidents which he narrates. Even De Foe's deficiencies in style, his homeliness of language, his rusticity of thought, seem to . . . claim credit for him as one who speaks the truth, the rather that we suppose he wants the skill to conceal or disguise it. (pp. 172-73)

It is greatly to be doubted whether De Foe could have changed his colloquial, circuitous, and periphrastic style for any other, whether more coarse or more elegant. We have little doubt it was connected with his nature, and the particular turn of his thoughts and ordinary expressions, and that he did not succeed so much by writing in an assumed manner, as by giving full scope to his own. (p. 175)

The air of writing with all the plausibility of truth must, in almost every case, have its own peculiar value; as we admire the paintings of some Flemish artists, where, though the subjects drawn are mean and disagreeable, and such as in nature we would not wish to study or look close upon, yet the skill with which they are represented by the painter gives an interest to the imitation upon canvass which the original entirely wants. But, on the other hand, when the power of exact and circumstantial delineation is applied to objects which we are anxiously desirous to see in their proper shape and colours, we have a double source of pleasure, both in the art of the painter, and in the interest which we take in the subject represented. Thus the style of probability with which De Foe invested his narratives, was perhaps ill bestowed, or rather wasted, upon some of the works which he thought proper to produce, and cannot recommend to us the subject of *Colonel Jack* and *Moll Flanders;* but, on the other hand, the same talent throws an air of truth about the delightful history of *Robinson Crusoe,* which we never could have believed it possible to have united with so extraordinary a situation as is assigned to the hero. All the usual scaffolding and machinery employed in composing fictitious history are carefully discarded. The early incidents of the tale, which in ordinary works of invention are usually thrown out as pegs to hang the conclusion upon, are in this work only touched upon, and suffered to drop out of sight. Robinson, for example, never hears any thing more of his elder brother, who enters Lockhart's Dragoons in the beginning of the work, and who, in any common romance, would certainly have appeared before the conclusion. We lose sight at once and for ever of the interesting Xury; and the whole earlier adventures of our voyager vanish, not to be recalled to our recollection by the subsequent course of the story. His father—the good old merchant of Hull—all the other persons who have been originally active in the drama—vanish from the scene, and appear not again. This is not the case in the ordinary romance, where the author, however luxuriant his invention, does not willingly quit possession of the creatures of his imagination, till they have rendered him some services upon the scene; whereas in common life, it rarely happens that our early acquaintances exercise much influence upon the fortunes of our future life.

Our friend Robinson, thereafter, in the course of his roving and restless life, is at length thrown upon his Desert Island, a situation in which, existing as a solitary being, he became an example of what the unassisted energies of an individual of the human race can perform; and the author has, with wonderful exactness, described him as acting and thinking precisely as such a man must have thought and acted in such an extraordinary situation.

Pathos is not De Foe's general characteristic, he had too little delicacy of mind; when it comes, it comes uncalled, and is created by the circumstances, not sought for by the author. The excess, for instance, of the natural longing for human society which Crusoe manifests while on board of the stranded Spanish vessel, by falling into a sort of agony, as he repeated the words, 'Oh, that but one man had been saved!—Oh, that there had been but one!' is in the highest degree pathetic. The agonizing reflections of the solitary, when he is in danger of being driven to sea, in his rash attempt to circumnavigate his island, are also affecting.

In like manner we may remark, that De Foe's genius did not approach the grand or terrific. The battles, which he is fond of describing, are told with the indifference of an old bucanier, and probably in the very way in which he may have heard them recited by the actors. His goblins, too, are generally a commonplace sort of spirits, that bring with them very little of supernatural terror; and yet the fine incident of the print of the naked foot on the sand, with Robinson Crusoe's terrors in consequence, never fail to leave a powerful impression upon the reader.

The supposed situation of his hero was peculiarly favourable to the circumstantial style of De Foe. Robinson Crusoe was placed in a condition where it was natural that the slightest event should make an impression on him; and De Foe was not an author who would leave the slightest event untold. When he mentions that two shoes were driven ashore, and adds that they were not neighbours, we feel it an incident of importance to the poor solitary.

The assistance which De Foe derived from Selkirk's history, seems of a very meagre kind. It is not certain that he was obliged to the real hermit of Juan Fernandez even for the original hint; for the putting mutineers or turbulent characters on shore upon solitary places, was a practice so general among the bucaniers, that there was a particular name for the punishment; it was called *marooning* a man. De Foe borrowed, perhaps, from the account in Woodes Rogers, the circumstance of the two huts, the abundance of goats, the clothing made out of their skins; and the turnips of Alexander Selkirk may have perhaps suggested the corn of Robinson Crusoe. Even these incidents, however, are so wrought up and heightened, and so much is added to make them interesting, that the bare circumstances occurring elsewhere, cannot be said to infringe upon the author's claim to originality. On the whole, indeed, Robinson Crusoe is put to so many more trials of ingenuity, his comforts are so much increased, his solitude is so much diversified, and his account of his thoughts and occupations so distinctly traced, that the course of the work embraces a far wider circle of investigation into human nature, than could be derived from that of Selkirk, who, for want of the tools and conveniences supplied to Crusoe by the wreck, relapses into a sort of savage state, which could have afforded little scope of delineation. It may, however, be observed, that De Foe may have known so much of Selkirk's history as to be aware how much his stormy passions were checked and tamed by his long course of solitude, and that, from being a kind of Will Atkins, a brawling dissolute seaman, he became (which was certainly the case) a grave, sober, reflective man. The manner in which Robinson

Crusoe's moral sense and religious feeling are awakened and brought into action, are important passages in the work. (pp. 179-82)

The continuation of Robinson Crusoe's history after he obtains the society of his man Friday, is less philosophical than that which turns our thoughts upon the efforts which a solitary individual may make for extending his own comforts in the melancholy situation in which he is placed, and upon the natural reflections suggested by the progress of his own mind. The character of Friday is, nevertheless, extremely pleasing; and the whole subsequent history of the shipwrecked Spaniards and the pirate vessel is highly interesting. Here certainly the *Memoirs of Robinson Crusoe* ought to have stopped. The Second Part, though containing many passages which display the author's genius, does not rise high in character above the *Memoirs of Captain Singleton,* or the other imaginary voyages of the author.

There scarce exists a work so popular as *Robinson Crusoe.* It is read eagerly by young people; and there is hardly an elf so devoid of imagination as not to have supposed for himself a solitary island in which he could act *Robinson Crusoe,* were it but in the corner of the nursery. To many it has given the decided turn of their lives, by sending them to sea. For the young mind is much less struck with the hardships of the anchorite's situation than with the animating exertions which he makes to overcome them; and *Robinson Crusoe* produces the same impression upon an adventurous spirit which the *Book of Martyrs* would do on a young devotee, or the *Newgate Calendar* upon an acolyte of Bridewell; both of which students are less terrified by the horrible manner in which the tale terminates, than animated by sympathy with the saints or depredators who are the heroes of their volume. Neither does a re-perusal of *Robinson Crusoe,* at a more advanced age, diminish our early impressions. The situation is such as every man may make his own, and, being possible in itself, is, by the exquisite art of the narrator, rendered as probable as it is interesting. It has the merit, too, of that species of accurate painting which can be looked at again and again with new pleasure.

Neither has the admiration of the work been confined to England, though Robinson Crusoe himself, with his rough good sense, his prejudices, and his obstinate determination not to sink under evils which can be surpassed by exertion, forms no bad specimen of the True-Born Englishman. The rage for imitating a work so popular seems to have risen to a degree of frenzy; and, by a mistake not peculiar to this particular class of the *servum pecus,* the imitators did not attempt to apply De Foe's manner of managing the narrative to some situation of a different kind, but seized upon and caricatured the principal incidents of the shipwrecked mariner and the solitary island. It is computed that within

Defoe on *Moll Flanders*:

The world is so taken up of late with novels and romances that it will be hard for a private history to be taken for genuine, where the names and other circumstances of the person are concealed; and on this account we must be content to leave the reader to pass his own opinion upon the ensuing sheets and take it just as he pleases.

The author is here supposed to be writing her own history, and in the very beginning of her account she gives the reasons why she thinks fit to conceal her true name, after which there is no occasion to say any more about that.

It is true that the original of this story is put into new words, and the style of the famous lady we here speak of is a little altered; particularly she is made to tell her own tale in modester words than she told it at first, the copy which came first to hand having been written in language more like one still in Newgate than one grown penitent and humble, as she afterwards pretends to be.

The pen employed in finishing her story, and making it what you now see it to be, has had no little difficulty to put it into a dress fit to be seen and to make it speak language fit to be read. When a woman debauched from her youth, nay, even being the offspring of debauchery and vice,

comes to give an account of all her vicious practices, and even to descend to the particular occasions and circumstances by which she first became wicked, and of all the progressions of crime which she ran through in threescore years, an author must be hard put to it to wrap it up so clean as not to give room, especially for vicious readers, to turn it to his disadvantage.

All possible care, however, has been taken to give no lewd ideas, no immodest turns in the new dressing up this story; no, not to the worst part of her expressions. To this purpose some of the vicious part of her life, which could not be modestly told, is quite left out, and several other parts are very much shortened. What is left 'tis hoped will not offend the chastest reader or the modestest hearer; and as the best use is to be made even of the worst story, the moral, 'tis hoped, will keep the reader serious, even where the story might incline him to be otherwise. To give the history of a wicked life repented of necessarily requires that the wicked part should be made as wicked as the real history of it will bear, to illustrate and give a beauty to the penitent part, which is certainly the best and brightest, if related with equal spirit and life.

Defoe, in a preface to *Moll Flanders*, 1722.

---

forty years from the appearance of the original work, no less than forty-one different *Robinsons* appeared, besides fifteen other imitations, in which other titles were used. . . . Upon the whole, the work is as unlikely to lose its celebrity as it is to be equalled in its peculiar character by any other of similar excellence. (pp. 182-83)

Walter Scott, in an extract from his *On Novelists and Fiction,* edited by Ioan Williams, Routledge & Kegan Paul, 1968, pp. 164-83.

W. C. ROSCOE

(essay date 1856)

[In the following excerpt, Roscoe explores characterization in Defoe's major works of fiction.]

The modern novel is the characteristic literature of modern times. It is not difficult to detect some of the leading sources of its growth in the conditions and tendencies of modern society, especially in England. Increase of personal liberty has given increased scope and a greater common importance to individual life and character. A diminishing political and social restraint over men's lives, and a less urgent necessity for active personal engagement in political affairs, combined with

a less formal and exigent code of manners in society, have endowed men with both more room and more leisure for the conscious determination of their own lives and characters. . . . An increased interest in our own characters has naturally given us an increased interest in the individual characters of others; and the examination and representation of character has been the most universal object of modern imaginative literature, its most special characteristic and its highest excellence. . . . Modern history, as we might expect tends too much to become biographical in its character; while biography is far less content than it used to be with stringing together the events of a man's life, and aims at as searching as possible an examination and exhibition of the whole nature of the man. The same reasons that have tended to make character a more universal subject of study have also tended to give it a form which has made newer and more exhaustive methods of treating it more necessary for its exhibition. There are fewer sharp diversities in character than there used to be. Men differ, not less completely, but less prominently, than they used to do: there is less one-sided individual development. When men are sharply constrained by an external power, which can grasp only a part of their nature, the very pressure there will make other parts of their nature start out in strange and abnormal excrescences. The more external restraint is removed, the more rounded and the more alike in their general aspects will be the forms of the single particles which together constitute society: differences of character become less apparent on the surface, and a finer discrimination, a more comprehensive insight, and a more delicate expression, are necessary to delineate its diversities.

Modern taste, accustomed to this more refined school of art, finds little to gratify it in the novels of De Foe. Neither his own genius nor that of his times was favourable to a compliance with its more recondite demands. The reigns of William and of Anne were any thing rather than adapted for the unhampered growth and quiet contemplation of character. They were filled with restless petty action. The liberties of the nation itself had been secured; but the respective rights and claims of the several parties within the nation were never more undecided. It was a time of discord and jangling. Arbitrary invasions on the general liberty of the subject were replaced by harassing restrictions on the free action of certain classes; and dangers important enough to unite the mass of the people in resistance had been replaced by a petty tyranny of disqualifications and fines over discordant minorities, which led an anxious life of mixed warfare and occasional conformity. In such times measures were more interesting than men, events occupied attention more than the study of character. And in such a time the natural bent of De Foe's genius to occupy itself with action and practical affairs was thoroughly confirmed by a long life of thankless political effort, conducted from so independent a point of view as to expose him to the persecution of both the great parties of the day.

Human existence, in all its varied forms and conditions, was the one thing which interested him: but he busied himself rather with what men were doing than with what they were; with how they influenced the external world, rather than with how the external world influenced them. The modes of human life had a curious fascination for him. The way in which people lived and did things, and other imagined ways in which they might live and do the same or other things, were the matters which occupied his attention. The administration of affairs, the conduct of wars, the management of trade, the control of a household,—these were his favourite objects of contemplation. Great or small, they pleased him alike. (pp. 380-82)

His novels set forth not so much the life of a particular person as some particular mode of life. They tell us something that happened, or how things happened. Often the hero is a mere mouth-piece for a mass of adventures, told for their *own* sakes, and carrying their interest entirely in themselves, not deriving any from the light they throw on the suppositious narrator. The *Memoirs of a Cavalier* is De Foe's notion of how the civil wars were carried on. *Captain Carleton* is only a device to tell us what he knows of some of the Low-Country campaigns, of Spain, and of Lord Peterborough's exploits there; and the *History of the Plague* is

interesting as history, not as a personal narrative. Of these sort of things one asks, as the children do, "But is it all true?" It professes to be so; every artifice is resorted to to make us believe it authentic; and there can be no doubt that De Foe deliberately intended to pass these narratives off upon the world as literally true, and to obtain the advantage of the interest so excited. But as soon as you get to learn that they are not authentic their main interest is gone. The great mass of the facts may be true, but you have not the slightest clue to enable you to distinguish between the truth and falsehood of any of the minor and characteristic details: we can be sure only of those broad facts which we know to be true from other sources. In the whole range of imaginative literature there is nothing less satisfactory and more useless than this inextricable mingling of truths and figments. It is not history; it is not fiction. . . . [When] a man bases the interest of his narrative on a mass of minute details about the real affairs of the world, professedly gathered by an eye-witness, the pleasure you derive from it is founded on the belief you have in its exact truth; and as soon as you find that the Cavalier who gives you the benefit of his personal experiences was really a tradesman in London of a generation later, the book loses its value. The element of invention destroys the interest you would have had in it as a record of fact, and the inextricable element of real fact destroys your pleasure in the invention. You wonder at it, and are perplexed in the perusal; if it retains any interest at all, it is due to the measure of probability that in the main it is still true.

And in De Foe's case this probability is very strong. His intense love for facts, and his very accurate and comprehensive knowledge and wide experience of the world of men, made him of all writers the one most able to give a true picture of, or at any rate a collection of true incidents relating to, any of the events either of his own times or of those sufficiently close to survive in the memory of the actors or their immediate descendants. On the other hand, his love of invention, his skill in giving the exactest air of reality to his fancied incidents, and his utter want of scruple in palming them off as truths, leave it quite uncertain in what proportion such narratives as the *History of the Plague* consist of real incidents, and in what of manufactured ones so closely resembling the others as not to be distinguishable from them by any test we now have it in our power to apply. (pp. 382-84)

Something similar to these quasi-historical pieces are such works as *Captain Singleton,* and the *New Voyage round the World;* but they differ from them in their interest lying in the invention displayed in fictitious narrative, to which a basis only of reality is given; and though the boundary which divides the two is as much obscured as possible, they are sufficiently distinguishable in the main; and while we look on the curious incidental revelations as to the trade in the Spanish seas and South-American settlements as no doubt embodying reliable information of its kind, and on the general picture of Singleton's career as giving us some insight (gathered probably from De Foe's confabulations with old Dampier, with whom he used to talk over these matters) into the sea-life of the times, we are not in danger of being misled to believe in those pearl-gatherings in undiscovered and undiscoverable South-Sea islands, or that marvellous journey across the continent of Africa.

The proper novels of De Foe—*Roxana, Moll Flanders, Colonel Jack,* and above all, the first part of *Robinson Crusoe*—are of a much higher class. They are pure fictions; any elements of fact which may be included in them being, as it were, entirely dissolved and incorporated in a homogeneous work of imagination. The most marked feature in them, the one which first strikes every reader that looks at them, is their reality, their lifelikeness. Perhaps this quality would have been less remarked had it been more balanced by other qualities more or less common in works of fiction. As it is, it stands sharply out as the characteristic of De Foe, and is the index to a genius not more remarkable for its wonderful power in this direction than it is for its absolute deficiencies in another. No where else does our literature show the trace of an imagination at once so vivid and so curiously limited. It is as if he had just one-half of that faculty we commonly call by this name. (p. 387)

[Defoe] abides in the concrete; he has no analytical perception whatever. Never was there a man to whom a yellow primrose was less or any thing more than a yellow primrose. He is always occupied with the absolute existent realities of the world; with men as he saw them move in actual life; with facts as they actually happened. He never conceives abstract passions: his only idea of anger is a particular man in a passion. He has an enormous reconstructive and a very narrow creative imagination. He takes up things just as he finds them; and when he wants to create, he resorts them, or at most makes others exactly like them. He loses much by these limits to his nature. What he gains on the other side is that life-likeness we spoke of in his art: the narrow range of his vision is compensated by its vividness. It is a mistake to say that the wonderful power he has of convincing you that his characters really lived in the flesh, and that all he tells you did really happen just as he says it did, arises from the minuteness of his detail. It is not the detail that causes the distinctness of the reflection in the reader's mind; it is the sharpness of the original image. A mind like De Foe's works by details; it is one of its defects that it does so. A greater genius can flash out as sharp and full an image of a concrete man as any of De Foe's, and unencumbered with useless minutiae. It can at once seize the very essence

of some special attribute of human nature, and embody it in a complete and individual man. It can give you Claudio, Angelo, Lucio, Isabella, within the limits of five acts; and in doing so it furnishes, under stringent restrictions of form and in limited space, a greater variety of character than can be found within the whole range of De Foe's novels, and leaves as distinct an image of each man as we can form of the heroes of his most laboured autobiographical narratives. We don't say as familiar; but as distinct and as complete. De Foe thus arrives by means of details at a result which may be reached independently of them; and his power lies not in his love of minute circumstance, but in the close and tenacious grasp of his imagination—in the constant and distinct presence before his own mind of the conception that controls and guides his minutiae. Richardson is far more detailed in his narration than De Foe, far more universally circumstantial, more diffuse, if possible, more tiresome; every matter that he has occasion to handle, whether important or unimportant, is elaborated with the same patient microscopic attention; he is thrice as tedious as De Foe; and yet his characters are infinitely inferior in life-likeness. Lovelace is a character more striking and more complex than Roxana or Robinson Crusoe; but you do not believe in his existence in the same way: he is more of a man in a book. De Foe's detail is a more partial and discriminating one than that of Richardson. True he loves it for its own sake, and it is sometimes superfluous; but it is always under control, and duly subordinated to the effect he wishes to produce. If we read him attentively, we shall be as much struck with what he omits as with what he inserts.

Totally destitute of the power to fathom any intricacies of human nature, Defoe is familiar with its external manifestations. He may have no conscious picture of *character;* but he has a keen eye for traits of character, and a very vivid idea of *persons.* He takes a man and his life in the gross, as it were, and sets them down in writing; but as it is his characteristic to be mainly occupied with the life, not the man, so this too becomes the main source of the reader's interest. It is not Robinson Crusoe we care about, but the account of his adventures, the solution of the problem of how to live under the circumstances. His name calls up the idea not of a man, but of a story. Say 'Lear,' and you think of a man; you have the image of the white-haired king— the central point, about which the division of his kingdom, the disaffection of his daughters, the terrors of the tempest, the soft pity and sad death of Cordelia, group themselves in subordinate place: say 'Robinson Crusoe,' and you see a desert island, with a man upon it ingeniously adapting his mode of life to his resources; the imagination of a solitary existence, reproduced in a special form with wonderful vividness, consistency, and particularity,—this is the source of our interest. It would be to impugn the verdict of all mankind to say *Robinson Crusoe* was not a great work of genius. It is a work of genius—a most remarkable one—but of a low order of genius. The universal admiration it has obtained may be the admiration of men: but it is founded on the liking of boys. Few educated men or women would care to read it for the first time after the age of five-and-twenty. . . . If a grown man reads the book in after years, it is to recall the sensations of youth, or curiously to examine the secret of the unbounded popularity it has enjoyed. How much this popularity is due to the happy choice of his subject, we may better estimate when we remember that the popular *Robinson Crusoe* is in reality only a part of the work, and the work itself only one of many others, not less well executed, from the same hand. No other man in the world could have drawn so absolutely living a picture of the desert-island life; but the same man has exercised the same power over more complex incidents, and the works are little read. *Moll Flanders* and *Roxana* and part of *Colonel Jack* are not inferior efforts of the same genius that wrote *Robinson Crusoe;* but the subject-matter is perhaps less well adapted for the sort of genius, and they are defaced by much both of narrated incident and expression which unfits them for the delicacy of modern readers. They are pictures of the career of vice. This is unfortunate; for had De Foe occupied himself with the domestic life of his period, and drawn his persons and incidents thence, he would have presented us with a more vivid glimpse into the life of his times than any author has ever done. Miss Austen is not unlike De Foe in some of the main aspects of her genius, though as much his superior in handling character as she is inferior in knowledge and vigour. Had he done as she has done . . . we should have gained a clearer idea of how people really lived in those days than can now be derived from all other sources of information put together. But De Foe as deliberately chooses his materials outside the field of ordinary social life as Miss Austen sedulously restricts herself within it. The latter deals with baronets, dyspeptics, young ladies, and amiable or self-sufficient clergymen. She represents the condition of man as regulated by marriage with settlements; her widest contrasts of life are between Bath and Wiltshire, Plymouth and the Hall; she walks gently through the well-trimmed "shrubberies" of existence, and does not trust herself ever to peep over the park-palings. De Foe goes down the ragged lanes, tramps through gorse and heather, sits by the side of the duckpond, and studies the aspect of the dunghill. Thieves and harlots, convicts, pirates, soldiers, and merchant-adventurers, are his *dramatis personae.* He has never attempted to draw a respectable man; or if the narrative of the *History of the Plague* be an exception, he is placed amid terrors that dislocate society and strip him of all the conventional proprieties which would naturally belong to him. He gives you no picture

of the manners and the life of his times except incidentally, and by showing what strange things were compatible with them, and what sort of life those led who were outcasts from them. (pp. 389-92)

De Foe puts his characters in degraded enough positions, and plunges them deep enough in the meanest criminality; but he was able to show them not absolutely dislocated from the regular order of society; they wind in and out from it, and retain some points of contact. There was then much less of a separate criminal class than now exists. It is still possible to use even the worst members of this class as subjects of fiction, but not if you work in the same way as De Foe does. You can't show *all* the life as he does. Dickens paints the Jew, Sykes, Nancy, and the Artful Dodger, but not their actual lives and daily habits. He never shows them as they really are: he only selects the terrible, the ludicrous, or the pathetic incidents and points of character, and shrouds the stained every-day career of wickedness in silence. But De Foe gives all this; to him one event is as important as another, nothing is too commonplace, nothing too revolting for his pen, he slurs over nothing, all is put down in its naked deformity, and, where it is dull and trivial, in its naked dullness and triviality. . . . [His] strokes are all the same thickness, and he labours on with line after line and touch after touch, intent only on exact copy, and careless of the expense either of time or labour. He never drops his subject for an instant to take it up again at a more interesting point; he tracks it like a slot-hound, with his nose close to the ground, through every bend and winding. He makes people talk as they really do talk. . . . When a man of De Foe's vivid powers of conception tracks out with this slow perseverance the history of a life, it is impossible that we should not gather a very distinct idea of the person who lived it; it grows up in a quiet and insensible manner out of the events. We are not expressly admitted by the author into the interior nature of such a person, but we know all of him which can be gathered from a complete acquaintance with the minutest circumstances of his actions, and often even of his thoughts. We must use our own insight and judgment if we wish to know what really was the interior character of Moll Flanders, just as we must have done had we met her in life,—not altogether a pleasant sort of person. None of his heroes or heroines are. Roxana is not pleasant; Colonel Jack is decidedly not pleasant; Robinson Crusoe is not the man to make a friend of; perhaps De Foe himself was not. (pp. 394-96)

In his novels we see what might have been the character of De Foe, had not the conscientiousness of his will raised it above the tendencies of his nature. Crusoe may be said to be only deeply self-engrossed; but Moll Flanders, Roxana, Colonel Jack, and Singleton, are selfish to the last extremes of baseness: their whole lives are only one struggle to secure their own interests, regardless not only of the welfare of others, but of gratitude, natural affection, and decency. It may be said that this is only what is to be expected if a man is writing with unsparing exactness and fidelity the lives of thieves and harlots; but this is a trait that pervades them all so universally, and shows itself so exactly in the same kind of way, that it evidently has a deeper root than mere appropriateness to the characters of those represented. Moreover De Foe is far from representing his characters as utterly depraved; and he is always anxious to point a moral. It seems strange to our juster notions of things,—and perhaps he wilfully deceived himself a little,—but he seems to have believed that he wrote these elaborate pictures of vice and wickedness with a direct moral purpose.

> Throughout the infinite variety of this book," says he in the preface to *Moll Flanders,* "this fundamental is most strictly adhered to: there is not a wicked action in any part of it, but is first or last rendered unhappy and unfortunate; there is not a superlative villain brought upon the stage, but either he is brought to an unhappy end, or brought to be a penitent; there is not an ill thing mentioned but it is condemned even in the relation, nor a virtuous just thing but it carries its praise along with it. Upon this foundation this book is recommended to the reader as a work from every part of which something may be learned; and some just and religious inference is drawn, by which the reader will have something of instruction, if he pleases to make use of it.

Thus (though these professions are not very adequately carried out) we see what the author's intentions were; but though vices and dishonesties meet with a thin share of reprobation, and are followed sooner or later by remorseful repentance, a depravity of selfishness, which to the reader seems far more abhorrent, is passed over in all the silence of complete unconsciousness. And with their selfishness and their insufficient affections, De Foe's characters have that solitary independent course through life which naturally results from these defects, and which reflects back in an exaggerated form the independent solitariness of De Foe's own life. Moll Flanders, Roxana, Singleton, Colonel Jack, all stand quite alone in the world. They are all single separate molecules, shifting to and fro in the wide sands of life—touching others, but never for a moment incorporated with them; they all live as using the world for themselves, and standing off from its binding influences; they grasp at others for a momentary assistance, but they never allow another's claim to interfere with their own liberty; they seize with the affections, but are never bound by them; they may cling to another life, but it is with a reserved power of disengagement, as a limpet clings to a rock; they never strike root in it, and grow from it, like a plant. (pp. 399-400)

In the substance of their constitution, still more than in special traits, do De Foe's fictitious personages echo back their creator. They have all a certain squareness and solidity; they are all of hardy and stubborn materials. They put you in mind of timber; they have no sensibility, no pliancy. The events of life make just such an impression as blows on a heavy balk of wood; they bear the brunt and carry the dent it leaves, but the blow has no perceptible effect on them. The roughest treatment does but blunt their edges and tear off a few splinters. Theirs is never the elasticity which recovers from a blow, but the tough fibrous nature which a blow cannot permanently injure. Robinson Crusoe is the only one of De Foe's heroes who is at all sensible to the injuries of fortune; and even he is only a little stunned by the worst that befalls him, and less by actual evils than the imagination of them—as when he sees the footprint on the sand. De Foe himself passed through a life crowded with troubles, but a small part of which would have shattered, or even killed, many men; but they neither broke nor bowed him. (pp. 403-04)

There must be something very singular in a work which the chimney-sweep and the peer both understand and both find interesting,—which the latter at any rate admires, and the former fully enjoys. This would be an easy triumph if it were gained by an appeal to, or a description of, the common feelings; but the characteristic of De Foe is, that he has written books universally popular, whose interest is quite independent of this universal resource. His memory was a remarkable one, and he was widely and accurately informed in all those matters which a man learns by observation; and he had a signal power of gathering up that sort of information which is knowledge at first-hand, without requiring to be digested, and which is got through eye and ear rather than through books. His education had been good, but he appears simply to have mastered languages for practical use; to have accumulated the facts, not to have studied the ideas, . . . can express himself as fully, and even as fast, as you please; but not concisely. His ideas are heavy malleable metal, and he loves to hammer them out; his mind moves easily, but without spring, and he is a heavy hand at a joke. No one likes to call him dull, and there is a vigour in all he writes which redeems him from the charge; but tedious and intolerably self-repeating he undeniably is. This is a defect, however, which shows less in his novels than elsewhere. He is a master in the art of narration, and for the mere telling of a story, does it better and more simply than any writer we have. His style in his novels is well adapted to the level of his subject. In itself it scarcely deserves the commendation it has received. It is like the manners of a farmer at an Inn: a man of the best breeding could not be more at his ease; but it is because he submits to no artificial restraint whatever. In his works, written expressly for amusement or instruction, the plainness of his writing suits well with his plain rude way of treating his subject, and his complete insensibility to, and disregard of, any of its refinements or less obvious aspects. His shortcomings in this respect have been one great cause of the popularity these works have obtained, especially among the less-highly cultivated classes. Every reader feels competent to say as he reads, "This is true and lifelike,"—to follow his arguments, and to comprehend his reflections. It is this which made Lamb say he was "good kitchen reading." Fielding is any thing but kitchen reading. A man must take pains with his education, and have a cultivated mind, if he intends to read *Tom Jones* so as to appreciate it. . . . Though a wide reader, [De Foe] was never interested in other men's thoughts,—if he cites them, it is simply as authorities. When he himself thinks, it is (with rare exceptions) to direct practical issues; then he is sagacious, acute—even wise in broad every-day matters. Only in one direction did he indulge in any speculative thought, and only in this one direction did his imagination break through its ordinary matter-of-fact boundaries. He had a singular interest in the world of spirits. He wrote a *History of the Devil;* and it is hard to say what object he proposed to himself in this amazingly tiresome, confused, lumbering work; a strange sort of half-serious, half-burlesque attempt to track the course of the great enemy's operations, criticising "Mr. Milton's" account of his fall, counting up how many names he has in Scripture, and apologising for still calling him "plain devil;" pursuing him through Jewish history, and partly through profane; inquiring—"What may probably be the great business this black emperor has at present upon his hands, either in this world or out of it, and by what agents he works;" and finally, discussing "his last scene of liberty," and "what may be supposed to be his end." His *Life of Duncan Campbell* is another extraordinary production of the same class. It professes to be the history of a famous deaf and dumb wise man, who in those days had set up as a fortune-teller in London; and seriously accounts for his powers of penetrating futurity as derived from the second-sight and intercourse with the spiritual world. What grains of truth there may be in the book as a biography, and how far it is jest or grave hoaxing, and how far serious; how much of it the author himself believed,—it is impossible to tell. One can never say of De Foe, whether he was so fond of fiction he could never write unmixed truth, or so fond of exact truth as to spoil his hoaxes by making them too real. (pp. 405-07)

[These] sort of stories, accompanied by direct strenuous assertions as to their truth in fact, and grave argument as to their bearing on unbelief, are chiefly remarkable for our present purpose as a further indication of the strange sort of confusion there seems to have been in De Foe's mind between real fact and pos-

sible fact. His imagination is so strong, that its facts seem to him of equal weight with those of memory or knowledge; and he appears scarcely to recognise the boundary between truth and fiction. His characters, as usual, carry the tendency a step further. They lie, to suit their purposes, at every turn, and without scruple or remorse.

De Foe was a man of strong religious convictions, and there is scarcely one of his writings which does not bear the impress of his deep sense of the all-outweighing importance of a religious life. . . . He had a strong sense of direct inspiration, even as guiding to or deterring from particular actions. Neither his genius nor his heart, however, were such as to give him any profound insight into a sense of spiritual relations. He had that sort of temperament which can feel and sympathise with sudden and violent accesses of somewhat coarse religious emotion, with too much sense and staidness on the one hand, and too much conscientiousness on the other, to make him guilty either of the unseemly excesses, or the discordant self-indulgence, which distinguish the debased forms of so-called Evangelicism. All his characters repent in the same way; they are suddenly stricken with an overwhelming sense, not so much of their guilt as of their crimes; they are appalled to think themselves outcasts from God; they lay down their evil habits generally when circumstances have removed the temptation to pursue them; repent in a summary manner, and become without difficulty sincere penitents and religious characters. He has no sense of the temptations, the trials, the difficulties with which the souls of most men find themselves surrounded after they have once left home with Bunyan's pilgrim. He knows that strait is the gate, and sharp the struggle necessary to pass it; but he always seems to forget that narrow is the way even after the gate is passed.

We have strict conventional rules in England as to what are to be considered readable books for society at large. It is scarcely necessary to say, that De Foe's novels are quite outside this pale. It is not that they were written with the least idea either of pandering to a vicious nature, or shocking an innocent one; but they deal frankly with matters about which our better modern taste is silent, and use language which shocks modern refinement.

It is only fair, however, to say, they are in their essence wholesome, decent, and, above all, cleanly. They have neither the varnished prurience of Richardson, the disgusting filth of Swift, nor the somewhat too indulgent and sympathising warmth of Fielding; they are plain-spoken and gross, but that is the worst of them; and though the obvious and hammered moralities of the author seem valueless enough, it is to be remembered that the class whose rudeness would make it impervious to injury from the absence of delicacy in

Nineteenth-century depiction of Defoe in the pillory.

these works, is just the one in a position to profit by their rough and primitive teaching. For those who seek it, they contain a deeper moral, not the less important because the writer was unconscious of its existence. They are warnings against the too common error of confounding crime and sin. They are the histories of criminals, who remind us at every page that they are human beings just like ourselves; that the forms of sin are often the result merely of circumstances; and that the aberration of the will, not the injury done to society, is the measure of a man's sinfulness. They show us among thieves and harlots the very same struggles against new temptations, the same slow declension and self-enfeebling wiles, which we have to experience and contend against in ourselves. We are too apt to think of the criminal outcasts of society as of persons removed from the ordinary conditions of humanity, and given up to a reprobate condition totally different from our own. One day we shall probably be surprised to find that, while right and wrong continue to differ infinitely, the various degrees of human sinfulness lie within much narrower limits than we, who measure by the external act, are at all accustomed to conceive. De

Foe is a great teacher of charity; he always paints the remaining good with the growing evil, and never dares to show the most degraded and abandoned of his wretches as beyond the pale of repentance, or unattended by the merciful providences of God; nay, he can never bear to quit them at last, except in tears and penitence and in the entrance-gate at least of reconciliation. (pp. 408-10)

W. C. Roscoe, in an originally unsigned essay titled "De Foe As a Novelist," in *The National Review,* London, Vol. III, No. VI, October 1856, pp. 380-410.

MARK SCHORER

(essay date 1950)

[Schorer is one of many twentieth-century critics who have interpreted Defoe's use of conventional morality in his works as a stricture forced upon him by an essentially Puritan public. In the following excerpt, he analyzes *Moll Flanders* as an allegory of middle-class virtue.]

In *Moll Flanders,* Defoe the bankrupt tradesman and Puritan moralist, Defoe the journalist and popular historian, above all, perhaps, Defoe the pilloried prisoner and Defoe the spy, come together. (p. x)

Everything about *Moll Flanders*—its kind and Defoe's extension of that kind, its literary method, its paradoxical morality—everything about it has a naively direct relation to his own world of experience and interests. The kind is the biography of a rogue, a conventional if low form of literary expression since Elizabethan times. Rogue biographies were usually the lives of real criminals fictionally foreshortened and sensationalized. Their ostensible purpose was to expose the operations of criminals and thereby to warn; their actual purpose was rather to thrill an undiscriminating audience with melodrama. The convention offered Defoe solid elements to which he would almost at once have responded. The world of crime he had experienced and observed with sufficient directness and even fascination to recognize as a subject matter that he was in a superb position to handle, and it is no accident that Moll's paralyzing fear of Newgate is her most forcibly urged emotion. At the same time, the journalist in Defoe would have responded to a subject that lent itself to exposure, and the Puritan, to the elements that allowed the expression of a ready impulse to admonish and exhort. Add to these the convention of the "secret history," which would be as attractive to the intriguing familiar of party ministers as it would be to the journalistic spy, and the several elements that the rogue biography offered to the special talents of Daniel Defoe should be evident.

The method that Defoe developed to animate the genre is perfectly calculated to his talents. The Puritan and the journalist together, the first out of genuine suspicions of the idle and the second out of his conviction that nothing is more persuasive than fact, lead Defoe to deny that he is writing fiction at all. On the contrary, he tells us, he is merely editing the diary of a real and notorious character who must, for reputation's sake, present herself under a pseudonym. Thus at once Defoe saves his conscience and puts himself into his favorite position, the assumed role. He is not telling us about Moll Flanders, he *is* Moll Flanders. The device comes easy to one whose own life had consisted of a series of conflicting roles, and he had had long practice not only in life but in his previous writings. He had written in the past as though he were a Turk, a Scotch soldier, a visionary Scotchman, a Quaker, a lonely but enterprising castaway. Why not now as a sexually abandoned thief? Once the role was assumed, it was easy, too, for the journalist to support the role, or, at any rate, for a journalist with Defoe's special feeling for the telling physical facts in any situation. Out of this gift grows his special kind of verisimilitude, that kind of realism best described as "circumstantial." It is a method that depends not on sensibility but on fact, not on description but on proof, as if a man, wishing to tell us of an excellent dinner, did not bother to say how his food tasted, but merely listed the courses that made up the meal, or, more likely, produced a canceled check to prove that he had paid a good deal for it. On such evidence, we would hardly doubt that he had eaten it. Thus the centrality in Defoe's method of the bolts of goods, the inventories, the itemized accounts, the landlady's bills, the lists, the ledgers, and the prose texture that such details generate.

Defoe's tone is hardly less important to this method than his persuasive details. How matter-of-fact all this is, for such an extraordinary life! Five marriages, a score of recorded lovers, and, if we can count, a score of children, twelve dead and eight alive when Moll's child-bearing ceased at last. *We* exclaim (we may even protest), but Defoe does not. In this story, the birth of a child or the acquisition of a new lover seem hardly as important as the hiring of a coach or the packing of a trunk. Defoe's prevailing matter-of-fact tone levels all incidents out on a straight narrative plane, and we are lulled into supposing that any account of a life that is so guilelessly without emphasis is necessarily true. Defoe's deepest guile, indeed, always lay in his appearance of being without guile. A narrator with an air of uncomprehending innocence or a narrator so innocent that he comprehends precisely the wrong things in a situation, had been among Defoe's great propagandistic devices throughout his career as a journalist, and over and over again, this device had been the basis of his satire. In *Moll Flanders,* the heroine, like Defoe's earlier narrators, is peculiarly innocent; the meaning of her experience seems to run off her moral skin like quicksilver; nothing touches her; at the end, a woman of seventy, she is almost exactly as bland as she was in the opening scenes, a small girl who wished to be a lady. And this quality again, this very imperceptiveness, lends itself to Defoe's purpose of persuasion. Isn't this, we ask ourselves, exactly what a woman like Moll would be, so wonderfully imperceptive that this is really a book about a remarkable self-deception?

But then the other question comes, and with it, the question whether this is a method adequate to the production of a novel. Whose deception is it—Moll's or Defoe's? And this question takes us into the third consideration, the paradoxical morality of the book. *Moll Flanders* comes to us professing that its purpose is to warn us not only against a life of crime but against the cost of crime. We cannot for very many pages take that profession seriously, for it is apparent all too soon that nothing in the conduct of the narrative indicates that virtue is either more necessary or more enjoyable than vice. At the end we discover that Moll turns virtuous only after a life of vice has enabled her to do so with security. The actualities of the book, then, enforce the moral assumption of any commercial culture, the belief that virtue and worldly goods form an equation. This is a morality somewhat less than skin deep, with no relation to motives arising from more than a legalistic sense of good and evil; having its relation, rather, to motives arising from the presence or absence of food, drink, linen, damask, silver, and timepieces. It is the morality of measurement, and without in the least intending it, *Moll Flanders* is our classic revelation of the mercantile mind: the morality of measurement which Defoe has apparently neglected to measure.

Defoe's announced purpose is probably a pious humbug, and he probably meant us to read the book as a series of scandalous events. His inexhaustible pleasure in excess (twenty children, not five; twenty lovers, not fifteen; five husbands, including a brother, not three)—this element in the book continues to amuse us. The book becomes indeed a vast joke, a wonderful kind of myth of female endurance, and like all tall tales, an absurdity. Yet it is not nearly as absurd as that other absurdity that Defoe did not intend at all, the notion that Moll could live a rich and full life of crime, and by mere repentance, emerge spotless in the end, a perfect matron. The point is, of course, that she has no moral being, and that the book has no real moral life. Everything is external. Everything can be weighed, measured, handled, paid for in gold, or expiated by a prison term. To this the whole method of the novel testifies: this is a morality of social circumstance, a morality in which only externals count since only externals show. Thus we may conclude that the real meaning of the book is to be discovered in spite of Defoe, whose point of view is, finally, indistinguishable from the point of view of Moll Flanders; and we may therefore conclude, further, that the book is not the true chronicle of a disreputable female, but the true allegory of an impoverished soul—the author's; not, indeed, an anatomy of the criminal class, but of the middle class striving for security.

Security and morality are almost identical in *Moll Flanders* and we today are hardly in a position to scorn Defoe's observation that it is easier to be pious with a bank account than without one. Like *Robinson Crusoe*, this is a desperate story of survival, a story that tries to demonstrate the possibility of success through unremitting native wit. Security, clearly, is the end of life. . . . But if security is the end of life, ingenuity, clever personal enterprise, is its most admirable quality, and, certainly, the only way to security. . . . (pp. x-xiv)

Strip *Moll Flanders* of its bland loquacity, its comic excess, its excitement, and we have the revelation of a savage life, a life that is motivated solely by economic need, and a life that is measured at last by those creature comforts that, if we gain them, allow us one final breath in which to praise the Lord. Yet this essence is not the book as we have it, as Defoe wrote it, any more than the acquisitive impulse is the whole of middle-class value. For there is also the secondary interest of the book, which is to reveal to us the condition of women, the small choice (there was only her needle; to be sure, there *was* her needle had she preferred it; but who would ask that she should have?)—the small choice that Moll could have made between disreputable and reputable enjoyment. The infant Moll, born in Newgate, becomes a public charge; education is an impossibility; independent work is likewise an impossibility; and as young men are by nature wolves, so the world at large is wolfish. Women, like men, are forced into the realm of trade, they offer such goods as they have for such prices as they can command.

This secondary interest suggests the softer side of Daniel Defoe, his will to create a less savage world than the world he knew. The paradox of the middle class has always been its hope to create, through its values of mere measurement, values that did not have to measure in its way. And the social pathos of *our* lives is largely to be traced to our illusion that we have done so. This is also the final pathos of Moll Flanders' life, whether Defoe was aware of it or not.

Sympathy exceeds awareness, and throughout *Moll Flanders* (this is probably the main reason that we continue to read it) we are charged by the author's sympathy. It shows as much in the gusto with which he enters Moll's life and participates in her adventures as it does in his tolerance of her errors and her deceits and self-deceits. It shows, furthermore, in a few moments of this vastly episodic narrative when genuinely novelistic values emerge, when, that is, the individual character somehow shines through the social automaton. One such moment occurs when Moll is reunited with her Lancashire husband. . . . Such genuinely moving scenes must be balanced, of course, against the long stretches of the book where the relentless narrative sense points up the totally deficient sense of plot, where the carelessness of time and causality destroys the illusion of actuality after all the pains to achieve it, where the monotonously summarizing method gives even the fine feeling for separate incident a pallor. These deficiencies all remind us that this is not, after all, the first English novel.

Yet it is very nearly the first English novel. It is the whole groundwork. Given twenty more years of literary convention and just a slightly different set of interests, Defoe would have freed himself from the tyranny of fact and the morality of circumstance and sprung into the liberties of formal fiction, where another morality must prevail. (pp. xv-xvi)

[Defoe] does not, finally, *judge* his material, as a

novelist must. He makes us sort out his multiple materials for him and pass our judgment. Our judgment must therefore fall on him, not on his creature, Moll. In her bland, self-deluded way, she asks us not to be harsh; and that again is the voice of Defoe, taking a breath at the end to beg posterity to be kind. As it has been. (p. xvii)

Mark Schorer, "Introduction," in *The Fortunes and Misfortunes of the Famous Moll Flanders & c.* by Daniel Defoe, The Modern Library, 1950, pp. v-xxii.

IAN WATT

(essay date 1957)

[Watt is best known for his 1957 study *The Rise of the Novel: Studies in Defoe, Richardson, and Fielding.* In the following excerpt from this work, he contends that the plot of *Moll Flanders* "flatly contradicts Defoe's purported moral theme."]

Moll Flanders is certainly, as E. M. Forster says, a novel of character; the plot throws the whole burden of interest on the heroine, and many readers have felt that she supports it triumphantly. On the other hand, Leslie Stephen has reproached Defoe with a lack of 'all that goes by the name of psychological analysis in modern fiction', and not altogether without justification, at least if our emphasis is on the word analysis. There is probably no episode in *Moll Flanders* where the motivation is unconvincing, but for somewhat damaging reasons—few of the situations confronting Defoe's heroine call for any more complex discriminations than those of Pavlov's dog: Defoe makes us admire the speed and resolution of Moll's reactions to profit or danger; and if there are no detailed psychological analyses, it is because they would be wholly superfluous. (p. 108)

Defoe does not so much portray his heroine's character as assume its reality in every action, and carry his reader with him—if we accede to the reality of the deed, it is difficult to challenge the reality of the doer. It is only when we attempt to fit all her acts together, and see them as an expression of a single personality, that doubts arise; nor are these doubts allayed when we discover how little we are told about some of the things we should need to know for a full picture of her personality, and how some of the things we are told seem contradictory. (pp. 108-09)

Usually when we attempt to make up our minds about anyone's total personality we take into account as many views about the person as possible, and by comparing them with our own are able to achieve a kind of stereoscopic effect.

No such enlightenment is forthcoming on Defoe's heroine. The episodic nature of the plot means that, although there are some two hundred characters in *Moll Flanders,* no one of them knows the heroine for more than a fraction of her career; while the autobiographical mode of presentation means that their attitudes to Moll Flanders are only given to us if and how she wishes. Their evidence actually reveals a unanimity of a very suspect kind—Defoe's heroine apparently excites in those best qualified to judge her—James, the Governess, Humphry, for instance—the most unqualified, and selfless devotion. On the other hand, the reader, observing that Moll Flanders herself is never wholly honest and disinterested in her dealings with them, or indeed with anyone else, may well feel inclined to interpret their apparent adoration as evidence of a paranoid delusion on Moll Flanders's part rather than as an accurate appraisal of her character on theirs. Everyone seems to exist only for her, and no one seems to resent it. One might have expected the Governess, for example, to regret Moll's reformation since it deprives her of a prize source of stolen goods; instead, she becomes 'a true penitent' as soon as the heroine has no further use for her services.

If none of those close to Moll Flanders seem at all aware of her true character, and if we continue to suspect that her own account of herself may be partial, our only remaining resource for an objective view of her personality is Defoe himself. Here again, however, we at once encounter difficulties. For Moll Flanders is suspiciously like her author, even in matters where we would expect striking and obvious differences. The facts show that she is a woman and a criminal, for example; but neither of these roles determines her personality as Defoe has drawn it.

Moll Flanders, of course, has many feminine traits; she has a keen eye for fine clothes and clean linen, and shows a wifely concern for the creature comforts of her males. Further, the early pages of the book undoubtedly present a young girl with a lifelike clarity, and later there are many touches of a rough cockney humour that is undeniably feminine in tone. But these are relatively external and minor matters, and the essence of her character and actions is, to one reader at least, essentially masculine. This is a personal impression, and would be difficult, if not impossible, to establish: but it is at least certain that Moll accepts none of the disabilities of her sex, and indeed one cannot but feel that Virginia Woolf's admiration for her was largely due to admiration of a heroine who so fully realised one of the ideals of feminism: freedom from any involuntary involvement in the feminine role.

Moll Flanders is also similar to her author in another respect: she seems fundamentally untouched by her criminal background, and, on the contrary, displays many of the attitudes of a virtuous and public-minded citizen. Here, again, there is no glaring inconsistency, but there is a marked pattern of attitudes which distinguishes Moll from other members of her class. . . . Moll Flanders obviously places criminals into two classes: most of them are vicious reprobates who richly deserve their fate; but she and a few of her friends are essentially virtuous and deserving people who have been unfortunate—she is even morally pure in her whoring since it is, as she assures us, by necessity and not 'for the sake of the vice'. Like Defoe, in fact, she is a good Puritan who, despite a few necessary and regrettable compromises, has, in the main and in defiance of illustrious precedent, lived in a world of pitch and not been defiled.

It is this freedom from the probable psychological and social consequences of everything she does which is the central implausibility of her character as Defoe has drawn it. It applies, not only to her crimes, but to everything she does. If we take the incest theme, for example, we find that although her half-brother becomes incapable in body and mind mainly because Moll Flanders has left him, after revealing her terrible secret, she herself is quite unaffected by the circumstance, once she has left Virginia. Nor are her son's feelings towards her influenced, apparently, by the fact that he is the offspring of an incestuous marriage; nor even by the fact that his mother, after deserting him for some twenty years, only returns because, having been transported back to his vicinity, she thinks that she may now have an estate to inherit, an estate which he would otherwise enjoy.

Moll Flanders's character, then, is not noticeably affected either by her sex, by her criminal pursuits, or indeed by any of the objective factors which might have been expected to set her apart from her author; on the other hand, she shares with Defoe and most of his heroes many of the character traits that are usually regarded as middle-class. She is obsessed with gentility and keeping up appearances; her pride is much involved in knowing how to get good service and proper accommodation; and she is in her heart a rentier, for whom life has no greater terror than when her 'main stock wastes apace'. More specifically it is apparent that, like Robinson Crusoe, she has, by some process of osmosis, picked up the vocabulary and attitudes of a tradesman. Indeed her most positive qualities are the same as Crusoe's, a restless, amoral and strenuous individualism. It is, no doubt, possible to argue that these qualities might be found in a character of her sex, station and personal vicissitudes; but it is not likely, and it is surely more reasonable to assume that all these contradictions are the consequence of a process to which first-person narration is peculiarly prone; that Defoe's identification with Moll Flanders was so complete that, despite a few feminine traits, he created a personality that was in essence his own.

The hypothesis of the unconscious identification between Defoe and his heroine seems equally valid when we come to analyse . . . [an] aspect of the total structure of *Moll Flanders*—its larger moral significance.

The 'Author's Preface' states that 'there is not a wicked action in any part of it, but is first or last rendered unhappy or unfortunate.' This moral claim for *Moll Flanders* amounts only to the assertion that it teaches a somewhat narrow kind of ethical lesson—vice must be paid for and crime does not pay. Even this, however, is not substantiated by the narrative itself. What seems to have happened is that Defoe succumbed to the eternal danger of the crime story: to be interesting the author has to project himself as completely as possible into the mind of the crook, but, having once donned the colours of crime, he plays to win. Defoe cannot bear to let Moll Flanders come on evil days. Her fortunes vary, it is true; but she never falls so low as to be forced to break her early resolve never to 'work housework', and she retains her middle-class status even in prison. For the most part, whether as wife, mistress or thief, she is exceptionally successful, and when the crash comes she saves enough of her ill-gotten gains to stock a plantation and yet retain a considerable balance in England.

Moll's penitent prosperity, then, is based on her criminal career, and the sincerity of her reformation is never put to the acid test of sacrificing material for moral good. The plot, in fact, flatly contradicts Defoe's purported moral theme. (pp. 112-15)

Whatever moral significance Defoe wished to attach to his story . . . had to spring directly from the moral consciousness of his heroine. This meant that she had to function both as a character and as an editorial mouthpiece and she therefore had to recount the story from the perspective of her later penitence. This also involved difficulties; partly because Moll's loves and larcenies would obviously lose most of their attraction for the reader if they were too heavily sprinkled with the ashes of repentance; and partly because such a perspective called for a very rigorous separation in time between the consciousness that had performed the evil deeds and the reformed consciousness that was responsible for their redaction. (p. 116)

[Defoe] failed to locate his didactic commentary convincingly in any particular period of his heroine's moral development; and this may stand as an example of his general failure to resolve the formal problems to which his moral purpose and his autobiographical narrative mode committed him. One reason for this is no doubt that Defoe did not give either his art or his conscience the searching attention which his moral aims involved; on the other hand, we must remember that he was in fact faced with a problem which was then new and has since remained the central problem of the novel: how to impose a coherent moral structure on narrative without detracting from its air of literal authenticity.

Formal realism is only a mode of presentation, and it is therefore ethically neutral: all Defoe's novels are also ethically neutral because they make formal realism an end rather than a means, subordinating any coherent ulterior significance to the illusion that the text represents the authentic lucubrations of an historical person. But the individual case-book is an arid study except in the hands of a skilled interrogator who can elicit the things we want to know, which are often the very things the person concerned does not know or is unwilling to admit: the problem of the novel was to discover and reveal these deeper meanings without any breach of formal realism.

Later novelists were to see that although formal realism imposed a more absolute and impersonal optical accuracy upon the manner in which literature performed its ancient task of holding the mirror up to nature, there were nevertheless ways in which a moral pattern could be conveyed, although they were perhaps more difficult and indirect than those of previous literary forms. . . . 'Point of view' was to become the crucial instrument whereby the writer expressed his moral sensibility, and pattern came to be the result of the hidden skill whereby the angles at which the mirror was held were made to reflect reality as the novelist saw it. No such pattern emerges from Defoe's treatment of plot and characterisation in *Moll Flanders;* as for the moral consciousness of his heroine, it continues to elude us in the infinite regress produced by the lack of co-ordination between the different aspects of his narrative purpose.

Those who, like John Peale Bishop, see *Moll Flanders* as 'one of the great English novels, perhaps the greatest', can hardly fail to notice this lack of co-ordination, but they discern behind it a firm grasp on the realities of human behaviour. As to the moralising, they assume that Defoe cannot have meant it seriously, and that the story belongs to that class of novel where the discrepancy between the apparent moral tenor and any intelligent understanding of it by the reader is a literary device by which the author tells us that his work must be interpreted ironically: the method may be called that of the conspicuous absence of authorial endorsement from first-person narration, and it has certainly been used successfully in such modern analogues of *Moll Flanders* as Anita Loos's *Gentlemen Prefer Blondes* and Joyce Cary's *Herself Surprised.* (pp. 117-18)

Moll Flanders has a few examples of patent and conscious irony. There is, first of all, a good deal of dramatic irony of a simple kind: for example in Virginia, where a woman relates the story of Moll's incestuous marriage, not knowing that she is addressing its chief figure. There are also some examples of much more pointed irony, as in the passage when, as a little girl, Moll Flanders vows that she will become a gentlewoman when she grows up, like one of her leisured but scandalous neighbours. . . . (p. 121)

These examples of conscious irony in *Moll Flanders,* however, fall far short of the larger, structural irony which would suggest that Defoe viewed either his central character or his purported moral theme ironically. There is certainly nothing in *Moll Flanders* which clearly indicates that Defoe sees the story differently from the heroine. There are, it is true, a few cases where such an intention seems possible: but on examination they are seen to have none of the hallmarks of the conscious examples of irony given above. . . . (pp. 121-22)

Whatever disagreement there may be about particular instances, it is surely certain that there is no consistently ironical attitude present in *Moll Flanders.* Irony in its extended sense expresses a deep awareness of the contradictions and incongruities that beset man in this vale of tears, an awareness which is manifested in the text's purposeful susceptibility to contradictory interpretations. As soon as we have become aware of the author's ulterior purpose, we can see all the apparent contradictions as indications of the coherent attitude underlying the whole work. Such a way of writing obviously makes severe demands upon the attention of the author and the reader: the implication of every word, the juxtaposition of every episode, the relation of every part to the whole, all must exclude any interpretation except the intended one. It is . . . very unlikely that Defoe wrote in this way, or that he had such readers; indeed, all the evidence points the other way. (p. 126)

Our crucial problem, therefore, would seem to be how we can explain the fact that a novel which was not intended ironically should be seen in such a light by so many modern readers. The answer would seem to be a matter not of literary criticism but of social history. We cannot today believe that so intelligent a man as Defoe should have viewed either his heroine's economic attitudes or her pious protestations with anything other than derision. Defoe's other writings, however, do not support this belief, and it may be surmised that the course of history has brought about in us powerful and often unconscious predispositions to regard certain matters ironically which Defoe and his age treated quite seriously.

Among these predispositions, these ironigenic attitudes, two at least are strongly aroused by *Moll Flanders:* the guilt feelings which are now fairly widely attached to economic gain as a motive; and the view that protestations of piety are suspect anyway, especially when combined with a great attention to one's own economic interest. But . . . Defoe was innocent of either attitude. He was not ashamed to make economic self-interest his major premise about human life; he did not think such a premise conflicted either with social or religious values; and nor did his age. It is likely, therefore, that one group of apparent ironies in *Moll Flanders* can be explained as products of an unresolved and largely unconscious conflict in Defoe's own outlook, a conflict which is typical of the late Puritan disengagement of economic matters from religious and moral sanctions. (p. 127)

There are other areas of conflict in Defoe's outlook which explain two further important difficulties in the critical interpretation of *Moll Flanders.* One reason for the feeling that Defoe cannot be serious about Moll's spiritual reformation is that her remorse and penitence are not supported by the action or even by any sense of real psychological change: as in *Robinson Crusoe,* the spiritual dimension is presented as a series of somewhat inexplicable religious breakdowns in the psychic mechanism, breakdowns, however, which do not permanently impair her healthy amorality. But this dissociation of religion from ordinary life was a natural consequence of secularisation, and the same feature of the life of Defoe's time is probably also the cause of the central confusion in Moll Flanders's moral consciousness—her tendency to confuse penitence for her sins with chagrin at the punishment of her crimes. (p. 128)

Many of the apparent discrepancies in *Moll Flanders,* then, are concerned with areas of individual morality where the last two centuries have taught us to make careful distinctions, but where the early eighteenth century tended to be a good deal less sensitive. It is natural, therefore, that we should be prone to see irony where there is more probably only a confusion—a confusion which our century is much better prepared to discern than was Defoe or his age. It is probably significant in this connection that the most ardent admirers of *Moll Flanders* are unhistorical in their outlook and interests. (pp. 128-29)

There is another historical explanation of a somewhat different kind for the modern tendency to read *Moll Flanders* ironically: the rise of the novel. We place Defoe's novels in a very different context from that of their own time; we take novels much more seriously now, and we judge his by the more exacting literary standards of today. This presumption, combined with Defoe's actual mode of writing, forces us to explain a great deal as ironical. We believe, for example, that a sentence should have unity; if we must invent one for

sentences which are really a random accumulation of clauses containing many disparate or incongruous items, we can impose unity only by an ironical subordination of some items to others. Similarly with the larger units of composition, from the paragraph to the total structure: if we assume on *a priori* grounds that a coherent plan must be present, we find one, and thereby produce a complex pattern out of what are actually incongruities.

Life itself, of course, is a suitable enough object for ironical contemplation, and so the tendency to regard *Moll Flanders* as ironic is in a sense a tribute to Defoe's vitality as a writer—it is partly because what he creates seems so real that we feel we must define our attitude to it. But, of course, such an attitude on the reader's part is excluded by genuinely ironical writing more than by any other: every way of looking at the events has been anticipated and either organised into the whole work, or made impossible. There is no evidence of such an exclusion in *Moll Flanders,* much less of a comprehensive control operating over every aspect of the work. If they are ironies, they are surely the ironies of social and moral and literary disorder. Perhaps, however, they are better regarded not as the achievements of an ironist, but as accidents produced by the random application of narrative authenticity to conflicts in Defoe's social and moral and religious world, accidents which unwittingly reveal to us the serious discrepancies in his system of values. (pp. 129-30)

We cannot but approach Defoe's novels through the literary expectations which later masters of the form made possible, and these expectations seem to find some justification as a result of our acute awareness of the conflicting nature of the two main forces in Defoe's philosophy of life—rational economic individualism and concern for spiritual redemption—which together held his divided but not, apparently, uneasy allegiance. Nevertheless, if we are primarily concerned with Defoe's actual intentions, we must conclude that although he reveals the sophistries whereby these dual allegiances are preserved intact, he does not, strictly speaking, portray them; consequently *Moll Flanders* is undoubtedly an ironic object, but it is not a work of irony. (p. 130)

Ian Watt, "Defoe As Novelist: 'Moll Flanders'," in his *The Rise of the Novel: Studies in Defoe, Richardson, and Fielding,* University of California Press, 1957, pp. 93-134.

SOURCES FOR FURTHER STUDY

Backscheider, Paula R. *Daniel Defoe: Ambition and Innovation.* Lexington: University Press of Kentucky, 1986, 299 p.

Analyzes the works of Defoe "in relation to the writing of his time," dividing his works into the genres of poetry, pamphlets and political writings, histories, and crime and adventure novels.

Bell, Ian A. *Defoe's Fiction.* London: Croom Helm, 1985, 201 p.

Attempts "to re-insert Defoe into his literary and paraliterary culture," which the critic views "as being corrective to all the critical efforts to place him in, or keep him out of, a literary tradition of a more exalted kind."

Elliott, Robert C., ed. *Twentieth Century Interpretations of "Moll Flanders": A Collection of Critical Essays.* Englewood Cliffs, N. J.: Prentice-Hall, 1970, 113 p.

Collection of twentieth-century interpretations of *Moll Flanders,* including essays by Virginia Woolf, Maximillian E. Novak, Cesare Pavese, and others.

Lee, William. *Daniel Defoe: His Life, and Recently Discovered Writings, Extending from 1716 to 1729, in Three Volumes.* London: John Camden Hotten, 1869.

Biography that includes a collection of Defoe's previously unpublished works.

Novak, Maximillian E. *Realism, Myth, and History in Defoe's Fiction.* Lincoln: University of Nebraska Press, 1983, 181 p.

Study by a noted authority on Defoe, who seeks to examine Defoe "as one of the greatest writers of his time and attempt to locate his excellence in his genius as a creator of fictions and in the often-underestimated complexities of his style and language."

Rogers, Pat, ed. *Defoe: The Critical Heritage.* London and Boston: Routledge & Kegan Paul, 1972, 228 p.

Collection of critical reviews and essays on Defoe's work from the eighteenth, nineteenth, and twentieth centuries.

Walter de la Mare

1873-1956

(Full name Walter John de la Mare, also wrote under pseudonym Walter Ramal) English poet, novelist, short story writer, critic, essayist, anthologist, and dramatist.

INTRODUCTION

*D*e la Mare was one of the chief exemplars of the romantic imagination in modern literature. In his poetry and fiction, he explored such romantic concerns as dreams, death, and fantasy worlds of childhood. His works often suggest the presence of a transcendent reality, subtly blending mystical experiences with ordinary objects and events. Although de la Mare's works have received recognition for their child-like, playful qualities, critics have also emphasized their frequent exploration of horror, evil, and the occult.

De la Mare was born in the village of Charleton in Kent. As a youth he attended St. Paul's Cathedral School, and his formal education did not extend beyond this point. Upon graduation he worked for the Anglo-American Oil Company, where he was employed for eighteen years. He began writing during this time, publishing his first book, *Songs of Childhood* (1902), which was recognized as a unique work of children's poetry for its creative imagery and variety of meters. Throughout his literary career, he produced collections of children's fiction and verse, as well as several highly praised anthologies. Critics often assert that a childlike richness of imagination influenced everything he wrote, emphasizing his frequent depiction of childhood as a time of intuition, deep emotion, and closeness to spiritual truth. Following the publication of his novel *Henry Brocken* (1904) and the poetry collection entitled *Poems* (1906), de la Mare received a government pension which enabled him to terminate his corporate employment and focus exclusively on a writing career. For the next fifty years, until his death, he wrote numerous short stories, novels, and poems, many of which reflect his interest in the supernatural. Among the most notable collections of his shorter works are *The Veil and Other Poems* (1921) and the posthumous *Ghost Stories* (1956).

De la Mare's fiction is often characterized by a mystical, dreamlike tone, rich imagery, poetic speech, slow, incantatory rhythms, and events conveyed by implication rather than direct action. By incorporating supernatural elements, including ghosts, it depicts veiled, elusive connections between life and death, and between dreams and consciousness. This motif is apparent, for example, in de la Mare's novel *The Return* (1910), in which elements of horror and the occult are intermingled with ordinary settings. At the opening of this work, a man falls asleep in a country churchyard near the tomb of a French exile who had committed suicide a century earlier. After returning home, the protagonist discovers that he has undergone an extensive physical and psychic transformation, assuming the appearance and personality of the dead Frenchman. Throughout the novel, he is increasingly fearful of becoming completely subsumed by the alien identity.

The characters of de la Mare's fiction reflect his motif of merging the mystical with the ordinary. Although the stories and novels frequently take place in a normal, placid setting, the characters often reflect peculiar or mysteriously sinister forces. While discussing de la Mare's characters, David Cecil observed that there is "always something odd about them. . . . The children are queer children, with their demure manners and solemn eyes and heads buzzing with fancies; the bachelors and old maids are solitary, eccentric, often a trifle crazy; the landladies and shopkeepers are 'character parts,' as full of grotesque idiosyncrasy as the personages of Dickens." Visibly bizarre characters are the focus of de la Mare's novel *Memoirs of a Midget* (1921), which has received praise for its examination of conflict between society and the individual. The protagonist of the work is Miss M., a woman so small she can barely climb stairs. Possessing a precocious intellect, she considers herself far superior to the "normal" people who surround her, and is often willful, sarcastic and aggressive. However, she is also troubled by a strong desire for belonging in spite of her scorn. Critics praised de la Mare's depiction of Miss M. as an ordinary person struggling to exist in a world of monstrous appearances. V. S. Pritchett asserted: "*Memoirs of a Midget* is a poet's book, perhaps a satire, perhaps a transposed confession, perhaps a fairy-tale in which people are either too large or too small." This work is often considered preeminent among de la Mare's novels.

As a poet de la Mare is often compared with Thomas Hardy and William Blake for their respective themes of mortality and visionary illumination. As in his fiction, de la Mare's poetry presents blurred states of reality, often juxtaposing such opposing images as night and day, death and life, sleep and wakefulness. Sleep is a prominent theme in his poetry, and in the introduction to his anthology *Behold, This Dreamer!* (1939), he defines dreams as "meaningful communings between self and self, revelations of the spirit within." He also speculates that "our senses are not our only trustworthy witnesses in this world, but that nature itself resembles a veil over some further reality of which the imagination in its visionary moments seems to achieve a more direct evidence." In his poem "Sleep" de la Mare asserts that through the visionary imagination of dreams, one may perceive a reality ordinarily concealed during waking life. Some critics have asserted that the style of his poetry suggests an intermingling of supernatural forces within the natural world through resonant, ambiguous language. Edward Davison observed that within de la Mare's poetry "is the atmosphere of a world hushed in mysterious, but slightly sinister calm, . . . thronged with invisible presences, unheard whispers. . . . Moreover, in this atmosphere there is frequently a vague sense of supernatural forces lurking invisibly. To Mr. de la Mare the gulf between reality and unreality is so small that he can doubt whether our waking life is more real than our dream life. The shapes and shadows of both lives enter into the world of his poetry."

For his extravagance of invention de la Mare is sometimes labelled an escapist, who retreated from accepted definitions of reality and the relationships of conventional existence. His approach to reality in his works, however, is not escapist; rather, it profoundly explores the world he considered most significant—that of the imagination.

(For further information about de la Mare's life and works, see *Contemporary Authors*, Vol. 110; *Dictionary of Literary Biography*, Vol. 19: *British Poets, 1880-1914; Something about the Author*, Vol. 16; and *Twentieth-Century Literary Criticism*, Vol. 4.)

CRITICAL COMMENTARY

STORM JAMESON

(essay date 1922)

[In the following excerpt, Jameson explores de la Mare's compassionate portrayal of humanity in *Memoirs of a Midget*, emphasizing the mystical nature of the author's writing.]

[Mr. de la Mare's] eyes catch the grotesque aspect of mortal loveliness, and his ears are attuned to the half-human note that underlies the human voice of the created world. Some part of him is often aloof and unresponsive to the human call, as if the listening spirit were half withdrawn. Throughout his work an elfin mockery peers through the words; with a sidewise glance for the mocker. It is not unkind, Mr. de la Mare is incapable of a sneer; it is the protective irony of a mind compelled to live awry in the procrustean bed of circumstance.

Viewed thus, from an angle only half human, the world of men and women shows faintly ridiculous, even while it keeps its aspects of courage and loving-kindness. Mr. de la Mare never insists upon the ridiculous aspect of humanity and rarely forgets it, looking at life with a smiling irony which is sometimes uncertain and always self-regarding. The Miss M. of [*Memoirs of a Midget*] shows often less like the elf she was than like an ordinary human adrift in a world of monstrous appearances, visited at times by a spirit far greater than her puny body, from which anon it departs, leaving her cowering, afraid, and wretched. She is mean and generous, capable of purest devotion and cruel egoism. Suffering teaches her, and joy escapes her, after the fashion of life. She worships beauty and sees it spoiled and self-defiled, craves kind love and loses that in the instant of achievement. It is as if her creator said: "This Midget is your mirror, discovering to you the whimsicalities of your bearing, which are my very own. Yet is it not a brave puppet?"

Gentle self-mockery pervades even Mr. de la Mare's mystical faith. A mystic he is, for whom the world of appearances exists as the transparent covering of things eternal. His imagination . . . , like Blake's, is rather a power of spiritual apprehension. . . . For him, as for Blake, "a Spirit and a Vision are not, as modern philosophy supposes, a cloudy vapour or a nothing"; they are passionate realities in a world of unreal show. (pp. 424-25)

There is a deep-rooted and seemingly involuntary

melancholy in his art. It is apparent behind his swift smile and behind his passionate adoration of beauty. He would be bitter were he a worse artist and a more worldly thinker. He is sad because he loves beauty with a sharp, intimate love, and can be hurt to the heart by loveliness. His sadness goes deeper than to the gentle Greek melancholy. He grieves little for the passing of beauty; that may be gracious, and at last is dignified by austere death. He grieves because most often beauty is betrayed by the heart that cherished it. It is slain by its own lovers, since human love grows weary and unkind. . . .

But if Mr. de la Mare is without illusion . . . he is indeed not without hope, having a sure refuge in humanity, which although mean and puny and cruel, is able to measure the paths of the stars, to suffer all things, to outface pain, to be kind, and to lay aside life for a dream or a word. Mr. de la Mare cannot always take mortal men seriously, but he does not forget that they are to be respected as well as to be pitied. . . . [He] sees through courage and meanness alike to the resolute secret dreamer which is man. (p. 426)

Memoirs of a Midget is the most notable achievement in prose fiction of our generation. A man writing of a woman with intent to penetrate through the shadow show of her adventures to the secret of her attitude to them, is hindered less by any inherent impossibility in the task than by the barriers which his own mind raises against his attempt. He will sometimes achieve complete understanding—when his mind has slipped into that world where all thought is one—and he will sometimes be baffled, imprisoned in his obstinate and inessential maleness. It may be that the diminutive size of Miss M., by allowing her creator to see her always as a little different from other women, removed one barrier. We do not and cannot know; but we do know that Mr. de la Mare has penetrated to the heart of this woman—never more woman that when her bodily insignificance is exaggerated by Fanny's triumphant charm—with an amazing and delicate audacity. He has divined, and conveyed with precision and a charming patience, the most subtle, emotional changes in one woman's adoring affection for another. (p. 427)

In an age of scamped and hurried work Mr. de la Mare has written a book of such exquisite and finished art that its words have the importance of threads in some tapestry of fabled beauty. (p. 430)

Principal Works

Songs of Childhood [as Walter Ramal] (poetry) 1902

Henry Brocken (novel) 1904

Poems (poetry) 1906

The Return (novel) 1910

The Listeners and Other Poems (poetry) 1912

Peacock Pie (poetry) 1913

Motley and Other Poems (poetry) 1918

Crossing (drama) 1921

Memoirs of a Midget (novel) 1921

The Veil and Other Poems (poetry) 1921

The Riddle and Other Stories (short stories) 1923

The Connoisseur and Other Stories (short stories) 1926

At First Sight (novel) 1928

On the Edge (short stories) 1930

Behold, This Dreamer! Of Reverie, Night, Sleep, Dream, Love-Dreams, Nightmare, Death, the Unconscious, the Imagination, Divination, the Artist, and Kindred Subjects [editor] (poetry and prose) 1939

Pleasures and Speculations (essays) 1940

The Burning Glass and Other Poems (poetry) 1945; published in the United States as The Burning Glass and Other Poems, Including The Traveler, 1945

Winged Chariot (poetry) 1951

Private View (essays) 1953

A Beginning and Other Stories (short stories) 1955

Complete Poems (poetry) 1969

Storm Jameson, "Mr. de la Mare and the Grotesque," in *The English Review*, Vol. XXIV, May, 1922, pp. 424-30.

J. B. PRIESTLEY

(essay date 1924)

[Below, Priestley examines de la Mare's major works, focusing on the theme of childhood imagination.]

[Mr. de la Mare] is one of those writers who have a few obvious characteristics known to everybody, characteristics that are complacently indicated by the reviewer whenever such writers publish a book; but if we wish to press forward and examine him more closely, he becomes curiously elusive, almost playing Ariel to our Caliban. There is no difficulty if we are simply prepared to enjoy and not to analyse, for we can always recognise his hand; the work is all of a piece. . . . Superficially, his work may appear somewhat fragmentary and casual, the spasmodic creation of a gifted dilettante—a few bundles of short lyrics, some short tales, and a fantasy or two, so many lovely and quaint odds and ends; but nothing could be further from the truth, for actually his work is one of the most individual productions this century has given us, every scrap of it being stamped with its author's personality and taking its place in the de la Mare canon. . . . Nevertheless, he remains to criticism an elusive figure, whose outline and gestures are not easily fixed in the memory—a shadowy Pied Piper.

One fairly common misconception must be brushed aside before we can begin to examine Mr. de la Mare, and that is the notion that he is primarily a creator of pretty fancies for the children. . . . Regarded as a general view this popular misconception is so preposterous that if we go to the other extreme, if we argue that Mr. de la Mare is a writer that no child should be suffered to approach, we shall not be further from the truth. We could point out that his work is really unbalanced, decadent, unhealthy, poisonous fruit for any child's eating. Consider his subjects. *The Return* is the story of a man who is partly possessed by an evil restless ghost, who comes back from a meditation among the tombstones in the local churchyard, wearing the face of a long-dead adventurer—a nightmare. The poetry is filled with madness and despair, wonders, and witchcraft, lit with a sinister moonlight; some crazed Elizabethan fool sitting in a charnel-house might have lilted some of these songs. The *Memoirs of a Midget* is the history of a freak who moves elvishly in the shadow of some monstrous spirit of evil; it is a long dream that never turns to the waking world, but only changes, when it does change, to nightmare. The tales in *The Riddle* are worse; they are the chronicles of crazed or evil spirits, Miss Duveen, Seaton's Aunt, and the rest; their world is one of abnormalities, strange cruelties and terrors, monstrous trees and birds and dead men on the prowl; their very sunlight is corrupt, maggot-breeding. And is this, we might ask, the writer of pretty fancies for the children; as well might we introduce [John] Webster, Poe, and Baudelaire into the nursery and schoolroom. Such an account of Mr. de la Mare as an unwholesome decadent is manifestly absurd, but on the whole it is probably less absurd than the more popular opinion of him as a pretty-pretty children's poet. (pp. 33-4)

The world he prefers to move in is one that has been pieced together by the imagination of childhood, made up of his childish memories of life and books, nursery rhymes, fairy tales, ballads, and quaint memorable passages from strange old volumes. Behind this, using it as so many symbols, is a subtle personality, a spirit capable of unusual exaltation and despair. There is nothing conscious and deliberate, I fancy, in all this; his mind instinctively seeks these forms in which to express itself; his imagination, when it is fully creative, instinctively avoids the world of common experience and runs back to this other world it created long ago.

The world we discover in Mr. de la Mare's poetry has some superficial resemblance to that in Mr. Yeats', but Mr. de la Mare could not casually wave away (as Mr. Yeats has done) his fairies and witches and ghosts and Arabias and Melmillos and Princess Seraphitas, not because they are really anything more than exquisite images and symbols, but because they are part of a world to which his imagination instinctively turns, in which it probably actually lives, not so much a beautifully embroidered coat that his Muse wears for a season, but her actual form and presence. One of the most beautiful and significant of Mr. de la Mare's earlier poems, *Keep Innocency,* puts before us the paradox of innocent childhood's love of what seems to its elders terrible and cruel, such as warfare. . . . And we may say that there is a central core in Mr. de la Mare's imagination that has "kept innocency," though his spirit should walk the awful borderlands and proclaim its despair; a man has *felt* the world he shows us, but a child's eyes have *seen* it, lit with strange stars or bright with unknown birds. (p. 36)

[It] is worth remarking that the later work is better and more personal, more characteristic than the earlier, both in poetry and prose. Thus, both the *Memoirs of a Midget* and the collection of short tales called *The Riddle* are better, on any count, than—to go no further back—*The Return.* This last is, of course, a fantasy, but it differs from the later work not so much in its theme as in its treatment, which brings it nearer to the ordinary realistic fiction of the time than the later stories are. The style is not so mannered, not so subtly cadenced and bright with imagery, as the style of the other two volumes, and it does not lure us on to forget this world of offices and the witness-box as the later one does, but really has the contrary aim of making the one fantastic stroke credible. Mr. de la Mare has not boldly entered his own world, and the result, for all the art he has plainly lavished on the story, is unfortunate; the story itself is one, or at least is of the kind, that we are more accustomed to seeing treated comically . . . than treated tragically as it is here, and though this would not have mattered in the least had the author lured us away into his own world, it matters a great deal when he is making terms with this one. . . . Mrs. Lawford, a commonplace, conventionally-minded wife, is the kind of character the ordinary realistic novelist sketches in between a few puffs of his (or her) cigarette; but just where such inferior chroniclers are happily in their depth, Mr. de la Mare is well out of his, and Mrs. Lawford is appalling, a crude monster from a first novel by a third-rate writer. Her friend and their

conversations are on the same level of crudity. In short, the conventional element, which would not be present at all in the later stories since the whole pack of characters, with their houses and furniture, would be subtly translated, is so badly done that it almost wrecks the fantasy, which is presented with some characteristic strokes of genius. Here, then, the normal, with its commonplace tangle of adult relations and interests, has baffled our author's imagination.

Then in his next story he boldly obliterated all the common relations and affairs of life by choosing a theme that was bristling with difficulties, that probably every other storyteller we have would have rejected at a glance, but that required just such an imagination as his and no other for its successful treatment. The *Memoirs of a Midget* overshadows *The Return* not so much because it is later and the author has improved his craft, but because he has now boldly entered his own world and has left off trying to come to terms with that of most novelists. Many people have wondered why Mr. de la Mare should choose such a queer subject, the history, in autobiographical form, of a year or so in the life of a freak, for what is easily his most ambitious single performance, a novel on the old heroic scale. But if our account of him has any truth in it at all, he could hardly have done better; the choice of subject itself, let alone his treatment of it, was a stroke of genius. (pp. 38-9)

At first sight it may appear that our theory of Mr. de la Mare's imagination will break down when we pass from the *Midget,* which triumphantly proclaims its truth, to the collection of short stories in *The Riddle.* In these tales the author creeps along the borderlands of the human spirit, and in a style that is even more artful, mannered and highly coloured than that of the *Midget,* he describes the corroding evils and moonstruck fantasies that visit those on whom the world's common burden of affairs presses most lightly, the very young and the very old, and those whose reason has been fretted away and whose ordinary faculties have fallen into desuetude; it is a book of "atmospheres," of adventures on the edge of things, crumbling away the homely and comforting reality, and confronting us with the heaving and crawling darkness. But not all the stories are set in this queer spiritual twilight; some of them seem little more than exquisite memories, clustered about some slight theme, and have something of the bright loveliness, the happy magic, of those clear dreams that only too rarely visit our sleep; their brightness and their suggestion of old ways and scenes point to their author's having made a poetical kind of camera obscura out of his memory. Many of them are related as the experiences of childhood, notably two of the most exquisite, *The Almond Tree* and *The Bowl,* both of which have the air of being fragments from some greater context (though perhaps existing only in the writer's mind); and none of these things could have been created by a man who had not kept alive his child-hood and never lost sight if its world. Some of the tales have the appearance of bright nursery pictures that have suffered some curious change and become sym-bolical representations of a spiritual life that no nursery ever knew. And even the stories that seem furthest away from anything we can connect with childhood re-veal, after some scrutiny, their indebtedness to the kind of imagination that has already been described. . . . There is a curious suggestion throughout these stories . . . that this world of Mr. de la Mare's is, as it were, the other half of the Dickens' world, the poetical, mysterious, aristocratic half that Dickens, with his eyes fixed on the democratic, humorous, melodramatic ele-ments, never gave us. This suggestion was something more than an odd fancy, for both these lovable genius-es (Mr. de la Mare is certainly a genius), different as they are in almost every essential, have at least one thing in common, their method of building up their worlds, the process of the creative imagination. (pp. 40-1)

[Mr. de la Mare] remains one of that most lovable order of artists who never lose sight of their childhood, but re-live it continually in their work and contrive to find expression for their maturity in it, memories and impressions, its romantic vision of the world; the artists whose limitations and weaknesses are plain for any passing fool to see, but whose genius, and they are never without it, never mere men of talent, delights both philosophers and children; the artists who re-member Eden. (p. 43)

J. B. Priestley, "Mr. de la Mare's Imagination," in *The London Mercury*, Vol. X, No. 55, May, 1924, pp. 33-43.

JOHN ATKINS
(essay date 1947)

[In the following excerpt, Atkins explores themes of horror and childhood mystery in de la Mare's novels, stories, and essays.]

[De la Mare's] obsession with the tomb and with life on the other side is apparent to even the most casual reader. His best novel, *The Return,* begins in a church-yard and is haunted by the churchyard throughout, as Shakespeare's *Julius Caesar* is haunted by the spirit of Caesar. The tendency came to a head when he devoted a whole book, *Ding Dong Bell,* to thoughts and emo-tions resulting from visits to cemeteries.

Put as baldly as this it might appear that de la Mare is an unnaturally morbid and unbalanced person. Nothing, of course, could be less true. His delightful

books on Childhood, Dreams and Desert Islands refute any such accusation. Despite his admiration for the writings of Poe, he is no Poe himself. (p. 8)

De la Mare's tomb points towards Egypt because the Ancient Egyptians preceded him in his absorption in the phenomenon of death. Their social lives were ruled by the never-forgotten fact that life was not eter-nal (in this world, at least) and that when life is impor-tant, so is death. . . . De la Mare is Egyptian in this re-spect, for he also can never forget it, although the con-ventions of our time force him to be less candid and more subtle. But any enclosed space reminds him of a tomb. Anything with walls is a grave-symbol. His walls are never on the defensive against the mind's ex-panding, roving spirit. Rather are they being battered from the outside by the unknown menace. (pp. 8-9)

The tomb is never far from de la Mare's active mind. It should be understood that the word "tomb" in this context stands for a great many more things than a sarcophagus. It is a symbol of all that belongs to the dividing line between life and death. No-one knows how fine this line is. The physiologist may be able to state that it is a matter of breath or heart-beats, but de la Mare, like his primitive ancestors, is suspicious of this simple explanation. He cannot forget, for instance, that the boundary between waking and sleeping is not a fine one. It is wide enough to contain daydreams; he himself refers to it as the territory between Dream and Wake. He is rather impatient with people who believe that physical definitions are sufficient to cover any-thing. (pp. 11-12)

[What] is the relation between [Poe and de la Mare]? On the outermost layer it is obviously one of teacher and taught, admired and admirer. But behind this is a subtle shift of ground. De la Mare is not con-tent merely to copy Poe's method. What he has done is to analyse Poe's work into its constituents of subject and atmosphere. But instead of retracing ground and adapting atmosphere and sensation to his own time, he has made them the subjects of his work. Thus most of his stories are really concerned, not with human beings in a particular psychic state, but with the psychic state itself. Naturally, he has to employ human beings, oth-erwise his stories would be essays and would not reach the public he wishes to reach—those readers who keep clear of psychological treatises. The atmosphere is the hero and, as is to be expected, the human characters are often no more than cyphers, unreal and not very human. Poe's first consideration was the individual, though always the individual under stress. De la Mare has used Poe as a stepping stone in his advance into the unknown land which lies somewhere between life, death, sleep, dream, wake and revery. That is all we know of its topography.

And now we come to that aspect of these two writers which is most obvious, and which has already been referred to. Few others have managed so efficiently the horror theme. It is this, more than anything else, that brings the two together. But it is only the subject that is common, for in its treatment and presentation they are in constant divergence. Poe's horror is visual and extremely objective; de la Mare's can only be sensed by some hidden instrument of the mind and is intensely subjective. This does not mean that he writes impersonally of horror, or tries to analyse states of mind of the horrible or horrified; he is never so explicit as this, never presents horror as does a film magnate, but allows a sensation of alarm and apprehension to creep across the reader's mind. Poe's situations are horrible to the least and most sophisticated minds; his devices, the living in the tomb, the pit and the pendulum, are frightening even to the most insensitive. But de la Mare, with his mastery of nuance and suggestion, palms his menace off on to the reader like an expert salesman. His harmless Victorian furniture and harmlessly eccentric old ladies (Seaton's aunt, for example) are objects and people we know and meet almost daily without the smallest shudder, yet he transforms them into dark threats and menacing witches.

What he has done, in effect, is to establish the existence of a subterranean link between horror and beauty. This Poe never did. In his world of maniacs we would be foolish to expect anything but the unnatural. . . . But there is nothing like this in the stories of de la Mare. Gradually one becomes conscious of an eeriness which it is impossible to attribute to any one trick, but which must derive somehow from an expert use of words. And that is about all that can be said. (pp. 14-17)

Two forms of beauty are to be found in de la Mare: the physical beauty of nature and the psychological beauty of character. As has been said, his horror is subjective and psychological. Although he makes effective use of objects and their properties, they never provide the horror sensations in themselves. They are always provided by the impact of these objects on impressionable minds *in the story*. The reader is led to sense the result of this impact, of this psychic relationship. None of the ingredients are evil, but the effect of their collusion is. In fact, de la Mare does not appear to recognise the existence of fundamental evil. He knows the stupid and the stubborn, but not the malevolent. But one of the disquieting facts of life is that the chance association of two goods often results in the production of an evil. This is the philosophic basis of his work. He goes further: evil is more likely to be produced by entities furthest removed in character from evil than by others which stand in closer proximity. Hence, the marriage of beauty and beauty can produce ugliness, and that of good and good can produce evil. This is an easily verifiable thesis. Intellectual marriages are some-

times spoiled by moronic offspring; the play of children is often marred by unfortunate accidents.

This is the explanation of de la Mare's apparently magic formula for the evocation of horror. It is based on a premiss that is so universal as to be universally ignored. It explains why a girl of ten, when placed in a certain environment, may appear repulsive. It is not the girl, and it is not the environment, but the association of the two. Association is both physical and psychic. Processes are set to work between the two poles, and they, the unseen epiphenomena of normal and everyday existence, provide the horror. They are the ghosts of de la Mare, they are the sinister influences, they are the pregnancy of his atmosphere. (pp. 17-18)

It is impossible to go any further with a portrait of de la Mare without entering more fully into the question of social criticism. Although many essays and biographies have been written of him, none that I know of is much concerned with this important aspect. It is not very difficult to see that his interest in subjects that are unpopular with and untouched by the majority of his contemporaries on the highest artistic and intellectual level is in itself a protest against the prevailing philosophy of our times. It is obvious that he must be extremely sceptical of the nineteenth century giants, the Darwins and Marxes. ("Marx is merely the boiled-up sentiment of a civilisation gone wrong".) It is a revolt against a philosophy rather than a system. De la Mare would probably say that the idea comes before the act, and that the hideous living of our times is an accurate reflection of shabby minds. To argue thus one is covertly comparing one's own times with other times—in other words, one is drawing on an implicit reservoir of history. In this de la Mare is distinguished from his younger contemporaries. He has a sense of history, of the march of civilisation, that impregnates all his work. It is a dark backcloth to his scenes—one can make out very little detail but one is always conscious of its presence. The reader is aware vaguely of a distant Golden Age; any concrete features of this Age are difficult to define. There was an "otherness" about it. An extra sense was in use, perhaps, and language was heartily alive and not the almost valueless old invalid it is becoming to-day. (pp. 20-1)

The position we have reached in this examination of the mind and beliefs of Walter de la Mare is roughly this: The human race once possessed to an extraordinary degree a faculty known as Imagination. In the course of its history, however, the use of this faculty largely lapsed and was replaced by another one called Reason. Reason is a poor substitute. It has meant the closer investigation of a part of our world with a corresponding loss of knowledge of another. Reason utilises the five senses, and by skilful manipulation and coordination has elicited many truths from dark corners. But there are certain other truths that cannot be elicited without the aid of a sixth sense. It is a familiar controversy. Imagination is the poet's weapon; its links with religious experience and the old Mysteries are more than fine; it is Pascal's platform. Reason belongs to the scientist; it first flowered among the Greek oligarchs; it is Descartes's platform. (pp. 31-2)

A lot of de la Mare's poetry is for and about the mystery of childhood. Implicit in his theme is, if you like, an alternative to the historical Descent of Man. Confining his philosophy to a single lifetime one is aware of a circle, beginning with childhood and ending with old age, but where the end and the beginning are the same point. It is the Platonic theory of historical cycles applied to the life-span. The age of childhood is one of dimly remembered mystery; at about the age of eighteen, when the world forces itself upon the individual in its crudest form, mystery is dissipated and replaced by reality; reality holds sway until the world looks upon the individual increasingly as a liability; there is a gradual return to mystery, which one feels is akin to the first stage in more respects than a common opposition to reality. The process represents the author's dislike of and impatience with utility as a measure of value. The process, seen from his viewpoint, is Appearance—Disappearance—Reappearance. Reappearance is a recurring form of Appearance, the two are one. This is expressed in his stories by the close links that exist between children and old people, while the middle-aged are either unaware that such links exist or cannot understand them when they are aware. (p. 39)

With his strong sense of isolation and individuality, de la Mare is never at ease with the profanity of love. Each person is an island fortress in a rough sea strewn with privateers. It is perhaps possible for a person to know himself, but to know others is out of the question. We make fumbling attempts to explore the minds of our friends, just as I am making a fumbling attempt to explore the mind of Walter de la Mare, but we never penetrate deeply and only then at random points. The ghosts within, the filibusters of the mind, elude us always. How can two people, a man and a woman, dovetail into each other like the fingers of locked hands, and be no longer two, but one?

The novels and stories of de la Mare are still readable, after the lapse of many years, for a number of reasons. One is simply literary, his ease in the language. Another is his psychological accuracy, his nuances which ring so true and say so much. Throughout his writings are to be found chance phrases, often enigmatical or seemingly unimportant, which yet are like little daggers pointing at the hidden heart of a problem. From the core of his work fly streamers of many colours, which, if followed through the maze, lead invariably to something which one instantaneously recognises as truth or authority or perception. These are the documents of his own mental experience. And yet,

with all this equipment, he never succeeds in creating a living character. In all his gallery—the Lawfords, Herberts, Bowaters, midgets and the thronging population of the stories—there is never a completely successful creation.

Here we have the greatness and shortcoming of de la Mare. Aesthetically he has no superior today; his mystic sense is of far greater value than most contemporary cerebration; his psychological perception is of a high order; but this perception extends only to parts, perhaps all the parts, yet never to the whole. The whole human being is as elusive to him as his ghosts are to us. (pp. 42-3)

John Atkins, in his *Walter de la Mare: An Exploration*, C. & J. Temple, Ltd., 1947, 45 p.

HENRY CHARLES DUFFIN
(essay date 1949)

[In the excerpt below, Duffin examines spiritual themes in de la Mare's poetry.]

[In his poetry de la Mare] exhibits, generally, a perfection of art as flawless as Tennyson's. It is interesting to observe how this was achieved. The first volume, *Songs of Childhood* . . . shows none of this perfection of craftsmanship, but is rich in those delights that presently came to be recognized as characteristic de la Mare, though the final magic of rhythm is there only as an undertone. *Poems* 1906 marks a great advance in art, and yet is deeply disappointing when read immediately after the [first] volume, because it contains so little of that entirely new thing—the spirit of Walter de la Mare—that made *Songs of Childhood* so precious. It seems that the poet was consciously disciplining himself to an exquisite artistry, but achieving this at a cost, giving us a greater number of excellent poems than were in the earlier volume, but very few to be remembered with equal pleasure. Yet the cost was well worth while. For in the first place, out of this conscious artistry was perfected the ultimate music of rhythmic form, embodied here in just one or two examples—*Age,* and *The Phantom.* . . . Moreover, the discipline of this volume was so effective that perfection of art became a habit, and in the next three volumes, far from being an obstacle to those special things this poet was born to create, it became the necessary medium and final voice of their utterance. (pp. 32-3)

De la Mare's ability to express in marvellous verse all the marvellous things he has to say is excelled by few even of the greatest poets. Moreover, it is progressive, and in *Motley* it is absolute. In this volume, as in

Hamlet, content and form are perfectly balanced, and not to be distinguished. Here we find profound imaginative vision given utterance in poem after poem of flawless art. . . . (p. 35)

[The] poetry of Walter de la Mare is not essentially either a criticism of life or (as some think it) an escape from life. It will fulfill both these functions for those who require them, but the primary end of de la Mare's poetry is to heighten life. Life is much too good that any but the very unfortunate or the very dull should want to escape from it, but there are times when the pressure, perhaps the preponderance, of its lower constituents creates a sense of insignificance in life itself. At such times a draught, a breath, of de la Mare, even a fleeting memory of one of his poems, effects a miraculous restoration, so that life again is full of meaning and beauty. If the lower levels are your choice, if your interests are "business" and "sport", exalting your ego or overreaching your neighbour, you will have no use for de la Mare; but all the major themes of life he ennobles by making them eternal, part of the world of spirit. It is not altogether a matter of his special insistence on the necessity of magic, but of course it is partly this. He makes us feel in our hearts the strangeness of a phantom world, its stillness answering our cry. Dark hints and intriguing voices come out of the sounds that break the silence of nature, and the silence of a wood or a still house is burdened with meaning. The vaguely, deliciously disturbing atmosphere of quiet places is interpreted for us. Enchantment is ever at hand. . . . (pp. 196-97)

The themes which excite the intensity of de la Mare's passion, and which in consequence he makes more passionately intense for us, are all spiritual. Of love he speaks as of something special and strange, so that those to whom he has spoken can never let love sink into commonplace, but must always see it as godlike, breathing a speechless grace; an inexpressible union of the spirits of man and woman, a "selfless solitude in one another's arms". (pp. 197-98)

Life itself, the all that we have, the grand sum of our being and knowing from birth to death, is marvellously transmuted, transfigured, heightened in value and beauty by the poetry of Walter de la Mare, as he listens in his heart for what is beyond the range of human speech. He, more than most poets, keeps alive an endless wonder in the visible world suspended between God and man. (pp. 198-99)

Of happiness, life's profoundest truth, de la Mare has little explicitly to say, and that little comes late, but when it comes, it comes with an emphasis born of knowledge, a finality that gives it special force. It has always been there, silent, in the poetry, for all creation, whether of God or of genius, is in essence happy. But his ultimate word is that love, beauty and happiness are the sacred triunity of life. Life so conceived, so lived,

is hard to abandon, and to the poet with his intense life doubly so. Loving the light, he is impatient of the advancing dark—for to him it is Good night, not "in some other clime" Good morning. . . . (pp. 199-200)

Henry Charles Duffin, in his *Walter de la Mare: A Study of His Poetry,* Sidgwick and Jackson Limited, 1949, 209 p.

W. H. AUDEN
(essay date 1963)

[In the following excerpt from a 1963 introduction to a collection of de la Mare's verse, English poet and critic Auden comments on the structure and technique of de la Mare's poetry.]

[De la Mare's] most obvious virtues, those which no reader can fail to see immediately, are verbal and formal, the delicacy of his metrical fingering and the graceful architecture of his stanzas. Neither in his technique nor his sensibility, does he show any trace of influences other than English, either continental, like Eliot and Pound, or Classical, like Bridges. The poets from whom he seems to have learned most are the Elizabethan songwriters, Christina Rossetti and, I would rashly guess, Thomas Hardy. Like Christina Rossetti, he is a master of trisyllabic substitution and foot inversion; the reader's ear is continually excited by rhythmical variations without ever losing a sense of the underlying pattern. . . . Like Hardy, he is a great inventor of stanzas and in command of every effect which can be obtained from contrasts between lines of different lengths, lines with masculine endings and lines with feminine endings, rhymed and unrhymed lines. (pp. 385-86)

Many poets have some idiosyncrasy or tic of style which can madden the reader if he finds their work basically unsympathetic, but which, if he likes it, becomes endearing like the foibles of an old friend. Hardy's fondness for compound and Latinate words is one example, de la Mare's habit of subject-verb inversion another. . . .

In his later work such inversions become much rarer. One can observe also a change in his diction. Though this continues to come from what one might call the "beautiful" end of the verbal spectrum—he never, like Yeats and Eliot uses a coarse or brutal word, and seldom a slang colloquialism—a chronological study of his poems shows a steady, patient and successful endeavor to eliminate the overly arty diction which was a vice of his Pre-Raphaelite forebears, and to develop a style which, without ceasing to be lyrical, has the directness of ordinary speech. (p. 387)

His late long poem, *Winged Chariot,* is a surprising performance. He still writes as a lyric poet, not as an epic or dramatic, and it is better read, perhaps, like *In Memoriam,* as a series of lyrics with a meter and theme in common, but readers who are only familiar with his early poetry will find something they would never have predicted, a talent for metaphysical wit. . . .

De la Mare wrote many poems with an audience of children specifically in mind. . . . [But] it must never be forgotten that, while there are some good poems which are only for adults, because they presuppose adult experience in their readers, there are no good poems which are only for children. (p. 388)

As a revelation of the wonders of the English Language, de la Mare's poems for children are unrivaled. (The only ones which do not seem to me quite to come off are those in which he tries to be humorous. A gift, like Hilaire Belloc's for the comic-satiric is not his; he lacks, perhaps, both the worldliness and the cruelty which the genre calls for.) They include what, for the adult, are among his greatest "pure" lyrics, e.g., *Old Shellover* and *The Song of the Mad Prince,* and their rhythms are as subtle as they are varied. Like all good poems, of course, they do more than train the ear. They also teach sensory attention and courage. Unlike a lot of second-rate verse for children, de la Mare's descriptions of birds, beasts, and natural phenomena are always sharp and accurate, and he never prettifies experience or attempts to conceal from the young that terror and nightmare are as essential characteristics of human existence as love and sweet dreams. (p. 389)

[De la Mare's] poems are neither satirical nor occasional; indeed, I cannot recall coming across in his work a single Proper Name, whether of a person or a place, which one could identify as a real historical name. Nor, though he is a lyric, not a dramatic, poet, are his poems "personal" in the sense of being self-confessions; the *I* in them is never identical with the Mr. de la Mare one might have met at dinner, and none are of the kind which excite the curiosity of a biographer. Nevertheless, implicit in all his poetry are certain notions of what constitutes the Good Life. Goodness, they seem to say, is rooted in wonder, awe, and reverence for the beauty and strangeness of creation. Wonder itself is not goodness—de la Mare is not an aesthete—but it is the only, or the most favorable, soil in which goodness can grow. (p. 393)

W. H. Auden, "Walter de la Mare," in his *Forewords and Afterwords,* edited by Edward Mendelson, Random House, Inc., 1973, pp. 384-94.

V. S. PRITCHETT
(essay date 1982)

[In the following excerpt, Pritchett examines plot and characterization in *Memoirs of a Midget.*]

'Away into secrecy frisked a pampered mouse'—a curdled Georgian sentence that leads one straight into one of Walter de la Mare's most plain and chilling tales about a boy's initiation into horror. The story is '**An Ideal Craftsman**'. In this genre he was a master—albeit a very literary master—of the riddles of sado-masochism, the dark underside of his 'magic'. So also was Stevenson—a predecessor in his 'sedulous ape' period; so too, later, is the bookish cross-bred Borges. Miss Angela Carter, whose preface speculates here on his famous novel *Memoirs of a Midget,* glances at Borges and goes on to the possibility that de la Mare may be the only English Surrealist, but one with a manner that has what she calls the 'sheen' of the Pre-Raphaelites. This 'sheen' on his best prose is of course

Walter de la Mare in 1922.

protective and is intended to give the false sense of safety in which we can play with unease. The rooms of his old country houses and their furniture gleam with malign assurance; the gardened Kentish landscape is rich and somnolent. Gardens are important to him—the shadows of trees or the cries of birds alarm a writer who feels himself to be watcher and watched. His 'normal' people are torpid, the class manners in which they are set are decorous and assured, even when they have the English acidity. 'A double-minded creature I was,' cries Miss M., the genuine midget in this novel. A freak she may be, precocious in her intellect and her retorts as she reads her Jane Austen, her Brontës, her Metaphysical poets, and studies astronomy, but she is vivacious and violent too: she is sarcastic rather than humbled, in her estrangement from the human norm. 'Foolish girl that I was,' she cries out again when she considers her self-will and her passions. Looking back on her failure to be anything more than a deviant, she eventually elects to see herself as nothing less than a damned soul—damnation is a kind of fame—and mysteriously speaks at the end of her story of being 'called away' out of loneliness into limbo—but not Hell. Miss Angela Carter, who is searching on the symbolism which seems basic to the *Memoirs,* thinks that its 'metaphysical subtext is a decoy'. De la Mare had a gift for the riddle within a riddle: but she thinks he offers 'a key to a door behind which there is only another door' and that he is shut up in Victorian reticence and sternly anti-Freudian. She quotes his own defence from his introduction to the Everyman edition of the novel in 1938: 'Feelings as well as thoughts may be expressed in symbols; and every character is not only a "chink" or "peep-hole" in the dark cottage from which his maker looks out at the world, but is also in some degree representative of himself, if a self in disguise.' This is a truism. What one notices are the 'peep-hole' and 'cottage': he was drawn to the small and unique because he applied a microscope to it and thereby turned it into the grotesque. He believed in the privacy of the imagination, regarding it as an anatomical part. We may think that Fancy rather than Imagination was his forte. Still, within these terms, he was an ingenious and marvellous architect of his elaborate drama. Immediately after the 1914 war, Angela Carter suggests, older readers may have been drawn to a nostalgia for the exclusive if staling comforts of a past that was safe: but there is no doubt that this novel is a minor masterpiece. He was an authentic connoisseur of manners, their spites and the price paid for their comedy.

How small was Miss M.? This is uncertain, but for years she was so tiny that she ran about on the dining table and stood there reading books that were taller than herself. When a child, born to embarrassed full-sized parents, she could sleep in a cat's basket. Even at the age of 20—the year of her personal crisis as a young lady—she could hardly manage stairs. She may have reached a height of two feet. She has a tiny safe income, until the crash comes. She might be a toy, an object, a mere collector's oddity but for the fact that she is aggressive, rash, sharp-tongued and carried away by adult passions, determined to be seen as far more alert than the normal people around her, at once scornful of them and craving to belong. She is sometimes arch, always demanding and a delightful talker. 'Aren't we becoming rather lugubrious?' she says to a love-sick clergyman. She is snobbish and very class-conscious—she knows she is superior to the homely country woman who becomes her landlady after the death of her parents—yet, more important, is infatuated with Fanny, her landlady's daughter, who is a schoolmistress and teaches English Literature. Miss M. picks up lower-class religious phrases and is proud of moments when she is 'a child of wrath', but can also preen herself on being 'the child of grace'. After the piquant opening chapters the central drama appears. She falls in love with Fanny, who is a beauty, noted for her greed, her social-climbing schemes and her heartlessness, and wonderfully well-drawn. Fanny is the placid cat who decides Miss M. is a useful victim and will torment and eventually set out to destroy her. Fanny is a 'vamp' with men. She has already driven that village clergyman to suicide—one of de la Mare's minutely documented suicides—and when Miss M. declares her love to her the girl turns on her and says: 'Do you really suppose that to be loved is new to me; that I'm not smeared all over with it wherever I go?'

Yet Miss M.'s infatuation lasts. What is its nature? Is it sexual? De la Mare is fortunately too reticent to say, though he grants her dislike of being touched. He either has no interest in sex or, at most, believes that it must be ingeniously disguised or disowned. Here we come to one of those doors which have no key—unless cruelty and the desire to suffer are more his interest. (There is a Plymouth Brother puritan in him and that perhaps prompted him to settle for 'the Romantic agony' of his period. Fanny may be Swinburne's strapping *dompteuse* reborn.) Fanny's object is solely to climb into Miss M.'s social world and get a rich husband. This is achieved when Miss M. is taken up by Mrs Monnerie, who collects freaks to show them off in her drawing-room, and gives Miss M. a London Season, no expense spared. Money will turn out to be Miss M.'s desperate temptation.

High Society turns Miss M.'s head. She confesses she became 'pranked up with conceit' in her intellectual superiority to the social crowd, many of whom had 'faces that looked as though they had been on an almost unbelievable long journey—and not merely through this world, though that helps'. They regarded her as a curio. A birthday party her rich hostess gives for her is of spectacular vulgarity. The menu is meant to flatter her: there is a frightful dish of nightingales' tongues, quails' wings and such, which was bad enough for one who could not eat meat, but a glass of some heavy green syrup does for her. She gets up on the table and trots over to her beloved Fanny, calling out, 'Holy Dying! Holy Dying! Sauve qui peut!' and passes out beside Fanny's plate.

Far stranger and elaborately symbolical events have occurred before this and are related by her quick and bookish tongue. To match the destructive Fanny there is the despised figure of one who is cut out to save her from spiritual ruin: it is Mr Anon, a revolting dwarf, who loves her. His name is distinctly coy. Miss M. loathes him and his devotion: he is a watcher! But he comes powerfully to the rescue when Mrs Monnerie and Fanny have turned on her and, being by now without money, she imitates a well-known rival midget and exhibits herself at a vulgar circus. In fact, Mr Anon is killed in a circus accident in attempting to save her life.

He completes the tragic riddle which de la Mare has so pawkily and poetically elaborated. He is gnomic in a touching and melancholy way, but de la Mare's gift of pampering the bleakness and horror of life gives him a dire force. There is a haunting metaphysical hint that, beyond Mr Anon, there may be a mysterious Guardian Spirit: but, as Angela Carter says, this does suggest that de la Mare was frightened by his own nerve at the end. It seems that he has some unbearable private agony, stoically borne, that has driven him to embed artifice so thoroughly into his tale that it becomes momentous as it glitters and gapes under his magnifying glass. *Memoirs of a Midget* is a poet's book, perhaps a satire, perhaps a transposed confession, perhaps a fairy-tale in which people are either too large or too small. One remembers that Hans Andersen said he wrote for adults. (p. 6)

V. S. Pritchett, "Falling in Love with Fanny," in *London Review of Books,* Vol. 4, No. 14, August 5-18, 1982, p. 6.

SOURCES FOR FURTHER STUDY

Barfield, Owen. "Poetry in Walter de la Mare." *The Denver Quarterly* 8, No. 3 (Autumn 1973): 69-81.

Analyzes structure and rhetorical devices in de la Mare's poetry.

Cecil, David. "The Prose Tales of Walter de la Mare." In his *The Fine Art of Reading and Other Literary Studies,* pp. 219-30. Indianapolis: Bobbs-Merrill Co., 1957.

Examines the style and structure of de la Mare's fiction.

Chesterton, G. K. "Walter de la Mare." *The Fortnightly Review* 138 (July 1932): 47-53.

Discusses the depiction of evil within de la Mare's fiction.

Davison, Edward. "Walter de la Mare." In his *Some Modern Poets and Other Critical Essays,* pp. 113-40. New York: Harper and Row, 1928.

Explores the magical, haunted atmosphere within de la Mare's poetry.

McCrosson, Doris Ross. *Walter de la Mare.* New York: Twayne Publishers, 1966, 170 p.

Critical study focusing on de la Mare's novels.

Wagenknecht, Edward. "News of Tishnar: Walter de la Mare." In his *Calvalcade of the English Novel: From Elizabeth to George VI,* pp. 533-46. New York: Henry Holt and Co., 1943.

Overview of de la Mare's major works of fiction.

Charles Dickens

1812-1870

(Also wrote under pseudonym Boz) English novelist, short story writer, dramatist, poet, and essayist.

INTRODUCTION

Dickens, a nineteenth-century English novelist, has achieved a degree of popular and critical recognition rarely equaled in English letters. Almost all of his novels display, to varying degrees, his comic gift, his deep social concerns, and his extraordinary talent for creating unforgettable characters. Many of his creations, most notably Ebenezer Scrooge, have become familiar English literary stereotypes. And though he has sometimes been criticized for creating caricatures rather than characters, he has been defended as a master of imaginative vision, forging whole character types out of tiny eccentricities. A frequent early criticism that his works are "formless" is not accepted by most modern critics. Many now see Dickens's novels as vast and complex denunciations of the bourgeois society that corrupts its members.

Dickens was the son of John Dickens, a minor government official and the model for the character Mr. Micawber in the novel *David Copperfield.* Like his literary counterpart, Dickens's father constantly lived beyond his means and was eventually sent to debtor's prison. This humiliation deeply troubled young Dickens, and even as an adult he was rarely able to speak of it. As a boy of twelve he was forced to work in a factory for meager wages. Although the experience lasted only several months, it left an indelible impression on Dickens. Late in his teens, he learned shorthand and became a court reporter, which introduced him to journalism and aroused his contempt for politics. His early short stories and sketches, which were published in various London newspapers and magazines, were later collected to form his first book, *Sketches by Boz* (1836). The book sold well and received generally favorable notices, setting the stage for a new, more unified series of fiction.

His next literary venture was *Posthumous Papers*

of the Pickwick Club (1837). By the time the fourth monthly installment was published, Dickens was the most popular author in England. His fame soon spread throughout the rest of the English-speaking world and eventually to the Continent. It has not diminished since. "The Pickwick Papers" are celebrations of individual character and full of Dickens's famous good-natured spirit and humor. The most loosely structured of his novels, *Pickwick* proved to be well suited for serial publication. Even as the structure of his novels grew more intricate, Dickens never abandoned this method of publication, for he cherished the constant contact with his readers through monthly or weekly installments. And the public returned his affection, lining up at bookstores for hours before a new number was distributed.

Success followed upon success for Dickens, and the number of his readers continued to grow during what is now regarded as his "early period," which includes the works *Sketches, Pickwick, Oliver Twist* (1838), *The Life and Adventures of Nicholas Nickleby* (1839), and *The Old Curiosity Shop* (1841). The last of these features one of his most famous and sentimental creations, Little Nell. As well as inspiring public grief, Little Nell's death was seen by most of Dickens's contemporary critics as a sublime example of pathos. Later critics, however, have viewed this scene as an example of crude sentimentalism; it prompted Oscar Wilde to remark that "one must have a heart of stone to read the death of Little Nell without laughing." But *The Old Curiosity Shop,* with a circulation of over 70,000, was Dickens's greatest early success.

In 1842 Dickens traveled to the United States, hoping to find an embodiment of his liberal political ideals. He returned to England deeply disappointed, dismayed by America's lack of support for an international copyright law, acceptance of the inhumane practice of slavery, and the vulgarity of the American people. Many critics consider the resulting *American Notes for General Circulation* (1842) ill tempered and superficial. His next novel, *The Life and Adventures of Martin Chuzzlewit* (1844), in which he satirized the American obsession with material possessions, was a popular book but a critical failure. Nevertheless, many commentators see the novel as a turning point in Dickens's career, claiming that he realized for the first time the failure of the bourgeois ideal: greed corrupted the human soul. Dickens was to become more and more concerned with avarice in what is called his "middle period," which began with the short story *A Christmas Carol in Prose* (1843).

An immensely popular work, *A Christmas Carol* chronicles the transformation of Ebenezer Scrooge from a miser to a generous being. Two other "Christmas books," *The Chimes* (1844) and *The Cricket on the Hearth* (1845), soon followed. His next full-length novel, *Dealings with the Firm of Dombey and Son*

(1848), more tightly composed than any of his previous novels, delineates the dehumanizing effects of wealth, pride, and commercial values. *Dombey and Son* was followed by the autobiographical *The Personal History of David Copperfield* (1850), which gives its readers a glimpse through fiction into Dickens's childhood and signals a change in his art of narration, for it is the first of his novels to be narrated wholly in the first person.

Dickens entered what critics call his "late period" with the powerfully pessimistic *Bleak House* (1853). This novel portrays a society in decay while its institutions gain frightening power and ruthlessness. The Chancery Court in *Bleak House* functions symbolically as a monolith hanging threateningly over the heads of the novel's characters. Dickens continued for the rest of his career to use in each novel one particular symbol to exhibit the overall decay of society. In *Little Dorrit* (1857) the Marshalsea Prison is juxtaposed with the internal prison in each character's mind; in *Great Expectations* (1861) Pip's inherent goodness is transformed into avarice by the prospect of inherited wealth; in Dickens's last completed novel, *Our Mutual Friend* (1865), the dust piles represent wealth that defaces the landscape of London.

While writing his last works, including *A Tale of Two Cities* (1859), *The Uncommercial Traveller* (1861), and *No Thoroughfare* (1867), Dickens experienced turmoil in his personal life. In 1858 he separated from his wife and formed a close relationship with the actress Ellen Ternan. He also gave a great number of public readings from his works in both England and America which left him exhausted. Many believe that increasing physical and mental strain led to the stroke Dickens suffered while working on *The Mystery of Edwin Drood* (1870), left unfinished at his death. When he died in 1870, England mourned the death of one of its favorite authors. His tombstone reads: "He was a sympathiser with the poor, the suffering, and the oppressed; and by his death, one of England's greatest writers is lost to the world."

Despite the growing pessimism of his later years, Dickens never lost faith in the essential goodness of the human soul. Though many of his characters are unjustly crushed by forces outside their control, some are able to triumph and achieve happiness. Perhaps his enormous popularity springs partly from the fact that he always valued humanity above society's artificial creations. As Edgar Johnson commented: "The world he created shines with undying life, and the hearts of men still vibrate to his indignant anger, his love, his glorious laughter, and his triumphant faith in the dignity of man."

(For further information about Dickens's life and works, see *Dictionary of Literary Biography,* Vols. 21, 55, 70; *Nineteenth-Century Literature Criticism,* Vols. 3, 8, 18, 26; and *Something about the Author,* Vol. 15.)

CRITICAL COMMENTARY

JOHN FORSTER
(essay date 1874)

[Forster was a Victorian biographer, historian, and critic who became Dickens's lifelong friend and literary advisor. His *Life of Charles Dickens* (1872-74), from which the following excerpt is drawn, is considered one of the greatest biographies of a literary figure in the English language. Here, he offers some personal reminiscences on the composition of *Great Expectations* and the dual endings to the novel.]

It may be doubted if Dickens could better have established his right to the front rank among novelists claimed for him, than by the ease and mastery with which, in . . . *Copperfield* and *Great Expectations,* he kept perfectly distinct the two stories of a boy's childhood, both told in the form of autobiography. A subtle penetration into character marks the unlikeness in the likeness; there is enough at once of resemblance and of difference in the position and surroundings of each to account for the divergences of character that arise; both children are good-hearted, and both have the advantage of association with models of tender simplicity and oddity, perfect in their truth and quite distinct from each other; but a sudden tumble into distress steadies Peggotty's little friend, and as unexpected a stroke of good fortune turns the head of the small protégé of Joe Gargery. What a deal of spoiling nevertheless, a nature that is really good at the bottom of it will stand without permanent damage, is nicely shown in Pip; and the way he reconciles his determination to act very shabbily to his early friends, with a conceited notion that he is setting them a moral example, is part of the shading of a character drawn with extraordinary skill. His greatest trial comes out of his good luck; and the foundations of both are laid at the opening of the tale, in a churchyard down by the Thames, as it winds past desolate marshes twenty miles to the sea, of which a masterly picture in half a dozen lines will give only average example of the descriptive writing that is everywhere one of the charms of the book. It is strange, as I transcribe the words, with what wonderful vividness they bring back the very spot on which we stood when he said he meant to make it the scene of the opening of his story—Cooling Castle ruins and the desolate church, lying out among the marshes seven miles from Gadshill!

My first most vivid and broad impression . . . on a memorable raw afternoon towards evening . . . was . . . that this bleak place, overgrown with nettles, was the churchyard, and that the dark flat wilderness beyond the churchyard, intersected with dykes and mounds and gates, with scattered cattle feeding on it, was the marshes; and that the low leaden line beyond, was the river; and that the distant savage lair from which the wind was rushing, was the sea. . . . On the edge of the river . . . only two black things in all the prospect seemed to be standing upright . . . one, the beacon by which the sailors steered, like an unhooped cask upon a pole, an ugly thing when you were near it; the other, a gibbet with some chains hanging to it which had once held a pirate.

Here Magwitch, an escaped convict from Chatham, terrifies the child Pip into stealing for him food and a file; and though recaptured and transported, he carries with him to Australia such a grateful heart for the small creature's service, that on making a fortune there he resolves to make his little friend a gentleman. This requires circumspection; and is so done, through the Old Bailey attorney who has defended Magwitch at his trial (a character of surprising novelty and truth), that Pip imagines his present gifts and "great expectations" to have come from the supposed rich lady of the story (whose eccentricities are the unattractive part of it, and have yet a weird character that somehow fits in with the kind of wrong she has suffered). When therefore the closing scenes bring back Magwitch himself, who risks his life to gratify his longing to see the gentleman he has made, it is an unspeakable horror to the youth to discover his benefactor in the convicted felon. If anyone doubts Dickens's power of so drawing a character as to get to the heart of it, seeing beyond surface peculiarities into the moving springs of the human being himself, let him narrowly examine those scenes. There is not a grain of substitution of mere sentiment, or circumstance, for the inner and absolute reality of the position in which these two creatures find themselves. Pip's loathing of what had built up his fortune, and his horror of the uncouth architect, are apparent in even his most generous efforts to protect him from exposure and sentence. Magwitch's convict habits strangely blend themselves with his wild pride in, and love for, the youth whom his money has turned into a gentleman. He has a craving for his good opinion; dreads to offend him by his "heavy grubbing," or by

*Principal Works

Sketches by Boz [as Boz] (sketches and short stories) 1836

Posthumous Papers of the Pickwick Club [as Boz] (novel) 1837

Oliver Twist (novel) 1838

The Life and Adventures of Nicholas Nickleby (novel) 1839

Barnaby Rudge (novel) 1841

The Old Curiosity Shop (novel) 1841

American Notes for General Circulation (travel essay) 1842

A Christmas Carol in Prose (short story) 1843

The Chimes (short story) 1844

The Life and Adventures of Martin Chuzzlewit (novel) 1844

The Cricket on the Hearth (short story) 1845

Pictures from Italy (travel essay) 1846

Dealings with the Firm of Dombey and Son (novel) 1848

The Haunted Man, and The Ghost's Bargain (short stories) 1848

The Personal History of David Copperfield (novel) 1850

Bleak House (novel) 1853

Hard Times for These Times (novel) 1854

Little Dorrit (novel) 1857

A Tale of Two Cities (novel) 1859

Great Expectations (novel) 1861

The Uncommercial Traveller (sketches and short stories) 1861

Our Mutual Friend (novel) 1865

No Thoroughfare [with Wilkie Collins] (drama) 1867

The Mystery of Edwin Drood (unfinished novel) 1870

*All of Dickens's novels were first published serially in magazines, usually over periods of from one to two years.

the oaths he lets fall now and then; and pathetically hopes his Pip, his dear boy, won't think him "low"; but, upon a chum of Pip's appearing unexpectedly while they are together, he pulls out a jack-knife by way of hint he can defend himself, and produces afterwards a greasy little clasped black Testament on which the startled new-comer, being found to have no hostile intention, is sworn to secrecy. At the opening of the story there had been an exciting scene of the wretched man's chase and recapture among the marshes, and this has its parallel at the close in his chase and recapture on the river while poor Pip is helping to get him off. To make himself sure of the actual course of a boat in such circumstances, and what possible incidents the adventure might have, Dickens hired a steamer for the day from Blackwall to Southend. Eight or nine friends and three or four members of his family were on board, and he seemed to have no care, the whole of that summer day (22 May, 1861), except to enjoy their enjoyment and entertain them with his own in shape of a thousand whims and fancies; but his sleepless observation was at work all the time, and nothing had escaped his keen vision on either side of the river. The fifteenth chapter of the third volume is a masterpiece.

The characters generally afford the same evidence as those two that Dickens's humour, not less than his creative power, was at its best in this book. The Old Bailey attorney Jaggers, and his clerk Wemmick (both excellent, and the last one of the oddities that live in everybody's liking for the goodheartedness of its comic surprises), are as good as his earliest efforts in that line; the Pumblechooks and Wopsles are as perfect as bits of

Nickleby fresh from the mint; and the scene in which Pip, and Pip's chum Herbert, make up their accounts and schedule their debts and obligations, is original and delightful as Micawber himself. It is the art of living upon nothing and making the best of it, in its most pleasing form. Herbert's intentions to trade east and west, and get himself into business transactions of a magnificent extent and variety, are as perfectly warranted to us, in his way of putting them, by merely "being in a counting-house and looking about you," as Pip's means of paying his debts are lightened and made easy by his method of simply adding them up with a margin. "The time comes," says Herbert, "when you see your opening. And you go in, and you swoop upon it, and you make your capital, and then there you are! When you have once made your capital you have nothing to do but employ it." In like manner Pip tells us, "Suppose your debts to be one hundred and sixty-four pounds four and two-pence, I would say, leave a margin and put them down at two hundred; or suppose them to be four times as much, leave a margin and put them down at seven hundred." He is sufficiently candid to add, that, while he has the highest opinion of the wisdom and prudence of the margin, its dangers are that in the sense of freedom and solvency it imparts there is a tendency to run into new debt. But the satire that thus enforces the old warning against living upon vague hopes, and paying ancient debts by contracting new ones, never presented itself in more amusing or kindly shape. A word should be added of the father of the girl that Herbert marries, Bill Barley, ex-ship's-purser, a gouty, bed-ridden, drunken old rascal, who lies on his back in an upper floor on Mill Pond Bank, by Chinks's Basin, where he keeps, weighs, and serves out the family stores or provisions, according to old professional practice, with one eye at a telescope which is fitted on his bed for the convenience of sweeping the river. This is one of those sketches, slight in itself but made rich with a wealth of comic observation, in which Dickens's humour took especial delight; and to all this part of the story there is a quaint riverside flavour that gives it amusing reality and relish.

Sending the chapters that contain it, which open the third division of the tale, he wrote thus:

> It is a pity that the third portion cannot be read all at once, because its purpose would be much more apparent; and the pity is the greater, because the general turn and tone of the working out and winding up, will be away from all such things as they conventionally go. But what must be, must be. As to the planning out from week to week, nobody can imagine what the difficulty is, without trying. But, as in all such cases, when it is overcome the pleasure is proportionate. Two months more will see me through it, I trust. All the iron is in the fire, and I have 'only' to beat it out.

One other letter throws light upon an objection taken not unfairly to the too great speed with which the heroine, after being married, reclaimed, and widowed, is in a page or two again made love to, and remarried by the hero. This summary proceeding was not originally intended. But, over and above its popular acceptance, the book had interested some whose opinions Dickens specially valued (Carlyle among them, I remember); and upon Bulwer Lytton objecting to a close that should leave Pip a solitary man, Dickens substituted what now stands. "You will be surprised," he wrote, "to hear that I have changed the end of *Great Expectations* from and after Pip's return to Joe's, and finding his little likeness there. . . . I have no doubt the story will be more acceptable through the alteration." This turned out to be the case; but the first ending nevertheless seems to be more consistent with the drift, as well as natural working out, of the tale. (pp. 285-89)

John Forster, in his *The Life of Charles Dickens, Vol. 2,* second edition, J. M. Dent & Sons Ltd., 1966, 480 p.

G. K. CHESTERTON

(essay date 1907)

[Chesterton was one of England's most prominent and colorful men of letters during the early twentieth century. Although he is best known today as a de-tective novelist and essayist, he was also an eminent literary critic. In the following excerpt, first published as part of an introduction to a 1907 edition of *Great Expectations*, he distinguishes the novel from Dickens's other works, pointing out that it is the author's only novel without a hero.]

Great Expectations, which was written in the afternoon of Dickens's life and fame, has a quality of serene irony and even sadness, which puts it quite alone among his other works. At no time could Dickens possibly be called cynical, he had too much vitality; but relatively to the other books this book is cynical; but it has the soft and gentle cynicism of old age, not the hard cynicism of youth. To be a young cynic is to be a young brute; but Dickens, who had been so perfectly romantic and sentimental in his youth, could afford to admit this touch of doubt into the mixed experience of his middle age. At no time could any books by Dickens have been called Thackerayan. Both of the two men were too great for that. But relatively to the other Dickensian productions this book may be called Thackerayan. It is a study in human weakness and the slow human surrender. It describes how easily a free lad of fresh and decent instincts can be made to care more for rank and pride and the degrees of our stratified society than for old affection and for honour. It is an extra chapter to *The Book of Snobs.*

The best way of stating the change which this book marks in Dickens can be put in one phrase. In this book for the first time the hero disappears. The hero had descended to Dickens by a long line which begins with the gods, nay, perhaps if one may say so, which begins with God. First comes Deity and then the image of Deity; first comes the god and then the demi-god, the Hercules who labours and conquers before he receives his heavenly crown. That idea, with continual mystery and modification, has continued behind all romantic tales; the demi-god became the hero of paganism; the hero of paganism became the knight-errant of Christianity; the knight-errant who wandered and was foiled before he triumphed became the hero of the later prose romance, the romance in which the hero had to fight a duel with the villain but always survived, in which the hero drove desperate horses through the night in order to rescue the heroine, but always rescued her.

This heroic modern hero, this demi-god in a top-hat, may be said to reach his supreme moment and typical example about the time when Dickens was writing that thundering and thrilling and highly unlikely scene in *Nicholas Nickleby,* the scene where Nicholas hopelessly denounces the atrocious Gride in his hour of grinning triumph, and a thud upon the floor above tells them that the heroine's tyrannical father has died just in time to set her free. That is the apotheosis of the pure heroic as Dickens found it, and as Dickens in some sense continued it. . . . But *Great Expectations* may be called, like *Vanity Fair,* a novel without a hero. Almost all Thackeray's novels except *Esmond* are novels without a hero, but only one of Dickens's novels can be so described. I do not mean that it is a novel without a *jeune premier,* a young man to make love; *Pickwick* is that and *Oliver Twist,* and, perhaps, *The Old Curiosity Shop.* I mean that it is a novel without a hero in the same far deeper and more deadly sense in which *Pendennis* is also a novel without a hero. I mean that it is a novel which aims chiefly at showing that the hero is unheroic.

All such phrases as these must appear of course to overstate the case. Pip is a much more delightful person than Nicholas Nickleby. Or to take a stronger case for the purpose of our argument, Pip is a much more delightful person than Sydney Carton. Still the fact remains. Most of Nicholas Nickleby's personal actions are meant to show that he is heroic. Most of Pip's actions are meant to show that he is not heroic. The study of Sydney Carton is meant to indicate that with all his vices Sydney Carton was a hero. The study of Pip is meant to indicate that with all his virtues Pip was a snob. The motive of the literary explanation is different. Pip and Pendennis are meant to show how circumstances can corrupt men. Sam Weller and Hercules are meant to show how heroes can subdue circumstances.

This is the preliminary view of the book which is necessary if we are to regard it as a real and separate fact in the life of Dickens. Dickens had many moods because he was an artist; but he had one great mood, because he was a great artist. Any real difference therefore from the general drift, or rather (I apologise to Dickens) the general drive of his creation is very important. This is the one place in his work in which he does, I will not say feel like Thackeray, far less think like Thackeray, less still write like Thackeray, but this is the one of his works in which he understands Thackeray. He puts himself in some sense in the same place; he considers mankind at somewhat the same angle as mankind is considered in one of the sociable and sarcastic novels of Thackeray. When he deals with Pip he sets out not to show his strength like the strength of Hercules, but to show his weakness like the weakness of Pendennis. When he sets out to describe Pip's great expectation he does not set out, as in a fairy tale, with the idea that these great expectations will be fulfilled; he sets out from the first with the idea that these great expectations will be disappointing. We might very well . . . apply to all Dickens's books the title *Great Expectations.* All his books are full of an airy and yet ardent expectation of everything; of the next person who shall happen to speak, of the next chimney that shall happen to smoke, of the next event, of the next ecstasy; of the next fulfilment of any eager human fancy. All his books might be called *Great Expectations.* But the only book to which he gave the name of

Great Expectations was the only book in which the expectation was never realised. It was so with the whole of that splendid and unconscious generation to which he belonged. The whole glory of that old English middle class was that it was unconscious; its excellence was entirely in that, that it was the culture of the nation, and that it did not know it. If Dickens had ever known that he was optimistic, he would have ceased to be happy.

It is necessary to make this first point clear: that in *Great Expectations* Dickens was really trying to be a quiet, a detached, and even a cynical observer of human life. Dickens was trying to be Thackeray. And the final and startling triumph of Dickens is this: that even to this moderate and modern story, he gives an incomparable energy which is not moderate and which is not modern. He is trying to be reasonable; but in spite of himself he is inspired. He is trying to be detailed, but in spite of himself he is gigantic. Compared to the rest of Dickens this is Thackeray; but compared to the whole of Thackeray we can only say in supreme praise of it that it is Dickens.

Take, for example, the one question of snobbishness. Dickens has achieved admirably the description of the doubts and vanities of the wretched Pip as he walks down the street in his new gentlemanly clothes, the clothes of which he is so proud and so ashamed. Nothing could be so exquisitely human, nothing especially could be so exquisitely masculine as that combination of self-love and self-assertion and even insolence with a naked and helpless sensibility to the slightest breath of ridicule. Pip thinks himself better than every one else, and yet anybody can snub him; that is the everlasting male, and perhaps the everlasting gentleman. Dickens has described perfectly this quivering and defenceless dignity. Dickens has described perfectly how ill-armed it is against the coarse humour of real humanity—the real humanity which Dickens loved, but which idealists and philanthropists do not love, the humanity of cabmen and costermongers and men singing in a third-class carriage; the humanity of Trabb's boy. In describing Pip's weakness Dickens is as true and as delicate as Thackeray. But Thackeray might have been easily as true and as delicate as Dickens. This quick and quiet eye for the tremors of mankind is a thing which Dickens possessed, but which others possessed also. George Eliot or Thackeray could have described the weakness of Pip. Exactly what George Eliot and Thackeray could not have described was the vigour of Trabb's boy. . . . It is the real unconquerable rush and energy in a character which was the supreme and quite indescribable greatness of Dickens. He conquered by rushes; he attacked in masses; he carried things at the spear point in a charge of spears; he was the Rupert of Fiction. The thing about any figure of Dickens, about Sam Weller or Dick Swiveller, or Micawber, or Bagstock, or Trabb's boy,—the thing about each one of these persons is that he cannot be exhausted. A Dickens character hits you first on the nose and then in the waistcoat, and then in the eye and then in the waistcoat again, with the blinding rapidity of some battering engine. The scene in which Trabb's boy continually overtakes Pip in order to reel and stagger as at a first encounter is a thing quite within the real competence of such a character; it might have been suggested by Thackeray, or George Eliot, or any realist. But the point with Dickens is that there is a rush in the boy's rushings; the writer and the reader rush with him. They start with him, they stare with him, they stagger with him, they share an inexpressible vitality in the air which emanates from this violent and capering satirist. Trabb's boy is among other things a boy; he has a physical rapture in hurling himself like a boomerang and in bouncing to the sky like a ball. It is just exactly in describing this quality that Dickens is Dickens and that no one else comes near him. No one feels in his bones that Felix Holt was strong as he feels in his bones that little Quilp was strong. No one can feel that even Rawdon Crawley's splendid smack across the face of Lord Steyne is quite so living and life-giving as the "kick after kick" which old Mr. Weller dealt the dancing and quivering Stiggins as he drove him towards the trough. This quality, whether expressed intellectually or physically, is the profoundly popular and eternal quality in Dickens; it is the thing that no one else could do. This quality is the quality which has always given its continuous power and poetry to the common people everywhere. It is life; it is the joy of life felt by those who have nothing else but life. It is the thing that all aristocrats have always hated and dreaded in the people. And it is the thing which poor Pip really hates and dreads in Trabb's boy.

A great man of letters or any great artist is symbolic without knowing it. The things he describes are types because they are truths. . . . Hence it is unavoidable in speaking of a fine book like *Great Expectations* that we should give even to its unpretentious and realistic figures a certain massive mysticism. Pip is Pip, but he is also the well-meaning snob. And this is even more true of those two great figures in the tale which stand for the English democracy. For, indeed, the first and last word upon the English democracy is said in Joe Gargery and Trabb's boy. The actual English populace, as distinct from the French populace or the Scotch or Irish populace, may be said to lie between those two types. The first is the poor man who does not assert himself at all, and the second is the poor man who asserts himself entirely with the weapon of sarcasm. The only way in which the English now ever rise in revolution is under the symbol and leadership of Trabb's boy. What pikes and shillelahs were to the Irish populace, what guns and barricades were to the French

populace, that chaff is to the English populace. It is their weapon, the use of which they really understand. It is the one way in which they can make a rich man feel uncomfortable, and they use it very justifiably for all it is worth. (pp. 197-205)

Of the other type of democracy it is far more difficult to speak. It is always hard to speak of good things or good people, for in satisfying the soul they take away a certain spur to speech. Dickens was often called a sentimentalist. In one sense he sometimes was a sentimentalist. But if sentimentalism be held to mean something artificial or theatrical, then in the core and reality of his character Dickens was the very reverse of a sentimentalist. He seriously and definitely loved goodness. To see sincerity and charity satisfied him like a meal. What some critics call his love of sweet stuff is really his love of plain beef and bread. Sometimes one is tempted to wish that in the long Dickens dinner the sweet courses could be left out; but this does not make the whole banquet other than a banquet singularly solid and simple. The critics complain of the sweet things, but not because they are so strong as to like simple things. They complain of the sweet things because they are so sophisticated as to like sour things; their tongues are tainted with the bitterness of absinthe. Yet because of the very simplicity of Dickens's moral tastes it is impossible to speak adequately of them; and Joe Gargery must stand as he stands in the book, a thing too obvious to be understood. But this may be said of him in one of his minor aspects, that he stands for a certain long-suffering in the English poor, a certain weary patience and politeness which almost breaks the heart. One cannot help wondering whether that great mass of silent virtue will ever achieve anything on this earth. (pp. 205-06)

G. K. Chesterton, " 'Great Expectations'," in his *Appreciations and Criticisms of the Works of Charles Dickens*, E. P. Dutton & Co., 1911, pp. 197-206.

DAVID CECIL
(lecture date 1931-32)

[Cecil—an important modern English literary critic who wrote extensively on eighteenth- and nineteenth-century authors—is highly acclaimed for his work on the Victorian era. In the following excerpt from a lecture given at Oxford University between 1931 and 1932, he proclaims Dickens the most typical of Victorian novelists. He proceeds to analyze Dickens's works, determining: "Lower- and middle-class life in nineteenth-century London as seen

Scene from *Oliver!,* a 1968 musical adaptation of *Oliver Twist.* Here, Oliver (Mark Lester) asks
Mr. Bumble: "Please, sir, I want some more."

from the angle of fantasy—this then is Dickens' range."]

[Dickens] is not only the most famous of the Victorian novelists, he is the most typical. If we are to see the distinguishing virtues and defects of his school at their clearest, we must examine Dickens.

This means, it must be admitted, that we see a great deal that is bad. The Victorian novelists are all unequal. But no Victorian novelist, no novelist of any period, is more sensationally unequal than Dickens. He cannot construct, for one thing. His books have no organic unity; they are full of detachable episodes, characters who serve no purpose in furthering the plot. Nor are these the least interesting characters; Mr. Micawber, Mrs. Gamp, Flora Finching, Mr. Crummles, Dickens' most brilliant figures, are given hardly anything to do; they are almost irrelevant to the action of the books in which they appear. We remember the story for them; but the story could perfectly well go on without them. Nor is this because there is not much story, because Dickens, like Tchekov, has eschewed the conventional plot in order to give freer play to his imagination. No, Dickens' books have only too much plot. More than any other novelist he is the slave of the formal conventions imposed on the novel by Fielding and Richardson: he cannot write a Christmas entertainment without

erecting a whole structure of artificial intrigue, disguised lover, mistaken identity, long-lost heir, and all the rest of the hoary paraphernalia of romance, on which to hang it. But this structure is, as it were, intermittent. After pages of humorous conversation Dickens will remember there should be a plot, and will plunge back for a paragraph or two into a jungle of elaborate intrigue; all the harder to follow from the fact that the fallible human memory has had to carry it unhelped through the long space of time since he let fall his thread. Very often he leaves a great many threads loose till the last chapter; and then finds there is not enough time to tie them up neatly. The main strands are knotted roughly together, the minor wisps are left hanging forlornly.

Again, he does not preserve unity of tone. His books are full of melodrama. This in itself is not a bad thing; and some of Dickens' melodrama is very effective. The murder of Nancy in *Oliver Twist,* Mr. Carker's last journey, haggard through the stormy night—these are masterpieces in their way. But they are melodrama. . . . They do not stir the emotions of pity and terror that they would awake if we came across them in real life. And they can only convince as long as they are not set against anything real. We can only believe in the limelight so long as we are not allowed to see the daylight. (pp. 37-9)

But his worst melodrama is less dreadful than his pathos. Pathos can be the most powerful of all the weapons in the novelist's arsenal. But it is far the most dangerous to handle. The reader must feel convinced that the story inevitably demands that a direct attack be made on his tender feelings. If he once suspects that his emotions are being exploited, his tears made to flow by a cold-blooded machination on the part of the author, he will be nauseated instead of being touched. The author must take the greatest care, therefore, first that the emotion he extracts from his pathetic situation is inevitably inherent in it; and secondly that he is not overstating it. . . . [Dickens] had a natural gift for homely pathos. But almost always he sins flagrantly against both the canons which govern its use. He overstates. He tries to wring an extra tear from the situation; he never lets it speak for itself. One would have thought the death of an innocent and virtuous child should be allowed to carry its own emotion; but Dickens cannot trust us to be moved by little Nell's departure from the world unassisted by church bells, falling snow at the window, and every other ready-made device for extracting our tears that a cheap rhetoric can provide. (pp. 39-40)

Finally Dickens often fails over his characters. His serious characters, with a few brilliant exceptions like David Copperfield, are the conventional virtuous and vicious dummies of melodrama. He cannot draw complex, educated or aristocratic types. And, what is more unfortunate, even in his memorable figures he shows sometimes an uncertain grasp of psychological essentials. He realizes personality with unparalleled vividness, but he does not understand the organic principles that underlie that personality. So that he can never be depended upon, not to make someone act out of character. (p. 41)

But if Dickens exhibits the Victorian defects in an extreme degree, so also does he exhibit the Victorian virtues. He may not construct his story well: but he tells it admirably; with his first sentence he engages our attention, and holds it to the end. He creates on the grand scale, covering a huge range of character and incident. Above all he has to the intensest degree possible that essential quality of the artist, creative imagination.

Of course, like that of every other artist, it has its limitations, its "range." The novelist's creative achievement is, as we have seen, born of the union of his experience and his imagination. But in any one writer there is only a certain proportion of his experience that can be so fertilized, only a certain proportion of what he has seen, felt and heard strikes deep enough into the foundations of his personality to fire his creative energy. (pp. 41-2)

Dickens is no exception to this rule. He was the child of poor middle-class parents, living mainly in and near London. And the range of his creative activity is, in the first place, limited to the world of his youth. All the vital part of his work is about it, all his living characters are members of it. As his own life in Border Scotland inspires Scott, so lower- and middle-class life in nineteenth-century London inspires Dickens. But— and here he parts company from Scott—it does not inspire him to give a realistic portrait of it. It is rather a jumping-off place for his fancy. . . . Dickens' stories may have the most realistic settings, their central figures be butchers and bakers and candlestick-makers in contemporary London. But butcher and baker and candlestick-maker and London are first of all characteristic of Dickens' world. And this means something not at all like the reality.

For his was a fantastic imagination. He was fascinated by the grotesque, by dwarfs and giants, by houses made of boats and bridecakes full of spiders, by names like Pumblechook and Gradgrind and Chuzzlewit. Any grotesque feature he noticed in the world came as grist to Dickens' mill. And such features as were not grotesque he tried to make so. This is how he modified his material; by accentuating its characteristic idiosyncrasies to a fantastic degree. . . . This is the second limitation of his range; it is confined to those aspects of life which are susceptible of fantastic treatment.

It is this which led to the old accusation made by Trollope fifty years ago and by less intelligent people since, that Dickens is exaggerated. Of course he is; it is the condition of his achievement. It would be as sensible to criticize a gothic gargoyle on the ground that it is an exaggerated representation of the human face as to criticize Mr. Pecksniff, for instance, on the ground that he is an exaggerated representation of a hypocrite. (pp. 42-4)

Dickens' London may be different from actual London, but it is just as real, its streets are of firm brick, its inhabitants genuine flesh and blood. For they have that essential vitality of creative art which is independent of mere verisimilitude. It does not matter that Dickens' world is not lifelike: it is alive.

Lower- and middle-class life in nineteenth-century London as seen from the angle of fantasy—this then is Dickens' range. And as long as he keeps within it his genius is always active. But it expresses itself especially in five ways. First of all in its actual appearance. Here indeed Dickens is not limited by the circumstances of his youth. Wherever they may take place, the settings of his stories have an extraordinary vividness. . . . The slums of *Oliver Twist,* the law-courts of *Bleak House,* the West End of *Little Dorrit,* the waterside of *Our Mutual Friend,* the suburbs whose privilege it was to provide a home for Mrs. Nickleby—all these form part of the same world, the world which is not London, but which London has stimulated Dickens' fancy to create. (pp. 44-5)

This power of realizing the actual setting never fails Dickens, even when everything else does. The plots of his dramas are often bad, the scenery is always admirable. . . .

It is as much a power of creating atmosphere as of actually describing appearance. And as such it is associated with Dickens' second distinction, his talent for horror. Dickens is one of the great masters of the macabre. It does not arise from character or situation; Dickens' figures of terror, Fagin, Bill Sykes, Jonas Chuzzlewit, Mr. Tulkinghorn, show Dickens at his most melodramatic and conventional, and the situations in which they are involved are as melodramatic and conventional as they are themselves. But they are shrouded in an atmosphere part sordidly realistic, part imaginatively eerie, of such sinister force as to shock the strongest nerves. We feel, as we read of them, both the ugly horror of a police-court report and the imaginative horror of a ghost story. (p. 48)

[Dickens' method of drawing characters] shows him once more as the typically Victorian. His great characters are all character parts. Mrs. Gamp and the rest of them are less intellectually conceived, their idiosyncrasies more emphatically insisted on even than those of the characters of Fielding or Scott or Smollett. As these were slightly caricatured, so are Dickens' figures startlingly caricatured. If they analyze them little, Dickens analyzes them less. . . . [As] Fielding and Scott and the others could fill their characters with an individuality beyond the power of meticulous realists, so much the more did Dickens.

It is here we come to the secret of Dickens' success. His was a fantastic genius. But fantasy, unless it is to be a mere ephemeral entertainment, must refer to reality: a good caricature is always a good likeness. Dickens' figures, for all that they are caricatures, derive their life from the fact that they do reveal, to an extraordinary degree, a certain aspect of real human nature—its individuality. As Trollope shows us living man in his social relations, and Dostoievski as a soul aspiring to God, so Dickens shows him as an individual. He had no special insight into the qualities which are characteristic of man as man; he had an acute discernment of those qualities which divide him from other men. In consequence he does not tell us much of the inner life; for it is in contrast with other men that individual characteristics reveal themselves most vividly. Nor has he much to tell us of human beings at the great crises of their lives, when individual differences are merged in common humanity. In those moments of death and despair when Tess or Meg Merrilies assume the sublime impersonal stature of man speaking for mankind, Dickens' characters dwindle to conventional

mouthpieces of conventional sentiment. But his power to perceive the spark of individuality that resides in everybody, is unequaled. (pp. 52-3)

Yet they are none of them types. No two are the same; and there are an enormous number of them. Of all the crowded Victorian canvases his is the most crowded. His books are like mobs; huge, seething, chaotic mobs; but mobs in which there is no face like another, no voice but reveals in its lightest accents a unique unmistakable individuality.

Finally, over a character, setting and horror, quivers always the shadow of Dickens' poetry, the light of his humor. It may seem odd to speak of poetry in connection with a writer so mundane and so grotesque. Where should poetry find its home in novels so conspicuously unsuccessful in the romantic and the sentimental? But poetry is the expression of the imagination at its most intense activity: and such an intense imagination as that of Dickens cannot fail to generate it. It is an Elizabethan sort of poetry. Not, indeed, like the Elizabethans in their tragic or lyrical moods: Dickens' poetry is of a piece with the rest of his genius, fantastic. And it is akin to the Elizabethans on their fantastic side; the quips and cranks, part comic, part macabre, part beautiful, with which Webster and Tourneur and Ford have let their fancies play round the drama of life and death. It is this poetry which gives their force to Dickens' descriptions. The fog in *Bleak House* is a sort of poetic fantasy on a London fog. The sinister waterside of *Our Mutual Friend,* with its black shadows and murdered secrets, and the desolate marsh which struck a chill to the heart of the boy Pip at the beginning of *Great Expectations:*—each of these is a poetic fantasy on its subject.

It may be noticed that all three passages deal with the gloomy, the sordid and the sinister. Dickens' poetic imagination is not stimulated by the sweet and the sunshiny. If he does write about them, he falls into the same error as when he writes about sweet and sunshiny characters: he becomes sentimental and a little vulgar. . . . Dickens' genius needed something harsh to bite its powerful teeth on; it grinds the tender and delicate to atoms. (pp. 54-5)

Dickens' poetry is secondary to his humor. He is not a great poet. He is perhaps the greatest humorist that England has ever produced. All sane critics have felt it, and most have said it; to expatiate at any length on Dickens' humor is unnecessary. A man might as well praise a bird for having wings. But it is to be remarked that Dickens' humor is of two kinds, satiric humor and pure humor; and both are highly characteristic. Both, of course, are fantastic. But the satire, like the character-drawing, owes its force to the fact that the satire has reference to reality. The absurdity of Mrs. Leo Hunter, of the Veneering family rising so laboriously in the social scale, of the Circumlocution Office, type of all government offices, of the cultured society who entertained Martin Chuzzlewit on his visit to America, of Bumble and Buzfuz and Chadband, is wildly exaggerated. But the wildness of the exaggeration is only equaled by its effectiveness. Dickens hits with a bludgeon, but he always touches his victims' weak spot. Only he emphasizes the weak spot as much as possible in order to make it as ridiculous as possible. The caricaturist, drawing a man with a big nose, makes it as big as his foot; that is the convention of his art; and it is the convention of Dickens' art. . . . (pp. 56-7)

Satire, however, is only one-half of Dickens' humor, and not the most characteristic half. After all, there have been other satirists. Dickens' unique position as a humorist lies in his mastery of "pure" humor, jokes that are funny not for the satirical light they throw, but just in themselves.

" 'But the words she spoke of Mrs. Harris,' " says Mrs. Gamp, expatiating on the wickedness of Mrs. Prig, " 'lambs could not forgive . . . nor worms forget.' "

" 'I wouldn't have believed it, Mr. Chuzzlewit,' declares Mr. Pecksniff magnificently, 'if a Fiery Serpent had proclaimed it from the top of Salisbury Cathedral. I would have said that the Serpent lied. Such was my faith in Thomas Pinch, that I would have cast the falsehood back into the Serpent's teeth, and would have taken Thomas to my heart. But I am not a Serpent, sir, myself, I grieve to say, and no excuse or hope is left me.' "

" 'Rich folks may ride on camels,' says Mrs. Gamp again, 'but it ain't so easy for 'em to see out of a needle's eye.' "

The humor does not illustrate anything or tell us anything; one needs no extraneous information to see its point; it is simply, self-dependently, intoxicatingly funny.

Dickens, then, in his merits and in his defects, is the typical Victorian novelist. And he is so, because more than Thackeray or Trollope or Charlotte Brontë, he is open to the influences whence these particular merits and defects arise. The defects came from the immaturity of the novel form and the uninstructed taste of that middle class who formed the bulk of his readers. Dickens was himself by birth and instinct a member of that middle class, nor had he the intellectual power to discern its faults. Indeed, he was not an intellectual at all. He observed life; he had no power to analyze and co-ordinate his observations. . . . The actual facts of his own experience he realized extraordinarily vividly; like a child he made no generalization on them. He unquestioningly accepted the general ideas held in the world in which he found himself.

And this, in his circumstances, meant a very inad-

equate sort of idea. It was not just that Dickens grew up among the comparatively uneducated. So did Burns; but Burns grew up amid the uneducated of an ancient civilization, developed for centuries in close and stable connection with nature and the great primary institutions of human life, soaked in an instinctive tradition. But Dickens' world had no instinctive tradition. He was a man not of the country but of the town, the town of a new-born changing industrial society. He sprang from the swift rootless life of the London streets. And except for his genius he is the typical representative of such a world. He was an average nineteenth-century Cockney, only he had genius. (pp. 57-9)

Dickens' intellectual weakness meant that he had no sense of form. He could not impose order on the tumult of his inspiration; figures and scenes swam into his mind in a colored confusion, he just strung them together on any worn thread of clumsy conventional plot he could think of. Intellectual weakness, again, is the cause of his uncertain grasp of character. He sees his figures and he can make the reader see them too; but he cannot reason from their external personality to discover its determining elements. . . .

On the other hand it is because he was uneducated that he fails over so many types. He did not know any aristocrats or intellectuals, just as he did not know about the French Revolution or the English eighteenth century; so he could not write about them. But he did.

And here we come to the major cause of his failures. Because he was both unintellectual and uneducated, he fell into the novelist's first error—he wrote outside his range. (p. 60)

He is always bringing in all sorts of types outside his range, aristocrats like Sir Mulberry Hawk and Sir Leicester Dedlock, French revolutionaries like Madame Defarge; and since the conventions of his time taught him that some types, like the hero and the heroine for instance, were essential to a novel, one if not both of these waxwork, wearisome, impeccable dummies deforms his every book. One sin leads to another; in order to give them something to do, he is forced to construct a conventional plot. And of course his lack of education made this disastrous to him. For when his inspiration fails him he has no good tradition of story-telling to fall back on. His conventional melodrama and his sentiment are the conventional melodrama and sentiment of the Cockney, no better and no worse than those which burgeon in flamboyant lusciousness from six-penny novelettes and supercinemas today; and indeed very like them.

Yet the same cause which is responsible for his defects is also responsible for his merits. Not indeed for his actual creative power; this is a gift. But circumstances do condition the particular mode of its expression. No polish of conventional culture has rubbed the fine fresh edge off his primary perceptions as it rubbed off that of Fanny Burney's; the free lightening-play of his instinct was never hampered as that of George Eliot's grew to be by the conscientious, intellectual criticism to which she subjected it. With the Cockney's crudeness and vulgarity he has his zest for life, his warm heart and racy wit. Dickens' unselfconscious crudeness provides a saving grace even for his pathetic moments; they have not the lifelessness of an unreal and superficial culture, they have the emotional energy of spontaneous feelings which have never been drilled into restraint. (pp. 61-2)

Dickens is the great democrat of English literature. His every book is a crowd; and it is the crowd of a democracy, the exuberant, restless, disorganized, clamorous, motley crowd of Hampstead Heath on a Bank holiday, with its charabancs and cocoanut shies and skirling mouth-organs and beery conviviality, squalid and sunny, domestic and indelicate, sharp and sentimental, kindly and undignified.

It is clearly impossible that so flawed a talent should ever produce a book of any consistent merit. But certain aesthetic conditions suit it better than others; the picaresque form, for instance. *Pickwick* is far from being Dickens' best book, but it is the freest from his structural faults. For since it is avowedly a story of heterogeneous adventures only connected together by a central figure, it does not require that framework of conventional intrigue with which Dickens has felt it necessary to cumber up the more "orthodox" novels of *Bleak House* and *Great Expectations.* If you have little gift for form, the wisest thing to do is to write a book with as little form as possible. Again, he does best when he writes from a child's point of view. Children are instinctive, they have strong imaginations, vivid sensations; they see life as black or white, and bigger than reality, their enemies seem demons, their friends angels, their joys or sorrows absolute and eternal. They do not look at life with the eye of the intellectual or of the instructed observer; they are not ashamed of sentiment: in fact they see life very like Dickens. (pp. 64-5)

The first halves of *Great Expectations* and *David Copperfield* are among the profoundest pictures of childhood in English letters. Who that has read it can forget the vast sinister marsh of *Great Expectations,* with the convict rising like a giant of fairy-tale from its oozy banks; and the forge with its entrancing sparks; and kindly clumsy Joe Gargery and Mrs. Gargery, that comic ogress, as they appear to the wondering, acute six-year-old gaze of Pip?

But better still are the first one hundred and sixty pages of *David Copperfield,* the best Dickens ever wrote, one of the very best things in the whole of English. Here for once Dickens seems not only living, but lifelike; for though the world that he reveals is more exaggerated, lighted by brighter lights, darkened by

sharper shadows than that of most grown-up people, it is exactly the world as it is seen through the eyes of a child. (pp. 65-6)

Indeed the whole episode of Mr. Creakle's school is an illustration of the inadequacy of mere realism. The school is unlike any modern school: and Dickens has taken no more trouble to make his description of it meticulously true to fact than he does anywhere else. But the essential features of school life, Steerforth's domination, David's devotion to him, Traddles' dislike of him; the cynical contempt of the pupils for the sycophantic Mr. Creakle, their arrogant contempt for the kindly, feeble Mr. Mell, show an insight into the nature of boys beside which all the conscientious and freespoken accuracy of later novelists [seems unreal]. (pp. 66-7)

But after one hundred and sixty pages David grows up; and with his childhood, Dickens' certainty of vision disappears. He still sees vividly and entertainingly, the rest of the book is crammed with good things: but the grasp on reality which marked its opening is there no more. Once again we are in the familiar Dickens world, where acute observation and brilliant fantasy and unctuous sentimentality and preposterous improbability tread on one another's heels. . . . And similarly cheap melodrama is the end of *Great Expectations.* It is always the way, always the reader endures the same series of impressions. He opens the book: easily, and irresistibly, in a paragraph, a line, a word, Dickens casts his spell; willingly we sink back on the strong wings of his imagination to be carried wherever he wishes. And then we are jolted and banged, now soaring to the central sun of the creative fancy, now falling with a bump on to a rock of ineptitude, now dragged through an oozing bog of false sentiment; till at the end we are only dazed. And when we close the book it remains in our memory, not as a clear, shapely whole, but as a gleaming chaos. Dickens is the most brilliant of all English novelists; but he is also one of the most imperfect. (pp. 68-9)

Creative imagination may not be the only quality necessary to the novelist, but it is the first quality. And no English novelist had it quite in the way Dickens had. Scott's imagination and Emily Brontë's were of a finer quality, Jane Austen's was more exactly articulated, but they none of them had an imagination at once so forceful, so varied and so self-dependent as Dickens. Indeed his best passages have the immediate irresistible force of music. Unassisted by verisimilitude or intellectual interest he sweeps us away, as Wagner does, by sheer dramatic intensity. This is why his popularity has not declined. Such intensity is not weakened by the lapse of time. Nor is Dickens' writing, even at his worst, ever wholly without it. His bad passages are more flagrantly faulty than those of Hardy or Scott; they are never so uninspired. The blaze of his towering imagination touches his most unreal scenes with a reflected light; bathed in its quivering glow the pasteboard figures seem for a moment to move, to be alive. (pp. 69-70)

David Cecil, "Charles Dickens," in his *Early Victorian Novelists: Essays in Revaluation,* 1934. Reprint by The Bobbs-Merrill Company, Inc., 1935, pp. 37-74.

EDMUND WILSON
(lecture date 1939)

[Wilson is considered one of America's foremost men of letters in the twentieth century. In the following excerpt from a lecture given at the University of Chicago in 1939 and later published in his *The Wound and the Bow,* he profiles the works of Dickens, "the greatest dramatic writer that the English had had since Shakespeare."]

Of all the great English writers, Charles Dickens has received in his own country the scantiest serious attention from either biographers, scholars, or critics. He has become for the English middle class so much one of the articles of their creed—a familiar joke, a favorite dish, a Christmas ritual—that it is difficult for British pundits to see in him the great artist and social critic that he was. (p. 3)

Chesterton asserted that time would show that Dickens was not merely one of the Victorians, but incomparably the greatest English writer of his time; and Shaw coupled his name with that of Shakespeare. It is the conviction of the present writer that both these judgments were justified. Dickens—though he cannot of course pretend to the rank where Shakespeare has few companions—was nevertheless the greatest dramatic writer that the English had had since Shakespeare, and he created the largest and most varied world. It is the purpose of this essay to show that we may find in Dickens' work today a complexity and a depth to which even Gissing and Shaw have hardly, it seems to me, done justice—an intellectual and artistic interest which makes Dickens loom very large in the whole perspective of the literature of the West. (pp. 4-5)

Of all the great Victorian writers, [Dickens] was probably the most antagonistic to the Victorian Age itself. He had grown up under the Regency and George IV; had been twenty-five at the accession of Victoria. His early novels are freshened by breezes from an England of coaching and village taverns, where the countryside lay just outside London; of an England where jokes and songs and hot brandy were always in order, where every city clerk aimed to dress finely and drink freely, to give an impression of open-handedness and gallantry. . . . When Little Nell and her grandfather on their wanderings spend a night in an iron foundry, it only has the effect of a sort of Nibelungen interlude, rather like one of those surprise grottoes that you float through when you take the little boat that threads the tunnel of the 'Old Mill' in an amusement park—a luridly lighted glimpse on the same level, in Dickens' novel, with the waxworks, the performing dogs, the dwarfs and giants, the village church. From this point it is impossible, as it was impossible for Dickens, to foresee the full-length industrial town depicted in *Hard Times.* (pp. 25-6)

But when Dickens begins to write novels again after his return from his American trip, a new kind of character appears in them, who, starting as an amusing buffoon, grows steadily more unpleasant and more formidable. On the threshold of *Martin Chuzzlewit* . . . , you find Pecksniff, the provincial architect; on the threshold of *Dombey and Son* . . . , you find Dombey, the big London merchant; and before you have got very far with the idyllic *David Copperfield* . . . , you find Murdstone, of Murdstone and Grimby, wine merchants. All these figures stand for the same thing. Dickens had at first imagined that he was pillorying abstract faults in the manner of the comedy of humors: Selfishness in *Chuzzlewit,* Pride in *Dombey.* But the truth was that he had already begun an indictment against a specific society: the self-important and moralizing middle class who had been making such rapid progress in England and coming down like a damper on the bright fires of English life—that is, on the spontaneity and gaiety, the frankness and independence, the instinctive human virtues, which Dickens admired and trusted. The new age had brought a new kind of virtues to cover up the flourishing vices of cold avarice and harsh exploitation; and Dickens detested these virtues. (pp. 26-7)

It is to be characteristic of Pecksniff, as it is of Dombey and Murdstone, that he does evil while pretending to do good. . . . Yet Pecksniff is still something of a pantomime comic whom it will be easy enough to unmask. Mr. Dombey is a more difficult problem. His virtues, as far as they go, are real: though he is stupid enough to let his business get into the hands of Carker, he does lead an exemplary life of a kind in the interests of the tradition of his house. He makes his wife and his children miserable in his devotion to his mercantile ideal, but that ideal is at least for him serious. With Murdstone the ideal has turned sour: the respectable London merchant now represents something sinister. Murdstone is not funny like Pecksniff; he is not merely a buffoon who masquerades: he is a hypocrite who believes in himself. (p. 27)

In such a world of mercenary ruthlessness, always justified by rigorous morality, it is natural that the exploiter of others should wish to dissociate himself from

Major Media Adaptations: Motion Pictures

Rich Man's Folly, 1931. Paramount. [Adaptation of *Dealings with the Firm of Dombey and Son*] Director: John Cromwell. Cast: George Bancroft, Frances Dee, Robert Ames, Juliette Compton, Dorothy Petersen.

Great Expectations, 1934. Universal. Director: Stuart Walker. Cast: Phillip Holmes, Jane Wyatt, Henry Hull, Florence Reed, Alan Hale, Francis Sullivan.

The Old Curiosity Shop, 1934. British International Pictures. Director: Thomas Bentley. Cast: Hay Petrie, Ben Webster, Elaine Benson, Beatrice Thompson, Gibb McLaughlin, Reginald Purdell, Polly Ward.

David Copperfield, 1935. MGM (David O. Selznick). Director: George Cukor. Cast: Freddie Bartholemew, Frank Lawton, W. C. Fields, Roland Young, Edna May Oliver, Lennox Pawle, Basil Rathbone, Violet Kemble Cooper, Maureen O'Sullivan, Madge Evans, Elizabeth Allen, Jessie Ralph, Lionel Barrymore, Herbert Mundin, Elsa Lanchester, Jean Cadell, Una O'Connor, Arthur Treacher.

The Mystery of Edwin Drood, 1935. Universal. Director: Stuart Walker. Cast: Claude Rains, Douglass Montgomery, Heather Angel, David Manners, E. E. Clive, Valerie Hobson.

Scrooge, 1935. Twickenham. [Adaptation of *A Christmas Carol*] Director: Henry Edwards. Cast: Sir Seymour Hicks, Donald Calthrop, Robert Cochran, Mary Glynne, Garry Marsh.

A Tale of Two Cities, 1936. MGM (David O. Selznick). Director: Jack Conway. Cast: Ronald Colman, Elizabeth Allan, Basil Rathbone, Edna May Oliver, Reginald Owen.

A Christmas Carol, 1938. MGM. Director: Edwin L. Marin. Cast: Reginald Owen, Gene Lockhart, Kathleen Lockhart, Terry Kilburn, Leo G. Carroll, Lynne Carver.

Great Expectations, 1946. Rank/Cineguild. Director: David Lean. Cast: John Mills, Jean Simmons, Alec Guinness, Finlay Currie, Martita Hunt.

Nicholas Nickleby, 1947. Ealing Studios. Director: Alberto Cavalcanti. Cast: Derek Bond, Cedric Hardwicke, Alfred Drayton, Sybil Thorndike, Stanley Holloway, James Hayter, Sally Ann Howes.

Oliver Twist, 1948. General Films Distributors. Director: David Lean. Cast: Alec Guinness, Robert Newton, Francis L. Sullivan, John Howard Davies, Kay Walsh, Anthony Newley, Henry Stephenson, Mary Clare, Gibb McLaughlin.

Scrooge, 1951. Renown/UA. Director: Brian Desmond Hurst. Cast: Alastair Sim, Mervyn Johns, Kathleen Harrison, Jack Warner, Michael Hordern, George Cole, Miles Malleson.

Pickwick Papers, 1952. Renown Pictures. [Adaptation of *Posthumous Papers of the Pickwick Club*] Director: Noel Langley. Cast: James Hayter, James Donald, Donald Wolfit, Hermione Baddeley, Nigel Patrick.

A Tale of Two Cities, 1958. Rank (Betty E. Box). Director: Ralph Thomas. Cast: Dirk Bogarde, Dorothy Tutin, Christopher Lee, Athene Seyler, Rosalie Crutchley.

Oliver!, 1968. Columbia. [Musical adaptation of *Oliver Twist*] Director: Carol Reed. Cast: Ron Moody, Oliver Reed, Harry Secombe, Mark Lester, Shani Wallis, Jack Wild, Hugh Griffith, Joseph O'Conor.

David Copperfield, 1970. Omnibus/Twentieth-Century Fox. Director: Delbert Mann. Cast: Richard Attenborough, Cyril Cusak, Edith Evans, Pamela Franklin, Susan Hampshire.

Scrooged, 1988. Art Linson-Mirage/Paramount. [Adaptation of *A Christmas Carol*] Director: Richard Donner. Cast: Bill Murray, Karen Allen, John Forsythe, John Glover, Carol Kane, Robert Mitchum, Jamie Farr, Robert Goulet, Lee Major.

the exploited, and to delegate the face-to-face encounters to someone else who is paid to take the odium. (pp. 27-8)

It is at the end of *Dombey and Son,* when the house of Dombey goes bankrupt, that Dickens for the first time expresses himself explicitly on the age that has come to remain:

The world was very busy now, in sooth, and had a deal to say. It was an innocently credulous and a much ill-used world. It was a world in which there was no other sort of bankruptcy whatever. There were no conspicuous people in it, trading far and wide on rotten banks of religion, patriotism, virtue, honor. There was no amount worth mentioning of mere paper in circulation, on which anybody lived

pretty handsomely, promising to pay great sums of goodness with no effects. There were no shortcomings anywhere, in anything but money. The world was very angry indeed; and the people especially who, in a worse world, might have been supposed to be bankrupt traders themselves in shows and pretences, were observed to be mightily indignant.

And now—working always through the observed interrelations between highly individualized human beings rather than through political or economic analysis—Dickens sets out to trace an anatomy of that society. *Dombey* has been the first attempt; *Bleak House* . . . is to realize this intention to perfection; *Hard Times,* on a smaller scale, is to conduct the same kind of inquiry.

Oliver gets caught. A scene from the 1948 movie *Oliver Twist,* starring Robert Newton, Alec
Guinness, and Kay Walsh.

For this purpose Dickens invents a new literary *genre* (unless the whole mass of Balzac is to be taken as something of the sort): the novel of the social group. The young Dickens had summed up, developed and finally outgrown the two traditions in English fiction he had found: the picaresque tradition of Defoe, Fielding and Smollett, and the sentimental tradition of Goldsmith and Sterne. (pp. 29-30)

In *Bleak House,* the masterpiece of this middle period, Dickens discovers a new use of plot, which makes possible a tighter organization. (And we must remember that he is always working against the difficulties, of which he often complains, of writing for monthly instalments, where everything has to be planned beforehand and it is impossible, as he says, to 'try back' and change anything, once it has been printed.) He creates the detective story which is also a social fable. It is a *genre* which has lapsed since Dickens. (pp. 30-1)

Bleak House begins in the London fog, and the whole book is permeated with fog and rain. In *Dombey* the railway locomotive—first when Mr. Dombey takes his trip to Leamington, and later when it pulls into the station just at the moment of Dombey's arrival and runs over the fugitive Carker as he steps back to avoid his master—figures as a symbol of that progress of

commerce which Dombey himself represents; in *Hard Times* the uncovered coal-pit into which Stephen Blackpool falls is a symbol for the abyss of the industrial system, which swallows up lives in its darkness. In *Bleak House* the fog stands for Chancery, and Chancery stands for the whole web of clotted antiquated institutions in which England stifles and decays. (pp. 31-2)

I go over the old ground of the symbolism, up to this point perfectly obvious, of a book which must be still, by the general public, one of the most read of Dickens' novels, because the people who like to talk about the symbols of Kafka and Mann and Joyce have been discouraged from looking for anything of the kind in Dickens, and usually have not read him, at least with mature minds. But even when we think we do know Dickens, we may be surprised to return to him and find in him a symbolism of a more complicated reference and a deeper implication than these metaphors that hang as emblems over the door. The Russians themselves, in this respect, appear to have learned from Dickens. (p. 32)

In *Little Dorrit* and *Great Expectations,* there is . . . a great deal more psychological interest than in Dickens' previous books. We are told what the characters think and feel, and even something about how they change. And here we must enter into the central question of the psychology of Dickens' characters.

The world of the early Dickens is organized according to a dualism which is based—in its artistic derivation—on the values of melodrama: there are bad people and there are good people, there are comics and there are characters played straight. The only complexity of which Dickens is capable is to make one of his noxious characters become wholesome, one of his clowns turn into a serious person. The most conspicuous example of this process is the reform of Mr Dombey, who, as Taine says, 'turns into the best of fathers and spoils a fine novel.' But the reform of Scrooge in *A Christmas Carol* shows the phenomenon in its purest form.

We have come to take Scrooge so much for granted that he seems practically a piece of Christmas folklore; we no more inquire seriously into the mechanics of his transformation than we do into the transformation of the Beast in the fairy tale into the young prince that marries Beauty. Yet Scrooge represents a principle fundamental to the dynamics of Dickens' world and derived from his own emotional constitution. It was not merely that his passion for the theater had given him a taste for melodramatic contrasts; it was rather that the lack of balance between the opposite impulses of his nature had stimulated an appetite for melodrama. For emotionally Dickens *was* unstable. Allowing for the English restraint, which masks what the Russian expressiveness indulges and perhaps overexpresses, and for the pretenses of English biographers, he seems almost as unstable as Dostoevsky. He was capable of great hardness and cruelty, and not merely toward those whom he had cause to resent: people who patronized or intruded on him. . . . There is more of emotional reality behind Quilp in *The Old Curiosity Shop* than there is behind Little Nell. If Little Nell sounds bathetic today, Quilp has lost none of his fascination. He is ugly, malevolent, perverse; he delights in making mischief for its own sake; yet he exercises over the members of his household a power which is almost an attraction and which resembles what was known in Dickens' day as 'malicious animal magnetism.' Though Quilp is ceaselessly tormenting his wife and browbeating the boy who works for him, they never attempt to escape: they admire him; in a sense they love him. (pp. 51-2)

Shall we ask what Scrooge would actually be like if we were to follow him beyond the frame of the story? Unquestionably he would relapse when the merriment was over—if not while it was still going on—into moroseness, vindictiveness, suspicion. He would, that is to say, reveal himself as the victim of a manic-depressive cycle, and a very uncomfortable person.

This dualism runs all through Dickens. There has always to be a good and a bad of everything: each of the books has its counterbalancing values, and pairs of characters sometimes counterbalance each other from the casts of different books. There has to be a good manufacturer, Mr. Rouncewell, and a bad manufacturer, Mr. Bounderby; a bad old Jew, Fagin, and a good old Jew, Riah; an affable lawyer who is really unscrupulous, Vholes, and a kindly lawyer who pretends to be unfeeling, Jaggers. . . . (p. 53)

Dickens' difficulty in his middle period, and indeed more or less to the end, is to get good and bad together in one character. He had intended in *Dombey and Son* to make Walter Gay turn out badly, but hadn't been able to bring himself to put it through. . . . In *Great Expectations* we see Pip pass through a whole psychological cycle. At first, he is sympathetic, then by a more or less natural process he turns into something unsympathetic, then he becomes sympathetic again. Here the effects of both poverty and riches are seen from the inside in one person. This is for Dickens a great advance; and it is a development which, if carried far enough, would end by eliminating the familiar Dickens of the lively but limited stage characters, with their tag lines and their unvarying make-ups. (p. 54)

Three years had passed since *Great Expectations* before Dickens began another novel; he worked at it with what was for him extreme slowness, hesitation and difficulty; and the book shows the weariness, the fears and the definitive disappointments of this period.

This story, *Our Mutual Friend* . . . , like all these later books of Dickens, is more interesting to us today than it was to Dickens' public. It is a next number in the Dickens sequence quite worthy of its predecessors, a development out of what has gone before that is in certain ways quite different from the others. It may be said Dickens never really repeats himself: his thought makes a consistent progress, and his art, through the whole thirty-five years of his career, keeps going on to new materials and effects; so that his work has an interest and a meaning as a whole. The difficulty that Dickens found in writing *Our Mutual Friend* does not make itself felt as anything in the nature of an intellectual disintegration. On the contrary, the book compensates for its shortcomings by the display of an intellectual force which, though present in Dickens' work from the first, here appears in a phase of high tension and a condition of fine muscular training. The Dickens of the old eccentric 'Dickens characters' has here, as has often been noted, become pretty mechanical and sterile. . . . Also, the complex Dickens plot has come to seem rather tiresome and childish. But Dickens has here distilled the mood of his later years, dramatized the tragic discrepancies of his character, delivered his final judgment on the whole Victorian exploit, in a fashion so impressive that we realize how little the distractions of this period had the power to direct him from the prime purpose of his life: the serious exercise of his art.

As the fog is the symbol for *Bleak House* and the prison for *Little Dorrit,* so the dust-pile is the symbol for *Our Mutual Friend.* It dominates even the landscape of London, which has already been presented by Dickens under such a variety of aspects, but which now appears—though with Newgate looming over it as it did in *Barnaby Rudge*—under an aspect that is new: 'A gray dusty withered evening in London city has not a hopeful aspect,' he writes of the day when Bradley Headstone goes to pay his hopeless court to Lizzie Hexam. (pp. 61-2)

Dickens' line in his criticism of society is very clear in *Our Mutual Friend,* and it marks a new position on Dickens' part, as it results from a later phase of the century. Dickens has come at last to depair utterly of the prospering middle class. We have seen how he judged the morality of the merchants. In *Bleak House,* the ironmaster is a progressive and self-sustaining figure who is played off against parasites of various sorts; but in *Hard Times,* written immediately afterward, the later development of Rouncewell is dramatized in the exploiter Bounderby, a new kind of Victorian hypocrite, who pretends to be a self-made man. In *Little Dorrit,* the one set of characters who are comparatively healthy and cheerful still represent that middle-class home which has remained Dickens' touchstone of virtue; but even here there is a distinct change in Dickens' attitude. Mr. Meagles, the retired banker, with his wife and his beloved only daughter, become the prey of Henry Gowan, a well-connected young man of no fortune who manages to lead a futile life (the type has been well observed) between the social and artistic worlds without ever making anything of either. But the smugness and insularity, even the vulgarity, of the Meagleses is felt by Dickens as he has never felt it in connection with such people before. (p. 63)

[The] resentment is to get the upper hand. The Meagleses turn up now as the Podsnaps, that horrendous middle-class family, exponents of all the soundest British virtues, who, however, are quite at home in a social circle of sordid adventurers and phony *nouveaux riches,* and on whom Dickens visits a satire as brutal as themselves. Gone are the high spirits that made of Pecksniff an exhilarating figure of fun—gone with the Yoho! of the stagecoach on which Tom Pinch traveled to London. The Podsnaps, the Lammles, the Veneerings, the Fledgebys, are unpleasant as are no other characters in Dickens. . . . One of the ugliest scenes in Dickens is that in which Fledgeby ascribes his own characteristics to the gentle old Jew Riah and makes him the agent of his meanness and sharp-dealing. And not content with making Fledgeby a cur, Dickens himself shows a certain cruelty in having him ultimately thrashed by Lammle under circumstances of peculiar

ignominy and then having the little dolls' dressmaker apply plasters with pepper on them to his wounds. This incident betrays a kind of sadism which we never felt in Dickens' early work—when Nicholas Nickleby beat Squeers, for example—but which breaks out now and then in these later books in a disagreeable fashion.

If the middle class has here become a monster, the gentry have taken on an aspect more attractive than we have ever known them to wear as a class in any previous novel of Dickens. If an increase of satiric emphasis turns the Meagleses into the Podsnaps, so a shift from the satirical to the straight turns the frivolous and idle young man of good family, who has hitherto always been exhibited as more or less of a scoundrel—James Harthouse or Henry Gowan—into the sympathetic Eugene Wrayburn. Eugene and his friend Mortimer Lightwood, the little old dinerout named Twemlow, the only gentleman in the Veneerings' circle, and the Reverend Frank Milvey, 'expensively educated and wretchedly paid,' the Christian turned social worker, are the only representatives of the upper strata who are shown as having decent values; and they are all the remnants of an impoverished gentry. Outside these, you find the decent values—or what Dickens intends to be such—in an impoverished proletariat and lower middle class: the modest clerk, the old Jew, the dolls' dressmaker, the dust-contractor's foreman, the old woman who minds children for a living. And the chief heroine is not Bella Wilfer, who has to be cured of her middle-class ideals, but Lizzie Hexam, the illiterate daughter of a Thames-side water-rat. Dickens has here, for the first time in his novels, taken his leading woman from the lowest class; and it will be the principal moral of *Our Mutual Friend* that Wrayburn will have the courage to marry Lizzie. (pp. 64-5)

Dickens has aligned himself in *Our Mutual Friend* with a new combination of forces. Shrinking from Podsnap and Veneering, he falls back on that aristocracy he had so savagely attacked in his youth, but to which, through his origins, he had always been closer than he had to the commercial classes. (p. 66)

There is, however, another element that plays an important rôle in the story: the proletarian who has educated himself to be a member of this middle class. Lizzie Hexam has a brother, whom she has induced to get an education and who, as soon as he has qualified himself to teach, drops his family even more callously than Pip did his; and the schoolmaster of Charley Hexam's school, another poor man who has advanced himself, is the villain of *Our Mutual Friend.* We are a long way here from the days when the villains and bad characters in Dickens, the Quilps and the Mrs. Gamps, could be so fascinating through their resourcefulness and vitality that, as G. K. Chesterton says, the reader is sorry at the end when they are finally banished from the scene and hopes that the discredited scoundrel will still open the door and stick his head in and make one more atrocious remark. Such figures are so much all of a piece of evil that they have almost a kind of innocence. But here Bradley Headstone has no innocence: he is perverted, tormented, confused. He represents a type which begins to appear in these latest novels of Dickens and which originally derives perhaps from those early theatrical villains, of the type of the elder Rudge or Monks in *Oliver Twist,* skulking figures with black looks and ravaged faces: a literary convention of which one would suppose it would be impossible to make anything plausible. Yet Dickens does finally succeed in giving these dark figures reality.

In Bradley Headstone's case, it is his very aspirations which have gone bad and turned the stiff and anxious schoolmaster into a murderer. . . . Bradley is the first murderer in Dickens who exhibits any complexity of character. And he is the first to present himself as a member of respectable Victorian society. There is a dreadful and convincing picture of the double life led by Headstone as he goes about his duties as a schoolmaster after he has decided to murder Eugene. In *Great Expectations* . . . Estella rejects the love of the hero. In *Our Mutual Friend,* Bella Wilfer rejects Rokesmith in much the same way—though less cruelly, and though she later marries him. But Rokesmith is a colorless character, and the real agonies of frustrated

passion appear in *Our Mutual Friend* in the scene between Bradley and Lizzie. This is the kind of thing—the Carker and Edith Dombey kind of thing—that is likely to be bad in Dickens; but here it has a certain reality and a certain unpleasant power. Who can forget the tophatted schoolmaster striking his fist against the stone wall of the church?

The inference is, of course, that Bradley, if he had not been shipwrecked in this way, would have approximated as closely as possible to some sort of Murdstone or Gradgrind. But his death has a tragic symbolism which suggests a different kind of moral. In order to escape detection, he has disguised himself at the time of the murder as a disreputable waterside character who is known to have a grievance against Eugene. When the man finds out what has happened, he makes capital of it by blackmailing Bradley. Headstone finally tackles him on the edge of the deep lock of a canal, drags him into the water, and holds him under until he is drowned; but in doing so, he drowns himself. It is as if the illiterate ruffian whom he would now never be able to shake off has come to represent the brutish part of Bradley's own nature. Having failed to destroy Eugene, he destroys himself with the brute. (pp. 67-8)

Edmund Wilson, "Dickens: The Two Scrooges," in his *The Wound and the Bow: Seven Studies in Literature,* 1941. Reprint by Farrar, Straus & Giroux, 1978, pp. 3-85.

SOURCES FOR FURTHER STUDY

Ackroyd, Peter. *Dickens.* New York: HarperCollins Publishers, 1990, 1195 p.

Exhaustive and somewhat controversial biography of Dickens. Ackroyd takes "imaginative" liberties to portray Dickens as a genius "whose public radiance gave little hint of the darkness of his private life."

Butt, John, and Tillotson, Kathleen. *Dickens at Work.* London: Methuen, 1957, 238 p.

Examines Dickens's novels in the light of their periodical publication. The critics state that Dickens followed in the tradition of the periodical essayist as well as that of Henry Fielding and Tobias Smollett.

Hardy, Barbara. *The Moral Art of Dickens.* New York: Oxford University Press, 1970, 155 p.

Centers on Dickens as a moral novelist. The first part of the book discusses "the changing shape of his moral art"; the second examines form, character, and

symbolism in *Pickwick Papers, Martin Chuzzlewit, David Copperfield,* and *Great Expectations.*

House, Humphry. *The Dickens World.* London: Oxford University Press, 1941, 231 p.

Examines both the internal world of Dickens's novels and the external world in which they were created. This important book claims that Dickens's works should not be used as reliable sources for history: "Dickens history is inseparable from Dickens reformism."

Johnson, Edgar. *Charles Dickens: His Tragedy and Triumph.* 2 vols. New York: Simon & Schuster, 1952.

The definitive modern biography. Johnson makes use of much previously unavailable material.

Monod, Sylvère. *Dickens the Novelist.* Translated by Sylvère Monod. Norman: University of Oklahoma Press, 1967, 512 p.

A seminal work. Monod rejects the notion that Dickens was a negligent stylist and examines his manner of conceiving and writing novels.

Emily Dickinson

1830-1886

(Full name Emily Elizabeth Dickinson) American poet.

INTRODUCTION

Dickinson is regarded as one of the greatest American poets. Although almost none of her poems were published during her lifetime and her work drew harsh criticism when it first appeared, many of her short lyrics on the subjects of nature, love, death, and immortality are now considered among the most emotionally and intellectually profound in the English language. Dickinson's forthright examination of her philosophical and religious skepticism, her unorthodox attitude toward her gender, and her distinctive style—characterized by elliptical, compressed expression, striking imagery, and innovative poetic structure—have earned widespread acclaim, and, in addition, her poems have become some of the best loved in American literature. Thomas Wentworth Higginson, Dickinson's mentor, commented that "the main quality of [her] poems is that of extraordinary grasp and insight, uttered with an uneven vigor, sometimes exasperating, seemingly wayward, but really unsought and inevitable." Today an increasing number of studies from diverse critical viewpoints are devoted to her life and works, thus securing Dickinson's status as a major poet.

Dickinson was born in Amherst, Massachusetts, where she lived her entire life. Dickinson's father, Edward Dickinson, was a prosperous lawyer who served as treasurer of Amherst College and also held various political offices. Her mother, Emily Norcross Dickinson, has been described as a quiet and frail woman. Dickinson's formal education began in 1835 with four years of primary school. She then attended Amherst Academy from 1840 to 1847 before spending a year at Mount Holyoke Female Seminary. Her studies, including courses in the sciences, literature, history, and philosophy, were largely informed by New England Puritanism, with its doctrines of a sovereign God, predestination, and the necessity for personal salvation. Dickinson, however, was unable to accept the teachings of the Unitarian church attended by her family and, despite her desire to experience a religious awakening, remained agnostic throughout her life.

Following the completion of her education, Dickinson lived in the family home with her parents and younger sister, Lavinia, while her older brother, Austin, and his wife, Susan, lived next door. Although the details of her life are vague, scholars believe that Dickinson first began writing poetry seriously in the early 1850s. Her otherwise quiet life was punctuated by brief visits to Boston, Washington, D.C., and Philadelphia in the years from 1851 to 1855. Biographers speculate that during one stay in Philadelphia Dickinson fell in love with a married minister, the Reverend Charles Wadsworth, and that her disappointment in love triggered her subsequent withdrawal from society. While this and other suggestions of tragic romantic attachments are largely conjecture, it is known that Dickinson became increasingly reclusive in the following years, spending her time primarily engaged in domestic routine and long solitary walks.

Biographers generally agree that Dickinson experienced an emotional crisis of an undetermined nature in the early 1860s. Her traumatized state of mind is believed to have inspired her to write prolifically: in 1862 alone she is thought to have composed over three hundred poems. In the same year, Dickinson initiated a correspondence with Higginson, the literary editor of the *Atlantic Monthly.* During the course of their lengthy exchange, Dickinson sent nearly one hundred of her poems for his criticism. While Higginson had little influence on her writing, he was important to her as a sympathetic adviser and confidant. Dickinson's reclusiveness intensified during 1869, and her refusal to leave her home or to meet visitors, her gnomic remarks, and her habit of always wearing white garments earned her a reputation for eccentricity among her neighbors. Her isolation further increased when her father died unexpectedly in 1874 and she was left with the care of her invalid mother. The death of her mother in 1882, followed two years later by the death of Judge Otis P. Lord, a close family friend and Dickinson's most satisfying romantic attachment, contributed to the onset of what Dickinson described as an "attack of nerves." Later, in 1886, she was diagnosed as having Bright's disease, a kidney dysfunction that resulted in her death in May of that year.

Only seven of Dickinson's poems were published during her lifetime, all anonymously and some apparently without her consent. The editors of the periodicals in which her lyrics appeared made significant alterations to them in an attempt to regularize the meter and grammar, thereby discouraging Dickinson from seeking further publication of her verse. Subsequently, her poems found only a private audience among her correspondents, family, and old school friends. Her family, however, was unaware of the enormous quantity of verse that she composed. After Dickinson's death, her sister Lavinia was astounded to discover hundreds of poems among her possessions. Many were copied into "fascicles," booklets formed from sheets of paper stitched together, but a large number appeared to be mere jottings recorded on scraps of paper. In many instances Dickinson abandoned poems in an unfinished state, leaving no indication of her final choice between alternate words, phrases, or forms.

Despite the disordered state of the manuscripts, Lavinia Dickinson resolved to publish her sister's poetry and turned to Higginson and Mabel Loomis Todd, a friend of the Dickinson family, for assistance. In 1890 *Poems of Emily Dickinson* appeared and, even though most initial reviews were highly unfavorable, the work went through eleven editions in two years. Encouraged by the popular acceptance of *Poems,* Todd edited and published two subsequent collections of Dickinson's verse in the 1890s as well as a two-volume selection of her letters. Family disputes over possession of manuscripts hindered the publication of further materials, yet over the next fifty years, previously unprinted poems were introduced to the public in new collections. It was not until 1955, with the appearance of Thomas H. Johnson's edition of her verse, that Dickinson's complete poems were collected and published together in an authoritative text.

Nearly eighteen hundred poems by Dickinson are known to exist, all of them in the form of brief lyrics (often of only one or two quatrains), and few of them titled. In her verse, Dickinson explores various subjects: nature, her preoccupation with death, her skepticism about immortality, her experience of love and loss, the importance of poetic vocation, and her attitude toward fame. Drawing on imagery from biblical sources, particularly from the Book of Revelation, and from the works of William Shakespeare, John Keats, and Elizabeth Barrett Browning, Dickinson developed a highly personal system of symbol and allusion, assigning complex meanings to colors, places, times, and seasons. Her tone in the poems ranges widely, from wry, laconic humor to anguished self-examination, from flirtatious riddling to childlike naïveté. Dickinson's diction is similarly diverse, incorporating New England vernacular, theological and scientific terminology, and archaisms. The meters of her poems are characteristically adapted from the rhythms of English hymns or nursery rhymes. Dickinson's experimentation with half rhyme, slant rhyme, assonance, consonance, and tonal harmony defied the poetic conventions of her day, as did her idiosyncratic capitalization and punctuation, especially her use of dashes for emphasis or in place of commas. The terse, epigrammatic, and elliptical aspects of Dickinson's style further distinguish her poetry from the mainstream of nineteenth-century American verse.

Most nineteenth-century critics viewed Dickinson's poetry with a combination of disapproval and bewilderment, objecting to her disregard for conventional meter and rhyme, her unusual imagery, and her apparent grammatical errors. By the turn of the century, Dickinson had acquired an enthusiastic popular following, but she was still regarded as a sentimental poet of minor importance. Interest in her eccentric life-style and alleged love affairs was the main focus of Dickinson scholarship over the next several decades, but there were also some serious critical assessments, especially by the New Critics, who concentrated on the technical aspects of her poetry. The single most important development in Dickinsonian scholarship was Johnson's 1955 edition of the complete poems. Numerous studies of her works have followed, utilizing linguistic, psychological, philosophical, historical, and feminist approaches. Studies of Dickinson's language and style often center on the complex interplay of her diction and imagery with her innovative meter and rhyme. Her adept use of images drawn from nature and literature has also been widely examined. Dickinson's unorthodox religious beliefs, her relation to the Romantic and Transcendental movements, and her personal philosophy of skepticism as expressed in her poems have been the main concerns of other research. In the 1970s and 1980s, feminist critics have explored such issues as the difficulties Dickinson encountered as a woman poet, the significance of her decision to withdraw from society, her use of language as a means of rebellion, and her importance to contemporary women writers.

Although Dickinson engendered no particular school of poetry, poets as diverse as Amy Lowell, Hart Crane, and Adrienne Rich have acknowledged her verse as an influence on their writings. Dickinson has continued to elicit fascination for both readers and scholars. For her originality, range, and emotional depth, Dickinson is now among the most universally admired and extensively studied figures in English literature. As Joyce Carol Oates has written, "Here is an American artist of words as inexhaustible as Shakespeare, as vigorously skillful in her craft as Yeats, a poet whom we can set with confidence beside the greatest poets of modern times."

(For further information about Dickinson's life and works, see *Concise Dictionary of American Literary Biography: Realism, Naturalism, and Local Color, 1865-1917*; *Dictionary of Literary Biography*, Vol. 1: *The American Renaissance in New England*; *Nineteenth-Century Literature Criticism*, Vol. 21; *Poetry Criticism*, Vol. 1; and *Something about the Author*, Vol. 29.)

CRITICAL COMMENTARY

ALLEN TATE

(essay date 1928-32)

[Tate is considered one of the most influential American critics of the twentieth century. In the following excerpt, he explores Dickinson's poetry as a mirror of the mind and era of the author herself.]

Great poetry needs no special features of difficulty to make it mysterious. When it has them, the reputation of the poet is likely to remain uncertain. This is still true of Donne, and it is true of Emily Dickinson, whose verse appeared in an age unfavorable to the use of intelligence in poetry. Her poetry is not like any other poetry of her time; it is not like any of the innumerable kinds of verse written today. In still another respect it is far removed from us. It is a poetry of ideas, and it demands of the reader a point of view—not an opinion of the New Deal or of the League of Nations, but an ingrained philosophy that is fundamental, a settled attitude that is almost extinct in this eclectic age. Yet it is not the sort of poetry of ideas which, like Pope's, requires a point of view only. It requires also, for the deepest understanding, which must go beneath the verbal excitement of the style, a highly developed sense of the specific quality of poetry—a quality that most persons accept as the accidental feature of something else that the poet thinks he has to say. This is one reason why Miss Dickinson's poetry has not been widely read.

There is another reason, and it is a part of the problem peculiar to a poetry that comes out of fundamental ideas. We lack a tradition of criticism. There were no points of critical reference passed on to us from a preceding generation. I am not upholding here the so-called dead-hand of tradition, but rather a rational insight into the meaning of the present in terms of some imaginable past implicit in our own lives: we need a body of ideas that can bear upon the course of the spirit and yet remain coherent as a rational instrument. We ignore the present, which is momently translated into

---

Principal Works

Poems of Emily Dickinson (poetry) 1890

Poems by Emily Dickinson, second series (poetry) 1891

Letters of Emily Dickinson (letters) 1894

Poems by Emily Dickinson (poetry) 1896

The Single Hound: Poems of a Lifetime (poetry) 1914

The Complete Poems of Emily Dickinson (poetry) 1924

Further Poems of Emily Dickinson (poetry) 1929

Emily Dickinson Face to Face: Unpublished Letters with Notes and Reminiscences (letters) 1932

Unpublished Poems of Emily Dickinson (poetry) 1935

Bolts of Melody: New Poems of Emily Dickinson (poetry) 1945

The Poems of Emily Dickinson. 3 vols. (poetry) 1955

The Letters of Emily Dickinson. 3 vols. (letters) 1958

The Complete Poems of Emily Dickinson (poetry) 1960

---

the past, and derive our standards from imaginative constructions of the future. The hard contingency of fact invariably breaks the standards down, leaving us the intellectual chaos which is the sore distress of American criticism. Marxian criticism has become the latest disguise of this heresy.

Still another difficulty stands between us and Miss Dickinson. It is the failure of the scholars to feel more than biographical curiosity about her. We have scholarship, but that is no substitute for a critical tradition. Miss Dickinson's value to the research scholar, who likes historical difficulty for its own sake, is slight; she is too near to possess the remoteness of literature. Perhaps her appropriate setting would be the age of Cowley or of Donne. Yet in her own historical setting she is, nevertheless, remarkable and special.

Although the intellectual climate into which she was born, in 1830, had, as all times have, the features of a transition, the period was also a major crisis culminating in the war between the States. After that war, in New England as well as in the South, spiritual crises were definitely minor until the First World War.

Yet, a generation before the war of 1861-65, the transformation of New England had begun. When Samuel Slater in 1790 thwarted the British embargo on mill-machinery by committing to memory the whole design of a cotton spinner and bringing it to Massachusetts, he planted the seed of the "Western spirit." By 1825 its growth in the East was rank enough to begin choking out the ideas and habits of living that New England along with Virginia had kept in unconscious allegiance to Europe. To the casual observer, perhaps, the New England character of 1830 was largely an eigh-

teenth-century character. But theocracy was on the decline, and industrialism was rising—as Emerson, in an unusually lucid moment, put it, "Things are in the saddle." The energy that had built the meeting-house ran the factory.

Now the idea that moved the theocratic state is the most interesting historically of all American ideas. It was, of course, powerful in seventeenth-century England, but in America, where the long arm of Laud could not reach, it acquired an unchecked social and political influence. The important thing to remember about the puritan theocracy is that it permeated, as it could never have done in England, a whole society. It gave final, definite meaning to life, the life of pious and impious, of learned and vulgar alike. It gave—and this is its significance for Emily Dickinson, and in only slightly lesser degree for Melville and Hawthorne—it gave an heroic proportion and a tragic mode to the experience of the individual. The history of the New England theocracy, from Apostle Eliot to Cotton Mather, is rich in gigantic intellects that broke down—or so it must appear to an outsider—in a kind of moral decadence and depravity. Socially we may not like the New England idea. Yet it had an immense, incalculable value for literature: it dramatized the human soul.

But by 1850 the great fortunes had been made (in the rum, slave, and milling industries), and New England became a museum. The whatnots groaned under the load of knick-knacks, the fine china dogs and cats, the pieces of Oriental jade, the chips off the leaning tower at Pisa. There were the rare books and the cosmopolitan learning. It was all equally displayed as the evidence of a superior culture. The Gilded Age had already begun. But culture, in the true sense, was disappearing. Where the old order, formidable as it was, had held all this personal experience, this eclectic excitement, in a comprehensible whole, the new order tended to flatten it out in a common experience that was not quite in common; it exalted more and more the personal and the unique in the interior sense. Where the old-fashioned puritans got together on a rigid doctrine, and could thus be individualists in manners, the nineteenth-century New Englander, lacking a genuine religious center, began to be a social conformist. The common idea of the Redemption, for example, was replaced by the conformist idea of respectability among neighbors whose spiritual disorder, not very evident at the surface, was becoming acute. A great idea was breaking up, and society was moving towards external uniformity, which is usually the measure of the spiritual sterility inside.

At this juncture Emerson came upon the scene: the Lucifer of Concord, he had better be called hereafter, for he was the lightbearer who could see nothing but light, and was fearfully blind. He looked around and saw the uniformity of life, and called it the routine of tradition, the tyranny of the theological idea. The death of Priam put an end to the hope of Troy, but it was a slight feat of arms for the doughty Pyrrhus; Priam was an old gentleman and almost dead. So was theocracy; and Emerson killed it. In this way he accelerated a tendency that he disliked. It was a great intellectual mistake. By it Emerson unwittingly became the prophet of a piratical industrialism, a consequence of his own transcendental individualism that he could not foresee. He was hoist with his own petard.

He discredited more than any other man the puritan drama of the soul. The age that followed, from 1865 on, expired in a genteel secularism, a mildly didactic order of feeling whose ornaments were Lowell, Longfellow, and Holmes. "After Emerson had done his work," says Mr. Robert Penn Warren, "any tragic possibilities in that culture were dissipated." Hawthorne alone in his time kept pure, in the primitive terms, the primitive vision; he brings the puritan tragedy to its climax. Man, measured by a great idea outside himself, is found wanting. But for Emerson man is greater than any idea and, being himself the Over-Soul, is innately perfect; there is no struggle because—I state the Emersonian doctrine, which is very slippery, in its extreme terms—because there is no possibility of error. There is no drama in human character because there is no tragic fault. It is not surprising, then, that after Emerson New England literature tastes like a sip of cambric tea. Its center of vision has disappeared. There is Hawthorne looking back, there is Emerson looking not too clearly at anything ahead: Emily Dickinson, who has in her something of both, comes in somewhere between.

With the exception of Poe there is no other American poet whose work so steadily emerges, under pressure of certain disintegrating obsessions, from the framework of moral character. There is none of whom it is truer to say that the poet *is* the poetry. Perhaps this explains the zeal of her admirers for her biography; it explains, in part at least, the gratuitous mystery that Mrs. Bianchi, a niece of the poet and her official biographer, has made of her life. The devoted controversy that Miss Josephine Pollitt and Miss Genevieve Taggard started a few years ago with their excellent books shows the extent to which the critics feel the intimate connection of her life and work. Admiration and affection are pleased to linger over the tokens of a great life; but the solution to the Dickinson enigma is peculiarly superior to fact.

The meaning of the identity—which we merely feel—of character and poetry would be exceedingly obscure, even if we could draw up a kind of Binet correlation between the two sets of "facts." Miss Dickinson was a recluse; but her poetry is rich with a profound and varied experience. Where did she get it? Now some of the biographers, nervous in the presence of this discrepancy, are eager to find her a love affair, and I think

this search is due to a modern prejudice: we believe that no virgin can know enough to write poetry. We shall never learn where she got the rich quality of her mind. The moral image that we have of Miss Dickinson stands out in every poem; it is that of a dominating spinster whose very sweetness must have been formidable. Yet her poetry constantly moves within an absolute order of truths that overwhelmed her simply because to her they were unalterably fixed. It is dangerous to assume that her "life," which to the biographers means the thwarted love affair she is supposed to have had, gave to her poetry a decisive direction. It is even more dangerous to suppose that it made her a poet.

Poets are mysterious, but a poet when all is said is not much more mysterious than a banker. The critics remain spellbound by the technical license of her verse and by the puzzle of her personal life. Personality is a legitimate interest because it is an incurable interest, but legitimate as a personal interest only; it will never give up the key to anyone's verse. Used to that end, the interest is false. "It is apparent," writes Mr. Conrad Aiken, "that Miss Dickinson became a hermit by deliberate and conscious choice"—a sensible remark that we cannot repeat too often. If it were necessary to explain her seclusion with disappointment in love, there would remain the discrepancy between what the seclusion produced and the seclusion looked at as a cause. The effect, which is her poetry, would imply the whole complex of anterior fact, which was the social and religious structure of New England.

The problem to be kept in mind is thus the meaning of her "deliberate and conscious" decision to withdraw from life to her upstairs room. This simple fact is not very important. But that it must have been her sole way of acting out her part in the history of her culture, which made, with the variations of circumstance, a single demand upon all its representatives—this is of the greatest consequence. All pity for Miss Dickinson's "starved life" is misdirected. Her life was one of the richest and deepest ever lived on this continent.

When she went upstairs and closed the door, she mastered life by rejecting it. Others in their way had done it before; still others did it later. If we suppose—which is to suppose the improbable—that the love-affair precipitated the seclusion, it was only a pretext; she would have found another. Mastery of the world by rejecting the world was the doctrine, even if it was not always the practice, of Jonathan Edwards and Cotton Mather. It is the meaning of fate in Hawthorne: his people are fated to withdraw from the world and to be destroyed. And it is one of the great themes of Henry James.

There is a moral emphasis that connects Hawthorne, James, and Miss Dickinson, and I think it is instructive. Between Hawthorne and James lies an epoch. The temptation to sin, in Hawthorne, is, in James, transformed into the temptation not to do the "decent thing." A whole world-scheme, a complete cosmic background, has shrunk to the dimensions of the individual conscience. This epoch between Hawthorne and James lies in Emerson. James found himself in the post-Emersonian world, and he could not, without violating the detachment proper to an artist, undo Emerson's work; he had that kind of intelligence which refuses to break its head against history. There was left to him only the value, the historic rôle, of rejection. He could merely escape from the physical presence of that world which, for convenience, we may call Emerson's world: he could only take his Americans to Europe upon the vain quest of something that they had lost at home. His characters, fleeing the wreckage of the puritan culture, preserved only their honor. Honor became a sort of forlorn hope struggling against the forces of "pure fact" that had got loose in the middle of the century. Honor alone is a poor weapon against nature, being too personal, finical, and proud, and James achieved a victory by refusing to engage the whole force of the enemy.

In Emily Dickinson the conflict takes place on a vaster field. The enemy to all those New Englanders was Nature, and Miss Dickinson saw into the character of this enemy more deeply than any of the others. The general symbol of Nature, for her, is Death, and her weapon against Death is the entire powerful dumbshow of the puritan theology led by Redemption and Immortality. Morally speaking, the problem for James and Miss Dickinson is similar. But her advantages were greater than his. The advantages lay in the availability to her of the puritan ideas on the theological plane.

These ideas, in her poetry, are momently assailed by the disintegrating force of Nature (appearing as Death) which, while constantly breaking them down, constantly redefines and strengthens them. The values are purified by the triumphant withdrawal from Nature, by their power to recover from Nature. The poet attains to a mastery over experience by facing its utmost implications. There is the clash of powerful opposites, and in all great poetry—for Emily Dickinson is a great poet—it issues in a tension between abstraction and sensation in which the two elements may be, of course, distinguished logically, but not really. We are shown our roots in Nature by examining our differences with Nature; we are renewed by Nature without being delivered into her hands. When it is possible for a poet to do this for us with the greatest imaginative comprehension, a possibility that the poet cannot himself create, we have the perfect literary situation. Only a few times in the history of English poetry has this situation come about, notably, the period between about 1580 and the Restoration. There was a similar age in New England from which emerged two talents of the first order—Hawthorne and Emily Dickinson.

There is an epoch between James and Miss Dick-

inson. But between her and Hawthorne there exists a difference of intellectual quality. She lacks almost radically the power to seize upon and understand abstractions abstractions for their own sake; she does not separate them from the sensuous illuminations that she is so marvelously adept at; like Donne, she *perceives abstraction* and *thinks sensation.* But Hawthorne was a master of ideas, within a limited range; this narrowness confined him to his own kind of life, his own society, and out of it grew his typical forms of experience, his steady, almost obsessed vision of man; it explains his depth and intensity. Yet he is always conscious of the abstract, doctrinal aspect of his mind, and when his vision of action and emotion is weak, his work becomes didactic. Now Miss Dickinson's poetry often runs into quasihomiletic forms, but it is never didactic. Her very ignorance, her lack of formal intellectual training, preserved her from the risk that imperiled Hawthorne. She cannot reason at all. She can only *see.* It is impossible to imagine what she might have done with drama or fiction; for, not approaching the puritan temper and through it the puritan myth, through human action, she is able to grasp the terms of the myth directly and by a feat that amounts almost to anthropomorphism, to give them a luminous tension, a kind of drama, among themselves.

One of the perfect poems in English is **"The Chariot,"** and it illustrates better than anything else she wrote the special quality of her mind. I think it will illuminate the tendency of this discussion:

Because I could not stop for death,
He kindly stopped for me;
The carriage held but just ourselves
And immortality.

We slowly drove, he knew no haste,
And I had put away
My labor, and my leisure too,
For his civility.

We passed the school where children played,
Their lessons scarcely done;
We passed the fields of gazing grain,
We passed the setting sun.

We paused before a house that seemed
A swelling of the ground;
The roof was scarcely visible,
The cornice but a mound.

Since then 'tis centuries; but each
Feels shorter than the day
I first surmised the horses' heads
Were toward eternity.

If the word great means anything in poetry, this poem is one of the greatest in the English language. The rhythm charges with movement the pattern of suspended action back of the poem. Every image is precise and, moreover, not merely beautiful, but fused with the central idea. Every image extends and intensifies every other. The third stanza especially shows Miss Dickinson's power to fuse, into a single order of perception, a heterogeneous series: the children, the grain, and the setting sun (time) have the same degree of credibility; the first subtly preparing for the last. The sharp *gazing* before *grain* instills into nature a cold vitality of which the qualitative richness has infinite depth. The content of death in the poem eludes explicit definition. He is a gentleman taking a lady out for a drive. But note the restraint that keeps the poet from carrying this so far that it becomes ludicrous and incredible; and note the subtly interfused erotic motive, which the idea of death has presented to most romantic poets, love being a symbol interchangeable with death. The terror of death is objectified through this figure of the genteel driver, who is made ironically to serve the end of Immortality. This is the heart of the poem: she has presented a typical Christian theme in its final irresolution, without making any final statements about it. There is no solution to the problem; there can be only a presentation of it in the full context of intellect and feeling. A construction of the human will, elaborated with all the abstracting powers of the mind, is put to the concrete test of experience: the idea of immortality is confronted with the fact of physical disintegration. We are not told what to think; we are told to look at the situation.

The framework of the poem is, in fact, the two abstractions, mortality and eternity, which are made to associate in equality with the images: she sees the ideas, and thinks the perceptions. She did, of course, nothing of the sort; but we must use the logical distinctions, even to the extent of paradox, if we are to form any notion of this rare quality of mind. She could not in the proper sense think at all, and unless we prefer the feeble poetry of moral ideas that flourished in New England in the eighties, we must conclude that her intellectual deficiency contributed at least negatively to her great distinction. Miss Dickinson is probably the only Anglo-American poet of her century whose work exhibits the perfect literary situation—in which is possible the fusion of sensibility and thought. Unlike her contemporaries, she never succumbed to her ideas, to easy solutions, to her private desires.

Philosophers must deal with ideas, but the trouble with most nineteenth-century poets is too much philosophy; they are nearer to being philosophers than poets, without being in the true sense either. Tennyson is a good example of this; so is Arnold in his weak moments. There have been poets like Milton and Donne, who were not spoiled for their true business by leaning on a rational system of ideas, who understood the poetic use of ideas. Tennyson tried to mix a little Huxley

and a little Broad Church, without understanding either Broad Church or Huxley; the result was fatal, and what is worse, it was shallow. Miss Dickinson's ideas were deeply imbedded in her character, not taken from the latest tract. A conscious cultivation of ideas in poetry is always dangerous, and even Milton escaped ruin only by having an instinct for what in the deepest sense he understood. Even at that there is a remote quality in Milton's approach to his material, in his treatment of it; in the nineteenth century, in an imperfect literary situation where literature was confused with documentation, he might have been a pseudo-philosopher-poet. It is difficult to conceive Emily Dickinson and John Donne succumbing to rumination about "problems"; they would not have written at all.

Neither the feeling nor the style of Miss Dickinson belongs to the seventeenth century; yet between her and Donne there are remarkable ties. Their religious ideas, their abstractions, are momently toppling from the rational plane to the level of perception. The ideas, in fact, are no longer the impersonal religious symbols created anew in the heat of emotion, that we find in poets like Herbert and Vaughan. They have become, for Donne, the terms of personality; they are mingled with the miscellany of sensation. In Miss Dickinson, as in Donne, we may detect a singularly morbid concern, not for religious truth, but for personal revelation. The modern word is self-exploitation. It is egoism grown irresponsible in religion and decadent in morals. In religion it is blasphemy; in society it means usually that culture is not self-contained and sufficient, that the spiritual community is breaking up. This is, along with some other features that do not concern us here, the perfect literary situation.

Personal revelation of the kind that Donne and Miss Dickinson strove for, in the effort to understand their relation to the world, is a feature of all great poetry; it is probably the hidden motive for writing. It is the effort of the individual to live apart from a cultural tradition that no longer sustains him. But this culture, which I now wish to discuss a little, is indispensable: there is a great deal of shallow nonsense in modern criticism which holds that poetry—and this is a half-truth that is worse than false—is essentially revolutionary. It is only indirectly revolutionary: the intellectual and religious background of an age no longer contains the whole spirit, and the poet proceeds to examine that background in terms of immediate experience. But the background is necessary; otherwise all the arts (not only poetry) would have to rise in a vacuum. Poetry does not dispense with tradition; it probes the deficiencies of a tradition. But it must have a tradition to probe. It is too bad that Arnold did not explain his doctrine, that poetry is a criticism of life, from the viewpoint of its background: we should have been spared an era of academic misconception, in which criticism of life meant a diluted pragmatism, the criterion of which was respectability. The poet in the true sense "criticizes" his tradition, either as such, or indirectly by comparing it with something that is about to replace it; he does what the root-meaning of the verb implies—he *discerns* its real elements and thus establishes its value, by putting it to the test of experience.

What is the nature of a poet's culture? Or, to put the question properly, what is the meaning of culture for poetry? All the great poets become the material of what we popularly call culture; we study them to acquire it. It is clear that Addison was more cultivated than Shakespeare; nevertheless Shakespeare is a finer source of culture than Addison. What is the meaning of this? Plainly it is that learning has never had anything to do with culture except instrumentally: the poet must be exactly literate enough to write down fully and precisely what he has to say, but no more. The source of a poet's true culture lies back of the paraphernalia of culture, and not all the historical activity of an enlightened age can create it.

A culture cannot be consciously created. It is an available source of ideas that are imbedded in a complete and homogeneous society. The poet finds himself balanced upon the moment when such a world is about to fall, when it threatens to run out into looser and less self-sufficient impulses. This world order is assimilated, in Miss Dickinson, as medievalism was in Shakespeare, to the poetic vision; it is brought down from abstraction to personal sensibility.

In this connection it may be said that the prior conditions for great poetry, given a great talent, may be reduced to two: the thoroughness of the poet's discipline in an objective system of truth, and his lack of consciousness of such a discipline. For this discipline is a number of fundamental ideas the origin of which the poet does not know; they give form and stability to his fresh perceptions of the world; and he cannot shake them off. This is his culture, and like Tennyson's God it is nearer than hands and feet. With reasonable certainty we unearth the elements of Shakespeare's culture, and yet it is equally certain—so innocent was he of his own resources—that he would not know what our discussion is about. He appeared at the collapse of the medieval system as a rigid pattern of life, but that pattern remained in Shakespeare what Shelley called a "fixed point of reference" for his sensibility. Miss Dickinson, as we have seen, was born into the equilibrium of an old and a new order. Puritanism could not be to her what it had been to the generation of Cotton Mather—a body of absolute truths; it was an unconscious discipline timed to the pulse of her life.

The perfect literary situation: it produces, because it is rare, a special and perhaps the most distinguished kind of poet. I am not trying to invent a new critical category. Such poets are never very much alike on the surface; they show us all the varieties of poetic feeling; and like other poets they resist all classification but that of temporary convenience. But, I believe, Miss Dickinson and John Donne would have this in common: their sense of the natural world is not blunted by a too rigid system of ideas; yet the ideas, the abstractions, their education or their intellectual heritage, are not so weak as to let their immersion in nature, or their purely personal quality, get out of control. The two poles of the mind are not separately visible; we infer them from the lucid tension that may be most readily illustrated by polar activity. There is no thought as such at all; nor is there feeling; there is that unique focus of experience which is at once neither and both.

Like Miss Dickinson, Shakespeare is without opinions; his peculiar merit is also deeply involved in his failure to think about anything; his meaning is not in the content of his expression; it is in the tension of the dramatic relations of his characters. This kind of poetry is at the opposite of intellectualism. (Miss Dickinson is obscure and difficult, but that is not intellectualism.) To T. W. Higginson, the editor of *The Atlantic Monthly,* who tried to advise her, she wrote that she had no education. In any sense that Higginson could understand, it was quite true. His kind of education was the conscious cultivation of abstractions. She did not reason about the world she saw; she merely saw it. The "ideas" implicit in the world within her rose up, concentrated in her immediate perception.

That kind of world at present has for us something of the fascination of a buried city. There is none like it. When such worlds exist, when such cultures flourish, they support not only the poet but all members of society. For, from these, the poet differs only in his gift for exhibiting the structure, the internal lineaments, of his culture by threatening to tear them apart: a process that concentrates the symbolic emotions of society while it seems to attack them. The poet may hate his age; he may be an outcast like Villon; but this world is always there as the background to what he has to say. It is the lens through which he brings nature to focus and control—the clarifying medium that concentrates his personal feeling. It is ready-made; he cannot make it; with it, his poetry has a spontaneity and a certainty of direction that, without it, it would lack. No poet could have invented the ideas of **"The Chariot";** only a great poet could have found their imaginative equivalents. Miss Dickinson was a deep mind writing from a deep culture, and when she came to poetry, she came infallibly.

Infallibly, at her best; for no poet has ever been perfect, nor is Emily Dickinson. Her precision of statement is due to the directness with which the abstract framework of her thought acts upon its unorganized material. The two elements of her style, considered as point of view, are immortality, or the idea of permanence, and the physical process of death or decay. Her diction has two corresponding features: words of Latin or Greek origin and, sharply opposed to these, the concrete Saxon element. It is this verbal conflict that gives to her verse its high tension; it is not a device deliberately seized upon, but a feeling for language that senses out the two fundamental components of English and their metaphysical relation: the Latin for ideas and the Saxon for perceptions—the peculiar virtue of English as a poetic language.

Like most poets Miss Dickinson often writes out of habit; the style that emerged from some deep exploration of an idea is carried on as verbal habit when she has nothing to say. She indulges herself:

> There's something quieter than sleep
> Within this inner room!
> It wears a sprig upon its breast,
> And will not tell its name.
>
> Some touch it and some kiss it,
> Some chafe its idle hand;
> It has a simple gravity
> I do not understand!
>
> While simple hearted neighbors
> Chat of the "early dead,"
> We, prone to periphrasis,
> Remark that birds have fled!

It is only a pert remark; at best a superior kind of punning—one of the worst specimens of her occasional interest in herself. But she never had the slightest interest in the public. Were four poems or five published in her lifetime? She never felt the temptation to round off a poem for public exhibition. Higginson's kindly offer to make her verse "correct" was an invitation to throw her work into the public ring—the ring of Lowell and Longfellow. He could not see that he was tampering with one of the rarest literary integrities of all time. Here was a poet who had no use for the supports of authorship—flattery and fame; she never needed money.

She had all the elements of a culture that has broken up, a culture that on the religious side takes its place in the museum of spiritual antiquities. Puritanism, as a unified version of the world, is dead; only a remnant of it in trade may be said to survive. In the history of puritanism she comes between Hawthorne and Emerson. She has Hawthorne's matter, which a too irresponsible personality tends to dilute into a form like Emerson's; she is often betrayed by words. But she is not the poet of personal sentiment; she has more to say than she can put down in any one poem. Like Hardy and Whitman she must be read entire; like Shakespeare she never gives up her meaning in a single line.

She is therefore a perfect subject for the kind of criticism which is chiefly concerned with general ideas. She exhibits one of the permanent relations between personality and objective truth, and she deserves the special attention of our time, which lacks that kind of truth.

She has Hawthorne's intellectual toughness, a hard, definite sense of the physical world. The highest flights to God, the most extravagant metaphors of the strange and the remote, come back to a point of casuistry, to a moral dilemma of the experienced world. There is, in spite of the homiletic vein of utterance, no abstract speculation, nor is there a message to society; she speaks wholly to the individual experience. She offers to the unimaginative no riot of vicarious sensation; she has no useful maxims for men of action. Up to this point her resemblance to Emerson is slight: poetry is a sufficient form of utterance, and her devotion to it is pure. But in Emily Dickinson the puritan world is no longer self-contained; it is no longer complete; her sensibility exceeds its dimensions. She has trimmed down its supernatural proportions; it has become a morality; instead of the tragedy of the spirit there is a commentary upon it. Her poetry is a magnificient personal confession, blasphemous and, in its self-revelation, its honesty, almost obscene. It comes out of an intellectual life towards which it feels no moral responsibility. Cotton Mather would have burnt her for a witch. (pp. 197-213)

Allen Tate, "Emily Dickinson, in his *On the Limits of Poetry: Selected Essays, 1928-1948,* The Swallow Press and William Morrow & Company, Publishers, 1948, pp. 197-213.

LOUISE BOGAN
(lecture date 1959)

[Bogan was an American poet and critic. In the following excerpt from a 1959 lecture, she discusses Dickinson's qualities as a visionary poet.]

It has been suggested that I develop, on this occasion, a statement I made in 1945, in an article published in that year—that the time had come "to assess Emily Dickinson's powers on the highest level of mystical poetry, where they should be assessed." Since then, the appearance of the *Collected Poems* and of the *Collected Letters,* superbly edited by Thomas H. Johnson, has made such an assessment less difficult than it formerly had to be. For now, with the existence of these definitive works, the stages of the poet's development are connected and clarified. We are now faced, as we should be, with the career of a writer who—we now realize—throughout her life made the most difficult kind of choices, many directed toward the protection of her sensitive nature and of her remarkable poetic gift. It is the poet Dickinson who has advanced into the full light of literary history and now belongs not only to Amherst, not only to America, but to the world that reads her either in English or in translation.

Now, the term "mystical poetry" is a difficult one to deal with. The words "mystic" and "mysticism" have become rather suspect in modern, materialist society. So it is important to define and place this term, at the outset. Mystics have appeared, it would seem, with fair frequency at many periods, in many cultures; but there is no doubt that when, in the West, we speak of true mysticism, we have in mind the example of the Christian saints. "In Christianity," says Evelyn Underhill, "the 'natural mysticism' . . . which is latent in humanity and at a certain point of development breaks out in every race, came to itself; and attributed for the first time true and distinct personality to its Object"— namely, God. True mystics do not indulge in diffuse pantheism or hold to the aim of "the occult," which wishes to wrench supernal power to human uses. In the words of another commentator: "The aim and content of Christian mysticism is not self or nature, but God."

We can see at once that there is a difference between the character, as well as the aims, of true mystics and of poets; and we know that to come upon the two gifts in one person is extremely rare. But close points of resemblance do exist between the mystic experience, at its purest and best, and the experience of poetic—or indeed, any creative—expression. Poets down the centuries, visited by that power which the ancients call *the Muse,* have described their experience in much the same way as the mystic describes his ecstatic union with Divine Truth. This experience has been rendered at length, and dramatically, by Dante, as well as by St. John of the Cross; and certain poems in the literature of every language attest to moments when, for the poet, "the deep and primal life which he shares with all creation has been roused from its sleep." And both poets and mystics have described with great poignance that sense of deprivation and that shutting away from grace which follows the loss of the vision (or of the inspiring breath), which is called, in the language of mysticism, "the dark night of the soul."

Certainly one of the triumphs brought about by the emergence of the Romantic spirit, in English poetry, at the end of the eighteenth century, was a freeing and an enlargement of poetic vision, and in the nineteenth century we come upon a multiplication of poets whose spiritual perceptions were acute. Beyond Vaughan and Herbert (who, in the seventeenth century, worked from a religious base) we think of Blake, of the young Wordsworth; of Keats and Shelley; of Emily Brontë; of Gerard Manley Hopkins; and we can extend the list into our own day with the names of Yeats and T. S. Eliot. By examining the work of these poets—to whom the imagination, the creative spirit of man, was of ut-

most importance—we find that the progress of the mystic toward illumination, and of the poet toward the full depth and richness of his insight—are much alike. Both work from the world of reality, toward the realm of Essence; from the microcosm to the macrocosm. Both have an intense and accurate sense of their surroundings; there is nothing vague or floating in their perception of reality; it is indeed as though they saw "through, not with, the eye." And they are filled with love for the beauty they perceive in the world of time— "this remarkable world" as Emily Dickinson called it; and concerning death they are neither fearful nor morbid—how could they be, since they feel immortality behind it? They document life's fearful limitations from which they suffer, but they do not mix self-pity with the account of their suffering (which they describe, like their joy, in close detail). They see the world in a grain of sand and Heaven in a wild flower; and now and again they bring eternity into focus, as it were, in a phrase of the utmost clarity. In the work of Emily Dickinson such moments of still and halted perception are many. The slant of light on a winter day, the still brilliance of a summer noon, the sound of the wind before the rain—she speaks of these, and we share the shock of insight, the slight dislocation of serial events, the sudden shift from the Manifold into the One.

One of the dominant facts concerning Emily Dickinson is her spirit of religious unorthodoxy. Her deeply religious feeling ran outside the bounds of dogma; this individualism was, in fact, an inheritance from her Calvinist forbears, but it was out of place when contrasted to the Evangelicanism to which, in her time, so many Protestants had succumbed. She early set herself against the guilt and gloom inherent in this revivalism. She avoided the constrictions which a narrow insistence on religious rule and law would put upon her. She had read Emerson with delight, but, as Yvor Winters has remarked, it is a mistake to think of her as a Transcendentalist in dimity. Here again she worked through to a standpoint and an interpretation of her own; her attitude toward pain and suffering, toward the shocking facts of existence, was far more realistic than Emerson's. As we examine her chief spiritual preoccupations, we see how closely she relates to the English Romantic poets who, a generation or so before her, fought a difficult and unpopular battle against the eighteenth century's cold logic and mechanical point of view. The names of Blake and Coleridge come to mind; we know that to both these poets the cold theory of Locke represented "a deadly heresy on the nature of existence." It is difficult to look back to this period of early Romantic breakthrough, since so much of that early boldness and originality was later dissipated in excesses of various kinds. But it is important to remember that Blake attached the greatest importance to the human imagination as an aspect of some mystery be-

A manuscript copy of "Safe in their Alabaster Chambers," in Dickinson's hand.

yond the human, and to listen to his ringing words: "The world of Imagination is the world of Eternity. . . . The world of Imagination is Infinite and Eternal, whereas the world of generation is Finite and Temporal . . ."—and to remember, as well, that "Blake, Wordsworth, Coleridge, Shelley and Keats shared the belief that the imagination was nothing less than God as he operates in the human soul." C. M. Bowra, writing of the Romantic ethos in general, brings out a fact which has been generally overlooked: that, although Romantic poetry became a European phenomenon, English Romantic poetry "almost alone . . . connected visionary insight with a superior order of being." "There is hardly a trace of this [insight]," Bowra goes on to say, "in Hugo, or Heine or Lermontov. They have their full share of longing, but almost nothing of Romantic vision. . . ." Hölderlin, in Germany tried to share a lost vision of Greece, but on the whole it was the English who accomplished a transformation in thought and emotion "for which there is no parallel in their age." It is surely in the company of these English poets that Emily Dickinson belongs. At

its most intense, her vision not only matched, but transcended theirs; she crossed the same boundaries with a like intransigence; and the same vigorous flowers sprang from different seeds, in the spirit of a woman born in 1830, in New England, in America.

The drawing of close parallels between the life and circumstances of poets is often an unrewarding task. But in the case of Emily Dickinson because hers was for so long considered a particularly isolated career, it is interesting to make certain comparisons. It has been pointed out that there is a close resemblance between the lives, temperament and works of Emily Brontë and Emily Dickinson. And one or two resemblances between Emily Dickinson and Blake (Blake taken as a lyric poet rather than as a prophet) can be traced (quite apart from the fairly unimportant fact that Miss Dickinson, in her apprenticeship, closely imitated Blake's form in at least two poems). Both took over the simplest forms of the song and the hymn and turned this simplicity to their own uses. Both seemed to work straight from almost dictated inspiration (Blake, indeed, claimed that his poems were dictated to him intact and entire) but we now know, from an examination of their manuscripts, that both worked over their original drafts with meticulous care. Both had to struggle against hampering circumstances: Blake against poverty and misunderstanding, and Dickinson against a lack of true response in the traditionally stiffened society in which she found herself. To both poets, limitation and boundary finally yielded originality and power; they were sufficiently outside the spirit of their times so that they were comparatively untouched by the vagaries of fashion; they both were able to wring from solitary contemplation sound working principles and just form. T. S. Eliot, in his essay on Blake, speaks of Blake's peculiarity "which can be seen to be the peculiarity of all great poetry. . . . It is merely a peculiar honesty, which, in a world frightened to be honest, is particularly terrifying. It is an honesty against which the whole world conspires, because it is unpleasant. Blake's poetry has the unpleasantness of great poetry. Nothing that can be called abnormal or perverse, none of the things which exemplify the sickness of an epoch or a fashion, have this quality; only those things which, by some extraordinary labor of simplification, exhibit the essential sickness or strength of the human soul." Eliot then remarks that the question about Blake the man "is a question of the circumstances that concurred to permit this honesty in his work. . . . The favoring conditions probably include these two: that, early apprenticed to a manual occupation, he was not compelled to acquire any other education in literature than he wanted, or to acquire it for any other reason than he wanted it; and that, being a humble engraver, he had no journalistic-social career open to him. There was, that is to say, nothing to distract him from his interests or to corrupt these interests—neither . . . the standards of society, nor the temptation of success; nor was he exposed to imitation of himself or anyone else. . . . These circumstances are what make him innocent."

The circumstances which led to Emily Dickinson's very nearly complete seclusion are, of course, different from those which Eliot mentions as applying to Blake. It was physical frailty which put an end to her formal education. But later, as we read the record of her withdrawal, as this record appears in the *Letters* (and, of course, the full reasons are not given) we can detect the element of choice working. By the time she wrote to Higginson in 1862 she had made that choice, and only wanted to have it confirmed. She wished to know whether or not her poems were "alive"—if they "breathed." She received a certain confirmation that they were and did; and she kept to her solitude. This solitude was not harsh. Her love for her friends never diminished, nor her delight in their occasional presence; her family ties were strong; her daily round sustained her; and the joy she felt in the natural world—particularly in flowers and in children—continues. Until a series of tragedies (beginning with the death of her father) began to break down her spiritual balance, she held to that balance over a long period of years. Balance, delicacy and force—fed by her exquisite senses and her infinitely lively and inquisitive mind—these are the qualities which reinforce her vision into the heart and spirit of nature, and into her own heart.

An added pleasure is given us, as we read Emily Dickinson's poetry from beginning to end, by the openness and inclusiveness of the work. Every sort of poem has been preserved; no strict process of self-editing has taken place, and we are not faced with periods in which much has been suppressed. The failures and the successes stand side by side; the poems expressing the poet's more childish and undeveloped characteristics and the poems upon which the sentimentality of her time left its mark, are often followed or preceded by poems which define and express the very nearly indefinable and inexpressible. There is no professionalism, in the worst sense, here; and it is interesting to note that, although she sought out Higginson's advice and named herself his "scholar," she never altered a poem of hers according to any suggestion of his. She had, at one time, perhaps been willing to be published, but, later, she could do without print.

We have, then, in Johnson's edition of the poems published in 1955, as complete a record of the development of a lyric talent as exists in literature. Scholars have busied themselves with the record; we know what color she names most frequently (purple) and what books she read (Shakespeare and the Bible well in the lead). We ourselves can discover, in the index to the three volumes, that her favorite subject was not death, as was long supposed; for life, love and the soul are also

recurring subjects. But the greatest interest lies in her progress as a writer, and as a person. We see the young poet moving away, by gradual degrees, from her early slight addiction to graveyardism, to an Emersonian belief in the largeness and harmony of nature. Step by step, she advances into the terror and anguish of her destiny; she is frightened, but she holds fast and describes her fright. She is driven to the verge of sanity, but manages to remain, in some fashion, the observer and recorder of her extremity. Nature is no longer a friend, but often an inimical presence. Nature is a haunted house. And—a truth even more terrible—the inmost self can be haunted.

At the highest summit of her art, she resembles no one. She begins to cast forward toward the future: to produce poems in which we recognize, as one French critic has said, both the *voyant* faculty of Rimbaud and Mallarmé's feeling for the mystery and sacredness of the word. This high period begins in the early 1860s, and is not entirely consistent; the power seems to come and go, but it is indubitably there. And when it is present, she can describe with clinical precision the actual emotional event, the supreme moment of anguish, and even her own death itself. And she finds symbols which fit the event—terrible symbols. The experience of suffering is like dying of the cold; or it resembles the approach of a maelstrom, which finally engulfs the victim; one escapes from suffering as from the paws of a fiend, from whose grasp one emerges more dead than alive. One poem, written about 1863, defies analysis: the poem which begins **"My life had stood—a loaded gun."** . . .

> My life had stood—a Loaded Gun
> In Corners—till a Day
> The Owner passed—identified—
> And carried Me away—
>
> And now We roam in Sovreign Woods—
> And now We hunt the Doe—
> And every time I speak for Him—
> The Mountains straight reply—
>
> And do I smile, such cordial light
> Upon the Valley glow—
> It is as a Vesuvian face
> Had let its pleasure through—
>
> And when at Night—Our good Day done—
> I guard My Master's head—
> 'Tis better than the Eider-Duck's
> Deep Pillow—to have shared—
>
> To foe of His—I'm deadly foe—
> None stir the second time—
> On whom I lay a Yellow Eye—
> Or an emphatic Thumb—
>
> Though I than He—may longer live

He longer must—than I—
For I have but the power to kill,
Without—the power to die—

Is this an allegory, and if so of what? Is it a cry from some psychic deep where good and evil are not to be separated? In any case, it is a poem whose reverberations are infinite, as in great music; and we can only guess with what agony it was written down.

This power to say the unsayable—to hint of the unknowable—is the power of the seer, in this woman equipped with an ironic intelligence and great courage of spirit. The stuff of Emily Dickinson's imagination is of this world; there is nothing macabre about her material (in the manner of Poe) and there is very little of the labored or artificial about her means. If "she mastered life by rejecting it," she mastered that Nature concerning which she had such ambivalent feeling by adding herself to the sum of all things, in a Rilkean habit of praise. "She kept in touch with reality," someone has said of her, "by the clearest and finest of the senses—the sense of sight. Perhaps the great vitality of contact by vision is the essence, in part, of her originality." How exactly she renders the creatures of this earth! She gives them to us, not as symbols of this or that, but as themselves. And her lyrical notation is so precise, so fine and moves so closely in union with her mind, that she is continually striking out aphorisms, from Plotinus to Blake. And as her life goes on, everything becomes whittled down, evanescent. Her handwriting becomes a kind of fluid print; her poems become notations; all seems to be on the point of disappearing. And suddenly all disappears.

"She was a visionary," says Richard Chase, "to whom truth came with exclusive finality [and] like her Puritan forbears she was severe, downright, uncompromising, visionary, factual, sardonic."

"My business is to create," said the poet Blake. "My business is circumference," said the poet Dickinson. And we know that the physical center of that circumference was to remain the town of Amherst, which almost exactly one hundred years ago (on December 10th, 1859) Miss Dickinson described with great charm and deep affection, in a letter to Mrs. Samuel Bowles: "It storms in Amherst five days—it snows, and then it rains, and then soft fogs like vails hang on all the houses, and then the days turn Topaz, like a lady's pin . . ."—as delicate a description as a New England town and New England winter weather have ever received. (pp. 27-34)

Louise Bogan, "A Mystical Poet," in *Emily Dickinson: Three Views* by Archibald MacLeish, Louise Bogan and Richard Wilbur, Amherst College Press, 1960, pp. 27-34.

CHERYL WALKER
(essay date 1982)

[In the following excerpt from her book-length study of American women poets before 1900, Walker details the hallmarks of Dickinson's poetic style.]

[What] distinguishes Emily Dickinson from other women poets is her skill with words, her use of language. She retained her compression despite pressure from her closest friends and critics, people like Samuel Bowles and T. W. Higginson, who would have made her more discursive. She introduced unusual vocabulary into women's poetry—vocabulary borrowed from various professions mainly closed to women, like law, medicine, the military, and merchandising. I agree with Adrienne Rich that she knew she was a genius. Nothing else could explain her peculiar invulnerability to contemporary criticism of her work.

Dickinson wrote many poems about violation. The integrity of some poems was literally violated by editors who made unauthorized changes before printing them. But the poet triumphed in the end. She created a unique voice in American poetry and would not modulate it, even for Higginson who directed her to writers like Maria Lowell and Helen Hunt Jackson as models.

Like Lowell and Jackson, Dickinson did not look down on the female poetic subjects of her day. She used them; but she used them in what would come to be perceived as a poetic assault on the feminine conventions from which they sprung. She was not, for instance, taken in by the propaganda of "true womanhood." She saw behind the virtue of modesty the caricature of the double-bind.

A Charm invests a face
Imperfectly beheld—
The Lady dare not lift her Vail
For fear it be dispelled—

But peers beyond her mesh—
And wishes—and denies—
Lest Interview—annul a want
That Image—satisfies—

Perhaps Dickinson's ambivalent relation to the world has more to do with this lady "who dare not lift her Vail" than has previously been perceived. What this poem captures is the feelings of a woman who must obtain what she wants through deception and manipulation. Thus it does not simply represent the familiar Dickinson wisdom that hunger tantalizes where satiety cloys. This woman's feelings become part of the substance of the poem. They are fear (of male rejection), curiosity, and desire. The lady must finally deny her desires, sublimate her will to power, and assume a passive role. **"A Charm"** might also serve as a commentary on a poem written three years earlier.

> Our lives are Swiss—
> So still—so Cool—
> Till some odd afternoon
> The Alps neglect their Curtains
> And we look farther on!
> *Italy* stands the other side!
> While like a guard between—
> The solemn Alps—
> The siren Alps
> Forever intervene!

We recognize the theme of the unattained, so close to the hearts of women like Lucy Larcom and Elizabeth Oakes-Smith. Here, however, the barriers both forbid assault and invite it. They are both awesome and enticing. Like the lady who "peers beyond her mesh," this speaker hasn't accepted the limitations on her experience. Though undemonstrative, she remains unreconciled.

The insights made available by the comparision of these two poems can help us even when we examine the particular language that made Dickinson unique. Take, for example, the following poem written during her most creative period.

> I had not minded—Walls—
> Were Universe—one Rock—
> And far I heard his silver Call
> The other side the Block—
>
> I'd tunnel—till my Groove
> Pushed sudden thro' to his—
> Then my face take her Recompense—
> The looking in his Eyes—
>
> But 'tis a single Hair—
> A filament—a law—
> A Cobweb—wove in Adamant—
> A Battlement—of Straw—
>
> A limit like the Vail
> Unto the Lady's face—
> But every Mesh—a Citadel—
> And Dragons—in the Crease—

This is a poem about the forbidden lover, and as such it reminds us of what Dickinson could do with conventional female subjects. Although this is not one of Dickinson's best poems, it exhibits many of her characteristic innovations and therefore makes an interesting focus for discussion. Does this poem have roots in real experience or was it merely an exercise?

In the second Master letter, probably composed about this time and intended for a recipient we can no longer identify, the poet asked: "Couldn't Carlo [her dog], and you and I walk in the meadows an hour—and nobody care but the Bobolink—and *his*—a *silver* scruple? I used to think when I died—I could see you—so I died as fast as I could—but the 'Corporation' are going Heaven too so [Eternity] wont be sequestered—now [at all]—". Here we find the familiar impossible attachment forbidden by "the Corporation," the constituted powers. It is an attachment that can only be indulged in secret, in some "sequestered" place. This Master letter has too much unrefined feeling in it to be the product of a merely literary pose, and I suggest that the poem was also written out of felt experience, although the structural properties this experience assumed may well have been influenced by the vocabulary of secret sorrow.

Dickinson begins "I had not minded—Walls" in the subjunctive, one of her characteristic modes. Thus, she establishes the initial grounds of the poem as those of the nonreal, the if. The first two stanzas posit a set of circumstances that would allow for fulfillment, the enticement of the view. . . . The last two stanzas, in contrast, describe the limitations on fulfillment that forever intervene.

Typical of Dickinson's language, the poem contrasts short Anglo-Saxon words with longer Latinate ones. "Block," "eyes," "groove," "law," and "mesh," for example, are all Anglo-Saxon and convey even in their brevity a sense of abrupt limitation. "Recompense," "universe," "filament," "citadel," and "dragon," on the other hand, are Latinate words: softer and more excursive. They have feminine endings. Using the same short vowel sounds as the Anglo-Saxon words, they nevertheless convey an opposite sense of possibility. Although the words themselves do not always mean what their sounds convey ("citadel" being used to suggest an obstacle instead of a possibility), there is at the levels of both meaning and sound a sense of opposition: desire vs. frustration. Dickinson's language operates on the basis of paired antitheses. Other pairings include the concrete vs. the abstract (face/recompense), the material vs. the immaterial (rock/silver call), and the hard vs. the soft (adamant/cobweb). Her code is conflict.

Thus far we might compare her use of language to Shakespeare's, which also depends upon doublings, paradoxes, contrasts. However, Dickinson, though she loved Shakespeare, chose to be more obscure, and she did this largely by breaking linguistic rules out of a commitment to compression. The first stanza, for instance, might be paraphrased: I would not have minded walls. Were the universe to have been entirely made up of rock and were I to have heard his call from afar, it would have seemed to me merely a short distance, the other side of the block. This, of course, reduces the impact of Dickinson's compression. "Block" in her poem affects one like a pun, reminding us of "rock" earlier, as well as of the geographical meaning of "block," a city street division.

Dickinson was criticized in her day for this kind of compression. It flew in the face of most contemporary poetry, which aimed at comprehensiveness through discursive exposition. Emerson was probably her closest friend here, but even he did not break rules as flagrantly as she. Her editors also grumbled at her rhymes. "His" and "eyes" did not seem like rhyming words to them.

The structure of this poem represents a final contrast to the conventions of her time. In "Acquainted with Grief," Helen Hunt Jackson posits an unnatural occurrence by personifying grief. However, once this given is accepted, the poem never departs from its established world. Dickinson, however, reverses expectations everywhere. She begins in the realm of "if," making all the details of this realm concrete and existential: *walls, rock, block, tunnel, groove,* and *face* are part of her real world of experience. Nevertheless, when the tense shifts from the subjunctive to the present, suddenly we have paradoxes that do not belong to an experiential realm: a cobweb woven in adamant, a mesh that is a citadel, and finally, dragons, mythical beasts belonging to the world of imagination.

Furthermore, in the sequence filament/law, cobweb/adamant, and battlement/straw there is a reversal of terms in the final pair. The first two move from the insubstantial to the substantive, the last one from the substantive back to the insubstantial. "Adamant" is echoed in "battlement," but the "law" becomes "straw."

The structural progression from the real to the surreal is recognizably characteristic of Dickinson. And here the lines, "A limit like the Vail / Unto the Lady's face," become significant. Like the veil, the limitations Dickinson describes are restrictive in the real world. The seemingly insubstantial "hair" is tougher than rock, and like the veil of restrictions women must accept, to pass beyond these limitations forces one to encounter terrible dragons. However, a citadel, the *Oxford English Dictionary* tells us, is a "fortress commanding a city, which it serves both to protect and to keep in subjugation." Like the prison, this image reminds us of Dickinson's Houdini-like ability to wriggle out of confining spaces, to convert limitations into creative resources. Dragons are at least interesting to contemplate. The lady's veil—the symbol of Dickinson's sense of social, legal, and literary restrictions—provided her with a certain recompense. Thus the reversal in the third stanza, where limiting law becomes insubstantial straw, works.

Ultimately, Emily Dickinson transformed her closed world into a creative space. If there is a disap-

pointment in this poem, it comes in the second stanza where "the looking in his eyes" seems a rather weak way of describing this triumph. But whatever its limitations, this poem shows us the way an artist like Dickinson could make interesting use of motifs such as the secret sorrow and the forbidden lover. Her vision was "slant," and therefore to us thoroughly refreshing.

Recently it has become fashionable to see Emily Dickinson as a woman who lived in the realm of transcendence, secure in the space she created for the exercise of her power. Although I am sympathetic with this view, I would like to add a word of caution. No one can read Dickinson's poems and letters in their entirety without a sense that the ground for security was forever shifting under her feet. She did not resort to references to fear only out of coyness. She felt it. She wrote: "In all the circumference of Expression, those guileless words of Adam and Eve never were surpassed, 'I was afraid and hid Myself ' ". And elsewhere: "Your bond to your brother reminds me of mine to my sister— early, earnest, indissoluble. Without her life were fear, and Paradise a cowardice, except for her inciting voice." To rejoice that she found ways of evading the subjugation of the spirit that her society enforced upon its women should not mean ignoring her sense of vulnerability, which was real, which was tragic. In Dickinson's preoccupation with the imagery of royalty, we find her desire to exercise the full range of her talents; we find her will to power. In her preoccupation with falling, surrendering, confinement, and violation, we find her fears. Knowing what she had to give up, recognition within her lifetime, the chance to remain within the world she devoured information about through her friends and her newspaper, we can only be glad that at moments she had the perspective to write:

The Heart is the Capital of the Mind—
The Mind is a single State—
The Heart and the Mind together make
A single Continent—

One is the Population—
Numerous enough—
This ecstatic Nation
Seek—it is Yourself.

The puzzle of Emily Dickinson's work is finally not a question of the identity of the Master or the extent of her real experience, but one of tradition and the individual talent. Although the concern with intense feeling, the ambivalence toward power, the fascination with death, the forbidden lover and secret sorrow all belong to this women's tradition, Emily Dickinson's best work so far surpasses anything that a logical extension of that tradition's codes could have produced that the only way to explain it is by the single word, genius. She was "of the Druid." That a great many poems like **"I tie my Hat—I crease my Shawl"** are in places not much above the women's poetry of her time is only to be expected. What Emily Dickinson did for later women poets, like Amy Lowell who wanted to write her biography, was remarkable: she gave them dignity. No other aspect of her influence was so important. After Emily Dickinson's work became known, women poets in America could take their work serious-ly. She redeemed the poetess for them, and made her a genuine poet. (pp. 111-16)

Cheryl Walker, "Tradition and the Individual Talent: Helen Hunt Jackson and Emily Dickinson," in her *The Nightingale's Burden: Women Poets and American Culture before 1900,* Indiana University Press, 1982, pp. 87-116.

SOURCES FOR FURTHER STUDY

Bloom, Harold, ed. *Emily Dickinson.* Modern Critical Views. New York: Chelsea House Publishers, 1985, 204 p.

A collection of previously published essays on Dickinson by Charles R. Anderson, Albert Gelpi, David Porter, Robert Weisbuch, Sharon Cameron, Margaret Homans, Joanne Feit Diehl, and Shira Wolosky.

Ferlazzo, Paul J. *Emily Dickinson.* Twayne's United States Authors Series, no. 280. Boston: Twayne Publishers, 1976, 168 p.

A general introduction to Dickinson's life and poetry.

———, ed. *Critical Essays on Emily Dickinson.* Critical Essays on American Literature, edited by James Nagel. Boston: G. K. Hall & Co., 1984, 243 p.

Reprints criticism by important Dickinson critics.

Nathan, Rhoda B., ed. *Nineteenth-Century Women Writers of the English-Speaking World.* Contributions in Women's Studies, no. 69. New York: Greenwood Press, 1986, 275 p.

Includes essays on Dickinson by Peggy Anderson, Tilden G. Edelstein, Vivian R. Pollak, and Anna Mary Wells.

Sewall, Richard B. *The Life of Emily Dickinson.* 2 vols. New York: Farrar, Straus and Giroux, 1974.

A respected biography.

———, ed. *Emily Dickinson: A Collection of Critical Essays.* Twentieth Century Views, edited by Maynard Mack. Englewood Cliffs, N.J.: Prentice-Hall, 1963, 183 p.

A collection of Dickinson criticism reprinted from earlier publications.

John Donne

1572-1631

English poet, epigrammist, and sermonist.

INTRODUCTION

Donne is considered one of the most accomplished, if controversial, poets of the seventeenth century. His life and work are often perceived as a study in contrasts, evincing both a sensual rake who celebrated the joys of lovemaking in his secular verses and a severe Christian humanist who contemplated mortality and the subservience of humanity to God in his divine poems. Donne inspired the School of Donne, also known as the metaphysical school of English verse, whose members include Andrew Marvell, Henry Vaughan, George Herbert, and Richard Crashaw, among others. Reacting against the traditions of Elizabethan love poetry, the School of Donne poets eschewed classical or romantic allusions, attempting instead to portray the complexities and uncertainties of everyday life. Their poetry is characterized by complex, witty conceits, sudden, even jarring paradoxes and contrasts, strong imagery that combines the ornate with the mundane, and contemplations melding the natural world with the divine. Modern scholars consider Donne a gifted, versatile poet and laud such works as "A Valediction: Forbidding Mourning," "Death Be Not Proud," and "Hymn to God My God, In My Sicknesse" for their wit, religious sensitivity, and profound insight into human nature.

Donne was born into a Roman Catholic family in 1572. His father was a prosperous London merchant and his mother was the daughter of dramatist John Heywood and a relative of Catholic martyr Sir Thomas More. Donne began studies at Oxford in 1584 but was forced to leave in 1587 without taking a degree because of his faith. For several years thereafter Donne pursued a legal career at the Inns of Court in London, and it was there that the duality of his temperament and interests first became evident. Donne was known both as a free-spending libertine and as a serious scholar of legal and religious issues of the day. While studying law, Donne wrote his *Elegies* and *Satyres,* which reflect variously his wit, dandyism, and gravity. Upon completing his degree in 1596, Donne accompanied the earl of Essex on two naval expeditions against the Spanish, after which he wrote of his experiences in the poems "The Storm," "The Calm," and "The Burnt Ship." Donne returned to England the following year and embarked upon a promising career, serving as secretary to Sir Thomas Egerton. His hopes for success vanished, however, after he secretly married Egerton's sixteen-year-old niece, Ann More, in 1601. More's father was enraged and ordered Donne dismissed from his brother-in-law's service and imprisoned. Sometime afterward, Donne sadly wrote an epigram describing his lot: "John Donne / Ann Donne / Undonne."

Released from prison in 1602, Donne had little chance of obtaining gainful employment. He spent the next thirteen years undergoing long stretches of grinding poverty broken by brief periods of modest gain, desperately seeking patronage to support his wife and rapidly growing family. (Ann Donne died while giving birth to their twelfth child in 1617.) At first he lived on charity, and then he came under the patronage of three influential peers: Sir Thomas Morton; Lucy, Countess of Bedford; and, finally, Sir Robert Drury. Having embraced the Church of England, Donne was enlisted by Morton to aid him in writing anti-Roman Catholic broadsides. *Pseudo-Martyr* (1610), Donne's first published work, was thus written to persuade English Catholics to foreswear their allegiance to Rome and instead take the oath of allegiance to the British crown. This work, which brought the author to the attention of King James I, was followed by the anti-Jesuit polemic *Ignatius His Conclave,* published in 1611, and a treatise arguing for the lawfulness of suicide, *Biathanatos,* which Donne withheld from publication. (This work was later published in 1646.) He also wrote two of his longest (and, in later years, critically controversial) poems, *An Anatomie of the World* (1611) and *Of the Progres of the Soule* (1612). These works, also known as the *Anniversaries,* were composed for Drury on the first two anniversaries of his fifteen-year-old daughter's death. Drury took Donne with him to France on a long diplomatic mission from 1611 to 1612, during which time Donne wrote one of his most praised and critically discussed love poems, "A Valediction: Forbidding Mourning," at being parted reluctantly from his wife. Upon his return to England, Donne sought to secure a diplomatic post with the help of Robert Carr, Viscount Rochester, a court favorite of the king—who himself had other plans for Donne.

Believing that Donne could be of greatest service to the Crown in a much different capacity, King James soon began to pressure Donne to take clerical orders.

After some resistance, Donne acquiesced to the monarch's wishes and was ordained in early 1615. After his ordination Donne wrote little poetry, instead devoting his time to writing sermons and devotions and attending to other priestly duties. By all accounts, Donne took his new vocation seriously, acquiring a great reputation as an impressive deliverer of insightful sermons. During the years immediately following his ordination, he held several important posts, culminating in his appointment—again at King James's insistence—as Dean of St. Paul's in 1621. Two years later he suffered an attack of spotted fever, during which he apparently believed himself dying and wrote his renowned *Devotions upon Emergent Occassions, and Severall Steps in My Sickness* (1624), a collection of somber meditations which includes the prose work "No Man Is an Island." At this time he also wrote two poems of hopeful resignation, "Hymn to God the Father" and "Hymn to God My God, in My Sicknesse." Donne's last and most famous sermon, *Deaths Duell,* was preached before Charles I during Lent, 1631 and was published the following year. Izaak Walton stated that Donne, by then clearly a dying man, appeared so gaunt before the congregation and spoke in such a weakened voice that many believed they had witnessed a man who *"preach't his own Funeral Sermon."* Walton also recorded that shortly after delivering this final sermon, Donne commissioned a portrait rendered of himself dressed in his burial shroud. Lying thus enshrouded upon his sickbed, Donne meditated upon the completed likeness during the few remaining weeks of his life. After his death, his body was interred in St. Paul's beneath a monument modeled on the deathbed portrait. (This statue was the only such monument to survive the fire that swept St. Paul's in 1666, and it may still be viewed today.)

Commentators note that Donne excelled in both poetry and prose. There was no definitive edition of Donne's poetry until H. J. C. Grierson's edition appeared in 1912. While settling questions of spelling, authenticity, and misattribution, Grierson's *Poems of John Donne* also divided the poems into the categories by which they are discussed today: among them *Songs and Sonets, Elegies,* and *Holy Sonnets.* Having studied the poems, N. J. C. Andreasen described Donne as a "conservative revolutionary," demonstrating that as a poet he worked firmly within a Christian and traditional framework throughout his career. Those poems deemed his best, the *Songs and Sonets*—notably "The Canonization," "The Ecstasie," "A Valediction: Forbidding Mourning," and "The Flea"—abound in the unexpected metaphors, original imagery, startling paradoxes, and avoidance of poetic diction for which the Metaphysicals are known, all voiced in a tone of immediacy and passion in which thought and feeling are intimately melded. In "The Flea," for example, the speaker seeks to coax a desirable woman to his bed, telling her that the flea she just caught has sucked her blood as well as his; their blood has already been mixed within the flea, foreshadowing—he hopes and hints—a more complete and enjoyable intercourse to come. Donne's *Elegies* are praised for similar qualities, as are the *Anniversaries,* "A Valediction: Forbidding Mourning," and "Goodfriday 1613: Riding Westward," with this last-named poem being considered one of the poet's most richly symbolic meditations upon mortality. Also considered intriguing in its use of imagery is "Hymn to God My God, in My Sicknesse," in which Donne likens his prone, diseased body to a map which doctors, like explorers, have been recently and intimately scrutinizing.

Donne's sermons and devotions are considered eloquent witnesses to a mind attuned to Christian orthodoxy, the style demanded of seventeenth-century religious writing, and the imagery and concerns congenial to the common man of the day. At times the imagery evoked is shocking to twentieth-century readers unaccustomed to the strict doctrines and pulpit style of Jacobean Anglicanism. *Deaths Duell,* with its relentless return to the theme of life as a deceptive prelude to death, is sometimes considered especially so. As with the poetry, though, cultural allowances must be made to enable readers to discern Donne's skill—in this case, in introducing, developing, illustrating, and concluding his exposition in *Deaths Duell* and the other religious writings. As a seventeenth-century divine, Donne has been judged a worthy successor to the accomplished Lancelot Andrewes, with some calling him Andrewes's superior.

The critical history of Donne's works is a checkered one. The first collection of Donne's poetry was not published until two years after the author's death, the poems having previously circulated in manuscript only. Entitled *Poems* (1633), this collection was prefaced with elegies by Walton, Thomas Carew, and other contemporaries of Donne. These writers represented one side of early criticism of Donne's poetry—those who honored Donne as a master—with Carew eloquently lamenting the passing of *"a King, that rul'd as hee thought fit / the universall Monarchy of wit,"* and Walton later writing his insightful—if perhaps overly reverent—life of Donne as a preface to the latter's *LXXX Sermons* (1640). Another early view was first voiced by Ben Jonson in his famous recorded conversations with William Drummond of Hawthornden. While giving much praise to Donne's poetry, Jonson also faulted it for its profanity and innovative meter and disparaged the first *Anniversarie* as obsequious. Jonson's criticisms, expressed to Drummond in 1618 or 1619, were adopted and developed by critics of Donne's poetry for nearly the next two centuries. In his "A Discourse on the Original and Progress of Poetry" (1693), John Dryden used the term "metaphysical" for the first time to describe Donne's poetry, characterizing Donne as more a wit than a poet. Other critics seized upon this criticism over the next decades, with Samuel Johnson eventually writing a crushing critique of Donne's poetry in his "Life of Cowley" (1779). In this famous essay, Johnson used the term "metaphysical" as a term of abuse to describe poets whose aim, he believed, was to show off their own cleverness and learning and to construct paradoxes so outlandish and inadvertantly pretentious as to be ludicrous, indecent, or both. Predominantly negative assessments of Donne's poetry continued into the early nineteenth century, with William Hazlitt, writing in 1819, being one of the last major critics to affirm Johnson's condemnation of Donne's work.

The early nineteenth century saw growing critical and popular interest in and acceptance of Donne's poetry. Samuel Taylor Coleridge, Robert Browning, and Thomas De Quincey were especially instrumental in focusing a favorable light on the works: Coleridge praised the power and vivacity of the poems; Browning wrote what G. K. Chesterton later described as "poetry which utters the primeval and indivisible emotions" in a manner reminiscent of Donne—whom Browning acknowledged publicly as a major influence; and De Quincey turned aside Johnson's arguments, hailing Donne's skill as a rhetorician. Donne's complete works were published in 1839, and thus the sermons and devotions began to be discussed, while several editions of the poems appeared throughout the century. Edmund Gosse's *Life and Letters of Dr. John Donne, Dean of St. Paul's* (1899), the first biography of Donne since Walton's "Life" of 1640, prepared the way for Grierson's definitive edition of the poems, published in 1912. Major literary figures—including Arthur Symons, Leslie Stephen, Lytton Strachey, Walter de la Mare, and Rupert Brooke—reviewed these works at length, bolstering a period of popular and critical interest in Donne. In 1921, T. S. Eliot wrote a major article, "The Metaphysical Poets," in which he focused attention on Donne and the Metaphysicals as poets of signal stature who had been to their age what the twentieth-century Modernists were to theirs. Like the Modernists, who were constructing complex, distanced poetry to reflect the spiritual vacuum at the center of modern life, Eliot argued, the Metaphysicals had written complex, emotionally charged celebrations of the joys, sorrows, and dilemmas of their own age, an age of both fleshliness and faith. Not all criticism of Donne's work was favorable at this time, however. C. S. Lewis, for example, a literary traditionalist and longtime nemesis of Eliot, found the love poetry vastly overrated, while several other commentators faulted the meter, structure, and subject matter of selected poems.

From mid-century to the present day, Donne's canon has been scrutinized according to the methods of various critical schools, with representatives of the New Critics, the deconstructionists, and others offering diverse interpretations of the works. Critics of the stature of Lionel Trilling, I. A. Richards, and Cleanth Brooks have commented on Donne's poetry. In addition, twentieth-century writers have used phrases from Donne's poetry to adorn their own works in the form of epigrams and titles. A phrase from Donne's best-known religious devotion was adopted by Ernest Hemingway as the title of his novel of the Spanish Civil War, *For Whom the Bell Tolls.* (Hemingway later told one correspondent that Donne's works were rife with such lines for use by authors searching for titles for their works.) And as the title of one of his better-known essays on the Christian life, Lewis used the last four words of one poem's opening line, "What if this Present were the world's last night?"—and used the entire line as his essay theme.

Once considered the story of an abrupt transformation from worldly audacity to Christian conformity, Donne's life and career are today seen in terms of an artistically sensitive man's spiritual growth in a lifelong search for meaning and wholeness. That there was a break between the younger Donne who wrote the gay *Songs and Sonets*, the Donne of middle years who wrote to please his patrons and gain favor with influential readers, and the older Donne so much concerned with the meaning of sanctification is undeniable. But there is evidence that Donne was deeply interested in spiritual truths throughout his life, and it is certain that he did not abandon poetry altogether after taking clerical orders. Further, it has been emphasized that the modern reader of Donne's poems and the interpreter of his life must take into account the cultural mores and atmosphere of Donne's age: a time when the sensual and the solemnly spiritual were comfortably married in English society; a time of devastating plagues in which a widespread sense of life's brevity and fleeting beauty was acknowledged; a time of schism and doubt as people in a once-Roman Catholic nation searched for certainty in a land now under the control of a state church and a spiritual leader of questionable spiritual authority. As a poet, Donne served as the inspiration to an entire school of poets—"the School of Donne"—who collectively wrote some of the most accomplished religious poetry in English history. He is seen as the forerunner of many modern poets, notably those Modernist innovators of the first half of the twentieth century. Frank Kermode has praised Donne as "at least as original and idiosyncratic" as his near-contemporaries Edmund Spenser and William Shakespeare. Perhaps Carew, writing three centuries earlier, wrote the most succinct and eloquent summary of Donne's accomplishment, concluding his elegy: *"Here lie two Flamens, and both those, the best, / Apollo's first, at last, the true Gods Priest."*

(For further information about Donne's life and works, see *Literature Criticism from 1400 to 1800*, Vol. 10 and *Poetry Criticism*, Vol. 1.)

CRITICAL COMMENTARY

JOHN DRYDEN
(essay date 1693)

[Regarded by many as the father of modern English poetry and criticism, Dryden dominated literary life in England during the last four decades of the seventeenth century. By deliberately and comprehensively refining the language of Elizabethan England in all his works, he developed an expressive, universal diction that has had immense impact on the development of speech and writing in Great Britain and North America. In the following excerpt from his 1693 "Discourse on the Original and Progress of Satire," an essay dedicated to Charles, Earl of Dorset and Middlesex, Dryden first compares the poetry of Dorset and Donne—to Donne's disadvantage. He then faults Donne's skill as a Horatian satirist, finding him more a wit than a poet.]

There is not an English writer this day living, who is not perfectly convinced that your Lordship excels all others in all the several parts of poetry which you have undertaken to adorn. (p. 18)

Donne alone, of all our countrymen, had your talent; but was not happy enough to arrive at your versification; and were he translated into numbers, and English, he would yet be wanting in the dignity of expression. That which is the prime virtue, and chief ornament, of Virgil, which distinguishes him from the rest of writers, is so conspicuous in your verses, that it casts a shadow on all your contemporaries; we cannot be seen, or but obscurely, while you are present. You equal Donne in the variety, multiplicity, and choice of thoughts; you excel him in the manner and the words. I read you both with the same admiration, but not with the same delight. He affects the metaphysics, not only

Principal Works

Pseudo-Martyr (essay) 1610

Ignatius His Conclave; or His Inthronisation in a Late Election in Hell: wherein many things are mingled by way of satyr; concerning the disposition of Jesuits, the creation of a new hell, the establishing of a church in the moone (essay) 1611

*The First Anniversarie. An Anatomie of the World. Wherein By Occasion Of the untimely death of Mistris Elizabeth Drury, the frailtie and decay of this whole World is represented (poetry) 1611

*The Second Anniversarie. Of the Progres of the Soule. Wherein, By Occasion Of the Religious death of Mistris Elizabeth Drury, the incommodities of the Soule in this life, and her exaltation in the next, are Contemplated (poetry) 1612

Devotions upon Emergent Occasions, and Severall steps in my sickness (devotions) 1624

Deaths Duell; or A Consolation to the Soul against the Dying Life, and Living Death of the Body (sermon) 1632

Juvenilia; or, Certaine paradoxes, and problems (prose) 1633

†Poems (poetry) 1633

LXXX Sermons (sermons) 1640

ΒΙΑΘΑΝΑΤΟΣ. A declaration of that paradoxe, or thesis, that self-homicide is not so naturally sinne, that it may never be otherwise. Wherein the nature, and the extent of all those lawes, which seeme to be violated by this act, are diligently surveyed (essay) 1646

‡Essayes in Divinity (essays) 1652

Works. 6 vols. (poetry, essays, sermons, devotions, epistles, and prose) 1839

Selected Passages from the Sermons (sermons) 1919

The Showing forth of Christ: Sermons of John Donne (sermons) 1964

*These works are collectively referred to as The Anniversaries.

†In later centuries, this first edition of Donne's poetry was succeeded by other, more authoritative editions, notably those issued in 1895 and 1912. H. J. C. Grierson's 1912 edition is considered definitive. It contains Songs and Sonets, Epigrams, Elegies, Heroicall Epistle, Epithalamions, Satyres, Letters to Severall Personages, An Anatomie of the World, Of the Progresse of the Soule, Epicedes and Obsequies upon the Deaths of Sundry Personages, Epitaphs, Infinitati Sacrum, Divine Poems, Holy Sonnets, Donne's Latin poems and translations, and poems of questionable authorship attributed to Donne in early editions.

‡This work was published with a 1652 printing of Juvenilia; or, Certaine paradoxes, and problems.

---

in his satires, but in his amorous verses, where nature only should reign; and perplexes the minds of the fair sex with nice speculations of philosophy, when he should engage their hearts, and entertain them with the softnesses of love.

• • • • •

'Tis but necessary, that after so much has been said of Satire some definition of it should be given. Heinsius, in his dissertations on Horace, makes it for me, in these words: 'Satire is a kind of poetry, without a series of action, invented for the purging of our minds; in which human vices, ignorance, and errors, and all things besides, which are produced from them in every man, are severely reprehended; partly dramatically, partly simply, and sometimes in both kinds of speaking; but, for the most part, figuratively, and occultly; consisting in a low familiar way, chiefly in a sharp and pungent manner of speech; but partly, also, in a facetious and civil way of jesting; by which either hatred, or laughter, or indignation, is moved.'—Where I cannot but observe, that this obscure and perplexed definition, or rather description, of satire, is wholly accommodated to the Horatian way; and excluding the works of Juvenal and Persius, as foreign from that kind of poem. The clause in the beginning of it *without a series*

of action distinguishes satire properly from stage-plays, which are all of one action, and one continued series of action. The end or scope of satire is to purge the passions; so far it is common to the satires of Juvenal and Persius. The rest which follows is also generally belonging to all three; till he comes upon us, with the excluding clause *consisting in a low familiar way of speech,* which is the proper character of Horace; and from which the other two, for their honour be it spoken, are far distant. But how come lowness of style, and the familiarity of words, to be so much the propriety of satire, that without them a poet can be no more a satirist, than without risibility he can be a man? Is the fault of Horace to be made the virtue and standing rule of this poem? Is the *grande sophos* of Persius, and the sublimity of Juvenal, to be circumscribed with the meanness of words and vulgarity of expression? If Horace refused the pains of numbers, and the loftiness of figures, are they bound to follow so ill a precedent? Let him walk afoot, with his pad in his hand, for his own pleasure; but let not them be accounted no poets, who choose to mount, and show their horsemanship. . . . Would not Donne's *Satires*, which abound with so much wit, appear more charming, if he had taken care of his words, and of his numbers? But he followed Horace so very close, that of necessity he must fall with him; and I may safely say it of this present age, that if we are not so great wits as Donne, yet certainly we are better poets. (pp. 100-02)

John Dryden, "A Discourse Concerning the Original and Progress of Satire," in his *Essays of John Dryden, Vol. II,* edited by W. P. Ker, Oxford at the Clarendon Press, 1900, pp. 15-114.

SAMUEL JOHNSON
(essay date 1779)

[Johnson wrote two landmark works in the history of English thought and criticism: *Dictionary of the English Language* (1755) and *Prefaces, Biographical and Critical, to the Works of the English Poets* (10 vols., 1779-81; reissued in 1783 as *The Lives of the Most Eminent English Poets*). In the following excerpt from an essay originally published in the first edition of his *Lives,* Johnson describes and denigrates the metaphysical poets, using "metaphysical" as a term of abuse. He illustrates his argument with examples from Donne's poetry.]

Wit, like all other things subject by their nature to the choice of man, has its changes and fashions, and at different times takes different forms. About the beginning of the seventeenth century appeared a race of writers that may be termed the metaphysical poets; of whom, in a criticism on the works of Cowley, it is not improper to give some account.

The metaphysical poets were men of learning, and to show their learning was their whole endeavour; but, unluckily resolving to shew it in rhyme, instead of writing poetry, they only wrote verses, and very often such verses as stood the trial of the finger better than of the ear; for the modulation was so imperfect, that they were only found to be verses by counting the syllables.

If the father of criticism has rightly denominated poetry *an imitative art,* these writers will, without great wrong, . . . lose their right to the name of poets; for they cannot be said to have imitated any thing; they neither copied nature nor life; neither painted the forms of matter, nor represented the operations of intellect.

Those, however, who deny them to be poets, allow them to be wits. Dryden confesses of himself and his contemporaries, that they fall below Donne in wit, but maintains that they surpass him in poetry. (pp. 12-13)

Critical remarks are not easily understood without examples; and I have therefore collected instances of the modes of writing by which this species of poets,

for poets they were called by themselves and their admirers, was eminently distinguished.

As the authors of this race were perhaps more desirous of being admired than understood, they sometimes drew their conceits from recesses of learning not very much frequented by common readers of poetry. (p. 16)

Thus *Donne* shews his medicinal knowledge in some encomiastick verses ['**To the Countesse of Bedford. "Madame, reason is"** ']:

In every thing there naturally grows
A Balsamum to keep it fresh and new,
If 'twere not injur'd by extrinsique blows;
Your youth and beauty are this balm in you.
But you, of learning and religion,
And virtue and such ingredients, have made
A mithridate, whose operation
Keeps off, or cures what can be done or said.

Though the following lines of Donne [from '**To the Countesse of Bedford "This twilight of "** '], on the last night of the year, have something in them too scholastick, they are not inelegant:

This twilight of two years, not past nor next,
Some emblem is of me, or I of this,
Who, meteor-like, of stuff and from perplext,
Whose what and where, in disputation is,
If I should call me any thing, should miss.

I sum the years and me, and find me not
Debtor to th' old, nor creditor to th' new,
That cannot say, my thanks I have forgot,
Nor trust I this with hopes; and yet scarce true
This bravery is, since these times shew'd me
    you. . . .

Yet more abstruse and profound is *Donne's* reflection upon Man as a Microcosm [in '**To Mr. R. W. "If as mine is"** ']:

If men be worlds, there is in every one
Something to answer in some proportion
All the world's riches: and in good men, this
Virtue our form's form, and our soul's soul is.

(p. 17)

The tears of lovers are always of great poetical account; but Donne has extended them into worlds. If the lines [which follow, from '**A Valediction: of weeping**'] are not easily understood, they may be read again.

On a round ball
A workman, that hath copies by, can lay
An Europe, Afric, and an Asia,
And quickly make that, which was nothing, all.

So doth each tear,
Which thee doth wear,
A globe, yea world, by that impression grow,
Till thy tears mixt with mine do overflow

This world, by waters sent from thee my heaven
dissolved so.

On reading the following lines [from **'An Epithalamion, Or mariage Song on the Lady Elizabeth, and
Count Palatine being married on St. Valentine's
day'**], the reader may perhaps cry out—*Confusion worse
confounded.*

Here lies a she sun, and a he moon there,
She gives the best light to his sphere,
Or each is both, and all, and so
They unto one another nothing owe.

(pp. 19-20)

Who but Donne would have thought that a good
man is a telescope?

Though God be our true glass, through which we see
All, since the being of all things is he,
Yet are the trunks, which do to us derive
Things, in proportion fit, by perspective
Deeds of good men; for by their living here,
Virtues, indeed remote, seem to be near.

(p. 20)

That prayer and labour should co-operate, are
thus taught by Donne:

In none but us, are such mixt engines found,
As hands of double office: for the ground
We till with them; and them to heaven we raise;
Who prayerless labours, or without this, prays,
Doth but one half, that's none.

By the same author, a common topick, the danger
of procrastination, is thus illustrated:

—That which I should have begun
In my youth's morning, now late must be done;
And I, as giddy travellers must do,
Which stray or sleep all day, and having lost
Light and strength, dark and tir'd, must then ride
post.

All that Man has to do is to live and die; the sum
of humanity is comprehended by Donne in the following lines:

Think in how poor a prison thou didst lie;
After, enabled but to suck and cry.
Think, when 'twas grown to most, 'twas a poor inn,
A province pack'd up in two yards of skin,
And that usurp'd, or threaten'd with a rage
Of sicknesses, or their true mother, age.
But think that death hath now enfranchis'd thee;
Thou hast thy expansion now, and liberty;
Think, that a rusty piece discharg'd is flown
In pieces, and the bullet is his own,
And freely flies: this to thy soul allow,
Think thy shell broke, think thy soul hatch'd but
now.

They were sometimes [as in **'Twicknam garden'**]
indelicate and disgusting. (pp. 24-5)

Hither with crystal vials, lovers, come,
And take my tears, which are Love's wine,
And try your mistress' tears at home;
For all are false, that taste not just like mine.

This [from **'Elegie VIII. The Comparison'**] is yet
more indelicate:

As the sweet sweat of roses in a still,
As that which from chaf'd musk-cat's pores doth
trill,
As the almighty balm of th' early East;
Such are the sweat-drops of my mistress' breast.
And on her neck her skin such lustre sets,
They seem no sweat-drops, but pearl coronets:
Rank sweaty froth thy mistress' brow defiles.

(p. 26)

To the following comparison [in **'A Valediction:
forbidding mourning'**] of a man that travels, and his
wife that stays at home, with a pair of compasses, it
may be doubted whether absurdity or ingenuity has
the better claim:

Our two souls therefore, which are one,
Though I must go, endure not yet
A breach, but an expansion,
Like gold to airy thinness beat.

If they be two, they are two so
As stiff twin-compasses are two;
Thy soul the fixt foot, makes no show
To move, but doth, if th' other do.

And though it in the centre sit,
Yet when the other far doth roam,
It leans, and hearkens after it,
And grows erect, as that comes home.

Such wilt thou be to me, who must
Like th' other foot, obliquely run.
Thy firmness makes my circle just,
And makes me end, where I begun.

In all these examples it is apparent, that whatever
is improper or vicious, is produced by a voluntary deviation from nature in pursuit of something new and
strange; and that [Donne and the metaphysical] writers
fail to give delight, by their desire of exciting admiration. (p. 28)

Samuel Johnson, "Cowley," in his *Lives of the English Poets, Vol.
I,* 1906. Reprint by Oxford University Press, 1955-56, pp.
1-53.

T. S. ELIOT

(essay date 1923)

[An Anglo-American critic, Eliot is closely identified with many of the qualities denoted by the term Modernism: experimentation, formal complexity, artistic and intellectual eclecticism, and a classicist's view of the artist working at an emotional distance from his creation. He was one of the key revivifiers of modern critical interest in metaphysical poetry, thanks largely to his seminal essay "The Metaphysical Poets," originally published in 1921 and later reprinted in his *Selected Essays* (1932; see Sources for Further Study). In the following excerpt from a review of *Love Poems of John Donne*, he argues that in his works Donne reflected the preoccupations and intellectual tone of his day in a manner that foreshadows the work of the twentieth-century Modernists.]

One of the characteristics of Donne which wins him, I fancy, his interest for the present age, is his fidelity to emotion as he finds it; his recognition of the complexity of feeling and its rapid alterations and antitheses. A change of feeling, with Donne, is rather the regrouping of the same elements under a mood which was previously subordinate: it is not the substitution of one mood for a wholly different one.

Impossible to isolate his ecstasy, his sensuality, and his cynicism.

With sincerity in the practical sense, poetry has little to do; the poet is responsible to a much more difficult consciousness and honesty. And it is because he has this honesty, because he is so often expressing his genuine whole of tangled feelings, that Donne is, like the early Italians, like Heine, like Baudelaire, a poet of the world's literature.

There are two ways in which we may find a poet to be modern: he may have made a statement which is true everywhere and for all time (so far as "everywhere" and "for all time" have meaning), or there may be an accidental relationship between his mind and our own. The latter is fashion; we are all susceptible to fashion in literature as in everything else, and we all require some indulgence for it. The age of Donne, and the age of Marvell, are sympathetic to us, and it demands a considerable effort of dissociation to decide to what degree we are deflected toward him by local or temporary bias.

The age objects to the heroic and sublime, and it objects to the simplification and separation of the mental faculties. The objections are largely well grounded, and react against the nineteenth century; they are partly—how far I do not inquire—a product of the popularization of the study of mental phenomena. Ethics having been eclipsed by psychology, we accept the belief that any state of mind is extremely complex, and chiefly composed of odds and ends in constant flux manipulated by desire and fear. When, therefore, we find a poet who neither suppresses nor falsifies, and who expresses complicated states of mind, we give him welcome. And when we find his poetry containing everywhere potential or actual *wit*, our thirst has been relieved.

Neither the fantastic (Clevelandism is becoming popular) nor the cynical nor the sensual occupies an excessive importance with Donne; the elements in his mind had an order and congruity. The range of his feeling was great, but no more remarkable than its unity. He was altogether present in every thought and in every feeling. It is the same kind of unity as pervades the work of Chapman, for whom thought is an intense feeling which is one with every other feeling. Compared with these men, almost every nineteenth-century English poet is in some way limited or deformed.

Our appreciation of Donne must be an appreciation of what we lack, as well as of what we have in common with him. What is true of his mind is true, in different terms, of his language and versification. A style, a rhythm, to be significant, must embody a significant mind, must be produced by the necessity of a new form for a new content. . . . The dogmatic slumbers of the last hundred years are broken, and the chaos must be faced: we cannot return to sleep and call it order, and we cannot have any order but our own, but from Donne and his contemporaries we can draw instruction and encouragement. (p. 332)

T. S. Eliot, "John Donne," in *The Nation and the Athenaeum*, Vol. XXXIII, No. 10, June 9, 1923, pp. 331-32.

KATHLEEN RAINE

(essay date 1945)

[Raine is an English poet, essayist, autobiographer, and translator. In the following excerpt, she examines Donne's poetry as a reflection of a life lived at the intersection of the medieval age of faith and spirituality and the modern age of doubt and materialism.]

It is now for an entire literary generation that the metaphysical poets have seemed to have the clue to our own situation. It is not difficult to see why. For we, probably the most unhappy, and certainly the most torn by conflict, of all the generations since the seventeenth century, have to make a choice, as they had, between the desirable but doomed, and the less desirable but inevitable. To make a choice, or to find a solution. Whether one sees in Baroque art a resolved or an unresolved conflict, a consideration of what that conflict essentially was, cannot fail to compel our respect for the intellectual courage, not to say heroism, of the poet John Donne, who among other great figures of the Baroque period felt its full impact, and held in equipoise, even if only for a moment, those forces of change that in a few years transformed the medieval into the modern world. (p. 371)

Those who saw the turn of the sixteenth century, saw the passing of the Renaissance into the first dawning of the centuries of the Common Man, in the beginnings of Puritanism; they saw the last, superb expression of the ancient faith in Spanish Baroque art, and the Spanish Baroque saints; the highest point ever attained in Christian mysticism, in the period of Saint Teresa of Avila and Saint John of the Cross (both also poets) came late in the sixteenth century. Saint Teresa died in 1582, St. John in 1591. But Copernicus had already set the round earth in motion, and the little world of his new astronomy was already a diminished part in an expanding universe, and Europe itself a diminishing part of a world in which America was already appearing on the western horizon. The medieval world and the modern, the setting and the rising stars, were in the sky together, for those who would to compare the values that had shaped the human world of the past, with those that were to shape its future.

As the rift between the spiritual and the material values widened, the Great picked sides. England was then the great protagonist of the modern, Spain of the ancient, order. And in this polarity, English thought and poetry were strong influenced by Spanish for the first and last time in history. The metaphysical poets are the fruits of this close contact with Spain, and that at a time when both countries were in their golden age. (p. 372)

What was great in the Baroque poets was that they did not underrate either kind of truth. They tried to hold the two hemispheres (the very word is characteristic of Baroque poetry) together, and if even partially they succeeded, their achievement was a tremendous one. Then, as now, the price of seeing too clearly both systems of value, was conflict and unhappiness. But then, as now, neither the revolutionary nor the reactionary, both of whom see things more simply, was wholly civilized.

The greatness of Baroque art, therefore, may be seen to be not in its destructive element, but in its attempt to reconcile those kinds of knowledge that at certain times seem impossible to reconcile, except in art.

Professor Edouardo Sarmiento, writing of Spanish Baroque art, point out how, the counter-reformation notwithstanding, even in Catholic Spain, this sense of strain reveals a latent doubt, disbelief, and loss of faith. 'If we may believe', he writes, 'the involuntary evidence of the art-style of an age for the state of its soul, then we cannot doubt that some such diagnosis of the Spanish counter-reform is true. The Baroque bears the stigmata of disbelief, anxiety and decadence, as certainly as the Gothic bears marks of faith, joy, and vigour.'

The strain characteristic of Baroque art is typically expressed in the use of perspective. In Baroque painting, the human figure is by this means seen to stand not firmly anchored to the earth, but is represented in often tormented and sensational attitudes rising towards heaven, or some other infinite point introduced into the composition by this exaggeration of perspective. (p. 374)

This may seem to be a digression from the subject—the metaphysical poetry of John Donne. But it is not so. For in poetry, a comparable attempt to bring together into focus the finite and the infinite, is the typical metaphysical figure, common to English and Spanish baroque poets, the conceit. Like the Baroque façade, this is not, as it might appear, a merely decorative device, but an attempt, in poetry, to harness together the tremendous forces of the temporal and the eternal, felt, as they were at the time, to be pulling apart. Here is a piece of John Donne from the poem **'Goodfriday 1613—Riding Westward'**, in which the space—the literal physical poles of the earth—are straining against the Christian image.

> Let mans Soule be a Spheare, and then, in this,
> The intelligence that moves, devotion is,
> And as the other Spheares, by being growne
> Subject to forraigne motions, lose their owne,
> And being by others hurried every day,
> Scarce in a yeare their naturall forme obey:
> Pleasure or businesse, so, our Soules admit
> For their first mover, and are whirld by it.
> Hence is't, that I am carryed towards the West
> This day, when my Soules forme bends towards the
>   East.
> There I should see a Sunne, by rising set,
> And by that setting endlesse day beget;
> But that Christ on this Crosse, did rise and fall,
> Sinne had eternally benighted all.

In this poem, Donne achieves something, in poetic terms very like the *Transparente* of Spanish Baroque architecture. The static image of Christ, the earth's fixed centre, is harnessed to the whirling image of the Copernican movement of the revolving earth, the moving spheres.

> Could I behold those hands which span the Poles,

And tune all spheares at once, pierc'd with those
   holes?
Could I behold that endless height which is
Zenith to us, and our Antipodes,
Humbled below us? or that blood which is
The seat of all our Soules, if not of his,
Made durt of dust, or that flesh which was worne
By God, for his apparell, rag'd, and torne?

The tension is immense. But the poem holds as it intends to hold, the two orders of reality together, not scientifically, or theologically, but as poetry—the only force perhaps that can harness together truths of different orders.

That is an extreme example of the constant characteristic of the conceit, which is to bring together, using as a focal point some light similarity between them, sharply contrasting images, belonging, often, to different orders of reality (as in the passage just quoted). Other figures are commonly used to accomplish the same end. Of metaphysical poems it is less the figures used than the purpose they serve that is characteristic.

In this other quoted passage from **'The Relique'**, it is not science and the image of Christ that pull apart and are held by the conceit, but that other basic conflict that tormented the Baroque period, the paradox of life and death, sex and corruption.

When my grave is broke up againe
Some second ghest to entertaine,
(For graves have learn'd that woman-head
To be to more than one a Bed)
And he that digs it, spies
A bracelet of bright haire about the bone,

Will he not let'us alone,
And thinks that there a loving couple lies,
Who thought that this device might be some way
To make their soules, at the last busie day,
Meet at this grave, and make a little stay?

There are other subsidiary antitheses; there is the juxtaposition of the old half-legendary medievalism, Adam and Eve in the Garden of Eden, Noah and the flood and the rest—with the new Copernican pattern of the world (pp. 375-77)

Or again, the microcosm and the macrocosm are harnessed together in an image that recurs often in Donne, of life as land, death as sea:

Man is the world, and death the ocean
To which God gives the lower parts of men.
This sea invirons all land though as yet
God hath set marks and bounds twixt us and it,
Yet doth it rore and gnaw, and still pretend,
And breaks our banks whenere it takes a friend,
Then our land waters (tears of passion) vent,
Our waters, then above the firmament
(Tears which our Soul doth for her sins let fall)

Take all a brakish taste, and funerall.

'My America, my newfound land,' Donne called his mistress. One meets everywhere images of latitude and longitude, lengthening and shortening shadows: the new Copernican framework of the universe. Superimposed on the human measure of the Christian myth with eternity and infinity, God-in-man, at the centre, is a new order in which eternity and infinity are being banished to the circumference of an expanding universe, no longer infinitely present, but infinitely remote. (p. 377)

Want of beauty is a charge that has been made against Donne's poetry; and in a certain sense with justice. For the worlds of beauty and of reality, too, were pulling apart at the turn of the century. Shakespeare wrote in a language at once near the real speech of men, and equally capable of speaking for that inner voice of the soul (heard all too often in the nineteenth century), for the two were not very different in an age when soldiers like Sydney and Essex, and seamen like Sir Walter Raleigh found it natural to be poets. But at the turn of the century, Shakespeare himself wrote:

Truth may see, but cannot be,
Beauty brag, but 'tis not she,
Truth and beauty buried be.

Donne spoke a language stripped of magic, bare, in that sense, of beauty. Milton inherited the beauty, but no longer wrote poetry in a language that men spoke. One might see in this division, too, another symptom of the repression of the soul. (p. 379)

Each poem that he wrote is like a finely poised needle, suspended between the great magnets of science and religion, action and learning, the pleasures of love, the call to martyrdom; the infirm glory of the greatest court on earth; and the annihilation of all in death. The needle, for Donne, comes to rest only when it points to the one true North—that of love. And for Donne, as for Dante, it was through woman's love that his way lay towards the divine love that was his final point of rest.

In two of his longer works, we can see Donne's speculative mind at work in a way essentially modern, on changes of the medieval pattern of thought. **'The Progresse of the Soule,'** written in 1601, and one of Donne's finest poems, combines the Garden of Eden myth with a fine intuitive forecasting of modern biological theory. The transmigration of a 'soul', beginning its life in an apple on the tree of Eden, and ending just as it reached the human level (rather in mid-air, as Donne did not finish the poem as he had originally planned it) are traced from plant to bird, to fish, whale, elephant, dog, ape, and finally to man. Donne having no theory of science to prove cannot be blamed if the order is a little out at one or two places. But that the 'progresse' in the poem is so close to the picture that

Darwin later established, is a measure of the natural scientific bent of Donne's mind. And all this is combined in a series of Duerer-like pictures of plant and animal life, suggesting the herbals and bestiaries of the middle ages, in which walks Eve herself, as true to life as detail can make her; her mythical figure pulls up a real mandrake plant to give, as medicine, to a real baby. Like Duerer, Donne makes the myth credible by the realism of the detail.

Nine years later; in 1610, Donne wrote *Ignatius his Conclave.* This satire is amusing reading even now; Donne describes his 'vision', in which

> I had liberty to wander through all places and to survey and reckon all the roomes, and all the volumes of the heavens, and to comprehend the situation, the dimensions, the nature, the people, and the policy, both of the swimming Islands, the *Planets* and of all those which are fixed in the firmament. Of which, I thinke it an honester part as yet to be silent, than to do *Galileo* wrong by speaking of it, who of late hath summoned the other worlds, the Stars to come nearer to him and give him an account of themselves. Or to *Keppler,* who as himselfe testifies of himselfe, ever since Tycho Braches death hath received it into his care, that no new thing should be done in heaven without his knowledge.

'In the twinkling of an eye', writes Donne,

> I saw all the roomes in Hell open to my sight. And by the benefit of certaine spectacles, I know not of what making, but I thinke, of the same, by which *Gregory,* the great, and *Beda* did discerne so distinctly the soules of their friends, when they were discharged from their bodies, and sometimes the soules of such men as they knew not by sight, and of some that never were in the world, and yet they could distinguish them flying into Heaven, or conversing with living men, I saw all the channels in the bowels of the Earth; and all the inhabitants of all nations, and of all ages were suddenly made familiar to me. I think truely, *Robert Aquinas* when he tooke *Christs* long Oration, as he hung upon the Crosse, did use some such instrument as this, but applied to the eare; And so I thinke did he, which dedicated to *Adrian* 6, the Sermon which *Christ* made in prayse of his father *Joseph;* for else how did they heare that, which none but they ever heard?

To proceed, Donne describes how (in Hell that is) 'I saw a secret place, where there were not many, beside Lucifer himselfe; to which, onely they had title, which had so attempted any innovation in this life, that they gave an affront to all antiquitie, and induced doubts, and anxieties, and scruples, and after, a libertie of beleeving what they would; at length established opinions, directly contrary to all established before.'

Here we recognize, in comic dress, the same Baroque conflict of ideas, of new and uncontrollable ideas that are far-reaching enough quite to overturn the foundations of the world. There is very little comic Baroque art, but *Ignatius his Conclave* may be claimed as a rare example of this category.

In this imaginary 'hell' the Jesuits take a high place as the arch equivocators. Here Donne 'saw' St. Ignatius (like Jouvet, in monk's habit) standing very close to Lucifer himself, advising him on the cases of those pretenders who sought admission to Hell's most exalted rank, as distorters of the universe.

The pretenders and their claims are interesting. Copernicus puts his case: 'Shall these gates be open to such as have innovated in small matters? and shall they be shut against me, who have turned the whole frame of the world, and am thereby almost a new "Creator"?' Ignatius opposes his claim. 'Who cares', Ignatius asks, 'whether the earth travell, or stand still? Hath your raising up of the earth into heaven, brought men to that confidence, that they build new towers or threaten God againe? Or do they out of this motion of the earth conclude, that there is no hell, or deny the punishment of sin? Do not men beleeve? do they not live just, as they did before?' Also 'those opinions of yours may very well be true'—and that in itself must exclude Copernicus from the highest honours of Hell. In the light of subsequent history, one is inclined to think that Donne's Ignatius was premature in his conclusion that men went on living 'just as they did before' after Copernicus.

Paracelsus was excluded likewise, because such as his discoveries were, they were of minor importance. Machiavelli had a better case:

> although the entrance into his place may be decreed to none but the Innovators, and onely such of them as have dealt in *Christian* businesse; and of them also, to those only which have had the fortune to doe much harme, I cannot see but that next to the Jesuites, I must bee invited to enter, since I did not onely teach those wayes by which, through *perfidiousness* and *dissembling of Religion,* a man might possesse, and usurpe upon the liberty of free *Commonwealths;* but also did arme and furnish the people with my instructions, how when they were under this oppression, they might safeliest conspire, and remove a *tyrant* or revenge themselves of their *Prince,* and redeeme their former losses; so that from both sides, both from *Prince* and *People,* I brought an abundant harvest, and a noble increase to this kingdome. By this time I perceived *Lucifer* to bee much moved with this Oration, and to incline much towards *Machiavel.* For he did acknowledge him to bee a kind of *Patriarke,* of those whom they call *Laymen.* And he had long observed, that the *Clergie* of *Rome* tumbled downe to *Hell* daily, easily, voluntarily, and by troupes, because they were accustomed to sinne against their conscience, and knowledge; but that the *Layitie* sinning out of a slouthfulnesse, and negli-

gence of finding the truth, did rather offend by ignorance, and omission. And therefore he thought himselfe bound to reward *Machiavel,* which had awakened this drowsie and implicite *Layitie* to greater, and more bloody undertakings.

'Vision' or not, what Donne wrote had this much truth in it. These were ideas whose conflict was on an earthly plan 'inducing doubts, and anxieties, and scruples, and after, a liberty of believing what they would'. (pp. 381-84)

Donne's middle period—the years of poverty and worry that drove him to the necessity of a servility to possible patrons that became him very ill; in a series of always frustrated attempts to get back into a career of some sort—produced no poems as fine in their kind as the early *Songs and Sonnets,* or later *Holy Sonnets* and religious verse. But those he wrote at that time are revealing, bringing to light as they do the measure of the spiritual maladjustment of Donne to his world, and that world to itself; and the growing seriousness with which the poet now sought to find a solution for a problem whose implications he increasingly realized. The clue is to be found in **'The Anatomie of the World'** and the **'First and Second Anniversaries.** These ambitious poems, full of fine passages, have something deeply wrong about them, and are embarrassing reading even now. This is not so much because they were written to some extent (possibly, or partly) with an eye to getting a patron (which they did), but because they open a religious void that it is saddening to contemplate.

These Rilke-like poems were written, like the *Duino Elegies,* on the occasion of the untimely death of a young girl—a girl whom the poet had never seen—Miss Elizabeth Drury, only daughter of that Sir Robert Drury who was to be Donne's patron for a number of years. And if ever poems rang false, these do. 'If it had been written of the Virgin Mary it had been something,' Ben Jonson said of the **'Anatomie of the World'**—and he has put his finger on the very point of the weakness. They were not written of the Virgin Mary. They were, however (as Donne said), written 'of the idea of a woman, not as she was'. They were, in fact, a lamentable, trumped-up attempt to put a personal image and personal 'idea of a woman' in the place of the old and universal Christian pantheon—even of the Mother of God herself—who were gone from the empty niches of the reformed churches of England. This pompous, inflated, home-made improvisation tagged on to the corpse of Miss Elizabeth Drury reveals just how far adulation falls short of canonization. The root of medieval faith had been severed. Not one of the elegies that Donne wrote in succeeding years, attributing to the nobility and to princes virtues that they may have possessed, or may not, ever could bridge that gulf between the scepticism of the reform and the lost me-

dieval faith. They remain mere epitaphs: these poems, and all Donne's poetry of the grave and the dead, is like a dark after-image of the light of faith and bears to the medieval faith the skull-like resemblance that the negative photograph bears to the positive.

Donne did indeed, like an apostle not of faith but of mortality, put something in those empty niches, in those churches deserted by their saints. But not the carved angels, not the shrines of gothic saints. He hung those empty walls with emblems of mortality, urns, marmoreals, symbols of death and physical corruption; the pomp of the grave, not the symbols of life. These silent testimonies of doubt have, in the English churches, replaced the saints in their shrines. Donne was, of that tradition, one of the orginators, who left imprinted on the English Church its characteristic grand, but essential, though reluctant, scepticism. (pp. 386-87)

And yet there is greatness in the scepticism of the reform—for it is a relative, not an absolute scepticism that we find in the English Baroque; a scepticism that would fain believe, not one that belittles, with the diabolical 'spirit that denies'. One that does still, in fact, hold to the desirability of faith, and therewith, some faith also. (p. 388)

Two years after Donne's ordination, and four before his appointment as Dean of St. Paul's, Anne Donne died in giving birth to their twelfth child. If one sees the events of a life as stages of a pilgrimage, it is difficult not to see in Anne Donne's death as the departure of one of those legendary guides—like Dante's Virgil, or Beatrice, who stayed with the poet only until her work was accomplished, for now Donne had entered the last stage of his strange development. Henceforth his inner life was to be lived in relation only to God.

Look at the beginning of Donne's life—those love-poems, so subtly introspective, yet so worldly, so far from serious; at the portrait of Jack Donne at eighteen, the young man with the earrings, at the end of his three years at Cambridge; and look at the end—the eloquent divine, who, in the words of one critic, now 'put a trumpet to his lips'; who himself chose that posterity should remember him in the aspect of his death, the features burned out, the winding sheet tied about his face. How did the one change into the other? It happened imperceptibly, naturally. It is the same man. That unmistakable personal idiom, the rapid ardent sentences, the very imagery of the early love poems are found in the *Holy Sonnets*. The very imagery of erotic love is retained, and amplified into a symbolic language to speak of God, and to God.

Take mee to you, imprison me, for I
Except you enthrall mee, never shall be free,
Norever chast, except you ravish mee.

The first and the last poems that he wrote, use almost precisely the same images.

Donne indeed put a trumpet to his lips in those later years, when he preached at Paul's Cross, to the people, and before two kings—James I, and later King Charles—at Whitehall; when he summoned up the angels in Baroque imagery of unsurpassed grandeur—

> At the round earth's imagin'd corners, blow
> Your trumpets, Angells, and arise, arise
> From death, you numberlesse infinities
> Of soules, and to your scattred bodies goe,
> All whom flood did, and fire shall o'erthrow,
> All whom warre, dearth, age, agues, tyrannies,
> Despaire, law, chance, hath slaine, and you whose eyes,
> Shall behold God, and never tast deaths woe.

But a trumpet does not necessarily mean a release from doubts. With Donne, the light and shade was deeper, that was all, as his life declined from evening into night. In his youth, that we cannot know all seemed reason to doubt God; in his maturity, a reason for trusting Him. But as the noon of love darkened into the shadow of death, the witty scepticism of youth darkened into the agonizing doubts of age. It is still a poetry of doubt, of decline from faith, struggling to find certainty at the brink of the grave, that no other times of life, neither the love nor the learning of his prime, had yielded the poet. For all Donne's doubts gradually focused on one point—Death. As in loving women he was introspective, analysing his love, so in his sickness he analysed himself as thoroughly as Freud could ever have searched the submerged regions of instinct and the unconscious. If only he could have found the soul, and brought it out like an undiscovered organ! But deep as he might search, it was not to be found. The *Devotions on Sundrie Occasions* are in their way as searchingly introspective as the *Ascent of Mount Carmel*. But they are the voice of the body, the unconscious, the dark chaos of man, not his incandescence, as is St. John's great introspective analysis.

To pass over the twenty years of his preaching and ministry, we reach the story of Donne's death. In the winter of 1630, Donne was a dying man. He was too ill to preach at Christmas, but at the beginning of Lent, knowing that it was for the last time, he rose from his bed to preach perhaps his greatest sermon of all— *Death's Duell, or A Consolation to the Soul against the Dying Life, and Living Death of the Body.* This sermon was 'Delivered at Whitehall, before the King's Majesty' on 25 February, 1630, 'Being his last Sermon and called by His Majesties' Household, the Doctor's owne Funerall Sermon'. He took as his text the terrible sentence 'And unto God the Lord, belong the issues of death'. Here at its most sublime is that 'metaphysical shudder', the horror of mortality. (pp. 390-92)

But in the very toils of this death, Donne was to portray, as it has never before or since been portrayed in England in poetry, or in any other art, the scene of the Crucifixion, in a baroque magnificence comparable only to the painting of El Greco:

> There now hangs that sacred Body upon the Crosse, rebaptized in his owne teares and sweat, and embalmed in his owne blood alive. There are those bowells of compassion, which are so conspicuous, so manifested, as that you may see them through his wounds. There those glorious eyes grew faint in their light: so as the Sun ashamed to survive them, departed with his light too. And then that Sonne of God, who was never from us, and yet had now come a new way unto us in assuming our nature, delivers that soule (which was never out of his Father's hand) by a new way, a voluntary emission of it into his Father's hands; For though to his God our Lord, belong'd these issues of death, so that considered in his owne contract, he must necessarily die, yet at no breach or battery, which they had made upon his sacred Body, issued his soule, but emisit, hee gave up the Ghost, and as God breathed a soule into the first Adam, so this second Adam breathed his soule into God, into the hands of God. There wee leave you in that blessed dependancy, to hang upon him that hangs upon the Crosse, there bath in his teares, there suck at his woundes, and lie downe in peace in his grave, till hee vouchsafe you a resurrection, and an ascension into that Kingdome, which hee hath purchas'd for you, with the inestimable price of his incorruptible blood.

Here indeed we have doubt at its most heroic, redeemed by its own intensity, and achieving the stature of faith. For greater than a complacent belief in something trivial, is the doubt of something great. For to doubt is in itself to assert and establish the values doubted. So Baroque art takes its stature from medieval faith. Never again, perhaps, will a decline of faith produce anything comparable, for never again will the world have so much to lose, as the medieval Christian faith. Compared with the struggle with which then were relinquished the values of a passing age, it is frightening to see, in our period, with what ease, what lack of spiritual struggle, values are discarded. For the gulf that opens for us (in *Mein Kampf*, the Communist Manifesto, and our own and the American materialist Utopias) is as much deeper than Donne's relative doubt as medieval Christianity was higher than the liberal humanism that succeeded it, and is now in its turn the vanishing faith.

The image of Christ crucified is, of all the Christian images, the one that in itself contains the full paradox of human doubt and human faith, the focal point of temporal and eternal, at which the eternal is at once most essentially challenged, and most essentially triumphant. For Donne, the pull was not only away from faith, but also, with equal, and perhaps finally with greater strength, towards it. At the end of his life only two magnets retained any power over him—the image of the grave and the image of God.

In the seven weeks that lay between the preaching of *Death's Duell* and death itself, Donne prepared for his promised end, still seeking God with a courage equal to that of any saint who ever battled his way out of this world. (pp. 392-93)

To these last weeks also belong two of the greatest of his lyrical poems—the **'Hymne to God my God, in my sicknesse'**, and **'A Hymne to God the Father'**.

In the first Donne, for a moment echoing the faith of Saint John of the Cross who wrote of the soul:

Oh night more lovely than the day
Oh night that joined the beloved with her lover,
and changed her into her love,

writes like a mystic 'Since I am coming to that Holy roome Where, with thy Quire of Saints for evermore *I shall be made thy Musique'.*

He takes his last backward look on the world. How long ago it was that he had written of his mistress' body,

without sharp north, without declining west.

How long ago those voyages with Essex, long dead, to

P O E M S,

By J. D.

WITH

E L E G I E S

ON THE AUTHORS

D E A T H.

LONDON.
Printed by *M. F.* for I O H N M A R R I O T,
and are to be fold at his fhop in St *Dunftans*
Church-yard in *Fleet-ftreet.* 1 6 3 3.

Title page of Donne's first collection of poems.

Cadiz and the Azores! Now these images of life are seen down the lengthening perspective of death:

Whilst my Physitians by their love are growne
Cosmographers, and I their Mapp, who lie
Flat on his bed, that by them may be showne
That this is my South-west discoverie
Per fretum febris, by these streights to die,

I joy, that in these straits, I see my West;
For, though theire currants yeeld returne to none,
What shall my West hurt me? As West and East
In all flatt Maps (and I am one) are one,
So death doth touch the Resurrection.

And for the last time for centuries to come, the natural and the spiritual orders are brought together in a Baroque image of unsurpassed power; for one last time the poles of the natural world, of the human measure and of supernatural truth, were one:

We thinke that Paradise and Calvarie,
Christs Crosse, and Adams tree, stood in one place;
Looke Lord, and finde both Adams met in me;
As the first Adams sweat surrounds my face,
May the last Adams blood my soule embrace.

But to his very death, doubt and faith struggled for the soul of John Donne. His last written words were these:

I have a sinne of feare, that when I have spunne
My last thred, I shall perish on the shore;
Sweare by thy selfe, that at my death thy sonne
Shall shine as he shines now, and heretofore;
And, having done that, Thou haste done,
I feare no more.

It has remained for a painter of our own tormented age, Stanley Spenser, to paint the scene that the monument he himself designed has for so long obscured, of 'John Donne arriving at the Gates of Heaven'. For though much had perished in doubt, enough faith finally remained to bring within their reach that heroic soul who welded together in his poetry the hemispheres of broken truth. (pp. 394-95)

Kathleen Raine, "John Donne and the Baroque Doubt," in *Horizon,* London, Vol. XI, No. 66, June, 1945, pp. 371-95.

A. ALVAREZ
(essay date 1961)

[Alvarez is a prominent British critic, editor, poet, and novelist. In his writings of the early 1960s, he campaigned against what he viewed as the excessive gentility of British poetry since World War II, advocating instead a poetry of extreme personal, emotional, and political import. In his insistence upon seeing the whole individual, Alvarez stands as a modern Metaphysical, himself a follower of 'the school of Donne.' " In the following excerpt, he appropriates and sharpens the thematic focus of one of T. S. Eliot's assessments of Donne (see excerpt dated 1923), outlining the nature of Donne's poetic realism.]

Donne was not only one of the most supremely intelligent poets in the language, he was also the first Englishman to write verse in a way that reflected the whole complex activity of intelligence. A number of Elizabethan poets embodied the philosophical truths of their period in verse of considerable elegance and power. But Donne created a poetic language of thought, a mode of expression which so took for granted the intellectual tone and preoccupations of his time that it made of them, as it were, the stage on which the intimate give-and-take of personal poetry was played. He was, in short, the first intellectual realist in poetry.

Eliot first made much the same point as early as 1923 in an article that has, to my knowledge, never been reprinted [see excerpt dated 1923]. . . . The difference between the time at which Eliot wrote this and our own lies in the way in which psychology can now be taken more or less for granted. The complexity and contradictoriness of the emotions are no longer fighting subjects. Instead, the contemporary problem is to write with an intelligence that recognizes this complexity and controls it in all its baffling fragmentariness.

Eliot's insights into Donne's originality were largely sidetracked by later critics in their search for a technique to produce certain effects. Hence the inordinate concentration on the 'outlandish conceit', as though the whole of Metaphysical poetry were reducible to a single, rather ostentatious trick of style. I simply want to replace the stress on the element of realism in Donne, the skill by which he created a poetic language in which technique was at the service of a fullness of the intelligence.

Nowadays 'realism' usually means a certain wilful harping on the facts of life, an insistence on the short, frank word and the daringly, or drearily, sordid detail. There is, of course, an element of this kind of frankness in Donne's poetry, but, as often as not, it enters when he is most classical: in, say, 'Elegie XIX. Going to Bed', where he is being a kind of new English Ovid. The realism I am referring to is, however something more diffused and its effect is distinctly not of grinding the reader's nose into the dirt. On the contrary, the final impression is one of a peculiarly heightened dignity.

This sense of personal dignity is at the centre of Donne's work. At the simplest level, it is his perennial theme:

She'is all States, and all Princes, I,
Nothing else is:

is an extreme but typical way of putting it. This dignity measures his distance from the more conventional Elizabethans . . . [and] it is at the root of his 'masculine', 'strong' style. More important, it makes for the cohesion of his work, that unity and strength which give his collected poems an importance difficult to pin down in any single one of them. He is, after all, one of the few major poets before this century whose achievement is not summed up in any one really extended work.

Yet despite this unity there is considerable variation in his style. The *Elegies,* for example, seem definably younger work than the best *Songs and Sonets.* This is due to something more than their occasional self-consciousness, which was the young Donne's fatal Cleopatra. It is a question of technique. The key to Donne's mature style is his use of logic: the more subtle and complex the emotion, the greater the logical pressure. The mature Donne organizes his poems in such a way that each shift of feeling seems to be substantiated logically. In the *Elegies,* however, the emotions are simpler and are sustained in their singleness. He adopts a stance and then develops it dramatically, not logically. So instead of a piece of elaborate human dialectics, he leaves you with a situation presented in the vivid colouring of a more or less single strong feeling.

Even the best of the *Elegies,* in fact, are more uncomplicatedly assertive than most of Donne's other work of the same standard. 'Elegie IV. The Perfume', for instance, is perhaps the most inventive of all Donne's poems, but its wit is more ornamental than profound: it has gone into the puns, into the dramatic detail, into maintaining the overriding masculine independence. It is, in short, less analytic than energetic. The only deepening of tone comes at the moment when his masculinity itself is threatened:

Onely, thou bitter sweet, whom I had laid
Next mee, mee traiterously hast betraid . . .

It may seem odd that the perfume should inspire a couple of lines which are as moving and as moved as anything Donne ever wrote on the theme of the inconstant mistress. But the reason comes a few lines later:

By thee, the greatest staine to mans estate
Falls on us, to be call'd effeminate . . .

The perfume, in fact, has undermined the whole basis of this and most of the other *Elegies:* the almost belligerent masculinity of the young Donne who was 'a great visitor of ladies'. The difference between the *Elegies* and Donne's maturest technique [exemplified by 'A nocturnall upon S. Lucies day, Being the shortest day'] is large and clear. . . . This is the only one of Donne's poems which might validly be called 'modern'. As in *The Waste Land,* the poet is on the rack to define a complex negative state which he apparently cannot fully understand and, what is even more pertinent to Donne's difficulty, which he cannot properly dramatize. The theme is a depression so deep as to verge on annihilation (he wrote, after all, a defence of suicide). And its root, I think, is inaction, or the impossibility of action, as he described it in the famous letter to Goodyer:

> Therefore I would fain do something; but that I cannot tell what is no wonder. For to chuse, is to do: but to be no part of any body, is to be nothing.

He tries to force some kind of clearing through this swaddling depression by bringing to bear upon it an extraordinarily tense logic and a great concentration of learning. Each stanza moves forward to its own temporary resolution; the twisted, pausing, in-turning movement clears to make way for a direct but invariably negative statement:

> "The worlds whole sap is sunke"
> "Compar'd with mee, who am their Epitaph"
> "For I am every dead thing"
> " . . . things which are not"
> " . . . made us carcasses"
> "But I am None" . . .

Unlike most of his other lyrics, the logic of the **'Nocturnall'** does not exorcise his troubles. Despite all the dialectic and the learning, despite the invocation of the outside lovers and even, in the third stanza, the invocation of his own more dramatic love poems, he is left with the blank fact of his isolation. Yet although whatever pressure he brings to bear on the situation produces no clear answer, it does help him to achieve some kind of balance. The last lines of the poem—"since this / Both the yeares, and the dayes deep midnight is"—may simply be a restatement of the first—"Tis the yeares midnight, and it is the dayes, *Lucies*"—but they are a restatement with a difference: the difficult, questioning movement of the start has been resolved into a clearer, more measured statement. He finishes, that is, by *accepting* the depression, instead of trying, with all the intellectual ingenuity at his command, to wriggle through it. So the poem ends with his facing the adult necessity of living with grief and depression, instead of giving in to them. Donne's logic and learning, in short, were the prime forces in his emotional maturity *as a poet.*

It is the absence of this quality, incidentally, which marks off Shakespeare's formal verse from Donne's. . . . Like the **'Nocturnall'**, 'Sonnet XCIV' is also, in its way, a rather modern poem: its mode is complex, negative and founded perhaps on the same sexual anger and frustration that produced Othello's "O thou weed / Who art so lovely fair and smell's so sweet / That the sense aches at thee, would thou hadst ne'er

been born!" But unlike Donne's, Shakespeare's compression is all in the imagery rather than the argument. Where Donne often begins with a straightforward situation (those famous, or infamous, dramatic openings) and then produces infinitely complicated arguments to justify it, Shakespeare begins with the abstractions and then gives them body. (pp. 12-21)

However far, of course, Donne seems from the usual Elizabethan rhetoric, he did produce a rhetoric of his own. He produced it for his rare public performances—the two *Anniversaries,* for example—and it was the rhetoric of the intellectual, abstract and analytic. Hence, Ben Jonson's irritated declaration "That Dones *Anniversarie* was profane and full of Blasphemies. That he told Mr. Done, if it had been written of ye Virgin Marie it had been something to which he answered that he described the Idea of a Woman and not as she was." In the *First Anniversarie* Donne dissects 'the idea of a woman' in order to produce *An Anatomie of the World,* a theological and political analysis of the state of corruption; that is, he was using the occasion to be deliberately less Donne the poet than Donne the learned wit, author of *Pseudo-Martyr.* The *Second Anniversarie: The Progresse of the Soule,* is less abstract, more dramatic and, seemingly, more deeply felt. It is possible, indeed, that its roots were much more personal than those of the *First Anniversarie.* Donne apparently wrote it well before the date it was due, while he was staying with Sir Robert Drury in Amiens. He had gone abroad unwillingly, full of anxiety for his wife whom he left ill and pregnant. It was at Amiens that he had the terrible dream in which his wife appeared to him with a dead child in her arms. It may be, then, that 'the idea of a woman' was, in this instance, his wife, not Elizabeth Drury. Be that as it may, the dramatic meditation on death and the after-life is closer to the style of Donne the preacher or Donne the author of the *Devotions* than to that of the more analytic theologian of the *First Anniversarie.* In both poems, his public personality is foremost. Their rhetoric is formally and formidably that of the intellectual, the debater.

Yet fundamentally it is the same rhetoric which, on less public occasions, is used to heighten a personal strength and richness. Philosophy, science, logic, divinity, poetry itself are all means of enhancing the dignity of the individual. His realism lies in the richness of the resources he brings to bear upon more or less conventional subjects and his ability to falsify the full range of his response. Donne's achievement was to take a poetry over which the academic theorists were fiercely haggling, and break down the constrictions of mere aesthetic criteria; to take a dialectical form which had become rigid in centuries of scholastic wrangling, and break down its narrow casuistry; to take the sciences in all the imaginative strength of the new discoveries, and bring them all together as protagonists in the inward drama of his own powerful experience. He substantiated less a poetic technique than a form of intelligence which the most talented men of the following generation could use without, at any point, belying their natural gifts outside the realm of poetry. As a result, the style of Donne lasted until, under the imperative stresses of the Civil War, the whole mode of intelligence changed. We are now far enough removed from the tensions that split the seventeenth century to be able to judge Donne's monarchy of wit not as a trick or a fashion but as one of the greatest achievements of the poetic intelligence. (pp. 21-3)

A. Alvarez, in his *The School of Donne,* 1961. Reprint by Pantheon Books, 1962, 211 p.

TERRY G. SHERWOOD
(essay date 1984)

[Sherwood is a Canadian educator and literary essayist. In his *Fulfilling the Circle: A Study of John Donne's Thought* (1984), he stressed that "there can be no absolute separation between the importance of epistemological and psychological principles for Donne and his personal consciousness that infuses his works. That these principles are manifested in writings clearly enlivened by Donne's own experience simply adds convincing evidence of their importance in his thought. And the fact that these writings define the experience of consciousness according to shaping metaphysical forces makes them characteristic of Donne's thought in general." In the following excerpt from this work, Sherwood examines *Deaths Duell* as "the final part added to a consistent whole": a work that completes a lifelong cycle involving "Donne's own person as a factor in his works."]

The event of *Deaths Duell* was remarkable even by the standards of Donne's day. He had been appointed to preach on 'his old constant day, the first *Friday* in *Lent,*' at Whitehall before the king. Though wasted by illness, Donne 'passionately denied' the requests of concerned friends that he not preach. His text was Psalm 68:20: *'And unto God the Lord belong the issues of death. i.e. from death.'* Isaak Walton captures a very special drama: 'Many that then saw his tears, and heard his faint and hollow voice, professing they thought Text prophetically chosen, and that Dr. Donne *had preach't his own funeral Sermon.*' But it is not just the drama of a wasted, dying man who embodies his own words about death that is remarkable. Even more so is that the event of Donne's delivery and the sermon itself, taken together, represent a coherent and fulfilling conclusion to his life and thought.

The vivid sight of the dying man could have made the sermon itself anticlimactic if not for its own powerful effects. A forceful statement of omnipresent mortality and vivid images of putrefaction and vermiculation relentlessly aggravate fear of death. Donne's dying body becomes only the most immediate example of the principle of mortality and of the inevitability of material decay and putrefaction. . . . And the portrayal of the crucified Christ that concludes the sermon remains amongst the most powerful statements in Donne's religious prose.

To say that the sermon itself was not anticlimactic is not to say that it can have the same power for us as for the actual audience. Both the dying man and the artifact would have been important. Even for a spellbinder like Donne, his presence in the pulpit then would have been a rare moment; and in his very self-conscious staging of it can be found much of the intended effect on his audience. Walton's account of Donne's final days—his return from Essex to deliver the sermon, the delivery itself before the king and the Whitehall audience, his order that a life-size burial effigy be drawn prematurely, his contemplation of that drawing as his 'hourly object'—reveals parts of a whole. There is a consciousness of the interrelationship between his own person, the artifacts embodying or expressing it, and the communal Body including both person and artifacts. Familiar assumptions here reach back to Donne's beginnings. His abiding sense of the body as a legitimate medium of truth and of the human need to read it . . . were revealed in the conception of the body as a 'book' as early as the love poetry in **'To his Mistris Going to Bed'** and **'The Exstasie'** and later in the verse letter **'To Sir Edward Herbert, at Julyers.'** The body's experience must be understood and known by an attentive reason. Likewise, we find the assumption that artifacts are surrogate bodies necessary for expressing truth. Such diverse works as **'The Canonization,' 'The Relique,'** *The Anniversaries,* the verse letters, and the *Devotions* reveal this assumption.

Walton's nervous estimate of Donne's order for the burial effigy as showing 'a desire of glory or commendation . . . rooted in the very nature of man' is not the only interpretation that can be given of Donne's motives. In the *Devotions* Donne assumes that his own diseased body has significance for other members of the participating Body. This significance is embodied in the literary artifact, which must be considered rationally by members of Donne's audience just as Donne must consider the events of his immediate experience. In *Deaths Duell* Donne's own person is not explicitly expressed in the artifact, but it would have been tangibly present. As members of the same Body as Donne, his auditors could have participated, in a very immediate way, in the significance of his dying body. (pp. 193-94)

At bottom is operating the elemental bodily consciousness that . . . [is] one key factor in Donne's epistemology and psychology and which, in *Deaths Duell,* provokes the fear of physical death and dissolution of bodily identity. The imminence of Donne's own death would exacerbate that fear in members of his audience. The fearful appeal to this bodily consciousness is answered by the climactic image of the crucified Christ, with its assurance that through identification with death itself, in the pattern of Christ's suffering death, fear can be transformed into hope. Only through conformity to Christ that bends man's will to God's through penitentially crucifying sin, in humility, obedience, and patience, can one escape the fear of death. Donne's assurance of his own resurrection from sin through conformity to Christ in the *Devotions* and Walton's account of his joyful assurance of salvation during the days before his death suggest that Donne would have viewed his own wasted body as an example of penitential conformity to Christ's suffering death. Thus, the vivid image of the dying man is fulfilled in the vivid depiction of the suffering God as its pattern. The audience is invited, implicitly, to participate in Donne as one exemplary member of the Body and, explicitly, to conform to the suffering and death of Christ the Head. In accordance with his Lenten purposes, 'Crucifying of that *sinne* that *governes thee*' to achieve conformity, Donne pulls tight the strings of bodily consciousness with his image of the suffering incarnate Word: 'There wee leave you in that *blessed dependancy,* to *hang* upon *him* that *hangs* upon the *Crosse,* there *bath* in his *teares,* there *suck* at his *woundes,* and *lye downe in peace* in his *grave,* till hee vouchsafe you a *resurrection,* and an *ascension* into that *Kingdome,* which hee hath *purchas'd for you,* with the *inestimable price* of his *incorruptible blood.* Amen.' Only this palpable image of Christ can change bodily fears into hope through acceptance of the body's own necessary death and resurrection.

Donne keeps our attention on Christ's bodily suffering as, increasingly, the sermon, like the development of Donne's own thought, converges on the Cross. Divine love inspires Christ's freely given love:

> *Many waters quench not love,* Christ's tryed many; He was *Baptized* out of his *love,* and his love determined not there; He wept over *Jerusalem* out his love, and his love determined not there; He *mingled blood* with *water* in his *agony* and that determined not his love; hee *wept pure blood,* all his blood at all his eyes, at all his pores, in his *flagellation* and *thornes (to the Lord our God belong'd the issues of blood)* and these *expressed,* but these did *not quench his love.*

Love of Christ, in return, inspires penintential conformity in body and tripartite soul, thereby converting the forces of annihilation and recreating man the damaged goal of Creation. In the suffering of the Cross that pays sin's debt, God shows to man the pattern in body and soul that mortifies sin. Donne's emphasis upon the humanity of the Word, his very palpable physical and psychological suffering, brings the specifically human together with the larger metaphysical power of the Word. In the explicit conformity built on love, humility, obedience, patience, and acceptance of suffering and death, being is recreated. And Donne, in offering his own accomplished suffering to the audience, exemplifies this recreation for others, thereby, like Paul, fulfilling the suffering of Christ in his own flesh for the Body's sake.

Consistent with his earlier works, Donne stresses that this meeting of the personal and metaphysical occurs in time. Donne ends *Deaths Duell* at the end of his own circle with yet another meditation on time that places importance on the given moment. In the sermon the movement from fear to conformity with Christ, from death of the body to the resurrection of hope, recreates time. The sermon's initial weight on the omnipresence of death points to the negativity of fallen time: 'We celebrate our owne funeralls with cryes, even at our own birth, as though our *threescore and ten years life* were spent in our mothers labour, and our circle made up in the first point thereof.' Similarly, the progression of fallen time is crippled and reversed: 'That which we call life, is but *Hebdomada mortium, a week of deaths,* seaven dayes, seaven periods of our life spent in dying, *a dying seaven times over,* and there is an end. *Our birth dyes in infancy,* and our *infancy* dyes in *youth,* and *youth,* and the rest dye in *age,* and *age* also dyes, and *determines all.*'

Against the degeneration of time through death, Donne, fittingly himself a dying man nearing his own last day, offers the model of Christ's last day. Gradually, the sermon conforms time itself to Christ, thereby re-informing time according to the Incarnate Word:

> Take in the *whole day* from the *houre* that *Christ received* the *passeover* upon *Thursday, unto* the *houre* in which hee *dyed* the *next day.* Make *this* present *day* in thy *devotion,* and consider what *hee did,* and remember what *you have done.* Before hee *instituted and celebrated* the *Sacrament,* (which was *after* the *eating of the passeover*) hee proceeded to that *act* of *humility,* to *wash his disciples feete,* even, *Peters,* who for a while *resisted* him; In thy *preparation* to the holy and blessed *Sacrament,* hast thou with a sincere *humility* sought a *reconciliation* with all the *world,* even with those that have been *averse* from it, and *refused* that *reconciliation* from thee? If so (and not else) thou hast spent that *first part* of this his *last day* in a *conformity* with him.

The day of Donne's sermon and the day before Christ's death are both special days. For Donne, it is his last sermon before an expected and welcome death, a point close to the Omega of his circle of time. For Christ, it is the period of a single day immediately before his Crucifixion, likewise a point close to the Omega of his exemplary circle. The auditors, like

Donne and Christ, must face the continuing possibility that each day may end their circles. Each day is a *'criticall* day' that must be regarded as potentially man's last to be brought into conformity with Christ's last day. Donne's visible conformity to Christ's pattern will dilate this particular moment in the respective lives of his listeners. Thus, *Death Duell* speaks to the immediate moment, to both individuals and to the communal Body, applying these special days of Donne and Christ. As in the *Devotions* Donne is speaking to members of the Body, the Church, invoking the image of Christ the Head; and he is speaking to members of the Body, the Kingdom, here in the presence of its regal Heart. All members hear the same pattern for fulfilling time.

As elsewhere in Donne's works, time is fulfilled within the human soul. The reference points are psychological and epistemological; and the guiding conformity to Christ, which is so crucial in Donne's theology of participation, works within a larger conformity of the tripartite human soul to the tripartite God, In the *divisio* in preparation for 'these three considerations' of the three meanings of *exitus mortis* that make up the sermon, Donne establishes parallels to the three Persons of the Trinity:

> In all these three lines then, we shall looke upon these words; *First,* as the *God* of *power,* the *Almighty Father* rescues his servants from the jawes of death: *And then,* as the *God* of *mercy,* the glorious *Sonne* rescued us, by taking upon himselfe this *issue of death: And then* betweene these two, as the *God of comfort,* the *Holy Ghost* rescues us from all discomfort by his blessed impressions before hand, that what manner of death soever be ordeined for us, yet this *exitus mortis* shall be *introitus in vitam* our *issue in death,* shall be an *entrance into everlasting life.*

Similarly, the sermon works on all members of the tripartite Image in the human soul: on the reason in the frequent request that the auditors consider the matter of the sermon, especially the experience of Christ; on the will in the stimulation of love for Christ's loving sacrifice; and on the memory in the request that believers remember their own sinful actions in comparison with Christ's example. The recreation of time requires attentive efforts by the entire soul.

In the *Devotions* reason considers each moment in time according to the principles informing it. The same assumption in *Death Duell* makes conformity to Christ dependent on the soul's keen rational awareness. The audience is asked to consider the significance of moments in Christ's 'day' ending with his death. 'Make *this* present *day* that *day* in thy *devotion,* To consider what *hee did,* and remember what *you have done.* Donne repeatedly points to the importance of considering the matter of the sermon, 'to consider with mee how to *this God the Lord belong'd the issues of death,* explicitly sharpening the audience's rational attention. Implicitly, the audience is

also being asked to consider the dying preacher standing before them, just as they are asked to consider his diseased body in the *Devotions.* The dramatic force of the given moment in Donne's works develops in these later works into a full-blown sense of temporal events as a form of communication from God to man, to be understood and known. When Donne speaks of God as Logos, who necessarily proceeds logically, for whom a minute in time is a 'syllogisme' he is emphasizing the rational dimension in that communication. The audience in *Death Duell* must consider not only Donne's spoken words, but also his presence in the pulpit as a form of temporal communication from God. This is necessarily the domain of reason's same bright attention emphasized throughout Donne's works as the condition for fulfilling temporal life. Reason must also attentively arbitrate the will's experience in love and examine anew what memory comprehends.

That Donne would expect the members of his audience to consider not only his words but also himself as part of the same event [brings us to a crucial matter in understanding Donne's works] namely, Donne's own person as a factor in his works. The complexities of Donne's nature have set off varied and, times, conflicting responses. Clearly, Donne was unsettled as a young man; it is nonetheless possible to determine those elements which dominate his essential nature even at that time. Merritt Hughes's clear warning against 'kidnapping' Donne in our own modern preconceptions still exhorts us to see Donne as he wished to be seen. Behind the restlessness and the chafing in Donne there was a yearning for constancy. . . . In Donne's restatement of Paul's joyous fulfilment of Christ suffering in his own flesh for the Body's sake, Donne expressed a Calling that, in the received forms of his Faith, fulfilled his yearning for constancy.

Walton's chronicle of Donne's final days, an account which his modern counterpart R. C. Bald regards as unexceptional, suggests that Donne's faith was fulfilled in his death. But death does not compromise his abiding sense that the Body of Christ, the physical and spiritual community that contributes to the constancy of Donne's mature being, would continue to span heaven and earth after his death. Though Donne himself was spiralling closer to his circular God, whose mercy ever moved perpendicularly above the believer, he recognized even in his last acts the responsibility to other participating members. Donne's relationship to the community was not always so resolved, and his life on the circumference of his temporal circle was not always so fulfilled. In the third satire there is the incompleted search for a 'true religion,' the injunction to 'doubt wisely' in a progress spiralling upward ('about must goe') to Truth on a 'huge' hill. In **'A Valediction: forbidding Mourning,'** its calmness a marked contrast to other love poems of Donne, is expressed the conviction that mutual love bonded by spiritual union can make an individual, private circle just. And in **'Good-friday, 1613. Riding Westward'** he affirms the need for affliction to turn his sinful soul in its circular, westward movement back to its eastern origin, in conformity with the suffering Christ. However, in Donne's maturity, in his priestly Calling, he did achieve a personal assurance and constancy that fulfilled life along the circumference of his circle. In his assurance of his conformity with Christ, he offered his bodily presence to fulfil Christ's suffering for the sake of the communal Body. And in his literary works he embodied his sense of the epistemological and psychological immediacies that make up that confirmity.

To conclude, it is in the two major artifacts in his last remains, the sermon *Deaths Duell* and the death effigy in St Paul's, that we can find the final measure of the Calling that fulfilled his life. The sermon, although it now lacks the startling ambience centred in the dying man, still leaves its deep imprint on readers in the way it emboldens the problems of mortality and time. The death effigy likewise leaves its imprint, with its composed face accepting the inevitability of death. Donne would have appreciated time's witty justification of his personal value for the Body; the marble effigy remains, but the original building was destroyed by fire. Many modern readers would say that both the sermon and the effigy, like his other literary works, have outlasted the system of belief that inspired Donne. Yet it is not too fanciful to suggest—and we can perhaps appreciate this irony better than Donne—that his artifacts still inform a kind of Body in so far as they unite us in asking that we know and feel the large forces that shape us. That Donne's own works accomplish this successfully, often in the most immediate ways, make them a coherent and understandable achievement that can be said to help fulfill life on the circumference of time's circle. (pp. 195-200)

Terry G. Sherwood, in his *Fulfilling the Circle: A Study of John Donne's Thought,* University of Toronto Press, 1984, 231 p.

SOURCES FOR FURTHER STUDY

Bald, R. C. *John Donne: A Life.* New York and Oxford: Oxford University Press, 1970, 627 p.

Detailed, highly esteemed biography.

Cathcart, Dwight. *Doubting Conscience: Donne and the Poetry of Moral Argument.* Ann Arbor: University of Michigan Press, 1975, 199 p.

Explores the questions of conscience evident in Donne's verse.

Eliot, T. S. "The Metaphysical Poets." In his *Selected Essays,* pp. 241-50. New York: Harcourt, Brace & World, 1950.

Considered one of the signal works of twentieth-century poetry criticism, this study was markedly influential in stirring interest in Donne and his school. Eliot's essay, originally published in 1921 as a review of H. J. C. Grierson's *Metaphysical Lyrics and Poems of the Seventeenth Century,* seeks to reveal to contemporary readers the value of metaphysical poetry.

Gardner, Helen, ed. *John Donne: A Collection of Critical Essays.* Englewood Cliffs, N. J.: Prentice-Hall, 1962, 183 p.

Reprints key essays on Donne's works by such scholars as George Saintsbury, Louis L. Martz, and J. B. Leishman.

Lewis, C. S. *English Literature in the Sixteenth Century, Excluding Drama,* pp. 469ff. Oxford: Oxford University Press, Clarendon Press, 1954.

Expresses harsh criticism of Donne's *Satyres, Elegies,* and verse *Letters,* but reserves high praise for the *Songs and Sonets.*

Roston, Murray. *The Soul of Wit: A Study of John Donne.* Oxford: Oxford at the Clarendon Press, 1974, 236 p.

Textual analysis of Donne's poetry in which Roston reconciles the seemingly paradoxical natures of Donne's secular and religious poetry.

John Dos Passos

1896-1970

(Full name John Roderigo Dos Passos) American novelist, essayist, poet, dramatist, travel writer, historian, biographer, and journalist.

INTRODUCTION

*B*est known for his sociopolitical novels of pre-World-War-II America, Dos Passos is considered a master novelist and chronicler of twentieth-century American life. His central concerns, including such social injustices as the exploitation of the working class, the loss of individual freedom, and the harmful emphasis upon materialism in American society, have been hailed in his novels *Manhattan Transfer* (1925) and those which comprise the trilogy *U.S.A.: The 42nd Parallel* (1930), *1919* (1932), and *The Big Money* (1936). In these and his other novels, Dos Passos often employed experimental techniques such as inserting actual news items, prose poem passages, and biographical excerpts into the narrative to evoke multiple layers of detail and realism. Strongly political, he moved from the left-wing revolutionary philosophy he held during the 1920s and 1930s, when his works were widely praised, to a later conservative stance. Although the reputation of Dos Passos declined in the 1940s and 1950s, in recent years scholars have reaffirmed the artistic merit of his innovative methods and consider him a significant voice in twentieth-century literature.

Dos Passos was born in Chicago to John Roderigo Dos Passos, a wealthy Portuguese immigrant, and Lucy Addison Sprigg Madison, who did not wed until their son was fourteen. Dos Passos spent most of his youth traveling in Europe and the United States with his mother. At the age of fifteen, Dos Passos was accepted at Harvard and began classes the following year. As an undergraduate he edited the *Harvard Monthly* and wrote poetry which was later published in *Eight Harvard Poets* (1917) along with poems by E. E. Cummings and Robert Hillyer. He traveled to Spain upon graduating in 1916 and, eager to become involved in World War I, volunteered for service the following year as an ambulance driver in France, joining a host of other volunteers—including Cummings, Hillyer, and Ernest Hemingway—who would later gain recognition as writers. (Dos Passos recorded his wartime experiences in the novel *One Man's Initiation—1917* (1920), an impressionist work which had begun as a collaboration with Hillyer, though the published novel includes only those chapters written by Dos Passos.) In late 1917 Dos Passos transferred to the American Red Cross Ambulance Corps in Italy, where he was dishonorably discharged in 1918 for his antiwar sentiments. Returning to France, he joined the U.S. Army Medical Corps, in which he served until his enlistment expired in 1919. At that time Dos Passos was already at work on his next novel, *Three Soldiers* (1921), which initiated his prominence as a writer and became the first important war novel of World War I. Clearly a condemnation of the social and political mechanisms behind the war, *Three Soldiers* quickly drew critical attention for its frank portrayal of the war's destructive effects on its three protagonists. Despite its romantic tone evoking impressionistic images and sounds, the novel denotes a passage from Dos Passos's early, impressionistic aesthete philosophy to one of anger and rebellion against what he perceived as the power of industrial capitalism to crush individual freedom.

Dos Passos traveled throughout Europe and the United States during the 1920s. He also grew increasingly active in leftist political causes and explored various artistic movements, incorporating such influences as cubism and expressionism into his own works. Dos Passos was both prolific and diverse, publishing novels, dramas, poetry, travel books, and essays. In the late 1920s he joined the New Playwrights Theatre, an experimental left-wing theater group. His dramas—*The Garbage Man* (1926), *Airways, Inc.* (1928), and *Fortune Heights* (1933)—contain strong political themes protesting against the ill effects of American capitalism and democracy. He also wrote for the *New Masses,* a radical-Left periodical he helped found in 1926. His disillusionment over the injustices against the individual in a capitalist society culminated in 1927 when he covered the trial of Nicola Sacco and Bartolomeo Vanzetti, immigrants and anarchists who, Dos Passos firmly believed, had been wrongfully accused of murder. He was arrested and jailed after taking part in demonstrations on behalf of the accused men; and in his pamphlet *Facing the Chair: Story of the Americanization of Two Foreignborn Workmen* (1927) he attempted to present evidence of the men's innocence. The eventual execution of Sacco and Vanzetti embittered Dos Passos and strengthened his distrust of the government.

During the late 1920s and early 1930s Dos Passos continued his involvement with the Left, contributing essays to the *New Masses,* the *New Republic,* and *Common Sense.* Although he never publicly claimed allegiance to the Communist party, his writings and activities—a visit to the Soviet Union in 1928 and to the coal fields in Harlan, Kentucky in 1931 to assess miners' working conditions—aligned him with communism. His novels during this time—*Manhattan Transfer; The 42nd Parallel* (1930); *1919* (1932); and *The Big Money* (1936), of which the latter three comprise the *U.S.A.* trilogy—portray the failure of the American Dream but, as critics note, do not overtly support any political program or party. Following the completion of *U.S.A.,* Dos Passos journeyed to Spain in 1937 with Hemingway to report on events of the Spanish Civil War between Marxist-backed Republican and Fascist-backed Falangists groups. There he became disillusioned with the Left when he learned that his friend José Robles, a Republican supporter, had been executed by Republican forces under an alleged Communist command. When Hemingway refused to question the integrity of the Republican cause, Dos Passos broke off his friendship with him and severed ties with Europe, returning to the United States with a new-found devotion to his homeland.

His dissatisfaction with leftist political groups is evident in his next novel, *Adventures of a Young Man* (1939), which delineates an idealistic protagonist who goes to Spain to fight for his vision of individual freedom only to be killed under the order of the political group he had supported. The other two novels, which with *Adventures of a Young Man* form the *District of Columbia* trilogy, *Number One* (1943) and *The Grand Design* (1949), continue to depict corruption that results from power and the devastating effects exercised by institutions and governments over the individual. *The Grand Design,* generally considered the best work of the trilogy, satirizes Franklin Roosevelt's New Deal policies as an impractical failure of centralized government. However, *District of Columbia* was poorly received, partly because the novels no longer evinced support for leftist causes and also because the narratives were regarded as straightforward and one-dimensional, unlike Dos Passos's accomplishment in *U.S.A.* His nonfiction also markedly shifted from radical-Left beliefs toward those of the conservative Right, generating consternation among many of his former supporters. Nevertheless, Dos Passos maintained that he had not betrayed his former beliefs. Townsend Ludington summarizes Dos Passos's position: "His point was that he adhered to the political point of view which seemed to him most promising of personal freedom at a given moment in history." From the 1940s through the rest of his life, Dos Passos lived mainly at Spence's Point, Virginia, on a farm he had inherited from his father, and in Provincetown, Massachusetts, gaining the reputation of a country squire who was now devoted to the ideals of Jeffersonian democracy and the study of American history and order. In his well-received historical works—which include *The Ground We Stand On*

(1941), *The Head and Heart of Thomas Jefferson* (1954), *The Men Who Made the Nation* (1957), *Prospects of a Golden Age* (1959), and *Mr. Wilson's War* (1962)—Dos Passos examines United States history from the roots of American government, with its traditions of self-government and individual freedom, to the era of World War I, when industrial capitalism strongly influenced the government.

Dos Passos's later fiction also reveals his changing attitudes. His earlier fiction, noted for its highly objective viewpoint, was replaced by novels evincing personal narratives closely akin in their details to Dos Passos's own life. Several critics maintain that this shift resulted after Dos Passos lost his wife, Katy, in an automobile accident in 1947. *Chosen Country* (1951), a nostalgic novel—or "chronicle" as Dos Passos had begun calling his fictions—offers a sentimental portrait of Lulie, a character based on Katy, and Jay Pignatelli, Dos Passos's own double. His most significant late novel, however, was *Midcentury* (1961), a despairing account of the corruptions of labor unions. In this novel Dos Passos returned to a cross-section narrative reminiscent of *U.S.A.*, through juxtapositions of fiction, biography, news stories, and authorial reflections, to delineate a broad representation of American society. The work was praised for displaying artistic sophistication that many critics had found lacking in Dos Passos's fiction since *U.S.A.*. Dos Passos continued to write histories, memoirs, travel essays, and journalistic works through his later years. At the time of his death at age seventy-four, he was at work on the novel *Century's Ebb: The Thirteenth Chronicle*, which was published posthumously in 1975. Intended as a record of American lives from the time of the Spanish Civil War to the lunar landing and described by Dos Passos as his "last forlorn Chronicle of Despair," the work evokes negative observations of American society as well as an underlying sense of hope in the nation's potential for good.

Despite Dos Passos's extensive literary canon, critical attention has focused predominantly upon *Manhattan Transfer* and the *U.S.A.* trilogy. In *Manhattan Transfer* Dos Passos drew upon his interests in avant-garde painting and literature as well as film for his technical innovations, juxtaposing prose poems against popular songs and varied images to create a cinematic collage that delineates a cross section of New York City. The multiple layers of Dos Passos's depiction of the city heightens its realism, as he thus presented all classes of society. George J. Becker commented that "this type of novel does not have fixed rules but can be described as a kind of mosaic, or, better, a revolving stage that presents a multitude of scenes and characters which, taken together, convey a sense of the life of a given milieu and by extension give the tone of contemporary life generally." Although the novel illustrates

the lives of numerous people living in New York City from the beginning of the century to the early 1920s, several central characters do emerge, such as the protagonist Jimmy Herf, a reporter who, like Dos Passos, is the objective observer of the events and characters of the novel. Dos Passos eschewed authorial intrusion by his kaleidoscopic presentation of characters pursuing the American Dream, allowing the reader to infer the novel's moral implications as all but a few are corrupted by their pursuit of material success.

Dos Passos further refined the technical innovations of *Manhattan Transfer* in the trilogy *U.S.A.*. Shaped by Dos Passos's fascination with history, the novels portray twentieth-century American society from 1900 to the early 1930s while presenting ironic juxtapositions of myriad details to broaden the trilogy's overriding theme of the failure of the American Dream. The first novel of *U.S.A.*, *The 42nd Parallel*, contains twenty narrative sections interspersed with the three unconventional perspectives that became Dos Passos's signature of the trilogy—"Newsreels," "Camera Eye," and biography. The Newsreels include actual clips from newspaper headlines and stories as well as portions of popular songs; the Camera Eye is, as described by Donald Pizer, "a form of autobiographical symbolic poetry" in which Dos Passos reveals his "state of mind, feeling, or spirit at a specific moment of his development"; the biographies recount the lives of famous Americans through often-ironic layerings of various details that culminate in the final, telling portraits of Dos Passos's subjects. Within the fictional narratives Dos Passos returns to many of the same characters introduced elsewhere in the trilogy. For instance, in *The 42nd Parallel* the reader is introduced to J. Ward Moorehouse, a public relations man who, in *1919*, will appear at the Versailles Peace Conference to ensure that the terms of the agreement benefit American money interests, and will be seen finally in *The Big Money* in his decline from power. This overlapping of characters and events contributes to the unity of the three works, as do the Newsreel, autobiographical Camera Eye, and biography sections so that the fiction merges with real events both from the world and from Dos Passos's own life. Pizer concludes that "*U.S.A.* is a kind of cubistic portrait of America. . . . It is Dos Passos's relentless pursuit of juxtapositional relationships in the seemingly disparate and fractured modal ordering of the trilogy that is largely responsible for the integral vision of American life in *U.S.A.*."

In 1938 Jean-Paul Sartre praised Dos Passos as "the greatest writer of our time"; however, Dos Passos never again achieved such recognition after the publication of his masterpiece *U.S.A.*. Much of the critical condemnation of Dos Passos's later works was based largely upon the perception that he had abandoned his political and social beliefs and had failed to maintain the artistic and innovative standards that *Manhattan Transfer* and *U.S.A.* had established. Critics also fault much of Dos Passos's later fiction for his characters' lack of psychological depth, though others maintain that Dos Passos's strength was in writing collective novels in which he delineated a wide range of character types, and that he purposively did not explore the inner lives of his characters. While several commentators have admonished Dos Passos for portraying an overly grim and pessimistic vision of American society, many assert that he still held an intrinsic belief in the good of the individual, with his intention being, according to Ludington, to "awaken other Americans with his words." Regardless of these critical differences, Dos Passos is recognized as a major chronicler in fiction of twentieth-century American life and as an important literary innovator for his imaginative experiments in narrative.

(For further information about Dos Passos's life and works, see *Concise Dictionary of American Literary Biography, 1929-1941; Contemporary Authors*, Vols. 1-4, rev. ed., 29-32, rev. ed.; *Contemporary Authors New Revision Series*, Vol. 3; *Contemporary Literary Criticism*, Vols. 1, 4, 8, 11, 15, 25, 34; *Dictionary of Literary Biography*, Vols. 4, 9; and *Dictionary of Literary Biography Documentary Series*, Vol. 1.)

CRITICAL COMMENTARY

DELMORE SCHWARTZ

(essay 1938)

[Schwartz, an American poet, short story writer, critic, and dramatist, was closely associated with a 1940s group of leftist writers and critics known as "the New York Intellectuals." In the following excerpt, he assesses the four different "forms" of *U. S. A.*]

In *U.S.A.,* Dos Passos uses four "forms" or "frames," each of them deriving directly from his representative intention, his desire to get at the truth about his time with any available instrument. . . .

There is the camera eye, an intermittent sequence of prose poems in an impressionist style. . . . The writing takes on the lyricism of a quasi-Joycean stream-of-consciousness and the emphasis is almost always upon the look and feel of things, mostly apart from any narrative context. At first glance the texture seems the crudity of an undergraduate determined to be modern, but upon examination this entirely disappears and one finds that all is based on faithful observation and is never pretentious, nor false. But these passages have no direct relation to the main story, although at times there is some link. . . .

Secondly, there are the newsreel passages which are inserted just as the camera eye panels are, between narratives. They consist of quotations from newspapers of a given time and period and also of its popular songs. Many amusing juxtapositions of headlines and stories are made by means of clever arrangements, and the lyrics are (where the present reader is able to judge) perfectly reminiscent. But the central intention of this form—to suggest the quality of various years and its public events—is not fulfilled for the most part. The newsreels are sometimes merely frivolous and trivial. (p. 355)

A third form is the "Biography." Here we are provided with concise recitatives in a Whitmanesque diction which is used at times with power. Each biography concerns a great figure of the period. . . . [On] the whole the biographies are as representative as one could wish and are written with a fine power of generalization and concision—the gist abstracted from the life of a man and presented in four or five pages, concluding very well at times in the form of a simple contradiction, Henry Ford's nostalgic desire for the horse-and-buggy days, which his whole career, of course, worked to destroy, and Andrew Carnegie's bestowal of millions for world peace, the millions being acquired, of course, by the manufacture of steel used in munitions and battleships.

The major part of the novel . . . is, however, constituted by direct narratives of the lives of eleven leading characters and perhaps three times as many minor ones who are notable. In creating a mode in which to present the lives of these characters, Dos Passos has definitely extended the art of narration. It is difficult to describe what he has accomplished because it is so much a matter of the digestion of a great many details and the use of facts which rise from the historical sense—all caught into a smooth-running story which, taken in itself, cannot fail to hold the reader's attention. The narratives are always in the third person and yet have all the warm interior flow of a story presented through the medium of a stream-of-consciousness

Principal Works

One Man's Initiation—1917 (novel) 1920; also published as First Encounter, 1945

Three Soldiers (novel) 1921

Rosinante to the Road Again (travel essays) 1922

Manhattan Transfer (novel) 1925

*The Moon is a Gong (drama) 1925; published as The Garbage Man, 1926

Facing the Chair: Story of the Americanization of Two Foreignborn Workmen (pamphlet) 1927

*Airways, Inc. (drama) 1928

†The 42nd Parallel (novel) 1930

†1919 (novel) 1932

*Fortune Heights [first publication] (drama) 1933

†The Big Money (novel) 1936

‡Adventures of a Young Man (novel) 1939

The Ground We Stand On (history) 1941

‡Number One (novel) 1943

‡The Grand Design (novel) 1949

The Prospect before Us (nonfiction) 1950

Chosen Country (novel) 1951

The Head and Heart of Thomas Jefferson (biography) 1954

The Theme Is Freedom (essays) 1956

The Men Who Made the Nation (history) 1957

Prospects of a Golden Age (history) 1959

Midcentury (novel) 1961

Mr. Wilson's War (history) 1962

The Best Times: An Informal Memoir (memoirs) 1966

The Shackles of Power: Three Jeffersonian Decades, 1801-1826 (history) 1966

Easter Island: Island of Enigmas (nonfiction) 1971

The Fourteenth Chronicle: Letters and Diaries of John Dos Passos (letters and diaries) 1973

Century's Ebb: The Thirteenth Chronicle (unfinished novel) 1975

*These works were published as Three Plays: The Garbage Man, Airways, Inc., Fortune Heights in 1934.

†These works were published as U.S.A. in 1938.

‡These works were published as District of Columbia in 1952.

first-person. One remarkable achievement is the way in which the element of time is disposed. With no break or unevenness at all, the narrative passes quickly through several years of the character's life, presenting much that is essential briefly, and then contracts, without warning, without being noted, and focuses for several pages upon a single episode which is important. It is an ability which an apprentice writer can best appreciate and comes from the indispensable knowledge of how very much the writer can *omit* . . . and a knowledge of how each sentence can expand in the reader's mind to include a whole context of experience. Another feature to be noted is Dos Passos' immense command of details which seem to come from a thousand American places and to be invested with a kind of historical idiom at all times. (pp. 356-57)

[In] the main, what we get is the typical life of the lower middle-class between 1900 and 1930. Typical indeed, for there is a constant "averaging," a constant effort to describe each character in terms which will reduce him to a type. . . . Their chief values, which they do not examine or question in the least (except for the radicals), are "love" and "money." . . . And the fate of almost all the characters is defeat, inhuman, untragic defeat—either defeat of a violent death without meaning or the more complete degradation of "selling out"—selling one's friends, one's integrity, one's earnest am-

bition and hope, for nothing more than "the big money." By the conclusion of the book, every character with the exception of Ben Compton, the radical leader, has come to the point where self-respect is not remote, but a term as of a dead language. (pp. 358-59)

Whatever else we may say of American life as represented in these narratives, there is one statement which we must make first: it is so, it is true; we have seen this with our own eyes and many of us have lived in this way. This is a true picture of the lives of many Americans, and anyone who doubts the fact can learn for himself very quickly how accurate Dos Passos is. But there is, on the other hand, a great deal more to be said about the truth which the novel as a form is capable of presenting.

To begin the attempt at a thorough judgment, the formal inadequacy of *U.S.A.,* taken as a whole, is the direct experience of every reader. . . . No reader can go from page one to page 1449 without feeling that the newsreels, camera eyes, and biographies, however good they may be in themselves, are interruptions which thwart his interest and break the novel into many isolated parts. Even in the central narratives, where, as in the greatest pure prose . . . the reader passes without an awareness of style to the intense, ragged actuality presented, even here the novel falls into separate parts, even though there is an occasional interweaving of lives. The unity, the *felt* unity, is only the loose grab-bag of time and place, 1919 and the U.S.A. The binding together of lives (and thus of the reader's interest and gaze) into the progress of a plot—an element present even in a work of the scope of *War and Peace*—is wholly lacking. This heaping together of fragments of valuable perception is a characteristic of the best poetry of our time and the connection is interesting. . . . [The] capacity for a narrative framework has gradually disappeared from poetry of the first order: modern poetic style can bear the utmost strain of sensibility, but it cannot tell a story. In the medium of poetry, however, a unity of tone and mood and theme can substitute, although imperfectly, for other kinds of unity. *U.S.A.* cannot be considered a poem, however, and even if it could, Dos Passos does not rise to the level of [poets such as Auden and Pound]. As a narrative, it becomes a suite of narratives in which panels without direct relation to the subject are inserted. . . . As a novel, it is not in any careful sense a novel, but rather an anthology of long stories and prose poems. And it is to be insisted that the unity and form in question are not the abstractions of the critic, but the generic traits of the actual experience of reading fiction.

But form is not, of course, applied to a novel as a press to a tennis racket. It is, on the contrary, the way in which the writer sees his subject, the very means of attempting to see. And thus it is obvious that the formal gaps in *U.S.A.* spring from Dos Passos' effort to see his world in conflicting ways. (pp. 359-61)

The root of the inadequacy [of the novel] is, I think, an inadequate conception of what the truth, the whole truth about the U.S.A., for example, is. The term, truth, is used merely in its common-sensical meaning, of an accurate report of that which is. The truth about the whole of experience is precisely what is more than the truth about any actual standpoint. It is merely the truth about the life of an individual person, as it appeared to the person himself, that we get from Dos Passos. The truth about the whole of experience is more than the sum of many or all standpoints, of many blind and limited lives. The whole truth includes what might have been and what may be and what is not (as not being). It includes the whole scale of imaginative possibilities and the nameless assumptions and values by which a society lives. It is exactly because the whole truth is so complex and various that the imagination is a necessity. And this is the reason why fiction is full of the fictitious and the imaginative. (p. 362)

But furthermore the whole truth is involved in literature in what seems to me a still more basic way. One fundamental postulate of literature seems to me to be here in question. It . . . cannot be argued about because it is the assumption by means of which we are enabled to speak. One can merely point to examples—all literary judgment and analysis being, in the end,

comparative—and as it happens, Dos Passos himself provides his own examples in this novel.

The unquestionable postulate—or presumption—of all literature is the individual of the fullest intelligence and sensibility—at least with respect to the circumstances of the work itself. Perhaps one can call this individual not the omniscient, but the multiscient individual. He is the one who in some one of many quite different fashions *transcends* the situation and the subject. . . . In some form or other the subject is transcended by a superior standpoint, and the superior standpoint reduces itself to one thing, a human being of the greatest intelligence and sensibility, who views all that occurs and is involved in the action, and who is best able to grasp the whole truth of the subject.

What we want of literature is the truth, and the truth is the only intention of *U.S.A.* But, to repeat, the truth is not merely the way in which human beings behave and feel, nor is it wholly contained in their conscious experience. . . . The facts represented are always there, but a good many of them can never be consciously known by any actor involved up to his neck in the present moment, as the characters of *U.S.A.* usually are. Only through the focus of the imagination can the relevant facts be brought into the narrative. In Dos Passos, however, there is a beautiful imaginative sympathy which permits him to get under the skin of his characters, but there is no imagination, and no Don Quixote. Dos Passos testifies to all this by his use of newsreels, just as he seeks the full sensibility in the impressions of the camera eye and the heroic character in the biographies; but in his central narratives the standpoint is always narrowed to what the character himself knows as the quality of his existence, life as it appears to him. And this leveling drags with it and tends to make rather crude and sometimes commonplace the sensibility shown in the other panels. If Dos Passos were not so wholly successful in grasping this level of experience, then, undoubtedly, he would be less aware of the need to jump back to the other levels of truth, and his novel would not break into four "eyes" of uncoördinated vision. Or to shift the metaphor, his novel attempts to achieve the whole truth by going rapidly in two opposite directions—the direction of the known experience of his characters, in all their blindness and limitation, and on the other hand, the direction of the transcendent knowledge of experience, the full truth about it. And thus the formal breakdown was scarcely avoidable.

The view of literature, of the truth, and of the individual assumed by Dos Passos may be attributed to two sources. First to the tradition of naturalism. . . . (pp. 363-65)

But naturalism and its external sources are merely effects of that society which has degraded the human being and his own conception of himself to the point where Dos Passos' presentation of him in his own terms is, in fact, perfectly true. One can only add that it is not the whole truth. The primary source of the formal breakdown of this novel is the U.S.A. It is only by distinguishing between the actual and the remotely potential that one can conceive of a different kind of life from that which Dos Passos accurately presents, on the part of most of the living. It is this mixture of the actual and the potential, however, which has made literature so precious to the human spirit. (p. 366)

One is sure that Dos Passos knows this, since it is the reason for his four forms and his discontinuity. His novel is perhaps the greatest monument of naturalism because it betrays so fully the poverty and disintegration inherent in that method. Dos Passos is the gifted victim of his own extraordinary grasp of the truth. He is a victim of the truth and the whole truth. (p. 367)

Delmore Schwartz, "John Dos Passos and the Whole Truth," in *The Southern Review,* Louisiana State University, Vol. IV, No. 2, Autumn, 1938, pp. 351-67.

JOSEPH WARREN BEACH
(essay date 1947)

[Beach was an American critic and educator. In the following excerpt, he appraises Dos Passos's literary reputation at the midpoint of his career.]

[We] have now had more than twenty years to digest *Manhattan Transfer* and fully ten years to come to terms with the completed trilogy of *U.S.A.* In books like *Journeys between Wars, The Ground We Stand On,* and *State of the Nation,* Dos Passos has exhibited his personal outlook upon the world, furnishing us the context in which to consider his "dramatic" representations of life. We should now be in a position to challenge this figure and ask ourselves what and how great is his significance for literary art.

The first thing we can say with a considerable degree of confidence is that his work before *Manhattan Transfer* is negligible, that his volumes of travel and commentary are relatively negligible, and that his place in literature (thus far) must rest on four novels, *Manhattan Transfer* and the three parts of *U.S.A.* The poems are negligible except as a reminder, important for understanding him, that this man is by natural inclination distinctly "esthetic"—drawn to the picturesque, the decorative, the exotic, and to the romantic in the sense in which that term applies to Amy Lowell and John Gould Fletcher. . . . The influence of Sandburg is strongly felt in *Manhattan Transfer* in the language and arrangement of the prose poems prefixed to the chapters. But the influence of Sandburg means a passage from the mere cult of the exotic to a more robust grappling with the familiar,—from the esthetic as evasion to the esthetic as significant composition.

The early fictions are negligible for similar reasons, and equally interesting for the light they throw on the author's temperament. *One Man's Initiation* and *Streets of Night* show us a young man fastidious and sensitive, shrinking from cruelty and ugliness physical and moral, and acutely conscious of the presence of ugliness in war and in sex. *Three Soldiers* . . . is in line with many novels following the first World War in jealous concern for the individual soul trying vainly to save itself from the clutches of the military (the social) machine. One thing more that is clear from these fictions is that their author is not a born storyteller in the traditional sense, being more concerned with the relation of the individual to society than he is with the idiosyncrasy and personal exploits of the individual.

The volumes of commentary on the state of the world are relatively negligible from the point of view of literary art. But they are of great importance for the understanding of Dos Passos' social philosophy, and they have many sturdy merits. They are good reporting in the sense that they render what he has seen—in interbellum Russia, in the United States during the second war, in Spain, in the Pacific—with a minimum of interference by the author. Dos Passos is patient and humble before the facts. He shows no *parti pris.* His ideology is that of one seeking to understand. He is, I suppose, some kind of socialist; which means, in effect, that he abhors the tyrannies and impersonal cruelties of our industrial machine. He can record the feeling of the Spanish peasant that in America men are not able to live their own lives. He is indignant over "justice denied in Massachusetts" or to the Harlan miners. He is sympathetic toward industrial experiments under the New Deal. He is for the American way, but he does not feel that contemporary capitalism favors the ideals of Tom Paine and Roger Williams. In 1945, in the preface to *First Encounter,* he is as safe in his political pronouncements as a candidate for a college presidency.

Perhaps the disillusionments of the last quarter of a century have taught us that there are no short cuts to a decent ordering of human affairs, that the climb back up out of the pit of savagery to a society of even approximate justice and freedom must necessarily be hard and slow. The quality of the means we use will always determine the ends we reach.

There is nothing in the style of this to suggest any kind of literary distinction. The only distinction it has is that of earnestness and mild good sense. The last sentence, to be sure, is radical, and if taken seriously would mean a revolution in human behavior, being as it is a reversal of Machiavelli's doctrine. But it is pitched so low that few will hear it, let alone take it to heart. The merit of Dos Passos' own style, when he is not trying for esthetic expressiveness, is the ingratiating humbleness of spirit which it displays. His sole ambition is to be the self-effacing medium of what he has to render. And that is, in his best fiction, a merit of very high order.

The turn from one of these books of commentary to *Manhattan Transfer* or *U.S.A.* is like the turn from Victor Bergen to Charley McCarthy, so much more vivid and colorful is the creature than the creator. (pp. 406-09)

Dos Passos has always been a "collectivist" writer. Of the two sciences that preside over the modern literary heaven he has taken sociology rather than psychology for his guiding star. The individual interests him, but mainly as a member of the social body; and his aim is always to give a cross-section of this body so as to show the structure of its tissues. In *Manhattan Transfer* it is the entire urban center that he shows; in *U.S.A.* the entire country, from Hollywood to Washington, from a Fargo boarding house to a New Orleans garage. In both cases he covers the period from the Boer War to the great boom following the first World War. In *Manhattan Transfer* the system is to present a prodigious number of persons of the most representative groups in short shots, without transition, each going his own way; some of them appearing once, just for the record, some several times over a course of years, some frequently enough to give the impression of leading characters, especially when their orbits cross in marriage, business, or other social contact.

In more or less remote ways they all affect one another; but they hardly seem aware of this, and when they do become more closely involved, this hardly amounts to a plot, with its clearly marked issues, critical scenes, and dramatic resolution. The time element is not there for the sake of a plot, but simply to furnish a measure of process in the social body. What the characters say and do is thematic and illustrative of sociological principles. (pp. 410-11)

In *U.S.A.* there is even less of plot in the conventional sense, but fewer characters are featured and the course of their lives is given in greater detail with less frequent interruptions. Each case is more fully documented. But these *are* case histories for a social worker's filing cabinet. (p. 411)

Many readers object to the unconventionality of Dos Passos' narrative method, as they do to that of Joyce in *Ulysses* and Eliot in *The Waste Land.* The simplest way to meet this objection is to point to the principle of abstract composition as it appears in various schools of post-impressionist painting as well as in poetry and fiction. The object here is not the complete and literal reproduction of a scene now present to the bodily eye and according to the laws of optics. It is rather the assembling within the frame of one picture of representative portions of many scenes related to one another not by their simultaneous presence in the same spot but by mental association—of contrast, analogy, irony, symbolic correspondence—and given significance and esthetic effectiveness by their planned arrangement in the new visual pattern. The application of this principle in the novel obviously does away with the "dramatic" type of narrative (with its neatly articulated "beginning, middle and end") that has dominated fiction from the beginning. There is no reason to suppose that this principle of abstract composition will displace the established tradition in fiction,—which has the advantage of following what we may call the standard or commonsense way of arranging human life in the imagination. It is sufficient to remind readers that Dos Passos is working on a new and in some ways more rewarding line, and suggest that they look for his effects in the direction in which they were sought by him.

The same readers who object to this narrative technique are likely to be repelled by the inconclusiveness of the story, and by the little meaning and little value in the lives presented. Well, that of course is Dos Passos' theme. If he does not offer examples of generous souls pursuing and achieving noble ends, it is because his main impression of contemporary life is of ordinary people caught in the mechanism of a soulless society, and exceptional cases would be irrelevant to the point he is making. If he does not make the point himself in personal commentary, it is because he is a modern objective realist, who does not want to risk the artistic integrity of his performance by mounting the soapbox.

The technical novelties of his narrative procedure are all intended to take the place of personal commentary, as well as to relieve the tedium of the conventional. (pp. 412-13)

The incoherencies of stream-of-consciousness in the Camera Eye [sections of *U.S.A.*] are a perfect rendering of the naïveté of early childhood, the confused gropings of conscious manhood. The tonelessness and uneventfulness of the case histories correspond to the sheer behaviorism exemplified in these lives, which are made up of reaction to stimuli rather than of the voluntary pursuit of significant ends. Perhaps the furthest triumph of art in Dos Passos is the virtually complete submergence of his own personal style in that of his characters. All that is left here of the author-as-author is the somewhat greater concern with color and form in the outward scene than can be plausibly attributed to Mac and Margot. Vocabulary and idiom, rhetoric and grammar are those of the several characters; and above all what may be called the moral tone is that of the people who go through these undramatic adventures. In some cases, where the spiritual confusions are particularly dense, as with Eleanor Stoddard and J. Ward Moorehouse, the effect is an irony all the more destructive because it is free from burlesque ventriloquism. The dialogue has not the point and resonance of Hemingway's, but serves well the rather different purpose of Dos Passos. Here we acknowledge with delight in an objective artist that gift for yielding himself wholly to his subject which, in the volumes of personal commentary, left us with some sense of let-down.

Altogether Dos Passos has given us the most comprehensive and convincing picture of American life in certain highly characteristic phases that is anywhere to be found. And if we shrink from the frosty glitter of the exhibit, we must yield to its fascination as a work of imaginative art. We are held by the teeming fertility of his invention, the colorfulness of his appeal to the senses, and by the bold originality and stark impressiveness of his structural composition.

But this brings us to the most radical of all objections that may be urged against Dos Passos. It may be urged that his representation of human nature is purely external and superficial, that he actually implies as his own philosophy the very behaviorism of which his characters are victims, that he has no conception of anything other than man political and economic. (pp. 414-15)

Dos Passos is not aiming at depth psychology, and must deny himself much of the fascination of a Joyce or Proust. He is not aiming to expose the dialectical complexities of European culture. . . . The only riddle he poses is the simple relation of the individual to the group history of his own time. Above all he has chosen to present men not self-conscious and deliberately seeking for answers and solutions, but men passive to the commonest impulses of instinct. If one's taste is for poetry and metaphysics and for nothing else, one will deny the appeal of Dos Passos and will rate him as distinctly inferior.

But if one's taste is more catholic, one will at least consider the nature of his artistic intention. He has, one may assume, no love for flat souls; but his *theme* is souls made flat by something in the culture-complex in which they have their being. To have presented them in other terms would have been to betray his subject. To complain that his representation is two- or at best three-dimensional is simply to characterize the method and medium which best suit his artistic intention. The thing to note is the brilliant virtuosity with which this method is applied and the inescapable impressiveness of the effect. One can be a passionate devotee of Proust and still admit the esthetic importance of Dos Passos.

But then, one says, his study is not "religious," and he can therefore have no standard of values, no moral sense, without which human nature becomes an unedifying subject of contemplation. Well, that is the moot question of our time, and not to be decided by the testimony of a horde of poets and critics, some of them deliberately unacquainted with the intellectual culture of our age, and many of them inclined to confusing double-talk—employing such terms as religion and myth in senses that would never have been admitted by Dante, Milton, or Swift, let alone St. Augustine or St. Thomas. (pp. 415-16)

There is one quasi-religious concept of which Dos Passos is strongly aware. It is what Kenneth Burke calls "piety." This, he says, is the desire, the impulse of the human being to identify himself with the group. And this, one would suppose, is a human development of what in the lower animals is called gregariousness. Dos Passos' characters, while reasonably gregarious, are singularly lacking in the type of piety that Jesus calls love. But this again is his *theme;* he is depicting a society unaware of what it takes to make a society. And the atomistic lovelessness of his people is a reminder of what he considers the great desideratum. If the reader misses this, it is because he is given objective realism where what might be expected is a tone of obvious satire.

But there is something missing to make these characters full-fledged human beings, and that is the conscious sighting and willed pursuit of ends conceived as having value. Here again we must give Dos Passos the benefit of the doubt and assume that this is precisely what he has in mind. His aim is to depict a society of people passively drifting without benefit of inner controls. His people are for the most part likeable and easily understood, but they are seldom lovable or admirable, and for that reason they are individually unimportant to the reader. And that is the head and front of his offense. His people are not "sympathetic" like those of Tolstoi, Dickens, Henry James, or André Malraux. They do not have the psychological interest of Dostoevsky's or Proust's, or the poetic interest of Kafka's. His vision of man is not religious but rationalistic. And most modern readers prefer psychology and the religious vision, along with reasonably sympathetic characters.

The reader will consult his taste, as ever. But tastes change and broaden. Dos Passos is now a standard though unpopular writer, like Henry James. He is an artist of bold originality, ingenuity and dash. He has covered the American scene more adequately than any other novelist. His social commentary is sharply defined and mordant. He has survived some twenty years of critical scrutiny. . . . Another twenty years and he may need no apologia. Our children may positively relish his flavor and take him for granted as an American classic. (pp. 417-18)

Joseph Warren Beach, "Dos Passos 1947," in *The Sewanee Review,* Vol. LV, No. 3, Summer, 1947, pp. 406-18.

JEAN-PAUL SARTRE
(essay date 1947)

[A French philosopher, dramatist, novelist, and essayist, Sartre was one of the chief contributors to the philosophical movement of Existentialism. In the following excerpt from an essay that first appeared in print in French in 1947, he analyzes Dos Passos's narrative technique, commending what he perceives as the contradictory essence of Dos Passos's art and denoting him "the greatest writer of our time."]

A novel is a mirror. So everyone says. But what is meant by *reading* a novel? It means, I think, jumping into the mirror. You suddenly find yourself on the other side of the glass, among people and objects that have a familiar look. But they merely look familiar. We have never really seen them. The things of our world have, in turn, become outside reflections. You close the book, step over the edge of the mirror and return to this honest-to-goodness world, and you find furniture, gardens and people who have nothing to say to you. The mirror that closed behind you reflects them peacefully, and now you would swear that art is a reflection. There are clever people who go so far as to talk of distorting mirrors.

Dos Passos very consciously uses this absurd and insistent illusion to impel us to revolt. He had done everything possible to make his novel seem a mere reflection. He has even donned the garb of populism. The reason is that his art is not gratuitous; he wants to prove something. But observe what a curious aim he has. He wants to show us this world, our own—to *show* it only, without explanations or comment. . . . We recognize immediately the sad abundance of these untragic lives. They are our own lives, these innumerable, planned, botched, immediately forgotten and constantly renewed adventures that slip by without leaving a trace, without involving anyone, until the time when one of them, no different from any of the others, suddenly, as if through some clumsy trickery, sickens a man for good and throws a mechanism out of gear.

Now, it is by depicting, as we ourselves might depict, these too familiar appearances with which we all put up that Dos Passos makes them unbearable. (pp. 61-2)

Dos Passos' hate, despair and lofty contempt are real. But that is precisely why his world is not real; it is a created object. I know of none—not even Faulkner's or Kafka's—in which the art is greater or better hidden. I know of none that is more precious, more touching or closer to us. This is because he takes his material from our world. And yet, there is no stranger or more distant world. Dos Passos has invented only one thing, an art of story-telling. But that is enough to create a universe. . . .

Dos Passos' time is his own creation; it is neither fictional nor narrative. It is rather, if you like, historical time. (p. 62)

The fictional event is a nameless presence; there is nothing one can say about it, for it develops. . . . In Dos Passos, the things that happen are named first, and then the dice are cast, as they are in our memories. . . .

The facts are clearly outlined; they are ready for *thinking about.* But Dos Passos never thinks them. Not for an instant does the order of casualty betray itself in chronological order. There is no narrative, but rather the jerky unreeling of a rough and uneven memory, which sums up a period of several years in a few words only to dwell languidly over a minute fact. Like our real memories, it is a jumble of miniatures and frescoes. There is relief enough, but it is cunningly scattered at random. One step further would give us the famous idiot's monologue in *The Sound and the Fury.* But that would still involve intellectualizing, suggesting an explanation in terms of the irrational, suggesting a Freudian order beneath this disorder. Dos Passos stops just in time. As a result of this, past things retain a flavour of the present; they still remain, in their exile, what they once were, inexplicable tumults of colour, sound and passion. Each event is irreducible, a gleaming and solitary *thing* that does not flow from anything else, but suddenly arises to join other things. For Dos Passos, narrating means adding. This accounts for the slack air of his style. (p. 63)

Passions and gestures are also things. Proust analysed them, related them to former states and thereby made them inevitable. Dos Passos wants to retain only their factual nature. . . . Dos Passos imposes upon us . . . the unpleasant impression of an indeterminacy of detail. Acts, emotions and ideas suddenly settle within a character, make themselves at home and then disappear without his having much to say in the matter. You cannot say he submits to them. He experiences them. There seems to be no law governing their appearance.

Nevertheless, they once did exist. This lawless past is irremediable. Dos Passos has purposely chosen the perspective of history to tell a story. He wants to make us feel that the stakes are down. In *Man's Hope*, Malraux says, more or less, that "the tragic thing about death is that it transforms life into a destiny." With the opening lines of his book, Dos Passos settles down into death. The lives he tells about are all closed in on themselves. . . . We constantly have the feeling that these vague, human lives are destinies. . . . [Beneath] the violent colours of these beautiful, motley objects that Dos Passos presents there is something petrified. Their significance is fixed. Close your eyes and try to remember your own life, try to remember it *that way;* you will stifle. It is this unrelieved stifling that Dos Passos wanted to express. In capitalist society, men do not have lives, they have only destinies. He never says this, but he makes it felt throughout. He expresses it discreetly, cautiously, until we feel like smashing our destinies. We have become rebels; he has achieved his purpose. (pp. 64-5)

[The] narrator often ceases to coincide completely with the hero. The hero could not quite have said what he does say, but you feel a discreet complicity between them. The narrator relates from the outside what the hero would have wanted him to relate. By means of this complicity, Dos Passos, without warning us, has us make the transition he was after. We suddenly find ourselves inside a horrible memory whose every recollection makes us uneasy, a bewildering memory that is no longer that of either the characters or the author. (pp. 65-6)

Dos Passos reports all his characters' utterances to us in the style of a statement to the Press. Their words are thereby cut off from thought, and become pure utterances, simple reactions that must be registered as such, in the behaviourist style upon which Dos Passos

Dos Passos in a sketch by Adolph Dehn.

draws when it suits him to do so. But, at the same time, the utterance takes on a social importance; it is inviolable, it becomes a maxim. . . . Dos Passos makes a pretence of presenting gestures as pure events, as mere exteriors, as free, animal movements. But this is only appearance. Actually, in relating them, he adopts the point of view of the chorus, of public opinion. (pp. 66-7)

In order to understand the words, in order to make sense out of the paragraphs, I first have to adopt his point of view. I have to play the role of the obliging chorus. This consciousness exists only through me; without me there would be nothing but black spots on white paper. But even while I *am* this collective consciousness, I want to wrench away from it, to see it from the judge's point of view, that is, to get free of myself. This is the source of the shame and uneasiness with which Dos Passos knows how to fill the reader. I am a reluctant accomplice (though I am not even sure that I am reluctant), creating and rejecting social taboos. I am, deep in my heart, a revolutionary again, an unwilling one.

In return, how I hate Dos Passos' men! I am given a fleeting glimpse of their minds, just enough to see that they are living animals. Then, they begin to unwind their endless tissue of ritual statements and sacred gestures. For them, there is no break between inside and outside, between body and consciousness, but only between the stammerings of an individual's timid, intermittent, fumbling thinking and the messy world of collective representations. What a simple process this is, and how effective! . . . [Dos Passos] can give all his attention to rendering a single life's special character. Each of his characters is unique; what happens to him could happen to no one else. What does it matter, since Society has marked him more deeply than could any special circumstance, since *he is* Society? Thus, we get a glimpse of an order beyond the accidents of fate or the contingency of detail. . . . (pp. 67-8)

Dos Passos' man is a hybrid creature, an interior-exterior being. We go on living with him and within him, with his vacillating, individual consciousness, when suddenly it wavers, weakens, and is diluted in the collective consciousness. We follow it up to that point and suddenly, before we notice, we are on the outside. The man behind the looking-glass is a strange, contemptible, fascinating creature. Dos Passos knows how to use this constant shifting to fine effect. . . .

Dos Passos' world—like those of Faulkner, Kafka and Stendhal—is impossible because it is contradictory. But therein lies its beauty. Beauty is a veiled contradiction. I regard Dos Passos as the greatest writer of our time. (p. 69)

Jean-Paul Sartre, "John Dos Passos and '1919'," in *John Dos Passos: A Collection of Critical Essays,* edited by Andrew Hook, Prentice-Hall, Inc., 1974, pp. 61-9.

EDMUND WILSON

(essay 1952)

[An important American critic, Wilson wrote on cultural, historical, and literary matters and was a tireless promoter of writers of the 1920s, 1930s, and 1940s. In the following excerpt from an essay that first appeared in his *Shores of Light* in 1952, he discusses the play *Airways, Inc.*, maintaining that it embodies Dos Passos's broad-reaching social, political, and economic philosophy.]

John Dos Passos's *Airways, Inc.,* was produced in March as the last play of the second season of the New Playwrights' Theater, and almost entirely failed to attract attention. (p. 31)

Airways is, like the group's other plays, a social-political-economic fable; but Dos Passos is more intelligent than most of his associates—he is able to enter into more points of view—and he is a much better artist. His play is neither a naturalistic study nor a vaudeville in the manner of John Howard Lawson, though it has some of the elements of both; it is rather a sort of dramatic poem of contemporary America. With great ingenuity, Dos Passos had assembled on a single suburban street-corner representatives of most of the classes and groups that go to make up our society. We concentrate upon the life of a single middle-class household, but this is submerged in a larger world: its fate is inextricably bound up with a current real estate boom; a strike that eventually gives rise to a Sacco-Vanzetti incident; and the promotion of a commercial aviation company. Nor, as is likely to be the case in this kind of play, are the social types merely abstractions which never persuade the imagination. Dos Passos has succeeded in producing the illusion that behind the little suburban street-corner of the Turners lies all the life of a great American city—all the confusion of America itself; and *Airways* made the meager stage of the bleak little Grove Street Theater seem as big as any stage I have ever seen. Dos Passos has also given the household of the Turners an extension in time as well as in space: he has provided a chorus of two old men, an American inventor and a Hungarian revolutionist, whose role is to relate what we see to what has gone before in history and to what may be expected to come after.

It is in the construction of this sort of sociological fable that Dos Passos particularly excels. The strength of his novel, *Manhattan Transfer,* lay in the thoroughness and the steady hand with which he executed a similar anatomy on the city of New York as a whole.

As a dramatist he is less expert; and *Airways* suffers in certain ways from comparison with *Manhattan Transfer.* Dos Passos sometimes interrupts his action with long passages of monologue, which, though they might go down easily in a novel, discourage our attention in the theater; and his last act, though the two separate scenes are excellent in themselves, fails to draw the different strands together as we expect a third act to do. But, on the other hand, *Airways,* at its best, has an eloquence and a spirit that *Manhattan Transfer* largely lacked. It is one of the best-written things that Dos Passos has so far done—perhaps freer than any other of his productions both from rhetoric doing duty for feeling and from descriptions too relentlessly piled up. Dos Passos is probably only now arriving at his mature prose style.

So much for the purely artistic aspect of *Airways.* It is impossible to discuss it further without taking into account Dos Passos's political philosophy. Dos Passos is, one gathers from his work, a social revolutionist: he believes that, in the United States as elsewhere, the present capitalistic regime is destined to be overthrown by a class-conscious proletariat. And his disapproval of capitalist society seems to imply a distaste for all the beings who go to compose it. In *Manhattan Transfer,* it was not merely New York, but humanity that came off badly. Dos Passos, in exposing the diseased organism, had the effect, though not, I believe, the intention, of condemning the sufferers along with the disease; and even when he seemed to desire to make certain of his characters sympathetic, he had a way of putting them down.

Now, in *Airways,* there are several characters whom Dos Passos has succeeded in making either admirable or attractive, but these are, in every case, either radicals or their sympathizers. His bias against the economic system is so strong that it extends beyond its official representatives to all those human beings whose only fault is to have been born where such a system prevails and to be so lacking in courage or perspicacity as not to have allied themselves with the forces that are trying to fight it. (pp. 31-3)

Now, the life of middle-class America, even under capitalism and even in a city like New York, is not so unattractive as Dos Passos makes it—no human life under any conditions can ever have been so unattractive. Under however an unequal distribution of wealth, human beings are still capable of enjoyment, affection and enthusiasm—even of integrity and courage. Nor are these qualities and emotions entirely confined to class-conscious workers and their leaders. There are moments in reading a novel or seeing a play by Dos Passos when one finds oneself ready to rush to the defense of even the American bathroom, even the Ford car—which, after all, one begins to reflect, have perhaps done as much to rescue us from helplessness, ignorance and squalor as the prophets of revolution. We may begin to reflect upon the relation, in Dos Passos, of political opinions to artistic effects. Might it not, we ask ourselves, be possible—have we not, in fact, seen it occur—for a writer to hold Dos Passos's political opinions and yet not depict our middle-class republic as a place where no birds sing, no flowers bloom and where the very air is almost unbreathable? For, in the novels and plays of Dos Passos, everybody loses out: if he is on the right side of the social question, he has to suffer, if he is not snuffed out; if he is on the oppressors' side, his pleasures are made repulsive. When a man as intelligent as Dos Passos—that is, a man a good deal more intelligent than, say, Michael Gold or Upton Sinclair, who hold similar political views—when so intelligent a man and so good an artist allows his bias so to falsify his picture of life that, in spite of all the accurate observation and all the imaginative insight, its values are partly those of melodrama—we begin to guess some stubborn sentimentalism at the bottom of the whole thing, some deeply buried streak of hysteria of which his misapplied resentments represent the aggressive side. And from the moment we suspect the process by which he has arrived at his political ideas, the ideas themselves become suspect.

In the meantime, whatever diagnosis we may make of Dos Passos's infatuation with the social revolution, he remains one of the few first-rate figures among our writers of his generation, and the only one of these who has made a systematic effort to study all the aspects of America and to take account of all its elements, to compose them into a picture which makes some general sense. Most of the first-rate men of Dos Passos's age—Hemingway, Wilder, Fitzgerald—cultivate their own little corners and do not confront the situation as a whole. Only Dos Passos has tried to take hold of it. In the fine last speech of *Airways,* he allows the moral of his play to rise very close to the surface. The spinster sister of the Turner household has just received the news that the strike leader, with whom she has been in love and who has been made the victim of a frame-up, has finally been electrocuted: "Now I'm beginning to feel it," she says,

> the house without Walter, the street without him, the city without him, the future that we lived in instead of a honeymoon without him, everything stark without him. Street where I've lived all these years shut up in a matchwood house full of bitterness. City where I've lived walled up in old dead fear. America, where I've scurried from store to subway to church to home, America that I've never known. World where I've lived without knowing. What can I do now that he is gone and that he has left me full of scalding wants, what can I do with the lack of him inside me like a cold stone? The house I lived in wrecked, the people I loved wrecked, around me there's nothing but words stinging like

wasps. Where can I go down the dark street, where can I find a lover in the sleeping city? At what speed of the wind can I fly away, to escape these words that burn and sting, to escape the lack that is in me like a stone?

It is true that the lack of real leadership is felt by us today as a stone. It is Dos Passos's recognition of this—his relentless reiteration of his conviction that there is something lacking, something wrong, in America—as well as his insistence on the importance of America—that gives his work its validity and power. It is equally true, of course, of H. L. Mencken that he finds something lacking and something wrong; but the effect of Mencken on his admirers is to make them wash their hands of social questions. Mencken has made it the fashion to speak of politics as an obscene farce. And Dos Passos is now almost alone among the writers of his generation in continuing to take the social organism seriously. (pp. 34-5)

Edmund Wilson, "Dos Passos and the Social Revolution," in *Dos Passos: A Collection of Critical Essays,* edited by Andrew Hook, Prentice-Hall, Inc., 1974, pp. 31-5.

MALCOLM COWLEY
(essay date 1973)

[Cowley is best known for his literary criticism and for his critical editions of American authors Walt Whitman, Nathaniel Hawthorne, Ernest Hemingway, William Faulkner, and F. Scott Fitzgerald. In the following excerpt, he addresses the changing literary stature of Dos Passos following the publication of *U. S. A.*]

The trilogy of novels recording what he learned from his travels is an impressive work that embodies a paradox. Dos Passos was primarily interested in presenting his *material*—that is, in offering a panorama of American life at all levels over a period of thirty years. But no previous novelist had found a method of painting such a panorama. Tolstoy? one asks. His *War and Peace* had achieved a breadth beyond the dreams of other novelists, but even Tolstoy had devoted most of his attention to four great families of the Russian nobility. Dos Passos wanted to present typical persons from many levels of society, giving sharp attention to each—even using their special idioms—while suggesting the movement of society as a whole. To do so he was forced to invent devices of his own. . . . There were to be hundreds of characters, but the substance of the novel would be the life stories of twelve more or less typical men and women. . . . At this point . . . [he] was setting out to make himself a master technician.

The paradox is that the technique, much more than the observed material it was designed to present, has had an effect on literary history in more than one country. Dos Passos' picture of America succumbing to decay as competitive capitalism gave way to monopoly capitalism is powerful, but in the end subjective; one is not obliged to accept his notion of a catastrophic decline and fall. One has to acknowledge, however, that his technical inventions soon reappeared in the mainstream of fiction. *The Grapes of Wrath, The Naked and the Dead,* and scores of other American novels . . . have owed a debt to Dos Passos for solving some of their problems in advance. So have novels by famous Europeans, as Jean-Paul Sartre explained in the *Atlantic Monthly:*

> . . . it was after reading a book by Dos Passos that I thought for the first time of weaving a novel out of various, simultaneous lives. . . .

(pp. 10-12)

[Nothing] he wrote after *U.S.A.* had the same widespread and lasting effect. . . . (p. 14)

His loss of literary stature might tempt one into making a false generalization about fiction and politics. Dos Passos was a radical and wrote works of great inventiveness and power; then he became conservative and produced such bald, embittered tracts as *Most Likely to Succeed* and *The Great Days;* so therefore—but that is entirely too simple. The history of fiction seems to show that great novelists can hold almost any sort of position, radical or conservative, aristocratic or egalitarian; they can be monarchists like Balzac or angry reformers like Dickens, or they can shift positions like Dostoyevsky without necessarily harming their work—but on one absolute condition, that they should believe in their characters more firmly than they hold to their opinions. Dos Passos in his later work often failed to meet that condition, and there too he broke another rule that seems to have been followed by great novelists. They can regard their characters with love or hate or anything between, but cannot regard them with tired aversion. They can treat events as tragic, comic, farcical, pathetic, or almost anything but consistently repulsive. (p. 16)

In . . . books he published during the later years there are admirable passages, though it must be added that almost all of them are retrospective. . . . It is as if [he] were saying that the best times were all in the past, or as if, in the various prospect of desolation, he could not bear to contemplate his literary decline and fall. (p. 17)

Malcolm Cowley, "Dos Passos: The Learned Poggius," in *The Southern Review,* Louisiana State University, Vol. IX, No. 1, Winter, 1973, pp. 88-9.

GEORGE J. BECKER
(essay 1974)

[Becker was an American educator, critic, and translator. In the following excerpt, he surveys Dos Passos's literary career, focusing on the author's dual role of novelist and chronicler of his times.]

[Dos Passos'] preparation as a writer may be seen as four separate rites of passage, subjection to major ordeals of mind and spirit, which determined and tempered his view of the world and therefore the nature of his art.

He had, first of all, to come to grips with the actualities of life in the United States, from which he was isolated by the unusual circumstances of his birth and upbringing. Beyond that, World War I was to him a genuine initiation, a quick—and safe—plunge into the stream of real life that expunged the conventional expectations and beliefs of sheltered youth. The war also brought to a head the forces of socialism—communism, largely theoretical up to that point, in revolutions which were to provide a major cultural and intellectual referent for at least a generation. Siren song, intellectual pitfall, liberating vision, whatever the Russian experiment was, it had to be faced. Statesmen, artists, thinkers, above all historians of the twentieth century had to come to terms with that shattering phenomenon. Finally, for the aspiring writer there was the new milieu of the arts, somewhat belated in the United States, but when it did come as important for the development of the American writer as the ferment of the nineteenth century had been for his European counterpart.

In addition to these four major involvements there were two particular predilections of John Dos Passos that helped to direct his thought and to determine the way he would synthesize his experience. He was from an early age an indefatigable traveler and was avid to report what he saw. And, controlling his observation of social structures and events was a political-philosophical bias that may most simply be identified as Jeffersonian. Without stretching truth too far, we may see in Dos Passos a man with the simplistic vision of the Enlightenment let loose in the dynamic chaos of the twentieth century. There is bound to be difference of opinion as to the accuracy of his judgment of that world, but there can be no doubt that in viewing and reporting it he was consistently his own man. (pp. 2-3)

A slight work, [*One Man's Initiation—1917*] bears much the same relation to his later writings as Tolstoy's *Sevastopol* bears to *War and Peace.* In each case there is an evident desire to bear truthful witness to the facts of war without much in the way of technical expertise. Certainly Dos Passos' work is not the great war novel that he said he was planning in his mind a few weeks after he arrived in France with the ambulance corps (and before he had any real experience of war). Rather it is an unpretentious series of impressions held together by the experiences of the fictional Martin Howe and his sidekick Tom Randolph in their noncombatant role as ambulance drivers. The novel is highly visual, made up of scores of vignettes of war. The narrative diction is unduly poetic, but the dialogue mostly rings true, and over all there is little arty straining for effect. (p. 23)

Three Soldiers (1921) brought [his] capacity for registering experience into play on a broader and more comprehensive scale. It was timely, and its success was immediate. There had never been a war novel like it. To a large extent it set the pattern of realistic war novels for the next thirty years, until relief from the grimness of war was sought by demonstration of its absurdity, as in *Catch 22*. . . . [Dos Passos shifted] the focus from men at war to war itself.

He did this in two ways: by means of a comprehensive metaphor and by means of a realistic cross section. The metaphor states bluntly that the army is a machine that dehumanizes men, that it is without mind and feeling and destroys mind and feeling in all whom it touches. . . . The metaphor is obvious—once someone thought of it—and the author makes the most of it, contrasting mechanical process with the rhetorical camouflage by which the machine is concealed and ennobled. Patriotism, making the world safe for democracy, punishing the Hun—myriad slogans to manipulate men's minds—all of these are meaningless and irrelevant when one looks at the inexorable grinding away of the machine. (pp. 24-5)

Three elements in this early novel point forward to the mature works. Trivial but significant is the use of contemporary songs, documentary in that they are what the soldiers sang, but also broadly evocative of time and place and feeling. More important is the novelist's control of dialogue. Each soldier speaks his particular kind of language, cleaned up a bit but very accurate. Most important of all is the fact that the major characters tend to be types rather than individuals. They embody characteristic states, or attitudes, rather than significant particular responses. At this point in his writing Dos Passos was not yet committed to the precise kind of characterization he wished to employ. He started with stereotypes but allowed John Andrews to become an individual. Yet over all we can discern a disposition not to render characters fully but to give them the outlines and functions of figures in a frieze. (p. 30)

In spite of this auspicious beginning Dos Passos

had not clearly found his direction. In fact, he backslid in a distressing way, trying to consolidate his reputation as new authors often do by publishing earlier, and inferior, works which are better left in oblivion. Though not published until 1923, *Streets of Night* belongs to the period of green apprenticeship and is a depressing indication of the path the author might have followed if he had remained in the cocoon of faded preciosity. The novel is abstract, conventionally symbolic, and bloodless, setting up a contrast between those who are afraid of life and those who plunge into it and try to meet it on its own terms. (p. 31)

[*Streets of Night*] states a recognizable human dilemma, but in unexciting and hackneyed terms. His Bostonians are conventionally anemic; his real life is nothing but a few recognizable pictures at an exhibition.

The same criticism must be directed at *A Pushcart at the Curb*, a collection of poems published in 1922, verse that belongs to the author's salad days of touristic emotion, though the "Quai de Tournelle" section derives from the months in Paris in 1919 when he was writing *Three Soldiers* and had presumably moved beyond sentimental prettiness. As the title suggests, the poems seek out the picturesque in foreign settings. They are modest and uninflated, but they show no awareness that a revolution in poetry had been going on for the past ten years. (p. 33)

Dos Passos also had his fling at writing plays. While his interest in the theater was as much social as literary, he did write three plays which are, in their way, important for their attempt to do something original in that form. His first play, *The Garbage Man* . . . [produced as *The Moon Is a Gong*] is an experimental effort to portray the life of the Twenties in an expressionistic manner and has something in common with *Manhattan Transfer* by reason of its kaleidoscopic format. . . . The discontinuity of the play makes it hard to follow. The individual scenes are sometimes interesting, sometimes opaque. Over all, it lacks coherence and has only visual appeal. (p. 34)

[*Airways, Inc.*] develops a contrast between the little people and the coercive forces of capitalist society: jerrybuilt housing, wage slavery, corporate sharp practice, strike breaking (a Jewish labor leader goes to the chair, recalling the Sacco-Vanzetti case), the tawdry enjoyments of the young, the deprivation of the old, cant phrases and attitudes that cripple thought and action—these are the content. The most interesting dimension of the play, though confused in presentation, comes in the figure of the Professor, a European revolutionary whose best friend sold him out. His comments make the spectator realize that all this has happened before, that history is a repetitious treadmill and exploitation the common fate of man, which undermines the play's polemic immediacy. (pp. 34-5)

[The third and longest of these plays, *Fortune Heights*] was never produced in the United States but appears to have been put on in Russia. It is a depression play in advance of the depression, focusing on a real-estate promotion scheme in a vague locale on a national highway where the extent of the dream actually realized is presented by an unprepossessing filling station. The latter is the locus for the coming and going of a large and varied cast of people who are rootless, poverty-stricken, and without any system of human values. At the end the service-station owner and his family have been evicted and the property has been repossessed. New owners come in, imbued with their own dreams. The same sorry round of inhumanity and greed is about to be played over again.

All three plays are in fact more novelistic than dramatic. They are diffuse; they practice no economy; they have little of the heightened tension which is the basis of drama. The characters are stereotypes who somehow do not come even half alive, as they do in the novels. Both the scattershot expressionism of presentation and the stereotyped doctrinal conceptions in plot and character militate against these works as plays. There is none of the poignancy or illumination of tragedy, though they are clearly intended to point up the tragic nature of the times. There is more drama in the vignettes of *Manhattan Transfer* than there is in these plays, just as there is more poetry in the "Camera Eye" sections of *U.S.A.* than is to be found in Dos Passos' formal efforts at poetry. By trial and error he found that conventional literary forms were not for him. By good luck he found his medium in what he ultimately called the "contemporary chronicle." (pp. 35-6)

While the cross section was by no means Dos Passos' invention, with *Manhattan Transfer* (1925) he brought it to a perfection not matched by any of his predecessors. At the same time he created the paramount novel of the big city. This accomplishment represented the full implementation of nineteenth-century realism in the American novel, though with a difference. . . .

This type of novel does not have fixed rules but can be described as a kind of mosaic, or, better, a revolving stage that presents a multitude of scenes and characters which, taken together, convey a sense of the life of a given milieu and by extension give the tone of contemporary life generally. The strategy is to move the reader through a varied series of actions involving a broad and representative cast of characters. It is inductive, a sort of Gallup poll, by which the meaning is the sum of all the parts. (p. 38)

This type of novel almost automatically exhibits unity of place. . . . It handles the dimension of time in a variety of ways. Dos Passos opts here for the predominant time pattern, that of a period of years approximating a generation, a sufficient span of growth and change to demonstrate the effects of a given milieu. While *Manhattan Transfer* is not a chronicle of public events to the same extent as *U.S.A.* is, it does have a sufficient time scheme to assist the reader's orientation. (p. 39)

[The] lack of detailed chronological reference is important in that it directs attention not to people's subjection to major external forces such as wars, ideologies, and economic crises, but to something more subtle, a changing psychosocial ambiance, a revolution in life styles and values. (pp. 39-40)

[The broad and varied scenic presentation of the individuals] indicates the basically inductive nature of the cross-section technique. The author provides what he thinks is an adequate sampling; the reader contemplates it, as he would the people whom he encounters in real life. He is left to draw his own conclusions without overt authorial intervention or moralizing, though we cannot deny that there is an intelligence, however, unobtrusive, which has chosen and arranged the elements on which the reader is to pass judgment. (pp. 43-4)

There is a fair amount of commentary on the nature of success and failure made by the characters themselves. To this extent the novel has an ideological or social focus, for the point seems to be that success as conceived within the existing social framework means conformity and a kind of progressive dehumanization. (p. 46)

[Certain] passages show the strong influence of Joyce's *Ulysses* in their intricate verbal play. (p. 48)

These experiments do not, on the whole, greatly change the texture of the work. We see almost entirely through the eyes of the impersonal narrator. But he is selective, even impressionistic. Characters rarely appear in full outline: a salient characteristic stands for the whole, and nine times out of ten that characteristic is a hat. The sensory experience of his people is dominated by smell; the novel contains an immense catalogue of the smells of the city. Auditory and tactile sensations are comparatively rare. Sight concentrates on sky, light, flashing color, silhouettes of light and darkness.

Manhattan Transfer goes beyond traditional realism in other important respects. It has often been called expressionistic; that is, it attempts to externalize essences, meanings, significant realities that lurk beneath the surface of observed reality. (p. 49)

[Through] imagistic emphases and contrasts we get the essence of New York City as siren and destroyer, promising and not keeping her promises, as in the case of the immigrants who are destroyed or who are deported because of their belief in freedom.

This novel contains little of what we call social criticism in terms of institutional malfunction or ideological argument. . . . It is changing mores and moral values, without much concern for the forces that produce such change, that are the objects of observation in *Manhattan Transfer*. (p. 52)

By its intricacy and by its comprehensive sweep the trilogy *U.S.A.* comes close to being the great American novel which had been the aspiration of writers since the turn of the century. It is one of the ironies of our times that when the great American novel did arrive, it turned out to be condemnatory and pessimistic rather than a celebration of the American way. Yet there is an underlying affirmation in Dos Passos' denial. The American dream, battered and corrupted by men of ill will, or little will, still manifests itself—though in anguish—not completely stifled by the trappings of empire and the machinations of self-interest that the author describes.

What first aroused the enthusiasm of readers and critics was the technical virtuosity of the work. . . . [The] techniques he employed and the balance of elements he achieved are his own and stamp him as the last of the great inventors in the field of the social novel. (p. 58)

U.S.A. in the jargon of some critics has been called a "collective" novel. The term is unfortunate in its ideological implications and fails to convey the central fact that this is a novel without a protagonist, one in which no single life provides a center of interest and meaning. This work exhibits multiple parallel lives on a scale never before attempted. Its form is radial; that is, each spoke has the same importance as the others, all converging on a common center. If the reader's mind could, indeed, focus on all these characters at once he would perceive that unity. But since the experience of the novel is temporal, not spatial, simultaneity is not possible, except in brief passages, and the reader must keep the various characters in suspension until he can weigh them as a group. (p. 69)

The actual narrative, while more conventional than the other dimensions of the novel, does not lack technical interest. In comparison with *Manhattan Transfer*, *U.S.A.* makes very little use of dialogue and dramatic scene. What gives the various life histories impact is the use of summary stream of consciousness in language appropriate to the character. (p. 71)

When we consider whether this cast of characters is representative, we must concede at once that it does not present an adequate cross section and that the selection is clearly and deliberately slanted in the direction of vacuity and failure. These lives may be exemplary, but most readers agree that they are exemplary of only one aspect of human endeavor. The very fact that these are hollow men and women whose course is downward constitutes an inescapable indictment of American life and institutions in their time. (p. 72)

The three novels use the full gamut of their techniques to emphasize [the theme of denial of freedom of speech and action]. We see a man being run in in San Francisco for reading the Declaration of Independence to a crowd. We are present with Ben Compton at a riot in Everett, Washington. We are told of the hounding of Thorstein Veblen. The examples are legion. The weakest part of this is the attempt to show in Ben Compton how a revolutionary is made. The lack of psychological depth characteristic of Dos Passos' people is fatal here. It is not enough to see Ben pushed and broken by external forces. We need to feel the generation of internal resolution and an anguished perception that the system is out of joint. The interlarded quotations from Marx that attend Ben's development are not enough, unless indeed the author is already being ironic about the claims of socialist doctrine. (pp. 75-6)

There is a unified progression of ideas as we move through the three parts of *U.S.A.* The first presents a fairly kindly, innocent America, where the ordinary man's aspirations are usually blocked but where he can dream of controlling his own destiny and throwing off the shackles which he feels but does not analyze. The war brings an end to innocence. It is in part a diversionary action to stifle dissent at home. President Wilson becomes the villain of the piece: *1919* is an ironic contrast between the idealistic promises he made to make the world safe for democracy and the actualities of power politics as they are revealed at the peace conference. The third novel shows the fruits of this deception, of the moral and social debacle that the war is seen to have brought. The opportunities for the average man narrow. As he resists, coercion is more and more overt. The hysteria of war years becomes an habitual state of mind directed at exaggerated or imaginary dangers. . . . *U.S.A.* is a chronicle of promises betrayed or forgotten, of a diminution of human dignity and liberty, of a basic disregard for human worth.

The overall statement is a pessimistic one. The "American Century" proudly announced in the opening Newsreel turns out to be a fatal misadventure. (pp. 76-7)

After *U.S.A.* Dos Passos wrote eight more novels. Three of them, *Chosen Country* (1951), *Most Likely to Succeed* (1954), and *The Great Days* (1958), have chiefly a biographical interest, indirectly reflecting certain aspects of the author's experience but telling us very little about the development of his thought. The other five are serious, if not always successful, works, continuing into the second third of the century the social chronicle that is the substance of the great trilogy.

One thing that strikes us in these later works, which the originality and technical virtuosity of the earlier ones caused many to overlook, is that Dos Passos is not a novelist of the traditional kind. That is, he is not capable of creating a fictive world that is self-subsistent or of creating characters who are interesting in their own right by reason of their rich and varied humanity. What we come to recognize, if it is not already apparent, is that he is a writer of exemplary tales which, under the guise of fiction, analyze, comment on, and increasingly lambaste developments in American society. There are two things about these later novels that dampen the reader's enthusiasm. There is little that is new in technique to arouse interest, and the heat of a consuming idealism that sustains the chronicle of failure in *U.S.A.* gives way to an almost weary arraignment of one malfunction after another in contemporary life. From an ideological point of view Dos Passos has had second—and third—thoughts about the aspirations of the liberal left and is disenchanted with all programs for social regeneration, making on them a comprehensive assault for the falsity of their rhetoric and their corrupt pursuit of power as an end in itself.

Though the three novels *Adventures of a Young Man* (1939), *Number One* (1943), and *The Grand Design* (1949) are grouped together as a trilogy under the covering title *District of Columbia,* they have none of the cohesiveness or concentrated impact of *U.S.A.* They are loosely linked by the presence of members of the Spotswood family in all of them. . . . Each novel is a study of the failure of idealism in a different public context. (pp. 82-3)

Glenn Spotswood [in *Adventures of a Young Man*] is very much a stereotype, and we cannot get around the fact that he is a wooden and unconvincing figure. He exists to demonstrate the difference between genuine radical idealism and cynical communist exploitation of that idealism. We never know how he thinks or how he feels as an individual. He has no substance except for what is useful for his role as fall guy in the arena of radical politics. His development as a radical is too mechanical, his ruthless destruction by the communist hierarchy is too perfunctory. The whole novel is obviously controlled by polemic purpose. (p. 86)

Number One, by contrast, is extraordinarily well done. In part this is because it is less programmed and is almost out of time. It is a simple and deadly demonstration of the corruptness of power with minimal attention to broad social chronicle. This is not a new subject in American fiction, but Dos Passos' treatment deserves to stand in the front rank between Robert Herrick's *The Memoirs of an American Citizen,* which preceded it by nearly forty years, and Robert Penn Warren's *All the King's Men,* which came out a few years after *Number One.* (p. 87)

The Grand Design, which completes this trilogy, is unfortunately a blurred and unsatisfactory piece of work. Like its predecessors it has as its target the arrogation of power to one man or to a self-designated group, with consequent subordination of the individual to impersonal and unresponsive authority, in this case the bureaucracy of the New Deal from its beginnings in 1933 to its gradual dismantling under the pressure of World War II. This canvas is too broad for the author to handle it with any clarity of outline. He is unable to mass detail effectively or to give his usual two-dimensional characters even minimal definition. The best he can do is to give a satiric picture of big and little Caesars, big and little Messiahs hopping ineffectually around Washington like chickens with their heads off. (p. 90)

Dos Passos' next fictional volley at the coercive force of bigness came eleven years after the second trilogy. *Midcentury* (1960), which he described as being in the modified manner of *U.S.A.,* is impressive for its technical originality and for the incisiveness of its statement, even though that statement is one-sided. It gave no comfort to the author's former associates and admirers since it is an attack on labor unions. When we consider that in *U.S.A.* those who devoted their lives to unionization were among the author's heroes, this attack represents an even more dramatic turnabout than his repudiation of the Communist Party and the New Deal. It is as though he has now gone back on the last article in his liberal creed. (p. 94)

As novelist Dos Passos is unequivocal in what he shows about human perfectibility. He may hold the dream in his heart, but the actuality of his fiction contradicts it. There is a persistent plea that the little man, weak and defenseless, be given a better break; yet we see his major figures consistently overborne by external pressures and their own inadequacies. (p. 112)

His two vocations of novelist and observer of institutions are ultimately one.

It is that duality that sets his work apart. Individually his novels must be read as chronicles of the times. In their totality they chart an individual's response to those times. (p. 114)

George J. Becker, in his *John Dos Passos,* Ungar, 1974, 133 p.

DONALD PIZER

(essay 1988)

[Pizer is an American educator and critic. Below, in an excerpt from his *Dos Passos' "U.S.A.": A Critical Study,* he interprets *U. S. A.* as a modern American epic novel.]

Like many twentieth-century fictional masterpieces—*Ulysses,* for example, or Faulkner's Yoknapatawpha saga—*U.S.A.* seeks to portray a culture in both historical depth and social breadth by means of modernistic techniques. There is thus a modern epic convention, to which *U.S.A.* belongs, in which the traditional aim of the epic to make manifest the history and values of a culture is achieved, not by conformity to a prescribed set of epic rules, but by the author's individual adaptation of the complex fictional devices that have arisen in the twentieth century for the depiction of the interaction of self and society. The success of works in this convention derives not only from the depth of the author's insight into his culture but from the appropriateness and effectiveness of the modernistic fictional forms that he has chosen to render his vision.

Which is to say that *U.S.A.* can be discussed meaningfully in a number of ways but that the final test of its value and centrality in twentieth-century art lies in its nature and quality as a modernistic epic American novel. Dos Passos' model for the epic was principally Whitman as *U.S.A.* seeks to depict in full detail the "varied strains" that are the American experience. To Whitman, too, can be attributed Dos Passos' belief in a semimystical oneness in the multiplicity of America, a oneness that to Dos Passos was above all the nation's history of democratic idealism. There is also of course a Whitmanesque element in the deep exploration of self in the Camera Eye, an exploration that, in the end, is an exploration of what America should be and isn't. Thus, one of the most pervasive and central sources of relatedness, of unity, in *U.S.A.* is in its character as a self-reflexive novel in which the Camera Eye persona's search for identity and role results simultaneously in a vision of self and a vision of America that is the remainder of the trilogy.

As an epic novel, *U.S.A.* is also a historical work, with history—like autobiography—simultaneously both a subject matter and a source of experimental form. In the pseudochronicle modes of the Newsreels and biographies Dos Passos consciously shapes a documentary base, through impressionistic selection and surreal juxtaposition, into an indictment of twentieth-century American life. The underlying motive for this distortion of the "factual" lies in Dos Passos' powerful ironic and thus satiric vision of the immense distance between verbal construct and actuality in twentieth-century America. *U.S.A.* is thus throughout, and not merely in the Newsreels and biographies, the work of a satiric moralist. Dos Passos' caricature of American types, beliefs, and language in the narratives through free indirect discourse and his portrayal of journeys of the self toward self-betrayal and self-destruction are above all a reflection of his condemnation of the failure of America to accept the heritage of its "old words."

Each of the four modes of the trilogy is therefore both a modernistic fictional form and a contribution toward an epic rendering of twentieth-century American life. One of Dos Passos' major achievements in the trilogy arises from his recognition that the four modes could be linked not only by their common reference to an overarching epic intent but by constant juxtapositional allusiveness of epic matter, event, theme, and symbol. *U.S.A.* is a kind of cubistic portrait of America—one in which the effect is of a multiplicity of visions rendering a single object, with every angle of vision related both to the object and to every other angle of vision. It is Dos Passos' relentless pursuit of juxtapositional relationships in the seemingly disparate and fractured modal ordering of the trilogy that is largely responsible for the integral vision of American life in *U.S.A.*

The extraordinary holding power of *U.S.A.* for most readers—the ability of the work to compel attention throughout its extreme length and its complex variety of modes—thus has its origin both in the single-minded intensity of Dos Passos' vision of American life as a whole and in his ability to engage us, as in the death-of-the-self motif that runs through the narratives and the counter rebirth theme in the Camera Eye, in the deepest level of meaning of the relationship of self to community. *U.S.A.* is about a nation of individuals, and in that Whitmanesque paradox Dos Passos found his form and his theme. (pp. 184-85)

Donald Pizer, in his *Dos Passos' U. S. A.: A Critical Study,* University Press of Virginia, 1988, 209 p.

SOURCES FOR FURTHER STUDY

Carr, Virginia Spencer. *Dos Passos: A Life.* Garden City, N. Y.: Doubleday & Co., 1984, 624 p.

   Well-documented biography.

Clark, Michael. *Dos Passos's Early Fiction, 1921-1938.* London: Associated University Presses, 1987, 171 p.

   Analyzes American cultural and intellectual influences on Dos Passos's early fiction.

Hook, Andrew, ed. *Dos Passos: A Collection of Critical Essays.* Englewood Cliffs, N. J.: Prentice-Hall, 1974, 186 p.

   Includes essays by such critics as Granville Hicks, Malcolm Cowley, Lionel Trilling, and Alfred Kazin, highlighting various interpretations of Dos Passos's works and reflecting the changing critical reception toward his writings.

Fyodor Dostoyevsky

1821-1881

(Full name Fyodor Mikhailovich Dostoyevsky; also transliterated as Fedor, Feodor; also Mikhaylovich; also Dostoevski, Dostoievsky, Dostoevskii, Dostoevsky, Dostoiewsky, Dostoiefski, Dostoievski, Dostoyevskiy, Dostoieffski) Russian novelist and short story writer.

INTRODUCTION

Dostoyevsky is considered one of the greatest writers in world literature. Best-known for his novels *Prestupleniye i nakazaniye* (1866; *Crime and Punishment*) and *Bratya Karamazovy* (1880; *The Brothers Karamazov*), he attained profound philosophical and psychological insights which anticipated important developments in twentieth-century thought, including psychoanalysis and existentialism. In addition, Dostoyevsky's powerful literary depictions of the human condition exerted a profound influence on modern writers, such as Franz Kafka, whose works further develop some of the Russian novelist's themes. The writer's own troubled life enabled him to portray with deep sympathy characters who are emotionally and spiritually downtrodden and who in many cases epitomize the traditional Christian conflict between the body and the spirit.

Dostoyevsky grew up in a middle-class family in Moscow. His father, a doctor, was a tyrant toward his family, and his mother was a mild, pious woman who died before Dostoyevsky was sixteen. Partly to escape the oppressive atmosphere of his father's household, the boy acquired a love of reading, especially the works of Nikolai Gogol, E. T. A. Hoffmann, and Honoré de Balzac. At his father's insistence, Dostoyevsky trained as an engineer in St. Petersburg. While the youth was at school, his father was murdered by his own serfs at the family's small country estate. Dostoyevsky rarely mentioned his father's murder, but Oedipal themes are recurrent in his work, and Sigmund Freud suggested that the novelist's epilepsy was a manifestation of guilt over his repressed wish for his father's death.

Dostoyevsky graduated from engineering school but chose a literary career. His first published work, a translation of Balzac's novel *Eugénie Grandet*, appeared in a St. Petersburg journal in 1844. Two years later, he published his first novel, *Bednye lyudi* (1846; *Poor Folk*), a naturalistic tale with a clear social message as well as a delicate description of life's tragic aspects as manifested in everyday existence. The twenty-four-year-old author became an overnight celebrity when Vissarion Belinsky, the most influential critic of the day, praised Dostoyevsky for his social awareness and declared him the literary successor of Gogol. Dostoyevsky joined Belinsky's literary circle but later broke with it when the critic reacted coldly to his subsequent works. Belinsky judged the novel *Dvoynik* (1846; *The Double*) and the short stories "Gospodin Prokharchin" (1846; "Mr. Prokharchin") and "Khozyayka" (1847; "The Landlady") as devoid of a social message.

In 1848 Dostoyevsky joined a group of young intellectuals, led by Mikhail Petrashevsky, which met to discuss literary and political issues. In the reactionary political climate of mid-nineteenth-century Russia, such groups were illegal, and in 1849 the members of the so-called "Petrashevsky Circle" were arrested and charged with subversion. Dostoyevsky and several of his associates were imprisoned and sentenced to death. As they were facing the firing squad, an imperial messenger arrived with the announcement that the Czar had commuted the death sentences to hard labor in Siberia. This scene was to haunt the novelist the rest of his life. Dostoyevsky described his life as a prisoner in *Zapiski iz myortvogo doma* (1862; *The House of the Dead*), a novel demonstrating both an insight into the criminal mind and an understanding of the Russian lower classes. While in prison the writer underwent a profound spiritual and philosophical transformation. His intense study of the *New Testament,* the only book the prisoners were allowed to read, contributed to his rejection of his earlier liberal political views and led him to the conviction that redemption is possible only through suffering and faith, a belief which informed his later work.

Dostoyevsky was released from the prison camp in 1854; however, he was forced to serve as a soldier in a Siberian garrison for an additional five years. When Dostoyevsky was finally allowed to return to St. Petersburg in 1859, he eagerly resumed his literary career, founding two periodicals and writings articles and short fiction. The articles expressed his new-found belief in a social and political order based on the spiritual values of the Russian people. These years were marked by further personal and professional misfortunes, including the forced closing of his journals by the authorities, the deaths of his wife and his brother, and a financially devastating addiction to gambling. It was in this atmosphere that Dostoyevsky wrote *Zapiski iz podpolya* (1864; *Notes from the Underground*) and *Crime and Punishment*. In *Notes from the Underground* Dostoyevsky satirizes contemporary social and political views by presenting a narrator whose "notes" reveal

that his purportedly progressive beliefs lead only to sterility and inaction. Dostoyevsky's portrayal of this bitter and frustrated "Underground Man" is hailed as the introduction of an important new type of literary figure. *Crime and Punishment* brought him acclaim but scant financial compensation. Viewed by critics as one of his masterpieces, *Crime and Punishment* is the novel in which Dostoyevsky first develops the theme of redemption through suffering. The protagonist Raskolnikov—whose name derives from the Russian word for "schism" or "split"—is presented as the embodiment of spiritual nihilism. The novel depicts the harrowing confrontation between his philosophical beliefs, which prompt him to commit a murder in an attempt to prove his supposed "superiority," and his inherent morality, which condemns his actions.

In 1867, Dostoyevsky fled to Europe with his second wife to escape creditors. Although they were distressing due to financial and personal difficulties, Dostoyevsky's years abroad were fruitful, for he completed one important novel and began another. *Idiot* (1869; *The Idiot*), influenced by Hans Holbein's painting *Christ Taken from the Cross* and by Dostoyevsky's opposition to the growing atheistic sentiment of the times, depicts the Christ-like protagonist's loss of innocence and his experience of sin. Dostoyevsky's profound conservatism, which marked his political thinking following his Siberian experience, and especially his reaction against revolutionary socialism, provided the impetus for his great political novel *Besy* (1871-72; *The Possessed*). Based on a true event, in which a young revolutionary was murdered by his comrades, this novel provoked a storm of controversy for its harsh depiction of ruthless radicals. In his striking portrayal of Stavrogin, the novel's central character, Dostoyevsky described a man dominated by the life-denying forces of nihilism.

Dostoyevsky returned to Russia in 1871 and began his final decade of prodigious literary activity. In sympathy with the conservative political party, he accepted the editorship of a reactionary weekly, *Grazhdanin* (*The Citizen*). In his *Dnevnik pisatelya* (1873-1877; *The Diary of a Writer*), initially a column in the *Citizen* but later an independent periodical, Dostoyevsky published a variety of prose works, including some of his outstanding short stories. Dostoyevski's last work was *Bratya Karamazovy* (1880; *The Brothers Karamazov*), a family tragedy of epic proportions, which is viewed as one of the great novels of world literature. The novel recounts the murder of a father by one of his four sons. Initially, his son Dmitri is arrested for the crime, but as the story unfolds it is revealed that the illegitimate son Smerdyakov has killed the old man at what he believes to be the instigation of his half-brother Ivan. Ivan's philosophical essay, "The Legend of the Grand Inquisitor," is a work now famous in its own right.

Presented as a debate in which the Inquisitor condemns Christ for promoting the belief that mankind has the freedom of choice between good and evil, the piece explores the conflict between intellect and faith, and between the forces of evil and the redemptive power of Christianity. Dostoyevsky envisioned this novel as the first of a series of works depicting "The Life of a Great Sinner," but early in 1881, a few months after completing *The Brothers Karamazov*, the writer died at his home in St. Petersburg.

To his contemporary readers, Dostoyevsky appeared as a writer primarily interested in the terrible aspects of human existence. However, later critics have recognized that the novelist sought to plumb the depths of the psyche, in order to reveal the full range of the human experience, from the basest desires to the most elevated spiritual yearnings. Above all, he illustrated the universal human struggle to understand God and self. Dostoyevsky was, Katherine Mansfield wrote, a "being who loved, in spite of everything, adored life, even while he knew the dank, dark places."

(For further information about Dostoyevsky's life and works, see *Nineteenth–Century Literature Criticism*, Vols. 2, 7, 21 and *Short Story Criticism*, Vol. 2.)

CRITICAL COMMENTARY

OSCAR WILDE

(essay date 1887)

[One of the most important literary figures of Victorian England, Wilde was a poet, essayist, novelist, playwright, and a brilliant representative of the aestheticist world view. His writings include the highly acclaimed comedy *The Importance of Being Earnest* (1895). In the following excerpt, he comments on *Injury and Insult*, praising Dostoyevsky as a master of characterization.]

Doistoieffski differs widely from both his rivals [Tourgenieff and Tolstoi]. He is not so fine an artist as Tourgenieff, for he deals more with the facts than with the effects of life; nor has he Tolstoi's largeness of vision and epic dignity; but he has qualities that are distinctively and absolutely his own, such as a fierce intensity of passion and concentration of impulse, a power of dealing with the deepest mysteries of psychology and the most hidden springs of life, and a realism that is pitiless in its fidelity, and terrible because it is true. Some time ago we had occasion to draw attention to his marvellous novel *Crime and Punishment,* where in the haunt of impurity and vice a harlot and an assassin meet together to read the story of Lazarus and Dives, and the outcast girl leads the sinner to make atonement for his sin; nor is the book entitled *Injury and Insult* at all inferior to that great masterpiece. Mean and ordinary though the surroundings of the story may seem, the heroine Natasha is like one of the noble victims of Greek tragedy, she is Antigone with the passions of Phaedra, and it is impossible to approach her without a feeling of awe. . . . Aleosha, the beautiful young lad whom Natasha follows to her doom, is a second Tito Melema, and has all Tito's charm, and grace, and fasci-nation. Yet he is different. He would never have denied Baldassare in the square at Florence, nor lied to Romola about Tessa. He has a magnificent, momentary sincerity; a boyish unconsciousness of all that life signifies; an ardent enthusiasm for all that life cannot give. There is nothing calculating about him. He never thinks evil, he only does it. From a psychological point of view he is one of the most interesting characters of modern fiction, as from an artistic standpoint he is one of the most attractive. As we grow to know him, he stirs strange questions for us, and makes us feel that it is not the wicked only who do wrong, nor the bad alone who work evil. And by what a subtle objective method does Doistoieffski show us his characters! He never tickets them with a list, nor labels them with a description. We grow to know them very gradually, as we know people whom we meet in society, at first by little tricks of manner, personal appearance, fancies in dress and the like; and afterwards by their deeds and words; and even then they constantly elude us, for though Doistoieffski may lay bare for us the secrets of their nature, yet he never explains his personages away, they are always surprising us by something that they say or do, and keep to the end the eternal mystery of life. Irrespective of its value as a work of art, this novel possesses a deep autobiographical interest also, as the character of Vania, the poor student who loves Natasha through all her sin and shame is Doistoieffski's study of himself. . . . [Almost] before he had arrived at manhood Doistoieffski knew life in its most real forms; poverty and suffering, pain and misery, prison, exile, and love were soon familiar to him, and by the lips of Vania he has told his own story. This note of personal feeling, this harsh reality of actual experience, undoubtedly gives the book something of its strange fervour and ter-

Principal Works

Bednye Lyudi (novel) 1846
  [Poor Folk, 1894]
Dvoynik (novel) 1846
  [The Double, 1917]
Unizhonnye i oskorblyonnye (novel) 1861
  [The Insulted and Injured, 1887; also published as Injury and Insult, 1887]
Zapiski iz myortvoga doma (novel) 1862
  [Buried Alive; or, Two Years Life of Penal Servitude in Siberia, 1881; also published as The House of the Dead; or, Prison Life in Siberia, 1911]
Zapiski iz podpolya (novel) 1864
  [Notes from the Underground, 1912; also published as Letters from the Underworld, 1913]
Igrok (novel) 1866
  [The Gambler, 1915]
Prestupleniye i nakazaniye (novel) 1866
  [Crime and Punishment, 1886]
Idiot (novel) 1869
  [The Idiot, 1887]
Besy (novel) 1871-72
  [The Possessed, 1913; also published as The Devils, 1953]
Podrostok (novel) 1875; published in journal Otechestvennye Zapiski [Notes of the Fatherland]
  [A Raw Youth, 1916]
Dnevnik pisatelya (essays and short stories) 1873-77
  [The Diary of a Writer, 1949]
Bratya Karamazovy (novel) 1880
  [The Brothers Karamazov, 1912]

rible passion, yet it has not made it egotistic; we see things from every point of view, and we feel, not that Fiction has been trammelled by fact, but that fact itself has become ideal and imaginative. Pitiless too though Doistoieffski is in his method, as an artist, yet as a man he is full of human pity for all, for those who do evil as well as for those who suffer it, for the selfish no less than for those whose lives are wrecked for others, and whose sacrifice is in vain. Since "Adam Bede," and *Le Père Goriot,* no more powerful novel has been written than [*Injury and Insult*]. (pp. 77-9)

Oscar Wilde, "Dostoevsky's 'The Insulted and Injured'," in *The Artist as Critic: Critical Writings of Oscar Wilde,* edited by Richard Ellman, W. H. Allen, 1970, pp. 77-9.

SIGMUND FREUD
(essay date 1928)

[Freud was an Austrian neurologist, psychologist, and educator who founded psychoanalysis. His writings include numerous discussions of literary works. In the following excerpt, he compares *The Brothers Karamazov* with Shakespeare's *Hamlet* and Sophocles' *Oedipus Rex,* observing that all three works deal with the subject of parricide.]

Four facets may be distinguished in the rich personality of Dostoevsky: the creative artist, the neurotic, the moralist and the sinner. How is one to find one's way in this bewildering complexity?

The creative artist is the least doubtful: Dostoevsky's place is not far behind Shakespeare. *The Brothers Karamazov* is the most magnificent novel ever written; the episode of the Grand Inquisitor, one of the peaks in the literature of the world, can hardly be valued too highly. Before the problem of the creative artist analysis must, alas, lay down its arms.

The moralist in Dostoevsky is the most readily assailable. If we seek to rank him high as a moralist on the plea that only a man who has gone through the depths of sin can reach the highest summit of morality, we are neglecting a doubt that arises. A moral man is one who reacts to temptation as soon as he feels it in his heart, without yielding to it. . . . He has not achieved the essence of morality, renunciation, for the moral conduct of life is a practical human interest. . . . Dostoevsky threw away the chance of becoming a teacher and liberator of humanity and made himself one with their gaolers. The future of human civilization will have little to thank him for. (pp. 222-23)

To consider Dostoevsky as a sinner or a criminal rouses violent opposition, which need not be based upon a philistine assessment of crime. The real motive for this opposition soon becomes apparent. Two traits are essential in a criminal: boundless egoism and a strong destructive impulse. Common to both of these, and a necessary condition for their expression, is absence of love, lack of an emotional appreciation of (human) objects. . . . [It] must be asked why there is any temptation to reckon Dostoevsky among the criminals. The answer is that it comes from his choice of material, which singles out from all others violent, murderous and egoistic characters, thus pointing to the existence of similar tendencies in his own soul, and also from certain facts in his life, like his passion for gambling and his possible admission of a sexual assault upon a young girl. The contradiction is resolved by the realization that Dostoevsky's very strong destructive instinct, which might easily have made him a criminal, was in his actual life directed mainly against his own person (inward instead of outward) and thus found expression as masochism and a sense of guilt. Nevertheless, his personality retained sadistic traits in plenty, which show themselves in his irritability, his love of tormenting and his intolerance even towards people he loved, and which appear also in the way in which, as an author, he treats his readers. Thus in little things he was a sadist towards others, and in bigger things a sadist towards himself, in fact a masochist, that is to say the mildest, kindliest, most helpful person possible.

We have selected three factors from Dostoevsky's complex personality, one quantitative and two qualitative: the extraordinary intensity of his emotional life, his perverse instinctual predisposition, which inevitably marked him out to be a sadomasochist or a criminal, and his unanalysable artistic endowment. . . . But the position is obscured by the simultaneous presence of neurosis, which, as we have said, was not in the circumstances inevitable, but which comes into being the more readily, the richer the complication which has to be mastered by the ego. For neurosis is after all only a sign that the ego has not succeeded in making a synthesis, that in attempting to do so it has forfeited its unity. (pp. 223-25)

[The] formula for Dostoevsky is as follows: a person of specially strong bisexual predisposition, who can defend himself with special intensity against dependence on a specially severe father. This characteristic of bisexuality comes as an addition to the components of his nature that we have already recognized. His early symptom of death-like seizures can thus be understood as a father-identification on the part of his ego, permitted by his super-ego as a punishment. 'You wanted to kill your father in order to be your father yourself. Now you *are* your father, but a dead father'—the regular mechanism of hysterical symptoms. And further: 'Now your father is killing *you*.' For the ego the death symptom is a satisfaction in phantasy of the masculine wish and at the same time a masochistic satisfaction; for the super-ego it is a punishment satisfaction, that is, a sadistic satisfaction. Both of them, the ego and the super-ego, carry on the role of father.

To sum up, the relation between the subject and his father-object, while retaining its content, has been transformed into a relation between the ego and the super-ego—a new setting on a fresh stage. (p. 232)

It can scarcely be owing to chance that three of the masterpieces of the literature of all time—the *Oedipus Rex* of Sophocles, Shakespeare's *Hamlet*, and Dostoevsky's *The Brothers Karamazov*—should all deal with the same subject, parricide. In all three, moreover, the motive for the deed, sexual rivalry for a woman, is laid bare. (p. 235)

It is a matter of indifference who actually committed the crime [in *The Brothers Karamazov*], psychology is only concerned to know who desired it emotionally and who welcomed it when it was done. And for that reason all of the brothers, except the contrasted figure of Alyosha, are equally guilty, the impulsive sensualist, the sceptical cynic and the epileptic criminal. . . . Dostoevsky's sympathy for the criminal is, in fact, boundless; it goes far beyond the pity which the unhappy wretch might claim, and reminds us of the 'holy awe' with which epileptics and lunatics were regarded in the past. A criminal is to him almost a Redeemer, who has taken on himself the guilt which must else have been borne by others. There is no longer any need for one to murder, since *he* has already murdered; and one must be grateful to him, for, except for him, one would have been obliged oneself to murder. . . . This may perhaps be quite generally the mechanism of kindly sympathy with other people, a mechanism which one can discern with especial ease in the extreme case of the guilt-ridden novelist. There is no doubt that this sympathy by identification was a decisive factor in determining Dostoevsky's choice of material. He dealt first with the common criminal (whose motives are egotistical) and the political and religious criminal; and not until the end of his life did he come back to the primal criminal, the parricide, and use him, in a work of art, for making his confession. (pp. 236-37)

Sigmund Freud, "Dostoevsky and Parricide," translated by D. F. Trait, in his *Collected Papers: Miscellaneous Papers, 1888-1938, Vol. 5,* edited by Ernest Jones, M. D. and James Strachey, Basic Books, 1959, pp. 222-42.

JANKO LAVRIN
(essay date 1947)

[A Slovenian-born British critic, essayist, and biographer, Lavrin is best known for his studies of nineteenth- and twentieth-century Russian literature. In the following excerpt, he discusses Dostoyevsky's technique as a novelist, lauding the Russian writer's ability to include profound psychological and spiritual insights into his complex narratives.]

Ideas which had been lived, i.e. tested through one's entire consciousness and then embodied in living characters, were the mainspring of Dostoevsky's novels. (p. 29)

Dostoevsky's love of involved mysterious plots was [a] feature which connected him with romanticism. So was his love of extreme antitheses and particularly his interest in the irrational which he combined, however, with an uncanny psychological sense. Prying into the most hidden recesses of man's soul and spirit, he was the first European novelist to explore the unconscious and to annex it wholesale to modern literature. Yet he was too much of a brooding analyst to be a reliable observer of externals. Nor did he care for the traditional homogeneity of character, since he was only too familiar with the contrasts and contradictions of the human ego. What attracted him above all was that inner chaos which compels one to look for some outlet from among the greatest antinomies. (pp. 29-30)

Dostoevsky usually starts with some vital inner problem which determines the trend of his intuitions, observations and ideas. But instead of pasting the ideas upon his characters, he makes them an organic part of their inner make-up, no matter whether he himself agrees with what they say or not. Moreover, during the creative process his leading idea itself becomes split into its own conflicting antitheses which open up dramatic possibilities of a new kind. The very form of a Dostoevskian novel results from the dynamic tension between several contradictory planes and trends of one and the same consciousness—each of them with its own conclusions.

The principle of fugue, of 'symphonic' treatment, is possible in a novel only if the author gives the most opposite themes and motives an equal chance. And this is what Dostoevsky does. His favourite methods are those in which not only the inner life, but also the personal tone of the characters described comes out to the best advantage in the relationship to their own opposites. (pp. 30-1)

Dostoevsky confronts dramatically not only antinomic characters, but antinomic features in one and the same character. In doing this, he preserves complete spiritual and intellectual fairness, no matter how acute or how personal his own attitude may be. Entire chapters of his have a power of their own precisely because they are so ambiguous. (p. 31)

Only an author capable of projecting his own inner chaos and travail into living characters, in order to achieve a kind of *katharsis,* could have written as Dostoevsky did. For him art was a relentless urge, perhaps an alternative to madness. This explains why some of his creations are so intense as to haunt the reader's imagination like spooks. Sometimes they affect one as nightmares and symbols in one—even symbols of forces which seem to transcend our ordinary plane of existence. It is at this point that Dostoevsky's 'realism' asserts itself in a peculiar and original fashion.

We may perhaps find a clue to his realism by drawing a line between reality and actuality. The two are often regarded as identical. Yet reality is more than actuality. It includes all the hidden forces and agents of life, whereas actuality is confined to its external or else 'topical' aspects. The proportion between these two planes varies and is reflected in the two different although complementary directions in art, especially in the novel: the horizontal and the vertical.

The 'horizontal' novel is concerned with manners, with life as expressed in terms of external contacts and relationships of the persons described. But it must not stop here. Unless it has a fringe, suggestive of something more important and universal than what it shows, it will remain only a picture or document of a certain period—nearer to journalism than to art. The 'vertical' novel, however, concentrates above all upon human destinies as they work in and through the characters presented. Hence it is predominantly psychological. It is more intensive than extensive; for which purpose it reduces the number of characters, as well as the area of their background, to a minimum. If the 'horizontal' novel is analogous to the old epic on the one hand and to comedy on the other, the 'vertical' novel finds its counterpart in the drama. And as for social manners, it is interested in them in so far as they can be a matter of conflict with the individual who turns against tradition in the name of his own vision of life, or of his own inner freedom. The entire problem of evil, for example, with its ultimate metaphysical implications, is dealt with by Dostoevsky only on this plane. And so intensely, too, that some of his characters may even strike one as agents of cosmic forces of good and evil.

He thus enlarged and deepened the scope of the European novel. (pp. 31-3)

If a label were necessary at all, we could perhaps call his art *visionary* realism, as distinct from mere visual realism. He strains the actual and the average to its utmost limits mainly in order to reach that reality which lies beyond it. His wildest and cruellest situations are often but experiments upon the human soul with the object of extracting its 'inmost essence'. Hence there is something paradoxical about Dostoevsky's exaggerated characters: they are most real when they seem least realistic from the standpoint of the mere visual realism.

Dostoevsky's work (like that of any great author) can best be understood if regarded in the perspective of his general perception and intuition of life. Yet in his case we must take into consideration the three planes which he usually intermingles. The first is the plane of *byt* or the social background. The second is the purely psychological plane. And the third—the most important among them—is the one in which 'psychology' passes into the sphere of spiritual experience and valuations.

The first of these three planes matters in so far as it expresses a complete absence of fixed or stable social forms. In Dostoevsky's writings everything is in a 'flux', including the social classes which are chaotically mixed up. His principal heroes are taken, as it were, out of all social causality—a fact which gives the author an even greater freedom in dwelling upon the fundamentals of human life, upon the tragic conflicts of mind and spirit. Yet while stripping his characters of external bonds and conventions, Dostoevsky adopted a number of external devices to keep the attention of his readers. A study of his technique may reveal tricks which resemble those of the sensational 'lower' fiction: the criminal or detective novel, the melodramatic newspaper serial, and even the penny shocker. . . . Only Dostoevsky could permit himself such cheap tricks and yet create great novels. He often adjusted his external plots to the level of the average reader; but at the same time he made them only scaffoldings for what lay beyond them. Thus the 'thrilling' detective element in *Crime and Punishment* is almost irrelevant as compared with the principal 'idea-force' of the novel: the idea of moral self-will.

Another reason why Dostoevsky loved to pile up so many unusual plots and events was his tendency to experiment with the human self: to put it into the most incredible situations, and watch its reactions. He was drawn towards such plots as would enable him to study the farthest limits of consciousness. Yet however complicated his plots may be, they develop with and through the characters. The motives of action thus remain internal. And once these motives have reached the intensity suggestive of supra-human agencies (whether of good or evil), Dostoevsky magnifies his characters accordingly; or at least his male characters, because his women are never treated on the same spiritual scale as his men. (pp. 33-5)

Dostoevsky had so much to say that the forms of the old novel proved inadequate. He had to work out a 'symphonic' form of his own whose style is often jerky, and composition uneven. . . . Most satisfactory, formally, are some of his smaller novels, such as *The Gambler* and *The Eternal Husband,* written at one sitting as it were. Among the big novels *Crime and Punishment* is best in construction, although the crime itself takes place before the motivation of the crime is given. The action begins right in the middle and then is gradually unravelled in concentric circles—from the periphery towards the focus. (pp. 35-6)

[A balance between art, psychology, and dynamic ideas is evident] in *The Brothers Karamazov,* Dostoevsky's last and longest novel. Each part of this monumental work is almost a novel in itself, yet they all converge towards the denouement in the finale. The contrast between the brothers is worked out with unsurpassed subtlety. Moreover, while reading this masterpiece, we actually follow its parallel development on the three mentioned planes. We watch the background of a Russian town, the involved psychological experiences of the main characters, and the spiritual import of it all. One of its great features is the delightful gal-

lery of boys, each of them depicted with consummate understanding of a child's mind. In addition, Ivan Karamazov's **'Legend of the Grand Inquisitor'** gives us the most dramatic philosophy of history ever presented in literary form. (p. 36)

[Dostoevsky's] significance is enhanced by the manner in which he approached man's basic dilemmas, and at the same time refused all facile and superficial solutions. He never tired of fighting, and fiercely so, the facile optimism with regard to our progress, for example. Nor was he inclined to make any truce with those theories (whether socialistic or otherwise), the aim of which is to make human beings 'happy' by lowering their consciousness; by standardizing them into mere units of an efficient ant-hill.

His *Notes from the Underworld* was his first protest against such optimistic rationalism. At the same time it was an indirect defence of human personality as something autonomous; something which must insist on its own rights, without isolating itself, however, from the collective group or groups. An individual who remains exclusively in the group, within the sphere of social taboos and conventions, cannot develop into a personality. On the other hand, an isolated personality which has lost its organic contact with the collective or with the rest of mankind, is bound to become starved through its very isolation. The problem of personality thus becomes inseparable from the problem of mankind as a whole. The two are in fact one and the same problem, approached from its opposite ends. (pp. 55-6)

[Many] of Dostoevsky's characters are haunted by the question: 'Does God exist or not?' Dostoevsky himself tackled the problem not on the plane of theological formulae, but primarily as a psychologist interested in God as an active element in man's consciousness—an element which fills the latter not only with the highest longings, but also with the bitterest doubts and torments. . . . Unable to separate man's fundamental problems from the problems of God, Dostoevsky was anxious to explore the degree of reality of that 'mighty activity' in our soul. He wanted to know whether God exists also objectively, i.e. apart from and outside that activity. He demanded certainty in this matter mainly in order to see how the answer (one way or the other) would affect the fate of man. The search for God he thus identified primarily with the question as to whether there exists an incontestable, absolute Value towards which one's will and efforts could be directed for the sake of one's highest self-realization and 'way of life'. And since such a Value can only be given or sanctioned by an absolute Being, the answer as to whether God exists or not is bound to affect us. If the latter is in the negative, then our existence—taken not from the social, but from the spiritual angle—is turned into something accidental and devoid of any ultimate meaning. Once cognizant of that, an uncompromising conscience must either reject life and the world, or else proclaim man's will as the only law, and his ego as the only divinity on earth. (pp. 57-8)

Among the religious teachers it was Christ in particular who abolished the purely legalistic conceptions of God, by transferring Him from outside into the consciousness of man: 'The Kingdom of God is within you.' But this mystical attitude, even when practised whole-heartedly, failed to destroy the rebellious 'magical' element in man, since both attitudes represent the two polar unconscious tendencies of every human self. Hence the duality of man's inner life, and even of mankind's development as a whole. The antagonism between the spiritual and the secular aspects in our historical life may partly be traced back to this split. The latter can occur, however, also on the plane of spirit alone—a phenomenon which often leads to unexpected conflicts, culminating in the antithesis of God-man and man-God, of Christ and Zarathustra.

The inner struggle of Dostoevsky's heroes, from Raskolnikov to Ivan Karamazov, is mainly due to this dilemma and to its two opposite sets of valuation, pushed to their final conclusions. During this process Dostoevsky realized that Christ has revealed to us the highest possible Value. In his opinion 'there is nothing lovelier, deeper, more sympathetic, more manly and perfect than the Saviour'. He even makes his 'superman' Kirillov exclaim that Christ is the One who gave the meaning to life, and that 'the whole planet, with everything in it, is mere madness without that Man'. Yet to see in Christ the Value and the meaning of life is not enough for an inquiring mind. One step farther, and we are confronted by the question: Does Christ Himself correspond to truth? Where is the certainty that the Value and the Way of Life, revealed by Him, are incontestable, with a reality behind, and not a mere illusion? In other words, is Christ Himself inside or outside the Truth? (p. 62)

Questions of this kind, prompted by incurable scepticism, crop up in all the chief novels of Dostoevsky, not as 'philosophy', but as living experience, as torments of the spirit. (p. 63)

He was so much afraid of the inner devastation, caused by modern scepticism, that he fought it with all the means at his disposal. . . . [He] asserted the priority of the irrational over the rational, and began to cling to Christ even in spite of reason. 'If any one could prove to me that Christ is outside the truth, and if the truth really did exclude Christ, I would prefer to stay with Christ and not with the truth,' he confessed candidly. On the other hand, he was too much of a dialectitian and a sharp thinker to be able to accept his religious intuitions without a rational sanction. As the two proved incompatible, he had to fight for his faith, step by step, during the whole of his creative life. (pp. 63-4)

The fight for belief is accompanied in [Dostoevsky's writings] by the most vigorous apology for unbelief. But for this very reason they are all the more poignant both as literature and as human documents. (p. 64)

Janko Lavrin, in his *Dostoevsky: A Study,* The Macmillan Company, 1947, 161 p.

F. F. SEELEY
(essay date 1983)

[In the following excerpt, Seeley analyzes the existential questions posed in *The Brothers Karamazov.* Focusing on the character of Ivan, the rationalist sceptic, the critic explains Dostoyevsky's world view as a reflection of titanic struggle to resist nihilism and unbelief.]

It is widely agreed that *The Brothers Karamazov* represents the 'synthesis' and culmination of Dostoyevsky's work, in which we are presented with the latest and richest developments and combinations of themes and types which have evolved through his earlier writings. Thus Ivan Karamazov is the last of a line sometimes designated in Russian 'philosophizing doubles' because of their intellectual preoccupations and split personalities. His genealogy can be traced back through such 'heresiarchs' as Kirillov and Raskolnikov to the Underground Man, and beyond him, in Dostoyevsky's pre-Siberian period, to such progenitors as Golyadkin (in *The Double*) and Ordynov (in **'The Landlady'**). However, it may be argued that this literary ancestry is less interesting and significant than his biological inheritance.

Though it is often claimed that Dostoyevsky wrote in terms of 'coexistence and interaction' as opposed to 'becoming', this formula will not fit *The Brothers Karamazov,* in which we can follow not only the processes of heredity working itself out from one generation to another, and not only the psychological maturation of, at any rate, Mitya Karamazov, but the evolution of Ivan's thinking over a six-year period. (p. 115)

By most critics the character and content of Ivan's thinking are examined mainly within the limits of his 'Legend of the Grand Inquisitor'. This is hardly surprising: the 'Legend' forms the climax of Book V of the novel and Dostoyevsky himself declared Books V and VI to be of pivotal importance.

Some critics have vouchsafed a glance at Ivan's article on the ecclesiastical courts. This, like the **'Legend'**, is summarized by Ivan himself and is the subject of comments by other personages in the novel; but it occupies so few paragraphs, and is sandwiched so modestly between much more vivid and dramatic scenes, that very little has been made of it.

But the **'Legend'** and the article represent only two out of the four recorded stages of Ivan's thinking, and the four need to be considered together and in sequence if one is to obtain an over-all view of its evolution. Dostoyevsky does nothing to encourage such an enterprise: he presents them to his readers out of chronological order and puts two of them into the mouth of a personage whose reliability may be a matter of dispute.

In chronological order—that is in the order in which they were produced in Ivan's mind—the four phases of Ivan's thought are embodied in the 'legend' of the 'philosopher' who refused to believe in paradise, the **'Legend of the Grand Inquisitor'**, the article on the ecclesiastical courts and the **'Geological Upheaval'**. These span the period between Ivan's high-school days and his father's murder, that is between his eighteenth and his twenty-fourth year. As might be expected, there is continuity between all four phases, especially in the problems addressed, but there are radical differences between the hypotheses propounded as solutions to the problems—and between Ivan's self-image in his teens and in his twenties.

The 'legend' of the philosopher who refused to believe in a future life; refused for a thousand years to accept the penalty imposed on him for his unbelief; and finally, after walking a quadrillion kilometres in darkness, became convinced that two seconds in paradise was worth a walk of a quadrillion quadrillions raised to the quadrillionth power—is related not by Ivan in his own person, but by his 'devil'. But since this devil is also our main source for Ivan's final construct, the **'Geological Upheaval'**, it is necessary to consider his credibility as a source.

Ivan's Mysterious Visitor complains that he is a 'much maligned person'; if he could have foreseen how Dostoyevsky's critics would treat him, his complaint might have been even louder! Most of them approach him either in religious terms, as the Father of Lies, or else in psychological terms, as Ivan's 'double', but uncritically swallowing Ivan's assertion that this double comprises only the basest and the stupidest, the most vile and vulgar elements of his self, and mainly of his past self at that.

However, this is grossly unfair to Ivan's devil, who is a most interesting personage in his own right. It is true that he embodies some of Ivan's characteristics of which Ivan is ashamed, such as 'Romanticism'; but he also criticizes or mocks such characteristics in Ivan, if not in himself too. Certain other characteristics of Ivan's, to which Ivan clings in spite, perhaps, of some underlying ambivalence, are unhesitatingly deplored

by the devil in relation to himself: what Ivan calls 'my Euclidean mind' becomes, in the devil's terminology, 'common sense . . . that most unhappy attribute of my nature'. Indeed, the devil has positive qualities of his own: he is sociable and equable, which Ivan is not; and, above all, he reveals a homely sense of humour, of which Ivan shows no trace in any other context.

Of course, as an emanation of Ivan, he cannot have in him any element which is not in Ivan; so we must posit in Ivan a 'repressed' sense of humour. And we may wonder just when that sense of humour was repressed. Was Ivan still capable of laughing at himself at the time when he thought up the legend of the unbelieving philosopher? From what we know of his childhood and adolescence, most probably not. The way in which the story is told in Ivan's nightmare is, in that case, the devil's; but we have Ivan's word for it that the story is his own, and he lays particular stress on its originality: it had emerged from the depths of his being.

So too we have at least partial corroboration of the devil's account of the **'Geological Upheaval'**, where Ivan confirms, in Zosima's cell, that belief in God and in the immortality of the soul is an indispensable basis for morality, and the lack or destruction of such belief a sanction for immorality. Moreover Ivan does not, in his nightmare, challenge any part of the devil's account of the **'Geological Upheaval'**; so we must assume that—in regard to these two myths—the 'Father of Lies' is a 'witness of truth'.

Ivan's teenage 'legend' of the unbelieving philosopher marks a stage just short of the 'dead point' in his struggle between faith and unbelief. Faith is still able to tip the balance—but only barely able: it takes a thousand years and a quadrillion miles to bow that stiff neck and subdue that stubborn heart. The 'philosopher' is, like Ivan, a scientist (he is, in fact, Ivan), and it is clearly implied that it is modern science which has destroyed faith. Science believes it has all the answers: our 'philosopher'-scientist values the *a priori* principles of his science above his direct experience—of life after death. Only the direct experience of paradise does, at last, overwhelm the arrogance of the *a priori* and burst the bounds of mathematics and cosmology. The way the devil tells the story foreshadows—or rather, parodies—the way Ivan had told the story of the Grand Inquisitor. This myth of the unbelieving philosopher is also a 'legend', and as Ivan prefaced his **'Legend'** with references to mediaeval literary models, so the devil claims that his 'legend' dates from the Middle Ages of hell: for hell, like earth, has had its Middle Ages and has its religious fanatics. Ironically, the devil defines his mission as the very opposite of that of the Grand Inquisitor, who claims to provide happiness for billions at the price of the unhappiness of one hundred thousand elect: the devil sees himself as appointed to 'destroy thousands so that one may be saved'. And the pi-quancy of the parody is further enhanced by the total difference in content and style between the two 'leg-ends'.

The **'Legend of the Grand Inquisitor'** dates from about a year before Ivan declaims it to Alyosha. So there had been an interval of five years between the composition of the first and the composition of the sec-ond legend. Studies and interpretations of the **'Legend of the Grand Inquisitor'** are legion; at this point, three comments are in order as germane to our outline of the evolution of Ivan's thought.

First: although the **'Legend'** is almost everywhere treated as the measure and peak of Ivan's intellectual achievement, it does not in fact represent the ultimate stage of his thinking, and it is interesting that he should present it to Alyosha as if it did. At the date when the two brothers met for their fateful conference, the **'Leg-end'** had been supplemented, or modified, by Ivan's ar-ticle on the ecclesiastical courts, and had been—or was about to be—virtually superseded by the **'Geological Upheaval'**. Ivan is driven to bring up his Grand Inquis-itor in order to meet Alyosha's challenge: how would your rebel against God's world deal with the person and teaching of Christ?

Secondly: who can fail to be struck by certain dis-sonances or incongruities between the revolt against God's world of Ivan himself in the chapter entitled **'Re-volt'** and the rebellion of the Grand Inquisitor—just such incongruities as would be likely if the **'Legend'** expresses attitudes and assumptions which Ivan had partly, or largely, transcended in the intervening year. The Grand Inquisitor rebels against Christ's teaching out of love and compassion for humanity; Ivan revolts against the order of the universe out of love and com-passion for little children. It would seem that in the course of twelve months Ivan's revolt has broadened in scope while his sympathies have narrowed. The Grand Inquisitor proclaims the happiness of mankind as his objective; Ivan's clamour is for justice, without which his life will not be worth living. The Grand Inquisitor will devote his energies and his life to organizing soci-ety in peace and prosperity; Ivan returns his ticket to eternity and proposes to spend his life, or at least his youth, in the pursuit of personal satisfactions. Within the last year, he has exchanged the humanitarian goals of utopian socialism for the individual goals of private hedonism.

And thirdly: Ivan, who at eighteen had imaged and projected himself as a unitary figure bent on mas-tering experience with the armoury of science, was im-aging and projecting himself at twenty-two as irreme-diably split into a would-be rational and realistic vota-ry of order (heir to Vergil's Rome!) and a prisoner, a forlorn victim of his own romantic cult of freedom.

The article on the ecclesiastical courts, written and published within months of the composition of the **'Legend of the Grand Inquisitor'**, can hardly have in-volved any significant changes of position: the time in-terval was too short. It seems plausible to regard it as an appendix or supplement to the **'Legend',** or per-haps—better still—as an experiment to find out how society might react to an adumbration of the regime of the Grand Inquisitor. Such testing of his theory or 'idea' is characteristic of each of Dostoyevsky's heresiarchs, but is, of course, doubly appropriate in Ivan, whose training had been in the natural sciences.

Finally, our hero is caught up in the **'Geological Upheaval'** consequent upon the breakdown of belief in the existence of God and the immortality of the human soul. Our main source here is again Ivan's devil; we are entitled, if not bound, to accept his account as reliable, but unfortunately it is only fragmentary.

Like the **'Legend of the Grand Inquisitor',** the **'Geological Upheaval'** offers two fundamentally irrec-oncilable answers to the question 'How is Man to live?' Only, in the latter myth the answers are presented not as simultaneous alternatives—not in confrontation—but as sequential, so that their contradiction is blurred or masked. The two answers are re-evoked from earlier writings of Dostoyevsky's: Versilov's vision of men's ultimate state in a sort of Elysium or Isles of the Blessed, preceded, during an interim period of indefi-nite duration, by Kirillov's fantasy of the 'man-god' who is bound to substitute his will as the supreme law for the law which has prevailed hitherto.

Ivan's thought has come a long way in these six years of emergence from boyhood into manhood. He envisions himself first as a scientist, who rejects God and immortality as incompatible with his science, but who ends by capitulating to the direct experience of immortality and God. Five years later he has concluded that questions such as those of the existence of God and the immortality of the soul are not to be resolved by feeble human wits; the most that man can hope to do is so to organize human society as to do away with the worst of human suffering. A year after this, during or shortly before his visit to his father's house, he has lost confidence in the possibility of such a utopia. He plays with a dream of individual salvation in the form of at least a respite of private joys—'till the age of thir-ty'. But he is one 'to whom the miseries of the world/Are misery and will not let him rest'; and he is torn apart between the urge to live and the need to un-derstand what life is for. As his prospects of achieving either purpose appear more and more dubious, his hold on reality weakens: he is standing on the brink of an abyss, over which he projects new fantasies in desper-ate attempts to light up the darkness beyond.

On a superficial view it might seem as if this six-year mental struggle could be fitted into a dialectic, or at least a spiral pattern. At first there is the psychological unity and assurance, the life lived out and 'justified' in the pursuit of the one 'Truth' (with the collapse into faith relegated to some quite inconceivably remote future); next, the antithesis of the Euclidean (or Aristotelian) 'either—or': the stark choice between the 'happiness' of peace provided by order and the suffering which is a necessary condition of freedom, which in turn is a necessary condition of love; then, Euclid/Aristotle transcended in a 'both—and': both the freedom of the man-god, to whom 'all is permitted', and the happy peace and togetherness of the future Golden Age.

But on closer inspection, this synthesis is seen to be just a pseudo-synthesis. Not only is there no place for the man-god in the earthly paradise, but the era of the man-god cannot possibly lead up to an era of earthly paradise. For the essence of the man-god is 'self-will', whilst at the core of the earthly paradise is a harmony of wills, minds and hearts. How, then, could such a society ever be evolved out of any proliferation of man-gods?

The devil himself raises the question how far his host could truly believe in the realization of an earthly paradise with nothing beyond (and it does indeed fly in the face of Ivan's conviction that it is impossible to love one's neighbour here on earth), and caps this query with the barbed suggestion that the concept of the man-god is merely what would today be called a 'rationalization' of Ivan's urges to escape from the shackles of traditional morality.

Ivan's reply to these insinuations is none the less eloquent for dispensing with words: he hurls a glass of tea at his visitor. This is evidently to admit that the devil has a point—or even, that his taunt has struck home. But what Ivan is acknowledging is not necessarily the charge of bad faith; what would be apt to enrage him even more would be the opening of his eyes to the incoherence to which his proud intelligence is being reduced by the human relations and problems in which he has involved himself. To clarify these relations and problems, we must turn back to his heredity and upbringing.

Dostoyevsky was opposed, on principle, to all varieties of psychological determinism: that is, to any theory claiming that individual behaviour is determined by character which is itself determined by external material factors, whether environmental or genetic. In the 1860s, his main attack is on theories which cite environment as the prime cause of crime and antisocial personalities. And accordingly, till the mid-1870s we never have a portrait of both parents of any of his major characters; in many cases, we learn virtually nothing of either parent.

But in the wake of Darwinism, heredity came to be widely regarded as a second major factor—beside, or before, environment—in shaping character. And *The Adolescent* is the first work in which Dostoyevsky gives us full-length portraits of his protagonist's father and mother. But the stress here is not yet on heredity; this was a year or more before Dostoyevsky is supposed to have 'discovered' Zola, who had defined his Rougon-Macquart series as 'Histoire naturelle et sociale d'une famille . . . '. . . . (pp. 115-21)

It seems obvious that Alyosha is predominantly his mother's son; indeed, if it were not for his confidences to Rakitin and Mitya, few readers would charge him with any resemblance to his father; even the confidences are sometimes discounted as a fine concern not to seem better than other people, not to wound their susceptibilities. But this is to overlook the 'absurd, frantic modesty and chastity' (*dikaya, isstuplennaya stydlivost' i tselomudrennost'*), a transparent reaction-formation, into which he had 'sublimated' his inheritance of sensuality. Dostoyevsky, who must have destined Alyosha for sins of the flesh as well as other sins in the unwritten second volume of the Karamazovs' history, was far too good a writer not to have supplied advance evidence of his hero's latent disposition. Nor is sensuality, perhaps, the only trait which Alyosha may have owed to his father. There is a strange lability in his religious faith, even before it has been really severely tested by life. To Lise he says, 'Now, perhaps I don't even believe in God'. At the first demonstration that the world is not run according to his idea of justice, he is ready to rise up against its Maker and is saved from sin only by a chance complex of circumstances. Old Karamazov's beliefs about God, the Devil, and the next world are obviously much more shallow-rooted and kaleidoscopic; but at Alyosha's age and in his circumstances, even the minor fluctuations are noteworthy.

In Smerdyakov, one could say that his father's amorality has combined with his mother's idiocy to produce a moral idiot, or psychopath, devoid of moral sense and human affections (though he does, oddly, claim to have 'loved' Ivan: this may perhaps connote a mixture of fascination with a superior intelligence and attraction to a figure perceived as a potential ally). In a combination of such disparate elements, it makes little sense to try to quantify the respective contributions of father and mother.

But Mitya—contrary to his own assumptions, to those of the other personages in the novel, and to those of most critics—has more in him of Adelaida Miusova than of Fyodor Karamazov. The Karamazov elements are by no means as limited in Mitya as they are in Alyosha, but they appear to account for a good deal less than half of his psychic make-up. This widespread misconception is all the more curious because a majority of personages and critics, if asked directly, 'Do you, then, see Mitya as the same kind of man as his father?'—would almost certainly answer, 'No: a very different kind of man.'

Why, then, this general obsession with Mitya's 'Karamazov inheritance'? To understand this, it is necessary to draw a distinction which is blurred everywhere in the novel, and subsequently in a good deal of the critical literature (although it was noticed by at least one critic [namely, L. Alekseyev] over a hundred years ago). All the Karamazov boys use the same word, *sladostrastiye*, to designate their father's instinctual disposition and their own. This is a mistake (which Dostoyevsky shares with them—or which, at any rate, he does nothing to challenge). Old Karamazov *is* a *sladostrastnik*—a voluptuary. His lust for pleasure is both exorbitant and undiscriminating; it has swamped his inhibitions, his respect for higher values, his capacity for love (not quite completely, as is shown by his attitude to Alyosha): in short, it impoverishes and destroys rather than enhances life. Mitya is not a voluptuary, but a sensualist, greedy for life and enjoyment, but by no means without inhibitions and discrimination. We see him capable of devoted, even chivalrous love—which would seem to have been beyond Fyodor Pavlovich even in his youth. Admittedly, there is in Mitya's sensuality a streak of excess and a streak of obsession; but, from his infancy up, he had been starved of affection, and such starvation is apt to engender such avidity: in a happy marriage Mitya has every chance of achieving a more normal emotional range and balance.

With *sladostrastiye* safely out of the way—what has Mitya taken from his father, and what from his mother? From both parents, 'le débordement des appétits'. The dissipation of Mitya's army days is the male analogue of the 'life of complete emancipation' into which Adelaida had plunged in St Petersburg: Mitya, like his mother, is simply following the fashion of his time and place. It is perhaps only when he encounters Katya and, later, Grushenka, that Karamazov elements are superadded.

From his father, the vein of meanness (*podlost'*) that brings Katya to his rooms and toys with the idea of humiliating her there; the vein of silliness or muddleheadedness (*bestolkovost'*) which however does not in Fyodor, as it does in Mitya, extend to business affairs; and the shamed sense of his own 'foulness' (*bezobraziye*), which drives both men to misbehave, though in quite different ways.

From his mother: the physical courage and aggressiveness displayed in her fights with her husband; the careless generosity with which she abandoned her dowry to him; the impulsiveness and the inability to respect or conform to social norms; the warm-heartedness; and the Romantic 'idealism'.

Ivan's inheritance differs from that of his brothers, Alyosha and Mitya, in two crucial and fateful respects. If Alyosha's psychic make-up is overwhelmingly, and Mitya's is predominantly, derived from their respective mothers, Ivan's nature is compounded about equally of paternal and maternal elements. This would be the almost inescapable inference from the intellectual and emotional deadlock in which he comes before us; but it is actually corroborated in the text of the novel also. . . . Smerdyakov, having a good deal of Fyodor in him, recognizes Fyodor's traits in Ivan, and stresses them, both because he senses that this will be odious to Ivan and, perhaps, by way of hinting at Ivan's affinities with himself. Fyodor, who has just discovered that he is even more afraid of Ivan than of Mitya, now perceives him as wholly alien; he does not connect this alien character with his second wife, Ivan's mother, because, as he had shown only the day before he does not think of Ivan as Sofya's son. So Smerdyakov sees Ivan as essentially Karamazov, while Fyodor sees him as essentially not-Karamazov.

But Ivan's predicament is even more tragic. Not only is he split 'fifty-fifty' between his father's nature and his mother's, but he is unwilling to accept either half as his own. Alyosha is quite content to have inherited his mother's nature, and struggles against such marginal traits in himself as lust or doubt—not because they come from his father, but because they threaten the unity of his being and the system of his values. Mitya's position is more difficult. The paternal component in his nature, though not predominant, looms large; and not only is Mitya aware of it, but he exaggerates its scope, is ashamed of it and detests it. On the other hand, he has no knowledge or clear remembrance of his mother; and though he has, romantically, enshrined an image of her in his heart, so that in a supreme crisis he can attribute his sparing of his father's life to his mother's intervention, yet that image is doubtless too shadowy to serve as a stable focus for identification or a strong counter-centre in his struggles for 'the ideal of the Madonna' against the 'ideal of Sodom'. In fine, Mitya consciously rejects his father while unconsciously identifying with his mother.

Ivan's loathing and rejection of his father is much more intense than Mitya's, in proportion as the Karamazov elements occupy a greater part of his psyche: Ivan wants his father dead, whereas Mitya only wants to neutralize his rival with Grushenka.

Ivan's rejection of his father is direct, open, unambiguous. His rejection of his mother is indirect and probably unconscious in the main. He rejects the world made by (his mother's) God. He strives to reject (his mother's) God. He mobilizes his Karamazov 'love of life' in plans to bury or shelve—at least till the age of thirty—all consideration of ultimate questions (*proklyatyye voprosy*). Above all, he chooses and sets out to adopt a life-style—science, writing, scepticism—equally remote from his mother's simple religion as from his father's debauchery, avarice and laodiceanism. He sets one half of his nature against the other—Karamazov earthy passion against Sofya's otherworldliness and passivity, and Sofya's muted rebelliousness against Karamazov licence and foulness (*bezobraziye*)—and aims to transcend both.

What, then, are the attributes which Ivan owes to his parents? To Sofya, his involvement with religion, his powers of attraction and his rebelliousness. Obviously, they appear in him transmuted. In Sofya, religion is 'natural', a force pervading her being and her life, from which she draws comfort and the strength to endure her sufferings. In Ivan, religion is under constant attack, both from his intellect and from his Karamazov passions, battling for survival, if not at times completely submerged. To him it is a source not of comfort, but of torment. Sofya arouses in rough Grigory a devotion which nerves him to stand up to his master on her behalf. Reactions to Ivan are more various. He is 'loved' by personages as different from him and from one another as Alyosha, Katya and—Smerdyakov. But Mitya is awed by him, old Karamazov is afraid of him, Lise is fascinated by him, and Katya's aunt dislikes him. In Sofya, revolt against the constant outrages to her heart and human dignity are muted by her religion or converted by her helplessness into hysteria (*klikushestvo*); only on one occasion—when her husband lets Belyavsky come courting her and submits to his blow in her presence—does it become overt and explicit. Ivan's revolt stops at nothing: it condemns his father, challenges Christ's teaching, indicts the order of the universe.

The qualities in Ivan which may be traceable to his father are also transmuted, and usually intensified and refined. It is a far cry from Fyodor's uglier appetites to Ivan's ardent thirst for life and joy, from Fyodor's, mainly practical, shrewdness to Ivan's speculative intelligence, from Fyodor's desultory reading to Ivan's scientific and literary culture, from Fyodor's random fantasies to Ivan's creativity in writing and myth-making. The shame to which Zosima, endorsed by Fyodor himself, attributes Fyodor's clowning and general misbehaviour, has in Ivan become excruciating: he is ashamed of his father, ashamed of his father's spirit in himself (and arguably, of more than his father's spirit), and he vents this shame in rage: against his father, against Mitya and Smerdyakov with whom he shares so much of that abhorred spirit, and against himself. Zosima also warned Fyodor against 'the lie in the soul', self-deception. And on two capital issues at least—his feelings for Katya and his desire for his father's death—Ivan is caught up in such a tissue of contradictions that it is a moot point how far he is deluded and how far self-deluded: that is, whether he is shutting his eyes to what he could see if he wanted to, or whether these are 'blind spots' due to repression of key materials into his unconscious.

And it may be relevant to recall here that, in Zosima's cell, old Karamazov allows himself to wonder whether he may not have a devil—if only a low-grade one, since he deserves no better!—and that when Ivan's devil makes his appearance, it is in the guise of a parasite, that is, in the very role in which Fyodor Karamazov had taken the first steps in his career. Thus symbolically Ivan identifies his devil with his father, and rams the point home by insisting (mistakenly, as we have argued) that this devil embodies only the basest and stupidest, the most vile and vulgar elements of his self.

Finally, one might discern in Ivan's pride a composite of his mother's integrity and sense of honour (as evidenced, for example, in the Belyavsky incident) and his father's arrogance, which is the obverse of his shame at his own *podlost'* and *bezobraziye*. The maternal aspect of it is most evident in his refusal to indulge his passion for Katya at Mitya's expense (that is till Mitya is definitely out of the running) and in the bitter struggle with his false pride which issues in his testimony at the trial; but it may be recognized too in the demand for independence (*nikomu ne klanyat'sya*) attested to by Smerdyakov.

It is a truism among educationists that it is the first seven years of life which set an indelible stamp upon the character and personality of the individual; and the rule certainly proves valid in regard to Ivan Karamazov. Though we are told nothing of how Ivan lived through those years, there can be no question of their effects on the formation of his character and thinking. (pp. 121-26)

Ivan must have been a highly intelligent and sensitive child, and he cannot have failed to sense and 'understand'—with his heart, if not with his head—how unhappy his mother was, that his father was the cause of her unhappiness, and how ugly his father's behaviour was. The seeds of his hatred of his father and of all cruelty, of his compassion for victims of human cruelty, and of his revolt against an order of things which gave such fathers unlimited power to inflict such cruelty—were certainly sown in those years, irrespective of whether his memories of them remained conscious or not and irrespective of whether he identified with his mother or rejected her also in his heart. If he identified with her, then his later rebelliousness was rooted in an instinctive grasp of the significance of her hysteria and a transmutation of it, later, in terms of his own powers and circumstances. But it is more likely that he 'rejected', or tried to 'reject' her (if he had identified with her, he should, like Alyosha, have had no difficulty in 'accepting' her God) and, despising what seemed her submission to tyranny, adopted his revolt not as a variation on her attitude, but as an alternative to it.

Of course, in those seven years Ivan's emotional and intellectual development was being conditioned not only by the relations between his parents, but equally if not more profoundly by his own plight and that of little Alyosha. From his father he will have had neither affection nor attention; and though Fyodor may never have punished nor even shouted at his children, Sofya's fear of him cannot but have communicated itself to the growing boy. His mother will have loved him, and, in his earliest years at least, with a full, warm, healthy love, however it may have been chequered later by preoccupation with the baby and by the fits of hysteria during which the servants felt that even the baby was not safe in her hands.

But what is remarkable is how closely Ivan's adult conception of the world is patterned on the experiences of his first seven years. He cannot conceive the possibility of loving one's neighbour, i.e. the people around one, because there had been so blighting a lack of love between the adults in his childhood world. Yet he loves children—because his mother loved him. But not all children—not all who are young and inexperienced and vulnerable; his attitude to Lise, whom Alyosha sees as a sick child, is one of brutal cynicism. He loves only children under seven, that is up till the age at which he lost his mother and, with her, all love. And these little children he not only loves, but idealizes. Under seven there are no ugly children. And children under seven are innocent: they have no knowledge of good and evil. There is a terrible gulf (*strashno otstoyat*) between them and the rest of humanity: they seem quite different beings, with a quite different nature. And so it is their sufferings (not those of wicked adults) which are intolerable, for which Ivan must and will call God to account, for which he must have justice and, since justice is impossible in regard to them, because of whom he will return his ticket to eternity. But surely it was Ivan himself who (in his unconscious memories) was, till the age of seven, beautiful and innocent, because loved—but not happy, for he suffered with his mother's sufferings—and at the age of seven was stripped of all he had and cherished. Like Job, he was delivered by God into the hands of Satan, for no fault of his; but unlike Job, he does not bless the name of the Lord in his affliction. When he rejects God's world on account of the suffering of little children—it is, unconsciously, his own sufferings, his own wrongs that he cannot forgive.

But at seven, revolt is not practicable. Ivan withdrew into himself. In Grigory's primitive home, in the grand but loveless house of the General's widow, in the family circle of Polenov, he held aloof, nursing his grief and his shame: shame for his father, shame for his own dependence. He concentrated on study, perhaps as the quickest path to independence, and proved a brilliant student; later, left to work his way through university on his own resources, he not only achieved independence, but developed new talents—literary and critical—which brought him notice and the respect he craved.

Still, his mind is a battlefield. At eighteen he had imagined he could find in science an escape route, at least for the duration of his life, from the 'frenzied and indecent' thirst for life of the Karamazovs and the religious obsession and precarious mental and emotional balance of Sofya. But university and the world beyond have extended his perspectives. The problem of his own salvation is now seen to be bound up with the destinies of humanity. Who among men is capable of freedom? The masses are not, and left to themselves, they will perish miserably. They can be saved only by the rule of superior intelligences; and would it not be nobler for these to devote themselves to establishing their weaker brethren in security and 'happiness' than selfishly to seek their own salvation either in the 'serene temples' of scientific wisdom or in the solitude of a desert? And so the Grand Inquisitor is conjured up. Here too the main features of the picture—the opposition between unlimited paternal power and helpless childlike submission—are extrapolations from Ivan's first seven years. But the Grand Inquisitor is a 'good' father: he uses his authority and power to make his children 'happy' and he takes the sufferings of the world upon himself.

This fantasy does not satisfy Ivan for long, though as a good scientist he proceeds immediately to test the 'idea' by writing and publishing his article on the ecclesiastical courts. His own doubts about the basic conception may be inferred from the ambiguity of his presentation, which leaves room for the most varied interpretations. And Ivan hardly waits to study the reactions before starting to search for another creed.

Reasons for this switch of interest are not far to seek. The **'Legend'** was likely to occur only to a solitary such as Ivan then was. It presents in the foreground only the two selves of Ivan, with the mass of mankind somewhere in outer darkness. But within a few months Ivan had become involved, for the first time since his childhood, in personal, emotional relations with other human individuals. He had been drawn into Mitya's imbroglio with Katya and had fallen passionately in love with her. And to follow up this affair—to mediate between Mitya and his father—he had returned to his childhood home. What was needed now was a myth, or rather, two myths: one for the immediate present, the other for the near future. Ivan hated his father with a deadly hatred (perhaps, largely unconscious); he detested, despised, and was jealous of, Mitya; and he loved Katya. He wanted Katya for himself; so he wanted Mitya out of the way, as he would be if he married Grushenka, and he did not want the old man to marry Grushenka, which would have made it more difficult for his pride to woo Katya, in view of the disparity be-

The St. Petersburg of Crime and Punishment

Places important in *Crime and Punishment*

1. Raskolnikov's room (No. 9, Srednaya Meshchanskaya Street).
2. The pawnbroker's room.
3. Sonya's room.
4. Haymarket Square (where Raskolnikov bows and kisses the earth).
5. Place of Svidrigaylov's suicide.
6. Tuchkov Bridge.
7. Yusupov Gardens.

Important Petersburg Locations

A. St. Isaac's Cathedral.
B. The Admiralty Building.
C. The Winter Palace and the Ermitage (Tsar's Palaces).
D. The Bourse (Stock Exchange).
E. Academy of Sciences.
F. Leningrad University.
G. Falconnet's statue to Peter the Great.
H. The Senate.

General Note

Petersburg was built early in the eighteenth century by Peter the Great, close to the Gulf of Finald, in a marshy region around the river Neva, which flows westward to the sea. A system of canals and small rivers drained the location of Petersburg; the city continued (and continues to this day) to have the character of a city criss-crossed by rivers and canals, with many bridges.

The area around the Haymarket, where Sonya and Raskolnikov lived, was a slummy section. Most of the locations which Dostoevsky had in mind have been identified; artists have painted the houses and even the doorways important in the novel. For the identification of houses referred to in *Crime and Punishment*, the editor is indebted to an unpublished radio script prepared, for Leningrad Radio, by Dostoevsky's grandson, Andrey Fyodorovich Dostoevsky, who is a specialist in the study of the Petersburg backgrounds of Dostoevsky's writings, and to *Literaturnye pamyatnye mesta Leningrada* (Leningrad, 1959), a book edited by A. M. Dokusov, which discusses Leningrad places important in literature.

On the map, it is possible to trace exactly Raskolnikov's various walks (his three trips from his room to the pawnbroker's, as well as his usual route to the university, with a view of the city from the bridge), Sonya's route from Raskolnikov's room to her own, and Svidrigaylov's last journey before his suicide.

The observant reader will note that "Kameny Bridge" (p. 1 in our text of the novel) ought to read "Kokushkin Bridge." (Dostoevsky's text used only the initial, "K—— Bridge." Somewhere along the line, an editor substituted "Kameny"—erroneously, as the map makes clear, since Dostoevsky's text shows that Raskolnikov must have turned towards Kokushkin Bridge on his way to Alena Ivanovna.)

A map of St. Petersburg indicating locales significant in *Crime and Punishment*.

tween her wealth and his prospects. So what was required was, first, a myth to legitimize the removal of Mitya and Fyodor and his own union with Katya; and then, a myth to establish that, although love of one's neighbour has been impossible until now, a time is at hand when it will become possible for humans to love one another and to be happy in doing so. Hence the twin myths—of the man-god, to whom 'everything is permitted', and of the earthly paradise to follow. If it be objected that this is to assimilate Ivan's myth-making *ante litteram* to Freud's theory of dreams, objectors might reread the exposition, by no less an authority than Ivan's devil, of the scope and artistry of 'dream-work'.

Did he actually want Mitya to kill their father, which would have removed both of them from his path, perhaps no less effectually? The evidence here is complicated and contradictory. On the one hand, we have Alyosha's categorical and repeated 'It wasn't you who killed him', which can only mean, 'You didn't intend to have him killed', for the intention would have been equivalent to the sin. On the same side we have Ivan's assurance to Smerdyakov at their last meeting:

'I swear I was not as guilty as you thought, and perhaps I wasn't inciting you at all'. The most that Ivan will admit here is that he may have had an unconscious desire (*taynoye zhelaniye*) for his father's death. But on the other hand, there are his words to Alyosha before the murder: 'One reptile will devour the other, and serve them both right!'; and: 'who has not the right to desire . . . even the death [of another]? . . . As to my desires, I allow myself full scope in this matter'.

To harmonize these pronouncements, especially in the light of Book V ('Pro and Contra'), one might assume that the sensual rationalistic Ivan wanted his father dead, while the would-be Christian Ivan did not, and that the desire continued to play hide-and-seek with Ivan's consciousness, as it is not uncommon in neurosis for 'unacceptable' desires to remain in consciousness so long as they carry no emotional charge (and therefore no potential for action), but to fade from consciousness in proportion as they become emotionally charged, and to disappear from consciousness completely when the emotionally charged desire, or intention, is ripe for translation into action. Thus after Mitya's assault on their father Ivan can speak coolly to

Alyosha of desiring the old man's death, while assuring him that he will not allow any killing to take place, and be perfectly sincere in this. Whereas next day, in his colloquy with Smerdyakov outside the gate, Ivan is in effect talking with two voices, of which he himself hears only one, while Smerdyakov hears only the other: Ivan thinks he is only satisfying his curiosity by his detailed questions about the danger to his father, while Smerdyakov, intent on not mistaking his young master's meaning, clearly hears behind the spoken words unspoken signals of approval for the crime.

What has happened within the last twenty-four hours to convert Ivan's conscious wish into unconscious will? Only two things: his break with Katya and his communion with Alyosha, which immediately precedes this splitting of his consciousness. The process must actually have begun during that meeting of the brothers, for the chapters entitled 'The Brothers Get Acquainted' and 'Revolt' are full of contradictory utterances; but at that point Ivan is still conscious of everything he says and means what he says while he is saying it. Whereas in the talk with Smerdyakov, there are no contradictions, but the unitary utterance is so refracted that one part of the spectrum of meaning is perceived by Ivan, the other part by his interlocutor. No doubt, Smerdyakov hears what he wants to hear, but he does not want to misunderstand Ivan. Ivan wants to understand his father's situation; but part of the meaning of his words is screened from his consciousness (though not from his unconscious: hence the repeated flares of temper). And the splitting of consciousness continues to the end of the novel, escalating into hallucination in 'Ivan's Nightmare' and lapsing ultimately into something like brain fever.

For sixteen years, since the death of his mother, Ivan has remained locked up inside himself, avoiding all close personal ties (as witness his admission to Alyosha that he has no friends). Suddenly fate throws him up against a girl and three men who arouse powerful emotions in him. But he distrusts emotions—positive ones even more than negative—and he will not give his free play now. He insists on treating Katya as his brother's fiancée, and for months he keeps Alyosha at arm's length, ignoring the boy's mute appeals for a *rapprochement.* Yet he believes himself in love with Katya and declares more than once that he 'loves' Alyosha.

These emotions, churning inside him, have been eroding the fragile unity of the personality he had so long striven to construct on the basis of the two disparate halves of his nature. The Karamazov elements, in particular, have been straining to break loose and establish an ascendancy over the rest. This is evidenced in the **'Geological Upheaval'**:whereas the myth of the earthly paradise, like the earlier myths of the unbelieving philosopher and the Grand Inquisitor, are creations of the whole personality, the myth of the man-god is

essentially a Karamazov myth. (And, in accordance with his usual practice, Ivan has started to test it, flaunting the principle that 'all is permitted' before society and before Smerdyakov, in whom he finds an apt pupil. Mitya too is interested, but finally cannot stomach the major premiss, the non-existence of God.)

Now, the dykes are breached. In a single day the emotions held down and caged in for months have burst out and found utterance, first in his declaration of love for Katya, then, more abundantly, in his 'confession' to Alyosha. And this release of feeling into expression marks a turning-point: from here on, the Karamazov in Ivan will have a voice of its own, an 'independent' voice—outside the purview of Ivan's central consciousness. That is what we hear in the colloquy with Smerdyakov at the gates, in Ivan's three visits to Smerdyakov after he returns from Moscow and in his final appearance in court. And not for nothing is the headlong passion for Katya, to which he 'abandons himself totally' after his return from Moscow, defined by the epithets 'burning' (*plamennoy*), 'insane' (*bezumnoy*) and—'new' (*novoy*). The devil in Ivan's nightmare expresses—despite Ivan's endeavours to equate him with Fyodor—not one but all sides of his nature; but in the following chapter, **'It Was He Who Said That'**, in which Ivan attributes to his vanished devil a series of sneers designed to deter Ivan from proclaiming his guilt in court next day, this invented (as distinct from hallucinated) devil is a Karamazov product.

From the time he leaves home (at the end of Book V) to the end of the novel, Ivan is engaged in strenuous if sporadic efforts to re-establish the integrity of his being. . . . (pp. 127-32)

In his meeting with Alyosha in Book V Ivan sets out to 'make himself known' to his 'little brother', to pour out before him his inmost thoughts and feelings. What erupts is a bewildering chaos of contradictions: 'acceptance' of God while rejecting His Creation; thirst for life and repudiation of the world; exaltation of 'stupidity' and of 'facts' while he castigates intelligence and disowns understanding; although love of one's neighbour is an impossibility, there will be individuals he will love; no one is guilty, but he will kill himself if he cannot see justice done on whoever inflicts suffering on the innocent; he is convinced that the eternal harmony can and will 'undo the done', yet he must return his ticket, 'even though I be wrong'. Even on the level of immediate practicalities: he does not want to subvert Alyosha's faith—but he will not yield him to Zosima. Perhaps this study should be rounded off by a consideration of some of the more puzzling or paradoxical terms and antinomies in Ivan's confession.

To start with the least difficult: love of one's neighbour is 'impossible' to a Karamazov and in terms of Ivan's childhood experience; but his adult experience has recently taught him that it is possible for him to love—in different modes—Alyosha and Katya. What he does not yet know is whether he, warped as he is, will be capable of constructing a close and enduring relationship on the basis of those feelings; and since he is on the point of abandoning both Katya and Alyosha, his hopes of love must be, at best, tenuous.

Next: as a scientist, he can accept that nobody is guilty, that men are what life has made them; as Sofya's son, he can accept that the eternal harmony will—like the paradise of his teenage myth—bring complete and perfect compensation for all suffering; yet he will kill himself, he must return the ticket! It is worth quoting his own, startlingly revealing words: 'I would rather remain with my [*sic!*] suffering unavenged and my indignation unappeased, *even if I were wrong!*'. Whatever the healing power of the harmony, he will not forgive what was done to him (and to his mother?) in the first seven years of his life. This is a measure of the rebelliousness he has developed as a transmutation of his mother's covert revolt—or as a protest against her overt meekness.

The stupidity-intelligence and facts-understanding antinomies are more intricate. On the face of it, one would expect intelligence to go with understanding and with facts, and all three to be opposed to stupidity. And indeed, elsewhere in the novel Ivan's attitude to stupidity and intelligence is the reverse of his attitude here. In his nightmare, for instance, he showers his devil with cries of 'Fool!', 'Ass!' and the like; the word 'stupid' and equivalents occur a dozen times or more in as many pages, and the devil snipes back deriding the excessive value Ivan sets on intelligence as the mark of a very young man. And Ivan's last significant words, at Mitya's trial, are, 'Why is everything that exists so stupid!'. With his life in ruins and his reason about to desert him, the most damning word he can find to sum up his world is 'stupid'. For Ivan the scientist and philosopher intelligence *is* the measure of worth. But in the chapter **'The Brothers Get Acquainted'** Ivan has shed, for a brief half-hour, his science and philosophy. It is a half-hour of unprecedented—and unrepeated—tenderness, in which he presents himself as an inexperienced boy, confides in lyric tones his surging love of life, exults in his freedom (from love and Katya), appeals for Alyosha's friendship, and ends up with the paradox about accepting God but not His world. In such a context one can, and Ivan does—for half an hour—find intelligence to be an encumbrance and 'stupidity'—that is, artlessness, directness, simplicity—the shortest and therefore best way to the heart of his problems.

But, at a deeper level, this new attitude has other ramifications. It connects with Ivan's words in the following chapter (**'Revolt'**): 'The world is founded on absurdities, and perhaps without them nothing would come to pass in it'. And these are in the same key as the devil's admonition that the truth is very seldom 'clever' (*ostroumna*), as his scorn for Ivan's cult of intelligence (after all, the devil is part of Ivan), and as his dream of achieving faith in the body of an eighteen-stone merchant's wife, which is a caricature of Ivan's unavowed yearning for religious certainty. There is scriptural warrant for a link between religion and 'stupidity' ('Blessed are the poor in spirit'); and if the 'stupidity' extolled by Ivan in **'The Brothers Get Acquainted'** is a metonym for 'religion', surely there could be no directer way to Alyosha's heart. All this is the spirit of Sofya speaking through Ivan, whether he knows it or not.

For the opposition of 'fact' to 'understanding' ('I don't understand anything . . . and now I don't want to understand anything. I want to stay with facts . . . If I try to understand anything, I shall immediately be false to the facts') and Ivan's refusal to understand, the context is different and his mood has changed between chapters. But it is still to his childhood we must turn for explanation. Facts are the materials of science and the food of the scientist, and Ivan has here reverted to his role of scientist. But the scientist does not 'understand' facts: he discovers, collects, knows, accepts them. He asks: 'What? when? where? how?'—not: 'Why?' 'Why?' involves the heart; it is the heart that pants to understand, as the child Ivan must have laboured to understand his mother's sufferings, and her death, and the collapse of his seven-year-old world. The facts feed not only Ivan's scientific brain, they feed too his 'unslaked indignation'. Understanding might soften his anger, might take the edge off his will to justice—and that must never be. He is committed to clamour for justice for his wrongs, and his mother's wrongs; and so he is doomed to be the eternal rebel, as his devil is doomed eternally to negate.

And lastly: what does Ivan mean when he says he 'accepts' God, and why does he accept Him? Since he does not accept God's Creation, it is clear that he does not accept God with his heart, with love. Does he, then, accept God intellectually? That would mean: either as a 'working hypothesis' or as a 'fact'. But from the presentation of Christ in the **'Legend'** and from Ivan's paean to the eternal harmony etc., it is plain that God is much more to Ivan than a working hypothesis. Yet He cannot be a fact either: from the viewpoint of a scientist of the mid-1860s, God cannot be fitted into the world of facts (any more than the devil could, when he tried to get his tribute to Hoff 's malt extract published). But if God is to Ivan neither an object of love nor a fact (i.e. an object of knowledge-that-it-is-so)—what is He? To answer this, we must look again at Ivan's attitude to the world. Or rather, not at Ivan's attitude, but at Ivan's attitudes. The child Ivan rejects the Creation because it is defiled by the sufferings of innocent children, and because it is unintelligible; the man Ivan loves 'life'—the sticky little leaves, the blue sky, a man here, a woman there, great human achievements.

Ivan's judgement condemns the Creation; Ivan's 'inside and belly' cleave to life—or would do, if they were not paralysed by the judgement. So too Ivan seeks and 'accepts' God—not with his heart, not with his head, but with his deepest, visceral instincts. He needs God, and with a twofold need: as a focus for his 'unslaked indignation' and rebellion, and as the indispensable condition of morality, Who, as such, can alone save him from his nightmare of turning into another—perhaps more bestial, perhaps more criminal—Fyodor Karamazov.

Ivan Karamazov is the most complex, the most richly gifted and the most tragic of Dostoyevsky's 'split thinkers'. Staggering under the load of his heredity, haunted by the spectres of his childhood, he wages a heroic fight, in utter loneliness, against despair: seeking to transcend, since he cannot reconcile, the warring halves of his nature, to evolve a faith to live by, and to relate himself to life through joy and love. The first and second acts of his drama end in disaster, and Dostoyevsky did not live to narrate what followed. (pp. 132-35)

F. F. Seeley, "Ivan Karamazov," in *New Essays on Dostoyevsky*, edited by Malcolm V. Jones and Garth M. Terry, Cambridge University Press, 1983, pp. 115-36.

SOURCES FOR FURTHER STUDY

Berdyaev, Nicholas. *Dostoevsky*. Translated by Donald Atwater. Cleveland, New York: The World Publishing Co., 1957, 227 p.

> Discusses the depth of Dostoyevsky's religious and philosophical concerns, stressing the novelist's Christian world view.

Frank, Joseph. *Dostoevsky*. 3 vols. Princeton, N. J.: Princeton University Press, 1976-86.

> The first three installments of a proposed five-part literary biography that studies the writer in the context of the "social-cultural life of his period." Frank judges Dostoyevsky's work a "brilliant artistic synthesis of the major issues of his time."

Ivanov, Vyacheslav. *Freedom and the Tragic Life: A Study in Dostoevsky*, edited by S. Konovalov. Translated by Norman Cameron. New York: The Noonday Press, 1952, 166 p.

> A Study of Dostoyevsky's life and work. Ivanov calls Dostoyevsky's books "vehicles of Dionysus."

Milosz, Czeslaw. "Dostoevsky and Swedenborg." In his *Emperor of the Earth: Modes of Eccentric Vision*, pp. 120-43. Berkeley: University of California Press, 1977.

> An examination of the theme of self-love as manifested in the struggle between good and evil in Dostoyevsky's characters.

Mirsky, D. S. "The Age of Realism: The Novelists (1)." In his *A History of Russian Literature*, edited by Francis J. Whitfield, pp. 169-204. New York: Alfred A. Knopf, 1973.

> A discussion of Dostoyevsky's early work, with particular emphasis on Gogol's influence.

Troyat, Henri. *Firebrand: The Life of Dostoyevsjy*. New York: Roy Publishers, 1946, 438 p.

> A detailed and well-documented biographical study.

Frederick Douglass

1817?-1895

(Born Frederick Augustus Washington Bailey) American lecturer, autobiographer, editor, essayist, and novella writer.

INTRODUCTION

Douglass is recognized as one of the most distinguished black writers of nineteenth-century America. Born into slavery, he escaped in 1838 and subsequently devoted his considerable rhetorical skills to the abolitionist movement. Expounding the theme of racial equality in stirring, invective-charged orations and newspaper editorials in the 1840s, 50s, and 60s, he was recognized by his peers as an outstanding orator and the foremost black abolitionist of his era. Douglass's status as a powerful and effective prose writer is based primarily on his 1845 autobiography *Narrative of the Life of Frederick Douglass, an American Slave, Written by Himself.* Regarded as one of the most compelling antislavery documents produced by a fugitive slave, the *Narrative* is also valued as an eloquent argument for human rights. As such, it has transcended its immediate historical milieu and is now regarded as a landmark in American autobiography.

The son of a black slave and an unidentified white man, Douglass was separated from his mother in his infancy. Raised by his maternal grandmother on the Tuckahoe, Maryland estate of Captain Aaron Anthony, he enjoyed a relatively happy childhood until he was pressed into service on the plantation of Anthony's employer, Edward Lloyd. There Douglass endured the rigors of slavery. In 1825, Douglass was transferred to the Baltimore household of Hugh Auld, who inadvertantly provided Douglass with an important critical insight into the slavery system. In an incident that Douglass described as a "revelation," he overheard Auld rebuke his wife for teaching the boy the rudiments of reading. Deducing that ignorance perpetuated subjugation, Douglass undertook reading as an avenue to freedom. His secret efforts to educate himself—aided by *Webster's Spelling Book* and the random instruction of white playmates—were fruitful: obtaining a copy of *The Columbian Orator,* a popular collection of writings on democratic themes, he avidly studied the speeches of Richard Brinsley Sheridan, Charles James Fox, and other advocates of liberty. Douglass grew restive as his desire for freedom increased. In 1838, he realized his long-cherished goal by escaping to New York.

Once free, Douglass quickly became a prominent figure in the abolitionist movement. In 1841, he delivered his first public address—a moving extemporaneous speech at an antislavery meeting in Nantucket, Massachusetts—and was invited by William Lloyd Garrison and other abolitionist leaders to work as a lecturer for the Massachusetts Antislavery Society. Sharing the podium with such renowned orators as Garrison and Wendell Phillips, he served successfully in that capacity for four years. Douglass's eloquent and cogent oratory led many to doubt that he was indeed a former slave. When urged by supporters to authenticate his experiences, he responded with a detailed account of his slave life, the *Narrative of the Life of Frederick Douglass,* which was an immediate popular success. Liable to capture under the fugitive slave laws, Douglass fled the United States in late 1845 and traveled to Great Britain, where he was honored by the great reformers of the day. Returning to the United States in 1847, he received sufficient funds to purchase his freedom and establish the *North Star,* a weekly abolitionist newspaper.

During the 1850s and early 1860s, Douglass continued his activities as a journalist, abolitionist speaker, and autobiographer. After splitting with Garrison over the issue of disunion, he aligned himself with Gerrit Smith's conservative Liberty Party and marked the change by rechristening his periodical *Frederick Douglass' Paper.* By the outbreak of the Civil War, Douglass had emerged as a nationally-recognized spokesman for black Americans and, in 1863, he advised President Abraham Lincoln on the use and treatment of black soldiers in the Union Army. Douglass then founded the *New National Era,* a short-lived newspaper, and delivered numerous addresses on the lyceum lecture circuit, but his last years were chiefly devoted to political and diplomatic assignments. When he revised his final autobiographical work, the *Life and Times of Frederick Douglass, Written by Himself,* (1881), he was able to record numerous political honors, including presidential assignments as assistant secretary to the Santo Domingo Commission, marshal of the District of Columbia, and United States minister resident and consul-general to the Republic of Haiti. Douglass died at his home in Anacostia Heights, D.C., in 1895.

In his speeches on abolition, Douglass frequently drew on his first-hand experience of slavery to evoke pathos in his audience. He is most often noted, however, for his skillful use of scorn and irony in denouncing the slave system and its abettors. One of the stock addresses in his abolitionist repertoire was a "slaveholder's sermon" in which he sarcastically mimicked a pro-slavery minister's travesty of the biblical injunction to "do unto others as you would have them do unto you." His most famous speech, an address delivered on 5 July 1852 in Rochester, N.Y., commonly referred to as the "Fourth of July Oration," is a heavily ironic reflection on the significance of Independence Day for slaves. Douglass was described by a contemporary critic as being "particularly obnoxious to . . . those in general who mix up character and color, man and his skin—to all, in short, who have little hearts and muddy heads," and he is occasionally criticized for indiscriminate severity and humorlessness. In general, however, his polemical techniques are praised as commendable attributes of reformist oratory. Douglass's postbellum orations are regarded as more intellectual—and by many critics as less artistic—than his abolitionist addresses. In J. Saunders Redding's words, he had become a "finished public speaker" by the 1880s, "more concerned with intellectual than emotional responses."

A similar estimate has been made of Douglass's powers as an autobiographer. Critics generally agree that, in retelling and updating his life history in *My Bondage and My Freedom* (1855) and the *Life and Times of Frederick Douglass,* Douglass provided a classic American story of struggle and achievement but failed to recapture the artistic vitality of the *Narrative.* Valued by historians as a detailed, credible account of slave life, the *Narrative* is widely acclaimed as an artfully compressed yet extraordinarily expressive story of self-discovery and self-liberation. Recording his personal reactions to bondage in such simply-written yet moving passages as his apostrophe to the vessels sailing free on the Chesapeake Bay, Douglass distinguished himself from most other slave narrators.

Appealing variously to the political, sociological, and aesthetic interests of successive generations of critics, Douglass has maintained an enviable reputation as an orator and prose writer. Douglass's contemporaries, who were influenced by Garrison and other abolitionist sympathizers, viewed him primarily as a talented antislavery agitator whose manifest abilities as an orator and writer refuted the idea of black inferiority. This view persisted until the 1930s, when both Vernon Loggins and J. Saunders Redding called attention to the "intrinsic merit" of Douglass's writing and acknowledged him to be the most important figure in nineteenth-century black American literature. In the 1940s and 1950s, Alain Locke and Benjamin Quarles respectively pointed to the *Life and Times of Frederick Douglass* and the *Narrative* as classic works which symbolize the black role of protest, struggle, and aspiration in American life. Led by Albert E. Stone, Robert B. Stepto, and Houston A. Baker, Jr., Douglass's critics have become far more exacting in recent years, for they have analyzed—and usually praised—the specific narrative strategies that Douglass employed in the *Narrative* to establish a distinctly individual black identity. Stepto's recent examination of Douglass's novella *The Heroic Slave* (1853) testifies to the growing recognition of Douglass's narrative skills.

Distinguished by praise and diversity, the history of critical response to Douglass's works may be taken as an indication of their abiding interest. As G. Thomas Couser has observed, Douglass was a remarkable man who lived in an exceptionally tumultuous period in American history. By recording the drama of his life and times in lucid prose, he provided works that continue to attract the notice of literary critics and historians.

(For further information about Douglass's life and works, see *Black Literature Criticism; Concise Dictionary of American Literary Biography, 1640-1865; Dictionary of Literary Biography*, Vols. 1, 43, 50; *Nineteenth-Century Literature Criticism*, Vol. 7; and *Something about the Author*, Vol. 29. For related criticism, see the entry on American Slave Narratives in *Nineteenth-Century Literature Criticism*, Vol. 20.)

CRITICAL COMMENTARY

WILLIAM LLOYD GARRISON

(essay date 1845)

[Garrison was a nationally recognized leader in the abolitionist movement and a key figure in Douglass's rise to public prominence. In the following essay, which was originally published as the preface to the 1845 edition of the *Narrative of the Life of Frederick Douglass*, he records his passionate reaction to Douglass's first public address, praises Douglass's influence and skill as a public speaker, and recommends the *Narrative* as an authentic and unexaggerated account of slave life.]

In the month of August, 1841, I attended an anti-slavery convention in Nantucket, at which it was my happiness to become acquainted with Frederick Douglass, the writer of the [*Narrative of the Life of Frederick Douglass*]. He was a stranger to nearly every member of that body; but, having recently made his escape from the southern prison-house of bondage, and feeling his curiosity excited to ascertain the principles and measures of the abolitionists, . . . he was induced to give his attendance, on the occasion alluded to. . . . (p. 3)

Fortunate, most fortunate occurrence!—fortunate for the millions of his manacled brethren, yet panting for deliverance from their awful thraldom!—fortunate for the cause of negro emancipation, and of universal liberty!—fortunate for the land of his birth, which he has already done so much to save and bless! . . . [Fortunate] for himself, as it at once brought him into the field of public usefulness, "gave the world assurance of a MAN," quickened the slumbering energies of his soul, and consecrated him to the great work of breaking the rod of the oppressor, and letting the oppressed go free!

I shall never forget [Douglass's first speech at an anti-slavery convention in Nantucket in 1841]—the extraordinary emotion it excited in my own mind—the powerful impression it created upon a crowded auditory, completely taken by surprise. . . . I think I never hated slavery so intensely as at that moment; certainly, my perception of the enormous outrage which is inflicted by it, on the godlike nature of its victims, was rendered far more clear than ever. There stood one, in physical proportion and stature commanding and exact—in intellect richly endowed—in natural eloquence a prodigy—in soul manifestly "created but a little lower than the angels"—yet a slave, ay, a fugitive slave,—trembling for his safety, hardly daring to believe that on the American soil, a single white person could be found who would befriend him at all hazards, for the love of God and humanity! Capable of high attainments as an intellectual and moral being—needing nothing but a comparatively small amount of cultivation to make him an ornament to society and a blessing to his race—by the law of the land, by the voice of the people, by the terms of the slave code, he was only a piece of property, a beast of burden, a chattel personal, nevertheless! (pp. 4-5)

As soon as he had taken his seat, filled with hope and admiration, I rose, and declared that Patrick Henry, of revolutionary fame, never made a speech more eloquent in the cause of liberty, than the one we had just listened to from the lips of that hunted fugitive. So I believed at that time—such is my belief now. (p. 5)

As a public speaker, [Douglass] excels in pathos, wit, comparison, imitation, strength of reasoning, and fluency of language. There is in him that union of head and heart, which is indispensable to an enlightenment of the heads and a winning of the hearts of others. May

Principal Works

Narrative of the Life of Frederick Douglass, an American Slave, Written by Himself (autobiography) 1845

Oration, Delivered in Corinthian Hall, Rochester, by Frederick Douglass, July 5th, 1852 (speech) 1852

The Heroic Slave (novella) 1853; published in Autographs for Freedom

The Claims of the Negro Ethnologically Considered (speech) 1854

My Bondage and My Freedom (autobiography) 1855

Men of Color, to Arms! (essay) 1863

"What the Black Man Wants" (speech) 1865; published in The Equality of All Men before the Law Claimed and Defended in Speeches by Hon. William D. Kelley, Wendell Phillips, and Frederick Douglass

John Brown (speech) 1881

Life and Times of Frederick Douglass, Written by Himself (autobiography) 1881; revised edition, 1892

The Life and Writings of Frederick Douglass. 5 vols. (letters, speeches, and essays) 1950-75

The Frederick Douglass Papers. 2 vols. (speeches and debates) 1979-82

his strength continue to be equal to his day! May he continue to "grow in grace, and in the knowledge of God," that he may be increasingly serviceable in the cause of bleeding humanity, whether at home or abroad! (p. 7)

Mr. Douglass has very properly chosen to write his [*Narrative of the Life of Frederick Douglass*], in his own style, and according to the best of his ability, rather than to employ some one else. It is, therefore, entirely his own production; and, considering how long and dark was the career he had to run as a slave,—how few have been his opportunities to improve his mind since he broke his iron fetters,—it is, in my judgment, highly creditable to his head and heart. He who can peruse it without a tearful eye, a heaving breast, an afflicted spirit,—without being filled with an unutterable abhorrence of slavery and all its abettors, and animated with a determination to seek the immediate overthrow of that execrable system,—without trembling for the fate of this country in the hands of a righteous God . . .—must have a flinty heart, and be qualified to act the part of a trafficker "in slaves and the souls of men." I am confident that it is essentially true in all its statements; that nothing has been set down in malice, nothing exaggerated, nothing drawn from the imagination; that it comes short of the reality, rather than overstates a single fact in regard to SLAVERY AS IT IS. The experience of Frederick Douglass, as a slave, was not a peculiar one: his lot was not especially a hard one. . . .

Many have suffered incomparably more, while very few on the plantations have suffered less, than himself. Yet how deplorable was his situation! what terrible chastisements were inflicted upon his person! what still more shocking outrages were perpetrated upon his mind! with all his noble powers and sublime aspirations, how like a brute was he treated, even by those professing to have the same mind in them that was in Christ Jesus! (pp. 9-10)

This *Narrative* contains many affecting incidents, many passages of great eloquence and power; but I think the most thrilling one of them all is the description Douglass gives of his feelings, as he stood soliloquizing respecting his fate, and the chances of his one day being a freeman, on the banks of the Chesapeake Bay—viewing the receding vessels as they flew with their white wings before the breeze, and apostrophizing them as animated by the living spirit of freedom. Who can read that passage, and be insensible to its pathos and sublimity? Compressed into it is a whole Alexandrian library of thought, feeling, and sentiment—all that can, all that need be urged, in the form of expostulation, entreaty, rebuke, against that crime of crimes,—making man the property of his fellow-man! (p. 11)

So profoundly ignorant of the nature of slavery are many persons, that they are stubbornly incredulous whenever they read or listen to any recital of the cruelties which are daily inflicted on its victims. . . . Such will try to discredit the shocking tales of slaveholding cruelty which are recorded in this truthful *Narrative;* but they will labor in vain. Mr. Douglass has frankly disclosed the place of his birth, the names of those who claimed ownership in his body and soul, and the names also of those who committed the crimes which he has alleged against them. His statements, therefore, may easily be disproved, if they are untrue. (pp. 11-13)

The effect of a religious profession on the conduct of southern masters is vividly described in the following *Narrative,* and shown to be any thing but salutary. In the nature of the case, it must be in the highest degree pernicious. The testimony of Mr. Douglass, on this point, is sustained by a cloud of witnesses, whose veracity is unimpeachable. "A slaveholder's profession of Christianity is a palpable imposture. He is a felon of the highest grade. He is a mansteeler. It is of no importance what you put in the other scale."

Reader! are you with the man-stealers in sympathy and purpose, or on the side of their down-trodden victims? If with the former, then are you the foe of God and man. If with the latter, what are you prepared to do and dare in their behalf ? Be faithful, be vigilant, be untiring in your efforts to break every yoke, and let the oppressed go free. Come what may—cost what it may—inscribe on the banner which you unfurl to the breeze, as your religious and political motto—"NO COM-

PROMISE WITH SLAVERY! NO UNION WITH SLAVEHOLDERS!'' (pp. 14-15)

William Lloyd Garrison, in a preface to *Narrative of the Life of Frederick Douglass, an American Slave* by Frederick Douglass, edited by Benjamin Quarles, Belknap Press, 1960, pp. 3-15.

FREDERICK DOUGLASS
(essay date 1855)

[In the following excerpt from a letter to the editor of *My Bondage and My Freedom*, Douglass explains his reasons for writing this second autobiographical work.]

In my letters and speeches, I have generally aimed to discuss the question of Slavery in the light of fundamental principles, and upon facts, notorious and open to all; making, I trust, no more of the fact of my own former enslavement, than circumstances seemed absolutely to require. I have never placed my opposition to slavery on a basis so narrow as my own enslavement, but rather upon the indestructible and unchangeable laws of human nature, every one of which is perpetually and flagrantly violated by the slave system. I have also felt that it was best for those having histories worth the writing—or supposed to be so—to commit such work to hands other than their own. To write of one's self, in such a manner as not to incur the imputation of weakness, vanity, and egotism, is a work within the ability of but few; and I have little reason to believe that I belong to that fortunate few.

These considerations caused me to hesitate, when first you kindly urged me to prepare for publication a full account of my life as a slave, and my life as a freeman.

Nevertheless, I see, with you, many reasons for regarding my autobiography as exceptional in its character, and as being, in some sense, naturally beyond the reach of those reproaches which honorable and sensitive minds dislike to incur. It is not to illustrate any heroic achievements of a man, but to vindicate a just and beneficient principle, in its application to the whole human family, by letting in the light of truth upon a system, esteemed by some as a blessing, and by others as a curse and a crime. I agree with you, that this system is now at the bar of public opinion—not only of this country, but of the whole civilized world—for judgment. Its friends have made for it the usual plea—"not guilty;" the case must, therefore, proceed. Any facts, either from slaves, slaveholders, or by-standers, calculated to enlighten the public mind, by revealing the true nature, character, and tendency of the slave sys-

tem, are in order, and can scarcely be innocently withheld.

I see, too, that there are special reasons why I should write my own biography, in preference to employing another to do it. Not only is slavery on trial, but unfortunately, the enslaved people are also on trial. It is alleged, that they are, naturally, inferior; that they are *so low* in the scale of humanity, and so utterly stupid, that they are unconscious of their wrongs, and do not apprehend their rights. Looking, then, at your request, from this stand-point, and wishing everything of which you think me capable to go to the benefit of my afflicted people, I part with my doubts and hesitation, and proceed to furnish you the desired manuscript. . . . (pp. vi-vii)

Frederick Douglass, in a letter to an unidentified recipient on July 2, 1855, in his *My Bondage and My Freedom,* 1855. Reprint by Dover Publications, Inc., 1969, pp. v-viii.

J. SAUNDERS REDDING
(essay date 1939)

[Redding was a distinguished American authority on African-American literature and history. He is remembered for a number of important studies of black culture, including *To Make a Poet Black* (1939), *They Came in Chains: Americans from Africa* (1950; revised edition, 1973), and *The Lonesome Road: The Story of the Negro's Part in America* (1958). In the following excerpt from the first-named work, he calls attention to the artistic qualities of Douglass's works and accords the author an important place in the history of American literature.]

The 1845 autobiography, *Narrative of the Life of Frederick Douglass,* came at a time when the writing of slave narratives, real or fictitious, was popular propaganda, but Douglass's book is in many ways too remarkable to be dismissed as mere hack writing. . . . In utter contrast to the tortured style of most of the slave biographies, Douglass's style is calm and modest. Even in this first book his sense of discrimination in the selection of details is fine and sure. The certainty of the book's emotional power is due in part to the stringent simplicity of style and in part to the ingenuous revelation of the author's character. (p. 32)

The same dignity with which [Douglass's letters to the press] answered malicious attacks or set forth his arguments marked his speeches. Indeed, reading his letters now, one feels that they were written for speech, that Douglass made no difference between the written and the spoken word. (p. 33)

The speeches [that Douglass] made between 1849

and 1860 were never equaled in logic, in emotional force, or in simple clarity. His peculiarly stony denunciation, the calm bitterness of his irony, and his frequent use of the simple and emotional language of the Bible make the speeches of this period memorable examples of the oratorical art. (pp. 33-4)

In 1855 the autobiographical *My Bondage and My Freedom* was published. His style, still without tricks, proves surer. Considerably longer than his first book, its length is amply justified by its matter. Though the first part follows in general the simple plan of the *Narrative,* he acquaints us more intimately with slavery and expresses his more mature thoughts on the problems which he faced. It is evident, especially when he writes of his English trip, that his knowledge of men had grown. Equally evident in the logic and sincerity of his arguments is the growth of his knowledge of issues. . . . *My Bondage and My Freedom* is the high mark of the second stage of Douglass's career. Indeed, though for many years after 1865 he was active as both speaker and writer, and though his thoughts steadily matured, he did not exceed the emotional pitch of this second period. As his intellectual vigor increased (and became, it may be said, a little warped by the overdevelopment of his capacity for irony), his emotional and artistic powers fell off. By the 1880's he was not an orator speaking with a spontaneous overflow of emotion: he was a finished public speaker, more concerned with intellectual than emotional responses. (p. 35)

[*Life and Times of Frederick Douglass*] was published in 1881. Its interest comes authentically from the man's life and thought. It has been called properly the most American of American life stories. Unconsciously, with no fanfare of self-satisfaction, the story develops the dramatic theme from bondage to the council tables of a great nation. It is written with the same lucid simplicity that marks all of Douglass's best work, but there is still the lack of differentiation between speaker and writer. *Life and Times* is his best book. (pp. 36-7)

[The larger edition of *Life and Times,* issued in 1892,] is slow and repetitious. [Douglass's] powers had waned, but he was still aware that all was not finished. He had mellowed with only slight decay; grown into acceptance without resignation. To the last, he wrote as he spoke. (p. 37)

The literary work of Douglass is first important as examples of a type and period of American literature. Many of his speeches rank with the best of all times. . . . That at least two of his books, *My Bondage and My Freedom* and the first *Life and Times,* have not been recognized for what they are is attributable more to neglect than to the judgment of honest inquiry. Certainly no American biographies rank above them in the literary qualities of simplicity, interest, and compression of style. They delineate from an exceptional point of view a period in the history of the United States than which no other is more fraught with drama and sociological significance. By any standard his work ranks high.

That he was easily the most important figure in American Negro literature at the time of his death goes without saying. He was the very core of the For Freedom group, fitting his art more nearly to his purposes than any of the others—and suffering less intrinsically for doing it. Without him the For Freedom group would be destitute of true greatness, Negro literature would be poorer, and American literary fields of oratory and autobiography would be lacking a figure in whom they might justly claim pride. (pp. 37-8)

J. Saunders Redding, "Let Freedom Ring: Charles Remond, William W. Brown, Frederick Douglass, Frances Ellen Watkins, James Madison Bell," in his *To Make a Poet Black,* 1939. Reprint by McGrath Publishing Company, 1968, pp. 19-48.

JOHN SEKORA
(essay date 1985)

[In the following essay, Sekora pronounces the *Narrative of the Life of Frederick Douglass* "the most comprehensive personal history of slavery in the language."]

Because it is one of the most important books ever published in America, Frederick Douglass' *Narrative* of 1845 has justly received much attention. That attention has been increasing for a generation at a rate parallel to the growth in interest in autobiography as a literary genre, and the *Narrative* as autobiography has been the subject of several influential studies. Without denying the insights of such studies, I should like to suggest that in 1845 Douglass had no opportunity to write what (since the eighteenth century) we would call autobiography, that the achievement of the *Narrative* lies in another form.

Elsewhere I have argued the uniqueness of the antebellum slave narrative as an American literary form, a signal feature of which is the conditions under which it was printed. Briefly put, eighteenth-century narratives like those of Hammon, Gronniosaw, and Equiano were published only when they could be fitted to such familiar patterns as the captivity tale or the tale of religious conversion. In the abolitionist period when slavery was the central issue, once again printers and editors determined the overall shape of the narrative. Lundy, Garrison, Tappan, and Weld sought to expunge a vile institution, not support individualized Afro-American life stories. They had set the language of abolition—its vocabulary as well as social attitudes and philosophical presuppositions—in place by the early 1830s. Former slaves were wanted primarily as lecturers, later as authors, not for their personal identities as men and women, but for their value as eyewitnesses and victims. (It was significant to Douglass that his white associates tended to see slaves as passive victims.)

Against these conditions, one must place current conceptions of autobiography. Traditionalists and poststructuralists seem to agree that autobiography comes into being when recollection engages memory. Recollection engages people, things, events that at first appear fragmented and unrelated. As an essential part of its activity, recollection brings sequence and/or relation to the enormous diversity of individual experience; it emplots the stages of the subject's journey to selfhood. Meaning emerges when events are connected as parts of a coherent and comprehensive whole. Meaning, relation, and wholeness are but three facets of one characteristic: a narrative self that is more a literary creation than a literal, preexisting fact. The self of autobiography comes into being in the act of writing, not before. This said, the contrast with the antebellum narrative is apparent. From Hammon's *Narrative* of 1760 to Harriet Jacobs's *Incidents* in 1861, the explicit purpose of the slave narrative is far different from the creation of a self, and the overarching shape of that story—the

facts to be included and the ordering of those facts—is mandated by persons other than the subject. Not black recollection, but white interrogation brings order to the narration. For eighteenth-century narratives the self that emerges is a preexisting form, deriving largely from evangelical Protestantism. For the abolitionist period, the self is a type of the antislavery witness. In each instance the meaning, relation, and wholeness of the story are given before the narrative opens; they are imposed rather than chosen—what Douglass in *My Bondage and My Freedom* (1855) calls "the facts which I felt almost everybody must know."

This approach would seem to resolve some persistent questions about the *Narrative:* why its structure is so similar to earlier (and later) abolitionist narratives, why Douglass subordinates so much of his emotional and intellectual life to the experience of slavery, why Garrison and Phillips are at such pains to make it appear a collective enterprise. At the same time it raises at least two others: if not autobiography, what kind of book is the *Narrative?* And how does it succeed so thoroughly?

White Americans, it would seem, have long attempted to cloak the raw experience of slavery—in the eighteenth century masking it in the language of triumphal Christianity, for most of the nineteenth century transmuting it into the language of abolition. For the years between 1870 and 1950, even this genteel transmutation was too raw, too threatening. Thus the slave narratives remained the most important and the most neglected body of early American writing. A consequence of that neglect is that we lack a distinctive term for a unique genre. For one example, most critics use the term *slave narrative* to refer to stories of oppression under slavery; yet before 1830 very few of the narratives concerned themselves with the injustices of the institution. Related to captivity tales, Franklinesque success stories, modern autobiographies, and other forms, the slave narrative is essentially different from all. It resembles other forms, but other forms do not resemble it.

In the absence of a distinguishing critical category, we must make do with that phrase used in authors' prefaces and advertisements as synonymous with abolitionist narrative—"personal history of slavery." Douglass was clearly aware in 1845 of the terms for such a history, for he had referred to them in his lectures earlier and wrote about them at length later. Before he became an antislavery agent, he had been questioned frequently concerning his life under slavery; once selected as an agent, he was coached concerning those aspects of slavery most likely to appeal to an ignorant or indifferent Northern audience. He had read the earlier separately published narratives and followed the shorter tales printed in the *Liberator* and other periodicals. He knew, he said, of the abolitionist emphasis upon facts, verifiable facts; upon instances of cruelty, repression, and punishment; upon the depth of Christianity in the owner's household; and so on. Overall, he knew that he was being woven into a network of clergymen, politicians, tradesmen, writers, editors, sponsors, and societies that was transatlantic in scope and resources. On any given day of lecturing, for example, he knew he would be introduced and followed by white speakers who would testify to his candor, character, and authenticity. And he knew he would conclude his address with an appeal to the audience to do as he had done—become absorbed in the abolitionist crusade.

Douglass was thus situated at the intersection of collectivizing forces. On both sides of the political divide, white people were busy defining and hence depersonalizing him. Apologists for slavery were doing their utmost to discredit him as a fraud; Garrison's agents were doing their best to publicize him as a representative fugitive slave. The issue over which they fought was not Douglass the lecturer or Douglass the author. Rather it was a narrower issue of their own defining. Douglass was important insofar as he embodied the experience of slavery. As author he was therefore caught in a genuine dilemma. He was indeed an individual human being with a particular story to tell, but if he were to discover personalizing words for his life, he must do so within the language of abolition. His success in resolving that dilemma, as arresting today as when it was first published, makes the *Narrative* the most comprehensive personal history of slavery in the language.

It embodies comprehension on several levels and in several successive stages, as intellectual apprehension of the many influences of slavery and narrative compassing its equally many forms. In the beginning Douglass as narrator comprehends the world that slaveholders have made, and Douglass as actor comprehends the power of language to transform that world. In his mature years he apprehends the eloquence of silence as well as the liberating power of words. Finally, as at once actor and narrator, he comprehends his own situation in the tradition of the slave narrative. Douglass highlights these levels with a series of gemlike sentences of Enlightenment irony and compression. Two are notable as preliminary illustrations of his modes of comprehension. Recalling his entrance into the Auld household in Baltimore twenty years before, he reports: "Little Thomas was told, there was his Freddy. . . ." In eight short words of indirect quotation, he signals both the effect of chattel slavery upon the Auld family and his intellectual apprehension of his place in the system. The Auld child is "Little Thomas"—an exalted owner of human property; Douglass is diminished in name as well as status—"*his* Freddy." In the kind of Enlightenment balance and compression

sought by Hume and Johnson (but not surpassed by them), two adjectives modifying two nouns carry all the weight of significance: analysis enveloped by description. The Aulds address not Douglass but the child. Douglass is deployed as an object—in the sentence, the child's mind, the household, and the system—and so employs himself to convey his awareness of that situation. The burden of the narrative will be to reveal the necessary reversal of that situation. The Aulds are too vacuous and vulnerable, Douglass too penetrating, for it to hold. In what Albert Stone has rightly called the key sentence of the *Narrative,* Douglass again unites balance, reversal, and narrative time to embody what an abolitionist narrative should be: "You have seen how a man was made a slave; you shall see how a slave was made a man." These two sentences suggest the depth of his enterprise. While operating within the abolitionist code, his adroit use of language would give his narrative a greater personal imprint, a wider historical compass, and a surer view of slavery than had ever been presented before.

That code prescribed that the opening portions of a narrative (as of a lecture) be heavily factual, containing if possible verifiable accounts of birth, parentage, and slaveholders. Douglass provided that—and much more. His opening paragraphs indicate a concern for accuracy designed to satisfy even the most hostile or scrupulous hunter of details. No one can do it better, he says in effect. He is then in position to portray the world of slaveholders and their minions, the world into which he was born. His plays upon the names of "Captain" Anthony, Mr. Severe, and Mr. Freeland are instances of his reduction of diverse personalities to their precise roles in an economic system they barely understand. With Austin Gore he provides a more elaborate description and a more powerful form of comprehension:

> Mr. Gore was proud, ambitious, and persevering. He was artful, cruel, and obdurate. He was just the man for such a place, and it was just the place for such a man.

With two trinities of adjectives and another sentence of finely wrought symmetry, the character of this baneful overseer is caught and reduced as if he were an overweening functionary in Molieere or Ben Jonson. With Gore's employer, Colonel Lloyd, Douglass's irony is at full stretch. In Lloyd's callousness toward men and women and his sensitivity toward horses, he finds an apt sign of his owner's true worth. Because he is so utterly insecure with people, Lloyd's threat is shown to be hollow and his stature petty. When we learn that on his plantation only horses are treated with regard, we understand the social situation he has created and its underlying structure. He and his class are like the petty gods of Greek myth, absurd whichever way they turn.

In comprehending his own and their assistants, Douglass establishes his grasp of a type representing the most powerful families in the South. In a sense he has *defined* the type, as a dramatist does his primary actors. But he does not stop there, as earlier narrators had done. For his interweaving of interpretation with description has all along recognized the economic machinery of which Anthony and Lloyd are but small cogs. Slavery, he shows, wishes to control more than the labor and physical being of slaves—even to their words, their very language. His first owner must be addressed as Captain Anthony: " . . . a title which, I presume, he acquired by sailing a craft on the Chesapeake Bay." Like the many slaveholders who insisted upon being called "General" or "Colonel," Anthony demands that he be known by a self-conferred military title. Slaves alone could entitle masters, this artifice seems to say. Likewise, Colonel Lloyd rode out to outlying farms—where he wasn't known by sight—to question field slaves about how kindly their master was. For a candid answer, a slave would be sold South. Reporting these episodes, Douglass makes clear that what is being revealed is larger than his owner's self-deception. Slaveholders, by seeking to control slave language, sought to exact slave complicity in their own subjugation. Their self-conceptions required the right words, the correct words. With the proper words, a slave could keep his life intact. With the proper words, a slaveholder could keep his self-esteem intact. In each case, the owner compels the slave to authorize the owner's power. Slavery and the language of slavery are virtually coextensive.

In comprehending the equation of words and power, Douglass relates not only the workings of slavery as a system, but also the advent of his personal history within it. He describes his initial situation in Chapter II as a well of ignorance, typified by his insensitivity to the words of work songs:

I did not, when a slave, understand the deep meaning of those rude and apparently incoherent songs. I was myself within the circle; so that I neither saw nor heard as those without might see and hear. They told a tale of woe which was then altogether beyond my feeble comprehension. . . .

This memory and the image of incomprehension spurred by it testify that for his life, as for the narrative we are reading, there will be no stop, no comforting return until his comprehension is complete. In one of the passages blending past and present at which he is so adept, he remarks:

The mere recurrence to those songs, even now, affects me; and while I am writing these lines, an expression of feeling has already found its way down my cheek. To those songs I trace my first glimmering

conception of the dehumanizing character of slavery.

The next stage in his understanding of the language of slavery takes Douglass to Baltimore, the Auld household, and the forbidden seduction of reading. Auld's diatribe on the danger of language is well known as the impelling force for Douglass' climbing the ladder to literacy. Yet it is equally significant as a further sketch of the effects of slavery upon white people. Because they do not know what slavery is doing to them, the Aulds understand far less what it is doing to him. The exercise of petty power is for Mrs. Auld as corrupting as the possession of great wealth has been for Colonel Lloyd. (It is also possible to see in her decline features of those Garrisonians who turned on Douglass.) It is through them that Douglass gains his penultimate lessons of the perversions of slavery.

In most abolitionist narratives the quest for freedom through literacy would conclude here, the story redirected toward plans for escape. With Douglass, however, simple literacy is merely the ground upon which a complex psychological drama will be played. Although he has learned much from earlier narratives, he will not provide exactly the same kind of straight-line narrative found in, say, Moses Roper, James Curry, Lunceford Lane, or Moses Grandy. His war with slavery through language consists not of a single battle with clear-cut victory on either side. Rather it is a sustained series of costly skirmishes, with losses following hard upon gains. As Auld had predicted, Douglass at twelve years of age is beset by discontent. His fall is occasioned by his hunger for language, for while his readings "relieved me of one difficulty, they brought on another even more painful than the one of which I was relieved." The more he learns of slavery, the farther freedom seems to recede. The condition is temporary since he refuses to be satisfied. The discontent brought on by language will be relieved by language: in this instance by a single word—*abolition*—and its resonance. The pain that is aggravated by language is also palliated by language. As he came to apprehend the meaning of abolition, he records, "The light broke in upon me by degrees."

The predicament recurs at a higher lever when he is broken by Covey's demands of incessant labor: "I was broken in body, soul, and spirit. . . . [T]he dark night of slavery closed in upon me. . . ." The language of abolition he has been learning possessed the power to inspire longing and to instill despair when that longing is thwarted. And once again a call in words evokes a powerful response, in the apostrophe to the ships on the Chesapeake so well analyzed by Stone. His predicament is resolved in a form of blues sermon that raises all doubts and answers all: "There is a better day coming." Douglass's career has been an ascent toward freedom through literacy. His comprehension of the language—first of slavery, then of abolition—has been the ladder of his climb. Structurally, he himself marks his rise to the top by his battle with Covey and the pivotal sentence, "You have seen how a man was made a slave; you shall see how a slave was made a man." Thematically it is the "protections" he writes for himself and others in 1835 that signal his position. With the protections he can *write* his way North, the ultimate verification of his victory over slavery and a final proof of his comprehension of language.

Although the contest with Covey has made Chapter X the most famous portion of the *Narrative,* it is the final chapter that most reveals its distinction as a personal history. In half the length of the preceding section, Chapter XI accomplishes three very large tasks of comprehension. First, he exercises an eloquence of silence fully as powerful as his brilliance of language. When he forgoes an account of his escape, he relinquishes an element of the narrative that had made it one of the most popular literary forms in America in the 1840s. For example, in Moses Roper before him, William Wells Brown, Henry Box Brown, the Crafts, and John Thompson after him, the escape is an exciting adventure story in itself, uniting ingenuity, suspense, courage, and endurance. It is, in short, precisely the kind of story Northeastern audiences would pay to hear and read. Douglass' decision to withhold that part of his story is an assertion of personal control within a mandated form. Only he can write this section, not Garrison or Phillips; only he knows what is being withheld. Only he can decide the proper time for its release. At the moment of writing he is painfully aware of the short distance (political as well as temporal) that separates past from present. Hence his silence is evoked by a communal regard for fellow slaves still seeking means of escape: he must "not run the hazard of closing the slightest avenue by which a brother slave might clear himself of the chains and fetters of slavery."

Second, what he does choose to include equally bears his personal stamp, the language of a free man. The two sentences in which he dates his escape and destination are models of laconic understatement, conspicuous in their restraint. By this point he has comprehended the art of the oxymoron, as he provides readers with poised anxiety and loud softness—eloquent silence. Also conspicuous is his inclusion of a second document (the first being the protections), the only one not of his own composition. The certificate of marriage to Anna Murray, subscribed by James W. C. Pennington, appears to be Douglass' proof in language of a new existence. Socially, legally, sexually, religiously, he is indeed a man—in the eyes of most Americans, for the first time. It was to this need for documentation that Pennington returned in his narrative, *The Fugitive Blacksmith,* in 1849. In his preface, he wrote:

Whatever may be the ill or favored condition of the slave in the matter of mere personal treatment, it is the chattel relation that robs him of his manhood, and transfers his ownership in himself to another. . . . It is this that throws his family history into utter confusion, and leaves him without a single record to which he may appeal in vindication of his character, or honor. And has a man no sense of honor because he was born a slave? Has he no need of character?

Douglass has ensured that his new family will be recorded, will from its inception possess a sense of honor.

In his final narrative gesture, Douglass establishes that he comprehends the tradition of the slave story and attempts to subvert a portion of that tradition. By closing with his address to the Nantucket convention in 1841, Douglass—as Stone and Stepto have cogently argued—brings the narrative full circle, to the opening sentence of Garrison's Preface. Garrisonians, he explains in *My Bondage and My Freedom,* often sought to limit his scope: "Give us the facts . . . we will take care of the philosophy" (1855 ed.). Here he makes no mention of Garrison and reverses a persistent abolitionist tactic. Garrison and his associates often spoke as if former slaves were minor characters in *their* great antislavery story. Douglass deftly ensures that Phillips and Garrison will, in this narrative, be minor characters in *his* story. He authenticates them.

It is a bold gesture. For on a philosophical level, one might say that the slave narrative as a form is defined paradoxically by a suppression of the personal voice of the slave. Most sponsors regarded the slave by stipulation as primitive and then proceeded to use the narrative to address other white people. Many sponsors condescendingly saw the narratives as essentially a political form for their own use and said that fugitive slaves had no stories until the abolitionists gave them one. Douglass by 1845 is certainly aware of the complex of attitudes surrounding him: "The truth was, I felt myself a slave, and the idea of speaking to white people weighed me down." Humility and restraint are poised in this final paragraph, for it gains dignity by using Enlightenment language when explosive effusion seems called for. Like his audience in Nantucket, his readers acknowledge the effort, the discipline of his control. Slavery is far worse than anything he can say about it. The tension created between the cruelties which he recounts and his manner of recounting them he will use communally, not to win applause, but to go on working. The surplus of tension will be spent in the future and in language; "engaged in pleading the cause of " his "brethren." Whatever his sponsors intend, he will not be distracted. His tension will be active, always on the move, always renewing and being renewed.

The *Narrative,* I would contend, is the first comprehensive, personal history of American slavery. Autobiography would come a decade later, in *My Bondage and My Freedom.* If many readers prefer the earlier volume, the reasons are not far to search. The *Narrative* is as tightly written as a sonnet, the work of years in the pulpit and on the lecture circuit. It comprehends all major aspects of slavery as Douglass knew it in a narrative that is as dramatically compassing as any first-person novel. It is at the same time a personal history of the struggle with and for language—against words that repress, for words that liberate. It is for author and reader alike a personalizing account of a system that would depersonalize everyone. It is the retelling of the most important Christian story, the Crucifixion, in the midst of the most important American civil crisis, the battle over slavery.

In *The Fugitive Blacksmith* Pennington asked if a slave had no need of character. He answered the question in the following way: "Suppose insult, reproach, or slander, should render it necessary for him to appeal to the history of his family in vindication of his character, where does he find that history? He goes to his native state, to his native county, to his native town; but nowhere does he find any record of himself *as a man.*" It is an acute question, one he is eager to raise, I believe, because of Douglass's example. Douglass renewed the conservative form of the slave narrative at a critical time. He gave record of himself as an anti-slavery man. And the magnitude of that achievement is difficult to overestimate. For in moral terms the slave narrative and its postbellum heirs are the only history of American slavery we have. Outside the narrative, slavery was a wordless, nameless, timeless time. It was time without history and time without imminence. Slaveholders sought to reduce existence to the duration of the psychological present and to mandate their records as the only reliable texts. Whatever the restrictions placed upon them, Douglass and the other narrators changed that forever. To recall one's personal history is to *renew* it. The *Narrative* is both instrument and inscription of that renewal. (pp. 157-170)

John Sekora, "Comprehending Slavery: Language and Personal History in Douglass' 'Narrative' of 1845," in *CLA Journal,* Vol. XXIX, No. 2, December, 1985, pp. 157-70.

WILLIAM S. MCFEELY

(essay date 1991)

[McFeely is an American educator and critic and the author of *Frederick Douglass* (1991), a massive, extensively researched account of Douglass's life and time. In the following excerpt from that work, he discusses Douglass's principal published works.]

The Tuckahoe is a quiet creek. Frederick Douglass, when he was a child, lived on its low banks. When he was a man, he walked boldly and talked clearly in a world noisy with hatred, but the country he first knew was tranquil. The Eastern Shore, the long peninsula that puts its back to the Atlantic and faces the great, broad Chesapeake Bay, is gentle. Wrested ruthlessly from the Indians in the seventeenth century, it had long been cleared and farmed when Frederick was born in February 1818. Streams, shaded with trees, divided the fields and flowed to join slow, meandering rivers that, in turn, met tidal waters reaching deep into easy terrain. Frederick's first home was a solitary cabin in the woods bordering a brook that separated the farther fields of two farms owned by the man who owned him. . . .

There was no being alone here; a rough-runged ladder led to a rail-bottomed loft that provided added sleeping quarters for his family of cousins and an infant uncle in this house of his grandparents, Betsy and Isaac Bailey. (p. 3)

His earliest memory was of swinging on a rung of the ladder to the loft. As he put his early sensations together into a narrative, he recalled (moving backwards in time) mimicking farm animals, splashing into the creek without having to take off any clothes (because all he had on was a shirt), and being fed "corn-meal mush" with an oyster shell for a spoon. Douglass made the events of his childhood, like almost all the experiences of his early life that he described in his three autobiographies, into parables of slavery. Ostensibly telling how the slave child escaped "many troubles which befall and vex his white brother," such as being "chided for handling his little knife and fork improperly," he made it clear that the slave child was deprived of all implements of gentility. But in this instance, as in too few others, private and sensuous recollections break through the moral he sought to point. "His days, when the weather . . . [was] warm," he wrote (and we confidently believe him), were "spent in the pure, open air, and in the bright sunshine," running "wild."

Betsy, his grandmother, was the central presence in his early life. He reported no memory of his mother from the period before he was six years old. Both the records (which he never saw) and his family's traditional history, as he understood it, leave no doubt that Harriet Bailey was his mother. But he had no recollection of seeing her during his years in Betsy's cabin, even though she appears to have been nearby, working in Aaron Anthony's fields or hired out to work on a neighboring farm. He could only recall her from the "four or five" visits she later made, at night, when he was living twelve miles away on the Lloyd plantation. She may not even have walked there specifically to see him.

As if to insist that she was real, Douglass wrote

that her "personal appearance and bearing are ineffaceably stamped upon my memory." She was, he said, "tall, and finely proportioned; of deep black, glossy complexion; had regular features, and, among other slaves, was remarkably sedate in her manners." He chose to see her as grander than her peers. Years after she died, reading James Cowles Prichard's *Natural History of Man,* he came across a picture of an Egyptian pharaoh with a striking likeness to her. This handsome portrait became his image of Harriet Bailey—of his mother. It was a heroic and androgynous way for her to be remembered, but the image does nothing to dispel the mystery of this dimly known tragic figure.

Douglass wrote chillingly, "I cannot say I was very deeply attached to my mother." He placed the blame squarely on slavery: "The slave-mother can be spared long enough from the field to endure all the bitterness of a mother's anguish, when it adds another name to a master's ledger, but *not* long enough to receive the joyous reward afforded by the intelligent smiles of her child." A look at the roster of Betsy's descendants in the estate inventory of her master in large part confirms this contention. But nothing prevented slaves, living close by, from visiting. To be sure, even frequent visits would have been a poor substitute for the constancy of a daily life together, but Harriet did not make them at all. Perhaps Frederick knew she could have done so; his insistence that his smile would have been intelligent conveys not only his sense of his own superiority but also a suggestion that, whatever the reason, his mother had not appreciated him as she should have.

There is no question about the importance that he gave in retrospect to the absence of a strong relationship to his mother. His coolness toward her was not, he thought, the natural feeling he should have had: "I never think of this terrible interference of slavery with my infantile affections, and its diverting them from their natural course, without feelings to which I can give no adequate expression." In the first of his autobiographies, telling of his mother's death, which occurred when he was about seven—Harriet Bailey has been denied even a firm death date—he wrote, "I received the tidings of her death with much the same emotions I should have probably felt at the death of a stranger."

This stark account was softened with sentimentality in his later versions. In the second, he wrote, "Death soon ended the little communication that had existed between us; and with it, I believe, a life—judging from her weary, sad, downcast countenance and mute demeanor—full of heartfelt sorrow." In his final telling, he omitted the reference to her "downcast countenance and mute demeanor," and instead credited "the natural genius of my sable, unprotected, and uncultivated mother," who he was told could read, with somehow instilling in him his "love of letters."

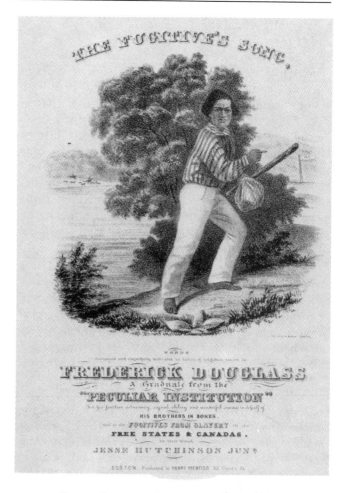

Cover of a piece of antislavery sheet music.

The differences between these three accounts illustrate as sharply as anything could the difficulty of knowing Frederick Bailey. Most of what we can learn about him is what Frederick Douglass chose to tell us in his three unidentical autobiographies. *Narrative of the Life of Frederick Douglass* (1845) is the brief, pungent declaration of freedom of a runaway slave writing a powerful antislavery tract. In *My Bondage and My Freedom* (1855) a mature writer gives deeper reflections on slavery. By then, Douglass could pause longer over the story of his life as a slave, but voids in it suggest that there were unbearable memories that had to be omitted. *Life and Times of Frederick Douglass* (1881, revised 1892) is the memoir of a famous man relishing his honors while smarting from those denied him. Like *Bondage,* it brings his story forward to the time of its writing, but the slavery days are still there, as if to remind an America eager to forget that slavery cannot be purged from the national memory.

Throughout his life, Frederick Douglass was obsessed with an eagerness to know about his origins—to know who he was. Dickson Preston, a meticulous and sympathetic historian, has brought together an astonishingly rich cluster of facts confirming Douglass's account of his early life [in *Young Frederick Douglass: The Maryland Years,* 1980], firmly establishing the family lineage, and determining from an inventory of his master's slaves the time of Frederick's birth—February 1818 (a year later than the date that Douglass himself calculated). But Preston's diligent scholarship has not revealed the fact Douglass most wanted to know—who his father was.

"My father was a white man. He was admitted to be such by all I ever heard speak of my parentage," he wrote in *Narrative of the Life of Frederick Douglass.* Doubtless he remembered such talk from Betsy's cabin, as people accounted for his difference in color from his brothers and sisters. This talk would have led to his first consciousness of what is termed racial difference; he would have looked at his body and learned that he was "yellow"—had a muted, dull complexion lighter than that of his "quite dark" grandparents and, he would observe later, that of his still "darker" mother. He also heard talk of a legendary and perfectly plausible Indian ancestor; something in the bone structure and the set of the eyes suggested this, not only in Frederick but in his mother and grandmother. He was probably still too young, in Betsy's cabin, to articulate any queries about his paternity although it is more than likely that he had already heard it "whispered," even if he had not understood what he heard, "that my master was my father."

Douglass wrote later of his boyhood in Betsy's cabin as "spirited, joyous, uproarious, and happy," but drew a picture of the surrounding area that does not just reflect what he saw as a child. His description of the "worn-out, sandy, desert-like appearance of its soil," the "general dilapidation of its farms," and the "ague and fever" that rose from the Tuckahoe is more a metaphor for the barrenness of slavery than the recollection of a six-year-old. It does, however, return attention from the idyllic to the realities of carving out a living in this remote country. (pp. 6-8)

• • • • •

In his writing, Douglass outran being a runaway. Never satisfied with the degree to which a nineteenth-century white world took the ex-slave seriously as an intellectual, he would have been profoundly gratified by the attention paid his work in the twentieth century. Read now only secondarily for what they tell us about slavery, his *Narrative* (1845) and *My Bondage and My Freedom* (1855) have earned the regard of critics, such as William L. Andrews, who see them as two in the series of great "I" narratives of that most remarkable of all decades of American letters. The *Narrative* carries none of the poetry of Whitman's first edition of *Leaves of Grass* (1855), but it too is a song of myself. There is not the epic tragedy of Melville's *Moby-Dick* (1851), and yet it is a story—not wholly unlike Ishmael's—of survival in a world at sea with evil. On the other hand,

with its message of growing self-confidence, of self-reliance, the *Narrative* is kin to Emerson's essays. But perhaps Douglass's telling of his odyssey is closest cousin to Thoreau's account of his altogether safe escape to Walden Pond. That quietly contained, subversive tale has reverberated ever since its telling with a message of radical repudiation of corrupt society. Thoreau heard a Wendell Phillips lecture describing Douglass's exodus—and reporting that a written account was on its way—in the spring of 1845 as he was planning his sojourn outside Concord. Robert D. Richardson, Jr., who wrote Thoreau's intellectual biography, has said that it is not "an accident that the earliest stages of Thoreau's move to Walden coincide with . . . the publication of Douglass's narrative of how he gained his freedom. *Walden* is about self-emancipation."

In all three of his autobiographies, Douglass tantalizes us with the many things he leaves out; not the least of these is discussion of why and how he wrote them. His correspondence is equally void of references to what must have been a compelling exercise for him. We know that Phillips and others in the Anti-Slavery Society urged him to put his story into print, but whom did he talk to about the project, who helped, who was its editor? His later quarrels with his British publisher make it clear that he cared not only about the content—he resisted any censoring of material thought to be offensive to Christians—but also about the appearance of the front matter and the cover. Such concerns must have been with Douglass even at the time of the first printing of the first book.

But perhaps not. To a remarkable degree *Narrative of the Life of Frederick Douglass* does seem to have simply sprung from a man who had been telling the same story in much the same language from the anti-slavery platform for four years. And once he had created, with his voice and then his pencil, the Frederick Douglass of the *Narrative,* the author never altered either the character or the plot significantly. This, more than the fact that speaking came easier than writing for Douglass, explains why he wrote no books other than the autobiographies. He had but one character to craft, one story to tell. The two later books, *My Bondage and My Freedom* and *Life and Times of Frederick Douglass,* reveal important shifts in approach and detail, but the Frederick Douglass of the *Narrative* remains inviolate.

The *Narrative* is short and direct, from the "I was born" of its first line to its closing account of the Nantucket speech, describing how Douglass "felt strongly moved to speak" and was urged to do so as well: "It was a severe cross, and I took it up reluctantly. The truth was, I felt myself a slave, and the idea of speaking to white people weighed me down. I spoke but a few moments, when I felt a degree of freedom." The person we come to know in these brief pages is unforgettable. From the *Narrative* and the many other accounts of runaways published in Douglass's day, right down to Toni Morrison's *Beloved* in ours, there has been no escape from the slave in America letters. And for the fifty years following publication of the *Narrative* in 1845, there was no escape for the author from the runaway he had created.

It is easy when reading the *Narrative* to misjudge the reason for the author's many omissions—the nature of his relationships with his brothers and sisters, for example. His focused concentration on himself does invite the charge of insensitivity to others. But there were other, deeper reasons for such voids. We get a hint of them when he tells of slaves on a Wye House farm singing "most exultingly" when "leaving home: . . . they would sing, as a chorus, to words which to many would seem unmeaning jargon, but which, nevertheless, were full of meaning to themselves." There were some sounds of slavery that Douglass could not render in words that his readers would hear, private torments and horrors too deep in the well to be drawn up.

The book was published by the "Anti-Slavery Office" in Boston in June 1845 and priced at fifty cents. The *Liberator* had announced its publication in May, and Phillips and his allies in the literary world saw to it that reviews appeared promptly. By fall, 4,500 copies had been sold in the United States; soon there were three European editions, and within five years 30,000 copies were in the hands of readers. The inevitable charge appeared that a slave boy could not have written the book—Lydia Maria Child (also falsely credited with having written Harriet Jacobs's *Incidents in the Life of a Slave Girl*) was one of many suspected of having been the ghost writer. But anyone who had heard Douglass—and by 1845 thousands of people had—knew that the language of the *Narrative* was the same as that of the man who so passionately told his tale from the platform.

The famous "Preface" by William Lloyd Garrison and the "Letter" by Wendell Phillips, both preceding Douglass's text, had a double purpose. The great white fathers of the antislavery movement sought to authenticate the book—"Mr. DOUGLASS," Garrison wrote, "has very properly chosen to write his own Narrative, in his own style, and according to the best of his ability, rather than to employ someone else"—and to commandeer it for the cause. By 1845, the ex-slave they had sent out to carry their message was displaying troubling signs of independence, but the leaders of the American Anti-Slavery Society knew that his fiery oratory was an asset of incalculable value. "Go on, my dear friend," wrote Phillips in his "Letter," exhorting Douglass to carry the word to reach "every hut in the Carolinas, and make the broken-hearted bondman leap up at the thought of old Massachusetts." (pp. 115-17)

• • • • •

[Douglass's novella *The Heroic Slave*], his only attempt at fiction, is a curious mirror of his *Narrative of the Life of Frederick Douglass* and a way station on the road to his second telling of his own heroic life, *My Bondage and My Freedom.*

In *The Heroic Slave,* a Northern traveler, Listwell, listens attentively to the ruminations of a slave musing over the philosophical problems that confront him. He moves from despair over his "aimless" life to a passionate pursuit of *"Liberty."* The slave in this work of historical fiction is named Madison Washington, after the leader of a revolt on the brig *Creole* in 1841. (Irony in American history knows no bounds.) Physically, the slave resembles if not Douglass himself, then Henry Harris: "Madison was of manly form, tall, symmetrical, round, and strong. In his movements he seemed to combine, with the strength of the lion, a lion's elasticity. His torn sleeves disclosed arms like polished iron." For him, "those distant church bells have no grateful music"; he wants to run away, and is held back, he tells the Northerner, only by the thought that he would have to leave his wife behind.

Five years later, back in Ohio, Listwell finds at his door a tall, weary traveler—Madison, on his way to Canada. The fugitive is invited into the best bedroom rather than the barn, and helped on his way to a successful escape. A year later still, Listwell is back in Virginia, in a tavern that in its decrepitude is a metaphor for the decay of the slaveholding society—it is a meeting place for "gamblers, horses-racers, cock-fighters, and slave-traders." He hears the doleful sound of chained slaves marching, and looking out, he sees Madison among the miserable people pressed on by loathsome slave traders. Unable to enjoy freedom without his wife, Madison had returned to try to rescue her, and had been caught and sold south.

As the slaves are driven onto the "Baltimore built American Slaver," the *Creole,* for the journey to New Orleans, Listwell slips three sharp files to Madison, whom, he has confessed, "he loved as well as admired." Off the Virginia coast, the files are put to good use; the slaves, led by Madison, attack, and the captain and the slaves' owner are killed. Madison spares the life of the first mate, and after stalwartly facing a great storm, orders him to take the ship into Nassau, in the Bahama Islands. There, when Madison is confronted with the responsibility for the deaths, he replies, "You call me a *black murderer.* I am not a murderer. . . . Liberty . . . is the motive of this night's work." Hearing his cry, the black officials in the British West Indies port refuse to send this "property"—these "barrels of flour"—back to Virginia: "Uttering the wildest shouts of exultation," the mutineers and the island's armed black soldiers march "amidst the deafening cheers of a multitude of sympathizing spectators, under the triumphant leadership of their heroic chief and deliverer, MADISON WASHINGTON."

There are echoes here of Nat Turner, with Madison having a sojourn in the Dismal Swamp, in which Turner hid after the failure of the uprising he led in 1831. And in addition to the *Creole* revolt, the story recalls the *Amistad* mutiny of 1839, when black slaves on board a ship seized it and sailed to New England in quest of their freedom. All of these actions had deep resonance for black Americans; Martin Delany's novel *Blake,* published in 1859, is another work telling of a black revolt. Such events stirred and somewhat frightened white abolitionists as well; in 1856 Harriet Beecher Stowe's *Dred: A Tale of the Great Dismal Swamp* appeared, as did Herman Melville's *Piazza Tales,* which includes "Benito Cereno," with its hauntingly ambiguous portrait of a black mutineer threatening a captured white ship captain. Douglass's Madison, with no ambiguity and far less depth than Melville's rebel, is in part the philosophizing slave that he remembered from *The Columbian Orator.* But there was more than memory; *The Heroic Slave* was its author's fantasy of his own heroism. (pp. 173-75)

• • • • •

[In 1855 Douglass] published the strongest of his three autobiographies, *My Bondage and My Freedom.*

His crisp 114-page telling of his story in the *Narrative of the Life of Frederick Douglass* ten years earlier has so grasped the imagination of American readers that the richer, deeper, and far more ambiguous *Bondage* has not been fully appreciated. But students of literature, William L. Andrews prominent among them, have now taken the lead in a reevaluation of Douglass's autobiographies; Andrews views *Bondage* as far more than just an extension of the *Narrative,* bringing up to date the account of Douglass's life after he reached the North. Rather, it is a different and much more penetrating look into the heart of slavery. And yet, *Bondage* suffers from some of the constraints and distortions that have beset virtually all works that seek to convey the experience of slavery from within the consciousness of the slave. Even Harriet Jacobs's *Incidents in the Life of a Slave Girl* (1860), with its extraordinarily candid telling of her sexual strategies for coping with slavery, is cloaked so tightly in the rhetoric of reform that for well over a century—until literary historian Jean Fagan Yellin made us look at it afresh—we did not see the immense psychological complexity of the slave experience that Jacobs struggled to express.

Douglass's problems had several sources. In the first place, there was the absurd but real business of white readers either refusing to believe that a black person could be a writer or being so amazed at the performance that all they could see was the ball on the seal's nose. In the second place, there was the political necessity of making the book work in the antislavery cause, which resulted in his unavoidable urge to climb onto a hortatory soapbox. Furthermore, when he told the story of slave experiences with graphic particularity—with names and descriptions of the things that happened to these real people—he could not be sure how much intellectual response he would get. His account of his aunt's whipping by their owner, Aaron Anthony—the woman bared to the waist, the taunts, the snap of the whip, the screams at the slicing of the leather into her "plump and tender" flesh—went not to his readers' brains, but to their groins. The long reach of racist sexuality made the story for them an exercise in sadomasochistic eroticism, rather than an exploration of the complexities of the sadistic but also self-interested lustful motivation of the man who did the whipping. In *Bondage,* Douglass gave three full pages to this episode, which occupied just one paragraph in the *Narrative,* but it seems unlikely that he succeeded in getting many readers to credit fully the humanness of the dilemma of a woman so determined to have her own man that she would defy—and be cruelly tortured for defying—another.

When it came to appealing to the other emotional response that his friend Harriet Beecher Stowe had so brilliantly exploited in *Uncle Tom's Cabin*—sympathy with the trauma of forcible separation of a child from its mother—Douglass was at a loss. Unlike Eliza, his mother had not crossed a river on ice floes to hold onto him; he was forced to report that he had scarcely known his mother, saying now not that she had been a stranger, but that they were "separated . . . when I was but an infant." When his grandmother, for whom he professed a great sense of closeness, had been forced to abandon him, she did so. And he could not point to successful, heroic deeds. Even his own escape didn't fill the bill; the first try, potentially heroic, was aborted; his actual escape from slavery came almost as an anticlimax. He hinted at the psychological scars of slavery in his descriptions of the Harris brothers and Sandy Jenkins (who, technically, was free), but he could not fully explore this realm of the slave experience. Had he done so, he would have played into the hands of two contradictory white audiences, both of whom saw African Americans as inferior beings. Members of the first group seized on any evidence of deficiency to justify slavery's continuance. A person forced to repress immense grief can become psychologically injured, but these white observers often saw—or chose to see—in the resulting seemingly submissive behavior only proof of black inferiority. Other white observers, opposed to slavery, preferred to think of the slaves as helpless victims, whom only white Northern benevolence could carry toward a happier existence. But if in Douglass's time readers distorted the book into just another runaway's tale, it stands today as one of the most suggestive inquiries into the heart of slavery that we have.

Bondage was also its author's declaration of independence. Douglass recanted none of the heartfelt praise for William Lloyd Garrison that was in the *Narrative,* but gone, now, were the prefatory essays by Garrison and Wendell Phillips that had introduced the earlier book. And there was in the saccharine effusion of a long dedication celebrating the "Honorable Gerrit Smith" for his "Genius and Benevolence" and for "Ranking Slavery with Piracy and Murder" and "Denying It Either a Legal or Constitutional Existence" a not very subtle slap at his former champions, who deplored Smith's political activities and his belief that slavery could be ended through constitutional means. This dedication scarcely leaves the impression of an author unimpeded by obsequiousness, but the reader who leaps past it into the text will find a Frederick Douglass of a far more critical and analytical mind than the one in the *Narrative.*

Strangely, for a man not loath to stand in the full light of praise for his accomplishments, Douglass has left almost no record of how he went about writing his books. We have no notes, no correspondence, concerning the travails of composition. . . . The best clue we have to the process of creating the work lies in its tone; it carries the voice of the best of Douglass's speeches, particularly those which have been described for us by people who heard them given. A surging, probing imagination is at work in *Bondage;* an "I" cries out and is heard. (pp. 180-82)

• • • • •

In 1881, Douglass published *Life and Times of Frederick Douglass.* In many ways, including the vanity of the title, the work was tired. Its time had passed—or so thought the public, which did not buy it. Douglass must have been aware that he was cranking out many-told tales yet again; his expression of frustration with his publisher over the poor physical quality of the volume suggests a more general dissatisfaction. But the book does have interesting differences from his *Narrative of the Life of Frederick Douglass* and *My Bondage and My Freedom,* and he brought his story up to date with observations on the Civil War, its coming, and its aftermath. Despite his distance from workers in the postwar world, it also includes curious, valuable insights into his experiences as a day laborer and a skilled caulker.

But the book's real message—which few people received—was that the story of slavery should not be purged from the nation's memory. White America wanted to hear no more of the subject; emancipation had taken care of it. Many black Americans, reacting to this weariness, had become almost apologetic about their slave past. His friend Harriet Beecher Stowe had

once awakened the nation with a great saga of slavery. Now his story might rouse people to the plight of the former slaves who were not fully free. He saw his life as a metaphor for a second emancipation, but he offered no plan that would meet the needs of a desperate people. Even if he had had a plan, few would have learned of it; the book sold few copies. And yet that book remains a cry from the heart that his slave experience, and the experiences of all American slaves, must not be forgotten.

Several of his friends had been encouraging him to branch away from autobiography in his writing. Ottilia Assing had urged him to tell the John Brown story, write of his relations with "Lincoln, Grant, Sumner, and other prominent men," describe his returning to Baltimore and the Eastern Shore, and tell of his trip to the Dominican Republic. All of these subjects found their way into *Life and Times,* but as part of his self-narrative. His own was, in the end, his only story. (pp. 311-12)

• • • • •

[In 1892 Douglass] told an old friend that he was bringing *Life and Times of Frederick Douglass* up to date only at the "bidding of my publisher"; there was a painful compulsion within him that drove the narrative on. "When I laid down my pen a dozen years ago I thought . . . I had reached the end, not of life, but of autobiographic writing, and was glad to have done with it. I have always found it easier to speak than to write. These ten or twelve years have not been cheerful," he wrote to Marshall Pierce, another old abolitionist who understood that the needs of the generation born since slavery were being ignored in the way that the slaves' needs had once been. "They have been years of reaction and darkness. The air has been filled with reconciliations between those who fought for freedom and those who fought for slavery. We have been . . . morally obscuring the difference between right and wrong. The Ship of State has been swinging back to its ancient moorings."

This doleful assessment led inevitably to a task: "I am now seventy five years, and though my eyes are failing and my hand is not as nimble as it once was I hope to do some service in writing [of] this period." The assignment sent his mind back to better, more vigorous periods and a sad reverie: "Three men [older than he] are now left of the old guard: John G. Whittier, Robert Purvis and Parker Pillsbury. They stand in the open field where once was forrest. Dear battered and scarred Parker, though he is now over eighty three, is still erect and active. You [Pierce] and I have seen the trees falling all around us."

After aggravating delays, his book, again called *Life and Times of Frederick Douglass,* was published in the fall of 1892. Douglass had added better than a hundred pages to the 1881 autobiography, telling of his trip to Europe and Africa and of his personal accomplishments. There was again an eloquent call for civil rights, but no direct attack on the new evils of the decade in which he was now living. There was nothing to match the fervor of the antislavery message of *Narrative of the Life of Frederick Douglass* or *My Bondage and My Freedom,* nothing, for example, on the scourge of lynching that had fallen on his people.

Douglass was disappointed in the appearance of the book, finding the paper "inferior and the binding slovenly, imperfect and unattractive," and it did not sell well. This telling of his story, his valedictory, did not invigorate him as the first two autobiographies had. (p. 360)

• • • • •

Frederick Douglass was one of the giants of nineteenth-century America. And in the end, he stood as tall as any. . . . In an age of oratory, some judged him to have had the greatest voice. As a writer, he created an unforgettable character named Frederick Douglass; as a citizen, he struggled in a winning cause to rid his homeland of its most grievous social flaw. . . . (p. 385)

William S. McFeely, in his *Frederick Douglass,* W. W. Norton & Company, 1991, 465 p.

SOURCES FOR FURTHER STUDY

Baker, Houston A., Jr. "Revolution and Reform: Walker, Douglas, and the Road to Freedom." In his *Long Black Song: Essays in Black American Literature and Culture,* pp. 58-83. Charlottesville: University Press of Virginia, 1972.

> A discussion of Douglass's use of humor, verisimilitude, animal imagery and other narrative devices in the *Narrative of the Life of Frederick Douglass.*

Chesnutt, Charles W. *Frederick Douglass.* 4th ed. Beacon Biographies of Eminent Americans, edited by M. A. DeWolfe Howe. Boston: Small, Maynard & Co., 1899, 141 p.

> An early biography that focuses on Douglass's career as an abolitionist and civil rights advocate. Chesnutt is recognized as a pioneer in African-American fiction.

Gates, Henry Louis, Jr. "Frederick Douglass and the Language of the Self." In his *Figures in Black: Words, Signs, and the "Racial" Self,* pp. 98-124. New York: Oxford University Press, 1987.

> Argues that Douglass was deeply concerned with presenting a public, fictive self in his autobiographies and that he himself carefully shaped the public image by which he wanted to be remembered. Gates notes: "When I choose to call these selves fictive ones, I do not mean to suggest any sense of falsity or ill intent; rather, I mean by fictive the act of crafting or making by design, in this instance a process that unfolds in language, through the very discourse that Douglass employs to narrate his autobiographies."

Preston, Dickson J. *Young Frederick Douglass: The Maryland Years.* Baltimore: Johns Hopkins University Press, 1980, 242 p.

> Extensively researched account of Douglass's early years as a slave in Maryland.

Quarles, Benjamin. *Frederick Douglass.* Washington, D.C.: Associated Publishers, 1948, 378 p.

> Important early biography that has been supplemented but not superseded by later scholarship.

——, ed. *Frederick Douglass.* Englewood Cliffs, N.J.: Prentice-Hall, Inc., 1968, 184 p.

> Collection of biographical and critical essays by and about Douglass grouped under the headings "Douglass Looks at the World," "The World Looks at Douglass," and "Douglass in History." The editor supplies an introduction, a chronology, afterword, and bibliographic note about editions of Douglass's works.

Arthur Conan Doyle

1859-1930

English short story writer, novelist, essayist, historian, poet, and dramatist.

INTRODUCTION

*A*lthough as Ivor Brown has noted "there was far more in Doyle's literary life than the invention of his fascinating and volatile detective," it is as the creator of Sherlock Holmes that Doyle is remembered. The volumes of historical explication for which he was knighted have been virtually forgotten; his extensively researched historical novels have not endured. Likewise, his other stories and novels, including some works of early science fiction, are largely overshadowed by the exploits of Holmes, the world's first consulting detective and one of the most famous literary creations of all time.

Doyle was born in Edinburgh to an English father and Irish mother and educated at strict Jesuit schools in Scotland and Austria. He thrived on the harsh regimen at these institutions and especially enjoyed the emphasis on sport. Despite his early religious training, as a young man he left the church and during a period of financial hardship declined aid that was conditional on his return to Roman Catholicism. In 1876 he entered Edinburgh University to study medicine. One of his professors, Dr. Joseph Bell, impressed his students with his ability to diagnose his patients' habits and occupations, as well as medical conditions, through telltale clues, and Doyle later patterned Holmes's methods of deduction on those of Bell. While still a medical student Doyle began to write fiction; he sold his first short story, "The Mystery of Sasassa Valley," to *Chambers's Journal* in 1879. Doyle earned his medical degree in 1881 and voyaged to Africa as ship's surgeon on a passenger vessel. After a partnership with a former fellow medical student ended in a disagreement in 1882, Doyle established his own practice. He continued to write fiction, completing two novels for which he could not find a publisher and engaging in historical research for others. The novel *A Study in Scarlet,* the first Sherlock Holmes adventure, appeared in *Beeton's Christmas Annual* in 1887 and as a book the following year. "A Scandal in Bohemia," the first short story featuring the detective, appeared in the *Strand* magazine in 1891. Holmes quickly became Doyle's most popular and profitable creation, despite his own preference for historical fiction; it was Holmes for whom readers clamored and publishers offered enticingly large payments. Doyle wrote that he found the Holmes stories as difficult to write as full-length novels because of the intricate plotting, and began to resent the amount of time spent on work that he considered relatively unimportant. In 1893 he depicted Holmes's death in "The Final Problem," and for the next ten years wrote only an occasional story about the detective, carefully establishing the putative date of each adventure as prior to the detective's death. It was during this period—in 1902—that the novel *The Hound of the Baskervilles,* perhaps the most famous of the Holmes adventures, appeared. Eventually Doyle was persuaded to resurrect Holmes, and in 1903 "The Adventure of the Empty House" revealed that Holmes had narrowly escaped death in the earlier story and was still thriving. Doyle resigned himself thereafter to Holmes's popularity; two additional volumes of Holmes adventures subsequently appeared, *His Last Bow: Some Reminiscences of Sherlock Holmes* in 1917 and *The Case-Book of Sherlock Holmes* in 1927.

Doyle volunteered for military service during the Boer War, and when turned down because of his age, volunteered as a surgeon at a field hospital near the front. He was knighted in 1902 for this wartime medical service and for his explication of Britain's part in the war in *The War in South Africa: Its Cause and Conduct.* In later years he became involved in politics and was twice narrowly defeated in bids for election to Parliament. Following the loss of several relatives in World War I Doyle became a firm believer in spiritualism and wrote extensively on the subject. He died in 1930.

Of Doyle's historical novels, *Micah Clarke* (1889) and *The White Company* (1891) were the first and best, possibly because they were written before the character of Holmes became widely popular and Doyle confidently expected to have his greatest success in this field. Doyle's historical fiction was meticulously researched and the narratives, in the style of Walter Scott and Thomas Macaulay, dense with vividly depicted, accurate detail. During the decade-long hiatus between the publication of "The Final Problem" and the resurrection of Holmes, Doyle had some success with two volumes of stories featuring a gallant Napoleonic soldier, *The Exploits of Brigadier Gerard* (1896) and *The Adventures of Gerard* (1903). Also successful was a novel about prizefighting, *Rodney Stone* (1896) and a volume of adventure stories, *The Croxley Master* (1907). Doyle wrote several science-fiction novels fea-

turing the dashing scientist-explorer, Professor Challenger, as well as several novels and stories of supernatural horror; his later work in this genre reflected his interest in spiritualism.

Holmes was not the first fictional detective—his antecedents include Edgar Allan Poe's Auguste Dupin and Emile Gaboriau's M. Lecoq. However, Doyle's creation is universally acclaimed as the first significant development in the genre since its inception in 1841 with Edgar Allan Poe's "The Murders in the Rue Morgue." According to Dorothy Leigh Sayers, "Doyle took up the Poe formula and galvanised it into life and popularity. He cut out the elaborate psychological introductions, or restated them in crisp dialogue. He brought into prominence what Poe had only lightly touched upon— the deduction of staggering conclusions from trifling indications in the Dumas-Cooper-Gaboriau manner. He was sparkling, surprising, and short. It was the triumph of the epigram." In his 1956 essay "From 'Phèdre' to Sherlock Holmes," Jacques Barzun noted some other qualities of Doyle's detective fiction: "In him for the first time since Poe (and for a long time to come) detection holds the center of the stage; yet it cannot be said of any of the Holmes tales that it is entirely a puzzle or a trick. . . . Though not profound, there is an air of philosophy about the Holmes-Watson ménage, a sense of the heights and depths of life, of the bustle of business and the oddities of character. . . . Doyle has the right humor of style and situation as none of his imitators had. . . . In Doyle, all is sharp, worldly, adult, contrasted, memorable and, where needed, sinister. And his imagination of the physical is so rich that he leaves one wondering whether the short story is not, after all, the true form of detective fiction."

Holmes retains a powerful hold on the public imagination. A large literature has grown up around this character, often to the exclusion of Doyle. Scholars all over the world, calling themselves "Sherlockians" or "Holmsians," produce masses of secondary literature drawing from sometimes contradictory information in the Holmes stories and novels in attempts to establish definitively, for example, which college Holmes attended and the number and order of Watson's marriages. Holmes also enjoys a vigorous extraliterary existence. He has become an intrinsic part of Western culture: much like the figures of Don Quixote or Hamlet, the name and nature of the great detective are known to people who have never read a Holmes story and cannot identify their author. Doyle vitalized and popularized the detective story, bringing fresh interest to a genre which has remained vigorous through the twentieth century. His transcendent achievement, according to Colin Wilson, was his creation of Holmes, a figure who "was more than a fictional character; he was a response to a deep-rooted psychological need of the late Victorians, a need for reassurance, for belief in the efficacy of reason and for man's power to overcome the chaos produced by this new disease of alienation. The need is as strong today as it was in 1890, which no doubt explains why Holmes is still so very much alive."

(For further information about Doyle's life and works, see *Contemporary Authors*, Vols. 104, 122; *Dictionary of Literary Biography*, Vols. 18, 70; *Something about the Author*, Vol. 24; and *Twentieth-Century Literary Criticism*, Vols. 7, 26. For related criticism, see the entry on Detective Fiction in *Twentieth-Century Literary Criticism*, Vol. 38.)

CRITICAL COMMENTARY

G. K. CHESTERTON

(essay date 1907)

[One of England's premier men of letters during the first half of the twentieth century, Chesterton is best known today as a colorful bon vivant, witty essayist, and creator of the Father Brown mysteries and the fantasy *The Man Who Was Thursday* (1908). In the following excerpt from a 1907 *Daily News* essay, he commends the literary quality of Doyle's Sherlock Holmes stories and discusses their wide popularity.]

The return of Sherlock Holmes to the *Strand Magazine* some years after his death, put a finishing touch to the almost heroic popularity of a figure whose reality was like the universally admitted reality of some old hero of medieval fable. Just as Arthur and Barbarossa were to return again, men felt that this preposterous detective must return again. He had emerged out of the unreality of literature into the glowing reality of legend, and in proof of this he has inherited the most widespread and pathetic of the characteristics of legendary heroes; that characteristic which makes men incredulous of their death. A slight and fantastic figure in a fugitive and ironical type of romance, he may seem too insignificant a subject for such a description. Nevertheless the fact remains that Mr. Conan Doyle's hero is probably the only literary creation since the creations of Dickens which has really passed into the life and language of the people, and become a being like John Bull or Father Christmas. It is remarkable to notice that although we possess many writers whose popularity is attested by enormous sales and general discussion, there is hardly one of them except Conan Doyle in this instance whose characters are familiar to everyone as types and symbols, as Pecksniff was the type of hypocrisy or Bumble of officialism. Rudyard Kipling, for example, is undoubtedly a popular writer. But if we were

to go up to any man in the street and say that a particular problem would have puzzled Strickland he would receive it with a very different expression of countenance to that which he would wear if we said that it would puzzle Sherlock Holmes. Mr. Kipling's stories give inexhaustible intellectual delight, but the personality which we remember is the personality of the story, not the personality of the character. We remember the action, but forget the actors. In no other current creation except Sherlock Holmes does the character succeed, so to speak, in breaking out of the book as a chicken breaks out of the egg. (pp. 168-69)

The fact that Sherlock Holmes alone has succeeded in familiarising himself at once with the cultured and the uncultured and turned his name into almost as descriptive a word as Dr. Guillotin or Captain Boycott, involves certain conclusions, which are for the most part worthy and reassuring. The phenomenon corrects finally, for example, much of the foolish and foppish talk about the public preferring books because they are bad. The stories of Sherlock Holmes are very good stories; they are perfectly graceful and conscientious works of art. The thread of irony which runs through all the solemn impossibilities of the narrative gives it the position of a really brilliant addition to the great literature of nonsense. The notion of the greatness of an intellect, proved by its occupation with small things instead of with great, is an original departure; it constitutes a kind of wild poetry of the commonplace. The intellectual clues and cruces upon which the development of each story turns are perhaps incredible as fact, but they are thoroughly solid and important as logic; they are such problems as a great lawyer might extract from two bottles of champagne; they are full of the very revelry of reason. The figure of Conan Doyle's detective is, in its own wild and trifling way, good literature.

Principal Works

A Study in Scarlet (novel) 1888

Micah Clarke (novel) 1889

The Captain of the Pole-Star and Other Tales (short stories) 1890

The Sign of Four (novel) 1890

The White Company (novel) 1891

The Adventures of Sherlock Holmes (short stories) 1892

Mysteries and Adventures (short stories) 1893

The Memoirs of Sherlock Holmes (short stories) 1893

Round the Red Lamp: Being Facts and Fancies of Medical Life (short stories) 1894

The Exploits of Brigadier Gerard (short stories) 1896

Rodney Stone (novel) 1896

Songs of Action (poetry) 1898

The Great Boer War (nonfiction) 1900

The Hound of the Baskervilles (novel) 1902

The War in South Africa: Its Cause and Conduct (history) 1902

The Adventures of Gerard (short stories) 1903

The Return of Sherlock Holmes (short stories) 1905

Sir Nigel (novel) 1906

The Croxley Master (short stories) 1907

Songs of the Road (poetry) 1911

The Lost World (novel) 1912

The Poison Belt (novel) 1913

The Valley of Fear (novel) 1915

The British Campaign in France and Flanders. 6 vols. (history) 1916-19

His Last Bow: Some Reminiscences of Sherlock Holmes (short stories) 1917

The New Revelation (essays) 1918

The Wanderings of a Spiritualist (essays) 1921

Memories and Adventures (autobiography) 1924

The Land of Mist (novel) 1925

The History of Spiritualism. 2 vols. (nonfiction) 1926

The Case-Book of Sherlock Holmes (short stories) 1927

The Maracot Deep (short stories) 1929

The Edge of the Unknown (essays) 1930

The Annotated Sherlock Holmes: The Four Novels and the Fifty-Six Short Stories Complete (short stories and novels) 1967

Sir Arthur Conan Doyle: The Historical Romances. 2 vols. (novels) 1986

Now, there are in London more than nine hundred and ninety-nine detective stories and fictitious detectives, nearly all of which are bad literature, or rather not literature at all. If, as the saying goes, the public likes books because they are bad, it would not be the fact that the one fictitious detective who is familiar to the whole public is the one fictitious detective who is a work of art. The fact of the matter is that ordinary men prefer certain kinds of work, good or bad, to certain other kinds of work, good or bad, which they have a perfect and obvious right to do. . . . But, preferring a certain thing, they prefer it good if they can get it. (pp. 169-70)

All English people have read the stories about Sherlock Holmes. Work like this is so good of its kind that it is difficult to endure patiently the talk of people who are occupied only in pointing out that it is not work of some other kind. The specific quality of a story of this sort is strictly what may be called wit; it is obliged to have some definite invention, construction and point, like a joke in the comic papers. Such work is inexpressibly superior to most mediocre serious work. There has to be something in it; it cannot be an entire imposture. A man can pretend to be wise; a man cannot pretend to be witty. His jokes may be much worse in your opinion than they are in his opinion; but after all they must be jokes; they cannot be entirely

shapeless mysteries, like many modern works of philosophy.

Many men can make an epic who could not make an epigram. What is true of the comic anecdote is true also of that extended anecdote, the sensational story with a point to it. All real philosophy is apocalyptic, and if a man can give us revelations of heaven it is certainly better than giving us horrible revelations of high life. But I would rather have the man who devotes a short story to saying that he can solve the problem of a murder in Margate than the man who devotes a whole book to saying that he cannot solve the problem of things in general.

Sir Arthur Conan Doyle certainly weakened his excellent series of stories by being occasionally serious; especially he weakened it by introducing a sort of sneer at Edgar Allan Poe's Dupin, with whom he sustained no comparison. Sherlock Holmes's bright notions were like bright Cockney flowers grown in very shallow soil in a suburban garden; Dupin's were flowers growing on a vast, dark tree of thought. Hence Dupin, when he quits the subject of crime, talks in the tongue of permanent culture of the relations of imagination to analysis or of the relations of the supernatural to law. But the greatest error of the Sherlock Holmes conception remains to be remarked: I mean the error which represented the detective as indifferent to philosophy and poetry, and which seemed to imply that philosophy and poetry would not be good for a detective. Here he is at once eclipsed by the bolder and more brilliant brain of Poe, who carefully states that Dupin not only admired and trusted poetry, but was himself a poet. Sherlock Holmes would have been a better detective if he had been a philosopher, if he had been a poet, nay, if he had been a lover. It is remarkable to notice (I assume that you are as intimate with Dr. Watson's narratives as you should be)—it is remarkable to notice that the very same story in which the biographer describes Holmes's inaccessibility to love and such emotions, and how necessary it was to the clear balance of his logic, is the very same story in which Holmes is beaten by a woman because he does not know whether a certain man is her fiancé or her lawyer. If he had been in love he might have known well enough.

The only real danger is that Conan Doyle, by spreading the notion that practical logic must be unpoetical, may have encouraged the notion, too common already, that imagination must be absent-minded. It is a false and dangerous doctrine that the poet must be absent-minded. The purely imaginative man could never be absent-minded. He would perceive the significance of things near to him as clearly as he perceived the significance of things far off. (pp. 171-72)

The real moral of the popularity of the adventures of Sherlock Holmes lies in the existence of a great artistic neglect. There are a large number of perfectly legitimate forms of art which are almost entirely neglected by good artists—the detective story, the farce, the book of boyish adventure, the melodrama, the music-hall song. The real curse of these things is not that they are too much regarded, but that they are not regarded enough; that they are despised even by those who write them. Conan Doyle triumphed and triumphed deservedly, because he took his art seriously, because he lavished a hundred little touches of real knowledge and genuine picturesqueness on the police novelette. He substituted for the customary keen eyes and turned-up collar of the conventional detective a number of traits, external and pictorial, indeed, but honestly appropriate to the logical genius, traits such as an immeasurable love of music and an egotism which was abstract and, therefore, almost unselfish. Above all, he surrounded his detective with a genuine atmosphere of the poetry of London. He called up before the imagination a new and visionary city in which every cellar and alley hid as many weapons as the rocks and heather-bushes of Roderick Dhu. By this artistic seriousness he raised one at least of the popular forms of art to the level which it ought to occupy.

He wrote the best work in a popular form, and he found that because it was the best it was also the most popular. Men needed stories, and had been content to take bad ones; and they were right, for a story in itself is a marvellous and excellent thing, and a bad story is better than no story, just as half a loaf is better than no bread. But when a detective story was written by a man who refused to despise his art, who carried all their dreams to fulfilment, they preferred him to the bungling and irresponsible authors who had catered for them before. (pp. 173-74)

G. K. Chesterton, "Sherlock Holmes," in his *A Handful of Authors: Essays on Books & Writers,* edited by Dorothy Collins, Sheed and Ward, 1953, pp. 168-74.

DOROTHY L. SAYERS

(essay date 1929)

[Sayers, an English writer and critic, was an accomplished medievalist as well as the creator of Lord Peter Wimsey, the sophisticated detective-hero of such acclaimed mystery novels as *Murder Must Advertise* (1933), *The Nine Tailors* (1934), and *Gaudy Night* (1935). She is regarded as a preeminent authority on detective and mystery fiction. In the following excerpt, she examines the place of Doyle's Sherlock Holmes stories in the development of detective fiction.]

In 1887 *A Study in Scarlet* was flung like a bombshell into the field of detective fiction, to be followed within a few short and brilliant years by the marvellous series of Sherlock Holmes short stories. The effect was electric. Conan Doyle took up the Poe formula and galvanised it into life and popularity. He cut out the elaborate psychological introductions, or restated them in crisp dialogue. He brought into prominence what Poe had only lightly touched upon—the deduction of staggering conclusions from trifling indications in the Dumas-Cooper-Gaboriau manner. He was sparkling, surprising, and short. It was the triumph of the epigram.

A comparison of the Sherlock Holmes tales with the Dupin tales shows clearly how much Doyle owed to Poe, and, at the same time, how greatly he modified Poe's style and formula. Read, for instance, the opening pages of "The Murders in the Rue Morgue," which introduce Dupin, and compare them with the first chapter of *A Study in Scarlet.* Or merely set side by side the two passages which follow and contrast the relations between Dupin and his chronicler on the one hand, and between Holmes and Watson on the other:

I was astonished, too, at the vast extent of his reading; and, above all, I felt my soul enkindled within me by the wild fervour, and the vivid freshness of his imagination. Seeking in Paris the objects I then sought, I felt that the society of such a man would be to me a treasure beyond price; and this feeling I frankly confided to him. It was at length arranged that we should live together . . . and as my worldly circumstances were somewhat less embarrassed than his own, I was permitted to be at the expense of renting, and furnishing in a style which suited the rather fantastic gloom of our common temper, a time-eaten and grotesque mansion . . . in a retired and desolate portion of the Faubourg Saint Germain . . . It was a freak of fancy in my friend (for what else shall I call it?) to be enamoured of the Night for her own sake; and into this *bizarrerie,* as into all his others, I quietly fell, giving myself up to his wild whims with a perfect abandon. ["The Murders in the Rue Morgue"]

An anomaly which often struck me in the character of my friend Sherlock Holmes was that, though in his methods of thought he was the neatest and most methodical of mankind, and although also he affected a certain quiet primness of dress, he was none the less in his personal habits one of the most untidy men that ever drove a fellow-lodger to distraction. Not that I am in the least conventional in that respect myself. The rough-and-tumble work in Afghanistan, coming on the top of a natural Bohemianism of disposition, has made me rather more lax than befits a medical man. But with me there is a limit, and when I find a man who keeps his cigars in the coal-scuttle, his tobacco in the toe-end of a Persian slipper, and his unanswered correspondence transfixed by a jack-knife into the very centre of his wooden mantelpiece, then I begin to give myself virtuous airs. I have always held, too, that pistol-practice should distinctly be an open-air pastime; and when Holmes in one of his queer humours would sit in an arm-chair, with his hair-trigger and a hundred Boxer cartridges, and proceed to adorn the opposite wall with a patriotic V.R. done in bullet-pocks, I felt strongly that neither the atmosphere nor the appearance of our room was improved by it. ["The Musgrave Ritual"]

See how the sturdy independence of Watson adds salt and savour to the eccentricities of Holmes, and how flavourless beside it is the hero-worshipping self-abnegation of Dupin's friend. See, too, how the concrete details of daily life in Baker Street lift the story out of the fantastic and give it a solid reality. The Baker Street ménage has just that touch of humorous commonplace which appeals to British readers.

Another pair of parallel passages will be found in "The Purloined Letter" and "The Naval Treaty." They show the two detectives in dramatic mood, surprising their friends by their solution of the mystery. In "The Adventure of the Priory School," also, a similar situation occurs, though Holmes is here shown in a grimmer vein, rebuking wickedness in high places.

Compare, also, the conversational styles of Holmes and Dupin, and the reasons for Holmes's popularity become clearer than ever. Holmes has enriched English literature with more than one memorable aphorism and turn of speech.

"You know my methods, Watson."
"A long shot, Watson—a very long shot."
"—a little monograph on the hundred-and-fourteen varieties of tobaccoash."
"These are deep waters, Watson."
"Excellent!" cried Mr. Acton.—"But very superficial," said Holmes.
"Excellent!" I cried.—"Elementary," said he.
"It is of the highest importance in the art of detection to be able to recognise out of a number of facts which are incidental and which vital."
"You mentioned your name as if I should recognise it, but beyond the obvious facts that you are a bachelor, a solicitor, a Freemason and an asthmatic, I know nothing whatever about you."
"Every problem becomes very childish when once it is explained to you."

Nor must we forget that delightful form of riposto which Father Ronald Knox has wittily christened the "Sherlockismus":

"I would call your attention to the curious incident of the dog in the night-time."
"The dog did nothing in the night-time."
"That was the curious incident."

So, with Sherlock Holmes, the ball—the original nucleus deposited by Edgar Allan Poe nearly forty years earlier—was at last set rolling. As it went, it swelled into a vast mass—it set off others—it became a spate—a torrent—an avalanche of mystery fiction. It is impossible to keep track of all the detective-stories produced to-day. Book upon book, magazine upon magazine pour out from the Press, crammed with murders, thefts, arsons, frauds, conspiracies, problems, puzzles, mysteries, thrills, maniacs, crooks, poisoners, forgers, garrotters, police, spies, secret-service men, detectives, until it seems that half the world must be engaged in setting riddles for the other half to solve. (pp. 24-6)

Dorothy L. Sayers, in an introduction to *The Omnibus of Crime,* edited by Dorothy L. Sayers, 1929. Reprint by Harcourt Brace Jovanovich, 1961, pp. 9-38.

A. E. MURCH
(essay date 1958)

[In the following excerpt, Murch pronounces Doyle's Sherlock Holmes adventures a pivotal point in the development of detective fiction.]

There are in literature certain characters who have

come to possess a separate and unmistakable identity, whose names and personal qualities are familiar to thousands who may not have read any of the works in which they appear. Among these characters must be included Sherlock Holmes, who has acquired in the minds of countless readers of all nationalities the status of an actual human being, accepted by many in the early years of the twentieth century as a living contemporary, and still surviving fifty years later with all the glamour of an established and unassailable tradition, the most convincing, the most brilliant, the most congenial and well-loved of all the detectives of fiction. (p. 67)

The reasons for the immense popularity of Sherlock Holmes are not hard to establish, and lie chiefly in Conan Doyle's inspired blending of two contrasting elements, the old and the new; mingling familiar, almost by that time traditional, features of the *genre* with startling, even sensational innovations. The time was exactly right in the 1890's for the appearance of a fresh detective hero of outstanding individuality, and to create him Doyle took the most notable characteristics of earlier fictional detectives and added to them the very qualities that the late Victorian general public admired most. Sherlock Holmes not only possessed far greater mental brilliance than his predecessors, but also a good social and cultural background, perfect respectability and integrity, the status of a "scientist," and an international reputation as a celebrity in his own field. Above all, he was an Englishman, while for the past fifty years, indeed ever since the time of Vidocq, all the celebrated detectives of fiction—Dupin, Père Tabaret, Monsieur Lecoq, Rocambole—had been French.

Sherlock Holmes's skill in following a trail is a legacy from the Three Princes of Serendip, inherited through Voltaire's *Zadig,* a novel which Conan Doyle acknowledged as one of his sources of inspiration. The same faculty characterised the Indian trackers of Fenimore Cooper and of his successor in the same sphere, Captain Mayne Reid, who was Doyle's favourite author in his boyhood days. Sherlock Holmes could perform even more masterly feats of tracking, deriving remarkable information from footprints on a garden path or a snow-covered lane, the wheelmarks of a cab, or the traces left by a small bare foot on a windowsill. Holmes's kinship with the Redskin hunters is also apparent from his habit of silent laughter, his ability to go without food or rest when on the trail, and that "immobility of countenance" which made Dr. Watson more than once compare him to a Red Indian.

Like the almost legendary Vidocq, Holmes is a master of disguise, an accomplished actor and a man of great physical strength. They both have a sound grasp of criminal psychology and an encyclopaedic knowledge of criminal history which serves them well. Holmes once referred disparagingly to Dupin, calling

him "a very inferior fellow, . . . showy and superficial," yet Dupin is the literary ancestor whom he most closely resembles. Like Poe's hero, Holmes is "unemotional," reasons with "ice-cold logic" and regards detection as "an exact science"; has a brilliant mind stored with all sorts of technical information; sometimes uses a newspaper advertisement to bring a suspect within his reach; can break in upon a friend's train of thought with an apropos remark after a quarter of an hour's silence. Both detectives express the opinion that when all impossibilities have been eliminated, what remains, however improbable, must be the truth; that an article is best hidden when left in full view; that an "abstract thinker" is the most formidable of all opponents, especially if he is a mathematician; that the more grotesque a mystery seems, the easier it will be to explain, while an apparently commonplace problem is the most difficult of all. They are both heavy smokers, take long walks through city streets at night, and hold a poor opinion of the police, whom they assist on occasion with brilliant deductions or inspired advice. Both are men of good family, bachelors with no interest in the opposite sex, and very little in their fellowmen, except as factors in a problem calling for the exercise of their analytical powers. They have their individual eccentricities, and while Poe comments on Dupin's "Bi-part soul," Dr. Watson mediates on Sherlock's "dual nature."

Both Dupin and Holmes are fortunate in having a faithful, long-suffering companion to chronicle with unfailing amazement and delight their various activities, their discourses on detective topics, but whereas Dupin's friend reveals little or nothing of his own individuality, Dr. Watson conveys his own character as clearly as he does the temperament and perspicacity of his famous colleague. He plays an active, if secondary, rôle in almost every story, serving not only as a foil to his brilliant friend but also as a figure with whom the reader feels a comforting comradeship when he, too, "sees but does not observe," and needs to have the implications of a clue explained. Dr. Watson, with his sturdy common sense and sincerity, his patient cheerfulness and instant readiness to face any danger beside his friend, stands almost as high as Holmes in the reader's affection. **"The Lion's Mane,"** which lacks his presence, has lost an appreciable part of the characteristic savour, even though it is related by Holmes himself. The important part played by Watson, so different from the minor rôle of the narrator in Poe's tale of Dupin, is one of Conan Doyle's most pleasing innovations.

In spite of the similarities between Dupin and Holmes, the contrast between Poe and Conan Doyle, as writers of detective stories, could hardly be more striking than it is. Poe's tales are purely analytical discussions of the science of detection, argued out like a geometric theorem with no irrelevant detail. Though the subjects may be sensational, in their treatment we find little excitement and less romance. The characters, other than Dupin himself, are so lightly drawn that they have no personality, often not even a name, and the interest lies not in the people but in the things that have happened to them and the bonds of logic that link cause and effect. Of action or normal conversation there is practically none. Dupin moves in logical steps from the stated problem to its solution, and he is never wrong, never at a loss, never misled by a false clue. Doyle's stories are full of movement and animation. Men and women bring their personal troubles to Holmes (as they never did to Dupin) and the reader shares their dramatic moments, for much of the action takes place before his eyes. Sherlock Holmes is not merely an abstract logician, and is sometimes baffled, if only temporarily, or misled by conflicting evidence, even by unforeseen human reactions. On some occasions, as in "The Yellow Face," he is completely in error, but he loses no prestige thereby, his mistake making him seem still more convincingly human, and serving also to throw his almost invariable success into stronger relief. Poe was unfamiliar with Paris, and the French background he gave to his Dupin stories had no special significance in the plot. Victorian London, which Conan Doyle knew so well, gives its own characteristic atmosphere to the tales of Sherlock Holmes, so much so that the mere thought of that hero conjures up the great metropolis of the period, with its November fogs and August heat, its hansom cabs and gaslight, the docks and railway stations, the dignity of Westminster, the humdrum suburbs, the squalor of an East End opium den.

Conan Doyle admired Gaboriau for "the neat dove-tailing of his plot," and in his first novels of Sherlock Holmes (as distinct from the short stories) he followed Gaboriau's example of plot-construction, and found himself in the same technical difficulty, needing to break the thread of the detective interest to interpolate a long account of events that had taken place at some distant time or place. In *A Study in Scarlet* it is so abruptly done as to seem the opening of an entirely different story. In *The Sign of Four* it comes about more naturally, in the form of Jonathan Small's confession of his share in looting the Agra treasure during the Indian mutiny. Only once more, in *The Valley of Fear,* written a quarter of a century later, does Conan Doyle follow the same plan of construction, and this time he carefully reassures his readers, before transferring his story to America, that in due course they will "return to those rooms in Baker Street" for the conclusion of the tale. In this novel Doyle improved upon Gaboriau, and took an original step by making the interpolation another complete detective story with a different hero, "one of Pinkerton's best men, Birdy Edwards."

At the time when Conan Doyle began to write, detective fiction consisted mainly of two distinct groups, each designed to appeal to very different types of reader. The great majority of such stories were sensational, written for the uncritical general public, and seldom able to read with interest a second time, once the secret was known. Side by side with these there was a growing popularity among more intellectual readers for the closely reasoned, more abstruse detective stories of Poe, which were repeatedly issued in new editions in this country and in France, as well as in his own country, especially from 1875 onwards. Conan Doyle contrived to combine the best features of both groups, and, by restraining the sensational within acceptable limits and explaining Holmes's deductions in such entertaining fashion, he evolved a new kind of detective story that pleased both types of reader. Sherlock Holmes's exploits are not simply tales of crime, nor mere puzzles that lose their interest as soon as they are solved. They can be read over and over again with renewed, even increased, appreciation for Holmes's detective acumen and the artistry with which the tale is unfolded.

When the reading public came to appreciate Holmes's powers in the *Adventures* they accorded him an affection that has scarcely diminished with the passing of more than a half a century. If, now and then, a plot contained some debatable statement, as, for example, Holmes's interpretation of the bicycle tracks in **"The Priory School,"** or his inaccurate impressions of the rules of horse-racing in **"Silver Blaze,"** Conan Doyle quickly learned about these discrepancies from readers' letters, or even from articles in the Press, but such comments did not ruffle his robust good humour. It is characteristic of well-written detective fiction that it stimulates the reader's mind almost equally to intelligent participation and analytical criticism. Mental effort on his part is essential to full enjoyment of the story, and he likes to increase his pleasure by exercising inductive reasoning upon the incidental details, provided always that the tale itself is sufficiently absorbing. The Sherlock Holmes stories quickly evoked this responsive interest, an interest which they still arouse in many critical minds seeking diversion.

Conan Doyle was singularly well equipped to produce fiction of this type. His prose was clear and factual, and he was mentally in tune with the spirit of sensational romance, for he loved action, adventure and tales of exciting quests. When little more than a youth, being troubled by religious doubts, he formulated for himself the rule: "Never will I accept anything which cannot be proved to me," and he made it his guiding principle through life, a principle that might well have served as a motto for Sherlock Holmes. . . . His long training in medicine enriched his mind in ways that had an important bearing on his work as a

Sherlock Holmes as conceived by Sidney Paget, whose illustrations became for many the definitive visual image of Holmes.

writer of detective fiction, giving him an intimate knowledge of all types of men and women and sharpening his inductive skill, his perception of the vital importance of *minutiae*. It also gave him, in the person of Dr. Joseph Bell, a prototype for the new "scientific" detective he was to create.

Holmes is introduced to the world as an expert in chemical research, a choice of profession very much in tune with the spirit of an age that was reaching out into scientific fields. On the historic occasion when Dr. Watson meets Sherlock Holmes for the first time, in the chemical laboratory at Bart's Hospital, Holmes has "just discovered a re-agent which is precipitated by haemoglobin and nothing else." "Practical?" cries Holmes in response to Watson's comment, "It is the most practical medico-legal discovery for years. Don't you see that it gives us an infallible test for bloodstains?" The same note is struck repeatedly. We hear of Holmes "spending seven weeks working out a few experiments in organic chemistry"; "settling down to one of those all-night researches which he frequently indulged in . . . stooping over a retort and test-tube"; "spending months on research into the coal-tar derivatives"; or discovering the decisive clue to a murder by testing a solution with litmus paper.

But it was not yet time for the appearance in fiction of a really scientific detective, such as Dr. Thorndyke and other specialists in this field who came later, for the average reader in the 1890's was scarcely able to appreciate chemical analysis as evidence. In spite of this flourish of test-tubes in the background, Holmes's experiments do little more than create the illusion of a scientific approach. He does not reason as a scientist in the cases related in detail, or make use of chemistry to solve the problems that form the framework of the plots. In *A Study in Scarlet* he believes that Enoch Drebber was murdered by poison, but he does not analyse the pills found later by the police. He tries them on his landlady's dog, and the little terrier's instant death satisfies the reader that the drug was lethal. The actual identification of the poison is a superfluous detail to him, as it is to Holmes. When, in **"The Devil's Foot,"** Holmes at last comes to suspect that the burning of a mysterious brown powder has killed Brenda Tregennis and driven her brothers insane, he does not turn to his test-tubes, or, since he was on holiday in Cornwall at the time, send the powder to a local analyst. Instead, he arranges a rough and ready experiment to discover how the fumes would affect himself and Dr. Watson, with all but fatal results—a dramatic, rather than a scientific course of action.

In his early days of research at Bart's Hospital, Holmes was once seen "beating the subjects in the dissecting room with a stick, to verify how far bruises may be produced after death," but he is nowhere reported as using such knowledge, or, indeed, examining a body in a mortuary. The public was not yet ready for the detective with a scalpel, or for post mortem investigations such as were later performed so brilliantly by Sir Bernard Spilsbury in real life and Reginald Fortune in fiction. Holmes found his famous magnifying glass sufficiently informative for his purpose in most cases, though he sometimes used a microscope, as other detectives had done before him. He was, however, the first fictional detective to use a microscope for examining the dust extracted from his suspect's clothing, and this is perhaps his closest approach to "scientific detection."

In most cases, his successes depend far less upon science than upon his wide general knowledge, his quick perception of informative trifles, and in such matters the average reader can grasp his arguments with full appreciation. It needs no scientific training to perceive (or to agree) that a man writing on a wall usually does so at his own eye level, thus indicating his height; that only a strong man with special training could drive a harpoon through a human body; or that there is something sinister about a coffin which "took longer to make, being out of the ordinary." No one will deny that there are grounds for suspicion when a first-class workman accepts a job at half the usual wages, or when a governess is offered a situation at three times the normal salary. All through the series it is such clues as these, placed in passing before the reader, that enable Holmes to solve apparently inexplicable mysteries. Doctor Watson once exclaimed: "I had heard what he had heard, I had seen what he had seen, and yet from his words it was evident that he saw clearly not only what had happened, but what was about to happen, while to me the whole business was still confused and grotesque!" The reader feels the same mingling of frustration and curiosity, and not until he learns just where and when he has failed to notice the clues can he put the story down. (pp. 178-84)

It seems odd that Sherlock Holmes, who scrutinized footprints with such minute care on so many occasions, was so contemptuous of fingerprints—an indication that the Red Indian out-weighed the scientist in him! In only one of his cases, **"The Norwood Builder,"** is a fingerprint mentioned in any detail, and then it is a forgery, misleading to the police but not to Holmes, who "writhes with inward merriment" before explaining how simply such a print could be counterfeited. On a later occasion, in **"The Three Gables,"** a pompous Inspector presumed to advise Holmes "never to pass anything, however trifling. There is always the chance of fingermarks or something." The remark was coldly ignored, and apart from these disparaging references there is scarcely a hint in all the Sherlock Holmes stories of this method of identification, and none of that familiarity with and respect for the work of fingerprint experts which became such a generally accepted feature in later detective fiction.

Conan Doyle, whose love for France was deep-rooted and sincere, repeatedly linked Sherlock Holmes with that country. His faculty of observation and deduction may have been inherited, he says, from his French grandmother, "the sister of Vernet, the French artist." Holmes was often engaged with French cases which are referred to in passing, that of the unfortunate Mme. Montpensier, for example, or of Huret, the boulevard assassin, "an exploit which won for Holmes a letter of thanks from the French president and the order of the Legion of Honour." Holmes frequently worked closely with the French police, and Dr. Watson records that one eminent detective, François le Villard, was so impressed with Sherlock Holmes's many monographs on technical aspects of detection that he translated them into French for the benefit of his colleagues.

The English police also valued Holmes's advise, and throughout his long career his services were available to help the professionals with any difficult case, from *A Study in Scarlet* (1887) to **"The Retired Colourman"** (1927). He had no great opinion of "the Scotland Yarders," in spite of their "quickness and energy," considering them "shockingly conventional," "lacking in imagination," sometimes even "obtuse to

the point of imbecility," but he appreciated their persistence and their powerful organisation, and eventually found it a great convenience to be able to say: "Thanks to the telephone and the help of the Yard, I can usually get my essentials without leaving this room."

The numerous police officials who worked with him in turn, always began by distrusting his "far-fetched theories" and unconventional methods, but quickly came to value his cooperation, especially since he wanted no publicity, and never identified a criminal to them without at the same time giving them such clear proofs of his guilt that they ran no risk of losing their case in court. On occasion, however he deliberately refrained from revealing the entire truth to the police, reserving the right to with-hold information when he saw fit, though he never hampered or misled the official force. In **"The Devil's Foot"** he was scrupulous in leaving every clue for the police to find, if they could, but decided that in view of the special circumstances he was "not called upon to interfere." In **"The Abbey Grange,"** also, he kept silence from similar motives, and never did Holmes let the police know that he and Watson had actually been present when a certain noble lady shot the blackmailing Charles Augustus Milverton.

In other murder cases when Holmes identifies the murderer, the guilty man may die of some long-standing disease, as in *A Study in Scarlet* and **"The Boscombe Valley Mystery,"** or by some avenging stroke of Fate, as in **"The Speckled Band"** or *The Hound of the Baskervilles*. If he is to stand trial, the story closes with his arrest, and no more is heard of him. Apart from one brief newspaper report of an inquest in one of the early stories there are no court-room scenes, no dramatic trials such as had been popular in earlier detective fiction and would be so again; no attempt to follow a murderer along the sombre paths that lead from arrest to conviction and on to execution, that harrowing, inevitable sequence in the administration of justice which has disturbed the peace of mind of many sensitive investigators, from Walter Lester in *Eugene Aram* to Lord Peter Wimsey in *Busman's Honeymoon*. While recognising that some readers might wish to know what happened to the criminal, Watson dismissed the matter with the brief comment:—

It has been difficult . . . to give those final details which the curious might expect. Each case has been the prelude to another, and, the crisis once over, the actors have passed for ever out of our busy lives.

Most of Sherlock Holmes's problems, in any case, are not concerned with murder but with less sensational crimes—burglary, fraud, blackmail, or the theft of important documents. Some of the most interesting do not treat of crime in the legal sense at all, but with human perplexities outside the scope of the law. Conan Doyle is unique among writers of detective fiction in the skill with which he so repeatedly weaves a fascinating mystery around some personal dilemma brought to Holmes by a distressed client—a missing fiancé, for instance, a husband's worry about his wife's health, or the disappearance of a rugby footballer on the eve of an important match. The reader finds additional pleasure in Holmes's frequent, intriguing little impromptu deductions about irrelevant matters, Dr. Watson's watch or Grant Munro's pipe, Dr. Mortimer's walking stick, or the profession of a casual passer-by; and a further savour is provided by the many tantalising hints of other mysteries which, for reasons of discretion, cannot yet be told, such as "The Case of the Two Coptic Patriarchs," "the truth about the Amateur Mendicant Society," or "the dreadful business of the Abernetty family."

In every story of Sherlock Holmes, the reader's interest is captivated not only by the detective's "unique methods," but perhaps to an even greater degree by "the singular personality of this remarkable man." Discussing his family link with Vernet, the French painter, Holmes commented that "Art in the blood is liable to take the strangest forms," and it may well have accounted for more than that hereditary aptitude for perception and deduction which he shared with his elder brother, Mycroft. There is artistry in his sense of the dramatic and in his skill as an actor. His impersonations deceive even his closest friend, and the reader is as amazed as Dr. Watson when Sherlock Holmes's voice is heard from a figure that till that moment has been fully accepted as a French workman, an elderly lady, a rough looking groom or a venerable Italian priest. (pp. 185-88)

Sherlock Holmes had many interests outside his professional activities, philology, for instance, and his study of ancient manuscripts or the music of the Middle Ages. He was an ardent lover of music, a composer as well as a capable performer, and the author of scores of treatises on abstruse subjects. Rather surprisingly, he was "one of the finest boxers of his weight," and it is a tribute to Conan Doyle's mastery of convincing detail that the reader can without hesitation accept Holmes in all these widely differing capacities. He had his eccentricities, his habit of countering boredom with cocaine, and now and then, like some of his French predecessors, he allowed his thoughts to stray to the other side of the fence. One of his particular hobbies was the opening of safes, and in idle moments he would remark: "I have always had an idea that I could have made a highly efficient criminal," or "Burglary was always an alternative profession had I cared to adopt it." Yet his honour remained clear, and if, once or twice, he did break the letter of the law when all other means of achieving his purpose had failed, his motive was al-

ways to further the ends of justice, and he could say in all sincerity, "In over a thousand cases I am not aware that I have ever used my powers upon the wrong side."

The popularity of the Sherlock Holmes stories inevitably inspired many imitations and even burlesques, in none of which is the central character more than a puppet without life or personality, lacking everything except eccentricity. Such productions attested the vogue for detective fiction without affecting its development and they need not be examined here. . . . (p. 189)

Sherlock Holmes is a focal point in the evolution of the detective hero. He not only embodied the characteristics of his most notable predecessors, but also became the ancestor of almost all the outstanding twentieth-century detective heroes in English fiction, who reflect one or more of the varied facets of his personality, widely though they differ from him, and from each other, in other respects. Father Brown, with his intuition and his psychological flair; the scientist, Dr. Thorndyke, specializing in chemical analysis; Poirot, that neat little Belgian, and the burly French official, Hanaud, who so much enjoyed mystifying their friends, Captain Hastings and Mr. Ricardo, and arranging a dramatic denouement; Lord Peter Wimsey, who collected rare volumes and was a skilled musician; Reginald Fortune, enigmatic and sarcastic, who loved to work on his own and keep the regular police in suspense; all these and many others have a certain kinship with Sherlock Holmes.

With Conan Doyle, the detective story came at last to full fruition. His sincerity, his great skill as a writer, gave it a new distinction and won for it a wider, almost universal, acceptance as a literary form. It was by no means his only, or to him his most important, work, but the reading public of his generation recognised him as unquestionably a master of this type of fiction, which in his hands became a force potent enough to influence world trends in popular literature. For the first time, English detective fiction, which had received so much in earlier years from American and French sources, repaid that debt fully and created a new standard for developments in the twentieth century. (pp. 190-91)

A. E. Murch, "Sherlock Holmes," in her *The Development of the Detective Novel*, Philosophical Library, Inc. 1958, pp. 167-91.

C. P. SNOW
(essay date 1974)

[Snow is best known for his popular *Strangers and Brothers* (1940-70), an eleven-novel series that examines questions of morality and power in contemporary England. In the following excerpt, he discusses the artistry of the Holmes stories, terming them the best of Doyle's literary work.]

Conan Doyle had a singularly powerful romantic imagination. One can see it, not only in the Holmes stories, but in the books which, as with *Sir Nigel*, have not lasted so long (where Doyle, as modest as a successful writer can be, for once felt that he was being badly treated). One can see it in his life, the gallant crusades, the spiritualism, even his second marriage. In literature, to the depth and richness to which he possessed it, it is a rare quality, much rarer than most of those which we are inclined to venerate more. Balzac had it, so had Dickens, but other fine novelists, even some of the greatest, to nothing like the same extent.

It is probably impossible to capture a world audience without it. It is certainly impossible without it to produce a fictional person whose name becomes far better known than that of the author himself. How many people all over the planet could say something significant about Sherlock Holmes but would not have the faintest idea who created him! The number must be large. It is difficult to think of any similar case; perhaps the nearest equivalent would be the relation of Cervantes and Don Quixote.

The essence of an imagination such as Doyle's is that it simplifies and heightens. It can be benign, and give us a feeling of a desirable world—which most of the time he did. As I shall say in a moment, that is one of his delights. With some darker and more tormented souls (c.f. Dickens) it can be Gothic, or plain sinister. This quality was not entirely lacking in Doyle. No one could write **"The Copper Beeches"** or **"The Speckled Band"** without sadistic undercurrents disturbing him somewhere. But that does not leave a lasting effect as one reads. It is more like being taken back to childhood, hearing a storm thrashing about outside, and feeling comforted in a warm bed.

It is a mistake to think of his two great characters as caricatures. They are amiable archetypes—archetypes of what, in different moods, most of us would like to be, as brave and solid as Watson, as clever and superlatively effective as Holmes. These are, of course, desires which will never be fulfilled, but some-

how we are safe. The whole environment gives us ultimate security. Adventure, risk, however timid we are, we have all had our flights of fancying them for ourselves—provided we come back intact, and bask in the comfort which is always residing deep down in the stories.

Remember, one feature of the author's imagination is that much of the grit of everyday life is washed away. Holmes and Watson aren't troubled about money. They have unqualified faith in each other's loyalty. They are not troubled about women, despite Watson's over-frequent marriages. Their attitude to women is chivalrous in the high Victorian manner (which incidentally, is a reason why Doyle's women are not satisfactory). Though their bachelor existence is happy-go-lucky and free from *Angst*, it is also respectably connected, again in the high Victorian manner. They have their place in the hierarchy, and it is a respected and influential place. Although Holmes sometimes produces admirable liberal sentiments about Board-schools as the lighthouses of the future, they take an entirely unaffected, unenvious pleasure in their connection with the eminent, especially with miscellaneous royalty. Note Watson's stupefied enthusiasm, in "The Adventure of the Illustrious Client," . . . when he catches sight of the brougham outside the door, and recognizes the armorial bearings. "It is a loyal friend and a chivalrous gentleman," says Holmes. "Let that now and for ever be enough for us."

Their pleasures are as unselfconscious and good-natured as that. Such pleasures have more charm than, with the top of our minds, we allow ourselves to think. Holmes and Watson are as unrancorous, as well-adjusted to turn-of-the-century England, as they are to their delectable cold suppers, presumably sent in from Fortnum's, after a successful case—though Holmes's choice of wine is sometimes distinctly eccentric. In spite of all the dramas and the occasional dangers, their lives are curiously soothing to read about. There is very little in any kind of literature which, in the last resort, bestows such reassurance and peace.

The truth is—this is often obscured—that the Holmes stories are a great artistic triumph, of a very strange kind, achieved without the writer's full engagement. That, of course, has happened to others. One of the most wonderful scenes in all literature, where Ivan Karamazov talks to his brother Alyosha in the garden, seems to have been written right against the grain, certainly against the conscious grain. Perhaps Doyle had one of those strokes of luck, which all writers know. After things which one has tried hardest to bring off have stayed half-dead, something else—maybe written without excitement or even interest—comes off with a dash, surprising the writer more than anyone else.

There is much more luck, sheer luck, in any kind of art than we care to recognize. A born professional like Doyle, slogging away, was likely to have it visit him once or twice. Before one or two suggestions why it visited him in the Holmes stories, it is perhaps as well to get rid of some illusions about them. They are not specially ingenious detective stories, and they didn't get much worse in that respect, simply because they were never very good. . . . **"The Illustrious Client,"** **"The Retired Colourman"** and **"The Sussex Vampire"** are rather better than the average of the first two volumes. Doyle had nothing like the inventive skill of plenty of twentieth-century practitioners: compare Ellery Queen, John Dickson Carr, for psychological sleight-of-hand, Agatha Christie. There are dozens of others more cunning in these respects than Doyle. He was not a master of plot. His themes are nearly always more interesting than his plots, and his narrative, which rarely failed him, came more naturally than either.

Further, he was not a scientific innovator. He calms us with a faith in rationality: but, working in his period, anyone with a little curiosity about science could have done that. With enough self-hypnotism, it is possible to argue that he anticipated all scientific detective techniques. With enough self-hypnotism, it is possible to argue that he anticipated almost the whole of modern thought. You can make a plausible case, for instance, that he got in before Sir Karl Popper and Sir Peter Medawar on the hypothetico-deductive basis of the scientific process. All this belongs to the cheerful and agreeable Sherlockian fake scholarship, which is fine, so long as it doesn't detract from what Doyle could really do.

Some of that scholarship, though, does have a value in effectively revealing how often he was quite uncommitted to, or uninvolved in, the Holmes stories. One of my favourite pieces of this type is Mr. Michael Harrison's deadpan remark that Dr. Moriarty had three brothers, all rather surprisingly called James. (pp. 7-10)

Nevertheless, in these stories, uncommitted and careless as he often was, Doyle's temperament and gifts fused as they never did in anything else he wrote. His imagination needed tying down. He hadn't quite enough sense of the actual to make the fourteenth century concrete. His own London gave him just the sense of fact which he required. He had a beautiful gift for mood which, when Holmes and Watson were about, did not often run away with him. He shared their assumptions and their virtues, and, without effort, his own admirable personality showed through. Personalities as admirable as his are not common among writers, or, as far as that goes, anywhere else. Perhaps that is one reason why his work has inspired such affection. He was an extremely brave man, as Holmes and Watson are. He was as honourable as they are. He was generous and open-hearted. He was a specimen of Victorian England at its best. Incidentally, he was superlative-

ly credulous, and even that leaves some endearing traces in the Holmes stories.

He was a good man, and somehow, with unusual percipience, first seduced by his restless imagination, his talent for atmosphere, the snugness of privileged London in the 'nineties, readers all over the world seem to have divined that goodness of his as a kind of subtext.

It is a credit to public taste. (pp. 10-11)

Doyle understood a lot about evil, not so much about venality and corruption and shabbiness. That is another reason why the Holmes stories are nobler than this mortal life of ours. (p. 12)

C. P. Snow, in an introduction to *The Case-Book of Sherlock Holmes* by Sir Arthur Conan Doyle, Jonathan Cape, 1974, pp. 7-12.

E. F. BLEILER
(essay date 1979)

[Bleiler is an American critic, editor, and bibliographer who has contributed extensively to scholarship in the fields of detective, fantasy, and horror literature. In the following excerpt, he assesses some of Doyle's supernatural horror fiction.]

Today we think of Doyle primarily as the foremost writer of detective stories since Poe, but he was also preëminent in historical fiction, science fiction, adventure and sports stories, topical stories, historical works and journalism. In his own opinion, with which I concur, his best work was the fascinating novel of events in the 13th-century Europe of the Black Prince, *The White Company.*

Doyle also moved much in public life and had opinions, often worth listening to, on many contemporary matters, including military science, in which he was a generation ahead of his day. A staunch supporter of the Establishment in most things, he received a knighthood for his work as an apologist for the British side in the Boer War. In World War I he was semiofficial chronicler of the British Army. A remarkably generous man, sincerely moved by abuses of power, he also devoted much time to correcting two judicial injustices, the famous Slater and Edalji cases.

In later life, around 1915-6, Doyle became converted to Spiritualism, and most of his activity thereafter was concerned with missionary work. He travelled and lectured, wrote pamphlets and books, and considered himself bound to defend every aspect of his creed against all comers. (p. vi)

Doyle wrote only fourteen supernatural short

Major Media Adaptations: Motion Pictures*

The Speckled Band, 1931. British and Dominions. Director: Jack Raymond. Cast: Raymond Massey, Athole Steward, Angela Baddeley.

Sherlock Holmes, 1932. Fox. Director: William K. Howard. Cast: Clive Brooke, Reginald Owen.

Silver Blaze, 1937. Twickenham. Director: Thomas Bentley. Cast: Ian Fleming, Lyn Harding.

The Adventures of Sherlock Holmes, 1939. TCF. [Released in Great Britain as *Sherlock Holmes*] Director: Alfred Werker. Cast: Basil Rathbone, Nigel Bruce, Ida Lupino, Mary Gordon.

The Hound of the Baskervilles, 1939. Director: Sidney Lanfield. Cast: Basil Rathbone, Nigel Bruce, Wendy Barrie, Lionel Atwill, John Carradine, Ralph Forbes, Mary Gordon.

Sherlock Holmes and the Secret Weapon, 1942. Universal. Director: Roy William Neill. Cast: Basil Rathbone, Nigel Bruce, Lionel Atwill, Mary Gordon.

Sherlock Holmes and the Voice of Terror, 1942. Universal. Director: John Rawlins. Cast: Basil Rathbone, Nigel Bruce, Mary Gordon.

Sherlock Holmes Faces Death, 1943. Universal. Director: Roy William Neill. Cast: Basil Rathbone, Nigel Bruce, Mary Gordon.

Sherlock Holmes in Washington, 1943. Universal. Director: Roy William Neill. Cast: Basil Rathbone, Nigel Bruce, George Zucco, Marjorie Lord.

The Hound of the Baskervilles, 1959. United Artists/Hammer. Director: Terence Fisher. Cast: Peter Cushing, Christopher Lee, André Morell.

The Lost World, 1960. TCF/Saratoga. Director: Irwin Allen. Cast: Claude Rains, Michael Rennie, David Hedison, Fernando Lamas, Jill St. John.

A Study in Terror, 1965. Compton-Tekli. Director: James Hill. Cast: John Neville, Donald Houston, Robert Morley.

The Hound of the Baskervilles, 1977. Hemdale/Michael White Ltd. Director: Paul Morrissey. Cast: Peter Cook, Dudley Moore, Denholm Elliott, Terry-Thomas, Roy Kinnear, Prunella Scales, Spike Milligan.

*Several of the motion pictures listed use characters created by Arthur Conan Doyle but are not based on specific works.

Other Adaptations:

American actor William Gillette premiered a three-act drama entitled *Sherlock Holmes* in New York in 1899. The play was Gillette's own adaptation of a drama written by Doyle. Seeking permission to revise Doyle's text, Gillette reportedly cabled to the author: "May I marry Holmes?" Doyle's reply: "You may marry him or murder him or do what you like with him."

Britain's Granada Television produced a series of faithful adaptations of the Holmes stories and novels beginning in 1984 and running through 1986. The series starred Jeremy Brett as Sherlock Holmes and David Burke as Dr. Watson; Edward Hardwick assumed the role of Watson in 1985.

In addition, there have been innumerable other television, film, radio, and stage adaptations of Holmes adventures.

---

stories and four supernatural novels, three of which are short. This is not a large production, especially when one compares it with his writings in other areas. He wrote some sixty stories about Sherlock Holmes and sixteen about Brigadier Gerard of the Napoleonic Army, while his literary corpus comes to more than four hundred works, not counting individual poems and minor journalism.

Yet these few stories reflect his inner personality and interests, just as his sport stories reflect his bouncing athleticism. While his earlier supernatural stories were journalistic, they did not fall into the easy path of the conventional Victorian ghost story, but introduced ideas that he had picked up during his serious reading. His later stories, on the other hand, were often frankly propaganda for the Spiritualist cause. (pp. vi-vii)

Most of the stories in [*The Best Supernatural Tales of Arthur Conan Doyle*] originated in ideas that can be traced without too much difficulty either in Doyle's life or in the cultural atmosphere of the day. The earlier stories show an apt journalistic versatility that was able to seize on concepts that were already fairly familiar and channel them into new stories.

["**The American's Tale**"], Doyle's second published story, is probably based on the wonderful man-eating plant of Madagascar. This was a traveller's tale familiar to Victorian readers and often retold in popular articles about natural wonders, true or otherwise. (p. ix)

More personal to Doyle is the pellucid horror of "**The Captain of the *Polestar***" . . . , with the darkless brilliance of endless day and the horrors of night. It obviously draws on Doyle's experiences in the whaler *Hope*, even to the personalities of the Scottish crew members, who are recorded in Doyle's papers. As for the ghost that pursues and lures, is there perhaps an echo of *Frankenstein*? (p. x)

["**J. Habakuk Jephson's Statement,**"] is in a class

by itself as a fantasy of history. Like Arthur Machen's "Angels of Mons" or [Wilhem] Meinhold's *Amber Witch,* it is one of the few pieces of fiction that have been taken seriously as fact and have been hotly refuted or defended by persons who should have known better.

This story, which appeared anonymously, was based on the historical incident of the *Mary Celeste,* one of the great mysteries of the sea. (p. xi)

While most of Doyle's readers probably had enough sense to recognize that Mr. J. Habakuk Jephson was a Yankee of literature and that his adventures on board the *Marie Celeste* (Doyle's spelling) were unlikely, Mr. Solly Flood, Her Majesty's Advocate-General and Proctor at Gibraltar, who had handled the salvage of the *Mary Celeste,* sent public telegrams denouncing the story as untrue. He followed this with an official report to the Admiralty proclaiming Jephson to be a hoaxer. Needless to say, the press, when details emerged, was delighted, as was Dr. Doyle.

Less likely to be taken for current events are Doyle's two Egyptological stories . . . ["The Ring of Thoth" and "Lot No. 249"]. Both good thrillers, they show the intense interest in ancient Egypt that arose during the last part of the 19th century after the findings of the Egypt Exploration Society. (pp. xi-xii)

Arthur Conan Doyle, it must be admitted, was not the towering figure in supernatural fiction that he was in the detective story or the historical novel. No one places his name with those of his contemporaries Bram Stoker, M. R. James, Algernon Blackwood, Arthur Machen or Ambrose Bierce. His was not a new vision, as was theirs; his was merely respectable accomplishment.

This is not to say that his supernatural stories are not worth reading. Doyle was one of the finest storytellers in modern English literature, and the dynamism of his better work often appeared in his lesser writings. If his weak area is idea, the zest and vitality with which his stories are told, the clear and forceful expression outweigh deficiencies. The situation in **"The Great Keinplatz Experiment"** is farcical, yet the reader is likely to remember Professor von Baumgarten, while the strange, immortal Egyptian of **"The Ring of Thoth"** may haunt the memory corridors of our mind-museums long after Doyle's "better" stories are forgotten. (pp. xiii-xiv)

E. F. Bleiler, in an introduction to *The Best Supernatural Tales of Arthur Conan Doyle* by Arthur Conan Doyle, edited by E. F. Bleiler, Dover Publications, Inc., 1979, pp. v-xvi.

JULIAN SYMONS

(essay date 1979)

[Symons is highly regarded as a biographer and writer of detective fiction. In the following excerpt, he surveys Doyle's principal literary works.]

Conan Doyle's output as an imaginative writer, distinct from factual histories and pamphlets, falls into three groups: the Sherlock Holmes and other mystery stories, the historical and sporting novels and short stories, and what we would now call the science fiction. There are also a few books that do not fit into any of these categories, and a number of plays. (p. 83)

The first three collections of short stories [about Holmes], *The Adventures, The Memoirs* and *The Return,* are much superior to the last volumes, *His Last Bow* and *The Case-Book.* The first two belong to the eighteen nineties, and the stories in *The Return* had been completed by 1904. *His Last Bow* appeared in 1917, and *The Case-Book* ten years later. There are good stories in these last volumes, along with some weak ones, but the enthusiastic delight in his own creations that marked the early books is missing. The old master is going through the motions, and doing so with skill, but no longer with pleasure. In part no doubt this comes from the fact that the later stories deal with a time long past. **"His Last Bow"**, which was set in August 1914 just at the beginning of the War, was actually written in 1917, and this was the nearest thing to a contemporary setting in the later stories. The tales written in the nineteen twenties deal with a Victorian or Edwardian England that was by now only a memory to their creator.

Some of the other mystery stories written at intervals over the years make lively reading, and in two cases carry a faint echo of Sherlock Holmes. Both **"The Last Special"** and **"The Man with the Watches"** are railway mysteries, the first of them being particularly ingenious, and both contain references to the theories of "an amateur reasoner of some celebrity" in one story, and "a well-known criminal investigator" in the other. These theories get near to the truth of the puzzle in the stories, although they do not uncover it.

The four Sherlock Holmes novels all have their partisans, particularly *The Hound of the Baskervilles* . . . , but not many people would place them on the same level as the short stories. Conan Doyle's genius was expressed in the short detective tale, not the novel. Both [*A Study in Scarlet* and *The Valley of Fear*] . . . give up detection part of the way through, to deal with life in an American Mormon community and in a miners' settlement. One reason for this was that Conan Doyle liked writing adventure stories, but he had also run out of detective steam. *The Hound* does not err in this way, but we know the villain's identity two-thirds of the way through the book, something that is displeasing to most modern detective story readers. Conan Doyle lacked the skill in spacing out clues and red herrings throughout a novel which became a commonplace of detective stories in the nineteen twenties. The Sherlock Holmes novels were, from the point of view of plotting, enlarged short stories. (pp. 83, 85-6)

It was upon [the historical novels], in particular *The White Company* . . . and *Sir Nigel* . . . that Conan Doyle placed his chief hopes of being remembered as a writer. He thought, as he said later, that they "would live and would illuminate our national traditions". He was disappointed by critics' reaction to *The White Company* even though it was praised, because they treated it "too much as if it were a mere book of adventure . . . whereas I have striven to draw the exact types of character of the folk then living and have spent much work and pains over it, which seems so far to be quite unappreciated by the critics." *Sir Nigel* seemed to him his high-water mark in literature, and again he was disappointed that the novel received no particular critical recognition.

These books, upon which he spent so many pains, are of all his imaginative writings the least congenial to modern taste. We value his "mere tales of adventure" more highly than he did, because they are so well told. The books he took more seriously, on the other hand, seem to most readers now rhetorical and wooden in much of the writing, and to take an idealistic view of the past that we cannot share. *Micah Clarke* . . . is an agreeable although conventional historical novel about Monmouth's rebellion, but in *The White Company* Conan Doyle attempted more and achieved less. The picture of fourteenth century life, with its insistence on patriotism and the importance of team spirit seems to be viewing the Middle Ages in Victorian terms, the author's passionate support of the ruling order in society would be disagreeable if it did not seem a little absurd, and most of the characterization is as stiff as the writing. There are fine scenes in the book, like the account of the siege of Villefranche and the discussion of the importance of the English archers in the campaign, but they are produced by the writer of adventure stories. The idea of a company of knight-errants moved by the mediaeval conception of chivalry even as they fight seems to us today simply to ignore the realities of history. The same criticism applies to the high romanticism of *Sir Nigel,* which shows us characters already met in *The White Company* at an earlier period in their lives. Conan Doyle took great trouble to get right the details

about armour and archery, but the people drawing the bow and inside the suit of armour are not human beings as we know them. (pp. 86, 89)

One or two of the less-regarded historical novels are more interesting, partly because their author tried less hard with them. *Uncle Bernac* . . . has found few admirers, and Conan Doyle himself always felt that there was something wrong with it, but the book has a marvellous opening. Young Louis de Laval, who has escaped to England during the French Revolution, is asked by his Uncle Bernac to return. He does so, ignoring the words "Don't come" written above the letter's seal, and is plunged into a series of misadventures which are brilliantly maintained without complete explanation for a full fifty pages. The book falls away, but the portrayal of Uncle Bernac is a good deal more interesting than anything in the two novels Conan Doyle valued so highly. The picture of Napoleon in the final chapter is done in a distinctly starry-eyed manner, alien from the rest of the book. There were times when Conan Doyle tended to identify heroes with dictators.

Most of the other historical novels need little comment because they are inferior versions of those already discussed. *Rodney Stone* . . . , however, is something different. Conan Doyle's love of sport and games shows comparatively seldom in his writing. He wrote very little about cricket or football, almost nothing about billiards, fishing or golf. But he did write a novel and some good short stories about boxing, and both *Rodney Stone* and the long short story **"The Croxley Master"** display his narrative and descriptive powers at their peak.

Conan Doyle said that he thought nobody but a fighting man could fully appreciate some of the detail in *Rodney Stone,* and the book gives scope to his feelings that the old bare-knuckle fighting of the prize ring was "an excellent thing from a national point of view". Its success depended upon people who like himself loved what he called the chivalry of sport, and he noted that the standards of British boxing had been corrupted during the nineteenth century by "the villainous mobs" who were concerned only with making money by betting. *Rodney Stone* is set in the chivalric time and it views the great fighters of the early nineteenth century, like Gentleman Jackson, Mendoza and Jim Belcher, with the awe-struck eyes of a boy—a boy, however, who knows what he is writing about in a technical sense, and is able to create the visual background of the period with great skill. **"The Croxley Master"** is just as good on a smaller scale. The picture of the Master, who might have been one of the great fighters of his time but for an accident which broke his thigh and left one leg shorter than the other, ungainly as a crab in advance or retreat but able to pivot on his bad leg with extraordinary speed, is brilliantly done. The success of these stories emphasizes again that his mastery as a writer was mostly in rendering the external surface of things, whether it was a boxing match or the investigation of a crime.

This exultant acceptance of physical exertion and struggle is to be found, together with a typical love of extrovert characters, in *The Exploits of Brigadier Gerard* . . . and *The Adventures* that followed. . . . The Brigadier is an officer in Napoleon's army, a swaggering vain braggart who is also brave, imaginative and resourceful. He is based fairly closely on the Baron de Marbot, whose memoirs show him to have been a real life Gerard so far as boastfulness went, and whose dash and skill were acknowledged even by those who most disliked him. Conan Doyle did not think very much of the Gerard stories. They sprang from his absorption for three years in things Napoleonic, an absorption responsible for *Uncle Bernac* and also for what the author deprecatingly called his little book of soldier stories. (pp. 89, 91-3)

[The Gerard stories] have the life and verve that is missing in *The White Company* and *Sir Nigel*. Perhaps it is an exaggeration to say, as one critic does, that he never wrote anything else as good as these tales, but they do show what he could achieve in the way of characterization. Gerard . . . was the kind of character he could perfectly understand. All Gerard's qualities show upon the surface. From his boastfulness and courage, his unquenchable self-satisfaction and its frequent humiliation, his disastrous mistakes and adroit recoveries from them, there is built a comic character who is still not absurd. It would be too much to call Gerard one of the great comic characters of literature, but on his own level he is unmatchable. (p. 93)

Most of the stories are anecdotes . . . , but they are marvellously well told, with a humour and good humour that carries a reader along. Brigadier Gerard is, after Holmes and Watson, Conan Doyle's most successful literary creation. (p. 94)

[Science fiction was a] development that came late in Conan Doyle's writing career, and is represented by three novels [*The Lost World, The Poison Belt* and *The Maracot Deep*] . . . , as well as some short stories. The first, and much the best, of these novels is about a journey to Amazonia, where Professor Challenger claims to have traced some prehistoric animals still living on a great plateau. The irascible Challenger, a figure based on the professor of anatomy at Edinburgh, takes a party of adventurous spirits to look for this lost world. Their adventures are marked by that speculative ingenuity which was one of Conan Doyle's most engaging marks as man and writer, and by an imaginative quality that came into play most fully when he was dealing with scenes outside everyday life. The description of the Amazonian forest obviously owes something to the author's travels, yet it has a kind of spectral quality that removes it from literal reality.

Challenger is also the central figure in *The Poison Belt,* which starts from the not unusual science fiction premise that by some means (in this case the earth moves into a poison belt) human life comes to an end. Challenger gathers together wife and friends in an airtight shelter, and hopes to survive. Most modern stories would be concerned with what happened to them after the extinction of civilised life, but Conan Doyle was too optimistic a man to consider seriously the end of life as we know it. It turns out that the poison belt through which the earth passed has induced unconsciousness, not death. Everybody wakes up, and life goes on as before. It is a feeble, unsatisfying ending. In *The Maracot Deep* the people of Atlantis are discovered by submarine explorers to have survived the flooding of the city. Wireless, television and nuclear energy are introduced into a story containing many inventive effects, unhappily largely dissipated by the introduction of such unlikely creatures as a giant caterpillar armed with a death ray.

The two books that conspicuously fail to fit into any category of Conan Doyle fiction are *The Stark Munro Letters* . . . and *A Duet, with an Occasional Chorus* . . . The first of these is a fairly direct autobiographical narrative, put in the form of sixteen letters from the young doctor of the title to a friend in America. . . . The book is far from a perfect novel, but it is infused throughout with Conan Doyle's energetic temperament and over it all broods the spirit of Dr. Budd, the badhat whose reckless daring fascinated Conan Doyle to the end of his life.

The book is important to anybody interested in understanding the author's character, and so is *A Duet,* a story which shows a flippancy and lightness unique in Conan Doyle's work. . . . The book's lightness of tone is not successful, yet the author was not altogether wrong when he wrote to [his mother]: "My inmost soul tells me that it is not a failure." *A Duet* is a gesture, never repeated, in the direction of a novel of social manners, and as an experiment it is certainly not without interest.

That is the sum of Conan Doyle's activities as a literary man, with the exception of his plays and poems. The published texts of his plays make it clear that he was not a natural dramatist, and the collected poems show that he was a competent maker of verses rather than a poet. Anybody who wants to approach him as a man of letters should read the Sherlock Holmes stories, the major historical novels, the Brigadier Gerard tales, one of the science fiction novels, and a selection of the short stories. Only the scholar will want to go further. Conan Doyle was a skilful writer, with a real gift for narrative, but in the end he was a fine craftsman rather than an artist. (pp. 94, 98, 100)

Julian Symons, in his *Portrait of an Artist: Conan Doyle,* Whizzard Press, 1979, 138 p.

SOURCES FOR FURTHER STUDY

Baring-Gould, William S. *Sherlock Holmes of Baker Street: A Life of the World's First Consulting Detective*. New York: Bramhall House, 1962, 336 p.

Uses implicit and explicit material from the Holmes stories and novels to compose a plausible life of the fictional detective. Baring-Gould includes bibliographies of the Holmes fiction, of Sherlockian scholarship, and of writings attributed to Holmes.

——, ed. *The Annotated Sherlock Holmes*. 2 vols. New York: Clarkson N. Potter, 1967.

Profusely illustrated and extensively annotated edition of the Holmes stories and novels. An introductory section includes essays on Doyle's life, the characters and possible inspirations for Holmes and Watson, notable illustrators of the stories, stage and screen adaptations of the adventures, and other aspects of the stories and their settings.

Carr, John Dickson. *The Life of Sir Arthur Conan Doyle*. New York: Harper & Brothers, 1949, 304 p.

Thorough biography.

Pearsall, Ronald. *Conan Doyle: A Biographical Solution*. London: Weidenfeld and Nicholson, 1977, 208 p.

Biographical and critical study focusing on the Holmes adventures.

Pearson, Hesketh. *Conan Doyle: His Life and Art*. London: Methuen & Co., 1943, 193 p.

Excellent critical biography.

Van Doren, Mark, and others. "A. Conan Doyle: 'The Adventures of Sherlock Holmes'." In *The New Invitation to Learning,* edited by Mark Van Doren, pp. 236-51. New York: Random House, 1942.

Lively round-table discussion of various aspects of the Holmes stories and novels, with Van Doren, Rex Stout, Jacques Barzun, and Elmer Davis.

Theodore Dreiser

1871-1945

(Full name Theodore Herman Albert Dreiser) American novelist, essayist, autobiographer, journalist, short story writer, dramatist, and poet.

INTRODUCTION

*A*s one of the principal American exponents of literary Naturalism at the turn of the century, Dreiser led the way for a generation of writers seeking to present a detailed and realistic portrait of American life. In such novels as *Sister Carrie* (1900) and *An American Tragedy* (1925), he departed from traditional plots in which hard work and perseverance inevitably yield success and happiness, instead portraying the world as an arena of largely random occurrences. His works have often been criticized for their awkward prose style, inadequately conveyed philosophy, and excessive length and detail. Nevertheless, Dreiser retains critical regard for presenting powerful characterizations and strong ideological convictions in novels that are considered among the most notable achievements of twentieth-century literature.

Dreiser was born in Terre Haute, Indiana, the twelfth of thirteen children. His father, a German immigrant, had been a successful businessman, but a series of reversals left the family in poverty by the time of Dreiser's birth, and the family's members were often separated while they sought work in different cities. While Dreiser did not excel as a student, he received encouragement from a high school teacher who paid his tuition when he entered the University of Indiana in 1889. Dreiser was acutely self-conscious about differences between himself and wealthier, better-looking classmates, and he attended the university for only one year. On leaving, he worked at a variety of jobs, including a part-time position in the offices of the Chicago *Herald* which kindled in him an interest in journalism, and in April 1891 he obtained a post with the Chicago *Globe*. After several years as a reporter in Chicago, Dreiser pursued a career as a newspaper and magazine writer in St. Louis, Pittsburgh, and New York. Commentators maintain that his years as a journalist were instrumental in developing the exhaustively detailed literary style that is the hallmark of his fiction.

In New York, Dreiser supported himself—and, after 1898, his wife—with free-lance magazine writing and editing, while working on the manuscript of *Sister Carrie*. Published in 1900, the novel was not promoted by the publisher, and it sold poorly. Marital difficulties and failing health further contributed to Dreiser's suffering from severe depression. After not working for several years, he was aided by an older brother, who had become a successful music hall performer and songwriter under the name Paul Dresser. Dresser arranged for his brother to recuperate at a health resort and then helped him find work. Dreiser later credited several years of light manual labor with restoring his mental as well as physical health. In 1905 he resumed free-lance magazine writing and editing, and over the next two years rose to the editorship of three prominent women's magazines. He lost this position in 1907 because of a scandal involving his romantic pursuit of a coworker's teenage daughter; that same year *Sister Carrie,* which had been received favorably in England, was reissued to positive reviews and good sales in the United States. Over the next eighteen years Dreiser published a succession of novels to widely varied but rarely indifferent critical notice; the publication of *An American Tragedy* in 1925 established him as the country's foremost living novelist. Dreiser subsequently became involved in social and political affairs. He went to Russia in 1927 to observe the results of the revolution, publishing his findings in *Dreiser Looks at Russia* (1928), and he joined investigations of labor conditions in Kentucky coal mines in 1931. At the time of his death in 1945 Dreiser was better known as a social and political activist than as a novelist.

Sister Carrie departed sharply from the gentility and timidity that characterized much realistic fiction during the nineteenth century. Dreiser uncompromisingly detailed the events that led his protagonist first into prostitution and then, as if pointedly avoiding a moral, to the attainment of success and financial security as an actress. The novel illustrates Dreiser's interpretation of complex human relationships as purely biological functions: Carrie exhibits what has been called "neo-Darwinian adaptability," surviving and prospering because she is able to adjust with equanimity to whatever advantageous situations develop. The deterioration and death of Carrie's second lover, Hurstwood, is generally agreed to be one of the most powerful and moving portraits of human defeat ever written. Critics of *Sister Carrie* have noted an apparent contradiction, which many find persists throughout Dreiser's works, between his professed determinism and his sentimentalism: although he portrayed their unhappy fates as inevitable, Dreiser evoked considerable sympathy for his defeated characters.

Dreiser's next novel was *The Financier* (1912), the first in the Cowperwood trilogy, or Trilogy of Desire, detailing the life and career of businessman Frank Algernon Cowperwood. Both *The Financier* and *The Titan* (1914), the second volume of the trilogy, utilize imagery based on Darwinian evolutionary theory, and offer somewhat didactic presentations of Dreiser's deterministic philosophy. In these novels Dreiser outlines his "chemicomechanistic" concept of life as little more than a series of "chemisms," or chemical reactions. Cowperwood's rise, fall, and second triumph in the world of high finance are recounted with journalistic attention to detail that some commentators contend becomes a too extensive listing of discrete facts. The third volume of the trilogy, *The Stoic* (1947), is considered vastly inferior to its predecessors. It concludes with the death of Cowperwood and the dispersal of his fortune, ending on an incongruous note of Eastern mysticism, which was a concern of Dreiser's second wife.

Dreiser's fifth novel, *The "Genius"* (1915), was controversial for its portrayal of the artist as a Nietzschean superman who is beyond conventional moral codes. Commentators maintain that this semiautobiographical work is Dreiser's thinly veiled self-justification of his own behavior, and view some unflatteringly portrayed characters as Dreiser's revenge upon those who, he believed, had mistreated or misunderstood him. Sales of *The "Genius"* were initially good and early reviews largely favorable; however, in the year following its publication *The "Genius"* came to the attention of the New York Society for the Suppression of Vice, which labeled the book immoral and sought to block its distribution. H. L. Mencken, who disapproved of the book on artistic grounds, nevertheless circulated a protest against the suppression of *The "Genius"* or any literary work. The protest was signed by hundreds of prominent American and British authors, including Robert Frost, Sinclair Lewis, Ezra Pound, and H. G. Wells. Although *The "Genius"* is considered one of Dreiser's weakest novels, Charles Shapiro has noted that it "achieved historical importance as a result of the famed fight over its suppression, a struggle that ranks with the *Ulysses* case as a pivotal victory in the fight for American literary freedom."

An American Tragedy, published in 1925, is considered Dreiser's most important work. Although critics deplored Dreiser's stylistic and grammatical flaws— what Mencken labeled his lack "of what may be called literary tact"—they considered *An American Tragedy* a powerful indictment of the gulf between American ideals of wealth and influence, and the opportunities available for their realization. The entire American system is blamed for the destruction of Clyde Griffiths, a weak-willed individual who aspires to the American dream of success. The journalistic style of Dreiser's prose, frequently assessed as a weakness of his earlier works, was found by many critics to benefit *An American Tragedy.* Grant C. Knight, for example, wrote that while it "is true that Mr. Dreiser is always at pains to spread out every fact that sometimes he even transgresses relevance, . . . in the instance of *An American Tragedy . . .* nothing short of full documentation would have been convincing."

In his final novel, *The Bulwark* (1946), Dreiser seemingly repudiated both Naturalism and the pessimistic determinism that informs his earlier novels. In *The Bulwark* the moral scruples of a Quaker businessman, Solon Barnes, conflict with the reality of American business dealings. In a reversal for Dreiser, Barnes, who upholds traditional mores and values, is portrayed sympathetically.

Dreiser published four autobiographical works, *A Traveler at Forty* (1913), *A Hoosier Holiday* (1916), *A Book about Myself* (1922), and *Dawn* (1931), as well as volumes of poetry, short stories, sketches, and essays, many of the latter pertaining to his social and political activism. Attention to this aspect of Dreiser's life exceeded the critical attention given his literary works during the 1930s and 1940s. At the time of his death he had not published a novel in twenty years, and his career as a novelist was considered to have ended with *An American Tragedy.* Reevaluation of Dreiser's literary reputation began with the posthumous publication of *The Bulwark* and *The Stoic* in 1946 and 1947. Widely varied critical opinions still stand regarding the merit of Dreiser's individual novels, with the exception of *An American Tragedy,* which is assessed as a masterpiece of American literature. Many commentators contend that Dreiser's chief importance is one of influence. His sprawling, flawed, but powerful novels helped to establish the conventions of modern Naturalism. Jack Salzman has noted that Dreiser's "significance in the history of American letters is no longer a matter for dispute. We may continue to debate his merits as an artist, but his importance to American literature has been well established."

(For further information about Dreiser's life and works, see *Contemporary Authors,* Vol. 106; *Dictionary of Literary Biography,* Vols. 9, 12; *Dictionary of Literary BiographyDocumentary Series,* Vol. 1; *Concise Dictionary of American Literary Biography,* 1865-1917; and *Twentieth-Century Literary Criticism,* Vols. 10, 18, 35.)

CRITICAL COMMENTARY

STUART P. SHERMAN
(essay date 1915)

[Sherman wrote one of the best-known attacks on Dreiser and his work, the 1915 essay "The Barbaric Naturalism of Mr. Dreiser." Here, in an excerpt from this study, he identifies Dreiser as "a novelist of the new school." For a response to this essay, see the excerpt below by H. L. Mencken.]

The layman who listens reverently to the reviewers discussing the new novels and to the novelists discussing themselves can hardly escape persuasion that a great change has rather recently taken place in the spirit of the age, in the literature which reflects it, and in the criticism which judges it. (p. 85)

The present age is fearless and is freeing itself from illusions. Now, for the first time in history, men are facing unabashed the facts of life. . . . Rejecting nothing, altering nothing, it presents to us—let us take our terms from the bright lexicon of the reviewer—a "transcript," a "cross-section," a "slice," a "photographic" or "cinematographic" reproduction of life. The critic who keeps pace with the movement no longer asks whether the artist has created beauty or glorified goodness, but merely whether he has told the truth.

Mr. Dreiser, in his latest novel [*The Genius*], describes a canvas by a painter of this austere modern school: "Raw reds, raw greens, dirty gray paving stones—such faces! Why, this thing fairly shouted its facts. It seemed to say: 'I'm dirty, I am commonplace, I am grim, I am shabby, but I am life.' And there was no apologizing for anything in it, no glossing anything over. Bang! Smash! Crack! came the facts one after another, with a bitter, brutal insistence on their so-ness." If you do not like what is in the picture, you are to be crushed by the retort that perhaps you do not like what is in life. Perhaps you have not the courage to confront reality. Perhaps you had better read the chromatic fairy-tales with the children. Men of sterner stuff exclaim, like the critic in this novel, "Thank God for a realist!"

Mr. Dreiser is a novelist of the new school, for whom we have been invited off and on these fourteen years to thank God—a form of speech, by the way, which crept into the language before the dawn of modern realism. He has performed with words what his

---

Principal Works

Sister Carrie (novel) 1900

Jennie Gerhardt (novel) 1911

*The Financier (novel) 1912; revised edition, 1927

A Traveler at Forty (autobiography) 1913

*The Titan (novel) 1914

The "Genius" (novel) 1915

A Hoosier Holiday (autobiography) 1916

Plays of the Natural and the Supernatural [first publication] (dramas) 1916

Free, and Other Stories (short stories) 1918

Twelve Men (sketches) 1919

Hey Rub-A-Dub-Dub: A Book of the Mystery and Wonder and Terror of Life (essays) 1920

A Book about Myself (autobiography) 1922; also published as Newspaper Days, 1931

The Color of a Great City (essays) 1923

An American Tragedy (novel) 1925

Moods, Cadenced and Declaimed (poetry) 1926; enlarged edition, 1928; also published as Moods, Philosophic and Emotional, Cadenced and Declaimed [revised edition], 1935

Chains (short stories and novellas) 1927

Dreiser Looks at Russia (essays) 1928

The Aspirant (poetry) 1929

A Gallery of Women. 2 vols. (sketches) 1929

Dawn (autobiography) 1931

Tragic America (essays) 1931

America Is Worth Saving (essays) 1941

The Bulwark (novel) 1946

The Best Short Stories of Theodore Dreiser (short stories) 1947

*The Stoic (novel) 1947

Letters of Theodore Dreiser. 3 vols. (letters) 1959

Theodore Dreiser: A Selection of Uncollected Prose (essays and journalism) 1977

American Diaries, 1902-1926 (diaries) 1982

†An Amateur Laborer (autobiography) 1983

Journalism, Volume One: Newspaper Writings, 1892-1895 (journalism) 1988

*These works are collectively referred to as the Cowperwood trilogy or the Trilogy of Desire.

†This work was written in 1903.

---

hero performed with paint. He has presented the facts of life "one after another with a bitter, brutal insistence on their so-ness," which marks him as a "man of the hour," a "portent"—the successor of Mr. Howells and Mr. James. . . . He has laid reality bare for us in five novels published as follows: [*Sister Carrie, Jennie Gerhardt, The Financier, The Titan,* and *The Genius*]. . . . These five works constitute a singularly homogeneous mass of fiction. I do not find any moral value in them, nor any memorable beauty—of their truth I shall speak later; but I am greatly impressed by them as serious representatives of a new note in American literature, coming from that "ethnic" element of our mixed population which, as we are assured by competent authorities, is to redeem us from Puritanism and insure our artistic salvation. They abundantly illustrate, furthermore, the methods and intentions of our recent courageous, veracious realism. Before we thank God for it, let us consider a little more closely what is offered us.

The first step towards the definition of Mr. Dreiser's special contribution is to blow away the dust with which the exponents of the new realism seek to becloud the perceptions of our "reverent layman." In their main pretensions, there are large elements of conscious and unconscious sham.

It should clear the air to say that courage in facing and veracity in reporting the facts of life are no more characteristic of Theodore Dreiser than of John Bunyan. These moral traits are not the peculiar marks of the new school; they are marks common to every great movement of literature within the memory of man. Each literary generation detaching itself from its predecessor—whether it has called its own movement Classical or Romantic or what not—has revolted in the interest of what it took to be a more adequate representation of reality. No one who is not drunken with the egotism of the hour, no one who has penetrated with sober senses into the spirit of any historical period anterior to his own, will fall into the indecency of declaring his own age preëminent in the desire to see and to tell the truth. The real distinction between one generation and another is in the thing which each takes for its master truth—in the thing which each recognizes as the essential reality for it. The difference between Bunyan and Dreiser is in the order of facts which each reports. (pp. 85-8)

Let us, then, dismiss Mr. Dreiser's untenable claims to superior courage and veracity of intention, the photographic transcript, and the unbiassed service of truth; and let us seek for his definition in his general theory of life, in the order of facts which he records, and in the pattern of his representations.

The impressive unity of effect produced by Mr. Dreiser's five novels is due to the fact that they are all illustrations of a crude and naïvely simple naturalistic philosophy, such as we find in the mouths of exponents of the new *Real-Politik.* Each book, with its bewildering masses of detail, is a ferocious argument in behalf of a few brutal generalizations. To the eye cleared of illusions it appears that the ordered life which we call civilization does not really exist except on paper. In reality our so-called society is a jungle in which the struggle for existence continues, and must continue, on terms substantially unaltered by legal, moral, or social conventions. (p. 91)

The idea that civilization is a sham Mr. Dreiser sometimes sets forth explicitly, and sometimes he conveys it by the process known among journalists as "coloring the news." . . . Righteousness is always "legal"; conventions are always "current"; routine is always "dull"; respectability is always "unctuous"; an institution for transforming schoolgirls into young ladies is presided over by "owl-like conventionalists"; families in which parents are faithful to each other lead an "apple-pie order of existence"; a man who yields to his impulses yet condemns himself for yielding is a "rag-bag moralistic ass." Jennie Gerhardt, by a facile surrender of her chastity, shows that *"she could not be readily corrupted by the world's selfish lessons* on how to preserve oneself from the evil to come." Surely, this is "coloring the news."

By similar devices Mr. Dreiser drives home the great truth that man is essentially an animal, impelled by temperament, instinct, physics, chemistry—anything you please that is irrational and uncontrollable. Sometimes he writes an "editorial" paragraph in which the laws of human life are explained by reference to the behavior of certain protozoa or by reference to a squid and a lobster fighting in an aquarium. His heroes and heroines have "cat-like eyes," "feline grace," "sinuous strides," eyes and jaws which vary "from those of the tiger, lynx, and bear to those of the fox, the tolerant mastiff, and the surly bulldog." One hero and his mistress are said to "have run together temperamentally like two leopards." The lady in question, admiring the large rapacity of her mate, exclaims playfully: "Oh, you big tiger! You great, big lion! Boo!" Courtship as presented in these novels is after the manner of beasts in the jungle. Mr. Dreiser's leonine men but circle once or twice about their prey, and spring, and pounce; and the struggle is over. A pure-minded servingmaid, who is suddenly held up in the hall by a "hairy, axiomatic" guest and "masterfully" kissed upon the lips, may for an instant be "horrified, stunned, *like a bird in the grasp of a cat.*" But we are always assured that "through it all something tremendously vital and insistent" will be speaking to her, and that in the end she will not resist the urge of the *élan vital.* I recall no one of all the dozens of obliging women in these books who makes any effective resistance when summoned to capitulate. "The *psychology of the human animal,* when confronted by these tangles, these ripping tides of the

heart," says the author of ***The Titan,*** "has little to do with so-called reason or logic." No; as he informs us elsewhere with endless iteration, it is a question of chemistry. It is the "chemistry of her being" which rouses to blazing the ordinarily dormant forces of Eugene Witla's sympathies in ***The Genius.*** If Stephanie Platow is disloyal to her married lover in ***The Titan,*** "let no one quarrel" with her. Reason: "She was an unstable chemical compound."

Such is the Dreiserian philosophy.

By thus eliminating distinctively human motives and making animal instincts the supreme factors in human life, Mr. Dreiser reduces the problem of the novelist to the lowest possible terms. I find myself unable to go with those who admire the powerful reality of his art while deploring the puerility of his philosophy. His philosophy quite excludes him from the field in which a great realist must work. He has deliberately rejected the novelist's supreme task—understanding and presenting the development of character; he has chosen only to illustrate the unrestricted flow of temperament. He has evaded the enterprise of representing human conduct; he has confined himself to a representation of animal behavior. He demands for the demonstration of his theory a moral vacuum from which the obligations of parenthood, marriage, chivalry, and citizenship have been quite withdrawn or locked in a twilight sleep. At each critical moment in his narrative, where a realist like George Eliot or Thackeray or Trollope or Meredith would be asking how a given individual would feel, think, and act under the manifold combined stresses of organized society, Mr. Dreiser sinks supinely back upon the law of the jungle or mutters his mystical gibberish about an alteration of the chemical formula.

The possibility of making the unvarying victoriousness of jungle-motive plausible depends directly upon the suppression of the evidence of other motives. In this work of suppression Mr. Dreiser simplifies American life almost beyond recognition. Whether it is because he comes from Indiana, or whether it is because he steadily envisages the human animal, I cannot say; I can only note that he never speaks of his men and women as "educated" or "brought up." Whatever their social status, they are invariably "raised." Raising human stock in America evidently includes feeding and clothing it, but does not include the inculcation of even the most elementary moral ideas. Hence Mr. Dreiser's field seems curiously outside American society. Yet he repeatedly informs us that his persons are typical of the American middle class, and three of the leading figures, to judge from their names—Carrie Meeber, Jennie Gerhardt, and Eugene Witla—are of our most highly "cultured" race. Frank Cowperwood, the hero of two novels, is a hawk of finance and a rake almost from the cradle; but of the powers which presided over his cradle we know nothing save that his father was a competent official in a Philadelphia bank. . . . Jennie Gerhardt, of course, succumbs to the first man who puts his arm around her; but, in certain respects, her case is exceptional.

In the novel *Jennie Gerhardt* Mr. Dreiser ventures a disastrous experiment at making the jungle-motive plausible without suppressing the evidence of other motives. He provides the girl with pious Lutheran parents, of fallen fortune, but alleged to be of sterling character, who "raise" her with the utmost strictness. . . . "Gerhardt and his wife, and also Jennie," says Mr. Dreiser, "accepted the doctrines of their church without reserve." Twenty pages later Jennie is represented as yielding her virtue in pure gratitude to a man of fifty, Senator Brander, who has let her do his laundry and in other ways has been kind to her and to her family. The Senator suddenly dies; Jennie expects to become a mother; Father Gerhardt is brokenhearted, and the family moves from Columbus to Cleveland. This first episode is not incredibly presented as a momentary triumph of emotional impulse over training—as an "accident." The incredible appears when Mr. Dreiser insists that an accident of this sort to a girl brought up *under the conditions stated* is not necessarily followed by any sense of sin or shame or regret. Upon this simple pious Lutheran he imposes his own naturalistic philosophy, and, in analyzing her psychology before the birth of her illegitimate child, pretends that she looks forward to the event "without a murmur," with "serene, unfaltering courage," "the marvel of life holding her in trance," with "joy and satisfaction," seeing in her state "the immense possibilities of racial fulfilment." This juggling is probably expected to prepare us for her instantaneous assent, perhaps a year later, when a healthy, magnetic manufacturer, who has seen her perhaps a dozen times, claps his paw upon her and says, "You belong to me," and in a perfectly cold-blooded interview proposes the terms on which he will set her up in New York as his mistress. Jennie, who is a fond mother and a dutiful daughter, goes to her pious Lutheran mother and talks the whole matter over with her quite candidly. The mother hesitates—not on Jennie's account, gentle reader, but because she will be obliged to deceive old Gerhardt; "the difficulty of telling this lie was very great for Mrs. Gerhardt"! But she acquiesces at last. "I'll help you out with it," she concludes—"with a little sigh." The unreality of the whole transaction shrieks.

Mr. Dreiser's stubborn insistence upon the jungle-motive results in a dreary monotony in the form and substance of his novels. Interested only in the description of animal behavior, he constructs his plot in such a way as to exhibit the persistence of two or three elementary instincts through every kind of situation. He finds, for example, a subject in the career of an American captain of industry, thinly disguised under the name of Frank Cowperwood. He has just two things to tell us about Cowperwood: that he has a rapacious appetite for money, and that he has a rapacious appetite for women. In *The Financier* he "documents" those two truths about Cowperwood in seventy-four chapters, in each one of which he shows us how his hero made money or how he captivated women in Philadelphia. Not satisfied with the demonstration, he returns to the same theses in *The Titan,* and shows us in sixty-two chapters how the same hero made money and captivated women in Chicago and New York. He promises us a third volume, in which we shall no doubt learn in a work of sixty or seventy chapters—a sort of huge club-sandwich composed of slices of business alternating with erotic episodes—how Frank Cowperwood made money and captivated women in London. Meanwhile Mr. Dreiser has turned aside from his great "trilogy of desire" to give us *The Genius,* in which the hero, Witla, alleged to be a great realistic painter, exhibits in 101 chapters, similarly "sandwiched" together, an appetite for women and money indistinguishable from that of Cowperwood. (pp. 92-9)

If at this point you stop and inquire why Mr. Dreiser goes to such great lengths to establish so little, you find yourself once more confronting the jungle-motive. Mr. Dreiser, with a problem similar to De Foe's in "The Apparition of Mrs. Veal," has availed himself of De Foe's method for creating the illusion of reality. The essence of the problem and of the method for both these authors is the certification of the unreal by the irrelevant. If you wish to make acceptable to your reader the incredible notion that Mrs. Veal's ghost appeared to Mrs. Bargrave, divert his incredulity from the precise point at issue by telling him all sorts of detailed credible things about the poverty of Mrs. Veal's early life, the sobriety of her brother, her father's neglect, and the bad temper of Mrs. Bargrave's husband. If you wish to make acceptable to your reader the incredible notion that Aileen Butler's first breach of the seventh article in the decalogue was "a happy event," taking place "much as a marriage might have," divert his incredulity by describing with the technical accuracy of a fashion magazine not merely the gown that she wore on the night of Cowperwood's reception, but also with equal detail the half-dozen other gowns that she thought she might wear, but did not. If you have been for three years editor-in-chief of the Butterick Publications, you can probably perform this feat with unimpeachable verisimilitude; and having acquired credit for expert knowledge in matters of dress and millinery, you can now and then emit unchallenged a bit of philosophy such as "Life cannot be put in any one mould, and the attempt may as well be abandoned at once. . . . Besides, whether we will or no, theory or no theory, the large basic facts of chemistry and physics remain."

None the less, if you expect to gain credence for the notion that your hero can have any woman in Chicago or New York that he puts his paw upon, you had probably better lead up to it by a detailed account of the street-railway system in those cities. It will necessitate the loading of your pages with a tremendous baggage of irrelevant detail. It will not sound much like art. It will sound more like one of Lincoln Steffens's special articles. But it will produce an overwhelming impression of reality, which the reader will carry with him into the next chapter where you are laying bare the "chemistry" of the human animal.

It would make for clearness in our discussions of contemporary fiction if we withheld the title of "realist" from a writer like Mr. Dreiser, and called him, as Zola called himself, a "naturalist." While asserting that all great art in every period intends a representation of reality, I have tried to indicate the basis for a working distinction between the realistic novel and the naturalistic novel of the present day. Both are representations of the life of man in contemporary or nearly contemporary society, and both are presumably composed of materials within the experience and observation of the author. But a realistic novel is a representation based upon a theory of human conduct. If the theory of human conduct is adequate, the representation constitutes an addition to literature and to social history. A naturalistic novel is a representation based upon a theory of animal behavior. Since a theory of animal behavior can never be an adequate basis for a representation of the life of man in contemporary society, such a representation is an artistic blunder. When half the world attempts to assert such a theory, the other half rises in battle. And so one turns with relief from Mr. Dreiser's novels to the morning papers. (pp. 99-101)

Stuart P. Sherman, "The Barbaric Naturalism of Theodore Dreiser," in his *On Contemporary Literature,* Holt, Rinehart and Winston, 1917, pp. 85-101.

H. L. MENCKEN

(essay date 1917)

[One of the most influential social and literary critics in the United States during the early twentieth century, Mencken was a persistent defender of Dreiser's fiction. He and Stuart P. Sherman (see excerpt above dated 1915) were bitter enemies in print; each held critical theories that were totally antagonistic to those of the other. Below, in an excerpt from an article that appeared in *The Seven Arts* in 1917, Mencken defends Dreiser against Sherman's earlier attack.]

[What] is Sherman's complaint? In brief, that Dreiser is a liar when he calls himself a realist; that he is actually a naturalist, and hence accursed. That "he has evaded the enterprise of representing human conduct, and confined himself to a representation of animal behavior." That he "imposes his own naturalistic philosophy" upon his characters, making them do what they ought not to do, and think what they ought not to think. That he "has just two things to tell us about Frank Cowperwood: that he has a rapacious appetite for money, and a rapacious appetite for women." That this alleged "theory of animal behavior" is not only incorrect, but immoral, and that "when one half the world attempts to assert it, the other half rises in battle" [see excerpt above]. . . . (pp. 74-5)

Only a glance is needed to show the vacuity of all this irate flubdub. Dreiser, in point of fact, is scarcely more the realist or the naturalist, in any true sense, than H. G. Wells or the later George Moore, nor has he ever announced himself in either the one character or the other—if there be, in fact, any difference between them that anyone save a pigeon-holing pedagogue can discern. He is really something quite different, and, in his moments, something far more stately. His aim is not merely to record, but to translate and understand; the thing he exposes is not the empty event and act, but the endless mystery out of which it springs; his pictures have a passionate compassion in them that it is hard to separate from poetry. If this sense of the universal and inexplicable tragedy, if this vision of life as a seeking without a finding, if this adept summoning up of moving images, is mistaken by college professors for the empty, meticulous nastiness of Zola in "Pot-Bouille"—in Nietzsche's phrase, for "the delight to stink"—then surely the folly of college professors, as vast as it seems, has been underestimated. What is the fact? The fact is that Dreiser's attitude of mind, his manner of reaction to the phenomena he represents, the whole of his alleged "naturalistic philosophy," stem directly, not from Zola, Flaubert, Augier and the younger Dumas, but from the Greeks. In the midst of democratic cocksureness and Christian sentimentalism, of doctrinaire shallowness and professorial smugness, he stands for a point of view which at least has something honest and courageous about it; here, at all events, he is a realist. (p. 75)

As for the animal behavior prattle of the learned headmaster, it reveals on the one hand only the academic fondness for seizing upon high-sounding but empty phrases and using them to alarm the populace, and on the other hand, only the academic incapacity for observing facts correctly and reporting them honestly. The truth is, of course, that the behavior of such men as Cowperwood and Eugene Witla and of such women as Carrie Meeber and Jennie Gerhardt, as Dreiser describes it, is no more merely animal than the behavior of such acknowledged and undoubted human beings as Dr. Woodrow Wilson and Dr. Jane Addams. The whole point of the story of Witla, to take the example which seems to concern the horrified watchmen most, is this: that this life is a bitter conflict between the animal in him and the aspiring soul, between the flesh and the spirit, between what is weak in him and what is strong, between what is base and what is noble. Moreover, the good, in the end, gets its hooks into the bad: as we part from Witla he is actually bathed in the tears of remorse, and resolved to be a correct and godfearing man. And what have we in *The Financier* and *The Titan*? A conflict, in the ego of Cowperwood, between aspiration and ambition, between the passion for beauty and the passion for power. Is either passion animal? To ask the question is to answer it.

I single out Dr. Sherman, not because his pompous syllogisms have any plausibility in fact or logic, but simply because he may well stand as archetype of the booming, indignant corrupter of criteria, the moralist turned critic. . . . What offends him is not actually Dreiser's shortcomings as an artist, but Dreiser's shortcomings as a Christian and an American. (pp. 75-6)

The Comstockian attack upon *The 'Genius'* seems to have sprung out of the same muddled sense of Dreiser's essential hostility to all that is safe and regular—of the danger in him to that mellowed Methodism which has become the national ethic. The book, in a way, was a direct challenge, for though it came to an end upon a note which even a Methodist might hear as sweet, there were provocations in detail. Dreiser, in fact, allowed his scorn to make off with his taste. . . . The Comstocks arose to the bait a bit slowly, but none the less surely. Going through the volume with the terrible industry of a Sunday-school boy dredging up pearls of smut from the Old Testament, they achieved a list of no less than 89 alledged floutings of the code—75 described as lewd and 14 as profane. An inspection of these specifications affords mirth of a rare and lofty variety; nothing could more cruelly expose the inner chambers of the moral mind. When young Witla, fastening his best girl's skate, is so overcome by the carnality of youth that he hugs her, it is set down as lewd. . . . Every kiss, hug and tickle of the chin in the chronicle is laboriously snouted out, empanelled, exhibited. Every hint that Witla is no vestal, that he indulges his unchristian fleshliness, that he burns in the manner of I Corinthians, VII, 9, is uncovered to the moral inquisition.

On the side of profanity there is a less ardent pursuit of evidence, chiefly, I daresay, because their unearthing is less stimulating. (Besides, there is no law prohibiting profanity in books: the whole inquiry here is but so much *lagniappe*.) On page 408, describing a character called Daniel C. Summerfield, Dreiser says that the fellow is "very much given to swearing, more

as a matter of habit than of foul intention," and then goes on to explain somewhat lamely that "no picture of him would be complete without the interpolation of his various expressions." They turn out to be *God Damn* and *Jesus Christ*—three of the latter and five or six of the former. All go down; the pure in heart must be shielded from the knowledge of them. . . . Also, three plain *damns*, eight *hells*, one *my God*, five *by Gods*, one *go to the devil*, one *God Almighty* and one plain *God*. Altogether, 31 specimens are listed. *The 'Genius'* runs to 350,000 words. The profanity thus works out to somewhat less than one word in 10,000. . . . Alas, the Comstockian proboscis, feeling for such offendings, is not as alert as when uncovering more savoury delicacies. On page 191 I find an overlooked *by God*. . . . On page 720 there is *as God is my judge*. On page 723 there is *I'm no damned good*. . . . But I begin to blush. (pp. 76-8)

[Dreiser] is an American like the rest of us, and to be an American is to be burdened by an ethical prepossession, to lean toward causes and remedies. Go through *The 'Genius'* or *A Hoosier Holiday* carefully, and you will find disqueting indications of what might be called a democratic trend in thinking—that is, a trend toward short cuts, easy answers, glittering theories. He is bemused, off and on, by all the various poppycock of the age, from Christian Science to spiritism, and from the latest guesses in eschatology and epistemology to *art pour l'art*. A true American, he lacks a solid culture, and so he yields a bit to every wind that blows, to the inevitable damage of his representation of the eternal mystery that is man. (pp. 78-9)

Struggle as he may to rid himself of the current superstitions, he can never quite achieve deliverance from the believing attitude of mind—the heritage of the Indiana hinterland. One half of the man's brain, so to speak, wars with the other half. He is intelligent, he is thoughtful, he is a sound artist—but always there come moments when a dead hand falls upon him, and he is once more the Indiana peasant, snuffing absurdly over imbecile sentimentalities; giving a grave ear to quackeries, snorting and eye-rolling with the best of them. One generation spans too short a time to free the soul of man. (p. 79)

[Dreiser] is still, for all his achievement, in the transition stage between Christian Endeavor and civilization; between Warsaw, Indiana, and the Socratic grove; between being a good American and being a free man; and so he sometimes vacillates perilously between a moral sentimentalism and a somewhat extravagant revolt. *The 'Genius,'* on the one hand, is almost a tract for rectitude, a Warning to the Young; its motto might be *Scheut die Dirnen!* And on the other hand, it is full of a laborious truculence that can be explained only by imagining the author as heroically determined to prove that he is a plain-spoken fellow and his own man, let the chips fall where they may. So, in spots, in *The Fi-*

nancier and *The Titan,* both of them far better books. There is an almost moral frenzy to expose and riddle what passes for morality among the stupid. The isolation of irony is never reached; the man is still a bit evangelical; his ideas are still novelties to him; he is as solemnly absurd in some of his floutings of the code American as he is in his respect for Bouguereau, or in his flirtings with New Thought, or in his naive belief in the importance of novel-writing. . . .

But his books remain, particularly his earlier books—and not all the ranting of the outraged orthodox will ever wipe them out. They were done in the stage of wonder, before self-consciousness began to creep in and corrupt it. The view of life that got into *Sister Carrie,* the first of them, was not the product of a deliberate thinking out of Carrie's problem. It simply got itself there by the force of the artistic passion behind it; its coherent statement had to wait for other and more reflective days. This complete rejection of ethical plan and purpose, this manifestation of what Nietzsche used to call moral innocence, is what brought up the guardians of the national tradition at the gallop, and created the Dreiser bugaboo of today. All the rubber-stamp formulae of American fiction were thrown overboard in these earlier books; instead of reducing the inexplicable to the obvious, they lifted the obvious to the inexplicable; one could find in them no orderly chain of causes and effects, of rewards and punishments; they represented life as a phenomenon at once terrible and unintelligible, like a stroke of lightning. The prevailing criticism applied the moral litmus. They were not "good"; *ergo,* they were "evil."

The peril that Dreiser stands in is here. He may begin to act, if he is not careful, according to the costume forced on him. Unable to combat the orthodox valuation of his place and aim, he may seek a spiritual refuge in embracing it, and so arrange himself with the tripe-sellers of heterodoxy, and cry wares that differ from the other stock only in the bald fact that they are different. . . . Such a fall would grieve the judicious, of whom I have the honor to be one. (pp. 79-80)

H. L. Mencken, "The Dreiser Bugaboo," in *Dreiser: A Collection of Critical Essays,* edited by John Lydenberg, Prentice-Hall, Inc., 1971, pp. 73-80.

ALFRED KAZIN

(essay date 1955)

[A highly respected American literary critic, Kazin is best known for his essay collections *The Inmost Leaf* (1955), *Contemporaries* (1962), and *On Native Grounds* (1942). In the following introduction to the 1955 essay collection *The Stature of Theodore Dreiser: A Critical Survey of the Man and His Work,* edited by Kazin and Charles Shapiro, he discusses Dreiser's critical reception. In his introduction, Kazin refers to several of the essays included in the collection.]

At a time when the one quality which so many American writers have in common is their utter harmlessness, Dreiser makes painful reading. The others you can take up without being involved in the least. They are "literature"—beautiful, stylish literature. You are left free to think not of the book you are reading but of the author, and not even of the whole man behind the author, but just of his cleverness, his sensibility, his style. Dreiser gets under your skin and you can't wait to get him out again: he stupefies with reality:

Carrie looked about her, very much disturbed and quite sure that she did not want to work here. Aside from making her uncomfortable by sidelong glances, no one paid her the least attention. She waited until the whole department was aware of her presence. Then some word was sent around, and a foreman, in an apron and shirt sleeves, the latter rolled up to his shoulders, approached.

"Do you want to see me?" he asked.

"Do you need any help?" said Carrie, already learning directness of address.

"Do you know how to stitch caps?" he returned.

"No, sir," she replied.

"Have you had any experience at this kind of work?" he inquired.

She answered that she had not.

"Well," said the foreman, scratching his ear meditatively, "we do need a stitcher. We like experienced help, though. We've hardly got time to break people in." He paused and looked away out of the window. "We might, though, put you at finishing," he concluded reflectively.

"How much do you pay a week?" ventured Carrie, emboldened by a certain softness in the man's manner and his simplicity of address.

"Three and a half," he answered.

"Oh," she was about to exclaim, but she checked herself and allowed her thoughts to die without expression.

"We're not exactly in need of anybody," he went on vaguely, looking her over as one would a package.

• • • • •

The city had laid miles and miles of streets and sewers through regions where, perhaps, one solitary house stood out alone—a pioneer of the populous ways to be. There were regions open to the sweeping winds and rain, which were as yet lighted throughout the night with long, blinking lines of gas-lamps, fluttering in the wind. Narrow board walks extended out, passing here a house, and there a store, at far intervals, eventually ending on the open prairie.

• • • • •

"He said that if you married me you would only get ten thousand a year. That if you didn't and still lived with me you would get nothing at all. If you would leave me, or if I would leave you, you would get all of a million and a half. Don't you think you had better leave me now?"

These are isolated passages—the first two from *Sister Carrie,* the third from *Jennie Gerhardt*—and normally it would be as unkind to pick passages from Dreiser as it would be to quote for themselves those frustrated mental exchanges that Henry James's characters hold with each other. For Dreiser works in such detail that you never really feel the force of any until you see the whole structure, while James is preoccupied with an inner meditation that his own characters always seem to be interrupting. But even in these bits from Dreiser there is an overwhelming impression that puzzles and troubles us because we cannot trace it to its source. "One doesn't see how it's made," a French critic once complained about some book he was reviewing. That is the trouble we always have with Dreiser. Carrie measuring herself against the immensity of Chicago, that wonderful night scene in which we see a generation just off the farms and out of the small towns confronting the modern city for the first time; the scene in which Hurstwood comes on Carrie sitting in the dark; Jennie Gerhardt's growing solitude even after the birth of her child; Clyde Griffiths and Roberta Alden walking around the haunted lakes when he is searching for one where he can kill her—one doesn't see the man writing this. We are too absorbed. Something is happening that tastes of fear, of the bottom loneliness of human existence, that just barely breaks into speech from the depths of our own souls; the planet itself seems to creak under our feet, and there are long lines of people bitterly walking to work in the morning dark, thinking only of how they can break through the iron circle of their frustration. Every line hurts. It hurts because you never get free enough of anything to ask what a character or a situation "really" means; it hurts because Dreiser is not trying to prove anything by it or to change what he sees; it hurts even when you are trying to tell yourself that all this happened in another time, that we are cleverer about life than Dreiser was. It hurts because it is all too much like reality to be "art."

It is because we have all identified Dreiser's work with reality that, for more than a half a century now, he has been for us not a writer like other writers, but a whole chapter of American life. From the very beginning, as one can see in reading over the reviews of *Sister Carrie,* Dreiser was accepted as a whole new class, a tendency, a disturbing movement in American life, an eruption from below. The very words he used, the dreaminess of his prose, the stilted but grim matter-of-fact of his method, which betrayed all the envy and wonder with which he looked at the great world outside—all this seemed to say that it was not art he

worked with but *knowledge,* some new and secret knowledge. It was this that the reviewers instantly felt, that shocked the Doubledays so deeply, that explains the extraordinary bitterness toward Dreiser from the first—and that excited Frank Norris, the publisher's reader (Dreiser looked amazingly like the new, "primitive" types that Norris was getting into his own fiction). Dreiser was the man from outside, the man from below, who wrote with the terrible literalness of a child. It is this that is so clearly expressed in Frank Doubleday's efforts to kill the book, in the fact that most literary and general magazines in the country did not review the book at all, that even some newspapers reviewed the book a year late, and that the tone of these early reviews is plainly that of people trying to accustom themselves to an unpleasant shock.

Sister Carrie did not have a bad press; it had a frightened press, with many of the reviewers plainly impressed, but startled by the concentrated truthfulness of the book. The St. Louis *Mirror* complained that "the author writes with a startling directness. At times this directness seems to be the frankness of a vast unsophistication. . . . The scenes of the book are laid always among a sort of people that is numerous but seldom treated in a serious novel." The general reaction was that of the Newark *Sunday News,* almost a year after the book had been published. "Told with an unsparing realism and detail, it has all the interest of fact. . . . The possibility of it all is horrible: an appalling arraignment of human society. And there is here no word of preachment; there are scarcely any philosophic reflections or deductions expressed. The impression is simply one of truth, and therein lies at once the strength and the horror of it."

This was the new note of the book, the unrelieved seriousness of it—but a seriousness so native, so unself-conscious, that Dreiser undoubtedly saw nothing odd about his vaguely "poetic" and questioning chapter titles, which were his efforts to frame his own knowledge, to fit it into a traditional system of thought, though he could not question any of his knowledge itself. Writing *Sister Carrie,* David Brion Davis comments, "was something like translating the Golden Plates." For Carrie was Dreiser's own sister, and he wrote without any desire to shock, without any knowledge that he could. Compare this with so "naturalistic" a book as Hardy's *Tess of the d'Urbervilles,* where the style is itself constantly commenting on the characters, and where the very old-fashioned turn of the prose, in all its complex urbanity, is an effort to interpret the story, to accommodate it to the author's own tradition of thought. Dreiser *could* not comment; so deeply had he identified himself with the story that there was no place left in it for him to comment *from.* And such efforts as he made to comment, in the oddly invertebrate chapter titles, were like gasps in the face of a reality from which he could not turn away. The book was exactly like a dream that Dreiser had lived through and which, in fact, after the failure of *Sister Carrie,* he was to live again, up to the very brink of Hurstwood's suicide.

It was this knowledge, this exclusive knowledge, this *kann nicht anders,* this absence of alternatives, that led people to resent Dreiser, and at the same time stunned the young writers of the period into instant recognition of his symbolic value to them. We never know how much has been missing from our lives until a true writer comes along. Everything which had been waiting for them in the gap between the generations, everything which Henry James said would belong to an "American Balzac"—that world of industrial capitalism which, James confessed, had been a "closed book" to him from his youth—everything free of "literature" and so free to become literature, now became identified with this "clumsy" and "stupid" ex-newspaperman whose book moved the new writers all the more deeply because they could not see where Dreiser's genius came from. To the young writers of the early twentieth century, Dreiser became, in Mencken's phrase, the Hindenburg of the novel—the great beast who pushed American life forward for them, who went on, blindly, unchangeably, trampling down the lies of gentility and Victorianism, of Puritanism and academicism. Dreiser was the primitive, the man from the abyss, the stranger who had grown up outside the Anglo-Saxon middle-class Protestant morality and so had no need to accept its sanctions. In Sherwood Anderson's phrase, he could be honored with "an apology for crudity"; and in fact the legend that *Sister Carrie* had been suppressed by the publisher's wife was now so dear to the hearts of the rising generation that Mrs. Doubleday became a classic character, the Carrie Nation of the American liberal epos, her ax forever lifted against "the truth of American life." So even writers like Van Wyck Brooks, who had not shared in the bitterness of Dreiser's early years, and who as socialists disapproved of his despair, now defended him as a matter of course—he cleared the way; in the phrase that was to be repeated with increasing meaninglessness through the years, he "liberated the American novel."

Dreiser now embodied the whole struggle of the new American literature. The "elderly virgins of the newspapers," as Mencken called them, never ceased to point out his deficiencies; the conservative academicians and New Humanists, the old fogeys and the young fogeys—all found in Dreiser everything new, brutal and alien they feared in American life. Gertrude Atherton was to say during the first World War that Dreiser represented the "Alpine School of Literature"—"Not a real American could be found among them with a magnifying glass"; Mary Austin was to notice that "our Baltic and Slavic stock will have an-

other way than the English of experiencing love, and possibly a more limited way. . . . All of Theodore Dreiser's people love like the peasants in a novel by Bojer or Knut Hamsun. His women have a cowlike complaisance such as can be found only in people who have lived for generations close to the soil"; Stuart Sherman, in his famous article of 1915 on "The Barbaric Naturalism of Theodore Dreiser" [see excerpt dated 1915], made it clear that Dreiser, "coming from that 'ethnic' element of our mixed population," was thus unable to understand the higher beauty of the American spirit.

So Dreiser stood in no-man's-land, pushed ahead like a dumb ox by one camp, attacked by the other. Everything about him made him a polemical figure; his scandals, miseries, and confusions were as well-known as his books. The "liberals," the "modernists," defended books like The *"Genius"* because "it told the truth"—and how delighted they must have been when John S. Sumner tried to get the book banned in 1915 and anybody who *was* anybody (including Ezra Pound, John Reed and David Belasco) rushed to its defense. To the English novelists of the period (and *Sister Carrie* owed its sudden fame to the edition Heinemann brought out in London) he was like a powerhouse they envied amid the Georgian doldrums of literary London. How much of that fighting period comes back to you now when you discover Arnold Bennett on his feverish trips to America identifying all the raw, rich, teeming opportunities of American life with Dreiser, or listen to Ford Madox Ford—"Damn it all, it *is* fun to see that poor old language, that vehicle for conveying moderated thoughts, having the guts kicked out of it, like a deflated football, over all the fields of the boundless Middle West." While Mencken, in Dreiser's name, slew William Lyon Phelps in his thousands, the young English discovered that Dreiser was the friend of art. Each side in the controversy used Dreiser, and each, in its own way, was embarrassed. How many times did the young Turks have to swallow Dreiser's bad books, to explain away his faults, and how clear it is from reading Paul Elmer More (who was a deeper critic than his opponents and would have been almost a great one if he had not always tried to arm himself against American life) that he was always more moved by Dreiser's cosmic doubts than he could confess. More settled the problem, as he settled every writer he feared, by studying the man's "philosophy"—where he could show up Dreiser to his heart's content, and, in a prose that could not have been more removed from the actualities of the subject, prove that he had disposed forever of this intellectual upstart.

This pattern remained to the end—Dreiser was the great personifier. When he went to Russia, even the title of the book he wrote had to begin with Dreiser rather than with Russia; when Sinclair Lewis praised

Dreiser in his Nobel Prize speech, he did so with all the enthusiasm of a Congressman trying for the farm vote; when Dreiser delivered himself of some remarks about Jews, the *Nation* was not so much indignant as bewildered that this son of the common people could express such illiberal sentiments; when he spoke against England at the beginning of the Second World War, there was a similar outcry that Dreiser was letting the masses down. It is typical of Dreiser's symbolic importance that a writer now so isolated as James T. Farrell has been able to find support for his own work only in Dreiser's example; that the word *plebeian* has always been used either to blacken Dreiser or to favor him; that Eisenstein suffered so long to make a film of *An American Tragedy* that would be the ultimate exposure of American capitalism. When Dreiser joined the Communists, his act was greeted as everything but what it really was—the lonely and confused effort of an individual to identify himself with a group that had taken him up in his decline; when he died in 1945, in the heyday of American-Soviet friendship, one left-wing poet announced that Dreiser's faults had always been those of America anyway, that he was simply America writ large—"Much as we wish he had been surer, wiser, we cannot change the fact. The man was great in a way Americans uniquely understand who know the uneven contours of their land, its storms, its droughts, its huge and turbulent Mississippi, where his youth was spent." Even Dreiser's sad posthumous novels, *The Bulwark* and *The Stoic,* each of which centers around a dying old man, were written about with forced enthusiasm, as if the people attacking them were afraid of being called reactionary, while those who honestly liked them reported that they were *surprisingly* good. And how F. O. Matthiessen suffered all through the last year of his life to do justice to Dreiser as if that would fulfill an *obligation* to the cause of "progressivism" in America.

But soon after the war all this changed—Dreiser was now simply an embarrassment. The reaction against him was only partly literary, for much of it was founded on an understandable horror of the fraudulent "radicals" who had been exploiting Dreiser before his death. And thanks not a little to the cozy prosperity of a permanent war economy, America, it seemed, no longer required the spirit of protest with which Dreiser had been identified. The writers were now in the universities, and they all wrote about writing. No longer hoary sons of toil, a whole intelligentsia, post-Communist, post-Marxist, which could not look at Alger Hiss in the dock without shuddering at how near they had come to his fate, now tended to find their new ideology in the good old middle-class virtues. A new genteel tradition had come in. Writing in America had suddenly become very conscious that literature is made with words, and that these words should look nice on the page. It became a period when fine writing was ev-

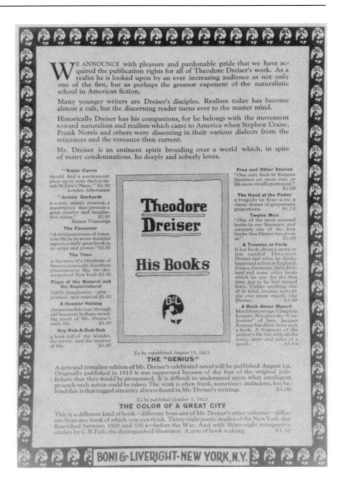

1923 advertisement for Dreiser's works.

erything, when every anonymous smoothie on *Time* could write cleaner prose about God's alliance with America than poor old Dreiser could find for anything, when even the *Senior Scholastic,* a magazine intended for high-school students, complained of Dreiser that "some of the writing would shock an English class." It is of this period, in which we live, that Saul Bellow has noted in his tribute to Dreiser:

I think . . . that the insistence on neatness and correctness is one of the signs of a modern nervousness and irritability. When has clumsiness in composition been felt as so annoying, so enraging? The "good" writing of the *New Yorker* is such that one experiences a furious anxiety, in reading it, about errors and lapses from taste; finally what emerges is a terrible hunger for conformism and uniformity. The smoothness of the surface and its high polish must not be marred. One has a similar anxiety in reading a novelist like Hemingway and comes to feel in the end that Hemingway wants to be praised for the offenses he does not commit. He is dependable; he never names certain emotions or ideas, and he takes pride in that—it is a form of honor. In it, really, there is submissiveness, acceptance of restriction.

The most important expression of the reaction

against Dreiser is Lionel Trilling's "Reality in America." This essay expresses for a great many people in America just now their impatience with the insurgency that dominated our famously realistic fiction up to the war, and not since Paul Elmer More's essay of 1920 has anyone with so much critical insight made out so brilliant a case against Dreiser; not since William Dean Howells supported Stephen Crane's *Maggie* and not *Sister Carrie* has anyone contrasted so sharply those notorious faults of style and slovenly habits of thought which our liberal criticism has always treated as "essentially social and political virtues" with the wonderful play of mind and fertility of resource one finds in Henry James. Never has the case against the persistent identification of Dreiser with "reality" in America—coarse, heavy, external reality—been put with so much intellectual passion. For Mr. Trilling is writing against the decay of a liberal movement ruined largely by its flirtation with totalitarianism, by its disregard of human complexity and its fear of intellect. No one who has followed the extent to which our liberal critics have always acknowledged that Dreiser *is* a bad thinker—and have excused it on the grounds that the poor man at least "told the truth about American life"—can help but share Mr. Trilling's impatience with what has recently passed in this country for liberal "imagination."

But may it not be suggested that Henry James as a cultural hero serves us as badly as Dreiser once did? What happens whenever we convert a writer into a symbol is that we lose the writer himself in all his indefeasible singularity, his particular inimitable genius. A literature that modeled itself on Dreiser would be unbearable; a literature that saw all its virtues of literature in Henry James would be preposterous. If one thing is clear about our addiction to Henry James just now, it is that most of our new writing has nothing in common with James whatever. For James's essential quality is his intellectual appetite—"all life belongs to you"—his unending inner meditation, and not the air of detachment which so misleads us whenever we encounter it on the surface of the society James wrote about—the only society he knew, and one he despaired of precisely because it was never what it seemed. Just now, however, a certain genteel uninvolvement is dear to us, while Dreiser's bread lines and street-car strikes, his suffering inarticulate characters, his Chicago, his "commonness"—are that bad dream from which we have all awakened. As Dreiser's faults were once acclaimed as the virtues of the common man, so now we are ashamed of him because he brings up everything we should like to leave behind us.

There is no "common man"—though behind the stereotype (how *this* executioner waits!) stand those who may yet prepare all too common a fate for us all. Literary people, as a class, can get so far away from the experience of other classes that they tend to see them

only symbolically. Dreiser as "common man" once served a purpose; now he serves another. The basic mistake of all the liberal critics was to think that he could ever see this world as something to be ameliorated. They misjudged the source of Dreiser's strength. This is the point that David Brion Davis documents so well in his study ["Dreiser and Naturalism Revisited"] of what Dreiser and the early naturalists really believed. For as Mr. Davis shows, these writers and painters were "naturalists" only in the stark sense that the world had suddenly come down to them divested of its supernatural sanctions. They were actually obsessed with the transcendental possibilities of this "real" world; like Whitman, they gloried in the beauty of the iron city. In their contemplative acceptance of this world, in their indifference to social reform, in their awe before life itself, they were actually not in the tradition of political "liberalism" but in that deeper American strain of metaphysical wonder which leads from the early pietists through Whitman to the first painters of the modern city.

This gift of contemplativeness, of wonder, of reverence, even, is at the center of Dreiser's world—who can forget the image of the rocking chair in *Sister Carrie*, where from *this* cradle endlessly rocking man stares forever at a world he is not too weak but too bemused to change? And it is this lack of smartness, this puzzled lovingness for the substance of all our mystery, that explains why we do not know what to *do* with Dreiser today. For Dreiser is in a very old, a very difficult, a very lonely American tradition. It is no longer "transcendentalist," but always it seeks to transcend. This does not mean that Dreiser's philosophy is valuable in itself, or that his excursions into philosophy and science—fields for which he was certainly not well equipped—have to be excused. It does mean that the vision is always in Dreiser's work, and makes it possible. Just as the strength of his work is that he got into it those large rhythms of wonder, of curiosity, of amazement before the power of the universe that give such largeness to his characters and such unconscious majesty to life itself, so the weakness and instability of his work is that he could become almost too passive before the great thing he saw out there, always larger than man himself. The truth is, as Eliseo Vivas says in his essay ["Dreiser, an Inconsistent Mechanist"], that Dreiser is "not only an American novelist but a universal novelist, in the very literal sense of the word. The mystery of the universe, the puzzle of destiny, haunts him; and he, more than any other of his contemporaries, has responded to the need to relate the haunting sense of puzzlement and mystery to the human drama. No other American novelist of his generation has so persistently endeavored to look at men under the aspect of eternity. It is no . . . paradox, therefore, that . . . while Dreiser tries to demonstrate that man's efforts are vain and empty, by responding to the need to face the problem of destiny, he draws our attention to dimensions of human existence, awareness of which is not encouraged by current philosophical fashions. . . ." To understand how this gets into Dreiser's work one must look not back of it but into it for that sense of "reality" which he thirsted for—that whole reality, up to the very shores of light, that made him cry out in *Jennie Gerhardt:* "We turn our faces away from the creation of life as if that were the last thing that man should dare to interest himself in, openly."

This is what makes Dreiser so painful—in his "atheism," his cosmology; this is what dismays us in our sensible culture, just as it bothered a generation that could never understand Dreiser's special bitterness against orthodox religion, against the churches; this is what drove Dreiser to look for God in the laboratories, to write essays on "My Creator." He may have been a "naturalist," but he was certainly not a materialist. What sticks in our throats is that Dreiser is outside the agreed boundaries of our concern, that he does not accept our "society" as the whole of reality, that he may crave after its fleshpots, but does not believe that getting along is the ultimate reach of man's effort. For we live in a time when traditionalists and "progressives" and ex-progressives alike are agreed that the man not to be trusted is the man who does not fit in, who has no "position," who dares to be distracted—when this great going machine, this prig's paradise in which we live just now, is the best of all possible worlds.

Dreiser committed the one sin that a writer can commit in our society—he would not accept this society itself as wholly real. And it is here, I think, that we can get perspective on his famous awkwardness. For what counts most with a writer is that his reach should be felt as well as his grasp, that words should be his means, not his ends. It is this that Malcolm Cowley noticed when he wrote that "there are moments when Dreiser's awkwardness in handling words contributes to the force of his novels, since he seems to be groping in them for something on a deeper level than language." This is what finally disturbs us about Dreiser in a period when fine writing is like a mirror that gives back our superficiality. Dreiser hurts because he is always looking to the source; to that which broke off into the mysterious halves of man's existence; to that which is behind language and sustains it; to that which is not ourselves but gives life to our words. (pp. 3-12)

Alfred Kazin, in an introduction to *The Stature of Theodore Dreiser: A Critical Survey of the Man and His Work,* edited by Alfred Kazin and Charles Shapiro, Indiana University Press, 1955, pp. 3-12.

LAWRENCE E. HUSSMAN, JR.
(essay date 1983)

[Hussman is an American educator and critic. In the following excerpt, he describes how Dreiser's experiences, philosophical principles, and personal characteristics helped shape his fiction.]

One of Dreiser's first jobs was as a reporter, assigned to the police beat, for the Chicago *Globe* in 1892. He became a daily witness to scenes of human degradation. The cruelty of the city was a vital primer in the doctrine which he was later to know by name as the survival of the fittest. The many examples of urban man's inhumanity made a joke of the world view taught him in the parochial schools. One might half believe in the widespread application of justice and mercy in rural Indiana, but not in Chicago in the 1890s. One trip through the slums would be enough to destroy the last vestiges of such illusions. Yet his first taste of life in the metropolis satisfied him immensely as spectacle and he never lost his romantic fascination with it. He resolved to be a fit survivor by making his way in a large city as a newspaperman. During the next few years he wrote for a number of dailies, working his way toward New York, the ultimate metropolis. On the way, he read several books which were to profoundly influence his own writing.

While working for the Pittsburgh *Dispatch* in 1894, Dreiser discovered the philosophical tracts of T. H. Huxley, John Tyndall, and Herbert Spencer. Already brooding over the apparent purposelessness of his own life and the failure of his previous education to provide him with a convincing world view, Dreiser was psychologically ready for the decisive impression that these philosophers made on him. He testified to the experience in an often quoted passage from *A Book about Myself:*

At this time I had the fortune to discover Huxley and Tyndall and Herbert Spencer, whose introductory volume to his *Synthetic Philosophy* (*First Principles*) quite blew me, intellectually, to bits. Hitherto, until I had read Huxley, I had some lingering filaments of Catholicism trailing about me, faith in the existence of Christ, the soundness of his moral and sociological deductions, the brotherhood of man. But on reading *Science and Hebrew Tradition* and *Science and Christian Tradition,* and finding both the Old and New Testaments to be not compendiums of revealed truth but mere records of religious experience, and very erroneous ones at that, and then taking up *First Principles* and discovering that all I had deemed substantial—man's place in nature, his importance in the universe, this too, too solid earth, man's very identity save as an infinitessimal speck of energy or a "suspended equation" drawn or blown here and there by larger forces in which he moved quite unconsciously as an atom—all questioned and dissolved into other and less understandable things, I was completely thrown down in my conceptions or non-conceptions of life.

Thus Dreiser records the central event in his conversion to philosophic naturalism and the touchstone used by several generations of critics to situate his books in literary history. Through his exposure to Huxley, Tyndall, and Spencer, Dreiser formulated his declared beliefs that life is without purpose or plan, that man has no soul, that free will and original sin are myths, that human morality and motivation are based on physiological and sociological fate and that the only discernible laws are the laws of change and chance.

But to pigeonhole Dreiser's art within the naturalistic movement is to stop far short of an understanding of that art at its deepest. The way he uses the naturalistic hypothesis to explore fundamental questions about man and his institutions constitutes Dreiser's unique contribution to our literature and to our understanding of ourselves. Having accepted the belief that was to become the common inheritance of the major writers of the twentieth century, the belief that "God is dead," Dreiser was among the first to explore the question of what to make of this seemingly diminished thing called existence. One might speculate on its meaninglessness for a time, but the question of how to organize oneself for living persisted. His fiction represents an implicit attempt to answer that question. Through it he explores various paths that might lead the modern pilgrim around the Slough of Despond to personal fulfillment. Furthermore, although Dreiser's negative experiences led him to embrace the precepts of naturalism intellectually, he was never able to accept them emotionally. We need only recall that he was given to speculating that man was no more important to the universe than an expiring beetle, yet he wrote four volumes of autobiography and an autobiographical novel. The exploration of alternative ways to live life coupled with the emotional need to believe in a transcendent reality led tortuously from *Sister Carrie* to *The Bulwark.* And the passage was made possible by Dreiser's fascinated observation of an ancient problem in its modern context, man's disillusioned longing for ultimate fulfillment and the moral questions which that longing raised.

In 1898, the year before he began *Sister Carrie,* Dreiser was working as a consulting editor for *Success* magazine, a monthly which high-lighted the accomplishments of the nation's prosperous and famous by describing how they became so. He interviewed a number of rich and celebrated men for *Success,* and though most of them piously professed that spiritual peace was far more important than material well being, a remark made by Thomas Edison during Dreiser's interview of him made a far more profound impression. Edison told Dreiser that his only pleasure came from the process of working on inventions and that he lost all interest when the work was completed. This remark crystallized for Dreiser his own vague feelings of disillusionment with things he had longed for and achieved. It became, along with other of Edison's ideas expressed in the interview, a source for character and theme in *Sister Carrie* and a subject for lifelong brooding. Dreiser had always been a dreamer of large dreams and intensely ambitious for financial security, material comforts, social acceptance, and the glamour of a writer's career. His sexual appetite was enormous. When he had secured some of his wants in Chicago, however, he remained curiously restless. By the time he came to interview Edison, this aspect of human nature which makes the attainment of an object of desire disappointing had stirred Dreiser's imagination. Since he believed from his reading that existence is meaningless and since he was naturally of a melancholy turn, he was concerned less with the pleasure in the pursuit of an object than with the disillusionment that attended its acquisition. And he found his insight prefigured in the era in which he lived. With the dawning of the age of conspicuous consumption in America had come the realization that material things do not bring fulfillment. The frenzied pursuit of an illusory happiness had already struck the young writer as the most fascinating and poetic phase of American city life around the turn of the century.

Ultimate fulfillment has always been seen as beyond man's grasp in his earthly state. A religious person might take the fact in stride, perform his duties and bide his time in anticipation of the perfect bliss promised in another world. But a mechanist could find this aspect of the human predicament another persuasive demonstration of life's essential senselessness. Dreiser began brooding about disillusionment at a time when his thinking was at least tacitly mechanistic. Furthermore, if man had overpowering yearnings that could be neither resisted nor satisfied, not only must life be purposeless but also free will must indeed by a myth. Some such interpretation surely played a part in Dreiser's reading of Huxley, Tyndall, and Spencer. Because they are in the grip of inscrutable desire, Carrie Meeber, Clyde Griffiths, and even Frank Cowperwood appear to be mere pawns of blind force. Each of Dreiser's books is remarkable for its author's profound preoccupation with frustrated desire. One of his most perceptive early critics, Randolph Bourne, remarked in a review of *The "Genius"* that "the insistent theme of Mr. Dreiser's works is desire, perennial, unquenchable."

Dreiser employs a variety of terms to describe and translate desire. At times he refers to mystic longing, unreasoning passion, or chemic compulsion, but always the reference is to the fact that his characters' desires are unquenchable. They are so because the objects of these desires are not sufficient to explain the intensity of the longing. This phenomenon was hardly a discovery of Dreiser's. Plato describes the inability of the objects of our desires to satisfy us through the analogy of a perforated vessel into which water is poured. Lucretius calls desire the "thirst for life" and observes that "so long as we have not what we crave, it seems to surpass all else; afterward, when it is ours, we crave something else, and the same thirst of life besets us as ever, open-mouthed." What makes Dreiser's treatment of desire new in his time and still fresh is its twentieth-century context. The naturalistic philosophers had cast doubt on the theological foundations of the western world, and the crumbling of the religious edifice would be so swift that by the twenties most of the books written by intellectuals would begin with the assumption that God was no longer an issue. Dreiser was among the first of American artists to try to make sense of a world in which science and religion seemed hopelessly split, a chasm which was to prove to be the foremost cultural fact of the first half of the twentieth century. Without a religious explanation of man's yearning for ultimate fulfillment, later writers would try to fill the void by establishing their own ersatz religions. Thus, Wallace Stevens wrote in "The Man with the Blue Guitar": "Art, surpassing music must replace empty Heaven and its hymns." James Joyce and Virginia Woolf agreed that art was the only surviving modern ideal. For D. H. Lawrence, the new faith was to be found in blood consciousness, for Ernest Hemingway, in modern stoicism, for John Steinbeck, in biological evolution. Dreiser's fiction transcribes through his characters his own relentless and vain search for a worthy reality. Carrie's aching need for material, social, and artistic success is answered with gowns, carriages, position, and career, but the end of the novel finds her still hopeful of release from "longings" and "heartaches." Frank Cowperwood, the robber baron hero of the Trilogy of Desire, acquires a succession of mansions, priceless paintings, and enchanting mistresses, but fulfillment eludes him. Eugene Witla, the artist hero of *The "Genius,"* is sustained neither by his art nor by the many liaisons that mark his frenzied pursuit of the "impossible she." Clyde Griffiths's doomed dream of money, importance, and sexual power leads inexorably to the electric chair.

Dreiser's autobiographies offer ample evidence that he was, himself, afflicted to an unusual degree with romantic desire that could never be satisfied. The absence of fulfillment intensified his brooding melancholy. For example, he writes of his youth:

I tell you, in those days, wonderful, amazing moods were generated in the blood of me. I felt and saw things which have never come true—glories, moods,

gayeties, perfections. There was a lilt in my heart and my soul. I wanted, oh! I wanted all that Nature can breed in her wealth of stars and universes—and I found—what have I found—? [*A Hoosier Holiday*]

The insatiable desire to experience all things simultaneously which stirs his characters stirred their creator as well. He often protested gloomily against what George Santayana called "the deepest curse of existence," the need of "rejecting and destroying some things that are beautiful," for in that direction Dreiser saw accommodation, compromise, decay, and death. His brooding over the extent to which mankind's reach extends beyond its grasp penetrates his very style, through which he conveys a sense of gnawing unrest.

Although Dreiser empathized with most people who seemed fated to strive for the objects of their personal desires, he admired those few who were able to transcend desire by dedicating themselves to a higher good, as he believed his mother had. He often regretted that most were essentially self-serving and that compassion and charity were not more widespread. As a consequence, his novels before *The Bulwark* seem curiously contradictory, for they are simultaneously deterministic and humanistic. Dreiser critics have frequently identified this seeming contradiction without tracing it to its source and relating it to the novelist's ongoing quest for moral as well as spiritual moorings in a postreligious world. The apparently incompatible impulses to take what one desires for personal happiness and to give of oneself for others were the alternatives that presented themselves as a result of the new freedom that attended Dreiser's loss of religious faith with its moral imperatives. In *A Book about Myself,* he wrote two long, contiguous confessional paragraphs in which he admitted to a ravenous appetite for the world's goods as well as a profound compassion for those whose possessions were minimal. Although he sometimes seemed simply to accept these two sides of himself, he continually explored them through fictional characters and situations as alternate paths to a possible secular salvation. Could a man or woman find true happiness by storing up treasures or by succoring those who had none? It must be remembered that although Dreiser thought of himself as a determinist, he did not consistently deny free will. In *A Hoosier Holiday,* for example, he cited historical precedence in the overthrow of monarchy as evidence of the people's will. And even the characters in a determinist novel must attempt to manage their lives by making moral choices, whether or not those choices are merely illusory against the backdrop of meaninglessness. Thus, the morally uncommitted heroine of *Sister Carrie* is motivated by her "guiding principle" of self-interest in her languid quest for position and possessions, but by the end of the novel she has begun to indulge her compassionate side. Jennie Gerhardt gives totally in an utterly selfless manner. Cowperwood shamelessly indulges his will to power. Clyde Griffiths follows his tawdry dreams to their tragic terminus and begins to see in prison that responsibilities to others might be a more crucial call than desire. Thus, Dreiser's novels scrutinize characters struggling to invest their lives with meaning by pursuing self-interested goals or by curbing their personal desires to devote themselves to others. Seen in this light, they have an existential dimension that has not been previously explored.

The relationships between men and women provided Dreiser with the most illuminating case studies for his examination of the conflict between the self and the other. He was himself a notorious womanizer whose affairs of the heart and exploits in the bedroom numbered in the hundreds and spanned his entire lifetime. In the give and take of these affairs he found a useful paradigm for abstract moral considerations. He returned to such relationships again and again in his fiction. The institution of marriage was an even richer source of moral speculation for Dreiser. He met his first wife in 1893. Assigned by the St. Louis *Republic* to escort a group of school teachers on a trip to the Chicago World's Fair, he picked Sara Osborne White (also known as "Jug") from among the twenty-five teachers as the most worthy of his attentions. Soon he was lost in romance, writing highly charged, emotional letters to her and constructing a miniature shrine in his room to display her picture. Despite the warnings of friends that Sara was too old for him (at nearly twenty-five she was two years his senior) and that as a conservative churchgoer she might be too narrow for him, Dreiser decided that he must marry her. Although he went East to further his career as a reporter, he resolved to return for Sara when he had sufficient money to support her. Their five-year courtship resulted in marriage late in 1898, even though his sojourn in the East had provided him with a succession of other women and the excitement of New York. Dreiser would later recall that the marriage was prompted by his obedience to "the pale flame of duty." He soon began to find his wife too conventional and possessive and himself too driven not to crave the "artistic" freedom to pursue younger women. His disillusionment grew incrementally, but Dreiser and Sara were not permanently separated until 1912. She refused him a divorce, preventing his remarriage until her death in 1942.

Dreiser often used marriage as a literary subject. His novels from *Sister Carrie* up to *The Bulwark* portray the institution with a mostly jaundiced eye. But it is in *The "Genius"* and in his "marriage group," a series of short stories including among others **"Married,"** **"The Second Choice,"** and **"Free,"** that he records his most subtle analysis of the concept of lifelong commitment to one sexual partner. In these works, marriage becomes a vehicle for discussing the struggle within the individual between the desire for the world's most alluring and abundant commodity—what Dreiser called "the show of soul in some passing eye"—and the wish to know that soul intimately and fully, possible only through an emotional expenditure and commitment which disallows our knowing as intimately and fully the souls that animate the many other equally tantalizing "passing eyes." Dreiser tried to resolve the dilemma through a series of intense, mostly short-lived relationships with a legendary number of women.

By 1899, he had contributed about forty articles and poems to magazines (most to *Metropolitan* and *Cosmopolitan*), had his first short story published by *Ainslee's*, and had seen his name appear in *Who's Who in America*. He began writing his first extended work in the autumn of that year, spurred by his newspaper colleague Arthur Henry's suggestion that they both attempt a novel. Dreiser confessed that he addressed himself to the task with no idea of how to proceed. He was probably indulging in his characteristic exaggeration when he said that he wrote the title on a blank sheet of paper with no conception of the story that was to follow. After writing about one third of the book, he was forced to abandon it for several months because he could not untangle the plot complications that had developed to that point. Although he ultimately managed to realize the narrative line of the novel in impressive fashion, his admitted amateurism was responsible for several flaws in the logical underpinning of *Sister Carrie*. But he was able to successfully transform into his first major work the experiences and conflicts that were to remain among the most important sources of all of his fiction. These included the grinding poverty of his youth, which stirred his sympathy for the poor as well as his resolve not to be among them; the contrasting examples of his father's narrow outlook and his mother's rich sympathy; his struggle for survival and recognition in Chicago; his Catholic schooling and the naturalistic precepts of Huxley, Tyndall, and Spencer; a growing hatred for the bondage of marriage, along with his sexual promiscuity and a paradoxical respect for the family; a minimal education and a voracious intellectual curiosity; a love-hate relationship with the American city; and a vivid lust for life linked to an uncommon love of people. William Faulkner noted, in his Nobel Prize acceptance speech, that "the conflict of the human heart within itself alone can make good writing." By this standard, Dreiser was well-equipped for his chosen profession. His novels record his characters' attempts to resolve profound conflicts that he deeply felt himself. At their best they constitute some of the most telling fiction of the twentieth century. (pp. 9-17)

Lawrence E. Hussman, Jr., in his *Dreiser and His Fiction: A Twentieth-Century Quest,* University of Pennsylvania Press, 1983, 215 p.

SOURCES FOR FURTHER STUDY

Dudley, Dorothy. *Dreiser and the Land of the Free.* New York: Beechhurst Press, 1946, 485 p.

> Revised edition of the 1932 biography *Forgotten Frontiers: Dreiser and the Land of the Free.* Dreiser worked closely with Dudley on both the original edition and the revision.

Hakutani, Yoshinobu. *Young Dreiser: A Critical Study.* Rutherford, N. J.: Fairleigh Dickinson University, 1980, 228 p.

> Examination of Dreiser's early life. The work focuses on Dreiser's youth, journalistic work, and his career as a magazine editor in an effort to demonstrate the significance of these experiences in the shaping of his earliest short stories and *Sister Carrie.*

Lehan, Richard. *Theodore Dreiser: His World and His Novels.* Carbondale, Edwardsville: Southern Illinois University Press, 1969, 280 p.

> Critical study of Dreiser's life and works.

Lydenberg, John, ed. *Dreiser: A Collection of Critical Essays.* Englewood Cliffs, N.J.: Prentice-Hall, 1971, 182 p.

> Compendium of previously published critical essays on Dreiser, including articles by Alfred Kazin, Malcolm Cowley, H. L. Mencken, and Irving Howe.

Pizer, Donald. *The Novels of Theodore Dreiser: A Critical Study.* Minneapolis: University of Minnesota Press, 1976, 382 p.

> Examines plot, characterization, and style in Dreiser's works.

Warren, Robert Penn. *Homage to Theodore Dreiser, August 27, 1871—December 28, 1945: On the Centennial of His Birth.* New York: Random House, 1971, 173 p.

> Analysis of the plots and major themes of Dreiser's novels.

John Dryden

1631-1700

English poet, critic, dramatist, and translator.

INTRODUCTION

*R*egarded by many scholars as the father of modern English poetry and criticism, Dryden dominated literary life in England during the last four decades of the seventeenth century. Through deliberate, comprehensive refinement of Elizabethan language, Dryden evolved an expressive, universal diction which has had immense impact on the development of speech and writing in the English-speaking world. Although initially famous for his numerous comedies and heroic tragedies, Dryden is today most highly regarded for his critical writings as well as his satirical and didactic poems. In the former, particularly *Of Dramatick Poesie* (1668), he originated the extended form of objective analysis that has come to characterize most modern criticism. In the latter, notably *Absalom and Achitophel* (1681), *The Hind and the Panther* (1687), and *Religio Laici* (1682), he displayed an irrepressible wit and forceful line of argument which later satirists adopted as their model. Dryden is also remembered as an inventive translator of the works of Virgil, Geoffrey Chaucer, and Giovanni Boccaccio. A precise, graceful, and vigorous style distinguishes nearly all his work and has helped earn him lasting fame as one of the greatest practitioners of English literature.

The eldest son of a large, socially prominent Puritan family, Dryden was born in Aldwinkle, Northamptonshire. A royal scholarship presented him at an early age allowed Dryden to attend Westminster School, where he received a classical education. At Westminster he published his first poem, "Upon the Death of the Lord Hastings," commemorating the life of a schoolmate who had recently died of smallpox. In 1650 Dryden was elected to Trinity College, Cambridge, where he earned a bachelor of arts degree. Shortly afterward his father died, leaving him to oversee the affairs of his family and of his own small estate. Dryden's activities and whereabouts during the next several years are unknown; in 1659, however, following the death of Oliver Cromwell, Lord Protector of England, Dryden returned to writing and published "Heroique Stanza's," a group of complimentary verses which portray Cromwell as architect of a great new age. In the following years Dryden continued to publish politically oriented poems, of which the most notable are *Astraea Redux* (1660) and *Annus Mirabilis: The Year of Wonders, 1666* (1667). The former, which celebrated the exiled Charles II's restoration to the English crown, incited libelous attacks in later years by Dryden's literary enemies, who charged him with political inconsistency and selfish motivation. But historians agree that Dryden maintained throughout his life a belief in religious tolerance and moderate government and switched allegiances from the republicans to the royalists at this time just as did the majority of the English people.

In 1663, following his marriage to Lady Elizabeth Howard, Dryden debuted as dramatist, a career which at the time held the most financial promise for an aspiring writer in England. His first play, *The Wild Gallant* (1663), combined the English comedy of humors with an emphasis on intricate plot structure characteristic of the Spanish theater. It was performed at the newly established Royal Theater but was unsuccessful. Dryden soon adopted a more sophisticated form of verse drama in collaboration with his brother-in-law Sir Robert Howard, and produced the heroic tragedy *The Indian Queen* (1664). He and Howard subsequently engaged in a lengthy literary debate on the merits of rhymed versus unrhymed plays, a debate which engendered Dryden's first critical essays and established Dryden as a champion of the rhymed verse drama. *The Indian Emperour* (1665), his sequel to *The Indian Queen*, represents his first entirely original play and was written wholly in rhymed couplets. This play was extremely popular and gave Dryden status in a field which he increasingly dominated during the next fifteen years. With the death of Sir William Davenant—the inventor of the English heroic play and, with Ben Jonson, a major influence on Dryden's dramas—Dryden assumed the post of poet laureate in 1668. The same year there appeared his most extended piece of literary criticism, *Of Dramatick Poesie*. Shortly thereafter Dryden reconsidered his earlier arguments in favor of the rhymed play and adopted blank verse, which he now recognized as a less constraining form for the drama. *All for Love; or, The World Well Lost* (1677), adapted from Shakespeare's *Antony and Cleopatra* and written in blank verse, was a great success, and solidified Dryden's reputation as the most talented and accomplished writer of the time.

But by then Dryden had wearied of writing for the stage (though a decade later he returned to the field for financial reasons after losing his laureateship following the deposition of James II), and had publicly acknowledged his belief that his talents were ill-suited to the field. The Popish Plot (1678-81), a thwarted attempt by the Earl of Shaftesbury and others to exclude Charles's Catholic brother, James, from his right of succession to the throne, provided Dryden with the topic for what critics consider his greatest work, *Absalom and Achitophel,* a satirical attack on Shaftesbury and his confederates. This work inaugurated a phase of satirical and didactic verse which directly influenced the development of Augustan poetry in the next century, especially that of Alexander Pope. Dryden's first major satire was followed in 1682 by *Mac Flecknoe,* a mock-heroic poem which had been circulating in manuscript for approximately four years and which was directed at the poet Thomas Shadwell, a literary antagonist of Dryden. Allied to *Absalom and Achitophel* in tone, *Mac Flecknoe* displays Dryden's mastery of word order, rhythm, and cunning verbal attack. The same year there also appeared a shorter, more serious satiric poem titled *The Medall,* which again was aimed at Shaftesbury, who escaped sentencing for treason despite Dryden's supposed attempt to influence the Grand Jury.

As political and religious matters repeatedly overlapped in Dryden's time, an era much concerned with the question of whether Protestant or Roman Catholic monarchs were the legitimate rulers of Britain, it is not surprising that Dryden also began to address religious issues during this period of national turmoil. *Religio Laici; or, A Laymans Faith* appeared when Whig plots to assassinate the king were being formed. In this didactic poem, Dryden promulgated a compromise between Anglican exclusivism and Roman Catholic belief in absolute papal authority, articulating the king's stance in favor of religious toleration. In 1685 James II ascended the English throne and soon enacted a declaration of toleration, while placing many of his sympathizers in high government positions. Within the first year of James's reign, Dryden converted to Catholicism, once again inciting his literary detractors to disparage his reputation as a man of conviction. But the question of any underhanded motives by Dryden has been dismissed, as scholars have demonstrated that the renewal of his laureateship by James occurred months before his conversion. The fact that Dryden did not renounce his conversion following James's abdication also gives evidence of his sincerity. The most unique of Dryden's works, *The Hind and the Panther,* stemmed from this occasion. Written in beast-fable form, the poem presents a long theological debate between a milk-white hind, representing the Roman Church, and a spotted panther, representing the Anglican Church. During his last years, in addition to completing five more plays, Dryden wrote the widely anthologized odes *A Song for St. Cecilia's Day* (1687) and *Alexander's Feast* (1697). However, it was as a translator that he spent most of his time, completing, in addition to several small projects, *The Works of Virgil* (1697) and *Fables Ancient and Modern* (1700). Dryden died in London in 1700 and was buried in Westminster Abbey.

Samuel Johnson, who first deemed Dryden the father of English criticism, also considered him the English poet who crystallized the potential for beauty and majesty in the English language: according to Johnson, "he found it brick, and he left it marble." In his early complimentary verses Dryden first began developing the language while experimenting with the traditional hexameter form. Although recognized for their artistic promise and innovation, these poems have been faulted for misplaced or excessive conceits and similes. *Annus Mirabilis,* an inspirational, heroic treatment of the great fire in London and of the Anglo-Dutch naval war, represents the capstone of Dryden's early period as a poet. With *Absalom and Achitophel* Dryden displayed his mastery of the heroic couplet and the suitability of his streamlined verse for political satire. Cloaked in allusive language and based on the biblical story of King David's rebellious son, the mock-heroic poem addresses the explosive political climate of the time through a string of character portraits, narrative, and speeches. Dryden's portrayals of Charles II, an inveterate philanderer; his illegitimate son Monmouth, who planned to dethrone his father; and Shaftesbury, the chief orchestrator of the Popish Plot; are admired by critics not only for their liveliness but for the judicious manner in which they are presented. The relentless movement of the poem, its delightful yet pointed commentary on the crucial situation, and its timeless appeal, establish it as one of the highest achievements in the heroic couplet form. That Dryden was an exemplary poet of the public event and was able to infuse even the most ordinary incident with dignified, original art is not disputed. But his poems have been charged with displaying a disturbing impersonality. Several modern critics, however, have revealed a clear, confessional tone in the later poems *Religio Laici* and *The Hind and the Panther.* Although the theological viewpoints in them are disparate, these works forcefully document Dryden's personal reactions to the political milieu and to the viability of religious faith in his age.

As translator, Dryden's greatest achievement is his *The Works of Virgil.* His intent, in all his translations, was less to reproduce than to paraphrase, while still capturing the individuality of the original. Hence, Virgilian and Chaucerian purists, for instance, have harshly criticized him for continually changing word order and narrative sense. Yet his translation of Virgil's works, particularly the *Aeneid,* is regarded as a monumental undertaking which, if not always exact, is nevertheless largely representative of the Latin original. *Fables Ancient and Modern* is similarly regarded as a lasting work

of translation. Critics agree that it embodies the finest examples of Dryden's narrative verse.

Of all Dryden's works, his dramas have been accorded the least acclaim since his death. With the exception of a few of his thirty-odd plays, such as *All for Love, Don Sebastian* (1689), and *Marriage-à-la-Mode* (1672), his productions have vanished from the English stage. This, according to critics, is perhaps largely due to his devotion to the heroic play, a form which attained its greatest expression through him but which has since radically declined in public appeal. In addition, Dryden's comedies, though held to possess fine examples of witty repartee and many memorable characters, have been found wanting in truly comic scenes or effective explorations of human emotion. Not until the early twentieth century, when studies by T. S. Eliot and Mark Van Doren as well as Montague Summers's six-volume collection of Dryden's *Dramatic Works* appeared, did the plays receive favorable reassessments, with Summers, in particular, extolling Dryden for his monumental contribution to Restoration drama. Yet, of most interest to the majority of critics of his plays are the numerous prologues, prefaces, and dedications, in which Dryden analyzed the works of John Fletcher, Francis Beaumont, Jonson, Shakespeare, and himself while perceptively expounding on the English theater, the difficulties of representing life on the stage, and the merits and drawbacks of rhyme. In so doing he inaugurated the English tradition of practical criticism. While critics of his time were characteristically preoccupied with issues of morality, immorality, and the edification of the reader or audience, Dryden wrote objectively and systematically of literature itself. Through a natural, conversational prose style—consummately demonstrated in *Of Dramatick Poesie,* a dialogue written in the skeptical tradition—he discussed works in the context of literary tradition, generic form, technical innovation, and effectiveness of presentation. Hence, his has been the standard for literary investigations to the present day.

In all fields of literary endeavor, though least so in drama, Dryden is considered to have attained a level of achievement rarely equalled or surpassed in English literature. Frequent comparisons with his most celebrated literary descendant, Pope, almost unanimously affirm Dryden's superiority in metrical innovation, imagination, and style, though the works of Pope are more widely known. But Dryden's importance is acknowledged to transcend the merits of any individual work. Through his lengthy, varied career he fashioned not only many memorable dramas, poems, and satires, but a vital, concise, and refined language which served as foundation for the writers of English prose and verse who followed him. For this reason Dryden has for centuries been considered one of the greatest forces in English literary history.

(For further information about Dryden's life and works, see *Dictionary of Literary Biography*, Vols. 80, 101 and *Literature Criticism from 1400 to 1800*, Vol. 3)

CRITICAL COMMENTARY

SAMUEL JOHNSON
(essay date 1779)

[A remarkably versatile and distinguished man of letters, Johnson was the major English literary figure of the second half of the eighteenth century; his monumental *Dictionary of the English Language* (1755) standardized for the first time English spelling and pronunciation, while his moralistic criticism strongly influenced contemporary tastes. In the following excerpt from an essay first published in 1779, he evaluates Dryden's oeuvre, establishing him as a preeminent literary critic and versifier of immense importance.]

Dryden may be properly considered as the father of English criticism, as the writer who first taught us to determine upon principles the merit of composition. Of our former poets, the greatest dramatist wrote without rules, conducted through life and nature by a genius that rarely misled, and rarely deserted him. Of the rest; those who knew the laws of propriety had neglected to teach them.

Two *Arts of English Poetry* were written in the days of Elizabeth by Webb and Puttenham, from which something might be learned, and a few hints had been given by Jonson and Cowley; but Dryden's *Essay of Dramatick Poesy* was the first regular and valuable treatise on the art of writing.

He who, having formed his opinions in the present age of English literature, turns back to peruse this dialogue, will not perhaps find much increase of knowledge, or much novelty of instruction; but he is to remember that critical principles were then in the hands of a few, who had gathered them partly from the Ancients, and partly from the Italians and French. The structure of dramatick poems was then not generally understood. Audiences applauded by instinct, and poets perhaps often pleased by chance. (p. 287)

To judge rightly of an author, we must transport ourselves to his time, and examine what were the wants of his contemporaries, and what were his means of supplying them. That which is easy at one time was difficult at another. Dryden at least imported his science, and gave his country what it wanted before; or rather, he imported only the materials, and manufactured them by his own skill.

The dialogue on the Drama was one of his first essays of criticism, written when he was yet a timorous candidate for reputation, and therefore laboured with that diligence which he might allow himself somewhat to remit, when his name gave sanction to his positions, and his awe of the public was abated, partly by custom, and partly by success. It will not be easy to find, in all the opulence of our language, a treatise so artfully variegated with successive representations of opposite probabilities, so enlivened with imagery, so brightened with illustrations. His portraits of the English dramatists are wrought with great spirit and diligence. The account of Shakespeare may stand as a perpetual model of encomiastick criticism; exact without minuteness, and lofty without exaggeration. The praise lavished by Longinus, on the attestation of the heroes of Marathon, by Demosthenes, fades away before it. In a few lines is exhibited a character, so extensive in its comprehension, and so curious in its limitations, that nothing can be added, diminished, or reformed; nor can the editors and admirers of Shakespeare, in all their emulation of reverence, boast of much more than of having diffused and paraphrased this epitome of excellence, of having changed Dryden's gold for baser metal, of lower value though of greater bulk.

In this, and in all his other essays on the same subject, the criticism of Dryden is the criticism of a poet; not a dull collection of theorems, nor a rude detection of faults, which perhaps the censor was not able to have committed; but a gay and vigorous dissertation, where delight is mingled with instruction, and where the author proves his right of judgement, by his power of performance.

The different manner and effect with which critical knowledge may be conveyed, was perhaps never more clearly exemplified than in the performances of Rymer and Dryden. It was said of a dispute between two mathematicians, 'malim cum Scaligero errare, quam cum Clavio recte sapere'; that *it was more eligible to go wrong with one than right with the other*. A tendency of the same kind every mind must feel at the perusal of Dryden's prefaces and Rymer's discourses. With Dryden we are wandering in quest of Truth; whom we find, if

Principal Works

"Upon the Death of the Lord Hastings" (poetry) 1649; published in Lachrymae Musarum; The Tears of the Muses: Exprest In Elegies

"Heroique Stanza's" (poetry) 1659; published in Three Poems upon the Death of his Late Highnesse Oliver Lord Protector of England, Scotland, and Ireland

The Wild Gallant (drama) 1663

The Indian Queen [with Sir Robert Howard] (drama) 1664

The Rival Ladies (drama) 1664

The Indian Emperour; or, The Conquest of Mexico by the Spaniards. Being the sequel of the Indian Queen (drama) 1665

Annus Mirabilis: The Year of Wonders, 1666. An Historical Poem: Containing the Progress and Various Successes of our Naval War with Holland, under the Conduct of His Highness Prince Rupert, and His Grace the Duke of Albamarl, and Describing the Fire of London (poetry) 1667

Sir Martin Mar-All; or, The Feign'd Innocence [with the Duke of Newcastle] (drama) 1667

The Tempest; or, The Enchanted Island [adaptor; from the drama The Tempest by William Shakespeare; with Sir William Davenant] (drama) 1667

An Evening's Love; or, The Mock-Astrologer [adaptor; from the drama Le feint astrologue by Thomas Corneille] (drama) 1668

*Of Dramatick Poesie (criticism) 1668

Tyrannick Love; or, The Royal Martyr (drama) 1669

Marriage-à-la-Mode (drama) 1672

Aureng-Zebe (drama) 1675

All for Love; or, The World Well Lost [adaptor; from the drama Antony and Cleopatra by William Shakespeare] (drama) 1677

"The Author's Apology for Heroic Poetry and Poetic License" (criticism) 1677; published in The State of Innocence, and Fall of Man

"The Grounds of Criticism in Tragedy" (criticism) 1679; published in Troilus and Cressida; or, Truth Found Too Late

Troilus and Cressida; or, Truth Found Too Late [adaptor; from the drama Troilus and Cressida by William Shakespeare] (drama) 1679

Absalom and Achitophel (poetry) 1681

The Duke of Guise [with Nathaniel Lee] (drama) 1682

Mac Flecknoe; or, A Satire upon the True-Blew-Protestant Poet, T. S. (poetry) 1682

The Medall. A Satyre against Sedition (poetry) 1682

Religio Laici; or, A Laymans Faith (poetry) 1682

The Second Part of Absalom and Achitophel [with Nahum Tate] (poetry) 1682

Miscellany Poems (poetry) 1684

Sylvae: or, The Second Part of Poetical Miscellanies (poetry) 1685

"To the Pious Memory of the Accomplisht Young Lady Mrs. Anne Killigrew" (poetry) 1686; published in Killigrew's Poems

The Hind and the Panther. 3 Vols. (poetry) 1687

A Song for St. Cecilia's Day (poetry) 1687

Don Sebastian, King of Portugal (drama) 1689

Examen Poeticum: Being the Third Part of Miscellany Poems (poetry) 1693

Alexander's Feast; or, The Power of Musique. An Ode, in Honour of St. Cecilia's Day (poetry) 1697

The Works of Virgil . . . Translated into English Verse [translator] (poetry) 1697

Fables Ancient and Modern; Translated into Verse, from Homer, Ovid, Boccace, & Chaucer: With Original Poems [translator and adaptor] (poetry) 1700

The Works of John Dryden. 18 Vols. (poetry, criticism, and dramas) 1882-93

Dryden: The Dramatic Works. 6 Vols. (dramas and criticism) 1931-32

Letters of John Dryden (letters) 1942

*This work is commonly referred to as Essay of Dramatic Poesy.

we find her at all, dressed in the graces of elegance, and if we miss her, the labour of the pursuit rewards itself; we are led only through fragrance and flowers: Rymer, without taking a nearer, takes a rougher way; every step is to be made through thorns and brambles; and Truth, if we meet her, appears repulsive by her mien, and ungraceful by her habit. Dryden's criticism has the majesty of a queen; Rymer's has the ferocity of a tyrant.

As he had studied with great diligence the art of poetry, and enlarged or rectified his notions, by experience perpetually increasing, he had his mind stored with principles and observations; he poured out his knowledge with little labour; for of labour, notwithstanding the multiplicity of his productions, there is sufficient reason to suspect that he was not a lover. To write *con amore*, with fondness for the employment, with perpetual touches and retouches, with unwillingness to take leave of his own idea, and an unwearied pursuit of unattainable perfection, was, I think, no part of his character.

His criticism may be considered as general or occasional. In his general precepts, which depend upon the nature of things, and the structure of the human mind, he may doubtless be safely recommended to the confidence of the reader; but his occasional and particular positions were sometimes interested, sometimes negligent, and sometimes capricious. (pp. 288-90)

When he has any objection to obviate, or any license to defend, he is not very scrupulous about what he asserts, nor very cautious, if the present purpose be served, not to entangle himself in his own sophistries. But when all arts are exhausted, like other hunted animals, he sometimes stands at bay; when he cannot disown the grossness of one of his plays, he declares that he knows not any law that prescribes morality to a comick poet. (p. 290)

It will be difficult to prove that Dryden ever made any great advances in literature. As having distinguished himself at Westminster under the tuition of Busby, who advanced his scholars to a height of knowledge very rarely attained in grammar-schools, he resided afterwards at Cambridge, it is not to be supposed, that his skill in the ancient languages was deficient, compared with that of common students; but his scholastick acquisitions seem not proportionate to his opportunities and abilities. He could not, like Milton or Cowley, have made his name illustrious merely by his learning. He mentions but few books, and those such as lie in the beaten track of regular study; from which if ever he departs, he is in danger of losing himself in unknown regions.

In his Dialogue on the Drama, he pronounces with great confidence that the Latin tragedy of *Medea* is not Ovid's, because it is not sufficiently interesting and pathetick. He might have determined the question upon surer evidence; for it is quoted by Quintilian as the work of Seneca; and the only line which remains of Ovid's play, for one line is left us, is not there to be found. There was therefore no need of the gravity of conjecture, or the discussion of plot or sentiment, to find what was already known upon higher authority than such discussions can ever reach.

His literature, though not always free from ostentation, will be commonly found either obvious, and made his own by the art of dressing it; or superficial, which, by what he gives, shews what he wanted; or erroneous, hastily collected, and negligently scattered.

Yet it cannot be said that his genius is ever unprovided of matter, or that his fancy languishes in penury of ideas. His works abound with knowledge, and sparkle with illustrations. There is scarcely any science or faculty that does not supply him with occasional images and lucky similitudes; every page discovers a mind very widely acquainted both with art and nature, and in full possession of great stories of intellectual wealth. Of him that knows much, it is natural to suppose that he has read with diligence; yet I rather believe that the knowledge of Dryden was gleaned from accidental intelligence and various conversation, by a quick apprehension, a judicious selection, and a happy memory, a keen appetite of knowledge, and a powerful digestion; by vigilance that permitted nothing to pass without notice, and a habit of reflection that suffered nothing useful to be lost. A mind like Dryden's, always curious, always active, to which every understanding was proud to be associated, and of which every one solicited the regard, by an ambitious display of himself, had a more pleasant, perhaps a nearer way, to knowledge than by the silent progress of solitary reading. I do not suppose that he despised books, or intentionally neglected them; but that he was carried out, by the impetuosity of his genius, to more vivid and speedy instructors; and that his studies were rather desultory and fortuitous than constant and systematical. (pp. 291-92)

Criticism, either didactick or defensive, occupies almost all his prose, except those pages which he has devoted to his patrons; but none of his prefaces were ever thought tedious. They have not the formality of a settled style, in which the first half of the sentence betrays the other. The clauses are never balanced, nor the periods modelled; every word seems to drop by chance, though it falls into its proper place. Nothing is cold or languid; the whole is airy, animated, and vigorous; what is little, is gay; what is great, is splendid. He may be thought to mention himself too frequently; but while he forces himself upon our esteem, we cannot refuse him to stand high in his own. Every thing is excused by the play of images and the spriteliness of expression. Though all is easy, nothing is feeble; though all seems careless, there is nothing harsh; and though, since his earlier works, more than a century has passed, they have nothing yet uncouth or obsolete.

He who writes much will not easily escape a manner, such a recurrence of particular modes as may be easily noted. Dryden is always *another and the same,* he does not exhibit a second time the same elegances in the same form, nor appears to have any art other than that of expressing with clearness what he thinks with vigour. His style could not easily be imitated, either seriously or ludicrously; for, being always equable and always varied, it has no prominent or discriminative characters. The beauty who is totally free from disproportion of parts and features, cannot be ridiculed by an overcharged resemblance.

From his prose, however, Dryden derives only his accidental and secondary praise; the veneration with which his name is pronounced by every cultivator of English literature, is paid to him as he refined the language, improved the sentiments, and tuned the numbers of English poetry.

After about half a century of forced thoughts, and rugged metre, some advances towards nature and harmony had been already made by Waller and Denham; they had shewn that long discourses in rhyme grew more pleasing when they were broken into couplets, and that verse consisted not only in the number but the arrangement of syllables.

But though they did much, who can deny that they left much to do? Their works were not many, nor were their minds of very ample comprehension. More examples of more modes of composition were necessary for the establishment of regularity, and the introduction of propriety in word and thought.

Every language of a learned nation necessarily divides itself into diction scholastick and popular, grave and familiar, elegant and gross; and from a nice distinction of these different parts, arises a great part of the beauty of style. But if we except a few minds, the favourites of nature, to whom their own original rectitude was in the place of rules, this delicacy of selection was little known to our authors; our speech lay before them in a heap of confusion, and every man took for every purpose what chance might offer him.

There was therefore before the time of Dryden no poetical diction, no system of words at once refined from the grossness of domestick use, and free from the harshness of terms appropriated to particular arts. Words too familiar, or too remote, defeat the purpose of a poet. From those sounds which we hear on small or on coarse occasions, we do not easily receive strong impressions, or delightful images; and words to which we are nearly strangers, whenever they occur, draw that attention on themselves which they should transmit to things.

Those happy combinations of words which distinguished poetry from prose, had been rarely attempted; we had few elegances or flowers of speech, the roses had not yet been plucked from the bramble, or different colours had not yet been joined to enliven one another.

It may be doubted whether Waller and Denham could have overborne the prejudices which had long prevailed, and which even then were sheltered by the protection of Cowley. The new versification, as it was called, may be considered as owing its establishment to Dryden; from whose time it is apparent that English poetry has had no tendency to relapse to its former savageness. (pp. 293-95)

The exigences in which Dryden was condemned to pass his life, are reasonably supposed to have blasted his genius, to have driven out his works in a state of immaturity, and to have intercepted the full-blown elegance which longer growth would have supplied.

Poverty, like other rigid powers, is sometimes too hastily accused. If the excellence of Dryden's works was lessened by his indigence, their number was increased; and I know not how it will be proved, that if he had written less he would have written better; or that indeed he would have undergone the toil of an au-

thor, if he had not been solicited by something more pressing than the love of praise. (p. 296)

The *Religio Laici,* which borrows its title from the *Religion Medici* of Browne, is almost the only work of Dryden which can be considered as a voluntary effusion; in this, therefore, it might be hoped, that the full effulgence of his genius would be found. But unhappily the subject is rather argumentative than poetical: he intended only a specimen of metrical disputation.

And this unpolish'd rugged verse I chose,
As fittest for discourse, and nearest prose.

This, however, is a composition of great excellence in its kind, in which the familiar is very properly diversified with the solemn, and the grave with the humorous; in which metre has neither weakened the force, nor clouded the perspicuity of argument; nor will it be easy to find another example equally happy of this middle kind of writing, which, though prosaick in some parts, rises to high poetry in others, and neither towers to the skies, nor creeps along the ground.

Of the same kind, or not far distant from it, is the *Hind and Panther,* the longest of all Dryden's original poems; an allegory intended to comprise and to decide the controversy between the Romanists and Protestants. The scheme of the work is injudicious and incommodious; for what can be more absurd than that one beast should counsel another to rest her faith upon a pope and council? He seems well enough skilled in the usual topicks of argument, endeavours to shew the necessity of an infallible judge, and reproaches the Reformers with want of unity; but is weak enough to ask, why since we see without knowing how, we may not have an infallible judge without knowing where. (p. 313)

His last work was his *Fables,* in which he gave us the first example of a mode of writing which the Italians call *refacimento,* a renovation of ancient writers, by modernizing their language. Thus the old poem of *Boiardo* has been new-dressed by *Domenichi* and *Berni.* The works of Chaucer, upon which this kind of rejuvenescence has been bestowed by Dryden, require little criticism. The tale of the Cock seems hardly worth revival; and the story of *Palamon and Arcite,* containing an action unsuitable to the times in which it is placed, can hardly be suffered to pass without censure of the hyperbolical commendation which Dryden has given it in the general Preface, and in a poetical Dedication, a piece where his original fondness of remote conceits seems to have revived.

Of the three pieces borrowed from Boccace, *Sigismunda* may be defended by the celebrity of the story. *Theodore and Honoria,* though it contains not much moral, yet afforded opportunities of striking description. And *Cymon* was formerly a tale of such reputation, that, at the revival of letters, it was translated into Latin by one of the *Beroalds*.

Whatever subjects employed his pen, he was still improving our measures and embellishing our language.

In this volume are interspersed some short original poems, which, with his prologues, epilogues, and songs, may be comprised in Congreve's remark, that even those, if he had written nothing else, would have entitled him to the praise of excellence in his kind.

One composition must, however, be distinguished. The ode for *St. Cecilia's* Day, perhaps the last effort of his poetry, has been always considered as exhibiting the highest flight of fancy, and the exactest nicety of art. This is allowed to stand without a rival. If indeed there is any excellence beyond it, in some other of Dryden's works that excellence must be found. Compared with the Ode on *Killigrew*, it may be pronounced perhaps superior in the whole; but without any single part, equal to the first stanza of the other.

It is said to have cost Dryden a fortnight's labour; but it does not want its negligences: some of the lines are without correspondent rhymes; a defect, which I never detected but after an acquaintance of many years, and which the enthusiasm of the writer might hinder him from perceiving.

His last stanza has less emotion than the former; but it is not less elegant in the diction. The conclusion is vicious; the musick of *Timotheus*, which *raised a mortal to the skies*, had only a metaphorical power; that of *Cecilia*, which *drew an angel down*, had a real effect; the crown therefore could not reasonably be divided.

In a general survey of Dryden's labours, he appears to have a mind very comprehensive by nature, and much enriched with acquired knowledge. His compositions are the effects of a vigorous genius operating upon large materials.

The power that predominated in his intellectual operations, was rather strong reason than quick sensibility. Upon all occasions that were presented, he studied rather than felt, and produced sentiments not such as Nature enforces, but meditation supplies. With the simple and elemental passions, as they spring separate in the mind, he seems not much acquainted; and seldom describes them but as they are complicated by the various relations of society, and confused in the tumults and agitations of life. (pp. 322-23)

Of Dryden's works it was said by Pope, that *he could select from them better specimens of every mode of poetry than any other English writer could supply.* Perhaps no nation ever produced a writer that enriched his language with such variety of models. To him we owe the improvement, perhaps the completion of our metre, the refinement of our language, and much of the correctness of our sentiments. By him we were taught *sapere et fari*, to think nat-

urally and express forcibly. Though Davis has reasoned in rhyme before him, it may be perhaps maintained that he was the first who joined argument with poetry. He shewed us the true bounds of a translator's liberty. What was said of Rome, adorned by Augustus, may be applied by an easy metaphor to English poetry embellished by Dryden, *lateritiam invenit, marmoream reliquit*, he found it brick, and he left it marble. (pp. 331-32)

Samuel Johnson, "Dryden," in his *Lives of the English Poets, Vol. 1*, 1779. Reprint by Oxford University Press, 1973, pp. 235-343.

JAMES RUSSELL LOWELL
(essay date 1868)

[Lowell was an American poet and essayist. In the following excerpt from an essay originally published in 1868, he evaluates Dryden's achievements as poet, critic, dramatist, and translator.]

English prose is indebted to Dryden for having freed it from the cloister of pedantry. He, more than any other single writer, contributed, as well by precept as example, to give it suppleness of movement and the easier air of the modern world. His own style, juicy with proverbial phrases, has that familiar dignity, so hard to attain, perhaps unattainable except by one who, like Dryden, feels that his position is assured. Charles Cotton is as easy, but not so elegant; Walton as familiar, but not so flowing; Swift as idiomatic, but not so elevated; Burke more splendid, but not so equally luminous. . . . Dryden undoubtedly formed his diction by the usage of the Court. The age was a very free-and-easy, not to say a very coarse one. Its coarseness was not external, like that of Elizabeth's day, but the outward mark of an inward depravity. What Swift's notion of the refinement of women was may be judged by his anecdotes of Stella. I will not say that Dryden's prose did not gain by the conversational elasticity which his frequenting men and women of the world enabled him to give it. It is the best specimen of everyday style that we have. But the habitual dwelling of his mind in a commonplace atmosphere, and among those easy levels of sentiment which befitted Will's Coffeehouse and the Bird-cage Walk, was a damage to his poetry. Solitude is as needful to the imagination as society is wholesome for the character. He cannot always distinguish between enthusiasm and extravagance when he sees them. (pp. 30-2)

The first poem by which Dryden won a general acknowledgment of his power was the **"Annus Mirabilis,"** written in his thirty-seventh year. Pepys, himself not altogether a bad judge, doubtless expresses the common opinion when he says: "I am very well pleased this night with reading a poem I brought home with me last night from Westminster Hall, of Dryden's, upon the present war; a very good poem." And a very good poem, in some sort, it continues to be, in spite of its amazing blemishes. We must always bear in mind that Dryden lived in an age that supplied him with no ready-made inspiration, and that big phrases and images are apt to be pressed into the service when great ones do not volunteer. (pp. 33-4)

Dryden himself, as was not always the case with him, was well satisfied with his work. He calls it his best hitherto, and attributes his success to the excellence of his subject, "incomparably the best he had ever had, *excepting only the Royal Family.*" The first part is devoted to the Dutch war; the last to the fire of London. The martial half is infinitely the better of the two. He altogether surpasses his model, Davenant. If his poem lacks the gravity of thought attained by a few stanzas of "Gondibert," it is vastly superior in life, in picturesqueness, in the energy of single lines, and, above all, in imagination. (p. 37)

The first part of the **"Annus Mirabilis"** is by no means clear of the false taste of the time, though it has some of Dryden's manliest verses and happiest comparisions, always his two distinguishing merits. Here, as almost everywhere else in Dryden, measuring him merely as poet, we recall what he, with pathetic pride, says of himself in the prologue to **"Aureng-Zebe"**:—

Let him retire, betwixt two ages cast,
The first of this, the hindmost of the last.

What can be worse than what he says of comets?—

Whether they unctuous exhalations are
Fired by the sun, or seeming so alone,
Or each some more remote and slippery star
Which loses footing when to mortals shown. . . .

Dear Dr. Johnson had his doubts about Shakespeare, but here at least was poetry! This is one of the quatrains which he pronounces "worthy of our author."

But Dryden himself has said that "a man who is resolved to praise an author with any appearance of justice must be sure to take him on the strongest side, and where he is least liable to exceptions." This is true also of one who wishes to measure an author fairly, for the higher wisdom of criticism lies in the capacity to admire. . . . The poet in Dryden was never more fully revealed than in such verses as these:—

And threatening France, placed like a painted Jove,
Kept idle thunder in his lifted hand;
Silent in smoke of cannon they come on;
And his loud guns speak thick, like angry men.
(pp. 38-9)

This is masculine writing, and yet it must be said that there is scarcely a quatrain in which the rhyme does not trip him into a platitude, and there are too many swaggering with that *expression forte d'un sentiment faible* ["strong expression of a weak feeling"] which Voltaire condemns in Corneille,—a temptation to which Dryden always lay too invitingly open. But there are passages higher in kind than any I have cited, because they show imagination. Such are the verses in which he describes the dreams of the disheartened enemy:—

In dreams they fearful precipices tread,
Or, shipwrecked, labor to some distant shore,
Or in dark churches walk among the dead;

and those in which he recalls glorious memories, and sees where

The mighty ghosts of our great Harries rose,
And armed Edwards looked with anxious eyes.
(p. 40)

It is now time to say something of Dryden as a dramatist. In the thirty-two years between 1662 and 1694 he produced twenty-five plays, and assisted [Nathaniel] Lee in two. I have hinted that it took Dryden longer than most men to find the true bent of his genius. On a superficial view, he might almost seem to confirm that theory, maintained by Johnson, among others, that genius was nothing more than great intellectual power exercised persistently in some particular direction which chance decided, so that it lay in circumstance merely whether a man should turn out a Shakespeare or a Newton. But when we come to compare what he wrote, regardless of Minerva's averted face, with the spontaneous production of his happier muse, we shall be inclined to think his example one of the strongest cases against the theory in question. He began his dramatic career, as usual, by rowing against the strong current of his nature, and pulled only the more doggedly the more he felt himself swept down the stream. His first attempt was at comedy, and, though his earliest piece of that kind (the **"Wild Gallant"**) . . . utterly failed, he wrote eight others afterwards. . . . In the reading, at least, all Dryden's comic writing for the stage must be ranked with the latter class. He himself would fain make an exception of the **"Spanish Friar,"** but I confess that I rather wonder at than envy those who can be amused by it. His comedies lack everything that a comedy should have,—lightness, quickness of transition, unexpectedness of incident, easy cleverness of dialogue, and humorous contrast of character brought out by identity of situation. The comic parts of the **"Maiden Queen"** seem to me Dryden's best, but the merit even of these is Shakespeare's, and there is little choice where even the best is only tolerable. The common quality, however, of all Dryden's comedies is their nastiness, the more remarkable because we have ample evidence that he was a man of modest conversation. (pp. 43-5)

It is pleasant to follow Dryden into the more congenial region of heroic plays, though here also we find him making a false start. Anxious to please the king, and so able a reasoner as to convince even himself of the justice of whatever cause he argued, he not only wrote tragedies in the French style, but defended his practice in an essay which is by far the most delightful reproduction of the classic dialogue ever written in English. Eugenius (Lord Buckhurst), Lisideius (Sir Charles Sidley), Crites (Sir R. Howard), and Neander (Dryden) are the four partakers in the debate. The comparative merits of ancients and moderns, of the Shakespearian and contemporary drama, of rhyme and blank verse, the value of the three (supposed) Aristotelian unities, are the main topics discussed. The tone of the discussion is admirable, midway between bookishness and talk, and the fairness with which each side of the argument is treated shows the breadth of Dryden's mind perhaps better than any other one piece of his writing. There are no men of straw set up to be knocked down again, as there commonly are in debates conducted upon this plan. The "Defence" of the Essay is to be taken as a supplement to Neander's share in it, as well as many scattered passages in subsequent prefaces and dedications. All the interlocutors agree that "the sweetness of English verse was never understood or practised by our fathers," and that "our poesy is much improved by the happiness of some writers yet living, who first taught us to mould our thoughts into easy and significant words, to retrench the superfluities of expression, and to make our rhyme so properly a part of the verse that it should never mislead the sense, but itself be led and governed by it." (pp. 49-50)

Dryden might have profited by an admirable saying of his own, that "they who would combat general authority with particular opinion must first establish themselves a reputation of understanding better than other men." He understood the defects much better than the beauties of the French theatre. Lessing was even more one-sided in his judgment upon it. Goethe, with his usual wisdom, studied it carefully without losing his temper, and tried to profit by its structural merits. Dryden, with his eyes wide open, copied its worst faults, especially its declamatory sentiment. He should have known that certain things can never be transplanted, and that among these is a style of poetry whose great excellence was that it was in perfect sympathy with the genius of the people among whom it came into being. But the truth is, that Dryden had no aptitude whatever for the stage, and in writing for it he was attempting to make a trade of his genius,—an arrangement from which the genius always withdraws in disgust. It was easier to make loose thinking and the bad writing which betrays it pass unobserved while the

ear was occupied with the sonorous music of the rhyme to which they marched. Except in **"All for Love,"** "the only play," he tells us, "which he wrote to please himself," there is no trace of real passion in any of his tragedies. This, indeed, is inevitable, for there are no characters, but only personages, in any except that. That is, in many respects, a noble play, and there are few finer scenes, whether in the conception or the carrying out, than that between Antony and Ventidius in the first act. (pp. 56-8)

It is as a satirist and pleader in verse that Dryden is best known, and as both he is in some respects unrivalled. His satire is not so sly as Chaucer's, but it is distinguished by the same good-nature. There is no malice in it. I shall not enter into his literary quarrels further than to say that he seems to me, on the whole, to have been forbearing, which is the more striking as he tells us repeatedly that he was naturally vindictive. It was he who called revenge "the darling attribute of heaven." "I complain not of their lampoons and libels, though I have been the public mark for many years. I am vindictive enough to have repelled force by force, if I could imagine that any of them had ever reached me." It was this feeling of easy superiority, I suspect, that made him the mark for so much jealous vituperation. (p. 67)

In his elegy on the satirist Oldham, whom Hallam, without reading him, I suspect, ranks next to Dryden, he says:—

For sure our souls were near allied, and thine
Cast in the same poetic mould with mine;
One common note in either lyre did strike,
And knaves and fools we both abhorred alike.

His practice is not always so delicate as his theory; but if he was sometimes rough, he never took a base advantage. He knocks his antagonist down, and there an end. Pope seems to have nursed his grudge, and then, watching his chance, to have squirted vitriol from behind a corner, rather glad than otherwise if it fell on the women of those he hated or envied. And if Dryden is never dastardly, as Pope often was, so also he never wrote anything so maliciously depreciatory as Pope's unprovoked attack on Addison. Dryden's satire is often coarse, but where it is coarsest, it is commonly in defence of himself against attacks that were themselves brutal. Then, to be sure, he snatches the first ready cudgel, as in Shadwell's case, though even then there is something of the good-humor of conscious strength. (pp. 69-70)

Dryden's prefaces are a mine of good writing and judicious criticism. His *obiter dicta* have often the penetration, and always more than the equity, of Voltaire's, for Dryden never loses temper, and never altogether qualifies his judgment by his self-love. "He was a more universal writer than Voltaire," said Horne Tooke, and perhaps it is true that he had a broader view, though his learning was neither so extensive nor so accurate. . . . Upon translation, no one has written so much and so well as Dryden in his various prefaces. Whatever has been said since is either expansion or variation of what he had said before. His general theory may be stated as an aim at something between the literalness of metaphrase and the looseness of paraphrase. "Where I have enlarged," he says, "I desire the false critics would not always think that those thoughts are wholly mine, but either *they are secretly in the poet,* or may be fairly deduced from him." Coleridge, with his usual cleverness of *assimilation,* has condensed him in a letter to Wordsworth: "There is no medium between a prose version and one on the avowed principle of *compensation* in the widest sense, i.e. manner, genius, total effect." (pp. 71-3)

[Has Dryden's] influence on our literature, but especially on our poetry, been on the whole for good or evil? If he could have been read with the liberal understanding which he brought to the works of others, I should answer at once that it had been beneficial. But his translations and paraphrases, in some ways the best things he did, were done, like his plays, under contract to deliver a certain number of verses for a specified sum. The versification, of which he had learned the art by long practice, is excellent, but his haste has led him to fill out the measure of lines with phrases that add only to dilute, and thus the clearest, the most direct, the most manly versifier of his time became, without meaning it, the source (*fons et origo malorum*) of that poetic diction from which our poetry has not even yet recovered. I do not like to say it, but he has sometimes smothered the child-like simplicity of Chaucer under feather-beds of verbiage. What this kind of thing came to in the next century, when everybody ceremoniously took a bushel-basket to bring a wren's egg to market in, is only too sadly familiar. (pp. 73-4)

Dryden has also been blamed for his gallicisms. He tried some, it is true, but they have not been accepted. I do not think he added a single word to the language, unless, as I suspect, he first used *magnetism* in its present sense of moral attraction. What he did in his best writing was to use the English as if it were a spoken, and not merely an ink-horn language; as if it were his own to do what he pleased with it, as if it need not be ashamed of itself. In this respect, his service to our prose was greater than any other man has ever rendered. (pp. 75-6)

He still reigns in literary tradition, as when at Will's his elbow-chair had the best place by the fire in winter, or on the balcony in summer, and when a pinch from his snuffbox made a young author blush with pleasure as would now-a-days a favorable notice in the "Saturday Review." What gave and secures for him this singular eminence? To put it in a single word, I think that his qualities and faculties were in that rare combination which makes character. This gave *flavor* to whatever he wrote,—a very rare quality.

Was he, then, a great poet? Hardly, in the narrowest definition. But he was a strong thinker who sometimes carried common sense to a height where it catches the light of a diviner air, and warmed reason till it had well nigh the illuminating property of intuition. Certainly he is not, like Spenser, the poets' poet, but other men have also their rights. Even the Philistine is a man and a brother, and is entirely right so far as he sees. To demand more of him is to be unreasonable. And he sees, among other things, that a man who undertakes to write should first have a meaning perfectly defined to himself, and then should be able to set it forth clearly in the best words. This is precisely Dryden's praise, and amid the rickety sentiment looming big through misty phrase which marks so much of modern literature, to read him is as bracing as a northwest wind. He blows the mind clear. In ripeness of mind and bluff heartiness of expression, he takes rank with the best. His phrase is always a short-cut to his sense, for his estate was too spacious for him to need that trick of winding the path of his thought about, and planting it out with clumps of epithet, by which the landscape-gardeners of literature give to a paltry half-acre the air of a park. In poetry, to be next-best is, in one sense, to be nothing; and yet to be among the first in any kind of writing, as Dryden certainly was, is to be one of a very small company. He had, beyond most, the gift of the right word. And if he does not, like one or two of the greater masters of song, stir our sympathies by that indefinable aroma so magical in arousing the subtle associations of the soul, he has this in common with the few great writers, that the winged seeds of his thought embed themselves in the memory and germinate there. If I could be guilty of the absurdity of recommending to a young man any author on whom to form his style, I should tell him that, next to having something that will not stay unsaid, he could find no safer guide than Dryden. (pp. 78-80)

James Russell Lowell, "Dryden," in his *Among My Books,* 1870. Reprint by Scholarly Press, 1969?, pp. 1-80.

WALTER RALEIGH
(essay date 1913)

[Raleigh was a renowned English lecturer and literary critic. In the following excerpt from the text of a lecture delivered in 1913, he commends Dryden's political satires.]

Dryden rose to his greatest in failure, and impressed himself most on his contemporaries when he was a sick and overtoiled man. His triumph was a triumph of character; so that his works cannot stand to us for all that the living man meant to his own generation. They were first collected in a single edition by Sir Walter Scott, more than a hundred years after Dryden's death. They vary enormously in merit. Some were written for money; some to oblige friends; on one page is a jingle of ephemeral trash, on another a whole succession of those magnificent couplets which he had at command when the occasion called forth all his powers. He belongs to the careless race of great writers, who do not correct their errors, but bury them under new achievement. They carry, and carry easily, a burden of faults that would crush a lesser man to the earth. (p. 159)

If Dryden had died just before he was fifty, he would have had a minor place in the annals of our literature; indeed, it may be doubted whether he would have been so highly esteemed as Shadwell, who died at that age. As a young man of decent family and small fortune he had followed the literary fashions of the time; not without great merit, yet it would be hard to discern the splendour of his matured powers in his heroic plays or in his eulogies of the great. Then came the last crisis of the fortunes of the Stuart dynasty, the crisis which gave us our constitutional monarchy and our modern party system. The proposal to exclude the Catholic Duke of York from the throne passed the House of Commons, and rent the nation in two. The Whigs, led by Shaftesbury, favoured the claims of the Duke of Monmouth, the natural son of Charles II, and a great popular favourite. The position was saved by the king, who having to choose between a son and a brother, became serious for once, and, neglecting his own ease and safety, declared himself immovable on the side of the lawful heir. To disinherit James was one thing; to override Charles quite another; for if he was not highly respected, he was much liked, and his just championship of his brother won the sympathy and admiration of the people. The leaders of the House of Commons drove their advantage too hard, and the reaction was swift. Shaftesbury was arrested and thrown into prison to stand his trial for high treason. His one chance of escape was that the Grand Jury of the City of London, which was a Whig stronghold, would refuse to find a true bill. It was while Shaftesbury lay in the Tower, awaiting his trial, that Dryden issued his first famous satire, *Absalom and Achitophel*. He meant it to do its work, and to procure the conviction of the Whig leader. It is the deadliest document in English literature, splendid in power, unrelenting in purpose. The lines in which he praises Shaftesbury's upright conduct on the bench did not appear in this first edition. Dryden was taking no risks. But his pamphlet failed in its immediate purpose; the Grand Jury threw out the bill; the

Whig party celebrated Shaftesbury's release by striking a medal in his honour, and Dryden, after returning to the charge in his satire called *The Medal,* had time to look about him and to deal out late vengeance on Shadwell, Settle, and the writers on the other side, who are crucified in *MacFlecknoe* and the Second Part of *Absalom and Achitophel.*

All four of these great satires fall within a single year. Dryden was a well-known dramatist and poet, but he issued them all anonymously. They produced a sensation greater than any printed pamphlet had ever produced in England. I do not remember any other case of a pamphlet designed to achieve a particular end, pointed to the occasion, topical and allusive in every line, which gained at once, and retained ever after, a place among our great national classics. The effect it produced may be well measured by the poems written in its praise, while yet the author remained unknown. The verse of *Absalom,* says Nathaniel Lee, is 'divinely good', each syllable is a soul. It is

As if a Milton from the dead arose,
Filed off the rust, and the right party chose.

Nahum Tate, who afterwards became Dryden's collaborator, discerned in the new author a great poet:

The rock obey'd the powerful Hebrew guide,
Her flinty breast dissolved into a tide;
Thus on our stubborn language he prevails
And makes the Helicon on which he sails;
The dialect, as well as sense, invents,
And, with his poem, a new speech presents.
Hail then, thou matchless bard, thou great unknown,
That give your country fame, yet shun your own!

What these praises mean is that Dryden was recognized at once, as he is recognized still, for the first of the moderns. He 'filed off the rust'; he discarded the antique poetic trappings, and proved that poetry could do work in the world. I confess that when I look through the collected poems of Dryden I am amazed by his completely modern attitude to all the old traditions. Take a trivial but significant instance. In *The Secular Masque* he introduces a chorus of the heathen divinities, who describe the changes that time has wrought in the world. Diana celebrates the sport of hunting beloved by the court of James I, and then joins with Janus, Chronos, and Momus, in a festive chorus:

Then our age was in its prime:
Free from rage and free from crime.
A very merry, dancing, drinking,
Laughing, quaffing, and unthinking time.

The whole masque resembles nothing so much as a Drury Lane pantomime. And Dryden's innovations in language were, to his own age, no less startling. He was content to make use of the colloquial speech of the day, the speech in which men traffic, and quarrel, and discuss, but he used it with such intensity and conciseness that he raised it to a higher power. The satirists who came before him had either beaten the air, like the Elizabethans, or had been fanciful, grotesque, and metaphysical, like Butler and Cleveland. They dressed themselves in cobwebs; Dryden wore a suit of armour. Men of the world had been accustomed to deal with poetry as a very good thing in its own place, when you have the time and the taste for it. You cannot deal thus with what you fear. Dryden compelled them to find the time.

If any one protests that the highest poetry, like the purest mathematics, can do no work, I do not desire to quarrel with him, so long as no attempt is made to deprive Dryden of the name of a great poet. Among the many definitions of poetry it is wise to choose the broadest. To exclude from the name of poetry work which is artistically ordered in strong and polished verse by an imagination of extraordinary scope and power, is a wretched impoverishment of thought and of speech.

The charge that has most frequently been brought against Dryden is that he was, to put it bluntly, a time-server. He celebrated Oliver Cromwell in ringing stanzas. He also celebrated the Restoration of King Charles II. He defended the position of the Church of England in a grave poem, full of weighty reasoning. When James II came to the throne he joined the Roman Communion, and, continuing in his office of Poet Laureate, wrote *The Hind and the Panther* in defence and praise of the Church of Rome. Men who change their religion after the age of fifty cannot expect to pass unchallenged, especially if the change happens to conduce to their material advantage.

Johnson and Scott were not puzzled or perturbed by these changes in Dryden, nor was their admiration for him, as man and poet, impaired at all. Indeed, I think that any one who takes the trouble to make acquaintance with Dryden's writings and the records of his life will find that there is no puzzle to solve. All through his life Dryden changed, or moved; steadily, in a single direction; he moved, and he never went back. Those who fiercely demand consistency in a political career commonly mean by consistency the repetition of a party cry. Their ideal character is the parrot, who never forgets what he was taught in youth, and never tires of repeating it. They make no allowance for experience, and none for thought—that bugbear of the drill sergeant, which will not stop when you cry 'Halt!' Dryden was born of a Puritan family and passed his youth in the religious and political chaos of the Commonwealth. It is not easy for us to realize what a lesson was there. (pp. 161-65)

Dryden believed in authority in religion, and monarchy in the State, even when the monarch's name was Cromwell. He was attracted, by the natural bent of his mind, to monarchy in religion—that is, to an indisputable power which should pronounce on all doubtful points. He never writes more vigorously or with more fervour of conviction than when he attacks the engineers of democracy. (p. 166)

Some wits of our own time have attempted to combine the advocacy of new views with satire directed against those who fail to be converted by them. The combination of the two professions, evangelist and buffoon, has a delightfully quaint air, but it robs the evangelist of all his efficacy. One simple soul makes more converts than many jesters. The terrible superstitious power of laughter is witnessed by this anxious care of nervous reformers to laugh first. They are afraid of ridicule, and try to intimidate their satirists by laughing at them. But this is a sign of weakness, for no one is hurt by laughter until he thinks he is hurt.

One of the great fascinations of Dryden's satire is its perfect ease of application to our own time. The divisions of opinion, the foibles, and the characters that he describes are alive among us to-day. Only the power and the will to satirize them have grown feebler. One reason of this, no doubt, is that our differences, for all their violence, are less fundamental and less tragic. A generation which had seen the king of England led to the block was in no danger of underestimating the gravity of political differences. Almost all the political problems of to-day bear a likeness to the problems of the seventeenth century; but the colours of that earlier picture are darker and stronger. We are perhaps humaner than they; we are certainly more humanitarian. We do not behead those who are opposed to us, we do not even condemn them; we explain them. Explanation is a subtler kind of satire, and it is touched, as Dryden insisted that all good satire should be touched, with concession, and even with sympathy. But we have to pay for our gains; and we have lost the grand style. When Richard Pigott, the informer, broke down, and took his own life, he was pitied more than he was hated. Far different was the case of Titus Oates, who, to work up Protestant frenzy against the Duke of York, invented a whole network of falsehoods concerning the Popish Plot. Titus Oates became an idol of the people for a time. Mr. Traill, summarizing the historical evidence, describes him as "a squat, misshapen man, bull-necked and bandy-legged, with villainous low forehead, avenged by so monstrous a length of chin that his wide-slit mouth bisected his purple face'. But he was worshipped as the defender of the faith. Dryden deals with him in lines that vibrate with scorn. Not even in the Roman satirists could you find four lines so packed with meaning and invective as the first four of Dryden's attack:

Yet, Corah, thou shalt from oblivion pass;
Erect thyself thou monumental brass:
High as the serpent of thy metal made,

While nations stand secure beneath thy shade.

And the controversies of modern authors, whether in verse or prose, are like the mewing of cats compared with Dryden's attack on Shadwell:

A double noose thou on thy neck dost pull
For writing treason and for writing dull. . . .
                                    (pp. 168-69)

I must not pass over Dryden's greatest enemy, the statesman and demagogue, Anthony Ashley Cooper, first Earl of Shaftesbury. To discuss his character and career would take me too far afield. It was not a simple character. If you do no more than take notice of Dryden's allowances and concessions, you will see at once that Shaftesbury can never be painted all black, or all white. He was a just and compassionate judge. He was of an indefatigable industry, and sought no private profit. He was courageous, even to rashness. Dryden's fiercest onslaught on him is directed against the demagogue. Shaftesbury took pleasure in the craft of statesmanship, and delighted in his own dexterity in handling public opinion. . . . The gist of Dryden's charge against Shaftesbury is not that he represented the people but that he deceived them. He encouraged opinions that he did not share, if he thought he could make use of them. He stirred up envy and hatred, which are more easily awakened than put to sleep again. . . . The warfare of party has raged on, with varying fortunes, for more than two hundred years since Dryden wielded his two-edged sword, and the honours are still divided. But it would be a mistake to regard Dryden as first and foremost a party man. No mere party pamphleteer ever has won, or ever could win, the place that he holds in English letters. He is of the centre; his party is the party of Aristophanes and of Rabelais. His best work is inspired by the sanity that inhabits at the heart of things. He lived in a turbulent age, and he was a fighter. But all extremists are his natural enemies. His weapons can be used, on occasion, by either side. He hated wrong-headed theorists and fanatics, who commonly impose their alliance, a heavy burden, on the reforming party in the State. He also hated all contented and self-sufficient dullards, who for the most part have to be supported, a grievous weight, by the party that stands for the established order. He makes war on both, with laughter that flashes and cuts. There are many provinces of poetry, some where poetry is most at home, that are strange to him. His love lyrics are, with very few exceptions, a miracle of banality. His best dramas just fall short of greatness. But in prose criticism, as in argumentative verse, and in metrical satire, he has not been surpassed. Not many authors have achieved the highest rank in three such diverse kinds.

If Dryden has failed to captivate some lovers of poetry it is perhaps because he deals, almost exclusively, with public affairs. Even religion is treated; through-

out his argumentative poems, in one aspect only, as a public interest. Were it not for one or two allusions to his advancing years, his works would give you no clue to his private life and retired meditations. If war, politics, and argument were banished from the face of the earth, nothing would be left for him to say, or at any rate he would say nothing. Congreve remarked that Dryden was the most modest man he ever knew; and certainly he is one of the most reserved of poets. He does not take his readers into his confidence; he has no endearing indiscretions. He is content to meet them in an open place, where there is business enough to bespeak their attention. A professional man of letters, especially if he is much at war with unscrupulous enemies, is naturally jealous of his privacy; he will be silent on his more personal interests, or, if he must speak, will veil them under conventional forms. So it was, I think, with Dryden; he is no bosom friend, to be the companion of those who keep the world and its noises at a distance. Those who do not care for Dryden may well care for poetry; it is difficult to believe that they can care for politics, war, or argument. And Dryden's resolutely public attitude has a purification of its own; it disciplines the more secretive and furtive passions by forcing them out into the light and air. War, after all, is the cleanest kind of hate; and, by its awful ordeal, often transforms hate altogether into pride and pity and sorrow. Something of the same kind may be said of great satire like Dryden's. The ugliness and squalor of personal hostility cannot live in that tonic atmosphere. The resentments of men are touched to larger issues, and raised above themselves. What is murky and little and obscene is drawn by the graving tool of the artist, with never a line in vain, and becomes a strong and noble thing, a possession for ever. (pp. 170-73)

Walter Raleigh, "John Dryden and Political Satire," in his *Some Authors: A Collection of Literary Essays 1896-1916*, Oxford at the Clarendon Press, 1923, pp. 156-73.

T. S. ELIOT

(essay date 1921)

[Perhaps the most influential English-speaking poet and critic of the first half of the twentieth century, Eliot introduced a number of terms and concepts that strongly affected critical thought in his lifetime, among them the idea that poets must be conscious of the living tradition of literature if they want their work to have artistic and spiritual validity. In general, Eliot upheld values of traditionalism and discipline, and in 1928 he annexed Christian theology to his overall conservative world view. In the following excerpt from an essay originally published in 1921, he favorably compares Dryden with the poets John Milton and Percy Bysshe Shelley.]

If the prospect of delight be wanting (which alone justifies the perusal of poetry) we may let the reputation of Dryden sleep in the manuals of literature. To those who are genuinely insensible of his genius (and these are probably the majority of living readers of poetry) we can only oppose illustrations of the following proposition: that their insensibility does not merely signify indifference to satire and wit, but lack of perception of qualities not confined to satire and wit and present in the work of other poets whom these persons feel that they understand. To those whose taste in poetry is formed entirely upon the English poetry of the nineteenth century—to the majority—it is difficult to explain or excuse Dryden: the twentieth century is still the nineteenth, although it may in time acquire its own character. The nineteenth century had, like every other, limited tastes and peculiar fashions; and, like every other, it was unaware of its own limitations. Its tastes and fashions had no place for Dryden; yet Dryden is one of the tests of a catholic appreciation of poetry.

He is a successor of Jonson, and therefore the descendant of Marlowe; he is the ancestor of nearly all that is best in the poetry of the eighteenth century. Once we have mastered Dryden—and by mastery is meant a full and essential enjoyment, not the enjoyment of a private whimsical fashion—we can extract whatever enjoyment and edification there is in his contemporaries—Oldham, Denham, or the less remunerative Waller; and still more his successors—not only Pope, but Phillips, Churchill, Gray, Johnson, Cowper, Goldsmith. His inspiration is prolonged in Crabbe and Byron; it even extends, as Mr. Van Doren cleverly points out to Poe. Even the poets responsible for the revolt were well acquainted with him: Wordsworth knew his work, and Keats invoked his aid. We cannot fully enjoy or rightly estimate a hundred years of English poetry unless we fully enjoy Dryden; and to enjoy Dryden means to pass beyond the limitations of the nineteenth century into a new freedom.

> All, all of a piece throughout!
> Thy Chase had a Beast in View;
> Thy Wars brought nothing about;
> Thy Lovers were all untrue.
> 'Tis well an Old Age is out,
> And time to begin a New.

* * *

> The world's great age begins anew,
> The golden years return,
> The earth doth like a snake renew
> Her winter weeds outworn:
> Heaven smiles, and faiths and empires gleam
> Like wrecks of a dissolving dream.

The first of these passages is by Dryden, the second by Shelley; the second is found in the *Oxford Book of English Verse,* the first is not; yet we might defy any one to show that the second is superior on intrinsically poetic merit. It is easy to see why the second should appeal more readily to the nineteenth, and what is left of the nineteenth under the name of the twentieth, century. It is not so easy to see propriety in an image which divests a snake of "winter weeds"; and this is a sort of blemish which would have been noticed more quickly by a contemporary of Dryden than by a contemporary of Shelley. (pp. 13-14)

Every one knows *MacFlecknoe,* and parts of *Absalom and Achitophel;* in consequence, Dryden has sunk by the persons he has elevated to distinction—Shadwell and Settle, Shaftesbury and Buckingham. Dryden was much more than a satirist; to dispose of him as a satirist is to place an obstacle in the way of our understanding. At all events, we must satisfy ourselves of our definition of the term satire; we must not allow our familiarity with the word to blind us to differences and refinements; we must not assume that satire is a fixed type, and fixed to the prosaic, suited only to prose; we must acknowledge that satire is not the same thing in the hands of two different writers of genius. The connotations of "satire" and of "wit," in short, may be only prejudices of nineteenth-century taste. Perhaps, we think, after reading Mr. Van Doren's book [*The Poetry of John Dryden;* see Sources for Further Study], a juster view of Dryden may be given by beginning with some other portion of his work than his celebrated satires; but even here there is much more present, and much more that is poetry, than is usually supposed.

The piece of Dryden's which is the most fun, which is the most sustained display of surprise after surprise of wit from line to line, is *MacFlecknoe.* Dryden's method here is something very near to parody; he applies vocabulary, images, and ceremony which arouse epic associations of grandeur, to make an enemy helplessly ridiculous. But the effect, though disastrous for the enemy, is very different from that of the humour which merely belittles, such as the satire of Mark Twain. Dryden continually enhances: he makes his object great, in a way contrary to expectation; and the total effect is due to the transformation of the ridiculous into poetry. (p. 15)

With regard to Dryden . . . we can say this much. Our taste in English poetry has been largely founded upon a partial perception of the value of Shakespeare and Milton, a perception which dwells upon sublimity of theme and action. Shakespeare had a great deal more; he had nearly everything to satisfy our various desires for poetry. The point is that the depreciation or neglect of Dryden is not due to the fact that his work is not poetry, but to a prejudice that the material, the feelings, out of which he built is not poetic. Thus Matthew Arnold observes, in mentioning Dryden and Pope together, that "their poetry is conceived and composed in their wits, genuine poetry is conceived in the soul." Arnold was, perhaps, not altogether the detached critic when he wrote this line; he may have been stirred to a defence of his own poetry, conceived and composed in the soul of a mid-century Oxford graduate. . . . Hazlitt, who had perhaps the most uninteresting mind of all our distinguished critics, says:

> Dryden and Pope are the great masters of the artificial style of poetry in our language, as the poets of whom I have already treated—Chaucer, Spenser, Shakespeare, and Milton—were of the natural [see excerpt dated 1818].

In one sentence Hazlitt has committed at least four crimes against taste. It is bad enough to lump Chaucer, Spenser, Shakespeare, and Milton together under the denomination of "natural"; it is bad to commit Shakespeare to one style only; it is bad to join Dryden and Pope together; but the last absurdity is the contrast of Milton, our greatest master of the *artificial* style, with Dryden, whose *style* (vocabulary, syntax, and order of thought) is in a high degree natural. And what all these objections come to, we repeat, is repugnance for the material out of which Dryden's poetry is built.

It would be truer to say, indeed, even in the form of the unpersuasive paradox, that Dryden is distinguished principally by his *poetic* ability. We prize him, as we do Mallarmé, for what he made of his material. Our estimate is only in part the appreciation of ingenuity: in the end the result *is* poetry. Much of Dryden's unique merit consists in his ability to make the small into the great, the prosaic into the poetic, the trivial into the magnificent. In this he differs not only from Milton, who required a canvas of the largest size, but from Pope, who required one of the smallest. If you compare any satiric "character" of Pope with one of Dryden, you will see that the method and intention are widely divergent. When Pope alters, he diminishes; he is a master of miniature. The singular skill of his portrait of Addison, for example, in the *Epistle to Arbuthnot*, depends upon the justice and reserve, the apparent determination not to exaggerate. The genius of Pope is not for caricature. But the effect of the portraits of Dryden is to transform the object into something greater. . . . Dryden is, in fact, much nearer to the master of comic creation than to Pope. As in Jonson, the effect is far from laughter; the comic is the material, the result is poetry. (pp. 17-18)

The great advantage of Dryden over Milton is that while the former is always in control of his ascent, and can rise or fall at will (and how masterfully, like his own Timotheus, he directs the transitions!), the latter has elected a perch from which he cannot afford to fall, and from which he is in danger of slipping.

> food alike those pure
> Intelligential substances require
> As doth your Rational; and both contain
> Within them every lower faculty
> Of sense, whereby they hear, see, smell, touch, taste,
> Tasting concoct, digest, assimilate,
> And corporeal to incorporeal turn.

Dryden might have made poetry out of that; his translation from Lucretius is poetry. But we have an ingenious example on which to test our contrast of Dryden and Milton: it is Dryden's "Opera," called *The State of Innocence, and Fall of Man,* of which Nathaniel Lee neatly says in his preface:

> Milton did the wealthy mine disclose,
> And rudely cast what you could well dispose:
> He roughly drew, on an old-fashioned ground,
> A chaos, for no perfect world were found,
> Till through the heap, your mighty genius shined.

In the author's preface Dryden acknowledges his debt generously enough:

> The original being undoubtedly, one of the greatest, most noble, and most sublime poems, which either this age or nation has produced.

The poem begins auspiciously:

LUCIFER.
> Is this the seat our conqueror has given?
> And this the climate we must change for Heaven?
> These regions and this realm my wars have got;
> This mournful empire is the loser's lot:
> In liquid burnings, or on dry to dwell,
> Is all the sad variety of hell.

It is an early work; it is on the whole a feeble work; it is not deserving of sustained comparison with *Paradise Lost.* But "all the sad variety of hell"! Dryden is already stirring; he has assimilated what he could from Milton; and he has shown himself capable of producing as splendid verse.

The capacity for assimilation, and the consequent extent of range, are conspicuous qualities of Dryden. He advanced and exhibited his variety by constant translation; and his translations of Horace, of Ovid, of Lucretius, are admirable. His gravest defects are supposed to be displayed in his dramas, but if these were more read they might be more praised. From the point of view of either the Elizabethan or the French drama they are obviously inferior; but the charge of inferiority loses part of its force if we admit that Dryden was not quite trying to compete with either, but was pursuing a direction of his own. He created no character; and although his arrangements of plot manifest exceptional ingenuity, it is the pure magnificence of diction, of poetic diction, that keep his plays alive. . . . In general, he is best in his plays when dealing with situations which do not demand great emotional concentration;

when his situation is more trivial, and he can practise his art of making the small great. . . . But drama is a mixed form; pure magnificence will not carry it through. The poet who attempts to achieve a play by the single force of the word provokes comparison, however strictly he confine himself to his capacity, with poets of other gifts. (pp. 19-21)

His powers were, we believe, wider, but no greater, than Milton's; he was confined by boundaries as impassable, though less strait. He bears a curious antithetical resemblance to Swinburne. Swinburne was also a master of words, but Swinburne's words are all suggestions and no denotation; if they suggest nothing, it is because they suggest too much. Dryden's words, on the other hand, are precise, they state immensely, but their suggestiveness is often nothing.

> That short dark passage to a future state;
> That melancholy riddle of a breath,
> That something, or that nothing, after death

is a riddle, but not melancholy enough, in Dryden's splendid verse. The question, which has certainly been waiting, may justly be asked: whether, without this which Dryden lacks, verse can be poetry? What is man to decide what poetry is? Dryden's use of language is not, like that of Swinburne, weakening and demoralizing. . . . Dryden lacked what his master Jonson possessed, a large and unique view of life; he lacked insight, he lacked profundity. But where Dryden fails to satisfy, the nineteenth century does not satisfy us either; and where that century has condemned him, it is itself condemned. In the next revolution of taste it is possible that poets may turn to the study of Dryden. He remains one of those who have set standards for English verse which it is desperate to ignore. (pp. 22-3)

T. S. Eliot, "John Dryden," in his *Homage to John Dryden,* Leonard and Virginia Woolf at The Hogarth Press, 1924, pp. 13-23.

EARL MINER

(essay date 1967)

[Miner, an American scholar, has written widely on the works of Dryden. In the following excerpt, he focuses on *Annus Mirabilis* and *All for Love*, noting especially their Christian humanist temperament.]

Dryden's historical sense is . . . neither unique nor first in time. But his is the first great poetic achievement embodying that sense and making it a norm of poetic eminence. He is the first really important English poet to bring contemporary history into poetry. So far is this the case that many of his greatest poems treat happenings not yet at their end. Such was the task he set himself in treating the naval war with Holland in *Annus Mirabilis.* And such the labor with the political events treated in *The Medal, Absalom and Achitophel,* and *The Hind and the Panther.* What enabled him to treat inchoate contemporary experience with assurance, what gave him the power to shape it into orderly structures, what furnished him with resources of metaphor, and what gave him immutable standards with which to imbue his writings was an older religious and royalist way of thought. The tradition, ritual, and myth of Christian humanism in its Renaissance royalist formulations provided him no less with the means of poetry than with faith in a divinely ordered world. In some respects, as in the belief in historical relativism and in historical progress . . . , he is more radically modern than Milton. In such others as . . . his enduring optimistic faith in divine Providence, and his conception of the divine essence as reason or wisdom, his beliefs antedate those of Milton and of his major contemporaries.

Dryden could not have foreseen the ways in which his later poems would dramatize the interplay in his thought between event and belief, between the modern and the old. Yet like the later works, *Annus*

John Dryden, ca. 1698, as painted by Sir Godfrey Kneller.

Mirabilis extols the triumph of public achievement wrought from personal and even national tragedy and celebrates the temporal in such a fashion that history is taken to a transcendent order above time. His earlier poems had moved with lesser or greater ease between these poles. It was essential that the paradoxes be resolved into a larger harmony. With all its faults, *Annus Mirabilis* achieves just that, and it does so by defining its purposes in terms that were to be basic to much of his subsequent poetry. *Annus Mirabilis* is a historical poem in narrative method, in subject, and in assumption. To this constellation of basic historical features are added the heroic and the panegyric, as he suggests in his **"Account"** of the poem. As everyone knows, all historical writing is in a sense dialectical, the past being directed toward the initial conceptions of it. For Dryden, history is the narrative of great events, epic in grandeur and revelatory of men deserving praise. Such optimism was to be closely tested in the public and personal crises of the seventies and eighties. Panegyric would turn to satire and epic grandeur to ironic posture, shifts accompanied and expressed by radical changes in technique. But the poetry would remain at root historical, the very satire would usually take forms of praise, and the epic aspirations would continue to be posed as a norm. With *Annus Mirabilis,* Dryden had discovered his New World of poetry. (pp. 34-5)

That world is one fashioned of the ideals of Christian humanism, imbued with history, public beyond merely private concerns, and affirmative of life for its potential. That world is the very one well lost in *All for Love: Or, The World Well Lost.* . . . It is lost with some regrets but triumphantly. What is gained is another world fashioned of the ideals of pagan passion, affirmative of an ecstatic moment above time, private in its exclusion of the larger world, and laudatory of gain in death. The two worlds seem as incompatible as might be; yet both are parts of the larger world of his poetry, and both are aspects of his values as a man. To the extent that they are contraries, they represent conflicting motives in the man, and themes that found expression in different genres.

The opposite pole to Dryden's public poetry is love poetry. Although he wrote a number of love lyrics, mostly songs for plays, that affirm the passions of private individuals, no one has ever taken them as the overflowings of his heart. The intimacy and ecstasy of private poetry at its intensest are absent, in part because the private individuals are dramatic fictions in the situations of plays, in part because the songs have a public audience. (p. 36)

Some twenty-eight plays make up Dryden's dramatic canon, a few of them falling outside generalizations that may be made about the majority. Among the lot there are such diverse forms as tragedy, comedy, tragi-comedy, the heroic play, and opera or masque.

Although such variety precludes a characterization at once simple and adequate, we may say that the major subjects of most of the plays are related in some fashion to those Dryden thought proper to the heroic play: "Love and Valour ought to be the subject of it." The love is usually that known in the century as heroical love, the passion overriding the limits that might bound it. Usually caught at first sight, it overturns reason and charges the will to seek its object, whatever the cost. "Valour" is similarly unbridled in its claims, and is often less a legitimate search for public trust than an exercise of its own pleasure. Dryden declared his grand fire-eater Almanzor to be descended from Achilles, through Tasso's Rinaldo and Calprenède's Artaban. It has been suggested that such a character is a type of the Herculean hero owed to remote antiquity through Roman drama and such earlier Renaissance types as Marlowe's Tamburlaine. Whatever his ancestry on one side or the other, Almanzor is—in love and valor—as voluntaristic a creature as ever lived on fire and words. Coextensive with his will, he resembles such other of Dryden's own characters as "little" Maximin, the tyrant of *Tyrannic Love.* The chief protagonists in the comedies match wills and words, usually brandishing challenges at the conventions of sexual behavior in the century.

At their worst, such characters will huff and puff. At their best, they are borne by the currents of their passionate wills. (pp. 37-8)

All for Love opens with ambiguous expression of alternatives—of the public, historical, and ethical values—and of the death-creation of passion. The famous opening speech by the Egyptian priest, Serapion, sets the possibilities in a way characteristic of Dryden's imagistic handling.

> Portents and prodigies are grown so frequent,
> That they have lost their name. Our fruitful Nile
> Flowed ere the wonted season, with a torrent
> So unexpected, and so wondrous fierce,
> That the wild deluge overtook the haste
> Ev'n of the hinds that watched it: men and beasts
> Were borne above the tops of trees, that grew
> On th' utmost margin of the water-mark.
> Then, with so swift an ebb the flood drove backward,
> It slipt from underneath the scaly herd:
> Here monstrous phocae panted on the shore;
> Forsaken dolphins there, with their broad tails,
> Lay lashing the departing waves: hard by 'em,
> Sea-horses flound'ring in the slimy mud,
> Tossed up their heads, and dashed the ooze about
> 'em. . . .

The initial line is one of those tragic portents our older playwrights use for poetic convenience; the next seven, concluding the first sentence, relate the rise of the Nile in its forward motion, as the second seven and another sentence its fall and backward motion. We begin with a "fruitful Nile"; we end with "slimy mud" and "ooze." (p. 41)

Most of the imagery of the play can be referred to the central integration of love and death. In this Dryden presents a version of one of the most abiding images of human experience, one that in Western literature may be called Romantic in view of its most characteristic expression in the medieval romances. (pp. 66-7)

Certainly without the "Romantic" identification in *All for Love* the play could not exist. There is nothing whatsoever in the play to show that death is a punishment of the two lovers; on the contrary, it brings their final and most exalted union. That fact is not controverted but modified by the presence in the play of a contrary image identifying the public world with life. This public image is not as significant to the play as the Romantic, but it is of great importance to a full view of it, and to our sense of the consistency of Dryden's interests. To pose the matter in terms of dramatic choice, Antony is faced with the alternatives of a vital public honor he has tired of and a mortal private desire which is insatiable. It is a question of will, of choice, of the extent to which—in the old faculty psychology—the will is directed by passion or reason. Yet, partly to make the lovers' triumph the magnificent thing it is, and perhaps partly as well to avoid a total commitment to the passionate will, Dryden makes the vital public honor and the mortal private desire accommodate themselves to each other part way by exchanging some of their values. What in the great nondramatic poems is a force of personal and even private feeling energizing a public mode, is in this play the private dignified by the public. This larger motion of the play is one factor in its claim to be Dryden's greatest, but it is typical of the motions of most of his plays. In all the will is to be seen choosing rightly or wrongly a private or public course, whether for a testing time or, with the finality of tragedy, choosing culpably, nobly, or in tragic ignorance of its true range of choice. (pp. 68-9)

[In each] there is a form of reconciliation managing by insight, acceptance, or yielding to bring into "perfect balance" a tragic or comic action of the human will. So much are these motions basic to Dryden's plays that it is difficult to find that conflict between a prevailing libertinism in most of the play and a final acceptance of convention which makes the tone of some Restoration comedies so difficult to assess. In his best plays, the reconciliation mingles the two worlds of private will and public reason or with opened eyes affirms the disparity between them.

In like fashion, the course of Dryden's dramatic career shows an increasing degree of protest and of awareness of the chasm between will and reason, even while leading to a higher reconciliation. The development from *The Indian Emperour* to *All for Love* and to *Don Sebastian* shows that he gradually found means of absorbing his own contrary motives in that blind tragedy, or comedy, of human life he had glimpsed as the fate of others in *Annus Mirabilis.* Similarly, his nondramatic poetry after his conversion affirmed in faith a faculty superior to reason and yet harmonious with it. Until that time he argued the reasons of the heart most eloquently in his plays and felt in his poetry outside the theatre the emotions of hope for a world meaningful in its rationality. In the plays we often find, whether in imagery of language, of action, or of both, that ages-old identification of love and death, the world of shadows and private desires. In works other than the plays, in their imagery and tone, we usually find a very different identification of meaningful action and civilized life, of the noonday world of light and personal achievement in a public arena. It may seem, then, that Dryden has two literary worlds, the dramatic and the nondramatic. Yet for all their concern with private shadows the plays finally submit to light, and for all their bright publicity the nondramatic poems take form in the obscure private reaches of Dryden's personality, whether his concern be with fate as in *Annus Mirabilis,* with that which causes bristling anger as in *The Medal,* or the salvation of his soul as in *Religio Laici* and *The Hind and the Panther.* For in both his dramatic and nondramatic works there is but one man responding, attempting to define his interests by exploring the limits of his forms and by searching for a "perfect balance" that could be struck in the writing only to the extent that it held between Dryden's inner needs and the values he could discover in his world. (pp. 72-3)

His poetry possesses some characteristic faults, especially of unevenness and carelessness. These may be readily forgiven for its virtues. It also possesses, especially in that intellectual remoteness revealed by comparison with the achievements of the Romantic poets, limitations that are more serious. Yet his achievement is a highly varied and dignified late expression of Christian humanism, and those who answer to his charge that we stand closer to it will continue to be taken by it. (p. 323)

Earl Miner, in his *Dryden's Poetry,* Indiana University Press, 1967, 354 p.

SOURCES FOR FURTHER STUDY

Eliot, T. S. *John Dryden: The Poet, the Dramatist, the Critic.* New York: Terence & Elsa Holliday, 1932, 68 p.

> Emphasizes the formative influence Dryden had on English poetry and prose.

Kinsley, James, and Kinsley, Helen, eds. *Dryden: The Critical Heritage.* London: Routledge and Kegan Paul, 1971, 414 p.

> Annotated selection of essays, from first reviews to early nineteenth-century criticism; contains a cross-section of Dryden's own criticism of his works.

Miner, Earl, ed. *John Dryden.* London: G. Bell & Sons, 1972, 363 p.

> Collection of critical essays on various aspects of Dryden's work, including "Dryden's Grotesque: An Aspect of the Baroque in His Art and Criticism," "Dryden and Satire: *Mac Flecknoe, Absalom and Achitophel, The Medall,* and *Juvenal,*" and "Dryden and Seventeenth-Century Prose Style."

Saintsbury, George, ed. *The Works of John Dryden.* 18 vols. Edinburgh: William Paterson, 1882.

> A revision and correction of Walter Scott's edition of the complete works of Dryden. The first volume comprises Scott's *The Life of John Dryden,* a pioneering biographical study which includes extensive critical commentary illuminating the historical and literary contexts of Dryden's works.

Van Doren, Mark. *The Poetry of John Dryden.* New York: Harcourt, Brace and Howe, 1920, 351 p.

> Seminal critical study evaluating Dryden's skill as a poet.

Ward, Charles E. *The Life of John Dryden.* Chapel Hill: University of North Carolina Press, 1961, 380 p.

> Complete, informative biography of Dryden.

W. E. B. Du Bois

1868-1963

(Full name William Edward Burghardt Du Bois) American historian, essayist, novelist, biographer, poet, autobiographer, and editor.

INTRODUCTION

Du Bois was a major force in helping define black social and political causes in the United States. He was both a leader and an outcast of his race, an intellectual who espoused controversial opinions early in his life and who in time earned himself the title of "prophet." He is widely remembered for his conflict with Booker T. Washington over the role to be played by blacks in American society—an issue that he treated at length in his famous *The Souls of Black Folk* (1903). Among his important works in many genres, he is particularly known for his historiography and for his pioneering role in the study of black history. According to Herbert Aptheker, however, Du Bois was more of a "history maker," and his works and ideas continue to attract attention and generate controversy today.

Du Bois had an almost idyllic childhood in Great Barrington, Massachusetts, where his family was part of a stable community of fifty blacks in the small town of 5,000. Born with "a flood of Negro blood, a strain of French, a bit of Dutch, but, thank God! no 'Anglo-Saxon'," Du Bois escaped outright racism and segregation in this small New England town. He and his mother, Mary Burghardt Du Bois, lived a meager existence; his father, Alfred Du Bois, left his mother about the time Du Bois was born. Class and race distinctions were slight in Great Barrington, however, and the town quickly recognized Du Bois to be a youth of exceptional intelligence and ability. When his mother died soon after his high school graduation, some residents of the town gave Du Bois a scholarship on condition that he attend Fisk University, a southern school founded for the children of emancipated slaves. Du Bois, however, had always dreamt of attending Harvard University. Some biographers maintain that the residents of Great Barrington thought their high school was ill-equipped to send students to Harvard. In 1885 Du Bois traveled to

Fisk in Nashville, Tennessee—his first journey to the southern United States.

"No one but a Negro going into the South without previous experience of color caste can have any conception of its barbarism," Du Bois later wrote in his *Autobiography* (1968). Yet Du Bois was "deliriously happy" at Fisk, where he met students of his own race. There he excelled at studies and during summers taught the young blacks who lived in destitute rural areas of Tennessee. After graduating with honors from Fisk in three years, Du Bois entered Harvard in 1888 to receive a second bachelor's degree and eventually his doctorate. Although fellow students greeted him with animosity, Du Bois found at Harvard professors who would provide lifelong inspiration—Josiah Royce, George Santayana, Albert Bushnell Hart, and William James, who became a mentor and friend. With only his dissertation to complete to receive his doctorate in history, Du Bois enrolled at the University of Berlin in Germany; there he studied philosophy, sociology, and history for two years. Upon return to the United States in 1894, however, he promptly rediscovered " 'nigger'-hating America," where the chances of a black history instructor finding a teaching position were slim. In 1895 Du Bois completed his dissertation, *The Suppression of the African Slave-Trade to the United States of America, 1638-1870.* The work became the first volume of the Harvard Historical Studies series, and Du Bois became the first black American to receive his doctorate from Harvard. In 1899 Du Bois published the sociological study *The Philadelphia Negro,* the product of interviews with 5,000 black persons living in the "dirt, drunkenness, poverty, and crime" of Philadelphia. The work, commissioned by the University of Pennsylvania, pioneered the scholarly study of black Americans. Yet the University did not give Du Bois a position on its faculty. Du Bois found this to be typical; despite his advanced degrees and important published works, he was denied key teaching positions time and again for no other reason than his color.

At the advent of the twentieth century the champion of black Americans was Booker T. Washington, then the principal of Tuskegee Institute in Alabama and the most powerful black man in America. In the preface to his *W. E. B. Du Bois: Negro Leader in a Time of Crisis,* Francis L. Broderick described Washington's accommodationist tactics as "speaking soft words to white men and careful words to colored men." Washington laid the blame for blacks' social positions on their inferior economic positions. As spokesman for his race, he was prepared to let black Americans be disenfranchised until they contributed to the economy by learning trades in agriculture and industry. Du Bois, however, could not abide by this stance. Broderick wrote of Du Bois: "Long restive under Washington's acquiescence in second-class citizenship, Du Bois or-

dered the Negro to be a man and demanded that white America recognize him as such." The two men, diametrically opposed in their views toward education, each found supporters, and the historic conflict began. In 1903 Du Bois published his best-known work, a collection of essays entitled *The Souls of Black Folk;* according to Arnold Rampersad in the *Dictionary of American Biography, Souls* became "perhaps the most influential work on blacks in America since *Uncle Tom's Cabin.*" Du Bois's critique of *Up from Slavery,* Washington's autobiography, was one of the essays in *Souls,* and with the work's publication Du Bois became inextricably involved with the fight for equality for blacks. In 1905 Du Bois formed the Niagara Movement, the first black protest movement of the twentieth century. Twenty-nine black men met on the Canadian side of Niagara Falls and planned to dismantle segregation and discrimination while opposing Washington. Du Bois helped institute a more lasting movement in 1909 when he became the only black founding member of the National Association for the Advancement of Colored People (NAACP). Du Bois also founded and edited *Crisis,* the official publication of the NAACP; at his editorial hand, it was the most important magazine directed at a black audience of its time. In it Du Bois wrote editorials condemning lynching and disenfranchisement, and his discussion of arts and letters in *Crisis* is considered the catalyst of the Harlem Renaissance. But in 1918 Du Bois lost credibility when he urged support for American involvement in World War I in the editorial "Close Ranks"; later, he discovered widespread racism in the armed forces in Europe. Many black Americans turned away from Du Bois's leadership at this time. As an intellectual and member of the middle class, he seemed at a distance from many of them. For instance, Du Bois was bewildered at the widespread popular appeal accorded to Marcus Garvey, Jamaican leader of the Universal Negro Improvement Association and "back-to-Africa" movement. His conflict with Garvey, whom he eventually called "the most dangerous enemy of the Negro race in America and the world," indicated his alienation from a large part of the black population in America.

"I would have been hailed with approval, if I had died at age fifty. At seventy-five my death was practically requested," said Du Bois of struggles later in his life, according to Addison Gayle, Jr. in *Dictionary of Literary Biography,* Vol. 50: *Afro-American Writers Before the Harlem Renaissance.* Although Du Bois continued to write great works, including his self-proclaimed magnum opus *Black Reconstruction* (1935), his popularity waned and resentment toward him grew. He was removed from the NAACP twice for ideological differences—he opposed the NAACP's idea of integration on the pages of *Crisis,* for example, and he supported Progressive party candidate Henry Wallace for president in the election of 1948 while the NAACP's executive secretary, Walter White, unofficially campaigned for Truman. In 1951 Du Bois was indicted as an unregistered "agent of a foreign principal" because of his involvement in the "subversive" Peace Information Center, an organization that sought to inform Americans about international events and to abolish the atomic bomb. Although Du Bois was acquitted, his passport remained in the custody of the United States government. In *Dictionary of Literary Biography*, Gayle wrote: "The black churches, the black press, the black educational institutions, and the NAACP were mostly silent during and after the period of his struggle." Du Bois found needed support instead from the "communists of the world." Awarded the International Lenin Prize in 1958, he became a member of the Communist Party of the United States in 1961, shortly before renouncing his American citizenship. He died at the age of ninety-five in Accra, Ghana.

"The problem of the twentieth century is the problem of the color line," said Du Bois to the Pan-African Congress in 1900, and his famous statement, which became the introduction to *The Souls of Black Folk*, has been hailed as prophetic. Despite the controversy that surrounded his ideas and actions throughout his embattled lifetime, Du Bois continued to fight for equality between races. As Rampersad wrote in his 1976 study *The Art and Imagination of W. E. B. Du Bois:* "Far more powerfully than any other American intellectual, he explicated the mysteries of race in a nation which, proud of its racial pluralism, has just begun to show remorse for crimes inspired by racism."

(For further information about Du Bois's life and works, see *Black Literature Criticism; Black Writers; Concise Dictionary of American Literary Biography, 1865-1917; Contemporary Authors,* Vols. 85-88; *Contemporary Literary Criticism,* Vols. 1, 2, 13; *Dictionary of Literary Biography,* Vols. 47, 50, 91; and *Something About the Author,* Vol. 42.)

CRITICAL COMMENTARY

J. SAUNDERS REDDING
(essay date 1948-49)

[Redding is a distinguished critic, historian, novelist, and autobiographer. His celebrated study *They Came in Chains: Americans from Africa* (1950) traces the history of black people in America. Written in a fluid style, the work has been called a creative story as opposed to a dry catalogue of historical facts—a style that closely mirrors Du Bois's own attitude toward the writing of history. In the following "portrait" of Du Bois, originally published in *The American Scholar* when Du Bois was eighty-one years old, Redding profiles the man and his thought.]

The first time I saw W. E. Burghardt Du Bois was on an occasion when he spoke in Philadelphia back in 1922 or '23. I remember that my father, who was then secretary of the Wilmington, Delaware, branch of the N.A.A.C.P., anticipated the event for days. I think he had never seen Du Bois either. But he had read him. He had read aloud to his uncomprehending offspring passages from *The Souls of Black Folk* and from *Darkeater,* and editorials from the *Crisis.* Indeed, though we could child-handle and mistreat the *Pathfinder,* the *Literary Digest,* and the *National Geographic* without fear of reprimand, the *Crisis* was strictly inviolate until my father himself had unwrapped and read it—often, as I have said, aloud. Afterwards it was turned over to us, and we

looked at the pictures of the colored babies, the handsome colored college graduates, and the famous colored college athletes, and read Effie Lee Newsome's "Children's Corner." Miss Newsome, we thought, was a fine writer. The name of W. E. B. Du Bois meant little to us as children.

But it had begun to mean something by the time I had reached my early teens. The meaning was purely emotional. We had a family friend whose sister had often danced with Du Bois in his Harvard days. In church on Sundays, the dark, passionate words of **"A Litany of Atlanta,"** which I had learned as a recitation, kept substituting themselves for the General Supplication. A speaker once told our small high-school assembly that we were of the "talented tenth," and somehow I remembered that the phrase was Du Bois'. So, when the opportunity came to see and hear this man, I was quite as eager as my father.

I did not know what to expect. Certainly, though, a man of giant stature—not the delicately structured man that Du Bois was: certainly a voice of thunder, and not merely the clear, clipped voice that Du Bois had: certainly an apostolic storm of wrath (for that is the way my father read him), and not the probing, deliberate, impersonal light that Du Bois' speech shed, like sparks struck off from tempered steel. I was disappointed. If my father was also, he did not tell me.

Principal Works

The Suppression of the African Slave-Trade to the United States of America, 1638-1870 (history) 1896

The Philadelphia Negro: A Social Study (essay) 1899

The Souls of Black Folk: Essays and Sketches (essays) 1903

The Negro in the South: His Economic Progress in Relation to His Moral and Religious Development; Being the William Levi Bull Lectures for the Year 1907 [with Booker T. Washington] (lectures) 1907

John Brown (biography) 1909

The Quest of the Silver Fleece (novel) 1911

The Negro (history) 1915

Darkwater: Voices from Within the Veil (poems, essays, and sketches) 1920

The Gift of Black Folk: The Negroes in the Making of America (history) 1924

Dark Princess: A Romance (novel) 1928

Africa: Its Georgraphy, People and Products (history) 1930

Africa: Its Place in Modern History (history) 1930

Black Reconstruction: An Essay Toward a History of the Part Which Black Folk Played in the Attempt to Reconstruct Democracy in America, 1860-1880 (history) 1935

Black Folk, Then and Now: An Essay in the History and Sociology of the Negro Race (history) 1939

Dusk of Dawn: An Essay Toward an Autobiography of a Race Concept (autobiography) 1940

Color and Democracy: Colonies and Peace (essay) 1945

The World and Africa: An Inquiry into the Part Which Africa Has Played in World History (criticism) 1947

In Battle for Peace: The Story of My 83rd Birthday (memoirs) 1952

*The Ordeal of Mansart (novel) 1957

*Mansart Builds a School (novel) 1959

*Worlds of Color (novel) 1961

†Selected Poems (poetry) 1964

The Autobiography of W. E. B. Du Bois: A Soliloquy on Viewing My Life From the Last Decade of Its First Century [edited by Herbert Aptheker] (autobiography) 1968

W. E. B. Du Bois Speaks: Speeches and Addresses [edited by Philip S. Foner] (speeches) 1970

W. E. B. Du Bois: The Crisis Writing [edited by Daniel Walden] (essays) 1972

The Emerging Thought of W. E. B. Du Bois: Essays and Editorials From "The Crisis" [edited by Henry Lee Moon] (essays) 1972

The Education of Black People: Ten Critiques, 1906-1960 [edited by Herbert Aptheker] (essays) 1973

*These works are collectively referred to as the Black Flame trilogy.

†The publication date of this work is uncertain.

Dr. Du Bois, of course, is tempered steel, and it is a matter of both character and mind. The bold outlines of his character—persistence, independence and a sort of realistic idealism—take their shape from a long line of down-East ancestors who were poor but never poverty-stricken, proud and self-contained but never self-centered. There were no particular subtleties in the characters of those ancestors; there are none in Du Bois. There was nothing of radiance; nothing mercurial, magnetic, gay. There is nothing of this in Du Bois either, except rarely. He is reserved, even aloof. His personality does not light up the place where he happens to be. Until he speaks on some subject that interests him, his presence in a room half full of people might go unnoticed by all save the artist, who would see the fine mold of the copper-colored features and the beautiful head.

The flexible sharpness of Du Bois' mind is due, at least in part, to the circumstance and experience of growing up a Negro in New England. In Great Barrington, Massachusetts, where he was born, he could cultivate the sensitiveness of perception that a town in Georgia would have dulled. There was little to stimulate emotionalism. The problem of color had some significance for him, but the tides of race ran calmly through the valley of the Berkshires, and the young Du Bois could breast them with a glorious disdain. He could be a competitor, without the beaten-in feeling of being a combatant against emotional forces too wild and unreasonable for understanding. The competition offered by his youthful associates was largely intellectual.

But the very mildness of the color problem in Great Barrington was teasing bait to Du Bois' expanding mind. Whenever he went to Albany, Hartford or Providence, he got "swift glimpses of the colored world," and had veritable seizures of awareness of that world's peculiar isolation, its slave heritage, its neurotic tensions, and its precarious clutch on the soiled hem of the economy. These things showed through the bright surface beauty and edged the gaiety with the icy lace of spiritual death. Du Bois came early to see the problem of color in impersonal terms as a matter of social condition, and this condition itself "as a matter of education, as a matter of knowledge; as a matter of scientific procedure in a world which had become scientific in concept."

Since before Fisk, which he entered in 1885, and through Harvard, the University of Berlin, and Harvard again, Dr. Du Bois has followed "knowledge like a sinking star." Now in his eighty-first year, he is still following it—not knowledge for its own sweet sake, which is a luxury of leisure his practical idealism would scorn, but knowledge purposeful, knowledge working. The pursuit has given him one of the most catholic minds of the century. It is not a difficult mind to know.

• • • • •

It is not a difficult mind to know, for it lies exposed in a dozen major books, hundreds of editorials and articles, and a thin scattering of poems. The writings of Du Bois have the lucidity of a series of anatomical drawings showing the progressive stages in the development of an organism. In this case the organism is truth—the truth of historics, which is both sociology and history. Du Bois sees this truth as a tool for the better performance of the scientific task of probing and assaying "the scope of chance and unreason in human action." That he has applied it to the limited area of race relations is partly because of the traditional "specialization" of modern scholarship, and partly because doing otherwise would have meant rejection of race and a consequent upsetting of the careful balance between intellect and emotion. Even a scientist need not be a monstrosity of sheer brain supported by the dehumanized mechanism, the body.

Certainly Dr. Du Bois is not. After *The Suppression of the African Slave Trade,* his doctoral dissertation, and *The Philadelphia Negro,* and in the midst of those Atlanta University Studies on the Negro, he published *The Souls of Black Folk.* This is perhaps as emotional and subjective a book as any written in the first decade of this century. Du Bois meant it to be that way. Four times in a long career devoted principally to investigation and research in material that *is* emotional—in material upon which he was one of the first to bring to bear the scientific method—he has had to give himself a thorough emotional housecleaning. *Darkwater* is a book like *The Souls of Black Folk: The Gift of Black Folk,* is another; and the novels, in a different way, are others.

What is remarkable is that these introspective sprees have come so seldom, and that they have not led to a pattern of introspective behavior, as with so many Negro leaders. Remarkable that his energies have not dribbled off in mere invective and condemnation, race chauvinism and apology and defense.

But the truth is that in spite of the general belief as to his purposes, Du Bois' professional commitment has been to a program of "scientific investigation into social conditions, primarily for scientific ends." One who reads his chief works must be convinced that their emotional overcast is inherent in the material, and is not a quality of the treatment. For almost twenty years Du Bois, alone among Negro spokesmen, believed that the basis for interracial change for the better was a knowledge of the facts and the broader truth they represented. Thirteen years of work at Atlanta University were posited upon this belief; this was at the heart of much that appeared in the *Crisis* and in *Phylon* under his editorship.

But Du Bois' scientific problem has been complicated in a way unknown to most professional scholars until recently. When a group of outstanding scientists came to realize the stake they had in the future application of their knowledge, atomic physics ceased to be a scientific problem merely: it became a freighted social problem too—and the physicists were social beings! Thus it has always been with Du Bois. Himself a Negro, he has been a socially responsible part of his problem; he has been concerned with the practical application of his discovered knowledge to the problem. This certainly accounts for his insistence upon a program of higher liberal education for Negroes; for his espousal of the "talented tenth" idea; for his connection with the N.A.A.C.P., and for the controversy with Booker T. Washington.

These interests and activities have been the logical consequences of Du Bois' concern. Higher education, especially for the talented tenth of Negroes, meant to him the training of leaders who could guide the race to cultural fulfillment. The controversy with Booker Washington, which increased in bitterness as it lengthen in years, started because Dr. Du Bois disdained the role of second class citizen which Washington thought the Negro ought to play. Du Bois has believed in political action, in the black world's fighting for equality "with the weapons of Truth, with the sword of the intrepid, uncompromising Spirit." Washington, who wished the Negro to remain politically passive, was a compromiser. He deplored agitation for equal rights. He was a gradualist. Du Bois has believed that the cultural contribution of the race to the nation was not less because it was different; Washington felt that the value of that contribution was doubtful. Du Bois remains certain that the autocratic power bestowed upon Washington by well-meaning but misguided whites was a danger and a thwart to Negro advancement.

Finally, Du Bois has believed in democracy, and his ultimate personal and spiritual commitment has been to this. He has never believed democracy impossible of attainment. As a social being, he has followed three paths that at one time or another seemed to lead to the ideal. The first, along which he started in his teaching days, was the path of objective Truth. He followed it on the assumption that once "the scientifically attested truth concerning Negroes and race relations" was realized, the world would act in accordance with the findings of science. The second was the path of Organization to propagandize and popularize the truth. This was in the early N.A.A.C.P. and the *Crisis* period. The third was the path of Security, to ensure "the survival of the Negro race" and the maintenance of its cultural advance, "not for itself alone, but for the emancipation of mankind, the realization of democracy and the progress of civilization." Du Bois has gone back to the first path now, and it is likely that he will remain in it until his journey's done.

The mind is not always perfectly the man and the personality. In spite of the tremendous respect which his high accomplishments have earned him, Dr. Du Bois is not generally liked. Many of the stories about him set him forth as a crusty, mordant-witted snob of both the intellectual and social varieties. He is, the stories say, a little too proud of himself. Negro and white people—and not just inconsequential people either—complain that they must be introduced to Du Bois time after time, because only the fifth or sixth introduction seems to "take" with him. Many think his preference for a certain brand of expensive cigarette an affectation, and they attribute the fact that he blends and generally brews his own coffee to a desire to maintain a social distance. Just below average in height, careful, even meticulous about his personal appearance, Dr. Du Bois gives some an impression of daintiness which does not fit into the popular concept either of scholar or dynamic leader. Yet it is the highest tribute, it seems to me, that even those who grumble about Du Bois in this wise acknowledge that he was indubitably their chosen leader, *the* Negro leader, from 1914 until the election of Franklin D. Roosevelt. He did not seek the place of leader. His intellectual honesty, his far length of vision, and a fundamental integrity destined him to it.

As a consequence of his position, Dr. Du Bois has few intimates, but these call him "Dubbie." They find him charming, witty and occasionally gay. Whatever sense of intellectual superiority he has never comes out in bombast or pomposity. When the mood strikes him, he can tell a fascinating story, though to call him a raconteur would stretch a point. His public addresses are usually brilliant and as carefully developed as works of art, but his delivery is deadpan, in-taking (as if he must reappraise his utterances), not out-giving. Because he has no oratorical flair, because he never talks down to an audience, and because audiences are what they are, he has been called a dull platform speaker. In 1931, after one of his lectures in Atlanta, where I was teaching at the time, a bright young college sophomore remarked, "The old man's lost his stride, hasn't he?" I do not remember what I answered besides the simple negative, but I know that Dr. Du Bois was not old then. He is not old now. Just three years ago, when he was reset-

tling in New York after a long absence, I heard him talk with glowing enthusiasm about the new furnishings for his apartment and about the years that lay ahead. At eighty he has still his hope and his dream, and his faith that one day truth will make men free. (pp. 93-6)

J. Saunders Redding, "Portrait . . . W. E. Burghardt Du Bois," in *The American Scholar,* Vol. 18, No. 1, Winter, 1948-49, pp. 93-6.

━━━━━

HERBERT APTHEKER
(essay date 1969)

[In 1946 Du Bois asked Herbert Aptheker to edit his correspondence and personal papers. According to J. Saunders Redding, Du Bois's choice was controversial. "Aptheker was white," wrote Redding in *Phylon,* "and editing the correspondence of a black American of Dr. Du Bois's stature and international prominence was a job for a Negro American, they said." The fact that Aptheker is an avowed Marxist further prejudiced black scholars against him. Nevertheless, Aptheker is widely recognized as the leading editor and scholar of Du Bois's works. In the following excerpt from a speech originally delivered to the American Historical Association in 1968 and published in an expanded version in 1969, he surveys Du Bois's career and contributions as a historian.]

Dr. Du Bois was more a history-maker than an historian. The two were intertwined, however; what interested Du Bois as a maker of History helped determine what he wrote, and what he wrote helped make history. (p. 249)

As historian, dedicated to the most rigorous standards of integrity, he remained, nevertheless, agitator-prophet; present was another fundamental ingredient in the man, namely, the poet. (pp. 249-50)

Du Bois' extraordinary career manifests a remarkable continuity. From his 1890 Harvard Commencement address to his posthumously-published *Autobiography,* the *essential* theme is the beauty, rationality, and need of service and of equality, and the ugliness, irrationality, and threat of greed and elitism. Because of the especially oppressed condition of the colored peoples of the earth—and particularly of the African and African-derived peoples—Du Bois believed in their capacity for compassion and comradeship, or, as he put it in the 1890 speech, "for the cool, purposeful *Ich Dien* of the African." (p. 250)

For Du Bois, history-writing was *writing;* one who produces a book should try, thereby, to produce *literature.* He drove himself hard on this. All authors, I think, are anxious to see their work in print; crusading authors probably feel this anxiety more than others. . . . Yet, Du Bois wrote and re-wrote his massive *Black Reconstruction* three times; and after that, revised and revised and cut and cut. . . . (p. 251)

Du Bois was explicit in his belief that while living behind the Veil might carry the danger of provincialism, it had the great advantage of helping disclose truth or neglected aspects of reality exactly because its point of observation differed. There was something else, too; Du Bois not only held that a new vantage point offered new insights. He held also that a racist viewpoint was a blighted one; that it could not fail to distort reality and that an explicitly anti-racist viewpoint was not only different but better. Hence, he insisted that the view—or prejudice, if one wishes—which he brought to data would get closer to reality not only because it was fresh but also because it was egalitarian. (p. 252)

Du Bois in practice resolved the difficult problem of objectivity and partisanship, of truth and justice, of the moral and the scientific by affirming—perhaps assuming would be more exact, for the argument is never quite explicit—that separating morals from science caricatures, the latter, that the just is the true, and that while objectivity in the sense of utter neutrality in any meaningful matter is absurd this does not rule out the describing of reality—of "telling it like it is"; that, rather, the solution to the apparent paradox has a paradoxical twist: it is intense partisanship—on the side of the exploited and therefore on the side of justice—that makes possible the grasping of truth. Or, at least, that such partisanship is the highway leading to that accumulation of knowledge which brings one closer and closer to the real but not reachable final truth. (pp. 254-55)

Du Bois had a towering sense of the Right, of the Just, a basic faith in reason and a passionate commitment toward achieving the just through the use of reason. Indeed, all this together is what Du Bois meant by that word which to him was most sacred: Science. And in his lifetime and in his experience the central lie was racism; this, therefore, received the brunt of his blows. (p. 256)

How shall we sum up Du Bois' conception of history? There is the facile technique of labels, normally unsatisfactory and in the case of a man as polemical, radical, and productive as Du Bois, bound to be, I suggest, especially unsatisfactory. (p. 259)

Having found Du Bois described as a confirmed Marxist, a plain Marxist, a quasi Marxist, and not a Marxist we have perhaps exhausted the possibilities.

Du Bois was a Du Boisite. His political affiliations or affinities varied as times changed, as programs altered, and as he changed. . . . (pp. 259-60)

While [*Black Reconstruction*] is weak insofar as

it tends to ignore the former nonslaveholding whites who were landed—*i.e.,* the yeomanry—and who therefore had class as well as racist differences with the black millions, and is weak, too, insofar as it accepts the concept of a monolithic white South from the pre-Civil War period to Reconstruction, it pioneered in a related area, for it called attention very forcefully to the neglect then, of the history of the poorer whites in the South.

The momentous impact upon the nature of U.S. society and therefore upon world history of the failure of the effort at democratizing the South—which is what the defeat of Reconstruction meant in Du Bois' view—is emphasized in *Black Reconstruction.* The consequent turn toward an imperial career, to which Woodrow Wilson pointed with delight, was a development which Du Bois denounced and concerning which he warned in prescient terms.

Du Bois also sought to make clear that Reconstruction was an episode in the entire—and worldwide—struggle of the rich versus the poor; in this connection he emphasized not only the specifics of the land question in the South but the whole matter of property rights; indeed, he called one of the most pregnant chapters in his volume, **"Counter-Revolution of Property."** He saw—as had Madison a century before him—that the right to and control of property was central to problems of the state and therefore of all forms of state, including that of democracy. Indeed, Du Bois—as Madison—emphasized the special connection between democracy and property insofar as the principle of universal enfranchisement meant political power in the hands of the majority and that majority normally had been and was the nonpropertied.

In this sense, Du Bois saw the story of Reconstruction—especially as it concerned the millions of dispossessed blacks—as an essential feature of the story of labor; not labor in the sense of industrial and/or urban working people, but labor in the more generic sense of those who had to work—to labor—in order to make ends meet. I think, too, that Du Bois' use of the term proletariat was more classical than Marxian. . . . (pp. 265-66)

Certainly, in the Marxian sense, Radical Reconstruction represented an effort to bring a bourgeois-democratic order to the South and in this effort—given the formerly slave-based plantation economy—the idea of "land to the landless" was fundamental; this meant not the elimination of the private ownership of the means of production—a basic aim of the dictatorship of the proletariat—but rather its wider distribution. From this point of view Du Bois' choice of words and expressions was confusing—and erroneous; but his perception of the relationship of particularly exploited black masses to any effort at making democracy real and to any secure advance of the deprived of all colors—which is what he was bringing forward—was a

---

Du Bois on race:

I do not for a moment doubt that my Negro descent and narrow group culture have in many cases disposed me to interpret my facts too favorably for my race; but there is little danger of long misleading here, for the champions of white folk are legion. The Negro has long been the clown of history; the football of anthropology; and the slave of industry. I am trying to show here why these attitudes can no longer be maintained. I realize the truth of history lies not in the mouths of partisans but rather in the calm Science that sits between. Her cause I seek to serve, and wherever I fail, I am at least paying Truth the respect of earnest effort.

Du Bois, in his 1939 study *Black Folk: Then and Now.*

---

profound one and remains a challenging one for today, not only in terms of history-writing but also in terms of history-making. (pp. 267-68)

It will be well . . . to allow Du Bois himself to state the basic theme of *Black Reconstruction;* presumably he is good authority for this. He stated this, in differing ways, several times; we shall for reasons of space, quote only one and that extremely brief:

To me, these propositions, extreme as they may sound, seem clear and true:

1. The American Negro not only was the cause of the Civil War but a prime factor in enabling the North to win it.

2. The Negro was the only effective tool which could be used for the immediate restoration of the federal union after the war.

3. The enfranchisement of the freedmen after the war was one of the greatest steps toward democracy taken in the nineteenth century.

4. The attempts to retrace that step, disfranchising the Negro and reducing him to caste conditions, are the deeds which make the South today the nation's social problem Number One.

(p. 269)

In the enormous body of Du Bois' writings, errors of fact will be found; almost always these are of a minor—even picayunish—nature. I think it is true that their occurrence is probably somewhat less uncommon than among historians of analogous scope. (p. 270)

Somewhat more serious was a kind of literary tendency on Du Bois' part which took the form of rather exaggerated assertions or a kind of symbolism that in the interest of effect might sacrifice precision. Professor Wesley in his . . . review in *Opportunity* (1935) gave several examples of this tendency; he called it "a

tendency to dismiss the explanation of some events with all too brief a wave of the hand." Exaggerations for effect would lead Du Bois to ascribe the Seminole Wars *purely* to the problem of fugitive slaves, or U.S. acquisition of the Louisiana Territory *solely* to the rebellion of Haitian slaves. A kind of poetic license would lead Du Bois to place John Brown's hopes as centering on the Blue Ridge Mountains—which was probably true—but he would add that it was in those same mountains "where Nat Turner had fought and died, [and] where Gabriel had sought refuge," which is simply not true; but probably this objection reflects the weaknesses of a pedestrian plodder before the canvases of an inspired poet-historian.

With such nitpicking I am reminded of Du Bois' **"Forethought"** to his immortal *The Souls of Black Folk:* "I pray you, then, receive my little book in all charity, studying my words with me, forgiving mistake and foible for sake of the faith and passion that is in me, and seeking the grain of truth hidden there."

His grains accumulated to a vast monument and precious heritage. It was Du Bois who began the scientific study of the Negro's history, who saw that it constituted a test of the American experience and dream, that it was a basic constituent in the fabric of United States history, that it was part of the vaster pattern of the colored peoples who makes up most of Mankind.

Even in detail, it was Du Bois who pioneered the study of the slave trade, who first offered new insights into the Freedmen's Bureau, who first pointed to the significance of the Negro in the Abolitionist movement, who contested the stereotype of the docile and contented slave, who helped illuminate the meaning of John Brown, who transformed approaches to the Civil War and Reconstruction, who pioneered in writing the history of African peoples, whose studies of Southern agriculture and of Northern cities—in particular Philadelphia—remain massive and—again—pioneering efforts in historiography. (pp. 270-71)

Herbert Aptheker, "The Historian," in *W. E. B. DuBois: A Profile,* edited by Rayford W. Logan, Hill & Wang, 1971, pp. 249-73.

ARNOLD RAMPERSAD

(essay date 1987)

[Rampersad is the author of the 1976 study *The Art and Imagination of W. E. B. Du Bois.* In the following essay, originally presented at the session on "Slavery and the Literary Imagination" at the 1987 English Institute, he analyzes Du Bois's concept of slavery in *The Souls of Black Folk*, noting how it differs from Booker T. Washington's in his autobiography *Up from Slavery*.]

W. E. B. Du Bois's *The Souls of Black Folk* was a controversial book when it appeared in 1903, but few readers opposed to it could deny its originality and beauty as a portrait of the Afro-American people. In the succeeding years, the collection of essays lost little of its power, so that it remains acknowledged today as a masterpiece of black American writing. In 1918, the literary historian Benjamin Brawley still could feel in Du Bois's book "the passion of a mighty heart" when he hailed it as the most important work "in classic English" published to that time by a black writer. About thirty years after its appearance, the poet, novelist, and NAACP leader James Weldon Johnson judged that Du Bois's work had produced "a greater effect upon and within the Negro race in America than any other single book published in this country since *Uncle Tom's Cabin.*" With admiration bordering on reverence for the book, Langston Hughes recalled that "my earliest memories of written words are those of Du Bois and the Bible." In the 1960s, the astute literary critic J. Saunders Redding weighed the impact of *The Souls of Black Folk* on a variety of black intellectuals and leaders and pronounced it "more history-making than historical." In 1973, Herbert Aptheker, the leading Du Bois editor and scholar, hailed the text as "one of the classics in the English language."

These are fervent claims for a book of thirteen essays and a short story written by an academic who had been rigidly trained in history and sociology (especially at Harvard and the University of Berlin, where Du Bois did extensive doctoral work), and whose previous books had been an austere dissertation in history, *The Suppression of the African Slave-Trade to the United States,* and an empirical sociological study of urban blacks, *The Philadelphia Negro.* Clearly, however, *The Souls of Black Folk* was something other than academic history and sociology. If white academics and intellectuals mainly ignored its existence (although Henry James called it "the only Southern book of distinction published in many a year"), its impression was marked on the class of black Americans who provided the leadership of their race. Among black intellectuals, above all, *The Souls of Black Folk* became a kind of sacred book, the central text for the interpretation of the Afro-American experience and the most trustworthy guide into the grim future that seemed to loom before their race in America.

The main cause of the controversy surrounding *The Souls of Black Folk* was its devastating attack on Booker T. Washington. The head of the Tuskegee Institute in Alabama was already a famous man when his autobiography *Up from Slavery* was published in 1901. His epochal compromise speech at the Atlanta Exposi-

tion in 1895 had catapulted him to the position of leading spokesman for his race before the white world, a friend of rich industrialists like Andrew Carnegie and a dinner guest in the White House of Theodore Roosevelt. Nevertheless, *Up from Slavery* reinforced Washington's authority to a significant extent. Above all, he has used the skeleton of the slave narrative form (that is, the story of a life that progresses from a state of legal bondage to a state of freedom and a substantial degree of self-realization) not only to describe his rise in the world but also to dramatize the heart of the Tuskegee argument that the salvation of Afro-America lay in self-reliance, conciliation of the reactionary white South, a surrender of the right to vote and the right to social equality, dependence on thrift and industriousness, and an emphasis on vocational training rather than the liberal arts in the education of the young. To these ideas, Du Bois and *The Souls of Black Folk* were unalterably opposed.

I wish to suggest here that perhaps the most important element in the making of Du Bois's book, which drew on his previously published material but also on fresh work, derived in significant degree from his full awareness of *Up from Slavery.* While this could hardly be an altogether novel suggestion—given Du Bois's attack on Washington in his book—the crucial area of difference between them has not been adequately recognized. I would argue that this crucial element involved Du Bois's acute sensitivity to slavery both as an institution in American history and as an idea, along with his distaste for Washington's treatment of the subject in *Up from Slavery.* To some extent Du Bois's book functions, in spite of its only partial status as an autobiography, as a direct, parodic challenge to certain forms and assumptions of the slave narrative (in all their variety) which had so aided Booker T. Washington's arguments. While it does so mainly to refute the major ideas in Washington's influential text, at the same time its contrariness of form is made obligatory by Du Bois's peculiar attitudes toward slavery.

The resulting book can be seen as marking Du Bois's sense (and that of the many writers and intellectuals influenced by him) of the obsolescence of the slave narrative as a paradigm for Afro-American experience, as well as the beginning of a reflexive paradigm, allied to the slave narrative, that leads the reader—and the race described in the book—into the modern Afro-American world. William L. Andrews has pointed out . . . in his essay on slavery and the rise of Afro-American literary realism, that postbellum slave narratives de-emphasized the hellishly destructive nature of slavery and offered it instead as a crucible in which future black manhood was formed. Du Bois's approach, I would argue, is in part a revival of the earlier, antebellum spirit of black autobiography and the slave narrative, but in more significant part also differs from that earlier spirit. In both the earlier and the later slave narratives there is progress for the black as he or she moves away from slavery. Du Bois's central point, as we shall see, is different.

For Booker T. Washington in *Up from Slavery,* slavery was not an institution to be defended overtly. Nevertheless, its evils had been much overstated, as he saw them, and its blessings were real. The evils, insofar as they existed, were to be acknowledged briefly and then forgotten. While this approach in some senses is to be expected of an autobiography by a man born only seven years before emancipation, it also underscores Washington's public attitude to American slavery in particular and to history in general. In Washington's considered view, neither slavery nor history is of great consequence—or, at the very least, of daunting consequence to any black man of sound character who properly trains himself for the demands of the modern world. In *Up from Slavery,* Washington writes flatly of "the cruelty and moral wrong of slavery," and he remarks conclusively about the former slaves that "I have never seen one who did not want to be free, or one who would return to slavery." "I condemn it as an institution," he adds. Tellingly, however, this condemnation springs from a need to clarify the major message about slavery in his chapter on his slave years, "A Slave among Slaves." The need itself springs from the patent ambiguity of Washington's view of slavery.

Whatever he intends to do, Washington stresses the fundamentally innocuous, almost innocent, nature of the institution. Of his white father (said to be a prosperous neighbor, who refused to acknowledge him) and of his poor, black mother (who sometimes stole chickens in order to feed herself and her children), Washington's judgment is the same. In lacking the courage or generosity to acknowledge his son, his father "was simply another unfortunate victim of the institution which the Nation unhappily had engrafted upon it at the time." In her thievery, his mother "was simply a victim of the system of slavery." Moreover, Washington's lack of hostility to his father allegedly reflected the complacent attitudes of other blacks to whites. There was no "bitter feeling toward the white people on the part of my race" about the fact that many whites were fighting as soldiers in the Confederate army to preserve slavery; where slaves had been treated "with anything like decency," they showed love and tenderness to their masters, even those in the military. The chapter "A Slave among Slaves" ends with a striking tableau of the day of emancipation. Whites are sad not because of the loss of valuable property but "because of parting with those whom they had reared and who were in many ways very close to them." Blacks are initially ecstatic, but the older freedmen, "stealthily at first," return later to the "big house" to consult their former masters about their future.

Doubtless sincere in his expressions of antipathy to slavery, Washington nevertheless emphasizes the benefits gained by blacks through the institution. "Notwithstanding the cruel wrongs inflicted upon us," he asserts, "the black man got nearly as much out of slavery as the white man did." With Afro-Americans comprising the most advanced community of blacks in the world (as Washington claimed), slavery was indisputably a fortunate act. Indeed, it was further proof of the notion that "Providence so often uses men and institutions to accomplish a purpose." Through all difficulties, Washington continues to derive faith in the future of Black Americans by dwelling on "the wilderness through which and out of which, a good Providence has already led us."

For Washington, the acknowledgment of Providence piously marks his negation of the consequences of forces such as those of history, psychology, economics, and philosophy at play in the field of slavery. (Providence does not perform a more positive function in his scheme, in which there is little room for religious enthusiasm or spiritual complexity. Of religion and spirituality in *Up from Slavery* he writes: "While a great deal of stress is laid upon the industrial side of the work at Tuskegee, we do not neglect or overlook in any degree the religious and spiritual side. The school is strictly undenominational, but it is thoroughly Christian, and the spiritual training of the students is not neglected.") Willing to share in the belief that economic competition and greed had been at the root of slavery, and that slavery itself was ultimately the cause of the Civil War, he pushes no further into causes and effects even as he everywhere, as a champion of pragmatism, lauds the value of "facts" and the "need to look facts in the face." In his scheme, the mental legacy of slavery to the black freedman is not conflict, but a blank, a kind of tabular rasa on which is to be inscribed those values and skills that would serve the freedman best in the new age. Although he offers a critical view of the past of his people, "who had spent generations in slavery, and before that generations in the darkest heathenism," Washington in fact invites a vision of the Afro-American as black Adam. This Adam is, in a way, both prelapsarian and postlapsarian. He is an Adam in the Eden of the South, with the world before him. He is also Adam who has fallen. The fall was slavery itself. Slavery, as seen in this context, is a "fortunate fall"— the fall by which Africans gained the skills and the knowledge needed for the modern world. But who is responsible for the fall? Who has sinned? The answer surely must be the black slave himself, since *Up from Slavery* places no blame on the white world. The failure to investigate the origins, the nature, and the consequences of slavery has led Washington to a subtle and yet far-reaching defamation of the African and Afro-American peoples.

The black American Adam, in his prelapsarian guise, and in the simplicity of his capabilities, must be protected from the fruit that would destroy him—in this case, knowledge in the form of classical learning. Otherwise, the black man may become a kind of Satan, excessively proud. Washington denounces the idea, apparently embraced eagerly by many blacks in the aftermath of the Civil War, "that a knowledge, however little, of the Greek and Latin languages would make one a very superior human being, something bordering almost on the supernatural." Inveighing against false black pride, he dismisses passionate black claims to the right to vote. The secret of progress appears to be regression. Deploring the mass black migration to the cities, he often wishes "that by some power of magic I might remove the great bulk of these people into the country districts and plant them upon the soil, upon the solid and never deceptive foundation of Mother Nature, where all nations and races that have ever succeeded have gotten their start." His garden is a priceless source of resuscitation. There, "I feel that I am coming into contact with something that is giving me strength for the many duties and hard places that await me out in the big world. I pity the man or woman who has never learned to enjoy nature and to get strength and inspiration out of it."

This refusal to confront slavery (or even the understandable association in the minds of many blacks of agricultural work with the terms of slavery) and this black variation on the myth of an American Adam make *Up from Slavery* an odd slave narrative according to either the antebellum or the postbellum model. Nevertheless, the hero moves from slavery to freedom and into his future as from darkness to light. Holding the story together is the distinction Washington quietly makes between himself and the other ex-slaves in general. He is the hero of a slave narrative. He sheds the dead skin of slavery, seeks an education, builds on it, and emerges as a powerful, fully realized human being, confident, almost invincible (within the bounds of discretion). This is seen as a possibility also for Washington's disciples, as the graduates of Tuskegee are represented. "Wherever our graduates go," he writes near the end of his book, "the changes which soon begin to appear in the buying of land, improving homes, saving money, in education, and in high moral character are remarkable. While communities are fast being revolutionized through the instrumentality of these men and women." The same cannot be said of the masses of blacks who have not been to Tuskegee or who have not come under the Tuskegee influence in some other way. In *Up from Slavery,* they remain blanks. This was hardly the first slave narrative in which the central character saw great distance between himself and other blacks. In Du Bois's *The Souls of Black Folk,* however, that distance would shrink dramatically.

When *The Souls of Black Folk* appeared in 1903, slavery had been officially dead in the United States for forty years. Du Bois himself, thirty-five years of age in 1903, had not been born a slave. Indeed, he had been born on free soil, in Great Barrington, Massachusetts, in a family that had lived there for several generations. One ancestor had even been a revolutionary soldier. Nevertheless, the shadow of slavery hangs powerfully over *The Souls of Black Folk.* Thus Du Bois acknowledged the fact that his book is about a people whose number included many who had been born slaves, and a vast majority who were immediately descended from slaves. On this central point, *The Souls of Black Folk* is a stark contrast to *Up from Slavery.*

In July 1901, shortly after the latter appeared, Du Bois reviewed it in *Dial* magazine. This was his first open criticism of Washington. In 1895, he had saluted Washington's compromising Atlanta Exposition speech as "a word fitly spoken." In the following years, however, he had watched with increasing dismay as the head of Tuskegee propagated his doctrine of compromise and silenced much of his opposition through his manipulation of elements of the black press and other sources of power. Du Bois's attack on him in *Dial* was decisive. The *Dial* review, followed by *The Souls of Black Folk* (where the review again appeared, in adapted from), created "a split of the race into two contending camps," as James Weldon Johnson later noted astutely. Cryptically noting that Washington had given "but glimpses of the real struggle which he has had for leadership," Du Bois accused him of peddling a "Lie." Surveying the various modes of black response to white power from the earliest days in America, he concluded that the vaunted Tuskegee philosophy for black self-improvement was little more than "the old [black] attitude of adjustment to environment, emphasizing the economic phase."

In *The Souls of Black Folk,* unable to fashion an autobiography to match Washington's, young Du Bois nevertheless infused a powerful autobiographical spirit and presence into his essays. From about three dozen of his published articles on aspects of black history and sociology, he selected eight for adaptation or reprinting as nine chapters in *The Souls of Black Folk.* The brief fifth chapter, **"Of the Wings of Atalanta,"** about commercialism and the city of Atlanta, was new, as were the last four chapters: **"Of the Passing of the First-Born,"** Du Bois's prose elegy on the death of his only son, Burghardt; **"Of Alexander Crummell,"** his tribute to an exceptional black man; **"Of the Coming of John,"** a short story; and **"Of the Sorrow Songs,"** an essay on spirituals. Holding these various efforts together is the central figure of Du Bois, who presents himself as a scholar and historian but more dramatically as an artist and a visionary who would not only depict the present state of black culture but also try to prophesy something about its future and the future of the nation.

Du Bois understood clearly that the representation of slavery was central to the entire task. Unlike Washington in *Up from Slavery,* he believed that slavery had been a force of extraordinary—and mainly destructive—potency. Destructive as it had been, however, slavery had not destroyed every major aspect of the African character and psychology (topics on which Washington had been silent); the African core had survived. But so had slavery. Where Washington saw opportunity on every hand for the black, if the right course was followed, Du Bois proclaimed that American slavery was not dead. In one guise or another, it still persisted, with its power scarcely diminished. The act of emancipation had been both a fact (such as Washington loved to fasten on) and a mirage: "Years have passed since then—ten, twenty, forty; forty years of national life, forty years of renewal and development, and yet the swarthy spectre sits in its accustomed seat at the Nation's feast. . . . The Nation has not yet found peace from its sins; the freedman has not yet found in freedom his promised land."

Although there were elements of agreement between Washington and Du Bois on the nature of slavery, *The Souls of Black Folk* portrays the institution in terms essentially opposite to those in *Up from Slavery.* Du Bois does not deny that slavery had its benign side, but in almost every instance his conclusion about its effects is radical when compared with Washington's. American slavery had not been the "worst slavery in the world," and had known something of "kindliness, fidelity, and happiness"; nevertheless, it "classed the black man and the ox together." Less equivocally, and more typical of Du Bois's view of slavery, black men were "emasculated" by the institution. Emancipation brought them "suddenly, violently . . . into a new birthright." The white southern universities had been contaminated by "the foul breath of slavery." Instead of the providential view of slavery espoused by Washington, for Du Bois the institution had amounted to "two hundred and fifty years of assiduous education in submission, carelessness, and stealing."

Du Bois's emphasis on slavery as a social evil is only one part of the scheme by which he measures the Afro-American and American reality. Central to his argument is his belief in the persistence of the power of slavery beyond emancipation. Many current ills had their start in slavery. The widespread tendency of white businessmen and industrialists to see human beings as property, or "among the material resources of a land to be trained with an eye single to future dividend," was "born of slavery." The "plague-spot in sexual relations" among blacks—easy marriage and easy separation—"is the plain heritage from slavery." Many whites in the South live "haunted by the ghost of an untrue dream." "Slavery and race-prejudice are potent if not sufficient causes of the Negro's position" today. Du Bois does not pretend, in the manner of a demogogue, that slavery and neo-slavery are absolutely identical. He sometimes proposes a new slavery as only a distinct possibility. The power of the ballot, downplayed by Booker T. Washington, is absolutely needed—"else what shall save us from a second slavery?" And yet, if the black man is not actually a slave, he is actually not free. "Despite compromise, war, and struggle," Du Bois insists, "the Negro is not free" and is in danger "of being reduced to semi-slavery." Repeatedly he invokes the central symbol of enslavement to portray the status of the modern black. Today, blacks are "shackled men."

In the final analysis, black Americans live in neoslavery. The race passed from formal slavery through an interim illusion of emancipation ("after the first flush of freedom wore off ") into a new version of slavery that in many respects continues the old. The law courts were used by the white South as the first means of "reenslaving the blacks." Examining estates that once were slave plantations, Du Bois marvels at how the design and disposition of the black cabins are "the same as in slavery days." While for Booker T. Washington the Tuskegee education eradicates the vestiges of slavery from students at the institute, Du Bois sees the legacy of slavery as inescapable: "No people a generation removed from slavery can escape a certain unpleasant rawness and *gaucherie,* despite the best of training." Even the Tuskegee philosophy, as has been pointed out, reflects for Du Bois, in its spirit of compromise, the timidity forced on blacks by slavery.

It is vital to recognize that, far from being the result of distorting bitterness or propaganda, Du Bois's position on neo-slavery at the turn of the century, which he amply documents with vivid examples (many drawn from his personal experience), is fully supported by a wide range of leading historians. Central to their analysis were not simply the repressive local laws but the even more confining decisions of the Supreme Court in *Plessy* v. *Ferguson* in 1896, which held that "separate but equal" facilities were constitutionally valid, and in *Williams* v. *Mississippi* in 1898, which endorsed that state's plan to strip blacks of the franchise given them after the Civil War. Rayford W. Logan dubbed the period before the end of the century the "Nadir" of the Afro-American experience. "When complete," C. Vann Woodward wrote of these segregationist laws, "the new codes of White Supremacy were vastly more complex than the ante-bellum slave codes or the Black Codes of 1865-66, and, if anything, they were stronger and more rigidly enforced."

Du Bois's attitude toward slavery, the black present, and the black future is heavily dependent on his attitude toward the preslavery situation of blacks—

that is, to Africa. In *The Souls of Black Folk* he does not dwell on the historical evidence of African civilization before slavery that twelve years later would form virtually the main subject of his Pan-Africanist volume, *The Negro* (1915). But where Washington writes only of heathenistic darkness in *Up from Slavery,* Du Bois concedes heathenism but also attributes to the slave a complex, dignified, and usable past. "He was brought from a definite social environment," Du Bois explains,"—the polygamous clan life under the headship of the chief and the potent influence of the priest. His religion was nature-worship, with profound belief in invisible surrounding influences, good and bad, and his worship was through incantation and sacrifice." In other words, the African lived in a stable, consistent, complex social order, complemented by strong and formal religious beliefs. Far from being a blank, the mind of the black, both in Africa and as a slave brought to the New World, was a remarkable instrument. And because of this background, the slave's natural reaction to slavery was not passivity—which was learned later—but revolt. "Endowed with a rich tropical imagination," Du Bois asserts, "and a keen, delicate appreciation of Nature, the transplanted African lived in a world animate with gods and devils, elves and witches; full of strange influences,—of Good to be implored, of Evil to be propitiated. Slavery, then, was to him the dark triumph of Evil over him. All the fateful powers of the Underworld were striving against him, and a spirit of revolt and revenge filled his heart."

In ascribing to the black in Africa and in the New World a mind that in its own way is as powerful as that of any other race in the world, Du Bois does more than merely try to boost his race's reputation. He shifts the terms of the debate toward the question of the black mind and character, and introduces questions of history, psychology, myth, and art. He also introduces into his scheme at least two other elements severely downplayed by Washington in *Up from Slavery.* One is the role of imagination; the other, that of memory. Otherwise derogatory of blacks, many white racial "scientists," including the Count de Gobineau, the author of the influential *Essay on the Inequality of Human Races,* had often credited them with remarkable imaginative and artistic faculties (the "rich tropical imagination" Du Bois ascribed to the transplanted African). Du Bois allows this credit to influence not only what he wrote about blacks but also how he wrote it.

Booker T. Washington, finding little that is useful in the African and the slave past, seems in *Up from Slavery* to harbor a deep suspicion of the black imagination, or even to be unaware that it exists. Indeed, his entire attitude toward the imagination contrasts with Du Bois's. While he reads books, or advocates the reading of books, he mentions no novels or poems. He is proud of the fact that his keenest pleasures are in the practical

world. "Few things are more satisfactory to me than a high-grade Berkshire or Poland China pig," he writes. "Games I care little for." Du Bois is different. From early in his life, he tells us, he has seen the development of his imagination as one possible key to simultaneous self-realization and the leadership of his race against the whites. "Just how I would do it I could never decide," he writes of his youthful dreams of racial and personal victory [in *The Souls of Black Folk*]; "by reading law, by healing the sick, by telling the wonderful tales that swam in my head,—some way."

In fact, Du Bois's greatest cultural claims for blacks are in the areas of art and imagination. In these claims, slaves play the decisive role. He lauds them as musicians, especially when music is blended with spirituality in the "sorrow songs." In a nation where "vigor and ingenuity" are prized, rather than beauty, "the Negro folk-song—the rhythmic cry of the slave—stands to-day not simply as the sole American music, but as the most beautiful expression of human experience born this side the seas." Of the three gifts from blacks to American culture, the first is "a gift of story and song—soft, stirring melody in an ill-harmonized and unmelodious land." (The other gifts are toil and "a gift of the Spirit.")

Recognizing imagination as a source of black strength, and confirming the power of the imagination in Africa, slavery, and thereafter, also freed Du Bois as a thinker and a writer. In his previous book, *The Philadelphia Negro,* he had warned fastidiously that the scholar "must ever tremble lest some personal bias, some moral conviction or some unconscious trend of thought due to previous training, has to a degree distorted the picture in his view." This timidity is abandoned in *The Souls of Black Folk,* which is full of impressionistic writing, including occasionally startling descriptions of people and places, and clearly subjective judgments. Du Bois based the book on his scholarly knowledge of history and sociology, but the eye and mind of the artist are given almost free play.

He was well aware of the possible price of indulging the imagination and even believed that he had paid a part of that price. A year after the book appeared, in a note about it published in the *Independent,* Du Bois conceded that "the style and workmanship" of *The Souls of Black Folk* did not make its meaning "altogether clear." He was sure that the book presented a "clear central message," but also that around this core floated what he called a shadowy "penumbra" of vagueness and partly obscured allusions. Similarly, in his preface, **"The Forethought."** Du Bois was restrained in outlining his plans. He will sketch, "in vague, uncertain outline," the spiritual world in which the ten million black Americans live." In both pieces, Du Bois is acknowledging the "tropic imagination" of blacks, of which he is one. His elite, formal, Western education has curbed this tropic imagination for too long; now it is free.

A crucial factor here is the connection thus proclaimed between the author of *The Souls of Black Folk* and the masses of American blacks, the despised slaves they had been or were descended from, and the Africans beyond the seas. Du Bois made this connection for all to see when he said of his book, in the note in the *Independent* just cited, that "in its larger aspects the style is tropical—African." In his **"The Forethought,"** too, he had linked himself to other blacks, and to slaves: "Need I add that I who speak here am bone of the bone and flesh of the flesh of them that live within the Veil?"

By indulging his imagination, Du Bois gains for his book much of its distinction. Where Booker T. Washington stresses cold facts, and avoids metaphors and similes, imagination leads Du Bois to the invocation of keen images to represent black reality, and to major insights. Chief among the images is that of "the Veil," which hangs between the black and white races, an apparently harmless fabric but one that the rest of the book shows to be in some respects an almost impregnable wall, and the prime source of misery. In one place he even links his image of the veil to the symbol of an ongoing slavery; at one and the same time, he records "the wail of prisoned souls within the veil, and the mounting fury of shackled men. Linked to the image of the veil, but going beyond it, and inscribed in the very title of the book, is the idea of black American "double consciousness." Taking the basic idea of double consciousness as a feature or a capability of the human brain from the reflections of leading psychologists of the time, such as his former professor William James, Du Bois applied the notion with telling force to the mental consequences of the social, political, and cultural conflicts that came with being Afro-American. Perhaps no more challenging single statement about the nature of the black American mind, about the psychological consequences of slavery and racism, has ever been offered. Both the notion of black invisibility and of innately conflicted Afro-American consciousness would be reflected powerfully in future black poetry and fiction.

The "souls" of the title is a play on words. It alludes to the "twoness" of the black American that Du Bois initially suggests in his first chapter. America, a predominantly white country, yields the black "no true self-consciousness, but only lets him see himself through the revelation of the other world." The result is "a peculiar sensation, this double-consciousness, this sense of always looking at one's self through the eyes of others, of measuring one's soul by the tape of a world that looks on in amused contempt and pity. One ever feels his twoness,—an American, a Negro; two souls, two thoughts, two unreconciled strivings; two warring ideals in one dark body, whose dogged

strength alone keeps it from being torn asunder." "Such a double life," Du Bois writes later, in his chapter on religion, "with double thoughts, double duties, and double social classes, must give rise to double words and double ideals, and tempt the mind to pretence or revolt, to hypocrisy or radicalism." Another way of seeing these two souls surely is as a contest between memory and its opposite, amnesia. American culture demands of its blacks amnesia concerning slavery and Africa, just as it encourages amnesia of a different kind in whites. For Du Bois, blacks may not be able to remember Africa but they should remember slavery, since it has hardly ended.

"In the days of bondage," he writes of the slaves, stressing their imagination, "they thought to see in one divine event the end of all doubt and disappointment; few men ever worshiped Freedom with half such unquestioning faith as did the American Negro for two centuries. . . . In song and exhortation swelled one refrain—Liberty; in his tears and curses the God he implored had Freedom in his right hand. At last it came,—suddenly, fearfully, like a dream." The first decade after the war "was merely a prolongation of the vain search for freedom, the boon that seemed ever barely to elude their grasp,—like a tantalizing will-o'-the-wisp, maddening and misleading the helpless host." Freedom never came, but something else did, very faintly, that "changed the child of Emancipation to the youth with dawning self-consciousness, self-realization, self-respect."

The fundamental progression of the Afro-American in history, as seen by Du Bois, is from a simple bondage to a more complex bondage slightly ameliorated by this "dawning" of "self-consciousness, self-realization, self-respect." "In those sombre forests of his striving, his own soul rose before him, and he saw himself,—darkly as through a veil; and yet he saw in himself some faint revelation of his power, of his mission." This realization, although "faint," facilitates Du Bois's shift toward what one might call cultural nationalism in the black: "He began to have a dim feeling that, to attain his place in the world, he must be himself, and not another." Cultural nationalism does not mean anti-intellectualism: "For the first time he sought to analyze the burden he bore upon his back, that deadweight of social degradation partially masked behind a half-named Negro problem."

The diminution of the myth of freedom, the elevation of the power of slavery, allows Du Bois to establish a continuum of African and Afro-American psychology. Times change and the nature and amount of data change, but the black mind remains more or less constant, for Du Bois sees it as irrevocably linked to its African origins. If that constancy is anywhere observable, it is for Du Bois in black Christian religion, which in the main is a product of slavery. For him, "the frenzy of a Negro revival in the untouched backwoods of the South" re-creates tellingly "the religious feeling of the slave." The full meaning of slavery "to the African savage" is unknown to Du Bois, but he believes that the answer is to be found only in "a study of Negro religion as a development" from heathenism to the institutionalized urban churches of the North. The black church is the key to knowing "the inner ethical life of the people who compose it." Then follows a venture in analysis that may be taken as the foundation of Du Bois's sense of the Afro-American mind, or soul.

By the 1750s, after the initial impulse to revolt had been crushed by white power, "the black slave had sunk, with hushed murmurs, to his place at the bottom of a new economic system, and was unconsciously ripe for a new philosophy of life." The Christian doctrine of passive submission facilitated this shift in which "courtesy became humility, moral strength degenerated into submission, and the exquisite native appreciation of the beautiful became an infinite capacity for dumb suffering." A century later, black religion had transformed itself once again, this time around the cry for abolition, which became a "religion to the black world. Thus, when Emancipation finally came, it seemed to the freedman a literal Coming of the Lord. His fervid imagination was stirred as never before, by the tramp of armies, the blood and dust of battle, and the wail and whirl of social upheaval." Forty years later, with the world changing swiftly, Du Bois sees "a time of intense ethical ferment, of religious heart-searching and intellectual unrest." This leads him, looking backward and forward, into history and into the future. "From the double life every American Negro must live, as a Negro and as an American, as swept on by the current of the nineteenth while yet struggling in the eddies of the fifteenth century,—from this must arise a painful self-consciousness, an almost morbid sense of personality and a moral hestitancy which is fatal to self-confidence." These are the secondary, but almost equally binding, shackles of neo-slavery.

The authenticity of slaveary as metaphor for the black experience is firmly underscored in the most "creative," or imaginative, areas of *The Souls of Black Folk.* These are the autobiographical passages of the book, the biographical chapter, on Alexander Crummell; and the short story, **"Of the Coming of John."** The sharpest focus of the autobiographical element occurs in **"Of the Passing of the First-Born,"** about the death of Du Bois's son (who died of dysentery in Atlanta). In certain respects this is an almost classical elegy, in impassioned and yet formal language. But it is one in which the central mourner, as a black, can find no consolation. Thus it is in truth anti-Christian, a bitter parody of the Christian elegy such as Milton's *Lycidas.* For Du Bois, unable to believe in Booker T. Wash-

ington's Providence, doubt completely infests his vision of his son's future: "If still he be, and he be There, and there be a There, let him be happy, O Fate!." Perhaps one day the veil will be lifted and the imprisoned blacks set free, but not in Du Bois's time: "Not for me,—I shall die in my bonds." The metaphor of black life as slavery preempts the annealing possibilities of the elegy.

This chapter underscores the memorable autobiographical impressions left by the first few pages of the book, in which Du Bois discusses his first, youthful encouter with racism: "Then it dawned upon me with a certain suddenness that I was different from the others [his white classmates]; or like, mayhap, in heart and life and longing, but shut out from their world by a vast veil." Taking refuge in fierce competitiveness, he wins small victories but understands at last that "the worlds I longed for, and all their dazzling opportunities, were theirs, not mine." Many of his black friends deteriorate into sycophancy or into hatred and distrust of whites. Du Bois does not, but "the shades of the prison-house closed round about us all; walls strait and stubborn to the whitest, but relentlessly narrow, tall, and unscalable to sons of night."

Thus, just as the acceptance of the idea of neo-slavery forbids Du Bois the writing of classical elegy, with its formal consolation, so does that acceptance also forbid Du Bois the writing of anything that resembles either the "classical" slave narrative—the account of a life that has passed from bondage to freedom, from darkness to light—or its white American counterpart, the rags-to-riches autobiographical tale built on the materialist base of the American Dream. Indeed, if one isolates Du Bois as the hero of *The Souls of Black Folk,* one sees the reverse pattern. He goes from light into darkness, from the freedom of infancy and childhood into the bondage of maturity. Each modern black American, he argues implicitly, re-creates this regressive journey. So too has the black race, in its New World experience, enacted a historical regression. Pres-lavery African manhood and womanhood have deteriorated into passivity, moral hesitancy, cyncicism, and rage.

Du Bois does not see all blacks as succumbing to pressure, but in any event those who resist have no hope of a lasting triumph. The most honored single figure in *The Souls of Black Folk* is Alexander Crummell (1819-1898), who struggled against tremendous odds but succeeded in being ordained as a priest in the almost entirely white Protestant Episcopal Church, earned a degree from Cambridge University, then went on to years of diligent service in Africa and the United States. Crummell also helped to found the American Negro Academy, in which Du Bois himself was involved. Clearly he stands as Du Bois's idea of the highest achievement among black Americans. Pointedly,

Crummell was born when "the slave-ship still groaned across the Atlantic." His life is one of trial and tribulation, but also of resistance to doubt, hatred, and despair. He decides early to live for his people: "He heard the hateful clank of their chains; he felt them cringe and grovel, and there rose within him a protest and a prophesy." But no great triumph followed. For all his service and achievement, Crummell's name is now barely known. "And herein lies the tragedy of the age: not that men are poor,—all men know something of poverty; not that men are wicked,—who is good? not that men are ignorant,—what is Truth? Nay, but that men know so little of men." Again, the consolation of faith is impossible: "I wonder where he is today?"

The short story **"Of the Coming of John"** (in a sense, one of "the wonderful tales that swam in my head" to which Du Bois alludes early in the book) further underscores the destructive force of neo-slavery. Black John, a simple country boy, comes to "Wells Institute" to be educated. But education cannot save him from racism, and his spirit deteriorates: "A tinge of sarcasm crept into his speech, and a vague bitterness into his life." Education alienates him from his own people; he returns home only to be struck by the "sordidness and narrowness" of what he had left behind. Unwittingly he tramples on the religious beliefs of the local blacks, and he preaches democracy in the black school although it is under the control of a reactionary white judge. Dismissed from his job there, he wanders in a daze until he sees his sister tussling with a white man he had known as a boy. He kills the man. John tells his mother he is is going away—"I'm going to be free." Not understanding, she asks if he is going north again. "Yes, mammy," John replies, "I'm going,—North." He is soon lynched by revengeful whites. Going north and freedom are meaningless for John and for blacks in America. Freedom does not exist, except in death.

Education is only one of the forces that, subverted by racism and neo-slavery, betray John when he should have been elevated by them. For a person of Du Bois's complicated and elite schooling, this must have been a particularly poignant aspect to the condition he describes. Education should lead to light and truth. Booker T. Washington rearranged the chronology of his life in *Up from Slavery* to end his book close to the dizzying personal height of a Harvard honorary degree awarded in 1896 to the former illiterate slave. With the invitation in hand, "tears came into my eyes." But education for John leads to darkness and death. The fate of Alexander Crummell and of the author of *The Souls of Black Folk* is not much more exalted.

The Souls of Black Folk offers no transcendent confidence in the future. Du Bois's essay on religion, **"Of the Faith of the Fathers,"** ends with an assertion of the existence of "the deep religious feeling of the real Negro heart, the stirring, unguided might of powerful human souls who have lost the guiding star of the past and seek in the great night a new religious ideal." Only in concluding the book does Du Bois appeal to the longest possible historical view. The assumption of whites that certain races cannot be "saved" is "the arrogance of people irreverent toward Time and ignorant of the deeds of men. A thousand years ago such an assumption, easily possible, would have made it difficult for the Teuton to prove his right to life." As powerful as it was, American slavery thus becomes for him, in the end, only an episode in the African people's history, not the history itself.

Before this point, however, he has engaged slavery valiantly in his text. His point of view is clear. Admitting and exploring the reality of slavery is necessarily painful for a black American, but only by doing so can he or she begin to understand himself or herself and American and Afro-American culture in general. The normal price of the evasion of the fact of slavery is intellectual and spiritual death. Only by grappling with the meaning and legacy of slavery can the imagination, recognizing finally the temporality of the institution, begin to transcend it. (pp. 104-23)

Arnold Rampersad, "Slavery and the Literary Imagination: Du Bois's 'The Souls of Black Folk'," in *Slavery and the Literary Imagination*, edited by Deborah E. McDowell and Arnold Rampersad, The Johns Hopkins University Press, 1989, pp. 104-24.

SOURCES FOR FURTHER STUDY

Broderick, Francis L. *W. E. B. Du Bois: Negro Leader in a Time of Crisis.* Stanford: Stanford University Press, 1959, 259 p.

    The first book-length biography of Du Bois. Broderick made use of Du Bois's private papers at the University of Massachusetts until Du Bois closed them to the public after his 1951 indictment as an unregistered agent of a foreign power.

Clarke, John Henrik; Jackson, Esther; Kaiser, Ernest; and O'Dell, J. H., eds. *Black Titan: W. E. B. Du Bois.* Boston: Beacon Press, 1970, 333 p.

Anthology by the editors of *Freedomways.* Includes tributes to Du Bois by Kwame Nkrumah, Langston Hughes, and Paul Robeson, among others; critical essays on Du Bois; selected essays and poems by Du Bois.

DeMarco, Joseph P. *The Social Thought of W. E. B. Du Bois.* Lanham, MD: University Press of America, 1983, 203p.

Studies Du Bois's evolving social thought throughout his lifetime.

Logan, Rayford W., ed. *W. E. B. Du Bois: A Profile.* New York: Hill and Wang, 1971, 324 p.

Collection of critical essays about Du Bois's life and works.

Rampersad, Arnold. "W. E. B. DuBois as a Man of Literature." *American Literature* 51, No. 1 (March 1979): 50-68.

Appraises Du Bois's career as a writer of fiction.

Tuttle, William M., Jr., ed. *W. E. B. Du Bois.* Englewood Cliffs, NJ: Prentice-Hall, Inc., 1973, 186p.

Brief biography, with essays by Du Bois, reactions from his contemporaries, and essays by scholars August Meier and Francis Broderick.

Alexandre Dumas, père

1802-1870

(Full name Alexandre Davy de la Pailleterie) French novelist, dramatist, memoirist, historian, essayist, and short story and travel writer.

INTRODUCTION

Dumas is regarded as one of the world's premier storytellers. Enormously popular and prolific, he wrote two of the best-loved and most widely read novels in literary history, *Les trois mousquetaires* (1844; *The Three Musketeers; or, The Feats and Fortunes of a Gascon Adventurer*) and *Le comte de Monte-Cristo* (1845; *The Count of Monte Cristo*). He also helped to inaugurate and popularize Romantic drama on the French stage with his two plays *Henri III et sa cour* (1829; *Henri III and His Court*) and *Antony* (1831).

Dumas was the child of Marie-Louis-Elisabeth Labouret, an innkeeper's daughter, and Thomas-Alexandre Dumas. The elder Dumas enjoyed a brilliant career as a general in the armies of the First Republic; but after repeatedly offending Napoleon Bonaparte with his outspoken criticism, he soon fell on hard times and, upon his death in 1806, left his family in dire financial circumstances. Dumas was subsequently raised by his mother in the town of Villers-Cotterêts and educated at a local parochial school. He worked as a clerk as a young man, but his growing interest in the theater brought him to Paris in 1822, where he was encouraged by the famous actor François Joseph Talma.

Dumas moved permanently to Paris in 1823. Soon after becoming a clerk for the duc d'Orléans, he collaborated with Adolphe de Leuven and Pierre-Joseph Rousseau on his first staged play, a one-act vaudeville entitled *La chasse et l'amour* (1825). But it was not until 1827, after he attended a British performance of William Shakespeare's *Hamlet,* that he discovered a direction for his dramas. "The battlement scene, the scene of the two portraits, Ophelia's madness, the gravedigger's scene, these shook me to the core," he later stated. "From this time on, but only then, did I have an idea of what the theater could be, and out of all the broken fragments of the past I glimpsed the possibility of creating a world." Thus inspired, he wrote a series of successful dramas. By investing his plays with a semblance of historical verisimilitude and by skillfully showcasing his melodramatic material, Dumas broke with the stagnating precepts Neoclassicism had imposed on the French stage for well over a century. His efforts made him an instant celebrity, winning even the praise of such illustrious contemporaries as Victor Hugo and Alfred de Vigny.

The year 1831 marked the first performance of three of Dumas's best-known plays: *Antony, Charles VII chez ses grands vassaux,* and *Richard Darlington. Antony* in particular was a triumph for Dumas; the first depiction of Romantic passion and defiance in a contemporary setting, the drama electrified audiences. Yet its notoriety was soon rivaled by his play *La tour de Nesle* (1832; *The Tower of Nesle*). Dealing with orgies and homicide among the aristocracy during the reign of Louis X, this lurid work became one of the playwright's most popular dramas. Because of his republican affiliations and activities, which the new king, Louis Philippe, regarded with disfavor, Dumas was advised to leave France for a time. In 1832, he embarked on a tour of Switzerland, recording his impressions in *Impressions de voyage: Suisse* (1851; *Travels in Switzerland*), a work that established his reputation as an innovative travel writer and anticipated a number of similar books covering his travels in Russia, Italy, and other lands. These works were later collected and published as "Impressions de voyage" in his *Oeuvres complètes.* Dumas also became involved with the actress Ida Ferrier at this time. Although the couple lived together for eight years before marrying in 1840, their marriage was unhappy and they separated in 1844. But Dumas was not long in seeking female companionship. Having had numerous affairs previous to his relationship with Ferrier and having fathered several illegitimate children (including the future playwright Alexandre Dumas, *fils*), he continued to lead an openly promiscuous life well into his old age.

Dumas achieved fame and fortune as a novelist in the 1840s. In collaboration with Auguste Maquet, he serialized *Le chevalier d'Harmental* in the periodical *Le siècle* in 1842. Compounded of history, intrigue, adventure, and romance, it is generally regarded as the first of Dumas's great historical novels. The years 1844 and 1845 were productive for the partners, distinguished by the serial and book publication of *The Three Musketeers* and *The Count of Monte Cristo.* Dumas subsequently collaborated with Maquet on a steady stream of historical romances, most of which were published serially in Parisian periodicals and eagerly consumed by the French public. Between 1840 and 1850, they produced two celebrated series of novels: the "D'Artagnan Romances," composed of *The Three*

Musketeers, Vingt ans après (1845; *Twenty Years After; or, The Further Feats and Fortunes of a Gascon Adventurer*), and *Le vicomte de Bragelonne; ou, Dix ans plus tard* (1848-50; *The Vicomte de Bragelonne; or, Ten Years Later*); and the "Valois Romances," composed of *La reine Margot* (1845; *Marguerite de Valois*), *La dame de Monsoreau* (1846; *Chicot the Jester; or, The Lady of Monsoreau*), and *Les quarante-cinq* (1847; *The Forty-Five Guardsmen*). Indeed, Dumas's productivity was so remarkable that the French journalist and writer Eugéne de Mirecourt publicly accused him of operating a literary "factory" and exploiting the services of slave-like collaborators. Mirecourt was eventually convicted of slander, but doubts concerning the authorship of his works beleaguered Dumas throughout his career. The author was well compensated, however, using the income from his writings to support an extravagant lifestyle epitomized by his opulent residence at Marly-le-Roi. Dubbed the "Château de Monte-Cristo," it was home to a menagerie of Dumas's pets and a parade of hangers-on until 1850, when their patron's finances collapsed.

Dumas's insolvency was closely linked to the closing of the Théâtre Historique. Begun by Dumas in 1847 as a vehicle for staging dramatizations of his historical novels, the theater's failure in 1850 left him destitute and precipitated a two-year retreat to Brussels to avoid his creditors. In addition, Dumas's partnership with Maquet dissolved at this time. However, with the help of his secretary in Brussels, who brought order to his financial affairs, Dumas returned to Paris in 1853. His voluminous memoirs had been published serially in his absence, and he subsequently devoted considerable energy to publishing and writing for a string of his own periodicals, including *Le mousquetaire* and *Le Monte-Cristo.* Dumas toured Russia in 1858-59 and lived in Italy from 1860 to 1864. Thereafter his life was relatively subdued. Although he enjoyed a flamboyant liaison with the young American actress Adah Isaacs Menken and published several collections of essays in the late 1860s, he was also beset by poverty and declining spirits. Dumas died in his sixty-eighth year at the home of his son Alexandre.

As Victor Hugo is considered the chief theorist of French Romantic drama, so Dumas is regarded as its chief popularizer. Most critics attribute this achievement to Dumas's peculiar ability to exploit the sensational: by using his peerless management of stagecraft and dramatic effect to magnify the high passion of Romanticism, he created some of the most powerful and popular dramas of his era. *Antony* was one of his greatest successes in this manner. Described by *Le constitutionnel* as "the most daringly obscene piece that has appeared in even these days of obscenity," the play features a Byronic hero who seduces his married lover and then kills her in a defiant attempt to disguise their relationship and save her reputation. The fact that Dumas challenged tradition by placing his inflammatory drama in a contemporary setting undoubtedly contributed to the play's success. *The Tower of Nesle* stands out as the most potent of Dumas's numerous historical melodramas. Yet many critics have remarked that the play also epitomizes the weaknesses of Dumas's dramaturgy. As with many of his plays, *The Tower of Nesle* is often criticized for its indiscriminate presentation of vice and violence—frequently at the expense of morality, probability, profundity, and good taste—and for its appeal to the baser instincts of the crowd. This tendency toward "popularizing" his works offended the moral standards of contemporary critics, and it continues to detract from Dumas's reputation as a serious dramatic author.

George Bernard Shaw reflected the consensus of critical opinion in his description of Dumas as "one of the best storytellers, narrative or dramatic, that ever lived." Although Dumas used his storytelling skills to great advantage in his memoirs and travel books, they are especially manifest in his novels. One of his ambitions as a novelist was to write a body of romances that would span French history from the Middle Ages to contemporary times. He nearly realized his goal, though more importantly his efforts established a unique brand of fiction that combines well-known events and historical personalities with characters and incidents of his own creation. Critics emphasize, however, that history is at the service of imagination in these works. Likewise, stylistic and thematic concerns are largely subordinated to the demands of fast-paced adventure and intrigue. Dumas's skill in managing his racing plots is acknowledged by many commentators and may well represent his greatest technical asset as a novelist.

Critics regard *The Three Musketeers* as one of Dumas's greatest and most representative works. Like many of his romances, the story is partly based on a quasi-historical document, in this case Gatien de Courtilz de Sandras's *Mémoires de M. d'Artagnan.* Dumas drew the character of D'Artagnan and the names of the famous trio of Athos, Porthos, and Aramis from this source and embroidered their fictional adventures around actual or reputed intrigues involving Louis XIII, Anne of Austria, Cardinal Richelieu, and the duke of Buckingham. While critics generally acknowledge the zest with which Dumas conducted his tale, they also focus on the factors that have contributed to the musketeers' continuing popularity. Most commentators praise the protagonists as well-wrought character types—D'Artagnan is commonly recognized as the adventurous type, Athos as the melancholic aristocrat, Porthos as the boastful strongman, and Aramis as the elegant schemer. They also acknowledge the musketeers' broad appeal as swashbuckling heroes en-

dowed with rather pragmatic morals. More complex interpretations of these figures have been suggested as well: Hippolyte Parigot described the adventurers as representatives of the "four cardinal points of French civilization," which he defines as "fierce determination, aristocratic melancholy, a somewhat vainglorious strength, [and] an elegance, at once delicate and gay"; André Maurois has explained their popularity in terms of the hunger among all societies for "action, strength, and generosity." Dumas's heroes also share the distinction of ranking among the favorite characters of William Makepeace Thackeray, Robert Louis Stevenson, and other eminent novelists.

The Count of Monte Cristo is an equally popular but somewhat more problematic work than *The Three Musketeers.* Inspired by Jacques Peuchet's account of François Picaud's search for vengeance in *Mémoires tirés des archives de la police de Paris,* Dumas devised the thrilling story of Edmond Dantès's unjust imprisonment in the Château d'If and his subsequent escape and search for revenge disguised as the mysterious and fabulously wealthy count of Monte-Cristo. Critics occasionally distinguish between the first and second "parts" of the novel, generally preferring the account of Dantès's victimization and captivity in the first part to the history of his revenge. Most troublesome to critics is the count's petty cruelty and the improbability of his escapades, which depend on his access to a hidden treasure on the island of Monte-Cristo. Yet commentators generally concede that the novel draws its power from these same sources. Critics agree that by exploiting Monte-Cristo's sudden wealth and lust for vengeance, Dumas evidently tapped potent, archetypal fantasies in the human psyche and thus created a story of near universal appeal.

Critical appreciation of Dumas's achievements has increased over time. During his lifetime, he was beset by accusations of plagiarism and outright fraud. He defended his practices, minimizing the contribution of his collaborators and arguing that he had reworked rather than copied the writings of others, but his reputation was severely damaged nonetheless. His tendency late in his career to pad his works for the sake of profit further jeopardized his fame. However, Dumas's literary stature rebounded shortly after his death, as critics showed a greater tolerance towards his authorial practices. Many of these commentators emphasized that Dumas was indeed responsible for the original quality of his works regardless of his borrowings and collaborations. Still, most critics grant that Dumas neither aspired to nor achieved profundity. Instead, he is usually discussed in terms of his unmatched storytelling ability and depicted as an entertainer *par excellence.* Recognition of these facts effectively excludes Dumas from the ranks of literary immortals, yet it has not prevented him from assuming an enviable position as one of the best-loved writers in world literature.

(For further information about Dumas's life and works, see *Nineteenth-Century Literature Criticism*, Vol. 11 and *Something about the Author*, Vol. 18.)

CRITICAL COMMENTARY

WILLIAM MAKEPEACE THACKERAY
(essay date 1840)

[A famed Victorian author, Thackeray is best known for his satiric sketches and novels of upper- and middle-class English life. He is also credited with bringing a simpler style and greater realism to English fiction. In the following excerpt from an essay originally published in 1840, he comments on Dumas's dramas, focusing on their excessive vice, violence, and specious morality. He particularly criticizes Dumas for debauching "sacred and sublime" aspects of Christianity, citing *Don Juan de Marana; ou, La chute d'un ange* and *Caligula* as examples.]

Victor Hugo and Dumas are the well-known and respectable guardians [of the *drame* in France]. Every piece Victor Hugo has written, since *Hernani,* has contained a monster—a delightful monster, saved by one virtue. There is Triboulet, a foolish monster; Lucrèce Borgia, a maternal monster; Mary Tudor, a religious monster; Monsieur Quasimodo, a humpback monster; and others, that might be named, whose monstrosities we are induced to pardon—nay, admiringly to witness— because they are agreeably mingled with some exquisite display of affection. And, as the great Hugo has one monster to each play, the great Dumas has, ordinarily, half a dozen, to whom murder is nothing; common intrigue, and simple breakage of the [seventh] commandment, nothing; but who live and move in a vast, delightful complication of crime, that cannot be easily conceived in England, much less described. (p. 359)

After having seen most of the grand dramas which have been produced at Paris for the last half-dozen years, and thinking over all that one has seen,— the fictitious murders, rapes, adulteries, and other crimes, by which one has been interested and excited,—a man may take leave to be heartily ashamed of the manner in which he has spent his time; and of the hideous kind of mental intoxication in which he has permitted himself to indulge.

Nor are simple society outrages the only sort of crime in which the spectator of Paris plays has permitted himself to indulge; he has recreated himself with a deal of blasphemy besides, and has passed many pleasant evenings in beholding religion defiled and ridiculed. (pp. 360-61)

The great Dumas . . . has brought a vast quantity of religion before the foot-lights. There was his famous tragedy of *Caligula,* which, be it spoken to the shame of the Paris critics, was coldly-received; nay, actually hissed by them. And why? Because, says Dumas, it contained a great deal too much piety for the rogues. The public, he says, was much more religious, and understood him at once.

"As for the critics," says he, nobly, "let those who cried out against the immorality of Antony and Marguérite de Bourgogne, reproach me for *the chastity of Messalina.*" (This dear creature is the heroine of the play of *Caligula.*) "It matters little to me. These people have but seen the form of my work: they have walked round the tent, but have not seen the arch which it covered; they have examined the vases and candles of the altar, but have not opened the tabernacle!

"The public alone has, instinctively, comprehended that there was, beneath this outward sign, an inward and mysterious grace: it followed the action of the piece in all its serpentine windings: it listened for four hours, with pious attention (*avec recueillement et religion*), to the sound of this rolling river of thoughts, which may have appeared to it new and bold, perhaps, but chaste and grave; and it retired, with its head on its breast, like a man who had just perceived, in a dream, the solution of a problem which he has long and vainly sought in his waking hours." (pp. 361-62)

We have people in England who write for bread, like Dumas . . . , and are paid so much for their line; but they don't set up for prophets. Mrs. Trollope has never declared that her novels are inspired by Heaven; Mr. Buckstone has written a great number of farces, and never talked about the altar and the tabernacle. Even Sir Edward Bulwer (who, on a similar occasion, when the critics found fault with a play of his, answered them by a pretty decent declaration of his own merits), never ventured to say that he had received a divine mission, and was uttering five-act revelations.

Principal Works

Henri III et sa cour (drama) 1829

[Catherine of Cleves published in "Catherine of Cleves" and "Hernani": Tragedies, 1832; also published as Henri III and His Court in Nineteenth Century French Plays, 1931]

Antony (drama) 1831

[Antony, 1880]

Charles VII chez ses grands vassaux (drama) 1831

La tour de Nesle (drama) 1832

[The Tower of Nesle, 1906]

Impressions de voyage. 5 vols. (travel sketches) 1833-37; also published as Impressions de voyage: Suisse, 1851

[The Glacier Land, 1848; also published as Travels in Switzerland, 1958]

Don Juan de Marana; ou, La chute d'un ange (drama) 1836

[Don Juan de Marana, 1939]

Les trois mousquetaires (novel) 1844

[The Three Musketeers; or, The Feats and Fortunes of a Gascon Adventurer, 1846]

Le chevalier de Maison-Rouge. 6 vols. (novel) 1845-46

[Marie Antoinette; or, The Chevalier of the Red House: A Tale of the French Revolution, 1846; also published as The Chevalier de Maison Rouge: A Tale of the Reign of Terror, 1859]

Le comte de Monte-Cristo (novel) 1845

[The Count of Monte Cristo, 1846]

[The Regent's Daughter, 1845]

La reine Margot (novel) 1845

[Margaret of Navarre; or, The Massacre of Saint Bartholomew's Eve, 1845; also published as Marguerite de Valois, 1846]

Vingt ans après (novel) 1845

[Twenty Years After; or, The Further Feats and Fortunes of a Gascon Adventurer, 1846]

La dame de Monsoreau (novel) 1846

[Chicot the Jester; or, The Lady of Monsoreau, 1857; also published as Diana of Meridor; or, The Lady of Monsoreau, 1860]

Mémoires d'un médecin: Joseph Balsamo. 19 vols. (novel) 1846-48

[Memoirs of a Physician, 1850?]

Impressions de voyage: De Paris à Cadix. 5 vols. (travel sketches) 1847-48

[From Paris to Cadiz, 1958]

Les quarante-cinq (novel) 1847

[The Forty-Five Guardsmen, 1848; also published as The Forty-Five, 1889]

Oeuvres complètes. 286 vols. (novels, short stories, travel sketches, memoirs, histories, and essays) 1848-1900

Le vicomte de Bragelonne; ou, Dix ans plus tard. 26 vols. (novel) 1848-50

†[The Vicomte de Bragelonne; or, Ten Years Later, 1857]

Le collier de la reine. 11 vols. (novel) 1849-50

[The Queen's Necklace, 1855]

Ange Pitou (novel) 1851

[Taking the Bastille; or, Six Years Later, 1859; also published as Ange Pitou, 1890]

La comtesse de Charny. 19 vols. (novel) 1852-55

[The Countess de Charny, 1894]

Mes mémoires. 22 vols. (memoirs) 1852-54

[My Memoirs. 6 vols., 1907-09]

Histoire de mes bêtes (essays) 1867

[My Pets, 1909]

The Romances of Alexandre Dumas. 60 vols. (novels) 1893-97

*Most of Dumas's prose works were originally published serially in periodicals. Due to the controversy surrounding the authorship of many of his works, Dumas's collaborators are not identified here.

†Portions of this work have frequently been translated and published as Ten Years Later, The Vicomte de Bragelonne, Louise de La Vallière, and The Man in the Iron Mask.

All things considered, the tragedy of *Caligula* is a decent tragedy; as decent as the decent characters of the hero and heroine can allow it to be; it may be almost said, provokingly decent: but this, it must be remembered, is the characteristic of the modern French school (nay, of the English school too); and if the writer take the character of a remarkable scoundrel, it is ten to one but he turns out an amiable fellow, in whom we have all the warmest sympathy. Caligula is killed at the end of the performance; Messalina is comparatively well-behaved; and the sacred part of the performance, the tabernacle characters apart from the mere "vase" and "candlestick" personages, may be said to be depicted in

the person of a Christian convert, Stella, who has had the good fortune to be converted by no less a person than Mary Magdalene, when she, Stella, was staying on a visit to her aunt, near Narbonne. (pp. 362-63)

Something "tabernacular" may be found in Dumas's famous piece of *Don Juan de Marana*. The poet has laid the scene of his play in a vast number of places: in heaven (where we have the Virgin Mary and little angels, in blue, swinging censers before her!)—on earth, under the earth, and in a place still lower, but not mentionable to ears polite; and the plot, as it appears from a dialogue between a good and a bad angel . . . , turns upon a contest between these two worthies for the possession of the soul of a member of the family of Marana.

Don Juan de Marana not only resembles his namesake, celebrated by Mozart and Molière, in his peculiar successes among the ladies, but possesses further qualities which render his character eminently fitting for stage representation: he unties the virtues of Lovelace and Lacenaire; he blasphemes upon all occasions; he murders at the slightest provocation, and without the most trifling remorse; he overcomes ladies of rigid virtue, ladies of easy virtue, and ladies of no virtue at all; and the poet, inspired by the contemplation of such a character, has depicted his hero's adventures and conversation with wonderful feeling and truth.

The first act of the play contains a half-dozen of murders and intrigues; which would have sufficed humbler genius than Monsieur Dumas's, for the completion of, at least, half a dozen tragedies. In the second act our hero flogs his elder brother, and runs away with his sister-in-law; in the third, he fights a duel with a rival, and kills him; whereupon the mistress of his victim takes poison, and dies, in great agonies, on the stage. In the fourth act, Don Juan, having entered a church for the purpose of carrying off a nun, with whom he is in love, is seized by the statue of one of the ladies whom he has previously victimized, and made to behold the ghosts of all those unfortunate persons whose deaths he has caused.

This is a most edifying spectacle. The ghosts rise solemnly, each in a white sheet, preceded by a wax-candle; and, having declared their names and qualities, call, in chorus, for vengeance upon Don Juan, as thus:—

> Don Sandoval *loquitur.*
> "I am Don Sandoval d'Ojedo. I played against Don Juan my fortune, the tomb of my fathers, and the heart of my mistress;—I lost all; I played against him my life, and I lost it. Vengeance against the murderer! vengeance!"—(The candle goes out.)

The candle goes out, and an angel descends—a flaming sword in his hand—and asks: "Is there no voice in favor of Don Juan?" when lo! Don Juan's father (like one of those ingenious toys called "Jack-in-the-box") jumps up from his coffin, and demands grace for his son.

When Martha the nun returns, having prepared all things for her elopement, she finds Don Juan fainting upon the ground.—"I am no longer your husband," says he, upon coming to himself; "I am no longer Don Juan; I am Brother Juan the Trappist. Sister Martha, recollect that you must die!"

This was a most cruel blow upon Sister Martha, who is no less a person than an angel, an angel in disguise—the good spirit of the house of Marana, who has gone to the length of losing her wings and forfeiting her place in heaven, in order to keep company with Don Juan on earth, and, if possible, to convert him. (pp. 366-68)

In spite, however, of the utter contempt with which Don Juan treats her, . . . the unfortunate angel feels a certain inclination for the Don, and actually flies up to heaven to ask permission to remain with him on earth. (p. 368)

[Her] request is granted, her star is *blown out* (O poetic allusion!) and she descends to earth to love, and to go mad, and to die for Don Juan!

The reader will require no further explanation, in order to be satisfied as to the moral of this play: but is it not a very bitter satire upon the country, which calls itself the politest nation in the world, that the incidents, the indecency, the coarse blasphemy, and the vulgar wit of this piece, should find admirers among the public, and procure reputation for the author? . . . The honest English reader, who has a faith in his clergyman, and is a regular attendant at Sunday worship, will not be a little surprised at the march of intellect among our neighbors across the Channel, and at the kind of consideration in which they hold their religion. Here is a man who seizes upon saints and angels, merely to put sentiments in their mouths which might suit a nymph of Drury Lane. He shows heaven, in order that he may carry debauch into it; and avails himself of the most sacred and sublime parts of our creed as a vehicle for a scene-painter's skill, or an occasion for a handsome actress to wear a new dress. (pp. 370-71)

William Makepeace Thackeray, "French Dramas and Melodramas," in his *The Paris Sketch Book of Mr. M. A. Titmarsh,* Estes & Lauriat, 1891, pp. 358-83.

GEORGE SAINTSBURY

(essay date 1878)

[Saintsbury was an English literary historian and critic. In the following excerpt, he assesses Dumas's handling of plot, description, characterization, and dialogue in his novels.]

For a novelist who is so prodigal of incident, Dumas is remarkably indifferent to a regular or cunningly entangled plot. In many of his works, indeed, there is really no particular reason why they should begin or end at the precise points of their beginning and ending. They are emphatically chronicles, slices from the history of the world or of certain individuals, the dimensions of which are determined merely by the arbitrary will of the carver. This is why they lend themselves so admirably to continuations, and why Dumas is one of the very few writers whose second parts do not disappoint us. It is true that in many of his books there is a central incident of some sort, but its development bears often no proportion to the extraneous matter introduced. What, for instance, is the central interest of *Les Trois Mousquetaires?* The quest for the diamonds? It finishes too soon. The wrath and discomfiture of Milady? It does not begin till too late. What is the central interest of *Vingt Ans Après?* The attempt to rescue Charles I perhaps, but yet this occupies but a very small part of the book. In *Le Vicomte de Bragelonne* there are two distinct themes—the restoration of Charles II, and the winning of Belleisle for Louis XIV—and the two might well have made two separate books. . . . The authorities at the disposal of the author or his own fertile imagination usually supply him with an inexhaustible store of moving incidents, and these he connects together as well as may be by the expedient of making the same personages figure in all or most of them. Nor is he any more to be called a novelist of description than a novelist of plot. Indeed he is less abundant and less successful in this respect than almost any other writer of great volume. Little bits of description of houses, dresses, and so forth are frequent enough, and the authorities are sometimes drawn upon largely for a festival or a battle. But Dumas seems to have felt that his readers did not want elaborate set-pieces from him, but plenty of "business" and lively speech. His characters, however, are a much more curious study. Those who call his general method scenepainting, of course, call his characters lay-figures. The appellation does not do their observation much credit. Dumas is nothing so little as an analyst, and he does not attempt to give us complicated or intricate studies of character, but his men and women are curiously adapted to their purpose and curiously lifelike of their kind. They are naturally types rather than individuals, and types of a somewhat loose and vague order, but still there is an amount of individuality about them which is very rarely found in novels of incident. No one will deny that the three, or rather four, musketeers are sustained in their contrast of dispositions throughout the score or so of volumes they occupy, with a good deal of skill. Nor are the repetitions of the types in different books merely *calqués* the one on the other. Chicot and D'Artagnan have remarkable points of contact, yet they are not mere duplicates. Ernauton de Carmainges is a clever variation of La Mole, rather than a mere reproduction of the character.

But it is in his dialogue that Dumas's real secret consists, and it is this which is the rosin that none of his imitators have ever succeeded in stealing, however confident they may be that they have got the fiddle. Its extraordinary volume would be the most remarkable point about it, if its goodness, considering its volume,

were not equally remarkable. The rapidity of it deprives it necessarily of much literary grace, and prevents it from supplying any jewels five words long. Indeed Dumas . . . is one of the least quotable of writers. But still, if not quotable, his dialogue is extraordinarily readable, and carries the reader along with it in a manner hardly to be paralleled elsewhere. Dumas possesses fully the secret of making dialogue express action, and this is where he is supreme. His gift, however, in this respect is of the kind which is almost necessarily a snare. He abuses his dialogic facility constantly, and the result is the exorbitant length of some of his books. It is absolutely impossible for him to be concise. He will make a single interview extend over half-a-dozen chapters, and give a volume to the talk of a single day. . . . [It is undeniable] that his situations have a tendency to repeat themselves, though, as in the case of his characters, the repetition is often very skilfully masked and coloured. But on the whole he succeeds not merely in rivetting the attention of the reader, but also in securing his affection for and interest in his characters. No one has ever managed the process called "working up" better than he has. In such scenes as that where the four princes wait at Marguerite's door, ready to assassinate La Mole, where the powder is found in the wine-casks, where D'Artagnan extracts the Queen and Mazarin from the clutches of the Parisians, and scores of others, it is impossible to avert the attention when once fairly engaged, and impossible to avoid identifying one's self with the characters. That is the triumph of this sort of novel-writing. (pp. 530-32)

[*La Reine Margot, La Dame de Monsoreau, Les Quarante-cinq,* and the D'Artagnan series] seem to me to be on the whole not merely the author's best [novels], but also the most characteristic of his genius. The period which they cover seems to have had a special faculty of inspiring him, or, perhaps, we may say that it was the only one with which he was sufficiently familiar to be able to employ his method with successful effect. In those of his historical novels which are earlier in date, the elements are less happily blended. . . . [In the *Bâtard de Mauléon,* for example,] the life is not in the characters in the same way as it is in Aramis and Porthos. One feels that the author is not so sure of his surroundings, and is chary of the little touches that make scenes and characters live. Nor do the novels whose scene is in more modern times please me much better. Almost all those of purely modern society may be swept away altogether. . . . They sink mostly to the level of mere recitals, interesting simply from the actual facts they contain. Nor, again, has he been happier than other novelists in treating the great revolution. Of the *Collier de la Reine* I shall speak presently. But the *Chevalier de Maisonrouge* adds, to my mind, only one more to the long list of failures which might be made up of French novels having '89 and its sequel for their subjects. . . . There are, however, two novels besides the *Collier de la Reine* and *Monte Cristo,* which lie outside the limits I have drawn, and which are usually ranked among the author's masterpieces. These are *La Tulipe Noire* and the *Chevalier d'Harmental.* With respect to *La Tulipe Noire,* I am inclined to think that, charming as it is in parts, it has been overpraised. . . . The tulip fancying and the loves of the excellent Cornelius Van Baerle make a perfect subject for a really short tale of a hundred pages or so. But Dumas's unfortunate prolixity is here especially unfortunate. The tale is choked up with irrelevant matter and spun out to an unconscionable length. . . . *Le Chevalier d'Harmental* contains detached passages of very striking merit. Le Capitaine Roquefinette, the last of the descendants of Dugald Dalgetty, is a great creation, though Dumas has been extremely hard on him. There is no reason whatever why the uninteresting chevalier should have been allowed to obtain such a victory, except the necessity, which Alexander the Great generally recognises, of making the end of his books melancholy. The caligraphist, Buvat, is another triumph; and his incarceration in the gilded captivity of the Palais Royal is most charmingly told. The Regent Philippe, again, is excellent; and the way in which Richelieu, Saint Simon, and other historical characters are made to play their part, is most artful. Lastly, it must be remembered, in favour of the *Chevalier d'Harmental,* that it is one of the very few books of its author that has a regular plot. The Cellamare conspiracy gives just enough framework for the book, and not too much, and the episodes and digressions are scarcely disproportionate in their extent. After allowing all these merits, which can certainly not be allowed in like measure to many others of Dumas's books, it might seem only reasonable to call it his masterpiece. Yet there is about it something wanting which is present elsewhere. The dialogue is not of the best, and the lack of interest which one feels in the hero is a serious drawback. For once, Dumas has let himself follow Scott in the mistake of making his hero too generally faultless and lucky, and this is the cause, I think, of failure, if failure there be, in the *Chevalier d'Harmental.* (pp. 532-34)

Le Collier de la Reine is one of Dumas's most popular works, but it seems to me to be very far from being one of his best. There is no single character in it of any particular excellence, and the endless scenes of intrigue between Jeanne de la Motte and the Cardinal de Rohan, between Oliva and Cagliostro, between the Queen and a half-a-dozen different personages, are altogether wearisome. The author has not succeeded in interesting us sufficiently to make his volume tolerable, and it is not tolerable in itself in virtue of any skill in handling the subject. This subject, moreover, is felt to be too much for Dumas. The stupendous interest of the French Revolution wants quite a different chronicler

and quite other modes of treatment. The particular episode, too, of the diamond necklace is one of those which have, in virtue of their special interest and strangeness, passed out of the class of subjects which can be successfully treated by fiction. All those who have studied the philosophy of novel-writing at all closely know that great historical events are bad subjects, or are only good subjects on one condition—a condition the steady observance of which constitutes one of the great merits of Sir Walter Scott. The central interest in all such cases must be connected with a wholly fictitious personage, or one of whom sufficiently little is known to give the romancer free play. When this condition is complied with, the actual historical events may be, and constantly have been, used with effect as aids in developing the story and working out the fortunes of the characters. Dumas himself has observed this law in his more successful efforts; he has not observed it here. . . . The character of Cagliostro as here given, moreover, is one which no writer could manage. He is at once too supernatural and not supernatural enough. (pp. 534-35)

Monte Cristo is said to have been at its first appearance, and for some time subsequently, the most popular book in Europe. . . . [It] still remains the book with which, with the possible exception of the *Three Musketeers,* more people connect the name of Dumas than with any other of his works. How far does it deserve this popularity? The answer of most critical persons would probably be, without any intention of flippancy, as far as the end of the first volume. The Château d'If indeed, as this section has sometimes been called, is almost faultless, and few persons can have found anything to object to in it except the rather dubious omniscience of the Abbé Faria. The style and character of the book, moreover, is so far all the author's own, and deals only with subjects which he can well manage. From the time, however, that Dantés has discovered the treasure, the case is altered. The succeeding scenes give indeed an opportunity of portraying what Dumas has always endeavoured and loved to portray, the rise of an adventurer to supreme power and importance. Nor is there any taint of the supernatural as in the case of Cagliostro; but, on the other hand, the scenes described and the characters attempted are scenes and characters in which the author is not himself at home, and which constantly recall to us scenes and characters in the work of other men who can manage them. Take, to begin with, Monte Cristo himself. Whether it is altogether fair for the generation which has come after him, and which he himself has helped to render *blasé* with persons of extraordinary attributes, may be answered in the negative by a fervent Alexandrian. But it cannot be denied that at the present day Edmond Dantès in his parts, of Lord Wilmore, or the Abbé Busoni, or the Count, appears to us a very tiresome and rather ludicrous player at providence. His use of his money seems ostentatious, and sometimes, as in the case of the horses bought from Danglars, intolerably vulgar. His mania for theatrical peripeteias—which might have resulted in the death both of Morrel and his son—is equally to be objected to, and the skimble-skamble stuff which so impresses his Parisian friends (for instance, in his first interview with Villefort) is pitiable enough. In few of the author's books, moreover, is the abuse of over-length greater, and the complicated series of intrigues, though managed with considerable skill, wearies the reader more than it interests him. But the involuntary comparisons that one makes in reading the book are the most unfortunate. No one, for instance, who knows Gautier's literary dealings with haschisch can avoid a sigh over the pages in which Franz d'Epinay's very commonplace experiences of the drug are described. I am not myself among those who consider Henri de Marsay, Bixiou, Blondel, and the rest as absolutely perfect creations beyond which the wit of man cannot go, but Châteaurenaud, Debray, the journalist Beauchamp, and others of De Morcerf 's set, certainly remind one but unpleasantly of Balzac's favourite cliques. The viscount himself would have been more acceptable if he had not in his excessive hospitality displayed "all the tobaccos of the known world" when he was expecting his visitors. Another point in which Dumas here fails is his description. This is, as I already said, probably his weakest point, and it is particularly noticeable in a book where description, one would have thought, was particularly in place. But the prevailing want all through is the want of a sufficient grasp of character to make scenes so familiar and modern as those of Parisian life in the middle of the present century tolerable. The plan is the plan of Balzac, the hand is the hand of Dumas, and it is impossible that the inefficiency of the workmanship should not be felt. There is no attempt at an impression of growing horror culminating in the horrible death of Madame de Villefort and her child. The interest is frittered away in endless details and episodes. The narrow escape of Valentine, and the burglarious attempt of Caderousse, are treated at the same length and on the same scale; and, above all, the dangerous method of introducing long recitals by various characters in order to help on the movement and join the intrigue is unscrupulously resorted to. The first impulse of the reader is to wish that the five last volumes had been condensed to at most two; it is to be feared that his last is to regret that they were ever written at all. (pp. 535-36)

That much of [Dumas's work] will go the way of all but the best fictitious literature, cannot for a moment be doubted. Whether any will survive is a question less easy to answer. The danger to which writers like Dumas are exposed, as a rule, is that there is not enough idiosyncrasy in their work to keep it fresh in

men's memory. Every age, or almost every age, produces for itself specimens of the talented improvisatore who has energy enough to produce enormously, and originality enough to launch his work in popular favour. Every age too naturally prefers its own practitioners in this manner, because they can hit its own tastes, and because the ephemeral adornments and fashion of their work are such as it understands and appreciates. The next age has no such inducements to read work of little permanent literary value. That Dumas is one of the princes of all such improvising writers I have no doubt whatever, and that he possesses the element of something better than improvisation must I think be evident to careful readers of him.

In order to estimate his deficiencies and at the same time the merits which accompany them, I do not know a more curious exercise than the comparison of one of these books, say *La Reine Margot* or the *Mousquetaires*, with Gautier's *Capitaine Fracasse*. They are in intention exactly similar. But Gautier had one thing which Dumas had not, an incomparable literary faculty, and Dumas had what Gautier had not, the knowledge how to *charpenter* a novel. The consequence is that, while *Le Capitaine Fracasse* is a magnificent piece of writing, it is only a second-rate story, and that *La Reine Margot*, though offering no special quotations or passages to the memory, is a book which it is impossible to put down till you have finished it. Such things as the Chateau de la Misère, as the description of the swordsman's garret and his tavern haunt, and above all as the wonderful duel between Lampourde and Sigognac, Dumas was utterly incapable of writing. He never wrote positively badly, but his writing never attracts admiration for itself. It is not negligent, but on the other hand it is not careful. The first word that comes into his head is used. Probably it is not a bad word, and serves very well to convey the impression intended. But of art, of careful choice, and laborious adaptation of words and phrases and paragraphs, there is none. It is even capable of being argued whether, consistently with his peculiar plan and object, there could have been or ought to have been any. The presence in a novel of incident of passages of the highest literary value may be plausibly contended to be a mistake, as well as an unnecessary extravagance. When the palate is tempted to linger over individual pages, to savour them slowly, and to dwell on the flavour, the continuity of interest of the story proper runs a danger of being broken. On the other hand, if the interest be strong enough to induce rapid reading, it is impossible to do justice to the vintage that it set before one. It is not, therefore, either accidental or from incapacity that the great masters of style in fictitious writing, like Merimée and Gautier, have usually preferred to write short stories. It is rather from a sense of incongruity. A story that takes at shortest half-an-hour to read may, without wearying the

G. K. Chesterton on Dumas's achievement as a novelist:

Dumas's fame is wrapped in similar clouds to those which wrap the fame of about half of the great Elizabethans. Nobody is quite certain that any idea which Dumas presented was invented by him. Nobody is quite certain that any line which Dumas published was written by him. But for all that, we know that Dumas was, and must have been, a great man. There are some people who think this kind of doubt clinging to every specific detail does really invalidate the intellectual certainty of the whole. They think that when we are in the presence of a mass that is confessedly solid and inimitable, we must refrain from admiring that mass until we have decided what parts of it are authentic; where the fictitious begins and where the genuine leaves off. Thus, they say that because the books of the New Testament may have been tampered with, we know not to what extent, we must, therefore, surrender altogether a series of utterances which every rational person has admitted to strike the deepest note of the human spirit. They might as well say that because Vesuvius is surrounded by sloping meadows, and because no one can say exactly where the plain leaves off and the mountain begins, therefore there is no mountain of Vesuvius at all, but a beautiful, uninterrupted plain on the spot where it is popularly supposed to stand. Most reasonable people agree that it is possible to see, through whatever mists of misrepresentations, that an intellectual marvel has occurred. Most people agree that, whatever may be the interpolations, an intellectual marvel occurred which produced the Gospels. To descend to smaller things, most people agree that whatever lending and stealing confused the Elizabethan Age, an intellectual marvel occurred which produced the Elizabethan drama. And to descend to things yet smaller again, most people agree that whatever have been the sins, the evasions, the thefts, the plagiarism, the hackwork, the brazen idleness of the author, an intellectual miracle occurred which produced the novels of Dumas.

G. K. Chesterton, in his 1902 *Bookman* essay "Alexandre Dumas."

---

appetite for it as a story, have a couple of hours spent upon it. But supposing that the time necessary to read *Les Trois Mousquetaires* is half a day, no one who has this appetite at all will consent to spend three days over it. Nor again in such a story is it possible, as it is with one of the analytic kind, to read first for the story and afterwards for the style. A novel of incident that allows itself to be treated in this way is a bad novel of incident, and if it be good it must be read just as rapidly the seventh time as it is the first. (pp. 540-41)

Dumas has the faculty, as no other novelist has, of presenting rapid and brilliant dioramas of the picturesque aspects of history, animating them with really human if not very intricately analysed passion, and connecting them with dialogue matchless of its kind. He can do nothing more than this, and to ask him for anything more is a blunder. But he will pass time for you as hardly any other novelist will, and unlike most novelists of his class his pictures, at least the best of them, do not lose their virtue by rebeholding. I at least find the *Three Musketeers* as effectual for its purpose now as I found it nearly twenty years ago, and [contrary to common belief,] I think there must be something more in work of such a virtue than mere scene-painting for a background and mere lay figures for actors. (p. 542)

George Saintsbury, "Alexandre Dumas," in *The Fortnightly Review,* n.s. Vol. XXIV, No. XVII, October 1, 1878, pp. 527-42.

BRANDER MATTHEWS
(essay date 1881)

[An American critic, dramatist, and novelist, Matthews wrote extensively on world drama and was a founding member and president of the National Institute of Arts and Letters. In the excerpt below, originally published in 1881 in the first edition of his *French Dramatists of the 19th Century,* he defends Dumas's authorial practices against those who accused him of freely plagiarizing and exploiting his collaborators.]

Ben Jonson, we are told, once dreamed that he saw the Romans and Carthaginians fighting on his big toe. No doubt Dumas had not dissimilar dreams; for his vanity was at least as stalwart and as frank as Ben Jonson's. To defend himself against all charges of plagiarism, the French dramatist echoed the magniloquent phrase of the English dramatist, and declared that he did not steal, he conquered. It is but justice to say that there was no mean and petty pilfering about Dumas. He annexed as openly as a statesman, and made no attempt at disguise. In his memoirs he is very frank about his sources of inspiration, and tells us at length where he found a certain situation, and what it suggested to him, and how he combined it with another effect which had struck him somewhere else. When one goes to the places thus pointed out, one finds something very different from what it became after it had passed through

Dumas's hands, and, more often than not, far inferior to it. It can scarcely be said that Dumas touched nothing he did not adorn; for he once laid sacrilegious hands on Shakespere, and brought out a *Hamlet* with a very French and epigrammatic last act. But whatever he took from other authors he made over into something very different, something truly his own, something that had *Dumas fecit* in the corner, even though the canvas and the colors were not his own. . . . In a word, all his plagiarisms, and they were not a few, are the veriest trifles when compared with his indisputable and extraordinary powers.

Besides plagiarism, Dumas has been accused of "devilling," as the English term it; that is to say, of putting his name to plays written either wholly or in part by others. There is no doubt that the accusation can be sustained, although many of the separate specifications are groundless. The habit of collaboration obtains widely in France; and collaboration runs easily into "devilling." When two men write a play together, and one of them is famous and the other unknown, there is a strong temptation to get the full benefit of celebrity, and to say nothing at all about the author whose name has no market-value. That Dumas yielded to it now and then is not to be wondered at. There was something imperious in his character, as there was something imperial in his power. He had dominion over so many departments of literature, that he had accustomed himself to be monarch of all he surveyed; and if a follower came with the germ of a plot, or a suggestion for a strong situation, Dumas took it as tribute due to his superior ability. In his hands the hint was worked out, and made to render all it had of effect. Even when he had avowed collaborators, as in *Richard Darlington,* he alone wrote the whole play. His partners got their share of the pecuniary profits, benefiting by his skill and his renown; and most of them did not care whether he who had done the best of the work should get all the glory or not. (pp. 66-8)

That Dumas plagiarized freely in his earliest plays, and had the aid of "devils" in the second stage of his career, is not to be denied, and neither proceeding is praiseworthy; but, although he is not blameless, it irks one to see him pilloried as a mere vulgar appropriator of the labors of other men. The exact fact is, that he had no strict regard for mine and thine. He took as freely as he gave. In literature, as in life, he was a spendthrift; and a prodigal is not always as scrupulous as he might be in replenishing his purse. Dumas's ethics deteriorated as he advanced. One may safely say, that there is none of the plays bearing his name which does not prove itself his by its workmanship. When, however, he began to write serial stories, and to publish a score of volumes a year, then he trafficked in his reputation, and signed his name to books which he had not even read. An effort has been made to show that even

Monte Cristo and the *Three Musketeers* series were the work of M. Auguste Maquet, and that Dumas contributed to them only his name on the titlepage. . . . I must confess that I do not see how any one with any pretence to the critical faculty can doubt that *Monte Cristo* and the *Three Musketeers* are Dumas's own work. That M. Maquet made historical researches, accumulated notes, invented scenes even, is probable; but the mighty impress of Dumas's hand is too plainly visible in every important passage for us to believe that either series owes more to M. Maquet than the service a pupil might fairly render to a master. That these services were considerable is sufficiently obvious from the printing of M. Maquet's name by the side of Dumas's on the titlepages of the dramatizations from the stories. That it was Dumas's share of the work which was inconsiderable is as absurd as it is to scoff at his creative faculty because he was wont to borrow. Señor Castelar has said that all Dumas's collaborators together do not weigh half as much in the literary balance as Dumas alone; and this is true. I have no wish to reflect on the talents of Dinaux, the author of *Thirty Years, or a Gambler's Life,* and of *Louise de Lignerroles,* or on the talents of M. Maquet himself, whose own novels and plays have succeeded, and who is so highly esteemed by his fellow-dramatists as to have been elected and re-elected the president of the Society of Dramatic Authors; yet I must say that the plays which either Dinaux or M. Maquet has written by himself do not show the possession of the secret which charmed us in the work in which they helped Dumas. It is to be said, too, that the later plays taken from his own novels, in which Dumas was assisted by M. Maquet, are very inferior to his earlier plays, written wholly by himself. They are mere dramatizations of romances, and not in a true sense dramas at all. The earlier plays, however extravagant they might be in individual details, had a distinct and essential unity not to be detected in the dramatizations, which were little more than sequences of scenes snipped with the scissors from the interminable series of tales of adventure. . . . Full as these pieces are of life and bustle and gayety, they are poor substitutes for plays, which depend for success on themselves, and not on the vague desire to see in action figures which the reader has learned to like in endless stories. These dramatizations were unduly long-drawn, naturally prolix, not to say garrulous. When his tales were paid for by the word, when he was "writing on space," as they say in a newspaper office, Dumas let the vice of saying all there was to be said grow on him. On the stage, the half is more than the whole. (pp. 69-72)

Brander Matthews, "Alexandre Dumas," in his *French Dramatists of the 19th Century,* third edition, Charles Scribner's Sons, 1901, pp. 46-77.

A. W. RAITT

(essay date 1965)

[Raitt is an English editor and scholar who has written extensively on nineteenth-century French literature. In the excerpt below, he examines Dumas's drama *Antony*.]

[*Antony* was produced] at the height of the great flowering of Romantic drama. . . . Its frantic emotionalism, its theatrical gestures, its exalted volubility make it a typical example of the dramatic literature of the time, with the important exception that, instead of a historical setting, it has a contemporary one. Dumas, no great theorist but well aware of the interest of this innovation, had the ingenious idea of drawing attention to his audacity and at the same time justifying it by inserting [a] conversation in the fourth act, during a party given by the Victomtesse de Lacy. Adèle, the heroine, asks Eugène, a dramatist, if he is still writing plays about the Middle Ages, and when he replies that he is, she inquires: 'Mais pourquoi ne pas attaquer un sujet au milieu de notre société moderne?' The Victomtesse agrees:

C'est ce que je lui répète à chaque instant: "Faites de l'actualité." N'est-ce pas que l'on s'intéresse bien plus à des personnages de notre époque, habillés comme nous, parlant comme nous?

Eugène is persuaded to explain his reasons, after which the discussion moves on and the plot resumes its headlong course. (pp. 37-8)

[One] is conscious of a faint self-irony when Dumas, hitherto a specialist in historical drama, makes Eugène admit that what he writes about is 'toujours du moyen âge'. Dumas seems to have realised sooner than most of his fellow-playwrights that the logical conclusion of the Romantic view of art was complete modernity, and that it was something of an accident that the return to modern times had become bogged down halfway through past history. And so, with commendable forthrightness, he set about writing a play with a wholly contemporary theme and setting. . . . (pp. 38-9)

It is true that Dumas was not the first dramatist to deal with modern themes, nor even the only one of his time. There was the precedent of Diderot's *drame bourgeois* in the eighteenth century, and numerous minor authors were busily scribbling mediocre plays on contemporary subjects in the 1830s and 1840s. Even the Romantics introduced topics of the same kind into their plays, albeit in disguised form. *Chatterton*, though set in

eighteenth-century England, contains some pertinent observations on industrial relations; *Ruy Blas* is, among other things, an impassioned plea for the emancipation of the lower classes; and *Angélo*, another costume drama by Hugo, . . . incriminates 'le fait social' for the injustices done to women in society. But Dumas is the only major dramatist among the Romantics to have faced the problem of the social responsibility of the theatre in the modern world by bringing the action of his play right up to the time at which he was writing. (p. 39)

[If] Dumas did not persuade the other Romantics to take to contemporary settings, he did foresee the course which the drama would be forced to follow, though not in the form which he expected. It was true that the spectator at a 'drame de passion' would soon complain that in real life people behaved more calmly and talked less poetically. . . . Eugène's argument that such an objection could be met if the actors were decked out in medieval costume failed to hold good for long. Ten years after *Antony*, the public was coming to think that at no time had anyone lived as depicted in *Hernani* or *Ruy Blas*, and was beginning to hanker after something closer to its own experience both in setting and in emotion. Even in *Antony*, Dumas has not solved that particular problem. The high-flown tirades jar with the modern costume and contrive to suggest that reality is still several removes away. Instead of people realising, as Dumas had hoped, that 'le coeur bat d'un sang aussi chaud sous un frac de drap que sous un corselet d'acier', they became sceptical about the possibility of its ever having beaten as hectically as the Romantic dramatists would have had them believe.

The result of this change in taste was the formation, by about 1850, of a realistic theatre in France, which depended for its effect on what Dumas aptly terms 'la ressemblance entre le héros et le parterre', and which dominated the stage until the last decade of the century. The leading writers of this school—Dumas *fils*, Augier, Labiche—not only brought their characters and settings up to date, but treated subjects which they knew to be close to the hearts of their audiences, and with a mentality which was also that of their audiences. So one finds the theatre transformed both into a mirror for the spectators and into a debating society where the topical talking-points of the day were aired—money in Dumas's *La Question d'argent* and Augier's *La Ceinture dorée*, difficulties of married life in Dumas's *L'Ami des femmes* and Meilhac and Halévy's *Froufrou*, questions of class prejudice in Augier's *Le Gendre de M. Poirier*, the social relations between the sexes in Dumas's *La Dame aux camélias* and *Monsieur Alphonse*, and so on. In so doing, they were fulfilling the programme sketched out for them in *Antony*, for though Dumas does not say so specifically here, the rest of the play makes it clear that he too envisages modern-dress drama as a suitable place for raising controversial issues. Indeed, the problems on which

Antony centres—the status of illegitimate children, the position of women in marriage, the social consequences of adultery—are precisely those which were to attract the writers of social plays thirty years later. (pp. 40-1)

[Dumas] was well aware of the dangers involved in adopting a combative position on current affairs. *Antony,* for all its contemporary trappings, is scarcely a committed play as we would understand the term nowadays. Yet even the relatively innocuous piece of dialogue [mentioned above] had awkward repercussions for the author. The Baron de Marsanne (a very minor figure in the play) is ridiculed by the fact that he never opens his mouth without making some absurdly flattering reference to *Le Constitutionnel,* the newspaper of the liberal middle classes, which, after having at one time lent lukewarm support to the Romantics, had since 1830 been among their sternest critics. But *Le Constitutionnel* took its revenge on Dumas in 1834, when *Antony* was due to be revived. It claimed that the play was immoral and succeeded in blackmailing Thiers, then Minister of the Interior, into banning it. Dumas went to law and won his case, but even this trifling incident illustrates the fact that the more authors take it upon themselves to comment on personalities and events of the day, the more they are liable to find their freedom interfered with. (pp. 41-2)

Dumas *père,* unlike his son, was not cut out to be a polemist, either in politics or in literature, and when the Baron de Marsanne says that 'les romantiques font tous des préfaces', Dumas is one of the few who could plead innocent. But he nevertheless had ideas of his own about the theatre, and what he used to call 'le feuilleton', that is to say, this page of dramatic criticism, 'l'apologie du drame moderne', is 'la vraie préface d'*Antony*'. For all its uncertain arguments, its oversimplifications and its fallacies, it might also be called the real preface to the post-Romantic theatre in France. (p. 42)

A. W. Raitt, "Alexandre Dumas père: 'Antony'," in his *Life and Letters in France: The Nineteenth Century,* Charles Scribner's Sons, 1965, pp. 36-42.

RENEE WINEGARTEN

(essay date 1991)

[Winegarten is an English literary critic and scholar. In the following excerpt, she analyzes Dumas's major dramatic works and novels, assessing reasons for the author's abiding popularity.]

If reading is a vice that goes unpunished, as the poet has it, then Alexandre Dumas *père* (1802-1870) offers one of

the principal means of access to that form of depravity for devotees too numerous to mention. Throughout the world, how many have tasted for the first time the refined pleasures, the ecstasies and thrills of reading, in *The Three Musketeers* and its sequels, or *The Count of Monte-Cristo?* How many have ventured to own that it was Dumas senior who set their feet on the primrose path, not just of dalliance, but of extremely serious liaisons with other novelists in the loftiest realms of literature? André Malraux, visiting Cayenne in his role as minister of culture, remembered a novel he had read as a small boy, Dumas's *Georges,* the adventures of a half-French mulatto with a will of steel who led a revolt against the British in the Caribbean. Malraux remarked elsewhere that he had passed when young from *The Three Musketeers* to Balzac, implying a kind of progress to higher things.

There, the word "judgment" is out. Malraux was far from alone in suggesting that Dumas was not a figure of the first order. It has long been customary to look askance at that prodigiously prolific writer: his early historical importance as a dramatist is readily admitted in manuals of literature, but his novels do not usually form part of the syllabus like those of Mérimée, Stendhal, or Balzac. All the same, Mérimée (who—like Dumas—also wrote historical fiction) said that he admired Dumas more than Sir Walter Scott, the doyen of historical novelists. Certainly, Dumas is greater fun: he does not linger over description or preachment, and he is very rarely tedious.

Can Dumas be mentioned in the same breath with Balzac (who started out by writing lurid adventure stories but moved on afterwards)? Certainly, Dumas did not think of himself as an "artist," sacrificing life to perfection in art in the manner of Flaubert. On the contrary, his contemporaries saw him as an elemental force, and he was intent on living life to the full. Claude Schopp, the noted authority on Dumas, rightly subtitles his biography of a man who was large in every sense, "the genius of life" [see Further Reading]. As for Dumas—surprising as it must seem nowadays—he considered himself to be a disciple of "the realist school" of Aeschylus and Shakespeare. He called himself a humanist and a popularizing novelist. "I am movement and life," he declared. Verve and vigor were certainly among his supreme qualities.

There may be a change in Dumas's posthumous fate, possibly because greater consideration is now being given to popular aspects of writing or culture in general, if not always with sensible results. Moreover, pressure is being exerted to eliminate so-called elitism or discrimination when discussing all forms of creativity. Perhaps certain elements in Dumas's work carry a charge that is in accord with current modes and moods, and especially with a taste for melodrama. (Has that taste ever been totally eliminated? Even great works, especially in the realm of opera, contain more than a modicum of melodrama.) It would appear that Dumas is actually enjoying a revival of sorts. In any case, he has always occupied a secret alcove in the hearts of lovers of pure narrative and narrative skills, and admirers of generosity of spirit.

Not so long ago, Dumas's play *Antony* (1831), which was a huge success in its own day, would have seemed unactable on the modern stage. Yet it was presented (in translation) in the spring of 1990 at the famous Citizens' Theatre, Glasgow, and was found to be worthwhile and highly enjoyable. It was, however, surely a serious mistake to move the setting from the 1830s to the 1880s. The current mania of stage directors for moving dramas and operas out of their historical context is often a token of laziness, conceit, or condescension toward the public. *Antony* encapsulates the spirit of the early 1830s. The reason why the play made so deep an impression in 1831 was because it depicted the passionate relationship between a man and a woman "realistically," that is, in contemporary speech, dress, and manners, without classical decorum or historical remoteness. The play's success also owed a great deal, as Dumas himself generously owned, to the talents of Marie Dorval and Pierre Bocage, who displayed a "natural" or unrhetorical style of acting that took Paris by storm and made their reputation as Romantic actors *par excellence*.

Antony, the doomed young Byronic hero or anti-hero, is illegitimate, and can discover nothing about his parentage. Thus, although he is superior in every way to the gilded youth of the age, he can have no place in good society. He rebels and rails against its conventions and prejudices. The damage done to his personality is manifest. What might be called the existential anguish caused by his non-status is exacerbated by his despair at the social impossibility of his union with Adèle, the woman he loves, who has been obliged to suppress her passion for him in a loveless marriage to the respectable Colonel d'Hervey.

The lovers meet again after the passage of years: Adèle now has a child; she reluctantly repulses Antony, and takes flight. At an inn on her route, whither he has pursued her, he takes her by force in a jealous frenzy. Their secret liaison becomes known in society, where only casual affairs (as distinct from grand passions) are commonplace. When the absent husband is at the door, Antony stabs Adèle as she herself wishes, in order to preserve her reputation. "She resisted me, I killed her!" cries Antony, throwing his dagger at the Colonel's feet. Curtain. Antony knows that he will be executed for her murder. The new theme of 1831 was middle-class adultery, regarded as an extremely serious matter, because it affected money and inheritance. Dumas was quite as much interested in money, or rather wealth, as Balzac, whom he regarded as his rival.

On the face of it, there would seem to be little in *Antony* to occupy a modern audience. The play was, as Dumas said, "a love scene in five acts." Nonetheless, Antony's revolt against social prejudice and society in general, his race to sexual gratification, the conflict in Adèle between being true to her passion and obedience to ideas of family, convention, and convenience—these have not altogether lost their force, as the welcome accorded to the Glasgow production made plain. Nor has Dumas's dramatic urgency, as he hurtles his prose drama along, despite the ill-timed tirade on the aim of modern theater being to reveal the human heart in all its nakedness.

When Dumas wrote the play he was in the throes of his passion for the writer Mélanie Waldor (married to a military man by whom she had a daughter). He gave his own retrospective sexual jealousy to Antony. All this, together with Dumas's curious ancestry (about which more will have to be said), made him declare that he was Antony minus the murder, as Mélanie was Adèle minus the flight. In a poem which he said was written two years before the play, and which he appended to it as a preface, Dumas cried, "Woe, woe to me, cast by heaven into this world a stranger to its laws!" Adèle, too, alludes to Antony as one who seemed a "stranger" or outsider in the world. This was over a hundred years before Camus's novel *L'Etranger*. The wild tones that can be heard in the poem and the play are to be found in Dumas's frenzied letters to Mélanie Waldor. What now often seems to be role-playing or excess was actually the way people liked to address each other in that era. (pp. 32-4)

[Dumas] made his name as a dramatist with historical plays, including *Henri III et sa cour* (1829), with its reminiscences of Shakespeare, Schiller, and Sir Walter Scott, a play that heralded the triumph of the French Romantic movement before its acknowledged dramatic advent with Victor Hugo's *Hernani*.

It was only afterwards that Dumas turned to writing novels, usually with the aid of a succession of collaborators, who included the helpful Auguste Macquet (or Augustus Mac Keat, as he liked to be known) and even the poet Gérard de Nerval. The wits used to refer to the enterprise as if it were a commercial firm, the House of Dumas and Company. Both *The Three Musketeers* and *The Count of Monte-Cristo*, for instance, were the work of Dumas and Macquet, though it would be difficult to see in them the presence of different hands—always supposing that the breathless reader could manage to stop to look for them. The two writers were often to be found working twelve hours a day, with at least two novels on the stocks at the same time. Indeed, when Dumas stood as a candidate in the elections of 1848, he put himself forward as "a worker," listing the sizable number of his works in justification of the title. According to him, these amounted to

Dumas with the American actress Adah Isaacs
Menken, 1867.

four hundred volumes and thirty-five dramas in twenty years. However, the electors decided not to revise their own more common notion of what constituted a proletarian and did not adopt him.

Not content with his huge output in fiction, Dumas often turned his novels into plays. It was common practice: George Sand took the same course (although, as Dumas thought, to less effect). Dumas employed collaborators and regurgitated his works in different genres because he needed money—for his mother, his wife, his children, his friends, all and sundry, including the extremely long line of his mistresses—though "line" inaccurately suggests succession rather than simultaneity. These last included numerous actresses, the opera singer Caroline Ungher (famous as Bellini's Norma and Donizetti's Parisina) and, in his declining years, the American Jewish equestrian performer Adah Isaacs Menken. Temperamentally, Dumas enjoyed the siege, but he was inclined to grow bored shortly after the surrender.

He lived extravagantly when he had money, ruining himself in building a château or mansion in various styles, including Gothic, Renaissance, and Moorish, with an English garden. He called it Monte-Cristo. It had a harem for his mistresses, and a menagerie of over two hundred animals. No fewer than six hundred friends were invited to the housewarming in July 1848, and there was always open house for numerous parasites. Dumas was wildly generous, and often in debt. "I have never refused money to anyone except to my creditors," he said once. It was the lordly attitude he gave to his Kean [in *Kean, on désordre et genie* (1836)]. The Count of Monte-Cristo himself, with his fabulous inexhaustible wealth and the immense power it gives him, is the wish-fulfillment of a writer who dreamed of riches. Dumas made money enough but it slipped through his fingers.

The list of Dumas's works is daunting. It seems unlikely that anyone could have read them all. Here are no slim volumes in the refined manner of a Jane Austen, but novels each consisting of eight or ten tomes. Dumas belongs with those who produced in such quantity that quality and reputation inevitably suffer. Yet Baudelaire (critic as well as poet), while regarding Dumas's facility or "fearful dysentery" with disfavor, could not refrain from lauding the novelist's prodigious imagination: "this man . . . seems to represent universal vitality," he wrote. The sheer energy involved is breathtaking. Dumas lived in an age when writers were "geniuses," larger than life, incredibly productive and energetic (Victor Hugo, Balzac, George Sand).

Besides being a playwright and novelist, Dumas was one of the founders of modern journalism, at a time when the cheap popular press was being launched in France. He wrote about anything and everything: drama criticism (often padded out with lengthy quotations), reminiscences (occasionally improved by invention), lively accounts of his travels (he would be an indefatigable traveler—to Italy, Germany, England, Spain, Russia, North Africa, and elsewhere). Dumas even wrote on gastronomy and fashion. He founded papers of his own like the charmingly named *Le Mousquetaire, Le d'Artagnan, Le Monte-Cristo,* none of which enjoyed a long life. Never one to hide his light under a bushel, Dumas also claimed to have invented the *roman-feuilleton,* the novel published in the popular press in installments. If he did not invent it, he was certainly one of its most admired and sought-after practitioners. His fiction has survived much more readily than that of Eugène Sue, the once popular author of *The Mysteries of Paris* and *The Wandering Jew.*

His ambitions were vast—quite as vast as those of Balzac, who aimed to capture an entire society in all its aspects in a series of novels. "My first wish has no limit," said Dumas. "My first aspiration is always for the impossible." (He once contemplated writing a novel that began with Jesus and ended with the last man!) In effect, what he sought to do was to re-create the whole of French history and make it live in drama and fiction. Many around the world have acquired their first notions of French history from Dumas, just as they have gained their idea of American history from the cinema.

In the early nineteenth century, historical inquiry was seen as resolutely modern. Dumas might treat documents or memoirs in a cavalier fashion, but they provided the starting point for imaginative re-creation and inventiveness. From the fourteenth century he took the subject of what is perhaps his most famous play, *La Tour de Nesle* (1832), about the secret scandalous goings-on of Queen Marguerite de Bourgogne. Concealed under a mask, she makes a habit of having each young lover murdered after a single night of pleasure and the body thrown in the Seine. It is a satisfyingly lurid melodrama of hidden and mistaken identities, passion, power, intrigue, and incest. The French cinema in its heyday could hardly miss an opportunity to film such a subject.

Dumas contributed to the revival of interest in the late sixteenth century with his novels about the last Valois kings and the Wars of Religion. He also stimulated curiosity about the early seventeenth century—an era with a romantic tinge of its own. Men and women were thought to live in those days a more energetic and exciting kind of life than was experienced in a bourgeois industrial era like his. It is difficult now to see the age of Louis XIII and Cardinal Richelieu, or the revolt of the nobles known as the Fronde, without something of Dumas coloring one's view.

For many, the period is forever associated with the three (or four) musketeers who fight in unquenchable friendship, all for one and one for all, in the struggle to outwit the dangerously clever Milady. *Les Trois Mousquetaires* (1844), based partly on the apocryphal memoirs of d'Artagnan, the impoverished Gascon who became Captain of the King's Guard, was surely in Edmond Rostand's mind when he charted the exploits of Cyrano, the (honorary) Gascon scholar-poet-dramatist, and the Gascon cadets, in *Cyrano de Bergerac* (1897). The fact that both d'Artagnan and Cyrano once lived and breathed cannot altogether remove the impression that they are more vivid on the page or the stage than they are in history.

Then there was an epoch-making event much closer to Dumas's own period: the Revolution of 1789. He must have heard a good deal about it from those who lived through the upheaval. His own father had risen rapidly from the ranks to become a general in the revolutionary armies. The Revolution dominated Dumas's imagination as a writer, just as it did the minds of many of his contemporaries, all seeking to grasp the causes and the significance of such a blood-stained phenomenon, to explain and sometimes even to justify its grislier manifestations. In 1845-46 Dumas published a strange novel, *Le Chevalier de Maison-Rouge,* based on the memoirs of the so-called Marquis de Rougeville, who had joined a secret society that made several vain attempts to rescue the imprisoned Queen Marie-Antoinette.

Some of the seemingly most far-fetched episodes in this novel had their models in actuality. For instance, the woman protagonist who offers to change clothes with the Queen, in order to facilitate her escape, recalls the generosity of an English lady who asked to take the Queen's place. A similar offer was made to the imprisoned Mme Roland who, like the Queen she hated, declined to accept the sacrifice. In the novel, the Chevalier de Maison-Rouge stabs himself under the guillotine at the moment when the Queen is executed, in a scene typical of frenetic Romantic excess and horror—and yet a man was actually found still alive under the scaffold when the Queen was guillotined. Like many of his contemporaries, Dumas was haunted by the guillotine and its victims. After this book he wrote a cycle of novels on the pre-revolutionary and revolutionary period: *Joseph Balsamo, Le Collier de la Reine, Ange Pitou, La Comtesse de Charny,* in an attempt to chart the decline and fall of the French monarchy. This cycle has recently been reprinted, doubtless to coincide with the bicentenary of the Revolution. Later in life, Dumas would return to the theme of the Revolution and its consequences.

Although the novelist had no great sympathy for the Bourbon dynasty, he did feel deeply for prisoners whatever their allegiance—not only the unfortunate Queen Marie-Antoinette, but also the earlier "Man in the Iron Mask" (supposedly the twin brother of Louis XIV) who spent a lifetime in prison. Most famously, perhaps, there is his own hero, the long-suffering Edmond Dantès, confined for years in the dungeons of the château d'If at Marseilles. Dantès's cruel fate and his later role as relentless avenger were drawn from an actual case of betrayal and wrongful imprisonment found in the police archives. Like the Count of Monte-Cristo, the original victim was a master of impenetrable disguise. He did not share with his fictional counterpart, though, the rare gift to be at home in many different countries and languages.

This fellow feeling with prisoners probably derived from the fact that the novelist's father, General Dumas, had been imprisoned in Naples under the Bourbons who ruled the Kingdom of the Two Sicilies. It happened when he was returning from Napoleon Bonaparte's Egyptian campaign, and he never fully recovered from the sickness he contracted in the Neapolitan prison. Indeed, he died in 1806 when Dumas was not yet four years old. In Egypt, General Dumas had made the grave mistake of expressing a different view from that of General Bonaparte, who saw to it that he was sent into retirement and deprived of the pension due to him.

While Dumas spoke of Napoleon as his father's "murderer," he could not help admiring the military genius who promoted French *gloire*. When, after Napoleon's downfall in 1815, the Bonapartists (in opposition under the Bourbon Restoration) adopted the Emperor's belated conversion to "liberalism," Dumas could be found among their number. Later, he would become a friend of Prince Napoleon (son of the Emperor's brother, Jérôme, former King of Westphalia), and would visit the island of Monte-Cristo with him. There is no way of following the political intricacies and intrigues that led to Edmond Dantés's long and terrible incarceration without some acquaintance with the effect of the rapidly changing regimes of the years 1814-15, or with the cynical and unscrupulous characters who (like Edmond's enemies) knew how to profit by those changes to rise to positions of power and wealth. Unjust imprisonment is not a theme that has become outdated.

Dumas's ancestry was more likely to make him another Antony or outsider than a figure of established society. He and Alexander Pushkin were (as far as I know) the only heirs of Byron to have Africans among their forebears. The mighty Russian creator of *Eugene Onegin* was at once proud of his African great-grandfather and unhappy at what he called his own "negroid ugliness." Dumas was sometimes teased in a thoughtless manner about his touch of the tarbrush (as it used to be called); sometimes he met with real animosity. One of Dumas's enemies, no doubt jealous of his popular success, wrote that his collaborators worked like "Negro laborers under the whip of a mulatto." There was a play on words here, for the word "négres" is used in French to mean not only blacks but literary assistants. When the electors of 1848 made it clear that they did not want a "Negro," Dumas thought of standing as a candidate for election in the Antilles. The writer's long-dead grandmother, Cessette Dumas, had been a black slave of Saint-Domingue (Haiti), at that time in part a French colony. She bore several illegitimate children to Colonel Antoine-Alexandre Davy de La Pailleterie, a Norman reprobate of noble but modest rank with the courtesy title of Marquis, who had gone to the colony to seek his fortune.

Three of the children were sold into slavery to help finance the father's return to France with his son, Thomas-Alexandre, whom he acknowledged. With the Revolution and careers open to talent, Thomas-Alexandre enlisted under his mother's name of Dumas in the army of the Republic, distinguished himself by performing singular feats of strength and heroic valor, and was rapidly promoted. He was able to marry the daughter of the former majordomo to the Ducs d'Orléans, first princes of the blood royal, who possessed a château at Villers-Cotterets, the town where the future writer was born. It was under the protection of the Duc d'Orléans (later King Louis-Philippe) and in

his offices in the handsome Palais-Royal that the young Dumas would begin his career in Paris as a copy clerk.

Notwithstanding his friendship with the ill-fated Duc de Chartres (elder son of the Duc d'Orléans), who was to die in a tragic accident, Dumas did not prove particularly loyal to the Orléans house, the younger branch of the Bourbon dynasty. When the Revolution of July 1830 broke out, sealing the fate of the elder branch, Dumas dashed off to Soissons, a town close to his birthplace, to obtain powder for the insurgents. He was not at all pleased when Louis-Philippe ascended the throne. As he wrote in his memoirs (which, despite numerous volumes, only reach to February 1833), the young men of the people who made the Revolution of 1830, that "ardent youth of the heroic proletariat," as he called them, are soon cast aside, and "the parasites of power" rise at their expense to position and command. There was never any doubt where his sympathies lay.

During the Revolution of 1848, Dumas was to be found in the streets, marching with the students and workers. Although in the beginning he supported Louis Napoleon (the first Emperor's putative nephew), Dumas was opposed to his presidency. The coup d'état of December 2, 1851, which set the scene for the Second Empire a year later, led to his departure for Brussels. However, he was not there as a political exile like Victor Hugo and so many others (with whom he sympathized), but rather because he was bankrupt. The construction and furnishing of his mansion, together with his lavish entertaining there, had largely contributed to his financial plight. He would be prosecuted in 1855 for public expressions of sympathy with the political exiles, and he visited Victor Hugo on his "rock" in Guernsey (in 1857)—a gesture of friendship much appreciated by the poet in exile.

By 1860, after obtaining a large advance for the publication of his complete works, Dumas was again in funds. He acquired a schooner and set sail for Sicily to join Garibaldi and the Thousand, who by then had taken Palermo. (The writer had encountered the popular liberator before, in Turin.) Dumas offered to obtain arms for Garibaldi who, having captured Naples, made him a freeman of the city where his father had once been incarcerated. In addition, the grateful Garibaldi appointed Dumas director of the Naples museums. The tireless novelist founded a paper, *L'Independente;* he also published a French version of Garibaldi's memoirs, and an account of the expedition of the Thousand. G. M. Trevelyan, the distinguished historian of the Sicilian campaign, observed that this account was "not inaccurate on the whole." Trevelyan also thought that the value of Dumas's edition of Garibaldi's memoirs as a historical document was "underrated."

As a result of his exploits and services for Garibaldi, Dumas was invited to join an insurrection in Albania, and was offered the rank of general, but he declined. He was by then over sixty. Those malicious observers, the brothers Goncourt, meeting him some years later, remarked on his marvelous talent as a raconteur. They said that he had an "enormous ego, as large as himself " but, they added, he was "overflowing with kindliness and sparkling with wit."

It is no wonder that Dumas is a name to conjure with among Italian writers. In Umberto Eco's recent novel, *Foucault's Pendulum,* for instance, the three friends, Casaubon, Belbo, and Diotallevi, have something of the three musketeers about them, with (it has been suggested) the computer named Abulafia making a fourth. In his inexhaustible, learned, and often hilarious variations on the vast theme of secret societies, Eco does not fail to mention Dumas's novel *Le Collier de la Reine,* echoing its author's view that the famous scandal over Queen Marie-Antoinette's necklace was prompted by a masonic plot to discredit the monarchy.

At the head of Eco's Chapter 97 is an epigraph from Dumas's novel *Joseph Balsamo.* Balsamo was a doctor and charlatan known as the Count of Cagliostro, born in Palermo in 1743, devotee of occultism and freemasonry, and exiled for his part in the scandal over the Queen's necklace. Readers will find in that chapter a discussion about the relative merits of the popular serial novel or *roman-feuilleton* and high art. This debate echoes current critical preoccupations. Where the *roman-feuilleton* "seems to speak in jest, basically it makes us see the world as it is, or at least as it will be. Women are much more like Milady than Clélia Conti," suggests Belbo. (The French translation names the idealized passionate Italian heroine of Stendhal's *La Chartreuse de Parme,* whereas the English version offers Dickens's sentimental Little Nell, who belongs to a different tradition entirely.)

How seriously are we meant to take Belbo's defense of the *roman-feuilleton* of Eugéne Sue and Alexandre Dumas? What credence should be given to his suggestion (after Dumas himself) that the novel of adventure and romance is fundamentally "realistic," or potentially so, if that is what he means? Are we supposed to agree to his proposition that the vengeful, resourceful, sexually independent Milady, who nearly outwits d'Artagnan (ever ready to fall "in love" at the sight of an attractive woman), is a more normal or recognizable representative of womanhood than a heroine like Clélia? Is Umberto Eco playing with current feminist criteria here?

There follows Belbo's satirical pastiche of Eugène Sue (with his belief in the malign powers of the Jesuits) and of Dumas and the historical adventure novel, with allusions to Joseph Balsamo/Cagliostro and to Jeanne de La Motte, who was branded for her part in the scandal of the royal necklace. All this is doubtless written tongue-in-cheek, or half in jest, as part of an intellectual game, designed—like the rest of the book—to stimulate the reader's wits, blur the frontiers of fact and fiction in the current style, and confound us all with the author's cleverness. Nonetheless, it may indicate a line that could lead to a certain revaluation of Dumas's writings, should anyone venture to pursue it, or believe it worthwhile to do so.

For the fact remains: Dumas was loved, and is still loved in a way that contemporaries of his like Vigny or Mérimée or Sue are not. He wanted to give pleasure and he succeeded. Imaginative and narrative skills like his are not to be despised. Besides, we are not obliged to stay on the heights all the time. (pp. 34-9)

Renee Winegarten, "Alexandre Dumas: Fact and Fiction," in *The New Criterion,* Vol. IX, No. 9, May, 1991, pp. 32-9.

SOURCES FOR FURTHER STUDY

Brandes, Georg. "The Drama: Vitet, Dumas, De Vigny, Hugo." In his *Main Currents in Nineteenth Century Literature: The Romantic School in France,* Vol. V, translated by Diana White and Mary Morison, pp. 339-56. London: William Heinemann, 1904.

> Discusses the unequal merits of Dumas's historical plays and describes *Antony* as the quintessence of Romantic passion and defiance.

Hemmings, F. W. J. *Alexandre Dumas: The King of Romance.* New York: Charles Scribner's Sons, 1979, 231 p.

> Biography surveying Dumas's literary development.

Marinetti, Amelita. "Death, Resurrection, and Fall in Dumas' *Comte de Monte-Cristo." The French Review* L, No. 2 (December 1976): 260-69.

> Discerns two mythic cycles of fall and resurrection at the structural and thematic core of *The Count of Monte Cristo* and contends that these cycles serve as vehicles for reflection on the theme of human competence and independence as arbiters of justice, a concern that Marinetti traces to social and political upheavals in Dumas's France.

Maurois, André. *The Titans: A Three-Generation Biography of the Dumas.* Translated by Gerard Hopkins. New York: Harper & Brothers Publishers, 1957, 508 p.

Respected biographical study of the three Dumas— General Thomas-Alexandre Dumas, Alexandre Dumas, *père,* Alexandre Dumas, *fils*—analyzing their relationships to one another, the vigorous Dumas "temperament," as well as literary works by Dumas, *père,* and Dumas, *fils.*

Schopp, Claude. *Alexandre Dumas: Genius of Life.* Translated by A. J. Koch. New York: Franklin Watts, 1988, 506 p.

Anecdotal biography.

Stowe, Richard S. *Alexandre Dumas 'père'.* Boston: Twayne Publishers, 1976, 164 p.

Critical biography tracing the wide variety of Dumas's contribution to world literature.

Paul Laurence Dunbar

1872-1906

American poet, short story writer, novelist, librettist, dramatist, and essayist.

INTRODUCTION

*B*est known for his poetry written in black American dialect, Dunbar is widely acknowledged as one of the first important black authors in American literature. In his writings he depicted the social conditions of emancipated slaves and expressed the emotions of black Americans during the late nineteenth century. Dunbar enjoyed his greatest popularity in the early twentieth century following the publication of two seminal books, *Majors and Minors* (1895) and *Lyrics of Lowly Life* (1896). Many of his poems and short stories pandered to the black stereotypes held by white society, for they were written at a time when appeasing white audiences was crucial to the literary success of black authors. Accordingly, Dunbar has been labeled an accommodationist by many reviewers, yet recent criticism has focused on Dunbar's attempts to insert strains of social protest into his works. The dialect poems which Dunbar is best known for constitute only a small portion of his canon, which is replete with novels, short stories, essays, and poems in standard English. In its entirety, Dunbar's literary body is an impressive representation of black life in turn-of-the-century America. As Dunbar's friend James Weldon Johnson noted in the preface to his *Book of American Poetry:* "Paul Laurence Dunbar stands out as the first poet from the Negro race in the United States to show a combined mastery over poetic material and poetic technique, to reveal innate literary distinction in what he wrote, and to maintain a high level of performance. He was the first to rise to a height from which he could take a perspective view of his own race. He was the first to see objectively its humor, its superstitions, its short-comings; the first to feel sympathetically its heart-wounds, its yearnings, its aspirations, and to voice them all in a purely literary form."

Born in Dayton, Ohio, Dunbar was the son of former slaves. As a child he listened to his mother's stories about her early life on Kentucky plantations, and later incorporated much of this information into his writing. However, because his mother had understandably omitted the more brutal aspects of slavery from her stories, Dunbar tended to glorify plantation life, an aspect of his work that has been widely criticized. He began writing stories and poems as a child, and teachers recognized and encouraged his talent. As a high school student, Dunbar continued to write, composing several plays for his drama club and acting as editor of the school newspaper. He also founded the *Dayton Tattler,* a short-lived black newspaper that was printed by his friend and classmate, the future aviator Orville Wright. Following graduation in 1891, Dunbar was unable to afford the expense of a college education, and so he applied for work at newspaper offices and other businesses. Despite his growing reputation in Dayton as a gifted writer, most jobs were closed to black applicants, and for several years Dunbar could only find work as an elevator operator. While on duty, he often recited his poetry to riders, and in his spare time he continued to write and publish poems and short stories, although he rarely received any payment for them.

During the early 1890s, Dunbar also gave occasional readings, one of which was enthusiastically received at a meeting of the Western Association of Writers (WAOW). Three members later visited Dunbar to find out more about his life and one, James Newton Matthews, appalled by the prejudice to which Dunbar was subjected, wrote a letter to the press praising Dunbar and his work that was reprinted in newspapers across the country. Shortly after the article appeared, Dunbar was admitted as a WAOW member, and his popularity as a speaker increased. Encouraged by this publicity, he privately published *Oak and Ivy* (1893), a collection of poetry that he sold from his elevator post. Much of the verse in this volume was black American dialect poetry, which was highly popular with white audiences. Dunbar believed that if he could win over white readers with the humor of his dialect verse, he could gradually display his abilities as a serious author.

In 1893 Dunbar left Dayton to work with Frederick Douglass in the Haitian Exposition of the Chicago World's Fair. On "Colored Day" he recited original compositions in standard English and was given a warm reception. Unfortunately, this reception was not to last. In the two years following the Chicago exhibition, Dunbar suffered career setbacks as his health, poor since childhood, worsened. Unable to support himself and his mother, he considered suicide. A Toledo attorney, Charles Thatcher, who had been avidly following Dunbar's career since the publication of *Oak and Ivy,* sent Dunbar enough money to sustain him, and later used his influence to help publish Dunbar's poetry collection *Majors and Minors.* William Dean

Howells, then the most prominent and influential critic in America, praised the dialect poems in this work, noting that Dunbar "reveals in these a finely ironical perception of the negro's limitations, with a tenderness for them which I think so rare as to be almost quite new. . . . It is this humorous quality which Mr. Dunbar has added to our literature, and it will be this which will most distinguish him." While Howells lauded the dialect verse, he was less impressed by the standard English poems: "Some of these I thought very good, but not distinctly his contribution to the body of American poetry"—a verdict that haunted Dunbar throughout his career. Initially overwhelmed by Howells's review and the fame that followed, Dunbar later confessed that he believed Howells had done him more harm than good; Dunbar's works written on contemporary themes and in standard English were never wholly embraced by white society, and he found himself trapped in the undesired role of dialect poet. He often described himself as "a black white man," and among papers found after his death was the note: "It is one of the peculiar phases of Anglo-Saxon conceit to refuse to believe that every black man does not want to be white."

After a trip to England, where he met and collaborated with the black composer Samuel Coleridge Taylor, Dunbar returned to the United States and married a poet and school teacher, Alice Ruth Moore, with whom he had been corresponding by mail for two years. During this period, Dunbar completed his first novel, *The Uncalled* (1898) and collaborated with songwriter Will Marion Cook on the musical *Clorindy; or, The Origin of the Cakewalk* (1898). A huge success, the show was the first to feature syncopated music and the first in which the chorus sang and danced simultaneously. Although Dunbar had agreed to collaborate on future projects with Cook, he was quickly disillusioned with his press reception as "king of the coon shows." Moreover, he was pressured to quit by his wife and mother, who were insulted by his association with the degrading minstrel tradition. Dunbar reluctantly fulfilled his obligations and in the process became acquainted with the artists, actors, singers, and musicians who frequented Harlem's popular theaters; he later included many of these colorful characters in his short stories and in the novel *The Sport of the Gods* (1902). While in New York, Dunbar contracted tuberculosis and began drinking to relieve his physical discomfort. The illness worsened in the last years of his life, necessitating intermittent retreats to milder climates. At the age of thirty-three, bitter, alcoholic, and tubercular, Dunbar died at his mother's home in Dayton.

Dunbar's dialect poetry has long been his most popular work. Dialect was a common literary device in the late nineteenth century, but Dunbar's work in the genre is considered especially realistic and sensitive. Like other dialect writers, Dunbar was primarily concerned with humorous situations; however, he portrayed these events with ironic tenderness that conveys the emotions and thoughts of his uneducated, inarticulate subjects. Even Dunbar's detractors admit that his dialect poetry vividly captures the folklife and beliefs of late nineteenth-century black Americans. This type of verse, however, constitutes only a small part of his creative achievement. Dunbar wrote many poems in standard English as well as four novels and several volumes of short stories. Unlike his dialect verse, his non-dialect poetry is chiefly concerned with his personal pain and anguish, not with created characters and situations. Similarly, Dunbar's fiction illuminates his struggle with artistic honesty and commercial success; his later work and its emphasis on social protest clearly reveal his choice for truth over popular themes.

Folks from Dixie (1898), Dunbar's first short story collection, strongly imitated the sentimental Southern plantation tradition of Thomas Nelson Page. Many of the tales, influenced by the stories Dunbar's mother told him, portray idealized master-slave relationships in the Civil War era. At the time of the book's publication, reviewers found the discussions of the spiritual, moral, and domestic lives of black people very revealing, and many commented on the stories in which Dunbar disregarded the plantation tradition and focused on psychological and social themes. His next volume, *The Strength of Gideon, and Other Stories* (1900), is considered by many critics to be his best collection of short fiction and his strongest statement of racial concerns. The few plantation stories that are included often focus upon the psychological dilemma of slaves who have been emancipated but are unsure of how to handle their new freedom. The most esteemed tales are those involving social or political injustice, and one, "The Ingrate," contains what is regarded as Dunbar's most forceful attack on slavery. Based on his own father's escape from a Southern plantation and set during the Civil War, this work revolves around Joshua, a slave who yearns for freedom, manages to flee to Canada, and then decides to join the Union army so that he can fight for the emancipation of all slaves. Although his later short story collections deal almost exclusively with racial oppression and exploitation, Dunbar understood the need to cater to white audiences and continued to accept and employ the limitations of the dialect story. *In Old Plantation Days* (1903) is a radical shift back to this style; Dunbar largely avoided racial themes in this collection, but wrote social protest articles for various newspapers and magazines during this time. Dunbar's final volume of short stories, *The Heart of Happy Hollow* (1904), chiefly contains tales of postbellum black life which, like those in *The Strength of Gideon*, are strongly concerned with racial problems. Included in *The Heart of Happy Hollow* are two stories

about lynching, one of which, "The Lynching of Jube Benson," is esteemed by contemporary critics as a courageous, moving work of social protest.

Overall, Dunbar's novels are considered failures. Critics largely rejected his first novel, *The Uncalled,* as dull and unconvincing in its portrait of Frederick Brent, a white pastor who had, in childhood, been abandoned by an alcoholic father and then raised by a zealously devout spinster, Hester Prime. Dunbar's second novel, *The Love of Landry* (1900), is about an ailing woman who arrives in Colorado for convalescence and finds true happiness with a cowboy. It was likewise deemed unconvincing in its presentation of white characters. Dunbar suffered further critical setback with his next work, *The Fanatics* (1901), about America at the beginning of the Civil War. Its central characters, from white families, differ in their North-South sympathies and spark a dispute in their Ohio community. Among the novel's many detractors is Robert Bone, who claimed that Dunbar resorted to "caricature in his treatment of minor Negro characters" and that his stereotypical portraits of black characters only served to reinforce prejudice. *The Sport of the Gods,* Dunbar's final—and most successful—novel, presents a far more disturbing portrait of black America. Written two years before his death, it is the only novel in which Dunbar depicted a black protagonist. Berry Hamilton, wrongly charged with theft by his white employers, is sentenced to ten years of prison labor. His wife, son, and daughter consequently find themselves targets of abuse in the southern community, and after being robbed by their local police they head north to Harlem. There they encounter further hardship; the son succumbs to alcoholism and crime; the naive daughter begins a "questionable" dancing career; and the wife, convinced her marriage to Berry is over, weds an abusive degenerate. When Berry is finally cleared of the crime, he travels north and finds his family in disarray. Matters are finally set right when, after a series of incidents, the Hamiltons are reunited in marriage.

In general, discussion of Dunbar's works has more often been a reflection of racial issues in American history than a dispassionate assessment of his literary production. It was not until the 1960s that critics began to pay more attention to Dunbar's achievements and, in doing so, resurrected Dunbar as an important voice in American literature. For Nikki Giovanni and other Dunbar scholars, his work constitutes both a history and a celebration of black life. "There is no poet, black or nonblack, who measures his achievement," Giovanni declared. "Even today. He wanted to be a writer and he wrote." Recent criticism has focused more on understanding Dunbar's compromises rather than simply attacking him for his accommodationist stance. Much of this criticism has demonstrated the tragedy of Dunbar's position—that of a man who was deeply ashamed of the only work he could sell, who perceived his own inadequacies, and who believed he collaborated in the defamation of his own people. A. Robert Lee stated: "Caught in the historical paradox of his time, endowed with invention but not genius, [Dunbar] was occasionally able to perceive and arrest the brutal particulars of black historical experience. Where he gave in to the costume formulas of romance and resorted to wooden dialogue he clearly writes fiction both weak and ineffective; but where he sought faithfully to portray the live psychology of race, he is able to break through, to seize his reader with a sense of place and time, of human beings bound up in racial calamity."

(For further information about Dunbar's life and works, see *Black Literature Criticism; Black Writers; Concise Dictionary of American Literary Biography, 1865-1917; Contemporary Authors*, Vols. 104, 124; *Dictionary of Literary Biography*, Vols. 50, 74, 78; *Short Story Criticism*, Vol. 8; *Something About the Author*, Vol. 34; and *Twentieth-Century Literary Criticism*, Vols. 2, 12.)

CRITICAL COMMENTARY

W. D. HOWELLS
(essay date 1896)

[Howells was the chief progenitor of American Realism and one of the most influential American literary critics of the late nineteenth century. He wrote nearly three dozen novels, few of which are read today. Despite his eclipse, he stands as one of the major literary figures of the nineteenth century: he successfully weaned American literature away from the sentimental romanticism of its infancy, earning the popular sobriquet "the Dean of American Letters." Through Realism, a theory central to his fiction and criticism, Howells sought to disperse "the conventional acceptations by which men live on easy terms with themselves" that they might "examine the grounds of their social and moral opinions." To accomplish this, according to Howells, the writer must strive to record impressions of everyday life in detail, endowing characters with true-to-life motives and avoiding authorial comment in the narrative. In addition to many notable studies of the works of his friends Mark Twain and Henry James, Howells reviewed three generations of international literature, urging Americans to read the works of Émile Zola, Bernard Shaw, Henrik Ibsen, Emily Dickinson, and other important authors. Dunbar was another writer that Howells introduced to the reading public. In the following excerpt from *Harper's Weekly*, he reviews *Majors and Minors*, praising Dunbar's dialect verse. This review proved to be a milestone in the poet's career. A year later, however, Dunbar sadly remarked: "I see now very clearly that Mr. Howells has done me irrevocable harm in the dictum he laid down regarding my dialect verse."]

[Mr. Dunbar] is a real poet whether he speaks a dialect or whether he writes a language. He calls his little book *Majors and Minors,* the Majors being in our American English, and the Minors being in dialect, the dialect of the middle-south negroes and the middle-south whites; for the poet's ear has been quick for the accent of his neighbors as well as for that of his kindred. I have no means of knowing whether he values his Majors more than his Minors; but I should not suppose it at all unlikely, and I am bound to say none of them are despicable. In very many I find the proofs of honest thinking and true feeling, and in some the record of experience, whose genuineness the reader can test by his own. . . .

Most of these pieces, however, are like most of the pieces of most young poets, cries of passionate aspiration and disappointment, more or less personal or universal, which except for the negro face of the author one could not find specially notable. It is when we come to Mr. Dunbar's Minors that we feel ourselves in the presence of a man with a direct and a fresh authority to do the kind of thing he is doing. . . .

One sees how the poet exults in his material, as the artist always does; it is not for him to blink its commonness, or to be ashamed of its rudeness; and in his treatment of it he has been able to bring us nearer to the heart of primitive human nature in his race than any one else has yet done. The range between appetite and emotion is not great, but it is here that his race has hitherto had its being, with a lift now and then far above and beyond it. A rich, humorous sense pervades his recognition of this fact, without excluding a fond sympathy, and it is the blending of these which delights me in all his dialect verse. . . .

Several of the pieces are pure sentiment, like **"The Deserted Plantation";** but these without lapsing into sentimentality recall the too easy pathos of the pseudo-negro poetry of the minstrel show. . . .

Mr. Dunbar's race is nothing if not lyrical, and he comes by his rhythm honestly. But what is better, what is finer, what is of larger import, in his work is what is

Principal Works

Oak and Ivy (poetry) 1893

Majors and Minors (poetry) 1895

Lyrics of Lowly Life (poetry) 1896

Clorindy; or, The Origin of the Cakewalk [with Will Marion Cook] (libretto) 1898

Dream Lovers: An Operatic Romance (libretto) 1898

Folks from Dixie (short stories) 1898

The Uncalled (novel) 1898

Lyrics of the Hearthside (poetry) 1899

The Love of Landry (novel) 1900

The Strength of Gideon, and Other Stories (short stories) 1900

Uncle Eph's Christmas (drama) 1900

Candle-Lightin' Time (poetry) 1901

The Fanatics (novel) 1901

In Dahomey: A Negro Musical Comedy [with others] (libretto) 1902

The Sport of the Gods (novel) 1902; also published as The Jest of Fate: A Story of Negro Life, 1903

In Old Plantation Days (short stories) 1903

Lyrics of Love and Laughter (poetry) 1903

When Malindy Sings (poetry) 1903

The Heart of Happy Hollow (short stories) 1904

Li'l Gal (poetry) 1904

Chris'mus Is a Comin', and Other Poems (poetry) 1905

Howdy, Honey, Howdy (poetry) 1905

Lyrics of Sunshine and Shadow (poetry) 1905

A Plantation Portrait (poetry) 1905

Joggin 'erlong (poetry) 1906

The Life and Works of Paul Laurence Dunbar (poetry and short stories) 1907

The Complete Poems of Paul Laurence Dunbar (poetry) 1913

Speakin' o' Christmas, and Other Christmas and Special Poems (poetry) 1914

The Best Stories of Paul Laurence Dunbar (short stories) 1938

The Letters of Paul and Alice Dunbar: A Private History (letters) 1974

The Paul Laurence Dunbar Reader (poetry, short stories, essays, journalism, and letters) 1975

I Greet the Dawn: Poems by Paul Laurence Dunbar (poetry) 1978

conscious and individual in it. He is, so far as I know, the first man of his color to study his race objectively, to analyze it to himself, and then to represent it in art as he felt it and found it to be; to represent it humorously, yet tenderly, and above all so faithfully that we know the portrait to be undeniably like. A race which has reached this effect in any of its members can no longer be held wholly uncivilized; and intellectually Mr. Dunbar makes a stronger claim for the negro than the negro yet has done. . . .

I am speaking of him as a black poet, when I should be speaking of him as a poet; but the notion of what he is insists too strongly for present impartiality. I hope I have not praised him too much, because he has surprised me so very much; for his excellences are positive and not comparative. If his Minors had been written by a white man, I should have been struck by their very uncommon quality; I should have said that they were wonderful divinations. But since they are expressions of a race-life from within the race, they seem to me indefinitely more valuable and significant. I have sometimes fancied that perhaps the negroes *thought* black, and *felt* black; that they were racially so utterly alien and distinct from ourselves that there never could be common intellectual and emotional ground between us, and that whatever eternity might do to reconcile us, the end of time would find us as far asunder as ever. But

this little book has given me pause in my speculation. Here, in the artistic effect at least, is white thinking and white feeling in a black man, and perhaps the human unity, and not the race unity, is the precious thing, the divine thing, after all. God hath made of one blood all nations of men; perhaps the proof of this saying is to appear in the arts, and our hostilities and prejudices are to vanish in them.

Mr. Dunbar, at any rate, seems to have fathomed the souls of his simple white neighbors, as well as those of his own kindred; and certainly he has reported as faithfully what passes in them as any man of our race has yet done with respect to the souls of his. It would be very incomplete recognition of his work not to speak particularly of the non-negro dialect pieces, and it is to the lover of homely and tender poetry, as well as the student of tendencies, that I commend such charming sketches as **"Speakin o' Christmas," "After a Visit,"** **"Lonesome,"** and **"The Spellin' Bee."** They are good, very good. . . . (p. 630)

W. D. Howells, in a review of "Majors and Minors," in *Harper's Weekly*, June 20, 1896, p. 630.

VERNON LOGGINS
(essay date 1931)

[In the review essay excerpted below, Loggins surveys Dunbar's novels, short stories, and poetry, noting: "The publication in 1896 of Dunbar's *Lyrics of Lowly Life* is the greatest single event in the history of American Negro literature."]

Dunbar's first collection of short stories, *Folks from Dixie* . . . , contains some of his most characteristic and best work as a writer of fiction. . . . Whatever unity the book as a whole has is told by the title, *Folks from Dixie;* the characters, not all of them colored, are either still in Dixie or once lived there. Two of the stories, **"The Ordeal at Mt. Hope,"** an argument for industrial education, and **"At Shaft II,"** an indirect plea for the Negro to stay out of labor unions, were designed for more than entertainment. The rest are pure tales. **"The Colonel's Awakening,"** the scene of which is laid in Virginia, follows so closely [Thomas Nelson] Page's method of extracting pathos out of the portrayal of the love and devotion of a faithful Negro servant that it might fit well into *In Ole Virginia*. A similar blending of kindliness and romance and sentimentality is in **"A Family Feud,"** a tale of ante-bellum days on two Kentucky plantations. The majority of the stories in the volume, however, show an indebtedness to [Joel Chandler] Harris rather than to Page. Dunbar's knowledge of plantation life in Kentucky probably came from his mother, who passed her childhood and early womanhood as a slave and who was throughout most of Dunbar's life his constant companion. At any rate, he had derived from some source a penetrating understanding of the primitive Negro's superstitions, religious zeal, romance, humor, and language. . . . And it was his intimate knowledge of the folk ways of Negroes which enabled Dunbar to do some of the strongest work found in his later volumes of short stories, [*The Strength of Gideon, In Old Plantation Days,* and *The Heart of Happy Hollow* . . .].

At the time of its appearance *Folks from Dixie* was by far the most artistic book of fiction which had come from an American Negro. But it was within a year superseded by Mr. Chesnutt's *The Conjure Woman.* Dunbar was certainly more skillful than Mr. Chesnutt as a recorder of dialect, and he perhaps got closer to the real heart of the plantation Negro. However, he created no such character as Uncle Julius, and he never attained Mr. Chesnutt's mastery of treating a folk tale from a subtle and intellectual point of view. Dunbar's stories appealed to the readers of such periodicals as *Lippincott's*

Magazine, while Mr. Chesnutt's met the requirements of the more critical *Atlantic Monthly* public.

Among the American writers who have been unable to judge what they could and could not do Dunbar is conspicuous. In 1898, the year of *Folks from Dixie*, he published his first novel, *The Uncalled.* It was to a certain extent autobiographical, an exposition of Dunbar's own ordeal in deciding whether he ought to enter the ministry. Since he was really writing about a personal experience, one cannot help wondering why he did not put himself into the story as a colored man. The action deals with the conflict in the mind of a white youth living in a small Ohio town who feels that he should not become a preacher but who is forced by circumstances into a seminary and then into the pulpit. There is not a single Negro character in the book. As a story about whites written by a Negro it introduces us to the second type of fiction which the Negro of the period attempted. Such a type Dunbar should have painstakingly avoided. All of the bubbling spontaneity which he showed in his tales on blacks is replaced in *The Uncalled* by cheap conventional story-telling, with echoes of Dickens and the popular magazine, and with an English which is often downright faulty. The book came as a great disappointment to Dunbar's admirers. Despite its weakness, it seems to have had some commercial success, and in 1900 Dunbar published a second novel in which all of the characters are whites, *The Love of Landry.* It is a story of Easterners, all treacly sentimentalists, who think that they find the sublime beauty of reality on a Colorado ranch. It was, if that is possible, even a poorer performance than *The Uncalled.* (pp. 314-17)

Dunbar's third novel, *The Fanatics* . . . , is a more successful treatment of white types. While it is a romance of the Civil War, emphasis is not on battle scenes, but on how the struggle affects a small Ohio town which is made up of sympathizers for the South as well as for the North. There is exciting narrative from the beginning. However, interest does not become strong until the "contrabands" come pouring in from across the Ohio River with their queer songs and delightful dialect. Yet entirely too little is made of them. With the exception of a minor character, who provides an interesting climax for the ending of the tale, the Negro appears for no more than atmosphere. (p. 317)

Two of the stories in Paul Laurence Dunbar's *Folks from Dixie*, **"The Ordeal at Mt. Hope"** and **"At Shaft II,"** have been pointed out as dealing with social problems. They belong to the . . . field in which the Negro novelists and short story writers between 1865 and 1900 ventured, that of fiction offering comment on the social status of the Negro, especially in relation to the white man. It was, as we might expect, the field in which the Negro was most voluminous, and, if not most pleasing, most vigorous. It was also the field in which he was most original.

In his later collections of short stories Dunbar dwelt more and more on racial problems. (p. 320)

Happy Hollow [the fictional setting of the short story collection *The Heart of Happy Hollow*] was not to Dunbar a place for nothing more than sentimental tears and spontaneous laughter. It had its serious side, its sense of wronged justice, its tragedy. In a story of an educated colored youth's ruthless disillusionment, **"One Man's Fortune,"** included in *The Strength of Gideon,* a white lawyer is made to say:

The sentiment of remorse and the desire for atoning which actuated so many white men to help Negroes right after the war has passed off without being replaced by that sense of plain justice which gives a black man his due, not because of, nor in spite of, but without consideration of his color.

The idea thus expressed was a guiding principle for Dunbar in writing stories on such themes as Negroes exploited by unscrupulous politicians, the economic relations existing between whites and blacks, and the effect of city life on country-bred Negroes. The deep pathos of the truth which it expresses is brought out with force in two stories on lynching, **"The Tragedy at Three Corners,"** in *The Strength of Gideon,* and **"The Lynching of Jube Benson,"** in *The Heart of Happy Hollow.*

But Dunbar's most complete and profound study of the true reality of Happy Hollow came in his fourth and last novel, *The Sport of the Gods.* . . . It is at the same time his most interesting and most imperfect novel. The title hints that Dunbar might have been reading Thomas Hardy, and the story itself more than once shows a naturalistic view of life. (p. 321)

The tragedy is attributed not so much to the wiles of the city as to the ignorant Negro's helplessness when in the clutches of circumstance aggravated by an unfair social system. The novel is structurally about as bad as it could be. A half happy ending is dragged in, and no temptation to submit to melodrama is resisted. Plausibility is in many situations strained to the shattering point. The style is nervous and uneven, typical of that which one might expect from the mind of a man who is suffering from tuberculosis. But there are many patches which are intense, serious, and telling. The description of the first evening which the country Hamiltons spend at a Negro theatre in New York is an effective blending of the Dickensian and the bitter. The horrid tinsel of life as it is portrayed in the Banner Club is saved from the nauseating and repelling only by a grim sort of humor. . . . [An] anonymous critic at the time of Dunbar's death [referred] to *The Sport of the Gods* as a compendium of information for the average American. If it was a revelation to white America, it

was a sermon to all America. Dunbar usually lost himself as an artist when he felt strongly the urge to preach, and *The Sport of the Gods* suffers extremely as a specimen of pure fiction. But with the exception of certain perfectly executed short stories, such as **"Jimsella"** in *Folks from Dixie* and **"The Finding of Zach"** in *The Strength of Gideon,* it is of all Dunbar's work in prose the book in which the modern reader would probably find greatest interest.

Dunbar's poetry . . . reveals that there was little bitterness in his nature. Moreover, he was a writer with a broad public to please. Bold and uncompromising fiction on the Negro problem was not to be expected from him. (pp. 323-24)

The publication in 1896 of Dunbar's *Lyrics of Lowly Life* is the greatest single event in the history of American Negro literature. Dunbar incorporated into the book the best selections from his earlier volumes, *Oak and Ivy* . . . and *Majors and Minors.* . . . Although some of his short stories were thoughtfully conceived and admirably constructed, and although one of his novels, *The Sport of the Gods,* contains such material as should be an inspiration to Negro fiction writers for years to come, his verse is the work which distinguishes him as the universally recognized outstanding literary figure who had by 1900 arisen from the ranks of the American Negro. And *Lyrics of Lowly Life* is in all respects his happiest and most significant volume.

"Ere Sleep Comes Down to Soothe the Weary Eyes," the poem which opens the volume, is a song of the man who sees in the "waking world a world of lies," a theme possibly inspired by Shelley, whom Dunbar counted as his favorite poet. But the book is not a lyrical arraignment of society. . . . One poem after another in the volume proves that Dunbar was a master of spontaneous melody. There is never intricacy of thought nor of imagery, but there is always the song that arouses mood. It was Shelley the melodist and not Shelley the humanitarian whom Dunbar worshipped. And he was natural and sincere enough to distinguish between thoughtful influence and slavish dependence. He came as near to Shelley in **"The Rising of the Storm"** as in any poem he wrote, but . . . he was not submitting to downright imitation. . . . Most of the pieces in *Lyrics of Lowly Life* are in Shelley's English. Many of the subjects—including definitions of life, the mysteries of love and passion, the appeal of nature, and the premonitions of death—are such as one finds often treated in the lyrics of Shelley. If the volume had contained no more, it would be accounted merely a collection of gentle sentiments sung in pure melody, far superior, to be sure, to anything which any other American Negro poet had done, but not sufficiently strong to be considered a contribution of merit to American literature.

Fortunately, the volume contains a number of selections written in what Howells called the Negro's "own accent of our English." The dialect poems justify the term "lowly life" used in the title. The first which one comes upon is **"Accountability,"** a monologue of an old "darky" who has stolen "one ob mastah's chickens" and who tries to rationalize the morality of the deed. . . . Too infrequently, follow more poems in the language which the Negro's unguided habits fashioned out of English. The soul of the black laborer satisfied with little is expressed with a pure art in **"When de Co'n Pone's Hot."** . . . **"When Malindy Sings,"** inspired, we are told, by the singing of the poet's mother, is another true expression of Negro character. . . . Equally expressive of the true nature of the lowly Negro are **"Discovered"** and **"A Coquette Conquered,"** humorous love poems; **"The Deserted Plantation,"** a sentimental song of reminiscence, suggestive of the mood of Thomas Nelson Page's "Marse Chan"; **"Signs of the Times,"** a pastoral of autumn; and **"The Party,"** an hilarious descriptive poem.

The dialect poems in *Lyrics of Lowly Life* made the book the artistic, as well as the popular, success which it became. They made the reputation of Dunbar. After all, the teacher who meant most to him was not Shelley, but James Whitcomb Riley. . . . His admiration for Riley led him to include in *Lyrics of Lowly Life* **"After a Visit," "The Spellin' Bee," "A Confidence,"** and a few other pieces written in the dialect of the middle western white farmer. Entertaining, humorous, and highly musical, they might easily be mistaken for Riley's own work. Therefore, there is little excuse for their existence. But in applying Riley's methods to the Negro, Dunbar achieved genuine originality. His strongest predecessors in the writing of Negro dialect verse, Sidney Lanier, Irwin Russell, and Joel Chandler Harris, were detached from their material; Dunbar was a part of his. His realism is better than theirs because it was inspired by sincere feeling and not by the search for novelty; his music appeals to us as more natural because we do not in any way have to associate it with white singers. His Negro dialect verse is today generally accepted as the best which has been written in America. It deserves that consideration, and will probably maintain it. For the picturesque and poetic Negro language which Dunbar knew so well is rapidly passing away; he preserved a record of it at the right time.

A type of pure English verse which Dunbar should have cultivated more intensively is represented in *Lyrics of Lowly Life* by such pieces as **"Frederick Douglass,"** undoubtedly more eloquent than any memorial poem produced by any one of Dunbar's Negro predecessors; **"The Colored Soldiers,"** a stirring tribute to the colored men who fell in the Civil War; and **"Ode to Ethiopia,"** perhaps the most significant of the poems which are not in dialect. . . . The gravest charge which can justly be brought against Dunbar as the author of *Lyrics of Lowly Life* is that he too often forgot the pledge which he made to his race in **"Ode to Ethiopia."** He was endowed by nature "to sing of Ethiopia's glory," but he crowded his first important volume with songs which have little relation to himself and none to his own people. Such songs can be estimated as no more than pretty exercises.

He was twenty-four years old when *Lyrics of Lowly Life* was published, and youthfulness might have been accepted as a reason for the shortcomings of the book. But Dunbar never fulfilled its unusual promise. . . . [Recognition] as a poet prepared the way for the attainment of an ambition which he had long cherished, that for publishing prose fiction. . . . Three volumes of verse followed *Lyrics of Lowly Life*: [*Lyrics of the Hearthside; Lyrics of Love and Laughter;* and *Lyrics of Sunshine and Shadow*]. . . . In spite of the odds which he had to fight against in writing the verse included in these volumes, no one of them falls below the standards which he set for himself in *Lyrics of Lowly Life*. Each, containing pure lyrics, occasional verses on the Negro written in straight English, and dialect poems, is similar in arrangement to the earlier volume. While his prose fiction was being printed in the popular magazines, his verse was appearing usually in such periodicals as the *Century, Harper's,* the *Outlook, Current Literature,* the *Bookman,* and the *Atlantic Monthly.* That he held himself true to the poet within him during the hectic nine years of life which were allotted him after his first great success is a sure mark of Dunbar's genius. If he had in the first place made poets of the soil, such as Burns and Riley, his exclusive masters, and if he had turned his back against popularity, his career would possibly be one of the most singular which American literature has to record.

But it is unfair criticism to expect too much of a Negro poet who lived in the United States in the days when Dunbar lived. The more one considers his work in verse, the more one wonders at his accomplishment. (pp. 344-52)

Vernon Loggins, "Fiction and Poetry, 1865-1900," in his *The Negro Author: His Development in America to 1900*, 1931. Reprint by Kennikat Press, Inc., 1964, pp. 305-52.

HUGH H. GLOSTER
(essay date 1948)

[In the following essay, Gloster offers a critical overview of Dunbar's novels and short stories.]

Catering to the demands of publishers and readers of

his time, Dunbar generally evaded themes such as those presented in Chesnutt's novels and usually specialized either in the treatment of white American life or in the perpetuation of the plantation tradition. Three of his novels—*The Uncalled* (1898), *The Love of Landry* (1900), and *The Fanatics* (1901)—deal almost entirely with white characters; and the fourth, *The Sport of the Gods* (1902), though a promising naturalistic study, illustrates the plantation-school concept that the Negro becomes homesick and demoralized in the urban North. With a few exceptions, moreover, the short stories comprising *Folks from Dixie* (1898), *The Strength of Gideon* (1900), *In Old Plantation Days* (1903), and *The Heart of Happy Hollow* (1904) follow the formulas of Thomas Nelson Page.

Dunbar's first novel, *The Uncalled* (1898), appeared complete in *Lippincott's Monthly Magazine* for May, 1898, and was published in book form later in the same year. Reflecting Dunbar's contemplation of a ministerial career, the novel traces the life of Frederick Brent, a small-town orphan boy who is compulsorily educated for the clergy. Brent obtains a Methodist pastorate voluntarily relinquished by the elderly father of his fiancée but resigns rather than preach openly against a woman who had digressed from virtue. In Cincinnati, where he later obtains a clerical position, he joins the Congregational Church.

Distinctly a shallow novel, *The Uncalled* attacks the religious bigotry of the small town. Discussing Hester's determination to train Brent for the church, Dunbar writes:

> Poor, blind, conceited humanity! Interpreters of God, indeed! We reduce the deity to vulgar fractions. We place our own little ambitions and inclinations before a shrine, and label them "Divine messages." We set up our Delphian tripod, and we are the priests and oracles. We despise the plans of Nature's Ruler and substitute our own. With our short sight we affect to take a comprehensive view of eternity. Our horizon is the universe. We spy on the Divine and try to surprise his secrets, or to sneak into his confidence by stealth. We make God the eternal a puppet. We measure the infinite with a foot-rule.

In the metropolitan environment of Cincinnati, however, Brent breathes a freer air, as the following passage from one of his letters shows:

> I feel that I am growing. I can take good full breaths here. I couldn't in Dexter: the air was too rarefied by religion.

Dunbar also answers the small-town concept of the immorality of the large city:

> It is one of the defects of the provincial mind that it can never see any good in a great city. It concludes that as many people are wicked, where large num-

bers of human beings are gathered together there must be a much greater amount of evil than in a smaller place. It overlooks the equally obvious reasoning that, as some people are good, in the larger mass there must be also a larger amount of goodness.

The Love of Landry (1900), the weakest of Dunbar's novels, is a tedious and pointless account of the journey of tubercular Mildred Osborne to Colorado for her health. While in the West, Mildred falls in love with Landry Thayer, a well-born Philadelphian. The only Negro character in the story is a train porter who thinks that white people delight in "trampling on, and making a fool of, the black man." Perhaps the main importance of *The Love of Landry* is its suggestion of Dunbar's residence in Colorado and sympathy for fellow-sufferers with lung ailments. Certainly the book has no literary distinction.

Of *The Fanatics* (1901), a more successful handling of white characters, Dunbar writes: "You do not know how my hopes were planted in that book, but it has utterly disappointed me." Mirroring intersectional strife among relatives and friends in a small Ohio town during the Civil War period, the novel opens with two former friends—Bradford Waters, a Unionist, and Stephen Van Doren, a Confederate supporter—alienated as a result of conflicting ideologies. When Van Doren's son Bob joins the Southern forces, Waters insists that his daughter Mary end her courtship with the young rebel; but the girl refuses:

> She loved Bob, not his politics. What had she to do with those black men down there in the South, it was none of her business? For her part, she only knew one black man and he was bad enough. Of course, Nigger Ed was funny. They all liked him and laughed at him, but he was not exemplary. He filled, with equal adaptability, the position of town crier and town drunkard. Really, if all his brethren were like him, they would be none the worse for having masters.

Exasperated by Mary's loyalty to her lover, Waters ejects his daughter. At the close of the war, however, the Waters and Van Dorens are reconciled; and Nigger Ed becomes more than the town buffoon:

> There were men who had seen that black man on bloody fields, which were thick with the wounded and dying, and these could not speak of him without tears in their eyes. There were women who begged him to come in and talk to them about their sons who had been left on some Southern field, wives who wanted to hear over again the last words of their loved ones. And so they gave him a place for life and everything he wanted, and from being despised he was much petted and spoiled, for they were all fanatics.

In his last and most promising novel, *The Sport of*

the Gods (1902), which had previously appeared in *Lippincott's Monthly Magazine* for May, 1901, Dunbar describes the misfortunes of a Negro family that migrates from a small Southern town to New York City. The first paragraph of the book suggests Dunbar's awareness of the repeated romanticizing of the ante-bellum South and his intention to depart from the tradition in portraying the family whose members are the main characters of the story:

> Fiction has said so much in regret of the old days when there were plantations and overseers and masters and slaves, that it was good to come upon such a household as Berry Hamilton's, if for no other reason than that it afforded a relief from the monotony of tiresome iteration.

Not all continues well with the Hamiltons, however, for Berry receives a ten-year sentence for the alleged theft of money from Francis, the irresponsible half-brother of his employer, Maurice Oakley. Because of community ill will, Fannie, Kit, and Joe Hamilton—Berry's wife, daughter, and son respectively—move to New York City. In Harlem, Joe disintegrates, and Dunbar comments as follows upon the change in his character:

> Whom the gods wish to destroy they first make mad. The first sign of the demoralization of the provincial who comes to New York is his pride at his insensibility to certain impressions which used to influence him at home. First, he begins to scoff, and there is no truth in his views nor depth in his laugh. But by and by, from mere pretending, it becomes real. He grows callous. After that he goes to the devil very cheerfully.

Becoming a frequenter of the Banner Club, "a social cesspool, generating a poisonous miasma and reeking with the stench of decayed and rotten moralities," Joe meets and later murders yellow-skinned Hattie Sterling. In contemplation of the fate of the youth, Dunbar states that "the stream of young Negro life would continue to flow up from the South, dashing itself against the hard necessities of the city and breaking like waves against a rock,—that, until the gods grew tired of their cruel sport, there must still be sacrifices to false ideals and unreal ambitions." After Joe is sent to the penitentiary, Francis confesses use of the money supposedly stolen by Berry and urges the acquittal of the Negro; but Maurice determines to protect the honor of his relative. Eventually, however, a New York newspaper reporter conducts an investigation which results in Berry's release. At the close of the novel Kit is dancing on the stage for a living, Maurice is mentally deranged because of an obsessive determination to maintain Francis' innocence, and Berry is living with his wife in their former home on the Oakley place. Of the old couple's re-establishment in the South, Dunbar writes fatalistically:

> It was not a happy life, but it was all that was left to them, and they took it up without complaint, for they knew they were powerless against some Will infinitely stronger than their own.

Though amateurish in execution, *The Sport of the Gods* is Dunbar's worthiest effort in fiction and suggests abilities which possibly did not achieve fruition because of the author's early death. Written under the influence of naturalism, which Parrington defines as "pessimistic realism," *The Sport of the Gods* follows Emile Zola's *Nana* (1880), Stephen Crane's *Maggie: A Girl of the Streets* (1893), Frank Norris' *McTeague* (1899), and other novels in which man is conceived as a powerless figure in an amoral and careless world. Showing race prejudice as an all-destructive virus, the book reveals social corruption in the South as well as in the North. In the Southern small town, interracial distrust is exposed, and the vaunted chivalry of Dixie gentlemen is debunked through the characterization of Francis and Maurice Oakley. In the New York setting, inexperienced Negro youth are pictured in a treacherous environment which deterministically produces degeneration and disaster. By treating the challenging and comparatively unworked Harlem low-life scene, Dunbar analyzed a background that was later to intrigue Claude McKay, Carl Van Vechten, and other writers of the 1920's. As a matter of fact, Van Vechten expresses the indebtedness of *Nigger Heaven* to *The Sport of the Gods* by saying that in the latter novel Dunbar "described the plight of a young outsider who comes to the larger New York Negro world to make his fortune, but who falls a victim to the sordid snares of that world, a theme I elaborated in 1926 to fit a newer and much more intricate social system."

To move from Dunbar's novels to his short stories is to enter a different field. Three of the novels sentimentally treat white characters in their conventional setting, and the fourth is a naturalistic study of a postbellum Negro family in a small Southern town and in Harlem. However, in most of the short stories comprising *Folks From Dixie* (1898), *The Strength of Gideon and Other Stories* (1900), *In Old Plantation Days* (1903), and *The Heart of Happy Hollow* (1904), Dunbar becomes a successful imitator of the plantation school. Like other resuscitators of the legendary South, he presents "the big house," peopled by highspirited and indulgent blue-bloods, and "the quarters," inhabited by spoiled and satisfied slaves whose lives are made picturesque by conjuration, gambling, feasting, rivalries, love affairs, mimicry, and primitive religion. In this environment move such familiar types as the proprietary mammy, the pompous butler, the pretentious coachman, and the plantation exhorter. A wide social gulf divides the slaves in "the big house" from those in "the quarters." The relationship between master and slave is idealized as one of mutual affection and loyalty, and the best masters do not buy and sell slaves unless forced to do so because of financial strain. Furthermore, the patricians generally avoid flogging by delegating this unpleasant assignment to overseers or supervised Negroes. The overseer, being in most cases a representative of "poor white trash," is not portrayed sympathetically. A purveyor of these expected themes, Dunbar avoids penetrating social analysis of the South and suggests that Negroes who migrate to the North become maladjusted and demoralized individuals who remember the years before emancipation with pitiable nostalgia.

Folks from Dixie, Dunbar's first collection of short stories, contains twelve tales treating action before and after the Civil War. The majority of the narratives conform to the postulates of the plantation tradition. **"Anner Lizer's Stumblin' Block"** presents a slave woman who will not become converted until sure of the marital intentions of her lover. **"A Family Feud"** is a story of ante-bellum days told to the author by Aunt Joshy. **"The Intervention of Peter"** shows how an old Negro prevents a duel between two Southern gentlemen. **"The Colonel's Awakening"** mirrors the loyalty of two ex-slaves to their elderly demented master who has lost his wealth and sons in the Civil War. **"The Ordeal at Mount Hope," "The Trial Sermons on Bull-Skin,"** and **"Mt. Pisgah's Christmas Possum"** furnish glimpses of Negro church life. Anticipating *The Sport of the Gods,* **"Jimsella"** describes the struggles of a Negro couple in New York, where "it was all very different: one room in a crowded tenement house, and the necessity of grinding day after day to keep the wolf—a very terrible and ravenous wolf—from the door." Several stories in *Folks from Dixie,* however, tend to diverge from plantation prescriptions. **"Aunt Mandy's Investment"** treats the machinations of a Negro shyster who fleeces gullible black folk. **"The Deliberation of Mr. Dunkin"** unfolds the wooing of a teacher by an affected member of the school board. **"Nelse Hatton's Revenge"** sets forth the kindness of an ex-slave to a former master whom he had earlier vowed to kill. Veering from plantation requirements more than any other story in the volume, **"At Shaft II"** recounts the heroic part played by Sam Bowles, a Negro foreman, in a West Virginia mine strike and race riot.

The imprint of the plantation tradition is also strong upon *The Strength of Gideon and Other Stories,* a collection of twenty narratives. The title story and **"Mammy Peggy's Pride"** depict the loyalty of ex-bondmen to their former masters. **"Viney's Free Papers," "The Fruitful Sleeping of the Rev. Elisha Edwards," "The Case of 'Ca'line': A Kitchen Monologue," "Jim's Probation,"** and **"Uncle Simon's Sun-**

day Out"** portray various experiences of plantation life. Illustrative of the unfitness of the Negro to cope with the inhospitable environment of the Northern metropolis are **"An Old Time Christmas," "The Trustfulness of Polly," "The Finding of Zach," "The Faith Cure Man," "Silas Jackson," "The Finish of Patsy Barnes"** and **"One Man's Fortunes."** The last-named story records the failure of a Negro lawyer who learns "that the adages, as well as the books and the formulas, were made by and for others than us of the black race." Several stories of the volume, however, break rather sharply from typical plantation subject matter. **"Mr. Cornelius Johnson, Office Seeker," "A Mess of Pottage,"** and **"A Council of State"** present the Negro in politics. **"The Ingrate"** portrays a slave who yearns for freedom:

> To him his slavery was deep night. What wonder, then, that he should dream, and that through the ivory gate should come to him the forbidden vision of freedom? To own himself, to be master of his hands, feet, of his whole body—something would clutch at his heart as he thought of it; and the breath would come hard between his lips.

Escaping to Canada, he rejoices in the work of the Abolitionists and joins the Union Army during the Civil War. A bloody tale of lynching and mob passion, **"The Tragedy of Three Forks"** is social protest that is a far cry from Dunbar's usual treatment of the Southern scene. After Jane Hunster, a white girl of a small Kentucky town, commits arson because of jealousy, her father hastily attributes the crime to a Negro:

> Look a here, folks, I tell you that's the work o'niggers. I kin see their hand in it.

Thereafter incendiary newspaper articles result in the seizure and lynching of two innocent Negroes. In a struggle for pieces of the mob's rope to be kept as souvenirs, Dock Heaters fatally stabs Jane's fiancé; and the one-sided justice of the South is indicated in the following persuasive reply to a demand that the murderer also be lynched: "No," cried an imperious voice, "who knows what may have put him up to it? Give a white man a chance for his life."

Most of the stories of *In Old Plantation Days* follow the pattern of those in Page's *In Ole Virginia* and have their setting on the plantation of Stuart Mordaunt, a typical master of the legendary South. **"Aunt Tempy's Triumph"** shows how a proprietary mammy, who thinks she owns the "plantation with all the white folks and niggers on it," succeeds in giving away the master's daughter in marriage. **"Dizzy-Headed Dick," "A Lady Slipper,"** and **"Who Stand for the Gods"** present slaves who intervene to assist white lovers. **"Aunt Tempy's Revenge," "The Trouble about Sophiny," "Ash-Cake Hannah and Her Ben," "The**

Conjuring Contest," "Dandy Jim's Conjure Scare," "The Memory of Martha," and "The Easter Wedding" deal principally with the love affairs of bondmen. The old-fashioned exhorter and plantation religious life are described in "The Walls of Jericho," "How Brother Parker Fell from Grace," "The Trousers," and "The Last Fiddling of Mordaunt's Jim." Slave loyalty is exemplified in "A Blessed Deceit" and "The Stanton Coachman." "The Brief Cure of Aunt Fanny" reveals the rivalry between two plantation cooks, while "A Supper by Proxy" pictures a lavish feast prepared by Negroes in "the big house" in the absence of the master. "Mr. Groby's Slippery Gift" unfolds the loyalty of two slave brothers and the cruelty of an overseer. The last five stories of the volume shift to post-bellum times and urban scenes. "The Finding of Martha," highly suggestive of Chesnutt's "The Wife of His Youth," sets forth the successful quest of a Negro preacher for his wife of slavery times. "The Defection of Mary Ann Gibbs," "A Judgment of Paris," "Silent Samuel," and "The Way of a Woman," all having their locale in the Negro ghetto of a Northern city, are chiefly concerned with competition in love.

In *The Heart of Happy Hollow* Dunbar gives the following description of the setting of the stories:

> Wherever Negroes colonize in the cities or villages, North or South, wherever the hod carrier, the porter, and the waiter are the society men of the town; wherever the picnic and the excursion are the chief summer diversion, and the revival the winter-time of repentance, wherever the cheese cloth obtains at a wedding, and the little white hearse goes by with black mourners in the one carriage behind, there—there—is Happy Hollow. Wherever laughter and tears rub elbows day by day, and the spirit of labour and laziness shake hands, there—there—is Happy Hollow, and of some of it may the following pages show the heart.

Though dealing chiefly with post-bellum Negro life, many of the sixteen tales of *The Heart of Happy Hollow* do not escape the influence of the plantation tradition. "Cahoots" sentimentalizes the life-long devotion of a slave to his master. "The Wisdom of Silence" portrays an ex-slave who, having grown prosperous and boastful, is humbled and thereafter aided by his former owner. "One Christmas at Shiloh" and "A Matter of Doctrine" present Negro ministers as suitors. "Old Abe's Conversion" traces the transformation of an old-fashioned exhorter into a progressive pastor. "A Defender of the Faith" and "The Interference of Patsy Ann" mirror the pathos of Negro life in a big city. "The Mission of Mr. Scatters," "The Promoter," and "Schwalliger's Philosophy" expose colored swindlers. "The Scapegoat" describes the craft of a Negro politician, while "The Home-Coming of 'Rastus Smith" limns a young Negro lawyer who adopts a supercilious

attitude toward his mother and former sweetheart. "The Boy and the Bayonet" illustrates a lesson in military discipline. Misleadingly titled, "The Race Question" is the soliloquy of an old colored man at a race track. In "The Lynching of Jube Benson" a white physician, defending his opposition to mob violence, recounts the murder of a loyal and innocent Negro friend.

In his short stories, therefore, Dunbar generally accepts the limitations and circumscriptions of the plantation tradition. Glorifying the good old days in the accepted manner, he sentimentalizes master-slave relationships and implies that freedom brings social misery to the black man. Negro migrants to the urban North are usually represented as nostalgic misfits, some of whom fall prey to poverty, immorality, or disease, and others to disillusionment occasioned by political or professional reverses. "The Ingrate" and "The Tragedy at Three Forks," both of which are effective examples of the use of irony, are possibly the only stories in the four volumes that entirely escape the tendency to idealize Dixie. Furthermore, the narratives give an unauthentic recording of life because of their neglect of the unpleasant realities of the Southland. These considerations lead directly to the observation that Dunbar usually catered to the racial preconceptions of his publishers and readers by employing the themes and stereotypes of the plantation tradition. Nevertheless, his literary reputation itself constituted a strong argument against Negro inferiority; and he helped to prepare the American audience for succeeding authors possessing greater originality and deeper social understanding. (pp. 46-56)

Hugh M. Gloster, "Negro Fiction to World War I," in his *Negro Voices in American Fiction*, 1948. Reprint by Russell & Russell, Inc., 1965, pp. 23-100.

DARWIN T. TURNER

(essay date 1967)

[Turner is an American educator, poet, and critic specializing in black and Southern literature. In the excerpt below, he explores the ironic nature of Dunbar's works, arguing that Dunbar was "far more bitter and scathing, much more a part of the protest tradition than his reputation suggests."]

[Dunbar's] image has been defaced by scholars who have censured him for tarnishing the symbol by perpetuating the derogatory caricatures of the minstrel show and the plantation tales. . . . His reputation has suffered also from those readers who, seeking to compress his thought into pithy phrases, have failed to reveal the significant changes in his subject-matter and attitudes. His reputation has suffered from those who have been blinded by a single work or who have failed to discern his attempts at ironic protest. The result has been the currently popular images of Dunbar as a disenchanted angel fluttering his wings against publishers' restrictions or as a money-hungry Esau willing to betray his birthright for a mess of popularity. Careful examination of Dunbar and of his works explains the reasons for his inability to write the kind of protest which some of his critics wish. Simultaneously, such scrutiny reveals Dunbar to be far more bitter and scathing, much more a part of the protest tradition than his reputation suggests.

Paul Laurence Dunbar's experiences, his political and economic philosophies, and his artistic ideals prevented his writing the acerbate criticism of the South which some readers desire. Paul Laurence Dunbar's cardinal sin is that he violated the unwritten commandment which American Society has handed down to the Negro: "Thou shalt not laugh at thy black brother" (Especially thou shalt not laugh at thy black brother who spoke dialect and was a slave). But Paul Laurence Dunbar could not identify himself with the slave or freedman about whom he wrote. . . . Dunbar judged the color of his skin to be a very thin bond linking him to the half-Christian, half-pagan slaves a mere two hundred years removed from savagery, in his opinion. That bond of color was insufficiently tight to gag his chuckles about some of their ridiculous antics which his mother, an ex-slave, had narrated.

Even if Dunbar had been completely free to write scathing protest about the South, he could not have written it, or would have written it ineptly. His experiences and those of his family had not compelled him to hate white people as a group or the South as a region. After Dunbar was twenty, every major job he secured, every publication, and all national recognition resulted directly from the assistance of white benefactors. It is not remarkable that Dunbar assumed that successful Negroes need such help or that, knowing the actuality of Northern benefactors, he believed in the existence of their Southern counterparts. (pp. 1-2)

Even had his experiences prompted protest against the South, his social and economic philosophies would have militated against it. Believing that America would prosper only if all citizens recognized their interdependence, he sought to win respect for Negroes by showing that, instead of sulking about the past, they were ready to participate in the joint effort to create a new America. In the poems of *Majors and Minors* . . . and the stories of *Folks from Dixie* . . . , he repeatedly emphasized the ability and willingness of Negroes to forgive white Americans for previous injustices.

Dunbar's noble sentiments and protagonists reveal not only a naive political philosophy but also a romantic and idealized concept of society. He believed in

Alice Moore Dunbar, Paul's wife, who despised her husband's association with minstrel shows and his black dialect poetry.

right rule by an aristocracy based on birth and blood which assured culture, good breeding, and all the virtues appropriate to a gentleman. He further believed that Negroes, instead of condemning such a society, must prove themselves worthy of a place in it by showing that they had civilized themselves to a level above the savagery which he assumed to be characteristic of Africa. Furthermore, having been reared in Dayton, Ohio, he distrusted big cities and industrialization.

Provincially, he assumed the good life for the uneducated to be the life of a farmer in a small western or mid-western settlement or the life of a sharecropper for a benevolent Southern aristocrat. Neither a scholar, political scientist, nor economist, he naively offered an agrarian myth as a shield against the painful reality of discrimination in cities.

Artistic ideals also restricted Dunbar's protest. Even Saunders Redding, generally extremely perceptive in his study of Dunbar, has regretted Dunbar's failure to criticize his society more frequently in his poetry. Dunbar, however, regarded poetry—in standard English—as a noble language, best suited for expressing elevated ideas. Prose was his voice of protest. Protest is missing even from his first two books of poetry, which were privately printed. . . .

Dunbar's experiences, his social and economic philosophies, and his artistic ideals limited his criticism of the South. This fact, however, should not imply, as some suppose, that Dunbar accepted the total myth of the plantation tradition. In reality, he was no more willing to assume the romanticized plantation to be characteristic of the entire South than he was willing to deny that some slaves had loved their masters or had behaved foolishly.

Nor should it be assumed that his hunger for fame and money silenced his protest against unjust treatment. Actually, he vigorously castigated [in his books and newspaper articles] conditions familiar to him in the North. (pp. 3-4)

[His] protests [in newspaper articles] had been mild. In *The Strength of Gideon and Other Stories* . . . , however, Dunbar slapped back. In **"A Mess of Pottage"** he pictured the Negro as an individual betrayed by both political parties. **"A Council of State"** is written in a similar tone. (p. 5)

Dunbar's characteristic irony occasionally seeps through the bitterness. . . . The irony, however, does not lighten the tone. These stories cannot be called pessimistic. The confirmed pessimist at least perceives an alternative outcome even while he positively affirms the inevitability of the undesired outcome. In these stories Dunbar, however, saw only destruction. (pp. 6-7)

In *The Strength of Gideon and Other Stories,* economic problems and injustice also harass the uneducated. . . .

Dunbar also examined injustices in the South. The popularity of lynchings inspired the ironic **"The Tragedy at Three Forks."** (p. 8)

Dunbar wedded his social criticism of Negroes and of America in a novel, *The Sport of the Gods.* . . . His savage attack upon stereotypes and myths of the plantation tradition has been blunted by critics who, observing the melodramatic occurrences and the diatribes against city life, fail to perceive the abject despair suggested by the ending. (p. 9)

Some critics argue that the attack on the evils of New York and the return to the South evidence Dunbar's inability to avoid the plantation tradition. Dunbar's ending, however, is far more bitter and hopeless than that. The alternatives he offers are the restraint of the body in the South and the festering of the soul in the North. . . .

If these two books had been published anonymously, they would be considered bitter protests and the author would be heralded as the first major ironist in literature by Negroes. Several reasons underlie the failure of many readers to recognize these qualities. Dunbar often phrased ideas ambiguously; consequently, his most successful irony is that which is heavily and fully developed. Second, some of his subtlety may have been overlooked by critics. Finally, his dark acerbity may have been missed by readers blinded by his bright image as a comic writer. (p. 11)

A muted voice of protest . . . was sounded in his poetry collection, *Lyrics of Love and Laughter*. . . . In two poems, **"The Haunted Oak"** and **"To the New South,"** he attacked lynchings and the ingratitude of the South.

In his final two works of protest fiction, **"The Wisdom of Silence"** and **"The Lynching of Jube Benson,"** he continued his criticism of the South. (pp. 11-12)

His writings evidence Dunbar's protests against both the South and the North. His position, however, is difficult to appraise exactly because he vacillated and assumed seemingly contradictory stances. Some of his attitudes are difficult to explain. (p. 12)

Perhaps the simplest explanation which offers any consistency is that readers have demanded too much of Dunbar as a symbol. Commanding him to speak for the Negro, they forget that Negroes speak with hundreds of different voices. Dunbar is merely one. Insensitive to the implications of creating comic Negro figures, he was extremely sensitive to the insults which a Northern society might inflict upon an educated Negro. Willing to criticize injustices of Northern or Southern society, he, nevertheless, supported outmoded economic and social ideals. Occasionally conscious of the ridiculous postures of white Americans, he was even more conscious and less tolerant of ridiculous behavior of Negro Americans. Ignorant of historical truths about Africa and about slavery, he respected as fact the myths current in his time. Because he recognized distinctions between Negroes he knew and Negro stereotypes of the plantation stories, he inferred the race's remarkable progress within a generation. In short, Paul Laurence Dunbar was a talented, creative, high school graduate whose views reflect the limited knowledge of many historians, economists, and social philosophers of his day. (pp. 12-13)

Darwin T. Turner, "Paul Laurence Dunbar: The Rejected Symbol," in *Journal of Negro History,* January, 1967, pp. 1-13.

ADDISON GAYLE, JR.

(essay date 1971)

[In the following excerpt from his biography of Dunbar, *Oak and Ivy*, Gayle examines Dunbar's lifelong concern with the possibility of attaining personal freedom and the resulting pessimism the poet felt when he was unable to direct his literary career or create the works of art he dreamed of. For Gayle, Dunbar's failure represents a personal and literary tragedy.]

In 1888, while [Dunbar] was still a student, the Dayton *Herald* published his poem **"Our Martyred Soldiers,"** which was followed five days later by another of his poems, **"On the River."** Neither of the poems was written in dialect. They were both written in standard English, as was the case with most of his early poetry. His first real attempts at creation were written in the English spoken by his mother, father, neighbors, and classmates. (p. 22)

As with most juvenalia, the early poems [in *Oak and Ivy*] foreshadowed the themes and conflicts of his later works. In such poems as **"October,"** the poet sang to nature with the passion and enthusiasm that would increase as he grew older. (pp. 28-9)

Here, too, could be found the first tribute to race. Dunbar's first call to his people to "strive ever onward" was given in **"Ode to Ethiopia."** Other poems hinted at what was to become the major conflict of his life. This can best be seen in **"A Career."** This poem is more than juvenalia; in a sense it is almost a prophecy—the young poet seemed able to see beyond the present and capable of knowing and analyzing the future. . . .

Despite the importance of *A Career* to Dunbar's development as a poet, few of his biographers have realized its full implication. Had they done so, they might have noted that Dunbar's most serious poems in *Oak and Ivy* were written in standard English and that the poet himself was less than pleased with the success of his dialect pieces. (p. 29)

Humorous and dialect poetry paid. It was what the editors wanted. One had confided to him at the Chicago World's Fair, "I'll take anything you write in dialect." And so he wrote dialect. More and more. Much of his new work was in the dialect vein. This decision was not made solely in the interest of making a quick profit. Most of his biographers have attributed to him a sophistication that he did not possess. He was, in reality, a small-town Midwesterner in thought and outlook. This accounts in part for his animosity towards the big city. He was incapable of divining the sinister forces at work in the society; and he believed that once he had established himself as a poet through the medium of dialect, his white audience would accept whatever he offered in a poetical vein. (pp. 37-8)

[*Majors and Minors*] was an improvement over *Oak and Ivy*. There were one hundred and forty-eight pages in *Majors and Minors*—more than twice the number in *Oak and Ivy*. . . . Of these seventy-four poems only eleven had previously appeared in *Oak and Ivy*. Once again, the poems in standard English dominated the book. Of the seventy-four, only twenty-six were in dialect, and these were placed in a special section entitled "Humour and Dialect." The title *Majors and Minors,* like the title *Oak and Ivy,* was meant to be a guideline for his readers.

Perhaps they would see, as he did, that the term majors, meant to designate the selections he considered serious works of art, reported, however subtly, the truth that burned with such volcanic fury within his breast. Perhaps they would feel something of the agony of spirit and mind suffered by those who were forced, as in the poem **"We Wear the Mask,"** to " . . . smile, [while] O Great Christ, our cries / to thee from tortured Souls arise." Perhaps they could understand his veiled plea for sympathy in the **"Poet and His Song"**. . . . Were there not readers whose souls were in tune with his? Could they mistake the despondent tones of **"Ere Sleep Comes Down to Soothe the Weary Eyes"** as an elegy for physical instead of creative death—that death of artistic sensibility, more meaningful to the poet than physical death. . . . (pp. 42-3)

But the world did not understand. It turned its attention to the minors—the humorous and dialect pieces—and, because of them, made the poet famous. **"The Party," "A Banjo Song," "When De Co'n Pone's Hot,"** and **"The Deserted Plantation,"** among others, became the overnight favorites of his readers. These poems received the heartiest applause during readings, while those "of deeper note" were accorded only polite, condescending recognition. Whatever his personal pain, whatever his private conflict, they were unimportant as long as he produced lines such as those from **"A Banjo Song,"** which spoke not of pain or conflict, but of contentment and joy. . . . (p. 43)

However, [*Lyrics of Lowly Life*] was important in a much more meaningful way: it brought him national fame and a national audience.

That a great deal of this acclaim was due to William Dean Howells is a point beyond dispute. . . . In terms of form, the book was a mixture of poems in standard English and dialect. The difference between this arrangement and that of the previous books—and it was probably due to the ingenuity of the editors—

was that the dialect pieces were not separated into special sections. (p. 71)

The book [*Lyrics of Lowly Life*] opens with a poem in standard English, **"Ere Sleep Comes Down to Soothe the Weary Eyes,"** and closes with the dialect poem from which Howells had quoted at length, **"The Party."** Perhaps the most important poem in the volume is **"Unexpressed."** It had previously appeared in *Majors and Minors* and received little notice by the critics. Yet, it is fundamental to an analysis of the crisis that Dunbar was undergoing. (p. 80)

In the summer of 1898, *Clorindy*, the musical which [Dunbar] had worked on with Will and John Cook, opened at the Casino Roof Garden in New York. Dunbar and his wife were present on opening night. . . . As Dunbar listened to the lyrics that he had helped to write, he felt a sense of embarrassment. The musical was in the worst of the minstrel tradition. Not only were black people laughing at themselves, they were also performing on stage, offering themselves as objects for the laughs of others. The tunes for which he had written the lyrics were not much more offensive than some of his dialect poems—although, in these he had avoided making his people into buffoons. Still there was a great deal of difference between writing a poem and reciting it, and watching the same poem acted out on a stage. The all-black cast, including the great Afro-American star Ernest Hogan, was very talented and performed well. However, the musical was not a serious work. The titles of the songs illustrate this fact: **"The Hottest Coon in Dixie," "Love in a Cottage Is Best," "Who Dat Say Chicken in a Crowd."** In addition, among his contributions was **"A Negro Love Song,"** which he had written in a humorous vein. Listening to it now, in this setting, it sounded not humorous, but ridiculous. *Clorindy* caused Dunbar to doubt the claim to fame which others made for him. In his own eyes he had not achieved success and never would. (pp. 87-8)

Dunbar desired freedom from restrictions above all else; as did his fictional counterpart, Freddie Brent [in *The Uncalled*]. Both were restricted by tradition, and neither thought he could win his fight against "blind fate." By the end of *The Uncalled*, however, Freddie would win his fight, and Dunbar, through identification with his character would win a victory also. As Saunders Redding has noted, Dunbar not only wrote about white characters, he became the white characters about whom he wrote. Paul Laurence Dunbar is Freddie Brent and Freddie Brent is Paul Laurence Dunbar. Freddie is trapped in the town of Dexter; he is forced to obey the dictates of Hester Prime; he attempts to live down his past. At the time *The Uncalled* was written Dunbar was forced to be the kind of poet he did not want to be; he was forced to obey the dic-

tates of his critics; he, too, was attempting to live down his past. (pp. 97-8)

The Uncalled fails as a novel because the events are unrealistic; for example, Freddie's accidental encounter with his father at the temperance meeting. In addition, the language is artificial and the characters are romanticized. However, these are the reasons for the failure of Dunbar's fiction in general. The collections of short stories, *The Strength of Gideon, Folks from Dixie,* and *In Old Plantation Days* all fail for the same reasons: none is true to life, the situations in each are implausible, the language is artificial, and the characters are way outside the range of possibility.

Folks from Dixie consisted of twelve short stories, and with the exception of **"At Shaft II,"** each deals with an aspect of the plantation tradition. **"At Shaft 11,"** which tells of a labor strike in a coal-mining town, and **"Jimsella,"** the story of a young married couple, who after leaving the South encounter great difficulty in the North, are the only two stories in the volume that contain elements of reality. (p. 99)

Lyrics of the Hearthside, dedicated to Alice, was released in February of 1899. . . . [Dialect] poems and those in standard English were separated from each other as they had been in the earlier books, *Oak and Ivy,* and *Majors and Minors.* The desperate struggle he waged with his own spirit—against a world he dared to fight openly—is here revealed more clearly than in the previous volumes. Here, in lines that tell of love, joy, melancholia, struggle, and death, is the stuff of his life, his inner-self, the material of his poetic essence. Of all these themes, he began to write most frequently of death. This was not a new theme for him. He had written of death, of the end of life, in *Oak and Ivy, Majors and Minors* and *Lyrics of Lowly Life.* However, for the most part, these poems had merely been speculations about death—youthful investigations of a world that attracts because it is unknown.

Now, his statements on death took on a maturity of form. He wrote of it with a passion and an understanding peculiar for a young man of twenty-seven. Death was still unknowable. Yet he looked upon it now as not being very far away, a mystery soon to be a mystery no more, the unknowable destined eventually to make itself known. Even in the love poems there is this longing for escape, for release from the earthly pain that only death can bring. No volume of his works is more despondent than *Lyrics of the Hearthside;* no lines appear in any of his other writings so filled with resignation and despair. (p. 110)

Lyrics of the Hearthside is the "fruitage" of the years spent wrestling with his conscience after Howells' review, of his experiences in England, and of the uncertainty concerning his marriage. At that time he had needed a love such as that called for in **"Love's**

Apotheosis," and there is little doubt that Alice fulfilled that need.

This belief that love might act as a barrier between him and the world is found in other poems in this volume. At times he seems to conceive of love as being more than emotion, more even than a bond between two human beings. With the world closing in on him, out of despair, he makes love an instrument—sometimes even a weapon—to be used in combating his many enemies. It is this sense of love as weapon that one finds in the poem, **"Love's Phases"**. . . . (pp. 111-12)

However, the poems that stand out in the first part of the book are those in which the poet looks at death through older eyes. The most beautiful, and perhaps the saddest of all his poems, is **"When All Is Done."** It is also the most personal. Here, more than anywhere else, the poet poured pain, anguish, despair, and heartbreak into one loud, long wail for the release which only death could bring. . . . (p. 113)

Beside such poems as these, those in dialect are mere ornament. Yet here, in this book, are included some of Dunbar's most popular dialect poetry: **"Little Brown Baby," "Angelina," "Whistling Sam," "At Candle-Lightin' Time," "Temptation,"** and **"How Lucy Backslid."** However, not even the dialect poetry was free of the theme of death. . . . (p. 114)

[He] worked diligently on the novel, *The Love of Landry.* The editor had asked for "a light novel," and this book filled the bill. It was a love story and took place in Colorado. (p. 120)

Once again, despite . . . a slight plot, Dunbar manages to impose his personal experiences on the novel. Each of the major characters represents some aspect of Dunbar's experiences: Arthur Heathclift, the English suitor for the hand of the heroine, a man who "smells of civilization," is a character modeled after Englishmen whom the poet had met during his stay in England. Heathclift is, to be sure, a poor stereotype of an Englishman, yet he represents Dunbar's idea of a civilized man. John Osborne is the kind, considerate father. He reminds one of the equally kind and considerate Doctor Tobey. Dunbar cherished Tobey's friendship as small boys cherish their relationship with their fathers. There is Aunt Annesley who attempts to interfere in the romance between Landry and Mildred, just as Alice's parents had attempted to interfere in their romance. Mildred, the heroine, suffers from tuberculosis. Like Dunbar, she is forced to come to Colorado to regain her health. Landry Thaler whose name, Landry, reminds one of land, is a man of the earth. Once a part of the frustration and chaos of the city, he has forsaken urban America and come back to nature. With such characters—each symbolizing different aspects of his

character—Dunbar wrote a novel in which he, once again, deals with the theme of personal freedom.

Like the characters in his first novel, *The Uncalled,* the characters in his second novel are also white. However, where Freddie Brent, the hero of *The Uncalled,* sought freedom from the iron grip of Hester Prime, Mildred and Landry, heroine and hero of *The Love of Landry,* seek freedom from the civilized world. The novel depicts a conflict between the civilized world and the world of nature: "Nothing," the author states in the novel, "is quite so conceited as what we call civilization. And what does it mean after all except to lie gracefully, to cheat legally and to live as far away from God and nature as the world limit will allow." (pp. 120-21)

The peace that [Dunbar] sought in life, the freedom, came only when he created out of a sense of reality as he knew it, when he created in his white characters images of himself. *The Love of Landry* is a poor novel. But as the account of a poetic spirit seeking escape, seeking release from the bars and cages of life, of a dying soul attempting to lessen the impact of pain upon the still living, it is a remarkable accomplishment.

The Strength of Gideon and Other Stories, with few exceptions, is not remarkable, although this second book of short stories is an improvement over the first. The improvement is due to the fact that Dunbar went beyond the plantation tradition and dealt with aspects of his own personal problems, and one story, **"One Man's Fortune"** is as close to an autobiography in the short story genre as Dunbar ever came.

There is no hint of a shift, however, in the opening story of the book. **"The Strength of Gideon,"** the title story, tells of the loyalty of the slave Gideon to his master during slavery and to his master's family after the abolition of slavery. (p. 125)

"One Man's Fortune" is [a] story based upon material of which the author had firsthand knowledge. The story deals with aspects of his own life and focuses on the disappointments of a young black man. Although the young man is educated, he still finds that the doors of opportunity are closed to him. (p. 128)

Not only is **"One Man's Fortune"** autobiographical, it also evidences the distance Dunbar had traveled since the optimistic days of *Oak and Ivy.* Like Halliday, he had believed that race was an artificial barrier. He had believed that men could rise above the limitations imposed because of race. Like Booker T. Washington, he had believed that one need only build a better mousetrap than his neighbor, and irrespective of color, the world would beat a path to his door. Yet, because of his skin, severe limitations had been placed upon him. He had been forced into special areas of the literary world just as his people had been forced into special jobs, special neighborhoods, and special associations. (p. 130)

The disappointments, the bitterness, the hostility—all were to be found in *The Strength of Gideon and Other Stories* neatly tucked between the narratives of the plantation tradition. (p. 131)

The Fanatics was published in 1901, and the reception it received was disappointing. He had spent countless painful and sleepless nights laboring over the plot of the story. He had crossed out phrases, torn up whole pages, and rewritten entire sections. He wanted the novel to stand as a monument to his contribution to literature. He had chosen his theme well. The sectional strife of the Civil War—when a nation was internally torn, when the conflict of loyalties between North and South were often reflected in private households, affecting the relationships between son and father, brother and brother—was not far from the memory of the reading public of 1901. (p. 137)

As he had done before in *The Uncalled* and in *The Love of Landry,* he sought to work out his personal problem through the medium of fiction. The theme, peculiar to his other novels, runs through this one also: the constant demand for freedom, the assertion that man must be released from all restrictions. (p. 138)

The Fanatics is a bad novel; it is far worse than *The Love of Landry.* The reason is that Dunbar was attempting to reconcile too many disparate elements. He wanted to reconcile North and South, Waters and Van Doren, Robert and Mary. In addition, he wanted to reconcile Nigger Ed with the town and, through Ed, the black men who sought refuge in the town. The result is that the attempt at reconciliation fails. For all of Dunbar's attempts to portray Nigger Ed as a changed character, he remains a buffoon at the end of the novel. More important, however, there is no reconciliation between the escaped slaves and the town. They are the most alienated group in *The Fanatics.* Unwanted by the North, mistreated by the South, they are men without a country. Whatever union may eventually come about as the result of peace between the two warring factions of the nation, there will be no union with the new freedom except on the terms that prevailed during slavery. (pp. 140-41)

[Dunbar] was forced to conclude that the world belonged not to the Nigger Eds or the escaped slaves, but instead to the Van Dorens and the Waterses. The blacks had places in it, but these places were selected and defined by others. The nation that had made Nigger Ed a buffoon was unlikely to raise him to the status of human being. The nation that had fooled itself into believing it had fought a war to free the slaves, was not likely to extend its generosity further.

The Fanatics was one of Dunbar's most fervent pleas in prose for compassion and understanding. It was his most eloquent appeal for peace. As a failure, therefore, the novel ranks among his most pessimistic.

In failing to reconcile the conflicting forces in the novel, he failed also to reconcile those within himself. (p. 141)

In 1902 he published what was to be his last novel. *The Sport of the Gods* is a product of the years of illness. (p. 150)

The Sport of the Gods marked a new turn for Dunbar in many ways. For the first time he dealt with blacks as major figures in a novel; he made the environment which produced crime and degeneracy the novel's chief villain. In no other novel does the city come under as fierce an attack from Dunbar's pen. The city is portrayed as the center of evil, vice, sin, and corruption. Into this hellhole falls the family of Berry Hamilton, a victim of the southern plantation system, whose daughter and son are ruined by this hostile environment. (p. 151)

The emphasis upon the city as a place of corruption is not new to Dunbar's fiction. In the short stories, **"The Truthfulness of Polly"** and **"Jimsella,"** he had already dealt with the evil influences of the city on his characters. Part of this animosity toward the city stemmed from his romance with nature, from a belief that the country life was far superior to that of the city. What is important in this book is that the emphasis on destiny is more pronounced here than in his other books; it is as though the poet had irrevocably resigned himself to "cruel fate." (pp. 152-53)

Within Dunbar, however, there remained elements of both the realist and the dreamer. The realist in him cried out in bitterness—in despair—as evidenced in . . . [his] poem to Frederick Douglass. . . . The dreamer cried out in hopeful if not optimistic tones: "Heart of the Southland, heed me pleading now," he began the poem, **"To the South,"** which he subtitled **"On Its New Slavery."** The poem is a plea. The poet enumerates the long list of deeds warranting better treatment for black men and women. . . . After . . . words of despair concerning lost love, he goes on to scale the heights of sentimentality. In lines that Du Bois would certainly have called whining and loathsome, Dunbar calls the South's attention to the former loyal servant in stanzas that rank among the most disgusting in black poetry. . . . (pp. 158-59)

The contradictions between these two poems are magnified in the volume *Lyrics of Love and Laughter.* . . . In it are included the poems of the years of depression and tension, of the sojourn in Colorado, of the search for health, of the breakup of his marriage. For the first time in a book of poetry, his dialect poems are almost as numerous as those in pure English. Unlike the poems in *Lyrics of the Hearthside,* they are intermingled. One finds, therefore, such poems as **"The Poet,"** Dunbar's most important statement on dialect poetry and the one that evidences his opposition to the writing of it, sandwiched in between two poems written in dialect, **"In the Morning"** and **"Li'l' Gal."** The bitterness and despondency illustrated in **"Douglass,"** by the lament that the hero is no longer present to lead the race, is obscured by the tribute to Booker T. Washington. . . . The most striking contradiction of all is that between **"To the South"** and **"The Haunted Oak."** **"The Haunted Oak"** paints a portrait of the South which no words can erase.

Despite serious shortcomings in selection, there were poems in *Lyrics of Love and Laughter* that rank among those in previous volumes. One of the most important is **"Life's Tragedy."** Here the poet weaves the twin tragedies of his life into a poetical pattern. Since the age of six when he first began to put words on paper in stanzaic form, his dream had been that of every poet:

to sing the perfect song, to write a poem so complete in meter, rhythm, and message that it would stand forever as a well-wrought work of art. (pp. 159-61)

"Life's Tragedy" laments his inability to attain these goals. Yet, he is despondent not because they were unattained, but because he had come so close to attaining them. . . .

Lyrics of Love and Laughter was not his last book. An illustrated volume of poems, *Howdy, Honey, Howdy,* and *Lyrics of Sunshine and Shadow* followed. However, neither measured up to its predecessors. . . . (p. 161)

Addison Gayle, Jr., in his *Oak and Ivy: A Biography of Paul Laurence Dunbar,* Doubleday, 1971, 175 p.

SOURCES FOR FURTHER STUDY

Baker, Houston A., Jr. "Paul Laurence Dunbar: An Evaluation." *Black World* XXI, No. 1 (November 1971): 30-7.

Discusses Dunbar's artistic environment, the critical ambivalence surrounding his works, and his overall contributions to black American literature.

Brawley, Banjamin. *Paul Laurence Dunbar: Poet of His People.* 1936. Reprint. Port Washington, N.Y.: Kennikat Press, 1967, 159 p.

Critical biography based on Dunbar's letters and on personal interviews with his mother, former wife, friends, and acquaintances.

Cunningham, Virginia. *Paul Laurence Dunbar and His Song.* New York: Dodd, Mead & Co., 1947, 283 p.

Considered one of the most authoritative biographies on Dunbar. The book, which contains dialogue attributed to letters, scrap books, and personal reminiscences, traces his life, presenting a picture of a dutiful son, loyal friend, and brilliant writer.

Martin, Jay, ed. *A Singer in the Dawn: Reinterpretations of Paul Laurence Dunbar.* New York: Dodd, Mead & Co., 1975, 255 p.

Collection of lectures and memorial poems read at the Centenary collects papers delivered at a conference on Paul Laurence Dunbar at the University of California, Irvine, in 1972. Contributors include Arna Bontemps, Addison Gayle, Jr., Nikki Giovanni, and Darwin T. Turner.

Story, Ralph. "Paul Laurence Dunbar: Master Player in a Fixed Game." *CLA Journal* XXVII, No. 1 (September 1983): 30-55.

Biographical and historical discussion of Dunbar's works and the difficulties he encountered as a black artist.

Williams, Kenny J. "The Masking of the Poet." In his *They Also Spoke: An Essay on Negro Literature in America, 1787-1930,* pp. 153-215. Nashville: Townsend Press, 1970.

Study of Dunbar's novels and short stories. The critic divides Dunbar's fiction into three traditions: romantic, plantation, and naturalistic; and assesses the strengths and weaknesses of each.

George Eliot

1819-1880

(Pseudonym of Mary Ann Evans; also Marian Evans)
English novelist, essayist, poet, short story writer, and
translator.

INTRODUCTION

*E*liot is considered one of the greatest novelists of
the English language. Her work is informed by
penetrating psychological analysis and profound
insight into human character and has been praised for
its realistic approach to character and skillful plot development. Staged against the backdrop of rural, nineteenth-century England, Eliot's novels explore moral
and philosophical issues that are associated with the
growing agnosticism and spiritual despair of nineteenth-century English society. Epitomizing Eliot's art
and thought, *Middlemarch* (1871-72), regarded by
most commentators as her greatest achievement, is
imbued with an intellectual vigor that enabled Eliot to
blend a profusion of complex ideas into an artistic
whole. *Middlemarch* is considered unsurpassed
among novels of the period in intellectual depth, and
it remains the work on which the author's reputation
most firmly rests.

Eliot was born and raised on a farm in Warwick-
shire, located in the English Midlands. The most important early influence on the author was her friendship
with Maria Lewis, one of her teachers at a boarding
school in Nuneaton. An ardent Evangelical, Lewis imparted her religious zeal to Eliot. However, after moving
to Coventry in 1841 and meeting the sceptical philosophers Charles Bray and Charles Hennell, Eliot began
to challenge her Evangelical beliefs. Though she became an agnostic, she continued to espouse the ethical teachings associated with Christianity. Critics frequently note that Eliot's religious crisis closely parallels
that of Dorothea Brooke, the heroine of *Middlemarch.*

In 1849, Eliot moved to London, where she met
John Chapman, the editor of the *Westminster Review.*
He hired Eliot in 1851 as the *Westminster's* assistant
editor, a post she retained until 1854. Through Chapman, Eliot met some of London's leading literary fig-

ures, including the versatile writer and intellectual George Henry Lewes, who profoundly affected both her life and her career. Lewes and Eliot fell deeply in love, but he was legally prohibited from divorcing his estranged wife. Defying the strict moral code of the Victorian era, Lewes and Eliot openly lived together from 1854 until his death in 1878. The two considered their union a marriage despite its lack of legal sanction; in fact, Eliot assumed the name Marian Evans Lewes. Her relationship with Lewes outraged her family, and she rarely communicated with them until a few months before her death, when she married John Walter Cross, a longtime friend.

Lewes's influence on Eliot's writings was great: he encouraged her first efforts at fiction and remained her most ardent supporter during their years together. In addition, it was Lewes who brought Eliot's first work of fiction, a collection of short stories entitled *Scenes of Clerical Life* (1858), to the attention of John Blackwood, who published it as well as most of her other books. *Scenes of Clerical Life* was followed by a number of extremely popular novels, all of which were written under the pseudonym George Eliot. Eliot's early novels—*Adam Bede* (1859), *The Mill on the Floss* (1860), and *Silas Marner* (1861)—are largely accounts of English rural life that display her characteristic interest in moral questions. In her later works—*Romola* (1863), *Felix Holt* (1866), *Middlemarch,* and *Daniel Deronda* (1876)—Eliot broadened the scope of her work to include concerns such as politics, aesthetics, history, psychology, and science.

A work so vast in scope that it is frequently compared to Leo Tolstoy's *War and Peace, Middlemarch* presents the most comprehensive picture of provincial life in English fiction. The breadth of the social world depicted in *Middlemarch* is paralleled by the variety of intellectual and moral issues treated in the novel. In developing the novel's main theme—the relationship of the individual to society—Eliot skillfully combined four separate plot strands that together reflect her wide-ranging interests. Throughout *Middlemarch,* Eliot scrupulously analyzes her characters and examines their effect upon the moral fabric of the community. Characteristically, themes of duty and the purification of the human heart through suffering are presented with pathos and understanding.

Daniel Deronda, Eliot's last novel, is regarded as her most ambitious yet perhaps her least successful work. In it she examines a broad spectrum of nineteenth-century European society—from the titled upper classes, whose leisure time is spent at continental resorts, to the shopkeepers and merchants of London's East End—and addresses such themes as spiritual growth, human potential for good and evil, and the idea of vocational calling. Composed of two distinct yet related narratives, the integration of which has usually been considered severely flawed, the novel is unusual in Victorian fiction in its positive portrayal of Jewish characters, culture, and nationalistic aspirations in the section of the work chronicling the history of Daniel Deronda. However, critical praise usually centers on the heroine of another portion of the work, Gwendolen Harleth. Eliot's subtle and insightful analysis of Gwendolen's character and motivations is judged by some critics to be one of her finest accomplishments.

While Eliot was regarded as the leading English novelist during the last years of her life, it was common at this time to differentiate between her early and late work and to prefer the former. Reviewers almost unanimously agreed that Eliot's later novels were overly philosophic and didactic, lacking the spontaneity and charm of her early autobiographical works. Consequently, the esteem in which she was held was already in decline by 1885 at the time of her death, and was further diminished by the late-Victorian revolt against "the-novel-with-a-purpose." As early as 1901, W. C. Brownell was able to ask, "How long has it been since George Eliot's name has been the subject of even a literary allusion?" During the next three decades, Eliot's works attracted very little scholarly attention. It was not until the 1940s that her novels, particularly the later ones, returned to favor, generating a resurgence of interest in her work and a body of criticism that rivals that of her fellow Victorian, Charles Dickens.

The variety and quantity of current critical response is perhaps the best measure of Eliot's complex genius. She continues to inspire analysis for her subtle psychological insight, broad philosophic vision, and mastery of a poignantly realistic narrative style.

(For further information about Eliot's life and works, see *Dictionary of Literary Biography,* Vols. 21, 35, 55 and *Nineteenth-Century Literature Criticism,* Vols. 4, 13, 23.)

CRITICAL COMMENTARY

VIRGINIA WOOLF

(essay date 1925)

[Woolf was an esteemed English novelist, essayist, and critic. In the following excerpt from a work that appeared in 1925 in her *The Common Reader*, she discusses several characteristics of Eliot's fiction, focusing especially on her portrayal of heroines.]

The beauty of [George Eliot's] first books, *Scenes of Clerical Life, Adam Bede, The Mill on the Floss,* is very great. It is impossible to estimate the merit of the Poysers, the Dodsons, the Gilfils, the Bartons, and the rest with all their surroundings and dependencies, because they have put on flesh and blood and we move among them, now bored, now sympathetic, but always with that unquestioning acceptance of all that they say and do, which we accord to the great originals only. The flood of memory and humour which she pours so spontaneously into one figure, one scene after another, until the whole fabric of ancient rural England is revived, has so much in common with a natural process that it leaves us with little consciousness that there is anything to criticise. We accept; we feel the delicious warmth and release of spirit which the great creative writers alone procure for us. As one comes back to the books after years of absence they pour out, even against our expectation, the same store of energy and heat, so that we want more than anything to idle in the warmth as in the sun beating down from the red orchard wall. If there is an element of unthinking abandonment in thus submitting to the humours of Midland farmers and their wives, that, too, is right in the circumstances. We scarcely wish to analyse what we feel to be so large and deeply human. And when we consider how distant in time the world of Shepperton and Hayslope is, and how remote the minds of farmer and agricultural labourers from those of most of George Eliot's readers, we can only attribute the ease and pleasure with which we ramble from house to smithy, from cottage parlour to rectory garden, to the fact that George Eliot makes us share their lives, not in a spirit of condescension or of curiosity, but in a spirit of sympathy. She is no satirist. The movement of her mind was too slow and cumbersome to lend itself to comedy. But she gathers in her large grasp a great bunch of the main elements of human nature and groups them loosely together with a tolerant and wholesome understanding which, as one finds upon re-reading, has not only kept her figures fresh and free, but has given them

an unexpected hold upon our laughter and tears. (p. 200)

But in the midst of all this tolerance and sympathy there are, even in the early books, moments of greater stress. Her humour has shown itself broad enough to cover a wide range of fools and failures, mothers and children, dogs and flourishing midland fields, farmers, sagacious or fuddled over their ale, horse-dealers, inn-keepers, curates, and carpenters. Over them all broods a certain romance, the only romance that George Eliot allowed herself—the romance of the past. The books are astonishingly readable and have no trace of pomposity or pretence. But to the reader who holds a large stretch of her early work in view it will become obvious that the mist of recollection gradually withdraws. It is not that her power diminishes, for, to our thinking, it is at its highest in the mature *Middlemarch,* the magnificent book which with all its imperfections is one of the few English novels written for grown-up people. . . . Those who fall foul of George Eliot do so, we incline to think, on account of her heroines; and with good reason; for there is no doubt that they bring out the worst of her, lead her into difficult places, make her self-conscious, didactic, and occasionally vulgar. Yet if you could delete the whole sisterhood you would leave a much smaller and a much inferior world, albeit a world of greater artistic perfection and far superior jollity and comfort. (pp. 201-02)

[The problem with all Eliot's heroines is that they cannot live] without religion, and they start out on the search for one when they are little girls. Each has the deep feminine passion for goodness, which makes the place where she stands in aspiration and agony the heart of the book—still and cloistered like a place of worship, but that she no longer knows to whom to pray. In learning they seek their goal; in the ordinary tasks of womanhood; in the wider service of their kind. They do not find what they seek, and we cannot wonder. The ancient consciousness of woman, charged with suffering and sensibility, and for so many ages dumb, seems in them to have brimmed and overflowed and uttered a demand for something—they scarcely know what—for something that is perhaps incompatible with the facts of human existence. George Eliot had far too strong an intelligence to tamper with those facts, and too broad a humour to mitigate the truth because it was a stern one. Save for the supreme courage of their en-

Principal Works

Scenes of Clerical Life (short stories) 1858

Adam Bede (novel) 1859

The Lifted Veil (short story) 1859

The Mill on the Floss (novel) 1860

Silas Marner, the Weaver of Raveloe (novel) 1861

Romola (novel) 1863

Felix Holt the Radical (novel) 1866

The Spanish Gypsy (poetry) 1868

Middlemarch: A Study of Provincial Life (novel) 1871-72

The Legend of Jubal, and Other Poems (poetry) 1874

Daniel Deronda (novel) 1876

Impressions of Theophrastus Such (essays) 1879

The George Eliot Letters. 9 vols. (letters) 1954-78

deavour, the struggle ends, for her heroines, in tragedy, or in a compromise that is even more melancholy. But their story is the incomplete version of the story of George Eliot herself. For her, too, the burden and the complexity of womanhood were not enough; she must reach beyond the sanctuary and pluck for herself the strange bright fruits of art and knowledge. Clasping them as few women have ever clasped them, she would not renounce her own inheritance—the difference of view, the difference of standard—nor accept an inappropriate reward. Thus we behold her, a memorable figure, inordinately praised and shrinking from her fame, despondent, reserved, shuddering back into the arms of love as if there alone were satisfaction and, it might be, justification, at the same time reaching out with 'a fastidious yet hungry ambition' for all that life could offer the free and inquiring mind and confronting her feminine aspirations with the real world of men. (pp. 203-04)

Virginia Woolf, "George Eliot," in her *Collected Essays, Vol. 1,* The Hogarth Press, 1966, pp. 196-204.

DAVID CECIL

(essay date 1934)

[Cecil was an English educator, critic, and biographer who wrote acclaimed studies of prominent nineteenth-century authors. In the following excerpt, he argues that Eliot's intellectual and moral didacticism impede full appreciation of her work.]

It is one of her principal claims to fame that [George

Eliot] is the first modern novelist. That first period of the English novel which begins with Fielding, ends with Trollope; the second—the period of Henry James and Meredith and Galsworthy and Wells, and which is hardly over today—begins with George Eliot. . . . George Eliot draws her picture in the Victorian way: objectively, with a careful attention to external features and without any excursions into the uncomfortable regions of the animal passions. All the same, her books are essentially different from those of Trollope and Mrs. Gaskell. For though she does not break with the tradition she had inherited, she develops it, and develops it in a direction which entails alteration of its fundamental character. She used the old formulas, but she used them for a new purpose. Her creative impulse was stimulated by a new sort of inspiration. (pp. 291-92)

[George Eliot] was something very unlike the typical Victorian novelists, she was an "intellectual" writer. Her mind was always active; experience set it immediately and instinctively analyzing and generalizing, to discovering why and how things happened. And when she turned her attention to the world around her it was this analysis that started her creative imagination working. It is inspired, not by what she felt or fancied, but by what she thought; not by a wish to convey her impressions of life but her judgments on it. And it embodied itself not in a picture but in a theme. . . . [She] had a vision of human society as the expression of certain principles, and then embodied it in a picture of a specific place—Middlemarch. Silas Marner did not come into her head like Mr. Pickwick as an individual, complete with face and manner and glinting spectacles, but as a representative of a type of human character, only later to be clothed in individual characteristics. She did not think of a man and then invent what sort of thing was likely to happen to him, she thought of what happened to him and from that evolved what sort of man he was likely to have been. Thus, though her story may include many of the same elements as those of the other Victorian writers, these elements have a different importance. . . . The separate scenes and characters which were the primary inspiration of the earlier Victorian novelists, are, in George Eliot, a secondary inspiration. For they are subsidiary to the central idea on which the story is built. And it is in the conception of this idea that her creative imagination primarily shows itself. (pp. 293-95)

George Eliot is an innovator, not only because her approach to her subject is intellectual, but also because her intellect took in a great deal of new country. . . . She was, unfortunately for herself in some ways, a "high-brow." Her mind was too massive and inquisitive to confine its incessant activities to the private practical area of experience which was all that was envisaged by the man in the street. It inevitably included in its view a great deal that her predecessors did not.

It regarded human life not just in its immediate particular but in its general ultimate aspects too. (p. 295)

Now so different an approach to her subject matter from that of Dickens or Trollope led to her writing a different sort of novel. It led her, indeed, to break with those fundamental conventions both of form and matter within which the English novel up till then had been constructed. . . . [Since] George Eliot began with an idea of character or situation, her plot was intended to follow not a standardized formula but what she conceived to be the logical development of that idea; and this might entail something quite different from the accepted Victorian notion of a plot. It might entail no marriage, no happy ending, no character answering to the Victorian conception of hero or heroine. Often it did not. Even in her earliest book, *Scenes of Clerical Life,* she ended her stories tragically, and in one of them, **"Amos Barton,"** she chose as a hero no gallant young man but a middle-aged, unattractive, married clergyman.

Later she sometimes departed still farther from the old conventions. In *Silas Marner* the hero is an elderly bachelor; *The Mill on the Floss* ends very badly and has no hero at all. In *Middlemarch* there is no central figure of any kind; the main interest is divided between four separate groups of characters; and none of these except Dorothea Brooke approaches the conventional "heroic" type. Finally, since the action of George Eliot's stories arises logically from the characters, those strokes of fortunes, coincidences, sudden inheritances, long lost wills, which are the stock-in-trade of the ordinary Victorian plot, are inevitably omitted. They are the first novels which set out to give a picture of life wholly unmodified by those formulas of a good plot which the novel had taken over from comedy and romance. Her story is conditioned solely by the logical demands of situation or character; it ends sadly or happily, includes heroes or omits them, deals with the married or the unmarried, according as reason and observation lead her to think likely. In fact, the laws conditioning the form of George Eliot's novels are the same laws that condition those of Henry James and Wells and Conrad and Arnold Bennett. Hers are the first examples in English of the novel in its mature form; in them it structurally comes of age.

It comes of age in spirit too. . . . It cannot be said that George Eliot dealt with the animal, her moral sensibilities were too Victorian for that. . . . Her wider intellectual interests did lead her to portray human life in those deeper, more general aspects that are omitted from the novels of Dickens and Thackeray. And this meant that it ceased to be primarily an entertainment. Like the novel today it is a medium for the discussions of the serious problems and preoccupations of mature life. (pp. 296-99)

Nor is it only in their matter that her novels aspire

to be a serious major form of art. It is also in their approach to it. George Eliot's active generalizing brain forbade her to confine herself merely to describe and observe, she must draw conclusions, construct a scale of values, evolve an attitude of mind. Like Thackeray she argues from the particular to the general, reasons from her observation of men to make judgments on man. Her novels, like his, are a criticism of life. But the fact that she envisages it against a larger background, makes it a different sort of criticism. . . . George Eliot's wider interests give her a wider vision. She sees man in relation to his own private ideals, not just in relation to society; and she sees both him and society in relation to what she considered the ideals of absolute truth and goodness. . . . [She] is like the great dramatists and poets—and the great continental novelists. Like *War and Peace* and *The Brothers Karamazov,* **Middlemarch** is concerned with how to live and what to think, not just as these problems present themselves to the man in the street, but to the artist and the philosopher.

All this should make George Eliot far easier for us to appreciate than Dickens. We can do it without having to accustom ourselves to unfamiliar conventions as we have to accustom ourselves before we can fully appreciate *Bleak House.* And George Eliot is worth appreciating. She may write a very different sort of novel from the other Victorians, but she is worth reading, and for the same reason,—she is a creative artist.

In some ways she is a characteristically Victorian artist. The nature of her genius is no more revolutionary than her choice of subject matter. Some of her chief merits are the merits of the tradition which she inherited. She had all the Victorian fertility and variety and vigor; she begins her books with the Victorian confidence, engages our attention in the first page, so that comfortable, unquestioning, we settle down to watch her build her world. Nor is it a small world. Of course it had its limitations. Like most writers, George Eliot could only create from the world of her personal experience—in her case middle- and lower-class rural England of the nineteenth-century Midlands. When, in *Romola,* she turns her hand to renaissance Florence, she comes a dreadful crash. This was not from want of care. George Eliot visited Florence, pencil and notebook in hand; she read every authority on her subject. Every detail of her settings is historically accurate, her costumes are monuments of archaeological research. But the human beings that wear them are inevitably the sort of human beings George Eliot knew, and these were the sort of human beings who inhabited the Victorian Midlands, narrow, prudish, steady and prosaic. . . . (pp. 299-301)

Nor did George Eliot see everything even within the world of her own experience. Her imagination was a sober earthbound affair; it had no fine frenzies, no brilliant capricious flights of fancy, no exquisite delicacy of observation. The world of its creation is not diversified by the volcanic conflagrations of the Brontës, the vivid miniature details of Mrs. Gaskell, the romantic byways of Dickens. Still, it is a big world, as big as that of any Victorian novelist, including in its substantial well-lighted area smiles and tears, thought and drama; and uniting them all is the level harmonious glow of an individual vision.

Her imagination triumphed too in some specifically Victorian fields. In humor, for instance. George Eliot keeps a tight rein on her humorous faculty. . . . Even at its brightest her humor is not exuberant. But within its limitations it is both individual and delightful. Intelligence gives it edge, good humor gives it glow; it sparkles over the comedy of rustic provincial life, a satire at once cool and mellow, incisive and genial. (pp. 301-02)

Finally, she has the Victorian power of making vivid the settings of her stories. They have more in common with Mrs. Gaskell's than with those of Dickens or the Brontës; they are straightforward, realistic pictures, undistorted by fantasy. But like hers they manage to have a marked character of their own. (p. 303)

Yet it must be repeated that George Eliot's is not a characteristically Victorian achievement. That intellectual interest which is the mainspring of her inspiration alters the angle from which she approaches every aspect of her subject matter: she cannot look at anything without analyzing and diagnosing. (p. 304)

[It] is not in her laughter or her tears, her setting or her social scene, that George Eliot's intellectual approach shows most clearly; it is in her drawing of character. (p. 308)

[She] did not begin with the personality that appeared to the outward world, but with the psychological elements underlying that personality. And this meant that her portrait is preeminently concerned with these elements. She may clothe them in outward idiosyncrasy, but this idiosyncrasy is never the principal thing about them as with Dickens or Trollope or Mrs. Gaskell. We do not remember her serious characters by their appearance or the way they talked, indeed we do not remember these things clearly at all. Her portraits are all primarily portraits of the inner man. . . .

[Her] books are a criticism of life. And this means that she conceives her vision of human existence only in those aspects that relate to her standard of criticism. Now this criticism was exclusively and consistently a moral criticism. George Eliot, though she was a thinker, was not a particularly original thinker. And her conception of life was that held by the dominant school of thought in "advanced" circles of her day. She was a thoroughgoing Victorian rationalist. (p. 309)

The second fundamental in her philosophy is a belief in free will. She thought every man's character was in his own hands to mold into the right shape or the wrong; and she thought that all his strength should be put forward to mold it right. (p. 310)

The third fundamental of her philosophy is a conviction that life is just. She was sure that those who live a virtuous life are essentially contented, that those who live a vicious are essentially discontented. (pp. 310-11)

It is in the light of these views that George Eliot constructs her novels. The "ideas" which are their germ are all moral ideas; the conflicts which are the mainspring of their action are always moral conflicts. They divide themselves into two classes. In some, **"Janet's Repentance,"** *Adam Bede, Silas Marner,* the moral course is clear. The characters are in a position to do what they think right, only they are tempted to do something wrong instead; and the conflict turns on the struggle between their principles and their weaknesses. . . . In *The Mill on the Floss* George Eliot confronts another problem. How should one act if one wants to do right but cannot find a satisfactory method of doing it? Maggie Tulliver thirsts after righteousness, but she finds no way to satisfy her thirst in the materialist provincial world in which she lives; and such efforts as she makes only result in annoying everyone around her. (pp. 311-12)

George Eliot's serious characters, then, are envisaged exclusively in their moral aspect. They are portraits of the inner man, but portraits not designed like Charlotte Brontë's to exhibit the color of his temperament, but the principles of his conduct—his besetting sin, his presiding virtue. Such a portrait inevitably omits many of those aspects of a man—his manner, his mood, his face—which make living most of the great figures of fiction. All the same, George Eliot's concentration on the moral side of human nature is the chief source of her peculiar glory, the kernel of her precious unique contribution to our literature. Her imagination is not a distorting glass like Dickens', vitalizing her figures by accentuating their personal idiosyncrasies, nor is it, like Charlotte Brontë's, a painted window suffusing them with the color of her own live temperament; it is an X-ray, bringing them to life by the clearness with which she penetrates to the secret mainspring of their actions. (pp. 312-13)

[This] clear-sighted vision of the essentials of character gives George Eliot certain advantages over the other Victorians. For one thing it means that her characters, unlike theirs, are always consistent. (p. 314)

But it is not only in this consistency that George Eliot's intellectual understanding of her characters gives her an advantage over the other Victorians. It also enables her to describe aspects of human nature which they cannot. It gives her the power which won her the admiration of Proust, the power to describe successfully how a character develops. This is very rare among novelists. . . . [George Eliot's perception of] these characteristics is the root of her whole conception. (p. 315)

George Eliot's grip on psychological essentials enables her to draw complex characters better than her predecessors. . . . Drawing from the inside out, starting with the central principle of the character, she is able to show how it reveals itself in the most apparently inconsistent manifestations, can give to the most varicolored surface of character that prevalent tone which marks it as the expression of one personality. Her characters always hang together, are of a piece, their defects are the defects of their virtues. (p. 317)

Her power to describe mixed characters extends to mixed states of mind. Indeed, the field of her most characteristic triumphs is the moral battle-field. . . . She is particularly good at showing how temptation triumphs. No other English novelist has given us so vivid a picture of the process of moral defeat, the gradual steps by which Mr. Bulstrode is brought to further Raffles' death, Arthur Donnithorne's gradual yielding to his passion for Hetty, Maggie Tulliver's to hers for Stephen Guest. With an inexorable clearness she reveals how temptation insinuates itself into the mind, how it retreats at the first suspicious movement of conscience, how it comes back disguised, and how, if once more vanquished, it will sham death only to arise suddenly and sweep its victim away on a single irresistible gust of desire when he is off his guard. . . . With equal insight George Eliot can portray the moral chaos that takes possession of the mind after wrong has been done. She exposes all the complex writhings of a spirit striving to make itself at ease on the bed of a disturbed conscience, the desperate casuistry by which it attempts to justify itself, its inexhaustible ingenuity in blinding itself to unpleasant facts, the baseless hopes it conjures up for its comfort; she can distinguish precisely how different an act looks before it is done, shrouded in the softening darkness of the secret heart, and after, exposed in all its naked ugliness to the harsh daylight of other people's judgment. (pp. 318-19)

This insight into the moral consciousness makes George Eliot's picture of human nature far more homogeneous than that of a writer like Dickens. She divides the world into saints and sinners quite as definitely as he does. But her sinners are not made of a different clay from her saints. They are for the most part amiable, well-intentioned people who mean to be good, just as much as the saints do; only they have not the same strength of mind, there is a flaw in the metal of their virtue. (p. 324)

George Eliot's structure is the very substance of her primary conception. She begins with her situation; her characters and scenes are developed from it. Each has its part to play in her general purpose and none is permitted to play more than this part. No minor character swells to gigantic proportions in George Eliot's novels, dwarfing the principals, her most memorable scenes are always turning points in the action. (p. 326)

In spite of the variety of her talents and the width of her scope, in spite of the fact that she is the only novelist of her time who writes on the scale of the great continental novelists, the only novelist who holds the same conception of her art which is held today, her reputation has sustained a more catastrophic slump than that of any of her contemporaries. It is not just that she is not read, that her books stand on the shelves unopened. If people do read her they do not enjoy her. It certainly is odd. All the same it is explicable. The temper of our time has something to do with it. For though she is nearer to us in form and subject than the other Victorians, in point of view she is quite as distant. Indeed, we find her point of view even more alien. This is natural enough. An exclusively moral point of view is, at any time, a bleak and unsatisfying affair. Life is altogether too complex and masterful and mysterious to be ordered into tidy little compartments of right and wrong; and any attempt so to order it inevitably leaves a good deal outside that is both interesting and delightful. Moreover, George Eliot's compartments are conspicuously inadequate ones. The virtues of her admiration, industry, self-restraint, conscientiousness, are drab, negative sort of virtues; they are school-teachers' virtues. George Eliot does confront human nature a little like a school-teacher; kindly but just, calm but censorious, with birchrod in hand to use as she thinks right, and lists of good and bad conduct marks pinned neatly to her desk. And when we see all the vivid disorderly vitality of human nature ranged before her for carefully measured approval or condemnation, we tend to feel rebellious and resentful.

Nor does she, like some Puritan writers, like Bunyan for instance, sweep away our antipathy to her moral system by the enthusiastic conviction with which she expounds it. It was impossible that she should; she did not feel enthusiastic about it herself. Victorian ethical rationalism is the least inspiring of creeds. (pp. 326-27)

All the same George Eliot's loss of reputation is not wholly undeserved. Even if we do strain ourselves to acquiesce in her point of view, we do not feel her the supreme novelist that her contemporaries did. Her books never give us that intense unalloyed pleasure we get from the greatest masters. Though like Tolstoy she is an interesting critic of life, though she constructs well like Jane Austen, though like Dickens she creates a world, yet when we set her achievement in any of these lines beside those of these famous competitors, we feel something lacking. Somehow we are dissatisfied.

It is easy to see why she fails to stand a comparison with Tolstoy. Her vision of life is smaller. She knows about life in provincial nineteenth-century England, life in Middlemarch, the life of merchants and doctors and squires and humble clergymen and small town politicians; she does not know about the savage or sophisticated, about artists and adventurers and the world of fashion and affairs. . . . *Middlemarch* may be the nearest English equivalent to *War and Peace,* but it is a provincial sort of *War and Peace.*

It is also easy to see why her form does not satisfy us as Jane Austen's does. Life is chaotic, art is orderly. The novelist's problem is to evolve an orderly composition which is also a convincing picture of life. . . . [George Eliot] sacrifices life to art. Her plots seem too neat and symmetrical to be true. We do not feel them to have grown naturally from their situation like a flower, but to have been put together deliberately and calculatedly like a building. For, in spite of her determination that her story should develop logically, she has not that highest formal faculty which makes development appear inevitable, she has to twist facts to make them fit her purpose. (pp. 329-31)

However, she might have constructed badly and criticized life inadequately and yet have been as satisfying an author as Dickens. He constructed much worse, and only offered us the most rudimentary criticism of life. Yet she is not as satisfying as he is. For she is as inferior to him in his distinguishing quality as she is to Tolstoy and Jane Austen in theirs: she is inferior to him in creative imagination. She had one, as we have seen. But, like Trollope's, it was a relatively mild imagination; it does not unite with its subject to generate the highest intensity of aesthetic life. So that when its creations are set beside those of a white-hot imagination like Dickens', they look pale and lifeless. (p. 332)

Indeed—and here we come to the root cause of her failure to attain that supreme rank to which she aspired—there was something second-rate in the essential quality of George Eliot's inspiration. Her genius was built on the same grand scale as that of the greatest novelists; but it was not, as theirs was, compounded of the best material. She had more talents than most writers; but they were none of them of the finest caliber. So that though she seeks success in so many fields—and never wholly fails to find it—in none, even at her best, does she reach the level of the masterpieces in that particular kind.

Still, this is not enough to account for the peculiar feeling of dissatisfaction that her books give us. . . . George Eliot is dissatisfying because, paradoxically, on one side she was much more gifted than Trollope, because she had so much more intellectual force. Her second-rate talents were strong enough to achieve success in a second-rate kind. But her intellect was always forcing her to attempt things that needed supreme talents for their achievement. (p. 334)

Yet we cannot regret her intellect. For it is the source of her most original characters and her most memorable passages. In it is engendered that penetration into the moral nature of man, which is her peculiar contribution to our literature. No, the truth is that there was a congenital disproportion in the original composition of George Eliot's talent. It had two sides, intellectual and imaginative. And they were inextricably connected. The intellect was the engine which started the machinery of the imagination working. But the engine was too powerful for the machine: it kept it at a strain at which it could not run smoothly and easily. So that it never produced a wholly satisfactory work of art.

All the same, her achievement is a considerable one, more considerable than that of many more accomplished writers. *Middlemarch* may never give us the same feeling of unalloyed pleasure as *Wives and Daughters* does, but rouses far deeper emotions, sets the mind far more seriously astir. For though she was not a supreme artist, George Eliot was not a minor one; laboriously but surely her insight, her integrity, her sad, mature wisdom, lifted her to the region of major art. When all is said and done she is a great writer; no unworthy heir of Thackeray and Dickens, no unworthy forerunner of Hardy and Henry James. She stands at the gateway between the old novel and the new, a massive caryatid, heavy of countenance, uneasy of attitude; but noble, monumental, profoundly impressive. (pp. 335-36)

David Cecil, "George Eliot," in his *Early Victorian Novelists: Essays in Revaluation,* 1934. Reprint by The Bobbs-Merrill Company, Inc., 1935, pp. 291-336.

JOAN BENNETT
(essay date 1948)

[In the following excerpt, Bennett examines theme and style in Eliot's best-known works.]

Despite all the differences between George Eliot's novels, certain broad resemblances mark them as the product of a single mind.

There is, first of all, a resemblance in the way she shapes her novels and consequently in the total impression any one of them leaves with the reader. When we try, after an interval, to recall any one of them we find ourselves thinking as much about the life of a village or a provincial town, or of the interrelation of groups of families, as about the central drama. (p. 78)

Adam Bede is the earliest and simplest example of the typical George Eliot form. The life of Hayslope envelops the tragedy. We come to know all grades of its society, artisans, labourers, farmers, rector, schoolmaster, innkeeper and squire. It is an active community in which most men or women have work to do and their character is affected by that work. That character is also the product of religious influences; we become aware of the impact of Methodism upon the inhabitants of Hayslope and of the more subtly pervasive influence of traditional Anglicanism. In the Third Book the whole community is assembled at Donnithorne Chase to celebrate the young squire's coming of age; by that time the pattern of living out of which the central characters emerge is clearly established and their drama is already under way. After the climax, when Hetty Sorrel has been condemned to death, reprieved and deported and another author would feel that the work was complete, there is a Sixth Book, balancing the Third. In it the rhythm of Hayslope life is re-established and, with the inevitable gaps made by the intervening event, a Harvest supper reassembles the same community as celebrated the young squire's birthday. . . . Although the impression while we read is of a leisurely sequence of naturalistic scenes of comedy or of pathos and of a world richly populated with entertaining characters, when we look back we find that every individual scene or character is directly or indirectly related to the simple story at the core of the book, of the carpenter's betrothed betrayed by the squire's grandson. In its setting this commonplace story becomes widely significant. The simple, well-contrived pattern conveys the sense of a social structure enclosing four human beings as completely as the soil encloses the roots of a growing plant and, in so doing, it illustrates one aspect of the author's vision of life.

Although the formal pattern is not elsewhere so simple and symmetrical as it is in *Adam Bede*— where the assembly of the villagers on the green to hear the preaching in Book I, their assembly at the birthday feast in Book III and at the Harvest supper in Book VI provide rests that divide the composition into almost equal parts—the general character of the design, an individual tragedy surrounded by the life of a community, is similar in all George Eliot's novels, except *Daniel Deronda*, where the absence of such an enclosing community is an important part of her conception. In her own view the lack of symmetry in *The Mill on the Floss* was responsible for her imperfect fulfilment of her intention, and for the dissatisfaction that most readers feel about the end of that novel:

> . . . the tragedy is not adequately prepared. This is a defect which I felt even while writing the third volume, and have felt ever since the MS. left me. The *Epische Breite* into which I was beguiled by love of my subject in the two first volumes, caused a want of proportionate fullness in the treatment of the third, which I shall always regret.

The regret is justified in so far as the compression

of the Maggie and Stephen episode contributes to its faulty presentation. Yet the epic breadth of the first two volumes is warranted by the completeness with which we come to understand the pressure of her surroundings on Maggie's developing personality which will, in turn, condition the central drama. We are brought to a full realization of those surroundings because, in a series of scenes, each with their own intrinsic value as social comedy, or drama, we grow familiar with a number of households and their way of life, which is both individual and representative. (pp. 79-81)

The difference in quality between George Eliot's novels is closely related to the degree of success with which she gives life to the social world surrounding her central characters. In her first period, from the *Scenes of Clerical Life* to *Silas Marner* she plants those characters in the environment with which she had been familiar since her childhood, and, for many readers, it is these novels that give the most delight. Certainly in them her characteristic humour, compounded of compassion, a sense of the incongruous, and an ear for dialogue that is both racy and individual, has the freest play. But when she returned, in *Middlemarch,* with a more assured command of her art, to the environment she most fully understood, she achieved her masterpiece. It is true that this great novel lacks some of the qualities of the first period; it has less spontaneous gaiety, partly because the provincial town gave her less scope for comedy than did the rural environment. There is also an aspect of her genius, absent here, which is more often found in the poet than in the prose artist, an ability to simplify without distorting human truths, so that they can be presented symbolically as they are in the legend of *Silas Marner.* (p. 82)

The relative failure of *Romola, Felix Holt* and *Daniel Deronda* is partly due to the fact that in these three works, for different reasons, the social background is imperfectly focussed. In *Romola* this is the result of transplanting her scene to a world that she needed to reconstruct with laborious intellectual effort. In *Felix Holt,* although the ingredients of a first-rate George Eliot novel are all there, they are not successfully integrated. The romance of Esther and Felix usurps the foreground of the book and the more serious and interesting study of Mrs. Transome and Jermyn, her son's father, is relegated to the background. The reader's interest oscillates between the political theme—the two contrasted radicals and their relations to the new voter—and the moral theme, illustrated by Mrs. Transome reaping the fruits of her former self-indulgence and Esther moving towards her self-abnegating choice of true love and modest means. Because the various threads of interest do not compose into a single pattern *Felix Holt,* though enjoyable, does not enlarge the field of understanding as do the major novels. The social en-

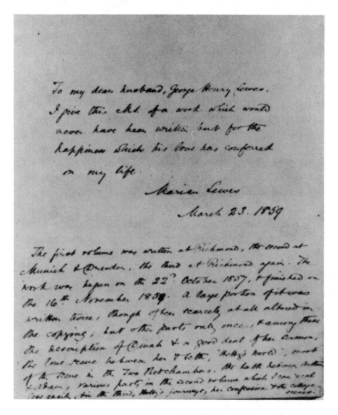

The first page of the manuscript of *Adam Bede,* inscribed
to G. H. Lewes.

vironment is not sufficiently convincing to provide a
unifying centre; whereas, in the vintage works, the
community has an identity as recognizable and persuasive as that of the central characters.

The case of *Daniel Deronda* is different. In this
book the absence of an enveloping society for either
Gwendolen or Daniel is a part of the author's central
conception. Both characters are incomplete because
they have been deprived of such a soil in which to
grow. Gwendolen's selfishness and narrowness of vision and Daniel's quest for some communal tie to direct
his altruistic aspirations are the outcome of a lack, in
the early life of each, of just such a background as
Hayslope provided for the characters in *Adam Bede,*
the Dodson-Tulliver world for Maggie, or Middlemarch for Dorothea. George Eliot's perception of the
dependence of human beings on one another and on
their social and religious traditions is as keen in *Daniel
Deronda* as elsewhere, but she attempts here to embody it by a process the reverse of the one she had mastered. . . . [In] *Daniel Deronda* the social scenes, often
vividly presented (for instance, the gambling scene; or
the family life of the Cohens; or the archery party) are
essentially disparate. They are of no service in fusing
the themes into a single whole. Some incoherence in
this last novel is due to the fact that the new approach
presented a new problem in composition which was
not successfully solved. The characteristic form of her

novels is the product of a vision of life the source of
which lay far back in her childhood. When she had
found herself unable to accept the Christian dogmas
she held fast to the ethical beliefs of which those dogmas had been the embodiment. She doubted the factual
truth of the miraculous story told in the Gospels, and
she doubted the factual truth of the theological dogma
elicited from that story and developed in the tradition
of the Church; but she had no doubt that human happiness and the full development of individual personality depend on mutual love and service. . . . Self-
sacrifice is good because human happiness depends on
it; man cannot live alone and social life is incompatible
with unrestrained self-indulgence. This truth was most
fully understood by her in relation to the English village and small town community life in which she had
been bred, and in such communities, impregnated with
social and religious traditions emerging in the conventions and observances of family and social life, it could
be clearly illustrated. The problems which face Hetty
and Arthur, Maggie and Stephen, Godfrey and Silas,
Lydgate and Dorothea, are all problems concerned with
the adjustment of the individual to the community, and
with the discovery of a mean point between complete
self-repression and unchecked self-indulgence. The
motive for self-sacrifice is the happiness of other people and George Eliot composed her fictions in such a
way as to set that motive in a clear light. But, by the
time she wrote *Daniel Deronda,* she herself had long
ceased to live in a community governed by traditions
slowly evolved through centuries and unquestionably
accepted by the majority. In the intellectual and artistic
world in which she and George Henry Lewes were ultimately made welcome, there was no such tradition,
woven of inherited beliefs, customs and conventions. . . . The unsatisfactory invention of Daniel's
discovery of a Jewish allegiance and a mission to his
people is an attempt to answer that question for him.
It is not an intellectually satisfactory answer; nor has
she successfully solved the artistic problem of linking
the rootlessness of Daniel with the differently derived
rootlessness of Gwendolen. The relationship between
the two characters is potentially interesting, but they
are arbitrarily brought together. Moreover, Daniel remains the symbol of an idea, whereas Gwendolen is the
product of creative insight. (pp. 83-5)

The humour in George Eliot's novels, more prevalent in the earlier than in the later works, is as direct a
product of her vision of life as is the way she shapes
her stories. It arises out of a profound and sympathetic
understanding of the world she creates and it expresses
itself predominantly in the dialogue which bears the
stamp both of the individual speaker and of the race
and class. Behind the words spoken and the characteristic idiom lie the accumulated misconstructions of inherited beliefs, or the complex of prejudices, experience

and common sense which make up rural wisdom. . . . The author's attitude towards these [characters] is not satirical. It is true that a sense of superior understanding contributes to the reader's enjoyment; but he is seldom allowed to feel contempt; and his amusement is often compatible with the reverse of this. (pp. 86-7)

When Marian first considered writing fiction Lewes was confident that she had some of the requisite gifts while he was doubtful about others. The requirements he names indicate what the Victorian novelist was expected to provide, while the particular stamp of George Eliot's own talent reveals itself in the way the demands are met. The gifts that Lewes believes a novelist must have are philosophy, wit, descriptive powers and a sense of the dramatic which includes the ability to write dialogue and to achieve pathos. He was confident about the first three qualifications. 'You have wit, description, and philosophy—those go a good way towards the production of a novel'; but both he and she were doubtful whether she could 'write good dialogue' and whether she could 'command any pathos'. By the time **'Amos Barton'** was finished Lewes was satisfied about both. But, although her first story has humorous, character-revealing dialogue and gives evidence of an aural imagination which was to remain one of her notable gifts, the pathos of Milly's death does not ring true. . . . But one suspects that the scene is literary rather than naturalistic. In any case there is an over-emphasis on pathos in the style. Tear-provoking adjectives are over-worked; 'the *little* footsteps on the stairs', 'the *poor, pale* child', '*pallid* lips', 'the *dear* child', '*tear-stained* cheeks', 'his *little* heart'—the italicized adjectives are from the trading-stock of pathetic writing. (pp. 92-3)

But though George Eliot's pathos was at first tainted with current literary fashion, or laid on too thick because of her mistrust of her powers in that line, she soon mastered the art of communicating her own sympathy with human suffering. The prison scene in *Adam Bede* when Dinah's passionate pity breaks down the barrier of bewildered bitterness that has kept Hetty silent, moves the reader far more deeply and lastingly than does Milly's death. . . . In the first half of the novel Hetty Sorrel is too often shown to the reader through the eyes of the author. Too often her moral and intellectual limitations are explained and her sensuous, kitten-like prettiness and selfishness demonstrated or reproved. But when the crisis comes George Eliot's creative genius takes command, and throughout the vivid scenes of Hetty's journey the reader becomes a participator in her misery instead of a superior person, merely measuring and pitying her moral and intellectual inadequacy. (p. 94)

When we part from Hetty at the end of [the 'Journey of Despair' (chapter 17)], our suspense and anxiety for her have obliterated all sense of moral superiority

or separateness. And it is only after four chapters in which we share the feelings of those who are searching for her, that the end of the story is revealed.

Consequently, the prison scene is no mere piece of pathetic writing, straining for the right emotional tone. It is the unfolding of the last scene of a drama we have watched with increasing participation. (p. 95)

The wide scope of the novel form as it was used in the nineteenth century is the result of the combination of dramatic with narrative presentation. The reader accepts the convention of an omniscient narrator who knows all the motives and all the consequences of the action he describes and whose assessment of the values involved he is invited to share. But the total effect depends upon the fact and discrimination of the author in his use of the two methods. Intellectual appreciation of character can be arrived at by analysis; but for full sympathy we need to participate as well as to understand, and the quickening and expansion of sympathy was what George Eliot hoped to achieve in her novels. . . . Sympathy for Hetty is almost choked by intellectual appreciation of her limitations and then, in the dramatic last scenes the 'broad fact' of our common humanity with her emerges. Even Tito Melema—who is in far greater danger of becoming merely a subject for speculation all the while the author dissects his character with relentless intelligence—evokes some fellow-feeling in dramatic scenes. The poverty of his nature and the gradual coarsening of his sensibility is not blurred—on the contrary it is particularly vivid when, for instance, he finds Baldassarre in Tessa's outhouse and hopes to propitiate him, or when he divulges to Romola the fact of his sale of her father's library. In both scenes the author's assessment of Tito's merits as a human being is confirmed. But the reader's position is no longer merely that of a disinterested judge weighing the evidence. When we are allowed to watch the criminal in action and to overhear his thoughts, the predominant emotion is sympathy for his uncomprehending isolation. What emerges most clearly in these scenes is that Tito, for all his cleverness, is utterly at sea. His habit of selfish casuistry has made him incapable of foreseeing the impact of the situation on the straightforward upright mind of Baldassarre or of Romola. He expects a gesture of reconciliation, he expects sympathy or, at worst, forgiveness, and his alarmed discovery of his loneliness extends the reader's capacity for sympathy.

In these cases dramatic presentation redresses or nearly redresses a balance. Analysis preponderates in the drawing of Hetty and Tito so as almost to defeat the author's declared intention. In the later books, however, the unlovely characters are seldom allowed to become mere case histories, coldly appraised by the reader with the help of the author's intellectual analysis. . . . In her first experiment with the traditional form of prose narrative George Eliot laid on her dramatic scenes as she laid on her pathos. She was as yet only fumbling towards the expression of her personal vision of life. In the presentation of **'The Sad Fortunes of the Rev. Amos Barton,'** along with the relatively assured recreation of a social background and the naturalistic portrait of Amos himself, including the characteristic effort to obtain the reader's sympathy for this ungainly, egoistic and intellectually limited human being, there is the contrived pathos of Milly's death. (pp. 96-8)

But in the later novels . . . the interest is focussed throughout on the mind and spirit of the protagonist. It does not matter whether Bulstrode was responsible for Raffles's death (in *Middlemarch*) or Gwendolen for Grandcourt's (in *Daniel Deronda*); what concerns us is what occurs in the mind of each. Each of them wills the death of a fellow-creature and in each case the dramatic tension is the result of the conflict in their minds which the reader witnesses through its whole evolution, before and after the death takes place. . . . The reader participates in the will to murder; his power of understanding and sympathy is stretched far enough to include that, and the total effect of the ensuing death on the mind of the would-be murderer. Moreover, because the author is wholly engaged in the act of creation—that is in participating imaginatively in the experience she presents—she is not lured into any literary clichés or exaggerations of style; the situation develops naturally towards its crisis. . . . When the moment comes in which the suspicions of the neighbours culminate in

Bulstrode's public disgrace it is again not so much what happens that holds the reader spellbound, but the reverberations of every act and speech in the minds of Bulstrode and Lydgate. Grandcourt's death scene is not so securely handled as Raffles's. In *Middlemarch* George Eliot is writing in a form she had completely mastered and this dramatic crisis is controlled by the whole pattern of the book. Its total effect depends upon the world in which it occurs, and the reader's response to the particular scenes of the 'murder' or of the public disgrace are involved with his total response to the novel. The relative failure of *Daniel Deronda* as a whole reflects itself in the crisis; we arrive at the central moment of Grandcourt's drowning in the scene in which Gwendolen confesses herself to Deronda and that scene suffers from the fact that Deronda himself is never wholly convincing. (pp. 98-100)

From one point of view [George Eliot's] novels continue in the tradition evolved from Fielding, but which had gradually become less picaresque and more strictly narrative. She tells a story with a beginning, middle and end. The main interest is focussed on a small group of characters the development of whose fortunes is laid out. They move towards a crisis or tangle which is unravelled before the end so that in the last chapter a *dénouement* is reached. All the fortunes with which the reader has been concerned are tidied up. The story ends in a marriage or a death and the future of the survivors in indicated. The reader is persuaded that the story is complete. Within this framework there is scope for the narrator to comment on the action and the characters and so to expound his 'philosophy' or sense of moral values. 'Wit', both in the commentary and in the dialogue, contributes to the reader's delight and communicates the author's sense of proportion; 'descriptive powers' evoke the surroundings in which the action takes place, while 'dramatic powers' enable the author to recreate the scenes of the story in terms of dialogue and action. But from another point of view George Eliot is an innovator. The organic or living form of her novels, within the expected framework, is different from anything that had gone before. It resembles, in some respects, Jane Austen's form in so far as the central characters are deeply rooted in their social environment which determines their story as much as does their individual character. The difference is that the social environment is wider, more complex, made up of a greater variety of minor characters drawn from many more social and economic levels, and also that the display of this outer circle or environment is more conscious. Jane Austen took her social *milieu* for granted; its manners and traditions were, for her, as little open to question as the laws of nature. George Eliot was aware of the ethical, religious and social conventions of the world she paints as a product of history, evolved in time and changing with time. She was consciously interested in the pressure all these exert on individual lives and in the existence of a problem concerned with resisting or succumbing to that pressure. She shares the modern consciousness of man in a changing and developing society. Consequently, the organic form of her novels—an inner circle (a small group of individuals involved in a moral dilemma) surrounded by an outer circle (the social world within which the dilemma has to be resolved)—is more significant than in any preceding fiction. Furthermore, her perception of individual human beings is more complex than that of her predecessors. She never suggests a simple division of characters into good and bad. The individual, like the environment, has evolved and is evolving; his or her behaviour at any given moment is the inevitable result of all that has gone before; therefore, while the action can itself be judged, both in relation to its consequences and to its aesthetic beauty (an action that pleases or displeases) the doer is not presented judicially but compassionately. In her discourse George Eliot sometimes deviates from this attitude and her novel suffers accordingly. But whenever her reflective powers are in due subordination to her creative gift, wherever, as usually happens in the dialogue, she responds to her characters rather than thinks about them, the reader feels with them and the total effect of her novel is an increase of understanding and of compassion. (pp. 100-01)

Joan Bennett, in her *George Eliot: Her Mind and Her Art,* Cambridge at the University Press, 1948, 202 p.

K. M. NEWTON
(essay date 1981)

[In the following excerpt, Newton analyzes Eliot's *Middlemarch*, noting its relationship to the Romantic tradition.]

[*Middlemarch* is] a much more ambitious work than anything George Eliot had attempted previously. It reflects to a greater extent than any of her other novels the wide range of her intellectual interests, in sociology, psychology, philosophy, science, religion and art, to name only the most obvious, and it is arguable that no other nineteenth-century novel can compete with it in terms of the breadth and complexity of the intellectual issues with which it deals. . . . [It] is one of the great artistic merits of *Middlemarch* that its interest in a wide range of intellectual issues does not diminish the quality of its human and social presentation, since George Eliot is largely successful in integrating the intellectual and philosophical aspects of the novel with the human and social. (p. 123)

In *Middlemarch,* George Eliot is concerned with the same fundamental problems in her study of character, as regards both individual psychology and human and social relationships, as she is in her other novels, but her characters are placed in a much more intricate and dominant environment and involved in a more complex social life than the characters in her other fiction. . . . With society being more at the centre of the novel and dominating character, such problems as the moral dangers of Romantic egotism or the conflict between strong impulse and the need for a sense of continuity of self, are treated more in a social context with less detailed concentration on individual psychology.

Despite the greater prominence of society in *Middlemarch,* which results in less emphasis being given to the individual problems of the main characters, at least in comparison with earlier novels such as *The Mill on the Floss* or *Romola* and her later novel, *Daniel Deronda,* there are important continuities between the characters in *Middlemarch* and those in her other novels, and their Romantic connections are equally clear. The most obvious similarity is between Dorothea Brooke and George Eliot's previous heroines. Dorothea possesses the same strength of feeling and potentially dangerous egotistic energies as Maggie Tulliver, Romola and Esther Lyon. Her Romantic affinities are suggested by the frequent use of the word 'ardour' in connection with her. This suggests the kind of idealistic enthusiasm associated with a figure like Shelley. She is seen in a Romantic light by Ladislaw, who thinks of the Aeolean harp, a key Romantic image, when he first meets her and again in Rome, and Naumann, a Romantic painter, sees her as 'a sort of Christian Antigone—sensuous force controlled by spiritual passion' . . . , a juxtaposition which again calls to mind Shelley. It seems clear that George Eliot intends Dorothea's ardent nature to be seen as Romantic.

The prime characteristic of Romantic feeling is that it operates as a means of spontaneous knowledge, prior to rational thought, and . . . [in an important passage Dorothea] tells Ladislaw that, for her, knowledge passes directly into feeling. Feeling and thought are inseparable for her, and it is natural for her to respond to experience with a unified consciousness: 'But in Dorothea's mind there was a current into which all thought and feeling were apt sooner or later to flow—the reaching forward of the whole consciousness towards the fullest truth, the least partial good'. . . . The word 'current', which is used several times in connection with her, suggests, like 'ardour', a Romantic sensibility.

But while the main problem for Maggie and Romola is that their strong feelings make them vulnerable to impulsive acts which contradict their past lives and past selves, Dorothea is at first faced with a different danger. Her most serious temptation is that form of idealism which longs for belief in an external order and meaning which one can serve with complete devotion because one believes utterly in its truth and value. Though Dorothea possesses such strong feelings, she at first distrusts what they tell her. She desires a form of knowledge and sense of truth which will be superior to subjective feeling. This is why she is so upset when Casaubon regards her only as a creature of feeling: 'She was humiliated to find herself a mere victim of feeling, as if she could know nothing except through that medium'. . . . She fears that what her feelings communicate to her may be wrong, and believes she needs a standpoint based on objective knowledge:

> Those provinces of masculine knowledge seemed to her a standing-ground from which all truth could be seen more truly. As it was, she constantly doubted her own conclusions, because she felt her own ignorance: how could she be confident that one-roomed cottages were not for the glory of God, when men who knew the classics appeared to conciliate indifference to the cottages with zeal for glory? . . .

Though this passage satirises her belief that knowledge is required to support feeling over the cottages, this does not solve the problem created by the over-subjective and unstable nature of feeling on its own. . . . Dorothea believes religion combined with knowledge will provide a sense of moral direction for the self which will be independent of subjective feeling.

Her desire to devote herself utterly to the service of a religious ideal is repeatedly stressed: 'Her mind was theoretic, and yearned by its nature after some lofty conception of the world which might frankly include the parish of Tipton and her own rule of conduct there'. . . . Dorothea longs 'for a binding theory which could bring her own life and doctrine into strict connection with that amazing past, and give the remotest sources of knowledge some bearing on her actions'. . . . This longing is not wrong in itself, but the form in which she hopes for its realisation is untenable. . . . Dorothea in her early idealistic stage desires a theory which will prove that there is a religious meaning in reality itself, and that knowledge will reveal this.

It is this religious longing that lies at the root of her attraction to Casaubon. It is his intellectual aim to provide the 'lofty conception of the world' and 'binding theory' which would create the basis for a unified Christian world-view similar to that which existed in the time of St Theresa, and which Dorothea could serve with certainty because knowledge had been used to establish in unquestionable terms the truth of Christianity. He says of himself: 'My mind is something like the ghost of an ancient, wandering about the world and trying mentally to construct it as it used to be, in spite

of ruin and confusing changes'. . . . This grandiose aim immediately appeals to Dorothea's Christian idealism: 'To reconstruct a past world, doubtless with a view to the highest purposes of truth—what a work to be in any way present at, to assist in, though only as a lamp-holder!' The theoretic side of her nature seeks an explanation of the world which will reveal the existence of a religious meaning and order external to the mind, and which would in consequence provide an absolutely firm basis for moral and social values. In other words, she sets her hopes on the establishment of a pre-Romantic world-view, as her Enlightenment faith in knowledge indicates: 'something she yearned for by which her life might be filled with action at once rational and ardent; and since the time was gone by for guiding visions and spiritual directors, since prayer heightened yearning but not instruction, what lamp was there but knowledge?' . . . (pp. 124-27)

It is natural then that she should be attracted to Casaubon. The aim of his 'Key to All Mythologies' is to counteract the fragmentation of man's knowledge and to provide the foundation for 'the coherent social faith and order' which a new St Theresa would require to give direction and purpose to her life. He will accomplish this by revealing that all mythologies are really only transformations or corruptions of the events in the Bible, which embodied religious truth. . . . Casaubon's aim makes him for Dorothea 'a living Bossuet, whose work would reconcile complete knowledge with devoted piety; here was a modern Augustine who united the glories of doctor and saint'. . . . Here again we see Dorothea interpreting Casaubon in pre-Romantic terms as someone who could use knowledge to establish the existence of a spiritual order in the world which could be the beginning of a new age of faith. (p. 127)

George Eliot should be seen as an advanced Romantic who rejects the pre-Romantic view that reality possesses a meaningful order and structure which exists independently of the mind. . . . For her, it was no longer possible to believe that there was an immanent order in the world identical in structure with human thought. Probably she believed that the key to all mythologies, if it existed, was to be found not by trying to find a coherent structure underlying the diversity of knowledge but by investigating the mind itself. The key that would unlock all mythologies and systems was to be discovered in psychology. This is implicit in the philosophies of Feuerbach and Lewes. Even if Casaubon had succeeded in finishing his 'Key to All Mythologies', he would only have created a closed system, incapable of being either proved or disproved, and so able to appeal only to the converted. This seems to be the point of the narrator's comment that his theory was based on 'a method of interpretation which was not tested by the necessity of forming anything which had sharper collisions than an elaborate notion of Gog and

Magog: it was as free from interruption as a plan for threading the stars together'. . . . George Eliot is perhaps suggesting that such a theory could never establish the objective truth of Christianity, and indeed that religion cannot be proved in scientific terms. Dorothea's hope that knowledge could reveal the existence of a religious order in the world, which everyone would have to recognise and accept, is misconceived, and she eventually realises this.

Her disillusionment with Casaubon and his work leads to a reluctant acceptance that the world lacks an immanent order which knowledge would discover and which would support Christian values. Her religious idealism seemed to her to justify moral action in the world, to create the foundation for a larger social faith, and to give her own life direction and purpose. Its breakdown, then, is a crisis in her life. She must come to terms with the failure of her pre-Romantic belief in a coherent order in the world, which revealed the existence of divine purpose. It is her experience in Rome which does most to make her aware of a disorder in the world that cannot be reconciled with her narrow religious principles. There she discovers a complexity and

A rare photograph of Eliot, taken by John Edwin Mayall in 1858.

sense of the contradictory in her experience which shatters the excess of order in her religious theories about the world, and causes severe disorientation. . . . (pp. 129-30)

It is implied that personal disenchantment with Casaubon is in part responsible for creating the frame of mind which makes her respond to Rome in this way, for George Eliot . . . brings together the philosophical and the human significance of Dorothea's experience. After discovering that the reality of marriage bears little resemblance to what she had expected, she 'found herself plunged into tumultuous preoccupation with her personal lot'. It is tempting to believe that George Eliot intends to suggest that Dorothea's experience of his physical impotence leads to an awareness of his intellectual impotence, though strictly speaking such an interpretation has to be read into the text. However, the crisis she suffers in Rome produces a state of mind in which she can see Casaubon's work critically instead of, as formerly, in the light of her religious hopes. Her loss of faith in him and his work undermines further her religious world-view; if her belief in him could have been sustained and he had been one of the wisest of men, 'In that case her tottering faith would have become firm again'. . . . But she eventually realises that the fragments he is trying to put together disintegrate again in his hands and can only support 'a theory which was already withered in the bud like an elfin child'. . . . She finally accepts that he will never be able to create a synthesis which will reconcile faith and knowledge, and it is implied that she believes it is impossible; after his death his notebooks resemble 'the mute memorial of a forgotten faith', and she must reject his request that she carry on his work: it would be 'working hopelessly at what I have no belief in'. . . . (p. 131)

Though it is not stated openly that she has lost her religious faith, these passages suggest that her belief that knowledge would reveal the presence of a Christian order in the world has gone. She does, however, preserve a religious world-view, even though she says she hardly ever prays. The following declaration she makes to Ladislaw suggests that she becomes a transcendentalist: 'That by desiring what is perfectly good, even when we don't quite know what it is and cannot do what we would, we are part of the divine power against evil—widening the skirts of light and making the struggle with darkness narrower'. . . . But her main problem now is how to confront life without the 'binding theory' she had hoped for. This creates for her the difficulty faced also by George Eliot's previous heroines, of supporting her sense of identity solely from her inner resources, without succumbing to negative egotistic forces in herself or to impulsive feeling. There are two important occasions in which the strongly egotistic side of her nature threatens to gain control:

when she is nearly overcome by an impulse of the moment and when she almost lapses into selfish despair.

The first of these occurs after Casaubon has snubbed her, having learned from Lydgate that he might not live long. All through her married life with Casaubon, Dorothea has restrained the strong feeling which is natural to her, and such feeling becomes transformed into egotistic revolt against her lot: 'She was in the reaction of a rebellious anger stronger than any she had felt since her marriage'. . . . Impulsive, resentful feeling threatens to overcome her more stable, sympathetic emotions. She wants to tell Casaubon 'the truth about her feeling' and to hurt him. But gradually she becomes aware of the danger of allowing 'her resentment to govern her', and that such feeling is false to her more persistent sense of self. She has to struggle hard to find an alternative feeling which is truer to her sense of whole self and not the expression of pent-up resentment. . . . Despite the loss of her religious idealism, in a moment of crisis in which she can rely only on her own resources, she is able to overcome a strong impulse. Her sympathy with how Casaubon must feel on learning that he might not have long to live and her own sense of continuity of self allow her to overcome a crisis, even though she is no longer supported by an external framework of Christian belief.

Her second serious crisis takes place when she sees Rosamond and Ladislaw together, believes that they are lovers, and that she has lost all hope of personal happiness through love. Like Romola when she has been forced to give up all affectionate feeling for Tito and lost her faith in Savonarola, Dorothea feels a sense of despair. While for Romola it had been Savonarola and religion which had provided her with greatest support after her original disillusionment with Tito, with Dorothea this process is reversed; it is her relationship with Ladislaw, which has developed into love, that has sustained her after the breakdown of her Christian idealism. In each case disappointment leads to despair, but as with Romola, Dorothea overcomes this and finds through feeling the means of reconstituting her life. She must come to terms with the fact that the world is indifferent to her own hopes and desires, just as she has had to accept already that reality does not conform to the structure of her Christian ideals. But the underlying feelings which were the real basis of her former Christian idealism are still valid, though she must not expect the world to conform with human ideals or take account of human hopes and desires. Her idealistic feelings remain valuable even if they must be projected onto an indifferent, unstructured world. This realisation comes to her when she recovers, after a night of conflict, the original sympathetic feelings which motivated her in the first place to visit Rosamond. These have not been shown to be false, despite what she thought she saw at Lydgate's house, and in her new

self-knowledge she can use them to overcome the egotistic feelings of anger, resentment, and despair aroused by the disappointment of her hopes and expectations. . . . Sympathetic feeling, with its basis in the human and social aspect of the self, triumphs over animal egotism and becomes her source of knowledge.

Even though she can no longer accept that there is religious meaning immanent in the world, and believes, mistakenly as it turns out, that events have frustrated her own hopes of happiness, this sympathetic feeling remains to give her life moral direction and to discipline egotistic impulse. It can be the foundation of an ideal value which can 'rule her errant will' and shape human action in the world. Dorothea also resembles Romola in that this inner moral feeling leads to a larger, more social vision when she opens the curtains of her room and looks out at the world beyond her own ego: 'Far off in the bending sky was the pearly light; and she felt the largeness of the world and the manifold wakings of men to labour and endurance'. During her Christian phase she had hoped that knowledge would reveal religious meaning in external reality, but now she discovers that though there may be no such meaning objectively in the world, it is present in her intense human feeling and vision. Her earlier Christian beliefs and idealism were the projection into objective form of this feeling, and despite the breakdown of her projection, the underlying feeling remains valid. She can go on to create a new orientation which supports her sense of identity and directs her life. (pp. 131-34)

The relationship between Dorothea and Ladislaw has been generally regarded as one of the artistic weaknesses of *Middlemarch,* primarily on the grounds that Ladislaw is too idealised or too lightweight to be worthy of Dorothea. It is probable that Ladislaw had to perform too many functions in the plot for George Eliot to succeed fully in creating both a complex psychological portrait and a character who plays an important part in the novel's philosophical structure. But he seems to me to be much more central to the novel and more successfully characterised than most previous critics have tended to think. His importance is closely connected with the novel's Romantic concerns. He is the character most obviously associated with the Romantics. For example, he has been educated at Heidelberg, one of the most important centres of German Romanticism; he is twice compared to Shelley by Mr Brooke: 'he has the same sort of enthusiasm for liberty, freedom, emancipation' . . . ; and he is described by Mrs Cadwallader as 'A sort of Byronic hero'. . . . His flamboyant appearance, his experiments with opium and his general attitudes all contribute to building up a picture of a Romantic, and this seems clearly to be George Eliot's intention.

But it is the development of Ladislaw as a Romantic that is important. At the beginning of the novel he is attracted towards the egotistic side of Romanticism. He sees himself as 'Pegasus' and he regards 'every form of prescribed work' as 'harness'. . . . The words 'pride', 'defiance', and 'rebellion', all of which have a Byronic connotation, are frequently associated with him. He tells Dorothea proudly that he comes 'of rebellious blood on both sides'. . . . Casaubon's opinion of him is 'that he was capable of any design which could fascinate a rebellious temper and an undisciplined impulsiveness'. . . . He is also Byronic in being an outsider and an alien, a role he takes some pleasure in: 'he was a sort of gypsy, rather enjoying the sense of belonging to no class; he had a feeling of romance in his position, and a pleasant consciousness of creating a little surprise wherever he went'. . . . He feels little connection with any country or social group, nor at the beginning of the novel does he wish to have any. He is a rootless wanderer, associated with gypsies and Jews.

In the dominating social world of *Middlemarch,* however, Ladislaw's rebellious and egotistic tendencies present little threat to society. The common criticism that Ladislaw is an insubstantial character perhaps does not take sufficient account of the fact that in the world of the novel the Romantic rebel is inevitably a lightweight figure. His egotistic rebellion expresses itself only in aestheticism and dilettantism. When Dorothea asks him what his religion is, he replies: 'To love what is good and beautiful when I see it. . . . But I am a rebel: I don't feel bound, as you do, to submit to what I don't like'. . . . Naumann believes he is incapable of devoting his attention to any one subject: 'His walk must be *belles-lettres.* That is wi—ide' . . . , and Casaubon considers him to be 'a man with no other principle than transient caprice'. . . . But his aestheticism and dilettantism are sufficient to alienate him from society or from any chosen vocation. Without the influence of Dorothea on his life, it seems certain that he would have remained a rootless aesthete.

The change that takes place in Ladislaw is an important element in the novel's structure. Dorothea's influence encourages him to direct his Romantic energies into social channels. He had previously believed that genius was 'intolerant of fetters' . . . , but his feeling for Dorothea makes him accept the 'harness' he had formerly rejected, 'having settled in Middlemarch and harnessed himself with Mr. Brooke'. . . . The same image is present in the following passage: 'Ladislaw had now accepted his bit of work, though it was not that indeterminate loftiest thing which he had once dreamed of as alone worthy of continuous effort. His nature warmed easily in the presence of subjects which were visibly mixed with life and action, and the easily stirred rebellion in him helped the glow of public spirit'. . . . The last part of this passage shows how his former rebellious energy is being socially directed. He no longer cuts himself off from society but devotes en-

ergies, once taken up by the study of art as a form of escape from society, to working for the social good: 'he studied the political situation with as ardent an interest as he had ever given to poetic metres or mediaevalism'. Dorothea has made him feel that Romantic ardour must be given a social expression. His transformation is shown in Dorothea's conversation with him when he is on the point of leaving Middlemarch: 'And you care that justice should be done to every one. I am so glad. When we were in Rome, I thought you only cared for poetry and art, and the things that adorn life for us who are well off. But now I know you think about the rest of the world'. . . . Significantly by the end of the novel this former Romantic rebel has become 'an ardent public man'. . . .

Dorothea's ardent desire to do some good in the world and her implied criticism of Ladislaw's attitudes are the most important factors in making him give up his rootless existence and involve himself in society. Her idealistic conception of him becomes part of his sense of self, and the need to earn her respect brings out tendencies in himself that might otherwise have been overwhelmed by his attraction to egotistic Romantic attitudes. . . . (pp. 136-37)

But though Ladislaw is able to play an active role in society and directs his energies in a socially responsible way, society is as little affected by this as it was by his period of rebellion and social alienation. The 'Finale' suggests that, like Dorothea, he is subject to the limitations that result from living in 'an imperfect social state'. Though he devotes himself energetically to trying to reform his society, this seems to lead to no obvious benefit: 'working well in those times when reforms were begun with a young hopefulness of immediate good which has been much checked in our days'.

It might be objected that despite Ladislaw's importance in the novel's philosophical structure, he is still an artistic failure. But in my view those who have criticised Ladislaw's characterisation have not sufficiently recognised that in *Middlemarch* George Eliot has made considerable progress in the dramatic presentation of what I have called sublimated egotism. In her previous novels, her positive characters often appeared to be idealised and one-dimensional in comparison with her negative egotists. In *Middlemarch* this artistic weakness is to a great extent overcome, particularly in the characterisation of Dorothea and Mary Garth. But even Ladislaw, though less convincing than Dorothea or Mary, is not the idealised figure many critics have seen him as being. Even after Dorothea's reforming influence on him, he remains strongly egotistic, and this is not merely stated but presented in dramatic terms. We see, for example, in a convincing and psychologically credible scene, how he succumbs to the egotistic temptation of going to church in Lowick to see Dorothea, realises his 'wretched blunder' when Casaubon and Dorothea enter, and feels 'utterly ridiculous, out of temper, and miserable' in the 'cage' he has created for himself. . . . We also see how his egotism shapes his interpretation of his relationship with Dorothea in their difficult meetings after Casaubon's death, and his vulnerability to a strong impulse of the moment in his cruel treatment of Rosamond when Dorothea surprises them together, an experience which makes him realise later that he is in danger of drifting into an affair with Rosamond and that he might not be capable of resisting

this. To see Ladislaw as merely an idealisation of the Romantic, as 'sentimental because he lacks the adult energies that would make his freedom problematic', is to overlook George Eliot's dramatic presentation of the tension between the egotistic and the idealistic sides of his character, even if this tension is not consistently maintained. (pp. 138-39)

K. M. Newton, in his *George Eliot, Romantic Humanist: A Study of the Philosophical Structure of Her Novels,* Barnes & Noble Books, 1981, 215 p.

SOURCES FOR FURTHER STUDY

Carroll, David, ed. *George Eliot: The Critical Heritage.* New York: Barnes & Noble, Inc., 1971, 511 p.

> Selected criticism and commentary by Eliot's contemporaries. Also included are George Henry Lewes's letter to John Blackwood, the editor of *Blackwood's Magazine,* in which he introduces his "friend," the pseudonymous "George Eliot." Blackwood's favorable response follows Lewes's letter.

Cross, J. W. *George Eliot's Life as Related in Her Letters and Journals.* New York: AMS Press, 1965, 646 p.

> The official biography, originally published in 1885. Cross, whom Eliot married shortly before her death, promoted the somber image of his wife which dominated Eliot biography and criticism for many years.

Fulmer, Constance Marie. *George Eliot: A Reference Guide.* Reference Guides in Literature, edited by Joseph Katz. Boston: G. K. Hall & Co., 1977, 247 p.

> A comprehensive annotated bibliography of published critical commentary on Eliot's life and works, 1858-1971.

Haight, Gordon S. *George Eliot: A Biography.* London: Oxford at the Clarendon Press, 1968, 616 p.

> The definitive biography.

Hardy, Barbara. *The Novels of George Eliot: A Study in Form.* London: The Athlone Press, 1959, 242 p.

> Considered "the best single critical study of George Eliot yet published." Hardy concentrates on Eliot's structural techniques, but comments on plot, character, and imagery as well.

——— ed. *Critical Essays on George Eliot.* New York: Barnes & Noble, Inc., 1970, 218 p.

> Essays on the individual novels, with commentary on Eliot's oeuvre by W. J. Harvey and John Bayley.

T. S. Eliot

1888-1965

(Full name Thomas Stearns Eliot) American-born English poet, critic, essayist, dramatist, and editor.

INTRODUCTION

As an eminent poet, critic, and playwright, Eliot has maintained an influence upon literature that some critics claim is unequaled by any other twentieth-century writer. His poetry and prose are frequently cited as having helped inaugurate the modern period in English and American letters. Eliot is best known for his distinctly erudite and innovative verse. Many of his poems combine classical references and concerns with elements drawn from contemporary culture in a format that often juxtaposes fragmentary, disjointed surfaces with underlying philosophical significance. Throughout his career, Eliot strongly advocated the development of a "historical sense," which, as he stated in his essay "Tradition and the Individual Talent," is "nearly indispensable to anyone who would continue to be a poet beyond his twenty-fifth year." Consequently, awareness and affirmation of his literary and cultural heritage is one of the most prominent features of Eliot's criticism and poetry. Eliot's verse also incorporates experiments with form, phrasing, and tone, as evidenced in such seminal works as "The Love Song of J. Alfred Prufrock," *The Waste Land* (1922) and *Four Quartets* (1943). Concurrently, the astute observations, terms, and definitions introduced in his essays are significant contributions to literary analysis and stress the importance of tradition, religion, and morality in art and society.

Eliot was born in St. Louis, Missouri, into a family of distinguished New England heritage; the importance of tradition and moral propriety informed Eliot's life early on. His family included Puritan ancestors who had been settlers of the original Massachusetts colonies; while his paternal grandfather, a Unitarian minister, had moved to St. Louis from Boston and founded Washington University. In 1906 Eliot entered Harvard, where he studied French literature and philosophy and also joined the staff of the *Harvard Advocate,* the university's literary journal, in which he first published segments of "The Love Song of J. Alfred Prufrock." He completed his undergraduate studies in 1909 and his masters degree in English literature the following year. Over the course of the next six years, Eliot pursued his graduate studies in philosophy at the Sorbonne, Harvard, Marburg, and Oxford, completing his dissertation on philosopher F. H. Bradley in 1916. During this time Eliot met Ezra Pound, who became his life long friend and an important literary influence. In 1915, while studying in England during the opening years of World War I, Eliot met and soon married an Englishwoman, Vivien Haigh-Wood; however, their relationship was greatly troubled by Vivien's neurotic illnesses and Eliot's sexual apprehensions, and the day-to-day, spiritually harrowing nature of their marriage is often seen as having contributed to the despair in the poetry Eliot wrote between 1915 and the early 1920s. The year of their marriage, Eliot and Vivien settled in London, and Eliot began teaching at a boy's school while also writing reviews for the *New Statesman* and the *International Journal of Ethics,* as well as publishing poems in *Blast* and *Poetry* magazines.

Eliot left teaching and began working at Lloyd's Bank in 1917, though he continued to follow his literary pursuits, publishing *Prufrock and Other Observations* (1917) and becoming an assistant editor for the journal the *Egoist,* all of which strengthened his reputation as a poet and literary critic. The combined strain of his failing marriage and the pressures from his banking and writing careers resulted in a breakdown in 1921, at which time he sought treatment at a sanitorium in Switzerland, where he completed *The Waste Land* in 1922. Returning to London, Eliot became the founding editor of a new literary journal, the *Criterion,* in which he published *The Waste Land* (itself judiciously edited at the poet's request by Pound) within a month of its publication in the American journal the *Dial* in late 1922. The *Criterion,* now recognized as one of the most distinguished twentieth-century periodicals, was founded on the assumption "that there existed an international fraternity of men of letters, within Europe: a bond which did not replace, but was perfectly compatible with, national loyalties, religious loyalties, and differences of political philosophy," as Eliot later wrote in *Notes towards the Definition of Culture* (1948). "And it was our business not so much to make any particular ideas prevail, as to maintain intellectual activity on the highest level." By the time it ceased publication in 1939, the *Criterion* had published work by such figures as Pound, W. B. Yeats, Virginia Woolf, Paul Valéry, Wyndham Lewis, C. P. Cavafy, Owen Barfield, Marcel Proust, and Lucien Lévy-Bruhl. The *Criterion* survived on patronage and subscriptions alone until 1925, when Eliot retired from his bank post and took a position as an editorial director at Faber and Gwyer (later Faber and Faber), which subsequently began subsidizing the periodical.

In 1927, having lived in England for over a decade, and affirming that he was essentially (as he later termed it) "Anglo-Catholic in religion, royalist in politics, and classicist in literature," Eliot became a British subject and a member of the Anglican Church. Five years later, he received a one-year appointment to the Charles Eliot Norton professorship at Harvard. His temporary move back to the United States to fulfill his academic responsibilities afforded him a definite separation from Vivien, with whom he had been emotionally estranged for many years. During the 1930s Eliot lectured at major universities throughout the United States, publishing his lectures in *The Use of Poetry and the Use of Criticism* (1933) and *After Strange Gods: A Primer of Modern Heresy* (1934), in which he elucidated his moral and religious theories of literary criticism. Also during the 1930s, Eliot began devoting much of his time to writing verse dramas. Such plays as *Murder in the Cathedral* (1935) and the later *The Cocktail Party* (1950) reflect his interest in the significance of the spiritual life—or lack of it—in modern society. During World War II, Eliot wrote his last major poetic works, *East Coker* (1940), *Burnt Norton* (1941), *The Dry Salvages* (1941), and *Little Gidding* (1942, together published as *Four Quartets*), which together affirm his belief in the vanity of human wishes and the need for complete submission to God in a world otherwise devoid of meaning.

Eliot experienced marked changes in his personal life beginning in 1947, when Vivien died after having spent several years in an institution. He subsequently met Valerie Fletcher, who became his secretary and later his wife, and with whom he enjoyed a stable and happy relationship for the rest of his life. In 1948 Eliot received both the Nobel Prize for Literature and the Order of Merit by George VI, both honors—along with his newfound popularity as a dramatist—augmenting his stature as a celebrated literary figure which he maintained until his death in 1965.

His first volume of poetry, *Prufrock and Other Observations,* established Eliot as an important new voice in English and American poetry. "The Love Song of J. Alfred Prufrock," in particular, encapsulates the distinctive techniques he employed throughout his career. James F. Knapp described the poem as "one which helped to change our conception of what kind of shape a poem might take." "The Love Song of J. Alfred Prufrock" is a lyrical, dramatic monologue spoken in the voice of a middle-class male persona who inhabits a physically and spiritually bleak environment. Although aware of the possibility of personal fulfillment, the speaker is afraid to act, unable to claim for himself a more meaningful existence. Many critics noted in the poems in *Prufrock and Other Observations*—including

"Preludes," "Rhapsody on a Windy Night," and "Portrait of a Lady"—the influence of the French symbolists, especially Jules Laforgue and Charles Baudelaire. These poets had impressed Eliot with their realistic portrayals of urban landscapes and their bold use of irony and symbolism. Eliot's early poems feature similar qualities: they are characterized by their often sardonic tone, strong rhythms achieved by blending formal and informal verse forms and speech, and vivid, startling metaphors.

Among the most innovative, influential, and controversial poems of the twentieth century, *The Waste Land* challenged conventional definitions of poetry upon its publication in 1922 and helped occasion the shifting of values that inaugurated the Modernist period in literature. The five sections of this book-length poem—"The Burial of the Dead," "A Game of Chess," "The Fire Sermon," "Death by Water," and "What the Thunder Said"—are composed of apparently random, disconnected images and scenes and are spoken by several different voices which blend together at various points throughout the poem. Compounded of numerous mythic allusions, varying voices, settings, and tones, colloquial, lyrical, and fragmented language, and quotations from works by other writers, *The Waste Land* develops a series of abruptly changing formats in which disillusionment, spiritual ennui, and casual sexuality are projected as representative elements of a post-World War I European sensibility. The meaning of *The Waste Land* is a subject of much debate, but scholars generally agree that it presents a metaphorical portrait of the modern world as dry and desolate and of humanity as emotionally, intellectually, and spiritually empty. Among the many themes in the poem are death and rebirth, time, sterility, and the failures of sexuality. The disjointed form of the poem accentuates bold metaphors and symbols that are often juxtaposed with deadpan irony, confronting readers with disparate and ambiguous images and narrative events. Among many factors, the work's seemingly chaotic structure and Eliot's inclusion of notes to elucidate and cite his various references have engendered charges of purposeful obscurity and contributed to the notoriety of *The Waste Land*. Acknowledging its complexity, Hugh Kenner contended that the poem's imposing structure and erudite references invite active and imaginative readings: "*The Waste Land* is suffused with a functional obscurity, sibylline fragments so disposed as to yield the utmost in connotative power, embracing the fragmented present and reaching back to that 'vanished mind of which our mind is a continuum.' "

Following Eliot's baptism into the Anglican church and his naturalization as a British subject, his work underwent a significant change. *The Journey of the Magi* (1927) and *A Song for Simeon* (1928) retain the basic elements of Eliot's style while introducing a religious dimension to his thematic concerns. The poems in these collections combine realistic detail with visionary imagery and biblical references, portraying the doubts and pain of the religious convert. Similarly, *Ash-Wednesday* (1930) has been interpreted as a direct declaration of Eliot's Christian orientation. It too describes the difficulties and indecision of his new commitment while emphasizing the value of spirituality in a highly secular age.

In the years immediately following the publication of *Ash-Wednesday*, Eliot wrote several plays in verse but produced little poetry, concentrating primarily on criticism, lectures, and his position as an editor at Faber and Faber. This relatively unproductive poetic period ended with the publication of *Four Quartets*, comprising four previously issued volumes: *East Coker, Burnt Norton, The Dry Salvages* and *Little Gidding*. The title of each section refers to a geographical landscape of significance to Eliot; these include his family's ancestral village in England and the Massachusetts coast where he spent his childhood summers. A long meditation on a variety of themes—most notably time and history—*Four Quartets* is marked by its attention to sound and music, its generally optimistic tone, and its skillful blending of philosophical complexity and lyricism. Although some critics claim that *Four Quartets* is weakly executed and pretentious, most consider it a fitting and powerful culmination of Eliot's poetic career, and Eliot himself believed it was his best work.

Eliot's work for the theater consists of plays written in verse rather than standard dialogue. His high regard for Elizabethan and Restoration drama led him to attempt a synthesis of modern theatrical techniques, classical poetic form, and mythical references and devices. Eliot's first effort, *The Rock: A Pageant Play* (1934), was commissioned by his church and is explicitly religious. Written in collaboration with E. Martin Browne, the play features Greek choruses whose speeches were Eliot's contribution. *Murder in the Cathedral*, widely recognized as Eliot's most successful play, was also commissioned by the church and again employs choral verse. This play recounts the martyrdom of Thomas á Becket, Archbishop of Canterbury, who was killed in 1170 by knights of Henry II. Eliot's later plays are generally considered less effective than *Murder in the Cathedral*. In *The Family Reunion* (1939), *The Cocktail Party* (1950), *The Confidential Clerk* (1954), and *The Elder Statesman* (1959), Eliot hoped to achieve philosophical depth in a context that would be appreciated by a wide audience by fusing contemporary settings, situations, and dialogue with classical forms and allusions.

Eliot has also exerted considerable influence on twentieth-century literary criticism. A. Alvarez claimed that "[our] interests and standards in literature are

Eliot's creation. . . . His critical pronouncements were made valid by his poetry. So he did more than change the standards of critical judgment; he altered the whole mode of expression in order to make room for his originality." Eliot's work is considered a major force behind the rise of New Criticism in England and the United States during the 1930s and 1940s. This movement advocated a move away from Romanticism toward a more intellectual and methodological evaluation of art. Two of Eliot's concepts are considered important contributions to critical analysis: "objective correlative" and "dissociation of sensibility." In the essay "Hamlet and His Problems" in *The Sacred Wood: Essays on Poetry and Criticism* (1920), Eliot defined the objective correlative as "a set of objects, a situation, a chain of events which shall be the formula of [a] particular emotion" and which have the ability to evoke that emotion in the reader. This idea, in its insistence on expression that is balanced and objective, runs contrary to Romantic tenets. Eliot first discussed dissociation of sensibility in his essay "The Metaphysical Poets." Dissociation of sensibility, as described by Eric Thompson, "is the dislocation of thought from feeling and feeling from thought that occurs when language orbits too far out from a metaphysical center." For Eliot, the dislocation of sensibility began in English literature in the early seventeenth century and he cites Dante and John Donne as poets whose works encompass metaphysical conflicts and who "possessed a mechanism of sensibility which could devour any kind of experience." In essays collected in such works as *The Use of Poetry and the Use of Criticism, After Strange Gods: A Primer of Modern Heresy* and *Notes towards the Definition of Culture,* Eliot stresses the importance of tradition, religion, and morality in literature and society.

Beginning in the 1950s, new experimental techniques in poetry, the revival of the Romantic belief in the primacy of the individual, and the emergence of personal or "confessional" poetry led to a decline in Eliot's authority and popularity. In his 1928 essay "For Lancelot Andrewes," Eliot had declared himself "an Anglo-Catholic in religion, a classicist in literature, and a royalist in politics," and this conservatism also contributed to his fall from favor. Most recent critics, however, while expressing occasional reservations about Eliot's personal ideology, agree that his profoundly innovative, erudite approach to poetry and criticism has had a permanent impact on literature. The divergence of critical opinion on the ultimate worth of Eliot's accomplishments continues, but, as Northrop Frye observed, "A thorough knowledge of Eliot is compulsory for anyone interested in contemporary literature. Whether he is liked or disliked is of no importance, but he must be read."

(For further information about Eliot's life and works, see *Concise Dictionary of American Literary Biography, 1929-1941; Contemporary Authors,* Vols. 5-8, 25-28; *Contemporary Literary Criticism,* Vols. 1, 2, 3, 6, 9, 10, 13, 15, 24, 34, 41, 55, 57; and *Dictionary of Literary Biography,* Vols. 7, 10, 45, 63. For related criticism, see the entry on New Criticism in *Twentieth-Century Literary Criticism,* Vol. 34.)

CRITICAL COMMENTARY

DELMORE SCHWARTZ
(essay date 1949)

[An American poet, short story writer, critic, and dramatist, Schwartz is frequently associated with a 1940s group of writers and critics known as "the New York Intellectuals." Members of this group were linked by their Jewish heritage, leftist political views, and endorsement of modernism. In the following 1949 revision of a 1947 lecture, he evaluates Eliot's literary criticism.]

When we think of the character of literary dictators in the past, it is easy to see that since 1922, at least, Eliot has occupied a position in the English-speaking world analogous to that occupied by Ben Jonson, Dryden, Pope, Samuel Johnson, Coleridge, and Matthew Arnold. It is noticeable that each of these dictators has been a critic as well as a poet, and we may infer from this the fact that it is necessary for them to practice both poetry and criticism.

Another characteristic is that each of these literary dictators has in some way reversed the judgments of his immediate predecessor. (p. 119)

When we come to Eliot's reign, we find that something has really been added: we have virtually two dictatorships from one literary dictator. Between 1922 and 1933 Eliot, in a series of unprecedented essays which were initially disguised as book reviews, revaluated the history of English poetry in one set of terms; between 1933 and 1946 he gradually reversed his whole evaluation. . . . Thus it is almost possible to say of Eliot, "The dictator has abdicated. Long live the dictator!" This is the only instance I know where anyone has

Principal Works

Prufrock and Other Observations (poetry) 1917

Poems (poetry) 1919

Ara Vos Prec (poetry) 1920

The Sacred Wood: Essays on Poetry and Criticism (criticism) 1920

The Waste Land (poetry) 1922

Homage to John Dryden: Three Essays on Poetry of the Seventeenth Century (criticism) 1924

Poems, 1909-1925 (poetry) 1925

The Journey of the Magi (poetry) 1927

For Lancelot Andrewes: Essays on Style and Order (criticism) 1928

Ash-Wednesday (poetry) 1930

Selected Essays, 1917-1932 (criticism) 1932

The Use of Poetry and the Use of Criticism: Studies in the Relation of Criticism to Poetry in England (criticism) 1933

After Strange Gods: A Primer of Modern Heresy (criticism) 1934

Murder in the Cathedral (drama) 1935

The Family Reunion (drama) 1939

The Idea of a Christian Society (criticism) 1939

Old Possum's Book of Practical Cats (poetry) 1939

*East Coker (poetry) 1940

*Burnt Norton (poetry) 1941

*The Dry Salvages (poetry) 1941

*Little Gidding (poetry) 1942

Notes Towards the Definition of Culture (criticism) 1948

The Cocktail Party (drama) 1950

The Complete Poems and Plays, 1909-1950 (poetry and dramas) 1952

The Confidential Clerk (drama) 1954

On Poetry and Poets (criticism) 1957

The Elder Statesman (drama) 1959

Collected Poems, 1909-1962 (poetry) 1963

To Criticize the Critic, and Other Writings (criticism) 1965

The Complete Poems and Plays of T. S. Eliot (poetry and dramas) 1969

The Letters of T. S. Eliot: Volume I, 1898-1922 (letters) 1988

*These works were published as Four Quartets in 1943.

abdicated and immediately succeeded to his own throne.

We can take 1922 as the approximate beginning of the first period, for in that year Eliot began to edit *The Criterion,* and *"The Waste Land"* was published in the first number, although it was in 1921 that Eliot published the reviews in the *London Times Literary Supplement* which were later collected as *Three Essays in Homage to John Dryden.* In the most famous of these essays, **"Metaphysical Poets,"** Eliot declared that English poetry had not been the same since the death of John Donne. . . . Since the time of Donne, according to this essay, there have been no poets in English who really enjoyed a unity of sensibility. What Eliot means by "unity of sensibility," a dubious psychological phrase, is difficult to make clear, but can perhaps best be stated by paraphrasing Eliot's remark that Donne felt his thoughts at the tips of his senses. All poets since Donne, with a few exceptional moments of unity, have permitted their thoughts and their emotions to be separated. (pp. 119-20)

By 1934 Eliot had fruitfully contradicted, modified or qualified practically all the literary and critical judgments implicit in this essay. . . . In 1937, when questioned during a radio interview on the British Broadcasting Company about what he regarded as great poetry, he replied that Wordsworth's "Independence and Resolution" and Coleridge's "Ode on Dejec-

tion" were probably "touchstones of greatness." This is a far cry from what Eliot said in 1922. . . .

I do not mean to imply in the least that Eliot is merely contradictory. It is true that no one could have guessed, by reading his essay on the **"Metaphysical Poets"** in 1922, that by 1937 he would admire Wordsworth and Coleridge very much and cite them, rather than Donne, as "touchstones of greatness." . . . But on the other hand, there is a real unity in back of all of these seemingly contradictory judgments. One basis of this unity is the admiration for Dante which obviously began when Eliot was still an undergraduate. If we understand Eliot's gradual and profound re-reading of Dante, then we can see how at one point, fascinated by one aspect of Dante, he would be likely to salute Donne, while at a later stage it would be natural for him to admire the characteristic directness and clarity of the poems by Wordsworth and Coleridge which he cited as touchstones of what is great in poetry. If we examine these poems carefully, we can see that in the most direct way they resemble the very beginning of *The Divine Comedy.* (p. 121)

[Five standards were] involved in Eliot's initial evaluation of the history of English poetry and his subsequent revaluation.

They can be named in a summary and incomplete way as follows: first, actuality; second, honesty . . . ;

third, the purification and maintenance of the English language; fourth, the dramatic sense . . . ; fifth, the quality of the versification. (p. 124)

Eliot makes it clear that a sense of the actual is really incomplete and warped without a sense of the past. . . . But we must be careful not to misunderstand Eliot's concern with a sense of the past as mere nostalgia for the days when knighthood was in flower. It is the past as actual, as an actual part of the present, which concerns Eliot. And one must have a strong sense of actuality in order to know just what of the past is alive in the present and what is merely a monument or a souvenir. Without a sense of the past, one's sense of the actual is likely to be confused with an obsessive pursuit of what is degraded, or idiosyncratic, or transitory, or brand-new. This is the dead-end of the naturalistic novelist who supposes that the slum is somehow more real than the library. Conversely, a sense of the actual enables one to understand the past itself as something which was not by any means Arcadian. Perhaps one can go so far as to say that one cannot have much of a sense of the past without a sense of the actual or much of a sense of the actual without a sense of the past. Thus, to use an example which can stand for much that is characteristic of Eliot, if one looks at a church, one does not really see very much of what one is looking at if one does not have both a sense of the actual, a sense of the past, and a sense of the past *as* actual in the present.

Let me turn now to a few instances of how Eliot uses the criterion of actuality in his criticism. Blake is praised because one of his poems expresses "the naked observation" and another "the naked insight." . . . In the same essay, which was written in 1920, Blake is praised because he possesses the peculiar honesty, which according to Eliot, is peculiar to all great poetry, an honesty which is to be found, Eliot says, in Homer, Aeschylus, and Dante, and an honesty which is, he adds, in a world too frightened to be honest, curiously terrifying, an honesty against which the whole world conspires because it is unpleasant. Here we can see how closely connected in Eliot's mind are the sense of the actual and the ability of a poet to be honest. (pp. 125-26)

There is [an] important negative instance. Eliot speaks of the images in the plays of Beaumont and Fletcher as "cut and slightly withered flowers stuck in the sand" in comparison with the images of Shakespeare, Donne, Webster, and Middleton, which have, he says, "tentacular roots" which reach down to "the deepest terrors and desires." In the same way, Tennyson is praised for his great technical skill but the quotations which Eliot cites, in 1936, when he reverses his judgment of Tennyson are praised because they are descriptions of a particular time and place. (p. 126)

[We] can see here the underlying unity which is involved in Eliot's revision of his first evaluation of English poetry. For in praising Blake as one who was unpleasantly honest and full of naked observations and insights, Eliot said that such honesty could not exist apart from great technical skill. In his first revaluation Eliot had praised Tennyson for his technical skill but dismissed him as one who merely ruminated. When Eliot came to revise his judgment of Tennyson in 1936, his revision was consequent upon a study of Tennyson's versification, which led him to see how that poet's great technical skill did in fact, at times, enable him to render the actual and not merely ruminate upon it. Thus, in a sense, Eliot is consistent throughout; the reason that a revision has been necessary is that Eliot was burdened by preconceptions which belonged to the period in which he was writing, and he had simply not read sufficiently in some of the poets he dismissed.

So too with the poetry of Milton, although I do not think that here it is a question of insufficient reading. When Eliot says in depreciation of some of Milton's poems that they are conventional, artificial, and enamelled, he is complaining again about the absence of the actual. . . . It seems to me likely enough that by now Eliot has perceived beneath the perhaps artificial and certainly grandiloquent surface of Milton's language precisely that peculiar honesty about the essential strength or sickness of the human soul, which he found in Dante, Shakespeare, Blake, and other of the very greatest poets. I should think that this desirable revision of opinion may also have come about as a result of the development of Eliot's own writing during recent years. (pp. 126-27)

Let us return now to the other touchstones, or criteria, of poetic genuineness.

Honesty is perhaps a shorthand term for a willingness to face the reality of one's emotions. . . . [A] poet's honesty is, in fact, very often a concern with morality, with the actuality of morality. Yet this moralism must be distinguished carefully from that overt didacticism which has spoiled the work of many great artists such as Tolstoy and resulted in the censorship of more than one masterpiece. Notice I have said the actuality of morality rather than simply morality as such. . . . [An] elucidation is to be found in Eliot's discussion of Hamlet. . . . To conclude that *Hamlet* is a failure, as Eliot does, though it is the most read, performed, and studied of all plays, seems to me to have a curious notion of success. To inquire as to why he wrote the play at all is incomprehensible in view of the remarks Eliot makes about the artist's effort to deal with emotions which are ecstatic, terrible, and inexpressibly horrifying. But I am not concerned so much with the wrongness of Eliot's judgment in an essay written as early as 1919 as I am concerned with the relation of these remarks to the honesty of the poet and the actuality of moral existence, to which these remarks point. The poet's honesty, and thus his morality, consists in his ability to face the ecstasy and the terror of his emotions, his desires, his fears, his aspirations, and his failure to realize his and other human beings' moral allegiances. Thus the morality of the poet consists not in teaching other human beings how to behave, but in facing the deepest emotional and moral realities in his poems, and in this way making it possible for his readers to confront the total reality of their existence, physical, emotional, moral and religious. (pp. 128-29)

[Eliot] looks always for those qualities in a poem which are likely to help the reader to see reality, if not to bear it. (p. 129)

The third of the standards with which Eliot has criticized poetry is language as such. . . .

In English poetry, . . . Eliot finds that two of the greatest masters of diction are Milton and Dryden and they triumph, he says, "by a dazzling disregard of the human soul." Here again there is an underlying consistency in the operation of Eliot's mind, for what he is saying of Dryden and Milton is close to what he had said in 1920 of Swinburne as being purely verbal, of using language really divorced from any reference to objects. And it should be noted that only by a very strong sense of the actual can we distinguish between poetry which explores the human soul and poetry which is largely verbal. There is an intermediate mode: poetry whose chief aim is that of incantation, of inducing a certain state of emotion. (p. 131)

If we take this concern with language in isolation it might seem that the chief purpose of poetry was to maintain and purify the language, and indeed Eliot's praise of Dryden often seems to be bestowed on that poet merely because he effected a reformation in the use of language, rather than for his intrinsic qualities. Throughout Eliot's own poetry there are references to the difficulties and trials of anyone who attempts to use language carefully. . . . [Throughout] Eliot's criticism the quality of the poet's language and its effect upon the future of the English language has always concerned Eliot very much. I think we can say that never before has criticism been so conscious of all that can happen to language, how easily it can be debased, and how marvelously it can be elevated and made to illuminate the most difficult and delicate areas of experience.

The fourth criterion is the dramatic sense, and Eliot maintains that all great poetry is dramatic. However, there is perhaps some confusion here, since Eliot means by dramatic the attitudes and emotions of a human being in a given situation. But when he comes to apply this broad definition, he is often influenced by his own love of Elizabethan drama, where the term, dramatic, narrows itself to the specific theatrical sense of the word, a sense in which it must be distinguished from meaning any human being's attitudes in any situ-

ation. . . . Eliot sometimes uses this criterion of the dramatic to enforce prejudices about poetry which he does not like for other reasons.

We come, finally, to the question of versification. It is here that Eliot has been most influenced by his own poetic practice. For at one time or another he has enunciated practically every possible theory of what the nature of versification is. In a late essay on the poetry of Yeats he says that blank verse cannot be written in the 20th century because it still retains its period quality. The period presumably is the Elizabethan one, and such a statement is belied by the fact that not only has some of Eliot's best poetry been written in blank verse, but such a statement disregards the triumphs of blank verse, the inexhaustible variety of this form of versification to be found in Milton, Wordsworth, in Keats' "Hyperion," in certain poems of Tennyson which Eliot himself has praised precisely for their technical mastery of blank verse, and in Browning; many other instances could be mentioned. Eliot's fundamental concern has been, however, with what he calls the "auditory imagination," "the feeling for syllable and rhythm, penetrating far below the conscious levels of thought and feeling, invigorating every word; sinking to the most primitive and forgotten, returning to the origin and bringing something back; seeking the beginning and the end." This should suggest that underneath the contradictory statements about the possibilities of versification which run throughout Eliot's criticism, there is a powerful intuition of how various, unpredictable, and profound are the possibilities of language when it is versified. (pp. 131-33)

If we examine Eliot's scrutiny of English versification from the time of Marlowe to the time of Hardy and Yeats, and are not seduced into glib and futile logic-chopping, we come upon a theory of the nature of versification which seems to do justice to the many different things that Eliot has said about it. Namely, the theory that the essence of metre and thus of versification is any repetitive pattern of words, and the endless arguments about versification from Campion to Amy Lowell and the Free Verse movement are caused by the curious feeling that some *one* repetitive pattern, or kind of pattern, is the only true method of versification. (p. 134)

Let me now try to place Eliot's criticism in terms of a classification which was first suggested by the late Irving Babbitt, and I believe misused by him. Babbitt speaks of impressionistic criticism, scientific criticism, neo-classic criticism, and a fourth kind to which he gives no name . . . : a kind of criticism which is sometimes called the test of time or the verdict of posterity. This fourth kind presents many difficulties, including the fact that the posterity of the past, the only posterity we know about, has changed its mind so often. . . . (pp. 134-35)

Babbitt's other three kinds of criticism are also, I think, inadequate classifications. For example, when Babbitt speaks of scientific criticism, what he really means is historical criticism, since he cites Taine as its leading exponent. What we ought to distinguish and emphasize is the purpose which each kind of critic has in mind when he takes hold of a literary work. The neo-classic critic looks in the new literary work for the specific characteristics which he has found in masterpieces of the past. . . . The historical critic is interested in the causes, social and biographical, of the literary work rather than in the work itself. The impressionistic critic is interested in the effects of the literary work upon himself as a delicate and rare sensibility rather than in the work as an objective and social phenomenon. The historical critic goes in back of the work to its causes; the impressionistic critic is concerned with himself rather than with the work itself. . . . Eliot's criticism fits none of these classifications, although it is to be regretted that there has not been more of the historical critic in him. He has proceeded, as I have said, by intuition and by seeking out what most interested him from time to time. Yet, at his best he has been what I would like to call the classic kind of critic, the critic who is expert precisely because he depends upon the quality of his own experience, while, at the same time being aware that the more experience of literature he has, the more expert he becomes. There are no substitutes for experience, a platitude which is ignored invariably by the neo-classic critic, whose essential effort is to deduce from classics of the past a ready-made formula for judging any new work. Eliot's classicism at its best is illustrated when he says that if a truly classic work were written in our time, it would not be recognized as such by most of us. It would seem so monstrous, so queer and horrifying. . . . [The] truly classical critic, the true expert, depends upon experience, and permits experience to correct his errors in appreciation. Experience is thus for the expert, or classical critic, not only the great teacher but the best text book. Eliot, in revising his initial revaluation of English poetry, has permitted experience to teach him as no theory and no authority possibly could.

Having reviewed this long and complex critical career, we come finally to the question of what conclusions we can draw and what lessons we can gain from it. It seems to me that we have reached a point in our knowledge of the history of taste, the history of literary reputation, and literary judgment, where we can clearly mark out some of the most important dangers and pitfalls involved in any kind of literary criticism. Is it not clear that the kind of action and reaction which characterizes so good a critic as Eliot may very well be the expense of spirit in a waste of false discrimination? Is it necessary, in order to praise poets A, B, and C, to condemn poets D, E, F, G, H, and the rest of the alphabet?

Perhaps it is necessary, but if we think concretely of the really shocking blunders in taste which prevail throughout literary history, then perhaps the very consciousness of these blunders can help us to arrive at a point of view in which there is no mere seesaw of praise and rejection. . . . The point is that the more we know about the history of literary reputation and literary opinion, the more conscious we are of how unjust and how stupid even the greatest critics can be, the more likely we are to avoid such errors in our own experience of literature. The matter is not merely a question of the reader's welfare; the creative writer himself is crucially involved. . . . [It] does not seem to me to be claiming too much for literary criticism when one declares that upon the goodness, the consciousness, and the justice of literary criticism the very existence of great works sometimes depends. . . . I should add at this point that it is only by a knowledge of the literary past that contemporary critical practice can be of much use in preventing new neglect, stupidity, unjustified admiration, and unwarranted blindness. Two of the best poets of the 19th century, Gerard Manley Hopkins and Emily Dickinson, went to their graves with hardly any external recognition; it is quite possible that they did not really know that they had written good poetry. . . . By reviewing Eliot's critical career we can envisage a point of view which will free our scrutiny of literature from many of the sins of the past, while at the same time illuminating anew all that we have inherited from the past. And we can, I think, see how it might be desirable to have no literary dictators. (pp. 135-37)

Delmore Schwartz, "The Literary Dictatorship of T. S. Eliot," in *Partisan Review,* Vol. XVI, No. 2, February, 1949, pp. 119-37.

JOHN BERRYMAN

(essay date 1949)

[Berryman was an American poet, biographer, novelist, and critic. He is best known as the author of *The Dream Songs* (1969), an unconventional, innovative poem sequence often compared to Walt Whitman's *Leaves of Grass*. In the excerpt below from a 1949 essay, he analyzes "The Love Song of J. Alfred Prufrock," discerning qualities that distinguish it as part of the genesis of modern poetry.]

To begin with Eliot's title, **"The Love Song of J. Alfred Prufrock,"** is the second half quite what the first led us to expect? A man named J. Alfred Prufrock could hardly be expected to sing a love song; he sounds too well dressed. His name takes something away from the notion of a love song; the form of the title, that is to say, is reductive. How does he begin singing?

Let us go then, you and I,
When the evening is spread out against the sky . . .

That sounds very pretty—lyrical—he does seem, after all, in spite of his name, to be inviting her for an evening; there is a nice rhyme—it sounds like other dim romantic verse. Then comes the third line:

Like a patient etherised upon a table . . .

With this line, modern poetry begins.

In the first place, the third line proves that the author of the first two lines did not mean them. They were a come-on, designed merely to get the reader off guard, so that he could be knocked down. The form, again, is reductive; an expectation has been created only to be diminished or destroyed. . . . And the word "then"—"Let us go *then*"—is really very unpromising; if he had only said, "Let us go," it would have sounded much more as if they were going to go; "Let us go then" sounds as if he had been giving it thought, and thought suggests hesitation. Of course he never goes at all: *the visit, involving the "overwhelming question," the proposal of marriage, is never made*. Here again we come on a reduction.

Also, the simile is not visual: it only pretends to be. No reader could possibly be assisted in seeing the evening spread out against the sky by having his attention suddenly and violently called to a patient laid out on an operating table. The device of simile is being put to a novel use, violating the ordinary logic of verse, just as the abrupt vision of a hospital violates the lyrical notion of an evening stroll.

What does the line mean? We are obliged to resort to suggestion, not to logic. The situation of a patient under ether is unenviable, risky: he is about to be cut into, soon he may be dead. This fear is basic to the poem: Prufrock finally says, in fact, "I was afraid." On the other hand, the situation of the patient can be regarded as desirable in that he *has* made a decision and now the result is out of his hands, he has no further responsibility, it is up to the surgeon to save him or not. This desire—to *have made* the proposal, and to have his fate left up to the woman—is also basic to the poem. We may think of that as quite a lot of work to get done in one line. Of course, the suggestion that Prufrock sees himself as *ill* is important also, and we will return to this.

Between the title, with its slight effect of double-take, and these opening lines, with their full effect of double-take, the poet has inserted an epigraph in Italian, six lines of it. A knowledge of Italian is of very little help. All the lines say is, "If I thought what I am going to tell you would ever get back to the world, you would hear nothing from me. But as it is," and so on. One has to know *who* is speaking in Dante's *Divine Comedy*. This is a lost soul, in Hell, damned in particular be-cause he tried to purchase absolution *before* committing a crime. We are obliged to consider, that is, as of Prufrock with his dilemma of whether or not to propose marriage, whether the fundamental reason he does not do so—his sin—is his refusal to take the ordinary, inevitable human risks: he wants to know beforehand whether he will be accepted or not—in fact, he does *think* he knows already what will happen—but this belongs later for us.

Everything we have been saying paints a picture as different as possible from that of a writer sitting down to entertain, beguile, charm, and lull a reader or readers. Obstacles and surprise, of no pleasant kind, are this poet's stock-in-trade. The reader's expectation that *one* thing will happen is the first to be attacked. Several things are going to be happening simultaneously. One feels, even, a certain hostility on the part of the poet. The modern poet, characteristically, has *lost confidence* in his readers . . . , but so far from causing him to reduce his demands therefore, this loss of confidence has led to an *increase* in his demands. Good poetry has never been easy to read with any advanced understanding, but it has seldom been made so deliberately difficult.

Shall we . . . suggest that the poet's impatience is based on the fact that the reader's mind is full of vague and grandiose assumptions which seem to the poet contemptible? The poet sees himself as a warning voice, like a Hebrew prophet calling on the people to repent, to understand better themselves and the world. . . . Eliot had pretty certainly not read Freud when he wrote this poem. In some ways, however, their thought is parallel, for the "you" whom Prufrock invites to go with him for the visit must be another part of his own personality, whom he vainly invites to join him in the great task before them. . . . (pp. 270-72)

But the "you" is perhaps also the reader, addressed thus surprisingly in this dramatic monologue; and this device is French, part of the general air of elaborate sophistication adopted by Eliot in this poem. This tone is not original; it is borrowed from the French symbolist poet Jules Laforgue (1860-87), under whose influence Eliot first found his own voice. Some of the characteristic properties in **"Prufrock"** are Laforgue's, allusions to Hamlet and the sirens. But there is influence also from Elizabethan drama, in the speech rhythms (the poem is written in what is called "free verse," which only means that the laws it obeys are different from those of traditional stanza or blank verse); and there is influence from prose works, especially the expatriate American novelist Henry James's. In any event, Laforgue could never have conceived or written the poem. He only supplied the *manner*, and anyway his music—very beautiful sometimes—is hardly Eliot's.

Eliot's manner is highly sophisticated, but perhaps we ought not to call the poem sophisticated. Let us call it primitive. The poem pretends to be a love song. It is something much more practical. It is a study—a debate by Prufrock with himself—over the *business* of proposing marriage. . . . The first half of the poem looks forward to the proposal, the second half looks back on how it *would* have gone if it had gone at all. The poem is intensely anti-romantic, and its extremely serious subject, in a so-called Love Song, is another rebuke to the [reader]. . . . It is clear that the poet sympathizes with Prufrock. It is also clear that the poet damns Prufrock. Some of the basic emotions of the poem are primitive also—fear, malice—but lust is absent, and the prevailing surface tone is one of civilized, overcivilized anxiety. Prufrock's feelings are rather abstract; he never makes the woman real at all, except in one terrible respect, which let us reserve a little. He is concerned with himself. He is mentally ill, neurotic, incapable of love. But the problem that he faces is a primitive problem.

Eliot brings to bear on Prufrock's dilemma four figures out of the spiritual history of man: Michelangelo, John the Baptist, Lazarus, and Hamlet. (pp. 272-73)

The resort to these four analogues from artistic and sacred history suggests a man—desperate, in his ordeal—ransacking the past for help in the present, and *not finding it*—finding only ironic parallels, or real examples, of his predicament. The available tradition, the poet seems to be saying, is of no use to us. It supplies only analogies and metaphors for our pain. (p. 275)

It must be obvious . . . that this extraordinarily ambitious poem, including as it does acrid sketches not only of man's spiritual but of his biological history, is not designed as entertainment, whatever the author may say to us (Eliot has defined poetry as "a superior amusement"), and whatever his mask *inside* the poem: the sophisticate, the disillusioned, the dandy with his particular social problem in Boston. . . . The poet has adopted the guise of light verse, but he writes as a prophet, without any trace of conciliation toward any possible audience. He does not write *directly*. He uses the mask of Prufrock—whose fate is like that of what are called the Vigliacchi in Dante. These sinners did neither good nor evil, and so they cannot be admitted even to Hell, lest the damned feel a certain superiority to them; they suffer eternally in what is called the vestibule of Hell. It is better, as Eliot says in one of his critical essays, to do evil than to do nothing. At least one exists in a relation to the moral world. Under this mask he sets up a ruinous antithesis to Victorian hope—in particular, to what must have seemed to him the vacuous optimism of the most recent master of dramatic monologue in English before him, Browning. Civilization is not condemned. The *results* of civilization are dramatized, that is all; above all, the destruction of the ability to love, and—in the well-meaning man—to be decisive. The poet speaks, in this poem, of a society sterile and suicidal. (pp. 277-78)

John Berryman, "Prufrock's Dilemma," in his *The Freedom of the Poet,* Farrar, Straus and Giroux, Inc., 1976, pp. 270-78.

RICHARD ELLMANN
(essay date 1971)

[Ellmann was an American critic, biographer, literary historian, and editor who wrote widely on early twentieth-century Irish literature and was an authority on the life and works of James Joyce. In the following excerpt, he studies *The Waste Land*, commenting on aspects of the poem inspired by events in Eliot's personal life as well as revisions made by Ezra Pound.]

Lloyd's most famous bank clerk revalued the poetic currency forty-nine years ago. As Joyce said, *The Waste Land* ended the idea of poetry for ladies. Whether admired or detested, it became, like *Lyrical Ballads* in 1798, a traffic signal. Hart Crane's letters, for instance, testify to his prompt recognition that from that time forward his work must be to outflank Eliot's poem. Today footnotes do their worst to transform innovations into inevitabilities. After a thousand explanations, *The Waste Land* is no longer a puzzle poem, except for the puzzle of choosing among the various solutions. To be penetrable is not, however, to be predictable. The sweep and strangeness with which Eliot delineated despair resist temptations to patronize Old Possum as old hat. Particular discontinuities continue to surprise even if the idea of discontinuous form—which Eliot himself was to forsake—is now almost as familiar as its sober counterpart. The compound of regular verse and vers libre still wears some of the effrontery with which in 1922 it flouted both schools. The poem retains the air of a splendid feat.

Eliot himself was inclined to pooh-pooh its grandeur. His chiseled comment, which F. O. Matthiessen quotes, disclaimed any intention of expressing "the disillusionment of a generation," and said that he did not like the word "generation" or have a plan to endorse anyone's "illusion of disillusion." To Theodore Spencer he remarked in humbler mood,

Various critics have done me the honor to interpret the poem in terms of criticism of the contemporary world, have considered it, indeed, as an important bit of social criticism. To me it was only the relief of a personal and wholly insignificant grouse against life. It is just a piece of rhythmical grumbling.

This statement is prominently displayed by Mrs. Valerie Eliot in her superb decipherment and elucidation of *The Waste Land* manuscript. If it is more than an expression of her husband's genuine modesty, it appears to imply that he considered his own poem, as he considered *Hamlet,* an inadequate projection of its author's tangled emotions, a Potemkin village rather than a proper objective correlative. Yet no one will wish away the entire civilizations and cities, wars, hordes of people, religions of East and West, and exhibits from many literatures in many languages which lined the Thames in Eliot's ode to dejection. And even if London was only his state of mind at the time, the picture he paints of it is convincing.

His remark to Spencer, made after a lapse of years, perhaps catches up another regret, that the poem emphasized his disgust at the expense of much else in his nature. It identified him with a sustained severity of tone, with pulpited (though brief) citations of Biblical and Sophoclean anguish, so that he became an Ezekiel or at least a Tiresias. (In the original version John the Divine made a Christian third among the prophets.) While Eliot did not wish to be considered merely a satirist in his earlier verse, he did not welcome either the public assumption that his poetic mantle had become a hair shirt.

In its early version *The Waste Land* was woven out of more kinds of material and was therefore less grave and less organized. The first two sections had an over-all title (each had its own title as well), "He Do the Police in Different Voices," a quotation from *Our Mutual Friend.* Dickens has the widow Higden say of her adopted child, "Sloppy is a beautiful reader of a newspaper. He do the Police in different voices." Among the many voices in the first version, Eliot placed at the very beginning a long, conversational passage describing an evening on the town, starting at "Tom's place" (a rather arch use of his own name), moving on to a brothel, and concluding with a bathetic sunrise. . . . This vapid prologue Eliot decided, apparently on his own, to expunge, and went straight into the now familiar beginning of the poem.

Other voices were expunged by Eliot's friend Ezra Pound, who called himself the *"sage homme"* (male midwife) of the poem. For example, there was an extended, unsuccessful imitation of *The Rape of the Lock* at the beginning of "The Fire Sermon." . . . The episode of the typist was originally much longer and more laborious. . . . (p. 10)

Pound persuaded Eliot also to omit a number of poems which were for a time intended to be placed between the poem's sections, then at the end of it. One was a renewed thrust at poor Bleistein, drowned now but still haplessly Jewish and luxurious under water. . . . Pound urged that this and several other mortuary poems did not add anything either to *The Waste Land* or to Eliot's previous work. He had already written "the longest poem in the English langwidge. Don't try to bust all records by prolonging it three

pages further." As a result of this resmithying by *il miglior fabbro,* the poem gained immensely in concentration. Yet Eliot, feeling too solemnized by it, thought of prefixing some humorous doggerel by Pound about its composition. Later, in a more resolute effort to escape the limits set by *The Waste Land,* he wrote "Fragment of Agon," and eventually, "somewhere the other side of despair," turned to drama.

Eliot's remark to Spencer calls *The Waste Land* a personal poem. His critical theory was that the artist should seek impersonality, but this was probably intended as not so much a nostrum as an antidote, a means to direct emotion rather than let it spill. His letters indicate that he regarded his poems as consequent upon his experiences. When a woman in Dublin remarked that Yeats had never really felt anything, Eliot asked in consternation, "How can you say that?" *The Waste Land* compiled many of the nightmarish feelings he had suffered during the seven years from 1914 to 1921, that is, from his coming to England until his temporary collapse.

Thanks to the letters quoted in Mrs. Valerie Eliot's Introduction, and to various biographical leaks, the incidents of these years begin to take shape. (pp. 10, 12)

The personal life out of which came Eliot's personal poem now began to be lived in earnest. Vivienne Eliot suffered obscurely from nerves, her health was subject to frequent collapses, she complained of neuralgia, of insomnia. Ezra Pound, who knew her well, was worried that the passage in *The Waste Land,*

My nerves are bad to-night. Yes, bad. Stay with me.
Speak to me. Why do you never speak? Speak.
What are you thinking of ? What thinking? What?
I never know what you are thinking. Think.

might be too photographic. But Vivienne Eliot, who offered her own comments on her husband's verse (and volunteered two excellent lines for the lowlife dialogue in "A Game of Chess"), marked the same passage as "Wonderful." She relished the presentation of her symptoms in broken meter. She was less keen, however, on another line from this section,

The ivory men make company between us,

and got her husband to remove it. Presumably its implications were too close to the quick of their marital difficulties. Years afterward Eliot made a fair copy of *The Waste Land* in his own handwriting, and reinserted the line from memory. (It should now be added to the final text.) But he had implied his feelings six months after his marriage when he wrote in a letter to Conrad Aiken, "I have lived through material for a score of long poems in the last six months."

Russell commented less sympathetically about the Eliots later, "I was fond of them both, and endeavoured to help them in their troubles until I discovered that their troubles were what they enjoyed." Eliot was capable of estimating the situation shrewdly himself. In his poem **"The Death of Saint Narcissus,"** which *Poetry* was to publish in 1917 and then, probably at his request, failed to do, he wrote of his introspective saint, "his flesh was in love with the burning arrows. . . . As he embraced them his white skin surrendered itself to the redness of blood, and satisfied him."

For Eliot, however, the search for suffering was not contemptible. He was remorseful about his own real or imagined feelings, he was self-sacrificing about hers, he thought that remorse and sacrifice, not to mention affection, had value. In the Grail legends which underlie *The Waste Land,* the Fisher King suffers a Dolorous Stroke which maims him sexually. In Eliot's case the Dolorous Stroke had been marriage. He was helped thereby to the poem's initial clash of images, "April is the cruellest month," as well as to hollow echoes of Spenser's *Prothalamion* ("Sweet Thames, run softly till I end my song"). From the barren winter of his academic labors Eliot had been roused to the barren springtime of his nerve-wracked marriage. His life spread into paradox.

Other events of these years seem reflected in the poem. The war, though scarcely mentioned, exerts pressure. In places the poem may be a covert memorial to Henry Ware Eliot, the unforgiving father of the ill-adventured son. Henry Eliot died in January, 1919, and Eliot's first explicit statement of his intention to write a long poem comes in letters written later in the year. The references to a father's death probably derive as much from this actual death as from *The Tempest,* to which Eliot's notes evasively refer. As for the drowning of the young sailor, whether he is Ferdinand or a Phoenician, the war furnished Eliot with many examples, such as Jean Verdenal, a friend from his Sorbonne days, who was killed in the Dardanelles. But it may be as well an extrapolation of Eliot's feeling that he was now fatherless as well as rudderless.

The fact that the principal speaker appears in a new guise in the last section, with its imagery of possible resurrection, suggests that the drowning is to be taken symbolically rather than literally, as the end of youth. Eliot was addicted to the portrayal of characters who had missed their chances, become old before they had really been young. So the drowned sailor, like the buried corpse, may be construed as the young Eliot, buried in or about *"i'an trentiésme de son eage,"* like the young Pound in the first part of *Hugh Selwyn Mauberley.*

It has been thought that Eliot wrote *The Waste Land* in Switzerland while recovering from a breakdown. But much of it was written earlier, some in 1914 and some, if Conrad Aiken is to be believed, even before. A letter to Quinn indicates that much of it was on paper in May, 1921. The breakdown or, rather, the rest

1938 portrait of Eliot by Wyndham Lewis.

cure did give Eliot enough time to fit the pieces together and add what was necessary. (p. 14)

The manuscript had its own history. In gratitude to John Quinn, the New York lawyer and patron of the arts, Eliot presented it to him. Quinn died in 1924, and most of his possessions were sold at auction; some, however, including the manuscript, were inherited by his sister. When the sister died, her daughter put many of Quinn's papers in storage. But in the early 1950s she searched among them and found the manuscript, which she then sold to the Berg Collection of the New York Public Library. The then curator enjoyed exercising seignorial rights over the collection, and kept secret the whereabouts of the manuscript. After his death its existence was divulged, and Valerie Eliot was persuaded to do this knowledgeable edition.

She did so the more readily, perhaps, because her husband had always hoped that the manuscript would turn up as evidence of Pound's critical genius. It is a classic document. No one will deny that it is weaker throughout than the final version. Pound comes off very well indeed; his importance is comparable to that of Louis Bouilhet in the history of the composition of

Madame Bovary. Yeats, who also sought and received Pound's help, described it to Lady Gregory, "To talk over a poem with him is like getting you to put a sentence into dialect. All becomes clear and natural." Pound could not be intimidated by pomposity, even Baudelairean pomposity:

> London, the swarming life you kill and breed,
> Huddled between the concrete and the sky;
> Responsive to the momentary need,
> Vibrates unconscious to its formal destiny.

Next to this he wrote "B-ll-S." (His comments appear in red ink on the printed transcription which is furnished along with photographs of the manuscript.) Pound was equally peremptory about a passage which Eliot seems to have cherished, perhaps because of childhood experiences in sailing. It was the depiction at the beginning of "Death by Water" of a long voyage, a modernizing and Americanizing of Ulysses' final voyage as given by Dante:

> Kingfisher weather, with a light fair breeze,
> Full canvas, and the eight sails drawing well.
> We beat around the cape and laid our course
> From the Dry Salvages to the eastern banks.
> A porpoise snored upon the phosphorescent swell,
> A triton rang the final warning bell
> Astern, and the sea rolled, asleep.

From these lines Pound was willing to spare only

> with a light fair breeze
> We beat around the cape from the Dry Salvages.
> A porpoise snored on the swell.

All the rest was seamanship and literature. It became clear that the whole passage might as well go, and Eliot asked humbly if he should delete Phlebas as well. But Pound was as eager to preserve the good as to expunge the bad: he insisted that Phlebas stay because of the earlier references to the drowned Phoenician sailor. With equal taste, he made almost no change in the last section of the poem, which Eliot always considered to be the best, perhaps because it led into his subsequent verse.

Eliot did not bow to all his friend's revisions. Pound feared the references to London might sound like Blake, and objected specifically to the lines,

> To where Saint Mary Woolnoth kept the time,
> With a dead sound on the final stroke of nine.

Eliot wisely retained them, only changing "time" to "hours." Next to the passage,

> You gave me hyacinths first a year ago;
> They called me the hyacinth girl,

Pound marked "Marianne," and evidently feared—though Mrs. Eliot's note indicates that he has forgotten—that the use of quotation marks would seem an imitation of Marianne Moore. But Eliot, for whom the moment in the hyacinth garden had obsessional force—it was based in part on an incident in his own life—made no change.

Essentially Pound could do for Eliot what Eliot could not do for himself. There was some reciprocity, because when the first three *Cantos* appeared in 1917, Eliot offered criticism which resulted in their being completely altered. It seems, from the revised versions, that he objected to the elaborate windup, and urged a more direct confrontation of the reader and the material. A similar theory is at work in Pound's changes in *The Waste Land.* Chiefly by excision, he enabled Eliot to tighten his form. Perhaps partially in reaction, he studied out means of loosening his own in the *Cantos.* (pp. 15-16)

Richard Ellmann, "The First Waste Land-I," in *The New York Review of Books,* Vol. XVII, No. 8, November 18, 1971, pp. 10, 12, 14-16.

HYATT H. WAGGONER

(essay date 1984)

[In the following excerpt, Waggoner surveys themes and techniques in Eliot's poems.]

In 1950, in the *The Heel of Elohim,* I could write, confident of general agreement, of T. S. Eliot as "the greatest poet writing in English today." My subject was American poetry, and the poets whose work I was comparing his with were Pound and Frost, Stevens not yet having been "discovered" by the critics I most respected. (p. 432)

Even by 1950 there had been some early signs of a poetic revolution to come that might have made me frame my judgment more cautiously. Delmore Schwartz in 1938 had already violated the cardinal Eliotic rule of "impersonal" poetry by doing without a persona and writing brilliantly of himself and his life, and Theodore Roethke in 1948 had published his autobiographic *The Lost Son;* but I did not yet realize Schwartz's immense promise, and it would be some years before Roethke's work was widely recognized for what it was and what it meant for the future of poetry.

By the end of the fifties there were unmistakable signs that Eliot's reign in modern poetry would not last much longer. Now the Beats were howling their discovery of Whitman and the open road, rejecting culture and tradition and taking to Zen and meditation. More significantly for poetry Lowell and Berryman were struggling to find their own voices, with Lowell's *Life Studies* (1959) being the first important, and ultimately the most influential, poetic rejection of the early Eliotic standard—a standard that Eliot himself of course had discarded in *The Four Quartets* and was busy now apologizing for in lectures. Meanwhile Randall Jarrell in *Poetry and the Age* (1953) had rescued several poets whose reputations had been hurt by Eliot's influence, especially Whitman, Frost, and Williams; and in 1960 we were urged by James Miller, Bernice Slote, and Karl Shapiro to "start with the sun" and rediscover Whitman and "the poetics of the cosmic poem."

After Eliot's death in 1965 rejection of him as man, poet, and critic quickly became the dominant fashion of the day, first among younger poets, then among younger critics. His Catholicism, at once religious and poetic, was swept aside as just as irrelevant as his announced "royalism" and "classicism" by the poetic reformers, along with all the rest that, rightly or wrongly, he was taken to stand for—cultural conservatism, "poetry of the library," and "impersonal poetry" particularly—in favor of poetry of the heart or of the psychiatrist's couch. The "invisible poet" was discovered to be visible behind his masks. To younger readers now Prufrock's trouble seemed to be not loss of belief but his excessive fastidiousness and his neurosis. . . . The New Critics might still occupy positions of power in English departments, but younger critics would soon make Stevens, not Eliot, the touchstone of the modern. A new romanticism was the order of the day, and any variety of classicism or formalism could be rejected without comment as we moved toward what one anthologist called the new naked poetry. (pp. 433-34)

Downward reassessments, after their deaths, of writers who have achieved great fame and influence during their lifetimes are commonplace; but the reaction against everything Eliotic was unusually strong, widespread, and uncritical. The effort was not to reach a more balanced judgment of his achievement but to reject, if necessary with ridicule and misreading, all that he had done and seemed to stand for. This man who had been, as John Ciardi called him, the literary equivalent of the Vatican's infallible Pope of our literature had become the enemy who must be routed if we were to move beyond modernism. Charles Olson urged his Black Mountain followers to get on with the job of "clearing away the junk of history"—religious, philosophic, and poetic. Eliot seemed to many, as he did to Williams, to be at once the spokesman for and the embodiment of that junk, so that what was called for was not a critical reassessment but a wholesale repudiation. The poetry could be ignored, but the authority of the man, with his values, attitudes, and commitments to the western tradition and particularly to an Anglo-Catholic version of that tradition, had to be rejected. The parallel with the Protestant Reformation is suggestive on several levels. The fierceness of the rejection was a measure not so much of the achievement of the poet as of the power he had wielded. (p. 434)

Enough time has now elapsed to allow young poets to find themselves as poets without being forced to choose between obedience and open rebellion and to permit the rest of us to read Eliot's poetry as we read Emerson's or Whitman's or Hardy's, not primarily as supporting or challenging our own views and values but as *poetry. . . .*

How good a poet was Eliot? What did he accomplish in his verse? Which poems seem likely to be remembered longest? His achievement as a critic seems to me to have been adequately discussed, but such questions as these seem seldom to have been addressed directly in this post-New Critical era.

What I think we should do is to follow the advice in the last words of Pound's brief contribution to the Eliot *Sewanee* issue, "READ HIM"—the poems, not the library of explications and source studies. (p. 435)

Many of the poems I once enjoyed have been spoiled for me now by too much explication. I have found it very hard, and sometimes impossible, to get a fresh impression of them when the margins of my books are cluttered with explanatory notes. But by using the one edition in my library with clean margins, I have arrived at an impression of which poems now seem to me the most rewarding to reread, volume by volume as they came out. The best of them strike me as very distinguished poetry indeed, fine enough to support the view that Eliot was one of the several greatest poets of the first half of our century, with no need for any help from all the adulatory criticism by those who not only admired the poetry without reservation but shared the poet's values and beliefs.

The poems in *Prufrock and Other Observations* (1917) that strike me as most likely to endure are ["**The Love Song of J. Alfred Prufrock**"], "**Portrait of a Lady**," and "**La Figlia che Piange.**" Many of the others seem, in varying degrees, dated, or derivative, or trivial, or, at best, not clearly superior to similar poems by other poets of about the same time or a little later. (Surely for example one could find more impressive Imagist poems than "**Hysteria**" or satirical portraits not surpassed by "**Aunt Helen.**") But the three I have named, all of which either start from the poet's personal experience—"**Portrait**"—or express feelings we can safely assume he had known, pass the test Eliot would much later, in "**A Note on War Poetry**," when he had ceased demanding "impersonal" poetry, express as "private experience at its greatest intensity / Becoming universal."

A writer need not have been as self-conscious and fastidious as Prufrock to suffer from a loss of direction and meaning in that—or our—time and to connect that loss with the loss of living myths. . . . Then and now Prufrock's problem of knowing too much to be able to believe in anything might be called the problem of the

well-educated for the last century or more. His monologue is at once that "confession" of an age that Emerson thought every generation needed from its poets and
an expression of the modern conflict between knowledge and commitment, fact and value, that put epistemology at the very center of philosophy in our century.

Of **"Portrait"** and **"La Figlia"** I would say only
this: that Eliot's **"Portrait"** is richer in meaning than
Pound's or Williams's poems of similar title, and that
"La Figlia" is a classic statement of the problem of the
artist at any time, Hawthorne's for example, as he is not
just tempted but in some sense required to *use* life, including other people and himself, as objectified material to be shaped into art. By contrast **"Morning at the
Window"** seems to me to express only depression and
snobbery, common enough of course but not interesting. It is too obvious that not all housemaids have damp
souls.

In *Poems, 1920* there are three poems I can still
read with real pleasure, the two Sweeney poems and
"The Hippopotamus"; one, **"Gerontion,"** that I can
admire without enjoying; and one, [**"Burbank with a
Baedeker: Bleistein with a Cigar"**], that I find positively distasteful. The others I should be happy never
to read again. Despite the Brahmin attitude toward the
South Boston Irish in the Sweeney poems, the speaker
in them seems to feel more pity than scorn for Sweeney, who is pictured as unaware but is not pushed
outside the human race, as Bleistein is. The poems are
an early and brilliant expression of that alienation of
intellectuals from the popular culture of the masses
that was noted by Unamuno and is still a feature of our
unhappy century. **"The Hippopotamus"** is still funny
and all the better because its satire of the church expresses the disappointment of a would-be convert.

"Gerontion" remains an historically important
poem, despite its antisemitic lines and its hints that sex
is nasty (there is much more of *this* in the parts of *The
Waste Land* that Eliot deleted from his final version),
for it gives powerful concrete expression to the alien
universe and knowledge-as-destructive-of-value-and-
meaning theme, the "nothing but" syndrome, that
would soon become so common in the work of many
of the greatest writers of the century. Reading it, we
can better understand Eliot's later conversion, as well
as the whole neoorthodox movement. Gerontion is
Prufrock as he will be in a few years, unless he can find
something to give more meaning to life than Henry
Adams's dynamo. **"Burbank"** I find simply too repulsive for comment, and not only because of its antisemi-
tism. The only possible reason for rereading it would
be to remind us of how far Eliot himself had to travel
in his effort to remake the man he found himself to be
in his youth.

The Waste Land has been far too much explicated
and discussed for me to feel that I have anything to add

about it, except as the perspective provided by sixty
years and the publication of Valerie Eliot's edition alter
our response or judgment. The poem both gave a name
to a period in literature and helped create that period.
Its diagnosis of the period, at least as far as intellectuals
and writers sensed it, was amazingly acute: the failure
of both love and belief to provide meaning for our lives.
Though Eliot would later dismiss it as no more than a
"personal gripe," the finished poem does rise to that
universality of meaning that Eliot demanded of poetry.
The passages in the early drafts that most strongly suggest merely personal gripes were omitted from the finished poem—mostly, it would seem, by Eliot himself,
not as a result of Pound's marginalia. The result is both
a less personal and a more unified, if perhaps superficially less coherent, poem suggesting that if life is taken
as a game, it's a game that can't be won. "Hurry up
please, it's time," but time is precisely what we won't
have when closing-time comes. The speaker at the end
is still fishing in the dull canal and waiting for rain, so
perhaps he will have time to profit by the words of the
thunder. (pp. 435-37)

The Hollow Men (1925) and *Ash-Wednesday*
(1930) both seem to me now to represent some falling-
off of power. *The Hollow Men* spells out at tiresome
length what had been more economically and memorably, if ambiguously, implied in **"Gerontion"** and *The
Waste Land,* and *Ash-Wednesday* is too dependent on
the Ash Wednesday service in the Book of Common
Prayer, rather thin by comparison with *The Waste
Land,* and finally expressive only of the new convert's
effort to put aside his learning and his pride and *really*
believe the words of the service he hears and says. (The
last section though I still find moving.)

Far better, it seems to me, are the two earlier post-
conversion dramatic monologues, **"Journey of the
Magi"** and **"A Song for Simeon,"** and the beautiful
lyric **"Marina."** Both the monologues seem at once
more formally "impersonal" than *The Hollow Men* and
Ash-Wednesday and yet more meaningfully revealing
of what we can suppose were the poet's own thoughts
and what he really felt. The biblical characters from
Matthew and Luke are fully realized figures, and it is
safe to assume that the poet felt a special affinity for
them, for the three kings or "wise men" whose long
and difficult journey had left them unsure of what the
birth meant, and for Simeon, who had to be content
with the knowledge that he would never be a saint, a
martyr, or a mystic granted the ultimate vision.

"Marina" seems to me the most rewarding short
poem to reread that Eliot ever wrote. Though the ambiguity first introduced by the title and the epigraph is
maintained throughout, yet this poem is a happy one,
even a joyous one. The images seem drawn not from
ancient myth but from the poet's early experience of
sailing off the coast of Cape Ann, with the mythologi-

cal Philomel replaced by the common woodthrush. The speaker finds the natural world no longer disgusting, boring, or ultimately threatening, even though the boat he has made for his journey is far from perfect, his exact location uncertain in the fog, and of course the whole feeling of being on the way may be only a dream: he cannot *know,* but seems content not to. Untypical of Eliot's poems though it is—except in the allusiveness of its title and epigraph—**"Marina"** is surely one of his greatest.

The Four Quartets may not be, as Randall Jarrell once called it, "the greatest long poem of the 20th century," but despite its unevenness it remains not only a very distinguished poem but a very moving one. . . . When it speaks to us most strongly, it could be described as a meditation on time and eternity, or life and death. Only in the lyrics that make up section four of each quartet does doctrine seem to be not only influencing but controlling the poem, and these parts may be skipped by readers who are not Anglo-Catholic without great loss to what I take to be the final impression left by the poem, of the limited value of "knowledge derived from experience" and the consequent need of a faith that goes beyond the "evidence."

Despite the explicitly doctrinal passages, the poem expresses feelings and attitudes that link it with the work of Emerson, especially in his journals, and of Whitman, especially in "Lilacs" and other late poems. We find Emerson's dissatisfaction with the quotidian and Whitman's late conviction that though grand is the seen, the unseen is grander still. Of course the dark view of life's possibilities, despite the work of "the wounded surgeon," is here also, to remind us both of how different Eliot's temperament was from Emerson's and Whitman's and of the fact that the poem was written in a less hopeful age, so that such abstract parallels must not be pressed too far. (pp. 437-39)

It was probably Bergson more than any other philosopher who prepared Eliot to write the meditative parts of the poem on time and memory (especially **"Burnt Norton"**) and matter and spirit, or spirit's involvement with nature (**"The Dry Salvages"**), as Bradley had been drawn on earlier for "the thousand sordid images" of which the soul was said to be constituted. In the Quartets we are beyond the Realism/Idealism choice, as Bergson had felt he was. Real time is not measurable in terms of space or in any way quantifiable, so that we cannot move beyond philosophic dualism. "The salt is on the briar rose" and "The river is within us." From Bergson to an Anglo-Catholic understanding of the meaning of the Incarnation is not an impossible leap, as the relation between Bergson's belief that it was necessary to affirm both that "we are, to a certain extent, what we do, and that we are creating ourselves continually" and many passages in the Quartets should illustrate. "Not fare well, / But fare for-

ward, voyagers," choosing freely within strict limits the kind of self we would be.

The voice we hear in *The Four Quartets* is Eliot's own, as there is no need to surmise when we note the pronouns on the first page of **"Burnt Norton"**—*my, I, we.* What this means we discover as we read on: no more "poetry of the library," no more personae, no more "mythological method"—in short a dropping of masks and defenses. The poet who in **"Prufrock"** and **"Gerontion"** had dramatized aspects of himself that he did not like now feels secure enough to speak to us directly from his experience and belief—though still, of course, without becoming "confessional" in Roethke's way.

I suspect that Eliot had found the myths of the Garden and the Fall expressive of his own experience and that his conversion helped him to see that experience as part of the human condition, not uniquely shameful. Earlier, feeling terribly vulnerable, he had adopted various stratagems to make himself invulnerable, both personally and poetically. He had been, as a man, highly mannered as well as fastidious and proud. . . . Aware of his vulnerability now but better able to accept it, as a poet he can stop hiding behind masks, and as a man he can dispense with the more outrageous mannerisms and the courteous arrogance that had once been his way of coping with his shyness.

After more than thirty productive years he could stop writing lyric poetry, except for an occasional poem. Having urged old men to be explorers, the "aged eagle" who had spent his youth anticipating the losses of age, fearing he might become a Gerontion, now explored the possibilities in verse drama, though here too, as in his occasional poems, the quality of his writing seems to me to have declined as the anxiety lessened. I find *Murder in the Cathedral* and *The Family Reunion* far more impressive than *The Elder Statesman,* in which I can applaud only the theme: love can save us. Or, again, a comparison of **"The Journey of the Magi,"** which expresses the disappointment of the convert at not finding himself suddenly "born again," with the late **"The Cultivation of Christmas Trees"** may secure my point: the better man has become the lesser poet. The weariness and disappointment of the Magi, along with the fatigue, boredom, and disgust of **"Preludes"** and **"Morning at the Window,"** are gone, replaced by healthier and more charitable attitudes and by greater wisdom; but the language of the early poems seems much more memorable, however we may deplore the attitudes. (pp. 439-40)

What Eliot has left us with is a volume of distinguished poems, long and short, a volume slender by comparison with Williams's or Stevens's total output but never filled with mere notes for unwritten poems like Williams's or repetitious and predictable like Stevens's: poems that give us still today the words to express, and thus be better able to understand and cope with, our own experience, our distress, our fears, and our occasionally possible hopes.

The "lost generation" was followed by a new generation equally or more desperately lost, as the lives and the work of Jarrell, Berryman, Lowell, and Roethke illustrate; then by several generations of poets unable to take seriously what Eliot, Hemingway, Faulkner, and others thought had been lost but also generally unable to find a satisfactory substitute, until today, when we may expect many of our most honored poets to indulge in word games or to remain locked within purely private experience. Eliot's way of retrieving what had been lost may be impossible for most poets today, but it offered him a way of living in and writing about the world we all briefly inhabit. Like the other modernists Eliot rejected popular culture, but unlike some other artists he did not rely on shock effect to express his radical rejection. His poems no longer shock us, but they still stand up under critical reading. Though reflecting wide learning, they do not require that we read the explications first, as many of the Cantos do, to find out what they are all about. Randall Jarrell was right . . . when he noted in 1962 that the poems were not really "classical," objective, impersonal, etc., but "subjective and daemonic." The best of them, early and late, free us from "the illusion of technique" and help us to know, if not what must be believed, at least what our choices are and in what direction we must travel if we are to find meaning for our lives in a time when all life on earth is threatened by the results of our knowledge and the power over nature it has given us. The great poet writes such poems of lasting "universal" significance whatever his poetic mode.

If we are to do T. S. Eliot's poetry justice in this time when the waste land is no longer a metaphor for cultural decline but is a literal physical possibility, we shall first of all, I think, have to reject Eliot's own early rejection of Emerson's half-truth—that the true poet, not just versifier, must first be a Seer in order to be a Namer and Sayer. What Eliot "saw" and gave us the words for in his poems has already outlasted the New Criticism and will I suspect outlast us, along with the best poems of Yeats, Frost, Stevens, and perhaps Pound. (pp. 440-41)

Hyatt H. Waggoner, "Eliot as Poet," in *The Sewanee Review*, Vol. XCII, No. 3, Summer, 1984, pp. 432-41.

MICHAEL DIRDA
(essay 1988)

[In the following excerpt, Dirda reviews two recent works, *The Letters of T. S. Eliot: Volume One, 1898-1922* (1988) and Lyndall Gordan's *Eliot's New Life* (1988), discussing biographical influences on Eliot's writings.]

During his lifetime T. S. Eliot bestrode the literary world like a colossus. From the publication of *The Waste Land* in 1922 until his death in 1965 he was the chief cultural poohbah of England and America; in 1956 over 14,000 people jammed into a stadium in Minnesota to hear him—or, more accurately, simply to see him; literary histories spoke reverently of "The Age of Eliot."

After all, he was the author of the most admired poem of the century, generally regarded as the greatest literary critic in English, and hearkened to as a social visionary and religious prophet. He received the outward signs of success too: the Nobel Prize, the Order of Merit, and a hit on Broadway (his play *The Cocktail Party*).

Which just goes to show that nothing fails like success. During the past 20 years Eliot's reputation has taken a beating on all fronts. In terms of poetic influence Wallace Stevens and William Carlos Williams divide contemporary American poetry between them. Virtually all of Eliot's literary judgments have been seriously challenged or strongly qualified. Modern verse drama came and went. Critics talk of "The Pound Era."

There's always a swing downward in reputation after the death of a giant. But then matters even out as scholarship starts to strip away the veneer of the smiling—or in Eliot's case, sad-faced—public man. In his centennial year (he was born on September 26, 1888) Eliot is currently enjoying, some might say enduring, that process. Memoirs, biographies, the discovery and publication of the *Waste Land* manuscript, and now his letters are altering our image of the Anglo-Catholic royalist and classicist into something much richer and stranger. Those are pearls that were his eyes. (pp. 1, 10)

In her introduction [to *The Letters of T. S. Eliot: Volume One, 1898-1922*] Valerie Eliot, the poet's widow, mentions that she had originally intended the first volume to go up to the end of 1926, that is, up to the moment of Eliot's religious conversion. This would have allowed a neat continuity with Lyndall Gordon's superb *Eliot's New Life*, which focuses on the poet's spiritual biography from 1927 till his death [see Sources for

Further Study]. But the years between these two books are in fact their hidden focus: the dissolution of Eliot's marriage to his first wife, Vivienne, and the reblossoming of his love for the girl he left behind, Emily Hale. It is the revelation of this human drama that is largely responsible for the image of Eliot as a confessional poet, somewhere between Baudelaire and Robert Lowell.

Admittedly, it is sometimes hard to find the human being in Eliot's correspondence. . . . Eliot simply is not in the class of his poet-friends Conrad Aiken and Ezra Pound, who made their lively correspondence an extension of their personalities and their poetic platforms. Happily, Valerie Eliot includes a few letters from these friends, as well as from Jean Verdenal, the mysterious dedicatee of *Prufrock and Other Observations,* who was killed in World War I. There was speculation at one time that he and Eliot were homosexual lovers; but Verdenal's letters are merely affectionate and nostalgic. However some of the correspondence with Aiken, Pound and other old friends displays a locker-room bawdiness: There are several excerpts from Eliot's obscene King Bolo poems, and lots of verbal towel-snapping about private parts and even more private acts.

Most of the time, though, these London letters show us Eliot the son (at times the mama's boy), the nurse-husband to neurotic wife Vivienne, and the ambitious young urban professional. In the early letters home Eliot stresses his accomplishments; only to his friends does he talk of emptiness and acedia, of the hollow man within: "In Oxford I have the feeling that I am not quite alive—that my body is walking about with a bit of my brain inside it, and nothing else."

This "aboulie," as Eliot calls it, may offer one reason why he suddenly and rashly married Vivienne Haigh-Wood—"the awful daring of a moment's surrender / Which an age of prudence can never retract." Emily Hale had not, apparently, made her feelings clear to Eliot before he left for England. Vivienne was vivacious, available; like characters in Henry James, they mistook each other's true selves. The result was a nightmare marriage. . . .

And yet, throughout this litany of woes, Eliot keeps saying things like "The present year has been, in some respects, the most awful nightmare of anxiety that the mind of man can conceive, but at least it is not dull . . . " One senses that the young Eliot's fear of the void within himself was so great that only by suffering and constant work could he keep it at bay. Eventually, I think, the ceaseless activity—both professional and social—became the workaholic's typical means of avoiding an impossible homelife.

Readers looking for Eliot the critic and poet in these pages will need to be highly imaginative. There are prefigurations of famous critical or poetic formula-

tions—"I like to feel that a writer is perfectly cool and detached, regarding other people's feelings or his own, like a god who has got beyond them . . . "—but such tidbits are few and never developed. No one reading these pages would believe that their author was at work on the critical pieces that would make *The Sacred Wood* a touchstone in the history of literary theory.

What is true of the essays is even more true of the poems. Eliot never talks about **"The Love Song of J. Alfred Prufrock"** or **"Gerontion"** except as products— as poems to sell to *Poetry* or *The Dial.* . . .

Even though Eliot's letters give us no direct glimpse into his poetic workshop, they do relate some telling and touching moments. The pathos of Eliot writing his mother, when he learns of his father's death, that he wants to hear her "sing The Little Tailor to me." The probably unconscious double-entendre of a note to Bertrand Russell, who has taken Viv on a little vacation: "I am sure you have done everything possible and handled her in the very best way—better than I" (Russell almost certainly slept with her). The personal plea behind the letter to *The Athenaeum* urging that the British Museum library should stay open in the evenings for people who had jobs during the day.

There are, of course, occasional signs of the "bad" Eliot. He refers callously to "our servant" and almost never calls her by name; he mentions "Siegfried Sassoon (semitic)"; he cuts old friends, including "Conrad Aiken, stupider than ever." And all the while he is smiling at the right people, keeping his name in the news, managing his literary career with Rommel-like cunning.

These letters leave us at the end with Eliot on the verge of his greatest success. He has finished *The Waste Land* (while on leave from Lloyd's bank for nervous exhaustion) and has inaugurated *The Criterion.* He has every reason to be proud, perhaps a little too proud: "There is a small and select public which regards me as the best living critic, as well as the best living poet, in England. . . . I really think that I have far more influence on English letters than any other American has ever had, unless it be Henry James."

He was right, of course, despite the snotty tone. But Lyndall Gordon's *Eliot's New Life* shows in part how little that public success came to mean to him. By 1925 Vivienne Eliot's neurasthenia started to pass over into delusional madness. In 1928 Eliot converted to the Church of England, eventually going so far as to make a private vow of chastity. Soon thereafter he began to live apart from his wife, keeping his whereabouts secret, sneaking out of his office when she appeared, dodging her in public and private.

Lyndall Gordon's *Eliot's Early Years* (1977) tried to understand Eliot's treatment of Vivienne, often taking her part against received history. *Eliot's New Life* chronicles the poet's "search for salvation," but focuses closely on the place of women in that search: the gnawing guilt over leaving Vivienne, the promise of renewed happiness with Emily Hale. Eliot wrote over 1,000 letters to Hale—all of them locked up at Princeton until the year 2020—and spent many springs and summers in her company. She was simply a New England-born school teacher, with an interest in drama, but she represented for Eliot an ideal love, his own lost innocence and purity. Ultimately she served as Beatrice to his Dante—and then was cruelly cast aside. . . .

In her brilliant analysis of the *Quartets*—a companion piece to the "autobiographical" reading of *The Waste Land* in her earlier book—Gordon links Eliot's spiritual search with that of his puritan forebears. Building on the classic studies by F. O. Matthiessen [see Sources for Further Study] and Helen Gardner, Gordon interprets the *Four Quartets* as a full-fledged spiritual autobiography—an attempt to understand how to live a religious life in a fallen world, how to achieve sanctity. These same highly personal themes recur in the plays of this era, not least in *The Cocktail Party* with its submerged homage to Emily Hale as Celia, whom the hero does not marry and instead sends to her martyrdom.

Which is what Eliot finally did. His family assumed that he and Emily would eventually wed; but when Vivienne died in 1947, after years in an asylum, Eliot looked within and found that all his desire for marriage had died too. He preferred his poetic dreams of the past and the lone path of the religious ordeal, di-

vesting himself of everything in his quest to know God. . . .

In his later years Eliot slept on a simple bed under a heavy iron cross. He took the bus every day to church, recited his prayers quietly in the crowded tube. He expected to retire to an abbey. As a lecturer he had gradually become something of a spiritual authority, talking about life and society, religion and literature with a voice beyond time, beyond place. And then, at age 68, he married his 30-year-old secretary, Valerie Fletcher.

This may seem almost a joke, the renunciation of a lifetime's habits. But this second marriage found Eliot surprised by joy, and his final years were, by all reports, extremely happy. He had journeyed from the inferno of his youth through the purgatory of his maturity to find an unexpected paradise in his last years.

For all his gifts and accomplishments, Eliot was for most of his life a haunted man, racked with a sense of sin, always yearning for "the peace that passeth understanding." In his self-obsession he sometimes treated others cruelly; he was often a holy prig; but knowing of his own purgatorial burning humanizes and transforms his poems, so perfectly beautiful, so terribly personal. Still, to read *The Waste Land* now is to hear the cries of Vivienne, as well as Philomel; and even though the end of **"Little Gidding"** may triumphantly unite the fire and the rose, it is hard to forget Emily Hale, ultimately left standing alone by the door that never opened. (p. 10)

Michael Dirda, "The Love Song of T. S. Eliot," in *Book World—The Washington Post*, September 25, 1988, pp. 1, 10.

SOURCES FOR FURTHER STUDY

Ackroyd, Peter. *T. S. Eliot: A Life.* New York: Simon and Schuster, 1984, 400 p.

Comprehensive study delineating Eliot's life and works.

Bush, Ronald. *T. S. Eliot: A Study in Character and Style.* New York: Oxford University Press, 1984, 287 p.

Traces Eliot's poetic and personal development and his relation to modernism.

Frye, Northrop. *T. S. Eliot.* Edinburgh: Oliver and Boyd, 1963, 106 p.

Analyzes influences on and characteristics of Eliot's writings.

Gordon, Lyndall. *Eliot's Early Years.* Oxford: Oxford University Press, 1977, 174 p.

Biography detailing Eliot's life and works up to his conversion to Anglo-Catholicism in 1927 and the years immediately following.

——. *Eliot's New Life.* Oxford: Oxford University Press, 1988, 356 p.

Sequel to *Eliot's Early Years*, chronicling the last thirty-eight years of Eliot's life and literary development.

Matthiessen, F. O. *The Achievement of T. S. Eliot: An Essay on the Nature of Poetry.* 3d ed. New York: Oxford University Press, 1958, 248 p.

Analysis focusing on the artistic technique of Eliot's poetry and dramas. The last chapter of this edition, written by C. L. Barber, examines Eliot's criticism.

Ralph Ellison

1914-

(Full name Ralph Waldo Ellison) American novelist, essayist, short story writer, critic, and editor.

INTRODUCTION

*E*llison is one of the most influential and accomplished American authors of the twentieth century. He is best known for his highly acclaimed novel *Invisible Man* (1952), a work that affirms the need for the individual to attain self-awareness. Honored with the National Book Award for fiction, *Invisible Man* is regarded as a masterpiece for its complex treatment of racial repression and betrayal. Shifting between naturalism, expressionism, and surrealism, Ellison combined concerns of European and African-American literature to chronicle an unnamed black youth's quest to discover his identity within a deluding, hostile world. Although critics have faulted Ellison's style as occasionally excessive, *Invisible Man* has consistently been praised for its poetic, ambiguous form, sustained blend of tragedy and comedy, and complex symbolism and characterizations.

Born in Oklahoma City, Oklahoma, Ellison was raised in a cultural atmosphere that encouraged self-fulfillment. After studying music from 1933 to 1936 at Tuskegee Institute, a college founded by Booker T. Washington to promote black scholarship, Ellison traveled to New York City, where he met author Richard Wright and became involved in the Federal Writers' Project. Encouraged to write a book review for *New Challenge*, a publication edited by Wright, Ellison began composing essays and stories that focus on the strength of the human spirit and the necessity for racial pride. Two of his most celebrated early short stories, "Flying Home" and "King of the Bingo Game," foreshadown *Invisible Man* in their portrayal of alienated young protagonists who seek social recognition. "Flying Home" is set during World War II and depicts a young black pilot whose obsessive desire to rid himself of stereotypes causes him to become contemptuous of his own race. After his airplane crashes, he is nursed back to health by a group of farmers who awaken his sense of cultural kinship and self-esteem. The anonymous protagonist of "King of the Bingo Game" is desperate to save his dying wife and enters a bingo tournament hoping to win enough money to hire a doctor. As the tournament proceeds, the bingo game becomes a symbol of his inability to control his destiny.

Although he originally envisioned writing a war novel, Ellison instead began work on *Invisible Man* following his honorable discharge from the United States Merchant Marines in 1945. His initial intention, to show the irony of black soldiers fighting for freedom who return to a civilian life of oppression, developed into a broader psychological study of the individual in society. Most critics consider the unspecified action of *Invisible Man* to take place between the early 1930s and 1950s. The novel's picaresque hero is often compared to Voltaire's Candide, who remains optimistic despite enduring betrayal, manipulation, humiliation, and the loss of his illusions. Narrating his story from an underground cell, the anonymous protagonist explains in the prologue that he is involuntarily invisible because society sees his social stereotype rather than his true personality. Establishing the novel's themes of betrayal and anonymity, the narrator recalls how he was raised in the South, named valedictorian of his high school graduation class, and invited to recite a speech for the community's prominent white citizens. This episode, which critics often refer to as Ellison's "battle royal" chapter, was originally published as a short story entitled "Invisible Man" in *Horizon* magazine. Among other degradations, the protagonist and several other black youths invited to the meeting are forced to participate in blind boxing matches and to crawl for money on an electrified carpet. Only after he has suffered these humiliations is the narrator allowed to recite his speech. Although largely ignored by the drunken gathering, Ellison's hero is presented with a college scholarship and assumes that education will help overcome the racial problems he encounters. The evening's brutality convinces him that he will be rewarded if he does what white people expect, and this naive assumption provokes an identity crisis.

While attending a Southern college that strongly resembles Tuskegee Institute, the protagonist is assigned to chauffeur Mr. Norton, a white philanthropist, and innocently takes him to visit Jim Trueblood, a disreputable sharecropper whom Norton believes to be a colorful storyteller in the folk tradition of Uncle Remus. Upon hearing Trueblood's account of incest with his daughter, Norton is both horrified and fascinated by the indulgence in moral taboos that he himself has secretly considered transgressing. Many critics claim that this episode contains some of Ellison's finest dialogue and characterizations. By evoking society's reactions to Trueblood, Ellison refuted stereotypes of ethical, principled whites and decadent, unscrupulous blacks. Following Trueblood's revelation, the narrator takes Norton to a saloon called the Golden Day. The saloon's name refers to the Era of Reform between 1830 and 1860, during which many citizens entertained idealistic hopes of social reform that were later thwarted by industrialism and materialistic values. Norton's visit occurs at a time when the saloon is crowded with American veterans of World War I who, after fighting overseas for the freedom of others, were institutionalized for refusing to conform to segregation laws. One patron, a brilliant brain surgeon, later gives the narrator advice for his future: "[The] world is possibility if only you'll discover it." The narrator contemplates the surgeon's comment as he travels north, a move reminiscent of the Great Migration of the 1920s, when displaced southerners journeyed to the industrialized northern United States to obtain employment.

Expelled from college for his misadventure with Mr. Norton, Ellison's protagonist travels to the Harlem district of New York City in search of a job. He possesses sealed letters of reference from Doctor Bledsoe, president of his former university, that are later revealed to contain character defamations. The narrator nonetheless obtains employment with Liberty Paints, a company that manufactures white paint to be used in the bleaching of national monuments. As the result of an accident for which he is held responsible, the protagonist is hospitalized and given a form of electroshock therapy intended to mimic the effects of a lobotomy. Although desensitized, he vividly recalls the folklore of his Southern boyhood and emerges with a new sense of racial pride, while the superficiality of his previous experience is erased. For the first time he is unashamed of his background and asserts his disdain for servile blacks by dumping a spittoon on a man whom he mistakes for Doctor Bledsoe.

Following an impromptu speech that he delivers on a street after discovering that an elderly couple have been evicted from their home, the narrator of *Invisible Man* attracts the attention of the Brotherhood, an organization that critics generally equate with American Communist associations of the 1930s. After briefly embracing the group's utopian ideals, he discovers that the Brotherhood merely feigns interest in civil rights while actually working to repress blacks and deny their individuality. The chaos that ensues in the black community following the frenzied exhortations of a fanatic nationalist develops into a hallucinatory treatment of the Harlem race riots of the 1940s and culminates in the protagonist's final rejection of false identities. Wright Morris asserted: "Mr. Ellison handles this surrealist evening with so much authority and macabre humor, observing the forces with such detachment, that the reader is justified in feeling that in the process of mastering his rage, he has also mastered his art."

Upon escaping the uproar of the riots, the narrator accidentally falls into a coal cellar that leads to the cell where he eventually achieves self-definition. Although he succumbs to anger by stealing electricity from the local power company, he deduces that his experiences have made him a unique individual. Despite his invisibility, the protagonist realizes that he must accept social responsibility and face the world.

Although attacked by black nationalists for lacking stringent militancy toward civil rights issues, *Invisible Man* garnered laudatory reviews immediately following its publication and has continued to generate scholarly exegeses. Many critics have commented on how the book's dexterous style, dense symbolism, and narrative structure lend intricacy to its plot. The narrator, who reflects on his past experiences, is observed as both an idealistic, gullible youth and as an enlightened, responsible man who actively addresses problems that may result from social inequality. Timothy Brennan declared: "[The] language and methods of the protest tradition are wielded by Ellison with an ambiguous voice, never finally pronouncing or judging, but building to a culmination of alternating hope and bitterness, rebellion and despair."

The most controversial issue concerning *Invisible Man* involves its classification as either a work written for and about blacks alone or as a novel with universal import. Critics who insist the book strictly concerns black culture maintain that the experiences, emotions, and lifestyles described could not possibly be simulated by white authors, while supporters of the more prevalent view that *Invisible Man* transcends racial concerns contend that the protagonist's problems of illusion, betrayal, and self-awareness are experienced by every segment of society. Ellison himself asserted that *Invisible Man* is a novel that attempts to provide a portrait of the American individual who must define his values and himself despite a transitory existence. Jonathan Baumbach observed: "Refracted by satire, at times cartooned, Ellison's world is at once surreal and real, comic and tragic, grotesque and normal—our world viewed in its essentials rather than its externals. Though the protagonist of *Invisible Man* is a southern Negro, he is, in Ellison's rendering, profoundly all of us."

Ellison is also highly regarded for his accomplishments as an essayist. *Shadow and Act* (1964) collects twenty-two years of reviews, criticism, and interviews concerning such subjects as art, music, literature, and the influence of the black experience on American culture. This acclaimed volume is often considered autobiographical in intent and is noted for its lucidity and insights into *Invisible Man. Going to the Territory* (1986), which contains speeches, reviews, and interviews written since 1957, echoes many of the concerns of *Shadow and Act.* Making use of ironic humor in the manner

of *Invisible Man,* Ellison here reflected on personal influences and payed tribute to such creative mentors as Richard Wright and Duke Ellington. Ellison's short stories remain uncollected but are anthologized in such volumes as *A New Southern Harvest* (1957), *The Angry Black* (1962), and *Soon, One Morning: New Writing by American Negroes, 1940-1962* (1963; published in Great Britain as *Black Voices*). The latter book contains "Out of the Hospital and under the Bar," a noted excerpt deleted from *Invisible Man.*

Ellison's influence as both novelist and critic, as artist and cultural historian, is enormous. A measure of his stature and achievement is his readers' vigil for his longawaited second novel. Although Ellison often refuses to answer questions about the work-in-progress, there is evidence to suggest that the manuscript is very large, that all or part of it was destroyed in a fire and is being rewritten, and that its creation has been a long and painful task. Most readers wait expectantly, believing that Ellison, who said in *Shadow and Act* that he "failed of eloquence" in *Invisible Man,* won't publish his second novel until it equals his imaginative vision of the American novel as conqueror of the frontier and answers the Emersonian call for a literature to release all people from the bonds of oppression.

Eight excerpts from this novel-in-progress have been published in literary journals. Set in the South in the years spanning the Jazz Age to the Civil Rights movement, these fragments seem an attempt to recreate modern American history and identity. The major characters are the Reverend Hickman, a one-time jazz musician, and Bliss, the light-skinned boy whom he adopts and who later passes into white society and becomes Senator Sunraider, an advocate of white supremacy. As Robert G. O'Meally noted in his 1980 study *The Craft of Ralph Ellison,* the major difference between Bliss and Ellison's earlier young protagonists is that despite some harsh collisions with reality, Bliss refuses to divest himself of his illusions and accept his personal history. Says O'Meally: "Moreover, it is a renunciation of the blackness of American experience and culture, a refusal to accept the American past in all its complexity."

Like *Invisible Man,* this novel promises to be a broad and searching inquiry into identity, ideologies, culture, and history. The narrative form is similar as well; here, too, is the blending of popular and classical myth, of contradictory cultural memories, of an intricate pattern of images of birth, death, and rebirth. In *Shadow and Act* Ellison described the novel's form as "a realism extended beyond realism." What the ultimate form of the novel will be—if, indeed, these excerpts are to be part of one novel—remains hidden. But the pieces seize the reader's imagination even if they deny systematic analysis.

One thing does seem certain about these stories.

In them Bliss becomes a traitor to his own race, loses his hold on those things of transforming, affirmative value. Hickman, on the other hand, accepts and celebrates his heritage, his belief in the timeless value of his history. The tone of these excerpts is primarily tragicomic, a mode well-suited to Ellison's definition of life. As he wrote in *Shadow and Act,* "I think that the mixture of the marvelous and the terrible is a basic condition of human life and that the persistence of human ideals represents the marvelous pulling itself up out of the chaos of the universe." Elsewhere in the book, Ellison argued that "true novels, even when most pessimistic and bitter, arise out of an impulse to celebrate

human life." As *Invisible Man* before and the Hickman novel yet to come, they celebrate the "human and absurd" commixture of American life.

(For further information about Ellison's life and works, see *Black Literature Criticism; Black Writers; Concise Dictionary of American Literary Biography, 1941-1968; Contemporary Authors,* Vols. 9-12; *Contemporary Authors New Revision Series,* Vol. 24; *Contemporary Literary Criticism,* Vols. 1, 3, 11, 54; *Dictionary of Literary Biography,* Vols. 2, 76; and *Major 20th-Century Writers.*)

CRITICAL COMMENTARY

WRIGHT MORRIS

(essay date 1952)

[A prolific American writer who has published works in a variety of genres, Morris is best known for novels that focus on such themes as the quest for identity, relationships between males and females, the effects of the past on people's lives, the relativity of knowledge, and the values associated with material success. In the following excerpt from an essay first published in *The New York Times Book Review* in 1952, he explores the concepts of "invisibility" and "the underground" in *Invisible Man.*]

The geography of hell is still in the process of being mapped. The borders shift, the shore lines erode, coral islands appear complete with new sirens, but all the men who have been there speak with a similar voice. These reports are seldom mistaken as coming from anywhere else. As varied as the life might be on the surface, the life underground has a good deal in common—the stamp of hell, the signature of pain, is on all of the inhabitants. Here, if anywhere, is the real brotherhood of man. . . .

[The title character of Ellison's *Invisible Man*] lives, he tells us, in an underground hole. To fill this dark hole with light, he burns 1,369 bulbs. He burns them free. A fine Dostoevskyan touch. In his *Notes From the Underground* Dostoevsky says: "We are discussing things seriously: but if you won't deign to give me your attention, I will drop your acquaintance. I can retreat into my underground hole."

The Invisible Man is also discussing things seriously. His report in this novel might be subtitled, "Notes From Underground America," or "The Invisible Black Man in the Visible White Man's World." That is

part of his story, but the deeper layer, revealed, perhaps, in spite of himself, is the invisible man becoming visible. The word, against all of the odds, becoming the flesh. Neither black nor white flesh, however, for where the color line is drawn with profundity, as it is here, it also vanishes. There is not much to choose, under the skin, between being black and invisible, and being white, currently fashionable and opaque. . . .

[The Invisible Man's] report begins the day that rich men from the North, white philanthropists, appear on the campus of a Negro college in the South. They are there for the ceremony of Founders Day. The Invisible Man, a student at the college, is chosen to act as the chauffeur for one of them. He shows him, inadvertently, the underground black world that should not be seen. Before the day is over, both the millionaire and the student have been disillusioned, and the student, expelled from the college, leaves for New York.

In the city he becomes increasingly invisible. Hearing him rouse the crowd at the scene of a Harlem eviction, a key party bigwig sees a bright future for him in the brotherhood. The mysteries of the Order, revealed and unrevealed, as they fall to the lot of the Invisible Man, have the authentic air of unreality that must have bemused so many honest, tormented men. The climax of the book, and a model of vivid, memorable writing, is the night of the Harlem riots. Mr. Ellison handles this surrealist evening with so much authority and macabre humor, observing the forces with such detachment, that the reader is justified in feeling that in the process of mastering his rage, he has also mastered his art. . . .

The reader who is familiar with the traumatic phase of the black man's rage in America, will find

---

Principal Works

"Flying Home" (short story) 1944; published in Cross Section; also published in Dark Symphony: Negro Literature in America, 1968

"King of the Bingo Game" (short story) 1944; published in periodical Tomorrow; also published in Dark Symphony: Negro Literature in America, 1968

Invisible Man (novel) 1952

"Out of the Hospital and under the Bar" (prose) 1963; published in Soon, One Morning: New Writing by American Negroes, 1940-1962

Shadow and Act (essays and interviews) 1964

Going to the Territory (essays, lectures, and interviews) 1986

---

something more in Mr. Ellison's report. He will find the long anguished step toward its mastery. The author sells no phony forgiveness. He asks none himself. It is a resolutely honest, tormented, profoundly American book.

"Being invisible and without substance, a disembodied voice, as it were, what else could I do?" the Invisible Man asks us in closing. "What else but try to tell you what was really happening when your eyes were looking through! And it is this which frightens me: Who knows but that, on the lower frequencies, I speak for you?"

But this is not another journey to the end of the night. With this book the author maps a course from the underground world into the light. *Invisible Man* belongs on the shelf with the classical efforts man has made to chart the river Lethe from its mouth to its source.

Wright Morris, "The World Below," in *The New York Times Book Review*, April 13, 1952, p. 5.

ANTHONY WEST

(essay date 1952)

[West was an English novelist, critic, biographer, and editor. In the following excerpt from a 1952 *New Yorker* review, he praises the vitality and depth of *Invisible Man*.]

Ralph Ellison's first novel, *Invisible Man,* is an exceptionally good book and in parts an extremely funny one. That is not to say that it is without defects, but since they are almost entirely confined to the intolera-

bly arty prologue and epilogue, and to certain expressionist passages conveniently printed in italics, they can easily be skipped, and they should be, for they are trifling in comparison with its virtues. What gives it its strength is that it is about being colored in a white society and yet manages not to be a grievance book; it has not got the whine of a hard-luck story about it, and it has not got the blurting, incoherent quality of a statement made in anger. What gives it its character is a robust courage; it walks squarely up to color the way seventeenth-century writing walks up to mortality and death, to look it in the face as a part of the human situation that has to be lived with. Mr. Ellison's hero is a Negro of the South who starts out with the naïve illusion that what stands between him and the whites is a matter of education. He is given a scholarship to a Southern college that has been endowed by Northern philanthropists, and he goes to it in great delight, thinking that what he will learn there will pare away all his disabilities and disadvantages. He finds that the college cannot do that for him and does not even try to do it; it is concerned only with helping him make realistic adjustments to things as they are. He gets into a mess of trouble and is expelled. Before expelling him, the dean tells him just what the facts of colored life are:

> You have some vague notions about dignity. . . . You have some white folk backing you and you don't want to face them because nothing is worse for a black man than to be humiliated by white folk. I know all about that too. . . . But you'll get over it; it's foolish and expensive and a lot of dead weight. You let the white folk worry about pride and dignity—you learn where you are and get yourself power, influence, contacts with powerful and influential people—then stay in the dark and use it!

He is too young and too nobly stubborn to believe that this is the best that can be done with his life, and the rest of the book deals with his attempts to force the world to accept him on a pride-and-dignity basis, and with his final realization that he has to stay in the dark as an invisible man. This could easily be a glum and painful performance, but Mr. Ellison has the real satirical gift for handling ideas at the level of low comedy, and when he is most serious he is most funny. The technique is that of which *Candide* is the supreme example, but there is nothing archaic about the writing, which has an entirely contemporary vitality and a quite unexpected depth.

The first chapter is a little slow, but the second and third, which describe the trouble that leads to the hero's expulsion, convince one that Mr. Ellison is a writer with much more than promise. (p. 93)

A good deal of [*Invisible Man*] is concerned with penetrating to the unease and self-consciousness that underlie a great many earnest white progressive approaches to The Question. After the student is kicked out of college, he goes North to try to make his way in New York, and his adventures are told in a highly imaginative, picaresque story, but, though the story-telling is excellent, in the end the impressive thing is the analysis of attitudes that rises out of each situation; there are always such sharpness of observation, such awareness of shades of feeling, at work. The hero is caught up in what is clearly an agit-prop apparatus of the Communist Party (Mr. Ellison does not, though, give it that name) that is exploiting the color situation in Harlem. He is a natural speaker and he is made use of in campaigns as a front for the white committee. There is not only perceptive writing about the feeling between Negro and white in this part of the book but there is also perhaps the best description of rank-and-file Communist Party activity that has yet appeared in an American novel. . . . At last, the hero discerns the rank stink of falsity in the Party line about color, partly through catching on to the way in which a white Comrade who has married a colored girl makes play with the fact to strengthen his hand in policy discussions of district tactics, partly through a realization that the white Comrades have used him as a lure, as a Negro gull to gull other Negroes. He sees that his district leader, Brother Jack, is just as much Marse Jack as a field boss in a white-supremacy state. The description of his disillusion with the Party, a true agon, which is also his final understanding that there is no external machine that can produce any readymade solution either to the color problem or to his own perplexities, is as moving and vivid a piece of writing on this difficult subject as one could wish to read.

The book ends with a . . . tour de force. . . . The Party has lost control of its agitation campaign as a result of what at first seems to the hero to be a typical tactical blunder, and the mass support that it has won drifts over to a straight anti-Communist and anti-white agitator called Ras, whose wild speeches bring on a wave of rioting and looting. The drift into disorder and the spread of violence are astonishingly well described in realistic terms, and through it all Mr. Ellison never loses touch with his gift for comic invention. As the riot builds up, the hero realizes that not only have the Communists an unfriendly interest in him but that he is due for unpleasantness from Ras's strong-arm men. . . . The hero's evasions as all Harlem comes apart have a real nightmare humor. And in the middle of it all, as the riot squads and the mounted police move in and shooting begins, he suddenly sees what is happening. The Party has not made a tactical blunder at all; it has deliberately surrendered its mass following to Ras in order to provoke violence, so that colored martyrs, shot down by the police, can be exploited in the next phase of agitation in the district. The hero emerges in his own identity to warn the innocents he has helped to fool what is being done to them. But Mr. Ellison has

a tight grip on his satiric comedy, and he is not going to let his buffoon hero escape into tragedy; martyrdom is not to be *his* fate. A gang of white looters chase him up a dark street, and he falls through an open manhole into a coal cellar. The whites, enraged by this surprising vanishing trick, slam the manhole cover down and leave him lying there helpless while the riot burns itself out above.

Few writers can have made a more commanding first appearance. Up to a point, *Invisible Man* resembles Céline's *Death on the Installment Plan*. Its humor recalls the jokes that hang on Céline's fraudulent scientist, with his ascents in worn-out and patched balloons, his absurd magazine, and his system of electromagnetic plant culture, but Ellison's jokes are on the whole funnier, and his satire is much more convincing because there is clearly visible behind it—as there is not in Céline—a positive alternative to the evils he is attacking, the knowledge of a better way without which all satire becomes merely an empty scolding. It is a pity that Mr. Ellison's direct statement of the better way takes the form it does in the prologue and the epilogue, since they are the two worst pieces of writing. But the ideas toward which they fumble are as dignified as they are impressive, and it is perhaps unnecessary to have this direct statement; as they are so plainly implied in the rest of the book. It is not merely the Negro who has to realize that the only escape from the rattrap of worry about what one is or is not is to abandon the constant tease of selfconsciousness. The Invisible Man of Mr. Ellison's title is the unattached man of Aldous Huxley's Perennial Philosophy, the man with courage to be utterly indifferent to himself and to his place in the world, the man who is alone free to be fully a man. (pp. 94-6)

Anthony West, "Black Man's Burden," in *The New Yorker*, Vol. XXVIII, No. 15, May 31, 1952, pp. 93-6.

DAVID LITTLEJOHN
(essay date 1966)

[In the following excerpt from his study *Black on White: A Critical Survey of Writing by American Negroes*, Littlejohn assesses theme, content, and motive in *Invisible Man*, labeling the novel "the supreme work of art created by an American Negro."]

Ralph (Waldo) Ellison stands at the opposite end of the writer's world from Richard Wright. Although he is as aware of the issues of the race war as anyone else, he is no more a consciously active participant than, say, Gwendolyn Brooks or William Faulkner. "I wasn't, and am not, primarily concerned with injustice, but with art." He achieves his extraordinary power through artistry and control, through objectivity, irony, distance: he works with symbol rather than with act. He is at least as much an artist as a Negro. He accepts both roles so naturally, in fact, that he has made them one. His one novel [*Invisible Man*], the supreme work of art created by an American Negro, is essentially a Negro's novel. It is written entirely out of a Negro's experience, and reveals its full dimension, I am convinced, only to the perfect *Negro* reader. But it is not a "Negro novel." Like Gwendolyn Brooks, like Faulkner, like most serious artists, he has transmuted himself and his experience almost entirely into his art. Only by turning to his essays and interviews can one discover the degree to which his own opinions, on racial issues or any other, are implicit in *Invisible Man*.

Invisible Man (1952) was not, Ellison insists, "an attack upon white society." . . . It is not, really, a race-war novel. But as no Negro's life in America, not even in the symbolic recreation, can be entirely free of racial combat, there are elements in the book that can be legitimately read in a race-war context. (pp. 110-11)

Several instances of direct propaganda occur, although each time in so organically convincing a situation that one does not think of attributing them to Ellison directly. They are simply taken as true, dramatically and substantially. (pp. 111-12)

[This] book is, among other things, a complete story of Negro life in America. By nature something of a pacifist, a quietist, Ellison is much more free than the embattled protestors like Wright to try to tell *all* of the Negro's story. It has been the theme of his entire creative life, in fact, that there is far, far more to the Negro's story in America than oppression, suffering, and hate: "The view from inside the skin," he insists, "is not so dark as it appears to be." (p. 113)

The focus of all [his] propaganda and history and ironic sociology is the nameless hero, the Invisible Man ("invisible," that is, to white men's eyes), the Negroes' Joseph K. It is his story, really, not the race's, not the war's, except insofar as he is of the race and in the war. (His non-naming, through five hundred pages, never becomes obvious or ominous—a testimony to the subtlety of Ellison's art. It is simply never needed.) The creation and loving sustenance of this narrator-hero, with all his follies and limitations, are among the triumphs of the book.

Reaching out from the central artifice of the narrator-hero are other displays of Ellison's art. His style, the "fine texture," is exact and acute, the language (usually) at fingertip control. Hear the crisp offhandedness of wicked ironies, the cool black humor; or . . . the needle-sharp evocations of sensation and interior pain. He can manipulate language, as he can character,

event, and design, for the optimum effects of irony, of a balanced double vision. Certain devices, tiny tricks, he leaves about like fingerprints: the strange selectivity of detail that leaves characters and objects and events undefinably charged, "off," ever so slightly left of real; the pre-announcement of a thing some lines before it is identified, giving to it an eerie surreality. Ellison has also, to move to items of slightly larger focus, the fullest sense of drama; he knows when to signal and advance a key moment, how to pace and position effects for the fullest buildup of artful tension or comedy or suspense: he can work up cool quiet horror like Harold Pinter, or handle the giant crescendo of effects needed for pageants like Clifton's funeral or the Harlem riots.

His rhetorical skill is prodigious, and he is not reticent about displaying its range. Not only does he indulge himself in perfect mimicry of the tall tale, the emotion-charged address, the Negro sermon; he also allows himself chances for Joycean word display, and makes his hero's hold on history a "way with words," a gift of tongues, an awesome and dangerous eloquence like his own.

Ellison's creative imagination, if such a talent can be singly regarded, is also more prolific than that of his peers. His exotic range of living characters, their vividness and magnitude; the extraordinary sequence of scenes and situations, each rendered with overflowing fullness—rooms, inner states, mob scenes, the fantasia of the hospital, the unforgettable battle royal at the Southern white men's smoker with which the novel opens: such independent creations bear witness to one of the most awesomely fertile living imaginations in American writing. (pp. 114-16)

His proper tradition *is* that of the great American novelists, as he so hoped it would be, and it is among them, rather than among the New Negroes, that he should be judged. Hawthorne and Melville, certainly, are of the family, and Faulkner and Fitzgerald: all the great ironists of the double vision, the half-romantic, half-cynical creators and retailers of the corrupted American dream. They are all symbolic artists, who charged their objects and events and effects with preternatural significance, who designed their fictions into national myths. He is not up *there*, of course; but I see no reason not to assign him a place—even for one unbalanced book—at least in the high second rank, with such other ironic idealists as Sherwood Anderson or Nathanael West. (p. 119)

David Littlejohn, in his *Black on White: A Critical Survey of Writing by American Negroes*, Grossman, 1966, pp. 101-37.

EDWARD MARGOLIES
(essay date 1968)

[A noted authority on African-American literature, Margolies has written widely on the life and works of novelist and autobiographer Richard Wright. In the following excerpt from his *Native Sons: A Critical Study of Twentieth-Century Negro American Authors*, he examines Ellison's depiction of black life in America in *Invisible Man.*]

[It] was not until the 1920's that Negro authors seriously attempted to deal with the folk materials in their culture. And when they did, the authors of the Harlem school treated Negro life self-consciously, as if somehow Negroness and poverty produced a superior kind of humanity, given to song and dance, and to a primitive, noble, exotic happiness as opposed to the corruption and neurosis of the surrounding white civilization.

The stark years of the thirties forced the Negro author to take a more realistic assessment of his situation. Frequently he labored under a structured ideology not altogether suited to his problems, but in any event he was required by this kind of discipline to relate what was unique in his culture to a broader over-all concept of history. During the first half of the decade the Communists appeared to champion an independent state located somewhere in the South, but after 1934 more and more stress was laid on full-fledged assimilation and integration into American life. This forced Negro intellectuals to examine even more closely their own ambivalent assimilationist and separatist views.

One of these was a young college student, Ralph Ellison, who came to New York in 1937 and began writing under the guidance and encouragement of a confirmed Party member, Richard Wright. Wright himself had written about the problem of Negro cultural identity and its place in a pluralistic society. Ellison almost immediately took up the dilemma, and in a sense devoted all his energies to its pursuit. (pp. 128-29)

No one could have been better suited, by virtue of his training and upbringing and experience, to undertake the challenge. Born in Oklahoma City in 1914, when caste lines were not yet so rigidly drawn as in other parts of the South, Ellison enjoyed a freedom to partake of the various crosscurrents of American life that were still sweeping across that near-frontier area. Not only did he encounter in his day-to-day experiences persons of different backgrounds, but he learned their songs, dances, and literature in the public schools. Moreover, he attended films and theater and read

books avidly, and none of these suggested to him the "limitations" of Negro life. (p. 129)

He knew best, of course, his Negro culture, and he projected on his vision of the outside world the specificities of a Negro outlook. . . . [Jazz] and especially blues provided him with the greatest sources of satisfaction. In his growing years, Kansas City jazz attained its ultimate refinement in the environs of Oklahoma City, and figures like Jimmie Rushing, Hot Lips Paige, Charlie Christian, and others became heroes to hosts of Negro boys. And if jazz was not regarded as being quite respectable in the schools he attended, he was given a rather impressive training in classical music so that he could make comparisons and perceive relationships. Thus for Ellison it was not simply a case of Negro culture standing apart, but a convergence in which Negro culture maintained its separate identity in a wider spectrum.

Not surprisingly, Ellison's understanding of his early life corresponds to his definition of Negro jazz. And ultimately it is jazz, and blues especially, that becomes the aesthetic mainspring of his writing. . . . [Music], however tragic its message, is an affirmation of life, a celebration of the indomitable human spirit, in that it imposes order and form on the chaos of experience.

> The delicate balance struck between strong individual personality and the group . . . was a marvel of social organization. I had learned too that the end of all this discipline and technical mastery was the desire to express an affirmative way of life through its musical tradition and that this tradition insisted that each artist achieve his creativity within its frame. He must learn the best of the past, and add to it his personal vision. Life could be harsh, loud and wrong if it wished, but they lived it fully, and when they expressed their attitude toward the world it was with a fluid style that reduced the chaos of living to form. (pp. 129-31)

The hero of *Invisible Man,* in the course of a journey from the deep South to Harlem, assumes a variety of poses, most of which he believes in at the time, to fit the white man's definition of a Negro. But each of these roles fails him, and a kind of chaos ensues . . . , for no one of them takes into account the fluidity and complexity of his individual being. At the end of the novel, hidden away in a forgotten basement room in an apartment building, the hero comes to no true resolution of his dilemma except the realization that his humanity is invisible to most persons, Negroes as well as white, and that he must discover for himself what he thinks, feels, and is. Yet the mere act of telling his story in novel form has given order to the meaninglessness of his experiences, and has thus become an affirmation, a celebration of life. He intends, he says, to ascend to the surface soon, to have another "go" at the world.

Ellison at the National Book Award presentation for *Invisible Man*, 1953. With him, left to right, are Archibald MacLeish, Frederick Lewis Allen, and Bernard DeVoto.

The novel is no more than a recapitulation of the pain the hero has suffered in his twenty or so years—the telling of which is its own catharsis. No social message, no system of beliefs, no intellectual conclusions arise from his tale other than his own consolation in telling it. Yet in the telling, he cannot but see the comically absurd aspects of his existence, of all Existence—and his narration is therefore not without humor. (Ellison told one interviewer that he thought he had written a very funny book.) *Invisible Man* is tragic in the sense that it celebrates the hero's capacity to endure, comic in the sense that he avers the fecundity of life, the wealth of the possibilities he may choose (and he often chooses wrongly) amidst the abundance of chaos.

Ellison has several times described this view of life as blues. In 1946 he wrote:

The blues is an impulse to keep the painful details and episodes of a brutal experience alive in one's aching consciousness, to finger its jagged grain, and to transcend it, not by the consolation of philosophy but by squeezing from it a near-tragic, near-comic lyricism. As a form, the blues is an autobiographical chronicle of personal catastrophe. . . .

Ellison also sees the blues as serving a ritual function.

The blues speak to us simultaneously of the tragic and comic aspects of the human condition and they express a profound sense of life shared by many Negroes precisely because their lives have combined these modes. . . . This is a group experience . . . and any effective study of the blues would treat them first as poetry and ritual.

Invisible Man opens with a prologue in which the hero, in his secret basement room, announces he is about to recite the catastrophic events of his life. . . . He has been playing a Louis Armstrong record, the refrain of which runs: "What did I do / To be so black / And blue?" In a sense, this refrain implicitly follows each of the major episodes of the novel. As his attempts to play out the roles that whites have assigned him (each of them different, but all of them dehumanizing, like variations on a theme) meet with disaster, the hero in effect asks himself Armstrong's punning question. He has tried to play the game according to the rules but has each time discovered himself more bruised. Thus each episode serves almost as an extended blues verse, and the narrator becomes the singer. The epilogue brings us back to the present; the reader is returned to the basement room, and the hero tells us that despite his psychic wounds (he has dreamt that he has been castrated), he has not yet given up on life. Hence the novel ends as it had begun, just as the last verse of a blues is frequently the same as the first.

Since the blues, according to Ellison, is by its very nature a record of past wrongs, pains, and defeats, it serves to define the singer as one who has suffered, and in so doing it has provided him with a history. As the novel develops, the hero takes on the role of a Negro Everyman, whose adventures and cries of woe and laughter become the history of a people. As a high-school boy in the South, he is a "Tom"—little better than a darky entertainer; in college, a Booker T. Washington accommodationist. When he moves North, he works as a nonunion laborer and then flirts for a while with Communism. Finally, he becomes a Rinehart, Ellison's word for the unattached, alienated, urban Negro who deliberately endeavors to manipulate the fantasies of whites and Negroes to his own advantage. But besides being a kind of symbolic recapitulation of Negro history, the blues structure of the novel suggests a philosophy of history as well—something outside racial determinism, progress, or various ideologies, something indefinably human, unexpected and perhaps nonrational.

In one sense the Negro since Emancipation has telescoped the American experience, passing from an agrarian existence to a highly industrialized urban life. In another sense this history is enigmatic—not only invisible but unformed—a history in which chance and accident act as principles in a designless universe. So long as men demand predetermined patterns of their universe, in order to reassure themselves that existence is not chaotic (which it is), they will demand that Negroes play out certain roles to conform to these patterns. But there is an issue of "necessity" involved. The Negro, like any other man, is unresolved nature, mysterious and complex, and cannot by the very exuberance of his being long play out these roles. When this occurs, illusion is then momentarily stripped away and chaos is seen for what it is. But the white man, terrified at these realities, proceeds to force upon the Negro still another role to suit yet another fancied pattern of existence. Does this mean that history and life need be perceived as unmitigated purposelessness? In effect Ellison never truly resolves the question aesthetically. But he seems to be saying that if men recognize first that existence is purposeless, they may then be able to perceive the possibility of shaping their existence in some kind

of viable form—in much the same manner as the blues artist gives form to his senseless pain and suffering. (pp. 131-34)

As the novel proper opens, the hero recalls his grandfather's dying words: "I never told you, but our life is a war and I have been a traitor all my born days, a spy in the enemy's country ever since I give up my gun in the Reconstruction." He goes on to advise, "I want you to overcome 'em with yeses, undermine 'em with grins, agree 'em to death and destruction, let 'em swoller you till they vomit or bust wide open." These then will be the tactics the Negro will employ for survival in years to come. He will pretend to agree to his invisibility until reality strikes down the white man for his obdurate blindness. The novel then proceeds to record the hero's various initiation rites into invisibility wherein the white man accords him several identities— none of them human. Ultimately his is a journey into self-recognition. He recognizes first that he is invisible—and second, that he is a man. (pp. 134-35)

The tone of the first half of the novel is that of an almost Gulliverlike innocence. [The hero] relates objectively how "sincerely" he attempts to fulfill his roles, how deeply he believes in them. As a high-school graduate, he is invited to deliver his valedictorian address on humility as being the "very essence of progress" to a smoker of the leading white citizens of the town. . . . The hero is finally allowed to give his speech (at first scarcely anyone appears to be listening), but there is very nearly an explosive situation when, by a slip of the tongue, he mentions social equality. At the end of his speech, he is given a briefcase in which, during the course of his subsequent adventures, he will place tokens and mementos of the various identities the Negro has assumed during his history.

The second major episode takes place in a Southern Negro college whose buildings and environs— magnolias, honeysuckle, moonlight—the hero describes in glowing (faintly satirical) terms. The college has been endowed in large part by Northern liberals who, since Reconstruction, have endorsed Booker T. Washington's twin principles of equality and caste submission—not only a logical contradiction, but, again, a kind of blindness to reality. But here Ellison is suggesting as well that the Northern white liberal philanthropist demands the invisibility of the Negro no less than his Southern racist counterpart, in order to conceal from himself his ancestors' complicity in Negro slavery. Ellison, in this portion of the novel, employs, in addition, constant allusion to Negro history as a means of discovering the Negro's present invisibility. The hero relates, for example, the presence on the campus of a statue of the Founder, a former slave, who is removing (or placing?) a veil from (or on?) the eyes of a kneeling Negro. Was Negro enlightenment simply another guise of keeping the Negro in the dark, invisible from himself ?

There are mellow scenes of students assembled in chapel singing symphonic and devitalized slave spirituals for white patrons. Or a moving and eloquent address by an ancient Negro minister rehearsing the life, trials, and achievement of the Founder. The Founder's immense sacrifices, the students are told (probably for the thousandth time) in wonderful old-fashioned ringing rhetoric, have made possible the progress and happiness they enjoy today. At the close of his speech, the minister stumbles as he leaves the rostrum and the students suddenly realize that the minister is himself blind.

Some of the best passages in the novel occur when the hero, an honors student, acting as chauffeur to one of the white patrons who has been visiting the college, inadvertently drives him beyond the picturesque manicured environs of the college campus past the old slave quarters. This is a part of the countryside Mr. Norton has never before seen and he is met with reality for the first time. The habitations are unchanged since ante-bellum days and the Negro peasants living thereabouts are regarded as little better than barbarians by the middle-class college community. Norton talks to one of them, Jim Trueblood, who recounts the fantastic events relating to his incest with his daughter, which has made him a celebrated figure among the whites in the county. (Respectable Negroes are ashamed.) . . . At the close of Trueblood's story, Norton apparently suffers a heart attack, and the hero takes him to a Negro roadhouse, the Golden Day, in order to revive him with whisky. As luck would have it, they arrive at about the same time as a group of Negro mental patients, shell-shocked veterans of World War I, who pay periodic visits under guard for a respite of drinks and disreputable women. A wild riot erupts and Norton is hurt and hustled out, but not before one of the veterans tells him that for all his vaunted philanthropy, the Negro is not a human being but a "thing," a cipher to satisfy his guilt and his cravings for adulation and love.

Here Ellison suggests the results of a hundred years of white liberal patrimony of the Negro. Large financial donations may afford the givers some illusion of having fulfilled their moral obligations, but failure to recognize the Negro's humanity has produced only a worsening of pain. . . . Although Norton would like to believe the college is a monument to his efforts, in reality the maddened rioting veterans of the Golden Day are his true fate. They represent the logical absurdity of his dream, for they are not, like Trueblood, Negro peasants bound to the soil, but testimonials to Negro progress—doctors, lawyers, teachers. Thus has Ellison married elements of the Negro's invisible past to the Negro's invisible present: slavery (Trueblood), Reconstruction (the college campus), philanthropy

(Norton), and World War I (the veterans)—all resulting in a chaos called The Golden Day. (pp. 135-38)

[As the novel ensues], Ellison moves from the white-Negro Southern power structure to the Negro's Northern plight. Bledsoe has ostensibly suspended the hero for the summer months but has provided him with letters of identity to important New York capitalists who might employ him. The journey North has a blues ring, especially when the hero discovers that Bledsoe too has deluded him with false promises. But the hero does manage to find work at the Liberty Paint Company, whose motto reads, "Keep America Pure with Liberty Paints." His first task is to infuse ten drops of a blackish substance into buckets of a white base liquid and stir, the result being a product called Optic White which is used in repainting national monuments. Here Ellison's allegory becomes a little too obvious.

The hero is next assigned to work at the furnaces of a basement, three levels underground, with a strange little Negro foreman named Lucius Brockaway. It develops that Brockaway, who has charge of all the immensely complicated machinery below ground— boilers, furnaces, cables, pipes, wires, and so on—is indispensable in running the plant. Efforts to displace him with white engineers have resulted in a total breakdown of production. . . . From simple allegory Ellison has moved to a more subtle kind of symbolism. Somewhere beyond the narrative level, he is saying that America has depended from the start on the unacknowledged skills and sacrifices of Negro labor.

But if Brockaway is the indispensable man, he is also the white capitalist's man as well. He is fiercely opposed to labor unions, and when he learns that the hero, during his lunch hour, inadvertently stumbled onto a union meeting (in which, incidentally, a discussion had been proceeding regarding the employment of nonunion Negro workers), he accuses the hero of treachery and betrayal. He attacks the hero and the two wrestle weirdly in the underground chamber—a Northern echo of the battle of the boys at the white citizens' smoker. Just when the hero believes that Brockaway has finally reconciled himself to his presence, a boiler explodes and the hero awakens to discover himself in the plant hospital. (pp. 138-40)

The hero is released from the hospital and dismissed from his job ("You just aren't prepared to work under our industrial conditions"), after an operation intended to produce in him a new and more docile personality. . . . Yet the operation does not altogether remove his identity. He remembers snatches of folklore and songs his grandmother had sung to him as a child which seem strangely applicable to his situation. The past lives on, then, in the present, and whatever else urban life and the Depression may have done to him, they have given him a greater sense of pride and an awareness of his history.

The hero now strides through the streets of Harlem somehow reassured by the swarming black life about him. He eschews the black middle class that hopelessly and ludicrously models itself on the white bourgeoisie—his first place of residence, Men's House, is a haven for such persons—and lives in a boarding-house run by Aunt Mary, a formidable mother-earth figure who cares warmly for the lost and bewildered children of her native Southland. Nor is the hero any longer ashamed of Southern Negro foods that identify him with a slave and peasant ancestry. On one occasion he stops to purchase a yam from a Southern street vender. "I am what I am," he says as he bites into the hot buttered delicacy.

But if urban life awakens the hero to emotions of a specific Negro historical identity, . . . the Depression expands these feelings to include an active sense of social responsibility the hero now shares with many other city Negroes. And the latter part of the novel deals with some of the forces that endeavored to make political use of the new awakening in Negro communities.

Black nationalism, the first of these, is represented in the figure of Ras the Exhorter, an exotic West Indian extremist. The hero sees Ras violently addressing a street corner gathering when he first arrives in Harlem from the South. He pays little attention at the time but when he later involves himself with the Brotherhood (the Communist Party), Ras and his followers play a distinct role in his experiences. Ras, who suggests something of the colorful Marcus Garvey, preaches a doctrine of complete black virtue coupled with an utter distrust of the white man. (pp. 140-41)

The hero is recruited by the Brotherhood when, after witnessing the physical eviction of an elderly Negro couple from their tenement, he delivers a fiery speech protesting the injustice of it all to a gathering street crowd. Even here, Ellison suggests the specific Negro history that has ultimately placed the unhappy pair on the dreary Harlem sidewalk. He cites the pathetic paucity of personal effects they are allowed to keep, among them a small Ethiopian flag, a tintype of Abraham Lincoln, a manumission paper dated 1859, a pair of "knocking bones" used in minstrel shows, some faded and void insurance policies, and a "yellowing newspaper portrait of a huge black man with the caption: 'MARCUS GARVEY DEPORTED.' " (pp. 141-42)

Ellison perhaps devotes too much space proportionally to the Communist wooing of the Negro, but these are experiences he knew, after all, firsthand, and the Marxist emphasis on Negro history as being part of a larger dialectical process must have appealed to Ellison's ingrained aesthetic sense. In any event, his hero's Communist experiences are too complicated to chronicle fully. He becomes an authentic Harlem "spokesman," but even when he is most blinded by his Marxist rhetoric, there persist in the marrow of his being some suspicions regarding the relevance of his Negro experience to the notions of history he publicly upholds. Indeed, Ras's violent and chauvinistic opposition to Brotherhood ideals is closer to what the hero knows to be true. What he finally learns in the course of his radical adventures is that even for the Brothers, the Negro is a thing, an object, an instrument of power politics and of preordained historical design, rather than a divinely complex and complicated human mystery. (p. 142).

Yet his experiences as a radical are not a total loss. For one thing, the hero, like his author, has acquired an education of sorts regarding the Negro's role in history. If what the hero learns is at considerable variance from what the Brotherhood wanted him to learn, he does nonetheless take away with himself an added sense of his own importance. Second, and possibly more important, is that in making him a Harlem leader, the Brotherhood has unwittingly given him access to his fellow Negroes on a level he had hitherto seldom achieved. He discovers to his astonishment (and to the chagrin of the Brothers) a bond of love and shared experience that the outside world can never know.

In one of his first performances for the Brothers, he addresses an assembly of Negroes on the question of rent evictions. (pp. 142-43)

As a result of his speech, his reputation is established. He begins to campaign against rent dispossessions, but then quite unexpectedly he is transferred downtown, ostensibly for further indoctrination. Upon his return several months later, he learns that the agitation he had begun so successfully has lost nearly all its momentum and that the community has become hostile to the Brotherhood for its betrayal. . . . His anxieties are further aroused when he learns that Tod Clifton, his closest Harlem comrade and a Brotherhood lieutenant, has vanished. . . . Later the hero witnesses Clifton being shot to death by a policeman who had been trying to arrest him.

On his return subway trip to Harlem, the hero ponders Clifton's death, and then as he observes a trio of zootsuited adolescent Negro boys sitting quietly in front of him, he realizes that:

They were men out of time—unless they found Brotherhood. Men out of time, who would soon be gone and forgotten. . . . But who knew (and now I began to tremble so violently I had to lean against a refuse can)—who knew but they were the saviors, the true leaders, the bearers of something precious? The stewards of something uncomfortable, burdensome, which they hated because, living outside the realm of history, there was no one to applaud their value and they themselves failed to understand it. What if Brother Jack were wrong? . . . What if history was not a reasonable citizen, but a madman full of paranoid guile and these boys his agents, his big surprise! His own revenge? For they were outside, in the dark with Sambo, the dancing paper doll; taking it on the lambo with my fallen brother, Tod Clifton (Tod, Tod) running and dodging the forces of history instead of making a dominating stand.

Here then is the blues theme as applied to history. The accidental, the unplanned, the unforeseen variables of history are symbolized by the presence of the Negro, who because of his invisibility should not logically exist, but who nonetheless endures and may, on some future occasion, transform events overnight. And the mere fact of his survival, despite sufferings, defeats and repressions, represents an affirmation of life that undercuts any "system" of history. Because human beings are involved, history, like blues, records only the possibilities of existence.

The hero organizes a huge procession for the dead Clifton on the streets of Harlem. . . . The Brotherhood at once makes plain its opposition to the hero's militancy and he is now finally convinced he has once more been betrayed. He intends as vengeance to delude them as they had all along been deluding him. He will follow his grandfather's advice: "overcome 'em with yeses, undermine 'em with grins" until the entire Harlem community erupts in their faces. He will pretend to them that their more pacific plans to organize the community are eminently successful, while in reality he knows that Harlem seethes with social and racial tensions, not the least of which are aimed at the Brotherhood.

Since much of the hostility of the community is directed toward him as being an instrument of a white man's organization, the hero determines to take a new identity. He settles for a wide-brimmed white hat and dark glasses—but the disguise works only too well. He is constantly being stopped on the street by persons who mistake him for someone named Rinehart. But on each occasion they know Rinehart as possessing a different occupation. . . . The hero is thus reborn as Rinehart, whose "world was possibility . . . [a] vast seething hot world of fluidity" in which Rinehart plays many roles. For the real Rinehart had evidently perceived the Negro's world as an undesigned Chaos in which he could have as many images as he wished. Is this not the white man's world as well, the hero wonders, since no understanding of history can have any validity if it fails to recognize the Negro's existence? Here Ellison and his hero stand at the brink of existential despair, where values such as love, honor, and integrity have no meaning.

But before he can resolve his disturbed vision, the hero is pulled back into a Harlem uprising of destruction and violence for which he is in part responsible. . . . [Pursued by a pair of white hoodlums he] dives into an open manhole and ultimately finds his way into the discarded basement room which will become his home.

In the basement room the hero decides that he has all along been invisible. But before he can determine who he is, Ellison makes him discard the contents of the briefcase he has been carrying ever since the night of the smoker. In the course of his life he has collected a number of objects which he has "unthinkingly" stuffed in his briefcase. In effect these represent not only his past identities but the roles the Negro has played in history. At one time or another, the briefcase has contained a small antique cast-iron bank for coins molded in the figure of a red-lipped, minstrel Negro (economic exploitation), a leg shackle (peonage), his high-school diploma (his Jim Crow education), Clifton's Sambo doll (his minstrel role), a letter from Jack identifying him as a Brother, and his dark Rinehart glasses. In jettisoning these, as it were, the hero can come to a true recognition of himself.

In isolating the historical theme of Ellison's blues, one does not, of course, begin to do justice to the novel. The narrative pace is swift and engaging, and the hero's adventures possess their own intrinsic interest. Moreover, Ellison's symbols seldom intrude as they explain, and yet are quite as original as they are functional. Nonetheless, splendid and ambitious as Ellison's novel is, it does not quite succeed. Perhaps one reason is that his hero, owning no identity or at best an invisible one, does not create in the reader any real empathy. He is not a lovable rogue, nor a goodhearted innocent, but merely a passive figure who, for the most part quite mindlessly, allows things to happen to him. This was of course Ellison's intention, but given the sustained length of the novel and the colorlessness of the protagonist, the reader is made more and more aware that he is reading a book. There is simply too much distance between the reader and the hero and one finds oneself subconsciously congratulating the author for the deftness with which he moves his character along, rather than paying attention to his troubles or his meaning. Secondly, there is a singleness of theme—the hero's invisibility—and episode after episode plays variations on this theme. It is as if one were compelled to listen to a marvelous blues extended to symphonic length. One may admire its various parts, but wish after a while for a different kind of movement—to catch oneself up in surprise or elation or another level of comprehension.

In all fairness, Ellison attempts to do this. The tone of the hero changes from that of a gullible innocent in the beginning to that of a straightforward narrator somewhere midway in the novel, to that of a somewhat more sophisticated observer of himself later on. And Ellison himself has said of his novel that it moves stylistically from naturalism to expressionism to surrealism—all of which is true. But these are, after all, effects, and the single idea still dominates. One somehow expects more, for all its richness, and the "more" is seldom forthcoming.

Which brings us once again to the thematic weakness of the novel. For Ellison's hero simply has nowhere to go once he tells us he is invisible. He does indeed, in the Epilogue, say that he intends to rise again and try his hand at life, that he has faith in democratic principles, and that life itself is its own excuse despite the blows it has dealt him. But there is no evidence in the text to fortify his beliefs. The blues singer has depths of feeling to begin with, but Ellison's hero has just begun to learn to feel as the novel ends. (pp. 143-48)

Edward Margolies, "History as Blues: Ralph Ellison's 'Invisible Man'," in his *Native Sons: A Critical Study of Twentieth-Century Negro American Authors*, J. B. Lippincott Company, 1968, pp. 127-48.

GEORGE SIM JOHNSTON

(essay date 1986)

[In the following essay, Johnston reviews *Going to the Territory*, commenting on Ellison's development as a writer and thinker.]

In 1965, the book-review supplement of the old New York *Herald Tribune* asked two hundred critics to pick the best American novels published since World War II. The resulting list of the "top twenty" was quite solid, as such lists go, and if it were to be revised today to take account of the novels published since then, it would, sad to say, require little revision. The first choice of the critics was Ralph Ellison's *Invisible Man,* which was published in 1952, and the book still stands as probably the best American novel to be published since—well, pick your favorite Faulkner.

Among Ellison's many accomplishments in that book was to demolish the Chinese Wall which critics like Philip Rahv had erected between the two main tendencies in American writing—between, as Rahv phrased it, the "palefaces" and the "redskins." Ellison's strategy was impeccably "literary"; he rejected the formulas of the social novelists of the 30's—given the story he wanted to tell, they must have suggested themselves as models—and took what he needed instead from the likes of Henry James and T. S. Eliot. The techniques of allegory and symbolism he learned from them gave his narrative both a depth and a surface texture which was beyond anything the writers in the naturalist camp were capable of. But at the same time, Ellison gave the impression that he was writing flat-out in

good "redskin" fashion; he not only injected his dialogue with the rhythms of jazz and Harlem street talk, but also seemed to draw on an enormous fund of raw, primary experience. It was as though Henry James were improvising riffs with Charlie Parker on the corner of Lenox and 125th Street.

Among the lessons which Ellison's novel would seem to hold for younger American writers today is that it is possible to explore the subject of alienation without writing about an adolescent off in a corner doing lines of cocaine. It is a lesson that Ellison tells us he first learned from André Malraux. For implicit in his novel is the idea that the identity and fate of an individual are inextricably tied to the public life of the society in which he lives.

Ellison has also told us that as a young writer he deliberately set about making himself familiar with "the major motives of American literature" and in the process discovered books like *Moby-Dick* and *Huckleberry Finn.* (And these books *were* a discovery for a writer starting out in the 30's. Joyce and Eliot did not become acquainted with *Huckleberry Finn* until they were past middle age.) Even more, perhaps, than the modernists, Hawthorne, Melville, and Twain helped Ellison to write a novel that, while deeply political in its implications, went far beyond any "protest" novel in its exploration of the social realities of America.

Ellison is much taken with his own biography, and in his new collection of nonfiction pieces, *Going to the Territory,* we learn a great deal about how he turned himself into a novelist. *Invisible Man* is a work of such high order that we do not begrudge the information. But Ellison's one novel appeared thirty-four years ago, and only a few fragments of the big (or at least very long) novel which he has been writing since then have been allowed to leave the workshop. So far as his public is concerned, then, we may say that Ellison's main work since *Invisible Man* has been the crafting of himself as a man of letters.

It has been very careful and measured work, and has produced one of the more dignified, if somewhat mannered, presences on the literary landscape. I do not think Ellison would object to my implication that there is an element of calculation in his public persona, for in the strongest essay in this new book, **"An Extravagance of Laughter,"** he quotes Yeats on the necessity of fashioning a "second self " if one is to do any work in this world. According to Ellison, Yeats's demand for a "mask," for a self-elected identity, applies doubly for an American, and triply for a black American like himself, because he lives in a fluid society in which the social identity of an individual is far more problematic than it is on the other side of the Atlantic.

Like *Shadow and Act,* which was published in 1964, *Going to the Territory* brings together some of the speeches, interviews, and articles which have come forth, at wide intervals, from the public Ellison. Like most artists who take it on themselves to instruct outside the medium of their art, Ellison turns out to have a few favorite hobby-horses which he mounts again and again. To begin with, he has a healthy obsession with the American writer's role as a continuator, as an improviser on the themes set down not only by past American writers, but also by the men who "conceived" America in documents like the Constitution and the Bill of Rights. Ellison understands American democracy much the way he understands literature—as a highly deliberate and self-conscious act. Like Emerson, he sees the writer as an energizer, teaching the possibilities of the individual in an open society. (Here, as elsewhere in these pieces, Ellison is playing the themes of *Invisible Man* in a different key. Early on in that novel, the nameless hero is told to read Emerson, and the epilogue contains phrases which might have been spun during a walk in the woods around Concord.)

Ellison, of course, is not the only postwar writer to have taken the American classics to heart and set up shop as a public "witness" to the democratic experience. There has been Robert Lowell, for example. When Lowell read his poem, "For the Union Dead," to a cheering crowd of thousands in the Boston Public Garden, he went about as far as a writer can go along these lines. But Lowell's most famous public act was his refusal to accept Lyndon Johnson's invitation to the White House Festival of the Arts in 1965 because of his disagreement with Johnson's policies in Vietnam. Ellison accepted the invitation, and in a subsequent interview he took Lowell to task for mixing art and politics. And here we come to another major theme which connects many of the pieces in this new book with one another and with *Invisible Man.* Ellison does not care for partisan politics, and he thinks that an artist contributes far more to the commonwealth by sticking to his work than by going public with an agenda.

Ellison's distaste for political activism, which seems to date from his involvement with the Communist party as a young man, caused him to be subjected to a fair amount of abuse during the salad days of the New Left. In the same year that Lowell and Norman Mailer marched on the Pentagon, Ellison tweaked the nose of the New York literary establishment by quoting in *Harper's,* with approval, a speech of Lyndon Johnson to the effect that art is not a political weapon. Like Saul Bellow (who is far more prickly on the subject), Ellison is impatient with those who would force him into the reductive certainties of a "position," and, again like Bellow, much of what he has put into print during the last few decades would seem to be an exasperated response to the sectarian clamor around him.

It would be a mistake, however, to say that Ellison rejects the use of political pressure to achieve ends

like racial equality. But for him, that goal is promoted far more effectively by powerful *non-political* forces which are at work in this country. America's vernacular culture, he points out, is a potent leveler. It is the great solvent of social disparities, constantly eating away at traditional barriers of class and race. And in relation to the cultural whole, he writes, "we are all minorities," anyway. The implication of Ellison's argument—that Stevie Wonder and Bill Cosby are the cutting edge leading to a successful multiracial society—is not likely to sit well with those who are still intrigued by various forms of social engineering; but Ellison is supremely confident that our pluralistic culture will always manage to "outflank" politics.

Ellison's sheer relish of American vernacular culture expresses itself in just about every piece in this book. He is really most at home writing about jazz and folk humor. He points out that from the beginning our general culture has been strongly influenced by blacks—Ellison prefers the term "Negro American"—and that even in the South before the Civil War, blacks and whites shared in a cultural relationship which was nothing less than organic. Black artists, he says, should not subscribe to "the myth of the Negro American's total alienation from the larger American culture—a culture he helped create in the areas of music and literature. . . ." Cold comfort, perhaps, to a black musician who finds himself on the less remunerative side of the so-called "crossover" line, where records do not go triple platinum, but Ellison is making the valid point, which again will not sit well with those who have not yet graduated from the 60's, that a minority artist unnecessarily handicaps himself if he surrenders to "sociological notions of racial separatism."

The pieces in this book deal with a variety of subjects, but many of them, even when they have titles like **"Remembering Richard Wright"** and **"Homage to Duke Ellington on His Birthday,"** are heavily autobiographical. The writing varies in quality. Ellison is crisp and engaging when he addresses a concrete topic—his own past, for example, or jazz—but he tends to get windy when dealing with abstractions like culture and democracy. His generalities have a way of drowning in a sea of five-dollar words. ("So perhaps the complex actuality of our cultural pluralism is perplexing because the diverse interacting elements . . . ," and so on.) But one thing Ellison never loses is his humor. It is constantly brought forth by his contemplation of the American scene. James Joyce complained that not one of the critics of *Ulysses* saw that the book was "damn funny," and Ellison in effect makes the same point to critics of America. For all its problems and incongruities, the country is blessed with a vernacular culture which produces "an extravagance of laughter," and in that laughter, Ellison tells us, much that is painful can be transcended. (pp. 71-4)

George Sim Johnston, "Man of Letters," in *Commentary,* Vol. 82, No. 6, December, 1986, pp. 71-4.

SOURCES FOR FURTHER STUDY

Hersey, John, ed. *Ralph Ellison: A Collection of Critical Essays.* Englewood Cliffs, N.J.: Prentice-Hall, 1964, 180 p.

> Collects previously published criticism of Ellison's major works. Essays include Saul Bellow's "Man Underground," Irving Howe's "Black Boys and Native Sons," James Alan McPherson's "Invisible Man," and William J. Schafer's "Ralph Ellison and the Birth of the Anti-Hero."

Nadel, Alan. *Invisible Criticism: Ralph Ellison and the American Canon.* Iowa City: University of Iowa Press, 1988, 181 p.

> Examines *Invisible Man* in light of contemporary notions of literary canon formation, maintaining that the work is "a perfect example of a novel which, through the use of allusions, can contain a literary-critical subtext."

McSweeney, Kerry. *'Invisible Man': Race and Identity.* Twayne's Masterwork Studies, No. 17. Boston: Twayne Publishers, 1988, 139 p.

> Book-length study of race awareness in *Invisible Man,* with commentary on psychological issues in the novel.

O'Meally, Robert G. *The Craft of Ralph Ellison.* Cambridge, Mass.: Harvard University Press, 1980, 212 p.

> Comprehensive study of Ellison's life and works.

———, ed. *New Essays on 'Invisible Man'.* Cambridge: Cambridge University Press, 1988, 190 p.

> Essay collection. Contributors include: John F. Callahan, "Frequencies of Eloquence: The Performance and Composition of *Invisible Man*"; Berndt Ostendorf, "Ralph Ellison: Anthropology, Modernism, and Jazz": Thomas Schaub, "Ellison's Masks and the Novel of Reality"; and Valerie Smith, "The Meaning of Narration in *Invisible Man.*"

Stepto, Robert B., and Harper, Michael S. "Study & Experience: An Interview with Ralph Ellison." *The Massachusetts Review* XVIII, No. 3 (Autumn 1977): 417-35.

> Text of an interview conducted at Ellison's Manhattan home in 1976. The discussion focuses on the critical reception given to *Invisible Man* as well as on Ellison's growth as a writer.

Ralph Waldo Emerson

1803-1882

American philosopher, essayist, lecturer, and poet.

INTRODUCTION

A founder of the Transcendental movement and the founder of a distinctly American philosophy emphasizing optimism, individuality, and mysticism, Emerson was one of the most influential literary figures of the nineteenth century. Raised to be a minister in Puritan New England, Emerson sought to "create all things new" with a philosophy stressing the recognition of God Immanent, the presence of ongoing creation and revelation by a god apparent in all things and who exists within everyone. Also crucial to Emerson's thought is the related Eastern concept of the essential unity of all thoughts, persons, and things in the divine whole. Traditional values of right and wrong, good and evil, appear in his work as necessary opposites, evidencing the effect of German philosopher G. W. F. Hegel's system of dialectical metaphysics. Emerson's works also emphasize individualism and each person's quest to break free from the trappings of the illusory world (maya) in order to discover the godliness of the inner Self.

The son of a Unitarian minister, Emerson spent a sheltered childhood in Boston. During his youth the publications of the German Higher Critics and their progeny, as well as translations of Hindu and Buddhist poetry, were causing controversy in American academic circles. Emerson's class at Harvard Divinity School was affected by these influences; consequently, upon assuming the pastorate of a Boston church in 1829, Emerson experienced many doubts concerning traditional Christian belief. He resigned from his pulpit in 1832, moved to nearby Concord, and then spent the next few years studying and traveling in Europe. After visiting a Paris botanical exhibition, Emerson resolved to be, as he termed it, a "naturalist." Upon returning to the United States, he began his career as a lecturer in the country's new lyceum movement. During the late

1830s and early 1840s, Emerson published the works that present his thought at its most idealistic and optimistic. The lyrical essay *Nature* (1836), a pamphlet repudiating both materialism and conventional religion, declares nature the divine example for inspiration and the source of boundless possibilities for humanity's fulfillment. *The American Scholar*, an address delivered before Harvard's Phi Beta Kappa Society in 1837, attacks American dependence on European thought and urges the creation of a new literary heritage. Emerson's *Divinity School Address*, delivered at Harvard in 1838, caused tremendous controversy for renouncing the tenets of historical Christianity and defining Transcendental philosophy in terms of the "impersoneity" of God. The doctrines formulated in these three works were later expanded and elaborated upon in his *Essays* (1841) and *Essays: Second Series* (1844), of which "Self-Reliance," "The Over-Soul," and "The Poet" are among the best-known.

Emerson became identified with the Transcendental movement in the 1840s, serving as its spokesperson, and as founder and guiding force of that group's quarterly periodical, the *Dial*. Conceived as "a medium for the freest expression of thought on the questions which interest earnest minds in every community," the *Dial* was published for a small readership from 1840 to 1844, when it folded. Introducing the public to the writings of Amos Bronson Alcott, Margaret Fuller, and Henry David Thoreau, a group who shared Emerson's philosophy, the journal also published Emerson's first poems. The merits of his poetry, collected in *Poems* (1847) and *May-Day, and Other Pieces* (1867), are subject to much critical debate. Prominent among them are "The Rhodora," "The Sphinx," "Brahma," "The Humble-Bee," and "Threnody." But the poem best known to the American public is one of his earliest works, the "Concord Hymn," which celebrates "the shot heard round the world" of the Battle of Concord, during the American Revolution.

Emerson's poetry written from the era of the *Dial* onward, as well as his prose works dating from *Essays: Second Series*, chart a steady decline in the author's idealism and give rise to an emerging recognition of mortal limitations. *The Conduct of Life* (1860) perhaps best expresses his humanistic acquiescence to the reality of worldly circumstances. Other important later works include *Representative Men: Seven Lectures* (1850), a series of essays on the men who most closely fit Emerson's ideals—including Plato, Napoleon, and Shakespeare—and *English Traits* (1856), a work hailed by his friend Thomas Carlyle as an accurate portrait of English social manners in the mid–Victorian era. *Society and Solitude* (1870) marks the beginning of Emerson's decline as an essayist. He spent his last years in Concord, writing little, but recognized throughout America as a philosopher of great stature.

Many American authors, including Herman Melville, Walt Whitman, Emily Dickinson, Nathaniel Hawthorne, and Thoreau are indebted to Emerson's thought. While some critics find in him the eternal naïf, a writer of pleasant-sounding but ultimately impractical essays, containing ideals that stale with the age of Emerson's works, others note his energizing influence on inquisitive minds as evidence of his lasting greatness.

(For further information about Emerson's life and works, see *Concise Dictionary of American Literary Biography, 1640-1865; Dictionary of Literary Biography*, Vols. 1, 59, 73; and *Nineteenth-Century Literature Criticism*, Vol. I.)

CRITICAL COMMENTARY

BLISS PERRY

(essay date 1931)

[Perry was an American critic, novelist, short story writer, editor, and lecturer. A proponent of the genteel tradition in American literature, which stressed morality, refined manners, and conventional forms in works of art, he edited several volumes of Emerson's poetry and prose. In the following excerpt, he discusses Emerson's poems and his aesthetics of poetry.]

Emerson's own estimate of his skill as a poet was extremely modest. "I, who am only an amateur poet,"—he wrote to Dr. Furness in 1844. In writing to Lydia Jackson, shortly before their marriage, he went more into detail:

I am born a poet,—of a low class without doubt, yet a poet. That is my nature and vocation. My singing, to be sure, is very husky, and is for the most part in prose. Still I am poet in the sense of a perceiver and dear lover of the harmonies that are in the soul and in matter, and specially of the harmonies between these and those.

Principal Works

Nature (essay) 1836

*An Oration, Delivered before the Phi Beta Kappa Society, at Cambridge, August 31, 1837 (lecture) 1837; also published as Man Thinking, 1844

†An Address Delivered before the Senior Class in Divinity College, Cambridge, Sunday Evening, 15 July 1838 (lecture) 1838

Essays (essays) 1841; enlarged edition, 1847

Essays: Second Series (essays) 1844

Poems (poetry) 1847; also published as Selected Poems [enlarged and revised edition, 1876]; enlarged and revised edition [Poems], 1884; revised edition, 1904

Nature; Addresses, and Lectures (lectures) 1849; also published as Miscellanies; Embracing Nature, Addresses, and Lectures, 1856; also published as Miscellanies, 1884

Representative Men: Seven Lectures (lectures) 1850

English Traits (travel essays) 1856

The Conduct of Life (essays) 1860

May-Day, and Other Pieces (poetry and essays) 1867

Society and Solitude (essays) 1870

Natural History of Intellect, and Other Papers (essays) 1893

The Complete Works of Ralph Waldo Emerson. 12 vols. (essays, lectures, travel essays, and poetry) 1903-04

The Journals of Ralph Waldo Emerson. 10 vols. (journals) 1909-14

*This work is commonly known as The American Scholar.

†This work is commonly known as The Divinity School Address.

That last sentence, roughly translated, means that we are to expect in his verse much of the characteristic thought of his prose; and there will always be some readers who discover the real Emerson in his poetry, as there will always be others who prefer to find their Emerson in his *Journals* or *Essays*. But everyone knows that he was a lifelong lover of verse. He rendered it in public readings, with singular beauty. He published an anthology of his favorite poems, entitled *Parnassus*. He wrote verse from boyhood, usually keeping a separate notebook for that purpose. Like Thoreau, he often scribbled the first draft of a poetical thought in rude blank verse, which was afterward turned into rhyme or honest prose. The prose draft of his rhymed poem **"Two Rivers,"** for instance, seems to many readers to possess a more delicate harmony than the metrical version. Emerson printed some of his verse in the *Dial* and elsewhere, and in 1847 and 1867 published two slender

volumes [*Poems* and *May-Day, and Other Pieces*] which neither raised nor lowered his reputation in his own generation.

The *obiter dicta* on poetry uttered by this veteran reader and writer are often memorable: "The great poets are judged by the frame of mind they induce"; "It is not metres, but a metre-making argument, that makes a poem"; "In poetry, tone: . . . the uncontrollable interior impulse which is the authentic mark of a new poem, and which is unanalyzable, and makes the merit of an ode of Collins, or Gray, or Wordsworth, or Herbert or Byron,—and which is felt in the pervading tone, rather than in brilliant parts or lines"; and finally, at the very end of his life, "The secret of poetry is never explained,—is always new. We have not got any farther than mere wonder at the delicacy of the touch, and the eternity it inhabits"; these are sayings worthy of Coleridge or Keats. (pp. 84-6)

Emerson's formal essays on poetry and the poetic art,—such as **"The Poet," "Poetry and Imagination," "Shakespeare, the Poet,"** and **"Persian Poetry,"**—while highly individual in their phrasing, present a curious blend of the theories of Platonism and the Persians, of Elizabethan and seventeenth century practice, and of conventional late eighteenth century aesthetics, as modified by Coleridge, Wordsworth and Blake. In such matters Emerson was an unashamed eclectic, and his enormously wide reading in poetry furnished him with examples of the most divergent theory and practice. In this field, as elsewhere, he has no theory to inculcate: he simply communicates an enthusiasm for poetry and interprets it with an insight denied to the system-makers.

The excellencies and defects of Emerson's own verse are so patent that schoolmasters deal with them swiftly. Whether one opens his *Poems* with the amused indifference of an undergraduate or with the affectionate loyalty of long acquaintance, certain superficial traits are clear. That exquisite choice of the right word,—sometimes a surprising, daring word,—which characterizes his prose style, often sparkles in his verse. "The Sphinx is drowsy"; "Devastators of the day"; "She spired into a yellow flame"; "His formidable innocence"; "Our sumptuous indigence"; "All the brags of plume and song." Such words fairly crackle. He is a master likewise, at times, of the full poetic phrase or line: "Voyager of light and noon"; "April cold with dropping rain"; "The eternal sky, Full of light and of deity"; "The vast skies fall, Dire and satirical"; "O tenderly the haughty day Fills his blue urn with fire." Emerson loves the tightly packed line as well as the master of his youth, Alexander Pope: "He builded better than he knew"; "And striving to be man, the worm Mounts through all the spires of form"; "And music pours on mortals Its beautiful disdain." Yet even these are no better in their way than his countless prose aphorisms, like "All the world loves a lover."

Some of the ringing lines of this cunning rhetorician are perhaps only oratory in disguise: "Things are in the saddle, And ride mankind"; "When half-gods go, The gods arrive"; "fired the shot heard round the world." His finest achievement in this oratorical *genre* is the stanza of the **"Boston Hymn"** read in Music Hall on January 1, 1863. His worried, anxious audience had been waiting for hours for the expected telegram from Washington telling them that Lincoln had at last signed the Emancipation Proclamation. Both Emerson and Lincoln had been at times advocates of the policy of compensated emancipation. But no orator ever caught his audience more completely off-guard than did Emerson with his unexpected climax:

> Pay ransom to the owner
> And fill the bag to the brim.
> Who is the owner? The slave is owner,
> And ever was. Pay him.

That brought the crowd to its feet, shouting, in the winter twilight.

The present-day advocates of *poésie pure,* that is to say, poetry unadulterated by any foreign substance, such as ethical content, are suspicious of Emerson's patriotic verse, like the **"Boston Hymn"** just mentioned, the **"Concord Ode,"** and **"Voluntaries"**—written in memory of fallen soldiers of the Civil War. It is true that in all these poems, and in Emerson's rhymed counsels of perfection for the individual, like **"Fate," "Sursum Corda," "To J. W.,"** and **"Give All to Love,"** there is an element of ethical admonition and appeal. But so there is in Milton's sonnets and in much of the most authentic poetry of the English race. The critic who would cut out the ethical, even the didactic, strain from English poetry would succeed only in emasculating it.

It is obvious, however, that though Emerson was undeniably an ethical teacher, he was by no means invariably in the pulpit, either as prose-man or poet. He could write purely objective poems about Nature, sometimes merely descriptive like **"The Snow Storm"** and **"Sea-Shore,"** and sometimes with the heightened lyric transport of **"The Humble-Bee"** and **"May-Day."** Now and again there will be a group of lines as detached from everyday reality, as haunting in their unearthly cadence, as anything in Poe:

> Subtle rhymes, with ruin rife,
> Murmur in the house of life,
> Sung by the Sisters as they spin;
> In perfect time and measure they
> Build and unbuild our echoing clay,
> As the two twilights of the day
> Fold us music-drunken in.

Emerson frequently composed poetic meditations based upon his chance experiences out of doors, like **"Each and All," "The Rhodora"** and **"The Titmouse"**; or upon growing old, as in **"Terminus"**; or upon sharp bereavement, as in the **"Dirge"** over his two brothers and the **"Threnody"** upon the death of his son. In such poems there is little attempt to generalize or to enforce any doctrine. They are poems of "occasion," in Goethe's sense of the word. (pp. 86-90)

Emerson is rich also in a sort of gnomic or wisdom verse, which in its mood is reflective rather than didactic, although we are free to apply the latent "morality"—as Chaucer says—if we will. **"Letters," "Days," "The Problem," "Brahma"** and **"Hamatreya"** belong here, as do **"Merlin"** and **"Saadi,"**—poems about poetry,—many verse mottoes and apothegms, and the **"Initial, Daemonic, and Celestial Love,"** where Emerson starts with Plato, but finding the final grade rather difficult, shifts gears expertly into Plotinus.

At this point the Devil's Advocate, who is always present at these "Assizes of the Poets," is getting restless and insists upon being heard. He admits,—being a sensible fellow and not without literary taste,—that Emerson has many interesting and indeed valuable things to say. But he insists that most if not all of them could be said in prose. The Devil's Advocate agrees that Emerson possesses a remarkable instinct for the brilliant single word or the pregnant phrase, but he points out coolly that the loveliest fragments of stained glass do not make a window unless there is a pattern, a controlling design. Emerson is a marvellous ejaculator of poetic phrases, no doubt, but is he a true builder of the lofty rhyme; has he the architectonic gift and training? And even as an artisan of the lesser units of verse-making, are not his words frequently harsh, his stresses grotesque, his rhymes abominable? Why could he not have employed a competent poetic secretary, like Christina Rossetti, to put his thoughts into impeccable verse?

I grant,—continues the Devil's Advocate,—that with good luck he may achieve a quatrain. The one beginning "So nigh is grandeur to our dust" and that other about "'Tis man's perdition to be safe" are indeed "excellent,"—if I recall rightly the adjective used by a Mr. Arnold, who has been frequently cited as a witness in this Court. Yet does not Emerson show a singular lack of sustained and symmetrical beauty? Could he by any possibility follow a complicated stanzaic pattern, or even turn out a respectable Petrarchan sonnet? Is not the "fatal facility" of his favorite octo-syllabic line really more fatal to him than it was to Scott or Byron, inasmuch as Emerson lacks utterly the narrative genius which held their lines together? Why should he be so incoherent, so wilful, so tantalizing? I believe he has read too much Donne and Cowley and Crashaw, and not enough Virgil and Dante. And yet for all his affectation of humility, I suspect that when he is wearing his singing robes he is really arrogant, even—if I may be pardoned the term—pontifical. In conclusion,—may it please the Court,—I like this gentleman personally, and have frequently been stimulated by his ideas, even if he does come out of a queer epoch and from a country as yet imperfectly civilized. But I can never submit to seeing him enthroned in the hierarchy of the great poets, or even beatified among the poets of the second class. And what is worse, he seems to be smiling at me in this very moment, as if this were not an extremely serious occasion! And with that, the Devil's Advocate sits down.

Now there is no doubt that Emerson is smiling a little,—with that baffling smile that always irritated his opponents. Perhaps he is thinking of Ben Jonson's remark about Shakespeare: "He wanted art." Or possibly he is thinking of his own dictum: "The great poets are judged by the frame of mind they induce." Let us take that sentence,—not as a mere rejoinder to the Devil's Advocate, for he has been asserting some indisputable truths,—but for a suggestion that an appeal may be taken to the jurisdiction of another court.

What, then, is the frame of mind induced in the reader of such poems as the **"Ode to Beauty," "Forerunners," "May-Day," "The Sphinx," "The World-Soul," "Woodnotes," "Monadnock," "Bacchus,"** and the second movement of the **"Threnody"?** In most of these poems there are traces, no doubt, of faulty drawing, unbalanced proportion, some obscurity and a strangely syncopated music. They are all mystical in their mood, built upon the perception of some endless Quest,—what the mystics call, in their various dialects, the Journey, the Way, the Life. These poems are profoundly spiritual, and to grasp their full meaning requires a degree of spiritual divination which few of us possess. And nevertheless, the man who is least like Emerson in his mental habits and range of perception can scarcely fail to become aware, in reading this group of poems, of certain truths about the world of appearance as related to the world of reality. He becomes conscious,—intimately and intensely conscious,—of beauty as it is revealed through the senses. (pp. 91-4)

Bliss Perry, in his *Emerson Today,* Princeton University Press, 1931, 140 p.

F. O. MATTHIESSEN

(essay date 1941)

[Matthiessen was an authority on American literature. Concerning his studies, he stated: "I wanted to place our master-works in their cultural setting, but beyond that I wanted to discern what constituted the lasting value of these books as works of art." In the following excerpt, he examines the philosophy underlying Emerson's major essays and lectures.]

'Mr. Coleridge has written well on this matter of Theory in his *Friend* . . . A true method has no more need of firstly, secondly, etc., than a perfect sentence has of punctuation. It tells its own story, makes its own feet, creates its own form. It is its own apology.'
—Emerson's *Journal* (1834)

'In a fortnight or three weeks my little raft will be afloat. Expect nothing more of my powers of construction,—no ship-building, no clipper, smack, nor skiff even, only boards and logs tied together.'
—Emerson to Carlyle just before the appearance of his first *Essays* (1841)

All of Emerson's books can be reduced to the same underlying pattern. They are hardly constructed as wholes. Even *Representative Men* (1850) and *English Traits* (1856) are collections of essays, written originally as lectures. Every lecture in turn, from *The American Scholar* to those published after his death, was made up by grouping together sentences from his journals. If his longer poems, 'Woodnotes,' 'Monadnoc' and 'May-Day,' are really strings of loosely connected verses, his constructive skills in prose were limited, as Woodberry saw, to the 'simple combination of the minister's old pulpit sermon and the man-of-letters' *pensée.'*

His work corresponds so naturally to his life that it constitutes the purest example of what individualism could produce. The sentence was his unit, as he recognized when confessing sadly to Carlyle (1838) that his paragraphs were only collections of 'infinitely repellent particles.' It is significant that he said the same thing when reflecting on society as 'an imperfect union': 'Every man is an infinitely repellent orb, and holds his individual being on that condition.' The sentence was the inevitable unit for the man who could say, 'A single thought has no limit to its value.' He was at his best when he could give both release and embodiment to one of his thoughts in a plastic image; but though he talked about the unexampled resources of metaphor and symbol, his staple device was analogy. As he said, 'All thinking is analogizing, and it is the use of life to learn metonymy.' His method was not induction, or logical persuasion of any kind, as even the relative infrequency of conjunctions in his paragraphs can show. In spite of his fondness for Montaigne, he had not a trace of skepticism in his being; and in spite of his profession of being a seeker, all his mature work proceeded from *a priori* deductive assertion. This would necessarily rely more on analogy than on the fresh discovery of metaphor; and the fact that Emerson seems to equate the value of the two modes is another instance of his concern with the idea to the partial neglect of its created vehicle.

His early attraction to Bacon was in keeping with his taste for the maxim, or as Bacon's age called it the 'sententia,' with its swift pithy compression of a thought. Such intensification of the moment in literature would be the natural instrument of the man for whom the intensification of the moment was the meaning of life. He expressed a kindred enthusiasm for proverbs, which he conceived differently from Franklin as 'the literature of reason, or the statements of an absolute truth without qualification. Proverbs, like the sacred books of each nation, are the sanctuary of the intuitions.' This definition has much in common with Coleridge's conception of the aphorism. One of Coleridge's main purposes in writing *Aids to Reflection* was 'to direct the reader's attention to the value of the Science of Words . . . and the incalculable advantages attached to the habit of using them appropriately, and with a distinct knowledge of their primary, derivative, and metaphorical senses.' In furtherance of this aim he provided his aphorisms, since 'exclusive of the abstract sciences, the largest and worthiest portion of our knowledge consists of *aphorisms:* and the greatest and best of men is but an *aphorism.*' This conception of the identity of the man with his work was integrally related to that of the word with the thing. It might be said that the sentences by which Emerson has become a living part of our language, the ones in which he showed a poet's delicate attention to the word and an equally poetic gift of phrase and of rhythmical balance, still contain a residue of the Yankee's respect for Franklin.

The problem of Emerson's prose was the same as that of his philosophy, how to reconcile the individual with society, how to join his sentences into a paragraph. Since his chief preoccupation was to demonstrate identity beneath all manner of variety, his formula for an essay was an abstraction instanced by an indefinite number of embodiments. His desire to get his whole philosophy into each essay led 'toward sameness and promiscuity at once; it made the sentences similar and the paragraphs diverse' [O. W. Firkins, *Ralph Waldo Emerson*, 1915]. Firkins was not thinking in social terms in that remark, but it corresponds with what many observers have noted as the consequences of our American theory of the self-sufficient individual—our double tendency towards standardization and anarchy. It was the philosophic anarchists among Emerson's contemporaries to whom his essays were principally addressed, though most of his audience, less daring than Thoreau, would hardly have recognized themselves under that description. They knew simply that they found the old conformities of their environment intolerable; and in an era when the abolitionists were attacking the state as morally defective, it was natural that the radicalism of the transcendentalists should have demanded the fullest freedom from all restraints.

Emerson himself visualized his solitary reader in his journal for 1839:

> In Massachusetts a number of young and adult persons are at this moment the subject of a revolution. They are not organized into any conspiracy: they do not vote, or print, or meet together. They do not know each others' faces or names. They are united only in a common love of truth and love of its work. They are of all conditions and natures. They are, some of them, mean in attire, and some mean in station, and some mean in body, having inherited from their parents faces and forms scrawled with the traits of every vice. Not in churches, or in courts, or in large assemblies; not in solemn holidays, where men were met in festal dress, have these pledged themselves to new life, but in lonely and obscure places, in servitude, in solitude, in solitary compunctions and shames and fears, in disappointments, in diseases, trudging beside the team in the dusty road, or drudging, a hireling in other men's cornfields, schoolmasters who teach a few children rudiments for a pittance, ministers of small parishes of the obscurer sects, lone women in dependent condition, matrons and young maidens, rich and poor, beautiful and hard-favored, without conceit or proclamation of any kind, have silently given in their several adherence to a new hope.

That hope itself was so sustaining that in Emerson's case at least it deferred the necessity of further radical action. He was uneasy at times in his detachment, as he was over his restricted audience when he compared the response of his few hundreds or thousands to the mass that greeted *Uncle Tom's Cabin.* He perceived also how it was that book's distinction to have been 'read equally in the parlor and the kitchen and the nursery.' But, as Eliot has observed, there are 'four ways of thinking: to talk to others, or to one other, or to talk to oneself, or to talk to God.' In the journals of Emerson and Thoreau we can participate in the shift from the fourth of those modes to the third. All of Emerson's work is illustrative of his early remark to Carlyle that 'the best poem of the Poet is his own mind.' That conviction put him in fundamental opposition to the norm of the previous century, as it had been made explicit, for instance, by Shaftesbury: 'I hold it very indecent that a man should publish his meditations or solitary thoughts. These are the froth and scum of writing, which should be unburdened in private and consigned to oblivion, before the writer comes before the world as good company.'

Nature was a Meditation, with some kinship to what the seventeenth century recognized as such, or at least to what Vaughan and Traherne had so recognized. Emerson gave its structure logical divisions, but they were somewhat stiff and arbitrary in contrast to his lyric unity of tone. Never again was he to succeed so well in clothing his abstractions in the colors of the visible world; or to sustain for so long the art of the rhapsode. No one could demand a composition more satisfactory for its purpose than that of *The American Scholar;* and the early essays still rely on the ordered skills of the preacher. In fact, at no time did Emerson lose his joy in such a device as the rhetorician's 'principle of iteration.' But, to paraphrase Firkins once more, Emerson's later work will sustain analysis better than perusal. With the inevitable loss of freshness in his repeated eloquence, the unity of tone—the method to which Coleridge had stimulated him—was no longer imaginatively compelling. Life remained for him primarily a flux and a becoming, and that flux and becoming were often carried over into his work. His essays tended to deliquesce, like that on the Over-Soul, which is compared to water no less than a dozen times.

As was the case with [his poem] **'Days,'** the paragraphs of his prose that assume wholeness in the reader's mind are those that grew from a pervasive theme. One of the most notable examples is the last paragraph of **'Illusions,'** the concluding essay in *The Conduct of Life* (1860). The theme of this essay can be traced to the conviction of Plotinus that appealed to Emerson most: 'This, therefore, is the life of the Gods, and of divine and happy men; a liberation from all terrene concerns, a life unaccompanied with human pleasures, and a flight of the alone to the alone.' He quoted the final image in his letters, and echoed it in **'The Over-Soul'** ('The soul gives itself, alone, original and pure, to the Lonely, Original and Pure'). He came back to it again when describing Swedenborg's mysticism, and developed his understanding of the flight as follows: 'This path is difficult, secret and beset with terror. The ancients called it *ecstasy* or absence—a getting out of their bodies to think.' That was also how Donne had described the process in his poem 'The Extasie,' which Emerson greatly admired, though he doubtless passed over Donne's insistence on the need to return to the body. Plotinus' image, transformed to Emerson's own usage and repeated at the beginning and the end of the paragraph in **'Illusions,'** helped to provide a frame for his Neo-Platonic thought and to condense it, as **'Days'** had been condensed, into an effective parable:

There is no chance and no anarchy in the universe. All is system and gradation. Every god is there sitting in his sphere. The young mortal enters the hall of the firmament; there is he alone with them alone, they pouring on him benedictions and gifts, and beckoning him up to their thrones. On the instant, and incessantly, fall snow-storms of illusions. He fancies himself in a vast crowd which sways this way and that and whose movement and doings he must obey: he fancies himself poor, orphaned, insignificant. The mad crowd drives hither and thither, now furiously commanding this thing to be done, now that. What is he that he should resist their will, and think or act for himself ? Every moment new

changes and new showers of deceptions to baffle and distract him. And when, by and by, for an instant, the air clears and the cloud lifts a little, there are the gods still sitting around him on their thrones,—they alone with him alone.

Without such condensation Emerson's writing was only too liable to exemplify the consequences of what he deemed the prevailing thought of his century, its reassertion of the Heraclitean doctrine of the Flowing. He saw himself, in a recurrent image, standing on the bank of a river watching the endless current upon which floated past him objects of all shapes and colors. He did not know whence they came or where they went, and he could not detain them as they passed, except by running beside them a little way along the bank. Similar images were the special signatures of nineteenth-century poets. Wordsworth felt that he escaped from uncertainty and understood the purpose of his own life by thus watching a river flow to the sea. By the time of Arnold the purpose was less clear, and his dominant thought was that the calm of the earlier stream was now lost in the incessant line of cities that crowded its edge. For Whitman these cities, as well as the river and the ocean itself, were all symbols for the movement that so exhilarated him while crossing Brooklyn ferry. For Baudelaire movement was more difficult, and the oppressiveness of the city overwhelming: a ship, with its white sails poised for flight, was his image of escape from the boredom and the horror. By the time of Rimbaud the ship had become *bateau ivre* whose pilot had lost all control and awaited the end in despair.

Emerson's work is as permeated with images of flowing as you would expect from his declaration that 'the philosophy we want is one of fluxions and mobility.' In *Nature* the earth becomes 'this green ball which floats him through the heavens.' Nothing solid is left secure, since all matter has been infiltrated and dissolved by thought. He noted himself how such images were the fitting expression of a mind most of whose values were continually varying, as in his estimate of America, 'which sometimes runs very low, sometimes to ideal prophetic proportions.' But unlike most poets who have contemplated mutability, Emerson found no cause for anguish even when he went to the length of saying that men's lives 'are spinning like bubbles in a river.' He was delighted that Swedenborg was 'a man who saw God . . . for a fluid moment.' Emerson's unshaken confidence lay in the river's progression onward, in the fact that 'God is a substance, and his method is illusion.' Consequently, when his images of flowing culminated in a paragraph of his **'Lecture on the Times'** (1841), he intended it to convey a hopeful tone. But out of its context and a century later than those times, the undertones now seem somber. This paragraph can serve as a final instance of how his strongest writing emerged from his recurrent themes:

> The main interest which any aspects of the Times can have for us, is the great spirit which gazes through them, the light which they can shed on the wonderful questions, What we are? and Whither we tend? We do not wish to be deceived. Here we drift, like white sails across the wild ocean, now bright on the wave, now darkling in the trough of the sea;— but from what port did we sail? Who knows? Or to what port are we bound? Who knows? There is no one to tell us but such poor weather-tossed mariners as ourselves, whom we speak as we pass, or who have hoisted some signal, or floated to us some letter in a bottle from far. But what know they more than we? They also found themselves on this wondrous sea. No; from the older sailors, nothing. Over all their speaking-trumphets, the gray sea and the loud winds answer, Not in us; not in Time . . .

The poignance of such isolation from any coherent community faded away in Emerson's sureness that he could step immediately out of time into the living moment of eternity. He could therefore delight in the flow, except when he tried to catch the meaning of the objects and events that drifted past him, and found himself alone with lonely fragments. (pp. 64-70)

F. O. Matthiessen, "The Optative Mood," in his *American Renaissance: Art and Expression in the Age of Emerson and Whitman,* Oxford University Press, 1941, pp. 3-75.

STEVEN E. WHICHER

(essay date 1953)

[Whicher was a noted authority on Emerson's life and literary works. In the following excerpt from an essay that first appeared in *The American Scholar* in 1953, he asserts that Emerson's works are informed by a fundamental conflict between transcendence and despair.]

There is something enigmatic about most American authors. Poe, Hawthorne, Melville, Thoreau, Whitman, Mark Twain, Emily Dickinson, Henry Adams, Henry James, Frost, Faulkner—each has his secret space, his halls of Thermes, his figure in the carpet, which is felt most strongly in his best work and yet eludes definition. Sometimes it is quite opposed to what its possessor thinks he is or wants to be: for example, Hawthorne, envying Trollope his sunshine and his sales, whose best story was "positively hell-fired"; or Whitman, affirmer of life, whose poetry is never more powerful than when it treats of death; Poe, who liked to think himself icily logical and who wrote best from a

haunted fantasy; Mark Twain, professional joker and amateur pessimist; or Frost, tough and humorous individualist, whose best poems are often his saddest. Generally this is linked with an obscure fear or grief, even despair: American literature, closely read, can seem one of the least hopeful of literatures.

To all this, Emerson, representative American author that he is, is no exception. The more we know him, the less we know him. He can be summed up in a formula only by those who know their own minds better than his. We hear his grand, assuring words, but where is the man who speaks them? We know the part he played so well; we feel his powerful charm: we do not know the player. He is, finally, impenetrable, for all his forty-odd volumes.

Yet no man can write so much and so honestly and not reveal himself in some measure. We can see enough to sense in him an unusually large gap, even a contradiction, between his teachings and his experience. He taught self-reliance and felt self-distrust, worshipped reality and knew illusion, proclaimed freedom and submitted to fate. No one has expected more of man; few have found him less competent. There is an Emersonian tragedy and an Emersonian sense of tragedy, and we begin to know him when we feel their presence underlying his impressive confidence.

Of course I must stress the word "Emersonian" here. As Mark Van Doren has remarked, "Emerson had no theory of tragedy," unless to deny its existence is a theory. His oblivion can be prodigious.

> The soul will not know either deformity or pain. If, in the hours of clear reason, we should speak the severest truth, we should say that we had never made a sacrifice. In these hours the mind seems so great, that nothing can be taken from us that seems much. All loss, all pain, is particular; the universe remains to the heart unhurt. Neither vexations nor calamities abate our trust. No man ever stated his griefs as lightly as he might.

As he explained in his lecture on **"The Tragic,"** the man who is grounded in the divine life will transcend suffering in a flight to a region "whereunto these passionate clouds of sorrow cannot rise."

Such transcendence of suffering is one of the great historic answers to tragedy and commands respect. To be valid, however, it must "cost not less than everything." Emerson seems to pay no such price. When, in the same lecture on **"The Tragic,"** he tells the "tender American girl," horrified at reading of the transatlantic slave trade, that these crucifixions were not horrid to the obtuse and barbarous blacks who underwent them, "but only a little worse than the old sufferings," we wonder if he paid anything at all for his peace. The only coin in which we can discharge our debt to suffering is attention to it, but Emerson seems to evade this obligation.

Yet this chilling idealism is not simple insensitivity. Emerson is teaching his tested secret of insulation from calamity: Live in the Soul. His famous assertion in **"Experience"** of the unreality of his devasting grief for his son is an impressive illustration of the necessity he was under to protect, at whatever human cost, his hard-won security. Yeats has said somewhere that we begin to live when we have conceived life as tragedy. The opposite was true of Emerson. Only as he refused to conceive life as tragedy could he find the courage to live.

By denying man's fate, however, Emerson did not escape it. His urgent need to deny it shows that his confidence was more precarious than he would admit. Who has not felt the insistence, the over-insistence, in such radical claims to freedom and power as **"Self-Reliance?"**

> Trust thyself: every heart vibrates to that iron string. Accept the place the divine providence has found for you, the society of your contemporaries, the connection of events. Great men have always done so, and confided themselves childlike to the genius of their age, betraying their perception that the absolutely trustworthy was seated at their heart, working through their hands, predominating in all their being. And we are now men, and must accept in the highest mind the same transcendent destiny; and not minors and invalids in a protected corner, not cowards fleeing before a revolution, but guides, redeemers, and benefactors, obeying the Almighty effort, and advancing on Chaos and the Dark.

What speaks here is self-*dis*trust, a distrust so pervasive that it must find an "absolutely trustworthy" seated at the heart before it can trust at all. Self-reliance, in the oft-cited phrase, is God-reliance, and therefore not self-reliance. Contrast the accent of a genuine individualist like Ibsen: "The strongest man in the world is he who stands most alone." Or recall a truly self-reliant American:

> It was about this time I conceiv'd the bold and arduous project of arriving at moral perfection. I wish'd to live without committing any fault at any time; I would conquer all that either natural inclination, custom, or company might lead me into. As I knew, or thought I knew, what was right and wrong, I did not see why I might not always do the one and avoid the other. . . . For this purpose I therefore contrived the following method. . . .

The free and easy assurance of Franklin is just what is missing in Emerson.

Certainly the first thirty years or so showed no great self-trust. A tubercular, like many in his family (two brothers died of the disease), he was engaged throughout his twenties in a serious battle of life and death in which he was not at all sure of winning. With his poor health went a disheartening self-criticism. He imagined he was incurably idle and self-indulgent, without force or worldly competence, constrained in the company of others, unresponsive in his affections. Though his early journals often show a manly courage and good sense, the dominant mood is a sense of impotence. He lacks all power to realize his larger ambitions and feels himself drifting, sometimes in humiliation, sometimes in wry amusement, before the inexorable flowing of time. He was the servant more than the master of his fate, he found in 1824; and later, in the depths of his illness, it seemed to him that he shaped his fortunes not at all. In all his life, he wrote, he obeyed a strong necessity.

The electrifying release of power brought to him by the amazing discovery, the start of his proper career, that God was within his own soul is understandable only against this early—indeed, this lifelong submission to a strong necessity. His subjection bred a longing for self-direction, all the stronger for his underlying sense of its impossibility. The force of his transcendental faith, and its almost willful extravagance, sprang from his need to throw off, against all probability and common sense, his annihilating dependence. He welcomed the paradoxical doctrine that "God dwells in thee" with uncritical delight, as the solution to all the doubts that oppressed him, and rushed in a Saturnalia of faith to spell out its revolutionary consequences for the solitary soul:

> . . . The world is nothing, the man is all; . . . in yourself slumbers the whole of Reason; it is for you to know all, it is for you to dare all. . . .

> . . . The height, the deity of man is, to be self-sustained, to need no gift, no foreign force. . . . All that you call the world is the shadow of that substance which you are, the perpetual creation of the powers of thought, of those that are dependent and of those that are independent of your will.

> . . . You think me the child of my circumstances: I make my circumstance. . . .

> . . . Every rational creature has all nature for his dowry and estate. It is his, if he will. He may divest himself of it; he may creep into a corner, and abdicate his kingdom, as most men do, but he is entitled to the world by his constitution. . . .

Yet this proclamation of the kingdom of man was always what he soon came to call it, a romance. He retained a common-sense awareness (and so retains our respect) that experience did not support it. Not merely were all manipular attempts to realize his kingdom premature and futile. The Power within, from which all capacity stemmed, was itself wayward. The individual relying on it was a mere pipe for a divine energy that came and went as it willed. With this hidden life within him, man was no longer hopeless, but he was still helpless. "I would gladly," Emerson wrote at the age of forty-one, " . . . allow the most to the will of man, but I have set my heart on honesty in this chapter, and I can see nothing at last, in success or failure, than more or less of vital force supplied from the Eternal."

When Emerson wrote *The American Scholar,* seven years earlier, his imagination had kindled to a blaze at the thought of the divine power latent in the soul. Give way to it, let it act, and the conversion of the world will follow. As this millennial enthusiasm inevitably waned, the old helplessness it had contradicted emerged unaltered from the flames. The result was a head-on clash of belief and fact. His vision of man as he might be only intensified the plight of man as he was. Something resembling the Fall of Man, which he had so ringingly denied, reappears in his pages.

It is not sin now that troubles him, but "the incompetency of power." One may accuse Providence of a certain parsimony.

It has shown the heaven and earth to every child, and filled him with a desire for the whole; a desire raging, infinite; a hunger, as of space to be filled with planets; a cry of famine, as of devils for souls. Then for the satisfaction,—to each man is administered a single drop, a bead of dew of vital power, *per day,*—a cup as large as space, and one drop of the water of life in it. Each man woke in the morning with an appetite that could eat the solar system like a cake; a spirit for action and passion without bounds; he could lay his hand on the morning star; he could try conclusions with gravitation or chemistry; but, on the first motion to prove his strength,—hands, feet, senses, gave way, and would not serve him. He was an emperor deserted by his states, and left to whistle by himself, or thrust into a mob of emperors, all whistling: and still the sirens sang, "The attractions are proportioned to the destinies." In every house, in the heart of each maiden and of each boy, in the soul of the soaring saint, this chasm is found,— between the largest promise of ideal power and the shabby experience.

This chasm is the Emersonian tragedy, a tragedy of incapacity. Man's reach must exceed his grasp, of course; that is not tragic. Emerson's chasm cuts deeper: between a vision that claims all power now, and an experience that finds none. Emerson's thought of the self was split between a total Yes and a total No, which could not coexist, could not be reconciled, and yet were both true. "Alas for this infirm faith, this will not strenuous, this vast ebb of a vast flow! I am God in nature; I am a weed by the wall."

There is an Emersonian skepticism as well as an Emersonian faith. Of the seven "lords of life" he distinguishes in his key essay, **"Experience,"** five are principles of weakness. A man is slave to his moods and his temperament, swept like a bubble down the stream of time, blinded and drugged with illusion, the captive of his senses—in a word, the creature of a strong necessity. To be sure, the God is a native of the bleak rocks of his isolation, and can at any moment surprise and cheer him with new glimpses of reality. But for all this miraculous consolation, he has no will or force of his own; self-reliant is precisely what he can never be. *The American Scholar*'s assurance of the unsearched might of man is a feat of faith in view of the actual humiliating human predicament, "with powers so vast and unweariable ranged on one side, and this little, conceited, vulnerable popinjay that a man is, bobbing up and down into every danger, on the other."

It goes without saying that one can easily overstate the case for a tragic sense in Emerson. **"Experience,"** for instance, is not a tragic-sounding essay. Perhaps "sense of limitation" would be more accurate; I have deliberately chosen a controversial term, in order to stress a side of Emerson often overlooked. For all his loss of millennial hope, Emerson in fact came to allow much to the will of man, as any reader of *The Conduct of Life* can see. Nor do I mean to suggest that he did not find the secret of a serene and affirmative life. The evidence is overwhelming that he did. My point is that his serenity was a not unconscious *answer* to his experience of life, rather than an inference from it (even when presented as such). It was an act of faith, forced on him by what he once called "the ghastly reality of things." Only as we sense this tension of faith and experience in him can we catch the quality of his affirmation. He *had* to ascribe more reality to his brief moments of "religious sentiment" than to the rest of life, or he could not live.

The way he did so altered sensibly, as his first excess of faith in man diminished. A gentle resignation came to settle over his thought of human nature, an elegiac recognition that life perpetually promises us a glory we can never realize. As it did so, the center of his faith traveled imperceptibly from man to the order that included him. In moments of faith, as he explained even in the midst of his essay on **"Self-Reliance,"** "The soul raised over passion beholds identity and eternal causation, perceives the self-existence of Truth and Right, and calms itself with knowing that all things go well." Such dogmatic optimism, always a part of his faith, became more and more its sole content as his first dream of a kingdom of Man dwindled into reasonableness.

Emerson the optimist said some shallow and callous things, as he did in his lecture on **"The Tragic."** To restore our sympathy with his humanity, we must glimpse the prisoner that now and then looked out of the eyes above the smile. Within, he was sovereign, a

Emerson on his poetry:

I am a bard least of bards. I cannot, like them, make lofty arguments in stately, continuous verse, constraining the rocks, trees, animals, and the periodic stars to say my thoughts,—for that is the gift of great poets; but I am a bard because I stand near them, and apprehend all they utter, and with pure joy hear that which I also would say, and, moreover, I speak interruptedly words and half stanzas which have the like scope and aim:—

What I cannot declare, yet cannot all withhold.

Emerson, in a December 1862 entry in *Journals of Ralph Waldo Emerson: 1856-1863.*

guide, redeemer, and benefactor; without, he was a lecturing and publishing old gentleman. Each time his inner promise of ideal power came up against the narrow limits of his experience, the response could only be the same—a renewed surrender to the Power that planned it that way.

He did not surrender to necessity because he found it good, so much as he found it good because he surrendered. Recurrently the Good he recognizes is more conspicuous for power than for goodness, a "deaf, unimplorable, immense fate," to which all man-made distinctions of good and ill are an impertinence. In some of his poems, particularly, those that have eyes to see may watch him swept into entranced submission to "the over-god" by the compulsion of his personal problems. This is how he meets the impossible challenge of social action, in the **"Ode"** to Channing. So the teasing evanescence of his moments of insight into reality is submerged in **"The World-Soul."** He bows to the same power for a bleak consolation in his **"Threnody"** for his son:

Silent rushes the swift Lord
Through ruined systems still restored,
Broadsowing, bleak and void to bless,
Plants with worlds the wilderness;
Waters with tears of ancient sorrow
Apples of Eden ripe to-morrow.
House and tenant go to ground,
Lost in God, in Godhead found.

In such poems we feel the hunger for strength that sent him first to his grand doctrine of Self-Reliance, and then swung him to its polar opposite, a worship of the Beautiful Necessity.

Like all puritans, Emerson was an extremist: he had to have entire assurance, or he had none at all. Though we have a tradition of mature tragedy in our literature, American authors have typically made the same demand. Either they have risen to his transcendental trust, like Thoreau and Whitman; or they have accepted shoddy substitutes, like Norris or Sandburg or

Steinbeck; or they have dropped into blackness, like Henry Adams or Jeffers. Emerson himself teetered on the edge of this drop, as did Thoreau and Whitman too, sustained by little more than their own power of belief. Since then the impulse to believe has become progressively feebler and the drop quicker and harder, until now, John Aldridge tells us, our honest writers *start* in the pit. If we are ever to have a great literature again, one would conclude, it will not be until we can break decisively with the whole extremist Emersonian pattern and find some means to face this world without either transcendence or despair. (pp. 39-45)

Stephen E. Whicher, "Emerson's Tragic Sense," in *Emerson: A Collection of Critical Essays,* edited by Milton R. Konvitz and Stephen E. Whicher, Prentice-Hall, Inc., 1962, pp. 39-45.

ALFRED S. REID

(essay date 1970)

[Reid was an American critic and educator who specialized in nineteenth-century American literature. Here, he discusses the prose style of Emerson's major essays and lectures.]

American students have little use for Emerson. If ordered to read him, they will. Otherwise they read fiction, and the more contemporary, the better. The reasons are obvious. Fiction touches a reader at more points of his being than essays; and fiction moves indirectly, whereas essays, especially those of the moralists, turn off today's readers by their garrulous preachiness. In short, the essay-moralist is out of favor. We do not read him, because he never concentrated his thought in powerful images and fictions. The scholar who chooses to write about an essayist's literary qualities has to be a trifle on the defensive or admit he has fallen into the wrong pew. Certainly no lover of literature can call anything but dull most of the dozen or more massive tomes that Emerson left, especially the journals and miscellaneous notebooks—no matter how meticulously edited. This sodden bulk belongs more to biography and cultural history than to literature. Plodding drearily through it all, we are constantly reminded of Emerson's statement: the pith of a man's genius contracts itself into a few short hours. How true! The bulk forcibly reminds us that Emerson's literary achievements reside in a few essays between 1836 and 1844 and that all the rest is preparation or residue. Our job is to define the quality of his style at his best and not mire ourselves in his exercises.

It goes without saying that we do not find Emerson's lasting literary qualities in his Romantic philosophy. Ringing assertions of human dignity cheer and uplift, but the metaphysics cloys. Nor do we find it in his practical ethics, which is more sturdy; we had the same preachments long before in the life and teachings of Jesus. We come closer to describing actual belief in the academy, if not the literal truth about his literary qualities, when we justify to diffident students our assignments in Emerson by saying that through his essays flow the vital currents of American culture. Here we find that fulsome blend of Puritanism, Enlightenment, and Romantic idealism that historically make up the early American character; here too the democratic idealism, the individualism, the contempt for tradition, and the practical sagacity. Emerson's fall from favor in recent decades is due as much to a shift away in American culture from precisely those middle-class values that he represents as to the decline of the essay.

Having made these patronizing remarks at the threshold of my generation's tromp on the moon in 1969, let me testify to an old-fashioned earthly appreciation for Emerson, who was no mere sublunar man himself, having long ago hitched his wagon to a star. Not for his mysticism, Romantic philosophy, his ethics, or his culture—gravity do I admire him, but as a writer, a skillful shaper of sentences, a composer of expository essays that move and give pleasure. A successful essay is no mean superfluity in America's literary history. Let us not fling stones at one of the few great craftsmen of the genre. We have had too few to risk one loss. Let us inquire instead into his distinctive qualities.

If we had to reduce them to a phrase, I would say it is a tone of moral earnestness, so that we experience a rare personality fulfilling his destiny. His writings record seriously a tall, if not rounded, personality who aspires upward to divine truth. A tone of rarefied earnestness pervades them—sober, sincere, austere, and straightforward. If we were permitted two phrases, I would add an oral art. For his essays speak to us, announce directly and forcefully, with all the instruments of oratory, those truths he discovered in the universal mind. Truths earnestly perceived find their own form. Emerson found the fit of his genius and times in the pulpit and the lyceum. He saw himself as prophet, priest, and law-giver, the world as a religious arena, art and literature as fixing "the divine boundaries of the human spirit." His writing is essentially lecturing and preaching, prophesying, announcing, exhorting, persuading. It is a sermonic art, designed to reveal truths, inspire belief, arouse confidence, cut through the crust of tradition and the rinds of lethargy, revitalize his hearers to the divine force in them, first, as to their capacities and possibilities as men, second, as to their roles as citizens of the United States. Next to living well, the highest art is this speech of the human voice in the service of truth-saying. He called it oratory or eloquence. Even when written as essays, the speech, sermon, address, or lecture partakes of grandness. Writing

does not "diminish inspiration;" it gives thought a chance to hone itself to its proper cutting edge. "Written composition can surpass any unwritten effusions of however profound a genius." He specifically defended "written composition in pulpit and academic eloquence."

To both distinctive traits, the moral tone and the sermonic art, I would append the phrase "with an edge." There is in Emerson's essays the righteousness of the cleaver. His goodness is not that of the beatitudes, which celebrate the meek and the mild, but that of a militant individualism, after the saying of Jesus that He came to bring not peace but a sword or after Paul's analogy of the Christian girded in armor. The attitude steadily increases in his style until in **"Self-Reliance"** he fixes his seal to it: "Your goodness must have some edge to it,—else it is none." The independent self-reliant man must go upright and vital, must chide malice, reprove vanity, reprimand affectation, be rough and graceless to bigotry, and, letting the chips fall where they may, speak the "rude truth" at all times. Integrity to self obliges one to be overweening, if need be, to establish boundaries, to put one's claims for integrity before family and friends and society, to go about as if everything were titular but oneself, to preach the doctrine of hatred if love be whining and pulling. "Let us affront and reprimand the smooth mediocrity and squalid contentment," he writes, and not be "decorous sayers of smooth things." Seeing the truth requires a scalpel just as acting the truth requires a sword. The eloquence of the orator depends upon detachment of parts from the divine consciousness, cutting them away for clear examination before reassimilating them to the whole. He must sever divine laws laboriously and speak them keenly so as to pierce and penetrate. The test of art as it is of truth is that it have an edge, be clear and cutting in its moral detachment, and thus shape its listeners to live starkly detached, independent lives, dedicated to Goodness, Truth, and Beauty.

Emerson came inevitably to this style of earnest oratory with an edge, and he devoted his life to mastering it. His essay-lectures grew from huge forests of family trees. They are the progeny of remarkable effort, first in the shapeless form of speculative musings in the journals beginning in the early 1820's when he was in college, then in the sermons of the late 1820's and early 1830's, then in the lectures for the rest of his life. Few writers have left such wide trails of their rigors. At first conventional in thought and undistinguished in sentence structure, the lectures of the mid-thirties gradually begin to take more liberties with sentence variation, introduce more personal anecdotes and opinions, and break out in rashes of metaphors and passages of wry acerbity. By 1835 we hear the sentences begin to pound, and we catch some of the famil-

Emerson's grave in Concord, Massachusetts.

iar urgency. The writing increases in pithiness and self-confidence. From the beginning Emerson sought diligently to reduce complex knowledge to manageable principles, to find the hard core of truth, to extract the living wisdom from inert matter. He relied on those authors who give us general truths and moral precepts in wise and quotable sentences: Plutarch, Shakespeare, Bacon. Very early he acquired a confidence in the potential of his genre. He knew how to catch interest, how to announce his topic, how to distribute its parts, usually by classification, and how to impale his audience with imperatives, direct address, and colorful maxims. He rewrote assiduously. Many of the same sentences and paragraphs in the journals and lectures, often carefully revised, reappear in his masterpieces.

After noticing that he prepared three or four major series of lectures in the mid-1830's—on natural history, travel, biography, and literature—we are not surprised to discover that his first published work, instead of being a single lecture, or even a collection of lectures, is a compendium of lectures, a series of nine addresses telescoped into one tightly unified ethical treatise, a digest of his previous writing in a form that partakes of the best of the speculative tendency in the journals and of the oratory of his lectures. It is a brilliant performance that we have come to regard as the

first fulfillment of his genius. I propose now to examine it in some detail and then to look more briefly at three subsequent works that belong to the main stream of Emerson's achievement, *The American Scholar, The Divinity School Address,* and **"Self-Reliance,"** which, with **"Experience,"** are his classics. We shall look at them as literary wholes and try to define the nuances of tone and variations of strategies in the context of their specific oral genres. We shall especially be on the lookout for the militant edge to goodness.

In his first book, *Nature* (1836), a unique blend of the personal meditative essay and the public lecture, Emerson struck the characteristic notes that give this edge to his style: a tone of earnestness, an art of eloquence, an affinity for dogmatism, a talent for aphorisms, an oracular cadence, and a vigorous metaphorical imagination. Next to the obvious oratorial features, which will emerge in the analysis, the most conspicuous of these traits is the earnest tone. "God never jests with us," he writes; "Nature never became a toy to a wise spirit. . . ." Emerson reciprocates. He neither jests with God nor toys with his subject. He is properly decorous. He writes with single-minded reverence, with few of those irreverent sallies of wit or whimsical perversities that characterize a later New Englander, Emily Dickinson, or his neighbor, Henry David Thoreau. Sublime subjects of nature, ego, creation, God, beauty, destiny, and the daily life deserve sublime treatment. He thus keeps the organ stops of his prose screwed to a high moral pitch, unrelieved by doubt, self-ridicule, or humor. He is often importunate. "Let us demand;" "Let us interrogate;" "Let us inquire." His curiosity is so earnest, and he is so intent on solving the big moral and spiritual questions, that he believes none can elude him. "Undoubtedly we have no questions . . . which are unanswerable." He knows he can know what is knowable if he will but rely on intuition. He thus approaches philosophical issues, the vague abstractions of God, Nature, the soul, and destiny, with reckless egotism, and before many pages he has reduced all wisdom to a few simple propositions—that man and nature are companion spirits, that nature serves man in several ways, among them the daily necessities, beauty, a symbolic language, and a discipline of his highest faculty, the Reason, whereby he comes to know the "Original Cause," the "central Unity" of being, and knows that God continuously creates Nature through man, and that each soul can share in its rightful divinity if it will but sally into the "unfound infinite."

These earnest simplifications, intuitively reached but backed by the authority of Western intellectual culture, emerge as dogmatisms. Emerson schematizes the universe and man. "Philosophically considered, the universe is composed of Nature and the Soul. Strictly speaking, therefore, all that is separate from us, all which Philosophy distinguishes as the NOT ME, that is both nature and art, all other men and my own body, must be ranked under this name, NATURE." The Mind of man has two faculties: "the Understanding and the Reason." His favorite modifiers are wholistic: *all* and *every;* or superlatives: *always* and *most.* His characteristic sentence is a sweeping generalization, as in the sentence above with three *all*'s, or below, as follows: "Every universal truth which we express in words, implies or supposes every other truth." "All science has one aim, namely, to find a theory of nature." "Nothing divine dies. All good is eternally reproductive."

More introspective than usual, the writing is largely amiable rather than edged with acid. Emerson has little cause to draw the sword. When he turns his gaze on society's failure to exercise its highest reason, however, he bristles to the attack, forced on by an earnest righteousness. He scoffs at divine teachers who dispute and hate. He deplores our tendency to use the "cinders of a volcano to roast our eggs," to expend our geniuses to convey "pepper-corn informations." Reliance on understanding makes one but half a man, imbruted and savage: "His relation to nature, his power over it, is through the understanding as by manure." Astringent phrases, such as this, come dressed in homely garb, colloquial, earthy, and barbed.

Not acerbity but dogmatism fathers his most brilliant stylistic feature—the aphorisms, those succinct insights, truths detached and clean-cut, that derive from his Romantic premises. The rifle fire of the introduction previews the barrage to come: "Our age is retrospective;" "The foregoing generations beheld God and nature fact to face; we, through their eyes." "Everyman's condition is a solution in hieroglyphic to those inquiries he would put. He acts it as life, before he apprehends it as truth." Dogmatisms thus shade into sententious art, and the *all*'s and *every*'s into figures of speech, carrying emotion and suggestion beyond the arid margins of dogma. Sentences are rhythmically rounded so as to fit the mouth and ear, and they are skillfully balanced by parallel words, alliterations, stress, and grammar: " . . . the most abstract truth is the most practical." "Nothing is quite beautiful alone; nothing but is beautiful in the whole." "Nature never wears a mean appearance." "A work of art is an abstract or epitome of the world." "Words are finite organs of the infinite mind. . . . An action is the perfection and publication of thought." "Beauty is the mark God sets upon virtue." The elegance of the latter lies in its careful adaptations of assonance and consonance to metrical stress. More basic to the thought of the book are two aphorisms in the final chapter: "A man is a god in ruins" and "Man is a dwarf of himself."

Often the aphorisms come in sequences of short, choppy sentences. "Nothing divine dies. All good is eternally reproductive. The beauty of nature reforms

itself in the mind, and not for barren contemplation, but for new creation." Even when sentences are not strictly aphorisms, they are frequently choppy; for the rhythm of one aphoristic or otherwise pithy sentence is often so pronounced that it tends to stand alone, separated from its context. Committed to slugs of wisdom, fit how they might, Emerson pushes his thought forward by strongly cadenced utterances. He pounds the wet mortar but does not smooth it into place. Pithy staccatoes resound, as Merlin, his poetic masque, says they should—strong and rude, vigorously attuned. As more than one commentator has remarked, this trait of style is oracular, or prophetic, or incantatory: "The wind sows the seed; the sun evaporates the sea; the wind blows the vapor to the field; the ice, on the other side of the planet, condenses rain on this; the rain feeds the plant; the plant feeds the animal; and thus the endless circulations of the divine charity nourish man."

The sermonic art that his doctrinaire caste of mind found congenial—earnest grappling with moral questions, dogmatic statements, aphoristic wit, and pithy, staccato-like, sentence clusters—is not incompatible with the commendable logic of his thought, the philosophical, analytic qualities of careful reasoning. The oral traits helped him reduce intellectual complexities to a confident creed of an indwelling divinity in man and nature, and this religious experience often swells into moving passages of religious ecstasy, especially in sections II and VII: "As a plant upon the earth, so a man rests upon the bosom of God. . . . Who can set bounds to the possibilities of man?" Just as dogmatism produces aphorisms, so rational analyses and passages of religious ecstacies are marked by vigorous metaphorical activity. The simile of the spirit putting forth nature through man as a tree puts forth branches and leaves is one of the most memorable, because thematically crucial, figures of speech. Even more memorable because not only intensely religious but bizarre, is the "transparent eyeball" image in the first passage of religious ecstasy. Figures soften the tone of dogmatism and give poetic intensity to the writing. The earth is a "green ball which floats" man "through the heavens." The sky and ocean are "splendid ornaments," the clouds a tent, the climates a "striped coat." "The field is at once [man's] floor, his work-yard, his playground, his garden, and his bed." The aphorisms themselves, sprinkled liberally throughout the work, are apt to be metaphors. Emerson was aware of the relationship of this imagery to his writing: fresh and vigorous thoughts require fresh and vigorous imagery. To detach divine wisdom and speak with prophetic fervor, the seer must be earnest. Then he will be a sayer: his speech will be aphoristic and metaphorical and pierce the heart of man. Reckless egotism and an unrestrained militancy are sometimes necessary.

Emerson's second major work, *The American*

Scholar, popularizes in concise form the ideas of *Nature* and carries the incipient eloquence of that piece into fiery oratory. As a decidedly oral piece, prepared for and delivered to the Phi Beta Kappa society at Harvard, it belongs to the genre of inspirational lectures. Whereas *Nature* is a hybrid genre, a digest of a lecture series, at times personal and rhapsodic, but in the main an extended philosophical treatise, *American Scholar* is a single genre, unified in texture. It shows how far Emerson has come in four years of lecturing, for he makes a masterwork out of a commonplace, sub-literary genre, the pep-talk or commencement speech. Consisting of personal testimony and national challenge, the work is a rare blend of practical philosophy, faith in the individual, and patriotic fervor: "If the single man," he concludes with a flourish, "plant himself indomitably on his instincts, and there abide, the huge world will come round to him. . . . A nation of men will for the first time exist." The tone of earnestness is all-pervasive, but the dogmatism is muted by the exuberance, by the vital conviction of the utterances, and by the more practical context of the implied occasion, a gathering of young persons setting forth to be scholars in a new country where possibilities for literary and scholarly achievement seem limitless. There is almost no let-up in this pitch of high excitement until the essay completes the discussion of influences on the scholar (nature, books, and work), the duties of the scholar (compressed into self-reliance), and thus begins the third and final section on the signs of the times (attention to the commonplace and importance of the individual). This final section then gradually rises to an ecstatic crescendo in which the relaxed prose rhythms become shorter and more repetitive, more cadenced and oracular: "Mr. President and Gentlemen, this confidence in the unsearched might of man belongs, by all motives, by all prophecy, by all preparation, to the American Scholar. We have listened too long to the courtly muses of Europe. . . . A nation of men will for the first time exist, because each believes himself inspired by the Divine Soul which also inspires all men."

This same ecstatic enthusiasm pervades the aphorisms, which are more artful, more imaginative, and more personal than those in *Nature.* They impress us as the central strategy in the carpet of his work. In addition to the usual rounded truism, unadorned—"one must be an inventor to read well" and "Each age, it is found, must write its own books"—there is the paradoxical aphorism—"Genius is always the enemy of genius by overinfluence"—the balanced parallelism—"There is a creative reading as well as a creative writing"—the doubly balanced antithesis, here inverted and with an internal rime—"Books are the best of things, well read; abused, among the worst"—the epigram, which, although not ironical or witty, is startling and supplies a pithy explanation—"Books are for the

scholar's idle times. When he can read God directly, the hour is too precious to be wasted in other men's transcripts of their readings"—the highly metaphoric—"Life is our dictionary" and "Life lies behind us as the quarry from whence we get tiles and copestones for the masonry of to-day"—and the usual, slightly incoherent, somewhat rhapsodic staccatoes, ambiguously succinct—"Character is higher than intellect. Thinking is the functionary. The stream retreats to its source. A great soul will be strong to live, as well as strong to think." Aphorisms, staccatoes, and rhythmical cadences carry with them the frenzied speech of the prophet, dogmatising fervently and unequivocally, slightly beyond mere mortal understanding, because he sees into the cause of things and reports as from Sinai.

With the dogma muted by exuberance, the rapier stays in its sheath. The swordsman is too enthusiastic to let his dyspepsia surface. Only in a word or phrase is he querulous, mainly when he suspects that scholars are not adequately self-reliant and easily quit their "belief that a popgun is a popgun." He is most acrid when most emotional, at the final climax, when he chides the "spirit of the American freeman" for being "timid, imitative, tame. Public and private avarice make the air we breathe thick and fat. The scholar is decent, indolent, complaisant. See already the tragic consequence. The mind of this country, taught to aim at low objects, eats upon itself. . . . Young men of the fairest promise . . . turn drudges, or die of disgust. . . ." He is not waspish and reverts immediately to formal optimism. Acerbity is not yet equal to the sharp-edged earnestness of his lecture style.

Not so with the third major work. In *The Divinity School Address* Emerson sharpens his righteousness to a finer edge than before. Beginning with a mystical calmness, brooded over by contemplative grace and reverence, the essay turns suddenly accusatory. The thought shifts from general to specific, from sweetness and light to condemnation. Harsh words in the transitional paragraphs, contrasting the living spirit with the closed church, grow more vehement when he charges the church with two specific errors: dwelling "with noxious exaggeration about the person of *Jesus*" and assuming that revelation has ceased "as if God were dead." He accuses church officials of building monarchies out of "indolence and fear;" he accuses preachers of being docile, timid, ignorant, lifeless, fearful, witless, and impotent; he labels preaching and worship as dull, creeds as petrifications, and sacraments, especially the Lord's Supper, as merely "hollow, dry, creaking formalities." The angry language is characterized by petulance, botheration, and embarrassment—that the "goodliest of institutions" has come to this, that Jesus be insulted, man degraded, the church sick and dying. "Courage, piety, love, wisdom, can teach; and every man can open his door to these angels, and they shall bring him the gift of tongues. But the man who aims to speak as books enable, as synods use, as the fashion guides, and as interest commands, babbles. Let him hush." After the accusatory outburst Emerson relaxes the tension, grows elegiac at the "passing away" of the Protestant force, and concludes in a conciliatory tone.

Contemplative mysticism effectively diminishes the aphoristic wit to moral platitudes or theological abstractions, and the accusatory tone throttles the imaginative energy so that potential brilliance fades into crabbed statements, specific and argumentative: "that which shows God in me, fortifies me. That which shows God out of me, makes me a wart and a wen." "Once man was all; now he is an appendage, a nuisance." "The doctrine of inspiration is lost. . . ." "Genius leaves the temple to haunt the senate or the market. Literature becomes frivolous. Science is cold." The oracular cadence is pronounced, but in the art of severing the truth and saying it sharply the seer may have honed the edges a bit too fine. After the severity of the *Address,* Emerson returns in **"Self-Reliance"** to the stirring, enthusiastic heart-thumping popular oratory of *The American Scholar.* Two traits that set it apart are the more richly exploited hortatory potentials of the sermonic-inspirational genre and the colorful extension of the aphoristic wit, more sharply self-righteous and metaphorical. Second-person speech, the imperative moods, modals of obligation, and a piquant militancy help advance the careful, easy-to-follow organization to a progressively rising climax: 1. "Trust thyself: every heart vibrates to that iron string. . . . Nothing is at last sacred but the integrity of your own mind. . . . 2. Two terrors frighten us from self-reliance: conformity and consistency. Whoso would be a man, must be a nonconformist. . . . Let us never bow and apologize more. 3. The basis of this faith is that self-reliance is God-reliance. 4. If we cannot at once rise to the sanctities of obedience and faith, let us at least resist our temptations; let us enter the state of war . . . by speaking the truth . . . obey[ing] no law . . . [but] my own. . . . It is easy to see that a greater self-reliance must work a revolution" in religion, education, artistic culture, and the whole state of society.

The essay is one pithy self-assertion after another. Nowhere in his writing are the aphorisms so integral a part of the structure and style. They come in all varieties, and then some, as cited in *The American Scholar.* And nowhere is the vinegar so thick, yet so essential. "Your goodness must have some edge to it—else it is none." He is not angry as in the *Address,* only militant and overconfident to the point of righteous arrogance. He speaks "the rude truth" about charities. He blasts reformers as bigots, students as fools, and beggars as sots. He counsels turning one's back on family and friends. As before, when he gets contemptuous, his language pricks and stings: "Let a man then know his worth, and keep things under his feet. Let him not peep or steal, or skulk up and down with the air of a charity-boy, a bastard, or an interloper." He is at the height of his linguistic skill. Not only does he stir by direct address and exhort by command; he prods by chiding and incites by grandstands of rudeness; he wheedles, cajoles, flatters, pontificates, scoffs, sneers, and eulogizes. His tonal nuances seem endless as he calls his audience to a greater self-reliance.

Emerson never again achieved such an artful balance of earnest goodness and pungent oratory. The dogma is instinctive. The self-righteous asperity pierces and coerces. We are not offended, because a self-reliant soul thrusts us into orbits of divinity. No other essay disentangles the truth from the universal soul as this one, or says it with such éclat. His treatment of militancy in "Heroism" is tame by comparison. The thought of **"The Over-Soul"** is stronger than the style. Perhaps **"The Poet"** comes closest, among all his subsequent works, to achieving a similar balance of earnest oratory with an edge. **"Experience,"** that remarkable exception to his prevailing oratorical style, nearly complements it. He is morosely acrid in his self-reproaches, but the piece is a series of elegies without compelling logic. It is a prose poem, an ode to dejection, and the least oratorical of his essays. The elegiac tone reverses his usual earnestness. Achilles no longer rallies his legions to self-assurance in the fray; he sits despondently in his tent, nursing his wounded ego, frustrated and stymied at the realization of a wide disparity between the theory of divine power in man and its practical realization. He has met his conquerors, the "lords of life." As we read the later essays, we find patches of eloquence, earnestness, and acidity; his goodness had an edge almost to the end. After the few years into which the pith of his genius contracted itself, he could not get these traits together. Nevertheless, let us give him credit for the pith rather than rebuke him for his preparations and residue. (pp. 37-42)

Alfred S. Reid, "Emerson's Prose Style: An Edge to Goodness," in *Style in the American Renaissance; a Symposium,* edited by Carl F. Strauch, Transcendental Books, 1970, pp. 37-42.

SOURCES FOR FURTHER STUDY

Arnold, Matthew. "Emerson." In his *Discourses in America,* pp. 138-208. New York: Macmillan, 1924.

> Extensive assessment of Emerson's poetry and prose by the nineteenth-century English poet and critic. In the essay, originally published in 1884, Arnold contends that Emerson "is the friend and aider of those who would live in the spirit" and particularly commends Emerson's essays.

Burkholder, Robert E., and Myerson, Joel. *Emerson: An Annotated Secondary Bibliography.* Pittsburgh, Pa.: University of Pittsburgh Press, 1985, 842 p.

> Offers chronologically ordered citations of Emerson's writings from 1816 to 1979 in "the first comprehensive annotated secondary bibliography of Ralph Waldo Emerson."

Konvitz, Milton R., and Whicher, Stephen E. *Emerson: A Collection of Critical Essays.* Englewood Cliffs, N.J.: Prentice-Hall, 1962, 184 p.

> Reprints significant critical essays on Emerson's works by such authors and critics as Robert Frost, William James, George Santayana, Stephen Whicher, Newton Arvin, and F. O. Matthiessen.

Rusk, Ralph L. *The Life of Ralph Waldo Emerson.* New York: Charles Scribner's Sons, 1949, 592 p.

> Seminal biography.

Waggoner, Hyatt H. *Emerson as Poet.* Princeton, N.J.: Princeton University Press, 1974, 211 p.

> Comprehensive study of Emerson's poems and his theories of poetry.

Yannella, Donald. *Ralph Waldo Emerson.* Boston: Twayne Publishers, 1982, 147 p.

> Study of Emerson's life and career designed "not for specialists in the literature of nineteenth-century America but for general readers."

William Faulkner

1897-1962

(Born William Cuthbert Falkner) American novelist, short story writer, poet, screenwriter, and essayist.

INTRODUCTION

A preeminent figure in twentieth-century American literature, Faulkner created a profound and complex body of work in which he often explored exploitation and corruption in the American South. Many of Faulkner's novels and short stories are set in Yoknapatawpha County, a fictional area reflecting the geographical and cultural background of his native Mississippi. Faulkner's works frequently reflect the tumultuous history of the South while developing perceptive explorations of the human character. In his acceptance speech for the Nobel Prize for literature in 1949, Faulkner stated that the fundamental theme of his fiction is "the human heart in conflict with itself," and he utilized a variety of narrative techniques to enrich his exploration of this struggle.

Faulkner was born into a genteel Southern family in New Albany, Mississippi. An indifferent student, he dropped out of high school in 1915 to work as a clerk in his grandfather's bank, began writing poetry, and submitted drawings to the University of Mississippi's yearbook. During World War I, Faulkner tried to enlist in the U.S. army, but was rejected because of his small stature. Instead, he manipulated his acceptance into the Royal Canadian Air Force by affecting a British accent and forging letters of recommendation. The war ended before Faulkner experienced combat duty, however, and he returned to his hometown, where he intermittently attended the University of Mississippi as a special student. On August 6, 1919, his first poem, "L'Apres-midi d'un faune," was published in *New Republic*, and later in the same year the *Mississippian* published one of his short stories, "Landing in Luck." After a brief period of employment as a bookstore clerk in New York, Faulkner returned to Oxford, Mississippi, where he was hired as a university postmaster. He resigned, however, when the postal inspector noticed that Faulkner often brought his writing to the post office and became so immersed in what he was doing that he ignored patrons.

After the end of his postal career, Faulkner traveled to New Orleans to visit his friend, Elizabeth Prall, who was married to acclaimed fiction writer Sherwood Anderson. Though Faulkner's primary ambition was to be a poet and his verse was published in his first full-length book, *The Marble Faun* (1924), he realized that his prose was more accomplished and was encouraged by Anderson to write fiction. Neither of Faulkner's first two novels, *Soldier's Pay* (1926) and *Mosquitoes* (1927), received much critical notice. *Soldier's Pay* is categorized as a "Lost Generation" novel because it centers on a physically and emotionally scarred young soldier who returns home and finds only further trauma and disillusionment. *Mosquitoes* is a mildly satirical study of the New Orleans literary scene. When his next work, *Sartoris* (1929), the first Faulkner novel set in Yoknapatawpha County, was rejected by numerous publishers, Faulkner became disgusted with the publishing industry and decided to write only for himself. He later stated: "One day I seemed to shut a door between me and all publishers' addresses and book lists. I said to myself, now I can write. Now I can make a vase like that which the old Roman kept at his bedside and wore the rim slowly away with kissing it." The resulting novel, *The Sound and the Fury* (1929), established the respect of numerous literary critics towards Faulkner's work.

The Sound and the Fury chronicles the disintegration of the Compson family, reflecting Faulkner's thematic interest in the deterioration of community. Philip Momberger stated that "Faulkner's recurrent dramatization of the decay of families, e.g., the deterioration of the Compson, Sutpen, and Sartoris lines—is an expression in the domestic sphere of a more general, public disintegration: the collapse of the ideal of 'human family' in the modern world and the resulting deracination of the individual." The novel's complex structure incorporates multiple narrative viewpoints, the incantatory repetition of certain words, long, convoluted sentences, and the intermingling of past and present. Reflecting many of Faulkner's works, the characters within *The Sound and the Fury* are obsessed with and even controlled by forces and events from their own pasts. For example, Quentin Compson commits suicide, partly as a result of his inability to relinquish an incestuous childhood relationship with his sister. With critical recognition established, Faulkner sought greater financial rewards from his writing. With an eye on the commercial market, he began composing what he called "the most horrific tale I could imagine." The result was *Sanctuary* (1931), a novel which had to be revised before final publication due to its graphic violence and the extravagant depravity of its

characters. An objective study of human evil, *Sanctuary,* even in its revised form, caused a minor uproar. While it became Faulkner's best-selling novel, a number of critics disparaged the work for its sensationalistic violence.

Faulkner's work grew increasingly complex during the 1930s, making even greater demands upon readers and eliciting mixed critical response. *As I Lay Dying* (1930), for example, is a novel composed of fifty-nine interior monologues providing various perspectives through constantly shifting, contrasting points of view. In *Light in August* (1932), Faulkner examines the origins of personal identity and the roots of racial conflicts. *Light in August* begins by introducing a few characters and then turns to the plight of Joe Christmas, who is trying to uncover his true identity by piecing together bits of hearsay information. Because this story is told in an extended flashback, many critics felt that the novel suffered from faulty structure. However, defenders of the novel claim that this structure is intentional and serves to enhance the thematic scope of the narrative.

Faulkner's next major novel, *Absalom! Absalom!* (1936), focuses on Thomas Sutpen, a tragic character with a monomaniacal passion for creating and controlling a self-contained world. Many of the "facts" regarding Sutpen, as well as other characters and events in the novel, are based on unreliable information, and the novel thus questions the human capacity to know the truth about anyone or anything. Upon publication of *Absalom! Absalom!,* many critics hailed Faulkner as a great artist, while others felt that his abstruse method of storytelling was confusing and ultimately ineffective. After publishing two subsequent novels that received lukewarm critical response, *The Unvanquished* (1938) and *The Wild Palms* (1939), and following a brief stint in Hollywood as a scriptwriter, Faulkner published *The Hamlet* (1940). According to some critics, this novel concludes Faulkner's "major period." *The Hamlet,* along with two later novels, *The Town* (1957) and *The Mansion* (1959), are collectively known as the "Snopes Trilogy." These novels center on Flem Snopes, whose single ambition in life is to acquire more and more property, and are a blend of tragedy and comedy. The Snopes trilogy also highlights another prominent theme in Faulkner's work—exploitation of land and people as a source of human misery.

In the opinion of some critics, Faulkner is most effective as a short story writer. He often used short stories to fill gaps in the historical development of Yoknapatawpha County as depicted in his novels. Many characters who appear in the novels also appear in the short stories, while new characters are also introduced. Even in isolation from his novels, Faulkner's short fiction provides the complete chronological development of Yoknapatawpha from the coming of white men, who introduced the concept of private property, up to the twentieth century, when the automobile becomes a common fixture in American society. *Go Down, Moses* (1942) is a short story collection that can also be considered a novel, with a thematic unity binding the separate sections of the work. Though Faulkner himself referred to this collection as a novel, many critics view "episodes" such as "The Bear" as fully realized short stories that are more concise and complete than many of Faulkner's novels.

During the 1950s, Faulkner spent much time traveling and lecturing both abroad and at American colleges. His novel *A Fable* (1954) won the Pulitzer Prize in fiction and the National Book Award, but received mixed reviews because of its rigidly structured prose. After completing the Snopes trilogy, Faulkner wrote his final novel, *The Reivers* (1962), which was published shortly before his death. *The Reivers* provides a final

glance at Yoknapatawpha County. Although written as a tall tale in the manner of the nineteenth-century Southwestern humorists, this work, like most of Faulkner's fiction, can also be read symbolically as a moral tale. Since his death, Faulkner's work has been extensively analyzed and is now more fully appreciated. Faulkner created a body of work that is distinctly American yet reflects, on a grander scale, the universal values of human life.

(For further information about Faulkner's life and works, see *Concise Dictionary of American Literary Biography, 1929-1941; Contemporary Authors*, Vols. 81-84; *Contemporary Literary Criticism*, Vols. 1, 3, 6, 8, 9, 11, 14, 18, 28, 52; *Dictionary of Literary Biography*, Vols. 9, 11, 44; *Dictionary of Literary Biography Documentary Series*, Vol. 2; *Dictionary of Literary Biography Yearbook: 1986*; and *Short Story Criticism*, Vol. 1)

CRITICAL COMMENTARY

CONRAD AIKEN

(essay date 1939)

[In the following excerpt from a 1939 essay, Aiken offers a descriptive analysis of Faulkner's writing style.]

[If] one thing is more outstanding than another about Mr. Faulkner—some readers find it so outstanding, indeed, that they never get beyond it—it is the uncompromising and almost hypnotic zeal with which he insists upon having a style, and, especially of late, the very peculiar style which he insists upon having. Perhaps to that one should add that he insists *when he remembers*—he can write straightforwardly enough when he wants to; he does so often in the best of his short stories (and they are brilliant), often enough, too, in the novels. But that *style* is what he really wants to get back to; and get back to it he invariably does.

And what a style it is, to be sure! The exuberant and tropical luxuriance of sound which Jim Europe's jazz band used to exhale, like a jungle of rank creepers and ferocious blooms taking shape before one's eyes— magnificently and endlessly intervolved, glisteningly and ophidianly in motion, coil sliding over coil, and leaf and flower forever magically interchanging—was scarcely more bewildering, in its sheer inexhaustible fecundity, than Mr. Faulkner's style. Small wonder if even the most passionate of Mr. Faulkner's admirers— among whom the present writer honors himself by enlisting—must find, with each new novel, that the first

fifty pages are always the hardest, that each time one must learn all over again *how* to read this strangely fluid and slippery and heavily mannered prose, and that one is even, like a kind of Laocoön, sometimes tempted to give it up. (p. 200)

Mr. Faulkner's style, though often brilliant and always interesting, is all too frequently downright bad. . . . But if it is easy enough to make fun of Mr. Faulkner's obsessions for particular words, or his indifference and violence to them, or the parrotlike mechanical mytacism (for it is really like a stammer) with which he will go on endlessly repeating such favorites as "myriad, sourceless, impalpable, outrageous, risible, profound," there is nevertheless something more to be said for his passion for overelaborate sentence structure.

Overelaborate they certainly are, baroque and involuted and in the extreme, these sentences: trailing clauses, one after another, shadowily in apposition, or perhaps not even with so much connection as that; parenthesis after parenthesis, the parenthesis itself often containing one or more parentheses—they remind one of those brightly colored Chinese eggs of one's childhood, which when opened disclosed egg after egg, each smaller and subtler than the last. It is as if Mr. Faulkner, in a sort of hurried despair, had decided to try to tell us everything, absolutely everything, every last origin or source or quality or qualification, and every possible future or permutation as well, in one terrifically con-

Principal Works

The Marble Faun (poetry) 1924

Soldiers' Pay (novel) 1926

Mosquitoes (novel) 1927

Sartoris (novel) 1929

The Sound and the Fury (novel) 1929

As I Lay Dying (novel) 1930

Sanctuary (novel) 1931

These Thirteen (short stories) 1931

Light in August (novel) 1932

A Green Bough (poetry) 1933

Pylon (novel) 1935

Absalom, Absalom! (novel) 1936

The Unvanquished (short stories) 1938

The Wild Palms (novel) 1939

The Hamlet (novel) 1940

Go Down, Moses and Other Stories (novel) 1942

Intruder in the Dust (novel) 1948

Knight's Gambit (short stories) 1949

Requiem for a Nun (drama) 1951
    [Drama was first performed in 1959]

A Fable (novel) 1954

The Town (novel) 1957

The Mansion (novel) 1959

The Reivers (novel) 1962

Essays, Speeches and Public Letters (nonfiction) 1966

---

centrated effort: each sentence to be, as it were, a microcosm. And it must be admitted that the practice is annoying and distracting.

It is annoying, at the end of a sentence, to find that one does not know in the least what was the subject of the verb that dangles *in vacuo*—it is distracting to have to go back and sort out the meaning, track down the structure from clause to clause, then only to find that after all it doesn't much matter, and that the obscurity was perhaps neither subtle nor important. And to the extent that one *is* annoyed and distracted, and *does* thus go back and work it out, it may be at once added that Mr. Faulkner has defeated his own ends. One has had, of course, to emerge from the stream, and to step away from it, in order properly to see it: and as Mr. Faulkner works precisely by a process of *immersion,* of hypnotizing his reader into *remaining immersed* in his stream, this occasional blunder produces irritation and failure.

Nevertheless, despite the blunders, and despite the bad habits and the willful bad writing (and willful it obviously is), the style as a whole is extraordinarily effective; the reader *does* remain immersed, *wants* to re-

main immersed, and it is interesting to look into the reasons for this. And at once, if one considers these queer sentences not simply by themselves, as monsters of grammar or awkwardness, but in their relation to the book as a whole, one sees a functional reason and necessity for their being as they are. They parallel in a curious and perhaps inevitable way, and not without aesthetic justification, the whole elaborate method of *deliberately withheld meaning,* of progressive and partial and delayed disclosure, which so often gives the characteristic shape to the novels themselves. It is a persistent offering of obstacles, a calculated system of screens and obtrusions, of confusions and ambiguous interpolations and delays, with one express purpose; and that purpose is simply to keep the form—and the idea—fluid and unfinished, still in motion, as it were, and unknown, until the dropping into place of the very last syllable.

What Mr. Faulkner is after, in a sense, is a *continuum.* He wants a medium without stops or pauses, a medium which is always *of the moment,* and of which the passage from moment to moment is as fluid and undetectable as in the life itself which he is purporting to give. It is all inside and underneath, or as seen from within and below; the reader must therefore be steadily *drawn in;* he must be powerfully and unremittingly hypnotized inward and downward to that image-stream; and this suggests, perhaps, a reason not only for the length and elaborateness of the sentence structure, but for the repetitiveness as well. The repetitiveness, and the steady iterative emphasis—like a kind of chanting or invocation—on certain relatively abstract words ("sonorous, latin, *vaguely* eloquent"), have the effect at last of producing, for Mr. Faulkner, a special language, a conglomerate of his own, which he uses with an astonishing virtuosity, and which, although in detailed analysis it may look shoddy, is actually for his purpose a life stream of almost miraculous adaptability. At the end extreme it is abstract, cerebral, time-and-space-obsessed, tortured and twisted, but nevertheless always with a living *pulse* in it; and at the other it can be as overwhelming in its simple vividness, its richness in the actual, as the flood scenes in *The Wild Palms.*

Obviously, such a style, especially when allied with such a *concern* for method, must make difficulties for the reader; and it must be admitted that Mr. Faulkner does little or nothing as a rule to make his highly complex "situation" easily available or perceptible. The reader must simply make up his mind to go to work, and in a sense to cooperate; his reward being that there *is* a situation to be given shape, a meaning to be extracted, and that half the fun is precisely in watching the queer, difficult, and often so laborious evolution of Mr. Faulkner's idea. And not so much idea, either, as form. For, like the great predecessor whom at least in this regard he so oddly resembles, Mr. Faulkner could say with Henry James that it is practically impossible to make any real distinction between theme and form. What immoderately delights him . . . and what sets him above—shall we say it firmly—all his American contemporaries, is his continuous preoccupation with the novel *as form,* his passionate concern with it, and a degree of success with it which would clearly have commanded the interest and respect of Henry James himself. The novel as revelation, the novel as slice-of-life, the novel as mere story, do not interest him: these he would say, like James again, "are the circumstances of the interest," but not the interest itself. The interest itself will be the use to which these circumstances are put, the degree to which they can be organized.

From this point of view, he is not in the least to be considered as a mere "Southern" writer: the "Southernness" of his scenes and characters is of little concern to him, just as little as the question whether they are pleasant or unpleasant, true or untrue. Verisimilitude— or, at any rate, *degree* of verisimilitude—he will cheerfully abandon, where necessary, if the compensating advantages of plan or tone are a sufficient inducement. The famous scene in *Sanctuary* of Miss Reba and Uncle Bud in which a "madam" and her cronies hold a wake for a dead gangster, while the small boy gets drunk, is quite false, taken out of its context; it is not endowed with the same *kind* of actuality which permeates the greater part of the book at all. Mr. Faulkner was cunning enough to see that a two-dimensional cartoon-like statement, at this juncture, would supply him with the effect of a chorus, and without in the least being perceived as a change in the temperature of truthfulness.

That particular kind of dilution, or adulteration, of verisimilitude was both practised and praised by James. . . . It was for him a device for organization, just as the careful cherishing of "viewpoint" was a device, whether simply or in counterpoint. Of Mr. Faulkner's devices, of this sort, aimed at the achievement of complex "form," the two most constant are the manipulation of viewpoint and the use of the flashback, or sudden shift of time-scene, forward or backward.

In *Sanctuary,* where the alternation of viewpoint is a little lawless, the complexity is given, perhaps a shade disingenuously, by violent shifts in time; a deliberate disarrangement of an otherwise straightforward story. Technically, there is no doubt that the novel, despite its fame, rattles a little; and Mr. Faulkner himself takes pains to disclaim it. But, even done with the left hand, it betrays a genius for form, quite apart from its wonderful virtuosity in other respects. *Light in August* . . . repeats the same technique, that of a dislocation of time, and more elaborately; the time-shifts alternate with shifts in the viewpoint; and if the book is a failure it is perhaps because Mr. Faulkner's tendency to what is almost a hypertrophy of form is not here, as well as in the other novels, matched with the characters and the theme. Neither the person nor the story of Joe

Christmas is seen fiercely enough—by its creator—to carry off that immense machinery of narrative; . . . for once Mr. Faulkner's inexhaustible inventiveness seems to have been at fault. Consequently what we see is an extraordinary power for form functioning relatively *in vacuo,* and existing only to sustain itself.

In the best of the novels, however—and it is difficult to choose between *The Sound and the Fury* and *The Wild Palms,* with *Absalom, Absalom!* a very close third—this tendency to hypertrophy of form has been sufficiently curbed; and it is interesting, too, to notice that in all these three (and in that remarkable *tour de force, As I Lay Dying,* as well), while there is still a considerably reliance on time-shift, the effect of richness and complexity is chiefly obtained by a very skillful fugue-like alternation of viewpoint. Fugue-like in *The Wild Palms*—and fugue-like especially, of course, in *As I Lay Dying,* where the shift is kaleidoscopically rapid, and where, despite an astonishing violence to plausibility (in the reflections, and *language* of reflection, of the characters), an effect of the utmost reality and immediateness is nevertheless produced. Fugue-like, again, in *Absalom, Absalom!,* where indeed one may say the form is really circular—there is no beginning and no ending properly speaking, and therefore no *logical* point of entrance: we must just submit, and follow the circling of the author's interest, which turns a light inward towards the center, but every moment from a new angle, a new point of view. The story unfolds, therefore, now in one color of light, now in another, with references backward and forward: those that refer forward being necessarily, for the moment, blind. What is complete in Mr. Faulkner's pattern, *a priori,* must nevertheless remain incomplete for us until the very last stone is in place; what is "real," therefore, at one stage of the unfolding, or from one point of view, turns out to be "unreal" from another; and we find that one among other thing with which we are engaged is the fascinating sport of trying to separate truth from legend, watching the growth of legend from truth, and finally reaching the conclusion that the distinction is itself false.

Something of the same sort is true also of *The Sound and the Fury*—and this, with its massive four-part symphonic structure, is perhaps the most beautifully *wrought* of the whole series, and an indubitable masterpiece of what James loved to call the "fictive art." The joinery is flawless in its intricacy; it is a novelist's novel—a whole textbook on the craft of fiction in itself, comparable in its way to *What Maisie Knew* or *The Golden Bowl.*

But if it is important, for the moment, to emphasize Mr. Faulkner's genius for form, and his continued exploration of its possibilities, as against the usual concern with the violence and dreadfulness of his themes—though we might pause to remind carpers on this score of the fact that the best of Henry James is precisely that group of last novels which so completely concerned themselves with moral depravity—it is also well to keep in mind his genius for invention, whether of character or episode. The inventiveness is of the richest possible sort—a headlong and tumultuous abundance, an exuberant generosity and vitality, which makes most other contemporary fiction look very pale and chaste indeed. It is an unforgettable gallery of portraits, whether character or caricature, and all of them endowed with a violent and immediate vitality. (pp. 201-06)

Conrad Aiken, "William Faulkner," in his *Collected Criticism,* Oxford University Press, Inc., 1968, pp. 200-07.

JEAN-PAUL SARTRE
(essay date 1955)

[A French philosopher, dramatist, novelist, and essayist, Sartre was a leading proponent of Existentialism. In the following excerpt from his 1955 collection *Literary and Philosophical Essays*, he examines Faulkner's metaphysics of time, focusing on his depiction of the past as a powerful force that consumes the present and future.]

Faulkner's metaphysics is a metaphysics of time.

Man's misfortune lies in his being time-bound. . . . Such is the real subject of [*The Sound and the Fury*]. And if the technique Faulkner has adopted seems at first a negation of temporality, the reason is that we confuse temporality with chronology. It was man who invented dates and clocks. (pp. 87-8)

Faulkner's present is essentially catastrophic. It is the event which creeps up on us like a thief, huge, unthinkable—which creeps up on us and then disappears. Beyond this present time there is nothing, since the future does not exist. The present rises up from sources unknown to us and drives away another present; it is forever beginning anew. "And . . . and . . . and then." . . .

In Faulkner's work, there is never any progression, never anything which comes from the future. The present has not first been a future possibility, as when my friend, after having been *he for whom I am waiting,* finally appears. No, to be present means to appear without any reason and to sink in. This sinking in is not an abstract view. It is within things themselves that Faulkner perceives it and tries to make it felt. (p. 88)

Quentin can say, "I broke my watch," but when he says it, his gesture is *past.* The past is named and related; it can, to a certain extent, be fixed by concepts or

recognized by the heart. . . . Faulkner's vision of the world can be compared to that of a man sitting in an open car and looking backward. At every moment, formless shadows, flickerings, faint tremblings and patches of light rise up on either side of him, and only afterward, when he has a little perspective, do they become trees and men and cars.

The past takes on a sort of super-reality; its contours are hard and clear, unchangeable. The present, nameless and fleeting, is helpless before it. It is full of gaps, and, through these gaps, things of the past, fixed, motionless, and silent as judges or glances, come to invade it. Faulkner's monologues remind one of airplane trips full of air-pockets. At each pocket, the hero's consciousness "sinks back into the past" and rises only to sink back again. The present is not; it becomes. Everything *was.* In *Sartoris,* the past was called "the stories" because it was a matter of family memories that had been constructed, because Faulkner had not yet found his technique.

In *The Sound and the Fury* he is more individual and more undecided. But it is so strong an obsession that he is sometimes apt to disguise the present, and the present moves along in the shadow, like an underground river, and reappears only when it itself is past. (p. 89)

This unspeakable present, leaking at every seam, these sudden invasions of the past, this emotional order, the opposite of the voluntary and intellectual order that is chronological but lacking in reality, these memories, these monstrous and discontinuous obsessions, these intermittences of the heart—are not these reminiscent of the lost and recaptured time of Marcel Proust? I am not unaware of the differences between the two; I know, for instance, that for Proust salvation lies in time itself, in the full reappearance of the past. For Faulkner, on the contrary, the past is never lost, unfortunately; it is always there, it is an obsession. One escapes from the temporal world only through mystic ecstasies. A mystic is always a man who wishes to forget something, his self or, more often, language or objective representations. For Faulkner, time must be forgotten. (p. 90)

But for Faulkner, as for Proust, time is, above all, *that which separates.* One recalls the astonishment of the Proustian heroes who can no longer enter into their past loves, of those lovers depicted in *Les Plaisirs et Les Jours,* clutching their passions, afraid they will pass, and knowing they will. We find the same anguish in Faulkner. . . .

To tell the truth, Proust's fictional technique *should have been* Faulkner's. It was the logical conclusion of his metaphysics. But Faulkner is a lost man, and it is because he feels lost that he takes risks and pursues his thought to its uttermost consequences. Proust is a

Frenchman and a classicist. The French lose themselves only a little at a time and always manage to find themselves again. Eloquence, intellectuality, and a liking for clear ideas were responsible for Proust's retaining at least the semblance of chronology.

The basic reason for this relationship is to be found in a very general literary phenomenon. Most of the great contemporary authors, Proust, Joyce, Dos Passos, Faulkner, Gide, and Virginia Woolf have tried, each in his own way, to distort time. Some of them have deprived it of its past and future in order to reduce it to the pure intuition of the instant; others, like Dos Passos, have made of it a dead and closed memory. Proust and Faulkner have simply decapitated it. They have deprived it of its future—that is, its dimension of deeds and freedom. . . . Faulkner's heroes . . . never look ahead. They face backward as the car carries them along. The coming suicide which casts its shadow over Quentin's last day is not a human possibility; not for a second does Quentin envisage the possibility of *not* killing himself. This suicide is an immobile wall, a *thing* which he approaches backward, and which he neither wants to nor can conceive. (p. 91)

Faulkner's entire art aims at suggesting to us that Quentin's monologues and his last walk *are already* his suicide. This, I think, explains the following curious paradox: Quentin thinks of his last day in the past, like someone who is remembering. But in that case, since the hero's last thoughts coincide approximately with the bursting of his memory and its annihilation, who is remembering? The inevitable reply is that the novelist's skill consists in the choice of the present moment from which he narrates the past. . . . [His] artistry and, to speak frankly, all . . . illusion are meant, then, merely as substitutions for the intuition of the future lacking in the author himself. This explains everything, particularly the irrationality of time; since the present is the unexpected, the formless can be determined only by an excess of memories. We now also understand why duration is "man's characteristic misfortune." If the future has reality, time withdraws us from the past and brings us nearer to the future; but if you do away with the future, time is no longer that which separates, that which cuts the present off from itself. "You cannot bear to think that someday it will no longer hurt you like this." Man spends his life struggling against time, and time, like an acid, eats away at man, eats him away from himself and prevents him from fulfilling his human character. Everything is absurd. "Life is a tale told by an idiot, full of sound and fury, signifying nothing."

But is man's time without a future? I can understand that the nail's time, or the clod's, or the atom's is a perpetual present. But is man a thinking nail? If you begin by plunging him into universal time, the time of planets and nebulae, of tertiary flexures and animal species, as into a bath of sulphuric acid, then the question is settled. However, a consciousness buffeted so from one instant to another ought, *first of all,* to be a consciousness and then, *afterward,* to be temporal; does anyone believe that time can come to it from the outside? Consciousness can "exist within time" only on condition that it become time as a result of the very movement by which it becomes consciousness. It must become "temporalized," as Heidegger says. We can no longer arrest man at each present and define him as "the sum of what he has." The nature of consciousness implies, on the contrary, that it project itself into the future. We can understand what it is only through what it will be. It is determined in its present being by its own possibilities. This is what Heidegger calls "the silent force of the possible." You will not recognize within yourself Faulkner's man, a creature bereft of possibilities and explicable only in terms of what he has been. Try to pin down your consciousness and probe it. You will see that it is hollow. In it you will find only the future. (pp. 91-2)

I am afraid that the absurdity that Faulkner finds in a human life is one that he himself has put there. Not that life is not absurd, but there is another kind of absurdity.

Why have Faulkner and so many other writers chosen this particular absurdity which is so unnovelistic and so untrue? I think we should have to look for the reason in the social conditions of our present life. Faulkner's despair seems to me to precede his metaphysics. For him, as for all of us, the future is closed. Everything we see and experience impels us to say, "This can't last." And yet change is not even conceivable, except in the form of a cataclysm. We are living in a time of impossible revolutions, and Faulkner uses his extraordinary art to describe our suffocation and a world dying of old age. I like his art, but I do not believe in his metaphysics. A closed future is still a future. [In the words of Heidegger:] "Even if human reality has nothing more 'before' it, even if 'its account is closed,' its being is still determined by this 'self-anticipation.' The loss of all hope, for example, does not deprive human reality of its possibilities; it is simply a way of *being* toward these same possibilities." (p. 93)

Jean-Paul Sartre, "On 'The Sound and the Fury': Time in the Work of Faulkner," in *Faulkner: A Collection of Critical Essays,* edited by Robert Penn Warren, Prentice-Hall, Inc., 1966, pp. 87-93.

MALCOLM COWLEY

(essay date 1956)

[Below, Cowley examines Faulkner's portrayal in his novels of values and attitudes characteristic of the Deep South.]

[Faulkner's] novels are the books of a man who broods about literature, but doesn't often discuss it with his friends; there is no ease about them, no feeling that they come from a background of taste refined by argument and of opinions held in common. (pp. 132-34)

Faulkner is a solitary worker by choice, and he has done great things not only with double the pains to himself that they might have cost if produced in more genial circumstances, but sometimes also with double the pains to the reader. Two or three of his books as a whole and many of them in part are awkward experiments. All of them are full of overblown words like "imponderable," "immortal," "immutable," and "immemorial" that he would have used with more discretion, or not at all, if he had followed Hemingway's example and served an apprenticeship to an older writer. (p. 134)

Faulkner's mythical kingdom is a county in northern Mississippi, on the border between the sand hills covered with scrubby pine and the black earth of the river bottoms. . . . It sometimes seems to me that every house or hovel has been described in one of Faulkner's novels, and that all the people of the imaginary county, black and white, townsmen, farmers, and housewives, have played their parts in one connected story. (pp. 135-36)

Sartoris . . . is a romantic and partly unconvincing novel, but with many fine scenes in it, such as the hero's visit to a family of independent pine-hill farmers; and it states most of the themes that the author would later develop at length. (p. 136)

Just as Balzac, who may have inspired the [Yoknapatawpha] series, divided his *Comédie Humaine* into "Scenes of Parisian Life," "Scenes of Provincial Life," "Scenes of Private Life," so Faulkner might divide his work into a number of cycles: one about the planters and their descendants, one about the townspeople of Jefferson, one about the poor whites, one about the Indians, and one about the Negroes. Or again, if he adopted a division by families, there would be the Compson-Sartoris saga, the continuing Snopes saga, the McCaslin saga, dealing with the white and black descendants of Carothers McCaslin, and the Ratliff-Bundren saga, devoted to the backwoods farm-

ers of Frenchman's Bend. All the cycles or sagas are closely interconnected; it is as if each new book was a chord or segment of a total situation always existing in the author's mind. (p. 137)

All his books in the Yoknapatawpha cycle are part of the same living pattern. It is the pattern, not the printed volumes in which part of it is recorded, that is Faulkner's real achievement. Its existence helps to explain one feature of his work: that each novel, each long or short story, seems to reveal more than it states explicitly and to have a subject bigger than itself. All the separate works are like blocks of marble from the same quarry: they show the veins and faults of the mother rock. Or else—to use a rather strained figure—they are like wooden planks that were cut, not from a log, but from a still-living tree. The planks are planed and chiseled into their final shapes, but the tree itself heals over the wound and continues to grow. (p. 138)

Although the pattern is presented in terms of a single Mississippi county, it can be extended to the Deep South as a whole; and Faulkner always seems conscious of its wider application. He might have been thinking of his own novels when he described the ledgers in the commissary of the McCaslin plantation, in *Go Down, Moses.* They recorded, he says, "that slow trickle of molasses and meal and meat, of shoes and straw hats and overalls, of plowlines and collars and heelbolts and clevises, which returned each fall as cotton"—in a sense they were local and limited; but they were also "the continuation of that record which two hundred years had not been enough to complete and another hundred would not be enough to discharge; that chronicle which was a whole land in miniature, which multiplied and compounded was the entire South." (p. 139)

More or less unconsciously, the incidents in [*Absalom, Absalom!* come] to represent the forces and elements in the social situation, since the mind naturally works in terms of symbols and parallels. In Faulkner's case, this form of parallelism is not confined to *Absalom, Absalom!* It can be found in the whole fictional framework that he has been elaborating in novel after novel, until his work has become a myth or legend of the South. . . .

Briefly stated, the legend might run something like this: The Deep South was ruled by planters some of whom were aristocrats like the Sartoris clan, while others were new men like Colonel Sutpen. Both types were determined to establish a lasting social order on the land they had seized from the Indians (that is, to leave sons behind them). They had the virtue of living single-mindedly by a fixed code; but there was also an inherent guilt in their "design," their way of life; it was slavery that put a curse on the land and brought about the Civil War. (p. 142)

After the war was lost, partly as a result of the Southerner's mad heroism . . . , the planters tried to restore their "design" by other methods. But they no longer had the strength to achieve more than a partial success, even after they had freed their land from the carpetbaggers who followed the Northern armies. As time passed, moreover, the men of the old order found that they had Southern enemies too; they had to fight against a new exploiting class descended from the landless whites of slavery days. In this struggle between the clan of Sartoris and the unscrupulous tribe of Snopes, the Satorises were defeated in advance by a traditional code that kept them from using the weapons of the enemy. As a price of victory, however, the Snopeses had to serve the mechanized civilization of the North, which was morally impotent in itself, but which, with the aid of its Southern retainers, ended by corrupting the Southern nation. In a later time, the problems of the South are still unsolved, the racial conflict is becoming more acute, and Faulkner's characters in their despairing moments foresee or forebode some catastrophe of which Jim Bond [a half-witted mulatto from *Absalom, Absalom!*] and his like will be the only survivors. (p. 143)

Faulkner presents the virtues of the old order as being moral rather than material. There is no baronial pomp in his novels; no profusion of silk and silver, mahogany and moonlight and champagne. . . . What [Faulkner] admires about [his Southern aristocrats] is not their wealth or their manners or their fine horses, but rather the unquestioning acceptance—by the best planters—of a moral code that taught them "courage and honor and pride, and pity and love of justice and of liberty." (pp. 143-44)

The old order was a moral order: briefly that was its strength and the secret lost by its heirs. But also— and here is another respect in which it differs from the Southern story more commonly presented—it bore the moral burden of a guilt so great that the Civil War and even Reconstruction were in some sense a merited punishment. (p. 144)

The men [Faulkner] most admired and must have pictured himself as resembling were the Southern soldiers—after all, they were the vast majority—who owned no slaves themselves and suffered from the institution of slavery. The men he would praise in his novels were those "who had fought for four years and lost . . . not because they were opposed to freedom as freedom, but for the old reasons for which man (not the generals and politicians but man) has always fought and died in wars: to preserve a status quo or establish a better future one to endure for his children." One might define the author's position as that of an anti-slavery Southern nationalist.

Faulkner's novels of contemporary Southern life [those written before 1945] continue the legend into a period that he regards as one of moral confusion and social decay. He is continually seeking in them for violent images to convey his sense of outrage. *Sanctuary* is the most violent of all his novels; it has been the most popular and is by no means the least important (in spite of Faulkner's comment that it was "a cheap idea . . . deliberately conceived to make money"). The story of Popeye and Temple Drake has more meaning than appears on a first hasty reading. . . . Popeye himself is one of several characters in Faulkner's novels who represent the mechanical civilization that has invaded and conquered the South. He is always described in mechanical terms: his eyes "looked like rubber knobs"; his face "just went awry, like the face of a wax doll set too near a hot fire and forgotten"; his tight suit and stiff hat were "all angles, like a modernistic lampshade"; and in general he had "that vicious depthless quality of stamped tin." . . . [He] was a compendium of all the hateful qualities that Faulkner assigns to finance capitalism. *Sanctuary* is not a connected allegory, as George Marion O'Donnell [see excerpt above] condemned it for being—he was the first critic to approach it seriously—but neither is it a mere accumulation of pointless horrors. It is an example of the Freudian method turned backward, being full of sexual nightmares that are in reality social symbols. It is somehow connected in the author's mind with what he regards as the rape and corruption of the South.

In his novels dealing with the present Faulkner makes it clear that the descendants of the old ruling caste have the wish but not the courage or the strength to prevent this new disaster. . . . Faulkner's novels are full of well-meaning and even admirable persons, not only the grandsons of the cotton aristocracy, but also pine-hill farmers and storekeepers and sewing-machine agents and Negro cooks and sharecroppers; but they are almost all of them defeated by circumstances and they carry with them a sense of their own doom.

They also carry, whether heroes or villains, a curious sense of submission to their fate. "There is not one of Faulkner's characters," says André Gide in his dialogue on "The New American Novelists," "who properly speaking has a soul"; and I think he means that not one of them exercises the faculty of conscious choice between good and evil. They are haunted, obsessed, driven forward by some inner necessity. (pp. 145-47)

Even when they seem to be guided by a conscious purpose, like Colonel Sutpen, it is not something they have chosen by an act of will, but something that has taken possession of them: Sutpen's great design was "not what he wanted to but what he just had to do, had to do it whether he wanted to or not, because if he did not do it he knew he could never live with himself for the rest of his life." In the same way, Faulkner himself writes, not what he wants to, but what he just has to write whether he wants to or not.

It had better be admitted that most of his novels have some obvious weakness in structure. Some of them combine two or more themes having little relation to each other, as *Light in August* does, while others, like *The Hamlet,* tend to resolve themselves into a series of episodes resembling beads on a string. In *The Sound and the Fury,* which is superb as a whole, we can't be sure that the four sections of the novel are presented in the most effective order; at any rate, we can't fully understand the first section until we have read the three that follow. *Absalom, Absalom!* though at first it strikes us as being pitched in too high a key, is structurally the soundest of all the novels in the Yoknapatawpha series—and it gains power in retrospect; but even here the author's attention seems to shift from the principal theme of Colonel Sutpen's design to the secondary theme of incest and miscegenation.

Faulkner seems best to me, and most nearly himself, either in long stories like **"The Bear,"** in *Go Down, Moses,* and **"Old Man."** . . . That is, he has been most effective in dealing with the total situation always

present in his mind as a pattern of the South, or else in shorter units which, though often subject to inspired revision, have still been shaped by a single conception. It is by his best that we should judge him, as every other author; and Faulkner at his best—even sometimes at his worst—has a power, a richness of life, an intensity to be found in no other American writer of our time. (pp. 148-49)

Moreover, he has a brooding love for the land where he was born and reared and where, unlike other writers of his generation, he has chosen to spend his life. . . . Here are the two sides of Faulkner's feeling for the South: on the one side, an admiring and possessive love; on the other, a compulsive fear lest what he loves should be destroyed by the ignorance of its native serfs and the greed of traders and absentee landlords. (p. 149)

Faulkner's novels have the quality of being lived, absorbed, remembered rather than merely observed. And they have what is rare in the novels of our time, a warmth of family affection, brother for brother and sister, the father for his children—a love so warm and proud that it tries to shut out the rest of the world.

Faulkner in Hollywood during the mid-1930s.

Compared with that affection, married love is presented as something calculating, and illicit love as a consuming fire. And because the blood relationship is central in his novels, Faulkner finds it hard to create sympathetic characters between the ages of twenty and forty. He is better with children, Negro and white, and incomparably good with older people who preserve the standards that have come down to them "out of the old time, the old days."

In the group of novels beginning with *The Wild Palms* (1939), which attracted so little attention at the time of publication that they seemed to go unread, there is a quality not exactly new to Faulkner—it had appeared already in passages of *Sartoris* and *Sanctuary*—but now much stronger and no longer overshadowed by violence and horror. It is a sort of homely and sobersided frontier humor that is seldom achieved in contemporary writing (except sometimes by Erskine Caldwell, also a Southerner). . . . In a curious way, Faulkner combines two of the principal traditions in American letters: the tradition of psychological horror, often close to symbolism, that begins with Charles Brockden Brown, our first professional novelist, and extends through Poe, Melville, Henry James (in his later stories), Stephen Crane, and Hemingway; and the other tradition of frontier humor and realism, beginning with Augustus Longstreet's *Georgia Scenes* and having Mark Twain as its best example.

But the American author he most resembles is Hawthorne, for all their polar differences. They stand to each other as July to December, as heat to cold, as swamp to mountain, as the luxuriant to the meager but perfect, as planter to Puritan; and yet Hawthorne had much the same attitude toward New England that Faulkner has to the South, together with a strong sense of regional particularity. . . . Like Faulkner in the South, [Hawthorne] applied himself to creating [New England's] moral fables and elaborating its legends, which existed, as it were, in his solitary heart. Pacing the hillside behind his house in Concord, he listened for a voice; one might say that he lay in wait for it, passively but expectantly, like a hunter behind a rock; then, when it had spoken, he transcribed its words—more cautiously than Faulkner, it is true; with more form and less fire, but with the same essential fidelity. . . . Faulkner is another author who has to wait for the spirit and the voice. He is not so much a novelist, in the usual sense of being a writer who sets out to observe actions and characters, then fits them into the framework of a story, as he is an epic or bardic poet in prose, a creator of myths that he weaves together into a legend of the South. (pp. 151-52)

In Faulkner's later novels, the Yoknapatawpha story is traced backward to the founding and naming of Jefferson, as well as being carried forward almost to the time of his death. Those novels might be regarded

as sequels to the earlier books, yet they almost seem to be written by a different man. The sense of doom and outrage that brooded over the early ones has been replaced by pity for human beings, even the worst of them ("The poor sons of bitches," Gavin Stevens says, "they do the best they can") and by the obstinate faith, expressed in the Nobel Prize address, "that man will not only endure; he will prevail"—all this combined with more than a touch of old-fashioned sentiment. In Faulkner's case, as in those of many other writers, there had been a return to the fathers. I respect the later author, with most of his demons exorcised, but the younger possessed and unregenerate Faulkner is the man whose works amaze us, as they never ceased to puzzle and amaze himself. (pp. 153-54)

Faulkner in his early novels is indubitably a Southern nationalist and an heir of the Confederacy—for all his sense of guilt about the Negroes—but he is something else besides. . . . What he regarded as his ultimate subject is not the South or its destiny, however much they occupied his mind, but rather the human situation as revealed in Southern terms—to quote from one of his letters, "the same frantic steeplechase toward nothing everywhere." He approached that steeplechase in terms of Southern material because, as he also said, "I just happen to know it, and dont have time in one life to learn another one and write at the same time." There was of course another reason, for it was the South that aroused his apprehensions, that deeply engaged his loyalties ("*I dont, I dont hate it!*"), and that set his imagination to work. He dreamed, however, that his Yoknapatawpha story might stand for the human drama everywhere and always. (pp. 154-55)

Malcolm Cowley, "Faulkner: The Yoknapatawpha Story," in his *A Second Flowering: Works and Days of the Lost Generation,* Viking, 1973, pp. 130-55.

PHILIP MOMBERGER
(essay date 1975)

[In the following excerpt, Momberger examines Faulkner's "master-theme" of the deterioration of community.]

Faulkner's master-theme is man's inescapable need to search for communal ties, a search on which the individual's achievement of authentic selfhood depends. If he is to complete himself, the Faulkner hero must move from his initial solitude toward some form of social engagement. He must accept the risks of involvement in the lives of his fellows, for only in so doing can he feel himself to be an integral part of "a human family, of the human family." Faulkner's metaphor points to the larger social ideal that lies behind all his fiction: a state of communal wholeness within which, as within a coherent and loving family, the individual's identity would be defined, recognized, and sustained.

It is precisely this sense of participation in a cohesive community that is lacking, however, in the lives of nearly all Faulkner's characters. In his fiction the ideal state of communal wholeness is usually implied by its absence, in the dramatization of its opposite. From the urban chaos depicted in his early New Orleans sketches (1925) through the anarchic violence rendered in the Snopes Trilogy (1940-1959), the fragmented world confronted by Faulkner's typical protagonist offers him no acceptable role, no sense of participation or purpose, and no religious or moral tradition that can guide and support him. Estranged from everything outside himself, a Darl Bundren, a Quentin Compson, or a Joe Christmas can look to no external authority for recognition and validation of his selfhood. Faulkner's recurrent dramatization of the decay of families—e.g., the deterioration of the Compson, Sutpen, and Sartoris lines—is an expression in the domestic sphere of a more general, public disintegration: the collapse of the ideal of "human family" in the modern world and the resulting deracination of the individual.

Only in section I of his *Collected Stories* (1950), subtitled "The Country," does Faulkner reverse his usual strategy. In these stories he offers an extended rendering of an organic community in which his social ideal is given positive definition and complete institutional embodiment. (pp. 112-13)

Occasional critical praise for the accuracy of Faulkner's depiction of the "plain folk" has suggested that the primary value of these tales is their contribution to a descriptive chronicle of the Southern experience.

To take that approach to the stories of the Country, however, would be to mistake their nature and function, impoverish their meaning, and praise them for demonstrably wrong reasons. Measured against the realities of the Southern farmer's lot, **"Shingles for the Lord," "A Bear Hunt,"** and the others hardly meet the test of strict historical or sociological accuracy. Indeed, Faulkner's frequent divergence from that standard helps point up the ideality of his fictional Country.

In economic terms, for example, the life of Faulkner's Country does not reflect conditions prevailing during the period in which these stories are set—the 'thirties and early 'forties, when President Roosevelt declared the rural South "the nation's number one economic problem." There is no agricultural depression in Frenchman's Bend, no grinding poverty, malnutrition, or unemployment, no drought, soil exhaustion, or crop failure, no absentee ownership or mortgaging of land,

and almost no labor migrancy or tenant farming—Abner Snopes, the wandering sharecropper of **"Barn Burning,"** being the lone exception.

Technological change and political responses to it have not affected the traditional economy of Faulkner's Country. The yeomen have no tractors, mechanical seeders, or chemical fertilizers, and they want no part of the farm relief programs sponsored by the New Deal. . . . The men of Frenchman's Bend continue to cultivate their ancestors' land with the same kinds of hand tools used there for generations, and they foresee no change in their manner of work. Since the Country seems immune to economic pressures, the members of the younger generation, unlike their actual prototypes, need plan no flight to the city. Personal roots run deep and hold firm in Frenchman's Bend. (pp. 114-15)

[Violence], physical or moral, has no place in the Country. In this respect, the socially harmonious world of these stories diverges not only from historical truth, but also from the Frenchman's Bend depicted in *As I Lay Dying* (1930), *Sanctuary* (1931), and *The Hamlet* (1940), where mutual distrust and savage conflict are usually the first laws of life. As the "sole owner and proprietor" of Yoknapatawpha County, Faulkner reserved the right to change a character's personality from book to book, as the exigencies of a particular fictional situation might demand. In section I of the *Collected Stories,* he takes the same liberty with all of Frenchman's Bend, transforming it from a world of violence to a realm of communal order.

Outwardly peaceful, the Country is also free of underlying class antagonism and racial tension. (p. 117)

Clearly, then, Faulkner's Country will hardly serve as a sociologically or historically accurate "mirror" of the rural South in this century. But while it is untenable to praise the strict verisimilitude of these stories, it would be equally wrongheaded to condemn them as "unrealistic"—as naive as to complain that there are no bandits in the Forest of Arden and no milking machines in Frost's New Hampshire. Like Frost's technique, Faulkner's obviously selective mode of presentation in these works is mythic, akin to pastoral idyll, and the stories function in the traditional manner of pastoral. The first part of the *Collected Stories* defines an ideal of communal health, wholeness, and peace against which the reader can measure the social and personal disintegration rendered in subsequent sections and throughout the Faulkner canon. (pp. 118-19)

The social and personal disintegration rendered in subsequent parts of the *Collected Stories* is the more vivid and appalling when contrasted with the organic union of self and community defined in the volume's opening section. . . . The normative function of Faulkner's Country extends far beyond his *Collected*

Stories, however. To juxtapose the ordered society of Frenchman's Bend with the anarchic worlds of *Sanctuary, Light in August,* and *The Sound and the Fury* is to heighten our awareness of the terrifying consequences that attend destruction of the communal spirit throughout Faulkner's works. Thus Faulkner's Country functions in the traditional manner of pastoral—to define an ideal vantage point from which to measure the corrupt realities of a fallen world, and to evoke a condition of social and personal fulfillment toward which men of moral imagination may strive. (p. 136)

Philip Momberger, "Faulkner's 'Country' as Ideal Community," in *Individual and Community: Variations on a Theme in American Fiction,* edited by Kenneth H. Baldwin and David K. Kirby, Duke University Press, 1975, pp. 112-36.

ELIZABETH M. KERR
(essay date 1979)

[In the following excerpt, Kerr examines the combination of realism, romanticism, and Gothic elements in Faulkner's fiction.]

Faulkner was *both* a realist and a romanticist and was positively Gothic: an artist can view life from various perspectives if his vision is sufficiently comprehensive and penetrating. Faulkner loved his land and his people too much to reject them in their everyday aspects, without romantic or Gothic makeup and lighting, and some of his characters share his love of the ordinary. He was enough of a romanticist to feel keenly the difference between the reality he observed and what his land and his people had been at their best, between the sometimes nightmarish present and the fine dreams they had cherished.

Faulkner achieved the fusion of dream and reality in his Yoknapatawpha novels. . . . By assuming many points of view and imaginatively sharing the experiences of many diverse characters, by showing the outer world as it appeared to the mentally deficient, the psychologically disturbed, or the romantic idealist, Faulkner revealed the inner worlds of dream and nightmare and the razor's edge which separated them. As the omniscient author or through a rational, humanistic central intelligence or narrator, he showed a world of everyday experience, cherished in its multiplicity and uniqueness. The scope provided by this fictional world, despite its short history and limited boundaries, accommodated a variety of approaches, within a single novel or within the Yoknapatawpha cycle. In this cycle, only *As I Lay Dying, The Town,* and *The Reivers* are more in the romance vein than some version of Gothic novel or romance. (Although *As I Lay Dying* has a ma-

cabre quality and a partially Gothic effect, I deal with it in my article as an ironic version of quest-romance.) For Faulkner, it is apparent, Yoknapatawpha was essentially a Gothic realm. (pp. 220-21)

Faulkner never abandoned the advantages of the omniscient author but tried various limitations of omniscience, always with the purpose of getting inside a character and involving the reader as fully as possible. With an inarticulate character or one of limited awareness and self-knowledge, such as Mink or Joe Christmas, the style must be the author's. The restriction or the relinquishment of authorial omniscience, however, had great advantages in securing reader cooperation and involvement in a Gothic tale. The most difficult and successful experiments with multiple points of view, with interior monologue or soliloquy, came early, in *The Sound and the Fury* and *As I Lay Dying.* Faulkner's predilection for the oral tradition, strong in *The Hamlet* and dominant in *The Town,* in much of *The Mansion,* and in all of *The Reivers,* is perhaps the most original feature of narrative method in his Gothic novels and the closely related romances. By never telling a Gothic tale in the first person from the point of view of the hero or heroine at the time of the action or in retrospect, Faulkner dissociated himself from the multitude of run-of-the-mill writers of Gothic romance.

In Yoknapatawpha the equivalents of the Gothic castles, symbols usually of past splendor and present decay, appear in most of the novels: the Sartoris plantation house in *Sartoris* and *Sanctuary;* the ruins of the Old Frenchman's place in *Sanctuary* and *The Hamlet;* the Compson house, in a state of dilapidation, in *Absalom, Absalom!* and *The Sound and the Fury;* Sutpen's Hundred in *Absalom, Absalom!* from creation to destruction; Miss Burden's house in *Light in August;* the McCaslin plantation, still a going concern, in *Go Down, Moses* and *Intruder in the Dust;* the Backus plantation in decline in *The Town* and as transformed by Mr. Harriss in **"Knight's Gambit"** and *The Mansion;* the old De Spain mansion as transformed by Flem in *The Town* and *The Mansion.* All these "castles" represent the plantation days of the past, and all of them had or have neighboring slave or servant quarters. Only one novel, *Intruder in the Dust,* lacks a "castle": the Mallison house is a comfortable middle-class residence in which the family live happily and usefully in the present. Although Will Varner's house, the only two-storey one in Frenchman's Bend, was scarcely a "castle," it housed a princess, Eula Varner, the Helen of Frenchman's Bend.

The scenes of enclosure, the "other rooms," in these "castles" or in other buildings, signify isolation, whether captivity or withdrawal or self-imprisonment. . . . External nature ranges from the waste land despoiled by man, in *The Hamlet* and *Sanctuary* and *Absalom, Absalom!* and *Light in August,* to the pastoral and elegiac views of nature in *The Hamlet* and *The Mansion,* respectively. Productive plantations in *Sartoris* and *Go Down, Moses,* small farms in *Sartoris* and *The Hamlet,* and worn-out sharecroppers' or tenants' acres in the Frenchman's Bend area epitomize the agricultural economy and in context may be either Gothic or realistic. The most extended views of the natural scene in Yoknapatawpha are Gavin's panoramic survey from Seminary Hill in *The Town,* in which nature is least often a setting, and Chick's observations of his land and his vision of its place in the continent in *Intruder in the Dust.* Both Gavin and Chick show the romantic sensitivity to nature which is typical of Gothic fiction, but neither lives close to the land. Conversely, Ike McCaslin, despite his mystique of the land and the wilderness, shows little feeling for the areas which provide a living for man. (pp. 226-28)

[We] not only find all the traditional Gothic character types, but we find them in every novel, played straight, ironically inverted, or parodied: the Romantic, Byronic, or Faustian heroes and, for good measure and medieval flavor, the courtly lovers; the tragic villain-heroes, the revenge villain-hero, the rational villains, the villain seducer, and the arch-villain of melodrama. The heroines, who may or may not be Persecuted Maidens, are less prominent than the heroes—in *The Sound and the Fury* Caddy appears only as a memory. What with adolescent heroes and heroes who can do without women, heroines would sometimes be as extraneous as in a horse opera. There is no traditional heroine in the action of *Intruder in the Dust* or *Go Down, Moses.* And *Snopes* makes do with two real heroines in three volumes, Eula Snopes and her daughter Linda, but they come closer to being romantic or romantic-Gothic heroines than do any other female characters. Evil Women or Temptresses are less numerous than villains and sometimes are disguised as heroines, like Narcissa, or beneath a bawdy exterior conceal a heart of gold, like Miss Reba. *Snopes* seems to lack a female villain until, at the end of *The Mansion,* Linda appears to qualify.

The parental figures who produced many of the heroes, heroines, and villains may be tyrannical or benevolent, but rarely were they successful as parents or grandparents. . . . In the record of ineffective or unloving parents, emotionally crippled children, and broken lives in Yoknapatawpha, Faulkner directly continued the Gothic tradition into the new American Gothic in which, Irving Malin said, "almost every work in the canon contains family terror."

The grotesques, which are the most easily recognizable of Gothic character types, appear in all the Yoknapatawpha novels, in part because Faulkner was both a Gothic and a comic novelist and combined the horror story with the comic tall tale. . . . The fact that Faulkner's grotesques, except those who are willfully

or insanely evil, are presented with sympathy distinguishes them from those of some other Gothic writers and suggests the influence of Dickens in this as in other aspects of Gothicism.

Visible grotesqueness may or may not indicate psychological abnormality or sexual perversion, but characters who display such deviations from normality usually are indicative of themes typical of Gothic fiction, especially southern Gothic. . . . Narcissism, homosexuality, incest, and miscegenation are the specifically sexual themes in Yoknapatawpha which reflect the southern concept of upper class white women. (pp. 228-30)

The strongest theme in this group is that of incest, involved in some characters . . . with narcissism and homosexuality. (p. 231)

The recurrence of these Gothic themes in Yoknapatawpha points to a basic weakness in the society, an inability of its members to enter into harmonious, vital relationships in family and social groups, which is confirmed in other Gothic themes. One group of themes deals with individual problems and the attempts to solve them. Isolation, alienation, and lack of love appear [in many of the works]. (p. 232)

In contrast to the themes of individuals but not necessarily irrelevant to them are the extremely Gothic themes of family relationships and family heritage, often a heritage of doom. Only rarely does the positive and un-Gothic aspect, a heritage of love and fidelity, occur. . . . In the Yoknapatawpha novels the Gothic theme of family and social heritage signals the doom of those who look to the past and glorify the dead and implies Faulkner's abiding concern for the continuance of the family by those who have love, vitality, and courage to face the future.

Transcending individual concerns are themes based on the community, such as the theme of Negro-white relationships in *The Unvanquished, Go Down, Moses,* and *Intruder in the Dust.* The theme of truth recurs in various aspects: the themes of truth and justice (*Sanctuary*), of the truth of history (*Absalom, Absalom!*) of life-saving and spirit-saving truth (*Intruder in the Dust*), of essential human truth (*The Town* **and** *The Mansion*). When these themes involve a search, it is not primarily self-centered or self-seeking. (p. 237)

The extent to which Faulkner retained essential Gothic elements is impressive. He also transformed the Gothic mode in significant respects: by reducing it, by inverting it, and by parodying it. In *Sartoris* he undercut the Gothic effect by counterpointing the story of young Bayard with that of old Bayard and by using Aunt Jenny to deflate the Sartoris vainglory; both these effects are stronger in *Sartoris* than in *Flags in the Dust,* where the romantic-Gothic and grotesque-Gothic characterizations of Horace and of Byron

Snopes divert attention from the Sartoris story. In *The Sound and the Fury* Faulkner provided a cheerful present scene in Benjy's and Quentin's sections and substituted psychological horror and pathos for mystery and suspense; the deaths take place offstage.

Omission of horror scenes is a favorite device with Faulkner. . . . In *Sanctuary* after the omission of the rape and the understatement of the two murders, the lynching scene is a devastating shock. Similarly, the omission of the actual murder of Joanna Burden in *Light in August* leaves the reader unprepared for the retrospective account of Joe's death in horrible detail. . . . The murders in *Intruder in the Dust* are distanced and understated, but the state of mind of Chick provides tension to lend Gothic suspense and mystery to setting and characters which in themselves are not Gothic. In *Snopes* the combination of Gothic and non-Gothic narrative sequences serves to modify the Gothic effects. Mink's two murders, of Houston and of Flem, admirably illustrate the two extremes of Faulkner's method, completely Gothic treatment and ironic understatement of violence.

In addition to diminishing some of the Gothic horror by such devices, Faulkner frequently, extensively, and significantly used ironic inversion, wherein characters and action are the reverse of what the Romantic or Romantic-Gothic tradition leads one to expect. This is done most completely in *Sanctuary,* to satirize the values and actions of respectable society. . . . (pp. 237-38)

Closely allied to ironic inversion is parody, which is inherent in Gothic romance. Parody is more comic in effect than irony, which may be bitterly satiric. (p. 239)

In addition to the ways in which Faulkner transformed or modified the Gothic elements he used are the ways in which he added new elements. First of all, he based the setting and characters on actual places and contemporary times or the relatively recent past, in an interrelated series of novels. He added individual characters which are not derived from traditional Gothic types. . . . In his experiments with point of view Faulkner covered all levels of intelligence, from speechless idiots to highly intelligent, sensitive, and articulate characters. . . . These are additions to the basic ingredients, as it were. Other additions are related to new purposes to which Faulkner adapted the Gothic.

These new purposes were rarely achieved in a single novel; the limited area and society made realistically possible the recurrence of characters, the repetition of incidents, the allusions to local legend, and the continued development of accounts of families and related themes. . . . The Gothic novel which deals with the more or less remote past or with a very limited scene and society in the present and with characters who are oriented to the past cannot attempt such a broad view

as Faulkner's of social change and its impact on successive generations. (p. 240)

Of all the failures and weaknesses with which he dealt, Faulkner seemed most concerned with the failure of the family and society to preserve and observe meaningful rituals by which to initiate the young into mature life. . . . One of the great strengths of Faulkner's characterizations in his Gothic novels is his intense sympathy with and understanding of young people; his indictment of families and society is that they have failed to give their children love and emotional security or to instill in them by precept and example sound moral and ethical principles, truths to live by.

By great good fortune Faulkner had at his disposal what the original Gothic novelists, and even those of the generation before his, had lacked: the insight into the unconscious provided by Freud. Thus, in dealing with the irrational and instinctual aspects of the psyche, Faulkner was able to combine the subjective techniques of modern fiction with knowledge of depth psychology. . . . To pour into a whole row of old bottles of Gothicism a new wine fermented by a powerful creative imagination, stimulated by technical knowledge, and irradiated by intuition, this was Faulkner's distinctive achievement in Gothic characterization.

The Gothic revival of interest in the irrational side of man's consciousness tended to undervalue the rational side which had been too exclusively the concern of the age of reason. This lack of balance Faulkner could avoid because the scope of the Yoknapatawpha cycle allowed him to include characters who combined imagination and sympathy with reason and whose lives were more satisfactory and useful than those of either the irrational or the too rational characters. . . . Such characters are naturally rare in Gothic novels but can be accommodated in the Yoknapatawpha cycle because, first, the ample scope permits non-Gothic elements, and, second, the point of view of normal characters under stress involves multiple levels of consciousness and irrational phenomena which serve to illuminate the dark and secret areas in man's psyche. (pp. 241-43)

As the omniscient author, Faulkner could express his moral and ethical convictions, or he could use normal characters as spokesmen or reflectors. . . . He could always convey his meaning through the narrative events and thematic ideas. Instead of the good-evil polarity that Gothic romance often took over from medieval romance . . . Faulkner represented evil as white. . . . The same principles, Faulkner showed, apply to all men, black or white, and human dignity must be respected, regardless of caste or class. *Intruder in the Dust* dramatizes both the American Dream and the American Nightmare by revealing the unconscious reasons for and the conscious reactions to race hatred which violates these principles. No more serious new purpose could be conceived for revitalizing the Gothic tradition. (p. 243)

Faulkner belonged naturally to the tradition that accepts change and will not be held in bondage to the past. By choosing the Gothic mode, he was recognizing that man's "moral conscience is the curse he had to accept from the gods in order to gain from them the right to dream." He recreated the motivating dreams of the past in a specific region and showed how its society was destroyed by what was wrong with its dreams or by its failure to attain and maintain what was right. (p. 244)

The influence of Faulkner is not necessarily the chief source of Gothicism in later writers; but his work, like that of Dickens, contributes significantly to the Gothic tradition and to its capacity to accommodate the dreams and nightmares of modern civilization. . . . (p. 248)

Elizabeth M. Kerr, in her *William Faulkner's Gothic Domain,* Kennikat, 1979, 264 p.

SOURCES FOR FURTHER STUDY

Beck, Warren. *Faulkner.* Madison: University of Wisconsin Press, 1976, 664 p.

> Collection of essays discussing controversial aspects of Faulkner's life and writing.

Blotner, Joseph. *Faulkner: A Biography.* 2 vols. New York: Random House, 1974.

> Definitive biography exploring the relationship between Faulkner's personal life and the development of his fiction.

Brooks, Cleanth. *William Faulkner: Toward Yoknapatawpha and Beyond.* New Haven: Yale University Press, 1978, 445 p.

> Considered one of the leading studies of Faulkner's early career.

Campbell, Harry Modean. *William Faulkner, a Critical Appraisal.* Norman: University of Oklahoma Press, 1951, 183 p.

> Approaches the body of Faulkner's work as a whole, identifying various structural and ideological phases.

Meriwether, James B., and Millgate, Michael. *Lion in the Garden: Interviews with William Faulkner, 1926-1962.* New York: Random House, 1968, 298 p.

> Collection of interviews in which Faulkner discusses literature and life.

Millgate, Michael. *The Achievement of William Faulkner.* New York: Random House, 1966, 344 p.

> Overview of Faulkner's career providing scholarly background on each of his works in chronological order.

Henry Fielding

1707-1754

(Also wrote under pseudonyms Conny Keyber and Scriblerus Secundus) English novelist, satirist, dramatist, journalist, essayist, and poet.

INTRODUCTION

*F*ielding is often considered the most important contributor to the development of the English novel in the eighteenth century. With *The History of the Adventures of Joseph Andrews* (1742) and *The History of Tom Jones, a Foundling* (1749) the genre matured as an art form. These carefully structured works represent the first attempts to aesthetically distinguish the novel from romance and epic traditions. While the works of his contemporaries featured didactic prose, larger-than-life characters, and exotic settings, Fielding depicted the natural world and designed his fiction to "laugh mankind out of their favourite follies and vices." Noted for their complexity, humor, and compassion, Fielding's novels are informed by what William Hazlitt termed a "profound knowledge of human nature," and they present a vivid, entertaining view of eighteenth-century English life.

Fielding was born in Somersetshire to aristocratic parents. He was educated at Eton, from which he graduated in 1725. Afterwards he moved to London and embarked on a career in the theater. His first effort, *Love in Several Masques,* was produced in 1728, and during the next nine years over twenty of his plays were performed. These burlesques and farces, which met with great success, satirize various literary, social, and political trends and figures. In 1734 Fielding married Charlotte Cradock, who later served as the model for the heroines of *Tom Jones* and *Amelia* (1751). Shortly after his marriage, Fielding became the manager and chief playwright of the Little Haymarket Theatre. His career ended abruptly after two of his political satires, *Pasquin* (1736) and *The Historical Register for the Year 1736* (1737), induced Prime Minister Robert Walpole to impose the Licensing Act, an ordinance that allowed government censorship of the stage, on the Little Haymarket. Fielding then studied law at the Middle

Temple and was called to the bar in 1740. According to his biographers, he was an honest lawyer with a solid but modest practice. To supplement his income, Fielding wrote and edited four periodicals, including *The True Patriot* and *The Covent-Garden Journal*.

In 1741 Fielding published the satire *An Apology for the Life of Mrs. Shamela Andrews;* his first novel, *Joseph Andrews,* appeared one year later. Both works ridicule Samuel Richardson's *Pamela; or, Virtue Rewarded,* a widely popular novel ostensibly written to advise and instruct young, working-class women against the ulterior motives of male employers. Fielding was both puzzled and alarmed by the success of this novel, which he considered superficial and pretentious. His attacks infuriated Richardson, who denounced Fielding and his work as coarse, vile, and immoral. There ensued a lifelong feud between the authors and a continuing debate over the merits of each among their critics.

While *Shamela* is a broad parody of the self-centered virtue of Richardson's heroine, utilizing mimicry and inversion of every character in Richardson's work, *Joseph Andrews* is a full-fledged novel of manners that did not directly parody the plot and characters of *Pamela* yet attacked Richardson's sanctimonious values and sentiments. Andrews is introduced as Pamela's brother, and like Richardson's heroine he is determined to remain chaste until marriage. However, unlike Pamela's, Joseph's virtue is sincere, not a facade calculated to advance or protect his social standing. He is fundamentally good, a kind and generous man guided by Christian ethics rather than by social mores or religious dogma. In *Joseph Andrews,* as in *Shamela* and *Tom Jones,* charity and goodness of heart are the touchstones of morality, while vanity, hypocrisy, and deceit characterize evil. Although it began as a satire of *Pamela, Joseph Andrews* evolved into what its author called a "comic epic-poem in prose," different in concept and form from previous fiction. Fielding's theory of the comic epic, which he set forth in his preface, is in effect one of the first theories of the English novel. Before *Joseph Andrews* the genre was mostly indistinguishable from pastoral romance and epic literatures. Implausible characters and adventures, didactic prose, and exotic settings dominated the literary landscape. Distinguishing himself from this tradition, Fielding depicted "real life"—natural, familiar settings, believable characters, and probable situations—and he couched his moral purpose in humor and irony. The structure of *Joseph Andrews* is equally innovative. Into the main narrative Fielding interpolated a series of stories. These tales work on several levels: they mimic particular literary vogues, such as traditional epics and romances; they reflect the design of the novel as a whole; or they offset the emotional intensity of the principal story line. Fielding also introduced the intrusive narrator, who controls the reader's response by commenting on the characters and action. Although highly inventive, *Joseph Andrews* is an apprentice work. Critics praise its originality and sustained humor, but they find that its interpolations and narrative intrusions obstruct the plot. In *Tom Jones* Fielding integrated these devices to create a more tightly structured novel.

The last ten years of Fielding's life were marked by professional achievement and personal tragedy. His wife died suddenly in 1744, and Fielding created a scandal by marrying her former maid, Mary Daniel. In 1748 Fielding was appointed a London magistrate and a justice of the peace for Westminster, and he wrote several essays on criminal and social reform. At this time he also composed and published his greatest work, *Tom Jones.* The quintessential comic novel and a classic of English literature, *Tom Jones* is renowned for its artistic unity, memorable characters, and vivid portrayal of life in eighteenth-century England. It chronicles the adventures and misadventures of a well-intentioned but imprudent orphan, Tom Jones, after he is banished from his guardian's estate. During the course of the novel, Jones pursues the daughter of a local squire, joins the army, is seduced by women of varied social standing, and is jailed. In the end he learns the truth about his parentage and is able to marry the squire's daughter, Sophia Western.

Fielding's experience in the theater is readily apparent in *Tom Jones:* the narrative is fast-paced, characters are defined by dialogue, and its three-part structure (the action takes place in the country, on the road, and in the city) resembles a three-act play. As in *Joseph Andrews,* a number of interpolated episodes thread through the main narrative. However, unlike the earlier work, these closely mirror and parody events in the novel, aiding in the development of theme and plot. The narrator intervenes with essays that summarize the action, discuss characters, and describe the art of writing and reading prose fiction. While some critics find the essays a hindrance, others contend that they effect a bond between the author and his reader, unify the novel, and highlight its philosophical theme. The philosophy of *Tom Jones* echoes that of *Joseph Andrews:* good will is the basis of morality, and indiscretion and intemperance, though wrong and punishable, are far less reprehensible than malevolence and self-interest. Jones is a kind, amiable figure who tries but usually fails to resist temptation, sexual and otherwise. His "sins," however, are pale in comparison to the greed, hypocrisy, and vanity exhibited by individuals like Blifil and Seagrim. Jones is inherently good, but he lacks discipline and judgment. As he gains these qualities through his experiences on the road and in society, he becomes truly moral.

For over two hundred years Fielding's achievement has been the subject of intense study and debate. Although widely popular with the reading public of his day, he suffered at the hands of his literary peers, who objected to the base natures of his characters and found his casual approach to sex morally offensive. Victorian commentators continued this line of attack. Moreover, believing the false anecdotes and half-truths recorded by Fielding's first biographer, Arthur Murphy, they formed an image of the author as a licentious drunkard whose work reflected an ignoble life. With few exceptions, eighteenth- and nineteenth-century critics read Fielding's supposedly base life into the characters and events of *Tom Jones, Joseph Andrews*, and *Amelia*. Nevertheless, they praised the verisimilitude and artistry of the novels, proclaimed Fielding a master craftsman and creative genius, and marveled that so dissolute an individual was able to produce such consummate works of art. The Fielding myth persisted until 1918, when Wilbur L. Cross published his voluminous biography, *The History of Henry Fielding*, which replaced popular anecdotes and speculation with facts. Cross's work dispelled the Fielding myth, allowing modern critics to concentrate on the moral, thematic, and structural complexity of Fielding's novels.

The elaborate, unified plot of *Tom Jones*, the comic narrative techniques introduced in *Joseph Andrews*, and the sustained irony and powerful satire of *Jonathan Wild* (1743) are frequently discussed by critics in the twentieth century, as are the humanism and tolerance of all of Fielding's work. However, not all commentators are convinced of Fielding's significance. F. R. Leavis contends that the attitudes and concerns expressed in his novels are too simple to warrant the attention of serious readers, and Frank Kermode argues that the contemporaries of Fielding and Richardson were correct in determining Richardson the better artist and a superior moralist. Other critics find Fielding's novels unnecessarily episodic and complain that his characters lack depth and dimension. Yet the great amount of interpretive and critical studies generated by his work attests to Fielding's importance. His themes, his theory of the novel, and his narrative innovations greatly influenced the course of English fiction and still provide thoughtful entertainment.

(For further information about Fielding's life and works, see *Dictionary of Literary Biography*, Vols. 39, 84 and *Literature Criticism from 1400 to 1800*, Vol. 1.)

CRITICAL COMMENTARY

AURELIEN DIGEON

(essay date 1923)

[In the following excerpt from a work first published in French in 1923, Digeon discusses *Journey from This World to the Next, Jonathan Wild, Tom Jones*, and *Amelia*.]

Chance plays a great part in literary history. It was pure coincidence that *Pamela* was published just at the moment when Fielding, prevented from writing freely for the theatre, was seeking a new outlet for his inspiration; and by another singularly happy chance, he was then, thanks to all his earlier experiments in literature, at the height of his talent. The *Miscellanies* . . . show the direction which he might have continued to follow, had he not been turned aside by Richardson's heroine. (p. 91)

The *Journey from this World to the Next* treats a theme as old as Lucian, and *Jonathan Wild* is essentially a picaresque novel, the offspring of an ancient tradition. It is strange that a writer of genius should hesitate for so long before finding the form of art which must allow him the fullest self-expression.

The *Journey from this World to the Next* describes a visit to Hades, and the avatars of a soul, that of the Emperor Julian, whom Minos has condemned to pass through a series of existences on earth. (pp. 92-3)

Fielding must often have abandoned and resumed his work on the *Journey*. Side by side with passages which frankly are dull and diffuse, he gives us better inspired pages, amusing characters, carefully, if superficially observed, with a feeling for the telling trait, which he had learnt in the service of the drama. (pp. 93-4)

The fact is that this tale, which I must persist in believing to be a youthful work, is mainly interesting for the promise which it shows. Many characteristics of the later Fielding are already there, and will only become more definite in the future. Hatred of the military, for whom there is no place in the Elysian Fields, a broad-minded and anti-Puritan morality which slams the gate in the face of a parson of strictly virtuous repute ("for no man enters that gate without charity"), and refuses eternal happiness to prudes; such ideas would bring no reproof to the lips of Parson Adams. (pp. 94-5)

Principal Works

Love in Several Masques (drama) 1728

The Author's Farce and the Pleasures of the Town (drama) 1730

The Temple Beau (drama) 1730

Tom Thumb (drama) 1730; also published as The Tragedy of Tragedies; or, The Life and Death of Tom Thumb the Great [enlarged edition], 1731

The Welsh Opera; or, The Grey Mare the Better Horse [as Scriblerus Secundus] (drama) 1731; also published as The Grub Street Opera, 1731

The Covent-Garden Tragedy (drama) 1732

The Modern Husband (drama) 1732

Don Quixote in England [adaptor; from the novel Don Quixote by Miguel de Cervantes] (drama) 1734

Pasquin: A Dramatick Satire on the Times; Being the Rehearsal of Two Plays, viz. a Comedy Called "The Election," and a Tragedy Called "The Life and Death of Common Sense" (drama) 1736

The Historical Register for the Year 1736 (drama) 1737

An Apology for the Life of Mrs. Shamela Andrews. In Which, the Many Notorious Falsehoods and Misrepresentations of a Book Called "Pamela" Are Exposed and Refuted; and All the Matchless Arts of That Young Politician, Set in a True and Just Light [as Conny Keyber] (satire) 1741; also published as Shamela in Joseph Andrews and Shamela, 1961

The History of the Adventures of Joseph Andrews, and of His Friend Mr. Abraham Adams. Written in Imitation of

Cervantes, Author of "Don Quixote" (novel) 1742; also published as Joseph Andrews, 1935

A Journey from This World to the Next (satire) 1743; published in Miscellanies, Vol. II

The Life of Mr. Jonathan Wild the Great (satire) 1743; published in Miscellanies, Vol. III; also published as Jonathan Wild, 1932

Miscellanies. 3 vols. (essays, satires, dramas, and poetry) 1743

The History of Tom Jones, a Foundling (novel) 1749; also published as Tom Jones, 1896

Amelia (novel) 1751

An Enquiry into the Causes of the Late Increase of Robbers, & c. with Some Proposals for Remedying This Growing Evil (essay) 1751

A Proposal for Making an Effectual Provision for the Poor (essay) 1753

The Journal of a Voyage to Lisbon (journal) 1755

The Works of Henry Fielding, Esq; With the Life of the Author. 4 vols. (dramas, novels, satires, and essays) 1762

The Complete Works of Henry Fielding, Esq. 16 vols. (novels, satires, dramas, essays, journalism, and poetry) 1903

The Works of Henry Fielding. 12 vols. (novels) 1928

The Complete Works of Henry Fielding; With an Essay on the Life, Genius, and Achievement of the Author. 16 vols. (novels, dramas, poems, essays) 1967

One has the impression that the *Journey* was abundantly, I might almost say desperately, touched up until the last moment. Some of the passages were certainly written at the same time as the best parts of *Jonathan Wild*. . . .

There are other pages which are probably contemporaneous with *Joseph Andrews*. (p. 95)

A few delightful touches are not, however, sufficient to save the book, which the reader will too often find dull. So did the author, for he never finished it. But does not this very fact allow us to observe how great was the progress made by Fielding? There is all the difference in the world between the loose construction of this *roman à tiroirs* and the more compact, judicious and self-imposed plan which we have admired in *Joseph Andrews*. And how wide is the gulf between this superficial observation, the current coin of the makers of literary 'portraits', and that rich picture of English life and English oddities.

The third volume of the *Miscellanies* is entirely occupied by the *Life of the late Jonathan Wild the Great.* It is the only first-class work which they con-

tain. The *genre* to which it belongs, the biography of thieves and vagabonds, was an old one in England, as the well-known books of Nash and Greene testify. But during the course of the seventeenth century the indigenous stock of romances of roguery was enormously enriched by the advent of the Spanish novelists and of their successor and popularizer, Le Sage. . . . There was a whole literary *genre,* and a very abundant one, which pandered to the same sort of curiosity as the columns of police court news in our daily papers. (pp. 96-7).

Because Jonathan Wild had been considered one of the most formidable of thieves, he was one of the most widely mocked. His biographers are pleased to jest; they tell how he asked, upon the eve of his execution, how the great men of Rome and Athens behaved on similar occasions; they relate his matrimonial misfortunes at length. (p. 99)

From the very beginning Fielding adopts towards him a determined attitude of severe irony. . . .

Jonathan Wild is a 'great man', a complete 'great man'. He is even more perfect than Alexander; for whereas Alexander is reported to have acted sometimes with comparative goodness, the wickedness, nay, the greatness of Wild is unblemished. His life from his birth to his death on the scaffold, is a perfectly harmonious work of art, unmarred by a single good action. Such is the philosophical basis of the book; a simple, clear and accessible idea, a development familiar to rhetoric.

The idea of the criminal conqueror is a commonplace, which is found here and there throughout antiquity. It occurs again in Boileau (Satire VIII) and the French classics; Maundeville (*Fable of the Bees* . . .) and Pope (*Essay on Man* . . .) call Alexander 'Macedonia's madman'. (p. 100)

Fielding found himself faced with two literary traditions, on the one hand, the joking tone of rogues' biographies, on the other, the commonplace of the criminal conqueror. He was the first to combine these two hitherto isolated elements into a new and consummate creation. The low joke, in the service of a general idea, is transmuted into philosophical irony, while the commonplace ceases at once to be banal.

Moreover, Fielding gives it a personal twist. The comparison of the conqueror to the thief was a convention of the school, but he reverses it. He gives us the inversion of the travesty à la Scarron, of which everyone was tired. No longer is Aeneas a rogue, it is the rogue who is Aeneas. The irony thus gains in subtlety. Mr Jonathan Wild is treated all through as a fine gentleman. The joke is aimed straight at him, but it rebounds from the poor devil, and strikes the fine gentleman, his neighbour. . . .

But none of this is yet enough to account for the virulence of the outburst. What was the point of attacking Jonathan Wild? He was dead. . . . Fielding envisaged a living figure, and that living figure was without any doubt the Minister, Walpole. (p. 103)

[Instead] of the picaresque novel, gay and copious, which might have been expected of him, a novelist's version of Gay's *Beggar's Opera,* Fielding writes a bitter book, full of corrosive irony, a novel so harsh that it has disturbed or frightened many of his readers. How are we to explain this remarkable exception to all the rest of his known work? (p. 104)

[Fielding's] irony may have been roused by the ephemeral actions of a Prime Minister, but it soon went further and higher. . . . Fielding begins by caricaturing Walpole in the figure of Wild, a notorious thief; but his personal anger is quickly transformed into a universal anger, the anger of humanity. One day he thinks of the great massacrer of men, Charles XII, whom he despises; then his thoughts turn to Charles I and he speaks of Wild in terms analogous to those which Clarendon applied to his king, making the thief leave, after his death, certain Maxims on greatness, which Fielding himself

compares with those which the author of *Eikon Basilike* claims to have found after the execution of Charles I.

But this is not all. After the elections of 1741, the fall of Walpole began to appear imminent. . . . [Suddenly] the satire takes a new direction. When Jonathan Wild arrives at Newgate he finds a certain Roger Johnson, who is king of the thieves. Wild makes an inflammatory speech, demanding 'the liberties of Newgate', overthrows Johnson and takes his place. The prisoners soon find to their disgust that the new master is worse than the old. Wild even wants to dress himself in the spoils of his predecessor but the fine velvet cap is too heavy for his head and the embroidered waistcoat is so big for him that it hangs in folds. Walpole has now become Roger Johnson and Wild represents Wilmington. The same mask now conceals another face. Walpole's successor was proverbially a nonentity. (pp. 107-08)

The miracle is that from all these scattered elements, there should emerge the harmonious unity of a book; a unity so vigorous and so perfect that some have thought that the book was written 'at a sitting'. . . . Fielding will take Wild as a type and will depict, he tells us, 'roguery and not a rogue'. This claim immediately places him on a different plane from Defoe. . . . [Fielding] is writing a novel and not pseudo-memoirs, a pseudo-correspondence or a pseudo-biography. Nor does he make use of any of these pretences which are designed to give an air of reality to such works; his aim is rather to reject reality when it proves a hindrance, to add to it at need, to be more true than nature. . . . Nor does the author hesitate, as Coleridge profoundly observes, to put into the mouth of his hero speeches which the real Jonathan Wild would never have uttered, for these speeches and reflections conform to the author's secret purpose of making his story unreal in order to give a transcendental reality to the truths which he wishes to convey. Everything which idealizes Wild, everything which lifts him out of the crapulous mediocrity of the real man, serves but to give more weight and universality to his example. This is a clear use, and possibly the first conscious one in literary history, of the synthetic method employed by the great realistic novelists of the nineteenth century. (pp. 109-10)

Fielding thus chooses and *composes* the life of his hero. (p. 111)

In *Jonathan Wild* Fielding, the novelist, bids farewell to pure satire. He has attacked Walpole bitterly, has seen him replaced by another and is now heartily sick of these struggles, the sole object of which is to put one 'great man' in the place of another. As for the small and the weak, they are always oppressed; it is from them that reform must come. . . . Henceforward Fielding hopes far more from moral reform than from any political change. The moralist emerges more and more clearly from the pure satirist. (pp. 126-27)

Jonathan Wild attacked the Pharisees, and some others, but its decent folk showed themselves such pitiable dupes that no one could possibly think of imitating them. Laughter in itself is negative; what ideal lay behind the author's mockery?

Tom Jones is the answer to this question. After this parody, after this destructive irony, it is a work of reconstruction, in which at last we have the moral ideal of Fielding.

Although the book is less polemical, it is by no means devoid of hostile intent. To begin with, the attack on Richardsonian tendencies is resumed. True, it is a more courteous battle, in which the insulting laughter of *Joseph Andrews* is no more heard. Fielding is greater now and has no need of weapons which are the resource of the weak. He merely asserts himself; but it is interesting to observe that he still asserts himself against Richardson. Richardson again! Yet I do not know a single biographer who has thought to point out, save by a few anecdotes, how close is the interaction between these two literary careers. *Joseph Andrews* follows *Pamela.* Then there is a long silence (1742-8). Within an interval of a few months *Tom Jones* follows *Clarissa Harlowe.* Two years pass and this time Fielding is ready first; *Amelia* precedes *Grandison.* These six great works go in pairs, and in order that nothing may be lacking in the picture, after two male portraits by Fielding had followed upon Richardson's two female portraits, Fielding was to end his career as a novelist with the picture of a woman, to which Richardson was to reply by that of a man. There is more here than mere coincidence. In these works two types of genius, two artistic conceptions, two techniques, two moral ideals and two conflicting temperaments, deliberately confront one another. But nowhere is the opposition as clear as in this: that while Fielding remains essentially "the author of *Tom Jones*", Richardson faces him, essentially "the author of *Clarissa Harlowe*". (pp. 129-31)

This preoccupation with Richardson is not the only one present in *Tom Jones.* . . . Richardson is but the symbol of a vast group of enemies, of all the moral prigs, all the Pharisees, whom Fielding shovels pell-mell into the common grave of ridicule.

Religious, philosophical and literary controversies pullulated in England during the eighteenth century. Three thick volumes were needed by Leslie Stephen to give a brief and accurate summary of them. For all these quacks and their panaceas, Fielding expresses the same scorn, which is professed without exception by all the humourists and best minds of his century. For half a dozen really great thinkers, such as Locke, Berkeley, and Hume, no century has ever seen such swarms of pedants. Hume and Gibbon both avowed their irritation at the 'sceptical fop'. Swift had already shut up all 'sages' in Laputa. Fielding, too, delivers blows on all sides with a fine impartiality: of his two 'thinkers',

Square and Thwackum, he says that they do not sing in the same key, but that the song which they sing is the same; and he nails theologian and deist to the same pillory. He had already, in true Swiftian style, ridiculed the commonplace refutation of deism in the Ordinary's speech to Jonathan Wild. In *Tom Jones* the hardest blows seem to be reserved for the deist, Square, but his enemy is not spared. On either side of Squire Allworthy, each appears as a pendant to the other, a little after the manner of Pangloss and Martin in *Candide;* and on every occasion they give opposite justifications for the same pharisaical morality. For such is Fielding's lesson: a mean soul, whatever ideas be presented to it, can only produce meanness. On every occasion Square gives a grotesque repetition of the same phrases, 'the eternal fitness of things,' 'the natural beauty of virtue'; Thwackum meets him with opposite formulae 'the divine power of grace', 'no religion exists independent of honour'. Both agree in heartily flogging an honest ne'er-do-well like Jones, and in predicting to Mr. Allworthy that the scamp will end on the gallows. But the Spirit of Comedy is preparing a series of joyful revenges for us. We shall find a hundred incidents, in the course of the narrative revealing the two parasites in most ignoble postures. One day Tom Jones comes to see Molly Seagrim, and finds the philosopher Square hidden in a corner of the room, in an odd and unseemly attitude. On another occasion Thwackum, seeing Tom disappearing in the distance with Molly, tries to surprise him in *flagrant délit,* and receives from his pupil the soundest thrashing which has ever reddened the back of a pedantic Grundy. Happy is the novelist who can thus distribute blows to antipathetic characters! He gives them no quarter. These detestable, grotesque gluttons, representative of a whole class, are overthrown in the final discomfiture of their protégé Blifil, while their martyr Tom Jones triumphs, thanks to the providential Allworthy. (pp. 151-53)

Our novelist, who has seen and described men, good, bad or worse, never loses an opportunity of proclaiming that he is a moralist. Yet from all these portraits is it possible to deduce a moral doctrine other than a somewhat negative hatred of hypocrisy? By what criterion can we replace the bourgeois, Christian traditionalism of Richardson, the Puritanism of Thwackum, or the rationalism of Square? What is Fielding's moral doctrine?

Its point of departure is feeling. Feeling has a moral value of its own, independent of its object. The man who feels very keenly is capable of great happiness whether imaginary or real. He feels the joys of others as deeply as he does his own. How then can he reject the happiness which a good action will bring him? Satisfy your feelings and they will lead you straight to goodness. Speak not of social prejudice nor of what the world thinks; "the truest honour is goodness". Can any success or prosperity equal the intimate joy which comes from the consciousness of having done a good action? The only way to be happy is to be good. Allworthy adopts a bastard and loves him as much as his own nephew, in spite of his friends' shocked faces. Tom Jones, at the height of his misfortunes, helps a scoundrel who has tried to rob him, because he finds that the poor wretch was stealing in order to feed his children.

In Fielding's novels none of this is entirely new. Some parts of *Joseph Andrews* are sentimental and effusive in much the same way. But in *Tom Jones* there is more method and above all, a new argument, that pleasure is to be experienced *in this world* by doing good. (pp. 161-62)

In the moral teaching of Fielding, feeling holds the first place; on the one hand happiness does not lie in outward prosperity but in inward contentment; and in the same way perfection does not consist in the accomplishment of actions which are reputed virtuous, but in the consciousness of a good intention. All Blifil's actions are outwardly virtuous, but Blifil is a rogue; all Tom Jones's actions appear to be vicious, but Tom Jones is an excellent fellow: "Tommy Jones was an inoffensive lad amidst all his roguery."

Such is the primary, and, one might say, the most frequent aspect of Fielding's morality, the aspect which best lends itself to an overflow of emotion. It is not yet the romantic motive of sincerity which redeems and passion which purifies; it is its prelude. I do not think it can often be met with in English literature prior to Fielding (save perhaps, without method, in Steele). In any case, there is no example of it before him in the novel. Richardson is full of feeling, much more so than Fielding, but he is at the same time rigidly Christian and, in his work, there will not be found that justification of feeling as a moral value, from which there will gradually emerge sentimentality, the *douceur de pleurer* (the characters in *Tom Jones* by no means deprive themselves of this pleasure) and the romantic eulogy of sentiment. (pp. 165-66)

[Fielding's] sentimentalism is never unbridled; it is always restrained and supported by his intelligence. Even when he attacks the moral standards of his age, his blows are methodically directed by the power of reason.

It is undoubtedly because of its intellectual character that although essentially practical, his morality is not one of worldly prudence. A bare trace of this may be observed here and there; more than once Fielding advises his reader to look to his reputation. He says, explicitly, that to be a good man is not enough, one must also think of the opinion which the world will have of one's actions. May we not recognize in this rather *terre à terre* ["commonplace"] advice the experience of a man

too heedless of calumny, who allowed his enemies to blacken him at will?

It is because he approaches everything from the standpoint of intelligence, that he sees all mankind as equal, men and women, rich and poor. He does not in any way fall a victim to that demagogic exaggeration which thinks that virtue can only be found among the lowly. Stupidity and wickedness seem to him vulgar wheresoever he may meet them, and he defines 'the mob' in a way which would have rejoiced the heart of Flaubert, that arch-enemy of the bourgeois in whatever social class he showed his face. (pp. 167-68)

Tom Jones often gives the impression of an epic. It is a picture of all England that we find there, and a picture of England at a moment when, suspended between her great past and her prodigious future, she was most limpidly herself. *Joseph Andrews* had not as yet given, and *Amelia* was not to give again this impression of a complete picture. *Tom Jones* is the England of the time. Rare have been the English who owned it and who confessed to their portraits, and they are still rare; *Tom Jones* still raises a furore, less because of a few somewhat improper scenes than because of the frank and faithful picture which it gives of that trivial life, lived without ideals, from day to day, in perfect self-satisfaction, which was the life led by long generations of Britons. *Tom Jones* is a 'common' book and is proud of the fact. It is the work of a man who paid no attention to social conventions and marks of respectability, but saw his compatriots as they were and told all he saw. His *mea culpa* is their *mea culpa*. He will never be forgiven, and the majority of his countrymen will always, like Richardson, bring against him that charge of vulgarity, which so often irritated when it did not amuse him. (p. 180)

[This] epic of Fielding is above all things comic. So far we have been mainly concerned to observe how truly comic it is in the highest sense of the word, the sense in which it is used by a Meredith, to express the intellectual contemplation of reality by a man who remains captain of his own soul. Let us try to carry our analysis a little further.

Fielding's comedy attains in *Tom Jones* its perfect equilibrium. Its most sure characteristic is sanity. More even than that of Molière, his gaiety leaves an impression of complete satisfaction and well-being. Perhaps the secret of this lies in the fact that in *Tom Jones* he is careful never to poke fun at one absurdity without also poking fun at its opposite. He jeers at Square but also at Thwackum. If Blifil is odious, Tom Jones is ridiculous. Here, Fielding's laughter is no longer the slave of a formula. His wide and fluid morality allows him to pardon all men, but also, by a natural corollary, commands him to laugh at them all. Neither the perfect Allworthy nor the author himself can always escape a gentle mockery.

We should certainly not escape it ourselves, were we to seek with pedantic pen to label and catalogue the divers examples of Fielding's comic genius. Laughter has wings, and we must watch Fielding's jests flying in the bright sunlight of his work, for pinned in a glass-case, they would lose their changing lustre and all the soft bloom of their delicate hues. We may, however, say that here again we frequently find that epic plentitude which is the general note of *Tom Jones. Joseph Andrews* and *Jonathan Wild* are at two extremes and Fielding's comic art moves, so to speak, between them. The first was essentially a work of humour, the second of irony: Adams is sympathetically ridiculous; Wild odiously ridiculous. *Tom Jones* unites and combines these two aspects of the comic genius. The broadly humorous portrait of Tom balances the caustically ironical sketch of Blifil. And this comic harmony is not the least of the factors which contribute to give this work its character of completeness. Besides being the complete expression of an epoch, *Tom Jones* is the complete expression of Fielding's genius. (pp. 184-85)

Amelia is purposely a moral novel, and its morality is Christian. "The following book is sincerely designed to promote the cause of virtue", states the dedication to Ralph Allen, in terms which would not have been disowned by Richardson. And, however different their manner of serving "the cause of virtue", it is obvious that in *Amelia,* Fielding's method came more near to that of the writer whom he now calls 'the ingenious author of Clarissa'. Amelia Booth is more sensitive and tender than Sophia Western; she is less virile, has the 'vapours', faints, and weeps copiously on the slightest pretext. Laughter for laughter's sake, disinterested comedy, has almost disappeared from this work. It is replaced, on the one hand, by a satire on "the most glaring evils, as well public as private, which at present infest the country", and, on the other, by an ever-encroaching sentimentality, moving descriptions inserted with the avowed intention of bringing tears to the eyes of the sentimental public, real *scènes de mouchoirs* which sometimes give the book a false air of belonging to the tribe of plaintive and tear-provoking tales. (pp. 219-20)

How far we have drifted from *Tom Jones* and his invocation to the gods of laughter. . . . [In] passing from *Tom Jones* to *Amelia,* we have passed from sentiment to sentimentality, from the moral to the moralizing novel. His contact as a magistrate with the daily realities of crime seems, little by little, to have made Fielding understand the practical usefulness of that bourgeois morality at which he used to scoff. Rabelais and Aristophanes now seem dangerous; as a judge, charged with the defence of public morality, he would consign their works to the hangman. And thus bit by bit the magistrate in him was killing the artist. (pp. 220-21)

Aurelien Digeon, in his *The Novels of Fielding,* George Routledge & Sons, Ltd., 1925, 225 p.

DOROTHY VAN GHENT
(essay date 1953)

[In the following excerpt, Van Ghent examines plot and characterization in *Tom Jones.*]

[The plot of *Tom Jones* is] elaborate not only in the sense that the book contains an immense number of episodes, but also in the sense that all these episodes are knit, as intimate cause and effect, into a large single action obeying a single impulse from start to finish. (p. 66)

Tom goes under and up Fortune's wheel from "low" to "high," and in this shape of his career lies one salient set of contrasts as boldly definitive of the design of the action as the "high" beginning and the "low" end of Oedipus in the Sophoclean tragedy. But in order that the action may evolve in its curve, the wicked Blifil is needed—Tom's "opposite," chief cause of his sorrows, and affording the chief character contrast in the book. For while the curve of tragedy is spun, like the spider's thread, from within the tragic protagonist, produced out of his own passions and frailties, the curve of comedy is spun socially and gregariously, as the common product of men in society. The tragic curve leads to the hero's "self-discovery," the comic curve sprouts a various ornament of "self-exposures" on the part of many men. Also in connection with this characteristic difference between tragic action and comic action, we may notice that while the tragic hero "changes" (that is, comes eventually to a new and revolutionary realization of what he is and what he has done), the characters of comedy are laid under no artistic obligation to "change," since the reason for their artistic existence is that they may be exposed, in their "true" natures, to the eyes of other men—to society. The point is rather important for a reader of Fielding, for the development of the modern novel has accustomed us to look for "change" in characters and to feel that the profundity and importance of a book is somehow connected with such change; and we may therefore be inclined to feel that Fielding's conception of his material is comparatively "shallow," however witty and engrossing. It is well for us, then, to bear in mind the generic characteristics of the comic mode, and the fact that the characters in comedy may remain relatively static while the broad social panorama of comedy need not for that reason be lacking in seriousness and depth of significance. We are confronted in *Tom Jones* with a picture of social interaction among souls already formed, already stamped with operative character, and out of this gregarious action the conflict between hero and villain is propelled to a resolution in which the rogue who appeared to be a good man is exposed in his true nature as rogue, and the good man who appeared to be a rogue is revealed in his true good nature, with many similar exposures of other people along the way.

We can thus indicate, in some degree, the aesthetic necessity of elaborate plot in Fielding's novel: the episodes must cumulate functionally toward a final, representative revelation of character; but, because the significance of this revelation is for all men in the given society, the episodes must illustrate subtle varieties of character and interaction, at the same time representing the complexities of human nature and contributing toward the final revelation which will be, although narrowed down to hero and villain, symbolic of all those complexities. The book must, therefore, have both variety of episode and "unity of action." But we must now describe the plot as it signifies a "theme" or "meaning." In *Tom Jones*, life is conceived specifically as a conflict between natural, instinctive feeling, and those appearances with which people disguise, deny, or inhibit natural feeling—intellectual theories, rigid moral dogmas, economic conveniences, doctrines of *chic* or of social "respectability." This is the broad thematic contrast in *Tom Jones*. Form and feeling ("form" as mere outward appearance, formalism, or dogma, and "feeling" as the inner reality) engage in constant eruptive combat, and the battlefield is strewn with a debris of ripped masks, while exposed human nature—shocked to find itself uncovered and naked—runs on shivering shanks and with bloody pate, like the villagers fleeing from Molly Seagrim in the famous churchyard battle.

But let us stop to weigh rather carefully what Fielding means by that "human nature" which he says is his subject matter, and which we see again and again exposed during that conflict we have described above. Its meaning is not univocal. Broadly it refers to that mixture of animal instinct and human intellection which is assumed to obtain in every personality. But, in many of the incidents in the book, its meaning tips to one side: it tends to lean heavily toward "animal instinct," simply for the reason that the animal and instinctive part of man is (in the *Tom Jones* world) so frequently disguised or denied by the adoption of some formal appearance. Instinctive drives must therefore be emphasized as an important constituent of "human nature." (pp. 66-8)

Fielding was a writer for the theater before he was a novelist, and one of the reader's strongest impressions is that of dramatic handling of scene and act (the chapters may be thought of as "scenes," a single book as an "act"): the sharp silhouetting of characters and their grouping in such a manner as to avoid any confusions

even in so populous a drama; the bright lighting of the individual episode; the swift pacing of scenes so that they flash past for the eye and ear at the same time that they maintain a clear system of witty contrast; and above all, the strict *conceptualizing* of the function of each scene, in relation to the larger unit of the "act" (or book) and to the over-all unit of the drama (the novel), as well as the *objectifying* of the individual scene as a subject in itself, a subject clear and significant in its own right. . . . In Book I, there are three definite shifts of scene (and time and place), correlated with three definite groups of characters, and Fielding prefaces each shift with a brief, sharp delineation of the new character, or characters, who are to contribute a new direction to the action. The first scene is that of the finding of Tom in Mr. Allworthy's bed, and so that we may have the fullest ironic understanding of the scene, we are first given (in the language of the table of contents) "a short description of Squire Allworthy, and a fuller account of Miss Bridget Allworthy," while Mrs. Deborah Wilkins quite adequately introduces herself during the action. The place of action is shifted now to the parish, upon which Mrs. Deborah descends as investigator of morals; and again we are given "a short account of Jenny Jones," before the scene gets under way. We move, then, back to Squire Allworthy's house, with the scene between the Squire and Jenny, after which Jenny is dispatched out of the book for the time being. Now the new group, composed of the Blifils, is introduced into the original group—the Squire and his sister—with, again, "a short sketch of the characters of the two brothers," before the action itself is released, the curtain goes up. This is the method of the theater. (pp. 72-3)

Fortune rules events in *Tom Jones*—that Chance which throws up event and counterevent in inexhaustible variety. Tom himself is a foundling, a child of chance. In the end, because he is blessed with good nature, he is blessed with good fortune as well. (p. 78)

The signature of Fortune's favor is wealth. Tom's blessings, at the end of the book, are not dissociable from the fact that he is Allworthy's heir: this is the center and fulcrum of all the rest of his good fortune. In *Moll Flanders*, the signature of the favor of Providence was also wealth, but the wealth had to be grubbed for with insect-like persistence and concentration; to obtain wealth, even with the help of Providence, one had to work for it and keep one's mind on it. In *Clarissa Harlowe*, again, wealth was to be worked for and schemed for: the Harlowe males work as hard and concentratedly, after their fashion, to acquire Solmes's wealth and the title it will buy for them, as Moll does for her gold watches, her bales, cargoes, and plantations. But in *Tom Jones*, wealth is not got by work or calculation or accumulation or careful investment. Blifil, who works shrewdly to obtain it, fails of his ends; Tom, who never thinks of it, is richly endowed with it. The benefits of money are as candidly faced by Fielding as they are by Defoe, or as they will later be by Jane Austen: people need money in order to live pleasantly, and though to be good and to be in love and loved are fine things, the truly harmonious and full life is possible only when one is both good and rich. . . . Also, we find in Fielding the more traditional, aristocratic attitude toward wealth: one simply has wealth—say, in landed properties, like Squire Allworthy—and how one got it is Fortune's business, a mysterious donation of free gifts to the worthy. But what we are fundamentally interested in here is the coherence of this attitude with other elements in the book: that is, the aesthetic coherence and integrity of the whole. We have considered the plot under the aspect of the surprise plays of Fortune, occultly working out its game with Nature, and it is clear that Tom's unsought blessing of financial good fortune in the end is consistent with, all-of-a-piece with, the other activities of Fortune that are exhibited in the action. (pp. 79-80)

We may think of *Tom Jones* as a complex architectural figure, a Palladian palace perhaps: immensely variegated, as Fortune throws out its surprising encounters; elegant and suavely intelligent in its details (many of Fielding's sentences are little complex "plots" in themselves, where the reader must follow a suspended subject through a functional ornament of complications—qualifying dependent clauses and prepositional phrases and eloquent pauses—to the dramatic predication or denouement); but simply, spaciously, generously, firmly grounded in Nature, and domed with an ample magnitude where Fortune shows herself as beneficent artisan. The structure is all out in the light of intelligibility; air circulates around and over it and through it. (p. 80)

Dorothy Van Ghent, "On 'Tom Jones'," in her *The English Novel: Form and Function*, Holt, Rinehart and Winston, 1953, pp. 65-81.

A. E. DYSON

(essay date 1957)

[In the excerpt below, Dyson distinguishes between satire and comedy in Fielding's major novels, concluding that Fielding was "not a genuine satirist."]

Satiric and comic elements mingle in all Fielding's works, but he is primarily a comic writer. He uses ridicule as a rule to point toward not an ideal but a norm. He warns his readers in *Tom Jones* that because a character is not "good," it does not follow that the character

is wholly bad. This, it will be seen, is a clear indication that he is going to forego the exaggeration appropriate to satire—the implied moral division of characters into blacks and whites—in favor of a more balanced comic view of human behavior. But it is obvious from *Jonathan Wild* as a whole, as well as from certain parts of all his other works, that he was also a satirist when he chose to be and was capable of making as damaging and vicious an analysis of human nature as Swift himself. For this reason I wish to distinguish between the satiric and comic elements in his major works and to suggest that the latter are nearly always more successful than the former. This, if I am right, is because Fielding has not sufficient indignation for satire. On the one hand, he does not have the genuine fervor of an idealist; on the other, he is not misanthropic enough to carry off the disgust which he sometimes pretends to feel. (p. 230)

Shamela Andrews makes two main satiric points: the first that servant girls are not as innocent as middle-class morality likes to think, and the second that Richardson's book (unknown perhaps to the author) offers a measure of vicarious experience that is quite the reverse of moral. But on the whole, the short parody of Richardson is a pure frivolity, and its raison d'être lies in its entertainment value. . . .

Joseph Andrews, which is also, among other things, a parody of *Pamela,* has a similar surface of flamboyant and irresponsible wit on top of its serious undercurrent. It is an exposure of human wickedness, and to this extent a satire, but the feeling is not "reformative," or anything like it. Though Fielding is genuinely disgusted by some men and amused by others, his main attitude is a benevolent acceptance of life and a disposition not to take anything too seriously. Parson Adams is a sympathetic character, a lovable personality, a religious teacher whom we are expected to admire, but he does not escape without his share of ridicule, especially for preaching harsh or stoic precepts that are happily belied in his own practice. The other characters in the book are dissected with similar impartiality. (p. 231)

At times in *Joseph Andrews,* Fielding's satire is more serious. The early life of West is an unpleasantly faithful picture of a prodigal's life among the swine; the character of Leonora is intended as an exposure of a scheming, superficial woman and is clearly worked out on a more serious level than *Shamela.* But more usually, Fielding foregoes the moral intensity of the satirist and allows himself to be amused as a man. The bedroom scenes exemplify a taste for bawdiness, with ironic situations that recall Boccaccio, but a robust good humor more reminiscent of Chaucer. The frequent attempts on Fanny's chastity are ostensibly a satiric commentary on human nature, but the real inspiration, once more, is a taste for bawdiness.

Hence we find the ambiguity of effect that I have

already referred to. Scenes which in a pure satire would have to be taken seriously are represented in a burlesque or mock-heroic style that makes them merely entertaining. (pp. 231-32)

Likewise, in a moral satire, the discourses on "virtue" by Parson Adams and the "good" characters would have to be implied obliquely, and not stated; for they are the positive values in the light of which the satire works, and toward which it points, and should not, therefore, be present in the text. By explicitly expressing them, in the same burlesque style that is used throughout, and through the mouths of fallible and often ludicrous characters, Fielding makes the standards of virtue seem absurd and their observance as amusing as their infringement. This is a superb stroke of irresponsible gaiety, but another stab in the back for satire.

This approach produces a new and distinctive type of humor, in which everything seems to be satirized in turn by reference to different sets of values. Fanny is the standard of chastity who exposes Betty on a moral level, but Betty the measure of unchastity who exposes Fanny on the level of the world's reaction to a prude. Fielding is clearly more interested in people than in ideas and more concerned to sympathize with his characters than to reform them. His comedy is touched, in fact, with the "sentimentalism" of the mid-eighteenth century and free from truly satiric ruthlessness.

In *Jonathan Wild,* the literary infirmity of purpose becomes apparent and is more obviously a source of weakness to the structure of the work. By the fierceness and consistency of its irony and the calculated polish of its style, *Jonathan* invites comparison with *Gulliver's Travels* and announces itself to be in the satiric tradition of Swift. But in fact, it is no such thing, for Swift works out a fierce indictment of humanity with unerring control of his medium, while Fielding merely sets out to be "clever" about human wickedness, without any driving bitterness or misanthropy to sustain him and with a consequent lack of control in his artistry. (p. 232)

Fielding depicts the character of Wild skillfully, and we can note how unpleasant he is. But it is hard for us really to believe in him or to feel him very relevant to life. Far from being alarmed on behalf of the human species to which he belongs (as we are alarmed on behalf of the species to which the supposed author of Swift's *Modest Proposal* belongs), we must regard him as an interesting exception. He is little more than a puppet—flawless in performance, but in the final analysis unconvincing. His villainy is supported by a twofold technique, which he normally applies in dealing with his victims—the first, a brilliant and persuasive rhetoric, based on psychological observation (and itself a satire on society), which has little effect; and the sec-

THE

HISTORY

OF

TOM JONES,

A

FOUNDLING

In SIX VOLUMES.

By HENRY FIELDING, Esq;

—— *Mores hominum multorum vidit.* ——

LONDON:
Printed for A. MILLAR, over-against Catharine-street in the Strand.
MDCCXLIX.

Title page of the first edition of *Tom Jones.*

ond, a direct threat of resorting to violence, which nearly always produces the desired effect. But his progress in crime is a mere accumulation of incidents, not a deepening insight into the nature of depravity. He has used all his best methods, and Fielding has expended his best irony on them, before a quarter of the novel is finished. The rest of it, therefore, tends to be unsatisfying. It is well enough executed in its own way, but increasingly tedious by repetition.

The good characters, too, suffer from the same disadvantages which I noted in *Joseph Andrews.* Mr. Heartfree's moral homilies, though apparently containing the positive standards toward which Jonathan is by satiric implication pointing, sound fantastically bombastic and unconvincing. The mock-heroic style reduces them, like Jonathan's words, to absurdity, and seems to suggest a further set of "man of the world" values to ridicule Christian idealism. . . . We are forced to conclude that Fielding, despite his pretensions, is not a genuine satirist, measuring the human race against an ideal and finding it wanting, but a good-natured, unpuritanical, and even rather pagan, observer, more amused than distressed by the habitual sins of men, and prepared to laugh at the best people almost as much as at the worst.

Tom Jones is, by common consent, Fielding's masterpiece, and here the ridicule in the broad outline of the book is fully comic. There is no consistent irony, as in *Jonathan Wild,* but at last we find a consistent moral purpose. The inconsistencies due to an insufficiently realized satiric technique are no longer in evidence. Instead, we find that all the major characters fit into a pattern, within the framework of which they are judged, and which is large enough to allow them to exist as complete and convincing people. (pp. 232-33)

Square and Thwackum represent purely intellectual conceptions of morality, which can be infinitely supported in disputation, but are divorced in both men from any genuine kindness or humanity. . . .

Square preaches the philosophic rationalism of the deists, maintaining that moral values antedate deity, that the light of reason guides men in their ethical actions, that human nature is the perfection of all virtue. Thwackum holds the more orthodox theological view, that man is totally fallen, wholly unable to perceive goodness without the aid of God's grace, and completely dependent for salvation and illumination upon the revelation given in Scripture. But both men are of mean character, selfish, bigoted, hypocritical, and both make moral judgments that habitually justify Master Blifil at the expense of Tom.

Fielding refuses to adjudicate between their respective philosophies and avows that his ridicule is aimed not at their ideas but at the men. But his repeated insistence on "good nature" proves that, in common with the prevailing opinion in the mid-eighteenth century, he regarded this quality as the key to virtue. Lack of "natural goodness of heart" invalidates any system of ethics, since such goodness alone can make morality work in practice, however impressive it may sound in theory. The central human virtues are sympathy, benevolence, warm-heartedness, and a life directed by these cannot go far astray.

Both Mr. Allworthy and Tom possess these virtues, though Mr. Allworthy adds to them the theoretic principles of morality and grace for which Square and Thwackum profess to stand, and tempers his mercy with justice. The moral purpose of the book centers upon a choice between these two. . . .

How far, we must ask, does Fielding identify himself with this view? It is clear that he has a great respect for Mr. Allworthy, who, although much imposed upon, is a man of honor and wisdom, one who can compose himself for death with perfect fortitude. But the tenor of the book, however, gives the final verdict to Tom, who is hasty and hotblooded and makes serious mistakes, but who lives by instinct rather than by reason, and is the more vitally alive of the two. (p. 234)

Tom's humanity and vigor, certainly, are at the opposite pole to the devitalized self-righteousness of the Pharisees; and Mr. Allworthy, though by no means a Pharisee, is imbued with the habit of intellectual calculation which obscures humane issues and tends in that direction. Throughout the novel, and emphasizing this impression, Mr. Allworthy's moralizing suffers, like that of Parson Adams and Mr. Heartfree before him, from the excessively burlesque style in which it is delivered. The very style of the book, as well as the general attitude of the author, vindicate Tom in his perfect naturalness. He is the "natural man," the idealized "noble savage," fulfilling his basically sound nature in the unnatural wilderness of civilization. And if things go wrong as a result of this, the fault is as much that of civilization as of Tom.

It would appear that Fielding regarded "reason" and "feeling" in ethics as two opposing principles, between which a choice had to be made. (p. 235)

A consistent antithesis is maintained in *Tom Jones* between Tom and Master Blifil, the former of whom is "warm" and the latter "cold," in their virtues and in their vices. Master Blifil excels in prudence and cool calculation and can use reason in the service of hypocrisy. But Tom is always passionate and impulsive and, for this reason, incapable of meanness or deception.

Though Tom's unchastity is in the end condemned, and Sophie produced as a truly balanced exemplar of virtue, this does not ring true to the feeling of the novel as a whole. Fielding's sympathies are with Tom, even when his reason is with Sophie, and this sort of bias constantly appears. He is at his happiest when making fun of people for being what they are rather than for not being what they ought to be, and his strength is above all to be found in the benevolent humanity which created such likable if imperfect characters as Parson Adams and Tom.

Tom Jones, then, is comic in its main outlines, but a mention must be made of the incidental satire, which is directed principally against the minor characters and tends toward a Hobbesian analysis of their motives. Fielding enjoys showing fear and self-interest behind all their actions, especially behind the supposedly disinterested ones. He uses the same techniques of irony as he used throughout *Jonathan Wild,* but keeps them now in a subsidiary position and does not pretend to too fierce an indignation behind them. The account of Bridget Allworthy's relationship with Captain Blifil is an excellent example of satiric observation. (pp. 235-36)

Tom's position as a bastard of high birth and with wide connections gives him a footing in all levels of society, and makes him a typical "picaresque" hero. This permits incidental picaresque satire of the sort particularly associated with Smollett—though in Fielding such satire is distinct from his comic purpose and not the main interest of the book. (pp. 236-37)

The ridicule in *Tom Jones* is used in support of a particular moral theory—one which prefers "good nature" to prudential calculation, "Feeling" to "Reason," warmly benevolent good will to coolly accepted sense of duty. This moral theory we associate with the later rather than the earlier part of the eighteenth century (though we should remember that it is firmly rooted in the teaching of Shaftesbury and can be thought of as a choice of his type of moralizing as against that of Butler). The theory clearly lends itself, however, to a comic and not a satiric criticism of human weakness, so that in turning more completely to the comic mode, Fielding was turning to a medium better suited to his particular sensibility and "content." This may help to account for the superiority of *Tom Jones* to any of his previous novels—which, fine though they are in many respects, are less consistently planned and executed as wholes. (p. 237)

A. E. Dyson, "Satiric and Comic Theory in Relation to Fielding," in *Modern Language Quarterly*, Vol. 18, No. 3, September, 1957, pp. 225-37.

JOHN LOFTIS
(essay date 1959)

[Loftis is an American critic who has written extensively on seventeenth- and eighteenth-century English drama. In the following excerpt, he surveys Fielding's dramatic comedies, farces, burlesques, and ballad operas.]

Henry Fielding's comedies, farces, burlesques, and ballad operas, in their forms and in their themes, provide an epitome of the dramatic activity from 1728 to 1737. . . . He was intensely in touch with his times: the contemporaneity of his plays is at once their merit and their limitation, the source of their vigor and their value as records of London life in the age of Walpole, Pope, and Hogarth, but the source also of the barrier to intelligibility that now limits the number of their readers to special students of the age. Fielding followed contemporary theatrical fashions and at the same time modified them: he wrote, but with a difference, comedies of fashionable life in the manner of Congreve; political and theatrical burlesques, some of them in the ballad opera form popularized by Gay; and farces, some in the native tradition and some in the French. Like nearly every other important writer of the 1730's he was caught up in the political debates; and like most of his fellow dramatists he wrote plays with political overtones. (p. 114)

In all of his plays he is censorious of the contemporary preoccupation with money, which other writers attributed to the rise in prominence of the business community. . . .

Yet his aversion to money-mindedness notwithstanding, Fielding did not satirize the merchants. (p. 115)

The central social antithesis of his plays as of his novels is not that between merchants and gentlemen, but that between residents in rural and in urban England. . . .

In *Love in Several Masques* and *The Temple Beau*, and to a more marked degree in *The Modern Husband*, *The Universal Gallant*, and *The Wedding Day* (all comedies of fashionable London), Fielding depicts the ugliness of a rich, sophisticated, but degenerate *beau monde*. (p. 116)

His five-act comedies published or produced before 1737 are [*Love in Several Masques, The Temple Beau, Rape upon Rape; Or, The Justice Caught in His Own Trap, The Modern Husband,* and *The Universal Gallant; Or, The Different Husbands*]. . . . All but *Rape upon Rape*, with its broadly farcical conception of characters and action, show a certain homogeneity. With the one exception, they portray characters of fashionable life. It is in them we may find Fielding's variations on the conventions of Restoration comedy.

Love in Several Masques and *The Temple Beau* focus on the love intrigues, including conventional guardian outwittings, of young couples who wish to be married; whereas *The Modern Husband* and *The Universal Gallant* focus on the illicit love intrigues of couples already married (though there is subordinate attention to licit courtships). An important difference in tone results: the two later plays are far more bitter than the earlier. Yet one theme runs through all (except perhaps *The Universal Gallant*): a sense of outrage at the subordination, actual or attempted, of love to money in marriage. (p. 117)

Love in Several Masques and *The Temple Beau* are conventional and competent, if quite undistinguished, comedies in the manner of Congreve (in their plotting, their attempted epigram, their satirical review of manners, and their characters) but with some notable differences in social values. Most conspicuously, Congreve's strong implied endorsement of prudence in financial affairs is absent here. In Congreve, the sympathetic characters conduct their love affairs with close attention to property settlements; in Fielding, by contrast, they protest the entanglement of mercenary considerations with marriage. (pp. 117-18)

In *Love in Several Masques* Fielding chooses as the subject of his strongest satire the affectations of the wellborn—notably their family pride. In doing so he dramatizes, more explicitly than any of his contemporaries, one of the most important hostilities created by the agricultural economy of the eighteenth century: that between the baronets and the lords, or, more precisely, between the lesser landowners, who as a group were becoming poorer, and the greater landowners, who as a group were becoming richer. (p. 118)

If in *Love in Several Masques* and *The Temple Beau* Fielding introduces variations in the formalized pattern of comedy deriving from the Restoration, in *The Modern Husband* he breaks abruptly with that pattern. In this comedy, which bears a resemblance to his novel *Amelia,* there is a departure from the customary stylization in character types, plotting, and dialogue sufficiently pronounced as to come as a jolt to readers long familiar with the plays of the earlier dramatists. All at once we seem to be entering the domain of the novel, so completely has stylization given way to natural dialogue and the gay love chase to the analysis of character, motive, and environment. . . . [The] play has none of the Restoration's distinctive excellencies and few of its distinctive qualities. The play has, to be sure, a concentration on sexual relations, as have the earlier ones, but even this in an altogether different spirit. There is no gaiety in sex in *The Modern Husband,* no witty transformation of animal attraction into an intellectual game; rather, sex remains an awkward fact of life, like poverty, which is a degrading and corrupting force. Fielding the embittered analyst of the personality and of society is too much in evidence here for the play to have the merits traditional to comedy.

The sex intrigue of the play is largely motivated, on one side at least, by money. . . . Mr. Modern, the title character, pimps for his wife. Having lost a fortune in the South Sea and other financial adventures, he and his wife nevertheless desperately maintain the appearance of fashion, by borrowing and gambling as well as by discreet prostitution. The railing review of the town in their conversation and in that of others would suggest that such a mode of life was far from uncommon. (pp. 119-20)

The Universal Gallant is in subject and tone a companion piece to *The Modern Husband,* though it has fewer of the novelistic qualities. Like the earlier play it conveys an impression of debauchery in fashionable life that is not softened by a surface wit: its subject, emphasized in intrigue and conversation alike, is marital infidelity in a corrupt London.

Fielding's corollary to London is, of course, the uncorrupted countryside, mentioned often even in the comedies of high life as a refuge for virtue. His most attractive dramatic portrayal of country life appears in *Don Quixote in England,* which in its locale, its tone, and its indebtedness to Cervantes has a special relationship to *Joseph Andrews. Don Quixote in England* is a sharply satirical play, a withering review of the machinery by which elections were bought. It is Squire

Badger, however, an earlier Squire Western, who with his fox-hunting songs and good spirits establishes the tone of the comedy, which is altogether English and conservative.

Satire notwithstanding, then, Fielding's writings reveal a certain conservatism, notably in their rather strict observation of the traditional relationships between classes. Yet he has an eye to the irony of social distinctions, the huge disparity often existing between rank and natural merit; and in at least two of his farces he expresses ideas that can bear an egalitarian interpretation—*An Old Man Taught Wisdom; Or, The Virgin Unmasked* . . . and *Miss Lucy in Town, A Sequel to the Virgin Unmasked.* . . . In the earlier farce there is perhaps the nearest approach in early-eighteenth-century drama to a misalliance: an heiress, worth ten thousand pounds, marries a footman. . . . In the sequel, which is only in part the work of Fielding, the young man asserts, in opposition even to a lord, his personal dignity: at one point he draws his sword against the lord, who attempts to corrupt his foolish wife. This young man is depicted as exemplary—and as remarkably different from the corrupt Londoners of various ranks whom he meets in his efforts to save his wife from the results of her foolish infatuation with town life and to take her back to the country, "where there is still something of old *England* remaining." . . . His father-in-law's pronouncement at the end of the play seems to embody Fielding's dramatic theme . . . : "Henceforth, I will know no Degree, no Difference between Men, but what the Standards of Honour and Virtue create: the noblest Birth without these is but a splendid Infamy; and a Footman with these Qualities, is a Man of Honour." Sententious platitudes, perhaps, but they still had something of novelty about them. (pp. 120-21)

John Loftis, "The Displacement of the Restoration Tradition, 1728-1737," in his *Comedy and Society from Congreve to Fielding,* Stanford University Press, 1959, pp. 101-32.

MARTIN C. BATTESTIN

(essay date 1959)

[Battestin is an American critic who has written extensively on eighteenth-century literature. In the following excerpt, he offers a close reading of *Tom Jones.*]

Henry Fielding wrote his first novel with such good humor and apparent artlessness that his more serious purpose, both as moralist and as craftsman, has been largely overlooked, or at best misapprehended. The old assumptions about the meaning and method of *Joseph Andrews* need to be reappraised. Perhaps the most prevalent and inhibiting supposition about the composition of the novel is the notion that it began simply as another parody of *Pamela* and somehow got gloriously out of hand. . . . The structure of *Joseph Andrews*, however, including the so-called digression of Mr. Wilson, was quite carefully designed—given substance and shape by Fielding's Christian ethic and by the principle of what he liked to call "that Epic Regularity." From the start the novel had a life and direction of its own. (p. 3)

Joseph Andrews was written, not in negation of *Pamela,* but in affirmation of a fresh and antithetic theory of the art of the novel. . . . Fielding recalls his rival not to mimic him as before, but rather to establish a sorry alternative, as it were, a kind of foil to the philosophic and esthetic intuitions that inform his own book from the first sentence to the last. What he offered in return was his own—and, for its time, a highly sophisticated—view of the art of fiction.

But what, precisely, is the moral basis of Fielding's art? Here, largely inspired by James A. Work's essay, "Henry Fielding, Christian Censor," recent scholarship has achieved some success in clearing away the old clouded notions. Though the arduous job of definition and clarification remains—a task that the present study in part essays—Fielding's ethic has been traced to its source in the popular latitudinarianism of his day. His writings, in fact, furnish such abundant evidence of his sympathies with orthodox Low Church doctrine that it seems odd that we have been so long in uncovering the obvious. (pp. 10-11)

The characters and plot of *Joseph Andrews* mutually function to illustrate the dominant thematic motifs of the novel, namely, the exposure of vanity and hypocrisy in society, and the recommendation of their antithetical virtues—charity, chastity, and the classical ideal of life. The journey in *Joseph Andrews* is not a mere picaresque rambling, a device solely for the introduction of new adventures such as we find in the *Roman comiqué, Gil Blas,* or *Don Quixote.* The wayfaring of Fielding's heroes is purposeful, a moral pilgrimage from the vanity and corruption of the Great City to the *relative* naturalness and simplicity of the country. In this respect Fielding, despite the hilarity of his comedy and his mock heroics, reminds us more of Bunyan or Fénelon than of Scarron, Le Sage, or Cervantes. (pp. 88-9)

In accord with the preference for Christian heroes found both in the tradition of the biblical epic and in the homilies (especially Barrow's "Of Being Imitators of Christ"), the careers of Joseph Andrews and Abraham Adams comprise brilliantly comic analogues to those of their Scriptural namesakes, likewise patterns, according to the divines, of the good man's basic virtues. Joseph chastely resists the charms of his mistress and is at last reunited with the father from whom he had been kidnapped as a child. Brandishing his crab-stick like a pilgrim's staff, Adams, the good patriarch and priest, travels homeward through strange and idolatrous countries, and is "tempted" by the near drowning of his son. The use of biblical analogues here, like the adaptation of the *Aeneid* in *Amelia,* is surprisingly subtle, contributing to the mock-heroic character of the novel while at the same time reminding readers of the function of Joseph and Adams as exemplars. Finally, Adams as the true Christian minister has a more specific role in Fielding's efforts to correct a growing popular contempt of the clergy. (p. 89)

For Fielding, town and country were always morally antithetical. They tended, respectively, to acquire values symbolic of the extremes of worldly vanity and vice, and true virtue and contentment. (p. 91)

The major thematic motif of *Joseph Andrews,* the doctrine of charity, principally informs Part II of the novel (Book I, chapter 11, through Book III), containing the adventures on the road and dominated, appropriately enough, by the figure of the good patriarch and priest, Abraham Adams. (p. 94)

The concept of charity presented in *Joseph Andrews* is the inevitable outgrowth of Fielding's latitudinarian sympathies. That Parson Adams, his author's spokesman, stands squarely with the Pelagian doctrines of the liberal divines—and especially with Fielding's admired friend Benjamin Hoadly—is most apparent from his vigorous criticism of Whitefield and of the High Church denigration of Hoadly's *A Plain Account of the Nature and End of the Sacrament of the Lord's Supper.* . . . Against Barnabas, a self-indulgent, pleasure-loving High Churchman, Adams concurs with Whitefield's efforts to restore the Church "to the Example of the Primitive Ages." (pp. 95-6)

For similar reasons Adams endorsed Hoadly's rationalistic conception of the eucharist against his more orthodox opponents, among them the pompous, punch-drinking parson Barnabas. . . . Hoadly's mystery-dispelling account of the sacrament as a simple communal memorial of Christ's sacrifice, a time for recognizing one's fellowship with the body of Christians and for dedicating one's life to "The Uniform Practice of *Morality,*" receives Adams' warmest praise. . . . Adams' recommendation of this controversial tract is in accord with the liberal Christianity of his author, who had lamented in *The Champion* (March 15, 1739/40) that "Religion and laws have been adulterated with so many needless and impertinent ceremonies, that they have been too often drawn into doubt and obscurity." His advocacy of a common-sense religion of practical morality against the principles of Methodism and the High Church places him directly in the latitudinarian tradition.

From Adams' frequent discussions of charity there emerges a definition of the concept that corresponds precisely to that of the liberal divines [Isaac Borrow, John Tillotson, Samuel Clarke, and Hoadly]. . . . True charity, which merits salvation, is not a matter of mere knowledge or profession or inclination, nor is it that self-centered, mercenary generosity cynically described by Hobbes and Mandeville. Rather, it is rooted in a good-natured, disinterested compassion, actively relieving the distresses and promoting the welfare of mankind. Fielding's satire of the Hobbesian man, whose altruism is constrained and selfishly motivated, is clearly implied in the "Good Samaritan" episode. By persuading the other passengers of the stage that Joseph must be rescued lest they be held legally responsible for his death, the lawyer—a "mean selfish Creature . . . who made Self the Centre of the whole Creation, would give himself no Pain, incur no Danger, advance no Money, to assist or preserve his Fellow-Creatures" . . .—perfectly exemplifies the moral worthlessness of a merely politic philanthropy. (pp. 97-8)

But the man of charity is truly honorable; he is heroic for virtue's sake. And this is so even if in his ardent pursuit of the good his simplicity sometimes makes us smile. . . . Adams' innocence or Joseph's militant chastity may excite laughter, but never the moral castigation and contempt implicit in Fielding's definition of the Ridiculous, which consists principally in the deviation from "the most golden of all Rules, no less than that of doing to all Men as you would they should do unto you"—the deviation, in other words, from the rules of charity and good breeding. A lack of charity, indeed, is the criterion of the Ridiculous. It is remarkable how often Fielding's satiric method is to oppose, in a given situation, the selfish and social passions and to direct our critical laughter against those whose avarice or lust or ambition or vanity subdues the requirements of compassion. (pp. 103-04)

Behind the conception of Parson Adams in his capacity as exemplar—his origin in fiction must be traced to Don Quixote—lies the whole homiletic tradition of the good man, whose biblical prototype, it will be recalled, was Abraham—father of the faithful, whose faith was proved (according to St. James) by good works; a pilgrim "adhering steadfastly to the *True Religion*, in the *midst* of idolatrous and corrupt Nations." Adams' name, character, and vocation, for example, combine Samuel Clarke's two examples of the good man, the patriarch Abraham and the true clergyman. (p. 104)

After his charity and goodness of heart, perhaps the most meaningful aspect of Adams' character as exemplar is his embodiment of Fielding's ideal of the true clergyman. As we shall see, it was a persistent aim of Fielding's writings both to rectify a widespread contempt of the clergy and to reform by ridicule the flagrant abuses within the Church that were the causes of that contempt. . . . For the moral health of society, Fielding felt, competent and dedicated clergymen and educators were indispensable. (pp. 104-05)

Fielding believed that much of the Ridiculous in society was owing to the prevalence of inadequate standards of education, promoting immorality by the indulgence of vanity and the encouragement of hypocrisy. (p. 110)

Of all Fielding's heroes, Parson Adams is the fullest personification of good nature. It is Adams' embodiment of the essential characteristics of this concept that permits Fielding to declare in his Preface—despite his hero's apparent likeness to Don Quixote—that "the Character of Adams . . . is not to be found in any Book now extant." The theory of good nature formulated in *The Champion* provided an ethical, rather than literary, basis for Adams' distinctive traits: his compassion, charity, and, above all, his simplicity. . . . Along with his moral idealism learned from the classics and primitive Christianity, however, the dominant feature of Adams' good nature, his simplicity, is consciously manipulated by Fielding to serve the ethical purpose of his satire. (pp. 111-12)

We may laugh at the parson's good-natured innocence and bookish idealism, but his honest bewilderment and shock at the great world imply a standard by which to measure the moral degeneracy of his age.

Pilgrim, priest, and patriarch, Abraham Adams maintains his faith in strange and idolatrous lands. Apparently following another of Barrow's suggestions, Fielding chose as his representative of chastity, symbolic of the rational discipline of the passions, a virtuous footman named Joseph, whose initial situation was not only sure to amuse by evoking the absurdities of *Pamela*, but was, in accord with the theories of the biblical epic, precisely parallel to the story of his "namesake" and Potiphar's wife. (p. 113)

Like their biblical prototypes, Abraham and Joseph, Fielding's good men exemplify the sum of the individual's duty to God, society, and himself. Adams' personification of true faith expressed through charity comprehends the first two and Joseph's chastity the last. Tillotson, we recall, had thus defined the head of our duty to ourselves: "That we govern our passions by reason, and moderate our selves in the use of sensual delights, so as not to transgress the rules of temperance and chastity." (p. 116)

Located at the heart of the book, the long biography of Mr. Wilson needs to be reckoned with. (p. 118)

[Most critics] look upon Wilson's story as another flaw—the most serious and glaring of all—in the random architecture of *Joseph Andrews*. . . . Far from being a needless or irrelevant interpolation, however, the Wilson episode is essential. It stands as the philosophic, as well as structural, center of *Joseph Andrews*, comprising a kind of synecdochic epitome of the meaning and movement of the novel. . . . *Joseph Andrews* represents the moral pilgrimage of its hero, guided by the good counsel and example of his spiritual father, Abraham Adams, from the folly and vice of London toward reunion in the country with the chaste and loving Fanny Goodwill. The digression focuses and moralizes this movement by depicting Wilson's progress—nearly disastrous because "without a Guide"—through the corrupting vanities of the town to a life of wisdom, love, and contentment in a setting reminiscent of the Golden Age. Under proper tutelage, Joseph has escaped the moral contamination of Wilson's London period and may profit from his hard-earned wisdom. The meaning of both the digression and the novel as a whole is largely a variation on the themes of Ecclesiastes, Juvenal's *Third Satire,* and Virgil's *Second Georgic,* controlled throughout, of course, by the doctrine of charity. (pp. 119-20)

On one level, what Fielding is attempting in the history of Mr. Wilson is a prose version of Hogarth's "progress" pieces. Specifically, the analogy between *The Rake's Progress* and Wilson's account of his London days is inescapable. The reason for this parallelism is not hard to find. In the Preface to *Joseph Andrews* Fielding virtually identifies Hogarth's conception of the comic art and his own. (p. 122)

The story of Mr. Wilson, however, is much more than an imitation of Hogarth. Its function within the novel gives it a direction and complexity of its own. As with *Joseph Andrews* as a whole, vanity of vanities is the message of Wilson's progress through London society, his hard-earned wisdom through adversity, and his retirement to a life according to the classical ideal. . . . While the emphasis throughout is on the exposure of fashionable folly and vice, Fielding is careful to suggest the moral dimension, tracing Wilson's spiritual degradation to its source in irreligion and a faulty education. (p. 123)

Wilson's spiritual impasse is also placed in a Christian context recalling the arguments for free will and the operation of Providence as against Fortune in Boethius' *Consolation of Philosophy* and the homilies. His brief flirtation with the "Rule-of-Right" club of deists and Hobbesian atheists is indicative of his state of mind. By blinding himself to the "Principles of Religion" and the operation of Providence, Wilson becomes caught up in the machinery of Fortune. "Prosperity" changes to "Adversity," and he sinks to a nadir of despair. (p. 124)

Wilson must earn his wisdom through the harsh discipline of adversity. As spiritual biography, his story dramatizes Fielding's recurrent insistence upon the operation of Providence and the moral responsibility of the individual. (p. 126)

More important for the novel as a whole, however, is the apparent lesson to be drawn from Wilson's history: *vanitas vanitatum* and its solution in "a retired life" of love and simplicity. (p. 127)

Mr. Wilson's long history, then, is not really a "digression" at all, but rather an integral part of the plan and purpose of *Joseph Andrews.* . . . While the main narrative exposes selfishness and hypocrisy along the highway, Wilson's rake's progress through the vanities of London completes the panoramic satire of English society. His own career depicts the nearly fatal consequences of immorality and irreligion, the twin results of a faulty education. It is what might have happened to Joseph Andrews himself had he lacked the good advice and good example of Parson Adams. With Wilson's wise adoption of the classical ideal of life his own pilgrimage is complete, symbolically reinforcing the movement of the novel as a whole, and a moral alternative is established in contrast to the ways of vanity. (p. 129)

Martin C. Battestin, in his *The Moral Basis of Fielding's Art: A Study of "Joseph Andrews,"* Wesleyan University Press, 1959, 195 p.

SOURCES FOR FURTHER STUDY

Blanchard, Frederic T. *Fielding the Novelist: A Study in Historical Criticism.* New Haven, Conn.: Yale University Press, 1926, 655 p.

Standard account of Fielding's literary reputation from the eighteenth through the early twentieth centuries.

Dudden, F. Homes. *Henry Fielding: His Life, Works, and Times.* 2 vols. 1952. Reprint. Hamden, Conn.: Archon Books, 1966.

Extensive biography containing discussions of Fielding's works and their historical backgrounds.

Johnson, Maurice. *Fielding's Art of Fiction: Eleven Essays on "Shamela," "Joseph Andrews," "Tom Jones," and "Amelia."* Philadelphia: University of Pennsylvania Press, 1961, 182 p.

Explicative essays on Fielding's literary devices.

F. Scott Fitzgerald

1896-1940

(Full name Francis Scott Key Fitzgerald) American novelist, short story writer, essayist, scriptwriter, and dramatist.

INTRODUCTION

*F*itzgerald was the spokesman for the Jazz Age, America's decade of prosperity, excess, and abandon, which began soon after the end of World War I and ended with the 1929 stock market crash. The novels and stories for which he is best known examine an entire generation's search for the elusive American dream of wealth and happiness. The glamour and insouciance of the youthful, affluent characters portrayed in *This Side of Paradise* (1920), *The Beautiful and Damned* (1922), and *The Great Gatsby* (1925) were derived from Fitzgerald's own life and that of his wife and friends. However, they reflect only one side of a writer whose second and final decade of work portrayed a life marred by alcoholism and financial difficulties, troubled by lost love, and frustrated by lack of inspiration. Much like his personal experience, Fitzgerald's works mirror the headiness, ambition, despair, and disillusionment of America in his lifetime.

Born in St. Paul, Minnesota, the son of well-to-do midwestern parents, Fitzgerald was a precocious child with an early interest in writing plays and poetry. As a young man he emulated the rich, youthful, and beautiful, a social group with whom he maintained a lifelong love-hate relationship. Following two years in an eastern preparatory school, he enrolled in 1913 at Princeton University. His first stories appeared in *Nassau Lit*, Princeton's literary magazine, which was edited by his friend and fellow student Edmund Wilson. Leaving Princeton for the army during World War I, Fitzgerald spent his weekends in camp writing the earliest draft of his first novel, *This Side of Paradise*. The acceptance of this work for publication by Charles Scribner's Sons in 1919 and the ensuing popular and financial success it achieved enabled Fitzgerald to marry Zelda Sayre, a socially prominent young woman he had met and courted during his army days. Zelda significantly affected her husband's life and career. During the 1920s she was Fitzgerald's private literary consultant and editor, while publicly she matched Fitzgerald's extravagant tastes and passion in living for the moment.

While continuing to illuminate the manners of the Roaring Twenties, Fitzgerald's second and third novels, as well as the story collections published between novels, evidenced a growing awareness of the shallowness and brutal insensitivity that are sometimes accoutrements of American society. These weaknesses and America's lost ideals are movingly described in Fitzgerald's strongest and most famous work, *The Great Gatsby.* Although it gained the respect of many prominent American writers and is now considered a classic, *The Great Gatsby* was not a popular success and marked the beginning of the author's decline in popularity. Another commercial disappointment, *Tender Is the Night* (1934) reflected the disillusionment and strain caused by the Great Depression and Zelda's gradual deterioration from schizophrenia and eventual breakdown. These events scarred Fitzgerald, contributing to a deep, self-reproaching despair that brought his career to a near standstill during the mid-1930s. Fitzgerald described his tribulations in detail in the three confessional "Crack-Up" essays of 1936, which brilliantly evoke his pain and suffering. Trying to start anew, he became a motion picture scriptwriter and began *The Last Tycoon,* a novel based on his Hollywood experiences, which remained unfinished when Fitzgerald died in late 1940.

In his first two novels, *This Side of Paradise* and *The Beautiful and Damned,* Fitzgerald examined the lives of young characters who much resembled Fitzgerald and his friends; hedonistic and acquisitive, yet also jaded and rebellious, these affluent Eastern youths helped secure the popular image of a "lost generation" both entranced and repelled by American materialism. Although most critics faulted both novels as sloppily constructed, sentimental, and laden with sophomoric philosophy, they also praised their lyrical, convincing bursts of emotional intensity. Much the same reception greeted the short stories which Fitzgerald prodigiously wrote for popular magazines during this period. Fitzgerald himself dismissed most of his stories as commercial pap written for strictly financial reasons; however, some of his more complex stories, notably "May Day," "The Rich Boy," and "Absolution," have received considerable critical praise and attention.

The Great Gatsby, considered a vastly more mature and artistically masterful treatment of Fitzgerald's early themes, scrutinizes the consequences of the Jazz Age generation's adherence to false values. In *The Great Gatsby,* Fitzgerald employed a first-person narrator, Nick Carraway, to tell the story of Jay Gatsby, a farmer's son turned racketeer, whose ill-gotten wealth is acquired solely to gain acceptance into the sophisticated, moneyed world of the woman he loves, Daisy Fay Buchanan. Gatsby's romantic illusions about the power of money to buy respectability and the love of Daisy—the "golden girl" of his dreams—are skillfully and ironically interwoven with episodes that depict what Fitzgerald viewed as the callousness and moral irresponsibility of the affluent American society of the 1920s. Set amid the glamour and the raucousness of that decade, Gatsby's tragic quest and violent end foretell the collapse of an era and the onset of disillusionment with the American dream.

In the decade before his death, Fitzgerald's marital troubles and the debilitating effects of his alcoholism limited the quality and amount of his writing. Nonetheless, it was also during this period that he attempted his most psychologically complex and aesthetically ambitious work, *Tender Is the Night.* Set against the backdrop of expatriate life in Europe in the 1920s, the novel presents the story of a brilliant young psychiatrist, Dr. Richard (Dick) Diver, and his schizophrenic wife Nicole. The victim of rape by her father when she was fifteen, Nicole steadily recovers through the care of her husband, who suffers disillusionment and emotional deterioration under the demands of the complex roles he must serve in the marriage as doctor, husband, and father. Broader in scope than the more introspective and poetic *Gatsby, Tender Is the Night* drew criticism from readers who considered it chronologically confusing and thematically unfocused. After Fitzgerald's death, however, the novel was accepted as exhibiting far more depth and narrative canniness than early critics perceived. In fact, later examinations of *Tender Is the Night* conclude that the circle of wealthy expatriates that Fitzgerald so knowledgeably depicted attains symbolic status as a microcosm of the Western world in decline.

At the time of his death, Fitzgerald was virtually forgotten and unread. But a growing Fitzgerald revival, begun in the 1950s, has led to the publication of numerous volumes of stories, letters, and notebooks. Since that time, critics have universally praised Fitzgerald's mastery of style and technique that renders even his most trivial efforts entertaining and well-executed. In his novels and stories, Fitzgerald displays what Kenneth G. Johnston termed an "ability to perceive the reality behind the glittering carnival, the face behind the mask." He is regarded as a profound and sensitive artist, as well as the unmatched voice of the Jazz Age.

(For further information about Fitzgerald's life and works, see *Authors in the News,* Vol. 1; *Concise Dictionary of American Literary Biography, 1917-1929; Contemporary Authors,* Vols. 110, 123; *Dictionary of Literary Biography,* Vols. 4, 9, 86; *Dictionary of Literary Biography Documentary Series,* Vol. 1; *Dictionary of Literary Biography Yearbook 1981; Major Twentieth-*

CRITICAL COMMENTARY

EDMUND WILSON
(essay date 1922)

[An American critic, novelist, short story writer, and essayist, Wilson was one of the most influential literary scholars of the twentieth century. A onetime classmate of Fitzgerald's, he continually corresponded with and advised the author, who termed Wilson his "intellectual conscience." In the following excerpt from an essay first published in 1922, Wilson discusses the technical flaws and aesthetic triumphs of Fitzgerald's early fiction.]

It has been said by a celebrated person [Edna St. Vincent Millay] that to meet F. Scott Fitzgerald is to think of a stupid old woman with whom someone has left a diamond; she is extremely proud of the diamond and shows it to everyone who comes by, and everyone is surprised that such an ignorant old woman should possess so valuable a jewel; for in nothing does she appear so inept as in the remarks she makes about the diamond. . . . (p. 27)

Scott Fitzgerald is, in fact, no old woman, but a very good looking young man, nor is he in the least stupid, but, on the contrary, exhilaratingly clever. Yet there *is* a symbolic truth in the description quoted above: it is true that Fitzgerald has been left with a jewel which he doesn't know quite what to do with. For he has been given imagination without intellectual control of it; he has been given the desire for beauty without an aesthetic ideal; and he has been given a gift for expression without very many ideas to express.

Consider, for example, the novel—*This Side of Paradise*—with which he founded his reputation. It has almost every fault and deficiency that a novel can possibly have. It is not only highly imitative but it imitates an inferior model. Fitzgerald, when he wrote the book, was drunk with Compton Mackenzie, and it sounds like an American attempt to rewrite *Sinister Street*. . . . [One] of the chief weaknesses of *This Side of Paradise* is that it is really not *about* anything: its intellectual and moral content amounts to little more than a gesture—a gesture of indefinite revolt. The story itself, furthermore, is very immaturely imagined: it is always just verging on the ludicrous. And, finally, *This Side of Paradise* is one of the most illiterate books of any merit ever published (a fault which the publisher's

proofreader seems to have made no effort to remedy). Not only is it ornamented with bogus ideas and faked literary references, but it is full of literary words tossed about with the most reckless inaccuracy.

I have said that *This Side of Paradise* commits almost every sin that a novel can possibly commit: but it does not commit the unpardonable sin: it does not fail to live. The whole preposterous farrago is animated with life. It is rather a fluttering and mercurial life: its emotions do not move you profoundly; its drama does not make you hold your breath; but its gaiety and color and movement did make it come as something exciting after the realistic heaviness and dinginess of so much serious American fiction. (pp. 27-9)

In regard to the man himself, there are perhaps two things worth knowing, for the influence they have had on his work. In the first place, he comes from the Middle West—from St. Paul, Minnesota. Fitzgerald is as much of the Middle West of large cities and country clubs as Sinclair Lewis is of the Middle West of the prairies and little towns. What we find in him is much what we find in the more prosperous strata of these cities: sensitivity and eagerness for life without a sound base of culture and taste; a structure of millionaire residences, brilliant expensive hotels and exhilarating social activities built not on the eighteenth century but simply on the flat Western land. And it seems to me rather a pity that he has not written more of the West: it is perhaps the only milieu that he thoroughly understands. When Fitzgerald approaches the East, he brings to it the standards of the wealthy West—the preoccupation with display, the appetite for visible magnificence and audible jamboree, the vigorous social atmosphere of amiable flappers and youths comparatively untainted as yet by the snobbery of the East. In *The Beautiful and Damned,* for example, we feel that he is moving in a vacuum; the characters have no real connection with the background to which they have been assigned; they are not part of the organism of New York as the characters, in, say, the short story **"Bernice Bobs Her Hair"** are a part of the organism of St. Paul. Surely F. Scott Fitzgerald should some day do for Summit Avenue what Lewis has done for Main Street.

But you are not to suppose from all this that the author of *This Side of Paradise* is merely a typical well-to-do Middle Westerner, with correct clothes and clear

Principal Works

Flappers and Philosophers (short stories) 1920

This Side of Paradise (novel) 1920

The Beautiful and Damned (novel) 1922

Tales of the Jazz Age (short stories) 1922

The Vegetable; or, From President to Postman (drama) 1923

The Great Gatsby (novel) 1925

All the Sad Young Men (short stories) 1926

Tender Is the Night (novel) 1934

Taps at Reveille (short stories) 1935

The Last Tycoon (unfinished novel) 1941

The Crack-Up (essays, notebooks, and letters) 1945

Afternoon of an Author (short stories and essays) 1957

Six Tales of the Jazz Age, and Other Stories (short stories) 1960

The Pat Hobby Stories (short stories) 1962

The Letters of F. Scott Fitzgerald (letters) 1963

Dear Scott/Dear Max: The Fitzgerald-Perkins Correspondence (letters) 1971

As Ever, Scott Fitz: Letters Between F. Scott Fitzgerald and His Literary Agent Harold Ober, 1919-1940 (letters) 1972

The Basil and Josephine Stories (short stories) 1973

*Bits of Paradise (short stories) 1973

The Notebooks of F. Scott Fitzgerald (notebooks) 1978

The Price Was High: The Last Uncollected Stories of F. Scott Fitzgerald (short stories) 1979

The Correspondence of F. Scott Fitzgerald (letters) 1980

Poems, 1911-1940 (poetry) 1981

*This collection also includes stories by Zelda Fitzgerald.

---

skin, who has been sent to the East for college. The second thing one should know about him is that Fitzgerald is partly Irish and that he brings both to life and to fiction certain qualities that are not Anglo-Saxon. For, like the Irish, Fitzgerald is romantic, but also cynical about romance; he is bitter as well as ecstatic; astringent as well as lyrical. He casts himself in the role of playboy, yet at the playboy he incessantly mocks. He is vain, a little malicious, of quick intelligence and wit, and has an Irish gift for turning language into something iridescent and surprising. He often reminds one, in fact, of the description that a great Irishman, Bernard Shaw, has written of the Irish: "An Irishman's imagination never lets him alone, never convinces him, never satisfies him; but it makes him that he can't face reality nor deal with it nor handle it nor conquer it: he can only sneer at them that do . . . and imagination's such a torture that you can't bear it without whisky. . . . And all the while there goes on a horrible, senseless, mischievous laughter."

For the rest, F. Scott Fitzgerald is a rather childlike fellow, very much wrapped up in his dream of himself and his projection of it on paper. For a person of his mental agility, he is extraordinarily little occupied with the general affairs of the world: like a woman, he is not much given to abstract or impersonal thought. Conversation about politics or general ideas have a way of snapping back to Fitzgerald. But this seldom becomes annoying; he is never pretentious or boring. He is quite devoid of affection and takes the curse off his relentless egoism by his readiness to laugh at himself and his boyish uncertainty of his talent. And he exhibits, in his personality as well as in his writings, a quality rare

today among even the youngest American writers: he is almost the only one among them who is capable of light-hearted high spirits. . . . His characters—and he—are actors in an elfin harlequinade; they are as nimble, as gay and as lovely—and as hardhearted—as fairies: Columbine elopes with Harlequin on a rope ladder dropped from the Ritz and both go morris-dancing amuck on a case of bootleg liquor; Pantaloon is pinked with an epigram that withers him up like a leaf; the Policeman is tripped by Harlequin and falls into the Pulitzer Fountain. Just before the curtain falls, Harlequin puts on false whiskers and pretends to be Bernard Shaw; he gives reporters an elaborate interview on politics, religion and history; a hundred thousand readers see it and are more or less impressed; Columbine nearly dies laughing; Harlequin sends out for a case of gin. (pp. 30-2)

Since writing *This Side of Paradise*—on the inspiration of Wells and Mackenzie—Fitzgerald has become acquainted with a different school of fiction: the ironical-pessimistic. In college, he had supposed that the thing to do was to write biographical novels with a burst of ideas toward the close; since his advent in the literary world, he has discovered that another genre has recently come into favor: the kind which makes much of the tragedy and what Mencken has called "the meaninglessness of life." Fitzgerald had imagined, hitherto, that the thing to do in a novel was to bring out a meaning in life; but he now set bravely about it to contrive a shattering tragedy that should be, also, a hundred-percent meaningless. As a result of this determination, the first version of *The Beautiful and Damned* culminated in an orgy of horror for which the reader was imperfectly prepared. Fitzgerald destroyed his characters with a succession of catastrophes so arbitrary that, beside them, the perversities of Hardy seemed the working of natural laws. (p. 33)

To conclude, it would be quite unfair to subject Scott Fitzgerald, who is still in his twenties and has presumably most of his work before him, to a rigorous overhauling. His restless imagination may yet produce something durable. For the present, however, this imagination is certainly not seen to the best advantage: it suffers badly from lack of discipline and poverty of aesthetic ideas. Fitzgerald is a dazzling extemporizer, but his stories have a way of petering out: he seems never to have planned them completely or to have thought out his themes from the beginning. This is true even of some of his most successful fantasies, such as **"The Diamond as Big as the Ritz"** or his comedy, *The Vegetable.* On the other hand, *The Beautiful and Damned,* imperfect though it is, marks an advance over *This Side of Paradise:* the style is more nearly mature and the subject more solidly unified, and there are scenes that are more convincing than any in his previous fiction.

But, in any case, even the work that Fitzgerald has done up to date has a certain moral importance. In his very expression of the anarchy by which he finds himself bewildered, of his revolt which cannot fix on an object, he is typical of the war generation—the generation so memorably described on the last page of *This Side of Paradise* as "grown up to find all gods dead, all wars fought, all faiths in men shaken." There is a moral in *The Beautiful and Damned* that the author did not perhaps intend to point. The hero and the heroine of this giddy book are creatures without method or purpose: they give themselves up to wild debaucheries and do not, from beginning to end, perform a single serious act; yet somehow you get the impression that, in spite of their fantastic behavior, Anthony and Gloria Patch are the most rational people in the book. Wherever they come in contact with institutions, with the serious life of their time, these are made to appear ridiculous, they are subjects for scorn or mirth. We see the army, finance and business successively and casually exposed as completely without point or dignity. The inference we are led to draw is that, in such a civilization as this, the sanest and most honorable course is to escape from organized society and live for the excitement of the moment. It cannot be merely a special reaction to a personal situation which gives rise to the paradoxes of such a book. It may be that we cannot demand too high a degree of moral balance from young men, however able or brilliant, who write books in the year 1921: we must remember that they have had to grow up in, that they have had to derive their chief stimulus from the wars, the society and the commerce of the Age of Confusion itself. (pp. 33-5)

Edmund Wilson, "F. Scott Fitzgerald," in his *The Shores of Light: A Literary Chronicle of the Twenties and Thirties,* Farrar, Straus and Giroux, 1952, pp. 27-35.

JOHN DOS PASSOS
(essay date 1945)

[An American novelist and essayist, Dos Passos is best known for his *U.S.A.* novel trilogy, a sweeping and vitriolic examination of American capitalism and politics. In the following excerpt, he praises the artistry of Fitzgerald's unfinished novel, *The Last Tycoon.*]

It is tragic that Scott Fitzgerald did not live to finish *The Last Tycoon.* Even as it stands I have an idea that it will turn out to be one of those literary fragments that from time to time appear in the stream of a culture and profoundly influence the course of future events. His unique achievement, in these beginnings of a great novel, is that here for the first time he has managed to establish that unshakable moral attitude towards the world we live in and towards its temporary standards that is the basic essential of any powerful work of the imagination. A firmly anchored ethical standard is something that American writing has been struggling towards for half a century. (p. 339)

The old standards just don't ring true to the quicker minds of this unstable century. Literature, who for? they ask themselves. It is natural that they should turn to the easy demands of the popular market, and to that fame which if it is admittedly not deathless is at least ladled out publicly and with a trowel.

Scott Fitzgerald was one of the inventors of that kind of fame. As a man he was tragically destroyed by his own invention. As a writer his triumph was that he managed in *The Great Gatsby* and to a greater degree in *The Last Tycoon* to weld together again the two divergent halves, to fuse the conscientious worker that no creative man can ever really kill with the moneyed celebrity who aimed his stories at the twelve-year-olds. In *The Last Tycoon* he was even able to invest with some human dignity the pimp and pander aspects of Hollywood. There he was writing, not for highbrows or for lowbrows, but for whoever had enough elementary knowledge of the English language to read through a page of a novel. (p. 342)

In *The Last Tycoon* he was managing to invent a set of people seen really in the round instead of lit by an envious spotlight from above or below. *The Great Gatsby* remains a perfect example of this sort of treatment at an earlier, more anecdotic, more bas relief stage, but in the fragments of *The Last Tycoon,* you can see the beginning of a real grand style. Even in their unfinished state these fragments, I believe, are of sufficient dimensions to raise the level of American fiction to follow in some such way as Marlowe's blank verse line raised the whole level of Elizabethan verse. (p. 343)

John Dos Passos, "A Note on Fitzgerald," in *The Crack-Up* by F. Scott Fitzgerald, edited by Edmund Wilson, New Directions, 1945, pp. 338-43.

CHARLES E. SHAIN
(essay date 1961)

[In the following excerpt, Shain provides an overview of Fitzgerald's literary career.]

This Side of Paradise is usually praised for qualities that pin it closely to an exact moment in American life. Later readers are apt to come to it with the anticipation of an archeologist approaching an interesting ruin. Its publication is always considered to be the event that ushered in the Jazz Age. (p. 20)

Today, the novel's young libertines, both male and female, would not shock a schoolgirl. Amory Blaine turns out to be a conspicuous moralist who takes the responsibility of kissing very seriously and disapproves of affairs with chorus girls. (He has no scruples, it must be said, against going on a three-week drunk when his girl breaks off their engagement.) At the end of the story he is ennobled by an act of self-sacrifice in an Atlantic City hotel bedroom that no one would admire more than a Victorian mother. For modern readers it is probably better to take for granted the usefulness of *This Side of Paradise* for social historians and to admire from the distance of another age the obviously wholesome morality of the hero. Neither of these is the quality that saves the novel for a later time. What Fitzgerald is really showing is how a young American of his generation discovers what sort of figure he wants to cut, what modes of conduct, gotten out of books as well as out of a keen sense of his contemporaries, he wants to imitate. (p. 21)

The novel is very uneven, and full of solemn attempts at abstract thought on literature, war, and socialism. It has vitality and freshness only in moments, and these are always moments of feeling. Fitzgerald said of this first novel many years later, "A lot of people thought it was a fake, and perhaps it was, and a lot of others thought it was a lie, which it was not." It offers the first evidence of Fitzgerald's possession of the gift necessary for a novelist who, like him, writes from so near his own bones, the talent that John Peale Bishop has described as "the rare faculty of being able to experience romantic and ingenuous emotions and a half hour later regard them with satiric detachment." (p. 22)

His success arrived almost overnight: 1920 was the *annus mirabilis*. In that year, the *Saturday Evening Post* published six of his stories, *Smart Set* five, and *Scribner's* two. (p. 23)

The first collection of Fitzgerald's stories in 1921 was timed by Scribner's to profit from the vogue of *This Side of Paradise*. It was called *Flappers and Philosophers*. A second collection, *Tales of the Jazz Age*, was published a year later in the wake of his second novel, *The Beautiful and Damned*. The nineteen stories in the two collections represent with more variety and perhaps more immediacy than the two first novels the manners and morals that have come to compose, at least in the minds of later historians, the Jazz Age. (p. 25)

The Beautiful and Damned was an attempt to write a dramatic novel about a promising American life that never got anywhere. . . . It was the first and least convincing of what were going to be three studies of American failures. As he started the novel in August 1920, Fitzgerald wrote to his publisher that his subject was " . . . the life of Anthony Patch between his 25th and 33rd years (1913-1921). He is one of those many with the tastes and weaknesses of an artist but with no actual creative inspiration. How he and his beautiful young wife are wrecked on the shoals of dissipation is told in the story." (p. 28)

The Beautiful and Damned is a novel of mood rather than a novel of character. The misfortunes of Anthony and Gloria are forced in the plot, but the mood in places is desperate. Fitzgerald does not know what to do with his hero and heroine in the end but make them suffer. The novel will place no blame, either on the nature of things or on the injustices of society. Anthony and Gloria are finally willing to accept all the unhappy consequences as if they had earned them, but the reader has stopped believing in the logic of consequences in this novel long before. The failure of *The Beautiful and Damned* suggests where the soft spots are going to occur in Fitzgerald's art of the novel, in the presentation of character and motivation. With Anthony Patch Fitzgerald assumes that if he has displayed a man's sensibility in some detail he has achieved the study of a tragic character. The "tragedies" suffered by Anthony and Gloria, Fitzgerald's members of the lost generation, lack a moral context as the characters in *The Sun Also Rises* do not. Fitzgerald's fears of his own weaknesses and the excesses that, according to his troubled conscience, he and Zelda were learning to like too easily, endowed the parable of the Patches with moral weight and urgency for its author; but the reader had to invent the worth of the moral struggle for himself. (p. 30)

The Great Gatsby has been discussed and admired as much as any twentieth-century American novel, probably to the disadvantage of Fitzgerald's other fiction. None of its admirers finds it easy to explain why Fitzgerald at this point in his career should have written a novel of such perfect art—though it is usually conceded that he never reached such heights again. (p. 32)

Gatsby's mingled dream of love and money, and the iron strength of his romantic will, make up the essence of the fable, but the art of its telling is full of astonishing tricks. To make the rise and fall of a gentleman gangster an image for the modern history of the Emersonian spirit of America was an audacious thing to attempt, but Fitzgerald got away with it. His own romantic spirit felt deeply what an Englishman has called the "myth-hunger" of Americans, our modern need to "create a manageable past out of an immense present." The poignant effect of the final, highly complex image of the novel, when Gatsby's dream and the American dream are identified, shows how deeply saturated with feeling Fitzgerald's historical imagination was. From his own American life he knew that with his generation the midwesterner had become the typical American and had returned from the old frontier to the East with a new set of dreams—about money. (p. 34)

The whole novel is an imaginative feat that managed to get down the sensational display of postwar America's big money, and to include moral instructions on how to count the cost of it all. *The Great Gatsby* has by this time entered into the national literary mind as only some seemingly effortless works of the imagination can. We can see better now than even some of Fitzgerald's appreciative first reviewers that he had seized upon an important set of symbols for showing that time had run out for one image of the American ego. Poor Gatsby had been, in the novel's terms, deceived into an ignorance of his real greatness by the American world that had for its great men Tom Buchanan and Meyer Wolfsheim, the Wall Street millionaire and his colleague the racketeer. The story does not pretend to know more than this, that Americans will all be the poorer for the profanation and the loss of Gatsby's deluded imagination.

The principal fact in Fitzgerald's life between his twenty-eighth and thirty-fourth year was his inability to write a new novel. (p. 35)

Between 1925 and 1932 he published fifty-six stories, most of them in the *Saturday Evening Post.* (pp. 36-7)

The best stories of those years he selected for two collections [*All the Sad Young Men* and *Taps at Reveille*]. . . . Two recently published collections, *The Stories of F. Scott Fitzgerald*, edited by Malcolm Cowley, and *Afternoon of an Author,* edited by Arthur Mizener,

have assured the modern availability of all the good magazine fiction of Fitzgerald's last fifteen years. (p. 37)

During three years beginning in 1928 he sent the *Saturday Evening Post* a series of fourteen stories out of his boyhood and young manhood. The first eight were based on a portrait of himself as Basil Duke Lee. The last six were built around Josephine, the portrait of the magnetic seventeen-year-old girl of his first love affair. It was characteristic of Fitzgerald to relive his youth during the frustrated and unhappy days of his early thirties. His characters always know how much of their most private emotional life depends upon what Anson Hunter calls the "brightest, freshest rarest hours" which protect "that superiority he cherished in his heart." (p. 38)

Fitzgerald's big novel *Tender Is the Night* was written in its final form while Fitzgerald was living very close to his wife's illness. . . . Their life together was over. It is astonishing that, written under such emotional pressures, *Tender Is the Night* is such a wise and objective novel as it is. (p. 39)

Tender Is the Night is Fitzgerald's weightiest novel. It is full of scenes that stay alive with each rereading, the cast of characters is the largest he ever collected, and the awareness of human variety in the novel's middle distance gives it a place among those American novels which attempt the full narrative mode. Arnold's assumption that how to live is itself a moral idea provides the central substance of the novel. The society Dick has chosen is a lost one, but Dick must function as if he is not lost. To bring happiness to people, including his wife, is to help them fight back selfishness and egotism, to allow their human imaginations to function. To fill in the background of a leisured class with human dignity does not seem a futile mission to Dr. Diver until he fails. For Fitzgerald's hero "charm always had an independent existence"; he calls it "courageous grace." A life of vital response is the only version of the moral life Fitzgerald could imagine, and when Dr. Diver hears the "interior laughter" begin at the expense of his human decency he walks away. He returns to America and his life fades away in small towns in upstate New York as he tries unsuccessfully to practice medicine again. (p. 41)

Nearly all the influential critics discovered the same fault in the novel, that Fitzgerald was uncertain, and in the end unconvincing, about why Dick Diver fell to pieces. . . . [Fitzgerald's] short stories in *Taps at Reveille*, the next year, were greeted by even more hostile reviews and the volume sold only a few thousand. . . . And between 1934 and 1937 his daily life declined into the crippled state that is now known after his own description of it as "the crack-up." (pp. 41-2)

Fitzgerald's public analysis of his desperate condition, published in three essays in *Esquire* in the spring of 1936, will be read differently by different people. (p. 42)

The crack-up essays have become classics, as well known as the best of Fitzgerald's short fiction. . . . The grace of the prose has made some readers suspect that Fitzgerald is withholding the real ugliness of the experience, that he is simply imitating the gracefully guilty man in order to avoid the deeper confrontation of horror. But his language often rises above sentiment and pathos to the pure candor of a generous man who decided "There was to be no more giving of myself" and then, in writing it down, tried to give once more. (pp. 42-3)

For several months in 1939 he was in a New York hospital but by July he was writing short stories again for *Esquire.* He wrote in all twenty-two stories in the eighteen months remaining to him, seventeen of them neat and comic little stories about a corrupt movie writer named Pat Hobby, and one little masterpiece, **"The Lost Decade,"** a sardonic picture of a talented man who had been drunk for ten years.

During the last year of his life Fitzgerald wrote as hard as his depleted capacities allowed him on the novel he left half-finished at his death, *The Last Tycoon.* It is an impressive fragment. (p. 44)

The Last Tycoon had the mark of the thirties on it as surely as his early novels had the American boom as their principal theme. The subject was Hollywood as an industry and a society, but also as an American microcosm. Instead of drawing a deft impression of American society as he had in his earlier fiction, Fitzgerald now wanted to record it. The first hundred pages of the novel take us behind the doors of studios and executive offices in Hollywood with the authority of first-rate history. The history fastens on the last of the American barons, Hollywood's top producer, Monroe Stahr, and we watch him rule a complex industry and produce a powerful popular art form with such a dedication of intelligence and will that he becomes a symbol for a vanishing American grandeur of character and role. "Unlike *Tender Is the Night,*" Fitzgerald explained, "it is not the story of deterioration—it is not depressing and not morbid in spite of the tragic ending. If one book could ever be 'like' another, I should say it is more 'like' *The Great Gatsby.* . . ." The plot was to show Stahr's fight for the cause of the powerful and responsible individual against Hollywood's labor gangsters and Communist writers. Violent action and melodrama were to carry the story, like a Dickens novel, to seats of power in Washington and New York. . . . The action is brilliantly conceived and economically executed. Fitzgerald's style is lean and clear. His power of letting his meanings emerge from incident was never more sharply displayed. At the center of his hero's last two years of life is an ill-starred love affair, like Fitzgerald's own, that comes too late and only reminds him of his lost first wife. But Fitzgerald kept his romantic ego in check in imagining Stahr. What obviously fascinated him was the creation of an American type upon whom responsibility and power had descended and who was committed to building something with his power, something that would last, even though it was only a brief scene in a movie. (pp. 44-5)

Charles E. Shain, in his *F. Scott Fitzgerald,* University of Minnesota Press, Minneapolis, 1961, 45 p.

ARTHUR MIZENER
(essay date 1964)

[An American educator and critic, Mizener is among the most respected of Fitzgerald's biographers and scholars. In the following excerpt from a 1964 lecture on *Tender is the Night,* he examines the characterization and collapse of the novel's protagonist, Dick Diver.]

The whole opening section of *Tender Is the Night,* I mean the opening section of the novel in its original form, which for all the deepest and most moving meanings of the novel is far the best form, the whole of this opening section is written to show us how people of great wealth, great imagination, and great self-discipline can create a magnificent life.

As is fairly well known Fitzgerald had actually observed this life. The little society that gathers on the beach of the Riviera and dines with the Divers is modeled closely on the group that actually lived there in the early twenties, around the Gerald Murphys, to whom *Tender Is the Night* is dedicated. That dedication, if you remember, reads "To Gerald and Sara Murphy." That remark, that dedication, referred to an observation Picasso once made after visiting the Murphys when he said, "Whatever Sara is, there's always a fête."

We see this beautiful life of the Divers through the eyes of Rosemary Hoyt who had learned what personal creativity is and, even more important, what self-discipline is from her experience as an actress. But she is still young enough not to understand what it costs to maintain these things all one's life. Thus she is aware of all the beauty of the dinner party at the Divers' when "the table seemed to have risen a little toward the sky like a mechanical dancing platform, giving the people around it a sense of being alone with each other in the dark universe." Then the Divers "began suddenly to warm, and glow and expand, as if to make up to their guests already so subtly assured of their importance, so flattered with politeness, for anything they might still miss."

What we see in the first part of *Tender Is the Night* is the ideal beauty of this life, the achieved perfection of this civilization (in the highest sense of that word) because that is all Rosemary Hoyt had the understanding to see. What we do not see is the cost in emotional energy, in selflessness, in self-discipline, because Rosemary is not experienced or old enough to understand that. Thus, this is the ideal opening for a book that wishes to make us feel the value of the fully imagined and completely civilized life. Nevertheless, even here in this first part, behind the intelligence and the controlled grace of the Divers that so dazzled Rosemary Hoyt, are hints of the cost. Afterward when Rosemary asked Dick Diver the time of day he said, "It's about half-past one. It's not a bad time. It's not one of the worst times of the day." For in fact Dick Diver has already begun to exhaust his emotional and imaginative nature. He has been carrying this world on his shoulders for six long years. Now he is approaching emotional exhaustion exactly as he approaches literal physical exhaustion at the end of the book, when he tries to lift a man on his shoulders on an aquaplane. "Did you hear I had gone into a process of deterioration?" he asks Rosemary. And when she denies it he says. "It's true. The change came a long way back, but at first it didn't show. The manner remains intact for some time after the morale cracks."

The reasons the task is so exhausting are also there for us to see in the book's first part if we only look. These are reasons that are represented for us by individual characters. But these characters are in turn carefully chosen to project something about a civilization. Not just American civilization, but Western culture as a whole. Where else could so representative a group of characters have been gathered as on the Riviera? There's the American social climber of another generation, Mama Abrams, "preserved," as Fitzgerald says, "by imperviousness to experience and a good digestion, into another generation." There is Luis Campion, the Spaniard, letting his monocle drop into the hair on his chest and saying to his friend, "Now, Royal, don't be too ghastly for words." There is the American McKisco who is writing a novel on the idea of *Ulysses* which "takes a decayed old French aristocrat and puts him in contrast with the mechanical age"; the McKiscos are belligerently anxious to keep up with what they called "what everybody intelligent knows." But McKisco is hopelessly defeated in his dinner-table argument by Tommy Barban, the extremely sophisticated, anarchic, European barbarian, who says with ruthless pleasantry, "I'm a soldier. My business is to kill people." He does it very well. There, finally, like a foreshadowing of what Dick Diver will become when his emotional energy is exhausted and his purpose in life gone, is Abe North, the brilliant musician who has written nothing for seven years and who is always with

great dignity quite drunk. Abe North is, incidentally, modeled after Fitzgerald's close friend, Ring Lardner. "I used to think until you're eighteen nothing matters," his wife says at one point. "That's right," Abe agrees, "and afterwards it's the same way." There, finally, is Nicole Diver's sister, Baby Warren, who concentrates in herself all the Warren arrogance and imperception. These are the rich from all parts of the Western world, representing all the characteristic types the West has produced, free to do anything they choose, and they choose to honor lack of moral imagination until they reduce all but the perverted and the stupid to despair.

These are the people who are gathered about the Divers. They are, by the heroic trick of the heart that Dick Diver works over and over again, lifted up as if by magic to something beautiful. "It was themselves," Fitzgerald says, "[Dick] gave back to them, blurred by the compromises of how many years."

But Fitzgerald does not leave to implication what this all means for the society as a whole. He tells us directly what has happened to Western civilization by showing us a scene of the battlefield of the First World War and by letting us listen to Dick Diver talk about that war. Dick says,

> "See that little stream; we could walk to it in two minutes. It took the British a month to walk to it—a whole empire walking very slowly, dying in front and pushing forward behind. And another empire walked very slowly backwards a few inches a day, leaving the dead like a million bloody rugs. No Europeans will ever do that again in this generation. . . . This kind of battle was invented by Lewis Carroll and Jules Verne and whoever wrote *Undine,* and country deacons bowling and marraines in Marseilles and girls seduced in the back lanes of Wurtemburg and Westphalia. . . . Why, this was a love battle—there was a century of middle-class love spent here."

This is a society that has spent its emotional capital and is living off borrowed energy—the inherited recollection of the honor, the courtesy, the courage of the previous age; keeping, as Dick says about himself, the manner intact for a little while after the morale has cracked.

A little later in the novel, Dick sees a group of elderly American women in a restaurant, a group of Gold Star mothers who have come over to visit the graves of their dead sons. Watching them, Fitzgerald says, "he perceived all the old maturity of an older America. They made the room beautiful, and almost with an effort he turned back to his two women, [that is, to Rosemary and Nicole] at the table, and faced the whole new world in which he believed." A little later again, at Gstaad, Dick, according to Fitzgerald, "relaxed and pretended that the world was all put together again by the gray-haired men of the golden nineties," and "for a moment . . . he felt they were in a ship with a landfall just ahead."

In moments like this Dick Diver remembers his father, an impoverished, beautifully mannered southerner who, above all, "had been sure of what he was," as Dick never has been. As the society of which Dick was a part had exhausted the accumulated energy of its culture in the First World War, so Dick was using up the emotional energy, the expenditure of which gives meaning to his life and a reason for his exercise of self-discipline and his powers of bringing out all that is best in the people around him.

Ultimately, Dick cracks up, to use the word Fitzgerald himself used when he came to describe his own personal experience with this kind of disease. Dick suffered what Fitzgerald called in *Tender Is the Night* a lesion of vitality. He had, as Fitzgerald puts it, "lost himself—he could not tell the hour when, or the day or the week, the month or the year. . . . between the time he found Nicole flowering under a stone on the Zurichsee and the moment of his meeting with Rosemary the spear had been blunted."

This crack-up first shows as little fissures. Dick notices a pretty, but insignificant girl at Gstaad and plays to her. He is appealed to in a random way by an unknown woman at Innsbruck; he lets his heretofore submerged unconscious judgments of the people around him come to the surface in bitterness, as when he says to Mary North, "You've gotten so damn dull, Mary." He does that because he is now drinking in an uncontrolled way. There are still occasional flashes of his old will to exercise his charm on people so that they become their best selves. One comes the last time he sees Rosemary on the beach; another comes when he talks for a last time there to Mary North; but he can't keep it up. "The old interior laughter," as the book says, "had begun inside him and he knew he couldn't keep it up much longer."

The greatest of all Dick's efforts to remake people into their best selves has been his struggle with Nicole. After six years, just about as he has exhausted himself, she is cured of her schizophrenia. Becoming whole again she becomes a more intelligent version of her sister, a Warren "who welcomed the anarchy of her lover," Tommy Barban, who can, when she chooses, speak in her grandfather's voice, slowly, distinctly, insultingly. The one thing Dick Diver can save from the wreckage of his own exhaustion is, he believes, Nicole. All that remains—now she is well—is to free her from her dependence on him. By a supreme effort of will, as he sits quietly on the terrace of their house, he drives her from him. When she finally walked away, a free woman, "Dick waited until she was out of sight. Then he leaned his head forward on the parapet. The case was finished. Dr. Diver was at liberty."

This is, I think, very beautiful. We remember that Baby Warren's idea had originally been to *buy* a doctor for Nicole until Nicole got well again. Dick had laughed helplessly at that idea originally, seeing everything that was going on in Baby's mind and knowing she would never see anything of what was going on in his. Twice during the engagement only his deep love for Nicole keeps him from throwing the marriage in Baby's face, as Fitzgerald says. But now at the end, Baby and her world have won. Dick's epitaph is pronounced by Baby Warren when Nicole says, "Dick was a good husband to me for six years. . . . He always did his best and never let anything hurt me." Baby sticks her jaw out in good arrogant Warren style and says, "That's what he was educated for."

Thus the hard, brutal, anarchic world of the unimaginative rich has won and the representative of the good life, of awareness, of kindness, of understanding, has been set adrift to wander like a ghost of his former brilliant self through the little towns of upstate New York. . . . "In any case," as the last sentence of the book says, "he is almost certainly in that section of the country, in one town or another," as are perhaps all the heroes of transcendentalist American idealists. *Tender Is the Night* is a book filled with despair because Fitzgerald begins it with such a high ideal of what the American individual and American society might be if they'd only take full advantage of their opportunities. (pp. 26-32)

Arthur Mizener, "On F. Scott Fitzgerald," in *Talks with Authors,* edited by Charles F. Madden, Southern Illinois University Press, 1968, pp. 23-38.

BARRY GROSS

(essay date 1970)

[In the following excerpt, Gross discusses the appeal of Jay Gatsby as a tragic hero.]

The Great Gatsby and the twenties are still, of course, inseparable. Published in 1925, the exact middle, the exact peak of the decade, the novel has become a cultural document. Without intending to, Fitzgerald wrote a love song to and a threnody for a time. Like Janus, he looked back and forward simultaneously, back to all the dreams that had impossibly come true, ahead to all the nightmares that were surely to come.

Yet, hand it to a college freshman who knows nothing about the twenties and he knows precisely what the novel is about. Unlike most critics, whose *Great Gatsby* is rarely the *Great Gatsby* one reads, he responds to it as it was meant to be responded to. Of all the responses to the novel Fitzgerald had heard, he thought that of Roger Burlingame, an editor at Scribners, best described "whatever unifying emotion the book has." Mr. Burlingame said the novel made him "want to be back somewhere so much."

But where? If the emotion the novel elicits is nostalgia, then today's college freshman cannot possibly feel anything akin to what Mr. Burlingame might have felt. The novel *does* elicit a nostalgic response, but not the sort of nostalgia we usually think of. It is not nostalgia for a time or a place. It is nostalgia for an attitude.

Listening to Gatsby, Nick Carraway is reminded of an elusive rhythm, a fragment of lost words, something heard somewhere a long time ago. Listening to Nick, so are we. We are reminded of an attitude toward life that we still stubbornly hold to despite the world's refusal to confirm it. We are reminded of heroism.

The Great Gatsby satisfies very basic needs that few contemporary novels can satisfy. It satisfies our need to see ourselves writ large. It satisfies our need to remember our infinite capacities. It satisfies our need to confirm our stubborn faiths in the ideals of courage and honor and love and responsibility. Like Gatsby's smile, the novel concentrates on us with an irresistible prejudice in our favor, believes in us as we would like to believe in ourselves, assures us that it has the impression of us that, at our best, we hope to convey. (pp. 331-32)

The Great Gatsby was an act of faith, an act of courage. At three o'clock in the morning [Fitzgerald] saw the dark night of the soul, but he also saw something else. He saw things as they were, what Lionel Trilling calls the condition, the field of tragedy, but he also saw things as they should be. It is this tension between realism and idealism, between knowledge and faith that lies behind all great tragedy. It is this tension that cannot be resolved, that can only be accepted, that Keats, his favorite poet, called negative capability, that Fitzgerald came to call the wise and tragic sense of life.

Fitzgerald gave it a peculiarly American twist. To those who would insist that America cannot, by definition, produce tragedy, Fitzgerald provided proof that it could. In the past such affirmation in the face of defeat was the prerogative of great men alone. Before him only Melville had succeeded in elevating an American to tragic height. But Ahab achieves the tragic height of a Macbeth, not of an Oedipus or a Hamlet or a Don Quixote. In *The Great Gatsby,* Fitzgerald was able to endow *two good* men with the wise and tragic sense of life.

He did not regard the attainment of such a perception as a mark of greatness. He regarded it as a necessity for any life at all. Without it, life would be an extinction up an alley. With it, life would at least be a journey, a journey of hope. The hope would, in the end, be dashed. The attempt to control one's destiny is fore-

doomed. But that really is no matter. Still the journey must be undertaken. Still the attempt must be made.

That is what *The Great Gatsby* is about and that is why we continue to cherish it. Our contemporaries tell us ours is an anti-heroic, anti-tragic age, but we do not really believe them. We persist in believing, despite all proofs to the contrary, the opposite. That is why we go out of our way to honor the hero and extol him when we think we recognize him, whether his name is John Kennedy or Martin Luther King or Che Guevara.

We are Nick Carraway, grown a little solemn with the feel of those long winters of our discontent, grown a little complacent from having been raised in the house of our security. Cautious, politic, wise, meant to swell a rout or two, but not Prince Hamlet. Yet we yearn to acknowledge our Hamlet, not just the Hamlet out there but the Hamlet in us. If Gatsby is the *great* Gatsby, it is because Nick thinks he is. (pp. 333-34)

Disillusioned and lonely, Nick finally meets Gatsby, who clearly represents everything Nick has been taught to scorn, to disapprove of. Gatsby's house is a huge and incoherent eyesore. His tastes run to pink suits and flashy cars. His parties follow the rules of the most vulgar amusement park. He is rumored to be a criminal, a killer.

Yet, against all logic, Nick finds himself attracted to Gatsby. He listens to Gatsby's preposterous autobiography with first incredulity, then fascination, and finally belief. He wants to believe Gatsby, wants to believe that this elegant roughneck, this proprietor of the elaborate roadhouse next door, is a person of consequence. And when Jordan tells Nick about Gatsby's five-year love for Daisy, Nick's beliefs are confirmed. Gatsby comes alive to him because Nick wants him to. Gatsby is the antidote to Nick's interior rules which keep him at a standstill, to his fear of involvement which keeps him from living.

Contrary to all his principles, he allows himself to become involved, allows himself to be used as a Pandarus to Gatsby's Troilus and Daisy's Cressida. But it is really Nick who uses Gatsby. He uses him as a model. There are only, Nick realizes, the pursued, the pursuing, the busy, and the tired. Gatsby is all of these and possessed by intense life. Nick is none of these and possessed by a fear of life. He overcomes his repulsion at life's inexhaustible variety long enough to commit himself to Jordan Baker.

But Nick discovers, as James Baldwin puts it, that connections *willed* into existence can never become organic. Gatsby has thrown himself into his dream of Daisy with a colossal vitality, a creative passion that Nick cannot begin to approximate. Unlike Nick's, Gatsby's commitment is not to a woman but to a vision. That is why, although Daisy is corrupt, Gatsby's dream of her is not. (pp. 335-36)

But to understand why Gatsby's dream of Daisy is incorruptible, we **must** go back to the night Gatsby saw that the blocks of the sidewalk really formed a ladder that mounted to a secret place above the trees. He knew he could climb to it and once there suck on the pap of life, drink down the milk of wonder. He also knew he could climb to it only if he climbed alone, only if he devoted all his energies, all his commitments to getting there. Such a climb could not be made halfheartedly.

But there was Daisy standing beside him, breathless, immediate. He knew that once he kissed her his mind would never romp again like the mind of God. Daisy could not be won by halves either. He must choose between the stars and a mortal flower. Against all logic, he weds his unutterable visions to her perishable breath and the incarnation is complete forever.

His commitment is to his Platonic conception of himself. To this he is faithful to the end. Gatsby's greatness resides in this vigil, in his protection of an internal flame. His vision comes from an inner light which he sustains and follows. He looks at life from a single window, an isolation that insures his purity. (pp. 336-37)

This is the greatness of the visionary and, as such, is inimitable. Nick cannot *be* Gatsby because he cannot *choose* to have a vision. And even if he could, he would not. The total commitment to an impossible dream is, of course, insane and very dangerous. Nick is too sensible to ever want to pay the price for living too long with a single dream. As an ideal, Gatsby is unapproachable. He can only be wondered at, not emulated.

Nevertheless, he is an ideal we need to recognize and affirm. For Gatsby represents nothing less than wonder itself, the heightened sensitivity to the promises of life, the extraordinary gift for hope, the romantic readiness that makes life something more than an extinction up an alley, that makes life a journey. Gatsby is one with the Dutch sailor whose boat was similarly propelled against the current by a fidelity to an impossible dream. (pp. 337-38)

Gatsby's morality may be nothing more than a chivalrous reflex, nothing more than what H. L. Mencken called it, the sentimentality of a sclerotic fat woman. But it is a morality nevertheless and in lieu of any other. In this too Gatsby atones for the world's failure, its failure to provide standards in terms of which human behavior may be measured and judged. Gatsby's moral response has to do with that Platonic conception of himself, with those ineffable dreams that permit him to transcend a brutal and materialistic world. In Gatsby Nick finds the connection between ideality and morality, between the capacity for wonder and the capacity for responsibility. The price for living too long with a single dream *is* too high. But the price

for living too long without one is even higher, not to the physical but to the spiritual life.

Although Nick must disapprove of Gatsby from beginning to end, he is able to recognize and affirm what Gatsby represents. In that recognition and affirmation lie Nick's heroism. He is able to affirm Gatsby in words when he tells him he is worth the whole damn bunch put together. He is able to affirm him in gestures when he erases the obscene word scrawled on Gatsby's steps. He is able to affirm him in deeds when he commits himself to and assumes responsibility for the dead Gatsby, when he invests his intense personal interest to which everyone is entitled at the end.

More important even, he is able, finally, to assume responsibility for himself. He left the Midwest without confronting the girl he was fleeing but before he leaves the East he confronts Jordan Baker. No longer able to lie to himself and call it honor, he admits his dishonesty and carelessness. He has learned not to be like the Buchanans who smash up things and people and then retreat back into their vast carelessness, leaving other people to clean up the mess they make. He has learned not to trust some obliging sea to sweep his refuse away. (pp. 338-39)

He wants, he says, no more riotous excursions with privileged glimpses into the human heart. He wants, he says, the world to be in uniform and at a sort of moral attention forever. He is no longer interested, he says, in the abortive sorrows and shortwinded elations of men.

But the only sort of moral order the world can create is the order of the inquisition which spares only children and the very old. The only order that is liberating is the one each man must create for himself. The riotous excursions are, at least, excursions, and not extinctions up an alley. The abortive sorrows and shortwinded elations of the human heart are what makes it beat.

In the final analysis, Nick knows all that. In telling Gatsby's story and his own, he does create an order, he does affirm the sorrows and elations of the heart. He becomes, in earnest, the guide, the pathfinder he fancied himself to be when he first arrived at West Egg. He captures the elusive rhythm, remembers the lost words, communicates the incommunicable something heard somewhere a long time ago.

Gatsby is the hero we need to acknowledge and affirm, but the hero we dare not be. Nick, who is, like us, within and without, simultaneously repelled and enchanted by the inexhaustible variety of life, is the hero we can and must become. (pp. 339-40)

Barry Gross, " 'Our Gatsby, Our Nick'," in *The Centennial Review,* Vol. XIV, No. 3, Summer, 1970, pp. 331-40.

BRIAN WAY
(essay date 1980)

[In the following excerpt, Way explores theme and structure in Fitzgerald's short fiction.]

Scott Fitzgerald has never received his due as a writer of short stories. His tales have been relegated to a minor position: they are too often discussed as if they mattered only as aids to the understanding of his major novels. It is symptomatic of this situation that some fifty of them remained uncollected for four decades after the author's death. And yet Fitzgerald deserves the same respect as the undisputed masters of the genre among his American contemporaries—Sherwood Anderson, Hemingway and Faulkner. (p. 72)

I shall not spend any time cataloguing the weaknesses of his poorer stories, but concentrate all my attention upon those tales which ought to have a secure place alongside the best short fiction of the twentieth century. Given this framework of analysis, his dislike of short-story writing instead of being an obstruction to the understanding of his work becomes potentially illuminating: it provides a deeper insight than any other aspect of his career into the difficulties he experienced because of his complex attitude to his role as an author; and it helps to draw attention to the exacting nature of his conception of short-story form.

Fitzgerald's ideas about the function of the artist . . . are divided by a central conflict: on the one hand he believes that the artist is a heroic figure, and the values of art supreme; and, on the other, that writing is a middle-class vocation which involves the author in a network of responsibilities and obligations to other people. (p. 73)

[In one sense], Fitzgerald's best tales have no plots at all; and it is here that we see the full significance of his claim that 'all my stories are conceived like novels, require a special emotion, a special experience.' The structure of any one of these is a matter of subtle connections and transitions, something too complex to be discussed adequately through any notion of plot. They differ from *The Great Gatsby* and *Tender is the Night* only in scale, not in kind. . . . Of all Fitzgerald's tales, it is **'The Rich Boy'** which most completely realizes his exacting sense of the possibilities of the genre, but even in a good commercial story like **'The Bowl'**, we find the same density of texture, a similar multiplicity of characters and episodes, and an extended time scale. It is surely no accident that three of his finest short stories, **'May Day'**, **'Absolution'** and **'One Trip Abroad'**, were

Fitzgerald and his wife, Zelda, photographed near the time of publication of *Tender Is the Night*.

fashioned out of material originally intended for inclusion in novels. (pp. 76-7)

In **'Echoes of the Jazz Age'** . . . , Fitzgerald names May Day, 1919, as the day on which the Jazz Age actually began, and in his story **'May Day'** . . . , he attempts, with an extraordinarily sure instinct for the shape of things to come, to evoke the atmosphere of the postwar era. The story is made up of the interwoven actions and feelings of several groups of characters, in New York, between early morning on 1 May 1919, and early the following morning. (pp. 77-8)

'May Day' not only conveys the atmosphere of a historical moment with incomparable vividness: it is also a triumph of artistic form. In order to write it, Fitzgerald had to find a way of representing social chaos which would, nevertheless, avoid condemning his story to a similar formlessness. He began with a device common to much naturalistic fiction—that of taking a single day in the life of a city—but went on to discover a far more subtle and creative structural principle: that the rhythms of city life could be made to function as the rhythms of his story. The various groups of characters are drawn together and flung apart again as these rhythms exert their influence. During the daylight hours, they are mostly apart, occupying themselves with their own private concerns: Philip Dean shopping and gossiping; Gordon worrying about money; Edith at the hairdresser's; the soldiers searching hopefully for liquor and entertainment. Then, during the climactic pleasure-seeking hours between ten and one, they are all brought together in the dance at Delmonico's, which is for that night the city's great revel, and therefore a centre of magnetic attraction. In the secret time between one and four, they disperse again, and then reassemble at Child's, Fifty-ninth Street, to refresh their tired bodies and jaded nerves with coffee and scrambled eggs. . . .

One of Fitzgerald's greatest gifts as a social novelist is this sensitivity to the rise and fall of nervous energy by day and night, which produces the rhythms of social life. His success in 'May Day' depends not merely on moving his characters through the right places and activities at the right times, but on a deep understanding of moods and atmospheres. A long night's revel, in particular, develops a subtly shifting pattern of sensations—anticipation, excitement, fatigue and depression. In order to give this pattern its full value, he had to master many contrasting modes of social comedy: the frothy absurdity of Edith's conversation with her dancing partners; the slapstick adventures of the two soldiers; and the bacchanalian fantasy of Mr In and Mr Out. This comedy has, in turn, to be balanced against other elements—unhappiness, strain, hysteria and despair—before the full complexity of the story can emerge. This is the artistry which enabled Fitzgerald much later in his career, to evoke the atmosphere of Gatsby's parties and Dick Diver's Riviera days. (p. 79)

In Fitzgerald's view, Americans, characteristically, attach more importance to dreams than to grasped experiences: their inner lives may be rich and colourful, even when their outer circumstances are conventional, drab or sordid. Their youth is filled with dreams of an 'orgastic' future (the word he uses on the closing page of *Gatsby*). Later, they become victims of nostalgia, and their lost youth, which slipped by in mere anticipation, now seems to them the period when they truly lived. Finally, with middle age, comes disillusionment: the inner life of dreams loses its power, and they find themselves alone in the emptiness of a purely material universe. The whole pattern, foreshortened in time though not in emotional fullness, is explored in *Gatsby*, but aspects of it form the basis for many of Fitzgerald's stories, particularly in the 1920s. . . .

['Absolution'] is a story about the origin of dreams. It has a Middle Western setting, though of a very different kind from those in 'Bernice Bobs her Hair' and 'The Ice Palace'. Its two principal characters, Rudolph Miller and Father Schwartz, are remote from the wealthy and comparatively sophisticated life of the country clubs and the big cities—they live in a lost Dakota prairie town. The habit of dreaming is born out of the circumstances of their lives. After the brief exciting drama of frontier life, the town stagnates in an atmo-

sphere of perpetual anticlimax. Theoretically, this is still a land of opportunity, but in fact the inhabitants are condemned to lives of isolation, monotony and inaction. Only dreams can fill the vast vacant spaces of their boredom. The brutal violence of the Middle Western climate, and the meagre but garish sensations of prairie life, ensure that their dreams take on a sensuous if not a directly sexual character. (p. 80)

By giving Father Schwartz's dreams a social, indeed a historical origin, Fitzgerald overcomes one of the main difficulties inherent in his theme. A story which deals with a man's hidden imaginative life is capable almost of vanishing through the sheer tenuousness and vagueness of its material. This had already happened in the case of a slightly earlier piece, 'Winter Dreams' . . . , where the hero has no tangible human existence at all. Such a story needs ballast in the form of precise social observation and intense poetic images. These elements, which are clear enough in Fitzgerald's portrayal of Father Schwartz, are still more apparent in his treatment of Rudolph Miller.

Rudolph's dreams are given an added dimension by the fact that he is eleven years old and on the brink of adolescence. He has been avoiding confession for a month because he is ashamed to tell Father Schwartz about his 'impure thoughts'; and yet these thoughts have become the most exciting part of his imaginative life. He manages to convey the external facts to the priest—how he lingered to eavesdrop on a pair of lovers in a barn—but he cannot tell him 'how his pulse had bumped in his wrist, how a strange, romantic excitement had possessed him when those curious things had been said.' Adolescence, as Fitzgerald sees it, intensifies and complicates a child's imaginative life, driving his thoughts inwards as he attempts to make sense of the turmoil of his feelings. Rudolph is torn between new, half-understood, romantic emotions and old idealisms. (pp. 80-1)

But when he goes to Father Schwartz the same afternoon, to ask for absolution from his mortal sin, his feelings are unexpectedly placed in a new light; and, by the end of the interview, he is led to believe that 'there was something ineffably gorgeous somewhere that had nothing to do with God.' Father Schwartz's behaviour is disconcerting to say the least. Having dismissed Rudolph's spiritual problems with a comically brusque scrap of pastoral theology, he begins to talk about that other forbidden world which so fascinates them both. The lonely, half-crazy, old man struggles incoherently to put into words thoughts he has never dared to acknowledge before. He speaks of people for whom things 'go glimmering', and of a great light in Paris bigger than a star; but it is in [the bright amusement parks of] the Middle West itself that he eventually finds the image he is groping for. . . . In 'Absolution', this image is the poetic and dramatic climax of the story: it draws Rudolph and Father Schwartz together in a new secret community of feeling; and it turns their dreams into something more than mere personal fantasies— into expressions of the American consciousness. For Rudolph in particular, it becomes a symbol of the future, hovering before him, leading him away from old allegiances towards the lure of a more expansive life.

'Absolution', a fairly early story, deals, appropriately, with the origin of dreams, but, by the late 1920s, Fitzgerald was becoming more interested in nostalgia as a fictional subject. Of the group of stories which reflect this concern, 'The Last of the Belles' . . . is very much the best. Superficially, it seems a mere reworking of some of his most familiar romantic properties—the War, the wayward aristocratic Southern girl, and the Northern suitor whom she rejects. In fact, however, he brings a more complex attitude, and a greater subtlety of narrative method to these materials than anywhere else except in *Gatsby*.

The design of 'The Last of the Belles' is like a woven fabric, with threads which go this way and that. The long threads of the warp are provided by its extended development in time. It tells the story of a beautiful Southern girl, Ailie Calhoun—how she is gradually transformed from a Southern belle of the old-fashioned type into a flapper of the later Jazz Age. At the same time, it conveys a sense of the more general changes in American manners which have formed the background to her career. More important still, it is the history of one man's dreams, of the narrator's growing nostalgia for the lost romance of his youth. The cross threads of the woof are woven into the story by the action of the narrator's own voice—his ironic and yet absorbed commentary upon all the changing elements of the situation. (pp. 81-2)

The narrator is saved from sentimental fatuity by his ironic self-awareness: he sees clearly that, in his infatuation with Ailie, genuine romance and tawdry illusion are inextricably mingled. Nevertheless, he achieves a fine balance in his feelings towards her: he is prepared to love her in spite of her defects—indeed, he realizes that he finds her defects an integral part of her charm. He regards with amused regret the very quirk of character which leads her to reject him. Throughout their acquaintance, he is puzzled by her insistence that her admirers should be 'sincere': it intrigues him that she should value a quality which she herself so evidently lacks, but at last he grasps what she means. In spite of her air of being an 'instinctive thoroughbred', she too has an accurate sense of her own deficiencies, and cannot believe that any man who sees them can really love her. . . . The complexity of attitude which makes the narrator interesting to us, is the very trait which renders him forever untrustworthy to her. (pp. 83-4)

Between 1920 and 1924, Fitzgerald lived almost continuously in New York or within commuting distance of it, and during this period the nature of his understanding of city life changed profoundly: in 'May Day' he had shown the insight of the brilliant outsider, but by the time he wrote 'The Rich Boy' in 1926, he possessed the deepened awareness of the settled resident. None of the characters in the earlier story actually belong to New York, and they experience only those sensations which are accessible to the casual visitor or the tourist. But Anson Hunter, the hero of 'The Rich Boy', is an entrenched member of the city's upper class, and his life is an expression of its underlying structure, not its glittering surface. (p. 84)

This is still substantially the world of *The House of Mirth* and *The Custom of the Country*: Anson Hunter, just like the Trenors, Dorsets and Van Degens of Edith Wharton's novels, owes his wealth, position and manners to the Gilded Age. Fitzgerald's narrative style, too, is remarkably close to Mrs Wharton's—indeed this seems to me a case where one can reasonably speak of a direct influence upon his work. As a rule, the most distinctive quality in his writing is the constant delicate play of atmospheric and poetic suggestion, but what impresses one particularly in 'The Rich Boy' is the sustained pressure of a fine moral intelligence. The tone is dispassionate, sober, analytical; it does not rise to high points of climactic intensity or wit, and so, unlike most of Fitzgerald's writing, it is not especially quotable. . . . Fitzgerald maintains this tone, with its carefully judged inflections of irony and sympathetic insight, throughout the story—a degree of artistic control which is unique in his short fiction.

The character of Anson Hunter is Fitzgerald's one unquestioned success in portraying the sophisticated Eastern rich. As a possible American aristocrat, Anson is a failure, but his inadequacies lurk beneath the surface of an apparently flawless good form. In this respect, it is interesting to contrast him with rich Middle Westerners like Tom Buchanan and Baby Warren: he could never be guilty of their crude and frequent lapses—Tom's outbreaks of uncouth violence, Baby's rudeness and her tantrums. Even his coarseness is of a subtler kind than Tom's. Tom's affair with Myrtle Wilson is merely sordid—it represents the breakdown of a style. Anson's gentlemanly dissipations, on the other hand—the ritualized college drunkenness he keeps up with his Yale Club friends, and his adventures with 'the gallant chorus girls'—are the expression of a style; he knows how to choose women of a certain class for a party, how much to spend on them, and how to get rid of them.

The essence of his failure lies still deeper, however, in that complex area where the psychology of an individual and the manners of a class become alternative expressions of the same situation. Fitzgerald believed that people who possess enormous wealth, particularly wealth acquired in an earlier generation, constitute a distinct psychological and moral type. . . . This inbred sense of superiority does not make Anson in any simple sense arrogant or snobbish: it is, rather, the basis of his cynicism and his indifference. Life has given him so much already, that he cannot believe that any of the remaining prizes are worth a serious effort. (pp. 84-6)

Anson finds himself increasingly alone with his own sense of superiority, and his story broadens into a further chapter in Fitzgerald's history of the Jazz Age. His class, the pseudo-aristocracy of the Gilded Age, are being rapidly engulfed in the [postwar decade's] onward rush of new conditions. When his father dies, Anson is disconcerted to find that the family isn't even particularly rich by current standards; and he is dismayed when his younger sisters insist on selling up the baronial country estate in Connecticut, which they regard as an irrelevance and a bore. His Yale Club cronies get married and disappear one by one, either to live abroad, or to settle into the new and unassuming style of domesticity which, even for the rich, has replaced the portentous splendours to which Anson is accustomed. One hot Saturday afternoon in New York, he finds himself a stranger and alone, in the city which once belonged, by dynastic right, to the Hunters and a handful of other leading families. As he gazes up at the windows of one of his clubs, he catches sight of a solitary old man, staring vacantly into the street. It is a portent of the future, an image of the isolation and neglect which await a man whose habits of thought and feeling no longer have any relation to the society he lives in.

But, although Anson's feelings of superiority are not supported by any external social reality, they are still psychologically necessary to him. At the end of the story, he leaves New York, the city which has forgotten him and his family, for a vacation in Europe. As soon as he boards the liner, he begins a flirtation with the most attractive girl on the ship, and it becomes clear that the admiration of women is his one remaining resource; only by making them respond to him and love him can he sustain a little of his accustomed sense of himself.

Anson Hunter's life in New York ends with his departure for Europe. Countless well-to-do Americans were to make the same journey by the end of the 1920s, as Paris and the Riviera, rather than New York, became the setting for the most extravagant manifestations of the Jazz Age. In Fitzgerald's fiction, this shift is reflected not only in *Tender is the Night,* but in an important group of short stories. (pp. 86-7)

[Impaired] or broken marriages are an important element in all of Fitzgerald's best international stories. **'One Trip Abroad'** . . . traces the gradual deterioration of Nelson and Nicole Kelly's relationship during a period of four years' travel overseas. Fitzgerald put the story together from a discarded early version of *Tender*

is the Night, and in both works, his sense of place is always made to serve a dramatic purpose or to strengthen his moral and social analysis—he is never merely picturesque or anecdotal. (pp. 89-90)

As in all Fitzgerald's best short stories, the form of **'One Trip Abroad'** is a particularly felicitous expression of the underlying structural necessities of its subject. Its episodes succeed each other like a series of moral tableaux—a kind of Jazz Age *Rake's Progress*—and within the broad canvas of each picture, there are striking vignettes, the excellent satirical sketches of minor expatriate types. Count Chiki Sarolai, the exiled Austrian nobleman who sponges on rich Americans in Paris, is a well observed case of the aristocratic confidence man. Better still are Mr and Mrs Liddell Miles, a pair of professional cosmopolitans, who turn even their ignorance and boredom into a pretext for feeling superior to their fellow travelers.

The expatriate life portrayed in . . . **'One Trip Abroad'** came to an end with singular abruptness: within a year of the Wall Street Crash of 1929, the swarms of Americans with their millions of dollars had vanished from the European scene. The opening pages of **'Babylon Revisited'** . . . are an evocation of the silence and emptiness in the Ritz bar, which had been filled only a year or so earlier with a shouting drunken crowd. When Charlie Wales asks the barman for news of old friends, the latter responds with a litany of ghosts—the names of men who have lost their health, their reason or their money. Later that same evening, he wanders through the city like a man in a state of shock, recognizing everything he sees and yet not feeling a part of it. He looks in at a Montmartre night club which had been one of his favourite haunts back in the 1920s. It is as quiet as the grave, but at his appearance, it explodes into a grotesque semblance of gaiety: the band starts to play; a couple of employees masquerading as patrons leap to their feet and begin to dance; and the manager rushes up to assure him that the evening crowd is about to arrive. In this macabre image of the unfamiliarity of the familiar, Fitzgerald conveys the first shock of the Depression more effectively than any other American writer. (pp. 90-1)

In many ways, as this account indicates, **'Babylon Revisited'** is a simple story, and its strength lies in its simplicity. Like a lyric poem or a folksong, it deals directly with deep and powerful emotions: a father's love for his daughter, the ugliness of family quarrels, the disturbing way in which ghosts may return from a seemingly buried past. In one important respect, however, the story is extremely subtle—in its treatment of the psychology of disaster and the nature of recovery. For Charlie, the suddenness of the Depression has produced a sense of dislocation, a feeling that he is living in two worlds at once: he is committed to the idea of recovery and to the new way of life he has painstakingly created, but he still clings half-consciously to many of the mental habits which he formed during the Boom. . . . Charlie's personal experience is a distillation of the social history of the age: during the period of economic chaos which followed the stock market collapse, President Hoover became notorious for his facile promise that recovery was 'just around the corner'; but Fitzgerald understood, with his usual fine instinct for the spirit of the age, that the Depression was going to last a long time. (pp. 91-2)

Most of the stories I have discussed so far deal with members of the leisure class, but during the 1930s Fitzgerald became increasingly concerned with people whose lives must be measured in terms of professional dedication or creative achievement. This is apparent in his novels—Dick Diver is a doctor and Monroe Stahr a film producer—and is also reflected in some of his stories. In these, the main characters are usually artists or entertainers, and the principal theme often arises from Fitzgerald's sense of the dual nature of the artist. . . . (p. 92)

Fitzgerald's best stories between 1920 and 1932 convey an overall impression of consistency rather than change. There are shifts of emphasis in his choice of subject matter, but few fundamental departures from the concerns already apparent in **'May Day'** and **'Absolution'**. From this point of view, his international stories are not so much an innovation as a variation within the pattern of his understanding of the Jazz Age. Similarly, his attitude to the form of the short story remains substantially the same, even though he made enormous advances (particularly in the earliest years of his professional career) in his mastery of fictional technique. But after 1932 the nature of his short fiction changed radically. (p. 95)

The most strikingly novel characteristic of these tales is how short they are—often no more than five or six pages. In the main, this was undoubtedly a response to . . . new commercial pressures . . . , and in particular to the fact that, after 1936, the main outlet for Fitzgerald's work was *Esquire,* whose editor preferred short pieces, and in any case paid such small fees that there was no incentive to write at length. These *Esquire* stories, however, are far from being mere truncated versions of Fitzgerald's earlier tales. They represent a fundamentally new approach on his part to the problem of short-story form, in which he was led to adopt a position very close to that of the modernist writers and critics. Like them, he now appeared to prefer the form of the sketch or episode, as practised by Chekhov and Joyce, Sherwood Anderson and Hemingway. This type of story is compressed and oblique; it relies on poetic evocation or outright symbolism, it eliminates authorial intervention and dispenses with fictional narrators; its rhetorical mode implies an attitude of complete objectivity. Joyce's 'Clay', Anderson's 'Hands', and Hem-

ingway's 'Hills Like White Elephants' are particularly clear examples. A number of Fitzgerald's most successful late stories conform to this pattern.

In subject matter, the contrast with his earlier fiction is less clear-cut . . . , stories like **'Three Hours Between Planes'** and **'News of Paris—Fifteen Years Ago'** carry forward old preoccupations into the new form. Nevertheless, there is one important development which it is impossible not to associate with his crack-up—a group of tales which deal with personal disaster and unhappiness, alcoholism, mental illness, psychological trauma, broken marriages, the sense of failure, and the increasing loneliness and declining vitality of middle age.

'Afternoon of an Author' . . . the best of all these stories, gives an almost unbearably painful sense of the author's exhaustion, discouragement and loneliness after some unspecified illness or breakdown. . . . Because of the dry, ironic impersonality and wit of its narrative style, this sketch does not have a trace of the self-pity and exhibitionism which frequently disfigure the crack-up essays.

In **'Afternoon of an Author'** (and other similar late stories), the extent to which Fitzgerald's attention is directed towards the inner, psychological condition of his characters has an interesting effect upon his treatment of the outer social reality which surrounds them. Here it is convenient to make use of an image from the story itself: as the author rides downtown, the overhanging branches of trees brush against the windows of the bus, and, in the same way, random impressions of the city flicker across his mind in vivid but unstable succession. In his shaky mental state, the disintegration within seems matched by fragmentation without. The real significance and value of this new way of looking at social life, however, is that it represents much more than simply the reflection of a sick mind. It corresponds very closely with Fitzgerald's conviction that the solid fabric of American wealth and American manners which he had made imaginatively his own, had collapsed in the Crash of 1929 leaving only shattered memories behind. He makes this view explicit in **'My Lost City'** and **'Babylon Revisited'**, and his late stories—**'The Lost Decade'**, **'Financing Finnegan'**, **'Afternoon of an Author'** itself—are filled with the reverberations of a vanished era. The new impressionistic technique which he began to develop in the last named of these, was admirably suited to the exploration of the unstable consciousness and shifting reality of recent American conditions. . . . (pp. 95-7)

There are several other excellent late stories—for example, [**'I Didn't Get Over,' 'An Alcoholic Case,'** and **'The Lost Decade'**] . . .—but there is one, **'Financing Finnegan'** . . . , which has a special interest. It reflects obliquely on those personal problems in the life of an author which became pressing for Fitzgerald after his crack-up, but its main concern brings us back full circle to the point where we began—to a renewed awareness of Fitzgerald's conflicting ideas about the artist's role. Finnegan himself, the hero of the story, is pre-eminently the artist as conqueror: half wayward genius and half confidence man, he rises superior to the conventions of professional reliability, financial probity and sexual morality, but does undeniably produce on occasion work which is incomparably fine. He never appears in person, but his mysterious doings, magnified by hearsay, are relayed to us through the conversations of his agent and publisher, who have invested so much in him in the form of loans and advances, that they have come to regard him with a mixture of infatuation and dread. The whole situation is described, with ironic disapproval, by a narrator who is in every way Finnegan's antithesis, a sober hard-working professional writer who possesses all the good qualities that Finnegan lacks, and is at the same time without a trace of the latter's genuine distinction. By pushing these alternative possibilities to the extreme, Fitzgerald is able to create a story which is at once a brilliant farce in the manner of **'News of Paris—Fifteen Years Ago',** and something more—a uniquely clearsighted view of the disturbing cross currents always present in his conception of art.

Indeed from several points of view, **'Financing Finnegan'** is a good story with which to conclude a discussion of Fitzgerald's short fiction. Like so many of the other tales we have considered, it shows his consummate skill at blending the social with the individual: Finnegan's obscure difficulties are set against the wider context of the Depression, and the problematic nature of recovery acquires a double sense. Above all, this story gives evidence of the strong element of continuity in Fitzgerald's development, his ability to keep returning to certain themes with a fresh awareness of their potentialities; and at the same time his adaptability, the way in which he could always respond creatively to new conditions both in his professional work and in the social life around him. (p. 97)

Brian Way, in his *F. Scott Fitzgerald and the Art of Social Fiction,* St. Martin's, 1980, 171 p.

SOURCES FOR FURTHER STUDY

Bruccoli, Matthew J. *Some Sort of Epic Grandeur: The Life of F. Scott Fitzgerald.* New York: Harcourt Brace Jovanovich, 1981, 624 p.

    Complete and highly informative biography.

Bryer, Jackson R., ed. *F. Scott Fitzgerald: The Critical Reception.* New York: Burt Franklin, 1978, 386 p.

    Anthology of a broad range of reviews of Fitzgerald's work, including essays by H. L. Mencken.

Kazin, Alfred, ed. *F. Scott Fitzgerald: The Man and His Work.* New York: Collier Books, 1962, 221 p.

    Collection of critical essays by such literary figures and scholars as Gertrude Stein, John Peale Bishop, Edmund Wilson, and T. S. Eliot.

Lockridge, Ernest H., ed. *Twentieth-Century Interpretations of "The Great Gatsby": A Collection of Critical Essays.* Englewood Cliffs, N.J.: Prentice-Hall, 1968, 119 p.

    Collection of writings about *The Great Gatsby,* including essays on the novel's themes and narrative strategies.

Mizener, Arthur. *The Far Side of Paradise: A Biography of F. Scott Fitzgerald.* Boston: Riverside Press, 1951, 362 p.

    First significant biography of Fitzgerald, written by one of the preeminent scholars of Fitzgerald's work.

Turnbull, Andrew. *Scott Fitzgerald.* New York: Charles Scribner's Sons, 1962, 364 p.

    The definitive Fitzgerald biography.

Gustave Flaubert

1821-1880

French novelist, short story writer, and dramatist.

INTRODUCTION

*T*he most influential French novelist of the nineteenth century, Flaubert is remembered primarily for the stylistic precision and dispassionate rendering of psychological detail found in his masterpiece, *Madame Bovary* (1857). Although his strict objectivity is often associated with the realist and naturalist movements, he objected to this classification, and his artistry indeed defies such easy categorization. Flaubert struggled throughout his career to overcome a romantic tendency toward lyricism, fantastic imaginings, and love of the exotic past. A meticulous craftsman, he aimed to achieve a prose style "as rhythmical as verse and as precise as the language of science."

Flaubert was born in Rouen, where his father was chief surgeon and clinical professor at the city hospital, the Hôtel Dieu, and his mother was a well-known woman from a provincial bourgeois family. Flaubert lived with his parents, brother Achille, and sister Caroline in an apartment at the hospital. As a youth he attended the Collège Royal de Rouen, traveled with his family throughout France, and spent summer vacations at Trouville. It was in Trouville that he first met Maria-Elisa Schlésinger, a married woman for whom he harbored a lifelong infatuation and who deeply influenced the character and direction of his third novel, *L'éducation sentimentale* (1870; *Sentimental Education*). Although Flaubert was interested in literature and began to write at an early age, upon receiving his baccalaureate he honored his parents' wishes and reluctantly began law school in Paris. In 1844 his studies were disrupted when he experienced the first attack of what is now believed to have been epilepsy. As a result, he abandoned his plans for a law career and devoted himself to writing. Both his father and sister died in 1846, and the author, his mother, and his infant niece moved to the family home at Croisset, near Rouen. Except for several trips abroad and to Paris, including one to the city in 1848 to observe the February Revolution "from the point of view of art," Flaubert remained at Croisset until his death.

The genesis of *Madame Bovary* is well known. In 1849, Flaubert completed the first version of *La tentation de Saint Antoine* (published 1874; *The Temptation of Saint Antony*), a novel inspired by a painting by Pieter Brueghel the elder. After reading the novel aloud to his friends Maxime Du Camp and Louis Bouilhet, Flaubert asked for their frank opinion. They declared the work a failure, saying, "We think you should throw it into the fire, and never speak of it again." According to Du Camp and Bouilhet, the subject of Saint Antony was an unfortunate choice because it encouraged Flaubert's tendency toward excessive lyricism and lack of precision, and they persuaded him to abandon historical subjects and begin a novel that would be contemporary in content and realistic in intent. In his *Souvenirs littéraires,* Du Camp contended that he then told Flaubert a true story about a local provincial couple. The wife, having disgraced herself within the community by incurring large debts and taking a lover, committed suicide; her husband, a doctor, killed himself soon after. In addition to Du Camp's commentary, scholars note several other sources that may have provided the inspiration for *Madame Bovary.* After Flaubert's death, a manuscript entitled *Mémories de Mme Ludovica* was found among his papers. This work is purportedly an autobiography of Louise Pradier, wife of the painter James Pradier and a friend of Flaubert, and some critics see in the events of her life a resemblance to the story of Emma Bovary. Others deny that Flaubert modeled his story after any specific source, pointing to his declaration, "Madame Bovary, c'est moi," or, Madame Bovary is myself. Because his letters demonstrate a fascination with stories of aspiring and frustrated women and because several early unpublished works include themes and prototypes of characters that appear in *Madame Bovary,* many conclude that Flaubert's imagination was in fact the primary source for the novel.

Often described as a satire on romantic beliefs and the provincial bourgeoisie, *Madame Bovary* relates the story of Emma Bovary, a bored housewife whose dreams of romantic love, primarily gathered from popular novels, are unfulfilled by her marriage to a simple country doctor. She attempts to realize her fantasies through love affairs with a local landowner and a law clerk, and later through extravagant purchases. Unable to pay her debts and unwilling to bear her disgrace or conform to bourgeois values, she commits suicide. This novel, Flaubert's first to be published despite years of writing and several completed manuscripts, initially appeared in installments in *La Revue de Paris.* Although serious critics immediately recognized in *Ma-*

dame Bovary a work of immense significance, the French government censored publication of the *Revue.* Flaubert, his printer, and his publisher were tried together for blasphemy and offending public morals. All were eventually acquitted, and both Flaubert and *Madame Bovary* acquired a certain notoriety. Flaubert came to resent the fame of *Madame Bovary,* which completely overshadowed his later works, saying he wished to buy all the copies, "throw them into the fire and never hear of the book again."

After *Madame Bovary,* Flaubert sought a new subject which would be far from the bourgeois provincial setting over which he had labored so long. Once again turning to the past, he traveled to Carthage to gather material for *Salammbô* (1863), a historical novel whose exotic subject matter and opulent setting are reminiscent of the romantic tradition but whose descriptive technique is rigorously objective. In 1859, well into the writing of *Salammbô,* he wrote to Ernest Feydeau: "The deeper I plunge into antiquity, the more I feel the need to do something modern, and inside my head I'm cooking up a whole crew of characters." Commentators agree that this "crew of characters" ultimately became the cast of *Sentimental Education.*

Beginning in 1840, *Sentimental Education* gives an account of Frédéric Moreau, an unenthusiastic law student in Paris. For years he has been in love with Madame Arnoux (believed to have been modeled on Schlésinger), a married woman he met by chance when he was eighteen. Madame Arnoux introduces him to a courtesan, Rosanette. He courts both women, but initially neither accepts his advances. Frédéric attempts to lure Madame Arnoux to his apartment by deception, but her son's illness forestalls the plan. As the February Revolution of 1848 rages in the streets, the angered Frédéric turns to Rosanette, with whom he then lives for a time. Later he takes a second lover, the rich and aristocratic Madame Dambreuse. On 2 December 1851, the day of Louis Napoleon's coup d'état, Frédéric learns that the Arnoux are bankrupt and that they have left Paris. Immediately, in apparent loyalty to the woman he desires most, he leaves his two lovers; but he does not go to Madame Arnoux. Nearly sixteen years pass before she visits him in March 1867. The two recall past times and walk in the streets of Paris before parting. As the novel concludes, Frédéric and his friend Deslauriers sit together and remember the dreams and companions of their youth.

Flaubert was tormented by doubts about *Sentimental Education.* While he intended to sketch bourgeois characters, he scorned the bourgeoisie and feared his readers would too. He also doubted his ability to depict the characters effectively. Flaubert's many misgivings about *Sentimental Education* were realized immediately after the work's publication. Critics derided the book: they accused him, as they had with *Ma-*

dame Bovary, of baseness and vulgarity; questioned his morality; attacked the novel's descriptive passages as tedious and redundant; deplored the absence of a strong hero; labeled the narrative awkward and disjointed; resented Flaubert's exposure of illusions held dear about the political events of 1848; and even claimed that Flaubert had lost forever what literary skills he may have once possessed. The reviews were so negative, in fact, that Flaubert suspected he was the victim of a plot to defame him. Yet modern scholars generally agree that the explanation is much simpler: most readers were not ready for what appeared to them to be a novel in which subject, plot, and character were merely background features, and few could easily bear its despairing tone and bleak atmosphere. Although not as well known or as widely read as *Madame Bovary*, *Sentimental Education* is currently regarded as one of his greatest achievements, both for its commentary on French life in the nineteenth century and for what it reveals, through its autobiographical content, about one of the greatest writers of France.

Flaubert was burdened in his last years by financial difficulties and personal sorrow resulting from the deaths of his mother and several close friends. He was also saddened by the feeling that his works were generally misunderstood. However, he enjoyed close friendships with many prominent contemporaries including George Sand, Ivan Turgenev, Henry James and Guy de Maupassant; the latter served as his literary apprentice. A complex personality, obsessed with his art, Flaubert is perhaps best understood through his voluminous *Correspondance* (published 1894-99). In these candid and spontaneous letters, Flaubert chronicles his developing literary philosophy and the meticulous research and writing of his works. Although some critics fault his pessimism, cold impersonality, and ruthless objectivity, it is universally acknowledged that Flaubert developed, through painstaking attention to detail and constant revision, an exquisite prose style which has served as a model for innumerable writers. Today, commentators consistently acknowledge Flaubert's contribution to the development of the novel, lauding *Madame Bovary* as one of the most important forces in creating the modern novel as a conscious art form. Recognized for its objective characterization, irony, narrative technique, and use of imagery and symbolism, *Madame Bovary* is almost universally hailed as Flaubert's masterpiece.

(For further information about Flaubert's life and works, see *Nineteenth-Century Literature Criticism*, Vols. 2, 10, 19.)

CRITICAL COMMENTARY

HENRY JAMES

(essay date 1902)

[James was an American-born English novelist, short story writer, critic, and essayist. As a young man, he travelled extensively throughout Great Britain and Europe; in France, where he lived for several years, he was part of the literary circle that included Emile Zola, Edmond de Goncourt, Guy de Maupassant, and Gustave Flaubert. In the following excerpt from his introduction to a 1902 edition of *Madame Bovary*, he discusses the novel's relationship to romanticism and realism and comments on its style.]

[Flaubert's] imagination was great and splendid; in spite of which, strangely enough, his masterpiece is not his most imaginative work. *Madame Bovary*, beyond question, holds that first place, and *Madame Bovary* is concerned with the career of a country doctor's wife in a petty Norman town. The elements of the picture are of the fewest, the situation of the heroine almost of the meanest, the material for interest—considering the interest yielded—of the most unpromising; but these facts only throw into relief one of those incalculable phenomena that attend the proceedings of genius. *Madame Bovary* was doomed, by circumstances and causes—the freshness of comparative youth and good faith on the author's part being perhaps the chief—definitely to take its position, even though its subject were fundamentally a negation of the remote, the magnificent and the strange, the stuff of his fondest and most characteristic dreams. It would have seemed very nearly to have excluded the play of the imagination, and the way this faculty of Flaubert's nevertheless comes in is one of those accidents, manoeuvres, inspirations—we hardly know what to call them—by which masterpieces are made. He, of course, knew more or less what he was doing for his book in making Emma Bovary a victim of the imaginative habit, but he must have been far from designing or measuring that total effect which renders the work so general, so complete, an expression of himself. His separate idiosyncrasies, his irritated sensibility to the life about him, with the power to catch it in the fact and hold it hard, and his hunger for style and history and poetry, for the rich and the rare, are here represented together as they are not in his later writings. . . . M. Faguet has, of course, excellently noted this—that the fortune and felicity of the book were assured by the stroke that made the central figure an embodiment of helpless romanticism. Flaubert himself but narrowly escaped, after all, being such an embodiment, and he is thus able to express the romantic mind with extraordinary truth. As to the rest of the matter, he had the luck of having been, from the first, in possession; having begun so early to nurse and elaborate his plan that, familiarity and the native air, the native soil, aiding, he had finally made out, to the last lurking shade, the small, sordid, sunny, dusty village-picture, with its emptiness constituted and peopled. It is in the background and the accessories that the real—the real of his theme—abides; and the romantic—the romantic of his theme—accordingly occupies the front. Emma Bovary's poor adventures are a tragedy for the very reason that, in a world unsuspecting, unassisting, unconsoling, she has herself to distil the rich and the rare. Ignorant, unguided, undiverted, ridden by the very nature of her consciousness, she makes of the business an inordinate failure, a failure which, in its turn, makes for Flaubert the most elaborate, the most *told* of anecdotes. (pp. xiii-xv)

And yet it is not, after all—and here comes in the curiosity of the matter—that the place the book has taken is so overwhelmingly explained by its inherent dignity. Here comes in especially its fund of admonition for alien readers. The dignity of its matter is the

dignity of Mme. Bovary herself as a vessel of experience—a question as to which, unmistakably, I judge, we can only depart from the consensus of French critical opinion. M. Faguet, for example, praises the character of the heroine as one of the most seized and rendered figures of women in all literature, praises it as a field for the display of the romantic spirit that leaves nothing to be desired. Subject to an observation that I shall presently make and that bears heavily, in general, I think, on Flaubert as a painter of life—subject to this restriction he is right; which is a proof that a work of art may be markedly challengeable and yet be perfect, and that when it is perfect nothing else particularly matters. *Madame Bovary* has a perfection that not only stamps it, but that makes it stand almost alone; it holds itself with such a supreme, unapproachable assurance as both excites and defies judgment. For it deals not in the least—as to unapproachability—with things exalted or refined; it only confers on its sufficiently vulgar substance a final, unsurpassable form. The form is *in itself* as interesting, as active, as much of the essence of the subject as the idea, and yet so close is its fit and so inseparable its life that we catch it at no moment on any errand of its own. That, verily, is to be genuine and whole. The work is a classic because the thing, such as it is, is ideally *done,* and because it shows that in such doing eternal beauty may dwell. A pretty young woman who lives, socially and morally speaking, in a hole, and who is ignorant, foolish, flimsy, unhappy, takes a pair of lovers by whom she is successively deserted; in the midst of which, giving up her husband and her child, letting everything go, she sinks deeper into duplicity, debt, despair, and arrives on the spot, on the small scene itself of her poor depravities, at a pitiful, tragic end. She does these things, above all, while remaining absorbed in the romantic vision, and she remains absorbed in the romantic vision while fairly rolling in the dust. That is the triumph of the book, as the triumph stands—that Emma interests us by the nature of her consciousness and the play of her mind, thanks to the reality and the beauty with which these things are invested. It is not only that they represent *her* state; they are so true, so observed, so felt, and especially so shown, that they represent the state, actual or potential, of all persons like her—persons romantically determined. Then her setting, the medium in which she struggles, becomes in its way as important, becomes eminent with the eminence of art; the tiny world in which she revolves, the contracted cage in which she flutters, is hung out in space for us, and her companions in captivity there are as true as herself.

I have said enough to show . . . [that Flaubert has], in this picture, expressed something of his intimate self, given his heroine something of his own imagination: a point, precisely, that brings me back to the restriction at which I just now hinted, in which M.

Faguet fails to indulge and yet which is immediate for the alien reader. Emma Bovary, in spite of the nature of her consciousness and in spite of her reflecting so much of that of her creator, is really too small an affair. That, critically speaking, is, in view both of the value and the fortune of her history, the wonderful circumstance. She associates herself with Frédéric Moreau in *L'Education* to suggest for us a question that can be answered, I hold, only to Flaubert's detriment. Emma taken alone would possibly not so directly press it; but, in her company, the hero of our author's second study of the "real" drives it home. Why did Flaubert choose, as special conduits of the life he proposed to depict, such inferior, and in the case of Frédéric such abject, human specimens? I insist only in respect to the latter—the perfection of *Madame Bovary* scarce leaving one much warrant for wishing anything different; even here, however, the general scale and size of Emma, who is small even of her sort, should be a warning to hyperbole. If I say that in the matter of Frédéric, at all events, the answer is inevitably detrimental, I mean that it weighs heavily on our author's general credit. He wished in each case to make a picture of experience—middling experience, it is true—and of the world close to him; but if he imagined nothing better for his purpose than such a heroine and such a hero, we are forced to believe it to have been by a defect of his mind. And that sign of weakness remains even if it be objected that the images in question were addressed to his purpose better than others would have been: the purpose itself then shows as inferior. (pp. xvii-xx)

Madame Bovary, subject to whatever qualification, is absolutely the most literary of novels—so literary that it covers us with its mantle. It shows us, once for all, that there is no *intrinsic* need of a debasement of the type. The mantle I speak of is wrought with surpassing fineness, and we may always—under stress of whatever charge of illiteracy, frivolity, vulgarity—flaunt it as the flag of the guild. Let us therefore frankly concede that to surround Flaubert with our consideration is the least return we can make for such a privilege. The consideration, moreover, is idle unless it be real, unless it be intelligent enough to measure his effort and his success. Of the effort as mere effort I have already spoken—of the desperate difficulty involved for him in making his form square with his conception; and I by no means attach a general importance to these secrets of the workshop, which are but as the contortions of the fastidious muse, the servant of the oracle. They are really, rather, secrets of the kitchen and contortions of the priestess of *that* tripod—they are not an upstairs matter. It is of their specially distinctive importance I am now speaking, of the light shed on them by the results before us.

They all represent the pursuit of a style—of the right one, and they would still be interesting if the style

had not been achieved. *Madame Bovary, Salammbô, Saint-Antoine, L'Education,* are so written and so composed—though the last-named in a minor degree—that the more we look at them the more we find in them, in this kind, a beauty of intention and of effect; the more they form, in the too often dreary desert of fictive prose, a class by themselves, a little living oasis. So far as that desert is our own English—by which I of course also mean our own American—province, it supplies with remarkable rarity this particular source of relief. So strikingly is that the case that a critic betrayed at artless moments into advocating the claims of composition is apt to find himself as blankly met as if he were advocating the claims of trigonometry. . . . For signal examples of what composition, distribution, arrangement can do, of how they can intensify the life of a work of art, we have to go elsewhere; and the value of Flaubert for us is that he admirably points the moral. This is the great explanation of the "classic" fortune of *Madame Bovary* in especial, as well as an aspect of that work endlessly suggestive. (pp. xxvi-xxvii)

I speak from the point of view of his interest to a reader of his own craft, the point of view of his extraordinary technical wealth—though, indeed, when I think of the general power of *Madame Bovary* I find myself desiring not to narrow the ground of the lesson, not to connect it, to its prejudice, with the idea of the "technical," so abhorrent, in whatever art, to the Anglo-Saxon mind. Without proposing Flaubert as the type of the newspaper novelist, or as an easy alternative to golf or the bicycle, we should do him an injustice in failing to insist that a masterpiece like *Madame Bovary* may benefit by its roundness even with the simple-minded. It has that sign of all rare works that there is something in it for every one. It may be read ever so attentively, enjoyed ever so freely, without a suspicion of how it is written, to say nothing of put together; it may equally be read under the excitement of these perceptions alone. Both readers will have been transported—which is all any reader can ask. Leaving the former, however that may be, to state the case for himself, I state it yet again for the latter, if only on this final ground. The book and its companions represent for us a practical solution—Flaubert's own troubled yet settled one—of the eternal dilemma of the painter of life. From the moment the painter deals at all with life directly, his desire is not to deal with it stintedly. It at the same time remains true that from the moment he desires to produce forms in which it shall be preserved, he desires that these forms, things of *his* creation, shall not be ignoble. He must make them complete and beautiful, intrinsically interesting, under peril of disgrace. . . . The question, for the artist, can only be of doing the artistic utmost, and thereby of *seeing* the general task. When it is seen with the intensity with which it presented itself to Flaubert, a lifetime is none too much for fairly tackling it. It must either be left alone or be dealt with, and to leave it alone is a comparatively simple matter. (pp. xxxvi-xxxviii)

Henry James, "Gustave Flaubert," in *Madame Bovary* by Gustave Flaubert, translated by W. Blaydes, P. F. Collier & Son, 1902, pp. v-xliii.

PERCY LUBBOCK
(essay date 1921)

[Lubbock was an English critic whose views were greatly influenced by Henry James. Like James, he considered dramatic presentation, rather than authorial narration and description, the best of all means of narrative expression in novels. In the following excerpt, he examines Flaubert's narrative technique in *Madame Bovary*.]

[Flaubert's *Madame Bovary*] remains perpetually the novel of all novels which the criticism of fiction cannot overlook; as soon as ever we speak of the principles of the art, we must be prepared to engage with Flaubert. (p. 60)

Flaubert handles his material quite differently from point to point. Sometimes he seems to be describing what he has seen himself, places and people he has known, conversations he may have overheard; I do not mean that he is literally retailing an experience of his own, but that he writes as though he were. His description, in that case, touches only such matters as you or I might have perceived for ourselves, if we had happened to be on the spot at the moment. His object is to place the scene before us, so that we may take it in like a picture gradually unrolled or a drama enacted. But then again the method presently changes. There comes a juncture at which, for some reason, it is necessary for us to know more than we could have made out by simply looking and listening. Flaubert, the author of the story, must intervene with his superior knowledge. . . . And so, for a new light on the drama, the author recalls certain circumstances that we should otherwise have missed. Or it may be that he—who naturally knows everything, even the inmost, unexpressed thought of the characters—wishes us to share the mind of Bovary or of Emma, not to wait only on their words or actions; and so he goes below the surface, enters their consciousness, and describes the train of sentiment that passes there. (pp. 64-5)

Flaubert is generally considered to be a very "impersonal" writer, one who keeps in the background and desires us to remain unaware of his presence; he places the story before us and suppresses any comment of his own. But this point has been over-laboured, I should

say; it only means that Flaubert does not announce his opinion in so many words, and thence it has been argued that the opinions of a really artistic writer ought not to appear in his story at all. But of course with every touch that he lays on his subject he must show what he thinks of it; his subject, indeed, the book which he finds in his selected fragment of life, is purely the representation of his view, his judgement, his opinion of it. The famous "impersonality" of Flaubert and his kind lies only in the greater tact with which they express their feelings—dramatizing them, embodying them in living form, instead of stating them directly. (pp. 67-8)

It is a matter of method. Sometimes the author is talking with his own voice, sometimes he is talking *through* one of the people in the book—in this book for the most part Emma herself. Thus he describes a landscape, the trim country-side in which Emma's lot is cast, or the appearance and manners of her neighbours, or her own behaviour; and in so doing he is using his own language and his own standards of appreciation; he is facing the reader in person, however careful he may be to say nothing to deflect our attention from the thing described. He is making a reproduction of something that is in his own mind. And then later on he is using the eyes and the mind and the standards of another; the landscape has now the colour that it wears in Emma's view, the incident is caught in the aspect which it happens to turn towards her imagination. Flaubert himself has retreated, and it is Emma with whom we immediately deal. (p. 68)

Furthermore, whether the voice is that of the author or of his creature, there is a pictorial manner of treating the matter in hand and there is also a dramatic. It may be that the impression—as in the case of the marquis's ball—is chiefly given as a picture, the reflection of events in the mirror of somebody's receptive consciousness. The reader is not really looking *at* the occasion in the least, or only now and then; mainly he is watching the surge of Emma's emotion, on which the episode acts with sharp intensity. The thing is "scenic," in the sense in which I used the word just now; we are concerned, that is to say, with a single and particular hour, we are taking no extended, general view of Emma's experience. But though it is thus a *scene*, it is not dramatically rendered; if you took the dialogue, what there is of it, together with the actual things described, the people and the dresses and the dances and the banquets—took these and placed them on the stage, for a theatrical performance, the peculiar effect of the occasion in the book would totally vanish. Nothing could be more definite, more objective, than the scene is in the book; but there it is all bathed in the climate of Emma's mood, and it is to the nature of this climate that our interest is called for the moment. The lords and ladies are remote, Emma's envying and wondering excitement fills the whole of the foreground. (pp. 69-70)

In *Madame Bovary* the scenes are distributed and rendered with very rare skill; not one but seems to have more and more to give with every fresh reading of it. The ball, the *comices,* the evening at the theatre, Emma's fateful interview with Léon in the Cathedral of Rouen, the remarkable session of the priest and the apothecary at her deathbed—these form the articulation of the book, the scheme of its structure. To the next in order each stage of the story is steadily directed. By the time the scene is reached, nothing is wanting to its opportunity; the action is ripe, the place is resonant; and then the incident takes up the story, conclusively establishes one aspect of it and opens the view towards the next. And the more rapid summary that succeeds, with its pauses for a momentary sight of Emma's daily life and its setting, carries the book on once more to the climax that already begins to appear in the distance.

But the most obvious point of method is no doubt the difficult question of the centre of vision. With which of the characters, if with any of them, is the writer to identify himself, which is he to "go behind"? Which of these vessels of thought and feeling is he to reveal from within? . . . [Which] *is* the centre, which is the mind that really commands the subject? . . . In Flaubert's *Bovary* there could be no question but that we must mainly use the eyes of Emma herself; the middle of the subject is in her experience, not anywhere in the concrete facts around her. And yet Flaubert finds it necessary, as I said, to look *at* her occasionally, taking advantage of some other centre for the time being. . . . (pp. 73-5)

If Flaubert allows himself the liberty of telling his story in various ways—with a method, that is to say, which is often modified as he proceeds—it is likely that he has good cause to do so. . . . [At] first sight it does seem that his manner of arriving at his subject—if his subject is Emma Bovary—is considerably casual. He begins with Charles, of all people. . . . (p. 77)

[His subject] is of course Emma Bovary in the first place; the book is the portrait of a foolish woman, romantically inclined, in small and prosaic conditions. She is in the centre of it all, certainly; there is no doubt of her position in the book. But *why* is she there? . . . Given Emma and what she is by nature, given her environment and the facts of her story, there are dozens of different subjects, I dare say, latent in the case. (p. 78)

Now if Emma was devised for her own sake, solely because a nature and a temper like hers seemed to Flaubert an amusing study—if his one aim was to make the portrait of a woman of that kind—then the rest of the matter falls into line, we shall know how to regard it. These conditions in which Emma finds herself will have been chosen by the author because they appeared

to throw light on her, to call out her natural qualities, to give her the best opportunity of disclosing what she is. . . . If he had thought that a woman of her sort, rather meanly ambitious, rather fatuously romantic, would have revealed her quality more intensely in a different world—in success, freedom, wealth—he would have placed her otherwise. . . . Emma's world as it is at present, in the book that Flaubert wrote, would have to be regarded, accordingly, as all a *consequence* of Emma, invented to do her a service, described in order that they may make the description of *her.* . . . All this—*if* the subject of the book is nothing but the portrait of such a woman.

But of course it is not so; one glance at our remembrance of the book is enough to show it. Emma's world could not be other than it is, she could not be shifted into richer and larger conditions, without destroying the whole point and purpose of Flaubert's novel. She by herself is not the subject of his book. What he proposes to exhibit is the history of a woman like her in just such a world as hers, a foolish woman in narrow circumstances; so that the provincial scene, acting upon her, making her what she becomes, is as essential as she is herself. Not a portrait, therefore, not a study of character for its own sake, but something in the nature of a drama, where the two chief players are a woman on one side and her whole environment on the other—that is *Madame Bovary.* (pp. 79-80)

Obviously the emphasis is not upon the commonplace little events of Emma's career. They might, no doubt, be the steps in a dramatic tale, but they are nothing of the kind as Flaubert handles them. He makes it perfectly clear that his view is not centered upon the actual outcome of Emma's predicament, whether it will issue this way or that; *what* she does or fails to do is of very small moment. . . . The *events,* therefore, Emma's excursions to Rouen, her forest-rides, her one or two memorable adventures in the world, all these are only Flaubert's way of telling his subject, of making it count to the eye. They are not in themselves what he has to say, they simply illustrate it.

What it comes to, I take it, is that though *Madame Bovary,* the novel, is a kind of drama—since there is the interaction of this woman confronted by these facts—it is a drama chosen for the sake of the picture in it, for the impression it gives of the manner in which certain lives are lived. . . . Let Emma and her plight, therefore, appear as a picture; let her be shown in the act of living her life, entangled as it is with her past and her present; that is how the final fact at the heart of Flaubert's subject will be best displayed.

Here is the clue, it seems, to his treatment of the theme. It is pictorial, and its object is to make Emma's existence as intelligible and visible as may be. We who read the book are to share her sense of life, till no uncertainty is left in it; we are to see and understand her experience, and to see *her* while she enjoys or endures it; we are to be placed within her world, to get the immediate taste of it, and outside her world as well, to get the full effect, more of it than she herself could see. Flaubert's subject demands no less, if the picture is to be complete. She herself must be known thoroughly—that is his first care; the movement of her mind is to be watched at work in all the ardour and the poverty of her imagination. . . . And then there is the dull and limited world in which her appetite is somehow to be satisfied, the small town that shuts her in and cuts her off. . . . [Accordingly] Flaubert treats the scenery of his book, Yonville and its odd types, as intensely as he treats his heroine; he broods over it with concentration and gives it all the salience he can. (pp. 81-5)

Such is the picture that Flaubert's book is to present. And what, then, of the point of view towards which it is to be directed? . . . Where is Flaubert to find his centre of vision?—from what point, within the book or without, will the unfolding of the subject be commanded most effectively? . . . Part of his subject is Emma's sense of her world; we must see how it impresses her and what she makes of it, how it thwarts her and how her imagination contrives to get a kind of sustenance out of it. The book is not really written at all unless it shows her view of things, as the woman she was, in that place, in those conditions. For this reason it is essential to pass into her consciousness, to make her *subjective;* and Flaubert takes care to do so and to make her so, as soon as she enters the book. But it is also enjoined by the story, as we found, that her place and conditions should be seen for what they are and known as intimately as herself. For this matter Emma's capacity fails.

Her intelligence is much too feeble and fitful to give a sufficient account of her world. . . . Her pair of eyes is not enough; the picture beheld through them is a poor thing in itself, for she can see no more than her mind can grasp; and it does her no justice either, since she herself is so largely the creation of her surroundings. (pp. 85-6)

[The] poor creature cannot tell the story in full. A shift of the vision is necessary. And in *Madame Bovary,* it is to be noted, there is no one else within the book who is in a position to take up the tale when Emma fails. There is no other personage upon the scene who sees and understands any more than she; perception and discrimination are not to be found in Yonville at all—it is an essential point. The author's wit, therefore, and none other, must supply what is wanting. This necessity, to a writer of Flaubert's acute sense of effect, is one that demands a good deal of caution. The transition must be made without awkwardness, without calling attention to it. (p. 87)

[Flaubert deals with the difficulty] by keeping Emma always at a certain distance, even when he appears to be entering her mind most freely. He makes her subjective, places us so that we see through her eyes—yes; but he does so with an air of aloofness that forbids us ever to become entirely identified with her. . . . A hint of irony is always perceptible, and it is enough to prevent us from being lost in her consciousness, immersed in it beyond easy recall. The woman's life is very real, perfectly felt; but the reader is made to accept his participation in it as a pleasing experiment, the kind of thing that appeals to a fastidious curiosity—there is no question of its ever being more than this. The *fact* of Emma is taken with entire seriousness, of course; she is there to be studied and explored, and no means of understanding her point of view will be neglected. But her value is another matter; as to that Flaubert never has an instant's illusion, he always knows her to be worthless. (p. 89)

His irony, none the less, is close at hand and indispensable; he has a definite use for this resource and he could not forego it. His irony gives him perfect freedom to supersede Emma's limited vision whenever he pleases, to abandon her manner of looking at the world, and to pass immediately to his own more enlightened, more commanding height. (pp. 89-90)

[*Madame Bovary*] is a book that with its variety of method, and with its careful restriction of that variety to its bare needs, and with its scrupulous use of its resources—it is a book, altogether, that gives a good point of departure for an examination of the methods of fiction. (p. 92)

Percy Lubbock, in a chapter in his *The Craft of Fiction,* Jonathan Cape Ltd., 1921, pp. 59-92.

ALBERT THIBAUDET
(essay date 1935)

[Thibaudet was a French literary critic and follower of the French philosopher Henri Bergson. In the excerpt below, which originally appeared in French in his 1935 study *Gustave Flaubert*, he investigates Flaubert's handling of the theme of fate in *Madame Bovary.*]

In the years around 1850, so decisive in the history of the novel, an inner logic was developed within the novel, from Balzac to Flaubert, just as an inner logic took form in French tragedy from Corneille to Racine. The novels of Balzac are constructed novels, sometimes excessively so; his imagination always remained lit, like the fire in the Cyclops' smithies. Balzac was a novelist endowed with the same natural power that inspired

Corneille as a dramatist. But Flaubert set out from the antipodes of the Balzacian novel when he wrote the following sentence, one which would certainly have been endorsed by [Racine,] the author of *Berenice*: "I would like to write books in which I have only to write sentences, if I may say so, just as I have only to breathe in order to remain alive; I am bored by the subtleties of composition, by combinations aimed at effect, by all the calculations involved in the design, but which, nevertheless, are art, for style depends on these and on these alone." Spontaneity of conception remains for him the highest value. This spontaneity, which is that of Racine, not that of Corneille or Balzac, does not prevent him from carrying out all the demands of his art with consummate skill. With cold detachment, he performs the technical machinations which bore him to tears; for Balzac, they would have been an inherent part of the work from its very beginning, a part of the original organic idea. The technique of *Madame Bovary* has become a model for all novels, as that of [Racine's] *Andromache* is considered the model for all tragedies. (p. 372)

And yet, Flaubert himself had serious misgivings about the organization of his novel. . . .

I think that the book will have a serious weakness, namely the relative length of the parts. I already have 260 pages that contain only preparatory action . . . The conclusion, which will narrate the death of my heroine, her burial and the ensuing distress of the husband, will take at least 260 pages. This leaves only 120 to 160 pages for the action properly speaking.

In his own defense, he states that the book is

a biography, rather than a developed dramatic situation. It contains little action: if the dramatic element remains thoroughly immersed in the general tone of the work, the lack of proportion between the different episodes and their development is likely to remain unnoticed. Moreover, it seems to me that life itself is a little like that.

Flaubert's choice of vocabulary is quite revealing here. "Action" and "dramatic element" are used as closely synonymous with composition or organization; it seems that the novel can do without them precisely because it is unlike the theater. The theater abstracts and retains privileged moments, moments of crisis; as such, it is forced to compose and to organize: it must group the moments in such a way that a maximum of useful effort is contained in a minimum of time and space. The dramatist is governed by time, whereas the novelist controls it; he can cut an entire life out of the cloth of time, and do so at his own will. Flaubert's novel is not a "human comedy" like Balzac's, but a pure novel. (pp. 372-73)

[Like Charles Dickens's] *David Copperfield* or George

Eliot's *The Mill on the Floss*, *Madame Bovary* can be called a biography. But rather than the biography of one individual, it is a sequence of interrelated life histories. From a certain point of view, the individual biography which delimits the novel's dimension in time, is that of Charles Bovary, not Emma's. The book opens with his entrance into college—and with his cap—and it ends with his death.

To be more accurate, *Madame Bovary* seems to be a biography of human life in general rather than of a particular person. . . . To be human is to feel oneself as a conglomeration of possibilities, a multiplicity of potential personalities; the artist is the one who makes this potential real. It would take some effort to apply so general a truth to all characters in Flaubert's novel— such as, for instance, Charles Bovary. The first pages of the novel consist of memories from school-life. They are a first introduction into this complex world. . . . [From] the school scene on, which is like a summary of existence, Charles's entire life is prefigured. Without realizing it, Charles had already been selected as a mate by the Emma Flaubert who was going to drag him into the light of notoriety and make him part of an inseparable couple. (pp. 373-74)

Flaubert's novel is entirely contained between Charles Bovary's cap and his profound statement at the end, the only one he will ever pronounce, after which nothing is left for him to do but drop to the ground like a ripe apple: "Fate willed it this way!" Such is Charles's beginning and his end. In a page of his early travel impressions entitled *Along Fields and Sea Shores* Flaubert had already revealed his intention of writing the chapter on hats that is still missing in literature; the passage on Breton hats is a prelude to Charles's famous cap. With its "dumb ugliness that had depths of expression like an imbecile's face," the whole of Yonville-l'Abbaye is already contained in the cap. A miserable life, but a life just the same; the novel of a miserable life, but nevertheless a life, is being prepared to crown the forehead of the same child, whose name is not Charles but Legion. (p. 374)

This type of lyricism or, rather, of counterlyricism is very typical of Flaubert. It demands some preparation to be appreciated and many a reader approves it with misgivings. The detail of the hat is as essential as it is gratuitous—a proper definition, be it said in passing, of pure lyricism and of spontaneous symbolism as well. (p. 375)

The development of the action, in *Madame Bovary,* does not occur by a simple succession of events but by the concentric expansion of a theme, first encountered in its simplest form, then gradually gaining in richness and complexity. The process reflects the very motion of fate. We call "fated" a development that was already contained in a previous situation but without being apparent. We have a feeling of fatality when we feel that life was not worth living, because we have come back to exactly the same point from which we started, and discovered that the road which was to be one of discovery turns out to be the circular path of our prison walls.

And yet, this novel of fate is a novel of life and of hope.

When we consider these creatures as completed and unified destinies, their lives are indeed heart-rending failures; but all of them have known the sacred moments after which there can only be decline and preparation for the grave. Charles experiences it when, hidden in a cartload, he sees the signal announcing from the window of Rouault's farmhouse that he has been accepted. Emma experiences it in the early phases of her love for Rodolphe. Seen as a whole, the novel is not onesidedly pessimistic; dark and light are evenly marked. Flaubert has not reached the total desolation of *Bouvard and Pécuchet.* Tostes and Yonville are like two concentric circles. Tostes is a more empty and cursory image than Yonville. The transition from one town to another, from one form of existence in the Bovary household to another which is yet the same, is a masterpiece of subtle progression. Tostes resembles Yonville as a sketch resembles the final picture. Flaubert takes pains not to fill in the details of his earlier outline, yet all the earlier characteristics of Yonville are already there, albeit in the general and abstract outline, without proper names, like an architectural model. "Every day at the same time the schoolmaster in a black skullcap opened the shutters of his house, and the village policeman, wearing his sword over his blouse, passed by." The two nameless figures suffice here to express the routine of a small town. (pp. 375-76)

The end of the story at Tostes also ends the actual marital life of Madame Bovary. Since all the attention is concentrated on Emma and Charles's joint existence, no other characters are needed; Flaubert introduces none, except for the servant. Tostes is no stage on which things are happening; Flaubert uses it to show how Charles lives, sleeps, dresses, and eats, how he gets on his wife's nerves and depresses her. The first part closes when she throws her bridal bouquet in the fire. "She watched it burn . . . the little pasteboard berries burst. . . ."

This sketch is followed by the completed picture, the stage on which characters and events will appear. Tostes was the small town; Yonville too is the small town but it is Yonville as well. Tostes lost itself to become the typical small town, but now the small town mingles with the reality of Yonville and becomes this reality; it is the usual transubstantiation of art. This is why the second part begins with a detailed description of Yonville, in the manner of Balzac. The purpose is to create a genuine setting, to set the stage, not for a human comedy but for the comedy of human stupidity

and suffering. Flaubert goes about this task with a quiet and merciless thoroughness: the notary's house, the church, the townhall, and facing the Golden Lion Hotel, M. Homais' pharmacy with its red and green bocals, which shine in the evening like Bengal fires. The dinner at the Golden Lion follows the typical, perhaps all too typical, technique of exposition, as in Racine's *Bajazet:* all the inhabitants of Yonville are successively described from the point of view that reveals them most clearly, and Homais is allowed to dominate the scene. This is the chosen setting in which all the characters, and especially Emma, will come to light and their destinies unfold.

Emma passes with good reason for one of the most masterful portraits of a woman in fiction; the most living and the truest to life. "A masterpiece," [the French prelate] Dupanloup told Dumas, "yes, a true masterpiece, for those who have been confessors in the provinces." Flaubert substituted his artistic intuition for the confessor's experience; he would not have created this masterpiece if he hadn't identified with his heroine and shared her existence. He created her, not only out of the recollections of his own soul, but out of the recollections of his own flesh. She is never seen from the same distant and ironic viewpoint as the other characters in the book. Women are well aware of this and recognize in her their inner beauty and their inner suffering, as a man endowed with a noble imagination is bound to recognize himself in Don Quixote. (pp. 376-77)

Emma is a true heroine—unlike Sancho and Homais, who are counterheroes—because she has senses. In trying to explain the superiority of *Madame Bovary* over the *Sentimental Education,* Brunetière said [in *Le roman naturaliste*] that Emma's character represents something "stronger and more refined than the commonplace" without which there can not be a truly great novel. "In the nature of this woman, commonplace as she is, there is something extreme and, for that reason, rare. It is the refinement of her senses." There is nothing extreme or rare in any of the characters in the *Education.* But Faguet writes [in the same work]: "Mme. Bovary is not exactly a sensuous person; she is above all a 'romantic,' a mental type, as the psychologists would call it; her first fault stems from an unbridled imagination rather than from a lack of control over the senses. The reason for the first downfall is her desire to know love; in her second downfall, she is moved by the desire to give herself to the man she loves."

Brunetière is right, not Faguet. Emma is first and foremost a person of sensuous nature; she is like the artist in that she is endowed with an unusual degree of sensuality. This is why, as an artist, Flaubert can identify with her and assert: I myself am Mme. Bovary. Whenever Emma is seen in purely sensuous terms, he speaks of her with a delicate, almost religious feeling, the way Milton speaks of Eve. He relinquishes his cold and detached tone and shifts to a lyrical voice, indicating that the author is using the character as a substitute for himself. So, for instance, when she has first given herself to Rodolphe:

> The shades of night were falling: the horizontal sun passing between the branches dazzled the eyes. Here and there around her in the leaves or on the ground, trembled luminous patches, as if humming-birds flying about had scattered their feathers. Silence was everywhere; something sweet seemed to come forth from the trees. She felt her heartbeat return, and the blood coursing through her flesh like a river of milk. Then far away, beyond the wood, on the other hills, she heard a vague prolonged cry, a voice which lingered, and in silence she heard it mingling like music with the last pulsations of her throbbing nerves. Rodolphe, a cigar between his lips, was mending with his penknife one of the two broken bridles.

If the novel itself is like a substance in motion, then Emma is the one who is being carried by the flow of this stream. She is the stream, whereas Rodolphe is only another pebble among the stones deposited on the riverbanks.

Flaubert was able to forestall his own critics, and he rightly showed that "intelligent readers want their characters all of a piece and consistent, as they only appear in books." For him, to the contrary, "Ulysses is, perhaps, the strongest character-type in all ancient literature, and Hamlet in modern literature, because of their complexity. Mme. Bovary is not simple. Her sensuality is combined with a vulgar imagination and a considerable degree of naïveté—or, in other words, of stupidity. Flaubert needed a character of this kind to satisfy his poetical as well as his critical instinct, his sense of beauty as well as his taste for a sad, grotesque incongruity.

Emma, like Don Quixote, doesn't place her desire and the things she desires on the same plane. Emma's sensuous desire, like Don Quixote's generous fantasies, are in themselves magnificent realities in which Flaubert and Cervantes project the best part of themselves. They admire desire and abandonment, but they have contempt for the things desired, the miserable bottle that comes out of a ridiculous pharmacy. Neither have any illusions about the value of the object desired by the imagination, and one half of their artistic nature—the realist half—mercilessly paints these mediocre and derisive objects.

Apart from her sensuous desire, everything else about Emma is mediocre. Flaubert marks her with this terrible trait: "She was incapable of understanding what she did not experience, or of believing anything that did not take on a conventional form." At heart, she is still the Norman peasant, "callous, not very responsive to the emotions of others, like most people of peas-

ant stock whose souls always retain some of the coarseness of their father's hands."

She is more ardent than passionate. She loves life, pleasure, love itself much more than she loves a man; she is made to have lovers rather than a lover. It is true that she loves Rodolphe with all the fervor of her body, and with him she experiences the moment of her complete, perfect and brief fulfillment; her illness, however, after Rodolphe's desertion, is sufficient to cure her of this love. She does not die from love, but from weakness and a total inability to look ahead, a naïveté which makes her an easy prey to deceit in love as well as in business. She lives in the present and is unable to resist the slightest impulse. . . . The final stages of her life that will lead her to her death are strictly personal, limited to the injustice and the criminality of the solitary self. Flaubert's novel is as Jansenist in spirit as Racine's *Phèdre,* and he has treated Emma's death as a damnation. He has made the devil present in the figure of the blind man, the grimacing monster she glimpsed during her adulterous trips to Rouen, the beggar to whom she throws her last piece of silver, as a lost soul is cast to the devil by the act of suicide. She dies with an atrocious laugh of horror and despair, as she hears him singing under her window, "thinking she saw the hideous face of the poor wretch loom out of the eternal darkness like a menace." This symbol of damnation was certainly present in Flaubert's mind; he wrote to Bouilhet that the blind man had to be present at Emma's death and that, for that reason, he needed to invent the episode of Homais' ointment. Lamartine, who was greatly disturbed by *Madame Bovary,* told Flaubert that he found the end of the book revolting: the punishment greatly surpassed the crime. It is true that we are here in a very different mood than in *Jocelyn.*

The fact is that Lamartine, in *Jocelyn,* was delighting in himself, while Flaubert, in *Madame Bovary,* subjects himself to the most scathing self-criticism. Emma symbolizes the double illusion which he has only very recently overcome. First, the illusion that things change for the better in time, an illusion as necessary to life as water is to plants: "She did not believe that things could remain the same in different places, and since the portion of her life that lay behind her had been bad, no doubt that which remained to be lived would be better." Then, the same illusion in spatial terms: "The closer things were to her, the more her thoughts turned away from them. All her immediate surroundings, the boring countryside, the stupid petty bourgeois, the mediocrity of existence, seemed to her to be exceptions in the world, a particular fate of which she was the victim, while an immense domain of passion and happiness stretched out beyond, as far as the eye could reach." When she is in the convent, she dreams of the outside world; later, she will remember these schooldays as her only moments of true happiness, because at that time the entire world was still a blank page and her heart full of infinite possibilities. On returning home to her father, she can no longer cope with country life and she accepts Charles, the healthy doctor who rides around on horseback, merely because he represents the outside world. When she marries him, she dreams of other places. It is true then, after all, that she is Brunetière's sensuous woman as well as Faguet's woman of imagination. But she is still something else besides.

She is also the person without luck. From a certain point of view, *Madame Bovary* is the novel of failure and bad luck, of a particularly unfortunate concentration of circumstances. Is Emma really altogether ridiculous and wrong when she believes that, in another setting and surrounded by different people, she might have been relatively happy? Don Quixote was bound to be disappointed, for he lives in a time and place when it is much easier to find windmills than knights-errant. His misadventures are not a matter of good or bad fortune; but, to a very considerable extent, Emma is a victim of circumstance. Considering how easily and thoroughly she is seduced by her lovers, it would seem that a certain kind of husband would conceivably have satisfied her heart and her senses. But Charles, one could say, has been systematically invented to be her undoer. She "made efforts to love him and repented in tears for having given in to another." It took the incident of the clubfoot to make her realize once and forever the incurable stupidity of her husband. In his failure, Charles becomes the cause and the symbol for all the failures in Emma's life. She could have experienced the great revenge and pride of women, to give birth to a man. "She hoped for a son; he would be strong and dark; she would call him Georges, and this idea of having a male child was like a revenge for all her impotence in the past." But it is a girl. In looking for religious help, she might have had better luck than with the unusually inept Bournisien, another character worthy of her bad luck. Her only acquaintance at Yonville is Mme. Homais who, by a refined irony of fate, is the female equivalent of Bovary himself. And Lheureux! with Homais, the one who ends up on top, as fortunate in life as his name suggests. ["Heureux" means happy in French; Lheureux is "the happy one" or, ironically, the one associated with happiness.] The walls against which she will finally dash herself to pieces have been erected around her as by an evil artist. When Charles says: Fate willed it that way! the reader acquiesces, and feels he has been reading the story of an ill-starred woman. *Madame Bovary*, like [Abbé Prévost's] *Manon Lescaut*, is a novel of love; like *Don Quixote*, it is a novel of the fictional imagination—but, aside from this, it is also, like Voltaire's *Candide*, a novel of fate.

A novel of fate, of destiny, can only exist in the absence of a strong will power. This is true in Emma's case. She is sustained by no will power, either from within herself, or from her husband. She is surrounded by the will of others, the will to seduce her in the person of Rodolphe, and the will to despoil her in Lheureux. In the absence of will power, she has enough passion, enough spontaneous excitement and somber selfishness to drive a man to criminal deeds. In her question: "Have you got your gun?" We see her willingness to make Rodolphe into a murderer; in her "At your office," that she would make Léon a thief. . . . (pp. 377-81)

Though she is a creature of passion, she doesn't kill herself out of love but for money; she is not punished as an adulterous woman, but as an untidy housekeeper. This has surprised some, who consider that the two parts of the novel are not consistent with each other. But logical consistency, in fiction, is a certain road to disaster; there is no need for the two parts to be logically connected. In the flesh and the blood of a living creature, they are perfectly coherent. For women, beauty is first of all a matter of décor and, for the bourgeois daughter of a farmer, the substance of life is likely to consist of a rather showy kind of cheap silverware. . . . In the nineteenth century, [the love of money] was a fundamental theme of the realistic novel. In the bourgeois world (as well as the other), love and money go together just as closely as love goes together with ambition, pride, and the affairs of the king in classical tragedy. In the final part of the novel, Léon and Lheureux are the two extremities of the candle that Emma is burning at both ends.

All this aspect of the novel is prefigured in the evening at Vaubeyssard. The soles of Emma's satin shoes "were yellowed with the slippery wax of the dancing floor. Her heart resembled them; in its contact with wealth, something had rubbed off on it that could not be removed." At first, in her schoolgirl dreams, she had dreamt of love as an almost otherworldly experience. The ball at the château convinces her that the world of the keepsakes and the novels really exists, and she identifies it with the world of wealth. She is left with the empty cigar case which she has picked up and by means of which, as with an archeological document, she reconstructs a world of love and luxury, joined like body and soul in the dream of an ideal life. "In her desire, she would confuse the sensuous pleasures of wealth with the raptures of the heart, the refinement of manners with the delicacy of sentiments." Her life will follow a parallel course on the financial and on the sentimental plane. The disappointments of the one coincide with the troubles of the other. Rodolphe and Lheureux are placed on either side of her life to exploit and destroy her, not through malicious intent, but because they act in accordance with the law of nature and society. They act according to the "right" of the seducer, which in France is always backed by established custom, and by the "right" of the usurer which is mistaken for law. After Rodolphe's letter, Emma falls ill and almost dies; after Lheureux's distraint, she dies in fact. The two faces of her destiny are symmetrical. This destiny is all of a piece. "The desires, the longing for money, and the melancholy of passion all blended into one suffering, and instead of putting it out of her mind, she made her thoughts cling to it, urging herself to pain and seeking everywhere the opportunity to revive it. A poorly served dish, a half open door would aggravate her; she bewailed the clothes she did not have, the happiness she had missed, her overexalted dreams, her too cramped home."

Like Sancho Panza and Molière's Tartuffe, Mme. Bovary is so real that she transcends reality and has become a type. The victim of love and the victim of usury do not seem a harmonious combination in the eyes of certain critics. . . . It seems, however, that a creature of fiction can only become a type when it exhibits such apparent anomalies of character; it seems that in this field also, as in the law of binocular vision, a perspective of real depth can only be achieved by the juxtaposition of two images. When Flaubert embarked on the gigantic *Temptation of Saint Anthony,* he had meant to write his *Faust.* He must have realized his mistake. It is striking, however, that it is precisely after his trip to the Orient, when he has given up his *Temptation* and embarked, at Bouilhet's advice, on the story of Delamarre and Delamarre's wife, that he succeeds in creating something close to a French *Faust.* (pp. 382-83)

Albert Thibaudet, "Madame Bovary," in *Madame Bovary: Backgrounds and Sources, Essays in Criticism* by Gustave Flaubert, edited and translated by Paul de Man, W. W. Norton & Company, Inc., 1965, pp. 371-83.

BENJAMIN F. BART
(essay date 1967)

[Bart has written extensively on Flaubert. His full-length 1967 study *Flaubert,* from which the following excerpt is taken, combines biographical detail, psychological investigation, and critical analysis. Here, Bart discusses the characterization of Emma in *Madame Bovary.*]

Emma Bovary is a very ardent woman who knows passion briefly but who discovers that sensual pleasure alone (Flaubert's "terrestrial love") cannot produce a complete and durable love. She is Don Juan, but Don Juan transposed into the bitter, ironic key of the antiromantic. So long as, in romantic fashion, she seeks her own, individual satisfaction, she is necessarily doomed in Flaubert's eyes. Complete love he envisaged as aspiration, outgoing rather than self-centered. But he made

Emma, from the very start, seek only a personal profit from any emotion, even from a landscape. This is what romanticism as she knew it in the convent invited her to desire. In facile, romantic novels the lover and his mistress are so much at one that all desires are held in common. Any romantic girl, Emma for instance, will then suppose that a lover is a man who wants what she wants, who exists for her. Nothing in Emma's character led her to doubt this, and nothing in her training could teach her otherwise. This, perhaps the most common and most serious of the romantic illusions, is at the core of *Madame Bovary* and helps to keep the book alive, for the succeeding years have not diminished the problem.

But Emma is more than that. Sensual, self-centered, vitiated by romanticism, she still carried to the grave some feeling of nobility and of grandeur. She has about her an aura of something extreme and rare. What she desires—furnishing her house, Léon, Rodolphe—may be petty, but her desire itself—to transcend Yonville—is neither tawdry nor wrong. The framework is akin to that of *Don Quixote,* in which Cervantes mocks the reality of what the knight wishes—the windmills, the real Dolores—but withholds his irony from the aspiration itself.

Flaubert once said that everything he was had its origin in *Don Quixote,* in which he admired the perpetual fusion of reality and illusion. But Don Quixote is deluded by his imagination; with Emma it is in large part her feelings which invalidate her perceptions. To some extent there is here a contrast between ideals and sentiments. Hence it is that Quixote's illusions have attained immortal life while Emma's feelings are forever damned. Quixote has misconceived reality but not his ideals; in some senses Emma misconceives both. Her surroundings are petty, it is true, but neither Léon nor Rodolphe is her equal; hence the objects of her desire are grotesque. Still, with the courage and violence of a Nero she drives toward her goals and gives of herself with generosity and grandeur, as Baudelaire points out. (pp. 317-18)

There is a further element to Emma, inherent in the determinism of Flaubert's philosophy. Since her specific fate is determined by her specific surroundings, it becomes possible to wonder whether other surroundings might not have let her have another fate. Contrast Don Quixote, who lives in a country with many windmills and no knights. Emma has no relatively harmless windmills against which to tilt and come out only bruised: she must confront Léon and Rodolphe and Lheureux. And Charles is so much of what she cannot stand: another husband might have alienated her less. Her child turns out to be a girl, when she longed for a boy. She could have had another priest than Bournisien. Homais's wife might have been a different sort of woman, capable of guiding her.

The issue the reader must decide is whether the determinism of *Madame Bovary,* the fated or inevitable quality the reader feels, depends in fact on a chance absence of anyone strong enough to break the chain of intellectual and moral conditioning. Flaubert was quite conscious of the problem and sought to transcend it by generalizing his portraits, by depicting not individuals but types. Bournisien is not a specific village parish priest, but the summation of all of them. Had he been more gifted, more sensitive, and hence more able to help Emma, his parish would no longer have been Yonville. Had he been less so, he would not have been in the priesthood. Similarly, Charles subsumes all possible husbands, Berthe all possible children. In each case the portrait is a type. For Flaubert the elements of Emma and Yonville were indispensable, but they had to be transcended. Emma is so real that she finally passes beyond immediate reality to become typical instead, and all specific examples of her type find themselves in her. And she is reacting to equally typical elements of provincial Normandy in her century. Finally, she reacts in a way which has thus far proved timeless.

The type Emma, as opposed to the person, is a strange one, relatively new in Flaubert's day and not to be confused with the woman whose problem is only that she has made the wrong marriage, a type common

Emma at the Hotel de Boulogne, at a clandestine meeting with Léon.

enough in all literature and especially frequent in Balzac and Mérimée in French fiction immediately preceding Flaubert. New in this novel, she has become steadily more common, once Flaubert gave her her classic formulation. She has sensuality, which is perennial. She has romantic illusions, which have shown no sign of disappearing. But she also has an uncontrollable desire for things, for material luxuries. And, with the lessening of her passionate involvement with Rodolphe and then with Léon, she finds less and less reason to control this latter passion. It is this, not her adulterous love affairs, which brings about her downfall. She is, in fact, the victim of a moneylender, not of a lover or an irate husband. Her materialism, not her sensuality, causes her death, although she does not so understand it.

Flaubert here interweaves his threads to give to his tapestry that almost inextricable confusion which suggests reality. Emma is in fact hopelessly caught by Lheureux as she returns from her fruitless visit to Rodolphe: her household furniture is about to be sold, and her husband will be there either already knowing all about the financial catastrophe or sure to learn of it within hours. But this is not why Emma takes arsenic! Rather, hopelessly disillusioned by the discovery that neither of her lovers will save her, she measures the extent of their devotion more truly than she ever had before. In the face of this despairing calculation, she forgets the cause of her visit to Rodolphe; financial matters disappear from her ken, and she commits suicide because of a world in which it is no longer possible to love.

Emma defiantly faces her world of Yonville, proclaiming her values over against its conventions. So long as her fantasies are not fatal, she and not Yonville controls them. Even outside of herself she is so strong that, a giant in her surroundings, she can dare to pile Pelion and Ossa on Mount Olympus to scale her heaven, though it is the tragedy of the modern world that not Hercules but Lheureux brings this latter-day giant down. Before this, however, and for some little time it is she who is dominant, even illuminating those about her so that they take their color only in reference to her.

It is she and not Charles who makes him what he becomes. Charles is, as Emile Zola pointed out, an author's *tour de force,* a completely mediocre person whose presence is always there from start to finish. As Zola notes, in reality such men are gray or colorless, with nothing to bring them to one's attention; but Charles is constantly in our view. Partly Flaubert makes him important by observing him closely. But to a far greater extent it is Emma who is responsible for Charles, his role, his importance, and his fate. In and of himself he is inoffensive at worst, and frequently he is very good. His regret for the death of his first wife showed sweetness; his present of a horse for his wife may have been disastrously blind, but it was, again, a gentle and loving gesture. The absolute confidence which he reposed in Emma made possible her adulteries; but it, too, was a virtue. Unfortunately, placed in the specific context of the husband of Emma all these pale to unimportance beside her need for flaming romanticism. That what she wanted does not exist is not quite the problem here: what matters is that Charles is totally unable to help her, and hence his very virtues become terrible weaknesses facilitating or even bringing on the destruction of his wife and hence his own. His was a limited world, all of which he could compass; hers was limitless, but she wished to experience at least more of it than Yonville and marriage to Charles could allow. And so she had, in the end, to shatter the bounds which limited Charles' world and let him see that more lay beyond. That view would ultimately break him. (pp. 318-21)

Rodolphe, who initiates an inexperienced Emma into adultery, does eventually dominate her, except for a momentary lapse during which he, too, envisages running away. Despite Emma's illusions, he is in fact the cold and calculating seducer, not the flaming visionary that Emma was. And this she will ultimately be unable to control. Like Leporello, Don Juan's uncomprehending servant, Rodolphe imagines that all women are alike and all loves the same. Flaubert had intended that the vulgarity of Leporello should display the superiority of Juan and his search for the ideal. When Rodolphe almost casually abandons Emma, he is bringing out the same contrast. His nature dominates, but when it has and he leaves Emma, he returns to his own tawdry and uninteresting self: his existence as an exhilarating and exciting personality is in Emma's mind and imagination alone.

Léon, too, comes to rich and full existence for a time, but only by virtue of a special relationship to Emma. Afterwards he will be no more interesting than Charles or Rodolphe. At the precise moments that he and Emma meet, particularly on the second occasion, he can appear to be the person she imagines. Hence she will lend to him the coloring he needs to play the role. It is only when familiarity has rubbed off these borrowed hues that Léon will revert to mediocrity.

What then is Emma, this ardent woman who is doomed herself yet who is able to give to her husband and her lovers a life which they hardly possess but which is wholly theirs so long as they are hers? Flaubert was conscious that he had something particular and special to say in the book, an account of the profoundly sad aspect of modern man. (pp. 321-22)

Emma dies, damned by Yonville. At the touch of reality her dreams must necessarily shatter. To be sure, she is wrong to dream them, and Flaubert castigates her for them. But what of this society which has brought her up this way? What of Yonville, which damns her? We cannot infer that it is right because she is wrong. This is why Flaubert could not close his book on the death of Emma or even on the death of Charles. In Emma there was virile strength and the willingness to sacrifice for an ideal; in Charles there was simple goodness, too simple perhaps, but still goodness. Both had been destroyed. It remained for Flaubert to have his final say on the destroyers.

Madame Bovary is a tale of destruction. For when Emma and Charles have been destroyed by Yonville, that destruction means the triumph of people who had already destroyed everything fine and noble in themselves. *Madame Bovary* has in it the internal driving power of life itself: the reader can readily prolong it and imagine a sequel at will, which would display the triumphant success of Homais and of Lheureux. On the debris of Emma and of Charles, even of Léon, Homais and Lheureux will build their structures—and this, to Flaubert, was even worse. That a living Emma Bovary was weeping in twenty villages of France distressed him, but it enraged him that uncounted men such as Homais were building futures that would give them the Legion of Honor. And this was Flaubert's ultimate message. It may have been unfortunate that his hatred of the bourgeoisie outweighed his affectionate understanding of Emma, for understanding is more important than hatred. But the Emmas and those associated with them all over the world have been grateful for the understanding and have, in general, been content to laugh off Homais, who does not read books anyway and whose triumph in the last pages disappears, somehow, from the memory of readers, who are overwhelmed by the grandeur of Emma's death or the pathos of Charles. (pp. 322-23)

Benjamin F. Bart, in his *Flaubert,* Syracuse University Press, 1967, 791 p.

MAURICE NADEAU

(essay date 1969)

[In the following excerpt from a work that originally appeared in French in 1969, Nadeau discusses theme, structure, and characterization in *Sentimental Education.*]

Some books arouse admiration and respect. Others one merely likes and keeps reading over again, building up a sort of secret relationship with them, though they are not necessarily masterpieces. Some excite an initial enthusiasm, but seem strangely faded ten or fifteen years later. It is only rarely that one likes and is impressed by a book to begin with, and then with every reading finds it more and more rich and moving and profound.

L'éducation sentimentale is like that—one of the great novels of its age, and one whose youth never fades.

The beauty here is less systematic than that of *Madame Bovary* with its purity of line; less stiff and showy than that of *Salammbô*. Instead of leaping to the eye, the beauty of *L'éducation sentimentale* hides behind what is said or, more often, suggested; it has to be found out.

Flaubert the painter is still there, laying on touch after touch to create a general color. Here it is the greyness of life in all its shades: blue for the voyage up the Seine aboard the *Ville-de-Montereau;* red for the revolution of 1848; ashen for the final scenes. Yet the neutral tone into which both private lives and great public events all fade never calls attention to itself. What one does perceive is a kind of music, already familiar to those who have read *Mémoires d'un fou, Novembre,* and the first *Education.* It forms part of a great symphony in a minor key, crossing the threshold of skin and nerve to penetrate right to the marrow of our bones. It is more heartrending than the plaints of earlier days, because the cry of despair is now serene.

A Novel of Failure

Flaubert used to talk of the *"grotesque triste* (dreary grotesqueness)"* of life, as if to exorcize and avenge himself on it rather than succumb to it. But now he speaks of the futility and hopelessness of any attempt to escape: every life is a failure in the long run for everyone in turn, the world rushes only downhill. There is no happiness except in the past, walled up in the memory and impossible to live over again. And a good thing too. "We'd have loved each other so well," say a couple who have never been able to belong to one another, and that could be the summing-up. But Flaubert insisted on making it fiercer still, and what survives of the ruined lives of Frédéric and his false friend Deslauriers, that "best thing" they have in common, is their farcical visit to the establishment of "La Turque."

Like the first *Education,* like *Madame Bovary,* like *Salammbô,* this is a novel of failure. The history of Frédéric Moreau belies both its title and its sub-title, *Histoire d'un jeune homme.* When his "education" is over, the "young man" from Nogent is neither stronger nor wiser nor more hardened than he was before, and when he leaves Paris he is thirty. He uses the next fifteen years to so little purpose they can be dealt with in ten lines. It is as if Frédéric were only waiting for the final confrontation with the great unfulfilled love of his youth to realize fully his own failure. Then, going over old times with Deslauriers, he accepts it. Once he was full of ambition and longed for fame, wealth, and love, but he was reduced to the common level by life, circumstance, and his own weakness. Now, in the "idleness of his mind and inertia of his heart," all that remains is for him to live and die a *petit-bourgeois,* existing

on unearned income. This is how great designs and ranging thoughts may end. At one time Flaubert thought of calling the book *Les Fruits secs* (literally dried or withered fruit, a figurative equivalent of "duds," "failures").

The Son of Madame Bovary

But, it has long been objected, Frédéric Moreau never really had any great design, was never really borne along by a splendid ideal. What fate had he then a right to, this "mediocrity" whom even Flaubert himself describes as a "man with every weakness"? He only wants what young bourgeois usually expect and consider their due, without their having to make any effort or show any perseverance. Frédéric left things to circumstance, and the fact that circumstance was unfavorable was enough to make him give up.

Why then does he win our sympathy? Why have so many young men recognized themselves in him? In the first place, he is not so mediocre as all that, either in his desires or in his intentions. He is not out for money—he has, or will have, sufficient—or honors, or for the power attached to high office and such careers, political and other, as dictate public opinion. It is as if as soon as he entered on life he saw the emptiness of what most men strive for. All he wants is to be recognized for what he is, to emerge from the anonymity of the crowd, and to live for himself, freely and independently. It is for this reason he is drawn by the glitter of Paris, rather than in order to read law and become a judge or a barrister. As he dreams of his future in his room at Nogent, or on the boat going back there, or in the country with Deslauriers, he never sees himself as exercising any profession, but following some occupation that lies outside common or garden society. He "thought of an outline for a play, subjects for paintings, future passions"—"he aspired to be one day the Walter Scott of France"—"above all else he valued passion; Werther, René, Franck, Lara, Lélia and others less distinguished aroused almost equal enthusiasm in him." He feels himself to be, and wants to be, an artist, though whether a musician, a writer, or a painter he does not know—he is attracted by every art in turn, sometimes several simultaneously. But the main thing for him is to experience a *grande passion.* "Love," he tells Deslauriers, "is the food, the atmosphere of genius. Unusual emotions produce sublime works . . ." Brought up on Byron, Chateaubriand, Victor Hugo and George Sand, he moves naturally among the great clichés of Romanticism. If he is the son of Madame Bovary, he is a son who has been educated into a "Parisian"; he is a cut or two above his mother.

"The Men of My Generation"

From the very first pages of the book we know he will fail all along the line, that he will not realize any of his ambitions, and that he will not have the strength or courage for the "grand passion" he aspires to. The symphony's main theme is stated in the opening bars, where the whole story is, as it were, already relegated to the past. "*J'aurais fait quelque chose avec une femme qui m'eût aimé* (I would have achieved something with a woman who loved me)." Deslauriers, who sees the funny side of this precocious world-weariness, laughs, and Frédéric recovers and adopts the only tense suitable for one of his age: the future. But he still comes to the same negative conclusions.

> *Quant à chercher celle qu'il me faudrait, j'y renonce! D'ailleurs, si jamais je la trouve, elle me repoussera. Je suis de la race des déshérités, et je m'éteindrai avec un trésor qui était de strass ou de diamant, je n'en sais rien.* (As to looking for the right woman, I shall not try! Anyhow, if ever I do find her she'll reject me. I am one of the outcasts of fortune, and when I die I shan't know whether the treasure I clasped was paste or diamonds.)

Once again the past encroaches on the future, and while Frédéric succumbs anew to Romanticism to the extent of affecting superiority to his own fate, at the same time he entrenches himself in renunciation, rejection, skepticism. It is not that he is exceptionally lucid about himself. He is too young; that will come later.

At present it is his dreams which see clearly for him and which already come up against reality. The time for grand passions is over. It is 1840, the age of *le roi bourgeois*, the Citizen King.

The practical-minded Deslauriers brings him rudely back to earth: since he has a black coat and white gloves, he ought to take up with M. and Mme Dambreuse. "Think of it, he's got millions! Set yourself out to please him, and his wife as well. Become her lover!" Frédéric is indignant: that is not the kind of success he is after. His friend tells him to remember Rastignac in *La comedie humaine.* But that is just what he does not want to be. Nevertheless, he does waver slightly and agree that his "despair is foolish." Forgetting Mme Arnoux, or including her in the prediction which had been made about the other, he could not help smiling." The novel has only just begun and Frédéric is already compromising mentally. He is not a "mediocrity," but he is impulsive and weak. He literally does not know what he wants. So he leaves it to circumstance, and hopes circumstance will prove favorable.

If he were the novel's only interest one might accuse the author of having made things too easy for himself. But Deslauriers is there as a corrective. He is a strong, ambitious character who means to "arrive" and has no scruples to stand in his way. He later tries to supplant Frédéric with Mme Arnoux, to get into the good graces of the Dambreuses, to influence opinion through a newspaper, and to play a part in politics. He does in fact hold office for a while under the provisional government, and makes a "good match," thereby doing

Frédéric out of this last chance. But his is a poor success. He is of such vulgar stuff, so steeped in greed and envy, that he overdoes it every time, and transforms into immediate or ultimate defeat all the possibilities of victory purchased by effort and ever-increasing degradation. His wife "runs away with a singer," and he too will die empty-handed.

Others—Hussonet, Cisy, Martinon—are different from both Frédéric and Deslauriers. They find their own level in society, as blackmailers, climbers, dowry-hunters. As lacking in character as Frédéric, they are also without the scruples and delicacy of mind and feeling which at least keep him from being abject. But abjection is too large a word for these air-balloons, these corks on the water. They are no more than foam on the wave which carries Frédéric along, and which he lets toss him from one situation to another, from Rosanette to Mme Arnoux, and from Mme Arnoux to Mme Dambreuse.

The only ones who see farther than their own interests and have some conviction or ideal belong to the "lower classes": Dussardier, a shop assistant whose magnanimity makes up for the simplicity of his ideas; Sénécal, the "mathematics tutor" who is spoken of as "a future Saint-Just." They are both republicans and socialists, Dussardier out of hatred for injustice and warmth of feeling, Sénécal out of cool rationalism. But alas, Dussardier, who believes in the fine words of Lamartine, fires on one of his class brothers in June 1848, considers himself half responsible for this betrayal, and by way of absolution gets himself killed by a policeman during Louis-Napoleon's *coup d'état.* Fate has arranged things well: in the policeman, Frédéric, "staring open-mouthed, recognized Sénécal." The wheel has come full circle, and if Flaubert's only purpose has been to write, as he said, "the moral history of his generation," these parallel destinies all ending in moral, intellectual, or political bankruptcy would be enough to show us why the Prince-President later became Emperor of the French.

A Vast Miscarriage

But *L'éducation sentimentale* is something very different from a moral history; its essence is to be found elsewhere. And yet Frédéric's unfulfilled passion for Marie Arnoux, the impossibility of its living and growing through everything shows it is requited; the faint-heartedness on one side and excessive reserve on the other which gave rise to so many *"intermittences,"* as Proust called them, so many eclipses, so much compromise, frustration and suffering; this unhealthy blighting of what should have flowered—all this would be less comprehensible if it did not take place against the background of an even vaster miscarriage. The generation of 1820, their ears still ringing with the loud exhortations of Romanticism, were reduced to inaction, confronted with a mean and cramping reality. Unable to live their dreams, they settled for dreaming their lives. Frédéric is the incarnation of this generation, and his behavior is typical, almost symbolic. He does not take part in the "February Days," he is merely "present." He enjoys the barricades, the riots, the sight of the people in arms, as a spectacle; the looting of the Tuileries he finds in bad taste. He is so afraid of being duped he will not believe in any change, and declares people will always be the same. When the provisional government massacres the proletarians in June he is at Fontainebleau with Rosanette. After the *coup d'état* he lets it be understood that that was not what he wanted. Most of his young bourgeois friends had thought and acted the same way.

L'éducation sentimentale would not possess the virtually inexhaustible richness it has without this political and social backcloth, this tapestry into which the story of Frédéric and Mme Arnoux is woven, this turmoil of events which reveals people as they are deep down—rich men, business men, republicans, artists, and even women of easy virtue. History confirms the accuracy and perfect objectivity of the picture, but that scarcely matters: Flaubert was not aiming at historical reconstruction. The truth he aimed at and attained was larger, more general, more typical. Dambreuse is our contemporary, and so is the sinister Père Roque, and you may pass Sénécal still in the Paris streets today, with his stubble haircut and his pseudo-priestly or professional air. More than one generation since 1820 has had its Days of February and June; more than one has been made up of disappointed dreamers and thwarted climbers. Many an adolescent, reading the *Education*, has learned to make his own self-examination. The truth as brought up to date by Flaubert is valid for all "lost" or "sacrificed" generations, and for all "angry young men." (pp. 175-81)

Flaubert's Problems

It took Flaubert five years to write *L'éducation sentimentale,* from 1864 to 1869. The work was long and hard. Though he complained less than before about "the throes of style," he experienced, as he had over *Madame Bovary,* moments of suffering, periods of discouragement, attacks of distaste at being tied to a "bourgeois subject." "It's about time I amused myself at last," he wrote to George Sand. He meant he would like to treat a more congenial subject, one which would require less research of all kinds, less hunting after details apparently unimportant but which for him had to be absolutely accurate. He had already expressed such a wish to Louise Colet. As the years went by bringing the death of friends, especially that of Bouilhet in 1869, and accentuating the fact that he was old before his time, he entrenched himself more firmly every day in pessimism, and, despite his social life in Paris, in solitude. He did not know the worst was yet to come.

His first concern in writing "the moral history of

the men of [his] generation" was to create a truthful work, *i.e.* one that was impartial and objective and did not betray his own sympathies and preferences. This concern derived from his theories about a "scientific and impersonal" art, and a novel which "should . . . remain within the limits of general plausibility." He wrote to George Sand: "Rich or poor, victors or vanquished, I don't accept any of all that"—meaning the exalting of the one and debasing of the other. "I don't want to have love or hate or pity or anger"; he hoped to "bring Justice into Art." Then, he went on, "the impartiality of description would have the majesty of law—and the precision of science."

He had to ask himself whether this concern was compatible with his wider aim of creating a work of art, and with the need to give form to what can only be called the author's opinion on "the things of this world."

On the theoretical plane he met with no answer to the first question. He believed what he was in the process of creating was "something useless, by which I mean contrary to the aim of Art, which is vague exaltation. But with the present scientific demands [*i.e.* his own] and a bourgeois subject, that seems to me fundamentally impossible. Beauty is not compatible with modern life. . . . "

This was one of the bees in Flaubert's bonnet. But there is more than one kind of artistic beauty, and while *L'éducation* does not observe the canons of classical art or of those of the novel as generally written in Flaubert's day, it is this very fact which lends it its eternal freshness and has made it a universal influence on the modern novel.

As to the "form" to be adopted "to express one's opinion now and then on the things of this world without running the risk of seeming an idiot later," one can only agree with Flaubert that it is "a tough question, *un rude problème.*" But to this question he did find an answer. Regarding the things of this world, "It seems to me the best is simply to paint them." Simply? What he did was paint them in his own way, with their good side and their bad, their causes and their effects, with a scalpel for instrument. "Dissection is revenge," or in other words the expression of opinion is revenge, because for a pessimist to dissect men is enough to show they are bad and that life drags us towards the void. *L'éducation,* like *Madame Bovary,* was to be a work of criticism, even of social criticism. When Flaubert wrote to George Sand, "I confine myself to showing things as they appear to me, to expressing what seems to me the truth," he added at once, "Damn the consequences!" showing how few illusions he had about what the reactions would be.

It was not the vanquished who were likely to be angry. They are dreamers rather than men of action, and Flaubert was irresistibly attracted to dreamers, and satisfied merely with showing their ludicrous side. But what would be the response to the picture of the frightened and cynical bourgeois at the Dambreuses', the shot fired by Père Roque at the prisoner in the Tuileries, and the murder of Dussardier by Sénécal? He had only had to show the characters as they were and describe the situations in detail to reveal the fundamental significance of the events. The impartiality and objectivity of the description add to its force and make it inexorable. Flaubert's powerful searchlight on events makes even those who, like Frédéric, are apathetic about them, appear different and in this respect less sympathetic.

Heroic Self-restraint

Another difficulty was how to insert individual stories into a picture of an age, with its great events dictated by history. First of all there was the love of Frédéric for Mme Arnoux, which with all its vicissitudes and consequences had to run right through the book and make its presence constantly felt. Then there were the adventures of dozens of other characters, which as in real life did not always fall into convenient groupings and were not sufficiently interesting to hold the limelight. Nevertheless the reader had to feel the presence of Hussonet, Cisy, Martinon, and many other minor figures. And how was Flaubert to confine himself to painting a back-cloth when public events erupted on to the front of the stage and monopolized attention? The author also had to be careful to preserve the overall greyness of tone he was aiming at.

All these problems Flaubert put to himself and to his correspondents. "Will character-descriptions interest you?" "Historical characters are more interesting than fictional ones, especially when the latter have moderate passions; one is less interested in Frédéric than in Lamartine." "I am afraid lest the backgrounds eclipse the foregrounds." And so on. He solved these difficulties by returning to them again and again, making changes like a painter muting his colors and transferring them from places where they catch the eye too much. He had to weave within the framework of his main tapestry without allowing himself any "embroidery" that might unbalance it. "No big scene, no purple passages, no metaphors even." He deliberately held back his abilities as a writer and the resources of his temperament, the whole skill of which a novelist is generally so proud, and by this heroic self-restraint he achieved the perfect work of art which is the *Education,* that long flow of dream, love, and nostalgia, the closest possible image of time which passeth and returneth not. (pp. 186-89)

Maurice Nadeau, in his *The Greatness of Flaubert,* translated by Barbara Bray, The Library Press, 1972, 307 p.

SOURCES FOR FURTHER STUDY

Cortland, Peter. *A Reader's Guide to Flaubert.* New York: Helios Books, 1968, 175 p.

> An introductory critical study of *Madame Bovary, Sentimental Education,* and *Three Tales,* including a brief guide to Flaubertian criticism and a critical biography.

James, Henry. "Gustave Flaubert." In his *Notes on Novelists with Some Other Notes,* pp. 65-108. New York: Charles Scribner's Sons, 1914.

> An analysis of Flaubert's literary style with particular emphasis on *Madame Bovary.*

Man, Paul de, ed. *"Madame Bovary" by Gustave Flaubert: Backgrounds and Sources, Essays in Criticism.* Translated by Paul de Man. New York: W. W. Norton & Co., 1965, 462 p.

> An edition of *Madame Bovary* that includes a summary of critical response to the novel and a collection of what de Man considers a representative sample of the most important essays.

Starkie, Enid. *Flaubert: The Making of the Master.* New York: Atheneum, 1967, 403 p.

> An extensive, well-documented portrait of Flaubert "the human being" as well as an informative analysis of Flaubert "the writer" up through the publication and trial of *Madame Bovary.*

——. *Flaubert the Master: A Critical and Biographical Study (1856-1880).* New York: Atheneum, 1971, 390 p.

> A continuation of Starkie's authoritative study *Flaubert: The Making of the Master* covering Flaubert's personal life and career from the year 1856 until his death. This volume "is intended to show Flaubert in full possession of his art and craft, and how he used them in different ways, without repeating himself; each novel being intended to solve a separate problem and to treat it in a different way, with a different style."

Steegmuller, Francis. *Flaubert and "Madame Bovary": A Double Portrait.* New York: Farrar, Straus and Co., 1950, 433 p.

> An excellent biography concentrating on the periods when Flaubert was writing *La tentation de Saint Antoine* and *Madame Bovary.* Steegmuller also provides an extensive account, primarily using Flaubert's letters and travel notes, of his oriental journey with Maxime Du Camp, taken between the composition of these two novels.

E. M. Forster

1879-1970

(Full name Edward Morgan Forster) English novelist, short story writer, critic, travel writer, biographer, dramatist, librettist, and nonfiction writer.

INTRODUCTION

*F*orster is best remembered as the author of *Howards End* (1910), *A Passage to India* (1924), and other novels of manners depicting Edwardian society and British morality. Similar in style to the novels of Jane Austen, Forster's works focus on three major themes: salvation through love, the deficiency of traditional Christianity, and the repressiveness of English culture. These themes are underscored by numerous allusions to paganism and mythology and are infused with Forster's liberal humanism and subtle wit. Forster's works are admired for their believable characterizations that simultaneously serve as representations of abstract ideas. Frederick P. W. McDowell noted: "A fascination exerted by characters who grip our minds; a wit and beauty present in an always limpid style; a passionate involvement with life in all its variety; a view of existence alive to its comic incongruities and to its tragic implications; and a steady adherence to humanistic values which compel admiration . . . such are the leading aspects of Forster's work that continually lure us to it."

Forster attended Cambridge University, where he was a member of the Cambridge Apostles, an intellectual student group that included Lytton Strachey and John Maynard Keynes. After leaving Cambridge, Forster participated in the lively circle of artists and writers that became known as the Bloomsbury Group. Informally led by Virginia Woolf, the group was strongly influenced by the Cambridge philosophers G. E. Moore and J. M. E. McTaggert. In his *Principia Ethica*, Moore expounded the value of social interaction and cultural stimuli, two crucial elements of Forster's ideology which, according to Claude J. Summers, also included "Forster's belief in individualism and the sanctity of personal relationships, his scorn for conventionality and religion, his passion for truth and friendship, his unaffected love for art, and his intellectual romanticism."

Forster's early novels derive from his experiences in the Cambridge and Bloomsbury coteries and examine the upper middle class of the Edwardian era. Both *Where Angels Fear to Tread* (1905) and *A Room with a View* (1908) are informed by Forster's travels to Italy and contrast European liberalism with more conservative English values. In these novels, the Italian characters are archetypes of instinct, spirituality, and imagination, whereas the British characters represent conventionalism and rational thought. Similarly, the protagonists of *The Longest Journey* (1907) personify opposite philosophies. Rickie Elliot, a Cambridge intellectual, and his half-brother, Stephen Wonham, respectively embody romantic and pagan ideals. *Howards End,* one of Forster's most acclaimed works, reveals the author's vision of a unified humanity. Many critics perceive Forster's renderings of Edwardian society to be among the most realistic in literature.

A Passage to India, which is widely regarded as Forster's masterpiece, is drawn on Forster's own experiences in India during visits there in 1912 and 1921. This novel's acclaim derives from its portrayal of widely diverse cultures—Muslim, Hindu, and Christian—and the difficulties inherent in their coexistence. Forster imbues *A Passage to India* with the Hindu principle of total acceptance, employing this philosophy to suggest an integrating force for which, as events in the novel suggest, the world is unprepared. The differences between Western and Eastern perceptions are exemplified by an episode in the Marabar Caves, where Mrs. Moore, an elderly British matron, presumably experiences nihilistic despair upon hearing an echo suggesting to her that "nothing has value." Mrs. Moore, unlike the Hindus, is unable to assimilate this despair into the totality of her religious sensibility, and she succumbs to spiritual passivity. This crucial scene represents, according to Philip Gardner, "The enigmatic and frightening side of spiritual experience, the sense of chaos and nothingness whose effects spill over and make the conclusion of the novel equivocal."

Forster published no more novels during his lifetime, concentrating instead on critical pieces, letters, biographies, and travel books. *Aspects of the Novel* (1927), Forster's seminal critical work, is his most highly regarded nonfiction volume. *Abinger Harvest* (1936) and *Two Cheers for Democracy* (1951) contain critical treatises as well as biographical portraits of other writers and essays outlining Forster's political beliefs. *Alexandria: A History and a Guide* (1922) and *Pharos and Pharillon* (1923) evidence Forster's knowledge of Egyptian locales, while *The Hill of Devi* (1953; republished as *The Hill of Devi and Other Writings*) collects his letters from India. Forster also published four collections of short stories: *The Celestial Omnibus and Other Stories* (1911), *The Story of the Siren* (1920), *The Eternal Moment and Other Stories* (1928), and *The Collected Short Stories of E. M. Forster* (1947). Forster's stories thematically resemble his novels but rely more heavily on supernatural and metaphysical elements.

Forster's reputation has been enhanced by the release of cinematic adaptations of several of his novels, as well as by the posthumous publication of *The Selected Letters of E. M. Forster: Volume I, 1879-1920* (1984), *The Selected Letters of E. M. Forster: Volume II, 1921-1970* (1985), and *Maurice* (1971), a previously suppressed novel centering on homosexual topics. Begun before *A Passage to India, Maurice* recounts a young man's growing awareness of his homosexuality and is generally considered to be autobiographical. In addition, *The Life to Come and Other Stories* (1972) and *The New Collected Short Stories of E. M. Forster* (1985) include such esteemed works as "Dr. Woolacott" and "The Road from Colonus." *Arctic Summer and Other Fiction* (1980) contains many unfinished pieces, including the title novel, which predates *A Passage to India* and anticipates its themes.

(For further information about Forster's life and works, see *Contemporary Authors,* Vols. 13-14, 25-28; *Contemporary Authors Permanent Series,* Vol. 1; *Dictionary of Literary Biography,* Vols. 34, 98; *Contemporary Literary Criticism,* Vols. 1, 2, 3, 4, 9, 10, 13, 15, 22, 45; and *Major Twentieth-Century Writers.*)

CRITICAL COMMENTARY

I. A. RICHARDS

(essay date 1927)

[Richards, an English poet and critic, has been called the founder of modern literary criticism. Primarily a theorist, he encouraged the growth of textual analysis and, during the 1920s, formulated many of the principles that would later become the basis of New Criticism, one of the most important schools of modern critical thought. In the following excerpt from a 1927 essay, he discusses Forster's moral concerns.]

Where another writer possessed of an unusual outlook on life would be careful to introduce it, gradually preparing the way by views from more ordinary standpoints, Mr. Forster does nothing of the kind. This very sentence tacitly assumes that the personal point of view is already occupied by the reader, who is left to orient himself as he can. This may lead to lamentable misunderstandings. For example, once we have picked up the author's position we see that the characters in his early books, Mrs. Herriton, Harriet, Gino, Mr. Eager, Old Mr. Emerson, are less to be regarded as social studies than as embodiments of moral forces. Hence the ease with which Miss Abbott, for example, turns momentarily into a goddess. *Where Angels Fear to Tread* is indeed far nearer in spirit to a mystery play than to a comedy of manners. This in spite of the astonishingly penetrating flashes of observation by which these figures are sometimes depicted. But to understand why, with all his equipment as an observer, Mr. Forster sometimes so wantonly disregards verisimilitude we have to find his viewpoint and take up toward them the attitude of their creator. (pp. 15-16)

Mr. Forster never formulates his criticism of life in one of those principles which we can adhere to or discuss. He leaves it in the painful, concrete realm of practice, presenting it always and only in terms of actuality and never in the abstract. In other words, he has no doctrine but only an attitude. . . . (p. 16)

Mr. Forster is a peculiarly uncomfortable author for [those] who are not content merely to enjoy the surface graces of his writing and the delicacies of his wit, but make themselves sufficiently familiar with his temper to see life to some degree with his eyes. His real audience is youth, caught at that stage when rebellion against the comfortable conventions is easy because the cost of abandoning them has not been fully counted. (pp. 16-17)

It is Mr. Forster's peculiarity that he offers his discomforting vision with so urbane a manner. He is no "holy howlstorm upon the mountains." He has no thunders, no hoots, no grimaces, nor any of the airs of the denunciating prophet, yet at the heart of his work there is less satisfaction with human existence as he sees it than in the work of any other living writer I can call to mind. The earliest of his books, *The Longest Journey,* is perhaps an exception to what has just been remarked about his manner. It has the rawness and crudeness and violence we should expect in the work of a very young writer. Those who have not realized the intensity of the dissatisfaction behind Mr. Forster's work would do well to read it. There is much there, of course, which time has mellowed. But the essential standards, the primary demands from life, which still make unacceptable to him so much that ordinary people find sufficient, have not altered.

Mr. Forster's peculiar quality as a novelist is his fiercely critical sense of values. What was, in the days of *Longest Journey,* a revolt, has changed to a saddened and almost weary pessimism. He has, in his later writings, in *Pharos and Pharillon* and in *A Passage to India,* consoled himself to some degree by a cultivation of the less militant and more humorous forms of irony. He has stepped back to the position of the observer from which in his *Where Angels Fear to Tread* he was at such pains to eject his Philip. But his sense of values remains the same. He has the same terribly acute discernment of and the old insuperable distaste for what he once called "the canned variety of the milk of human kindness" and for all the other substitute products that in civilized communities so interfere between us and our fellows. . . . [To] Mr. Forster life does seem constantly vitiated by automatism, by official action, by insincerity, by organization when it touches charity, or any of the modes of human intercourse which once were governed, in small communities, by natural human feeling alone. (pp. 17-18)

We can trace to this horror of automatisms in human affairs, to this detestation of the nonspontaneous, very much that might seem unconnected and accidental in his books. The passion for the Italian character which animates *Where Angels Fear to Tread* and *A Room with a View,* the unfairness to the medical profession which crops up so markedly from time to time, as in *Howards End,* the exaggeration which mars his depiction of schoolmasters apart from Fielding,

Principal Works

Where Angels Fear to Tread (novel) 1905

The Longest Journey (novel) 1907

A Room with a View (novel) 1908

Howards End (novel) 1910

The Celestial Omnibus and Other Stories (short stories) 1911

The Story of the Siren (short stories) 1920

A Passage to India (novel) 1924

Aspects of the Novel (criticism) 1927

The Eternal Moment and Other Stories (short stories) 1928

Abinger Harvest (criticism) 1936

Collected Short Stories of E. M. Forster (short stories) 1948

Maurice (novel) 1971

The Life to Come and Other Stories (short stories) 1972

Arctic Summer and Other Fiction (unfinished writings) 1980

clergymen, and others in authority, his sentimentalization of Old England, and his peculiarly lively flair for social coercion in all its forms—all these spring from the same source. And I believe that the theme which more than any other haunts his work and most puzzles his attentive readers has the same origin.

A special preoccupation, almost an obsession, with the continuance of life, from parent to child, with the quality of life in the sense of blood or race, with the preservation of certain strains and the disappearance of others, such is the nearest description of this theme which I can contrive. In itself it eludes abstract presentation. Mr. Forster himself refrains from formulating it. He handles it in the concrete only, or through a symbol such as the house, *Howards End.* (Mrs. Wilcox, the most mysterious of his creations, was a Howard, it will be recalled.) This preoccupation is extremely far removed from that of the Eugenic Society—which would be, precisely, the canned variety; the speculations and calculations of the geneticist do not bear upon it, for it is to Mr. Forster plainly a more than half mystical affair, a vision of the ultimate drift or struggle of the universe and the refuge into which an original strong tendency to mysticism has retreated. The supreme importance to him of this idea appears again and again in his books and it is when automatisms such as social pressures and insincerities threaten to intervene here that he grows most concerned—witness *A Room with a View.* In *Longest Journey,* Rickie's mother appears to him in one of the most dreadful dreams in fiction. "Let them die out! Let them die out!" she says. His son has

just been born a hopeless cripple. Gino in *Where Angels Fear to Tread* stands "with one foot resting on the little body, suddenly musing, filled with the desire that his son should be like him and should have sons like him to people the earth. It is the strongest desire that comes to a man—if it comes to him at all—stronger even than love or desire for personal immortality. . . . It is the exception who comprehends that physical and spiritual life may stream out of him for ever." Compare also the strange importance in *A Passage to India* of the fact that Mrs. Moore's children are Mrs. Moore's.

But the most fascinating example of the handling of this theme is in *Howards End,* the book that still best represents the several sides of Mr. Forster's worth, and in which its virtues and its occasional defects can best be studied. Two different aims are combined in *Howards End;* they have their interconnections, and the means by which they are severally pursued are very skilfully woven together; but it is true, I think, that the episodes which serve a double purpose are those which are usually regarded as the weakest in the book. One of these aims is the development of the half mystical, and inevitably vague, survival theme which we have been considering. The other is the presentation of a sociological thesis, a quite definite piece of observation of great interest and importance concerning the relations of certain prominent classes in Modern England. For that matter, they can be found without trouble in every present day community. To this second aim more than half the main figures of the book belong. A certain conflict between these aims is, I suggest, the source of that elusive weakness which, however high and distinguished a place we may find for *Howards End,* disqualifies it as one of the world's greatest novels. (pp. 18-19)

I. A. Richards, "A Passage to Forster: Reflections on a Novelist," in *Forster: A Collection of Critical Essays,* edited by Malcolm Bradbury, Prentice-Hall, Inc., 1966, pp. 15-20.

VIRGINIA WOOLF

(essay date 1942)

[Woolf was an English novelist, essayist, and critic. Along with Forster, Lytton Strachey, Roger Fry, and Clive Bell, she and her husband Leonard formed the literary coterie known as the "Bloomsbury Group." In the following excerpt from her essay "The Novels of E. M. Forster," she commends Forster's observations in his early novels and identifies *Howards End* and *A Passage to India* as triumphs of literary imagination.]

Mr. Forster is extremely susceptible to the influence of time. He sees his people much at the mercy of those conditions which change with the years. He is acutely conscious of the bicycle and of the motor-car; of the public school and of the university; of the suburb and of the city. The social historian will find his books full of illuminating information. . . . Mr. Forster is a novelist, that is to say, who sees his people in close contact with their surroundings. . . . But we discover as we turn the page that observation is not an end in itself; it is rather the goad, the gadfly driving Mr. Forster to provide a refuge from this misery, an escape from this meanness. Hence we arrive at that balance of forces which plays so large a part in the structure of Mr. Forster's novels. Sawston implies Italy; timidity, wildness; convention, freedom; unreality, reality. These are the villains and heroes of much of his writing. In *Where Angels Fear to Tread* the disease, convention, and the remedy, nature, are provided if anything with too eager a simplicity, too simple an assurance, but with what a freshness, what a charm! Indeed it would not be excessive if we discovered in this slight first novel evidence of powers which only needed, one might hazard, a more generous diet to ripen into wealth and beauty. . . . [Though] Mr. Forster may be sensitive to the bicycle and the duster, he is also the most persistent devotee of the soul. Beneath bicycles and dusters, Sawston and Italy, Philip, Harriet, and Miss Abbott, there always lies for him—it is this which makes him so tolerant a satirist—a burning core. It is the soul; it is reality; it is truth; it is poetry; it is love; it decks itself in many shapes, dresses itself in many disguises. But get at it he must; keep from it he cannot. (pp. 162-64)

Yet, if we ask ourselves upon which occasions this happens and how, it will seem that those passages which are least didactic, least conscious of the pursuit of beauty, succeed best in achieving it. When he allows himself a holiday—some phrase like that comes to our lips; when he forgets the vision and frolics and sports with the fact; . . . it is then that we feel that his aim is achieved. . . . But the second novel, *The Longest Journey,* leaves us baffled and puzzled. The opposition is still the same; truth and untruth; Cambridge and Sawston; sincerity and sophistication. But everything is accentuated. He builds his Sawston of thicker bricks and destroys it with stronger blasts. The contrast between poetry and realism is much more precipitous. And now we see much more clearly to what a task his gifts commit him. We see that what might have been a passing mood is in truth a conviction. He believes that a novel must take sides in the human conflict. He sees beauty—none more keenly; but beauty imprisoned in a fortress of brick and mortar whence he must extricate her. Hence he is always constrained to build the cage—society in all its intricacy and triviality—before he can free the prisoner. . . . At the same time, as we read *The Longest Journey* we are aware of a mocking spirit of fantasy which flouts his seriousness. No one seizes

more deftly the shades and shadows of the social comedy; no one more amusingly hits off the comedy of luncheon and tea party and a game of tennis at the rectory. His old maids, his clergy, are the most lifelike we have had since Jane Austen laid down the pen. But he has into the bargain what Jane Austen had not—the impulses of a poet. The neat surface is always being thrown into disarray by an outburst of lyric poetry. Again and again in *The Longest Journey* we are delighted by some exquisite description of the country; or some lovely sight—like that when Rickie and Stephen send the paper boats burning through the arch—is made visible to us forever. Here, then, is a difficult family of gifts to persuade to live in harmony together: satire and sympathy; fantasy and fact; poetry and a prim moral sense. No wonder that we are often aware of contrary currents that run counter to each other and prevent the book from bearing down upon us and overwhelming us with the authority of a masterpiece. (pp. 164-66)

[Mr. Forster's] concern is with the private life; his message is addressed to the soul. "It is the private life that holds out the mirror to infinity; personal intercourse, and that alone, that ever hints at a personality beyond our daily vision." . . . This belief that it is the private life that matters, that it is the soul that is eternal, runs through all his writing. . . .

[Let] us look for a moment at the nature of the problem he sets himself. It is the soul that matters; and the soul, as we have seen, is caged in a solid villa of red brick somewhere in the suburbs of London. It seems, then, that if his books are to succeed in their mission his reality must at certain points become irradiated; his brick must be lit up; we must see the whole building saturated with light. We have at once to believe in the complete reality of the suburb and in the complete reality of the soul. (p. 167)

[The problem confronting Mr. Forster seems to be] how to connect the actual thing with the meaning of the thing and to carry the reader's mind across the chasm which divides the two without spilling a single drop of its belief. . . . [At certain moments he succeeds, but in the] great scenes which are the justification of the huge elaboration of the realistic novel . . . we are most aware of failure. For it is here that Mr. Forster makes the change from realism to symbolism; here that the object which has been so uncompromisingly solid becomes, or should become, luminously transparent. He fails, one is tempted to think, chiefly because that admirable gift of his for observation has served him too well. (pp. 168-69)

The stories collected under the title of *The Celestial Omnibus* represent, it may be, an attempt on Mr. Forster's part to simplify the problem which so often troubles him of connecting the prose and poetry of life. Here he admits definitely if discreetly the possibility of magic. . . . The stories are extremely charming. They release the fantasticality which is laid under such heavy burdens in the novels. But the vein of fantasy is not deep enough or strong enough to fight single-handed against those other impulses which are part of his endowment. We feel that he is an uneasy truant in fairyland. Behind the hedge he always hears the motor horn and the shuffling feet of tired wayfarers, and soon he must return. One slim volume indeed contains all that he has allowed himself of pure fantasy. (pp. 169-70)

[None] of the books before *Howards End* and *A Passage to India* altogether drew upon the full range of Mr. Forster's powers. With his queer and in some ways contradictory assortment of gifts, he needed, it seemed, some subject which would stimulate his highly sensitive and active intelligence, but would not demand the extremes of romance or passion; a subject which gave him material for criticism, and invited investigation. . . . In *Howards End* the lower middle, the middle, the upper middle classes of English society are . . . built up into a complete fabric. It is an attempt on a larger scale than hitherto, and, if it fails, the size of the

Forster at the age of five, with his mother, Alice Whichelo Forster.

attempt is largely responsible. . . . The reason is suggested perhaps by the manner of one's praise. Elaboration, skill, wisdom, penetration, beauty—they are all there, but they lack fusion; they lack cohesion; the book as a whole lacks force. (pp. 170-71)

Yet in *Howards End* there are, one feels, in solution all the qualities that are needed to make a masterpiece. The characters are extremely real to us. The ordering of the story is masterly. That indefinable but highly important thing, the atmosphere of the book, is alight with intelligence; not a speck of humbug, not an atom of falsity is allowed to settle. And again, but on a larger battlefield, the struggle goes forward which takes place in all Mr. Forster's novels—the struggle between the things that matter and the things that do not matter, between reality and sham, between the truth and the lie. Again the comedy is exquisite and the observation faultless. But again, just as we are yielding ourselves to the pleasures of the imagination, a little jerk rouses us. We are tapped on the shoulder. We are to notice this, to take heed of that. Margaret or Helen, we are made to understand, is not speaking simply as herself; her words have another and a larger intention. So, exerting ourselves to find out the meaning, we step from the enchanted world of imagination, where our faculties work freely, to the twilight world of theory, where only our intellect functions dutifully. (p. 172)

[In *A Passage to India*] there is a change from *Howards End.* Hitherto Mr. Forster has been apt to pervade his books like a careful hostess who is anxious to introduce, to explain, to warn her guests of a step here, of a draught there. But here, perhaps in some disillusionment both with his guests and with his house, he seems to have relaxed these cares. We are allowed to ramble over this extraordinary continent almost alone. We notice things, about the country especially, spontaneously, accidentally almost, as if we were actually there. . . . No longer do we feel, as we used to feel in England, that [his characters] will be allowed to go only so far and no further lest they may upset some theory of the author's. Aziz is a free agent. He is the most imaginative character that Mr. Forster has yet created. . . . We may guess indeed that it has helped Mr. Forster to have put the ocean between him and Sawston. It is a relief, for a time, to be beyond the influence of Cambridge. Though it is still a necessity for him to build a model world which he can submit to delicate and precise criticism, the model is on a larger scale. The English society, with all its pettiness and its vulgarity and its streak of heroism, is set against a bigger and a more sinister background. And though it is still true that there are ambiguities in important places, moments of imperfect symbolism, a greater accumulation of facts than the imagination is able to deal with, it seems as if the double vision which troubled us in the earlier books was in process of becoming single. The saturation is much more thorough. Mr. Forster has almost achieved the great feat of animating this dense, compact body of observation with a spiritual light. The book shows signs of fatigue and disillusionment; but it has chapters of clear and triumphant beauty, and above all it makes us wonder, What will he write next? (pp. 174-75)

Virginia Woolf, "The Novels of E. M. Forster," in her *The Death of the Moth and Other Essays,* Harcourt Brace Jovanovich, Inc., 1942, pp. 162-75.

LIONEL TRILLING

(essay date 1943)

[Trilling has been called the single most important American critic to apply Freudian psychological theories to literature. The following excerpt is from his highly influential 1943 study *E. M. Forster.* Here, Trilling places Forster within a liberal literary tradition while identifying him as chiefly a moral realist.]

E. M. Forster is for me the only living novelist who can be read again and again and who, after each reading, gives me what few writers can give us after our first days of novel-reading, the sensation of having learned something. I have wanted for a long time to write about him and it gives me a special satisfaction to write about him now, for a consideration of Forster's work is, I think, useful in time of war.

In America Forster has never established a great reputation. Perhaps his readers are more numerous than I suppose, but at best they make a quiet band, and his novels—excepting *A Passage To India,* and that for possibly fortuitous reasons—are still esoteric with us. In England, although scarcely a popular writer, he is widely known and highly regarded; still, it is not at all certain whether even in England he is properly regarded and truly known. Some of the younger writers—among them Christopher Isherwood and Cyril Connolly—hold him in great esteem and have written well about him; I. A. Richards' remarks about Forster are sometimes perceptive [see excerpt dated 1927], Elizabeth Bowen has spoken of him briefly but well, and the late Peter Burra's essay (now the introduction to the Everyman edition of *A Passage To India*) is a sound appreciation. But both Rose Macaulay and Virginia Woolf [see excerpt dated 1942], who write of Forster with admiration, perceive the delicacy but not the cogency of his mind. As for the judgment canonized in *The Concise Cambridge History Of English Literature,* it is wholly mistaken; the "shy, unworldly quality" of work "almost diffidently presented" by a man who is "at heart a scholar" simply does not exist. The author of

this comment has taken an irony literally and has misinterpreted a manner.

It is Forster's manner, no doubt, that prevents a greater response to his work. That manner is comic; Forster owes much to Fielding, Dickens, Meredith and James. And nowadays even the literate reader is likely to be unschooled in the comic tradition and unaware of the comic seriousness. The distinction between the serious and the solemn is an old one, but it must be made here again to explain one of the few truly serious novelists of our time. Stendhal believed that gaiety was one of the marks of the healthy intelligence, and we are mistakenly sure that Stendhal was wrong. We suppose that there is necessarily an intellectual "depth" in the deep tones of the organ; it is possibly the sign of a deprivation—our suspicion of gaiety in art perhaps signifies an inadequate seriousness in ourselves. A generation charmed by the lugubrious—once in O'Neill, Dreiser and Anderson, now in Steinbeck and Van Wyck Brooks—is perhaps fleeing from the trivial shape of its own thoughts.

Forster is not only comic, he is often playful. He is sometimes irritating in his refusal to be great. Greatness in literature, even in comedy, seems to have some affinity with greatness in government and war, suggesting power, a certain sternness, a touch of the imperial and imperious. But Forster, who in certain moods might say with Swift, "I have hated all nations, professions and communities, and all my love is for individuals," fears power and suspects formality as the sign of power. "Distrust every enterprise that requires new clothes" is the motto one of his characters inscribes over his wardrobe. It is a maxim of only limited wisdom; new thoughts sometimes need new clothes and the seriousness of Forster's intellectual enterprise is too often reduced by the unbuttoned manner he affects. The quaint, the facetious and the chatty sink his literary criticism below its proper level; they diminish the stature of his short fiction and they even touch, though they never actually harm, the five novels; the true comic note sometimes drops to mere chaff and we now and then wish that the style were less comfortable and more arrogant.

But while these lapses have to be reckoned with, they do not negate the validity of the manner of which they are the deficiency or excess. Forster's manner is the agent of a moral intention which can only be carried out by the mind *ondoyant et divers* of which Montaigne spoke. What Forster wants to know about the human heart must be caught by surprise, by what he calls the "relaxed will," and if not everything can be caught in this way, what is so caught cannot be caught in any other way. Rigor will not do, and Forster uses the novel as a form amenable to the most arbitrary manipulation. He teases his medium and plays with his genre. He scorns the fetish of "adequate motivation," delights in surprise and melodrama and has a kind of addiction to sudden death. Guiding his stories according to his serious whim—like the anonymous lady, he has a whim of iron—Forster takes full and conscious responsibility for his novels, refusing to share in the increasingly dull assumption of the contemporary novelist, that the writer has nothing to do with the story he tells and that, *mirabile dictu,* through no intention of his own, the story has chosen to tell itself through him. Like Fielding, he shapes his prose for comment and explanation, and like Fielding he is not above an explanatory footnote. He summarizes what he is going to show, introduces new themes when and as it suits him to do so, is not awed by the sacred doctrine of "point of view" and, understanding that verisimilitude, which more than one critic has defended from his indifference, can guarantee neither pleasure nor truth, he uses exaggeration and improbability. As a result, the four novels up to *A Passage To India* all suggest that they have been written after a close application to the dramatic principles of *The Winter's Tale.*

In all this Forster is not bizarre. He simply has the certainty of the great novelists that any novel is a made-up thing and that a story, in order to stand firmly on reality, needs to keep no more than one foot on probability. Against this belief is opposed our increasingly grim realistic prejudice: we have learned to believe that *The Winter's Tale* is great poetry but bad dramaturgy. Our literal and liberal intelligence jibs at an interruption of sixteen years, at what we are convinced is an improbability not only of event but of emotion—we think it wrong that Mamillius and Antigonus should die so casually, or that anyone should "exit, pursued by a bear," or that Polixenes should fly into his brutal rage after having so charmingly taken part in Perdita's great flower scene, for it confuses us that good and evil should co-exist and alternate. To accept Forster we have to know that *The Winter's Tale* is dramatically and morally sound and that improbability is the guide to life.

This means an affirmation of faith in the masters of the novel, in James, Meredith, Dickens—and in Hawthorne, whose notion of the "romance" (for he was forced to distinguish his own kind of novel from the more literal kind) is here so suggestive.

When a writer calls his work a Romance, it need hardly be observed that he wishes to claim a certain latitude, both as to its fashion and material, which he would not have felt himself entitled to assume had he professed to be writing a Novel. The latter form of composition is presumed to aim at a very minute fidelity, not merely to the possible, but to the probable and ordinary course of man's experience. The former—while, as a work of art, it must rigidly subject itself to laws, and while it sins unpardonably so far as it may swerve aside from the truth of the human heart—has fairly a right to present that truth under circumstances, to a great extent, of the writer's own choosing or creation.

Hawthorne is no doubt the greater artist and perhaps the greater moralist, yet Forster stands with him in his unremitting concern with moral realism. All novelists deal with morality, but not all novelists, or even all good novelists, are concerned with moral realism, which is not the awareness of morality itself but of the contradictions, paradoxes and dangers of living the moral life. To the understanding of the inextricable tangle of good and evil and of how perilous moral action can be, Hawthorne was entirely devoted. Henry James followed him in this devotion and after James, though in a smaller way, comes Forster, who can say of one of his characters that he was "cursed with the Primal Curse, which is not the knowledge of good and evil, but the knowledge of good-and-evil."

It is here that the precise point of Forster's manner appears. Forster's plots are always sharp and definite, for he expresses difference by means of struggle, and struggle by means of open conflict so intense as to flare into melodrama and even into physical violence. Across each of his novels runs a barricade; the opposed forces on each side are Good and Evil in the forms of Life and Death, Light and Darkness, Fertility and Sterility, Courage and Respectability, Intelligence and Stupidity—all the great absolutes that are so dull when discussed in themselves. The comic manner, however, will not tolerate absolutes. It stands on the barricade and casts doubt on both sides. The fierce plots move forward to grand simplicities but the comic manner confuses the issues, forcing upon us the difficulties and complications of the moral fact. The plot suggests eternal division, the manner reconciliation; the plot speaks of clear certainties, the manner resolutely insists that nothing can be quite so simple. "Wash ye, make yourselves clean," says the plot, and the manner murmurs, "If you can find the soap."

Now, to the simple mind the mention of complication looks like a kind of malice, and to the mind under great stress the suggestion of something "behind" the apparent fact looks like a call to quietism, like mere shilly-shallying. And this is the judgment, I think, that a great many readers of the most enlightened sort are likely to pass on Forster. For he stands in a peculiar relation to what, for want of a better word, we may call the liberal tradition, that loose body of middle class opinion which includes such ideas as progress, collectivism and humanitarianism.

To this tradition Forster has long been committed—all his novels are politically and morally tendentious and always in the liberal direction. Yet he is deeply at odds with the liberal mind, and while liberal readers can go a long way with Forster, they can seldom go all the way. They can understand him when he attacks the manners and morals of the British middle class, when he speaks out for spontaneity of feeling, for the virtues of sexual fulfillment, for the values of intelligence; they go along with him when he speaks against the class system, satirizes soldiers and officials, questions the British Empire and attacks business ethics and the public schools. But sooner or later they begin to make reservations and draw back. They suspect Forster is not quite playing their game; they feel that he is challenging *them* as well as what they dislike. And they are right. For all his long commitment to the doctrines of liberalism, Forster is at war with the liberal imagination.

Surely if liberalism has a single desperate weakness, it is an inadequacy of imagination: liberalism is always being surprised. There is always the liberal work to do over again because disillusionment and fatigue follow hard upon surprise, and reaction is always ready for that moment of liberal disillusionment and fatigue—reaction never hopes, despairs or suffers amazement. Liberalism likes to suggest its affinity with science, pragmatism and the method of hypothesis, but in actual conduct it requires "ideals" and absolutes; it prefers to make its alliances only when it thinks it catches the scent of Utopia in parties and governments, the odor of sanctity in men; and if neither is actually present, liberalism makes sure to supply it. When liberalism must act with some degree of anomaly—and much necessary action is anomalous—it insists that it is acting on perfect theory and is astonished when anomaly then appears.

The liberal mind is sure that the order of human affairs owes it a simple logic: good is good and bad is bad. It can understand, for it invented and named, the moods of optimism and pessimism, but the mood that is the response to good-and-evil it has not named and cannot understand. Before the idea of good-and-evil its imagination fails; it cannot accept this improbable paradox. This is ironic, for one of the charter-documents of liberalism urges the liberal mind to cultivate imagination enough to accept just this improbability.

Good and evil we know in the field of this world grow up together almost inseparably; and the knowledge of good is so involved and interwoven with the knowledge of evil, and in so many cunning resemblances hardly to be discerned, that those confused seeds which were imposed upon Psyche as an incessant labor to cull out, and sort asunder, were not more intermixed. It was from out the rind of one apple tasted, that the knowledge of good and evil, as two twins cleaving together, leaped forth into the world. And perhaps this is that doom which Adam fell into of knowing good and evil, that is to say of knowing good by evil.

And the irony is doubled when we think how well the great conservative minds have understood what Milton meant. Dr. Johnson and Burke and, in a lesser way at a later time, Fitzjames Stephen, understood the mystery of the twins; and Matthew Arnold has always been thought the less a liberal for his understanding of them. But we of the liberal connection have always liked to play the old intellectual game of antagonistic principles. It is an attractive game because it gives us the sensation of thinking, and its first rule is that if one of two opposed principles is wrong, the other is necessarily right. Forster will not play this game; or, rather, he plays it only to mock it.

This indifference to the commonplaces of liberal thought makes the very texture of Forster's novels and appeared in the first of them. The theme of *Where Angels Fear To Tread* is the violent opposition between British respectability and a kind of pagan and masculine integration. D. H. Lawrence, who played the old game of antagonistic principles for all it was worth—and it was worth something in his hands—gave us many characters like Forster's Gino Carella, characters who, like Gino, were cruel (the scene of Gino's cruelty is, incidentally, one of the most remarkable in modern fiction) or, like Gino, indifferent to the "higher" and romantic emotions. But here Lawrence always stopped; from this point on all his effort went to intensifying his picture, and by this he no doubt gained, as against Forster, in sheer coercive power. For the poor, lost respectable British people, Gino may serve as the embodiment of the masculine and pagan principle, but Forster knows that he is also coarse, dull, vain, pretentious, facilely polite and very much taken with the charms of respectability.

And it is irritating to be promised a principle and then to be given only an hypothesis. The hypothesis, having led us to criticize respectability, is useful, but we had wanted it to be conclusive. And Forster refuses to be conclusive. No sooner does he come to a conclusion than he must unravel it again. In *A Room With A View*, to take another example, he leads us to make the typical liberal discovery that Miss Bartlett, the poor relation who thinks she is acting from duty, is really acting from a kind of malice—she has been trying to recruit the unawakened heroine into "the armies of the benighted, who follow neither the heart nor the brain." But Forster does not stop at this conventionality, even though in 1908 it was not quite so conventional. For when the heroine at last fulfills her destiny, deserts Miss Bartlett and marries the man she had unconsciously loved (this is, to all appearance, a very modest little novel), she comes to perceive that in some yet more hidden way Miss Bartlett had really desired the union. And we have been prepared for this demonstration of the something still further "behind" the apparent by the action of the tolerant and enlightened clergyman, Mr. Beebe, who has ceased to be the angel of light and has set himself against the betrothal.

Forster's insistence on the double turn, on the something else that lies behind, is sometimes taken for "tolerance," but although it often suggests forgiveness (a different thing), it almost as often makes the severest judgments. And even when it suggests forgiveness it does not spring so much from gentleness of heart as from respect for two facts co-existing, from the moral realism that understands the one apple tasted. Forster can despise Gerald of *The Longest Journey* because Gerald is a prig and a bully, but he can invest Gerald's death with a kind of primitive dignity, telling us of the maid-servants who weep, "They had not liked Gerald, but he was a man, they were women, he had died." And after Gerald's death he can give Agnes Pembroke her moment of tragic nobility, only to pursue her implacably for her genteel brutality.

So much moral realism is rare enough to be a kind of surprise, and Forster, as I have said, likes to work with surprises mild or great. "Gerald died that afternoon," is the beginning of a chapter which follows immediately upon a description of Gerald full of superabundant life. We have to stand unusually far back from Forster's characters not to be startled when they turn about, and the peculiar pleasure to be had from his books is that of a judicious imperturbability. He is always shocking us by removing the heroism of his heroes and heroines; in *A Passage To India,* Mrs. Moore, of whom we had expected high actions, lets herself be sent away from the trial at which her testimony would have been crucial; Cyril Fielding, who as a solitary man had heroically opposed official ideas, himself becomes official when he is successful and married; and Dr. Aziz cannot keep to his role of the sensitive and enlightened native. It is a tampering with the heroic in the manner not of Lytton Strachey but of Tolstoy, a kind of mithridate against our being surprised by life. Let us not deceive ourselves, Forster seems to say, it is with just such frailties as Mrs. Moore and Mr. Fielding, and with and for such unregeneracies as Dr. Aziz that the problem of, let us say, India must be solved. The moments of any man's apparent grace are few, any man may have them and their effects are not easily to be calculated. It is on a helter-skelter distribution of grace that Forster pins what hopes he has; but for years after *A Passage To India*—it is still his latest novel—he has had the increasing sense of possible doom.

Perhaps it is because he has nothing of the taste for the unconditioned—Nietzsche calls it the worst of all tastes, the taste that is always being fooled by the world—that Forster has been able to deal so well with the idea of class. The liberal mind has in our time spoken much of this idea but has failed to believe in it. The modern liberal believes in categories and wage-scales and calls these class. Forster knows better, and in *How-*

ards End shows the conflicting truths of the idea—that on the one hand class is character, soul and destiny, and that on the other hand class is not finally determining. He knows that class may be truly represented only by struggle and contradiction, not by description, and preferably by moral struggle in the heart of a single person. When D. H. Lawrence wrote to Forster that he had made "a nearly deadly mistake glorifying those *business* people in *Howards End.* Business is no good," he was indulging his own taste for the unconditioned. It led him to read Forster inaccurately and it led him to make that significant shift from "business people" to "business." But Forster, who is too worldly to suppose that we can judge people without reference to their class, is also too worldly to suppose that we can judge class-conditioned action until we make a hypothetical deduction of the subject's essential humanity. It is exactly because Forster can judge the "business people" as he does, and because he can judge the lower classes so without sentimentality, that he can deal firmly and intelligently with his own class, and if there is muddle in *Howards End*—and the nearly allegorical reconciliation is rather forced—then, in speaking of class, clear ideas are perhaps a sign of ignorance, muddle the sign of true knowledge; surely *Howards End* stands with *Our Mutual Friend* and *The Princess Casamassima* as one of the great comments on the class struggle.

To an American, one of the most notable things about Forster's work is the directness and consciousness of its connection with tradition. We know of Forster that he is a Hellenist but not a "classicist," that he loves Greece in its mythical and naturalistic aspects, that Plato has never meant much to him, perhaps because he mistrusts the Platonic drive to the absolute and the Platonic judgment of the body and the senses. He dislikes the Middle Ages and all in Dante that is medieval. He speaks of himself as a humanist and traces his descent to Erasmus and Montaigne. He is clearly in the romantic line, yet his admiration for Goethe and Shelley is qualified; Beethoven is a passion with him but he distrusts Schumann. He has no faith in the regenerative power of Christianity and he is frequently hostile to the clergy, yet he has a tenderness for religion because it expresses, though it does not solve, the human mystery; in this connection it is worth recalling that he once projected a book on Samuel Butler. I list these preferences of Forster's not because I wish to bound his intellectual life—so brief a list could not do that—but because enumerating them will help to suggest how hard it would be to name an American novelist whose connection with intellectual tradition is equally clear. In America the opinion still prevails, though not so strongly as it once did, that a conscious relation with the past can only debilitate a novelist's powers, dull his perceptions and prevent his experience of life.

Yet if we test the matter we must come to a contrary conclusion. Sherwood Anderson, for example, though at first it may seem strange to say so, had much in common with Forster. The original gifts of the two men, so far as we can measure such things, might for purposes of argument be judged nearly equal. Each set himself in opposition to the respectable middle class of his own country and each found a symbolic contrast in an alien and, as it seemed, a freer race. Each celebrated the salvation of the loving heart, the passionate body and the liberated personality. Yet as Anderson went on, he grew more and more out of touch with the life he represented and criticized, and it was as if, however much he might experience beyond a certain point, he had not the means to receive and order what he felt, and so ceased really to feel. In his later years he became, as gifted men of a certain temperament tend to become, symbolic and visionary, but, never understanding how to handle his ultimate hopes and his obscurer insights, he began to repeat himself and became increasingly vague. The vision itself began to fail when Anderson could not properly judge its importance and could not find for it the right symbols and the right language; and in his later years he made the impression, terribly touching, of being lost and alone.

He was indeed lost and alone, though he need not have been. But the men with whom he might have made community were not to be found where he thought they were, in the stable and the craftsman's shop. The men of Anderson's true community were the members of the European tradition of thought. But Anderson was either indifferent to the past or professionally contemptuous of it; he subscribed to the belief that American art must throw off the shackles of tradition and work only with intuition and observation. Anderson saw "culture" as gentility; and he saw it too, one feels, as a kind of homogeneous mass to be accepted or rejected only in totality; he did not know that it was a collection of individuals much like himself with whom he might claim kinship and equality, nor did he know that what he was demanding for life had been demanded by other men time out of mind. Anderson's books, like so many other American books, had at first a great and taking power; then, like so many other American books that have astonished and delighted us, they fell out of the texture of our lives, they became curiosities.

Let us say the worst we can of Forster—that beside a man like Anderson with his tumble of emotions and child-like questions, Forster might seem to have something donnish about him. But then we must at once say that Forster has a sense of the way things go which Anderson, for all his great explicit impulse toward actuality, never had—the sense of what houses, classes, institutions, politics, manners and people are like. Forster knows, as Anderson never knew, that things are really there. All his training has helped bring

his impulses to consciousness, and the play of consciousness over intuition and desire gives him his curious tough insight.

The great thing Forster has been able to learn from his attachment to tradition and from his sense of the past is his belief in the present. He has learned not to be what most of us are—eschatological. Most of us, consciously or unconsciously, are discontented with the nature rather than with the use of the human faculty; deep in our assumption lies the hope and the belief that humanity will end its career by developing virtues which will be admirable exactly because we cannot now conceive them. The past has been a weary failure, the present cannot matter, for it is but a step forward to the final judgment; we look to the future when the best of the works of man will seem but the futile and slightly disgusting twitchings of primeval creatures: thus, in the name of a superior and contemptuous posterity, we express our self-hatred—and our desire for power.

This is a moral and historical error into which Forster never falls; his whole work, indeed, is an implied protest against it. The very relaxation of his style, its colloquial unpretentiousness, is a mark of his acceptance of the human fact as we know it now. He is content with the human possibility and content with its limitations. The way of human action of course does not satisfy him, but he does not believe there are any new virtues to be discovered; not by becoming better, he says, but by ordering and distributing his native goodness can man live as befits him.

This, it seems to me, might well be called worldliness, this acceptance of man in the world without the sentimentality of cynicism and without the sentimentality of rationalism. Forster is that remarkably rare being, a naturalist whose naturalism is positive and passionate, not negative, passive and apologetic for man's nature. He accepts the many things the liberal imagination likes to put out of sight. He can accept, for example, not only the reality but the power of death—"Death destroys a man, but the idea of death saves him," he says, and the fine scene in *The Longest Journey* in which Rickie forces Agnes to "mind" the death of Gerald is a criticism not only of the British fear of emotion but also of liberalism's incompetence before tragedy. To Forster, as to Blake, naturalism suggests not the invalidity or the irrelevance of human emotions but, rather, their validity and strength: "Far more mysterious than the call of sex to sex is the tenderness that we throw into that call; far wider is the gulf between us and the farmyard than between the farmyard and the garbage that nourishes it." (pp. 17-23)

Lionel Trilling, "Introduction: Forster and the Liberal Imagination," in his *E.M. Forster,* 1943. Reprint by Harcourt Brace Jovanovich, 1980, pp. 7-24.

JOSEPH EPSTEIN
(essay date 1985)

[In the following essay, Epstein explores Forster's motives as a novelist.]

How did E. M. Forster manage to elude the Nobel Prize in Literature? He published his last novel, *A Passage to India,* at the age of forty-five in 1924 and died at the age of ninety-two in 1970. He must have been passed over, then, no fewer than thirty or forty times. Not winning the Nobel Prize put him in a select little club, Tolstoy, Henry James, Chekhov, and Proust being among its most distinguished members—rather a more select club, when one thinks about it, than that comprised by the winners. Still, one wonders, did Forster think much about it? . . .

True, Forster's work is relatively unmarked by the rather strenuous thinking on the cosmic level that Nobel Prize committees seem traditionally to favor. Yet E. M. Forster has long held a special place in the hearts of English-speaking readers. He is the novelist par excellence of modern liberalism, and during a period when the liberal point of view has been ascendant. If he had won the Nobel Prize, it would scarcely have been a surprise. On the contrary, it is rather surprising in retrospect that he did not.

The complicated truth is that E. M. Forster was probably better off without the Nobel Prize. It would have been unseemly, even slightly unbecoming to him, a man who made something of a specialty of claiming so little for himself in the way of literary aspirations. But aspirations are one thing, reputation another. Forster's reputation has never been other than high. Even today it sails in the literary stratosphere. The most consistent note in the often strident criticism of David Lean's recent film version of *A Passage to India,* for example, has been that Lean betrayed the richness and subtlety of Forster's novel. What has been almost universally judged to be a poor film has thus redounded to Forster's posthumous standing.

Not that this standing required much in the way of reinforcement. Apart from his attempt to write a homosexual idyll in the posthumously published novel *Maurice,* Forster's work has received no serious attacks, and his reputation has remained oddly inviolate. During his lifetime it appeared that the less he wrote, the higher his reputation rose. (p. 48)

I have called E. M. Forster the novelist par excellence of modern liberalism, but I am not the first to have done so. Lionel Trilling did it as early as 1943 in

a critical study that over the years has immensely aided E. M. Forster's reputation [see excerpt dated 1943]. As Trilling allowed in a preface to the second edition of this book, his study had "benefited by the special energies that attend a polemical purpose." Trilling had been attacking American writing for what he deemed its "dullness and its pious social simplicities," and against this he now posed Forster's "vivacity, complexity, and irony." Like many of those writers Trilling had attacked, Forster was a liberal, but a liberal with a difference—he was a liberal, in Trilling's view, "at war with the liberal imagination." Forster was of the liberal tradition yet at the same time would have nothing to do with its simple solutions, its crudities, its sentimentality, and its earnest belief in rationalism. In other words, without losing his idealism neither did Forster lose his head; never for a moment did Forster settle for received opinions and indeed, according to Trilling, he even "refuses to be conclusive." Forster possessed—a crucial element, this, for Lionel Trilling—"moral realism," which Trilling defined as not only "the awareness of morality itself but of the contradictions, paradoxes, and dangers of living the moral life." (p. 49)

E. M. Forster's intellectual ability was not of the ordinary kind. He never felt he had any commanding power of abstract thought. . . . His were the powers of serene observation, often oblique but usually telling. He had quiet wit and a lyrical streak and imaginative sympathy. He had a lucid mind and had early acquired a prose style of unobtrusive elegance that permitted him to state profound things with simplicity. In Forster, intellect united with sensibility, and their tethering in tandem produced the artist that, at Cambridge, he knew he would become. (p. 51)

Evelyn Waugh once remarked that most writers, even quite good ones, have only one or two stories to tell. The exceptions are the truly major figures; Balzac, Dickens, George Eliot, Tolstoy, James, Conrad. But E. M. Forster, I don't think many would wish to dispute, is not among their number. He was a one-story man. His is the story of the undeveloped heart. He told it four different times, then set it in India and told it again. In this story a character—an English man or woman of the middle class—is placed in a crucial situation, crucible of the spirit as it turns out, where his or her heart either develops or permanently stultifies. This crucible invariably entails a confrontation with the primitive, or the pre-literate, or the *déclassé.* In all Forster's novels culture is pitted against spirit, mind against feeling. It takes no deep reader to recognize that the author, though himself a habitué of the concert hall and of suburban teas upon English lawns, is on the side of spirit and feeling.

A paradigmatic E. M. Forster story is **"The Road from Colonus,"** a tale written when he was in his twenties. In it a group of English travelers are touring by mule in Greece. Mr. Lucas, the oldest member of the group, comes upon an enormous plane tree near a rather squalid Greek house. The center of the tree is hollowed out, and from it water flows, which irrigates and makes fertile the land below. The tree is a shrine from which little votive offerings hang. The sight of the tree stirs Mr. Lucas, who climbs into its hollow, the water flowing about him. In it he feels overpoweringly the urge to live. . . . He feels himself utterly at peace— "the feeling of the swimmer, who, after long struggle with chopping seas, finds that after all the tide will sweep him to his goal."

At which moment his daughter and the remainder of the party of English travelers arrive. They exclaim over the beauty of the tree, the crude little Greek dwelling, the entire scene. But Mr. Lucas "found them intolerable. Their enthusiasm was superficial, commonplace, and spasmodic." When Mr. Lucas announces that he plans to remain there, to stay as a guest in the house of the Greeks, his daughter and the members of the party humor him. . . . But of course he cannot be permitted to stay in any such place. In the end he is dragged off, brusquely set upon his mule by their guide. It is not to be.

In the second part of the story Mr. Lucas and his daughter are back in England. He is complaining about the disorderly behavior of their neighbor's children. She has just received a parcel from Athens containing asphodel bulbs, wrapped up in an old Greek newspaper. It happens that the newspaper carries a story about a small tragedy that occurred in the province of Messenia, where a large tree blew down in the night and crushed to death the occupants of a nearby house. It is of course the same tree and the same house from which Mr. Lucas had been forcibly removed. Now, in England, he is not much interested in the story. His daughter remarks upon what a near miss they have had. Had he stayed in the house as he wished, he might well have been killed, too. But Mr. Lucas is scarcely listening. Instead he rambles on about his neighbors and composes a letter of complaint to their landlord. "Such a marvelous deliverance," says his daughter, "does make one believe in Providence." But in fact Mr. Lucas had to all intents and purposes died the moment he had been dragged away; his heart had shriveled from that very moment and from that very moment, too, he had been consigned to live out his days in middle-class English suburban sterility.

To dwell on **"The Road from Colonus"** a bit longer, one grants Forster his concluding point: yes, it would have been better to have died happy, even that very night, in the rough-hewn Greek house, feeling oneself in touch with the spirit of the world, than to live out one's days a grumbly, grousing old man. That is conceded. What is less easy to concede is the validity of Mr. Lucas's mystical experience in the tree and the

Dust jacket of Forster's posthumously published novel about homosexuality.

wisdom of the Greek family, who, however squalid the conditions of their lives, had never lost the gift of living in nature and hence had retained the secret of the art of life. Clearly, Forster hated middle-class life, the sterility of its culture, the aridity of its relationships, but all he could pose against it was the superiority of those who, through whatever accidents of geography or social class, eluded it.

For an otherwise remarkably subtle novelist, E. M. Forster could be remarkably crude in his division of characters into those who either were or were not in touch with life. In the middle were those characters whose personal drama—supplying the drama of his novels—revolved around the question of on which side they would fall. Like many another artist and intellectual of his day, Forster suffered the condition known as *horror victorianus*; in his novels villains and villainesses are, not very far under the skin, uneminent Victorians: people who believe in progress, empire, the virtues of their social class. As he presents them they are not so much cardboard as metallic; they continually give off sharp pings of their author's disapproval.

Nor did Forster have great powers of invention.

All his novels are marred by unbelievable touches. Rickie Elliot in *The Longest Journey* falls in love with his wife-to-be when he sees her being passionately kissed by her fiancé; a bookcase topples onto the pathetic culture-hungry Leonard Bast in the crucial scene in *Howards End;* Lucy Honeychurch is kissed by George Emerson in a field of spring flowers in Italy, which is noted by a female novelist who later publishes a novel reproducing the scene, which causes a scandal that in turn forces the action in *A Room With a View;* a carriage crashes, killing a kidnapped infant in *Where Angels Fear to Tread;* characters regularly die on the instant ("Gerald died that afternoon," is an inspissated but not anomalous sentence in a Forster novel). I do not mean that such things don't happen in life, which provides the trickiest plots of all, but in Forster's novels there is a herky-jerky quality to his plots. If one of the things masterful novelists do is to make the unpredictable seem inevitable, in Forster the unpredictable tends to be expected, which is not at all the same thing. (pp. 54-5)

[If] E. M. Forster had few cards in his hand, he could nonetheless shuffle them brilliantly. He was an astute judge of character and a potent moralist, in the French sense of the word. Of Mr. Wilcox in *Howards End,* for example, he writes: "But true insight began just where his intelligence ended, and one gathered that this was the case with most millionaires." Adela Quested in *A Passage to India* fails to realize "that it is only hypocrites who cannot forgive hypocrisy." Forster's novels are studded with such small gems. Quite as much as for their action—perhaps rather more than for their action—one anticipates Forster's aphoristic commentary upon his characters.

In his book on Forster Lionel Trilling remarks that "in Forster there is a deep and important irresolution of whether the world is one of good and evil, sheep and goats, or one of good-and-evil, of sheep who are somehow goats and goats who are somehow sheep." Trilling refers here to Forster's propensity in his novels to allow good actions occasionally to derive from characters of whom he otherwise disapproves, and, going the other way 'round, to impute qualities of which he clearly disapproves to characters he clearly wishes us to admire. (p. 55)

Such curious turnings in character can lend Forster's novels verisimilitude, though sometimes, as in Charlotte Bartlett's radical turning to the side of good in *A Room With a View,* it can be quite unconvincing. But Trilling is at least partially correct in averring that E. M. Forster did not resolve the question of good and evil in his novels. I say partially because, with the exception of *A Passage to India,* I do not believe it loomed as a large problem for him. Forster seemed not to be greatly perplexed by questions of good and evil and of the meaning of life. He thought, within his own

set limits, he knew life's meaning. As Mr. Emerson, one of Forster's guru characters in *A Room With a View* says, "Passion is sanity"; and it is he who shows Lucy Honeychurch, the heroine of the novel, "the holiness of direct desire."

The only novel of Forster's in which obeisance to the instinctual life is not central is his most famous novel, *A Passage to India.* It is, interestingly enough, the novel Lionel Trilling liked least. . . . Certainly, as Forster himself felt, *A Passage to India* is the best-made of his novels: the most elegantly written, in some ways the most filled with wise comment—it is the only one of his novels written when he was in his forties—and the most solidly organized. At the center of the novel is that grand old favorite of symbol-hunting English professors, the scene at the Marabar Caves which Forster, it transpires, allowed that he had fuddled. Of this scene he wrote to William Plomer: "I tried to show that India is an unexplainable muddle by introducing an unexplained muddle—Miss Quested's experience in the cave. When asked what happened there, *I don't know.*" Still, muddle and fuddle, the novel is an impressive piece of work. . . .

So long has *A Passage to India* held the status of a modern classic that writing about it today one feels almost as if called to comment upon *The Rite of Spring* or *Sunday Afternoon on the Grande Jatte.* Rereading it after more than a quarter of a century, one is struck by how interesting a portrait it provides of the Indian character as viewed by Western eyes. One is also struck by its streak of unfairness. At various points in the novel it is difficult to determine which Forster felt more strongly: his love of India or his hatred of England's presence there. He gives the Anglo-Indians very short shrift, so short that there can be no doubt about his having taken sides. . . .

Books are created in history, and through the events of history is our reading of them influenced. Here it must be noted that history has dissipated much of the glory of *A Passage to India,* by revealing that the treatment of the Indians by the British had been nowhere nearly so cruel, indeed murderous, as the treatment of the Indians by one another, beginning with the massacres following upon independence and continuing even today with the bloody dispute between the Indian government and the Sikhs.

E. M. Forster probably never thought himself a very political writer. He tended, in fact, to think himself rather above politics. . . . To be above politics, to be seeking only truth, is ever the plaint of the emancipatory liberal. E. M. Forster, it is well to remember, was the author of a novel (*Maurice*) he could not publish and for the better part of his life was enmeshed in homosexual relationships he could not openly declare. The truth he sought was of a particular kind; it presupposed freedom. For him, indeed, without freedom, again of a particular kind, there could be no truth. And the particular kinds, both of truth and of freedom, were at their base political. (p. 56)

[The] novels upon which E. M. Forster's reputation rests now seem chiefly screens for their author's yearning for freedom for his own trapped instinctual life. He wrote about men and women, often commenting upon them brilliantly, yet other things must all the while have been at the forefront of his mind.

What these other things were are revealed less in the sadly sentimental novel *Maurice* than in a collection of posthumously published stories entitled *The Life to Come.* These are stories about the suppression of homosexuality and about giving way to it, about its costs so long as society disapproves of it and its pleasures nonetheless. One of them, **"Dr. Woolacott,"** T. E. Lawrence, to whom Forster showed it, thought the best thing he had ever written. Another, **"The Obelisk,"** has a touch of nastiness one would not have expected from the great proponent of personal relations. In it a husband and wife on holiday meet up with two sailors also on holiday. To make a short story even shorter, one sailor goes off into the bushes with the wife while, though we do not know this until the end, the other sailor has gone off into other bushes with the husband. It is arch and cruel, a stereotypical homosexual mocking of marriage, which is no prettier than heterosexual mocking of homosexuality. "Only connect," Forster famously wrote in an epigraph to *Howards End.* Indeed.

What *The Life to Come* along with the *Selected Letters* and P. N. Furbank's biography all conduce to make plain is that in E. M. Forster the emancipatory liberal appears to have hidden a homosexual utopian. Ironically, the victories of emancipatory liberalism, issuing in the breakdown of censorship and with it the freedom to know and publish hitherto private facts of writers' lives, have resulted in our having to reassess E. M. Forster's novels radically. It is no longer possible to think of Forster as a writer who happened to have been a homosexual; now he must be considered a writer for whom homosexuality was the central, the dominant, fact in his life. Given this centrality, this dominance, it hardly seems wild to suggest that the chief impulse behind Forster's novels, with their paeans and pleas for the life of the instincts, was itself homosexual. Given, again, all that we now know about his private life, it is difficult to read them otherwise.

In a curious way the effect of this is to render E. M. Forster's novels obsolete, and in a way that art of the first magnitude never becomes. Filled with wisdom though all of his novels are at their peripheries, ornamented though all of them are by his lucid and seductive style, at their center each conducts an argument. E. M. Forster was essentially a polemical and didactic novelist. He argued against the sterility of middle-class English life, he attempted to teach the beauty of the passionate instinctive life. In the first instance, he wrote out of his personal antipathies; in the second, out of his personal yearnings.

Viewed from the present, it can be said that in large part Forster won his argument. An English and vastly more sophisticated Sinclair Lewis (a writer whom Forster himself admired), with a sexual and spiritual twist added, he has, in his quiet way, been one of the most successful of those who in our time have written *pour épater les bourgeois.* As for his teaching about the instinctual life—the sanity of passion, the holiness of desire, and the rest of it—here, too, his side, that of emancipatory liberalism, has known no shortage of victories. If, then, his writing today seems so thin, so hollow, and finally so empty, can it be in part because we have now all had an opportunity to view the progress of emancipationism in our lifetimes, the liberation that was the name of Forster's own most ardent desire, and know it to be itself thin, hollow, and finally empty? (p. 57)

Joseph Epstein, "One Cheer for E. M. Forster," in *Commentary,* Vol. 80, No. 3, September, 1985, pp. 48-57.

SOURCES FOR FURTHER STUDY

Beer, J. B. *The Achievement of E. M. Forster.* New York: Barnes & Noble, 1962, 225 p.

A highly regarded examination of Forster's life and works.

Das, G. K., and Beer, John, eds. *E. M. Forster: A Human Exploration.* New York: New York University Press, 1979, 314 p.

Collection of twenty four essays on various aspects of Forster's works.

Furbank, P. N. *E. M. Forster: A Life.* New York: Harcourt Brace Jovanovich, 1981, 672 p.

An extensive biography of Forster's life.

Gardner, Philip, ed. *E. M. Forster: The Critical Heritage.* London and Boston: Routledge & Kegan Paul, 1973, 498 p.

Collection of short reviews of Forster's works from the time of their first appearance through 1971.

Stone, Wilfred. *The Cave and the Mountain: A Study of E. M. Forster.* London: Oxford University Press, 1966, 436 p.

  A respected examination of Forster's novels, short stories, criticism, and selected prose works. Includes many photographs that illuminate Forster's life and works.

Summers, Claude J. *E. M. Forster.* New York: Frederick Ungar Publishing Co., 1983, 406 p.

  Examines Forster's life and homosexuality in relation to his fiction.

Anne Frank

1929-1945

(Born Annelies Marie Frank) German-born Dutch diarist, fabulist, short story writer, and essayist.

INTRODUCTION

A nne Frank is known throughout the world for her diary *Het Achterhuis* (1947; *Anne Frank: The Diary of a Young Girl*), which documents her adolescence in German-occupied Amsterdam during World War II. The diary also describes the impact of Nazi anti-Semitism on both Jewish and non-Jewish Dutch individuals during that era. Her diary is at once a candid self-portrait, a portrayal of domestic life, an account of people threatened with imminent death, a depiction of experiences and problems common to young adults, and an examination of universal moral issues. This private journal, which she did not live to see published, sheds light on an episode in history that embodied extremes of both the degradation and the nobility of the human spirit.

Frank was born to an upper-class Jewish family in the city of Frankfurt. The early childhood of Frank and her elder sister, Margot, was secure, loving, and comfortable, but the year of Anne's birth also marked the onset of a worldwide economic depression, a catastrophic event that affected the lives of a great number of Europeans. In Germany, economic disaster, combined with the lingering effects of the harsh demands made on Germany after its defeat in World War I, led to the installation of Adolf Hitler as leader of the government. Through policies that stressed rearmament, nationalism, and racism, Hitler sought to restore his country to a position of preeminence in Europe. A primary target for Hitler's condemnation were Jews; by aggravating long-held antisemitic prejudice, Hitler sought to purge Germany of what he considered an exploitive group. In 1933, following Hitler's decree that Jewish and non-Jewish children could not attend the same schools, the Franks left their homeland and by 1934 were settled in Amsterdam, where Anne's father, Otto Frank, directed a food import business.

Despite the growing threat of war, Frank lived a normal life, much like any Dutch girl, for the next few years. She attended a Montessori school and was an average student, remembered by one teacher as being ordinary in many ways but as having the ability to draw more from her experiences than other children. In many respects, Frank remained absorbed in everyday life even after the Germans invaded Holland in 1940 and imposed harsh anti-Jewish measures. Under the German occupation, Frank was forced to leave the Montessori school and attend the Jewish Lyceum, where she adjusted well and soon became known for her pranks and her incessant talking. However, as Nazi horrors increased, including the roundup of Amsterdam's Jews in 1941 for incarceration in concentration camps, Otto Frank and his business partners secretly prepared a hiding place in some rooms located in the top, back portion of their company's combined warehouse and office building on Prinsengracht Canal. In June 1942 Anne celebrated her thirteenth birthday, receiving among her presents a small clothbound diary which she deemed "possibly the nicest of all" her gifts. Several weeks later, Margot Frank was notified to report to the reception center for the Westerbork concentration camp, and the family fled into the "Secret Annex." They were joined shortly thereafter by a Mr. and Mrs. Van Pelz (rendered as "Van Daan" in Anne's diary) and their fifteen-year-old son Peter, and several months later by Albert Dussel, a middle-aged dentist. Together they remained hidden and virtually imprisoned for over two years.

During her confinement, Frank continued her education under her father's guidance, and on her own initiative wrote the equivalent of two books: in addition to her diary she also wrote a number of fables, short stories, reminiscences, essays, and an unfinished novel. Life in the annex, a common concern in her diary entries, was strained by quarrels and tensions arising from the anxiety inherent in the situation, the frustrations of a monotonous, restrictive life, and personality clashes. The eight annex inhabitants shared cramped, drab quarters and had to remain stiflingly quiet during the day, at times refraining from using water faucets and toilet facilities to avoid being heard by other people in the building. Their very survival depended on remaining undiscovered. Through the generosity of four benefactors who risked their own lives, the annex inhabitants were provided with food and supplies, as well as companionship and news from the outside world. When on June 6, 1944 (D-Day), news came that the tide of war had turned in favor of the Allies, hope increased for the annex group. Then suddenly, on August 4, 1944, their hiding place was raided, and they became prisoners of the Nazis. All were sent first on a passenger train to Westerbork, and then in a cattle car among the last human shipment to Auschwitz. Anne

was remembered by a survivor of Auschwitz as a leader and as someone who remained sensitive and caring when most prisoners protected themselves from feeling anything. In March 1945, two months before the German surrender, Anne Frank died of typhoid fever in the Bergen-Belsen concentration camp.

Of the eight inhabitants of the secret annex, only Otto Frank survived. When he returned to Holland from Auschwitz, Anne's diary and papers were given to him. Anne's writings had been left behind by the secret police in their search for valuables, and were found in the hiding place by two Dutch women who had helped the fugitives survive. Frank kept her diary for nearly twenty-six months, capturing experiences which range from a visit to the ice cream parlor to her reflections about God and human nature. What emerges from Frank's diary is a multifaceted young person who is at once an immature young girl and a precocious, deep-thinking individual. Yet, her inner world and writing ability had hitherto remained unknown to anyone but herself. After reading her diary, Otto Frank confessed, "I never knew my little Anna was so deep." Shortly after the war's end, he circulated typed copies of the diary among his friends, who quickly recognized it as a meaningful human document which should not remain a private legacy. Published two years after Anne's death, the diary has since been translated into at least forty languages and adapted into the Pulitzer Prize–winning play *The Diary of Anne Frank,* which was made into a motion picture.

Although stylistic considerations are of minor importance when compared to the documentary value of the diary, some critics have described Frank as a "born writer," or as someone who could have become a professional writer. Annie Romein-Vershoor has expressed the view that Frank "possessed the one important characteristic of a great writer: an open mind, untouched by complacency and prejudice." Initially, Frank had considered her diary a private work that she might someday show to a "real friend." Motivated by her need for a confidant and by a strong desire to write, she disclosed her deepest thoughts and feelings to her diary, though she sometimes doubted that anyone would be interested "in the unbosomings of a thirteen-year-old schoolgirl." Conceiving of her diary as a friend, she named it "Kitty" and wrote her entries in the form of letters to Kitty. Throughout, the diary reveals Frank's sense of an unseen audience as well as her ambivalence toward the importance of her own experience. She also sensed the need for variety in her writing and was able to achieve it despite the repetitiveness of routine and paucity of stimulation in her life. The vivid, poignant entries range in tone from humorous to serious, casual to intense, and reveal Frank's ability to write narrative and descriptive accounts as well as to write about abstract ideas. The diary, often commended for its engaging style, is full of vitality.

Meyer Levin has praised the work for sustaining "the tension of a well-constructed novel," and attributes this to Frank's dramatic psychological development and to the physical dangers that threatened the group.

Because Frank's diary was not written as creative literature, and because of the extraordinary circumstances of the author's life, critics most commonly discuss the human and historical importance of the work rather than its aesthetic or structural elements. Most also express their personal responses to the diary, as well as to its worldwide success and its powerful impact on readers. Anne herself and her experiences in growing up are the primary focus of discussions about the diary as a human document. Henry Pommer has stated, "The chief literary merit of the diary is its permitting us to know intimately Anne's young, eager, difficult, lovable self," and other critics express similar opinions. John Berryman has underscored the significance of her diary as a frank account of growing up, explaining that, unlike other books which are merely about adolescence, Frank's diary makes available the mysterious, fundamental process of a child becoming an adult as it is actually happening. In simply being herself, Frank also succeeded in portraying the universalities of human nature and in touching millions. In particular, young people can at once identify with her zest for life and her typical adolescent problems and be inspired by her courage and ideals.

As a historical document the diary is an indictment against the Nazis' destruction of human life and culture. As Ilya Ehrenburg has stated, "One voice speaks for six million—the voice not of a sage or a poet but of an ordinary little girl." Critics have posited that while newsreels and books which explicitly portray Nazi atrocities have had a stupefying effect on people, Frank's story acquaints people with everyday, recognizable individuals, and has thus been phenomenally effective in communicating this enormous tragedy. In postwar Germany, for example, there were widespread expressions of guilt and shame in response to viewing the stage production of *The Diary of Anne Frank*, and an intense interest in Frank among German youth after years of repressive silence regarding Nazi crimes. Anne Birstein and Alfred Kazin have asserted that "the reality of what certain people have had to endure in our time can be grasped humanly and politically only because of the modulation of a document like *The Diary of a Young Girl*, which permits us to see certain experiences in a frame, in a thoroughly human setting, so that we can bear them at all." Recognized by some critics as a portrait of humanity in all of its varied aspects, Frank's diary has been used as a basis for considering other injustices in the world and for assessing moral responsibility in contemporary crises. Frank herself has become a symbol, not only of six million murdered Jews, but of other people who suffer persecution because of race or belief.

Frank's diary, which embodies the triumph of the human spirit in a destructive, dehumanizing system, has outlasted many other books about World War II. Although it has been suggested that her writing is an escape into the ideal, it may be this quality which partially accounts for the universal acceptance of the diary. Frank herself questioned her idealism in an often-quoted passage: "It's really a wonder that I haven't dropped all my ideals, because they seem so absurd and impossible to carry out. Yet I keep them, because in spite of everything I still believe that people are really good at heart." Her story and ideals have inspired many creative and constructive responses which reflect the timeless message of her diary: the importance, as stated by Rabbi Philip S. Bernstein, of keeping "pity and kindness and love alive in the world."

(For further information about Frank's life and works, see *Contemporary Authors*, Vol. 113 and *Twentieth-Century Literary Criticism*, Vol. 17.)

CRITICAL COMMENTARY

ANNIE ROMEIN-VERSHOOR

(essay 1947)

[In the following excerpt from an essay that first appeared in Dutch in 1947, Romein-Vershoor praises Anne Frank's diary as both a war document and as a testament of human feeling.]

Under the exceptional circumstances of life in the Annex, the growth of the lively, intelligent and impressionable child Anne Frank, from girl to woman, from child to adult, occurred in a remarkably brief time. The relationship of the growing young individual to the outside world, which in normal life is recorded in a great number of more or less fluctuating and varying lines, was here reduced to an extremely simple pattern, forcing her perceptive spirit to expand in depth rather than in width. In a continual process of rapprochement, collision, and wrestling with the seven people around

Principal Works

Het Achterhuis (diary) 1947
  [Anne Frank: The Diary of a Young Girl, 1952]
The Works of Anne Frank (diary, fables, reminis-
  cences, short stories, and essays) 1959
Tales from the House Behind (fables, reminiscences,
  short stories, essays, and unfinished novel) 1962
Tales from the Secret Annex (fables, reminiscences,
  short stories, and essays) 1984

her, in a constant state of inquisitive examination of these seven eternal close-ups, the child's knowledge of human character grew perceptibly. Through introspection forced upon her by circumstances, through a struggle with herself and her limited possibilities, the self-knowledge of the child playing at keeping a diary, evolved with unbelievable speed to sharp analysis, even of her own dreams and illusions, of her reactions to her surroundings, of her fate, and of her abandonment of all the beautiful little girl's dreams which were no longer a part of her life in hiding. . . .

There is much more to say about this diary. It is a war document, a document of the cruelty and heartbreaking misery of the persecution of the Jews, of human helpfulness and treason, of human adjustment and non-adjustment, of the small joys and the great and small miseries of life in hiding, written in a direct, non-literary, and therefore often excellent style, by this child who in any case possessed the one important characteristic of a great writer: an open mind, untouched by complacency and prejudice.

But for me the most important thing about this diary is not the documentation, which so often is and will be recorded elsewhere. When people in the tropics take a young plant from the temperate mountain zone and plant it in a very hot area, it will bloom once, richly and superabundantly, only to die soon after. That feeling is what touches me the most in this diary.

In the same way, this small, plucky geranium stood and bloomed, and bloomed, behind the shuttered windows of the Annex.

Annie Romein-Vershoor, "The Book that Started a Chain Reaction: Prefaces to the Diary," in *A Tribute to Anne Frank*, Anna G. Steenmeijer, Otto Frank, and Henri van Praag, eds., Doubleday & Company, Inc., 1971, p. 34.

MEYER LEVIN
(essay date 1952)

[An American Jewish writer whose career spanned fifty years, Levin was a novelist, playwright, short story writer, editor, journalist, and filmmaker. While on assignment as a war correspondent, he was with the liberators of Buchenwald, Dachau, and other concentration camps. In the following excerpt from a review of *Anne Frank: The Diary of a Young Girl*, he praises the work for successfully communicating, in classic form, the drama of puberty, and he recommends the diary be read both for insight and enjoyment.]

Anne Frank's diary is too tenderly intimate a book to be frozen with the label "classic," and yet no lesser designation serves. For little Anne Frank, spirited, moody, witty, self-doubting, succeeded in communicating in virtually perfect, or classic, form the drama of puberty. But her book is not a classic to be left on the library shelf. It is a warm and stirring confession, to be read over and over for insight and enjoyment.

The diary is a classic on another level, too. It happened that during the two years that mark the most extraordinary changes in a girl's life, Anne Frank lived in astonishing circumstances: she was hidden with seven other people in a secret nest of rooms behind her father's place of business, in Amsterdam. Thus, the diary tells the life of a group of Jews waiting in fear of being taken by the Nazis. . . .

This is no lugubrious ghetto tale, no compilation of horrors. Reality can prove surprisingly different from invented reality, and Anne Frank's diary simply bubbles with amusement, love, discovery. It has its share of disgust, its moments of hatred, but it is so wondrously alive, so near, that one feels overwhelmingly the universalities of human nature. These people might be living next door; their within-the-family emotions, their tensions and satisfactions are those of human character and growth, anywhere.

Because the diary was not written in retrospect, it contains the trembling life of every moment—Anne Frank's voice becomes the voice of six million vanished Jewish souls. It is difficult to say in which respect her book is more "important," but one forgets the double significance of this document in experiencing it as an intimate whole, for one feels the presence of this child-becoming-woman as warmly as though she was snuggled on a near-by sofa.

We meet Anne on her thirteenth birthday, "Quicksilver Anne" to her adored father, but "Miss

Chatterbox" and "Miss Quack-Quack," she tells us, to her teacher—for the family is still at liberty. Indeed, her teacher makes her write a self-curing essay on chattering; she turns in a poem that convulses teacher and class, and is allowed to remain her talkative self without further reprimand.

Yet, with the moodiness of adolescence, she feels lonesome. "Let me put it more clearly, since no one will believe that a girl of 13 feels herself quite alone in the world, nor is it so. I have darling parents and a sister of 16. I know about thirty people whom one might call friends—I have strings of boy friends, anxious to catch a glimpse of me, who . . . peep at me through mirrors in class. I have relations, aunts, uncles, who are darlings too, a good home, no—I don't seem to lack anything. But it's the same with all my friends, just fun and nothing more. We don't seem to be able to get any closer, that is the root of the whole trouble. Hence, this diary. I want this diary itself to be my friend, and shall call my friend Kitty."

What child of 13 hasn't had these feelings, and resolved to confide in a diary? Anne carried it through, never shrinking from revealing the ugly things about herself. . . .

A born writer, Anne zestfully portrays the Annex inhabitants, with all their flaws and virtues. . . . Anne Frank's diary probes far deeper than [John Hersey's] "The Wall" into the core of human relations, and succeeds better than "The Wall" in bringing us an understanding of life under threat.

And this quality brings it home to any family in the world today. Just as the Franks lived in momentary fear of the Gestapo's knock on their hidden door, so every family today lives in fear of the knock of war. Anne's diary is a great affirmative answer to the life-question of today, for she shows how ordinary people, within this ordeal, consistently hold to the greater human values.

The Frank's Dutch friends in the office on the other side of the secret door sustained them to the end. "Never have we heard *one* word of the burden which we certainly must be to them. . . . They put on the brightest possible faces, bring flowers and presents for birthdays, risking their own lives to help others." These Dutch friends, Miep, Elli, Kraler, Koophuis, even managed to smuggle in Chanukah gifts, and shyly offered their Christmas remembrances to the hidden Jews. (p. 1)

Most wondrous of all is her love affair. Like a flower under a stone fulfilling itself, she came to her first love in her allotted time. "I give myself completely. But one thing. He may touch my face, but no more." All is told, from her potato-fetching devices for going up to Peter's attic lair, to the first misplaced kiss, on her ear. And the parents worrying about the youngsters

trysting up there in the dusk, sitting by the window over the canal. And her fears that her older sister is lonely and jealous, leading to an amazing exchange of letters between the two girls, in those hidden rooms. Finally, there is even the tender disillusionment with Peter, as Anne reaches toward maturity, and a character understanding replaces the first tug of love. In all this there are perceptions in depth, strivings toward mother, father, sister, containing love-anguish of the purest universality.

As is arch-typical for a girl in this period, her relations with her mother are difficult. Unflinchingly, Anne records each incident. "Dear Kitty—Oh dear, I've got another terrible black mark against my name. I was lying in bed yesterday evening waiting for Daddy to come and say my prayers with me, and wish me good night, when Mummy came into my room, sat on my bed, and asked very nicely, 'Anne, Daddy can't come yet, shall I say your prayers with you tonight?' 'No, Mummy,' I answered.

"Mummy got up, paused by my bed for a moment, and walked slowly toward the door. Suddenly she turned around, and with a distorted look on her face said, 'I don't want to be cross, love cannot be forced.' There were tears in her eyes as she left the room.

"I lay still in bed, feeling at once that I had been horrible to push her away so rudely. . . . It is hard to speak the truth, and yet it is the truth: she herself has pushed me away, her tactless remarks and her crude jokes, which I don't find at all funny, have now made me insensitive to any love from her side."

But her understanding grew, until she could write, "The period when I caused Mummy to shed tears is over. I have grown wiser and Mummy's nerves are not so much on edge."

It is this unfolding psychological drama of a girl's growth, mingled with the physical danger of the group, that frees Anne's book from the horizontal effect of most diaries. Hers rises continuously, with the tension of a well-constructed novel. On the plane of physical suspense, a series of burglaries in the office-warehouse dreadfully endangers the hidden group. And there is the race of the Nazis' intensified hunt for victims, as against the progress of the Allied campaign, followed over a clandestine radio.

Psychologically, the diary contains the completely rounded story of the development of a social nature; one lives in suspense, watching it unfold: will she understand her mother? will she surmount her perplexities? will she comprehend her body-changes, so frankly described?

The girl's last entries rather miraculously contain a climactic summation, a maturing self-analysis: "If I'm quite serious, everyone thinks it's a comedy, and then

I have to get out of it by turning it into a joke," she remarks with typical adolescent self-consciousness. "Finally I twist my heart around again, so that the bad is on the outside and the good is on the inside. . . . I am guided by the pure Anne within, but outside I'm nothing but a frolicsome little goat who's broken loose."

This frolicsome little goat could write, "It's twice as hard for us young ones to hold our ground, and maintain our opinions, in a time when all ideals are being shattered and destroyed, when people are showing their worst side, and do not know whether to believe in truth and right and God.

"It's really a wonder that I haven't dropped all my ideals, because they seem so absurd and impossible to carry out. Yet I keep them, because in spite of everything I still believe that people are really good at heart. I simply can't build up my hopes on a foundation consisting of confusion, misery, and death. I see the world gradually being turned into a wilderness. I hear the ever-approaching thunder, which will destroy us too, I can feel the sufferings of millions and yet, if I look up into the heavens, I think that it will all come right, that this cruelty too will end, and that peace and tranquility will return again. . . . "

"I want to go on living even after my death," Anne wrote. "I am grateful to God for giving me this gift, this possibility of developing myself and of writing, of expressing all that is in me." Hers was perhaps one of the bodies seen in the mass grave at Bergen-Belsen, for in August, 1944, the knock came on that hidden door in Amsterdam. After the people had been taken away, Dutch friends found Anne's diary in the debris, and saved it.

There is anguish in the thought of how much creative power, how much sheer beauty of living, was cut off through genocide. But through her diary Anne goes on living. From Holland to France, to Italy, Spain. The Germans too have published her book. And now she comes to America. Surely she will be widely loved, for this wise and wonderful young girl brings back a poignant delight in the infinite human spirit. (pp. 1, 22)

Meyer Levin, "The Child behind the Secret Door," in *The New York Times Book Review,* June 15, 1952, pp. 1, 22.

ANN BIRSTEIN AND ALFRED KAZIN
(essay date 1959)

[In the following excerpt from their introduction to *The Works of Anne Frank*, Birstein and Kazin focus on the sensibility of the author: her ambivalence toward her own experience, her sense of an unseen audience, her interpretation of ordinary events, her emphasis on moral accountability, her compassion for suffering humanity, and her search for the meaning of life.]

For two years before her arrest [Anne Frank] wrote all the time. She wrote while she was in hiding from the Nazis and could not take one step outdoors or in the daytime speak above a whisper. She wrote although the bombs came down so heavily at night that she fled for comfort into her father's bed. She wrote so steadily that by the time she was fifteen she had finished the equivalent of two books, one the *Diary,* the other a collection of short stories, essays, and reminiscences. (pp. 9-10)

In a certain sense . . . it isn't fair to call *The Diary of a Young Girl* a diary at all, since from the very first it was more to her than a purely personal record of triumphs and defeats. Always she had toward her own experience the marvelous ambivalence of the born novelist, and immediately after claiming that "neither I—nor for that matter anyone else—will be interested in the unbosomings of a thirteen-year-old schoolgirl," on the very same page of her journal she has already chosen a literary form—the entries will be in the shape of letters to an imaginary girl named Kitty—and embarked on a concise sketch, not only of her own life, but of general conditions in Holland. This same uncanny sense of an unseen audience, actually of posterity, prevails throughout her work. Scared out of her wits as she must have been when she went into hiding, one of the first things she writes about it is a detailed description of the hiding place and the bits and pieces of furnishings that went into it. When new people arrive, first the Van Daans and then Dussel, the dentist, she has them down on paper practically the minute they are through the door. With a writer's eye for how much is implied in the ordinary events of an ordinary day, she describes a typical morning, afternoon, and evening in the annexe; how they went to the toilet; where they slept; what they talked about while they peeled potatoes and shelled peas and stuffed sausages. She fell in love with the boy upstairs, yearned desperately for her first kiss, and in the breathless moment before it finally came broke into tears—which she described meticulously: "I sat pressed closely against him and felt a wave of emotion come over me, tears sprang into my eyes, the left one trickled onto his dungarees. Did he notice? He made no move or sign to show that he did. . . . At half past eight I stood up and went to the window, where we always say good-by. . . . He came toward me, I flung my arms around his neck and gave him a kiss on his left cheek, and was about to kiss the other cheek, when my lips met his and we pressed them together."

To everything that happened to her, to everything that she felt, Anne gave a kind of permanence by transcribing it, and day after day she went on adding still another segment to the world she was creating. In the stories, where she chose her subjects, this world is not so real. But in her diary, where her subject chose her, its vividness and poignance are overwhelming. . . . What makes her achievement really amazing is how little, aside from her own natural gifts of observation and her sense of humor, she had to work with. Other people have countrysides and multitudes. For Anne, the one boy upstairs was love; a single chestnut tree seen from her window, nature; a patch of blue sky—heaven. No wonder that soon she began to think of her diary and some of her sketches as the basis for a book after the war. *Het Achterhuis* (*The House Behind*) she meant to call it—a perfect title for the first book of a young girl, suggesting mystery and suspense and excitement; she even had a list of pseudonyms for the people in it. . . . (pp. 11-13)

But the duality of Anne's nature, that quality of mind that made her turn to her writing for solace and relief, that made of her diary her "only friend" and the first thing she packed when she went into hiding, was exactly what would not let her rest. Like all young growing things, Anne, forced into a premature ripeness by the terrible intensity of events, yearned and struggled for the light. It was not enough to take her own little part in the day's happenings, to chatter and laugh and cry with everyone else; the spectator in her kept pressing her to ask the meaning of it all, kept goading her into a search that could only take her deeper and deeper into the most painful realms of solitude. We tend to think of Anne now as pure innocence in captivity. But her mind and heart were never held captive by herself or anyone, and as for her innocence—it was the last thing she ever thought about. On the contrary, she wanted to take it all on her own shoulders, she considered herself responsible for everything, not only her own destiny—if she was permitted to live it out—but also the fate of everyone else who suffered. " . . . I believe," she said, "that God wants to try me . . . " And this theme of being tested through confinement is repeated in her stories of Blurry, the Explorer, the bear who goes out to see the world and is locked up instead, and of Dora and Peldron, the two elves who are imprisoned by a wise dwarf and emerge improved by their experience. Somehow, Anne, too, would come out a better person, if only she were good and strong enough. Of course it was hard, agonizingly hard, to keep herself to such a strict moral accounting, especially when everything outside beckoned so sweetly: "The sun is shining, the sky is a deep blue, there is a lovely breeze and I'm longing—so longing—for everything. To talk, for freedom, for friends, to be alone. And I do so long . . . to cry!" . . . But still she kept at it, crying herself out when she could, and then trying to unloose her own pity for herself into a great stream of compassion

for all suffering humanity. How could she feel sorry for herself when just outside her door children were running about half naked, begging food from passers-by, and people did not dare leave their homes for fear that when they came back no one would be left in them? It was not enough to be glad of her own precarious safety; one had to ask why even this was denied others. (pp. 13-14)

Child or not, anyone who asks such questions can never find an answer, only the strength of spirit to go on searching. Anne found her strength in her love of the very world which was denied her. (p. 14)

Anne Frank has become a universal legend. Out of the millions who were gassed, burned, shot, hanged, starved, tortured, buried alive, the young girl who died so "peacefully" in Bergen-Belsen, almost in unconscious sympathy with her dead sister Margot, has become a prime symbol of the innocence of all those who died in the middle of the twentieth century at the hands of the most powerful state in western Europe. Perhaps more than any of the known dead, and certainly more than the now nameless ones who died scratching the ceilings of the gas chambers in the last agonized struggle against death, the girl born in Frankfurt of an upper-class Jewish family, whose father was a German officer in World War I, has become the personal example of the heartlessness, the bestiality, the still unbelievable cruelty of Germans in World War II. Upon her, at least, all agree; in her all peoples, in the uneasy peace since 1945 that is no peace, can find a moment's occasion for compassion and awareness. When *The Diary of Anne Frank* was produced on the Dutch stage, royalty wept; and . . . Germans who had wept for no one but themselves, who had not allowed themselves to recognize the horror in their midst, who laughed in derision when they were made to see films of Auschwitz and Buchenwald, have wept in theaters over Anne Frank. (pp. 17-18)

The production of *Das Tagebuch der Anne Frank* coincided with what in certain intellectual circles became a pro-Jewish philosophy, a return to the abstraction of the "noble Jew" among the German intellectuals of the Enlightenment. It is for this reason that Anne Frank has symbolized so much—so peculiarly much—in current German thought. (p. 19)

The figure of universally accepted innocence, a young girl, is so perfect a subject that young people can identify with her; older people can pity her; the world can almost believe that it has made peace with itself over the unknown grave of Anne Frank. During the height of the German emotion over the play, reports Alfred Werner, a few Germans protested that "the play might be letting the Germans off too lightly, that it did not even begin to suggest how frightful were the German actions." Yet it is also a fact that it is impossible to make artistic use of the worst horrors of the concentration camps. *The Diary Of Anne Frank* does not deal with horror—at least not directly; yet this, though it makes it too easy for all of us not to think of the horror at all, is also what makes both book and play *possible*. It was not only Germans who laughed derisively when shown the first films of the concentration camps; so did the English in Piccadilly newsreel theaters. The fact is that certain events in our time, prime and unforgettable images of human suffering and degradation, seem incredible to us even when we remember them, and are ungraspable even when we face them. (pp. 20-1)

Anne Frank's diary has rarely been subjected to criticism. The dramatic economy of the book has moved its readers just as much as the fate of its author has served as an occasion of emotion. Yet it has been suggested that Anne was unable to confront the hideousness of her experience, that her diary was an escape into the ideal. And in one sense this "evasion" of reality, if one may so call it, though improbable coming from people who have never had to face anything like Anne Frank's experience, is perfectly true. It may be that the "ideal" quality of the book accounts for the universal acceptance of the *Diary;* has made it possible for Germans to ease their souls sitting in a theater; for Jews to honor their dead; for the Dutch and the French to remember their suffering under the occupation; for adolescent children to take imaginative refuge from their problems. And yet it is a fact that Anne Frank's wholly domestic picture of life works toward the understanding of her true situation, rather than the other way around. For truthfully direct "war literature," naked shots of the ultimate horror, are hard for everyone to get down—this is as true for the victims' kin as it is for the Germans eager to evade responsibility; they stupefy instead of awakening us. The last shudder of death, the shriek of crucifixion—these really belong to death, not life. If we are still in danger of evading the full truth of Nazism, we are also in danger, when we think we are confronting the truth, of adding to the extreme abstractness and tension of the human spirit which represents Nazism, with its insatiable slogans and its monolithic sense of truth. The enemy of Nazism is its enemy because it is different from Nazism in kind, in intention, in the spirit with which it addresses itself to life. In the "ideal" world of Anne Frank's diary, in the preoccupation with potato peels, a young girl's discovery of puberty, there is the truth of life as human curiosity and sensitivity and fellowship—while outside, the green and gray German army lorries trundle past bearing their helpless Jewish victims to the slaughter heap.

The Diary of a Young Girl has survived its author and most of her family, as it has already survived so many books about the war, because the faithfulness with which it records an unusual experience reminds us—as opposition to Nazism on its own terms never

can—of the sweetness and goodness that are possible in a world where a few souls still have good will. The *Diary* moves us because its author had the strength to see, to remember, to hope. (pp. 22-3)

Ann Birstein and Alfred Kazin, in an introduction to *The Works of Anne Frank* by Anne Frank, Doubleday & Company, Inc., 1959, pp. 9-24.

FREDRIC MORTON
(essay date 1959)

[In the following excerpt from a review of *The Works of Anne Frank*, Morton commends Frank for following the platitude "Write whereof you know" but states that none of her essays or works of short fiction has the power of any single entry of her diary.]

It may well be that the single most enduring thing to be born during the entire course of the Nazi nightmare was a book a young Jewish girl wrote in the occupied Holland of the early Forties. Anne Frank's diary of the years spent in the few cubic feet of her family's hideout has become familiar to the world as an international best seller, as a dramatization that has moved audiences in every major country, and as a motion picture.

Now Anne is being published again; this time the diary together with all her other writings extant, and a deeply felt introduction by Anne Birstein and Alfred Kazin [see excerpt dated 1959]. The new writings [*The Works of Anne Frank*] consist of stories, fables, essays and reminiscences found by Dutch friends in notebooks.

Today many will be able to extend to Anne Frank that full critical justice they couldn't help withholding earlier. For the shock accompanying the first appearance of the diary was so great that it focused attention only on Anne the victim. It was almost easy to forget Anne the writer, who made her victimization so memorable. . . .

[The] illumination of these new pages is important. They show that Anne followed instinctively the best of all platitudes: Write whereof you know. Not even her little fairy tales are easy escapes into make-believe, but rather pointed allegories of reality—the two elves who are imprisoned together to learn tolerance; or Blurry the Baby who runs away from home to find the great, free, open world, and never does. At the other end of the gamut we find **"My First Article."** It is a thorough journalistic account of Peter Van Daan's small room (the Van Daans shared the hiding place with the Franks). Her infatuation for the boy sets aglow the skimpy catalogue of furnishings. Through her words glimmers the prisoner's secret fondness for the universe that is his cell.

Still none of these places, not even a charming little morality tale like **"The Wise Old Dwarf,"** has the power of any single entry in the diary. Anne's stories show an occasional leaning to rhetoric quite inevitable in a 15-year-old who sits down "to write." And the obligation she seems to have felt to give most efforts a didactic turn reflects her background as a rather stringently brought up child (by American standards) in a German-Jewish home. But the little author's ebullience keeps breaking through her stiffest intentions. In **"Kitty"** she sets out to write a rather formal composition about an imaginary girl next door. Before long she stops composing and simply bubbles on, with an entirely incidental perceptiveness about all girlhood.

Indeed, as I reread the diary in the light of her other works I realized that Anne, like any true writer, was at her best when, without self-consciousness or elaborate device, she poured out her own personality. Such enormously difficult simplicity is the hallmark of her journal. Not even terror or the most painful constraint could deprive her of a wonderfully feminine, young, vital responsiveness.

Somehow she preserved enough of the teenager's normal frivolities and irresponsibilities—enough to make her abnormal plight comprehensible to a generation who could read her in an armchair under an open sky. She has shown us that it is possible to remain human as long as we are alive.

Frederic Morton, "Her Literary Legacy," in *The New York Times Book Review,* September 20, 1959, p. 22.

First page of Anne's 29 March 1944 letter to Kitty.

HENRY F. POMMER
(essay date 1960)

[In the following excerpt, Pommer surveys critical response to Anne Frank's diary and traces Frank's development as a writer.]

The quality of both her death and her life have given Anne Frank an extraordinary status in our culture. Antigone represents a willingness to die for principles; Juliet's is the tragedy of ironic confusion; Marguerite was the victim of her own and Faust's sensuality; St. Joan was martyred by jealous institutions. Anne was destroyed by a pattern of evil perhaps not unique to our century, but at least unique within Western culture of the past two thousand years.

But her fame rests on knowledge of her life as much as of her death. She is not a fictional character like Juliet or Tolstoy's Natasha, nor a girl with widespread and immediate effects like St. Joan or the young Cleopatra. Yet she shares with Cleopatra and St. Joan the fact of being historical; and her life is already, like theirs, the source of a legend. As an historical figure relatively unimportant to her immediate contemporaries but affecting a larger and larger circle after her death, she is most like St. Thérèse of Lisieux. But over all these girls from Antigone to St. Thérèse, Anne has the great advantage that she left a diary. Therefore, we need not know her through the documents of her contemporaries or the professional imagination of middle-aged authors. Her legend lacks the support of patriotic and ecclesiastical power, but it has the strength of her authentic, self-drawn portrait. (p. 37)

Some writers have considered the diary as primarily "one of the most moving stories that anyone, anywhere, has managed to tell about World War II." At Oradour-sur-Glane, where Nazis wantonly destroyed the entire population, is printed "Remember," and in the ruins of bomb-destroyed Coventry has been carved "Father Forgive." Anne's diary helps us remember what there is to forgive. (p. 38)

[The] truths of Anne's history, the bitter as well as the sweet, are not about Germans alone or Dutchmen or Jews, but humanity. And these truths must be recalled whenever we try to measure human nature, to estimate its heights and depths, its capacities for good and evil. The extremes of cruelty temper all our hopes. On the other hand, a young person is supposed to have once asked Justice Felix Frankfurter "And how do you know that the human race is *worth* saving?" The Justice replied, "I have read Anne Frank's diary."

A second group of critics has praised the diary as primarily an intimate account of adolescence. For these it is of only secondary importance that Anne hid with her family in an attic of old Amsterdam; of primary importance is her frankness in telling what it is like to grow up. (p. 40)

Often she was difficult to live with. Tensions were almost inevitable for eight people living with so many restrictions in such cramped quarters, but Anne seems to have done more than her share to stir up ill will. She had a temper, and was not always either anxious or able to control it. At times she must have been obnoxiously precocious in telling the other hiders what they were like; she may have appeared very patronizing at times; particularly in dealing with Margot about Peter. She was very critical of her mother, very fond of her father, and from time to time hurt both of them deeply. Her sense of justice, her loathing of whatever was pompous or artificial, and her desire to be treated as an adult led to frequent quarrels with Mr. and Mrs. Van Daan, and with Mr. Dussel.

Bit by bit, however, these evidences of immaturity and of being difficult decrease. Mixed with them, yet gradually replacing them, came the actions and reactions of a more mature young woman. (pp. 40-1)

Any diary of a young girl who hid in Amsterdam during the Nazi occupation, who described her first protracted love affair, and who was a person of breeding, humor, religious sensitivity, and courage might well interest us. But Anne had one further trait of the utmost importance for her own maturity and for what she wrote: an unusual ability for self-analysis. She knew she had moods, and she could write eloquently about them—about loneliness, for example. But she could also step outside her moods in order to evaluate them and herself in them. (p. 43)

One of the clearest evidences of objectivity was her ability to see a moral ambiguity in her enjoying relative security while other Jews suffered worse fates:

I saw two Jews through the curtain yesterday. I could hardly believe my eyes; it was a horrible feeling, just as if I'd betrayed them and was now watching them in their misery.

This is the honesty concerning oneself out of which are

born humor, maturity, and one kind of ability to write well.

Anne could write well. Her self-consciousness and skill as an author receive only implicit acknowledgement if we regard her diary as no more than an educative historical document or an intimate disclosure of adolescence. W. A. Darlington is probably correct in predicting that

in time to come, when the horrors of Nazi occupation in Europe are no longer quite so fresh in quite so many minds and "The Diary of Anne Frank" comes to be judged purely on its merits as a play, the piece will . . . lose its place on the stage.

But Anne's diary may have a longer life. It is, to be sure, a mixture of good and bad writing—but so, too, are the diaries of Pepys, Samuel Sewall, and William Byrd.

Some people have combed the external record of Anne's life for evidence of her ability as a writer. (pp. 43-4)

It was to be expected that little external evidence of Anne's talent would be found. When she went into hiding, she was not a diarist worthy of much attention. During the twenty-five months in the Secret Annexe, the world of her thought was a secret within a secret—a secret so well kept that even her father confessed, when the diary was first published, "I never realized my little Anna was so deep." After she had left the Annexe, the brutality of guards, shortages of food, epidemics of disease, separation from loved ones, and the prospect of gas chambers must have left Anne little time to think about writing, and certainly gave her companions little interest in what her literary talents might be. Ever so much more important was whether she could beg a piece of zwieback.

When we turn to the diary itself, we find that if her affair with Peter is the most striking measure of her change towards maturity, the second most striking is the clarification of her desire to be a writer. The third entry begins the development.

I haven't written for a few days, because I wanted first of all to think about my diary. It's an odd idea for someone like me to keep a diary; not only because I have never done so before, but because it seems to me that neither I—nor for that matter anyone else—will be interested in the unbosomings of a thirteen-year-old schoolgirl. Still, what does that matter? I want to write, but more than that, I want to bring out all kinds of things that lie buried deep in my heart. . . .
There is no doubt that paper is patient and as I don't intend to show this . . . "diary," to anyone, unless I find a real friend, boy or girl, probably nobody cares. And now I come to the root of the matter, the reason for my starting a diary: it is that I have no such real friend. . . .

It's the same with all my friends, just fun and joking, nothing more. I can never bring myself to talk of anything outside the common round. . . .
Hence, this diary. In order to enhance in my mind's eye the picture of the friend for whom I have waited so long, I don't want to set down a series of bald facts in a diary like most people do, but I want this diary itself to be my friend, and I shall call my friend Kitty.

After this early entry the diary shows a progressively self-conscious artistry reflected in the beginnings of certain letters to Kitty such as

Now that we have been in the "Secret Annexe" for over a year, you know something of our lives, but some of it is quite indescribable. . . . To give you a closer look . . . , now and again I intend to give you a description of an ordinary day. Today I'm beginning with the evening and the night. . . . (August 4, 1943).
I asked myself this morning whether you don't sometimes feel rather like a cow who has had to chew over all the old pieces of news again and again, and who finally yawns loudly and silently wishes that Anne would occasionally find something new. . . . (January 28, 1944).
Perhaps it would be entertaining for you—though not in the least for me—to hear what we are going to eat today. . . . (March 14, 1944).

That her diary might itself be the basis of a published work may not have occurred to Anne before March 29, 1944, when

Bolkestein, an M.P., was speaking on the Dutch News from London, and . . . said that they ought to make a collection of diaries and letters after the war. Of course, they all made a rush at my diary immediately. Just imagine how interesting it would be if I were to publish a romance of the "Secret Annexe." The title alone would be enough to make people think it was a detective story.
But, seriously, it would seem quite funny ten years after the war if we Jews were to tell how we lived and what we ate and talked about here.

(pp. 44-5)

After the entry of March 29, Anne's expressed desires to be a journalist, and then a famous writer, grew more numerous. Writing would, she hoped, enable her to live after her death; she wrote short stories, even wanting to submit them for publication. (p. 45)

The chief literary merit of the diary is its permitting us to know intimately Anne's young, eager, difficult, lovable self. We follow the quick alternations of her great gaiety and sometimes equally great depression, and we benefit from the introspections generated by her sharply contrasting moods. Some pages read as though they had been written in the security of a Long Island suburbia; on the next page we are plunged into Nazi terror; and both passages use vivid details. Some-

times our delight is simply in her charm, as in "Daddy always says I'm prudish and vain but that's not true. I'm just simply vain." At other times her wisdom surprises us, as in her distinction that "laziness may *appear* attractive, but work *gives* satisfaction." She sensed the need for variety in reporting, and used effective techniques for achieving it. Life in the Secret Annexe was terribly repetitious, but there is little repetition in the diary itself.

Even if the last entry told of Jews liberated by the arrival of Allied armies in Amsterdam, the book would still have real interest and value. And it would still have its chief moral significance. Both diary and play illustrate D. H. Lawrence's contention that

the essential function of art is moral. Not aesthetic, nor decorative, not pastime and recreation. But moral. . . . But a passionate, implicit morality, not didactic. A morality which changes the blood, rather than the mind. Changes the blood first. The mind follows later in the wake.

Because of Anne Frank's art, this change in blood and then in mind sometimes takes the direction of brotherhood. At those moments her legend receives fresh life, and her adolescent record of history helps to make history less adolescent. (pp. 45-6)

Henry F. Pommer, "The Legend and Art of Anne Frank," in *Judaism*, Vol. 9, No. 1, Winter, 1960, pp. 37-46.

G. B. STERN
(essay date 1962)

[In the following excerpt, Stern surveys Frank's minor works.]

Let us for the moment remember Anne Frank as just a delightful child, a chatterbox, a flirt, and even with the characteristic childish need to invent an imaginary friend called Kitty to whom she addressed the now world-famous *Diary* found after she and her family had been taken away by the Nazis to die in concentration camps at Auschwitz and Belsen; and be glad that she lives again in [*Tales from the House Behind,* a] collection of fables, personal reminiscences, and short stories found in a notebook and on odd sheets of paper. . . . (p. 9)

Anne was a writer in embryo. Her title for the book she was planning to write after the war was *Het Achterhuis*, meaning the 'House Behind,' referring of course to the house in Amsterdam where they all lived cooped up and in hiding for over two years, but it could also have stood for an unconsciously symbolic title to indicate that behind her passionate zest for life, we should find wisdom and a deeply religious sense of values. For instance, in one of her fables, the elf who takes Eve on a tour of a big park dismisses the rose as too obviously the queen of flowers, lovely, elegant, and fragrant—"and if she wouldn't always push herself into the foreground, she might be lovable as well," and then completes the lesson by analogy between two of Eve's friends, Lena symbolising the rose, and little Marie, plain and poor, as a bluebell: "This flower is much happier than the rose. It doesn't care about the praise of others." Though the language of this fable may be immature, it reveals nevertheless that amazing sense of values which we have already noticed.

And according to Anne Frank, the overworked little flower-girl, Krista, is never dissatisfied so long as at the end of every day she might have a brief rest "in the field, amid the flowers, beneath the darkening sky. . . . Gone is fatigue . . . the little girl thinks only of the bliss of having this short while alone with God and nature"—as Anne herself found endless compensation in looking up at the sky or at the chestnut tree, from the attic window of *Het Achterhuis*.

And indeed, the more we read of her or by her, the more strange and incongruous it seems that she could combine in one human being the contradictory qualities of extrovert and introvert. In spite of her overflowing exuberance, her reputation as a chatterbox, unable to refrain from pouring out to her companions whatever might have danced into her head, in these fables we are allowed to penetrate into the House Behind—and aware of the end of Anne Frank, we can hardly bear to read the vivid fable called **"Fear,"** written, according to its date, only a few days before she was taken away to Belsen: she dreamed that bombs were falling and she ran outside the city and fell asleep in the grass under the sky—"Fear is a sickness for which there is only one remedy. Anyone who is afraid, as I was then, should look at nature and see that God is much closer than most people think." Like all the best fabulists, she applies her own experience to a universal need.

And that brings us to her last fable, of the **"Wise Old Dwarf"** who keeps captive two elves of widely different temperaments, Dora and Peldron, and would not let them go home until four months later: he explains his motive—"I took you here and left you together to teach you there are other things in this world beside *your* fun and *your* gloom . . . Dora has become somewhat more serious, and Peldron has cheered up a bit, because you were obliged to make the best of having to live together."

We have already seen that Anne Frank was by no means lacking in a subtle vein of humour; she concluded her story of Blurry, the little bear who set off to 'discover the world,' when after all his crowded experiences he had to admit that he had failed to discover it because—"You see, I couldn't find it!"

And so we pass on to the section of personal reminiscences, her school-days in retrospect, gay and entirely youthful, with no heartbreak for the reader until her fervent wish at the end that those happy days could come again. Among these reminiscences is a study of a certain Miss Riegel, a clever woman who gives them lectures in biology "starting with fish and ending with reindeer. Her favourite topic is propagation, which surely must be so because she is an old maid"—satire, pungent and mature, co-dweller in the House Behind with Anne's merry description of her six reprimands for talking incessantly in class, when she pleads that little can be done because her case is hereditary: "My mother, too, is fond of chatting and has handed this weakness down to me"; thus our young extrovert finds a plausible excuse for her fault. In **"Dreams of Movie Stardom"** she lapses again into the child day-dreaming of herself as a movie star—well, she had the looks, the exuberance and animation, but the world would have lost an author revealing already those infallible signs of genius, including the necessary flair for conveying personality; as where in **"My First Article"** she brings her friend Peter vividly before us with every touch.

The essay called **"Give"** strikes a note startlingly up to date and prophetic; since the date of its conception we have all read a hundred essays and leaders, heard a thousand sermons and speeches, on the theme of the true communal spirit of sharing—"Oh, if only the whole world would realise that people were really kindly disposed toward one another, that they are all equal and everything else is just transitory! . . . No one has ever become poor from giving! . . . There is plenty of room for everyone in the world, enough money, riches, and beauty for all to share! God has made enough for everyone. Let us all begin by sharing it fairly."

But more than all the rest of this collection, Anne Frank's fragment of a novel, which she called *Cady's Life,* corroborates all one has said about her potential powers. In it she combines a wisdom beyond her years, a sense of character and a feeling for religion, until at the very end a lapse from fiction into the grim reality of the danger to all Jews under Hitler's régime that autumn of 1942, though she still continues to call her heroine 'Cady' and Cady's friend 'Mary,' foreshadows what was shortly to prove the fate of her own family and herself.

Cady's Life starts straight into the story without unnecessary preliminaries: Cady had been knocked down and injured by a car, and opened her eyes in hospital—"The first thing she saw was that everything around her was white," and the first thing she felt was a panic that she would be a cripple for life. When she woke again, her parents had come to visit her, and immediately we get an impression that her father means far more to her than her mother, who—the nurse looking after her noticed—"tired the child out with her incessant nervous prattle." After a fortnight, Cady confided in the nursing sister, who was calm and always talked softly, her reactions towards her mother, and here Anne Frank's talent for drawing character emerges clearly: she longs for a mother who, as well as loving her, would truly and sensitively understand how to handle her. (pp. 10-14)

All this is psychologically perceptive to a marked degree; as far as can be surmised, Anne Frank would have developed into a subjective novelist, never objective.

After several weeks Cady's health slowly improves, and for a moment Anne Frank herself intrudes on fiction: "Her father bought her a diary. Now she often sat up and wrote down her feelings and thoughts."

In three months they sent her to a sanatorium in the country, where she began to learn to walk without support and then to go out alone into the gardens and grounds or into the wood, where she loved to sit and meditate "about the world and its meaning," and "suddenly realised that here in the wood and in the quiet hours in hospital she had discovered something new about herself, she had discovered that she was a human being with her own feelings, thoughts, and views, apart from anyone else. . . . What does a child know of the lives of others, of her girl friends, her family, her teachers, what else did she know of them but the outer side? Had she ever had serious talks with any of them?"

Enter romance and a panacea for loneliness both

in one—Hans Donkert, a boy of seventeen on holiday from school, who passed by her in the wood every morning on his way to visit his friends in the neighborhood. For some time they knew each other only by sight, until one day he stopped and introduced himself; after that, he came along earlier and sat and talked with her, though not profoundly . . . until on one occasion they looked at each other longer than they really wanted to and he asked her what she was thinking about. She could not at first bring herself to tell him, and then she suddenly said: "Do you also often feel lonely, even if you have friends, lonely inside, I mean?" Hans owned up to it and added that boys confide even less in their friends than do girls, and were even more afraid of being laughed at.

Again neither of them spoke for a long time, until: "Do you believe in God, Hans?" "Yes, I do firmly believe in God." And the discussion between them which followed this, although simply phrased, contained the essence of so much that one has read in profound theological works of the true nature of God and how He expresses Himself, that one is staggered at its maturity.

Yes, perhaps Cady and Hans were destined by their author, could she have completed the volume, to be *en route* for a happy marriage in a few years . . . when suddenly, as we noted earlier, Anne Frank was swept away from fiction into stark unbearable reality. (pp. 15-16)

G. B. Stern, in an introduction to *Tales from the House Behind: Fables, Personal Reminiscences and Short Stories* by Anne Frank, translated by H. H. B. Mosberg and Michel Mok, The World's Work (1913) Ltd., 1962, pp. 9-16.

SOURCES FOR FURTHER STUDY

Afterword to *Anne Frank: The Diary of a Young Girl*, by Anne Frank, pp. 245-58. New York: Pocket Books, 1967.

Provides the historical context of Frank's experiences, summarizing her final months in concentration camps.

Berryman, John. "The Development of Anne Frank." In his *The Freedom of the Poet*, pp. 91-106. New York: Farrar, Straus and Giroux, Inc., 1976.

Argues that the diary is most important as an account of a child's maturation into an adult. Berryman cites many examples from Frank's diary to illustrate the process of her maturation, and analyzes her experiences, sometimes in Freudian terms.

Lewisohn, Ludwig. "A Glory and a Doom." *Saturday Review* XXXV, No. 29 (19 July 1952): 20.

Cites the sobriety and clarity of Frank's vision as traits which contribute to the poignant quality of her chroni-

cles about the war and about her own personal development.

Schnabel, Ernst. *Anne Frank: A Portrait in Courage.* Translated by Richard and Clara Winston. New York: Harcourt, Brace and Co., 1958, 192 p.

A survey of people and places in Frank's life before and during her imprisonment in concentration camps. Schnabel interviewed forty-two people who describe experiences ranging from brief encounters to long-term relationships with Anne, including anecdotes and character sketches.

Stevens, George. Preface to *Anne Frank: The Diary of a Young Girl*, by Anne Frank, translated by B. M. Mooyaart-Doubleday, pp. vii-viii. New York: Pocket Books, 1958.

Focuses on Frank's enduring hopefulness.

Werner, Alfred. "Germany's New Flagellants." *The American Scholar* XXVII, No. 2 (Spring 1958): 169-81.

   States that romantic enthusiasm characterized both Nazi anti-Semitism and the German philo-Semitism of the mid-1950s. In addition Werner examines the aroused national conscience that followed the German stage production based on Frank's diary, and analyzes ceremonial and social phenomena that reveal the German people's desire to confront their responsibility for the Holocaust and atone for their guilt.

Robert Frost

1874-1963

(Full name Robert Lee Frost) American poet, essayist, and critic.

INTRODUCTION

*I*n his verse, Frost described natural scenes with vivid imagery, celebrated ordinary rural activities, and mused upon mysteries of existence, subtly developing dramatic tension he frequently left unresolved, ambiguous, and open to interpretation. Positing that humanity must constantly struggle against chaos and bewilderment, Frost stated that poetry, like all human-made forms, is a "momentary stay against confusion." His finely-crafted poems reflect this belief through thematic explorations of profound philosophical issues, the beauties and terrors of nature, conflicts between individual desires and social obligations, and the value of labor. Frost is particularly noted for his mastery of form and rhythm, through which his poems evoke distinct New England speech patterns. In order to achieve this quality he termed "sound of sense," Frost structured his verse in strict metrical, rhyme, line, and stanzaic arrangements and experimented with such conventional forms as blank verse, sonnets, lyrics, and masques. While viewed by detractors as a simple farmer-poet, Frost is among the most revered, honored, and popular of American writers.

Born in San Francisco, Frost was eleven years old when his father died, and his family relocated to Lawrence, Massachusetts, where his paternal grandparents lived. In 1892, Frost graduated from Lawrence High School and shared valedictorian honors with Elinor Wylie, whom he married three years later. After graduation, Frost briefly attended Dartmouth College, taught at grammar schools, worked at a mill, and served as a newspaper reporter. He published a chapbook of poems at his own expense, and contributed the poem "The Birds Do Thus" to the *Independent,* a New York magazine. In 1897, Frost entered Harvard University as a special student, but left before completing degree requirements because of a bout with tuberculosis and the birth of his second child. Three years later, the Frosts's eldest child died, an event which led to marital discord and which some critics believe Frost later addressed in his poem "Home Burial."

In 1912, having been unable to interest American publishers in his poems, Frost moved his family to a farm in Buckinghamshire, England, where he wrote prolifically, attempting to perfect his distinct poetic voice. During this time, he met such literary figures as Ezra Pound, an American expatriate and champion of innovative literary approaches, and Edward Thomas, a young English poet associated with the Georgian school of poetry then popular in Great Britain.

Frost's first major collection of verse, *A Boy's Will,* was published in England in 1913, and Pound wrote the first important review of the volume to appear in an American literary journal. Several recurring motifs in Frost's work are introduced in *A Boy's Will.* In "Into My Own," the opening poem, for example, the speaker yearns to enter a dark forest, which metaphorically represents the mysteries of self and life. "Storm Fear" presents a man awed and subdued by sublime natural forces, while "Mowing" describes a person cultivating a field and thus imposing a sense of order on the world.

Following the success of *A Boy's Will,* Frost relocated to Gloucestershire, England, and directed publication of his second collection, *North of Boston* (1914). This volume contains several of his most frequently anthologized pieces, including "Mending Wall," a meditation on individualism and community inspired by the annual springtime ritual of repatching walls of rock that divide New England farms; "Death of a Hired Man," a dramatic narrative in which a woman pleads for her husband to show sympathy toward an old, unreliable laborer who has returned to their farm; "After Apple-Picking," one of many Frost poems that promote the value of hard work, in which an apple harvest is recounted in reverie; and "Home Burial," in which a couple experience deep emotional conflict over their different manners of grieving for their dead child. Shortly after *North of Boston* was published in Great Britain, the Frost family returned to the United States, settling in Franconia, New Hampshire. The American editions of Frost's first two volumes won critical acclaim upon publication in the United States, and in 1917 Frost began his affiliations with several American universities as professor in literature and poet-in-residence.

Frost's next two collections, *Mountain Interval* (1916), which contains such famous poems as "Birches" and "The Road Not Taken," and the Pulitzer Prize-winning *New Hampshire* (1923), which includes "Fire and Ice," "Stopping by Woods on a Snowy Evening," and "The Witch of Coös," furthered his reputation as a major poet. The speaker in "Birches" wonders whether a bent birch branch was caused by a child at play or by natural elements and metaphorically links

tree-climbing with aspirations for heaven. Ruminations on earthly existence and paradise occur frequently in Frost's verse, which, along with his emphasis on self-reliance and his moral observations inspired by nature, led critics to associate his work with that of Ralph Waldo Emerson and other American Transcendentalists. In "Birches," Frost concludes that "Earth's the right place for love: / I don't know where it's likely to go better." "The Road Not Taken" and "Stopping by Woods on a Snowy Evening" are two of many Frost poems in which the speaker faces a dilemma of choosing between the unknown, represented by wild nature, or mundane life, represented by a clearing or town. In the former, the speaker chooses a road "less traveled by," while the latter piece, perhaps Frost's most frequently discussed work, ends inconclusively: "The woods are lovely, dark, and deep, / But I have promises to keep, / And miles to go before I sleep, / And miles to go before I sleep." Critics debate whether the speaker ultimately rejects the unfathomable, remains uncertain, or resolves to further explore the alluring mysteries of life. Typical of Frost's verse, "Stopping by Woods on a Snowy Evening" presents a speaker whose imagination has been activated by nature.

In *West-Running Brook* (1928) and *A Further Range* (1936), which also was awarded a Pulitzer Prize, Frost expanded upon his characteristic style and subject matter to comment upon social and political issues, including economic hardships of the Depression and turmoil surrounding the advent of World War II. John T. Oglivie observed: "[With these two collections], Frost becomes the more 'neighborly' poet who chats at length with his readers about the issues of the day, and less the objective dramatist and self-exploring lyricist of the earlier books. He becomes more outspoken about himself and about the world of men. He projects himself into the 'further ranges' of politics, science, philosophy, education, and theology. 'Ideas' as such become more important to him than the individual persons and objects of nature." However, Frost's lyrics on nature continued to receive the most attention and praise. These include "Spring Pools," which focuses on both the revivifying and ephemeral qualities of nature; "Tree at My Window," in which a speaker links his emotional fluctuations with the varying kinds of weather endured by a tree outside the speaker's room; and "Design," in which Frost develops a web of symbolic implications to contrast order and randomness, violence and beauty.

While Frost continued to write prolifically and received numerous literary awards as well as honors from the United States government and American universities, his critical reputation waned during the latter part of his career. His final three collections received less enthusiastic reviews, yet contain several pieces acknowledged as among his greatest achievements. *A*

Witness Tree (1942), which won Frost a third Pulitzer Prize, contains many brief nature lyrics as well as "The Gift Outright," a poem about the heritage and individual responsibilities of American citizens that he recited at the inauguration of President John F. Kennedy. *Steeple Bush* (1947) includes "Directive," in which the speaker expresses ambivalence toward nature but discovers means for reconciliation while undertaking a metaphorical quest through confusion and decay. "Directive" is generally considered Frost's most significant later poem, displaying his command of form to accomodate and accentuate fantasy elements, symbolism, and varying allusions. In "In Winter in the Woods," Frost's final poem in his final collection, *In the Clearing* (1962), the speaker is once again in a forest contemplating the relationship between nature and self.

Although Frost is generally recognized as a major American poet, many critics express reservations about his artistry. These commentators usually cite such shortcomings as simplistic philosophy, expression of stock sentiments, failure to delve deeply into thematic concerns, and inability to universalize distinct concerns of rural New England. Malcolm Cowley, in his essay "The Case against Mr. Frost," summarized these views: "[Frost] is concerned chiefly with himself and his near neighbors, or with the Yankees among his neighbors. . . . And Frost does not strive toward greater depth to compensate for what he lacks in breadth; he does not strike far inward into the wilderness of human nature. It is true that he often talks about the need for inwardness. . . . [Yet] still he sets limitations on the exploration of himself, as he sets them on almost every other human activity." Cowley added: "If he does not strike far inward, neither does he follow that other great American tradition . . . of standing on a height to observe the panorama of nature and society." Nevertheless, most critics praise the imagery, rhythmic qualities, dramatic tension, and synecdochical qualities of Frost's verse, and his poems are among the most widely studied and appreciated of American literature. Randall Jarrell stated: "Frost, along with [Wallace] Stevens and [T. S.] Eliot seems to me the greatest of the American poets of this century. Frost's virtues are extraordinary. No other [poet of his time] has written so well about the actions of ordinary men: his wonderful dramatic monologues or dramatic scenes come out of a knowledge of people that few poets have had, and they are written in verse that uses, sometimes with absolute mastery, the rhythms of actual speech." Added Robert Graves: "[Frost] reminds us that poems, like love, begin in surprise, delight, and tears, and end in wisdom. Whereas scholars follow projected lines of logic, [Frost] collects his knowledge undeliberately, he says, like burrs that stick to your legs when you walk through a field."

(For further information about Frost's life and works, see *Concise Dictionary of Literary Biography: The Twenties, 1917-1929*; *Contemporary Authors*, Vols. 89-92; *Contemporary Authors New Revision Series*, Vol. 33; *Contemporary Literary Criticism*, Vols. 1, 3, 4, 9, 10, 13, 15, 26, 34, 44; *Dictionary of Literary Biography*, Vol. 54: *American Poets, 1880-1945*; *Dictionary of Literary Biography Documentary Series*, Vol. 7; *Poetry Criticism*, Vol. 1; and *Something about the Author*, Vol. 14.)

CRITICAL COMMENTARY

ROBERT PENN WARREN

(essay date 1947)

[Warren was an American poet and novelist. In the following excerpt from a 1947 essay, he provides a thematic analysis of two of Frost's best-known poems, "Stopping By Woods on a Snowy Evening" and "After Apple-Picking."]

A large body of criticism has been written on the poetry of Robert Frost, and we know the labels which have been used: nature poet, New England Yankee, symbolist, humanist, skeptic, synecdochist, anti-Platonist, and many others. These labels have their utility, true or half true as they may be. They point to something in our au-

thor. But the important thing about a poet is the kind of poetry he writes. (p. 118)

In any case, I do not want to begin by quarreling with the particular labels. Instead, I want to begin with some poems and try to see how their particular truths are operative within the poems themselves. (p. 119)

As a starting point I am taking one of Frost's best-known and most widely anthologized pieces, **"Stopping by Woods on a Snowy Evening."** . . . It will lead us to the other poems because it represents but one manifestation of an impulse very common in Frost's poetry. (p. 120)

The poem does, in fact, look simple. A man driving by a dark woods stops to admire the scene, to watch

Principal Works

A Boy's Will (poetry) 1913

North of Boston (poetry) 1914

Mountain Interval (poetry) 1916

New Hampshire (poetry) 1923

West-Running Brook (poetry) 1928

The Cow's in the Corn: A One-Act Irish Play in Rhyme (poetry) 1929

A Further Range (poetry) 1936

Collected Poems of Robert Frost (poetry) 1939

A Witness Tree (poetry) 1942

A Masque of Reason (poetry) 1945

The Poems of Robert Frost (poetry) 1946

A Masque of Mercy (poetry) 1947

Steeple Bush (poetry) 1947

Deducation / The Gift Outright / The Inaugural Address (poetry) 1961

In the Clearing (poetry) 1962

The Letters of Robert Frost (letters) 1963

Selected Letters of Robert Frost (letters) 1964

The Poetry of Robert Frost (poetry) 1966

Selected Prose of Robert Frost (essays) 1966

Family Letters of Robert Frost and Elinor Frost (letters) 1972

Robert Frost on Writing (essays) 1973

Early Poems (poetry) 1981

the snow falling into the special darkness. He remembers the name of the man who owns the woods and knows that the man, snug in his house in the village, cannot begrudge him a look. He is not trespassing. The little horse is restive and shakes the harness bells. The man decides to drive on, because, as he says, he has promises to keep—he has to get home to deliver the groceries for supper—and he has miles to go before he can afford to stop, before he can sleep.

At the literal level that is all the poem has to say. But if we read it at that level, we shall say, and quite rightly, that it is the silliest stuff we ever saw. (p. 121)

With [the] first stanza we have a simple contrast, the contrast between the man in the village, snug at his hearthside, and the man who stops by the woods. The sane, practical man has shut himself up against the weather; certainly he would not stop in the middle of the weather for no reason at all. But, being a practical man, he does not mind if some fool stops by his woods so long as the fool merely looks and does not do any practical damage, does not steal firewood or break down fences. With this stanza we seem to have a contrast between the sensitive and the insensitive man, the man who uses the world and the man who contem-

plates the world. And the contrast seems to be in favor of the gazer and not the owner—for the purposes of the poem at least. In fact, we may even have the question: Who is the owner, the man who is miles away or the man who can really see the woods? (p. 122)

[In the second stanza] we have the horse-man contrast. The horse is practical too. He can see no good reason for stopping, not a farmhouse near, no oats available. The horse becomes an extension, as it were, of the man in the village—both at the practical level, the level of the beast which cannot understand why a man would stop, on the darkest evening of the year, to stare into the darker darkness of the snowy woods. In other words, the act of stopping is the specially human act, the thing that differentiates the man from the beast. The same contrast is continued into the third stanza—the contrast between the impatient shake of the harness bells and the soothing whish of easy wind and downy flake.

To this point we would have a poem all right, but not much of a poem. It would set up the essential contrast between, shall we say, action and contemplation, but it would not be very satisfying because it would fail to indicate much concerning the implications of the contrast. It would be a rather too complacent poem, too much at ease in the Zion of contemplation.

But in the poem the poet actually wrote, the fourth and last stanza brings a very definite turn, a refusal to accept either term of the contrast developed to this point. (pp. 122-23)

The first line proclaims the beauty, the attraction of the scene. . . . But with this statement concerning the attraction—the statement merely gives us what we have already dramatically arrived at by the fact of the stopping—we find the repudiation of the attraction. The beauty, the peace, is a sinister beauty, a sinister peace. It is the beauty and peace of surrender—the repudiation of action and obligation. The darkness of the woods is delicious—but treacherous. The beauty which cuts itself off from action is sterile; the peace which is a peace of escape is a meaningless and, therefore, a suicidal peace. There will be beauty and peace at the end of the journey, in the terms of the fulfillment of the promises, but that will be an earned beauty stemming from action.

In other words, we have a new contrast here. The fact of the capacity to stop by the roadside and contemplate the woods sets man off from the beast, but in so far as such contemplation involves a repudiation of the world of action and obligation it cancels the definition of man which it had seemed to establish. So the poem leaves us with that paradox, and that problem. . . . We must find a definition of our humanity which will transcend both terms.

This theme is one which appears over and over in

Frost's poems—the relation, to state the issue a little differently, between the fact and the dream. In another poem, **"Mowing,"** he puts it this way, "The fact is the sweetest dream that labor nows." That is, the action and the reward cannot be defined separately, man must fulfill himself, in action, and the dream must not violate the real. But the solution is not to sink into the brute— to act like the little horse who knows that the farmhouses mean oats—to sink into nature, into appetite. But at the same time, to accept the other term of the original contrast in our poem, to surrender to the pull of the delicious blackness of the woods, is to forfeit the human definition, to sink into nature by another way, a dangerous way which only the human can achieve. So our poem, which is supposed to celebrate nature, may really be a poem about man defining himself by resisting the pull into nature. There are many poems on this subject in Frost's work. (pp. 123-24)

[But let] us leave the dark-wood symbol and turn to a poem which, with other materials, treats Frost's basic theme. This is **"After Apple-Picking,"** the poem which I am inclined to think is Frost's masterpiece, it is so poised, so subtle, so poetically coherent in detail. (p. 127)

The items [in this poem]—ladder in apple tree, the orchard, drinking trough, pane of ice, woodchuck— all have their perfectly literal meanings—the echo of their meaning in actuality. And the poem, for a while anyway, seems to be commenting on that actual existence those items have. Now, some poems make a pretense of living only in terms of that actuality. For instance, **"Stopping by Woods on a Snowy Evening"** is perfectly consistent at the level of actuality—a man stops by the woods, looks into the woods, which he finds lovely, dark and deep, and then goes on, for he has promises to keep. It can be left at that level, if we happen to be that literal-minded, and it will make a sort of sense.

However, **"After Apple-Picking"** is scarcely consistent at the level of actuality. It starts off with a kind of consistency, but something happens. The hero of the poem says that he is drowsing off—and in broad daylight, too. He says that he has a strangeness in his sight which he drew from the drinking trough. So the literal world dissolves into a kind of dream world—the literal world and the dream world overlapping, as it were, like the two sets of elements in a superimposed photograph. (pp. 128-29)

The dream will relive the world of effort, even to the ache of the instep arch where the ladder rung was pressed. But is this a cause for regret or for self-congratulation? Is it a good dream or a bad dream? (p. 130)

[We] must look for the answer in the temper of the description he gives of the dream—the apples, stem end and blossom end, and every fleck of russet showing clear. The richness and beauty of the harvest— magnified now—is what is dwelt upon. In the dream world every detail is bigger than life, and richer, and can be contemplated in its fullness. And the accent here is on the word contemplated. Further, even as the apple picker recalls the details of labor which made him overtired, he does so in a way which denies the very statement that the recapitulation in dream will "trouble" him. For instance, we have the delicious rhythm of the line,

I feel the ladder sway as the boughs bend.

It is not the rhythm of nightmare, but of the good dream. . . . So even though we find the poet saying that his sleep will be troubled, the word *troubled* comes to us colored by the whole temper of the passage, ironically qualified by that temper. For he would not have it otherwise than troubled, in this sense. (p. 131)

[What] does the woodchuck have to do with it? . . . His sleep is contrasted with "just some human sleep." The contrast, we see, is on the basis of the dream. The woodchuck's sleep will be dreamless and untroubled. The woodchuck is simply in the nature from which man is set apart. The animal's sleep is the sleep of oblivion. But man has a dream which distinguishes him from the woodchuck. But how is this dream related to the literal world, the world of the woodchuck and apple harvests and daily experience? It is not a dream which is cut off from that literal world of effort—a heaven of ease and perpetual rewards, in the sense of rewards as coming after and in consequence of effort. No, the dream, the heaven, will simply be a reliving of the effort—magnified apples, stem end and blossom end, and every fleck, every aspect of experience, showing clear. (pp. 131-32)

[It] may be well to ask ourselves if the poet is really talking about immortality and heaven—if he is really trying to define the heaven he wants and expects after this mortal life. No, he is only using that as an image for his meaning, a way to define his attitude. And that attitude is an attitude toward the here and now, toward man's conduct of his life in the literal world. (p. 132)

What would be some of the implied applications [of such an attitude]? First, let us take it in reference to the question of any sort of ideal which man sets up for himself, in reference to his dream. By this application the valid ideal would be that which stems from and involves the literal world, which is arrived at in terms of the literal world and not by violation of man's nature as an inhabitant of that literal world. Second, let us take it in reference to man's reward in this literal world. By this application we would arrive at a statement like this: Man must seek his reward in his fulfillment through effort and must not expect reward as something coming at the end of effort, like the oats for the dray horse in the trough at the end of the day's pull. He must cherish each thing in his hand. Third, let us take it in reference to poetry, or the arts. By this application, which is really a variant of the first, we would find that art must stem from the literal world, from the common body of experience, and must be a magnified "dream" of that experience as it has achieved meaning, and not a thing set apart, a mere decoration.

These examples, chosen from among many, are intended merely to point us back into the poem—to the central impulse of the poem itself. But they are all summed up in this line from **"Mowing,"** another of Frost's poems: "The fact is the sweetest dream that labor knows." (pp. 132-33)

The process [Frost] has employed in all of these poems, but most fully and subtly I think in **"After Apple-Picking,"** is to order his literal materials so that, in looking back upon them as the poem proceeds, the reader suddenly realizes that they have been transmuted. . . . [In] these poems, Frost is trying to indicate, as it were, the very process of the transmutation, of the interpenetration. That, and what that implies as an attitude toward all our activities, is the very center of these poems, and of many others among his work. (pp. 135-36)

Robert Penn Warren, "The Themes of Robert Frost," in his *Selected Essays*, Random House, 1958, pp. 118-36.

C. M. BOWRA

(essay date 1950)

[Bowra, an English critic and literary historian, was one of the foremost classical scholars of the first half of the twentieth century. He also wrote extensively on modern European poetry. In the following excerpt, he examines themes and techniques in Frost's work.]

The achievement of the United States in poetry is undeniably paradoxical. This vast country, with its wide variety of landscape and human beings, has seldom found a truly national poet who speaks primarily of American experience from an American point of view. It has given Edgar Allan Poe to Europe and T. S. Eliot to England, but in the nineteenth century its only great national poet was Walt Whitman. . . . He was the poet of pioneers and explorers, of 1848 and the Civil War, but not of established American life, of the farms and villages which created the American people and gave to it some of its most notable characteristics. His more respectable and more respected contemporaries in

New England lacked his essentially American outlook. They put too much trust in European standards and models, and their work is American only in a limited sense. In Longfellow and Whittier, even in Emerson, we miss the local accent, the indigenous touch. In their desire to keep abreast of their time and to speak to the word, they fell too often into a standardised view of life which lacks colour and does not always carry conviction. The twentieth century has been more adventurous and more consciously American. If at times it has been too adventurous, it has at least tried to speak of a world that it knows and to make the most of it.

With the possible exception of Virginia, New England is the most individual region of the United States. With a history that goes back to the Pilgrim Fathers, with its old, if uneasy, connections with the British Isles, with its Puritan independence, with its peculiar dialect noted for its nasal inflections and its biblical turns of phrase, it has still in its country districts a homogeneity and an originality which can hardly be found elsewhere in the United States. Its white, wooden villages, with their array of rival church round a village green, have a character unlike anything in the Middle West, with its interminable main streets and its devotion to corrugated iron. Outside the large towns New England is a country of hills and rivers, of agriculture and forestry. . . . Here are a past and background and a richness of colour which we do not always associate with America. Such a society provides material for a special kind of poetry. It has those finer shades which come from long established habits and from local idiosyncrasies. The Puritan tradition is even now not broken and still gives a pattern and a style to village life. Such conditions may well produce a poet, and in Robert Frost, New England has at last come into its own. Through him New Hampshire and Vermont and the outlying parts of Massachusetts have found a voice—a voice not of Boston and its Brahmins but of the fields and the woods.

Frost was actually born in California, but he came of New England stock and has spent most of his life in New England. To it he owes nearly all his subjects, and its marks are clear on everything that he writes. He speaks for it with special knowledge and special authority. Just because he is a New Englander, he was slow to start. Though he was born in 1875, he did not publish his first book of poems, *A Boy's Will*, until 1913, when he was thirty-eight years old, and even then he had not found his essential gifts or his really personal utterance. There is still something conventional and artificial about most of these poems. The language is a little too careful, the tone too sweet, the music too tender, and too regular. But once or twice something unusual makes itself heard, and it is clear that Frost has begun to find his special gifts. (pp. 46-7)

Frost found himself with *North of Boston* and

Frost on poetry:

The figure a poem makes. It begins in delight and ends in wisdom. The figure is the same as for love. No one can really hold that the ecstasy should be static and stand still in one place. It begins in delight, it inclines to the impulse, it assumes direction with the first line laid down, it runs a course of lucky events, and ends in a clarification of life—not necessarily a great clarification, such as sects and cults are founded on, but in a momentary stay against confusion. It has denouement. It has an outcome that though unforeseen was predestined from the first image of the original mood—and indeed from the very mood. It is but a trick poem and no poem at all if the best of it was thought of first and saved for the last. It finds its own name as it goes and discovers the best waiting for it in some final phrase at once wise and sad—the happy-sad blend of the drinking song.

No tears in the writer, no tears in the reader. No surprise for the writer, no surprise for the reader. For me the initial delight is in the surprise of remembering something I didn't know I knew. . . .

More than once I should have lost my soul to radicalism if it had been the originality it was mistaken for by its young converts. Originality and initiative are what I ask for my country. For myself the originality need be no more than the freshness of a poem run in the way I have described: from delight to wisdom. The figure is the same as for love. Like a piece of ice on a hot stove the poem must ride on its own melting. A poem may be worked over once it is in being, but may not be worried into being. Its most precious quality will remain its having run itself and carried away the poet with it. Read it a hundred times: it will forever keep its freshness as a metal keeps its fragrance. It can never lose its sense of a meaning that once unfolded by surprise as it went.

Frost, in his preface to the 1939 edition of Collected Poems.

Mountain Interval. . . . His poetry is concerned not merely with his own corner of New England but, strictly and accurately, with what he actually knows of it. Since it deals in the first place not with fancies but with facts, it can fairly be called realistic. Its subjects are drawn from country life and often from its most familiar activities, and are presented with an experienced knowledge which proves that the poet is a true countryman. This realism is not a form of display but comes from a pleasure in the manifold aspects of life in farms and fields. Frost dwells on details because he loves them and what they stand for, and likes to honour them with careful sketches of them. He builds his verses on a precise observation of common things and common sights. (pp. 48-9)

Through his loving observation of otherwise unnoticed things Frost secures a special kind of success. Just because he himself is engaged so deeply by what he sees, he makes others feel that even the most modest sight may have a special interest. By the mere act of noticing something and turning his mind to it he suddenly makes it vivid. Everyone knows the familiar sight of broken walls in the country, nor does it usually excite comment. Frost, however, has his own view of the matter:

Something there is that doesn't love a wall,
That sends the frozen ground-swell under it,
And spills the upper boulders in the sun;
And makes gaps even two can pass abreast.

This is only the start for a poem which raises several original and pertinent questions and touches on several sides of life. But it is an excellent start because it is solidly grounded in fact. Again, many poets have written about the spring, but Frost has his own contribution to make in his precise account of April weather:

The sun was warm but the wind was chill.
You know how it is with an April day;
When the sun is out and the wind is still,
You're one month on in the middle of May.
But if you so much as dare to speak,
A cloud comes over the sunlit arch,
A wind comes off a frozen peak,
And you're two months back in the middle of
    March.

This is admirable, partly because the observation is so keen and sensitive, partly because it has more than observation. The poet not only notices the freakish moods of the sun but gives to each its exact quality and catches the whimsical atmosphere of such a day.

This observation of real things is presented in a gentle and unobtrusive style. Frost deals with familiar objects and does not try to pretend that they are essentially different from what they are to the common man. Frost may see more in them than others do, but they belong to the ordinary world and must not be presented in too grandiose a manner. This style may be a development of the language used by the Georgian poets, but it has more life and distinction than its origins would suggest. It is never flat or dull, and its quiet air is the product of accomplished art. Frost sets his tone at this pitch because he is concerned with real things in the same way as other men are. But his language has many half-concealed virtues. It responds exactly to Frost's moods; it is never lazy or verbose; its occasional flashes of conversational idiom are perfectly timed and produced with unerring tact: it has been severely pruned of literary echoes. Frost brings off his special effects because he operates with a style so natural and straight-forward that even the slightest shock or surprise seems almost violent in his level tones. He fulfils Wordsworth's requirements for the language of poetry but without either Wordsworth's reversions to a grand style or the sophisticated simplicity of such poems as "We are Seven". Frost writes as he speaks with complete ease and felicity in the natural language of other men.

This naturalness is guided by a sure sense of the value and force of words in relation to each other. In such a style any word which is at all unusual or unexpected has a redoubled power and draws the whole poem to itself. It may even overweight the poem and spoil its balance. How skillfully Frost avoids this danger can be seen from many places where he uses an unexpected word and makes it do its full work without asserting itself unduly. . . . More often Frost uses a more subtle art and plans his emphasis so well that we hardly notice it. Take, for instance the poem **"Acquainted with the Night."** . . . The charm of this poem largely depends on the slight heightening of tone in the phrase 'acquainted with the night'. Just because it is a little out of the ordinary, it carries a special burden, and its repitition both stresses the main idea of the poem and pulls the whole together.

Frost uses these slight variations to secure surprise. Since he operates in a limited and largely familiar field, they cannot be very violent or impressive, but they give the delightful shock which comes from something seen and enjoyed for the first time. Frost likes to make discoveries, to start from some quite usual situation and then to find in it an unanticipated excitement or paradox or pathos. He is clever at finding such situations. He knows that they need not be very impressive, nor does he wish to make them so. He sees their charm and presents it on its merits. In this poetry the slightest change of direction, the smallest variation of tone, may produce surprise enough, as in **"Stopping by Woods on a Snowy Evening"**:

Whose woods these are I think I know.
His house is in the village though;
He will not see me stopping here
To watch his woods fill up with snow.

My little horse must think it queer
To stop without a farmhouse near
Between the woods and frozen lake
The darkest evening of the year.

He gives his harness bells a shake
To ask if there is some mistake.
The only other sound's the sweep
Of easy wind and downy flake.

The woods are lovely, dark and deep.
But I have promises to keep,

And miles to go before I sleep,
And miles to go before I sleep.

The last verse is a complete surprise. Most of the poem is taken up with a situation which has its own charm, but this becomes much more interesting because it is the prelude to something else which is the more mysterious because very little is said about it. Frost marks this change in his subject with a slight change of technique in the last verse, where a single rhyme and the repetition of the last line show that something important is afoot. (pp. 49-52)

In Frost's narratives there is always a central point, a theme which appeals by its unexpected character, though it may not be at all sensational. Frost likes the odd, the unforeseen, the paradoxical, but he is quite content that it should be found in small ways and on a small scale. Yet he succeeds in making his subjects significant and in relating them to fundamental issues of human life. Behind the vivid special cases we can see universal rules at work and know that even the oddest behaviour rises from something fundamental in man. For instance, in **"The Code"** Frost illustrates how countrymen have their own kind of honour and feel insulted when they are told how to do something of which they are perfectly capable. In this case a farmer goes too far with one of his hands and patronises him when he makes a hayrick. The hand takes his revenge by smothering the farmer with hay in the barn and leaving him under an enormous pile, not caring what happens to him. The farmer emerges, but is next seen not in the barn picking peas in the garden, and the tale ends with a neat little crisis:

"Weren't you relieved to find he wasn't dead?"

"No! and yet I don't know—it's hard to say.
I went about to kill him fair enough."

"You took an awkward way. Did he discharge you?"

"Discharge me? No! He knew I did just right."

That is all. The question of honour is settled, and the drama which turns on it reaches an appropriate conclusion in the farmer's tacit admission that he has offended against the proprieties of his profession.

This is not to say that Frost avoids exciting and mysterious themes. More than once he assays them. The country has its full share of secrets and horrors and Frost makes a proper use of them. **"The Death of the Hired Man"** is a humble tragedy of a farmworker who is of very little use since he always leaves the farm at the busiest time or tries to cajole the farmer with boasts and promises which he cannot fulfil. Yet he has his own pathos, because he has no home other than the farm, and, despite his poor efforts to better himself, he always comes back to it. Now he comes back for the last time, and, as the farmer's wife sees, he is dying. The farmer resents his presence and refuses to believe that anything is wrong with him, and anyhow why cannot he go to his brother who is quite well off ? The wife feels differently and understands the situation, as she says to her husband:

"Warren," she said, "he has come home to die;
You needn't be afraid he'll leave you this time."

The husband resists the appeal to his sympathy, feels that anyhow he has done enough, and that anyhow the whole thing is a nuisance. Then he goes to look for the man and comes back quietly to say that he is dead. The poem is about the pathos of men who have no roots and no ties and no firm grip on life. Despite his defects and lack of character the hired man has his own minor tragedy, which emerges through the quite different views which the husband and wife take of him. (pp. 53-5)

New England has its traditions of witches and witchcraft, of which memories and more than memories still linger in the villages. In **"The Witch of Coos"** Frost touches on the subject. A mother and son whom he meets on a farm behind the mountains, talk freely to him. The son is proud of the mother, who, he claims, can do some unusual things:

Mother can make a common table rear
And kick with two legs like an army mule.

The mother is more reticent and claims no great powers for herself. She admits that she has spoken with spirits, but she is not very proud of it and thinks "there's something the dead are keeping back". But, none the less, she has her tale to tell. In her attic is a skeleton behind a nailed door. It is that of a man whom her husband killed when he tried to lay hands on her. In the night it can be heard in the attic trying to get back to the cellar where it came from. Then the story comes. The son, who was a baby at the time, gives his account of what happened:

It left the cellar forty years ago
And carried itself like a pile of dishes
Up one flight from the cellar to the kitchen,
Another from the kitchen to the bedroom,
Another from the bedroom to the attic,
Right past both father and mother and neither
    stopped it.

The mother confirms the story and adds other details, how she saw the creature coming upstairs, knocked its finger off when it approached her, and with her husband trapped it in the attic and locked it in. She used to keep the fingerbone in her button-box, and, though she cannot at the moment find it, her word is not disputed. It is all circumstantial and convincing, and its reality is the greater because we hear no more than what the mother and son themselves believe. It is

not clear that the mother is in any sense a witch. Beyond the mountains such things are quite plausible, and there Frost leaves it.

Frost's lyrical poetry is a different kind of art from these stories. It has the same loving observation and the same quiet surprises; but it has other qualities outside the scope of story-telling. It is in the first place the poetry of Frost's intimate acquaintance with the country. In its traditional activities he finds much that is new and enchanting, and this gives a special quality to his record of it. While he carries out the hum-drum duties of farm life, he notices all manner of small things and so gives himself up to his tasks that everything in them has a special vividness. (pp. 55-6)

Frost's observation is always accompanied by delight in what he sees. He asks no great rewards from nature because it has more than enough to offer. The small surprises of country life are an endless source of pleasure to him. He sees a runaway colt on a mountain pasture. It shies away from him:

And now he comes again with a clatter of stone,
And mounts the wall again with whited eyes
And all his tail that isn't hair up straight.
He shudders his coat as if to throw off flies.

He sees the countryside covered with snow and thinks of the time when it will thaw:

Nothing will be left white but here a birch
And there a clump of houses with a church.
(pp. 57-8)

Frost is much more than a recorder of what he sees. His visual powers are clear and exact, but they start other forces working in him and take him beyond description. In particular they evoke a special kind of fancy. A thing seen suggests something else, and Frost uses this second thing to bring out hidden qualities of the first, to make them clearer and to show what they mean. His fancy forms vivid pictures and no doubt owes much to sensations stored and matured in his memory. Some sight may so excite him that for the moment he believes it to be something else. This is not make-believe or even a momentary suspension of unbelief. It is real belief which transforms phenomena not usually associated with them. Frost seems to have had this faculty in childhood. In San Francisco, with its famous Golden Gate and its glittering atmosphere he heard tales of gold and told what these meant to him:

Dust always blowing about the town,
Except when the sea-fog laid it down,
And I was one of the children told
Some of the blowing dust was gold.

All the dust the wind blew high
Appeared like gold in the sunset sky,
But I was one of the children told
Some of the dust was really gold.

Such was the life in the Golden Gate;
Gold dust all we drank and ate,
And I was one of the children told,
"We all must eat our peck of gold."

This is of course a fancy, but a fancy based not only on a child's belief but on a real insight into actual conditions and an imaginative delight in them. This gift plays a large part in Frost's poetry and is responsible for some of its most striking qualities.

This fancy displays itself through the usual instruments of image and simile and always reflects Frost's discriminating insight. But it does more. Whole poems owe their success to it, because it provides them with just the moment that really counts, with the sudden thrill for which Frost prepares the way with sensitive care. (pp. 58-9)

Frost is for many reasons an unusual figure in the contemporary scene. He has hardly been touched by the modern desire to make poetry as intense and as suggestive as possible. His gifts are different. He is quite happy not to hint but to describe, to present not complex states of mind but simple emotions and moments of vivid insight into ordinary things. For his own ends he has evolved a truly adequate technique which secures those quiet and yet delightful effects which are his domain. He is fortunate in having New England behind him; for it gives to his work a background and a unity of character which are lacking to many more travelled and more cosmopolitan poets. But New England too is fortunate in having found an authentic voice in Frost. Perhaps this rural world of which he speaks with such love and knowledge will decay. The trees are already growing again in the clearings which the old colonists made, and ruinous farm-houses, deserted by men who have gone to richer pastures in the West, are the haunt of wild animals. Frost has caught the spirit of this world while it is still alive. He shows no sign of melancholy or fear of decay. This world is good enough for him. He knows its faults and its failures, but he trusts in the wisdom of men and wishes them to be happy. . . . (pp. 63-4)

C. M. Bowra, "Re-Assessments," in *The Adelphi,* Vol. XXVII, No. 1, November, 1950, pp. 46-64.

A. ZVEREV

(essay date 1976)

[Zverev is a literary historian and critic who has published reviews and essays on such American writers as James Baldwin, John Gardner, William Carlos Williams, and Denise Levertov. He is also the editor of *Contemporary American Poetry* (1975). In the following excerpt, he analyzes some of the major themes in Frost's poetry.]

To picture American poetry of the 20th century without Robert Frost would be as difficult as picturing 19th century poetry without Edgar Allan Poe or Walt Whitman. Poe, Whitman and Frost represent the three highpoints in American poetry. The significance of each has long since been acknowledged unanimously and universally. Even people who have no interest whatsoever in verse know these names. . . .

Frost's visit to the USSR in the autumn of 1962 was a memorable event for many. The eighty-eight-year-old poet astonished everyone not only with his youthful heart, his avid interest in the country he was shown and the people whose acquaintance he made, but also because here, as rarely happens, the real man coincided with the image of the poet conveyed in his verses. (p. 241)

A superficial reading of Frost's poetry may give the impression that he is an artist who has delved deeply into the law of eternal return: birth, flowering, death, new birth. Or an artist whose works are all authentic and autobiographical. Or an escapist philosopher, a Thoreau of the 20th century who has retreated from the soulless and cruel reality of the megalopolis and found refuge under the forest canopy of New England.

Each of these impressions is true and reveals some facet of Frost's poetic world. But let us try to read Frost not only as a poet who has given us marvellous examples of lyrical and dramatic poetry, but also as one who has left us with an uncommonly authentic artistic testimony of *our epoch.* In the stream of books on Frost issuing from his native land the poet's work is rarely viewed from such an angle. Yet such an approach might prove both important and useful. The fact is that Frost, like many other eminent writers, became a sort of legend in his lifetime, and his "public image", created by numerous critics, from the Georgians on down to the critics represented in Richard Thornton's anthology *Recognition of Robert Frost,* proved, it seems, to be rather distant from the essence of Frost as poet. (p. 244)

It is one thing to recognize an artist, but to understand his work is something far more difficult. Frost's earliest verses made it clear that here was a completely independent poet unlike any other. Frost was like an island, situated, it is true, not all that far from the mainland of American poetry, but separated from it by a sufficiently broad strait. It was necessary to understand what exactly distinguished Frost from his contemporaries. And the explanation was quickly found. Too quickly, in fact, for though it was based on actual features of Frost's poetic conceptions, it overlooked others, as a result of which Frost's creative temper was distorted. The explanation ran as follows: Frost in principle did not want to be a contemporary poet, did not want to respond to the "spirit of the times".

The situation in which American poetry found itself in the nineteen tens was complex, and it would be too perilous to outline this situation in a few words. Nonetheless one must observe that this was a period of decisive thematic and artistic renewal. Reality was saturated with sharp social conflicts. Life was changing at a headlong, abnormal pace. The tentacles of sprawling cities were sweeping aside the sleepy provinces. America was becoming a land of "smoke and steel", to quote the title of one of Sandburg's collections. The first harbingers of the "jazz age" were making their appearance.

The feverish tempo of life infected poetry, and its canons, which had only recently appeared unassailable, were now collapsing.

Looking for support to the discoveries made by Whitman, who had not been understood by his contemporaries, young poets strove to convey the dynamism of their stormy age. Industrial America found its voice in Sandburg. Lindsay expressed the confusion of the young as they faced a civilization of material wealth and spiritual poverty; later F. Scott Fitzgerald and John Dos Passos would write on the same theme. Anderson's *Winesburg, Ohio* and Lewis' *Gopher Prairie* traced their lineage back to [Masters'] *Spoon River*.

In another camp—this one headed by Ezra Pound—mind-boggling experiments with verse were taking place, and such avant-garde schools as Imagism, "Amygism" and Vorticism appeared and disappeared in rapid succession.

And what about Frost? He seemed to stand on the sidelines of these poetic movements, remaining a "conservative", an "archaist". He was not attracted by new themes or by *vers libre,* which was rapidly and decisively crowding out metrical verse. He learned far more from the English and American romantics than from *Leaves of Grass.* In many ways taking after Thoreau, Emerson and Keats, Frost reworked their favorite themes: he described nature, the farmer's labors, native scenes of rural New England. Among his favorite genres were those very ones which the "interim" poets had succeeded in hopelessly compromising—all those epigones in the Riley mold imitating the Victorians with their syrupy voices. Frost loved the ballad, the song, the landscape, the pastoral.

When the public, which had begun to take an interest in *A Boy's Will* and *North of Boston,* discovered that the author had spent his boyhood in the country, that he had devoted his life to farming and found time to write poetry only in the evening, they formed a permanent image of Frost in their minds as a "peasant poet" far removed from the distemper of his times, one who strove consciously to speak not of the transient, but of the eternal.

So it seemed that the "national American poet" was indifferent to the drama and conflicts which agitated the America of his times.

Thus already at the onset of Frost's literary career there arose the myth of "the quietest of poets", the "stubborn optimist" with a profound faith in the eternal spiritual values of the toiling farmer, the poet who had retreated from the "madding crowd" to the canopied shelter of the eternally lovely New England woods, and urged his readers to follow his example. Thus arose the widespread and still prevailing notion of Frost as a custodian of the traditions of lyrical poetry, singing of the "simple life". (pp. 245-47)

Such judgements of Frost are not, of course, without foundation—he really was a "peasant poet", a bard of patriarchal New England. His quest for a harmonious and integrated perception of the world was undoubtedly inherent to his artistic thought. His "Horatian serenity" was a unique phenomenon for an epoch in which poets "ran wild in the quest of new ways to be new", an epoch governed by the spirit of reckless poetic experimentation. [In his preface to Edwin Arlington Robinson's *King Jasper,* Frost wrote:] "Poetry, for example, was tried without punctuation. It was tried without capital letters. . . . It was tried without any images but those to the eye. . . . It was tried without content under the trade name of poesie pure. . . . It was tried without ability."

All these extremes of experimentation . . . were always in the poet's field of vision; in opposition to the coquettish "difference" of many of his contemporaries, he chose "the old-fashioned way to be new" and felt a keen responsibility for the poetic word. The "archaic" quality of Frost, who clung stubbornly to traditional forms and vocabulary and felt himself to be a direct heir of the New England poets—Thoreau and Emerson, was called to life in part by the fact that American poetry at the time needed someone who would preserve the great romantic tradition, in some ways related to social utopianism. Frost realized it was his calling to guard this tradition, to develop it, and to oppose tendencies which "sorely strained" the "limits of poetry". (pp. 247-48)

Frost called poetry "an effort to explain life", by which, of course, he meant contemporary life. He did not write free verse and said that he would rather play tennis without a net than employ *vers libre,* but this does not in the least imply that Frost's metrical verse was the same as Longfellow's. He did not strive along with his contemporaries "to include a larger material", for often as a result of such efforts the poet "gets lost in his material without a gathering metaphor to throw it into shape and order". In comparison to T. S. Eliot or Carl Sandburg Frost was a poet of "narrow", local and always traditional material. But does that mean that Frost's "metaphor", in other words his poetic image, is equivalent to James Russell Lowell's "metaphors" or those of Edwin Arlington Robinson, a poet incomparably closer to Frost? Does this mean that Frost's "narrow" material does not reveal some absolutely new artistic qualities to the reader, or appear in an absolutely new artistic dimension?

Frost is too strikingly different from his New England predecessors for us to explain away these differences simply in terms of the creative individuality or uniqueness which nature bestows on any outstanding talent. It would be difficult to solve the "riddle" of Frost by examining his poetics from the inside, as a closed system. In the first decades of the 20th century the American poetic tradition was being rejuvenated, and here Frost had a decisive role to play. The American literature of those years was realistic, and Frost belonged to the aesthetic movement of his times, regardless of how traditional and "timeless" he may have appeared to be.

Here we approach the very essence of the problem. A realistic artistic system does not, of course, presuppose photographic fidelity in its reflection of the surrounding world. It presupposes above all an attempt to grasp the true laws of life, to penetrate the essence of life processes—social and individual, spiritual and psychological. It demands an objective view of the world. It entails not only a new aggregate of expressive means, but also a reconsideration of various aesthetic and philosophical categories which have determined the specific features of poetry in earlier periods, in particular romantic poetry.

For Frost the most important of these categories was understanding the people and the life of the people.

The romantic tradition lay at the foundation of his art, but as an artist of realistic bent he gave new meaning to a principal aspect of this tradition—the way it reflected the people's life. For the romantics "the people" was an abstract and static spiritual substance. For Frost "the people" emerges as a category of historical existence. This was a great shift. Having apparently exhausted all its possibilities and now compromised in the "twilight interval", the romantic tradition received a powerful stimulus. Facing new aesthetic demands, the tradition proved its vitality, and the continuity of poetry was preserved.

In place of the mythologized and decorative "folk style" of the romantics Frost brought a peculiar artistic concept of "autochthony", to borrow the term from Mircea Eliade's *Myth, Dreams and Mysteries.* Speaking of "autochthony", Eliade implies a profound and frequently unconscious sense of belonging to the place: "men feel that they are *people of the place,* and this is a feeling of cosmic relatedness deeper than that of familial and ancestral solidarity".

This seems to be a relevant and true description of Frost's outlook too. In the context of literary history this "autochthonic" sense which is conveyed in his poetry is possibly Frost's greatest achievement. (pp. 248-50)

When I speak of Frost as the most "autochthonic" American poet of the 20th century, I have in mind not only such poems as **"The Gift Outright"** (which, however, are certainly worth rereading particularly at this point, when books like Gore Vidal's *Burr* are so astonishingly popular). Rather, I have in mind those poems which contain no outright declarations, poems which recreate with unique breadth and objectivity a picture of the people's life in all its diversity, its normal course, which for the poet is inseparable from the course of his own life; poems like the ones you find in Frost's two best collections—*North of Boston* and *New Hampshire.*

> I touch my tongue to the shoes now,
> And unless my sense is at fault,
> On one I can taste Atlantic,
> On the other Pacific, salt.

Here is a precisely formulated poetic motif, one which is repeated at various stages in Frost's artistic development. Though a "New England" poet, he often returned to this theme of the great American expanses, moving far beyond the immediate horizons of New England. When he was a child Frost crossed the American continent twice over, and as a poet he was keenly aware that this was his world, his universe; in his verses the most varied facets of the image of America are explored. But Frost's America is always a country that belongs to people capable of preserving the vital link that binds them to nature and to each other, of filling their lives with high ethical meaning, for this is an active, creative, morally pure and healthy life. And the major lyrical principle in all of Frost's books—from *A Boy's Will* to the last collection *In the Clearing*—is the feeling that the poet and his world are indivisible, that all men are brothers working together on this earth . . . , that nature and man and all men are united:

> I had for my winter evening walk—
> No one at all with whom to talk,
> But I had the cottages in a row
> Up to their shining eyes in snow.
>
> And I thought I had the folk within:
> I had the sound of a violin;
> I had a glimpse through curtain laces
> Of youthful forms and youthful faces.
>
> I had such company outward bound . . .
>
> (pp. 250-51)

In his time Malcolm Cowley severely rebuked Frost for his unwillingness to speak of life definitively and clearly, for the vagueness of his poetic judgements. . . . It would be hard to find a more unjust statement regarding the poet. In his brilliant essay **"The Figure a Poem Makes"** Frost asserts, "The possibilities for tune from the dramatic tones of meaning struck across the rigidity of a limited meter are endless." The poet's own experience led him to this conviction; a poem by Frost is always the most subtle interweaving of "dramatic tones of meaning", whereas graphic precision of line and clarity of meaning would only destroy the entire artistic structure of Frost's poetry.

Cowley's mistake consists in the fact that he immediately identifies the poetic device with the content of the lyric. But the content itself was never ambiguous or vague. Edward Thomas, a member of the Georgian circle, wrote that *North of Boston* was "one of the most revolutionary books of the time", and though Frost was never a revolutionary in his social views, one could nonetheless concur completely with this statement. Frost's epic canvas with its profound fidelity to life was very much a revolutionary event in American poetry. Frost's objective view on the life of the people, his effort to merge totally with the people and assume their view on life's fundamental problems—all these things were in fact revolutionary for the poetry of the time. (pp. 251-52)

"I had a lover's quarrel with the world," Frost said of himself, and he could not have expressed himself more exactly, for his truly was a lover's quarrel, a recognition of life's drama which did not lead to a rejection of this life in the name of some ideal, nor to the setting up of his own, isolated world in contrast to the life around him. Yes, Frost belonged to this world, but he never looked at it through the rose-colored glasses of superficially understood patriotism. He saw this world in its true light and linked himself irrevocably to it. Otherwise he would have proved incapable of that organic understanding of the world's anxieties which so astonishes us in Frost's lyrics. The call of the city, luring us with its tawdry splendors, the lost harmony of man and the earth on which he toils, the growing mistrust and alienation between people who were once united by common cares, and the poet's unflagging feeling of belonging to that great body known as the People—all this we find in Frost and his remarkably, profoundly realistic panorama of the people's life.

Frost's comments on "two types of realist" are well known: "There are two types of realist—the one who offers a good deal of dirt with his potato to show that it is a real one; and the one who is satisfied with the potato brushed clean. I am inclined to be the second kind. To me, the thing that art does for life is to clean it, to strip it to form." Another of his statements on the same subject is less well known: "Instead of a realist—if I must be classified—I think I might better be called a Synecdochist; for I am fond of the synecdoche in po-

Frost at John F. Kennedy's inauguration with the President and Dwight D. Eisenhower, January, 1961.

etry—that figure of speech in which we use a part for the whole."

It is this "synecdochism" which constitutes the basis for Frost's realistic poetics. The situations described in his dramatic verses sometimes come close to being casual, and in any case very commonplace. But they are imbued with genuinely poetic content, for behind the "individual" there is always the "general", the "autochthonic". In **"Mending Wall"** Frost talks about a most commonplace occurrence: the wall separating a farmer's land from that of his neighbor has crumbled and must be repaired. For the romantic poet this would serve as an occasion to embark on a poetical meditation on the passage of time; such a possibility is also hinted at in **"Mending Wall"**:

Something there is that doesn't love a wall,
That wants it down. I could say "Elves" to him,
But it's not elves exactly . . .

But Frost is a poet with a realistic bent; he discovers a completely different aspect in the motif "Something there is that doesn't love a wall", a rich image which serves to convey notions of true and false in the mind of the people. The "autochthonic" sense in this poem is not, of course, conveyed by the simple, peasant-like, practical considerations which Frost imputes to his hero ("My apple trees will never get across / And eat the cones under his pines"), nor by the abundance of folkish expressions. The poet, as it were, set himself the task of reproducing in detail the thought processes of an ordinary farmer, and every trifle is important for him—the fact that there is no livestock on the farm, and therefore that the wall serves no purpose, and the fact that in lifting up the stones he and his neighbor scrape their fingers raw: "The work of hunters is another thing: / I have come after them and made repair."

Frost's realism is based in large measure on his exact knowledge of the material at hand; but this is not the realism of the "particular", not the realism of details, but of the "universal", the people's point of view. The desire to fence oneself off from others, to shut oneself off in one's own little world, is a notion quite alien to the people. . . . (pp. 253-55)

The fact that a nearby farmer with such a motto as "Good fences make good neighbors" appears in Frost's poem is not mere coincidence. Even though for Frost's hero he is "like an old-stone savage armed", Frost himself realized that such neighbors on nearby farms were increasing in number. The tragic spirit that informs so many of Frost's poems consists in the fact that his attraction to the people clashes with his realization of the growing differentiation, particularly social differentiation, among the people. As an artist and realist Frost could not ignore this process. Throughout his works one can find images that speak of the passing of the village, that cradle of unity and "plebeian" democracy which was so dear to Frost, images telling us how this world has collapsed under the pressures of the 20th century, that it is undergoing a period of crisis and decline. (p. 255)

But Frost's importance consists, of course, not only in the fact that he recognized the "seeds of degeneration" which had fallen on New England soil. Perhaps he was even mistaken in defending the view that the village, despite all its internal conflicts (of which Frost was well aware), nonetheless remained the only firm foundation for democratic world order. But having accepted the "autochthonic" view of the state of things (even sometimes equating it with the viewpoint of the ordinary farmer—granted that to a certain degree he was a conventional figure), and having come to a realistic perception of life, Frost was able to grasp genuinely and subtly the changes taking place in his native rural America, and to defend, convincingly but without pretention, ideals shared by the people. Without this indivisibility of the poet and the people, Frost's artistic vision would lack that real originality which draws us in such masterpieces as **"The Pasture"**, **"October"**, **"Blueberries"**, **"Birches"**, or **"Stopping by Woods on a Snowy Evening"**. Amazing in their intensity of lyrical feeling and their musicality, all these verses are born of a perception of nature which would be impossible for a man who had not come into daily contact with it—like a farmer or laborer.

The feeling of distress over the changes taking place in his native region is sometimes expressed with surprising forcefulness in Frost's verses. His images are artless, but they are animated by an elevated sense of tragedy, as for example in **"The Woodpile"**, where a stack of firewood left lying outdoors becomes a symbol for neglect, for a land that is wasted, for disintegration. . . . (pp. 255-56)

Nonetheless it would hardly be accurate to describe Frost's poetry as "saturnine terror that creeps up unnoticed" (as Ivan Kashkin once described it). Yes, Frost felt deeply the tragedy of the land, how it had been reclaimed from the swamps and salinas and had flowered, and now, against the will of those who had made it bear fruit, it was once again reverting to a state of wildness and desolation. The poet felt himself a part of the drama of that disintegrating world out of which America had grown. But regardless of how distressing were the consequences of the onset of the "machine age" in world so dear to Frost, the poet saw that democratic ideals had not died, and his faith in the imperishability of the people's moral health lent even greater cogency to his work.

His poetry is imbued with this faith. Sometimes, immersed in his love for his native land, Frost seems not to notice that enormous world, replete with its own concerns, which extends beyond the horizons of New England. At times he resembles the hero of his poem **"The Mountain"**, who tries to fence himself off from the universe, to withdraw into the shell of his own monotonous existence, to limit himself to the confines of his own village. . . . (pp. 256-57)

But Frost had good reason to call his *North of Boston* a "Book of People". The character of this collection, like that of all of Frost's works, is defined by those poems in which the poet gazes intently on the people's life without taking "shelter from a wind", penetrating its drama and playing the role of an active participant. This distinguishing trait of Frost's poetry emerges with particular clarity in his dramatic works. Sometimes they are called "narrative", which is inaccurate. It is precisely the dramatic element which Frost valued so highly in poetry. He wrote, "Everything written is as good as it is dramatic." The form and subject of these stories and scenes written in blank verse, were for the most part taken directly from folk ballads. The folkloric base also makes itself felt in the devices Frost uses to develop character, and even in the choice of character (for example, the tight-fisted boss and the sharp farm-hand in the poem **"The Code"**). Perhaps the best known of all of Frost's dramatic works is **"The Death of a Hired Man"**. It is one of Frost's most brilliant poems. Here, perhaps, more than anywhere else, we find the fullest treatment of Frost's major themes—the disintegration of the once unified world of New England, and the search for what is undyingly human. (pp. 257-58)

In his books this world was examined in a unique and profound manner, and the ideals to which Silas [in **"The Death of a Hired Man"**] adhered and which were so dear to Frost himself were far from being reactionary ("back to patriarchal simplicity") but rather democratic in character. Frost's realism and sincere democratic impulses made him the greatest American poet of the 20th century.

And a broad range of readers (not only in the poet's homeland) have long since acknowledged Frost, the real Frost—not as an intellectual dressed in home-spun farmers' clothes, not as a conformist, not as an unthinking composer of idylls and pastorals, but as an artist who expressed the people's view on the complex, sharply contradictory world of America in the 20th century, one who believed in the people and shared their hopes, their democratic traditions and ideals. This is how he appears if we approach his work without prejudice. (pp. 259-60)

A. Zverev, "A Lover's Quarrel with the World: Robert Frost," in *20th Century American Literature: A Soviet View,* translated by Ronald Vroon, Progress Publishers, 1976, pp. 241-60.

ROBERT KERN

(essay date 1988)

[In the following excerpt, Kern challenges the contention that Frost was a traditional poet who contributed very little to the development of modern verse.]

Up until fairly recently, the conventional wisdom about the relation of Robert Frost to modernism, when it was considered at all, was that for the most part there was none—that between Frost's poetry on the one hand and a virtually monolithic phenomenon composed primarily of the work of Eliot, Pound, Stevens, and Williams on the other, there was and could be little commerce. But over the last several years, as the issue has begun to be addressed with greater seriousness and scrutiny (by such critics as Frank Lentricchia, Richard Poirier, William Pritchard, and others), it has become harder not only to maintain the separation between Frost and his contemporaries but to continue to regard modernism itself as a unified, homogeneous movement in literary history, as though it were an exclusive club with strict rules of membership and with no room for a poet who refused to abandon the formal and generic conventions of traditional verse. The insistence on Frost's difference from modernism, it has become clear, was based on an oversimplification of both.

Whether Frost himself would have welcomed the end of his exclusion from the company of the great modern poets is, of course, another question. His friendship with Pound, Frost once noted, lasted but six weeks, his relations with Stevens were always cool and distant, and Eliot and Williams he hardly knew at all and seemed to prefer it that way. But in spite of Frost's personal attitudes and antipathies, which probably

contributed to the general critical sense of his isolation from his contemporaries, one important result of this new attention to him in the context of modernism may well be a new understanding of modernism itself, of the different ways in which it was possible to be a modern poet. And such understanding may derive as much from considerations of what Frost in fact shares with his contemporaries as from an acknowledgement of the real differences between them. Indeed, in comparing Frost with "certified" modernists like Eliot and Joyce, Richard Poirier points out [in his *Robert Frost: The Work of Knowing,* 1977] that despite certain similarities and differences among all three, the differences between the latter two tend to shrink in importance when Frost is brought into the picture. But this is not to revive the idea that Frost cannot be regarded as an authentically modern writer. Poirier's point, instead, allows us to see that he is a different kind of modernist, or that he represents a different degree of modernism—that he is a writer, for example, for whom the pressure or "chaos" of history is less a determinant of poetic form than a provocation to reproduce it in its more or less established modes. "When in doubt," Frost says, "there is always form for us to go on with," as though form for him is always something stable and unproblematic in its relation to what lies outside it, a stay against doubt—whereas doubt for other writers may well include doubts about form itself.

The extent to which Frost's modernism is, in this way, qualified, although not to the point where it ceases to exist, shows up in the "Introduction" he wrote for Edwin Arlington Robinson's *King Jasper* (1935). Here Frost distinguishes between what he calls "new ways to be new," which involve stripping poetry of many of its conventional devices and traditional procedures, and "the old fashioned way to be new," with which he associates Robinson and is himself in sympathy. The new ways to be new, which are motivated, as Frost bluntly puts it, by "science," call for a process of subtraction or elimination, of trying to write poetry without everything from meter and rhyme to ability. But the interesting point that emerges from Frost's distinction here is that he thought of himself as "new," and, as Poirier reminds us, he was in fact considered "an exponent of the new" for the first quarter of the century. Although we have to look elsewhere in Frost's work for a more explicit account of what he might mean by "the old fashioned way to be new," it seems clear that it cannot simply be a matter of clinging to all the things that the pursuit of innovation for its own sake tries to do without. That would be *merely* old fashioned. Frost's newness, rather, as we learn from several letters written in 1913 and 1914 to his friend John Bartlett, consists in his radical renewal and revision of the Wordsworthian project of appropriating the language of everyday life for poetry. Or, as Poirier puts it, he finds ways of admitting English poetry, both its sounds and metaphors, into ordinary speech, principally that of New England. And what this involves, more than anything else, is his idea of "sentence-sounds," the seemingly idiosyncratic, ultimately primitivistic notion that sentences are sounds in themselves which can convey meaning above and beyond the collective meaning of the words of which they consist. In the most important of the letters to Bartlett, one that constitutes a virtual manifesto, Frost announces rather grandly:

I give you a new definition of a sentence:

A sentence is a sound in itself on which other sounds called words may be strung.

You may string words together without a sentence-sound to string them on just as you may tie clothes together by the sleeves and stretch them without a clothes line between two trees, but—it is bad for the clothes.

The number of words you may string on one sentence-sound is not fixed but there is always danger of over loading.

The sentence-sounds are very definite entities. (This is no literary mysticism I am preaching.) They are as definite as words. It is not impossible that they could be collected in a book though I don't at present see on what system they would be catalogued.

They are apprehended by the ear. They are gathered by the ear from the vernacular and brought into books. Many of them are already familiar to us in books. I think no writer invents them. The most original writer only catches them fresh from talk, where they grow spontaneously.

Despite the self-conscious extravagance of these remarks (subtended as they are, perhaps, by Frost's own sense that he may in fact be verging on a sort of "literary mysticism"), it would be a mistake, I think, not to take him seriously here. He refers several times in his letters to the possibility of collecting and cataloguing the sentence-sounds, and although such a project never materialized, it is clear that his thinking about what he also calls the "sound of sense" informs his poetic production in important ways, explicitly thematized, for instance, in such a later poem as **"Never Again Would Birds' Song Be the Same."** A sentence-sound, Frost is proposing, is something heard, "apprehended by the ear," rather than, primarily, something understood. The issue here is one not of meaning but of qualities of voice that link meaning to a specific human occasion or emotion. As the metaphor of the clothes line suggests, words without a sentence-sound to support them are mere abstractions, removed from the reality of actual utterance, and in this sense, sentence-sounds become Frost's means of countering the

abstract force of language or the "bookish" rhetoric that poetic modernism in general seeks to avoid. They are his way of making a poem *be* rather than just *mean*—which is why sound for Frost, as he puts it in **"The Figure a Poem Makes,"** is "the gold in the ore," the element of greatest value, humanly and aesthetically, in poetic structure. In addition, at a time when other modernists were responding variously to the lure of the primitive, or returning to origins as part of the enterprise to "make it new," Frost's notion of sentence-sounds bears an intriguing similarity to certain contemporary developments in linguistics. The Danish writer Otto Jespersen, for example, had recently described primitive language in terms of what he calls "sentence-words" and "sound conglomerations." These were complicated and often massive linguistic forms in which the elements of speech, which would later split off from each other in modern analytic languages, are fused together, and what these forms imply, at least hypothetically, is an original *language*-word, a mythic, undifferentiated word-mass containing within it the possibility of all utterance. In his own effort to make it new, at any rate, Frost seems to have invented a primitive or originary speech entirely on his own.

There are, moreover, other grounds for insisting on Frost's modernism (qualified as it may be), ranging from Lentricchia's emphasis on the centrality of post-Kantian and William Jamesian theoretical perspectives in Frost's poetics to Poirier's detailed demonstration of shared thematic concerns between Frost and a poet like Stevens. And yet, one suspects, there is still a stumbling block, a resistance, at least for some readers, in granting to Frost the full status of modern writer, whether it lies in the area of Frost's traditional formalism, or in the insistent ordinariness and conventionality of his subject matter, so firmly based in straightforward narrative, or in the lack in his work of what Poirier calls the "formal dislocation" characteristic of much twentieth-century literature, "the heady mixture of discontinuity and cultural allusiveness" whose supreme instances are Eliot's *Waste Land* and Pound's *Cantos*. To be sure, given Frost's own sense of himself as pursuing "the old fashioned way to be new"—which may mean, in part, that he does not tamper with the reading process—and given his attitudes toward the work of other modern poets in general, it is easy to see why some readers are led to wonder if there is ever a point, in fact, where his qualified modernism becomes *dis*qualified as modernism.

One way of bringing this issue into focus, if not completely to resolve it, is to consider Frost's response to imagism (regarded as an early or inaugural phase of the revolution in modern poetry), and to gauge the extent to which the imagist milieu that he encountered in London when he arrived there in 1912 may have affected his thinking about his own work. Frost, of course, has never been considered (and rightly so) an imagist.

His work never appeared in any of the imagist anthologies; and although he got on well with F. S. Flint (one of the reorganizers of the original "school of Images," as Pound called it) and attended some of the group's meetings, he apparently found himself at odds with certain imagist ideas. In any case, as one historian of the imagist movement reports, at these meetings Frost kept his silence. But increasingly, in letters and even in such later pieces as the Introduction to *King Jasper* and the obituary for Amy Lowell (1925—by which time the imagist movement was already part of literary history), Frost registered his sense of the inadequacies of imagism. In the summer of 1914, for instance, the year of Pound's *Des Imagistes*, Frost wrote to John Cournos, one of its contributors, that what he was most interested in cultivating was "the hearing imagination" "rather than the kind that merely sees things." This opposition between hearing and seeing, between ear and eye, which recurs in many of the letters and essays, developed into a small, continuing campaign against imagism, and became, as well, one of Frost's chief ways of distinguishing himself from his modernist contemporaries.

To see what he was up against, and to appreciate the loneliness of Frost's position, one need only recall the virtual hegemony of what might be described as visualist thinking, both in philosophy and poetics, during this period. In the work of such figures as Henri Bergson, Remy de Gourmont, and T. E. Hulme, among others, verbal language falls under increasing suspicion as a kind of systematic fraud, utterly out of touch with the reality it supposedly names, consisting largely of metaphors which have lost their communicative power and degenerated into the mere clichés of ordinary speech. Even what was assumed to be the purely literal language of philosophic discourse turned out, for Nietzsche, to be nothing but buried or forgotten metaphor. The remedy, as a number of writers were suggesting, lay in the cultivation of the concrete visual mind, as opposed to the abstract verbal mind. While the verbal mind, in Gourmont's definition, merely repeats sounds, the visual mind has the capacity to create new metaphors and thus to force language to achieve greater immediacy. (pp. 1-7)

Yet, for their part, the imagists among his early reviewers, primarily Flint and Pound, responded to Frost's first book, *A Boy's Will,* with enthusiasm when it appeared in April 1913. In his review in particular, which Frost included in one of his letters to Bartlett, Flint chooses terms of praise that have a distinctively imagist cast. "Each poem," he says, referring to the five or six he judges to be the best, "is the complete expression of one mood, one emotion, one idea. I have tried to find in these poems what is most characteristic of Mr. Frost's poetry; and I think it is this: direct observation of the object and immediate correlation with the emotion. . . ." Flint published these remarks in June 1913, just a few months after the appearance of Pound's "A Few Don'ts" in *Poetry,* and about a year after the formulation of the three famous principles of imagism, beginning with "Direct treatment of the 'thing' whether subjective or objective." As a critical response, they are somewhat vague, and they may tell us more about Flint's susceptibility to the power of abstract principles than about the poems themselves. What seems clear, at least, is that for Flint, Frost is working within an imagist orbit. But what is of greater interest, I think, than whether Flint was right or wrong about Frost's poems is the extent to which Frost's theory of sentence-sounds may ultimately have evolved as a deliberate, even defensive, reaction against imagism, prompted by Frost's own pursuit of what he calls "specific images to the ear," as opposed to "those to the eye," and prompted as well by his need for a countertheory at a time when the imagist ferment was at its most intense and he increasingly felt it necessary to fend off the influence of Pound in particular.

Regarding Pound himself, Frost wrote, in July 1913, that he "has taken to bullying me," and "He says I must write something much more like *vers libre* or he will let me perish of neglect. He really threatens." It may well be that Frost's negative sense of Pound's encroachments upon him led him not only to articulate his own theory in opposition to imagism, and in a more accelerated way than might otherwise have been the case, but to see that his place in modernism, especially those aspects of it identified with Pound, could not but be a limited one. At the same time, it may be equally true that Frost is a modernist by virtue of the very fact that he was forced to theorize, to define a position for himself, and thus to participate in the collective effort, "then going forward in London," as Hugh Kenner puts it, "to rethink the nature of an English poem."

Frost's rethinking, of course, is focused on issues of voice and sound, and the closest thing to an imagist poem by him is probably **"A Patch of Old Snow,"** the very poem he uses, in one of his letters to Bartlett (where it appears in a rough prose version), to illustrate his notion of sentence-sounds:

There's a patch of old snow in a corner
That I should have guessed
Was a blow-away paper the rain
Had brought to rest.
It is speckled with grime as if
Small print overspread it,
The news of a day I've forgotten—
If I ever read it.

It is precisely its closeness to imagist techniques, however, that allows us to see how far Frost diverges from imagist aims. Even in the prose version of it that Frost provides in the letter, the poem is organized, very much in the imagist manner, as a brief comparison of two images, a strategy close to what Pound called the "superposition" of one image upon another, and what T. E. Hulme called "the simultaneous presentation to the mind of two different images." With some editing it could be reduced to a plausible imagist text. But such reduction would eliminate a good deal of what Frost apparently intends to express, and as an instance of the "sound of sense," the poem seems less imagist finally than a critique of imagism, since it refuses to pursue any sort of simultaneity of presentation in favor of the consecutiveness of its speaker's language and the temporality of his experience.

In Pound's orthodox imagism, on the other hand, the goal is to present "the precise instant when a thing outward and objective transforms itself, or darts into a thing inward and subjective." The classic example is "In a Station of the Metro," a poem in which thirty lines, according to Pound's own testimony, were cut down to two:

The apparition of these faces in the crowd;
Petals on a wet, black bough.

This kind of poem, Pound tells us, "is a form of superposition," in which "one idea [is] set on top of anoth-

er," and although in such an arrangement the words "is like" or "are like" may be understood to occur between the two ideas, specifying their relation, to leave out the words creates a sense of fusion, or even confusion, between the ideas, which leads Pound to speak of the "one image poem." Here, for instance, the process of transformation is already under way as we begin to read, since what we encounter is not the "faces in the crowd" directly but their "apparition" in the mind of the speaker, and that "apparition" is then defined as "Petals on a wet, black bough." In its focus on "the precise instant" of transformation, the poem suppresses the temporality of the process, just as it suppresses any phrase of comparison at the end of the first line, all in the name of the instantaneity of the experience and the sense of "sudden liberation," the "freedom from time limits and space limits," that such poems are meant to evoke.

Frost's poem, by contrast, is constituted by the very time limits and space limits, in terms of its language and situation, that imagist poems like Pound's normally try to abolish. If anything, **"A Patch of Old Snow"** presents not the deliberate imagist confusion between figure and ground, between tenor and vehicle, characteristic of "In a Station of the Metro," but a recovery from such confusion, a moment of clarification or balance that is thoroughly typical of Frost. He is not interested in Pound's sense of "sudden liberation" but in its aftermath, which constitutes a different kind of liberation—a freedom from or resolution of the very ambiguity that Pound's poem generates in its refusal to specify precisely how its two images relate to one another. Frost's speaker makes it clear that his own confusion between a patch of old snow and a blow-away paper, which is what an imagist poem would focus on, was more potential than actual, and that in any case it has come and gone:

There's a patch of old snow in a corner,
That I should have guessed
Was a blow-away paper the rain
Had brought to rest.

His interest now lies in elaborating on the image, accounting for what would have been his mistake and to some extent justifying it, and spelling out the image's further implications.

It is speckled with grime as if
Small print overspread it,
The news of a day I've forgotten—
If I ever read it.

After admitting that what he has seen is not a blow-away paper, the speaker goes on, nevertheless, to explain why he "should have guessed" that he had, refusing to let go of the transformed patch of old snow. Then in the final two lines, he virtually reinstates the image of snow as a newspaper in order to make his point about the transitoriness and pathos of the "news." But that point is conveyed not so much by the image as by the speaker's intonation, the cadence or pacing of the lines themselves. Their effectiveness, Frost says, lies "in the very special tone with which you must say—news of a day I have forgotten—if I ever read it," where the speaker, in a kind of afterthought, passes beyond the image to a different level of insight, and to a use of language—discursive, reflective—of which imagism would not have approved.

This emphasis on tone, on the dynamics and sound of a voice, creates an effect very different from that cultivated by most imagist poems. Here the concern is not with "the thing itself" or its "direct treatment" but with the speaker and ultimately the reader, who is invited to enter into the speaker's experience by saying his words and then to recognize, through their intonation, his state of mind. We encounter, through his speech, the inwardness of a person, rather than just objects in the world, no matter how emotionally evocative. In this sense, Frost is working with images to the ear as well as to the eye, so that the reader experiences a voice as much as (if not more than) a thing. The effect is not the imagist avoidance of "rhetoric," the virtual displacement of linguistic conventions by sharply observed concrete particulars (or what Hulme refers to as the bodily handing-over of sensations), but a conscious indulgence in rhetoric, understood as the careful fashioning (or capturing and preserving) of speech-sounds that Frost ultimately identifies with the primitive origins of human language. Poetic speech is thus authorized for Frost not merely by the poet's adherence to the truth of things seen but by his fidelity to these sounds, which, he insists, are a permanent and original element of language. "They are always there," he says, "living in the cave of the mouth. They are real cave things: they were before words were." And he adds, still squaring off against imagism, "they are as definitely things as any image of sight." On the basis of these remarks, though, we may be justified in saying that Frost is not opposing imagism so much as attempting to redefine it, to extend its limits. If images to the ear are things, then Frost is an imagist. And in this way, too, Frost seems to be insisting, in spite of himself, on his own involvement in modernism—a modernism in which the "sound of sense" is as much an "objective reality" as the visual "thing itself," and in which the writer, keeping his "ear on the speaking voice," and believing that "the sentence-sound often says more than the words," is attempting to return to origins as deliberately as Eliot and Pound do, linking his poem to an originary substratum of language that is prior to literature, to tradition, and even to words.

Frost evokes that substratum, much later in his career, in **"Never Again Would Birds' Song Be the Same"** (1942), a poem that provides a good example of

what might be described as his more advanced modernist thinking—advanced, that is, beyond imagism—even as it demonstrates the extent to which his modernism continues to be bound up with his notion of sentence-sounds. It also demonstrates, I would argue, a modernism less or differently qualified than that projected in some of Frost's essays and letters, insofar as the poem raises problems of reading and interpretation that are normally less obtrusive or visible on the surface of his texts. While we do not quite encounter the "formal dislocation" of Eliot or Pound here, we are still presented with a speaker who, like Eliot's Gerontion or Tiresias, bridges great gaps of time and seems both ancient and modern, simultaneously one of us and an intimate of Adam in the garden of Eden. This quality, moreover, casually revealed in the speaker's own sentence-sounds, is completely taken for granted in the poem.

In several ways, in fact, **"Never Again Would Birds' Song Be the Same"** is a curious mixture of apparently unrelated motives and effects. For one thing, it is a sonnet. For another, despite its innocent guise of a pleasant "just so" story, it actually constitutes something like a meditation on origins, both linguistic and poetic. Set in Eden, scene of origins par excellence, the poem nonetheless imagines a time when a kind of fall seems already to have taken place, when Adam and Eve have already become aware of their difference from nature. Like Milton, however, Frost does not view this event entirely in terms of loss; it is, rather, the beginning of something else.

> He would declare and could himself believe
> That the birds there in all the garden round
> From having heard the daylong voice of Eve
> Had added to their own an oversound,
> Her tone of meaning but without the words.
> Admittedly an eloquence so soft
> Could only have had an influence on birds
> When call or laughter carried it aloft.
> Be that as may be, she was in their song.
> Moreover her voice upon their voices crossed
> Had now persisted in the woods so long
> That probably it never would be lost.
> Never again would birds' song be the same.
> And to do that to birds was why she came.

Here Adam is presented as the author of a myth about the human appropriation of nature, or the absorption, the transformation, of nature into language—an event which gives rise to the nostalgia of the poem's title even as it marks the beginnings of a full human awareness of nature. "Never again would birds' song be the same," says the speaker, although, by the poem's own logic, what "birds' song" was like before its transformation could not, strictly speaking, have been either knowable or nameable. In this sense, the speaker's nostalgia is misplaced; the poem elegizes the loss or absence of what Adam or the speaker could know *only as* loss or absence. Clearly, a break in continuity between

Adam and Eden has occurred, a break signalled by both his nostalgia and his myth-making. At the same time, however, there is a sense in which that myth-making, and perhaps poetry itself, are intended as compensations for the sense of loss, imaginary as it may be. To the extent that Eve came, as the poem's last line suggests, in order to humanize nature, it is to her coming that we owe whatever knowledge of nature we have, along with myth, poetry, and this very poem.

But the poem's complexity is not only thematic; it also lies in the manner of its telling, particularly in the relation of its speaker to Adam, whose thinking is reported to us in an apparently noncommittal indirect style that seems at odds with myth in its tentativeness and in its almost fussy reliance on terms that belong to logical discourse (itself, perhaps, a sign of the fall). Who, we must ask, is speaking here? As the poem proceeds, it becomes increasingly difficult to separate the speaker from Adam, to distinguish quotation from narration. Only the tenses of the verbs remind us that we are listening to a mediated discourse, a description of someone else's thinking; and in the last line of all, which could reasonably be understood as either Adam's or the speaker's, even that indication disappears. If the speaker begins at some distance from Adam, allowing for the possibility of an ironic account, one in which modern skepticism exposes or at least stands apart from primitive belief, such a gap narrows considerably, if not completely, by the end of the poem, where the speaker seems fully involved in Adam's vision. On the other hand, the speaker is careful to suggest that Adam himself is not entirely committed to what he nevertheless "would declare," and we have to wonder if the speaker, in speaking for Adam, is being more or less diffident about his myth than Adam himself would be. In other words, how faithful a version or translation of Adam's own language is this speaker providing (not a trivial question about a poem by Frost, famous for his remark that poetry is what gets lost in translation)? Do such terms and phrases as "Admittedly," "Be that as may be," and "Moreover" reflect the attitudes of Adam, or the speaker, or both? And does the rational tone that they convey work ultimately to undermine or to signal an acceptance of Adam's myth? In any case, the mythic is being viewed here, it would seem, from a decidedly "fallen" point of view, one characterized not by visionary or imaginative certainty but by a cautious and reasonable consideration of possibilities.

Adam's vision itself, of course, is focused most centrally on what the poem calls Eve's "tone of meaning" and its influence upon the birds. "From having heard the daylong voice of Eve," we are told, the birds in the garden "Had added to their own an oversound, / Her tone of meaning but without the words." By "tone of meaning" here we can understand, precisely,

Frost's sentence-sound. It is a kind of pure intonation, a substratum of speech that can apparently cross over from human beings to birds and be reproduced by them in a way that thereafter becomes meaningful to human ears, or at least perceptible as "song." This crossing over can take place, however, only because it is not meaning but sound that the birds pick up and convey. In Frost's conception, one which plays an interesting variation on traditional notions of linguistic origins, a language of spoken words is preceded or underlain by a language of sounds without words, and like most notions of an original or ideal language, this one is both *prior* to actual speech, and so free of the problems of signification, and somehow communicative nevertheless. This is the language that Adam hears as an "oversound" in the voices of the birds. Appropriately, since the poem is a sonnet, this language seems to be a language of love, of "call or laughter," in which meaning is conveyed by tone without the need for words. Strictly speaking, though, it is not meaning but the *sound* of meaning, the *sound* of sense, that Adam hears. What he responds to or recognizes in the sound is a meaning already identified with it in his relationship with Eve.

For the poem is not about the origin of language so much as it is about its humanizing power, its capacity to separate nature from itself and make it the reflection of human meanings. In this sense, in narrating the event of Adam's "discovery" of birds' song, the poem's speaker is locating the origin of a lyric tradition, the very tradition in which his poem participates by imagining that Eve is "in their song"; and again, it is Eve herself, by her coming, who has precipitated this event and who therefore stands as the ultimate cause not only of myth and poetry but of the human passage from nature to culture. In arriving at this realization in the poem's final line, the speaker seems, in addition, to be aware that what Eve has done to the birds she has also, in some sense, done to him—that he and his language, even with its "Admittedly" and "Moreover," are equally the results of her naturalizing/humanizing act. Thus the poem is not simply about Adam's myth; it is about itself in relation to that myth, and its final line, however obliquely, offers the speaker's awed recognition of the connection, of the way his poem is implicated in the very tradition whose origin it describes. What makes the poem modern, beyond the fact of the problematic nature of its speaker and his curiously indirect discourse, is precisely this sense of its connection with poetic origins, its speaker's sudden apprehension of the continuity of his own utterance with the mythic origin of poetic utterance in his own account of it.

Frost's stance in the poem, finally, with respect to myth and the primitive, is perhaps not unlike T. S. Eliot's attitude toward *The Golden Bough.* Frazer's great book, Eliot suggests, "can be read in two ways: as a collection of entertaining myths, or as a revelation of that vanished mind of which our mind is a continuation." Frost's poem, it seems to me, can similarly be read as an entertaining myth or as a revelation of the kind Eliot describes, a revelation of continuity. What I am suggesting, though, is that it is precisely the latter reading that allows for location of the poem in a modern context, one in which the poet discovers that his poem, and his very language, are conditioned if not caused by history. This is not, to be sure, the modernism of absolute beginnings, of Pound's "Make it new," but its other side—the modernism of Eliot's "Tradition and the Individual Talent" . . . , in which the writer comes to recognize that his task involves a struggle with meanings already inscribed in language. Indeed, to work in terms of this recognition may be just what Frost means by "the old fashioned way to be new." (pp. 7-16)

Robert Kern, "Frost and Modernism," in *American Literature,* Vol. 66, No. 1, March, 1988, pp. 1-16.

SOURCES FOR FURTHER STUDY

Burnshaw, Stanley. *Robert Frost Himself.* New York: George Braziller, 1986, 342 p.

Biographical and critical study.

Cox, James Melville, ed. *Robert Frost: A Collection of Critical Essays.* Englewood Cliffs, N.J.: Prentice-Hall, 1962, 205 p.

Representative collection of major essays on Frost and his poetry.

Frost, Robert. *Interviews with Robert Frost.* Edward Connery Lathem, ed. New York: Holt, Rinehart and Winston, 1966, 295 p.

Includes fifty-four interviews originally published between 1915 and 1962.

———. *Robert Frost on Writing.* Elaine Barry, ed. New Brunswick, N.J.: Rutgers University Press, 1973, 188 p.

Selection of letters, reviews, prefaces, and interviews in which Frost discusses writing and writers.

Tharpe, Jac L. *Frost: Centennial Essays II.* Jackson: University Press of Mississippi, 1976, 322 p.

Contains over twenty critical and biographical essays written by such critics as Joseph Kau, Walton Beachman, and Dorothy Tyler.

Wagner, Linda M. *Robert Frost: The Critical Reception.* New York: Burt Franklin, 1977, 280 p.

Collection of the major newspaper and periodical reviews of Frost's poetry collections. Includes bibliography.

Carlos Fuentes

1928-

Mexican novelist, dramatist, short story writer, script-writer, essayist, and critic.

INTRODUCTION

*F*uentes is widely regarded as Mexico's foremost contemporary novelist. His overriding literary concern is to establish a viable Mexican identity, both as an autonomous entity and in relation to the outside world. In his work, Fuentes often intertwines myth, legend, and history to examine his country's roots and discover the essence of modern Mexican society. Fuentes commented: "Our political life is fragmented, our history shot through with failure, but our cultural tradition is rich, and I think the time is coming when we will have to look at our faces, our own past." This tradition incorporates elements of Aztec culture, the Christian faith imparted by the Spanish conquistadors, and the failed hopes of the Mexican Revolution. Fuentes uses the past thematically and symbolically to comment on contemporary concerns and to project his own vision of Mexico's future.

Born in Panama City, Panama, Fuentes is the son of a Mexican career diplomat. As a child, he lived at several diplomatic posts in Latin America and spent much of the 1930s in Washington, D.C. He attended high school in Mexico City and later entered the National University of Mexico. While studying law there, he published several short stories and critical essays in journals. After graduating from law school, Fuentes traveled to Geneva, Switzerland to study international law and in 1950 began a long career in foreign affairs that culminated in his serving as Mexico's ambassador to France from 1975 to 1977.

Fuentes wrote throughout his diplomatic career, and in the late 1950s and early 1960s he gained international attention as an important contributor to the "boom" in Latin American literature. Along with such authors as Gabriel García Márquez and Julio Cortázar, Fuentes published works that received international acclaim and spurred the reassessment of the position

Latin American authors held in contemporary literature. Fuentes's work, like that of several writers associated with the "boom," is technically experimental, featuring disjointed chronology, varying narrative perspectives, and rapid cuts between scenes, through which he creates a surreal atmosphere. For example, in his first novel, *La región más transparente* (1958; *Where the Air Is Clear*), Fuentes uses a series of montage-like sequences to investigate the vast range of personal histories and lifestyles in Mexico City. This work, which provoked controversy due to its candid portrayal of social inequity and its socialist overtones, expresses Fuentes's perception of how the Mexican Revolution failed to realize its ideals. The frustration of the revolution, a recurring theme in his writing, forms the basis for one of his most respected novels, *La muerte de Artemio Cruz* (1962; *The Death of Artemio Cruz*). The title character of this work is a millionaire who earned his fortune by ruthless means. Using flashbacks, the novel shifts between depicting Cruz on his deathbed, his participation in the Revolution, and his eventual rise in business. Through this device, Fuentes contrasts the exalted aims that fostered the Revolution with present-day corruption. *The Death of Artemio Cruz* is generally considered a complex work that demands the reader's active participation.

In the novella *Aura* (1962), Fuentes displays less concern with social criticism and makes greater use of bizarre images and the fantastic. The plot of this novel involves a man whose lover mysteriously begins to resemble her aged aunt. Fuentes employs a disordered narrative in *Cambio de piel* (1967; *A Change of Skin*) to present a group of people who relive significant moments from their past as they travel together through Mexico. Fuentes's concern with the role of the past in determining the present is further demonstrated in *Terra nostra* (1975), one of his most ambitious and successful works. Many critics believe that this novel exceeds the scope of his earlier fiction, extending the idea of history as a circular force by incorporating scenes from the future into the text. *Terra nostra* is divided into three sections: "The Old World," which concerns Spain during the reign of Philip II; "The New World," about the Spanish conquest of Mexico; and "The Next World," which ends as the twenty-first century begins. By tracing the evolution of Mexico beginning with the Spanish conquest, Fuentes depicts the violence and cruelty that originated in the Mediterranean area and was perpetuated in Mexico through Spanish colonialism.

In *La cabeza de la hidra* (1978; *The Hydra Head*), Fuentes explores the genre of the spy novel. Set in Mexico City, this work revolves around the oil industry and includes speculations on the future of Mexico as an oil-rich nation. Fuentes's later fiction investigates Mexico's relationship with the rest of the world. *Una*

familia lejana (1980; *Distant Relations*), for example, involves a Mexican archaeologist and his son who meet relatives in France; on another level, however, this work is about the interaction between Mexican and European cultures. In this novel, an old man relates a tale to a man named Carlos Fuentes, who in turn relates the tale to the reader. Through the inclusion of ghosts and mysterious characters, Fuentes also introduces fantastic events into otherwise realistic settings, a technique prevalent in Latin American literature that is often termed magic realism. In the novel *El gringo viejo* (1985; *The Old Gringo*), which examines Mexican-American relations, Fuentes creates an imaginative scenario of the fate that befell American journalist Ambrose Bierce after he disappeared in Mexico in 1913. Michiko Kakutani commented: "[Fuentes] has succeeded in welding history and fiction, the personal and the collective, into a dazzling novel that possesses the weight and resonance of myth."

Cristóbal nonato (1987; *Christopher Unborn*), a verbally extravagant novel, continues Fuentes's interest in Mexican history. This work is narrated by Christopher Palomar, an omniscient fetus conceived by his parents in hopes of winning a contest to commemorate the quincentenary of Christopher Columbus's arrival in the Americas. According to contest rules, the male baby born closest to midnight on October 12, 1992 whose family name most closely resembles Columbus will assume leadership of Mexico at the age of twenty-one. The novel's nine chapters symbolize Christopher's gestation and allude to Columbus's voyage, which Fuentes views as a symbol of hope for Mexico's rediscovery and rebirth. Narrating from his mother's womb, Christopher uses wordplay, literary allusions, and grotesque humor, combining family history with caustic observations on the economic and environmental crises afflicting contemporary Mexico. *Christopher Unborn* satirizes Mexico's government as inept and its citizenry as complacent, warning that the country's collapse is imminent without change. Fuentes returns to the historical novel with *La campaña* (1990; *The Campaign*). Set in early nineteenth-century Latin America, this work chronicles the adventures of Baltazar Bustos, the naïve, idealistic son of a wealthy Argentinian rancher, who becomes embroiled in the revolutionary fervor then sweeping the region. Considered less complex than Fuentes's earlier works, *The Campaign* has been praised for its incisive portrait of a tumultuous period.

In addition to his novels, Fuentes has written several plays, including *Orquídeas a la luz de la luna* (1982; *Orchids in the Moonlight*), and has published the short story collections *Los días enmascarados* (1954), *Cantar de ciegos* (1964), and *Chac Mool y otros cuentos* (1973). Many of his short stories appear in English translation in *Burnt Water* (1980). Fuentes is also respected for his essays, the topics of which range from social and political criticism to discussions of Mexican art. In assessing Fuentes's career, Earl Shorris concluded that he "has been the palimpsest of Mexican history and culture separated into its discrete layers: Indian, Spanish, French, revolutionary, aristocratic, leftist, centrist, expatriate. In this analyzed presentation of the person, this soul shown after the centrifuge, Mr. Fuentes demonstrates the complexity of the Mexican character and the artistic difficulties peculiar to the novelist born in the Naval of the Universe, which is where the Aztecs placed Mexico."

(For further information about Fuentes's life and works, see *Artists and Authors for Young Adults*, Vol. 4; *Contemporary Authors*, Vols. 69-72; *Contemporary Authors New Revision Series*, Vol. 10; and *Contemporary Literary Criticism*, Vols. 3, 8, 10, 13, 22, 41, 60.)

CRITICAL COMMENTARY

LUIS LEAL
(essay date 1982)

[In the following excerpt, Leal examines Fuentes's narrative technique, concentrating on his use of history and myth.]

Carlos Fuentes has stated that fiction can be useful in looking at history from new perspectives, and this is precisely what he has done in most of his novels, wherein he has presented a vision of history that cannot be gathered from the reading of history books. And, even more, he has reinterpreted history to present a new version of its development, a version reflected by a mind keenly conscious of the significance of past events in the shaping of the contemporary course of human events. In most of his novels he has gone one step further, to the recreation of history by the combination of realistic and mythical structures. The purpose of this essay is to trace the intrusion of history and myth upon Fuentes' narrative, and to observe how he has solved the technical problems involved and yet has managed to produce novels that are aesthetically satisfying. (p. 3)

One of the characteristics of the writers of the new Spanish American novel . . . is the tendency to create pure fiction. One of the leaders of this trend has been Carlos Fuentes. He, like other new novelists (García Márquez, Cortázar, Rulfo, etc.), has moved in this direction by combining two narrative modes, the realistic (historical) and the mythical. Northrop Frye has discussed these two modes at length, and he differentiates between them by saying that realism is the art of verisimilitude, the art of implied similarity, and myth the art of implied metaphorical identity. However, he says that the presence of a mythical structure in realistic fiction "poses certain technical problems for making it plausible, and the devices used in solving these problems may be given the general name of *displacement*." (pp. 3-4)

[In the story **"Chac Mool"** from his first book, *Los días enmascarados*], Fuentes solves the problems of displacement by the use of realistic motifs: the action takes place in Mexico City and Acapulco; the two characters are clerks in a government office; and Filiberto, the protagonist, purchases a statue in a well-known market. To introduce historical fact, the technique of the diary, in which conversations are recorded, is used. The fictitious Filiberto writes about historical events in his diary, such as the introduction of Christianity after the Conquest and the effect it had on the conquered people. In the other aspect of the story Fuentes recreates the myth of the eternal return by the illusory transformation of the statue of the god which Filiberto had placed in the basement of his home. Chac Mool comes back to life with the coming of the rains and takes control of Filiberto's life, finally driving him to suicide. Thus Fuentes skillfully blends the historical and the mythical into a continuous narrative form which derives its structure from the tension created by the interaction between two different cultures, that of ancient Mexico, represented by Chac Mool, and the contemporary, represented by Filiberto.

The technique used in this early story was soon perfected and expanded in the novel, and it has become the distinguishing mark of Fuentes' fiction. The models that he followed for this mode of fiction he found principally in William Faulkner, Malcolm Lowry, and Miguel Angel Asturias. From them he learned the art of utilizing myth, either as form or theme in the context of the realistic novel. (pp. 5-6)

The novels of Fuentes, with some exceptions, can be considered as mythical approaches to history, or creative history. The success of his novels is due in great part to this use of myth to interpret history; for history, as Ernst Cassirer has observed, is determined by the mythology of a people. . . . In his first major work, *Where the Air Is Clear*, Fuentes presents a mythical history of Mexico City and its four million (1958) in-

Principal Works

Los días enmascarados (novel) 1954

La región más transparente (novel) 1958

[Where the Air Is Clear, 1960]

Las buenas consciencias (novel) 1959

[The Good Conscience, 1961]

Aura (novella) 1962

[Aura, 1965]

La muerte de Artemio Cruz (novel) 1962

[The Death of Artemio Cruz, 1964]

Cantar de ciegos (short stories) 1964

Cambio de piel (novel) 1967

[A Change of Skin, 1968]

Zona sagrada (novel) 1967

[Holy Place, 1972]

Paris: La revolución de mayo (essays) 1968

Cumpleaños (novella) 1969

Tiempo mexicano (essays) 1971

Chac Mool y otros cuentos (short stories) 1973

Terra nostra (novel) 1975

[Terra Nostra, 1976]

Cervantes: o la crítica de la lectura (essays) 1976

[Cervantes: or, The Critique of Reading, 1976]

La cabeza de la hidra (novel) 1978

[The Hydra Head, 1978]

Una familia lejana (novel) 1980

[Distant Relations, 1982]

Agua quemada (short stories) 1981

[Burnt Water, 1980]

Orquídeas a la luz de la luna: comedia mexicana (drama) 1982

[Orchids in the Moonlight: A Mexican Comedy, 1982]

El gringo viejo (novel) 1985

[The Old Gringo, 1985]

Cristóbal nonato (novel) 1987

[Christopher Unborn, 1989]

Myself with Others: Selected Essays (essays) 1988

La campaña (novel) 1990

[The Campaign, 1991]

habitants. The characters who represent the historical aspects of the novel are products of the Mexican Revolution and, at the same time, representative of Mexican society during the 1950s: Robles, the revolutionary turned into a conservative banker; his wife Norma, the social climber who marries for money; Zamacona, the brooding intellectual who becomes one of the sacrificial victims; the decadent Bobó, from the new upper middle class; Gabriel and Beto, the displaced *braceros* back from California; and the Ovando family, the impoverished representatives of the dethroned porfiristas.

In the novel, the representatives of its mythological counterpart are found in the old lady Teódula Moctezuma and Ixca Cienfuegos. They symbolize Mexico's past, a mythical Mexico that still survives and believes in ritual, in sacrifice as the only way for man to redeem himself. The Mexican people have been chosen by the gods to feed the sun and keep it moving so that mankind can survive. Without sacrifices this would be impossible. Displacement in the novel takes the form of parallel action in the fictional world representing history. Both Norma and Zamacona are sacrificed to modern gods. This revelation of the mythical nature of Mexican history is accomplished by the use of image and metaphor. The characters, the description of the city, the action, and the plot are all expressed by uniting two worlds, that of the remote past and that of the present. The interaction between the characters representing both cultures becomes the central technique of dis-

placement. Mythical episodes are used by Fuentes to give his work a pure, literary quality. History and myth balance each other to give the novel equilibrium. (pp. 6-7)

The Death of Artemio Cruz and *Aura* were published the same year, 1962. While in the latter work the mythical predominates, the historical elements surface in *The Death of Artemio Cruz,* but even here mythical aspects are evident in the structure of the subject matter and the characterization of the hero. After writing the social history of Mexico City in *Where the Air Is Clear,* Fuentes continued and recreated the history of modern Mexico in *La muerte de Artemio Cruz,* approximately from the era of Santa Anna to the 1950s, with the period of the Revolution receiving the most attention. Historical personages are freely mentioned, as are historical facts and events. . . . It is also a history, as seen through the eyes of Artemio Cruz, an unreliable character. The mythical structure is found in the use of the myth of the descent into hell to depict the career of the hero who recreates in his mind, just before he dies in the hospital, the twelve most important moments of his life. These twelve days represent the twelve circles of Dante's Inferno, as well as the twelve months of the year. This mythical motif is repeated in the temporal structure of the novel, in which the narrative time covers the last twelve days in the life of Artemio. (p. 8)

In the novels published after *The Death of Ar-*

temio Cruz—*Aura* (1962), *Zona sagrada* (1967), *Cambio de piel* (1967), *Cumpleaños* (1969), *Terra Nostra* (1975), *La cabeza de la hidra* (1978), and *Una familia lejana* (1980), Fuentes has given more emphasis to the mythical than to the historical, but never forgets history or the social condition, which underlies all his fiction.

In *Aura* he gives expression to the historical and the mythical by creating characters symbolic of both forms of thought. Two male characters—Llorente, a general of the period of Maximilian's Empire, and Felipe Montero, a young contemporary historian who later turns out to be the general's double—represent the historical component in the novelette. For balance, there are two additional archetypes, both female—Consuelo (Llorente's wife and a sorceress), who conquers time by recovering her youth, and Aura, her counterpart as a young girl. (pp. 8-9)

[Some of the mythical elements in *Zona sagrada* occur] in the thematic content, the relation between Claudia Nervo, the mother, and Guillermo (Guillermito, Mito), the son. The first chapter, entitled "Happily Ever After," narrates the myth of the sirens in the story of Ulysses, but in a present-day context—a football game which is played in a sacred zone, the staked field. In the last chapter, "Zona sagrada," Mito is transformed into a dog. While in *Where the Air Is Clear,* the beginning and the ending of the novel are in opposition (mythical introduction, historical epilogue), in *Zona sagrada* they are parallel. The novel ends with the episode of Circe, the sorceress who changes men into animals. Since Claudia Nervo is associated with Circe, the transformation of Mito into a dog becomes a part of the myth. As a theme, the myth of Ulysses has also been recreated, for the characters represent Penelope and her son Telemachus. Even Telegonus, the son of Ulysses and Circe, is there, under the name of Giancarlo. The historical part of the novel is based on the life story of a famous Mexican movie star.

Cambio de piel (*A Change of Skin*) signals a change of attitude in Fuentes as a novelist. Here for the first time he builds a purely fictional construct. . . . Displacement is achieved by introducing numerous realistic motifs, starting with the date when the events in the novel begin—Palm Sunday, April 11, 1965. On that precise, historical day two couples leave Mexico City in a Volkswagen on their way to Veracruz, taking the old road and stopping at Cholula, where the rest of the action takes place, at a second-rate hotel and inside the great pyramid. This, however, is preceded by a prologue with a displacement function and in which the destruction of Cholula by Cortés and his men is recreated. (p. 10)

[The theme of *A Change of Skin*] is the mythification of history. In history there is no progress, time has been abolished, as in myth. This explains why the violent acts occurring at the end of the novel—the death of Franz and Elizabeth in the center of the pyramid, the killing of Isabel by Javier in the hotel—are structured in parallel trajectories with some of the most violent events in history: the destruction of Cholula by Cortés, the massacre of the Jewish people. (p. 11)

Cumpleaños (1969) is the first novel by Carlos Fuentes in which the action takes place outside of Mexico. It is also the first that transcends his preoccupation with Mexican history and myth, being based, instead, on European history and myth. However, there are, as in his first novels, both historical and fictitious personages. Also, in *Cumpleaños,* as in previous novels, there is a sacred place, where the theologian, accused of heresy, takes refuge to escape his enemies. This place becomes a bedroom in a contemporary London house where the old man, Nuncia, and [a] boy live. Both places merge into one labyrinthian residence symbolic of the universe. In the bedroom the old man remembers his past life which extends back to the thirteenth century, since he is the reincarnation of Siger de Brabant, a theologian from the University of Paris persecuted for his ideas by Etienne Tempier and Thomas Aquinas. In the present he is George, an architect in London, husband of Emily and father of Georgie, whose tenth birthday they are celebrating that day. This novel is the least realistic of those written by Carlos Fuentes; yet, even here, there are historical elements in the plot, in the artistic motifs, and in the description of the milieu: books read by the boy (*Treasure Island, Black Beauty,* etc.); realistic descriptions of London. . . . (pp. 11-12)

In *Cumpleaños* all traces of Mexican history have disappeared, but the same is not true of *Terra Nostra, The Hydra Head,* and *Una familia lejana. Terra Nostra* deals with the history of Spain during the Renaissance period, but in the second of its three parts, "The New World," the subject is pre-Hispanic Mexican myth and the conquest of the land. By the use of history and myth Fuentes attempts to apprehend the meaning of the age of Philip II and, therefore, the destiny of the Hispanic people, both in the Old World and in the New World, and even in "The Other World," the title of the last part of the novel. As a technique he superimposes several historical periods, going back to the age of Tiberius and pre-Hispanic Mexico, and forward to the end of the century. By this means he creates a new historical reality which, although it is purely fictional, is based on empirical fact and real historical personages. The figure of Philip II, however, becomes an archetype, since it is a composite of several Spanish rulers who have exercised absolute power, and it is this obsession with power on the part of Philip II that gives universality to the novel.

Terra Nostra opens with a scene in Paris on a precise day, July 14, 1999, and ends there on the last day of the same year, the end of the millennium. Thus, the entire narrative partakes of the apocalyptic myth. In the second part, Fuentes creates a space in the New World where historical, fictional, and mythical characters act their roles in a purely mythical time. But even here are found the everpresent historical references, presented with the techniques of fiction. (p. 13)

[In] *The Hydra Head* and *Una familia lejana*, history plays a secondary role to fiction. A current event, the struggle for the control of Mexican oil deposits, is the subject of the first, a detective novel. The protagonist, Félix Maldonado, is patterned after a present-day mythical archetype, James Bond. In *Una familia lejana* Fuentes tries to establish, in a minor way, the cultural relations between Mexico and France, as he had done with Spain in *Terra Nostra,* but in a more personal way. The protagonist, Mexican archeologist Hugo Heredia, husband of a French girl, Lucie, and father of two sons, Víctor and Antonio, delivers a long, historical essay in the first part of chapter 20. At the same time, the author identifies himself with the protagonist, thus becoming the hero of his own novel. . . .

Mythical elements in [*Una familia lejana*], which predominate, are given expression by means of several devices: the association of the characters with the mythical past of Mexico (Lucie as La Llorona); the use of the double (Heredia and "Heredia"); the use of motifs related to the "Día de Muertos" (November 2); and, especially, the use of fiction itself as myth. (p. 14)

In general, then, it can be said that the narrative of Carlos Fuentes swerved strongly at the beginning toward the historical, and strongly after 1969 toward the mythical, but never in a pure form. His idea of history, however, is not that of the empirical historian, but goes beyond fact to a reality that includes myth and legend, so important in the shaping of the Mexican mind. Quite often he fills the lacuna of the historical record with oral history, legend, or myth. His fiction reveals that history itself often becomes myth; and although it is based on a collection of facts, the mythical consciousness of the author is ever present before the facts are verbalized. . . . By fusing history and myth in his novels (and the same can be said of his play, *Todos los gatos son pardos*), Fuentes has been able not only to reveal important aspects of the mind and character of the Mexican people, but also to project his own hopes and aspirations, one of which is not to kill the past. (pp. 15-16)

Luis Leal, "History and Myth in the Narrative of Carlos Fuentes," in *Carlos Fuentes: A Critical View,* edited by Robert Brody and Charles Rossman, University of Texas Press, 1982, pp. 3-17.

MALVA E. FILER
(essay date 1982)

[In the following excerpt, Filer discusses Fuentes's vision of contemporary Mexico.]

Octavio Paz writes in *The Labyrinth of Solitude* that Mexicans are, for the first time in their history, "contemporaries of all mankind." This claim to full membership in a world of expanding and diversified culture is also at the core of Carlos Fuentes' fiction and essays. The collected articles of *Tiempo mexicano* are a result of his concern with this subject, while the novel *A Change of Skin* attempts to recapture his Mexican experience as part of the universal historical drama. "We are contemporaries through the word," he says, echoing Paz's idea. "In order to name ourselves, we have to name the world; and the world, to name itself, has to name us." The effort to encompass an infinite reality makes of Fuentes' novel a labyrinth of time, such as the infinite novel left by Ts'ui Pên in "The Garden of Forking Paths." Its goal is unattainable, as acknowledged by a narrator who bears the family name and shares the madness of Balzac's character Louis Lambert. We are told, indeed, in Fuentes' novel, that "madness may be the mask too much knowledge wears." Freddy Lambert will leave us on "the morrow of an impossible feast," but his "personal happening" is, for him and for his readers, a forceful and transforming experience. The text, while discrediting itself as an adequate means of representing reality, claims none the less to be truthful to it. . . . *A Change of Skin* is Fuentes' most ambitiously designed work before *Terra Nostra.* The following pages analyze some aspects of this novel as they relate to the author's view of Mexico and that country's possible role in a culturally pluralistic world.

Fuentes' choice of time and setting points to the deeper meaning of his book. The day is Palm Sunday, April 11, 1965, on the eve of Holy Week; the place is Cholula, where Mexican history has deep roots and where voices of the past still break into the present. This is a unique stage on which to represent the drama of a Mexican history that has been made, says Fuentes, by the coexistence of diverse, even conflicting cultures: the mythic and cosmic conceptions of the Indians; the Spanish version of Christianity; the individualistic values of the European bourgeoisie; and the faith in science, reason, and progress borrowed from the industrially developed countries. . . . The novel's description of Cholula's church stresses the overlapping of traditions: Christ, as conceived by the natives, has his wounds covered with blood and feathers; the baptismal fonts are the ancient pagan urns where the hearts of the sacrificed were cast; the Arabic arches stand on the tezontle-stone floor; the sixteenth-century chapel combines an austere simplicity with the rich Renaissance-style ornamentation that was imposed by the Romantic spirit of the last century.

Religious syncretism also is evident at Cholula. In *Tiempo mexicano,* for instance, Fuentes refers to the Indians' concept of cyclical time and to their belief in a founding God, a belief which caused them to understand Christ not as the Savior but as the God of the Origins. According to Fernando Benítez, whose expertise in Mexican Indian culture Fuentes greatly admires, the ceremonies of the "coras" during Holy Week attribute the Creation to Christ. In the Indians' understanding of the Passion, Christ's sacrifice does not redeem humanity, but his blood assures that the sun will not die and Quetzalcoatl's maize will continue to grow on this earth. The ancient Mexican gods, says Fuentes, were conceived as protectors against change, for the Indians thought that the future could bring only destruction. In fact, memory of their origins and fear of the future dominated the society of the Aztecs. Religion, politics, and art were each a form of exorcism, a way to postpone the catastrophe. The Aztecs accepted the inevitability of change, but not without first building elaborate safeguards. Every fifty-two years, a cycle was closed, and the past had to be "cancelled, denied, destroyed or covered like the seven successive pyramids at the ceremonial center of Cholula." Human blood was required to win another reprieve, so that new life could grow.

A Change of Skin is clearly centered around this theme of a cyclical time (represented by the seven pyramids), the idea that "the end of a cycle required, as homage to the arrival of the new, that the old should disappear." Fuentes believes that Mexico has kept the original conception of sacrifice as necessary to maintain the order of the cosmos. This, he holds, is Moctezuma's real revenge, and the "final victory of the Indian world in Mexico." The novel summons the whole world to participate in the sacrificial exorcism of Cholula, for guilt is universal and the apocalypse can be averted only by cancelling the past. Western civilization is tried and convicted, as man seeks to free himself from "the old schizophrenias of the Greco-Christian-Judaeo-Protestant-Marxist-industrial dualism." The ceremony involves, as in the ancient ritual, the offering of human blood, here represented by the execution of one of the characters. An introduction to the last part of the book carries the announcement that the narrator, now identified as Xipe Totec, Our Lord of the Flayed Hide, is changing his skin. Finally, at the close of the novel, he indicates that he is an inmate of Cholula's asylum for the insane, a place symbolically named Our Lord Lazarus, "he of the resurrections."

In order to build up to its climax at the Gran Cu of Cholula, the text strives to produce a kaleidoscopic view of our own times. Frequent incursions into past centuries show that progress is mere illusion, that past and future exist here and now. Violence is presented as being the same, no matter who the perpetrators are or who their victims, in evocations that switch from the cruelties of both Spaniards and Indians to the atrocities of the Inquisition, the concentration camps, Hiroshima, and Vietnam. The open-ended, inexhaustible list also includes the Molotov-Ribbentrop pact, the Moscow trials under Stalin, and Trotsky's murder. Everybody is implicated, even the beatniks who judge and condemn the preceding generation. "There is no historical progress, . . . only a repetition of a series of ceremonial acts." This is part of Fuentes' intended message in the novel. (pp. 121-23)

Fuentes believes that Mexico, aware of its own overlapping of cultures, should avoid an illusion of progress that has proven self-destructive to those societies where it has succeeded most. In both *Tiempo mexicano* and *A Change of Skin,* he compares the United States' "mechanical ruins" of progress with the "natural ruins" of Mexican underdevelopment: "If Mexico is nature in ruin," says Javier in the novel, "the United States is machines in ruin. In Mexico everything is a ruin because everything is promised and no promise is kept. In the United States all promises have been kept. Yet it is a ruin just the same." The author clearly feels that his country still has time to avoid the mistakes of its more prosperous neighbor. Since their independence, Latin American nations have followed the "triumphant model" of progress, empiricism and pragmatism. By so doing, says Fuentes, they have adopted the ideologies of their exploiters, the "antiutopian time of progress, of being" as against the "moral time" of that which should be, and can only be desired or imagined. (pp. 123-24)

The narrator of *A Change of Skin* assembles memories that run through centuries of human experience and failure. He needs to take possession of the past before he can cancel it. His evocation of the characters' voices is an attempt to reenact and render meaningful his own Mexican experience made of Greek and Judeo-Christian tradition, of Indian myths and Spanish Catholicism, of European culture and the American manufactured world. Before the start of a new cycle, he tries to mold that experience into a totality. This is the novel's "impossible feast." In fact, the writer's immediate problem is, according to Fuentes: "How to employ a fragmented, sequential discrete medium—language— yet achieve the impression of totality of wholeness, and above all, of presence." Javier, mirroring the narrator, pursues his own elusive totality in *Pandora's Box,* only to discover that "words could not conquer the fragmentation of reality."

Although to recapture total reality is admittedly impossible, the novel does succeed in reviving the time of "being" and "progress," even though it falls short of imagining the new, utopian, Mexican time. The cyclical concept of life would seem not to allow for anything but the repetition of the past. In fact, Fuentes' narrative is consistent in presenting a pessimistic view of the world, according to which the new is always condemned to acquire the negative features of the old. From his first novel, *Where the Air Is Clear,* to *A Change of Skin,* he critically examines his country's past and present, decrying its inability to break away from old and self-destructive patterns. In *Terra Nostra* and *The Hydra Head,* his more recent novels, he imagines Mexico's future, but only as a fatalistic recurrence of the past. Yet, it would be incorrect to identify the author's own position with this pessimistic outlook. In essays and lectures Fuentes has expressed his belief in Mexico's ability to build "a generous and revolutionary utopia," based on the cultural realities resulting from its coexisting histories. To that effect, a "screening effort" must be made, to "effectively separate the oppressive, dead weight from the living and liberating realities." The aim should be a "creative recreation," as represented by two great poems of Mexican literature: *Death without End* by José Gorostiza and *Sun Stone* by Octavio Paz, where Western linear discourse struggles with the spirit of Indian cyclical time in order to reestablish reality on a new foundation. (pp. 124-25)

A Change of Skin may be read as an exploration of the possibilities of prose fiction to create its own synthesis of language and time. More specifically, the text can be interpreted as an effort to rescue the reality of Mexican experience by creating its fiction. "We are resolved to invent our own reality," says Octavio Paz. "Spanish American literature . . . is both a return and a search for tradition. In searching for it, it invents it. But invention and discovery are not terms that best describe its purest creations. A desire for incarnation, a literature of foundations." That desire, we believe, is Fuentes' main motivation in writing his novel. On the other hand, the "revolutionary utopia" must await its fiction; his characters are still going through the pains of their self-criticism.

The narrative is built on the recreated experiences of the protagonists: Javier, a Mexican intellectual who failed as a writer and became a United Nations bureaucrat; Elizabeth, his Jewish wife, who may be a Mexican but remembers herself growing up in the New York of the Depression; Franz, a Czech Nazi refugee, who designed the buildings of Terezin's concentration camp, and did not try to save his Jewish girl friend; Isabel, an uninhibited but somewhat faceless young Mexican woman. The ambiguity concerning Elizabeth's origin makes it possible for her to represent a feminine image of an American or Americanized view of reality, min-

gled with the complexities of her Jewish background. She is a product of mass education, increased intellectual and sexual awareness, and cosmopolitan life. Her frustration and neurosis are the price that she pays for these privileges. Isabel, the young and definitely Mexican woman, is presented as the least conflictive of the characters and, at the same time, as an unfinished product. She already lives in the sexually liberated world built by the older generation and takes it for granted. Not sharing and not understanding Javier's interpretation of Mexican life, she finds his writing laughable and his concern pointless. . . . She is a blasé, uprooted pursuer of her own pleasure. Her behavior typifies the imported and superficial sophistication that Fuentes considers a hindrance to the creation of Mexico's own future. Is she condemned to repeat Elizabeth's life, as Javier fears? In order to prevent this, he kills her, in one of the possible outcomes of the novel. Symbolically, Javier strangles Isabel with the shawl that Elizabeth had given to her. (pp. 125-26)

A Change of Skin has been compared to Cortázar's *Hopscotch,* an earlier attempt by a Latin American writer to convey his experience of contemporary life. Indeed, Javier shares with Oliveira a demolishing intellect and a total paralysis of will. While *Hopscotch* recaptures its author's Argentinian experience, *A Change of Skin* is, not surprisingly, a Mexican version of our time. Fuentes' intimate knowledge of his country's history and concern with its present realities emerge from within the book's universal framework. We find in these crowded pages numerous descriptions and critical comments dealing with Mexico City, the Mexican people and the unresolved conflicts of their way of life. The text, as much as the characters, repeatedly returns to modern Mexico from far away places and distant times. On one of these occasions, we are told: "Javier decided that the time had come to return to Mexico City, that he needed Mexico again, that if he did not face and overcome its terrible negations he would always believe that he had taken the easy road and his writing could have no value." Javier would go out and "roam all over the city," looking for contrasts, images, words, profiles, masks. He was trying to find his words in that world that belonged to him. However, despite a declared interest in Mexico's Indian past, he feels that his country's uneducated and mostly Indian citizens are like creatures of another species. To them, "we are Martians," Javier says. "We don't speak as they do or think as they do. . . . If we do see them, it's like the zoo. . . . We are their enemies and they know it." He tries to break the barrier by provoking a fight in which they beat him up. The humiliating experience, sought with masochistic determination, momentarily dissolves the social and intellectual distance that separates him from that group. He was now "on their side of the cage." Javier's attempt at sharing the experience of the oppressed is rather unconvincing, but sufficiently indicative of the guilt that is typical of socially concerned intellectuals. Most of the time, though, he is satisfied with his role of interpreter and critic of Mexican society. His remarks generally echo the author's views. They are also close to the ideas of Octavio Paz, whose friendship and works have been credited by the novelist with being an "original and permanent inspiration" for his own books.

Fuentes thinks of Mexico as a country wearing a series of masks in the course of its history: At its origin, "a skin of stone, mosaic and gold," then "the baroque and frozen order of liberalism and modernity," and the mask of "peace and progress" under Porfirio Díaz. They were the masks of slavery and hunger that were broken by the revolution. He says that the exceptional, unmasking moments of Mexican history force the country to see itself in its own "depth of latent myths, palaces in ruins, tragic miseries, grotesque coups, painful betrayals," and "useless deaths." . . . One wonders what our social critic can offer to that mass of people, marked by "centuries of humiliation and frustrated revenge."

"We cannot return to Quetzalcóatl," states Fuentes, "nor will Quetzalcóatl return to us." Mexico should not settle, however, for "Our Lady the Pepsicóatl," which is the time being forced upon it by the "modern world": "a technocracy without cultural values, without political liberties, without moral aspirations and without esthetic imagination." Javier knows, also, that the clock cannot and should not be turned back. "Or do you really think," he pointedly asks, "it would have been better if the Spaniards had been defeated and we had gone on living under the Aztec fascism?" His frustration and guilt feelings are evident, however, when he faces his own experience. Javier illustrates the limitations and agony of an intellectual whose social ideas have not made a dent in the fabric of reality. He is paralyzed by an excess of knowledge and destructive skepticism. This type of personality and behavior recurs in Fuentes' novels. He portrayed it for the first time in *Where the Air Is Clear* through his characterization of Rodrigo Pola, also an ineffectual writer. *A Change of Skin,* while exposing the selfishness and parasitism of Javier, suggests on the other hand the opposite model of Vasco Montero, a successful poet who is actively committed to the social and political struggles of his time. In the last pages of the novel, Javier admits his failure and condemns himself: "The world didn't change. It denied me and refused to notice me. . . ." He declares his passive, irrelevant life to be as guilty as Franz's Nazi past, and more cowardly: "What was action in him in me was only possibility, latency. In me it lacked all greatness, all courage. I have been a kind of larva Franz." "A soul of jelly, like Javier's, is far more guilty than mine," says Franz. This is also the opinion of the narrator who, unhappy with the turn of events leading to Franz's execution, would like to change his story.

The novel's verdict is clear: Javier should not survive, the possibilities of his experience have been exhausted. It is safe to assume also the author's agreement with a negative evaluation of this character. Lonely intellectual exercises, such as those engaged in by Javier, are not what culture is all about, according to Fuentes. He understands culture to be a collective and disciplined effort to address all the needs of human life, from economic satisfaction to the fullest development of each human being. Javier represents the type of "innocuous" intellectual that the author criticizes and rejects. Obviously, he is not the kind of human material with which to achieve a creative synthesis of the past and invent, as Fuentes envisions, Mexico's own model of development. Freddy Lambert knows it, as he knows it all, in his own mad wisdom.

Fuentes' novel, both through its narrator and through Javier himself, aims at a reality that is different from the one which Javier represents. As pointed out by Julio Ortega, *A Change of Skin* "pursues another world, another time: the new space where reality is invented." This was also Javier's ambition, stated at the beginning of his aborted book: "A novel discloses what the world has within itself but has not yet discovered and may never discover." However, Fuentes' narrator and characters are trapped by a text that, like the life it recaptures, devours its own creatures as well as their hopes. The future, symbolized by a bundle of rags (or a child), is swallowed and digested by the present, a yellow dog whose "hunger is far from being sated." Time is, in this novel, the eternal consumer that must, like the god Kronos, devour its children in order to exist. Freddy's narration remains, challenging death with the power of its own creation. Writing a story is, like the ceremony at Cholula, a way to postpone the final destruction. "The 'lies' we spinners of tales tell," says Lambert, "betray the 'true' . . . in order to hold away . . . that day of judgment when the beginning and the end shall be one." In Fuentes' novel, we may conclude, not only are Mexicans the contemporaries of all mankind, but all mankind has been made to participate in the exorcism, and the shaping, of a Mexican time. (pp. 127-30)

Malva E. Filer, " 'A Change of Skin' and the Shaping of a Mexican Time," in *Carlos Fuentes: A Critical View,* edited by Robert Brody and Charles Rossman, University of Texas Press, 1982, pp. 121-31.

GLORIA DURÁN
(essay date 1983)

[An American educator who specializes in Spanish literature, Durán is the author of *La magia y las brujas en la obra de Carlos Fuentes* (1976; *The Archetypes of Carlos Fuentes: From Witch to Androgyne*), a study of recurring female character types in Fuentes's novels. In the following excerpt, Durán analyzes *Orchids in the Moonlight*.]

Fuentes has been less than successful as a playwright possibly because the form of dramatic art that has influenced his fiction is not the stage play but the movie. Up to now he has written plays that create imposing technological problems in a stage presentation, problems that can be solved only by the magic of the screen.

But perhaps there is magic in the number three. His third play, *Orchids in the Moonlight,* seems clearly to be written for the stage, yet it is inspired by his overwhelming love for the movies. If we judge by conventional standards, it is his most successful play to date: it has enjoyed a six-week presentation by the American Repertory Theatre in Cambridge, Massachusetts. . . .

However, judging by both the production and the manuscript, I would not say that this is Fuentes's best play. . . .

How then, can we account for the play's relative success? A factor of some significance may be that the play was written by Fuentes directly in English. In view of his growing reputation in the United States, and especially in academic circles, we may suspect that the potential audience for his dramatic works is also growing. But another factor of some importance may be the interview with Fuentes by Arthur Holmberg, published in section 2 of the Sunday *New York Times* of 6 June 1982, three days before the play's premiere. In this prominent, illustrated interview, Fuentes describes his play and emphasizes its feminist content. Talking about his two protagonists, Dolores Del Río and María Félix, film stars of the thirties and forties, Fuentes says: "I loved these two actresses because they were strong and independent. They shattered all the macho myths. They were not what Latin American women were supposed to be. They were not little dolls men could cuddle. María Félix was a Pancho Villa in skirts." (p. 595)

Orchids is a play about the relationship between two women. But although this is a feminist play, at least on its most conspicuous level, *Orchids* is not readily understood by a public who may not be conversant with Fuentes's constant recourse to archetypal charac-

ters. . . . As in his earlier works, he is fascinated by all the physical attractions that turn women into symbols rather than people. He also makes feminists wonder how these women can be both sexy and anti-sexist symbols, archetypes of the glamorous female and also role models for average Latin American women. Yet in all fairness to Fuentes, in the Holmberg interview he warns us that this play will not be easily understandable: "My play is about the myth of culture and the culture of myths," he says as he describes movies as "bearers of the collective unconscious, the warehouse of modern myths."

The initiate, therefore, is forewarned that *Orchids in the Moonlight* will be feminism passed through the sieve of Jungian psychology. The feminist element will be supplied by the fact that now, for the first time, female archetypes are to be examined from their own viewpoints rather than from the perspective of a male protagonist. They will become the "we," not the "they." Fuentes accomplishes this transformation by intruding upon the sacred area inhabited by his archetypes. Possibly he is describing this process when he says in the playbill: "That is the thing about archetypes: they fascinate you but you dare not touch them. They nurture you but who nurtures them? Who is the archetype of the archetype, the star of the star, the model of the model? Who is Mother?"

In the above passage Fuentes shows that he is no longer using these archetypes in the classical Jungian sense of projections by our collective unconscious, projections which we incarnate in other people. Rather, his new archetypes will now generate their own archetypes, much as Borges's dream characters give birth to new dream characters and in so doing attempt to convince themselves of their own reality. In fact, the only female character in the play who remains a true archetype is the one who never appears—"Mummy." Mummy is the Great Mother, the unseen psychic presence against whom the protagonists must struggle in order to assert themselves as human beings rather than popular fantasies. Although Mummy may have nurtured them, as Fuentes indicates, she has nurtured only their public images, their *personas*. She stands in the way of human fulfillment. To a certain extent the dialogue of the two actresses can be seen as a psychoanalytical attempt to integrate the Great Mother archetype through a dialectical process. (pp. 595-96)

María is the more liberated of the two women. She is portrayed as an earthy Chicana with few illusions about her past. In realistic details she closely resembles Fuentes's earlier characterizations of María Félix in *Zona sagrada* (*Holy Place*). María is relatively free of the escapism of the older Dolores, who lives only for her memories. Dolores's memories, like Elizabeth's in *Cambio de piel* (*Change of Skin*), are apocryphal, a collage of movie make-believe. Dolores seems to be a Mexican version of Gloria Swanson in *Sunset Boulevard.* Enmeshed in her own narcissism, she is relatively passive to the professed love of María. María reiterates that she loves Dolores only for herself, and that she is the only person—not excluding Dolores—who loves her for what she is rather than for what she appears to be or to have been. Although in the archetypal image that she represents to others María is a femme fatale, in her love for Dolores she is all too vulnerable. When she imagines that she has lost Dolores, she commits suicide, like a modern Juliet. And yet ironically, Dolores, by her departure, finally shows that she has come to grips with María's love and is capable of reciprocating it. A brief reference to the plot as it unfolds in the second act should explain this cruel paradox in the play's conclusion.

The private world of the two actresses (a windowless apartment with huge mirrors, racks of clothes and oversize bed) is breached when Dolores, still playing the great actress, makes a telephone call. Stopped by María, Dolores does not manage to identify herself over the telephone, but nevertheless the call mysteriously summons forth a fan, an ardent admirer who has seen every one of Dolores's films. María, now torn by suspicion and jealousy, identifies the male intruder as a prying newspaperman whose real motive in seeking out Dolores is to do research for an obituary column. Reacting to María's accusations, the jovial intruder becomes menacing. He threatens to publicize a pornographic film once made by María and which she believed was destroyed. It is at this point that Dolores appears to forsake María by going off to marry the fan. But when she returns after María's dramatic suicide (accomplished by an overdose of sleeping pills as she attempts to reenter a film that is being projected on the boudoir walls), Dolores reveals that she had accompanied the fan only to kill him and thus save María's reputation. Her apparent betrayal of María was in fact her greatest proof of love.

Clearly, the only real similarity between *Orchids in the Moonlight* and *Zona sagrada* is that both deal with the life of María Félix. But in the play María loses her archetypal, magical properties. She is far more than a sex goddess. In fact, if we compare elements of plot, *Orchids* is far closer to an earlier work of Fuentes, the novelette *Aura* of 1962. In both this work and the play Fuentes deals with two exotic women of indeterminate age (the manuscript for *Orchids* suggests that they should appear to fluctuate between thirty and sixty years of age) who inhabit a mysterious, private world. The women's goals in both cases are love, youth and immortality. In both cases the moonlit world is breached by a young, male writer. In *Aura* the writer pays for his folly by a relinquishing of personality. In *Orchids* the penalty is greater; his very person is sacrificed on the altar of love.

Thus, in schematic terms, the basic elements of plot in both *Aura* and *Orchids* are similar. Yet in psychological terms, the two tales are poles apart. In *Aura* we see the world through the perspective of the male protagonist. He is mesmerized and immobilized by the archetypal female figure, incarnation of the Great Mother, and so succumbs to the power of the collective unconscious. Instead of achieving an integration of personality as a result of his struggle with his archetype, he accepts its total disintegration. In *Orchids,* on the other hand, a decisive difference is effected through change in point of view. Although the male character is still a victim, his fate becomes inconsequential. Instead it is the women who are the real protagonists; it is they who must struggle with their own archetypes, the foremost being Mummy. . . . María defies and fears Mummy. Dolores is constantly apprehensive about the possible reactions of this omnipresent figure who lives on "the upper floor." It is only at the play's end that she can call Mummy "the atrocious old lady, believing she can take life because she gave us our life, the hypocritical whore older than all the dead." . . . Her liberation from Mummy has been accomplished by the intervention of "the Fan."

Who is this character whom Fuentes identifies only as "the Fan"? We are told almost nothing about him. His motivations are uncertain. It is never made clear whether he imagines himself in love with Dolores or merely wishes to blackmail María. . . . [Fuentes] identifies him as a punster. The Fan enters the scene almost as a court jester, paying Dolores the lavish compliment of remembering every detail of each of her films. He is jovial and boisterous like a gust of fresh air that ripples across an ill-ventilated room. But when María accuses him of pretense, his ribald personality turns menacing. Eventually both women regard him as demonic. If we seek the Fan's identity in the archetypal world described by Jung, the Fan can be easily assimilated to the figure known as the Trickster.

Writing on the psychology of the Trickster figure, Jung describes him as a "shape-shifter" with a "dual nature, half animal, half divine," and traces him back beyond Hermes. (pp. 596-97)

[For Fuentes] movies are often both the seed and the fruit of literature. Instinctively he seems to know that the medieval fables about the sly fox who is eventually outfoxed have their modern cinematic counterpart in the "private eye" figure, the ethically ambiguous detective who often reveals truths that those who summon him would rather not accept and whose services, therefore, are not always fully appreciated. Some of Humphrey Bogart's famous roles have a true Trickster dimension; he is the tough guy who evokes both laughter and tears. (p. 597)

[The] appearance of the Trickster in the second act transforms *Orchids* from a play about memory, which is static and interesting mainly to those who share Fuentes's nostalgia for the two actresses, to one of dynamic action. The fantastically rapid pace of events in this act is probably welcomed by the average member of the audience, who sees the Fan as a dynamic third character. Yet for those familiar with Fuentes's work, third characters are suspect insofar as they often turn out to be new versions of existent characters. . . . Thus Fuentes cognoscenti may share my suspicions that the Fan is an incarnation of the unconscious of Dolores, the dreamer, or, as already suggested, a collective mirage for both actresses. If the latter is the case, the action may be regarded as taking place on two levels, as reality and as imagination.

This dual interpretation of the action enhances not only the metaphysical significance of the work but also its unity and esthetic value. If we do not give an oneiric interpretation to the second act, it becomes inexplicably different from the first one, where there is a Tennessee Williams atmosphere of escapism struggling against harsh reality. The second act, by way of contrast, seems to be a hybrid of film and dreams. The film is out of Del Río's early period, where action appears accelerated. The dream is also an actress's dream, where "real" life and film are intertwined. At the mo-

ment that the actresses sing their tango about dreams, the Fan knocks at their door, almost as if conjured out of their collective longing. Curiously, they both fear at first that the impossible apparition will turn out to be Mummy.

The first act of the play, therefore, broadly hints at the unconscious world dominated by archetypal characters. The second act immerses us in this world, where one such character, the Trickster, materializes and combats the other, the Great Mother. In keeping with the myth of the Trickster, the Fan becomes too clever for his own good and is himself tricked and sacrificed. Fuentes's female protagonists thus emerge as far more able to combat the emanations of the collective unconscious than his male protagonists. In this respect, if in no other way, we may say that *Orchids in the Moonlight* is a truly feminist play.

Yet *Orchids* is not only a feminist play. In his stage directions Fuentes even (jokingly?) suggests that the protagonists could be played by two men. Fuentes emphasizes that *Orchids* is a play about authenticity versus the role-playing which society forces upon us and which we come to accept as definitions of our personalities. He portrays a Del Río so identified with her public image as a movie star that loss of public recogni-

Gregory Peck, Jane Fonda, and Jimmy Smits starred in the 1989 film adaptation of *The Old Gringo*.

tion undermines her belief that she is still herself, necessitating constant confirmation by María for her to continue to exist. Thus the play continues to explore the theme of continuity of personality which has been a preoccupation of Fuentes in most of his fictional writings.

For critics attuned to social commentary in Fuentes's works, the character of Dolores may also be seen as a vehicle for the author's condemnation of Mexico's middle class, its self-deception, sentimentality and escapism. Against Dolores's genteel world of make-believe he contrasts the coarse realism of María, a lowly Chicana, who is innately generous in her capacity to love.

Beyond feminism and social commentary, *Orchids* is a drama about psychic growth, about maturing and facing death. Since the loss of youth and beauty is more painful to bear for those who have become identified with them, the two Mexican actresses make excellent protagonists. Dolores, moreover, with her suggestive name (*dolor*=pain), becomes a symbol of the human condition. *Orchids,* therefore, is a metaphysical play which Fuentes has packaged in the attractive allure of Hollywood, in part perhaps to draw an audience, but also because, as he has said, "movies are bearers of the collective unconscious." (pp. 597-98)

Gloria Durán, " 'Orchids in the Moonlight': Fuentes as Feminist and Jungian Playwright," in *World Literature Today,* Vol. 57, No. 4, Autumn, 1983, pp. 595-98.

MICHIKO KAKUTANI
(essay date 1985)

[In the following review, Kakutani praises *The Old Gringo.*]

[The title character of *The Old Gringo*] happens to be Ambrose Bierce, the American journalist and short-story writer who left for Mexico in 1913—presumably to join Pancho Villa's revolutionary army—and who mysteriously disappeared. What Mr. Fuentes has done is to imagine Bierce's subsequent life—and death—there in the desolate desert reaches of northern Mexico, and in doing so, he has succeeded in welding history and fiction, the personal and the collective, into a dazzling novel that possesses the weight and resonance of myth.

Mr. Fuentes, of course, has long been interested in the history of his homeland, and in such novels as *Where the Air Is Clear* and *The Death of Artemio Cruz,* he has already examined the effects of Mexico's 1910-20 revolution, and that country's tangled relationship

with America, the sprawling, imperialist giant to the north. None of his earlier works, however, illuminate those issues with the assurance evinced by *The Old Gringo* or use his gifts for magical realism with this book's passion and precision. In *The Old Gringo,* Mr. Fuentes has found a form and a subject that enable him to exploit his favorite techniques and explore some of his favorite themes (from cultural and Freudian determinism to the nature of reality and art) and give them their fullest expression.

Cutting back and forth in time, *The Old Gringo* is, on one level, the story of Bierce, as recollected by Harriet Winslow, an American spinster whose encounter with the journalist will have tragic consequences for both of them—as well as for their friend and adversary, a Mexican general named Tomás Arroyo. Yet if Harriet's attempts to come to terms with this experience through memory and imagination underline Mr. Fuentes's own concern with the uses of fiction, hers is hardly the only voice that compels our attention in *The Old Gringo.* Within her account, we also hear the voices of Bierce and Arroyo, and we listen to the voices, too, of assorted Mexicans—other officers in Villa's army, their women and their hangers-on, who together form a Faulkner-like chorus, articulating Mexico's past and present. . . .

Certainly the hard-bitten author of "The Devil's Dictionary" does not share the bright illusions of Harriet Winslow—this spirited Jamesian heroine, who has left behind her safe little home in Washington to teach young Mexican children, and who naively clings to her missionary faith, even in the midst of a chaotic revolution. And yet taken together, these two norteamericanos form a sort of composite portrait of America, an America that will come to stand in shadowy contrast to the Mexico of Tomás Arroyo and his people. America, a land of changing seasons, a country built upon the ideals of order and democracy and individual will, and so devoted to the notion of progress as to obliterate the past; and Mexico, a land of eternal summer and "memorious dust," a country unable to forget its history of conquest and unrequited blood—these two nations, so representative of our inability to comprehend the differentness, the plain otherness, of the foreign, will become the poles from which the tragic action in *The Old Gringo* springs.

Such a summary tends to make this book sound a good deal more schematic than it is, for while Mr. Fuentes is concerned with cultural and racial myths, he is even more interested in how those forces intersect with the private lives of individuals. Indeed, he makes it clear that the triangle among Bierce, Arroyo and Winslow is the product both of their idiosyncratic psychic and familial histories and larger, social movements beyond their control. By grounding the more symbolic actions of his story in a welter of biographical details and minutely imagined facts, Mr. Fuentes persuades us that the love Harriet Winslow inspires in both men—the old gringo, who believed that his cynicism protected his heart, and the young revolutionary, who believed that no woman could come between him and his cause—is as inevitable as it is real.

Although Mr. Fuentes's lyric tendencies occasionally result in rather clotted passages—there are a few too many vague, incantatory musings about the meaning of life and death—his gift for metaphor lofts *The Old Gringo* out of the realm of naturalism and invests its more didactic social impulses with the fierce magic of a remembered dream.

Michiko Kakutani, in a review of "The Old Gringo," in *The New York Times,* October 23, 1985, p. C21.

FERNANDA EBERSTADT
(essay date 1986)

[Eberstadt is an American novelist. In the following excerpt, she examines the influence of nineteenth- and twentieth-century literary traditions on Fuentes's novels and offers an unfavorable appraisal of his political views.]

Fuentes's first two novels, *Where the Air Is Clear* (1958) and *The Good Conscience* (1959), together form a crossroads, each marking his indebtedness to a different literary tradition. Though published later, *The Good Conscience* is clearly the author's first novel. It is set in the heavy, almost dyspeptically ornate colonial silver-mine town of Guanajuato, and tells of a family of Spanish merchants who came to Mexico in the 19th century to make good. Written in a deliberately archaic, period-piece manner, the novel opens with a leisurely history of the Ceballos family, nicely entwined with the history of their provincial capital as it is buffeted and scourged by Mexico's bloody uprisings and its unhappy brushes with empire.

The Good Conscience, however, is not the novel it starts out to be. From a tale of the provincial grand bourgeoisie, a class and generation which the historian Frank Tannenbaum has described as "locally bred colonists who for all purposes felt themselves to be living in a foreign country," *The Good Conscience* abruptly changes course when it reaches the 20th century and becomes instead a steamy coming-of-age story, charting the autoerotic and religious fervors of its hero, Jaime Ceballos. Now we are in a world of adolescent alienation and rebellion, as Jaime bucks his family's conformism by sheltering a union organizer on the lam, befriending an Indian scholarship student who dreams

of class warfare, working on the railroad (where he encounters his estranged mother operating as an alcoholic evangelist-hooker, but is too prissy to approach her), flagellating himself in the desert, and masturbating in church before the image of Christ.

The novel concludes with a discomfitingly abrupt reversal. On being told by the parish priest that his religious and (implicitly) political yearnings are not true imitations of Christ but rather manifestations of an overweening pride, Jaime embraces conformism with a vengeance, kissing off his Indian friend and cynically embarking on the moneygrubbing legal career for which his family has prepared him. In later Fuentes novels, Jaime Ceballos will reappear as a Mexico City sophisticate, a faceless figure at high-society soirées.

For all its headlong shiftings of gear, for all the glib cynicism of its denunciation of bourgeois values, and for all its crude lashings of self-pity, *The Good Conscience* is quite a gripping and colorful book. Anyone reading this youthful novel will feel himself in the hands of a confident and powerful if somewhat sensational writer, one gifted with abundant natural talents and not too much brain. The book is interesting, too, in that it suggests a course Fuentes's work might have taken: of fast-paced adventure writing in the 19th-century manner with a strong undercurrent of social criticism. Instead, as we shall see, Fuentes's desire to be not just a novelist but an intellectual heavyweight led him to work in fancy literary forms which make mincemeat out of his native gifts.

If *The Good Conscience* is a truncated revamping of the French tale of the provinces, *Where the Air Is Clear* . . . could be described as a flawed gem of high modernism. On the level of manifest content, *Where the Air Is Clear* sets out to portray post-revolutionary Mexican society in its full array of luxury, tyranny, and wretched inequality, and to herald its imminent collapse. On another level—for *Where the Air Is Clear* is also an unrelentingly mystical piece of work—the novel depicts the survival, beneath Mexico's overlay of internationalism and modernity, of its secret pagan gods with their insatiable demands for bloodshed and betrayal.

The "hero" of this novel, in unabashed homage to James Joyce's personification of Dublin in *Ulysses,* is Mexico City itself; the title refers, sardonically, to the capital's perennial smog. . . . Fuentes, in the person of Ixta Cienfuegos, a mysterious stranger who is simultaneously man-about-town and the reincarnation of the Aztec god of war, takes us through many layers of Mexico City by eliciting confessions from bankers, cabdrivers, cooks, kept girls, beggars, revolutionary heroes, accountants' wives, and dispossessed aristocrats.

Of these, by far the most compelling is the life story of Federico Robles, a ruthless and sentimental tycoon whose rise and fall form a cautionary symbolic tale of modern Mexico. Born on a dirt floor, the son of an Indian peasant whose wife was raped by the local landowner, Robles becomes, successively, a protégé of the local priest; a cavalry officer under the governor-turned-revolutionary-leader Venustiano Carranza, fighting first the dictator Victoriano Huerta (who in 1913 had wrested the presidency of Mexico from the freely-elected Francisco Madero) and then the brigand Pancho Villa; a provincial lawyer holding much credit with the new government; and, finally, one of the richest and most powerful men in Mexico. In the novel's obligatory reversal of fortune, Robles's financial empire collapses because of unsound speculations, his brittle wife dies in a fire, he marries his blind mistress, and, absolved of the sin of capitalism, becomes a humble cotton farmer up north.

Where the Air Is Clear is full of pungent evocations of the sights, sounds, smells, tastes, and textures of the city, exciting action, and freshly captured battle scenes. . . . But the novel is marred by authorial self-indulgence and pretentiousness. Fuentes here mimics the more exaggerated mannerisms of the modernist style, transposing to a Mexican setting that stylized clatter of sounds and traditions which one critic has aptly described as the juxtaposition of Bartók with bar-talk. Much of *Where the Air Is Clear* is a highly self-conscious mélange of advertising slogans, refrains from popular songs, and overheard fragments of cocktail-party chitchat. The pastiche is made more local but no more palatable by being interspersed with lyrical streams of consciousness about Aztec sacrifice, plumed serpents, and darkness—incantations which run on for ten pages at a clip without hope of a comma, let alone a full stop. That, despite these efforts to smother it in affectation, *Where the Air Is Clear* remains an energetic and engrossing book is a tribute to Fuentes's gifts as a storyteller.

Those gifts are most effectively displayed in *The Death of Artemio Cruz* (1962), a slighter but stronger brother to *Where the Air Is Clear,* being the story of a powerful financier's deathbed journey into his own past. Cruz is a man who was made by the Revolution and whose cynical cooptation of its ideals makes him in turn symbolic of the failures of modern Mexico. As a character he is also the most developed and the most stylized example of a type that recurs in Fuentes's fiction.

The resentful, barefoot bastard of a Veracruz landowner and a mulatto servant girl, the youthful Cruz runs away to join the Revolution after he accidentally murders his uncle. We follow his rise in the ranks of Venustiano Carranza's army by means of disguised acts of cowardice; his crazy, unmanning love for a young camp follower who is strung up by Huerta's Federalists; his capture by Pancho Villa's army, notori-

ous for its slaughter of prisoners and of innocents; and his escape from death when he betrays to his captors his own army's whereabouts. After the Revolution, Cruz marries the aristocratic Catalina Bernal and takes over her father's heavily mortgaged estate. At the time of his deathbed reminiscences, in 1959, Artemio Cruz's Mexican empire encompasses chains of newspapers and hotels, mines, timber concessions, pipe foundries, and (in a piece of characteristic Fuentes symbolism) the fish business. More importantly for Fuentes's purposes, Cruz is a front man for numerous American corporations seeking to evade Mexican restrictions on foreign holdings.

Artemio Cruz is elaborately constructed (thanks, this time, to the influence of the French *nouveau roman*) in three separate persons and tenses. The first-person present catalogues Cruz's silent sickroom excoriations of his spineless family . . . ; the rather strained second-person future, likewise in interior monologue, traces Cruz's physiological functionings and malfunctionings . . . ; the mercifully conventional third-person past retails Cruz's historical recollections. These last, constituting the most interesting portions of the book, move backward in time to 1903, when we are introduced to Cruz's natural grandmother, a lunatic harridan living in an abandoned Veracruz hacienda, who herself recollects the palmy days when she and her husband, a military man, had "glittered in the makebelieve court of His Most Serene Highness, General Santa Anna" (deposed by the Liberals in 1855). In this way is the history of the republic comprehended within the clotted brain of a rich mulatto bastard on his deathbed.

For Fuentes's final verdict on men like Artemio Cruz, and on the republic they helped to found, we turn to the end of the novel:

> You will bequeath this country: your newspaper, the hints and adulation, the conscience drugged by lying articles written by men of no ability; . . . You will bequeath them their crooked labor leaders and captive unions, their new landlords, their American investments, their jailed workers, their monopolies and their great press, their wet-backs, hoods, secret agents, their foreign deposits, fawning ministers, elegant tract homes, . . . their fleas and wormy tortillas, their illiterate Indians, unemployed laborers, rapacious pawnshops, fat men armed with aqualungs and stock portfolios, thin men armed with their fingernails: they have their Mexico, they have their inheritance. . . .

According to Fuentes, the failure of Mexico to translate the Revolution's original idealism into an honest, just, and equitable polity is to be blamed on this new class of military-men-turned-tycoons-and-politicians who have shielded themselves "behind glory to justify rapine in the name of the Revolution, self-aggrandizement in the name of working for the good of the Revolution," and who have perpetuated ancient cycles of exploitation and inequalities of wealth by selling out to North American imperialism. (That the Revolution might have been a corrupt or self-serving proposition from the start is a prospect he does not entertain.) Yet it must also be said that for the early Fuentes, these men also retain something irresistibly heroic about them. Complex, witty, divided, Artemio Cruz and Federico Robles possess a depth of feeling that outmatches everyone around them, including the insipid counter-heroes whom Fuentes introduces to remind us of the unmet spiritual needs of the masses.

The Death of Artemio Cruz is in many ways Fuentes's best work, and certainly his most disciplined and concentrated, notable for the richness of its prose and the subtlety of its insights into human relations, especially in their more devious modes. Yet it too suffers, like its predecessors, from its self-imposed formal constraints. Fuentes's mannered veerings from first person to second to third, his tricky allusiveness and ellipses, his unpunctuated prose poems (which sometimes seem to mimic a crafty old bully's determination to be boring on purpose) all serve to wreak in the name of art an unnecessary and finally debilitating havoc. That all this fragmentariness is intended to duplicate the movements of human consciousness itself is no consolation to the reader who comes to literature to see how true artists overcome fragmentation by a unifying effort of the imagination.

In the two decades following the publication of *The Death of Artemio Cruz,* Fuentes embarked on a succession of experiments with different voguish literary forms. In novellas like *Aura* (1962) and *Birthday* (1969), he adopted the southern offshoot of surrealism known as "magic realism". . . .

Fuentes's world outlook can be readily extrapolated from his views on Mexico. Taking into account the shifts and modifications of this outlook over the years, it can best be described as left-wing utopian with an overlay of sentimental anarchism. Primarily, his role in this hemisphere has been as a cultivated and (all things considered) rather patrician denouncer of American imperialism, colonialism, and big business. In addition to his role as nay-sayer to imperialist exploitation, Fuentes has served as a devout and ardent defender of revolution, making no distinction (at least for polemical purposes) in either aims or results between the American Revolution of 1776 and the Cuban Revolution of 1959—or, for that matter, the Paris student riots of May 1968, on which he published a slim volume, accompanied by photographs, declaring that "This revolution is ours, too."

Fuentes's habit of blurring distinctions is abetted by another habit, which is to deny the role that ideology plays in revolution. For example, he insists that Marxism-Leninism is simply a "label" for Latin Ameri-

can revolutionaries like the Sandinistas and the Salvadoran FMLN, a label covering the sorts of services formerly provided in the region by the Roman Catholic Church. That the Soviet Union might be involved in affixing this particular label is regarded by Fuentes as a canard, or a pretext for an American invasion.

In Fuentes's mind, it comes as no surprise to learn, the Soviet Union and the United States are "spectral siblings." The one has its Brezhnev Doctrine, the other its Monroe Doctrine; the one has Eastern Europe, the other its "Caribbean Warsaw Pact"; the one invaded Afghanistan, the other Grenada. The only difference is that while Russia is a stagnant gerontocracy unable and unwilling to lift a finger in the international arena, the United States is an active global slave-master.

The toll all this attitudinizing has taken on Fuentes's talents is painfully evident in his most recent novel, *The Old Gringo,* in which relations between the United States and Latin America, long an implicit theme of his fiction, become the main event.

The Old Gringo's point of departure is the disappearance into revolutionary Mexico of the American satirist, journalist, and short-story writer, Ambrose Bierce. The action unfolds in 1914 at a Chihuahuan hacienda occupied by Pancho Villa's rebel army, which is gathering strength for its march south to occupy Mexico City.

A brief and sparsely written novel, *The Old Gringo* describes the triangle formed among Ambrose Bierce—a lean, bitter, quixotic old man who, we are told repeatedly, has "come to Mexico to die"; Tomas Arroyo, a young general in Villa's army, out to avenge centuries of exploitation and oppression; and Miss Harriet Winslow, a headstrong young schoolmarm from Washington, D.C. who has been hired as a governess by the now-fled owners of the hacienda and whose determination to give her money's worth obliges her to stay on to teach Villa's Indian followers how to read and write.

For a Fuentes novel, the action is both fairly listless and elliptical. Much of it occurs offstage or in dreams while other characters sit in Arroyo's luxurious Pullman car, delivering soliloquies about Mexican destiny and North American wickedness. As in one of those reverse Westerns that are low on action and high on moralizing about the just grievances of the red man, *The Old Gringo* falls into the stock division of good guys vs. bad guys. "Haven't you ever thought, you gringos, that all this land was once ours? Ah, our resentments and our memories go hand in hand," sighs one *comandante,* gazing north at El Paso.

Pop psychologizing takes the place of character delineation in this novel, in which each protagonist is merely a type standing in for a particular political or cultural viewpoint. Arroyo, a stud whose private parts are described often and in lingering detail, is a spokes-man for the Revolution's new order; Harriet, rather a figure of fun, develops from a knee-jerk American pa-triot with a missionary zeal into a confused and guilty liberal who denounces U. S. policy in Cuba and Mexi-co—"the backyards of my country, occupied by my country because our destiny is to be strong with the weak"; Bierce, who most speaks for the author, is a rebel and cynic, embittered by North American crook-edness, hypocrisy, and ignorance and yearning after the dark, primitive soul of the Mexican Revolution. "Open your eyes, Miss Harriet, and remember how we have killed our Redskins and never had the courage to fornicate with the squaws and at least create a half-breed nation. We are caught in the business of forever killing people whose skin is of a different color. Mexico is the proof of what we could have been, so keep your eyes wide open."

The Old Gringo is almost deliberately indifferent to preserving historical propriety or avoiding anachro-nisms. Fuentes collapses chronology, misrepresents Ambrose Bierce's personal life, and confuses much of his career. The novel's historical liberties are most egre-giously apparent when it comes to the sexual front—for although all Fuentes's books are dirty, *The Old Gringo* is the most implausibly so.

But Fuentes has played fast and loose with histor-ical context for a reason. *The Old Gringo* is not really a novel about 1914, about Mexico, or even about Am-brose Bierce, but a weak and thinly disguised allegory of contemporary United States policy toward Central America, with Pancho Villa's charismatic rebellion a stand-in for the Nicaragua of men like Omar Cabezas, and Miss Winslow a little drummer girl in search of good sex and a revolutionary cause. "Ask yourself how many like me have taken up arms to support the Revo-lution," says a middle-class colonel in Villa's army. "We can govern ourselves, I assure you, *senorita*. . . . You don't think we're capable, then? Or do you fear the violence that has to precede freedom?" Thus *The*

Old Gringo, little more than a wan storefront excuse for stilted polemics and gratuitous pornography.

Carlos Fuentes's is altogether a sorry case. He is a born novelist, endowed with boundless energy, sharp senses, an appetite for life, and a heady instinct for sus-pense, adventure, heroism, melodrama. These strengths are displayed to best advantage in one partic-ular kind of writing at which Fuentes excels: the battle scene. Perhaps no other contemporary fiction writer has evoked with such gusto and such precision a charge of the cavalry.

Yet Fuentes's artistic gifts have been increasingly eroded over the years by what can only be described as an irresistible tendency toward derivativeness. Even Fuentes's best work has been pressed by him into a suc-cession of aesthetic molds which have obscured his vir-tues and inflamed his faults—those faults being self-indulgence and a certain cheapness of mind.

Similarly, the encroachment of politics upon Fu-entes's novels has led increasingly to the recession of character and thought. In a true novel of ideas—and whether or not the reader finds the ideas themselves persuasive—there always remains an inner sanctum of human life and character upon which theory-mongering cannot intrude. . . . Fuentes's earliest nov-els maintain such a place, in which social condemnation and social prescription do not yet smother the irre-pressibly natural longings of his characters to be rude to a dressmaker, to kiss a girl's neck, to lie in bed an extra hour, to chisel a cabdriver out of his fare, to own five acres of land. In his later work, however, and in-creasingly so as his career has progressed, human life with all its confusions and delights has receded, and the novel of ideas has instead turned into a kind of political demonstration, carefully marshaled by a very small and very loud party, with characters serving as banners and the sloganeering author as the only scheduled speaker.

Fernanda Eberstadt, "Montezuma's Literary Revenge," in *Commentary*, Vol. 81, No. 5, May, 1986, pp. 35-40.

SOURCES FOR FURTHER STUDY

Brody, Robert, and Rossman, Charles, eds. *Carlos Fuentes: A Critical View.* Austin, Texas: University of Texas Press, 1982, 221 p.

Fourteen interpretive essays on various aspects of Fu-entes's writing, focusing particularly on his novels.

Durán, Gloria B. *The Archetypes of Carlos Fuentes: From Witch to Androgyne.* Hamden, Conn.: Archon Books/The Shoe String Press, 1980, 240 p.

A revised and enlarged English translation of Durán's *La magia y las brujas en la obra de Carlos Fuentes* (1976). Durán explains the focus of her study: "[There] is at least one sorceress, implicit or explicit, who domi-nates nearly every one of Fuentes's novels. This sor-ceress stands as a guide to the subterranean world of the unconscious, which is the world that has increas-ingly preoccupied Fuentes. Therefore, a study of the witch and her multiple mutations—the final one being that of the androgyne—is critical to an understanding of Fuentes's works as a whole."

de Guzman, Daniel. *Carlos Fuentes.* New York: Twayne Publishers, 1972, 171 p.

Critical and biographical study, focusing primarily on Fuentes's novels.

Faris, Wendy B. *Carlos Fuentes.* New York: Frederick Ungar Publishing, 1983, 241 p.

Analyzes Fuentes's novels, short stories, dramas, and essays in separate sections devoted to each of his published volumes.

The Review of Contemporary Fiction. 8, No. 2 (Summer 1988): 147-291.

Special issue devoted to Fuentes and Claude Ollier with essays by Gabriel García Márquez, Octavio Paz, Milan Kundera, and others. This collection also features a new short story by Fuentes and an interview with the author.

World Literature Today. 57, No. 4 (Autumn 1983): 529-98.

Special issue devoted to Fuentes with essays by Gloria Durán, Margaret Sayers Peden, Wendy B. Faris, and others. Includes a selected bibliography.

John Galsworthy

1867-1933

(Also wrote under pseudonym John Sinjohn)
English novelist, dramatist, short story writer,
poet, and essayist.

INTRODUCTION

*A*n important figure in English literature of the early
twentieth century, Galsworthy is best known as
the author of "The Forsyte Chronicles," a collection of novels and short stories noted for its meticulous
depiction of upper-middle-class English life. Loosely
modeled on Galsworthy's relatives, the Forsytes are
members of a family of wealthy industrialists who value
material success above all else. During his lifetime
Galsworthy was also highly regarded as a dramatist for
his plays examining contemporary social problems.

Born on a family estate in Kingston Hill, Surrey,
near London, Galsworthy was the second child of an
upper-middle-class family. His father was a successful
solicitor who had a financial interest in mining companies in Canada and Russia; he later served as the
model for Old Jolyon Forsyte in "The Forsyte Chronicles." At the age of nine Galsworthy was sent to the
Saugeen Preparatory School, a boarding school in
Bournemouth. Five years later he entered the prestigious Harrow School in London, where he excelled in
athletics. In 1886 he went to Oxford University to study
law, graduating with second degree honors in 1889.
The following year he was called to the bar and began
writing legal briefs for his father's firm. Galsworthy,
however, had little interest in a legal career. In 1891 his
father sent him on an extended inspection tour of his
mining interests in Canada, and during the next few
years he traveled widely. During a two-month voyage
aboard the *Torrens* in 1893, he formed a close friendship with the first mate of the ship, Joseph Conrad, who
was then at work on his first novel. Conrad later encouraged and guided Galsworthy in his literary efforts.
Between 1897 and 1901 Galsworthy published two
novels and two volumes of short stories under the
pseudonym John Sinjohn. The last of these works, *A*

Man of Devon (1901), contains his first short story dealing with the Forsytes.

After his father's death in 1904, Galsworthy began publishing under his own name. In 1906 the first "Forsyte" novel, *The Man of Property*, appeared, and a production of his play *The Silver Box* was favorably reviewed by critics. Galsworthy wrote prolifically until his death, gaining international recognition for his works. During the First World War he donated the income from his writings to the war effort and volunteered as a masseur in a Red Cross hospital in France. In 1917 Galsworthy was offered a knighthood, which he declined; he later accepted the Order of Merit for his literary achievements. For twelve years he served as the first president of PEN, the international writers' organization. In 1932, shortly before his death, Galsworthy was awarded a Nobel Prize in literature.

Galsworthy first achieved prominence as a dramatist. His most esteemed plays are noted for their realistic technique and insightful social criticism. While working for his father, Galsworthy collected rents from the tenants of London slum properties, and several of his plays examine the contrast between the rights of the privileged upper classes and the poor. In *The Silver Box*, for example, the son of a wealthy member of Parliament steals a purse from a prostitute. Later, the husband of one of the family's servants steals a cigarette box from the purse. While the wealthy young man is released, the servant's husband is convicted and sent to prison. *Justice* (1910) examines the practice of solitary confinement in prisons and has been credited with prompting Winston Churchill to introduce legislation for prison reforms. Although a few critics consider Galsworthy's social plays his most important works, his accomplishments as a dramatist have been largely overshadowed by the renown of "The Forsyte Chronicles."

Publication of *The Forsyte Saga* (1922) established Galsworthy's reputation as a novelist. The works known as "The Forsyte Chronicles" include the novels and short fiction collected in *The Forsyte Saga* and *A Modern Comedy* (1929); the short story volume *On Forsyte 'Change* (1930); and several pieces of short fiction published in other works. Galsworthy modeled many of the characters in these works upon his ancestors and immediate family members. Soames Forsyte, the central figure of the "Chronicles," is based on Galsworthy's cousin Arthur. Tracing the rise and decline of the Forsyte clan, the narrative of the "Chronicles" begins in the 1820s with a short story included in *On Forsyte 'Change* and ends with the death of Soames in 1926 in *Swan Song* (1928). In *The Man of Property*, the first novel of *The Forsyte Saga*, Soames's wife, Irene, has an affair with an architect commissioned to build the Forsyte mansion. Soames takes revenge by ruining the architect and raping Irene. The architect later dies in a mysterious accident. Commentators have noted that while Galsworthy satirized the wealthy in his early works, his later works, especially those collected in *A Modern Comedy*, present a more sympathetic view of the Forsytes.

After completing "The Forsyte Chronicles," Galsworthy began working on a novel trilogy which was published posthumously as *End of the Chapter* (1934). His other works include fourteen volumes of short stories and sketches and several collections of essays and poetry. Although Galsworthy's dramas and novels were highly regarded during his lifetime, critical and popular interest in his works declined shortly after his death. In 1967 the British Broadcasting Corporation aired a twenty-six-hour serial adaptation of *The Forsyte Saga* for television. Repeated the following year and syndicated in more than forty countries around the world, this adaptation is credited with renewing interest in Galsworthy's novels. Today Galsworthy is recognized as an important chronicler of English life, with Sanford Sternlicht praising his works as "the finest written portrait of the passing from power of England's upper middle class."

(For further information about Galsworthy's life and works, see *Contemporary Authors*, Vol. 104; *Dictionary of Literary Biography*, Vols. 10, 34, 98; and *Twentieth-Century Literary Criticism*, Vol. 1.)

CRITICAL COMMENTARY

CONRAD AIKEN

(essay date 1928)

[An American man of letters best known for his poetry, Aiken is considered a master of literary stream of consciousness. In reviews noted for their perceptiveness and barbed wit, he exercised his theory that "criticism is really a branch of psychology." In the following excerpt from an essay that first appeared in *The New Republic* in 1928, he discusses Galsworthy's prose style and comments on his apparent literary forebears.]

What Trollope did for the "country family" in England in the early and middle parts of nineteenth century—taking up the theme about a generation after the point at which Jane Austen dropped it—Mr. Galsworthy has set out to do for the second half of the century, and the early years of the next. The three authors provide us, indeed, with an almost perfect *continuum.* Not only do they deal with the same scene and with the same kinds of people: they also share a common method. It is the "wholeness" of the social picture that interests them, and all three of them go about the presentation of this picture with something of the unexaggerative detachment of the sociologist. Allowing for individual differences—for the shrewder wit of Jane Austen, the generous urbanity of Trollope, the more inquisitive intellectualism of Mr. Galsworthy, and also his keener interest in the purely *dramatic* element in the architecture of fiction—the three authors are very obviously congeners.

[If] Mr. Galsworthy resembles his two predecessors in his comprehensiveness and in his predilection for a level and cumulative realism, he has also his striking differences. He is not as "pure" a literary phenomenon as either of the others: his talent is not, like Jane Austen's or Trollope's, a single and immediately recognizable thing, but rather a kind of synthesis, whether we regard it from the point of view of style or the point of view of method. We can, and should, grant immediately his greater intellectual grasp: he assumes for his purpose a far more complex scene, and this more complex scene he handles with admirable control. Nothing is left out, everything is adequately seen and rendered. If we take the picture as a whole, we can say that it is true and rich, and that in assembling so much material on one canvas he has achieved a remarkable feat of design.

It is when we look at the thing in detail that we begin, perhaps, to be here and there a little disquieted and to feel that for all its energy his talent is not quite so fine or deep, not so individual, as that of either of his literary forbears. (p. 214)

Mr. Galsworthy's prose is an adequate prose, but it is not a distinguished one. It is frequently awkward, frequently monotonous, to the point of becoming actively and obtrusively *not* a good medium for the thing said. . . . Mr. Galsworthy has always been somewhat disposed to purple passages. There are . . . times when he wants something a little better than his "mere medium" for the thing said; he desires to be poetic; an emotional scene or atmosphere is to be conveyed, and accordingly he attempts a prose more charged and ornate. These attempts are almost invariably failures: Mr. Galsworthy's taste fails him. What one usually feels on these occasions is that he is simply unable to express feelings delicately; and that is, perhaps, a definition of sentimentality.

One feels . . . that when one accepts, as one does, Mr. Galsworthy's place in English fiction, one does so with very definite reserves as to the quality of his style. And even the "wholeness" of his picture, which is his major virtue, is not without grave faults. If he gives us admirable scenes, sharp, quick, and living, and admirable portraits . . . he also gives us a good many scenes which we do not believe in for a minute, and more than a handful of portraits which do not belong at all in any such gallery as this, but rather in the category of the Jonsonian or Dickensian "humor." (p. 215)

One has the feeling, occasionally, that he is describing his characters rather than letting them live; that when they face a crisis, he solves it for them *intellectually:* and that again and again he fails to sound the real truth in the situations which he himself has evoked. Soames Forsyte, for example, is a real person, on the whole admirably drawn. But could Soames, granted the sensitiveness with which we see him to be endowed, possibly have lived four years with Irene in so total a blindness as to the real state of things between them? Here was a situation which could have been magnificent. A real "realism" would have luxuriated in the minute-by-minute analysis of this profound disaccord. But Mr. Galsworthy never comes to grips with it.

Something of this failure to get inside his characters shows again in *Swan Song,* the coda to the Forsyte Saga. . . . [We] are given the culmination of the interrupted affair of Fleur and Jon, and the death of Soames. The whole story moves toward, and is focused on, the

Principal Works

From the Four Winds [as John Sinjohn] (short stories) 1897

Jocelyn [as John Sinjohn] (novel) 1898

Villa Rubein [as John Sinjohn] (novel) 1900

A Man of Devon [as John Sinjohn] (short stories) 1901

The Island Pharisees (novel) 1904

*The Man of Property (novel) 1906

The Silver Box (drama) 1906

Justice (drama) 1910

*Awakening (short story) 1920

*In Chancery (novel) 1920

*To Let (novel) 1921

The Forsyte Saga (novels and short stories) 1922

The Works of John Galsworthy. 30 vols. (novels, dramas, essays, poetry, and short stories) 1923-36

†The White Monkey (novel) 1924

Caravan: The Assembled Tales of John Galsworthy (short stories) 1925

†The Silver Spoon (novel) 1926

†Two Forsyte Interludes: A Silent Wooing; Passers By (short stories) 1927

†Swan Song (novel) 1928

A Modern Comedy (novels and short stories) 1929

On Forsyte 'Change (short stories) 1930

‡Maid in Waiting (novel) 1931

‡Flowering Wilderness (novel) 1932

‡Over the River (novel) 1933; also published as One More River, 1933

The Collected Poems of John Galsworthy (poetry) 1934

End of the Chapter (novels) 1934

*These works and the short story "Indian Summer of a Forsyte" from Five Tales (1918) were published as The Forsyte Saga in 1922.

†These works were published as A Modern Comedy in 1929.

‡These works were published as End of the Chapter in 1934.

eventual love-scene between Jon and Fleur: . . . but when it comes, it is quite lamentably inadequate; it is as if the author had gone into a complete psychological funk about it, and had simply not *known* how two such people would have behaved on such an occasion. This scene needed to be the realest and richest and most moving in the book; and given the sufficient actuality of the two people, it could easily have been so. Mr. Galsworthy's failure to give us here anything but a stagey little scene of rhetorical melodrama suggests anew that his gravest fault is his habit of *thinking* his way, by sheer intelligence, into situations which he has not sufficient psychological insight to *feel*. (pp. 216-17)

Conrad Aiken, "John Galsworthy," in his *Collected Criticism*, Oxford University Press, Inc., 1968, pp. 213-17.

JOSEPH J. REILLY

(essay date 1932)

[In the following excerpt, Reilly offers an appraisal of Galsworthy's novels.]

When the distinguished English novelist John Galsworthy delivered a few lectures in Greater New York last spring, his appropriately heralded presence attracted large audiences in the metropolitan area. It did something even more important. It moved a large section of the American reading public to talk about him with some show of interest, and the discriminating minority to turn afresh to his books and, with their excellences and shortcomings in mind, attempt to decide upon his place among the masters of English fiction.

Everybody knows that Galsworthy was born in 1867, that he was educated at Harrow and at Oxford, that he studied law and was admitted to the bar in 1890, that he made a journey around the world, that he gave up law for literature, and that he has to his credit many distinguished essays, short stories, sketches, plays and novels, and even a volume of verse.

For the first years of his career as novelist (1898-1901) Galsworthy wrote under a pseudonym. In 1904 he published *The Island Pharisees* with his own name and followed it two years later with what is probably his masterpiece, his first Forsyte novel, *The Man of Property.* During the next fourteen years he wrote seven novels and in 1920, after a lapse of fourteen years, he returned to the Forsytes and produced a sequel, *In Chancery.* This move opened the way for further chronicles of the family, and the very next year Galsworthy produced *To Let,* a third volume in the Forsyte series. In 1922 these three novels, with two connecting Interludes, appeared in one volume under the title *The Forsyte Saga.*

Having gone so far and made a new generation of Forsytes his concern—with generous applause from critics and public—Galsworthy was tempted to continue, and for the next six years (1922-1928) his interest in fiction was centered on the further doings of that long-lived family. *The White Monkey, The Silver Spoon,* and *Swan Song* appeared biennially in succession, and, with two connecting Interludes, were published in 1929 as *A Modern Comedy.* It is with these two trilogies that Mr. Galsworthy's name is most intimately associated and on them that his reputation as a novelist chiefly rests.

With the evidence before us of such industry and skill as they unquestionably present, precisely what are we to think of Galsworthy?

Of his success there is no question. His books have sold widely, they have won him recognition at home and abroad, they have so impressed us in America that we consider him the foremost living English novelist and probably the superior of any living American. The ablest and best-balanced of American critics goes so far as to declare that only *The Forsyte Saga* among present-day novels in our tongue will last a century.

This celebrity as a novelist does not rest upon long fiction alone. It is paralleled by short stories, essays, sketches, often published in popular magazines, and by plays which have won Galsworthy a place with Barrie and Shaw. All these productions bear the impress of a single shaping hand and of a unique personality. They appear at frequent intervals, keep Galsworthy's name constantly in the public eye, and are, to a striking and (for Galsworthy) fortunate degree, mutually reinforcing.

Above all things else Galsworthy is a conscientious workman. He could not more indulge in the Arnold Bennett type of pot-boiler than he could make a balloon ascension in order to advertise his books. His work is never hastily done; in fact it is planned with the same forethought and executed with the same care as would have characterized the briefs of John Galsworthy, solicitor, charged with important litigation. Perhaps it is not merely an accident that his most important and most completely drawn character, Soames Forsyte, "the man of property", is a lawyer, and that he is painstakingly attentive to every detail of his life; that he has, in a word, the Galsworthian conscience. Soames's daughter Fleur has a similar sense of orderliness and efficiency despite the post-war environment in which she moves and it serves her equally in selecting the right sort of people to give atmosphere to her drawing-room and in operating a soup kitchen during the great strike. So too Michael, Soames's son-in-law, who must give business details his honest consideration and, on entering Parliament, must, in lieu of convictions, at least find and espouse definite principles.

Galsworthy's orderliness, his sense of conscience in all his work, is evident in his style no less than in the fashioning of his novels. It is an unusual style, smooth, graceful, supple, and in the competent hands of its master it is a skilful instrument. It lacks the point and precision of Shaw's and the virility of Bennett's. It is the reflex of a different type of mind, a more impressionable, a more sensitive, a less masculine type than theirs.

A mind like Galsworthy's, with its feminine side, is not necessarily lacking in vital interests or in the tenacity to cleave to them. His particular concern is with social conditions as affected by the injustice, selfishness, and lack of vision of the wealthy and aristocratic classes, and even his love episodes are coloured by that concern and projected against that background. With a quicker sensitiveness than his contemporaries and a deeper pity he sees poverty and its attendant evils not primarily as superscientific questions like Wells, not as merely personal conditions like Bennett, not things to be triumphed over by an imagination, a fairy godmother, or a happy turn of fortune like Barrie, but first of all as objects of human sympathy and after that as intolerable effects of a social and economic situation for which well-to-do Britons must be answerable.

In *The Forsyte Saga,* Galsworthy turns his attention to the well-to-do middle class in England whose roots were already struck deep at the beginning of the nineteenth century. The industrial revolution brought them property and wealth and from one generation to another they clung to both tenaciously, watching them increase by natural growth, by fortunate investments, and by far-sighted intermarriages with wealthy families of their own caste. They were narrow, self-satisfied, grasping, and unconscious of social obligations in any broad sense. Soames, man of property, who adds to an inheritance already great, whose possessive passion extends from lands to houses, to pictures, and even to his wife, exemplifies the instinct of his class, and his defeat at the hands of his wife Irene prefigures the downfall of the social order of which he is a part.

To the generation of Soames's daughter Fleur, the generation that has lived through the Great War and felt old ties loosed and social conventions flouted, Galsworthy turned to study further the evolution of the upper middle class. An unforeseen phenomenon greeted him. His social problem had ceased to be so arresting in its economic aspect and had become both arresting and frightening on its moral side. He beholds in Fleur the undying possessive passion of Soames and his forebears but diverted from the acquisition of property toward the gratification of merely social ambition, personal vanity, and even lust. The Decalogue has gone overboard and with it restraint, reverence, and even pity.

What is Galsworthy's attitude toward the two problems with which his overmastering interest in society confronts him? In *The Forsyte Saga* he implies with skilful irony and keen satire that conditions are economically impossible; in *A Modern Comedy* with irony no less skilful and satire no less keen he implies that they are morally chaotic. For the former he seems to have a nostrum. He speaks of art and says: "Art is the one form of human energy which really works for vision and destroys the barrier between man and man". About sixty years ago Matthew Arnold expressed similarly high hopes in the case of culture. It was going to assimilate what was "best in religion", provide yearning souls with an approach to God, turn the minds of the masses from a belief in "machinery", in coal mines and population, in railroads and exports, and transform them from Philistines to lovers of culture eager to make reason and the will of God prevail. There is a startling similarity between the nostrum suggested by Arnold and that advocated by Galsworthy, and it is as impossible to be sanguine of the one as it is of the other.

In *A Modern Comedy,* where the moral situation edges the economic conditions out of the limelight, it is through the lips of his most attractive character, Michael Mont, Fleur's husband, that Galsworthy speaks. Michael notes the self-consciousness of his generation, its poses, its affectation of cleverness, the joylessness which marks it, its restlessness, "the effort to escape from something that couldn't be got away from". Michael asks himself what his generation has put in the place of the things they discarded and finds no answer except, "We must be after something". When a son is born to Fleur and Michael they wonder in what creed they will bring him up. "Without faith", Michael asks himself, "was one fit to be a parent? Well, people were looking for faith again", but, warped as they were, would, he feared, fail to recover it. He talks it over with Fleur, but her bewilderment is scarcely less than his and in the end Fleur and Michael arrive nowhere.

And where does Galsworthy arrive? As a matter of fact he has no way out. To him life is a muddle and it is in an observation of one of his characters, Young Jolyon, that his philosophy is revealed: "To be kind, and keep your end up—there's nothing else in it". At the conclusion of *Swan Song* when Michael, aware that Fleur had played him false, seeks a brief refuge from his bewildering bitterness of soul out under the summer stars, he finds no thought to comfort him, no solution of the strange enigma of life.

Let us now turn to a consideration of Galsworthy as the artist in fiction. Without question we grant him the merits of a scrupulously careful craftsman, of an accomplished and resourceful stylist, of an ironist of the Addisonian tradition grown more obviously conscious, and finally the merit of a deep and sincere human sympathy. These assets have carried him far. It remains to ask: Have they carried him so far that *The Forsyte Saga* is the finest work of fiction produced by any living British novelist? Do they seem to assure to Galsworthy a distinguished place in the attention of our great-grandchildren?

Galsworthy has lost his only serious rival among recent English novelists. Arnold Bennett did more than his share of ephemeral work and was too often deaf to the protests of his artistic conscience. Occasionally, however, he gave ear to it and turned his undoubted talents to good purpose. Once inspiration came to his aid, he drew upon every resource of experience and art at his command, and "with an impressiveness unmatched since Thackeray" (to borrow a judgment from Dean Cross) achieved his only masterpiece, *The Old Wives' Tale.* Here is a novel entirely unconcerned with those social problems which Galsworthy has always found absorbing and which occupy so large a place in the world's thought today. It boldly turns its back on our generation, and its historical high point is not the nineteen-hundreds but 1870. Its concerns are limited, personal, almost petty. It is (you remember) merely the chronicle of the childhood, youth, marriage, subsequent fortunes, and death of two sisters, and it is about the same length as the three novels that make up *The Forsyte Saga.* The personages of *The Old Wives' Tale* are no whit less selfish, narrow and self-centered than the figures in Galsworthy's saga. And yet there is a difference emphatic enough in treatment, but even more emphatic in the result accomplished. Neither by conscience nor by inclination was Bennett bedevilled into attempting two rôles; he is completely the novelist dedicated to an all-absorbing task, and not even by a stroke of the pen or a flicker of the eye is he a conscious critic of society. Not even in his mind did he have a divided aim, but the abundance of his own vitality flowed into his story and he achieved that mysterious blood transfusion by which, so to speak, a novelist who pretends to greatness must fill the veins of his creatures and transform them into independent entities who think, will, and act for themselves.

Galsworthy's men and women lack this vitality. Annette, Soames's second wife, is only a name; Bosinney and Irene are scarcely more vital than the fog into which Bosinney walks to his death. Others—most of the older Forsytes in fact—are brought nearer to a three-dimensional existence by the device of a pet interest or a pet phrase in the Dickens manner. It is on Soames and Fleur that Galsworthy lavishes his skill as a creator of character and the result is significant. Only in *The Man of Property* does Soames emerge from the shaping hands of the novelist and appear upon the retina of the mind's eye, a breathing human creature capable of thought and action. Throughout the five subsequent novels he becomes constantly less corporeal and it is only at occasional moments, as in *Swan Song* when he rescues his pictures from the burning gallery, that he steps out of the shadows into reality or when (ironic fact!) dying, alone with Fleur, who peers into his dulling eyes, he declines her offer to bring in the others; he wants *her*. As for Fleur, the most successfully drawn of all his characters, she achieves life of her own thanks to the device of presenting her through Soames's and Michael's eyes; and her eager, selfish heart, with its passion to possess, awakens her pulses to a living response. She overshadows Michael whose veins are warm only in her presence, and neither of the two develops, but both, in the manner of Dickens, remain static. It is a singular fact that Galsworthy's women more nearly approach reality than his men. A certain feminine element in him, noticed before, an unvirility, revealed in his style, from which Wells, Bennett, and Barrie (for all his fancifulness) are free, gets in the way, and the elements that go to the making of his men fail to cohere and to harden. (You are aware of this also in his best short stories, **"The Apple Tree," "The First and the Last,"** and even in **"A Stoic."**)

Of course the Forsytes are commonplace people, but commonplace people may be as real as one's own brothers and as fascinating to read about as queens or adventurers. The people in *Vanity Fair,* the greatest of English novels, are commonplace; they are Forsytes of an earlier generation. The people are commonplace in *David Copperfield,* in *The Mill on the Floss,* in Hardy's *Tess of the D'Urbervilles,* and in *The Old Wives' Tale.* It is not the quality of the people but life that is important and everlastingly fascinating, and even commonplace men and women can command our interest once the creative genius of the novelist awakens them to life.

Saintsbury says finely of Thackeray: "He could not introduce a personage, no matter how subordinate, without making him a living creature. He may be introduced to say a couple of lines, and never appear again, but Thackeray has no sooner touched him than there is a human being—an entity. He could not introduce a footman, saying some half-dozen words, 'My Lady is gone to Bright*ing*' or something of that sort, without presenting the fellow for his trouble with life and immortality".

Fundamentally Galsworthy's weakness, despite (to say it once more) his undeniable virtues, is vital. It is to be found in a phrase used by Henry James when he said that the supreme virtue of a novel was to "produce the illusion of life". That is the secret—"the illusion of life"—and it sanctions any method (Bennett's, Galsworthy's, Hardy's, or any other) which can perform the miracle of producing it. How the novelist shall achieve this, whether by the use of description, dialogue, or incident, in addition to the clearness of character, no one can say. That is a secret, as James pointed out, "between the novelist and his good angel". In what proportions his elements are mixed is no man's concern provided only the novelist "catch the very note and trick, the strange irregular rhythm of life". To demand this is to demand much. True! It is to demand what only

the masters can give and what, when given, proves their genius. The greatest of British critics, paying tribute to the greatest of British romanticists, wrote: "All that portion of the history of his country that he has touched upon, the manners, the personages, the events, the scenery, lives over again in his volumes. Nothing is wanting—the illusion is complete. There is a hurtling in the air, a trampling of feet upon the ground, as these perfect representations of human character or fanciful belief come thronging back upon our imaginations. . . . His works, taken together, are almost like a new edition of human nature". And he adds, half between applause and envy: "This is indeed to be an author!"

Herein lies the secret of Galsworthy's failure to be a great novelist. In the phrase of Hazlitt and of Henry James, the "illusion of life" is wanting. At times we catch it as in that fine scene at Mrs. Magussie's rout in which the social duel between Fleur and Marjorie Ferrar reaches its climax and society takes its revenge on Fleur. Again we catch it in *Swan Song* when Fleur, denied an assignation by Jon, drinks to the dregs the bitterness of humiliation. But instances such as these are rare in Galsworthy. Not in his as in genuinely great novels, does the reader feel the tide of life flowing all about him, eddying at his feet, ebbing and returning, in never ending motion, like the sea. It is such a sense of life that Galsworthy attributes to Michael Mont; it is such an illusion of that life that his novels fail to provide.

The critics, deeply impressed by the many-sided talents of John Galsworthy, gentleman, have been highly generous to John Galsworthy, novelist. But in treating his works they have closed their eyes to the real function of fiction, and by emphasizing the wrong things have declared in effect that that function is to provide posterity with pictures of contemporary society rather than to create the illusion of life. Thus they have established the myth that Galsworthy, painstaking, conscientious, observant, with the temper of a critic and a propagandist rather than artist, is a great novelist.

But time will settle all that. We cannot, by a kind of mortmain, impose our idols on our grandchildren. Besides, our grandchildren may be too busy setting up idols of their own. (pp. 488-93)

Joseph J. Reilly, "John Galsworthy—An Appraisal," in *The Bookman,* New York, Vol. LXXIV, No. 5, January-February, 1932, pp. 488-93.

ALEC FRÉCHET
(essay date 1979)

[In the following excerpt from a study originally published in French in 1979, Fréchet discusses realism in Galsworthy's works and appraises his novels.]

A love story lies at the heart of nearly every Galsworthy novel. The hero's senses and temperament are completely involved, his mind and consciousness less so, or at any rate less immediately, less directly. The novels, then, offer several harmonics. But a lyrical poetic style, and a restless, nostalgic atmosphere predominate. The role Galsworthy attributes to woman, her beauty, the passions she arouses and experiences, is so great that it is even possible to talk of his romantic conception of life. Indeed, his various allusions to Don Quixote suggest the image of a knight errant, always ready to take up arms to defend the defenceless, and draw attention to the dreamlike element in his philosophical outlook.

His lyricism, which can be described as 'romantic' because of the lovely natural settings in which he places it, has nothing exotic, theatrical or gushing about it. There is no question of parading yearnings or conquests. There is never any posturing. It is a secretive, contemplative, delicate romanticism, almost religious, in that it turns love into a religion. This is when it is most genuine. When his inspiration falters, it can lapse into sentimentality.

He claimed to be realistic, in describing the arousal and growth of passion in reality, in other words in complete freedom. He was particularly fond of a definition of him put forward by a critic who called him 'a romantic realist'. He liked it because it suggested a distinction between what he regarded as his own realism and the vulgar materialism that he attacked in D. H. Lawrence's way of depicting love. He did not realise that his heroes required leisure and money for the way they loved. It never occurred to him that his way of drawing a veil over certain things would one day leave readers dissatisfied.

'Realism' does not seem to be the right term to define his work. [Examination shows] how limited and relative Galsworthy's realism is in every area, psychological analysis, description or choice of situation. Admittedly, the French Realist taught him certain value precepts, concision, the discretion of the narrator, avoiding any intrusion, any asides, any accentuation. But he did not know Zola, owed little to Flaubert, and even Maupassant's influence on him was restricted. He rejected his themes and crudeness. For Galsworthy, realism was no more than a device, a technique, a method, not a philosophy. He did not exploit the resources offered by the French Naturalists, as George Moore did in *A Modern Lover* or *Mummer's Wife.* As might be expected, not the slightest Surrealist influence is to be detected in his works.

The most obvious form of realism is the precision with which he notes time and place, and his descriptions of attitudes and gestures. This precision is not systematic, but selective and deliberate. The straightforwardness with which he describes the layout of places where action takes place is reminiscent of stage directions.

In general, he displays that most typically English quality of pragmatism, rather than realism. It has already been seen in his political attitudes, and is what made them so regrettably ambiguous. For Galsworthy, value and durability were inseparable. Whatever lasted, whatever possessed the power of survival, was good. This is where the source of his interest in families, and especially their older members, surely lay. Some old people are described admiringly (and admirably), though not all. He was capable of admiration and respect, but he measured them out according to each individual case and its circumstances. It would be wrong to talk of any faith in the family or cult of the family.

The main evidence of his detachment from realism is his principal characters' indifference to the material difficulties of life, and the choice of characters of the same standing in life as himself.

Galsworthy's outlook was not centred on objects and their possession. This is why he was so well placed to write *The Man of Property.* He had that sophisticated detachment from earthly goods conferred by the very fact of being a man of property himself, who had never known need, and had never nurtured material, social or political ambitions. At home, he ate and drank well, and may be assumed to have had an epicurean enjoyment of anything attractive and of good quality. His novels describe the heavy mahogany tables, silverware, sweet peas and thick carpets that create the muffled charm of those large upper middle-class houses where life is so pleasant. His characters include several Epicureans: Old Jolyon, Swithin, despite his vulgarity, Heythorp in **'A Stoic'.** But Galsworthy had a conscience, and his novels are, in his own words, 'conscience-stricken'.

They are the work of a gentleman, who did not write in order to make a living, but who lived in order to write. This is the basic argument: far from arising from the attitudes of a materialist, far from being encumbered with possessions, his novels above all evoke an inner world, the most complicated labyrinths and profoundest contradictions of which are painstakingly analysed. It was almost without his realising it that, in creating this world, he depicted the social class to which he belonged. Since this class held power and set the tone, his writings provide a glimpse of the whole of English society.

The essential question he asked himself was both personal and general. It related quite precisely to the 'gentleman', the man who continues to observe good form, whatever happens. Galsworthy was deeply attached to such an ideal, because only in self-respect did he hold any faith. For him, real moral force lay in a man's verdict on himself: social retributions represented an arbitrary usurpation of this force. Yet, seeing the injustices of a society run by gentlemen, he suspected the inadequacy of their ideals, and consequently of his own. This misgiving never led him to such a thorough critique as that of Ford Madox Ford in *The Good Soldier.* He never turned to any other belief. He rejected all religions and ideologies, and maintained firmly the primacy of individual judgement, in accordance with the liberal philosophy of John Stuart Mill, whose essay *On Liberty* probably influenced him. He was attacked from both sides for his obstinate attachment to independence. Yet his only response, using Young Jolyon as his mouthpiece, was to assert that what men lack above all else is imagination—not creative imagination or intelligence, but moral imagination, the capacity to feel compassion. The heroes of his early novels feel ill at ease because, without giving up their class privileges, they are incapable of enjoying them with a quiet mind. This is what makes them outsiders in their own world.

His strongest criticisms bear on the position of women in a society where laws are made by men, to justify and perpetuate male domination. Both his romanticism and his criticism thus share the same origin and object. In his conception of the role of woman in a man's life, he is in direct opposition to Balzac, and different from Meredith, Hardy, Conrad and Shaw. Far from regarding love as a deception, or a form of seduction fraught with perils, he regarded it, like a true romantic, as an enhancement of one's whole being, and one of the peaks of existence. If he had thrown off the other shackles of Victorian convention, his position would have been that of an extreme feminist. But all he demanded for women was equality with men in love, not full equality of social rights, particularly the right to work. His writings show him attached to the idea that above all a woman is beautiful and intended for love; at the most, she might play a little music and do charitable work. The Victorian conception of the family no longer holds sway, but the ambitions that women began to entertain in the Edwardian age are not yet reflected. Unlike several of his contemporaries, ultimately he was in favour of marriage, on the sole condition that divorce should be easier.

His attitude was a mixture of conservatism, re-

formism, and, on one or two points, such as religion and education, revolt against the prevailing state of affairs. With the passage of time, his criticisms of English society may seem timid, over-cautious, flimsy; like the humour of *Punch,* they are not really intended to hurt. But this interpretation of his work cannot really stand up to any examination of the early novels, and other forms of writing: plays, poetry, essays and articles. It is hard to avoid such an error of perspective, for the novels not belonging to the trilogies have always been neglected, and are likely to remain so. And even in his most successful books, Galsworthy does not succeed in expressing his ideas dynamically enough to make them properly reflect his philosophy. His discretion and reasonableness are appreciated by those primarily seeking honesty, as in Montaigne. But more often they are turned against him. He has been condemned for not offering a system, an all-embracing and coherent vision of the world. A few years ago, he was being compared most unfavourably with Graham Greene.

His most serious weakness as a writer may be seen as the inadequacy of his creative imagination, arising from a lack of exuberance, spontaneity, gaiety, or immediate contact with practical life and with people, an absence of fantasy and even, on occasion, of a sense of the ridiculous. There is nothing everyday or ordinary about the scenes he describes. It gives his effects great distinction, but they are also rather thin, and sometimes cloying. His characters have few vices but, except for stoical courage in the face of death, they also lack virtues.

Galsworthy does not lend himself to classifications, simplified, modish definitions. In his confidence in the good-heartedness of the middle classes, once their imagination is awakened, his reasoning is as optimistic as George Eliot's or Dickens'. He also belongs to the 19th century in his reservations about democracy, his doubts about its vulgarity. Yet the extreme sensitivity and generosity of his social consciousness make him the most modern of the Edwardians. David Daiches very accurately points out [in *The Present Age*] that 'Wells' scientific humanism was essentially late Victorian, and so too was Shaw's iconoclastic wit, but J. Galsworthy's humane worrying about society remained important for a decade at least after the first war'.

E. M. Forster [in his essay 'English Prose between 1918 and 1939' in *Two Cheers for Democracy*] puts Galsworthy among those authors who 'got their impressions and formed their attitudes in an earlier period, before the first of the two world wars'. This is also penetrating, and it is confirmed most strikingly in the letter to Garnett in which Galsworthy admitted that the First World War had deeply disturbed his beliefs.

[Analysis] of *A Modern Comedy* [shows] it to be more superficial than *The Forsyte Saga.* Yet there is a lot of truth in its image of an unstable generation, thrown off course by the First World War. In other words, Galsworthy did not feel in perfect sympathy with the Georgians, but neither was he a typical Edwardian nor a representative Victorian. His independence of mind has been emphasised. He was also sufficiently receptive to take something from every period in which he lived. His example suggests, incidentally, that the three periods involved should not be differentiated too dogmatically or arbitrarily.

His indifference, or even hostility, to trade and industry, his tendency to adopt an amoral attitude in matters of private life, his pessimism, scepticism and tolerance, distinguish him quite clearly from the Victorians. Yet his criticism of the Forsytes does not take the form of any virulent, all-embracing condemnation of the Victorian age. He seldom uses the adjective 'Victorian', indeed, and abstains from any criticism of the Queen.

His artistic and literary tastes . . . were rather those of an Edwardian. His preference for the Impressionists, his condemnation of modern art, his aversion for Dostoyevsky and his posthumous fame, his anger at the statue of Rima sculpted by the controversial artist Jacob Epstein in 1924, in memory of his friend W. H. Hudson, all go to show Galsworthy displaying rather orthodox tastes as the Edwardian age went on. The outline of his literary fortunes showed that it was in the first decade of the century that he was regarded as a spokesman and innovator.

Yet one must never forget that the most formative period of his mind began before Edward VII came to the throne. The decade of crisis in his personal life, which made him a writer, lay half in the 19th and half in the 20th century. Through an odd coincidence, the same was true of his life. He lived thirty-three years in the 19th century, and thirty-three in the 20th. If his position has to be defined in the history of art and ideas, the second half of the reign of Edward VII is probably the right choice.

It is no easier to situate him in the history of English literature. He believed that he had been little influenced by it. Consequently, he had no interest in establishing his precursors: in fact, he did the contrary. Leon Schalit [see Sources for Further Study], whom he knew personally and trusted, and who discussed the matter with him, wrote that 'except Dickens and perhaps Thackeray a little, no English writer has influenced him, unless it be Shakespeare'. There is every reason to believe that this remark was inspired directly by Galsworthy himself. His statements on the decisive influence of Maupassant and Turgeney on his art reveal how he saw himself: a pure-blooded Englishman (he prided himself on the absence of any Scots, Irish or Welsh ancestry), using a foreign art to depict his country. But although this might have seemed true at the

Eric Porter as Soames Forsyte in the BBC production of *The Forsyte Saga.*

start of his career, in time Galsworthy recognised that England also boasted stylists and artists: Stevenson, whom he liked, Pater, whom he mistrusted, Jane Austen, for whom he had little liking.

However, he never admitted, and probably never perceived, the full influence of English literature on his work. His art is far more English than he thought, although the many diverse influences on it never stifled his originality. The names of Shakespeare, Keats and the Pre-Raphaelites, Thackeray, Dickens, Carlyle, Ruskin, Arnold, Meredith, Butler, Hardy, Hudson, Conrad and others have been mentioned. The English authors to whom Galsworthy owed most are perhaps Thackeray, Meredith, Hardy and Conrad. A parallel can be drawn, not only between *Beauchamp's Career* and *The Patrician,* but between *The Ordeal of Richard Feverel* and *The Country House.* However, there are as many differences as similarities, perhaps more, so that such comparisons are of limited value. Conrad's moral or philosophical themes were probably more influential, despite obvious contrasts between the two writers. Do they not share the same sense of moral obligation, a taste for the irrational, even sometimes the supernatural, in spite of a similar hostility to Christianity? However, no literary and human influence was so strong on Galsworthy as that of Turgenev, from whom he borrowed frequently and extensively, thereby enriching the whole of his work. He could have been accused of parody, if the social context in England and Russia had not been so different, and if, despite these differences, there had not been a very great spiritual affinity between him and his master. Turgenev was the man he would have liked more than anyone else in the world to meet.

It is hard to see any meaningful similarities among the three Edwardians whom Virginia Woolf equally reproved, Galsworthy, Bennett and Wells. [Analysis] of *Beyond* [shows] the profound divergences between the novel and *The Old Wives' Tale.* Louis Tillier [in his *Arnold Bennett et ses romans réalistes*] has pointed out differences between Bennett and Wells. There is an even wider gulf between Wells and Galsworthy, in temperament, taste, talent and ideas. At most, the stature of both writers is comparable. Wells long appeared the greater, no doubt because of the wider and more universal nature of his work; but his reputation has not re-emerged in the same way as those of his two contemporaries. Of the three, I consider Galsworthy the greatest artist.

However, other terms of reference must be sought. The name of Trollope is sometimes mentioned, but Galsworthy is a better stylist and a more profound thinker. In a more recent period, the 'Georgians', particularly the Bloomsbury Group, have not thrust the Edwardians into oblivion as they expected and indeed appeared to do for several decades. Virginia Woolf and E. M. Forster both possess charms that are lacking in Galsworthy, but their inspiration is narrower. Other writers, like J. D. Beresford, Compton Mackenzie, or

Frank Swinnerton, so gifted in the twenties, failed to live up to their early promise.

This is why Galsworthy can no longer be depicted as the last executant of a dying *genre.* Other family novels or novel sequences have been published with success by other authors. J. D. Beresford published a trilogy between 1911 and 1915. The woman writer G. B. Stern described a family in *Children of No Man's Land* in 1919. R. H. Mottram's trilogy *The Spanish Farm* appeared from 1914 to 1926. Between 1924 and 1928, Ford Madox Ford published the quartet of 'Tietjens novels'. At the end of the Second World War, L. P. Hartley made his reputation with a trilogy.

J. B. Priestley's temperament and realism make him more a descendant of Bennett, but C. P. Snow's novel sequence *Strangers and Brothers* recalls the Galsworthian novel in several ways.

Without possessing the power and genius of Hardy, Conrad or Lawrence, Galsworthy may well be recognised as one of the leading English authors of the century. It may be that the renewed popularity of the *Forsyte* trilogies will encourage readers to discover the other novels and stories that best illustrate his humane outlook on life.

Deceived by the apparent facility of his style, critics have so far not taken the trouble to examine the more personal and innovatory aspects of Galsworthy's art. This is hardly surprising. But his two triumphs among the general public, nearly fifty years apart, and under very different historical conditions, suggest that real treasures may still lie hidden in his novels. (pp. 198-204)

Alec Fréchet, in his *John Galsworthy: A Reassessment,* translated by Denis Mahaffey, Barnes & Noble Books, 1982, 229 p.

SOURCES FOR FURTHER STUDY

Coats, R. H. *John Galsworthy as a Dramatic Artist.* New York: Charles Scribner's Sons, 1926, 240 p.

Examines themes and techniques in Galsworthy's plays.

Fisher, John. *The World of the Forsytes.* London: Martin Secker & Warburg, 1976, 224 p.

Discusses England's social and political climate from 1886 to 1926, a period that Fisher calls the "Forsyte Era." The critic provides photographs and illustrations of life during the era and comments on various passages from the "The Forsyte Chronicles."

Gindin, James. *John Galsworthy's Life and Art: An Alien's Fortress.* London: Macmillan Press, 1987, 616 p.

Biography of Galsworthy, focusing on the events and people that have shaped his life and work.

Kaye-Smith, Sheila. *John Galsworthy.* New York: Haskell House Publishers, 1972, 123 p.

Evaluates Galsworthy as a novelist, dramatist, poet, and short story writer. This study was originally published in 1916.

Marrot, H. V. *The Life and Letters of John Galsworthy.* New York: Charles Scribner's Sons, 1936, 819 p.

Authorized biography of Galsworthy.

Stevens, Earl E., and Stevens, H. Ray. *John Galsworthy: An Annotated Bibliography of Writings about Him.* De Kalb: Northern Illinois University Press, 1980, 484 p.

Comprehensive primary and secondary bibliography of
Galsworthy.

Federico García Lorca

1898-1936

Spanish poet, dramatist, critic, and essayist.

INTRODUCTION

*H*ailed as one of Spain's most important twentieth-century poets, García Lorca drew upon all elements of Spanish life and culture to create poetry at once traditional, modern, personal, and universal. Combining classical verse with folk and gypsy ballads, García Lorca sought to liberate language from its structural constraints and bring out the musicality inherent in Spanish dialect. While initially influenced by the Symbolists, who believed the function of poetry was to evoke and not describe, García Lorca began to experiment with startling imagery, scenic metaphors, and complex rhythms after coming in contact with filmmaker Luis Buñuel, poet Pablo Neruda, and artist Salvador Dalí. García Lorca's dramatic approach to poetry led him to devote the latter part of his life to playwriting. In his drama, like his verse, García Lorca wrote about death, frustrated sexuality, and the relationship between dream and reality. While his poetry and drama continue to be widely studied among literary scholars, García Lorca emphasized that he wrote for and about common people: "No true man still believes in that rubbish about pure art, art for art's sake. At this dramatic moment in the course of world events, the artist must weep and laugh with his own people. He must put aside the spray of lilies and wade waist-deep into the mud to help those who are looking for lilies."

García Lorca was born and raised in rural Andalusia, the southernmost province of Spain and a region greatly influenced by Arabic and gypsy culture. He attended schools in the nearby town of Almeria and studied law and literature at the University of Granada. After moving to Madrid in 1919, García Lorca continued his studies at the Residencia de Estudiantes, a center for writers, critics, and scholars of cultural liberalism. While there, he earned a law degree and came in contact with several emerging literary and artistic figures, many of whom would later comprise the Generation of 1927. The members of this group rejected what they considered to be the sentiment and superficiality of Romanticism and instead advocated hermetic expressionism. García Lorca's closest friend at the Residencia de Estudiantes was Salvador Dalí, whose dramatic surrealist paintings and "quest for joy for the sake of joy" would later inspire García Lorca to write "Ode to Salvador Dalí." Another prominent figure of this period was poet Juan Ramón Jiménez, whose use of symbolism influenced García Lorca's first volume of poetry, *Libro de poemas* (1921). This work is a compilation of gypsy folklore García Lorca heard during his youth in Andalusia. Although considered a conventional account of his childhood experiences, *Libro de poemas* is recognized for its vivid, accessible language and mythological imagery. After the publication of this volume, García Lorca organized Spain's first *cante jondo* festival. *Cante jondo*—or "deep song"—is a traditional form of Andalusian music that, according to Felicia Hardison Londré, "combines intensely emotional yet stylistically spare poetry on themes of pain, suffering, love, and death with a primitive musical form." García Lorca's continuing involvement in the *cante jondo* festival, at which Spain's most famous singers and guitarists performed, is reflected in *Canciones* (1927) and *Poema del cante jondo* (1931). These collections, which were directly inspired by composer Manuel de Falla, elevated the traditional ballad forms known as *siguiriya gitano* and *soleá* to new levels of stylization.

García Lorca's next collection, *Primer romancero gitano* (1928; *The Gypsy Ballads*), is widely regarded as a masterpiece of Spanish poetry. In this volume, comprised of eighteen poems written between 1924 and 1927, García Lorca incorporated images of gypsy village life with traditional ballad forms to create verse both thematically accessible and lyrically complex. Utilizing such dramatic elements as action, characterization, and dialogue, García Lorca created what Londré described as "symbolist dramas in miniature." Since its publication, *The Gypsy Ballads* has been popular in Spanish-speaking countries worldwide due to its focus on common people and its use of idiomatic language. C. M. Bowra explained: "[*The Gypsy Ballads*] is a book which has a special place in our time because it shows not only that the outlook of a highly civilized poet is in many ways that of the simplest men and women, but that the new devices which have been invented to express a modern sensibility are not restricted to urban and sophisticated subjects." Although *The Gypsy Ballads* brought García Lorca widespread acclaim, it also led both readers and critics to categorize him as strictly a "gypsy poet," a label which García Lorca would repudiate throughout his life: "Gypsies are a theme. Nothing more. I would be the same poet if I wrote about sewing needles or hydraulic landscapes. Besides, the gypsy myth makes me sound like an an uncultured, uneducated, *primitive poet*, which . . . I am not."

While not as well known as *The Gypsy Ballads*, *Llanto por Ignacio Sánchez Mejías* (1935; *Lament for the Death of a Bullfighter, and Other Poems*) is also considered a masterpiece. This four-part elegy was occasioned by the mauling death of Spain's most celebrated matador, Ignacio Sánchez Mejías, who was one of García Lorca's closest friends. A celebration of Spanish sound, rhythm, and assonance, *Lament* evidences García Lorca's unique blend of poetry and drama. In this work García Lorca combines a factual narrative with startling and macabre descriptions to present the matador as a symbol of vitality who confronted death with playful indifference. Repeating the refrain "at five in the afternoon," García Lorca evokes a sense of suspense and foreboding which caused Edwin Honig to observe, "*Lament* is the work of a poet in whose consciousness dramatic and poetic forms have interpenetrated."

Despite the fact that García Lorca's work was extremely popular throughout the 1920s, the poet suffered an emotional crisis in 1928, stemming from his belief that he was being stereotyped as a "gypsy poet." Leaving the Andalusian landscape with which he was so familiar, García Lorca traveled to New York City in 1929, where he came in contact with images directly contrasting those of his homeland. Deeply disturbed by the monotony of industrial life and America's reliance on mechanization, García Lorca began writing poems that were later collected in the posthumous volume *Poeta en Nueva York* (1940; *Poet in New York*), considered to be his most abstract and surrealistic volume due to its themes of chaos and alienation. Commentators initially castigated García Lorca for eschewing Spanish motifs in favor of horrific imagery and scathing commentary concerning the quality of life in New York City. However, recent views on *Poet in New York* have been more favorable, with critics citing the difficulties in translating García Lorca's unfinished manuscript as one reason for initial negative reaction. Although many of the poems contained in this volume are cynical, including "Landscape of the Vomiting Multitude" and "Sleepless City; Brooklyn Bridge Nocturne," many commentators agree that none approach the tragedy of "The King of Harlem," in which García Lorca laments the plight of poverty-stricken African-Americans living in New York: "Ay, Harlem, Harlem, Harlem! / There is no sorrow like your oppressed eyes."

Although García Lorca wrote the drama *El malefico de la mariposa* (1920; *The Spell of the Butterfly*) in 1920, it was not until he returned to Spain in 1930, shortly after the proclamation of the Spanish Republic, that he composed the majority of his dramatic works. Among his best known plays are *Bodas de sangre* (1933; *Blood Wedding*), *Yerma* (1935; *Yerma*), and *La casa de Bernarda Alba* (1945; *The House of Bernarda Alba*). *Blood Wedding*, which closely resembles a classical Greek tragedy, is the story of a bride who runs off with another man on her wedding day. The bridegroom, understanding that his honor is at stake, follows the bride and her lover into a forest where the two men eventually kill each other. Considered a violent and passionate account of peasant life, *Blood Wedding* addresses García Lorca's concerns with sexuality, death, and the relationship between tradition and modernism. *Yerma*, written two years later, is thematically similar to *Blood Wedding*. In this play, García Lorca chronicles three years in the life of young married woman, Yerma, who longs to have children despite being unsatisfied with her husband and her marriage. After taking part in an annual pilgrimage of childless women, Yerma angrily strangles her husband to death when he asserts that he does not want children. In this work, as in *Blood Wedding*, the wife struggles between passion and moral duty while the husband remains unresponsive and oblivious to her concerns. In contrast to *Blood Wedding* and *Yerma*, which are generally considered expressionistic and abstract, *The House of Bernarda Alba* is intensely realistic. This work focuses on Bernarda, a tyrannical woman who virtually imprisons her five daughters in her home. When Pepe, the only available male in the village, becomes engaged to the eldest daughter, the others attempt to express their own oppressed sexuality through flirtatious behavior. The play ends tragically when the youngest daughter, who has been having an affair with Pepe, commits suicide after being led to believe that her mother has killed the young man. While some critics suggest that the mother

symbolizes the cruelty of totalitarian governments, others concur that García Lorca was merely presenting a psychological study of women.

In 1936 political unrest forced García Lorca into hiding, despite the fact he had never aligned himself with any particular political party and referred to himself as a "catholic, communist, anarchist, liberal, conservative, and monarchist." García Lorca was eventually discovered at the home of a friend and arrested by General Francisco Franco's nationalists. After being detained by the Civil Government in Granada for several days, García Lorca was executed by a firing squad in an olive grove outside the tiny village of Viznár and buried in an unmarked grave. His murder is often considered a tragically ironic ending for an author who so frequently wrote about death. Scholars maintain, however, that although death is a prevalent theme in his works, García Lorca is perhaps more strongly esteemed for his abiding humanitarian concerns, deep affection for Andalusian culture and landscapes, and passionate dedication to all art forms. C. M. Bowra observed: "[García Lorca's] personality turned everything about him into poetry. . . . With him the landscape and the human beings in it took on an enchanted air and seemed different from what they had been before. His art was no mere department of his life; it filled and inspired everything that he did."

(For further information about García Lorca's life and works, see *Contemporary Authors*, Vol. 104; *Drama Criticism*, Vol. 2; *Poetry Criticism*, Vol. 3; and *Twentieth-Century Literary Criticism*, Vols. 1, 7.)

CRITICAL COMMENTARY

ÁNGEL DEL RÍO

(essay date 1941)

[Del Río was a Spanish critic and editor who wrote numerous works about Spanish literature. In the following excerpt from a work that first appeared in 1941, he provides a thematic and stylistic overview of García Lorca's drama.]

As is so often the case in Spanish literature, Lorca's dramatic work is inseparable from his poetry and is a natural emanation from it. We have many examples of this: Gil Vicente, Lope de Vega, the Duke of Rivas, Zorrilla; in modern times, Villaespesa, Marquina, Valle-Inclán, Unamuno, and the Machado brothers. In European Romanticism we frequently find the phenomenon of lyri-

cal poetry being turned into dramatic poetry. In this respect, as in so many others, Lorca can be placed within the framework of the Romantic attitude. But let us understand Romanticism not as a school of a certain period, but as a manner of feeling and artistic expression.

Lyricism and Romanticism seem to be fused from the start of his career. His first play, *El maleficio de la mariposa* (*The Spell of the Butterfly*) was written at the same time as his Symbolistic early verse and was animated by the same inspiration as his poems about insects and animals.

Leaving aside the dramatic intensity of his poetry, especially that of the *Gypsy Ballads*, his dramatic work developed side by side with his poetic work, both oscillating between the two magnetic poles of his inspira-

Principal Works

Impresiones y paisajes (sketches) 1918

El malefico de la mariposa (drama) 1920
  [The Spell of the Butterfly, 1957]

Libro de poemas (poetry) 1921

Canciones (poetry) 1927

*Mariana Pineda (drama) 1927

Primer romancero gitano (poetry) 1928
  [The Gypsy Ballads, 1953]

†La zapatera prodigiosa (drama) 1930

Poema del cante jondo (poetry) 1931

†Amor de Don Perlimplín con Belisa en su jardín (drama) 1933

Bodas de sangre (drama) 1933
  [Blood Wedding, 1939]

†Yerma (drama) 1934

El público (drama) 1934
  [The Audience, 1958]

†Doña Rosita la soltera (drama) 1935

Llanto por Ignacio Sánchez Mejías (poetry) 1935
  [Lament for the Death of a Bullfighter, and Other Poems, 1937]

† Así que pasen cinco años (drama) 1938

Retablillo de Don Cristóbal (drama) 1938
  [In the Frame of Don Cristóbal, 1944]

Obras completas. 7 vols. (complete works) 1938-1946

Poeta en Nueva York (poetry) 1940
  [Poet in New York, and Other Poems, 1940]

Selected Poems of Federico García Lorca (poetry) 1943

‡La casa de Bernarda Alba (drama) 1945

The Cricket Sings: Poems and Songs for Children (poetry) 1980

Deep Song and Other Prose (lecture, poetry, and essays) 1980

*Translated as Marian Pineda and published in Tulane Drama Review, 1962.

†These works were translated and published in Lorca's Theatre, 1941.

‡Translated as The House of Bernada Alba and published in Three Tragedies, 1947.

---

tion and his style, the poles of the select and the popular, the capricious and the tragic, the stylized grace whose art was close to the art of the miniature painter, and the anguished passion within a whirlwind of sensuality. (p. 140)

[Several] years after the premature *Spell of the Butterfly,* Lorca really began his dramatic career with *Mariana Pineda.* Conceived in the popular vein, the work suggests a childhood ballad: "Oh, what a sad day in Granada." It follows a technique similar to that of many of his first poems and songs. We see here the attempt, probably intuitive, to fuse elements of the classical and Romantic theater and to do so with a modern flair. From the classical tradition he takes the essential spirit, the dramatization of a popular ballad in whose verses the drama is suggested. On the other hand, from the Romantic era he takes the historic theme, the feeling of background, and above all the character of the heroine, an angel sacrificed on the altar of love. Judged on its own merit, the work lacks true dramatic dimensions. It is a static picture. Only in one or two dialogues between Pedrosa or Fernando and Mariana can we catch a glimpse of the clash of wills without which there can be no drama. As for the intimate conflict of the heroine, Mariana, it is barely sketched. From the very beginning she seems predestined to her end; she is the embodiment of sacrifice: neither the hope of saving herself, nor the certainty of Don Pedro's love for

her can change her tone of resignation. . . . She is revealed to us not through action nor in intimate dramatic soliloquies but in lyrical fugues, as in the beautiful ballad that begins with the lines, "With what an effort / the light leaves Granada!" In the rest of the play the same thing happens. The best moments are due to the presence of lyrical elements, either directly, separated from the action, as in the ballads describing the bullfight in Ronda and the arrest of Torrijos, or as a lyrical motif in contrast to the dramatic action. The latter we find in the ballad of Clavela and the children or the song in the garden, "Beside the water." In many scenes there is a pathetic, almost musical atmosphere. On the whole we detect throughout the play the lack of maturity of an author who is experimenting with a new technique. Even his verse has a naïve and occasionally clumsy cadence. Though doubtless inferior to the poetry of these years, in which Lorca had already written many of his *Gypsy Ballads, Mariana Pineda* is not without interest. In more than one way we can catch a glimpse in it of the great merit which the best dramatic work of Lorca was to exhibit. There is a clear feeling for the tragic and a faultless good taste: aesthetic dignity saves the most dangerously poor passages, those on the border of immature and trite melodrama, like the scene of the conspirators, the seduction attempt on the part of Pedrosa, and the chorus of novices. Above all, there is a conscious effort of innovation in his intention to synthesize in the theater the plastic, lyrical, dramatic, and musical arts into a superior unity. For this reason Lorca took great pains to "tune up" each scene within a stylized atmosphere of colors, lights, allusions, and constant musical interludes and backgrounds, until at the end of the play a sort of operatic and symbolic apotheosis is achieved. (pp. 140-42)

Far better constructed, although of less emotional intensity, are the works which followed *Mariana Pineda.* We find in them again the same qualities—expertness, self-confidence, stylization—as in his *Book of Songs,* but here enriched by a well-defined and conscious ironic grace.

Three farces in prose, written between 1929 and 1931, make up this phase of his work and constitute at the same time a group by themselves within his theatrical writings. The first is *Amor de Don Perlimplín con Belisa en su jardín (The Love of Don Perlimplín for Belisa, in His Garden)* . . . Then came *La zapatera prodigiosa (The Shoemaker's Prodigious Wife),* . . . and finally the delightful *Retablillo de Don Cristóbal (In the Frame of Don Cristóbal).* (pp. 142-43)

They have in common the same stylized popular background and a similar theatrical technique which results from the combination of elements taken from the courtly comedies at the end of the seventeenth and the beginning of the eighteenth centuries, from the Italian stage, from the puppet theater, and from the modern ballet. Each one, depending on which element predominates, has its particular character.

The Love of Don Perlimplín is the most cultivated of the group in technique and the most lyrical in spirit. Although not distinguished by the careful technique or the lively movement of *The Shoemaker's Prodigious Wife,* it is nevertheless superior in its poetic qualities. Always within the framework of irony, we can detect passages of beautiful lyricism, as in Perlimplín's lament: "Love, love, wounded love," and in Belisa's song: "Along the banks of the river." In the third scene—Perlimplín's suicide—buffoonery is raised to an atmosphere of delicate melancholy. The playfulness of the farce becomes impregnated by a pathetic aura, diffused in soft tones like the sonatas of Scarlatti, which were used by Lorca as melodic interludes, or like the poetic theater of Musset, which Lorca had read with great interest. We find ourselves at the limit of pantomime where an intentional dehumanization of characters takes place, and nevertheless we perceive in the comic profile of Don Perlimplín his sentimental anguish, caused by a love which is at the same time pure and grotesque.

The Shoemaker's Prodigious Wife is a stylization of pure folk charm, the most complete and successful work of this group. Directly inspired by folklore, the shoemaker and his wife, the chorus of neighbors, the

dialogue and the action are conceived with a picaresque, old Spanish flavor, which reminds us of certain short plays of the Golden Age. The popular ballad of the shoemaker preserves the common and clumsy flavor of the ballads commonly recited by blind men, refined through touches of the best poetic quality. The play is an exercise in wit: the few dramatic scenes are expressed in a knowing gradation through the contradictory feelings of the shoemaker's wife toward her husband. Throughout she is bad-tempered and tender, piquant and impudent. The farce is resolved in the triumph of love, when the shoemaker and the shoemaker's wife are reunited. Even within the framework of comedy Lorca places a trace of bittersweetness, when after the reconciliation of the couple the work closes with the half serious, half ironic lamentations and insults of the shoemaker's wife: "How unfortunate I am with this man that God has given me!" We should take notice of this ending, basically a happy one, because it is the only time that it occurs in Lorca's dramatic works, which are primarily concerned with frustrated love. As in his other plays, the music—song, rhythm, background—has an essential role, producing an effect of unreality and giving the play the subtlety, grace, and movement of a ballet.

In the Frame of Don Cristóbal, like *Los títeres de Cachiporra (Cachiporra's Puppets),* comes from the period of the first youthful experiments and was inspired directly by the puppet theater. It is not much more than a game, a folk Andalusian *divertissement;* it is important only as an example of Lorca's versatility, that constant search for a better integration of the arts which characterizes his theatrical writings as much as his poetry. It also reveals the piquant background of malicious country wit which was part of his mental makeup and added spice to his conversation. *In the Frame of Don Cristóbal,* full of naïve fantasy, is a magnificent example of "naughtiness" and spontaneity.

These short unpretentious plays illustrate typical aspects of Lorca's artistic personality; his more profound self we find in his treatment of anguish and tragedy, but even here we shall continue to find a counterweight of light and joyfulness, of pleasure generated by wit and innocent irony.

Así que pasen cinco años (If Five Years Pass) and some scenes from the drama *El público (The Public)* . . . belong to the period in which he was interested in Surrealism. This work comes a little after or at the same time as his poems about New York City. (pp. 143-44)

If Five Years Pass ("a legend about time in three acts and five scenes") is of greater interest than *El público.* Here the theme is a combination of two typically Lorcan preoccupations: the passing of time and the frustrations of love. The central characters, the young man and the fiancée, are new versions of Marfisa and Don Perlimplín and the waiting for a wedding which never takes place is almost a foretaste of *Doña Rosita la soltera* (**Doña Rosita the Spinster**). The technique and the atmosphere are, however, completely Surrealistic. It is an atmosphere of dreams, with masks, mannequins, clowns, or real people like the rugby player or the card players dehumanized in the manner of the characters of Gómez de la Serna, to whose influence his work is largely indebted. Lorca manages to sustain an unreal atmosphere suspended somewhere between humor and drama and with an undercurrent of mysterious sensuality. As in the best of his plays, the lyric elements are ever present. . . . The dialogue, whether in prose or in verse, almost always shows a growing mastery of the theatrical technique which the poet was slowly acquiring through his various experiments. Lorca never confined himself to a definite type of poetry or of drama nor to the inflexible formula of any fixed school. Thus, having learned all he could from it, he soon abandoned Surrealism and returned for inspiration to the feelings and themes of Spanish reality where his art finally found its focal point. (pp. 145-46)

If his tragedies represent a balance between lyricism and drama, *Doña Rosita* is the fusion of poetry and comedy, with subtle historical overtones.

The author describes the work as "a poem of Granada in 1900 divided into various 'gardens' with scenes of singing and dancing." Like *Mariana Pineda*, to which it bears a strong resemblance in technique and mood, it deals with the evocation of a period. But the shading of the poetic, plastic and emotional elements of the play is better achieved. The direct romanticism of the earlier work now becomes soft irony. The intense drama of love becomes diluted and is dissolved into lyrical fragrances. The somewhat artificial pathos of *Mariana Pineda* is replaced by a sweet melancholy, a pure and intense emotion. Doña Rosita, a woman (the most important characters in Lorca's plays are always women), is not a heroine but rather a symbol of womanhood in the Spanish provinces at the end of the century. Thus we have a lack of real dramatic intensity. In order to become a deep psychological play it would have had to delve into the individual soul of the characters. This is precisely one of the main shortcomings in all of Lorca's plays, including his tragedies, where passion never quite acquires full psychological embodiment and always remains skin deep, with no motivation other than a kind of tragic destiny before which the characters submit with hardly a struggle. What happens in *Doña Rosita* is that the poet turns this limitation into his main creative force. The drama of resigned love incarnated in Doña Rosita, the endless waiting for the sweetheart who will not return, is consciously subordinated to a more impersonal anguish: what moves the spectator is neither the passion nor the suffering of the protagonist but the bodiless presense

of time itself hovering over the stage and the life of every character. Lorca is a master of creating a lyrical atmosphere, and in this play he succeeds completely. The evocation of those quiet years from 1890 to 1910 in which Spanish life seemed to be at a standstill as if it had lost all its vital springs gives us a perfect picture of both reality and trite pathos, touching in its irony. All the sentimental mood of the play, all its lyrical quality find their maximum expression in the "language of flowers," a symbol of existence without desires and without ambitions, and a symbol at the same time of the slow withering of Doña Rosita. (pp. 146-47)

[In *Blood Wedding*] Lorca for the first time finds the right expression for the passionate intensity vibrating in the inner recesses of his best poetry: a peasant tragedy. At times the dehumanized, stylized art of his songs and stage artifices make us forget the frantic trembling of life and nature which the voice of this dark and passionate poet brought to us from the time of his earliest creations. This constantly present trembling of life can be found in the dramatic quality of his lyrical poetry as well as in his tragedies, where it comes to be felt with all its violence, subordinating the lyrical content to the dramatic tone in a perfect fusion which Lorca had to achieve if he wished to express fully his most complete self.

"I was," the Fiancée says, "a burnt woman, full of sores outside and within. And your son was a drop of water from whom I expected children, earth, health." Here is the essential element of tragedy: beings who are scorched by a deep passion against which it is futile to struggle. The situation is a simple one and an old one: the rivalry within a family, and the rivalry of two men for a woman who struggles between the attraction of a fiancé, who offers her peace of mind, and the more powerful attraction of her lover. (pp. 148-49)

Blood Wedding is a work of the highest artistic rank. In it we can detect the breath of classical influence, a touch of Mediterranean tragedy and even a certain Shakespearian quality. . . . [It] is impossible to doubt the exceptional value of this play. The unity of its poetic elements, the moving clarity of its drama, and the breath of folk life that animates it make it the most complete and beautiful masterpiece of Lorca's theater and place it well above the mediocre productions of today's Spanish dramatic literature.

Yerma, written two years later, is similar in its main idea and its technique to *Blood Wedding*. In many ways it is a more finished product. The subject is a more ambitious one. Lorca had been elaborating it for many years. It deals with a love frustrated because of man's powerlessness to respond to woman's passion. The subject appears in some of Lorca's earliest poems and reappears later as an obsession in *Mariana Pineda*, in some of the *Gypsy Ballads*, in *Don Perlimplín*, in *If Five Years Pass*, in *Doña Rosita*. Sometimes he deals with spiritual love, sometimes with sensuous lubricity. In *Yerma* the situation develops within the framework of frustrated motherhood, and the passion becomes intimate and spiritualized. The play's structure follows an order in which dramatic elements predominate. The lyrical elements—songs, washerwomen's chorus—are less important. The tragic conflict acquires greater density because within a primary climate of passion surrounding the characters there is a more complex hierarchy of forces. As in *Blood Wedding,* there is a suggestion of pagan forces struggling in Yerma's soul against her moral sense of duty, until she is incapable of giving in to either of the two forces and decides to kill her husband.

In spite of all this and perhaps because of its ambitious scope, Yerma does not quite reach the artistic level of *Blood Wedding.* It does not have the same artistic unity; the dramatic motivation is less clear. In *Blood Wedding* everything is concrete and basic, earthy, within a folk poetic atmosphere. In *Yerma* at bottom every element strains toward abstraction. We would well suspect that [Miguel de] Unamuno's presence hovered around Lorca's subconscious while he was writing *Yerma.* The very character of the heroine reminds us of Unamuno's literary creations. . . . Doubtlessly Lorca wanted to go beyond Unamuno's disembodied approach to tragedy; he wanted to add to it life, blood, individuality. He managed to do so up to a point, but in order to give to Yerma's intimate anguish all its pathos and its universal meaning he needed instruments for abstract reasoning and at the same time for subtle psychological penetration. These Unamuno possessed abundantly but Lorca lacked, being an intuitive spontaneous artist. Lorca's domain extended from direct speech to symbols, from folk elements to stylization. That is why the reading of *Yerma* is somewhat disappointing. We do not find in it the lyrical pathos or the burning dialogue of *Blood Wedding.* Perhaps on stage the effect would be more positive. Lorca's theater is in great measure a spectacular theater and words lose a great part of their meaning when read outside a total atmosphere that was posited at the very moment the work was written. Lorca was a past master in the rendering of dramatic elements in terms of visual details, rhythm, and lyrical symbols. (pp. 151-53)

Ángel del Río, "Lorca's Theater," translated by Gloria Bradley, in his *Lorca: A Collection of Critical Essays,* edited by Manuel Duran, Prentice-Hall, Inc., 1962, pp. 140-54.

EDWARD C. RILEY
(essay date 1952)

[Riley is an American educator, critic, and Hispanist. In the following excerpt, he asserts that García Lorca is essentially an apolitical poet whose genius lies in his use of Andalusian imagery, his awareness of the musicality of the Spanish language, and his emphasis on emotion and nature over rationality.]

Federico García Lorca is a legend. He was one of those rare persons who have something of legend about them while they live. His death added to that legend some of the mystery that invests the martyr, although he was in fact no more a martyr than any of the other million persons who died in the Civil War. But where does the myth end and the man begin? . . . He is the modern Spanish poet best known outside Spain. And yet how misrepresented both within and without! He has been the victim of his admirers more than of his detractors. He has been given political labels that he would have been the first to disavow. Now he is accepted as much by the Nationalist regime as by its opponents, who first adopted him after his death. At last, it seems, justice begins to be done him. For if ever there was an unpolitical poet, it is Lorca.

Passion, Mr. Pearse Hutchinson said in a recent article in *Envoy,* is what makes Lorca great. Articulate passion. That is, passion made words and the words made poetry. Genius is its own justification, and one may read, and be moved by Lorca's poetry without concerning oneself with anything save the poem in front of one. But he is occasionally bewildering; his language is sometimes obscure and often apparently extravagant. The foreign reader must have some comprehension of Lorca's Spanish background if Lorca is to mean to him even a part of what he can mean to a Spaniard. (pp. 14-15)

It is a peculiarity of Spanish literature that much of its greatest writing achieves greatness in proportion as it is an expression of certain national characteristics, of something that can only be called *lo español.* As with bull-fighting or *flamenco* singing, unless the foreigner will at least try to learn how to be an *aficionado,* he is, if not repelled, at any rate left cold. Of course there are exceptions. Cervantes is as universal as he is Spanish. But to how many who know all about Racine and Ronsard, say, are Lope de Vega and Góngora really anything more than names? (p. 15)

The *españolismo* of Lorca is as intense as that of Lope or Góngora, but inevitably outside the Spanish-speaking world it has been neglected. His fame abroad has rested on three main foundations: first, and principally, the passionate lyricism that knows neither frontiers nor barriers of time; second, such of his artistry as has survived translation; third—it is to be regretted—the sordid glamour of his death. But his *españolismo* cannot be rendered in another idiom at all.

To take first the most striking feature of his verse, the imagery. It is drawn very largely from the Spanish, and in particular the Andalusian landscape. Like that landscape in real life, it hits you with something almost like a physical impact. There is nothing mild or vague or half-tone about it. It is a compound of extremes—burning deserts and luxuriant gardens, snow-topped mountain ranges and slow red rivers. It is brutal, voluptuous, stark, delicate, fragrant, exuberant, melancholy. The air has a limpidity that is almost luminous. Abounding elemental vitality lies sunk in passive somnolence. (pp. 15-16)

The poet's feeling for his province is characteristic of any Andalusian. Sr. Ortega y Gasset, in his *Theory of Andalusia,* has some pertinent observations to make on this subject:

> Every Andalusian has the wonderful notion that to be an Andalusian is a piece of fantastic good luck with which he has been favoured. . . . One must insist on this primary root of the Andalusian character, this peculiar enthusiasm for its slice of the planet. . . . The union of man and earth is not a mere fact here, but is idealized and almost a myth. . . . The Andalusian transplanted cannot go on being an Andalusian; his peculiarity evaporates and disappears. Because being an Andalusian means living with Andalusian soil, responding to its cosmic favours, being obedient to its atmospheric inspirations.
>
> (p. 16)

Even to Spaniards Lorca's poetic imagery is sometimes bold and startling, like the landscape; but it is not usually obscure, and never silly. In translation it is frequently both. It is not *always* the translator's fault. What is he to do with "voz de clavel varonil" for instance?—"Voice of manly carnation"! What, in any case, is he to do with a word as hopelessly unmusical as "carnation," when Spanish offers you "clavel"! In Spanish such a phrase is not silly at all. A characteristic of ordinary Andalusian speech is the use of striking imagery. Words like "carnation," "bull," "rose," "moon," "blood," "silver," so abundant in Lorca, are not unusual images in popular speech and are commonplaces of songs and popular poetry. Andalusian verse as far back as the Arabs has a tradition of great plasticity, colour and luminosity.

Like all the great Spanish poets he exploits to the full the musical qualities of the language, and he will use words at times for the pure beauty of their sounds

alone. He even, on rare occasions, coins words. "Luna lunera" and "noche que noche nochera," he says, where "lunera" and "nochera," apart from their suggestive qualities and their obvious association with "moon" and "night" are meaningless. Or he repeats a word: "por el monte, monte, monte," again simply for the sake of the sound and the semi-hypnotic effect of the repetition. He is even more sensitive than most writers to the musical beauties of the language, for besides being a poet (as well as a painter of considerable talent), he is a musician of no mean order. . . . (p. 17)

The vocal nature of so much of his verse is evident too in his use of such devices as exclamation, where the speaker or singer is relied upon to invest the words with the necessary emotion and surcharge of suggestion. This is particularly so in the book of poems called *Poema del cante jondo* (*Poem of Cante jondo*), where the musical motif of Andalusian gipsy song is especially pronounced. . . . (pp. 17-18)

Lorca's complete identification of himself with his people is one of the principal features of his *españolismo*. It is another peculiar feature of poets of the past like Lope de Vega and Góngora. While preserving their individuality and their personal artistic integrity, they are able to merge themselves with that current of essentially anonymous popular poetry that has persisted in Spain since the Middle Ages and which, although at times the stream has dwindled to a trickle, has never entirely dried up. . . . [Lorca] brings the ballad back to life in his *Romancero gitano* (Gipsy Ballads) as it had not lived since the sixteenth century. There is nothing "arty-crafty" in his efforts. The diligent folklorist inspired him with horror. He found his material among a people for whom a tradition of popular verse still existed, a tradition more oral than written. He composed as one of these people for themselves, because he was a part of these people. He composed poems and songs which were often being recited and sung long before they were ever committed to print. People were sometimes at a loss to know whether a song of his was original or whether it was a piece he had unearthed from the store of age-old compositions. Such was his mastery of a traditional form.

Lorca's extraordinary facility, his powers of improvisation and his easy association with the traditional and popular have led many people to stamp him rather too blithely a "non-intellectual" poet. There is some truth in this, if by "intellectual" poet they mean such an one as Rubén Darío, say, or Gerardo Diego. But they also say that Lorca read little and thought less. I have the most serious doubts about this assertion. Can one really claim that Lorca had not an ample acquaintance with literature, ancient and modern, after reading one or two of his published lectures—the exquisite **"Teoría y juego del duende" ("Theory and practice of the Goblin")** for instance, or the brilliant appreciation of Góngora, which is a serious and valuable contribution of the study of that most difficult poet? Is it likely that he could have been the close friend of Salvador Dalí and Manuel de Falla, and have known well poets like Gerardo Diego, Rafael Albertí, Pedro Salinas, Jorge Guillén and Dámaso Alonso, without being well abreast of contemporary trends in the artistic and literary worlds? If he did not care to associate himself with any particular movement, any of the "isms" of the 'twenties and 'thirties, need he have been oblivious to them? He does not stand aloof and alone. He has his place among the Spanish poets of his generation.

"Lorca never *thinks*!" said an Argentine writer. This is one of those brilliantly half-true remarks. It is true to the extent that in his own poetry Lorca works far more from intuition and imagination than from ordered processes of reasoning. True to the extent that Lorca is no *theorist*, by which I mean that he scarcely ever composes to a theory. But not true to the extent that Lorca is an artist and therefore well aware of the exigencies of his poetic form of expression. Art is very rarely sacrificed by Lorca. It is very seldom quite drowned, even when the inner voice is overwhelmingly loud and insistent. Even in the poems of *El Poeta en Nueva York* (*The Poet in New York*), so often called chaotic and anarchical, there is, I believe, a great deal more deliberate art than is generally thought. His poetry is born in the heart, and, although he is aware that Reason must harness Inspiration, the conventionally rational is not *permitted* to impose itself on the strange processes of the unconscious mind any more than the necessities of Art demand.

As for being no theorist, the reason of that is, generally speaking, that Lorca expressly chooses not to theorise. I say 'generally speaking' because in fact he has two poems, both of an experimental nature (in hexameters)—exercises, the poet called them—the **"Oda a Salvador Dalí"** and the **"Oda al Santísimo Sacramento,"** which *are* concerned with aesthetics. His views on the whole subject of poetry he once stated in a recorded conversation with Gerardo Diego. By his words it is clear that for Lorca Poetry is ultimately a Mystery (the corollary of that being that if there is no Mystery there is no Poetry):

But what am I to say about Poetry? What can I say about those clouds, about that sky? Look, look, look at them, look at it and nothing more. You will understand that a poet cannot say anything about Poetry. Leave that to the critics and professors. But neither you nor I nor any poet knows what Poetry is. . . .

There we have the deliberately non-thinking, non-theorising Lorca. But it is the artist who thoroughly knows his metier that goes on:

In my lectures I have sometimes spoken of Poetry, but the one thing I cannot talk about is my own poetry. And not because I am unaware of what I am doing. On the contrary, if it is true that I am a poet by the grace of God—or the devil—it is also true that I am one by the grace of technique and of effort and of realising exactly what a poem is.

Naturally, no poet can keep himself out of his poetry. But he can control, to a certain extent, how much of himself he puts in. Lorca is an intensely personal poet. He insinuates himself in a thousand ways into his poems, where often—apart from his inevitable Godlike presence as creator of the poem—one does not suspect he is at all. This is, of course, closely connected with that power to be at once individual artist and anonymous poet of an age-old tradition.

Most of the poems of the exquisitely lyrical and musical *Canciones* and the tormented *Poeta en Nueva York* are intensely and obviously personal. Others are as intensely, but less obviously so. In these the poet often projects his state of heart as a landscape or renders it in some other concrete imagery. There is an extraordinary emotion behind what often looks like the most impersonal description. It is an *aesthetic* emotion, which is a great feature of much Spanish poetry. (pp. 18-21)

There is the same intensity of personal emotion when he speaks through other persons in his poems. Here is . . . [an] example from a poem in which is also found one of the constantly recurring motifs of his poetry: the longing to be something else. The poem is the deliciously nonsensical, but poignant **"Canción tonta" ("Silly Song")**:

Mother.
I want to be made of silver.

Son.
you'll be very cold.

Mother.
I want to be made of water.

Son.
you'll be very cold.

Mother.
Embroider me on your pillow.

That I will do!
Right away!

This identification with other people—who are not only the creatures of Lorca's imagination, but may also be identified in a wider sense with the actual Andalusian people themselves—is found especially in the *Poema del cante jondo*. And, perhaps above all, in the *Romancero gitano*. (pp. 21-2)

Edward C. Riley, "Considerations on the Poetry of García Lorca," in *The Dublin Magazine*, Vol. XXVII, No. 1, January-March, 1952, pp. 14-22.

ROY CAMPBELL

(essay date 1952)

[Campbell was a South African journalist, autobiographer, and translator who aligned himself with the Fascist rebels during the Spanish Civil War. He is known for his translations of Portuguese, French, and Spanish authors. In the following excerpt, he examines García Lorca's use of sound, nature imagery, and the theme of death in his works.]

Though not by any means the greatest Spanish poet of his time, Lorca is the most intensely and nationally Spanish. This, however, he does not express in patriotism, as an Englishman would do were he so extremely English as Lorca is Spanish. He is also one of the most narrowly regional of Spanish poets; and at the same time, paradoxically enough, he is the most popular and universal in his appeal both inside and outside Spain. His appeal is never more universal than when he is writing, at home, about his native Andalusia. It is never more parochial and provincial than when he is self-consciously trying to be 'cosmopolitan', under the influence of Whitman, in the poems written in, and about, New York and the Caribbean. Andalusia is Lorca's *querencia*. The *querencia* is the exact spot which every Spanish fighting bull chooses to return to, between his charges, in the arena. It is his invisible fortress or camp. It is not marked by anything but the bull's preference for it, and may be near the centre, near the barricade, or between the two, as the bull chooses. The nearer the bull is to his *querencia* or stamping-station, the more formidable he is, the more full of confidence, and the more difficult to lure abroad into the territory of the bullfighters, for their territory is wherever the bull is most vulnerable, and least sure of himself.

During Lorca's sojourns abroad, or in Madrid, he always returned for poetical strength to his native province; even when he did not return to it in person, he returned in imagination, memory, and dreams: and it never failed him as a source of strength and inspiration. It was from there that he was most difficult to lure abroad into the intellectual territory of the enemy, the territory of bad verse and of adverse criticism, where the critics can take advantage of the vulnerability of the poet, just as the 'toreros' do of the weakness of the bull when he stays outside of the magic and magnetic radius of his *querencia*. A poet can only get into that enemy ter-

ritory by writing poorly about things he cannot feel instinctively. That is what happens to Lorca when he leaves Andalusia. He is like his ancient fellow-countryman, the giant Antaeus, who rose with strength redoubled each time he touched his mother-earth.

The cities of Granada, Córdoba and Sevilla, the three capital cities of Andalusia, always recur in that order in the poems of Lorca. After Granada the ancient Roman Córdoba comes second in his heart. He is attracted by something shadowy, nostalgic, and melancholy in both these towns which have outlived their greatest splendour. Sevilla, the gay, beautiful, and ever young giantess with the huge carnation between her teeth is too powerful and raucous to engage the same tender and intimate love that he feels for Granada or Córdoba.

That Lorca, one of the most narrowly regional poets of modern times, should be at the same time one of the most universally appreciated among his contemporaries, is just one more of those delightful little paradoxes which make bearable the present stereotyping dehumanisation, unification, and bureaucratic centralisation of human life. (pp. 8-9)

A body without reaction is a corpse: so is any social body without tradition. 'Reactionary' Spain has, during this century, produced better poetry than any other country; and this is chiefly due to her preoccupation with spiritual necessities rather than immediate physical conveniences.

At first sight some of the great poetical plays of Lorca will seem far-fetched because his characters prefer broken pockets, broken bank balances, and even broken hearts, to broken spirits. But those characters are true to life in Spain: and if they were true to life here, there would be more poetry here. There are no substitutes for morality, honour, and loyalty, either in themselves (as we are so painfully learning) or as the substance of poetry and drama. (p. 12)

There is one poet in contemporary English literature who is deeply conscious, as Lorca was, of the *sound* of words; that is Dylan Thomas: he extracts the maximum of meaning from words through their sound. So does Lorca. They are both musicians: more than any poets of our times, they have studied the evocative force of sound in words. Thomas is a dealer in thunder and lightning, Lorca deals rather in the sound of rivers and leaves, and the irridescences of lights and waters. Strength is Dylan Thomas's salient quality, though he is by no means without subtlety. Subtlety is Lorca's chief quality though he is by no means without strength. They both derive from countries where there is a very strong musical and vocal tradition, and where singing is a natural function of the people. (The success of the Welsh miners' choirs in Spain was only equalled by that of the Spanish singers and dancers in Wales.) (p. 13)

[The] popular tradition is one of the main influences in Lorca's work; but it has been vastly exaggerated by some critics, excusably perhaps, since it is so rare in the modern world that it immediately distinguishes a living modern poet who is lucky enough to have undergone that influence. But Lorca grafted on to the tree of popular tradition his own gorgeous ramification of the sophisticated and highly *literary* Gongorine tradition, which is the very opposite of the simple popular folk-lore with which he blended it so harmoniously. Thus he performed the miraculous operation of combining the most cultivated artifice of baroque poetry with the ingenuous art of the people, and of reconciling the treasures of the library to those of the earth and sky of his native sierra. He was influenced in turn by many of the other great poets of the Golden Age . . . who formed a galaxy only equalled in literary history by that of our own Elizabethans and Jacobeans. (pp. 13-14)

Nearly all Lorca's most flowery work is vertebrated with a sinewy spinal-cord. However much he luxuriates externally into such sparkling froth . . . , it is the froth of good strong champagne—with a body to it. There is always a central design to his work. The two principles, that of luxuriation and that of economy, wrestle harmoniously in nearly all the best Andalusian art, as if a sort of tropical oriental luxuriance were being pruned and ordered by the cold hard axe of Romanity. (p. 21)

Lorca's achievement, throughout his career, is reflected, as by an infallible index, by the effectiveness of his images. His poems stand or fall by them. They are the pulses by which we measure his health, beating strongly and normally in his first poems, his best plays, the *Lament for the Bullfighter,* the *Canciones,* the *Cante Jondo,* but by fits and starts, irregularly, in his New York poems and his *Diván de Tamarit.* Whereas a Castilian poet like Gabriel y Galán can write a superb poem without a single metaphor, simile or image, they form both the glory and (sometimes) the weakness of Lorca's work. He has periods when they are consistently successful, other periods when they are not, and it is very rare that he ever mixes good and bad images in the same poem. (p. 24)

Latin 'nature poets' differ entirely from the German and English Romantics. When I read Wordsworth, I feel that all his rocks, trees, and mountains are more intelligent than human beings, whereas his human characters, wherever they can be unearthed, are almost without exception imbeciles and nit-wits. I feel that there is something deeply perverse, intellectually suicidal and misanthropic about this transposition of values. In fact I think the whole Romantic principle (in its bad sense) can be defined as something perverse, a sort

of centrifugal panic in which the poet escapes from himself: a principle that subordinates the immediate to the remote, the evident to the occult, the normal to the abnormal, the lucid to the obscure, the moral to the immoral, and the present to some Utopianised future or romanticised past. . . . The difference in the Latin-Mediterranean type of 'nature poetry', seen at its best in the *Georgics* of Virgil, is that there is no brown study, no Buddhistified blurring and blending with 'the Whole', to the detriment of all outlines and sane values. Where a Latin poet creates a darkness, as in Saint John of the Cross's *Dark Night of the Soul,* it is not for the sake of merging with that darkness alone, nor the losing of all contours in a brown study; it is simply to rid the mind of a less intense form of reality, so as to give it all the more power to seize the more intense reality of God. The proof is in the fact that this kind of mystical poetry makes you wide awake, and the other soothes you almost to sleep; and this is the difference between the mystic and the mistagogue. The nature poets of the Latin races tend to differentiate, to particularise, and even to anthropomorphise the objects about which they write, as Virgil did with his bees, bringing them out clearly from their background. The tendency of the northern poets is to let nature envelop them around with moss, clouds, weeds, and flowers, until we and they disappear in a dream of mental vegetation and vapour.

Lorca, who had known intense suffering in childhood and throughout the rest of his life, since he was never to know the normal command of his muscles and limbs, grew up amongst those countrymen who, different from the poetical excursionists, know the particular in nature, and not a single entity with a capital N. The things that attract his attention most as a poet are always in his immediate surroundings, with their peasants and their animal population of bees, butterflies, nightingales, cicadas, frogs, and lizards. . . . In dealing with the smaller creatures of the earth, he affects a sort of Lilliputian minuteness, almost Franciscan in its intimacy, which in its detail reminds one of the exquisite treatment of bees by Virgil and Góngora, or the even more perfect treatment of the fable of the Town and Country Mouse by Horace in his satires. We are reminded of the pre-Romantic poets in our own literature, the exquisite Drayton of the *Nymphidia,* the speech of Mercutio about Queen Mab, and certain passages of *A Midsummer Night's Dream.* The very important difference is that we are torn by Lorca between a comic grotesqueness and a heartrending pathos with which he invests these slightly humanised, tiny creatures of the fields. He notices on the lizards their 'little white aprons', calls them 'drops of crocodile', and 'dragons of the frogs', seeing their 'green frockcoat of a devil's abbot'. But Lorca's small animal and insect world, though conceived with a childish directness of vision, is no dream world of Titanias and fairies, but the real old world we inhabit ourselves, seen in miniature, with startling clearness, as through the wrong end of a telescope. Its fierceness remains undiminished by microscopic proportions, and becomes all the more startling because of them and because of a sort of Goyaesque and Bosch-like mixture of the human with the Lilliputian.

The description of the voices of the frogs 'freckling the silence with little green dots' is another uncanny but perfect image to those who have heard the frogs of the southern marshes, at sundown, start up their chorus with the twinkling of the stars. When I say Lorca partly humanises his creatures, I do not mean that he detracts from their peculiar frogginess, lizardliness, or whatever it may be. The touch of humanity seems to enhance and emphasize their innate quality as frogs, snails or ants, by the sheer force of contrast. [At the age of five] Lorca used to love harrowing and terrifying the peasants by imitating the priest's 'hell-fire sermons'. Some of his poems, of a seemingly trivial nature, are so poignant that one sometimes indignantly and resentfully accuses the poet of going out of his way to make one suffer. (pp. 26-8)

[The] disconsolate mood recurs with insistence and power in Lorca's early work: and it returns even more powerfully in his later plays in which he invariably deals with what we call 'unpleasant subjects'. But in these later plays, the cruelty which he flings in one's face almost aggressively, as if to relieve his own sufferings, is tempered and balanced by the Euripidean stature of the protagonists, their innate strength, their willingness to accept suffering (since there is always a way out of cowardice or compromise) and their capacity for resignation. We accept his plays as we would accept them from scarcely anyone else dealing with the same subjects. It is his sheer artistic mastery which makes us accept them, and the realisation that his compassion is, after all, one of the main motives for burning both himself and us with such anguish. (p. 30)

In the end it is clear that Lorca is not deliberately inflicting pain on the reader, in order to shock or annoy him; but that he feels so poignantly that he has to share this feeling with others. This is the motive underlying his insistence on themes of cruelty. We know that in his life he was cheerful, full of fun, a radiant and kindly personality, and that considering the extent and nature of what he had to suffer, there was not much perversity in his make-up, as modern poets go.

Together with this sense of pain one feels almost everywhere in Lorca's poetry, even at its gayest (and it can be very gay) there goes also the sense of a lurking, imminent and violent death. (p. 31)

His eternal wrestling with the theme of death had its justification, just as Keats's preoccupation with the same theme. It came out of strength rather than weakness. The event proved that it was no illusion. His own violent death, and that of nearly three million Spanish men, women, and children, could already be sensed in the air, like a coming thunderstorm, for many years before the Terror was unleashed. It was publicly threatened on all the walls. One could not escape from being confronted with skulls and crossbones with bloodthirsty inscriptions chalked up everywhere. . . . In the repeated wrestling with the idea of death, Lorca generally increases the stature of life, and intensifies it. All those people who repeatedly seek out death to risk their lives do so chiefly because they are overflowing with a surplus of life. They get a stimulus from the presence of death as a healthy body does from a cold bath. (pp. 37-8)

In Lorca's greatest sustained lyrical poem, the *Lament for the Death of the Matador* (*Llanto por Ignacio Sánchez Mejías*), we see a duel between Life and Death, enacted almost as a ritual dance between the superb, overflowing vitality of the matador and the cold shadow of Absence, while each augments and enhances the stature and the mystery of the other. In all his early poems in which he treats the subject of death we feel that the dual process is at work, which he carries to such a supreme triumph in the *Llanto*. Many of the earlier poems are rehearsals of this towering spiral in which the two forces contend in a sort of ecstasy; but there are also heights of serene lyrical contemplation which are exceptional in such a young poet. . . . (pp. 38-9)

'Romancero' means a collection of 'Romances'. This is by far the most famous and popular of all Lorca's collections of verse. . . . The romance is the Spanish equivalent of our ancient popular ballad-form; and the latter is the only means by which we can possibly translate it, since the Spanish 'romance', instead of rhyming, requires an assonance in every second line, which continues right through the whole poem, and, in the long run, produces a stronger effect than our rhyme. . . . Lorca, who while we are reading him appears to be a very spontaneous and facile writer, must have expended prodigious study and pains on the Romance form; his assonance is very much more pronounced than that of other Spanish poets. On analysing his use of vowel sounds, one finds that the extra emphasis which his own vowel assonance sounds acquire is usually due to their having been entirely suppressed from the rest of the line in which they occur. This is a true feat of profound technical engineering. (pp. 40-1)

[The] two books of his songs, or *Canciones*, . . . were written mostly between 1921 and 1924, but not revised or published till many years later. In some of these he sets out to capture half-meanings and impressions that are difficult, vague, and remote, and literally to give to 'airy nothing' a name and address. 'Rien que la nuance', Verlaine's motto, 'nothing but the mere shade', flickers like a will-o'-the-wisp over some of these pages. (p. 62)

In Lorca's work, as in that of his two friends Falla and Salvador Dali, the tradition finally balances perfectly with their revolutionary innovations, though there is a violent struggle at first to dominate the irruption of the new forces in their work. Of the four Spaniards who loom so great in the world of modern art, Picasso is the only one who remains an iconoclast, in a state of perpetual fission. (p. 66)

Lorca's chief public activity was concerned with the stage, in reviving the masterpieces of the Golden Age under his own direction, and in travelling round with puppet shows and companies of his own. He was responsible for a national revival of poetic drama. He wrote many plays which he produced himself. Some like *Así que pasan los Cinco Años* were experimental.

The best verse dramas of Lorca fill several volumes and are generally remarkable alike for their stagecraft and the quality of the verse that sustains them. (p. 67)

[While in the United States, Lorca] was unable to establish a real contact with the Americans or their way of life. The result on his poetry was entirely negative. He underwent while there the intellectual influence, if not domination, of Salvador Dali, his friend, who is also a great artist of international repute, but a far more complicated personality than Lorca, more resilient and aggressive, with a far wider range of sympathies and interests, and at home anywhere from the U.S.A. to Catalonia. Lorca attempted to follow the Catalonian into the complex world of surrealism, and lost his depth. In Lorca's New York poems, the *Poeta en Nueva York,* his metaphors and images fall out of focus; his verse becomes loose, plaintive, and slightly mephitic. It took him quite a long time to recover his poetical eyesight and insight after he returned to Spain. In his long **"Ode to Salvador Dali"** he applauds the clear vision of the Catalan painter, but seems to lose a grasp on his own; yet the poem nevertheless contains some fine lines. We are reminded, in Lorca's American venture, of Burns when he went into high society at Edinburgh and started to write like a courtier and gentleman of the world. It was a fiasco. Lorca's talent is not cosmopolitan, and it did not flourish far from the scent of the orange groves of the South. Even in his two **"Odes to the Sacrament,"** which were written under the intense stimulus of religion, Lorca fails to organise the chaos in his imagery and the impact on his mind of Dali's work.

Lorca reached the height of his achievement in his *Llanto por Ignacio Sánchez Mejías;* here he remained true to his native Andalusia, to the earth and the landscape from which his verse derived its strength, flavour and perfume; yet he was not under the restriction he imposed upon himself in the *Romancero,* that of the coldly impartial and ironic spectator. On the contrary, he was expressing his grief for a beloved friend, one of the greatest bullfighters of all time, who was also a cultured literary man, a good farmer, a great horseman, and a popular figure who was equally beloved by all for his goodness of heart, as well as for his prowess and valour. The death of Ignacio Sanchez Mejías was a public calamity in Andalusia. (pp. 71-2)

The fourth part of the *Llanto* in which he takes final leave of his friend, ends with a verse which might serve as an epitaph for the poet himself:

> It will be long before there is born, if ever,
> An Andalusian so frank, so rich in adventure;
> I sing your elegance with words that moan
> And remember a sad wind among the olive trees.
> (p. 77)

Roy Campbell, in his *Lorca: An Appreciation of His Poetry,* Yale University Press, 1952, 79 p.

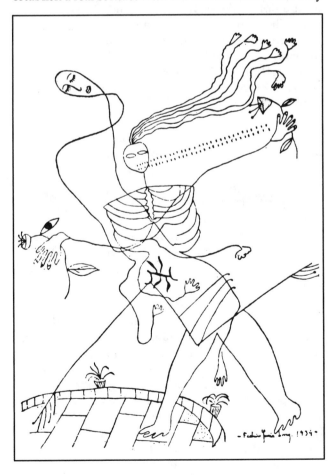

A depiction of Death by García Lorca.

EDWIN HONIG

(essay date 1963)

[Honig is an American poet, critic, and dramatist. In the following excerpt, he examines historical and thematic elements in García Lorca's work.]

Lorca was neither a "political" nor a "surrealist" poet—in whatever sense these terms are used nowadays. He was, however, a *popular* poet in that special sense reserved to Spain: a poet whose work is loved and acclaimed by the illiterate and the sophisticated alike for those immediately discernible characteristics through which the Spanish people identify themselves. And he was a *difficult* poet, in the modern phrase, because he attempted to create a personal idiom by relating his understanding of a folk world with the values of an industrial world. In this attempt, he adapted materials and techniques from sources as remote as the medieval Arabic poets and as recent as Breton and Dalí. Yet to recognize his poetry alone is to omit his important dramatic work, for which poetry was, in one sense, a preparation. Poetic and dramatic both, his genius grew not out of advance-guard literary or political movements, but out of a richly functioning Spanish tradition barely surveyed by most present-day criticism. To approach him as an artist at all, one must realize the extent of his integration with that tradition, and understand the kind of sensibility able to thrive so well within it. (pp. iii-iv)

Unlike Yeats, Lorca had no set poetic system; unlike Eliot, his poetry and plays show no line of religious or ideological development. And if a good deal of his early work (in *Libro de Poemas, Canciones* and *El Maleficio de la Mariposa*) is nurtured by Jiménez' exquisitism, Lorca never perfected the older poet's glittering style of expression, perhaps because he could not be contained by the kind of arduously cultivated objective perceptivity it required. Lorca was more like Unamuno and Dylan Thomas: a self-dramatist possessed by the effort to describe the conflict of natural forms seeking escape from death and thereby lighting up the intensest of living moments. And so behind the mask of the gypsy in *Romancero Gitano* and of the Negro in *Poeta en Nueva York,* Lorca succeeded in being more personal than in the subjective lyricism of *Canciones.* In the same way, his *Lament* for the bullfighter is perhaps more intensely Spanish than his strongly honor-ridden plays about women. We should expect of a poet whose temperament is dramatic an acutely personal way of speaking that is not at the same time merely confessional. And similarly, of someone possessed by

the idea of capturing reality in the conflicting flashes of the moment, we should expect a gradual discarding of ornament, poetic ritual and symbolism for the barest, most essential kind of prose, such as we find in *The House of Bernarda Alba.* (p. x)

Somewhere in a letter to Jorge Guillén, Lorca wrote that poetry is made out of love, force, and renunciation. The statement tells us something about the springs of his personality; it also says much about his literary procedures, his themes, and his problematical forcing of the door of the constant enemy, death. For what are these three paradoxical elements but a synthetic figure for human pride—a figure which attempts to assert the meaning of life against death? This is what *Mariana Pineda* stands for: in the end her triumphant love, her struggle to make it pervade her action, her self-sacrifice, and through this, her powerless fight against martyrdom and its dehumanizing consequence of being turned into an abstraction. The triple complex of love-force-renunciation appears in the "erotic aleluya" *Don Perlimplín,* in *Yerma,* in *Blood Wedding,* in a more diffuse form in *Bernarda Alba,* as a fight against sterility, false honor (the tyranny of "whiteness") which is both chastity and death. Human pride is the ability to declare through a course of self-sacrifice what human love, however misunderstood, must affirm in the teeth of death and its own destruction. The figure of human pride is present in the gypsy's contention against the weapons of the law, in his erotic code, and in his last disdainful encounter with death. It is also present in the ever-new, ever-repeated encounter between the bullfighter and the bull, which must end in death, and, if fought well, in glory.

Reality, Lorca said, is prose, what lives now, the present tense: *it is.* The beauty of truth is poetry, timeless, always existent, all tenses. To be made conceivable, reality requires the poet's strategy, and poetry needs for its truth what Lorca called "the opening of the veins"—the expression of human pride in love, force, and renunciation. Understood in this way, Lorca at the end of his life was writing for very high stakes—and the only ones by which he could sustain his vision of human pride. (pp. xii-xiii)

Before seeking to estimate the distinctively modern qualities of his poetry, we must understand his art as primarily an expression of national genius. The main aspects of the Spanish lyric tradition which find a new culmination in Lorca's poetry are: the medieval Arabic-Andalusian art of amorous poetry together with the early popular ballad; the Renaissance synthesis in Spain of the Greco-Latin poetic art, accomplished by the sophisticated "conceptist" poetry of Luis de Góngora; and the broad body of Andalusian gypsy art known as *cante jondo,* "deep song." (p. 20)

***Romancero Gitano* (*Book of Gypsy Ballads*) . . .**

is the realization of poetic sensibility which has achieved technical mastery over its materials. Here the poet's restless imagination has at last found a form in which to cast his personal cosmology. Less slavish to the letter of folkloric devices, Lorca has begun to create a respectable folklore of his own. The characteristic concentration upon a theme in single monotone, which occurs in the conventional Andalusian song, is replaced in *Romancero Gitano* by a solid variety of thematic materials. These are elaborated in subtle musical patterns with a personal emphasis which marks the matured poetic spirit. Written in the traditional octosyllabic meter, these ballads become a series of re-invented *cantares de gesta.* They partake of the anonymous folk character upholding a tradition distinctive for its magical recreation of language and its exaltation of natural phenomena and pagan feeling. Spanish poets beginning with Jiménez sought to eschew the anecdotal qualities of the old *romance* and to reshape the form according to new inventive techniques. And this is Lorca's first accomplishment in *Romancero Gitano.* He has re-created the classical style of the old ballad and given it a new tonal quality which is distinctly modern. (pp. 65-6)

The constant struggle of the gypsies is against a universal repression whose edict is death. They themselves, however, own the moon's proud body which they hammer on a forge in the intimacy of the surrounding night. (p. 67)

Lorca's use of the traditional ballad gradually merges with his whole esthetic procedure. This use is not the mere exploitation of a theme for the discursiveness of some folkloric poetaster; it is a marriage between the language of personal perception and the language of popular feeling. Lorca's esthetic demands continually enhance a subjective element of gypsy atmosphere in Andalusian life which others have overworked as an exotic attraction without particular spiritual significance. . . . But *Romancero Gitano* was in no sense a consummation of artistic purpose. Lorca's spirit was still hungry, as is the spirit of every poet who feels the burden of "the song I shall never sing." For Lorca was not interested in the popular elements of Andalusian culture alone. In his restless seeking of a bond between the habits of an older cultural perception and the values of the modern world, he felt compelled to experiment ceaselessly with different forms. (p. 77)

Just as Lorca discovered in Dalí's art a courageous instinct to deal with phenomena of pure form, so in the body and spirit of Christ he found committed the "love and discipline" by which he also sought to implement his poetry.

For Lorca, the Holy Eucharist was the religious counterpart of his own esthetic; in the unity of the godhead was the same concretization of form symbolized. Through this unity one might aspire to find "love and discipline" outside the characterless flux of the world. (p. 83)

Lorca speaks of his Odes as spiritual exercises, as attempts to overcome a sense of artistic irresolution and personal despair. (p. 84)

Lorca's short stay in New York resulted in the volume *Poeta en Nueva York.* It is the work of a new spiritual insight and of a largely incoherent prophetic vision. Tormented and mutilated, but still sensually realistic, the poems included in this volume carry a peculiarly important message to the modern age. It is easy to think of them as the fabrications of a mind which has lost its balance, as the outpourings of a surrealist gruesomely constructing an antihuman nightmare world. Certainly they are Lorca's most difficult poems. Musically discordant, disrupted in meter, poured into an arbitrary autonomous form, cascading with the fragments of exploded metaphor, they seem to contradict the whole of his previous procedure. But their secret is that a new world of imagery has been created to embody the fervid spiritual effort which informs them. The intricate imagistic and metaphoric terminology of *Poeta en Nueva York* proceeds from a vision of the world which, finding no expressive instrument in the traditions of any communicative medium, demands of the poet a new imaginative invention. (p. 85)

For Lorca, New York is a symbol of spiritual myopia, where man is unable to cope with the disease of body and soul because he cannot see the nature of his dislocation, because he has lost sight of those elemental natural forces which a people living close to the soil understand instinctively. (p. 87)

Lorca discovered a solid base for his poetic drama precisely in Lope and Calderón. Like Lope, he is essentially a lyric poet whose dramatic instinct grew out of a sense of communication he felt himself able to establish with the people. He too was possessed with the need to create spectacle, a visual and musical supplement to the art of the spoken word. Lorca's work also has a close moral affinity with Calderón's drama. Like Calderón, he seems to reduce life to a symbolic formula, holds that traditional Spanish respect for honor, and sees on life's flashing mosaic face the essential mask of death. But if on these terms Lorca's drama lacks the old unity, it is because he could not find grace, as Calderón did, in heaven, or absolution from the sins of human perversity on earth, the Catholic Church notwithstanding. He had no answer to the questions which most obsessed him. But he was fired with the fine musical imagination of a minstrel, and the sharp sense of death magnified—magnified as a garden in the clear morning light, to the least inconsiderable weed. With the first he wove out his dramatic idea; with the second he set his scene; and with both he opened the eyes of an audience which had not been stirred by such display for over two centuries.

Growing out of his consistent innovations in the lyric medium, Lorca's development as a dramatist fulfilled the imaginative pattern of his whole art. (pp. 108-09)

The positive dramatic thing which Synge was seeking and trying himself to do in the theatre was also the business of Garcia Lorca. For, like Synge and Yeats and Lady Gregory when they set out to create a national literature for the Irish theatre, Lorca was rebelling against the realistic middle-class drama, which in Spain had succeeded in shutting off from the stage the rich atmosphere of folk speech and imagination. Lorca tried to break through the commercialized theatre with its vulgar parades of life twisted into the neat cynical gesture, the always triumphant negative morality. What he, like those leaders of the Irish movement, proposed to put in its place was the sense of the magic of language to which only a people still attached to the rituals of the land could respond with authentic pleasure. (p. 110)

The strength of Lorca's folk drama lies precisely in his use of woman as bearer of all passion and earthly reality: the wild superb nature of which Synge had spoken. With Lorca it is not simply an accidental choice. The Spain which let its blood for Christ secretly admired the Virgin more. The Virgin prevailing over all early Spanish church art was the symbol of earthly fecundity as well as the mother of divine mercy. The Spaniard often seems to mistrust his male saints for not suffering enough or convincingly. Spanish women saints, however, were always known to suffer magnificent and terrible martyrdom. The character of the *dueña*, the woman chaperon, very early became a convention in the Spanish theatre. And she, as the repository of good earthy frankness, knew the world's tricks and provided the audience with the protective motherly domination which it sought in woman. The Don Juan legend has been a popular and recurrent theme in Spanish literature because it re-affirms the generously fertile nature of woman as distinct from the abstract and essentially barren male lover who finds no permanence except in the arms of death. The Spaniard has been somewhat contemptuous of his philandering Don Juan, who instead of conquering women should have been conquering the New World, or even his own small plot of ground.

Lorca's heroines are modern versions of the warm matriarchal type found in all Spanish literature. They are magnetic fields inevitably drawing tragedy to themselves from a too ardent faith in the right of their natural instincts. Again, they are islands which the world cannot touch with its soiled and makeshift logic. Because their humanity is such an extremely procreative answer to life, they threaten to disrupt the mere man-made machinery of social law, which is, finally, a substitution for life. They are the affirmation to the ques-

tion of the ultimate which man, with the beam of social exigency in his eye, is always begging. When they lose the sense of integration in life which is necessary to them, the world trembles and comes apart. Thus it is as martyrs of frustrated love, from the heroine of *Mariana Pineda,* who dies on the gallows, to the suicide of the youngest daughter in *La Casa de Bernarda Alba,* that Lorca's women uphold the insistent theme of his tragedies. (pp. 151-53)

The personal dilemma of the poet reflected in his plays, which to some extent are the enactment of that dilemma, is precisely that of his heroines in the folk dramas: frustrated love. In personal terms lack of fulfillment suggests a conflict of sexuality through its insistence on unresolved impasse in the plays, and through it increasingly an uncontainable eroticism which *wills* the impasse. . . .

Lorca's dramatic experiments like *Mariana Pineda, Don Perlimplín, Así Que Pasen Cinco Años,* etc., all treat the problem of romantic love ironically. (p. 195)

In the folk dramas which culminate with *La Casa de Bernarda Alba,* romance no longer exists even as an ironic statement. The poet, identified with all his heroines, perpetuates desire endlessly in an eroticism which, like Yerma's, ends in a metaphysical suicide, or like Doña Rosita's, spreads itself through the fields and wells and walls of Granada's circumambience. The refuges into which all his protagonists escape are in a sense fatally predetermined by the enormity of their excessive and unfulfillable need which they realize cannot be ratified by the society and situation in which they find themselves. And they correspond, in this way, to the poet in the jail of his richly surging world of sexuality which can neither be contained without a sympathy as gigantic as his own or broken through without catastrophe. But just as the first is never encountered, so the second gradually seems, as the dénouement of play after play, more a result of the same paralyzed circumstance than a revealing resolution of a many leveled tragic insight. It is the personal dilemma which prevents Lorca's folk dramas as well as his other plays from rising so often out of pathos to real tragedy. At the same time, however, it makes for Lorca's unique sincerity as an artist and shows why a tragedy of personal validity must fail in the modern world, where it remains unresolved finally in terms of social criticism, in terms of a society which inevitably degrades as it makes meaningless personal integrity. (p. 196)

The secret of Lorca's whole art is that as a poet he had an overwhelming impulsion to supplement the written word by a union of various artistic media; and that despite the consequences to which this led him, he succeeded in remaining primarily a poet. . . .

Few serious modern poets dealing with the heterodox world of the present are content to face it with so few original ideas. And most of the ideas in Lorca's work can be found embodied in the themes and conventions he adapted from Spanish literature. Notable in his folk plays are the insistence on themes of honor, the defeat of innocence when seeking justification in anarchic instinct, and the unconsummated love or marriage whose outcome is spilt blood and death. These appear in his poetry as the quest for spiritual permanence through sensual reality—a search peculiar to the Spanish temper with its mystical investment in what Unamuno has called "the tragic sense of life." (pp. 197-98)

In passing from the lyric-dramatic form of *Romancero Gitano* to the poetic form of his folk tragedies, he was repeating the process of dramatic adaptation as it occurred in the Golden Age. This was the transformation of the original epic into the popular ballad, and then directly into the drama, where both theme and character were continually preserved, though the literary forms had been changed. When Lorca made his gypsy the *modus vivendi* of *Romancero Gitano*, he proved that he could dramatize within a supple ballad form a well-recognized aspect of Spanish life; and in universalizing the gypsy so that the reader was able to identify himself, Lorca had found the hidden door which leads from poetry into the theatre. The same precise use of invention accompanies his entrance into the drama. For he was again transposing his subject into a recognizable traditional frame when he substituted for the silent, bronzed gypsy, agonized in his dream, the frustrated woman, agonized in her love. (pp. 199-200)

Lorca's use of musical motifs as dramatic support was another aspect of his poetry which emerged through imagery to assume a considerable part in his drama. (p. 201)

As still another esthetic complement, the ballet weaves its way into the plays. This is especially notable in sections of his "surrealist" attempts where certain characters exist only to mimic the main action of the play, as the Girl seeking her lover, who encounters the buffoons in the last act of *Así Que Pasen Cinco Años.* (p. 202)

Finally, there is in Lorca's art the imaginative dramatization of conflict between abstract and concrete forces, developing directly from his concerns as a poet into his inventions as a dramatist. There are at least three characteristic ways in which this dramatization occurs in Lorca's imagery.

The first is as a sudden awakening of animate or inanimate things to an awareness of heightened power which is not ordinarily prescribed in their nature. All Lorca's poetry is full of such imagery; but in his later work, through continual condensation, it becomes almost a stylistic habit, which is his particular signature in contemporary poetry. (p. 204)

A second way in which Lorca dramatizes the conflict between abstract and concrete forces is by revealing the compulsion of one element or quality of nature to become another and throw off its own inevitable form to live vicariously in one of its own choosing. Seeking such a change of identity, for instance, are glow-worms who want to be eagles. (p. 206)

The third facet of Lorca's imagistic inventions in this representation of conflict between abstract and concrete forces can be described as the achievement of a sense of halt in the rush of things forever in motion; the need of all life to find fixity, permanence, and its own endurability in rest. This is closely allied to the second process which deals with the complement of the same problem: the everlasting hunger for motion, change and illusion. Relevant here are Lorca's symbols of the mirror, the profile, the stone, and the backwater of a stream. (p. 208)

Edwin Honig, in his *García Lorca,* revised edition, New Directions, 1963, 239 p.

SOURCES FOR FURTHER STUDY

Adams, Mildred. *García Lorca: Playwright and Poet.* New York: George Braziller, 1977, 204 p.

Biographical and critical study. Adams concludes that García Lorca can be understood only through an objective study of his life and, in particular, by analyzing the effect his visits to North and South America had on his work and philosophy.

Campbell, Roy. *Lorca: An Appreciation of His Poetry.* New Haven: Yale University Press, 1952, 79 p.

Examines García Lorca's use of sound, nature imagery, and the theme of death within a narrow regionalistic context.

Crow, John A. *Federico García Lorca.* Los Angeles: University of California Press, 1945, 116 p.

Study of the biographical, thematic, formalistic, and historical elements which inform García Lorca's poetry and drama. Includes bibliography.

Durán, Manuel, ed. *Lorca: A Collection of Critical Essays.* Englewood Cliffs, N.J.: Prentice-Hall, 1962, 181 p.

Includes essays by such critics as William Carlos Williams, J. B. Trent, Roy Cambell, Edwin Honig, and Louis Parrot.

Loughran, David K. *Federico García Lorca: The Poetry of Limits*. London: Tamesis Books Limited, 1978, 219 p.

Extensive critical analysis of García Lorca's themes, symbols, and imagery. Focuses on the writer's approach to such subjects as dualism, fatality, and alienation. Also includes selective critical bibliography.

Morris, Brian C., ed. *"Cuando yo me muera . . . ": Essays in Memory of Federico García Lorca*. Lanham, M.D.: University Press of America, 1988, 339 p.

Collection of lectures given at a 1986 symposium on García Lorca occasioned by the fiftieth anniversary of his assasination. Includes essays by prominant García Lorca scholars, including Manuel Durán, Paul Ilie, and Virginia Higginbotham.